DATE DUE

Tibetan Nation

Tibetan Nation

A History of Tibetan Nationalism and Sino-Tibetan Relations

Warren W. Smith, Jr.

WestviewPress
A Division of HarperCollins*Publishers*

Copyright © 1996 by Westview Press, Inc., A Division of HarperCollins Publishers, Inc.

Published in 1996 in the United States of America by Westview Press, Inc., 5500 Central Avenue, Boulder, Colorado 80301-2877, and in the United Kingdom by Westview Press, 12 Hid's Copse Road, Cumnor Hill, Oxford OX2 9JJ

Library of Congress Cataloging-in-Publication Data
Smith, Warren W.
    Tibetan nation : a history of Tibetan nationalism and Sino-Tibetan relations / by Warren W. Smith, Jr.
        p.   cm.
    Includes bibliographical references and index.
    ISBN 0-8133-3155-2 0-8133-3280-X (pbk)
        1. Nationalism—China—Tibet.   2.Tibet (China)—Politics and government.   3. Tibet (China)—Relations—China.   4. China—Relations—China—Tibet.   I. Title.
DS786.S56   1996
951'.5—dc20   96-34206
                                                                              CIP

The paper used in this publication meets the requirements of the American National Standard for Permanence of Paper for Printed Library Materials Z39.48-1984.

10   9   8   7   6   5   4   3   2

If history were a chronicle of the voluntary association and disassociation of groups, there would be no need for a doctrine of self-determination. It is the distinct absence of such a peaceful evolution of mankind's social organization which ultimately gave rise to the principle of self-determination as the twentieth century's primary expression of disapproval of involuntary political association.

—Lee C. Buchheit, *Secession: The Legitimacy of Self-Determination*

Where the sentiment of nationality exists in any force, there is a prima facie case for uniting all the members of the nationality under the same government, and a government to themselves apart. This is merely saying that the question of government ought to be decided by the governed. One hardly knows what any division of the human race should be free to do if not to determine with which of the various collective bodies of human beings they choose to associate themselves.

—John Stuart Mill, *Utilitarianism, Liberty and Representative Government*

To us Tibetans the phrase "the liberation of Tibet," in its moral and spiritual implications, is based upon a deadly mockery. The country of a free people was invaded and occupied under the pretext of liberation — liberation from whom and what? Ours was a happy country with a solvent Government and a contented people till the Chinese invasion in 1950.

—"Manifesto by Tibetan Leaders,"
in *The Question of Tibet and the Rule of Law*

Tibet is far away, and other countries have their own fears and troubles. We can well understand that there may be a tendency to let the events in Tibet drift back into history. Yet Tibet is on this very earth; Tibetans are human; in their way they are very civilized; certainly they are sensitive to suffering. I would dare to say that no people have suffered more since the Second World War; and their sufferings have not ended, they are continuing every day, and they will continue until the Chinese leave our country, or until Tibetans have ceased to exist as a race or as a religious community.

—Dalai Lama, *My Land and My People*

Contents

Preface

Tibet's brief appearance on the international political stage in 1950-1951, at the time of the Chinese invasion, and in 1959, following the flight of the Dalai Lama into exile in India, was followed by long periods of the absence of any news on Tibet, except the glowing reports emanating from the PRC propaganda machine about the glorious progress of the Tibetan people in achieving "liberation," "democratic reforms," and "socialist transformation." Since 1980, however, the opening of Tibet to the outside world has revealed that Chinese rule in Tibet has been oppressive and destructive of Tibetan culture and civilization. In addition, Tibetan nationalism has not been eradicated but has been exacerbated by Chinese rule and repression. In a phenomenon typical of colonialism, Tibetan nationalism has grown under the conditions of foreign conquest and rule despite every effort by the Chinese to eradicate it.

The history of Tibetan nationalism and Sino-Tibetan relations involves immensely complicated historical and political issues. Tibetans and Chinese will never agree on whether Tibet was or even currently is a "part of China." In the Tibetan Empire period of the seventh to ninth centuries, a centralized Tibetan government dominated the entire Tibetan plateau and consolidated a Tibetan cultural and political identity over that area. In later centuries, however, with the demise of a centralized government and the rise of the Tibetan Buddhist state, which was dependent upon foreign political and military patronage, Tibet came under the foreign domination of Mongol and Manchu empires, both of which were also ruling dynasties of China. China, when it overcame its own foreign domination, was thus able to claim Tibet as part of China due to the legacy of Mongol and Manchu domination over Tibet. Tibetan nationalism, little developed under the politically benign conditions of indirect rule, was aroused by China's attempt to transform its previous "suzerainty" into direct sovereignty.

After the Chinese Communists' "liberation" of Tibet in 1950-1951, Tibetan "local nationalism" was targeted for eradication by Marxist-Leninist nationalities policies, which were purported to provide the "solution to the nationalities question." Marx and Lenin had realized that nationalism is inevitably aroused by foreign imperialism; however, because Marxists define themselves as anti-imperialists, they have not applied this lesson to nations under their own domination. Instead, Marxists have attempted to disguise their imperialist domination of other nations by claiming to have "liberated" those nations from their own ostensibly "feudal" and exploitative social and political systems, a type of justification typical of imperialism. The issue of Tibet is not the nature of its former social and political system, a system far more benign than the "hell on earth" described in Chinese propaganda. Instead, the issue is the legitimacy of China's invasion and conquest of Tibet, its continuing foreign imperialist rule over Tibet and its denial of Tibetans' right to self-determination.

The history of Tibetan nationalism and Sino-Tibetan relations may be divided into four main periods. The first period is that of the consolidation of the Tibetan state from the beginnings of Tibetan history up to the fall of the Tibetan empire in 842. The territory and peoples of the Tibetan plateau were politically unified by the Tibetan empire (630-842), the only time in history that all of Tibet was unified under an independent centralized Tibetan state. During the empire period, Tibet rivaled T'ang dynasty China (618-907) for influence in Inner Asia and along the frontier between the two countries. It is during this period that Tibetan cultural, territorial and political identities, the fundamentals of later Tibetan nationalism, were consolidated.

After the collapse of the Tibetan empire in 842, Tibet was not again politically unified until the mid-13th century, when Tibetan lamas established a political-spiritual relationship, known as *Cho-Yon*, or priest-patron relationship, with the Mongol empire. This arrangement averted a Mongol conquest of Tibet and established ecclesiastical rule in Tibet under the Sakya sect. Tibet was a dependent state under the Mongol Yuan (1260-1368) and Manchu Ch'ing (1644-1911) dynasties. Tibet was independent of Chinese influence during the native Chinese Ming dynasty (1368-1644). Tibet's relationship to China during the Yuan and Ch'ing may be characterized as indirect rule typical of feudal relationships. Tibetan feudal relations with the Mongol Yuan and the Manchu Ch'ing had little impact upon Tibetan ethnic, cultural or national identity.

In the third period, Tibet experienced modern imperialist pressures and Tibetan nationalism was aroused in response. Tibetan nationalism was stimulated in the early 20th century by British imperial interests in Tibet and Chinese attempts to impose more direct control over Tibet. Tibet managed to achieve *de facto* independence under the conditions of British patronage for Tibetan autonomy and Chinese impotence but failed to achieve international recognition of its independence.

In the fourth period, from 1950 to the present, Tibetan independence was forcibly eliminated. Tibetan national identity came under intense pressure from Chinese campaigns for repression of Tibetan resistance to Chinese rule and for the "socialist transformation" of Tibetan society.

Tibetan culture was subjected to extreme assimilationist pressure during the Cultural Revolution. Nevertheless, despite every effort at its eradication, Tibetan nationalism survived and grew under the conditions of Chinese rule and the threat to Tibetan cultural and national identity which Chinese rule represented. In the period of liberalized Chinese policies in Tibet after 1980, Tibetan culture and nationalism have revived and China has been confronted with evidence of Tibetans' continuing rejection of Chinese rule. During this period Tibetans have sought and gained international support for their cause.

The first three periods are examined by an extensive review and synthesis of secondary historical sources in European languages and, for the early twentieth century, some British and Chinese government documents. The modern period of Tibetan history has been examined by using Chinese, Tibetan and international primary documentary sources in English translation as well as extensive interviews with Tibetan subjects. The book ends with an examination of Tibet's legal case within international law, self-determination in international law and the prospects for Tibetan self-determination. My technique throughout has been to let the story tell itself rather than to excessively synthesize and analyze. This reflects the enormous amount of primary source material available in English translation, especially for the post-1950 period, and a preference for the reader to discover from those materials, as I did, the story contained within.

The volume of Chinese justificatory propaganda on Tibet has been tremendous, especially at the times when Tibet has come under international scrutiny. Much factual information is contained in that propaganda, often unintentionally, as well as many revelations about the realities of the Chinese conquest and rule of Tibet. For this reason, and for the obvious reason of availability, this book employs PRC propaganda on Tibet to a large extent; it is my contention and my experience that, if one is willing to read vast quantities of it, Chinese propaganda on Tibet reveals much of what it intends to obscure. This book is devoted to the limited task of revealing the truth about the injustice and tragedy of China's conquest of Tibet and the destruction of Tibetan civilization. The inescapable conclusion of this study is that Tibet has a remarkably distinct national identity and a desire for independence clearly and unmistakably expressed not only before the Chinese conquest but since, and is therefore undeniably deserving of the right to national self-determination, a right now egregiously denied by the Chinese state.

Note on transliteration: This book employs the common phonetic system for translation of Tibetan and Mongolian words. Chinese words are translated according to the Wade-Giles system for the period before 1979 and according to the Pinyin system thereafter. However, translations of Chinese words may vary by period and source. For instance, Ch'ing-hai, Chinghai, Tsinghai and Qinghai all refer to the Kokonor area of Tibet.

Acknowledgments

The immediate origins of this book lie in a Ph.D. dissertation at the Fletcher School of Law and Diplomacy completed in 1995. However, this is not an academic treatise divorced from personal experience; rather, it is the result of a pilgrimage undertaken in 1982 in an attempt to understand and to explain, to the best of my ability, all of the factors making up the complex historical, political and moral issues of Tibet. This book has its origins in my personal experience of Tibetan culture and politics during a ten year residence in Nepal, 1971-1981. In 1982 I embarked upon a Chinese language study program at the University of Inner Mongolia at Huhehaote in order to study another "minority nationality" region of the People's Republic of China and in the hope that I might somehow be able to make my way to Tibet. I was rewarded by being in the right spot when the Chinese government began an experiment with individual travel in previously restricted areas of the PRC, including Tibet, and gave out some 150-200 individual travel permits to Tibet in 1982 on an unofficial basis (individual travel was still officially prohibited). These permits were available in only three small cities in the PRC, one of which was Huhehaote (the "Blue City" of the Mongols where the Tibetan lama Sonam Gyatso met the Mongol Altan Khan in 1789 and acquired the title Dalai Lama). I immediately availed myself of one of these permits and set out for Tibet.

I was able to spend five months in Tibet in the summer and fall of 1982, at a time when the rubble of the Cultural Revolution had hardly been cleared, but when Tibet was experiencing the beginnings of a cultural rebirth. Those few individual foreign travellers who reached Lhasa that summer (there were never more than a dozen or so at any time) experienced both a Tibetan cultural revival and a simultaneous outpouring of revelations of the sufferings and oppression of the past. I arrived in Lhasa on the very day in early July when the Panchen Lama returned for the first time since his arrest in 1964 and, along with many thousand Tibetans, I received his blessing at the Jokhang temple. Lhasa that summer and fall was the scene of a testing by Tibetans of the limits of the Chinese state's newly liberalized policies on the practice of religion and freedom of speech and association, including association with foreigners. One of my first personal contacts was with a Tibetan on the steps of the

Potala; when I asked in my halting Tibetan a simple "how are things in Lhasa," the reply was an equally simple "*rangzen mindu*," or "no freedom."

Lhasa in the summer of 1982 was unprepared for an influx of foreigners. The Chinese and Tibetan authorities had not yet developed any means of enforcement of their rules and regulations for foreigners, therefore many of us traveled to parts of Tibet not yet open to foreigners, usually to return to Lhasa to be forced to write a "self-criticism" for our illegal activities and nonconformist attitudes. I was able to make a month-long hitchhiking journey to Kham via the southern route through Batang and Litang, and return to Lhasa via the northern route through Derge and Chamdo, at a time when many monasteries still lay in ruins or were in the initial stages of reconstruction. Few Tibetans in eastern Tibet had ever seen a foreigner. I was also privileged to witness the celebration of the Ganden *Serthang*, "Golden Thanka," ceremony at the ruins of Ganden monastery outside Lhasa which Tibetans were enthusiastically reconstructing, a ceremony which Tibetans were allowed to celebrate for the first time since 1959. Lhasa was full of pilgrims from other parts of Tibet, including eastern Tibet, Kham and Amdo, allowed to visit their own holy city for the first time since 1959.

Having lived in Nepal for the previous ten years and having been closely associated with Sherpas and Tibetans, I was already aware of Tibetan political issues. My experience in Inner Mongolia had increased my understanding of Chinese minority nationality policies and provided a vision of the future the Chinese planned for Tibet (Inner Mongolia is now only some ten percent Mongol). Living in China for any period of time tends to be a life-altering experience; my experience was no exception, especially in the realization that one gains of the realities of life under a communist system, even in that relatively liberalized time in the history of the PRC. But the experience that most altered my life and set me on a path of devotion to the study of Tibetan history and politics was my five months in Tibet in 1982. One would have to be spiritually, not to mention politically, blind not to see the evidence of Chinese oppression and cultural destruction in Tibet, even under a recently introduced more liberalized regime.

Many Tibetans and even a few Chinese befriended me that summer, but one person stands out as my political guru and inspiration at that time. Dolma Yudon Tenpa, a Tibetan-American who had returned to Lhasa for the first time since 1959, one of the first exiled Tibetans to return, took me in hand with the intention of instructing me in the intricacies and the sorrows of recent Tibetan politics. Dolma's bargain was that she would reveal all that she knew and all that was told to her by her many friends and relatives if I would promise to write a book about the recent history of Tibet. I spent several months at the old Phala mansion east of the Barkor in Lhasa at the home of Dolma's sister, Sonam Choedon, and her husband, Rinchen Paljor, a master thanka painter. A constant stream of people came to visit, each with their tale of suffering under the Chinese occupation. The Public Security Police became aware of these sessions, and of the fact that they were attended by a foreigner, and came by often to investigate, but Dolma was fearless, asserting that she was an American and I was her American friend and she would have me as a guest in her house as often as she pleased. Sonam Choedon and Rinchen Paljor were more apprehensive, but both said that they had already suffered so much that they were no longer afraid. Both had been imprisoned, Rinchen being released in the early 1970s only so he could begin the restoration of monasteries, including the Jokhang and Drepung. Both were subsequently able to leave Tibet for Dharamsala where they were able to realize their dream of living in the presence of the Dalai Lama before they died.

At the end of that year Dolma took me to Dharamsala where she introduced me to Tibetan Government in Exile officials and instructed them to assist me in my endeavor. Dolma had in 1963 been the first woman in Tibetan history to be appointed to a position in the Tibetan Government (in exile) and therefore had a certain amount of authority. This book has been many years in the making but Dolma never gave up hope that I would finally complete my part of the bargain. Dolma was my source and inspiration; therefore this book is dedicated to her. I also wish to thank all the Tibetans in Dharamsala who helped me in my research and endured my endless questions, in particular my good friends and political gurus Jamyang Norbu and Tashi Tsering.

From the beginning of my quest to comprehend and explicate the intricacies of Tibetan history and politics, I believed that the issue had to be framed not only within the context of Tibetan history, Tibetan political culture and Sino-Tibetan relations but also within Chinese history and political culture, traditional Chinese frontier policies, and Marxist-Leninist-Maoist nationalities theory and policy. I also wished to put the Tibetan issue within the context of modern international law as well as human rights and self-determination in international law. Therefore I returned to academia in order to become more competent in all these subjects, not because I thought that an academic degree in Tibetan politics was ever going to mean much in the academic or political job market (as it has not). I wish to thank all of my Fletcher School professors who were amazingly supportive of my somewhat unorthodox subject, in particular Professor Uri Ra'anan, my guru on the subject of ethnic nationalism and

Marxist-Leninist nationalities policies, and Professor Alfred P. Rubin, whose knowledge of Tibet's legal status and unselfish and untiring editing of my huge and unwieldy dissertation were of immense benefit to my endeavor. I also wish to thank Professor John Curtis Perry, who provided much needed support, and Professors Hurst Hannum and Phillip Alston.

The actual writing of this book was undertaken as a six year dissertation pilgrimage during which I was the beneficiary of several friends' generosity. My pilgrimage took me first to Moose, Wyoming, where I wintered in Dr. David Peterson's cabin. Next I luxuriated in the wine country of Sonoma County, California, courtesy of Judith Weitzner and Jim and Janet Roach. Again cross-country to Martha's Vineyard for a winter courtesy of Todd Stuart and Pam Putney. Then a year at Norway, Maine, at the cabin of Mike and Mary Amato. I would also like to thank those who have encouraged and supported me over these years, first of all Gay Browning, who has encouraged me in many ways, as well as Lhazang Tsering, Lhakpa Tsering, Tashi Tsering (Lhasa), Thupten Kalsang, Tsering Shakya, Tseten Wangchuk, Jigme Ngapo, Tenzin Tethong, Lodi Gyari, Tenzin Geyshe, Sonam Topgyal, Dawa Norbu, John Ackerly, Maura Moynihan, Matthew Kapstein, Mimi Church, Ian Alsop, Kathy Peterson, Brot Coburn, Hemanta Mishra, Ward Williamson, Judith Weitzner, Don Broderson, Pam Putney, Quee Josayma, and His Holiness the Dalai Lama. I would like to thank my friends at Westview Press, particularly the late Fred Praeger, and my editors, Susan McEachern and Carol Jones. I also want to thank my mother, Elizabeth Thompson Smith, whose support has been unconditional throughout my life.

Warren W. Smith, Jr.

Geographic Preface

Environment has been of the most primary significance in the evolution of the ethnic, cultural and national identities of both China and Tibet. Many characteristics of material and social culture are determined by the necessities of environmental adaptation. Both Chinese and Tibetan cultures are very strongly defined by their unique environments and their adaptations to their respective environmental conditions; each culture is also firmly delimited by its environmental geography. As the Chinese cultural area is defined by climate and hydrology, by the area in which intensive, irrigated agriculture is possible, so the Tibetan cultural area is defined by altitude.

The most significant event in Tibetan history may have occurred some 25 million years ago at the time when the Indian subcontinent collided with Eurasia. This event, occurring rather late and very rapidly in terms of geological time, changed the geographic and climatic environment of all of Eurasia. Before this time Tibet was beneath the Tethys Sea; winds from this sea created tropical and subtropical conditions in the whole of what are now Eastern Turkestan, Mongolia, Manchuria and China.[1] The geological plate carrying the Indian subcontinent arrived at the southern boundary of the Eurasian (or Laurasian) plate during the Miocene era (13-25 million years before present) after having drifted 6,000 miles over 50 million years. By the late middle Miocene (14-18 million years before present) Tibet had emerged from the Tethys sea as a hot and wet plain.[2] By the late Miocene (13-15 million years before present) uplift of the Himalayan mountain range had begun. The rise of the Tibetan plateau prior to that of the Himalaya is evidenced by the fact that the southern edge of the plateau, not the Himalaya, forms the watershed between

---

1. Robert Orr Whyte, "Evolution of the Chinese Environment," in *The Origins of Chinese Civilization*, ed. David N. Keightley (Berkeley: University of California Press, 1983), 4.

2. Liu Tungsheng and Han Jingtai, "The Role of Qinghai-Xizang Plateau Uplifting in the Shift of Monsoon Patterns over China," in *Proceedings of Sino-Japanese Joint Scientific Symposium on the Tibetan Plateau*, ed. T. Shidei (1989), 40.

3. Ibid., 42.

India and Tibet; south-flowing rivers cut through the Himalaya on their way to join the Ganges river in India.

The plateau reached an altitude of about 1,000 meters by the late Pliocene (2-4 million years before present).[3] From the late Pliocene to the present the Tibetan plateau rose to its present average altitude of 4,000 meters. Parallel, predominantly east-west mountain ranges arose, the Kun Lun in the far north, then the Nyenchenthangla to the south, and finally the southernmost and highest range, the Himalaya. On the western edge where the greatest geologic pressure was exerted by the Indian subcontinent, the Pamir and Karakoram ranges were formed. The eastern edge of the plateau drove western China northward 5 degrees in latitude.[4] Tremendous gorges were cut by rivers flowing south, southeast and east from the southeastern edge of the plateau.

The climate of Tibet during the Pliocene era (1-13 million years before present) was tropic or subtropic and was similar to that of North China at the time.[5] By the end of the Pliocene the rise of the Himalaya had begun to affect the climate to the north.[6] The Himalaya began to block the northward advance of the heavily laden airmass of the Indian Ocean monsoon. Poleward heat transfer was also blocked, creating high pressure, low temperature weather systems in Siberia. The climate of Tibet, which, consistent with its latitude, should be sub-tropic, became a frigid alpine zone. The boundary of the subtropic zone in China shifted from 42 to 35 degrees north latitude.[7] Inner Asia gradually became the area with the greatest degree of climatic "continentality" on the planet.[8]

With the continuous increase in the altitude of the Tibetan plateau, temperature and pressure differentials also increased. Air over the plateau is greatly responsive to heat radiation because of its low density (one-half that of sea-level). In summer a stable, high temperature, low pressure system is created which combines with terrain to block moisture and heat transfer from the south. In winter a stable, low temperature, high pressure system is created that exacerbates the physical effects of the Himalaya by preventing poleward heat transfer and contributes to the development of the Siberian low pressure system. Westerly winds are divided, both by terrain and the Tibetan high pressure system, into two streams, one south of the Himalaya and one north of the Tibetan plateau. The northern stream combines with the Siberian cold high pressure to create the cold dust-laden winter and spring winds in north China.

---

4. Ibid.
5. Ibid.
6. Ibid.
7. Ibid., 45.
8. Robert N. Taaffe, "The Geographic Setting," in *The Cambridge History of Early Inner Asia*, ed. Denis Sinor (Cambridge: Cambridge University Press, 1990), 21.

Geomorphic forces of the Indian subcontinent's collision with Eurasia, plus the subsequent environmental shifts, created three primary and two secondary geographical regions. These regions have had significant influence on the development of human cultures in each area. First, of course, is the Tibetan plateau, raised some 4,000 meters on average in relation to surrounding terrain and cut off in the south and west by the Himalaya, Karakoram and Pamir ranges, in the north by the desert of Takla Makan, and in the east by tremendous parallel gorges of the Salween, Mekong, Yangtze and Yellow rivers. Only in the northeast in the Kokonor area is the plateau easily accessible.

A second ecological region delimited by the uplift of the plateau was China, now subjected to a southeastern monsoon and cold arid winds from the northwest. These environmental factors had not only climatic but geographical effects. The geography of north China was changed due to the buildup of windborne loess soils transported by the Siberian winds from the deserts and steppes of Inner Asia. There were also possible biological effects due to the impacts on plant species of the conflicting climatic regimes between North China and the steppe. China has become, like the Tibetan plateau, effectively delimited by altitude, by the plateau in the east and by the 2,000-3,000 meter elevation of the steppe to the north.

The steppe formed the third major geographical region. The rise in altitude and aridity created steppe conditions over much of Inner Asia from north of the Caspian to eastern Mongolia. The ecological characteristics of the steppe and the form of human economic adaptation therein, nomadic pastoralism, were to have profound historical effects not only in the steppe but in all adjacent regions.

Subsidiary regions created were the Gobi and Takla Makan deserts. The Takla Makan, a true shifting-dune desert, was formed from the remnants of a large inland sea which occupied the Tarim depression until it evaporated under more arid climatic conditions. The oasis agriculture of the Takla Makan separates it in an ecological and cultural sense from the surrounding steppe. The Gobi, so named for the rounded stones which litter its surface, effectively separated China from Mongolia and, like the Takla Makan, divided the steppe itself.

The Tibetan plateau, at an average altitude of 4000 meters above sea level, is set apart from all adjacent areas as a distinct geographic, ecological and cultural region. The plateau is bounded by the Himalaya on the south, the Karakoram and Kun Lun on the west, the Kun Lun, Altyn and Qilian ranges on the north, and the boundary of altitude (approximately 3,000 meters) between Chinese and Tibetan ecological and cultural zones on the east. The plateau slopes from its highest point in the west, the virtually uninhabited high altitude desert Chang Thang, "northern plain," to the forests and gorges of Sichuan and jungles of Yunnan in the southeast. Tibetans refer to areas in the west in general as *toh*, or "upper" (*Toh* is also a proper name for the upper Tsangpo, or Brahmaputra River valley) and areas to the east as *mei*, "lower." All of the major rivers of Asia have their sources in Tibet. The Indus, Ganges, Sutlej and Brahmaputra all arise in the southwestern corner of upper Tibet at the Tibetan sacred mountain Kang Rimpoche, "precious snow mountain" (Meru or Kailash of Indian mythology). The Salween, Mekong, Yangtze and Yellow rivers all arise in the central and eastern Chang Thang.

The Tibetan plateau is 2,500 kilometers from east to west and 1,200 kilometers from north to south; its area of 2.5 million square kilometers is one-fourth the current total area of the People's Republic of China, approximately equal in area to Western Europe or the Rocky Mountain states of the United States. The geography of the Tibetan plateau is very similar to that of the Rocky Mountain states with the significant difference that the Tibetan plateau is on average twice the altitude. The plateau lies at mid-latitudes, which would normally indicate a subtropical climate; instead, altitude is the dominant environmental factor and produces a frigid alpine climate.

Ecological zones of the plateau vary with increasing altitude from southeast to northwest, from alpine meadow to alpine steppe and alpine desert. Relief varies from the deeply incised valleys of the southeast to barren high altitude plains punctuated by rounded peaks of the northwestern Chang Thang. Approximately 600,000 square kilometers in the northwest are an area of internal drainage; this area exhibits an undulating and undissected surface weathered mainly by wind action and glaciation rather than by flowing water. The plateau was not covered by a continental glacier but glaciers exist in most of the highest mountain ranges and were of greater extent in the past.

Perennially frozen earth covers 2.15 million square kilometers of the plateau.[9] Almost all of the Chang Thang area is affected by permafrost. The permafrost varies from a few meters thick in southern and eastern low altitude areas to more than a hundred meters in the northwestern Chang Thang. At the Kun Lun, where the present Qinghai-Tibet highway passes, permafrost is 140 to 170 meters thick with a seasonal thaw zone of 1-4 meters. The permafrost belt in this area extends 550 km from the

---

9. Ren Mei'e, Yang Renzhang and Bao Haosheng, *An Outline of China's Physical Geography* (Beijing: Foreign Languages Press, 1985), 19.

10. Ibid., 19.

Tangula to the Kun Lun.[10] In its rise from the sea the Tibetan plateau has become increasingly arid, but the plateau is still dotted with many hundred lakes, some of great extent, now mostly salty. The lakes show evidence of Tibet's more humid past in still-visible shorelines arranged like concentric shelves around the lakes' now much reduced extent. Numerous lakes and extensive areas of alpine marsh exist, despite high aridity, because low mean temperatures produce a low evaporation rate and permafrost in many areas prevents water from penetrating the surface.

The elevation of the plateau created a climatic zone that would make it appear that it has shifted 20 degrees north in latitude compared to the same latitude areas of China. However, solar radiation is very high due to high altitude and little cloud cover. Daily variation in temperatures is large, but seasonal variation is relatively small due to low mean temperatures at all seasons. The frigid climatic zone does not prevent agriculture in all places:

> Due to the ample sunshine, big daily temperature range, intense solar radiation and increased ultraviolet and infrared rays of the solar spectrum, the accumulated temperature value on the plateau has a different meaning for crop growth from the same values in lowlands of the same latitudes. . . . Long sunshine hours, intense solar radiation and a big daily temperature range all help to promote the synthesis of hydrocarbons in crops, and the low temperature at night helps to reduce the consumption of nutrients.[11]

Each of the successive east-west mountain ranges is formed along a fault line and creates separate geological regions. The main boundary fault of the plateau in the north is along the Kun Lun-Altyn Tagh-Qilian (Ch'i-lian) ranges. Between the northern boundary fault and the southern Kun Lun are the areas that enclose Qinghai (Chinghai), the Kokonor Lake and Tsaidam, "salt marsh" area. To the south is the Tangula range that separates the headwaters of the Yangtze and Mekong from the Salween. Further south is the Kailash-Nyenchentangla range, or Transhimalaya, which lies north of the Tsangpo and forms the geological divide, and the watershed, between India and Tibet. To the south again, enclosing the Tsangpo valley and central Tibet, is the Himalaya.

The plateau may be divided into five primary geographical and ecological regions: the Mountain Desert region of the western Qilian, Alytn and northern Kun Lun ranges and the Tsaidam Basin; the Alpine Desert region of the western Chang Thang; the Alpine Grassland Region which

---

11. Ibid., 423.
12. Zhao Songqiao, *Physical Geography of China* (Beijing: Science Press, 1986), 189-197.

stretches from the Kailash-Nyenchentangla ranges through the central and eastern Chang Thang all the way to the Qilian Range in the northeast; the Alpine Forest and Alpine Meadow region of the southeast (Kham); and the Montane Shrubby Steppe and Alpine Steppe region of the Tsangpo valley (central Tibet).[12]

The Mountain Desert-Kun Lun and Tsaidam region is geologically part of the Tibetan plateau but ecologically it is a desert more akin to the Kun Lun and Tarim to the north. The Tsaidam is a temperate desert, a transition ecological zone between the plateau and the Tarim Basin to the north. From west to east, the Kun Lun range has a crest line altitude of 5,000-6,000 meters, the Alytn 3,600-4,000 meters and the Qilian 4,000-5,000 meters. The Tsaidam Basin is 850 kilometers from east to west and 250 kilometers from north to south, covering an area of 220,000 square kilometers. The basin is a geological graben, an area that has been depressed or has fallen between geologic faults. The Tsaidam Basin lies at an altitude of only 2,600-3,000 meters, lower than the plateau to the south and west; therefore, mean temperatures in the Tsaidam are much higher, rainfall is very minimal and evaporation is great. The Tsaidam is the driest area of the plateau, dominated by a salt-crust surface and salt-marshes.

The Alpine Desert region of the western Chang Thang is bounded on the south, west and north by the high 5,500-6,000 meter peaks of the Himalaya, Karakoram and Kun Lun ranges. The area is dotted with hundreds of lakes, many of large extent and almost all salty. The lake basins of the western Chang Thang are at altitudes of 3,800-5,100 meters, increasing from southeast to northwest. The region is extremely arid and cold; permafrost prevails over the entire area. In the northwest the daily mean temperature in the warmest month is only 4-6 degrees centigrade and the daily minimum temperature is always below freezing. The northwest is almost uninhabited whereas the southern zone supports animal husbandry and even some agriculture in the southwest.

The Alpine Grassland region includes all of the lower altitude Chang Thang and the grasslands of northeastern Tibet (Amdo). The region begins at the Nyenchentangla range in central Tibet and sweeps across the central and eastern Chang Thang, south of the Tsaidam and north of the Nyenchentangla, to the Kokonor lake and the Qilian range to the north. This is the grassland and nomadic pastoralist area of Tibet. The western part of this area lies at altitudes between 4,500-4,800 meters and is relatively arid; there are many lakes, mostly salty, and drainage is internal. The eastern part of this zone is at the headwaters of the Salween, Mekong, Yangtze and Yellow Rivers; it is less arid, lower in altitude and warmer than to the west. The Kokonor lake at the eastern edge of this zone lies in a basin at 3,200 meters. The Alpine Grassland zone could also be divided into eastern and western sections along the line of internal drainage. The eastern zone supports some agriculture and is better grassland than the west. In general, the fertile eastern grasslands support horses and yak, whereas the more sparse western areas support greater proportions of sheep and goats.

The Alpine Meadow and Alpine Forest region of the southeast varies in relief and altitude from the north, where relief is glacially rounded and valleys are broad treeless grasslands only a few hundred meters below mountain ridges to the southeastern edge of the plateau, where the great rivers of Southeast Asia and South China — the Salween, Mekong and Yangtze — begin their descent to the Indian Ocean and South China Sea and the valleys are deeply cut and thickly forested. The southern valleys are sometimes gorges thousands of meters below adjacent terrain. This is the Tibetan region of Kham: the local name for the area, *Chushi Gangdruk*, "four rivers and six ranges," describes it well. This region receives some moisture from both southeast and southwestern monsoons and is richly forested. Chinese botanists describe it as "one of the richest areas of alpine flora in the world."[13] Agriculture exists but is sparse, located mainly on terraces and alluvial fans; animal husbandry is more important than agriculture, existing on alpine meadows in the north and in the south in areas like Lithang.

The Montane Shrubby Steppe and Alpine Steppe area of central Tibet is the upper Tsangpo valley between the Transhimalaya and the Himalaya. This is the main agricultural area of Tibet. Sixty percent of Tibet's agriculture is in this region. The region varies in climate from the east, where the Bay of Bengal monsoon penetrates up the lower Tsangpo valley, to the west, where monsoon penetration decreases and westerly winds increase aridity. Conditions for agriculture are good; the valley is at low latitude and relatively low altitude (3,500-4,500 meters) and solar radiation is very high. In the middle Tsangpo valley 70-80 percent of rainfall occurs at night, therefore most days are clear.[14]

The plateau is divided into two main cultural ecological regions, the high altitude plains, *thang*, and the lower level valleys, *rong*. The geological boundary between the northern plain, Chang Thang, and the southern valleys is also the cultural ecological boundary within the Tibetan ecosystem. Tibetans define themselves in cultural ecological terms as either *rongpa*, those who dwell in valleys, or *drokpa*, those who dwell on the plains.[15] The *rongpa* practice mixed agriculture and animal husbandry

---

13. Ibid., 192.
14. Ibid., 193.
15. *Drok* means "grassland," therefore *drokpa* is one who lives on the grassland.

while the *drokpa* are nomadic pastoralists. Although the territorial isolation of the Tibetan plateau unites the Tibetans culturally and politically, regional divisions also separate them. Besides the *rongpa-drokpa* division, the *rongpa*, who form the majority of the population, are divided by their mountain valleys into territorially isolated units typical of mountain cultures. As a Tibetan proverb puts it: "Each valley its own language; each lama his own teaching." The word for valley in this proverb, *lung*, can mean either valley or country.

Not only the Tibetan plateau but Tibet as a culture and a nation is defined by altitude; Tibetan cultural ecology has evolved in response to and is distinguished from surrounding areas by the high altitude of the plateau. The majority of the Tibetan population inhabits an area of valleys from about 3,000 to 4,500 meters on the eastern and southern edges of the plateau. The plateau is most accessible on the northeastern edge, in the Kokonor lake area, where lower level plains merge with Inner Asian steppe and Chinese border highlands. Both Chinese border peoples and steppe nomadic tribes have penetrated the plateau from this area; the most profound ethnic and political influences upon Tibet have derived from this area. Some penetration has also been possible via the river valleys of the southeast from the jungles of Yunnan. The Himalayan border is also far from impassable; Himalayan passes are often at low altitude due to the fact that the Himalaya is not the watershed; the watershed is far to the north and rivers have cut through the Himalaya to reach the Indian Ocean to the south.

Though the Tibetan climate is harsh in the extreme, exhibiting vast daily and seasonal variations in temperature, the Tibetans consider themselves possessed of an advantageous environment: "Tibet is a region where both in summer and winter the heat and cold are minimized, and the fear of famine, beasts of prey, poisonous serpents, poisonous insects, heat and cold, is not great."[16] In relation to neighboring countries such as India, of course, summers in Tibet are pleasantly cool, and the cold of the Tibetan winters is tempered by the warmth of the sun's rays at high altitude, unimpeded by atmosphere or cloud. The awesome scale and magnificence of the Tibetan environment, and the overwhelming superiority of nature over mankind exhibited there, has had the effect of emphasizing, both in ancient Tibetan religious beliefs and in Tibetan Buddhism, a reverence for, often fear of, the spirits of nature. The severity of the environment and the nature of the ecological adaptation required to survive

---

16. Lama Tsangpo, *The Geography of Tibet*, trans. Turrell V. Wylie, Serie Orientale Roma, XXV (Roma: Instituto Italiano per il Medio ed Estremo Oriente, 1962). 54.

in that environment have led to sparse settlement, reliance upon isolated family units, and an ideology of individualism unique among the usually densely populated societies of Asia.

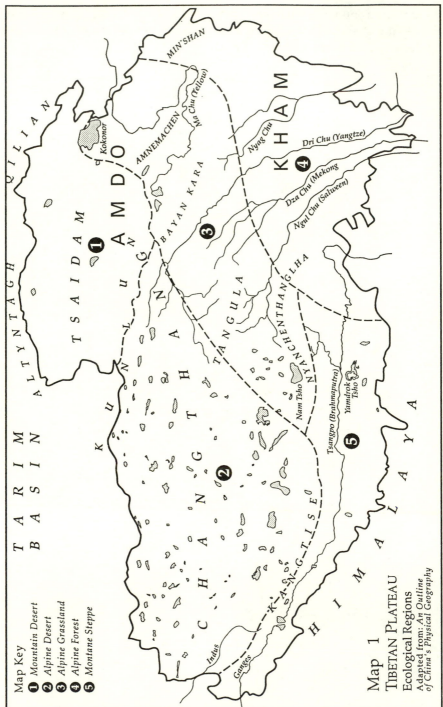

Map Key
1 Mountain Desert
2 Alpine Desert
3 Alpine Grassland
4 Alpine Forest
5 Montane Steppe

Map 1
TIBETAN PLATEAU
Ecological Regions
Adapted from: *An Outline of China's Physical Geography*

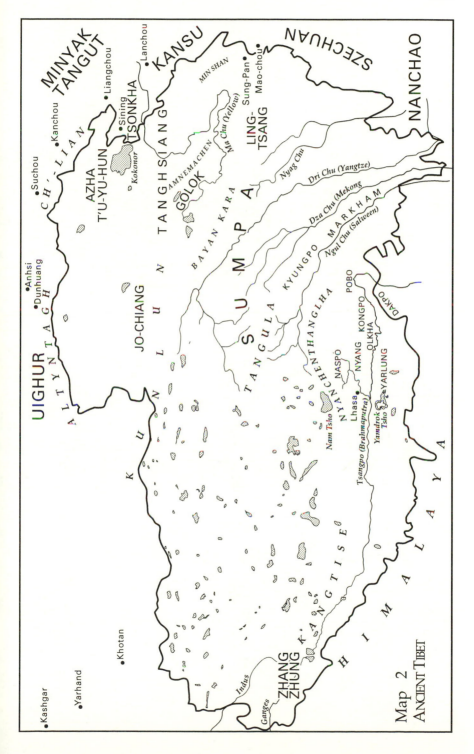

Map 2
ANCIENT TIBET

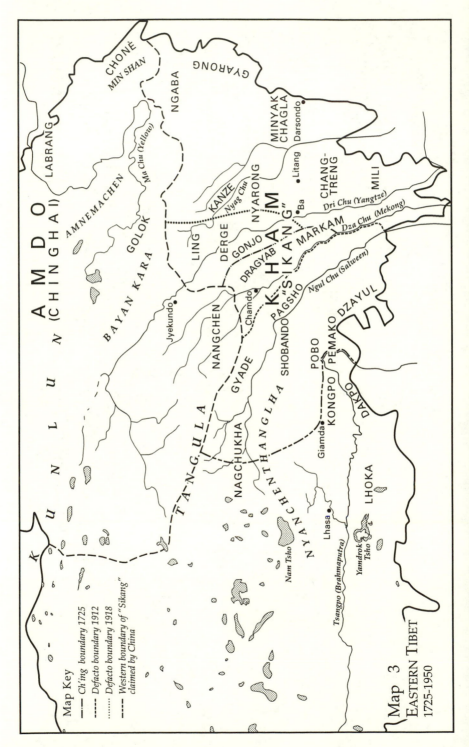

Map Key
—·— Ch'ing boundary 1725
----- Defacto boundary 1912
········· Defacto boundary 1918
—··— Western boundary of "Sikang"
          claimed by China

Map 3
EASTERN TIBET
1725-1950

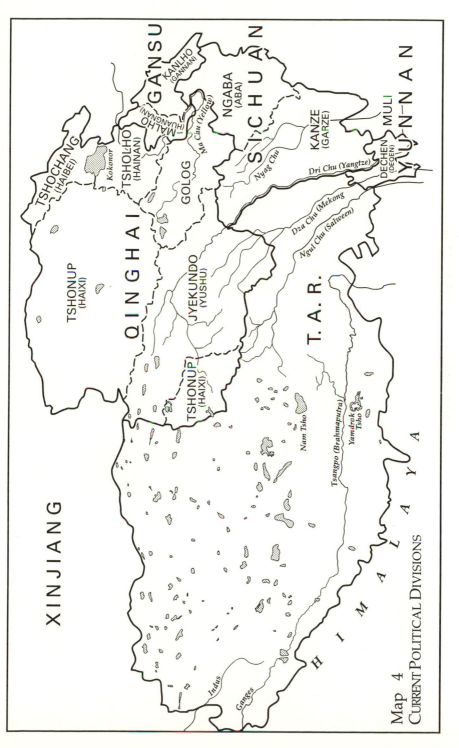

Map 4
CURRENT POLITICAL DIVISIONS

1

Tibetan Ethnic Origins and Sino-Tibetan Ethnic Relations

Tibetan Ethnic and Cultural Origins

Archaeological evidence indicates that peoples of the "Mongoloid" phenotype occupied all of North China, Mongolia and Manchuria during the Paleolithic.[1] In the south of China were peoples of the "Australoid" phenotype, although some consider the original inhabitants of south China and Indochina Southern Mongoloids.[2] The very early Mongoloids are distinguished from the modern Chinese, who are secondary or differentiated Mongoloids. Howells describes the early Mongoloid remains at the Peking Man cave site as akin to the "American Indian" phenotype.[3] The Soviet anthropologist Cheboksarov described Neolithic remains found in Kansu as preserving primary Mongoloid racial characteristics due to their isolation from the main body of the Mongoloids: "the Kansu skulls . . . preserve features peculiar to the late Paleolithic emigrants to the New World, for which reason this less differentiated form of the Mongoloid race could even be designated Americanoid."[4] Jettmar suggested that the Kansu "Americanoids" were "possibly the ancestors of the Tibetans."[5] According to this thesis, the "Americanoid," or primary Mongoloid types, continued to exist in some isolated areas in the New World, in parts of Siberia, and perhaps in Tibet, while the Chinese developed by mixture and environmental adaptations in divergence from the primary Mongoloids.[6]

---

1. Gordon T. Bowles, *The People of Asia* (New York: Charles Scribners Sons, 1977), 241. Mongoloids are considered one of the "primary races" of humanity. M.G. Levin, *Ethnic Origins of the Peoples of Northeastern Asia* (Toronto: University of Toronto Press, 1963), 44. Paleolithic is the Stone Age.
2. Levin, *Ethnic Origins*, 38.
3. W.W. Howells, "Origins of the Chinese People: Interpretations of the Recent Evidence," in *The Origins of Chinese Civilization*, ed. David N. Keightley (Berkeley: University of California Press, 1983), 301.
4. Karl Jettmar, "The Origins of Chinese Civilization: Soviet Views," in *The Origins of Chinese Civilization*, 220.
5. Ibid., 222.
6. Howells, "Origins of the Chinese People," 315.

Archaeological evidence indicates that a common Neolithic culture pervaded the area of northern China, Inner Asia and Mongolia. Originally uniform cultures of China and Inner Asia eventually differentiated in response to differing ecological conditions. In China, agriculture evolved into an intensive irrigated form. In the steppe, mixed agriculture and animal husbandry evolved into nomadic pastoralism. The first known Chinese agrarian culture was that of Yang-shao, which flourished in the loess region of the Yellow River valley from 5000-3000 B.C.[7] The Yang-shao culture was mainly concentrated in the area of loess soils in the bend of the Yellow River, where the river turns east toward the sea, and along the Wei tributary of the Yellow River in the west.

In *Archaeology of Ancient China*, Kwang-chih Chang states that the late Yang-shao culture of China spread as far to the west as the T'ao valley of Kansu and led to a subdivision known as the Kansu culture (3000-1850 B.C.). Geographically, Kansu is on the ecological frontier between the plains of China and the steppes of Inner Asia. Chang indicates that the Kansu culture may have received cultural influences from the northwest: "the Yang-shao stage in Kansu and eastern Chinghai [Kokonor] seems to have been gradually replaced by several new cultures whose origins remain unclear but which seem to have some sort of connection with the sub-Neolithic and possibly Neolithic peoples to the north and west in the steppe regions."[8] The peoples of Kansu, known as the Ch'i-chia culture (approx. 2150-1780 B.C.), were "possibly of a different ethnic strain and probably of a distinct cultural tradition."[9] Jaroslav Prusek emphasizes that while the Kansu cultures were probably related to Yang-shao, they preserved their neolithic forms of economy while the Shang developed in China: "Kansu was probably beyond the influence of the mature bronze culture of dynastic Shang."[10]

Some of the Neolithic peoples to the northwest of the Kansu culture were of probable Indo-European origins: "In the third millennium proto-Indo-Europeans were stretched all along the present political boundaries of China and perhaps even farther to the east." An ancient and fundamental language boundary between China and Inner Asia is apparent, indicating the existence of a foreign ethnic group on the northern border of China. Archaeological research in the Tarim Basin in the twentieth century revealed that the Indo-European Tocharian language was spoken

7. Kwang-chih Chang, *The Archaeology of Ancient China* (New Haven: Yale University Press, 1977), 119.

8. Ibid., 194.

9. Ibid., 398.

10. Jaroslav Prusek, *Chinese Statelets and the Northern Barbarians in the Period 1400-300 B.C.* (New York: Humanities Press, 1971), 71.

there at least from the early centuries A.D. Tocharian is considered an archaic Indo-European language that separated at a very early date from common Indo-European and was later subjected to "very considerable isolation and contact with non-Indo-European languages."[11]

These people of the Tarim, who referred to themselves as Tukhara, were in Chinese sources known as Yueh-chih.[12] The Yueh-chih were known to reside in the area between Dunhuang, at the eastern terminus of the Tarim, and the Ch'i-lian (Qilian or Nan Shan) mountain range, northeast of Kokonor.[13] The earliest Chinese historical references place them there as early as 1000 B.C., and definitely by the 3rd century B.C.[14] The Chinese describe them as nomadic, and the dominant power in the western steppes until the second century B.C.

Pulleyblank discussed the possibility that the Yueh-chih may be identified with the Ch'i-chia or successor cultures:

> When we know more about the prehistoric archaeology of the city-states of the Tarim we may be in a better position to tell whether it would be possible to identify as Tocharian the Ch'i-chia culture in Kansu and Chinghai. . . . Certainly it should ultimately be possible to identify the Yueh-chih either with some of the descendants of the Ch'i-chia culture or with some as yet undiscovered archaeological remains in those regions.[15]

The Yueh-chih territory lay to the west and adjacent to the territory of the Kansu cultures, but indefinite dates for the Yueh-chih prevent any certainty about cultural contacts between the Yueh-chih and the Kansu cultures. However, the Yueh-chih would definitely have come into contact with the successors of the early Kansu cultures. Successors to the Ch'i-chia in Kansu were several contemporary or overlapping cultures that Kwang-chih Chang indicates were not related to the proto-Chinese Yang-shao culture though they "might have been influenced by that culture." The burial customs of one of these cultures, the Ssu-wa, "indicate that the Ssu-wa-shan people were not Han Chinese but were possibly the Ch'iang recorded in Chinese annals."[16]

---

11. E.G. Pulleyblank, "Chinese and Indo-Europeans," in *Journal of the Royal Asiatic Society*, 1966, 15.

12. A.K. Narain, *On the First Indo-Europeans: The Tokharian-Yuezhi and their Chinese Homeland* (Bloomington: Indiana University, 1987), 2.

13. Pulleyblank believes that Ch'i-lian is a Yueh-chih word meaning "Heavenly Mountains." Pulleyblank, "Chinese and Indo-Europeans," 20.

14. A.K. Narain, "Indo-Europeans in Inner Asia," in *The Cambridge History of Early Inner Asia*, ed. Denis Sinor (Cambridge: Cambridge University Press, 1990), 155.

15. Pulleyblank, "Chinese and Indo-Europeans," 29.

16. Kwang-chih Chang, *Archeology of Ancient China*, 406.

The Ch'iang were known to the Chinese as early as the Shang dynasty (ca. 1700-1050 B.C.). Ch'iang appears as an "ethnic" name on the Shang oracle bones.[17] The name Ch'iang is composed of the characters for "sheep" and "man," meaning "shepherds." Pulleyblank states that the *Shuo-wen* identifies the Ch'iang as belonging to the Western Jung: "it makes good sense on a number of grounds to identify Jung as the general name for non-Chinese Tibeto-Burmans, including the Ch'iang and Ti, of Chou times."[18] Prusek tells us that "the Shang were constantly at war with the Ch'iang." The Ch'iang allied with the Western Chou (1122-771 B.C.) to overthrow the Shang. Ch'iang clans were rewarded by the Chou with titles and fiefs.[19]

There were more than 150 Ch'iang tribes; one tribe, named the Great Tsang-i, in Shu (Szechuan), was reported in A.D. 94 to have a population of over half a million. The Ch'iang peoples were shepherds but kept a variety of livestock, including oxen, horses, sheep, donkeys and camels.[20] The Ch'iang engaged in mixed agriculture and animal husbandry in areas of eastern Kansu until they were forced out of these lands by the Chinese. The earliest territory of the Ch'iang was described as bounded on the north by the Nan Shan (the Ch'i-lian or Qilian Shan, south of the Kansu corridor), and on the south by the Min Shan (on the current Qinghai-Kansu-Sichuan border).[21] Later, the Ch'iang were reported all along the western frontier of China: "While the largest single concentration was probably in the high plains of Chinghai and Tibet, individual groups were also scattered throughout the Western Regions, Kansu, Yunnan, and Szechuan."[22]

The Ch'iang tribes were notoriously fractious and disunited; they had "neither established a lord-vassal relationship nor developed a system of control and solidarity among themselves."[23] However, the importance of the Ch'iang to the Chinese was magnified in the 3rd century B.C. by the

---

17. E.G. Pulleyblank, "The Chinese and their Neighbors in Prehistoric and Early Historical Times," in *The Origins of Chinese Civilization*, 419. An ethnic group, or ethny, is usually defined as a group with actual or subjective belief in common kinship. A nation is a politically conscious ethny, possessed of territory (or territorial memory) and history. An ethny is a social category, whereas a nation has become a political entity.

18. Ibid.

19. Prusek, *Chinese Statelets and Northern Barbarians*, 38.

20. Yu Ying-shih, "Han Foreign Relations," in *The Cambridge History of China: The Chin and Han Empires*, ed. Denis Twitchett and Michael Loewe (Cambridge: Cambridge University Press, 1966), 422.

21. Rafe de Crespigny, "The Ch'iang Barbarians and the Empire of Han: A Study in Frontier Policy," in *Papers on Far Eastern History* (Canberra: The Australian National University, Department of Far Eastern History, 1977), 4.

22. Yu, "Han Foreign Relations," 422.

23. Ibid., 423.

appearance of the first political confederation of true steppe nomads under the leadership of the Hsiung-nu. The Ch'iang had some political relations with the Hsiung-nu, either because they were forced to submit to the Hsiung-nu or perhaps because they found they had greater cultural affinities with the Hsiung-nu than with the Han.[24] Alliance, or the potential for alliance, between the Hsiung-nu and the Ch'iang constituted the greatest threat to the Han dynasty.

The territorial proximity of early Chinese cultures and the Ch'iang indicate probable cultural affiliations. The Ch'iang may well have had some ethnic affiliations with the early Chinese but evidence does not permit any definitive conclusions. Other ethnic origins or influences on the Ch'iang are also possible. The Ch'iang are only very uncertainly identified with any of the Neolithic cultures of this area even though the Ch'iang appear in Chinese records in this area from a time contemporary with the later Kansu cultures. It must be remembered that the Chinese were unspecific about their barbarian neighbors, all the tribes to the west were "Jung," or "Ch'iang," both generic names. In the opinion of Pulleyblank:

> By the Later Han, there were certainly Tibeto-Burman peoples stretching all along the western side of what is now Szechuan province. The *Hou Han shu* [Later Han Annals] classifies them as separate branches of the Ch'iang which descended from the same ancestor as the primary group of Ch'iang in the upper reaches of the Huang Ho.

> If, as Chinese historians suggest, these southern Ch'iang tribes of the Han period were comparatively recent immigrants from farther north, one might conjecture that during Shang times Tibeto-Burmans had not penetrated much south of the watershed of the Huang Ho. If this is the correct picture, it further suggests that, looking back to still earlier times, we could find the heartland of the Sino-Tibetan peoples as a whole in the Yang-shao Neolithic, the Chinese being an easterly branch that evolved in the Central Plain.[25]

The Soviet anthropologist Kirukov favored a similar scenario:

> At the end of the fifth and the beginning of the fourth millennia B.C., a developed middle Neolithic, painted pottery, Yang-shao culture came into being in the Wei basin. This Neolithic population can probably be regarded as a branch of the tribes speaking Sino-Tibetan languages. In the fourth millennium B.C., the area of Neolithic culture that had emerged in the Wei valley expanded considerably. . . . Two groups of the population appeared; one

---

24. Ibid., 424.
25. Pulleyblank, "Chinese and Their Neighbors," 423.

was shifting to the east, the other to the west. The first while moving along the Huang Ho . . . laid the foundation for the shaping of the Shang (Yin) community. . . . The group of Yang-shao tribes that had spread west in the fourth millennium underwent further differentiation. One of its branches, which had come to the upper reaches of the Huang Ho (the present province of Kansu), later became known as Ch'iang (or Jung), whereas another branch became the backbone of the Chou.[26]

Owen Lattimore has described the process of cultural differentiation and assimilation whereby some of the Ch'iang became Tibetans while others became Chinese:

> The term *Ch'iang* or *Chiang*, written in a way that indicates the meaning "shepherd," is an old generic designation for non-Chinese tribes of the Kansu-Tibetan border. It appears probable that out of the early barbarians of this region, who were not yet true mounted nomads and probably had a mixed economy of herding, hunting, farming, and the gathering of wild plants, some were incorporated and "converted" into Chinese and some were crowded over to the north and northwest, up to the Kansu-Tibetan border. The general term Ch'iang was applied to those who withdrew to the uplands of Tibet, where some of them kept up at least a partial practice of agriculture in the border valleys, while others took to a pastoral nomadism comparable to that of the steppe.[27]

The Ch'iang and Tibeto-Burman languages are generally thought to be related. According to Pulleyblank, the words to a song in the native language of one of the Ch'iang groups of the Later Han period, transcribed in Chinese characters together with a Chinese translation, can be identified as Tibeto-Burman.[28] Gordon Bowles found similarities between Ch'iang languages and archaic Tibetan.[29] The language of the modern Ch'iang is classified as Tibeto-Burman.[30]

Tibeto-Burman is generally regarded as a branch of the Sino-Tibetan language family. Pulleyblank maintains that the relationship is clear, although he admits some uncertainty about the strength of the connections:

---

26. Kirukov, quoted in Jettmar, "Origins of Chinese Civilization," 224.

27. Owen Lattimore, *Inner Asian Frontiers of China* (American Geographical Society, 1940; Oxford: Oxford University Press, 1988), 215.

28. Pulleyblank, "Chinese and Their Neighbors," 422.

29. Gordon Bowles, "Racial Origins of the Peoples of the Central Chinese-Tibetan Border" (Ph.D. diss., Harvard University, 1935), 300.

30. Ma Yin, ed., *China's Minority Nationalities* (Beijing: Foreign Languages Press, 1989), 220-333. Many of the peoples of southwest China (Yunnan), Burma, Assam, Nepal and northern India speak Tibeto-Burman languages.

By common consent, the language family to which Chinese is most likely to be genetically related is Tibeto-Burman. Indeed, such a connection is regarded as well established by most scholars, even if there is still much disagreement about details. The primary evidence for such a genetic relation is provided by shared items of basic vocabulary. One can readily list a few dozen obvious cognates between Chinese, Burmese, and Tibetan. . . . Moreover, the phonetic correspondences are in many cases not so simple and transparent as to lead to a suspicion of borrowing . . . [but] the number of generally agreed upon cognates between Chinese and the other languages of the family remains fairly modest.[31]

However, some Tibetologists are skeptical of any but the most remote connections between Chinese and Tibetan. Beckwith describes attempts to force Tibetan into a "Sino-Tibetan family" of languages as predominantly due to "contemporary political-racial considerations":

The Tibetan verbal system is strongly reminiscent of Germanic tongues, but the language exhibits systematically entrenched proto-Indo-Iranian vocabulary. Together, these features indicate a relationship with the divergent "Indo-European" group, but the agglutinative grammatical structure, among other features (especially of modern spoken Tibetan), indicates a relationship with languages of the convergent "Altaic" group. Vocabulary and some other features do indicate a probable relationship of some sort with Burmese. Any divergent relationship with Chinese is unlikely— although still conceivable for the remotest prehistoric past.[32]

Certain themes of Tibetan and Ch'iang mythology indicate cultural contacts or possibly common ethnic origins. In Tibetan mythology, the earliest tribes are referred to as *mi'u*, a name that in its present form means "dwarf" or "little man," but which Stein suggests came from a Chinese term, "mi-hou," denoting the monkeys from whom the ancient Ch'iang were said to be descended.[33] The ethnonym of the modern Ch'iang of Szechuan, whom Stein agrees can be identified with the ancient Ch'iang, is *me*, *mi* or *ma*. *Mi* is the common word in Tibeto-Burman languages for "man."[34] Ch'iang and Tibetans share the belief in their descent from a monkey ancestor, whose name in the Ch'iang language is *mi* or *mu*, and in Tibetan is *mu*. The Tibetan for the sky-cord by

31. Pulleyblank, "Chinese and their Neighbors," 416.

32. Christopher Beckwith, *The Tibetan Empire in Central Asia: A History of the Struggle for Great Power among Tibetans, Turks, Arabs, and Chinese during the Early Middle Ages* (Princeton: Princeton University Press, 1987), 5.

33. R.A. Stein, *Tibetan Civilization*, trans. J.E. Stapleton Driver (London: Faber and Faber, 1972), 46.

34. Stein, "Les K'iang des Marches Sino-Tibetaines," unpublished paper, 4.

which the ancient Tibetan ancestral kings descended is *mu*, and the name *phya* means "sky god." Stein compares this to the Ch'iang *mu-pia* for "sky."[35] Stein claims that the link between the ancient Ch'iang and Tibetans via the monkey legend is well established. This is especially true, he maintains, because the monkey is indigenous to the areas from whence the Ch'iang derived, but not in central Tibet.[36] The Ch'iang and Tibetans also share the tradition of the use of sheep in ritual sacrifice and a correspondence of words relating to the sheep sacrifice ritual.[37]

Stein mentioned other probable connections between the Ch'iang and the Tibetans: "From the seventh century onward Chinese historians associate these people (the Ch'iang) with monumental stone structures, like towers or fortresses, which are still often found among them, but are also to be seen in Kongpo and Lhotrak, and are apparently the prototypes of Tibetan architecture in general."[38] All of the Tibeto-Burman peoples occupy areas of similar ecological character in the middle altitude valleys of the eastern, southeastern and southern edges of the Tibetan plateau.[39]

Although the peoples known as Ch'iang may tentatively be identified as an early component of the Tibetan ethnic mixture, they were not necessarily the earliest inhabitants of the Tibetan plateau. Tibetan legends indicate that there were indigenous peoples of the central valleys of Tibet who regarded the Ch'iang as foreigners. The early Tibeto-Burmans displaced, in their southward movement, peoples known as Mon:

> Tibetan tradition indiscriminately calls Mon the populations which Tibetans met with on their way, as they expanded southward and westward. Mon is, of course, a general term, applied to populations of various languages and descent; it is therefore difficult to investigate what ethnical groups may be hidden under this name.[40]

> Mon may be the same word as the Chinese Man which was used for all the barbarians to the south. The Chinese also mention that the Man inhabit areas of the Sino-Tibetan border.[41]

The Mon are identified by some as peoples of the Austro-Asiatic, Mon-Khymer race who inhabited southern China and South-east Asia. Thomas maintains that they were non-Ch'iang Tibeto-Burmans.[42]

---

35. Ibid., 12.

36. Ibid., 5.

37. Ibid., 13.

38. Stein, *Tibetan Civilization*, 29.

39. Bowles, "Chinese-Tibetan Border," 304.

40. Guiseppi Tucci, *Tibetan Painted Scrolls* (Rome: La Libreria dello Stato, 1949), 6.

41. Stein, *Tibetan Civilization*, 35.

42. F.W. Thomas, *Nam: An Ancient Language of the Sino-Tibetan Borderland, Publications of the Philological Society*, XIV (London: Oxford University Press, 1948), 66.

Pulleyblank mentions that "there is good historical evidence that the Yangtze region was non-Chinese in language and was only drawn into the circle of Chinese culture during the first millennium B.C." For example, he points out that the name of the Yangtze, *chiang*, is cognate with the Mon word for river: "The etymology of this word now definitely points to the original non-Chinese language having had Mon-Khymer affinities."[43] Bowles links these Mon with the Mon population of Assam and Burma and with the Mon-Khymer.[44] According to Chakravarti, "It is evident from the traditions, place names and legends that the Mons held considerable influence in the southern Himalayas before the immigration of the Tibetans and other races."[45]

The extent of settlement of the Mon in Tibet is not known. However, based on what is known of their very early inhabitation of Himalayan areas, it is possible that they were the earliest inhabitants of the southeastern and southern Tibetan plateau. In some sources, the Mon are described as carpenters and smiths who spread among the Ch'iang as craftsmen.[46] Their speciality as carpenters may be evidence that they were inhabitants of the forested areas on the fringes of the Tibetan plateau. They are known from such areas in Szechuan; their presence in contiguous areas in Kham and further west in Pobo and Kongpo seems possible if not probable. Tibetan scholars associate the Mon with the earliest Tibetan states of Kongpo, Pobo and Dakpo.[47] The Mon can reliably be identified as a population who were encountered, displaced, and to some extent absorbed by those migrants from the north who were to become the Tibetans. The Mon can be included with some certainty in the list of ethnic groups that contributed to the ethnic identity of the Tibetans.

Early Indo-European additions to the population of Tibet are also probable. The Tocharians or Yueh-chih were on the borders of the Tibetan plateau from as early as the beginning of the second millennium B.C.; their penetration into the northern and northeastern regions of the plateau is very possible. The plateau is most accessible at the northeastern corner; migration of nomads with their animals is easily accomplished from the Tarim via the Dunhuang area and from the Ch'i-lian mountain region via the Kokonor lake area. The Yueh-chih may have had

43. Pulleyblank, "Chinese and Indo-Europeans," 10.

44. Bowles, *People of Asia*, 190.

45. B. Chakravarti, *A Cultural History of Bhutan* (Chittaranjan, West Bengal: Hilltop Publishers, 1979), 4.

46. Thomas, *Nam*, 151.

47. Tashi Tsering, personal communication, Dharamsala, 1990.

an important ethnic influence on the Ch'iang. Chinese sources indicate that some of the Yueh-chih, the "Little Yueh-chih," migrated into the Ch'i-lian area in the second century B.C. and "settled among the Ch'iang."[48]

As a final candidate for the title of the earliest Tibetans, the "American Indian" impressional type observed in eastern Tibet must be mentioned. Anthropologists who have had access to Tibet usually distinguish two main impressional types: one of slight build, spread throughout Tibet, and the other, of taller build, typical of Kham.[49] The ethnic origins of these tall eastern Tibetans have been the subject of much speculation. As R. A. Stein has written, "The predominant strain in most cases is Mongoloid, but many travelers have been struck by the prevalence of what they describe as a 'Red Indian' type." These are only subjective impressional types; nevertheless, "it is obvious that different types exist and that different populations have occupied various parts of Tibet in the course of history."[50]

The only anthropometric survey that has been conducted in Tibet was that of the American anthropologist Gordon Bowles, who measured many of the people of the Sino-Tibetan frontier in eastern Kham in 1930. According to Bowles, the "Plains Indian" type forms "upwards of ten percent of the population of the eastern Tibetans," and also appears strongly among the Ch'iang of the Sino-Tibetan border zone. Bowles found a wide variety of Mongoloid traits among the Tibetans he measured:

> The epicalantic fold is considered a distinctly mongoloid characteristic. Accepting this premise, the Chinese of whom 90% have some degree internal fold are the closest to the typical mongoloid norm. The Ch'iang and Gyarong are strikingly alike and average 80%, while in Minya and Bawang the percentage reaches approximately 62%. Dawo and the Eastern Tibetans average the relatively low figure of 53%. More significant are the figures for the complete eyefold. The Chinese, Ch'iang and Gyarong average over 44%, Minya and Bawang over 18%, and the Eastern Tibetans 8%. Dawo reaches the low extreme of 2.56%.[51]

The low incidence of Mongoloid traits in eastern Tibet may be taken as evidence of early Mongoloid influence (the "typical" epicalantic fold is actually a relatively modern evolution),[52] or of some early non-Mongoloid, perhaps Indo-European, ethnic influence. This type may or may not be identical with the Ch'iang.

48. F. W. Thomas, *Ancient Folk Literature from North-Eastern Tibet*, (Berlin: Akademie Verlag, 1957), 6.
49. Bowles, "Chinese-Tibetan Border," 307.
50. Stein, *Tibetan Civilization*, 27.
51. Bowles, "Chinese-Tibetan Border," 307.
52. Ibid.

The ethnic identity of the plateau has also been significantly influenced by relatively modern migrations of peoples of Mongolian ethnicity (as distinguished from the Mongoloid phenotype). The Hsien-pi Tu-yu-hun settled in the Ch'i-lian area in the early fourth century, later moving to the south, displacing and absorbing Ch'iang tribes. Many Hsien-pi tribes followed, becoming dominant in Kansu and northeastern Tibet.[53] Substantial migrations of Mongol tribes to the northeastern plateau began during the period of the Mongol empire in the 13th century and increased upon the fall of the Mongol dynasty in China in the 14th century. Later conflicts between Mongol tribes forced many to seek refuge in the Kokonor area of northeastern Tibet. These Mongols, with a few exceptions, have been Tibetanized in language and culture. The overall influence of peoples of Mongol ethnicity has been relatively large, continuing from the fourth century until the eighteenth.

The Tibetanized Mongols of northern Tibet are referred to by Tibetans as Hor or Sok, both of which originally referred to Uighurs.[54] The more recent Mongol migrants to the plateau are known as Sok, a name which has come to refer to Mongols and to Mongolia (Sok), but which "seems to be derived from that of the ancient Sogdians (*Sog-dag* in early Tibetan)."[55] However, the name Hor has also come to be used to refer to almost all of the northern nomads. It is most likely that the vast majority of the nomads to whom the name Hor or Sok is now applied are the descendants of the Mongol tribes who migrated to the plateau after the fall of the Mongol Yuan dynasty (1260-1368) and during the early Manchu Ch'ing dynasty (1644-1912). The five Hor states of Kham apparently derive from the time of Kubilai Khan, not from the armies of Chingghis Khan as is sometimes claimed. The designation Hor derives from a Mongol prince who propagated a lineage in the area, but apparently does not represent a significant Mongol ethnic addition or designation.[56]

---

53. Gabriella Mole, *The T'u-Yu-Hun from the Northern Wei to the Time of the Five Dynasties* (Roma: Instituto Italiano per Il Medio ed Estremo Oriente, 1970), xii.

54. Stein, *Tibetan Civilization*, 34; "Mi-Nag et Si-Hia," *Bulletin Ecole Francaise d'Extreme Orient XLIV* (1951), 252. The Uighurs of Kanchou were absorbed in the Tangut kingdom in 1028. Rene Grousset, *The Empire of the Steppes: A History of Central Asia*, trans. Naomi Walford (New Brunswick: Rutgers University Press, 1970), 125. The Tangut state was destroyed by the Mongols under Chinggis Khan in 1227. Many Tanguts fled to Tibet, settling in the southeastern Kham and western Tsang areas, but the majority of these were the originally proto-Tibetan Minyak, by which name they are still known. Some Uighur may have been part of this migration, but otherwise there are no recorded instances or any reason to suggest the likelihood of any Uighur migrations to Tibet.

55. Stein, *Tibetan Civilization*, 34.

56. Elliot Sperling, "Some Remarks on Sga A-gnyan Dam-pa and the Origins of the Hor-pa Lineage of the Dkar-mdzes Region," in *Tibetan History and Language* (Wien: Arbeitskreis fur Tibetische und Buddhistische Studien Universitat Wien, 1991), 455.

Mythology of Tibetan Origins

Tibetan mythological sources speak of four or six original tribes of Tibet. The four tribes which appear in most sources, and to whom precedence is usually given, are the Don (*lDon*), Ton (*sTon*), Se and Mu (*rMu*).[57] Stein suggests that two additional tribes in some lists may indicate lateral branches of tribes or perhaps tribes more peripheral to central Tibet than the other four.[58] Even though these tribes are referred to as the "original" tribes, they are also spoken of as foreign, implying that they were not the indigenous populations of central Tibet, but rather those that migrated there and absorbed the indigenous peoples.[59] Each of these tribes is also associated with states foreign to the central Tibetan state, and they are often referred to in that connection: Don with Minyak; Ton with Sumpa; Se with Azha, and Mu with Zhangzhung.[60]

The Don tribe has a certain primacy; only the Don appear in all the lists of tribes in the texts that Stein examined. The Don are referred to as the ancestors of the Tibetan royal families, although they are also described as non-Tibetan.[61] Both Thomas and Stein came to the conclusion that the name Don referred in a generic sense to many of the tribes of the Sino-Tibetan frontier, similar to the Chinese use of the name Ch'iang for some of the perhaps same tribes.[62] The Don inhabited the northern plains (Chang Thang), from Kham to Zhangzhung.[63]

The mythological ancestry of the Don, as revealed in the Dunhuang manuscripts, indicates origins in the area east of the Yellow River gorges (the south to north course of the river in what is now Qinghai (Chinghai)), in the ancient land known as Nam or Skyi.[64] This country was bounded on the west and north by the Ma Chu (Yellow River), on the east by the T'ao River of Kansu, and to the south by the Jupar mountains (Min Shan).[65] *Ma*, the name of the Don ancestral deity is found in the Ma Chu and the mountain near its source that is considered to be the residence of the ancestral deity, Amne Machen.[66] This is also the area that the Chinese indicate as the original home of the Ch'iang.[67]

---

57. R. A. Stein, *Les Tribus Anciennes des Marches Sino-Tibetaines* (Paris: Imprimerie Nationale, 1959), 4; Eric Haarh, *The Yar-Lun Dynasty* (Kobenhavn: G.E.C. GAD's Forlag, 1969), 281.
58. Stein, *Les Tribus*, 17.
59. Ibid., 28, 40.
60. Ibid., 4. Haarh, 281.
61. Stein, *Les Tribus*, 4, 20, 64.
62. Thomas, *Nam*, 137; Stein, *Les Tribus*, 40.
63. Thomas, *Nam*, 32.
64. Ibid., 38; Stein, *Les Tribus*, 35.
65. Thomas, *Ancient Folk Literature*, 4.
66. Thomas, *Nam*, 1.
67. Ibid., 57.

Thomas says that the ancient texts mention the *Nam-pa Ldon*, (Don of Nam).[68] Stein indicates that the association of the Tibetan name *khrom* with the Nam, as *Nam-khrom*, may link the Nam, and therefore the Don, with the Ch'iang tribe known to the Chinese as Pailan. Both *Pai* in Chinese and *khrom* in Tibetan mean "white."[69] Thomas states that the territory of Nam "from about the middle of the 6th century had been advanced southward, under a Tanghsiang organization, so as to embrace the whole upper valley of the *Rma-chu* as far as its sources. This Ch'iang tribe can therefore be identified as the same as, or related to, the Don."[70]

Tanghsiang is the Chinese name for the Ch'iang tribe located to the east of Kokonor that formed a unified kingdom in Amdo in the sixth century, perhaps, as Thomas suggests, in response to pressure from the Tu-yu-hun.[71] The Tanghsiang apparently united several Ch'iang tribes, including the Pailan and Tangchang,[72] and controlled the territory of Amdo to the south of the Kokonor.[73] Tibetan texts of the seventh century refer to this area as Minyak.[74] Mythology of origins of the Minyak locates them in the area to the northeast of Kokonor, in Tsonkha and perhaps even as far as the northern slopes of the Ch'i-lian mountains in the Kansu Corridor.[75]

The Ton are first located in northern Kham and the grasslands of the Chang Thang from Amdo to the far west. Stein states that the Ton were related to the Sumpa, who are identified as the Ch'iang tribe known as *Sou-p'i* to the Chinese.[76] According to Hoffman, the Sumpa spoke a Tibeto-Burmese language.[77] Haarh states that "The Sum-pa . . . were named Su-p'i by the Chinese, and they lived in two main groups, one to the east and north of Central Tibet, at the western frontier of China, the other to the west, toward the Pamir . . . . They formed two states, which were characterized by a matriarchal constitution, for which reason the Chinese called them the Woman States."[78]

---

68. Ibid., 137.
69. Stein, *Les Tribus*, 40.
70. Thomas, *Nam*, 137.
71. Ibid., 28.
72. According to Bushell, based upon his translations of chapters relating to Tibet in the T'ang Annals, the Pailan, known as the Ting Ling to the Tibetans, were a tribe in Amdo to the south of the Kokonor who were said to be similar in customs to the Tanghsiang. The Tangchang are often mentioned by the Han as one of the prominent tribes of the Ch'iang. F.W. Bushell, "The Early History of Tibet from Chinese Sources," *Journal of the Royal Asiatic Society, New Series*, 12 (1980), 528.
73. Thomas, *Nam*, 29.
74. Stein, "Mi-nag et Si-hia," 228.
75. Ibid., 225, 231.
76. Stein, *Les Tribus*, 42.
77. Hellmut Hoffman, "Early and Medieval Tibet," in *The Cambridge History of Early Inner Asia*, 375.
78. Haarh, 347.

The Sumpa were located around Nagchukha in north-central Tibet in T'ang times and were known as the largest tribe on the northern plateau. They were located even as far west as Khotan.[79] The Sumpa are particularly associated with the yak.[80] Ironwork was the distinctive attribute of the Sumpa.[81] After their submission to the Tibetans, the Sumpa were assigned to guard the eastern frontier in Minyak, northeast of Kokonor, facing China.[82] In this way the Ton Sumpa most likely became mixed with the Don Minyak.[83]

The Se tribe is associated with Azha, the Tibetan name for the Tu-yu-hun. The Tu-yu-hun were a proto-Mongol Hsien-pi tribe that in the second century left their homelands in the Liao river area of southern Manchuria and, after travelling to the west, settled in the Yin (Ch'i-lian) Mountains, north of Kokonor.[84] Between 307 and 313, they are known to have moved to the south where they encountered Ch'iang tribes.[85] Hoffman says that "the Ch'iang of northeast Tibet, including the Kokonor region, came under the rule of a Hsien-pi group whose dynasty called itself A-ch'ai (found in Tibetan literature as A-zha) and the state was called Tu-yu-hun."[86]

Thomas thinks that the name Azha may be that of the tribes absorbed by the Tu-yu-hun, and that they may be the same as the Jo-Ch'iang, who are known as a prominent tribe of the Tsaidam area as far north as Dunhuang and Khotan in the period before the arrival of the Tu-yu-hun, but whose name disappears thereafter.[87] In another context, the Jo-Sumpa (*Mjo-sum-pa*) are mentioned, which may imply that the Jo tribe were Sumpa, or related to the Sumpa, or it may be an example of the interrelationships of all of the northern nomadic tribes.[88] The Tibetan names Se and Azha may then refer to these Ch'iang tribes that were partly absorbed by the Tu-yu-hun, rather than to the Hsien-pi Tu-yu-hun themselves. The Jo-Ch'iang, Se or Azha of this area likely absorbed some of the Little Yueh-chih who migrated to this area in the second century B.C.

Stein is of the opinion that the Se must be related to Se-hu, ancestor

79. Stein, *Les Tribus*, 42.
80. Haarh, 300.
81. Stein, *Les Tribus*, 44.
82. Stein, *Les Tribus*, 43; *Tibetan Civilization*, 31.
83. Stein, *Les Tribus*, 43.
84. Grousset, *Empire of the Steps*, 39, 61.
85. Mole, *T'u-Yu-Hun*, xii.
86. Hoffman, "Early and Medieval Tibet," 373.
87. Thomas, *Nam*, 45.
88. Thomas, *Ancient Folk Literature*, 6.

deity of the Minyak.[89] The Se, although later found in association with the Azha, are also related to the Minyak, which perhaps implies that some remnants of Azha were absorbed by the Minyak state, or that the Se independently contributed to the populations of both Azha and Minyak.[90] The Se clan is also associated with Khyungpo.[91] Se still survives as a clan name in Amdo.[92]

The Mu tribe is closely associated with Zhangzhung, the ancient kingdom of western Tibet that was conquered and absorbed by the Tibetan state in the mid-seventh century. *Mu-ca-med* is the local divinity of Zhangzhung. Mu is also connected with the Ch'iang terms *mu*, "skycord", *mu*, the ancestral monkey and *mi*, "man." Stein states that "The Don and the Mu are particularly associated with the *miu* aboriginals which would indicate that they were some of the oldest of the tribes deriving from the Ch'iang.[93] Hoffman states that "The Zhangzhung were unquestionably the Ch'iang and spoke a language similar to, but not identical with, Tibetan."[94] The Mu, like the Don, were considered to originally have been non-Tibetan.[95]

The Mu apparently migrated from their eastern area of origins to western Tibet. The mobility of nomadic groups and the availability of continuous pasturage across the northern Tibetan steppe zone makes such migrations feasible. The Mu tribe, upon their arrival in Zhangzhung, may have encountered other peoples already settled in this area. Mon peoples also inhabited the areas adjacent to Zhangzhung and may have been displaced by the Mu tribe in the Zhangzhung area itself. Stein points out that the king of the Mon is supposed to have been related to the Mu.[96]

In addition to the four primary tribes, there are several others that appear in different versions of the Tibetan legends. Some of these additional tribes are the Bra, Bru, Bro, Ba, Dro, Go, Ga and Khyung. Some of these may be homonyms, or lateral branches of the same tribes. A predominant characteristic of all of these tribes, including the four "primary" ones, is their interrelationships. Many tribes are said to be related to one another; sometimes one group is said to be the "leading clan" of another, or one is in a relationship of "maternal uncle" to another. The ancestor spirit of the Don and the Bra is said to be the mountain Machen

89. Stein, *Les Tribus*, 25.
90. Stein, "Mi-Nag et Si-Hia," 248.
91. Beckwith, *Pre-Imperial Tibet*, 212; Stein, *Les Tribus*, 25.
92. Stein, *Les Tribus*, 24.
93. Ibid., 20.
94. Hoffman, "Early and Medieval Tibet," 375.
95. Stein, *Les Tribus*, 64.
96. Ibid., 56.

Pomra (Amne Machen).[97] The Bru and Ga are said to be from the upper Jinsa Jiang (Yangtze) in Kham.[98] The Ga are also associated with Jyekundo and areas to the southeast near Ling in northern Kham, and further to the northeast as far as Choni.[99]

The mythological "original tribes" of Tibet can all be identified as of eastern Sino-Tibetan border area origins and most, if not all, can be identified as those same people known to the Chinese as Ch'iang.[100] The evidence of this comes from linguistic connections, similarities in the myths of origin of the Ch'iang and Tibetans, and the evidence from Tibetan history that the Tibetan population evolved by assimilation of groups who may be identified with the Ch'iang. The Ch'iang and Tibetans are definitely related, though Stein has concluded that "These two groups are not identical, though the latter are one of the principal elements which contributed to the formation of the former."[101] As late as the T'ang dynasty, the Chinese still distinguished the Ch'iang from the Tibetans (Tu-fan); the Ch'iang were described as more nomadic and pastoral than the Tu-fan.[102]

Summary of Tibetan Ethnic Origins

Historical and mythological sources indicate that a primary component of the Tibetan ethny were the tribes originating on the Sino-Tibetan border known to the Chinese as Ch'iang. Other probable components of the Tibetan ethny are the Mon, who were perhaps the original inhabitants of Tibet, and early Indo-European migrants from the north. Isolated groups of primary Mongoloids, similar to the American Indians, who may or may not be the same as the Ch'iang, are another possible ethnic influence.

The characterization of the Ch'iang in Tibetan mythology as the "original" tribes of Tibet, and simultaneously as "foreign," seems to indicate that the Ch'iang were not the indigenous population of Tibet. Rather, it appears that they prevailed over the original inhabitants to the extent that only remnants of the indigenous people's mythology survived to identi-

---

97. Ibid., 31.
98. Ibid., 44.
99. Ibid., 46, 48.
100. Ibid., 84; Haarh, *Yar-Lun Dynasty*, 281.
101. Stein, *Les Tribus*, 84.
102. Stein, *Tibetan Civilization*, 46. The nomadic Ch'iang of the northern plateau may have remained more distinguishable than the central Tibetan Tu-fan because the former were less assimilated to the Mon.

fy the Ch'iang as immigrants.[103] The Don, Ton, Se and Mu and their ethnic affiliates were very likely nomadic hunter-gatherers and primitive agriculturalists-pastoralists who migrated along a margin of similar ecological character on the eastern and southeastern edge of the Tibetan plateau. Some of these groups gravitated to the grasslands, where they adopted pastoral nomadism, while others settled as agriculturalists in the valleys of central Tibet.

Ethnic affiliations between the Ch'iang and the Chinese, and, consequently, between the Chinese and the Tibetans, are possible, given the territorial proximity of their areas of origin. Ethnic differences between the Chinese and the Ch'iang are also possible, due to original ethnic differences between the Ch'iang and the proto-Chinese or Indo-European influences upon the Ch'iang. Tibetan assimilation of the Mon is not a source of ethnic differences between Tibetans and Chinese since the Chinese also assimilated Mon peoples. Whatever original kinship relations may have existed between the earliest Chinese and Tibetans, adaptation to vastly different environments has resulted in populations of significantly different cultural ecology. Cultural ecology is a primary component of the subjective sense of ethnicity. A history of conflict between the two groups has also greatly contributed to this subjective ethnic differentiation.

Whatever their original connections—and these will probably remain unknown—the Chinese and Tibetans have differentiated to an extent that they formed two distinctly different ethnic groups from a relatively early time. This differentiation may date from the time when the Kansu cultures became isolated from the Yang-shao culture, at the end of the third or beginning of the second millennium B.C., or when the Ch'iang began to be influenced by Indo-Europeans from the steppes to the north, during the second millennium B.C., or, at least, from the former and later Han dynasties (206 B.C.-220 A.D.), when conflict between the Ch'iang and the Han resulted in large-scale Ch'iang migrations to the plateau.

---

103. Modern Chinese studies based upon surveys of blood antigens have indicated that Tibetan origins were in the northeastern Tibetan plateau area: "The Tibetans are descendants of people from southern Gansu [Kansu] and Qinghai [Chinghai] provinces who moved south to the Himalayas." This evidence was cited to prove that "the Tibetan people are inseparable members of the Chinese family." "Tibetans Related to Northern Chinese," *Beijing Review, 6 August 1990*, 30. However, Tibetan origins in Kansu and Chinghai do not prove that Tibetans are related to Chinese, only that they originated in areas of close proximity.

2

Chinese Frontier Policies

Sino-Barbarian Differentiation

Chinese society evolved by an amalgamation of peoples who shared in the homogenizing effects of a uniform economy and cultural ecology. Chinese society developed out of the cultural differentiation between extensive economies of hunting and gathering, which require a relatively extensive territory and can support only a limited density of population, and the more intensive economy of agriculture. The cultural developments associated with sedentary agriculture created a distinction between those who adopted this economy and those who retained the hunter-gatherer economy.

Sedentary agriculture first developed in the areas of loess soils of northern China rather than in areas of better climatic and soil conditions to the south and southeast. Loess is wind-blown soil stirred up by the "Siberian anticyclone" of Inner Asia and deposited in northwestern China. This soil is fertile to a great depth, porous, free of stones, and, due to its gradual deposition, usually not covered by dense forest. Unlike the more fertile soils to the south, the loess can be cleared and worked easily with primitive tools. Irregular rainfall, a characteristic of the climatic frontier zone, may have stimulated the first attempts at irrigation, to which loess soils respond extremely well due to their porosity. Lattimore speculates that irrigation may have been possible at an early time in the zone of loess soils using only stone, bone or wood tools.[1]

The introduction of irrigation to agriculture increased agricultural intensity and contributed to further cultural and political developments. The expansion of irrigation eventually required more intensive labor and greater social cooperation for water conservation and irrigation projects. The necessity for cooperative labor may have been an impetus to politi-

---

1. Owen Lattimore, *Inner Asian Frontiers of China* (Oxford: Oxford University Press, 1988), 32.

cal organization.[2] Intensive agriculture and a sedentary lifestyle also allowed for the accumulation of surplus food supplies, creating disparities of wealth in land and food and leading to economic class distinctions. Agricultural economy allowed permanent occupation of a territory, an increase in the density of population, and the creation of towns and cities. A uniform and exclusive style of agriculture also led to homogeneous economic and social structures. These particular forms of agriculture and social organization became characteristic of Chinese culture.

As agricultural society began to acquire a distinct cultural identity and to assume more definite political organization, it began to conceive of itself as distinct from pre-agricultural society. According to one estimate, the Chinese began to think of themselves as "Chinese" (*Hua*) from about the mid-second millennium.[3] This identification was based upon shared cultural attributes that excluded those without these attributes. Those excluded, predominantly by cultural criteria, were regarded as "barbarians."

Lattimore describes Chinese culture as developing by cultural differentiation of several similar ethnic groups. This differentiation was on an ecological and economic basis, as individuals or groups chose intensive agriculture, and the social organization that accompanied it, over the previous hunter-gatherer or agriculture-animal husbandry economy:

> While the proto-Chinese society first crystallized in the region of the Great Bend of the Yellow River, the spread of "China" from the Yellow River to the Yangtze and beyond did not mean the colonization by the Chinese of previously unpopulated lands. On the contrary, primitive populations were scattered throughout the area. The early Chinese form of society was first differentiated in the region of the Great Bend of the Yellow River. The subsequent spread of the Chinese society involved to some extent the expulsion and to some extent the conquest, without expulsion, of people who were either "non-Chinese" or "not yet Chinese." In the main, however, the growth of the Chinese society was accomplished by the acculturation and incorporation of homogeneous or kindred peoples who were not yet Chinese socially but became Chinese as soon as they acquired those cultural characteristics which made them Chinese.[4]

2. See Karl A. Wittfogel, *Oriental Despotism: A Comparative Study of Total Power* (New Haven: Yale University Press, 1957; New York: Vintage Books, 1981).

3. Wolfram Eberhard, *A History of China*, 4th ed., rev. (Berkeley: University of California Press, 1987), 2.

4. Owen Lattimore, "An Inner Asian Approach to the Historical Geography of China," in *Studies in Frontier History, Collected Papers 1928-1958* (London: Oxford University Press, 1962), 496.

Chinese culture spread to all areas of northern China where similar methods of intensive irrigated agriculture were possible, gradually expanding to the east along the lower Yellow River as new techniques of hydro management made possible the drainage of swamps and flood control. As Chinese techniques of irrigation became more sophisticated, the Chinese were able to make use of more marginal areas, where they pressured the non-Chinese, or "not yet Chinese," to either become Chinese by acculturation or to move to ever more marginal lands:

> As it [Chinese culture] spread, it drove out of the most-wanted land or con-
> quered and absorbed the tribes that it encountered. Only at a later time,
> when there began to be a shortage of optimum land, were the "Chinese"
> practices—by now more strongly developed, resourceful, and capable of
> raising the level of productivity of poorer land to a level formerly possible
> only on the best land—applied to taking over the territory of the "back-
> ward" groups scattered through the blocks of hilly land, marsh, jungle or
> forest in the same vast continental expanse as the Chinese themselves.
> These groups that had lagged behind in the culture that was once that of the
> people who had now become "the Chinese" were increasingly assigned
> now to the hostile category of "the barbarians"; but they were "inner" bar-
> barians, of the same matrix as the Chinese.[5]

The primary difference between the Chinese and the barbarians was Chinese culture's practice of sedentary agriculture. The Chinese regard-ed the pre-agricultural peoples as sub-human, or as not yet human because they pursued a lifestyle similar to wandering beasts:

> The basis of the difference between the Hans and the Barbarians was not
> originally of an ethnic nature, but rested on a relationship to Civilization,
> since for the Chinese there is Civilization and the Void. And the relevant cri-
> terion to establish this difference is sedentarization; the civilized one is the
> one who constructs towns and devotes himself to agriculture. . . . The
> nature of Barbarians is to wander like animals in zones unsuited to seden-
> tary culture such as steppes and mountains; animals are different from men
> precisely in that they have to wander in search of their subsistence, having
> only temporary lairs in which to rest their heads. Likewise with the
> Barbarians.[6]

During the process of Chinese cultural expansion, unassimilated bar-barians were confined to areas where Chinese-style agriculture was diffi-

5. Owen Lattimore, "The Frontier in History," in *Studies in Frontier History*, 475.

6. Francois Thierry, "Empire and Minority in China," in *Minority Peoples in the Age of Nation-States*, ed. Gerard Chaliand (London: Pluto Press, 1989), 78.

cult, non-productive or impossible. Barbarian territories formed islands within the territory occupied by the Chinese. These pockets of barbarism were often in hilly or mountainous areas but also in dense forests and swamp-lands and in the still unpenetrated jungles south of the Yangtze. The barbarians encountered on the frontiers of Chinese culture became "internal" barbarians as Chinese culture expanded to surround them.

Until the end of the first millennium B.C., Chinese culture expanded within an area that was relatively easily converted to agriculture. Chinese culture had not yet encountered geographical terrain that was so unsuited to Chinese-style intensive agriculture that Chinese cultural expansion was impeded; neither had Chinese culture encountered any unassimilable culture on its frontiers. Policies toward barbarians and the frontiers of Chinese culture were therefore exclusively assimilative.

Chinese cosmological schemes reflect the universality of Chinese cultural and political conceptions. The Chinese Mandate of Heaven ideology was universally applicable; the Chinese emperor was considered universal ruler and China the center of the cultural and political universe. Chinese cosmology consisted of concentric zones of cultural assimilation without territorial limitation. An early conception of universal Chinese cultural and political dominance or "levels of subjugation," had an Imperial center surrounded by five concentric zones: Royal Domains (*tien fu*); Princes' Domains (*hou fu*); Pacification Zone (*sui fu*); Zone of Allied Barbarians (*yao fu*); Zone of Cultureless Savagery (*huang fu*).[7]

There was no cognizance of any culture comparable to Chinese culture at whose territorial frontier Chinese cultural assimilation must stop. The only limit to Chinese culture was *Tien-hsia*, or "all under Heaven." Even the outer cultureless zone was assumed to be eventually assimilable. The only known peoples beyond the frontiers of Chinese culture were the barbarians, who might either remain barbarians or become Chinese, but whose independent cultural existence was inconceivable within Chinese cultural cosmology. There was no concept of Chinese culture and other cultures, only Chinese culture or no culture at all.

Even the concept of frontier was relative; the frontier was simply the limit of assimilation at any time, variable with time, until, with universal acculturation, the frontier itself would disappear. The Chinese character for feudal vassal, *fan*, means "a hedge, a boundary, a frontier" or "to screen or to protect." The same sound, *fan*, written with different radicals,

---

7. Michael Aris, *Bhutan* (London: Aris and Phillips, 1979), 18; Yu Ying-shih, "Han Foreign Relations," in *The Cambridge History of China: The Chin and Han Empires*, ed. Denis Twitchett and Michael Loewe (Cambridge: Cambridge University Press, 1966), 379.

also means "foreign" and "barbarian."[8] The two characters were used interchangeably, thus creating an ambiguity in the concepts of feudatory, foreign and barbarian, implying an identity in the terms. Thus, a foreigner or a barbarian is actually or potentially a feudatory and, once a feudatory, then eventually assimilated to Chinese culture. "Foreign" in Chinese thus does not mean "non-Chinese" but "not yet Chinese."

The early Chinese states developed policies for dealing with the barbarians within China and those constantly being encountered on the expanding frontiers. Feudalistic-type relations with the barbarians were established as the first step in their political and cultural assimilation.[9] Feudalistic organization is characteristic of early states that are able to conquer or dominate more territory than they can actually administer. It also reflects the often confederative nature of conquest, achieved with clan affiliates or allies, who had to be rewarded with fiefs. In the absence of a salaried bureaucracy in early states, fiefs were also a means for compensation for administrators.

Fiefs were of two main types: those awarded to allies or associates over subject territories and populations, and those of federated allies whose autonomous rule was merely confirmed and perpetuated. The second category might include federated Chinese states or barbarian tribes or confederations of tribes. Barbarian chieftains sometimes rendered service to the state, either in its original consolidation or its later defense, for which they were awarded recognition of autonomous rights in their own territories. The rulers of some fiefs, especially those of allied states, might be virtually independent of the sovereign. Such allies might continue to exercise autonomous rule, according only nominal allegiance to the central state and receiving nominal protection in return.

Indirect feudalistic rule had as its ultimate goal the imposition of direct Chinese rule and assimilation of the barbarians. The primary steps in that process were acculturation of barbarian elites, sedentarization, and, as

---

8. John K. Fairbank, ed., *The Chinese World Order* (Cambridge: Harvard University Press, 1968), 9.

9. We are using the term "feudalism" in the sense defined by Creel: "Feudalism is a system of government in which a ruler personally delegates limited sovereignty over portions of his territory to vassals. . . .Feudalism is primarily a method of government, not an economic or a social system, though it obviously modifies and is modified by the social economic environment." Herrlee G. Creele, *The Origins of Statecraft in China: The Western Chou Empire* (Chicago: University of Chicago Press, 1970), 32. This emphasis on the political aspects of feudalism may be more appropriate in the Chinese context than in European feudalism because, as Weber has observed, "In China, as far as one can judge, political feudalism was not primarily connected with landlordism in the occidental sense." Max Weber, *The Religion of China* (New York, The Free Press, 1951; Free Press Paperback, 1968), 33.

the barbarians became increasingly dependent on the Chinese, the appointment of Chinese civil and military officials. Internal barbarians were slowly assimilated; those encountered on the frontiers were treated as external feudatories until the Chinese frontier advanced and they became internalized.

China's Ethnic, Cultural and Political Frontier

As Chinese culture expanded to fill up terrain suitable for agriculture, it gradually encountered ecological boundaries beyond which expansion became difficult or impossible. In the south, the scope for Chinese expansion was limited only by the difficulties of the terrain and the resistance of indigenous peoples. The southern environment, once tamed, was suitable to agriculture, even more productive in fact than the northern areas of loess soils. In the north and northwest, however, Chinese culture encountered insurmountable ecological barriers. Aridity increased to the north and the growing season was shortened; temperature fluctuations of the climatic border zone were also encountered. The lack of surface water in this climatic zone made irrigated agriculture unfeasible.

Between the Chinese ecological zone and the northern steppe and western Tibetan plateau lay a intermediate ecological zone where a mixed economy of agriculture and animal husbandry was practiced. This was an extensive economy relative to the intensive economy of China, an economy that fostered a diversity of economic specializations or combinations, in contrast to the homogenizing effects of the more uniform ecological adaptation of Chinese intensive agriculture. The extensive economy of the borderlands allowed for only a low density of population and was conducive to only a low level of social and political organization. The society of the borderlands developed in a style determined by its own ecology; this style was sufficiently different from that of China to be unassimilable to Chinese economy or culture.

At the northern steppe boundary the Chinese encountered a true ecological, ethnic and cultural frontier. The appearance of mounted warriors in the steppe, and especially their first political confederations, began a new historical period for the steppe and for China. Chinese and steppe cultures came into contact at approximately the time when the latter were perfecting the techniques of mounted warfare. This event can be dated to the fourth and third centuries B.C., when Chinese states began to take steps to defend against steppe tribes.[10] The Chinese states of Ch'in and Chao (fourth century B.C.) adopted mounted warfare and even nomadic

---

10. Lattimore, *Inner Asian Frontiers*, 360.

dress to combat the nomads, and began building walls that later, during the Ch'in (221-207 B.C.), were connected to form the Great Wall. The Great Wall was not only a defense against the steppe nomads, but also a recognition of the limits of the Chinese ecological and cultural area.

The Chinese were uncertain about the origins of the inhabitants of the intermediate zone, the Ch'iang, or the first confederation of steppe nomads, the Hsiung-nu, or their possible affiliations. The Ch'iang were to the Chinese a group of barbarians with indefinite internal-external status. They had appeared before the steppe tribes and were not fully nomadic; they were similar to the barbarians of the past but they had some affinities with the new nomads of the steppe. The Chinese imagined that the Hsiung-nu and Ch'iang had more in common with each other than either had with the Chinese. In this they were correct; the Ch'iang often allied with the Hsiung-nu against the Chinese.

The unique characteristics of the frontier barbarians of the intermediate zone and the steppe required the Chinese state to develop a new policy for dealing with them. These "external barbarians" would have to be dealt with diplomatically as foreign tribes and states or they would have to be assimilated by moving them within Chinese frontiers or by expanding Chinese frontiers to encompass them. The first method led to the tribute system of Chinese foreign relations while the second led to a new type of frontier feudalism. Both had important implications for later Chinese policies toward Tibet.

Tribute System

The consolidation of the first unified Chinese state under the Ch'in dynasty (221-207 B.C.), and the first confederation of steppe nomads under the leadership of the Hsiung-nu, occurred contemporaneously at the end of the third century B.C. Ch'in Shi Huang-ti, the first emperor of the Ch'in, eliminated the autonomous power of Chinese feudatory states and feudal aristocracy, destroyed the records of the formerly autonomous states, repressed reverence for social and political forms of the past, burned historical books and executed scholars. Peasants were released from bondage to the feudal landlords and made directly responsible to the state for taxes and services. Direct taxation and access to peasant labor facilitated the military and political consolidation of the Chinese state, making possible massive construction projects such as the Great Wall.

The Ch'in dynasty was significant but short-lived. The Han dynasty (206 B.C.-8 A.D.) was established as a reaction to the draconian measures of the Ch'in, but it retained the legacy of centralized state organization.

The Han reverted to a Confucianist style of political and cultural philosophy in contrast to the "Legalist" ideology of the Ch'in. In frontier relations, this meant a shift from the military policy of the Ch'in to a policy of reliance upon the virtue of China to attract and transform the barbarians. This policy was necessitated by an early defeat of Han armies by the Hsiung-nu in 202 B.C., in which the Han emperor was surrounded and almost captured. After this humiliation, the Han decided to appease the Hsiung-nu by the traditional means of a marriage alliance and substantial annual "gifts." Opponents of this policy justifiably criticized it as "tribute in reverse."

The Han dynasty initiated a style and a policy of feudalistic relations with both internal and frontier barbarians known as *chi-mi*, "loose rein," or *ho-ch'in*, "harmonious kinship" (referring to marriage relations), which allowed barbarians a degree of self-rule under varying degrees of Chinese control and administration.[11] The *ho-ch'in* policy relied upon the attractions of Chinese civilization to achieve voluntary assimilation of the barbarians, who would come and be transformed (*lai-hua*) of their own accord. Confucian scholars favored a policy of sophisticated diplomacy that combined the attractions of China's cultural and material civilization with skillful appeasement to awe and flatter the barbarians while corrupting and pacifying them. The barbarians were rewarded for submission with gifts of the products of civilization such as silks and metal ornaments and implements, which they could use to establish their status within their own societies, and flattered by the award of high-sounding titles that they could also use to impress their own people. They might be favored by the bestowal of a Chinese princess in marriage. The purposes of the policy were frankly admitted:

> To give them [the barbarians] elaborate clothes and carriages in order to corrupt their eyes; to give them fine food in order to corrupt their mouth; to give them music and women in order to corrupt their ears; to provide them with lofty buildings, granaries and slaves in order to corrupt their stomach; and, as for those who come to surrender, the emperor should show them favor by honoring them with an imperial reception party in which the emperor should personally serve them wine and food so as to corrupt their mind. These are what may be called the five baits.[12]

As Chinese society was organized on the principles of social and ideological orthodoxy and conformity, so, it was supposed, would the bar-

---

11. Yu Ying-shih, *Trade and Expansion in Han China* (Berkeley: University of California Press, 1967), 36.

12. Ibid., 37, quoting the *Han Shu* (Han dynasty Annals).

barians be converted to civilization by the effects upon them of Chinese ceremony and ritual (*li*). Chinese society was supposed to function by conformity to the *Tao*, or the "Way of Heaven," as interpreted and exemplified by the emperor. The proper performance by the emperor of *li*, and the consequent harmony between Heaven and Earth, was supposed to create an aura of virtue (*te*) which would create and maintain harmony among the people and, secondarily, attract the barbarians to Chinese culture. Should *li* fail to subdue the barbarians, there were fa, or regulations, which implied the use of military force. The necessity for the imposition of *fa* implied that natural and social harmony was lacking and that the emperor's or the dynasty's virtue was insufficient to achieve harmony. *Fa*, or rule by positive law, therefore had negative connotations in Chinese society.

The policy of appeasement of the Hsiung-nu was rationalized as appropriate, even though it accorded equal status to the Hsiung-nu, because the Hsiung-nu were barbarians of the outer uncivilized zone, temporarily beyond the range of the emperor's mandate. The Han and Hsiung-nu states were to be regarded as equals, each with a sovereign territory, delimited by the Great Wall, not to be infringed upon by the other. However, this arrangement failed to prevent conflict. The Hsiung-nu were aware that occasional threats to the frontier consistently produced "gifts" or increased subsidies from the Han. The arrangement also failed to achieve Han political domination, a necessity for initiating the process of cultural assimilation of the barbarians.

The Han Emperor Wu-ti (140-87 B.C.) significantly altered the *ho-ch'in* policy by a military expansion into the Kansu Corridor in 121 B.C., intended to isolate the Hsiung-nu from the Ch'iang. The Han also began an expansion into Ch'iang territory in the valley of the Yellow River above Lanchou and the Sining Valley east of Kokonor. In 101 B.C., a Han army reached Ferghana. In 71 B.C., the Han, in alliance with nomadic enemies of the Hsiung-nu, inflicted a series of defeats on the Hsiung-nu in the Tarim, establishing Han control there. As part of his policy of confronting the Hsiung-nu, Wu-ti refused to renew the previous *ho-ch'in* treaties. Wu-ti hoped to impose relations upon the Hsiung-nu under which the barbarians would have to perform ceremonious acts of submission to the Han. The Hsiung-nu were to be required to pay homage by coming personally to the Han court to submit; a son of the Hsiung-nu chieftain, the *Shan-yu*, was to be retained as a hostage. In addition, the Hsiung-nu were to be required to submit symbolic tribute to the Han.

The Hsiung-nu refused these conditions. Frontier relations therefore remained confrontational during the reign of Wu-ti. After 60 B.C., however, the Hsiung-nu confederation broke up into factions that warred upon each other. The Southern Hsiung-nu sought protection from the Han in 53 B.C. to escape attacks from their kinsmen to the north. The *Shan-yu* of the Southern Hsiung-nu sent his son as hostage and travelled to the Han court himself in 51 B.C. to render homage. The *Shan-yu* was rewarded for his act with lavish gifts of money, silk and provisions. He was treated as a foreign dignitary, even being exempted from performing the kowtow. The act of submission to the Han having proven less humiliating, and considerably more profitable, than expected, the *Shan-yu* requested that he be allowed to pay homage again the following year and was even more lavishly rewarded.[13]

Han rewards to the Hsiung-nu under the new system were far in excess of those that they had provided previously. Hsiung-nu "tribute" to the Han was entirely symbolic, consisting of a few items of steppe provenance, whereas Han gifts to the Hsiung-nu amounted to a considerable economic subsidy for the entire tribe and lavishly rewarded Hsiung-nu elites for their symbolic "submission." Even though this policy was expensive and was admittedly "tribute in reverse," the Han were willing to continue the bribery of the Hsiung-nu because of the importance to them of the barbarians' symbolic political submission. Under the tributary system, the Han were able to initiate the theoretical process of transformation of the nomads from external barbarians of the "savage uncontrolled zone" (*huang-fu*) of Chinese political cosmology into controlled barbarians of the "allied zone" (*yao-fu*).

The tributary system incorporated the frontier barbarians within Chinese political cosmology. As Yu Ying-shih has written:

> The whole development from the *ho-ch'in* system to the tributary system may be viewed as a continuous quest on the part of the Han empire for a proper form in which Sino-barbarian relations could be regulated in keeping with the general imperial order. . . . The superiority of the tributary system over its *ho-ch'in* predecessor, from the point of view of the Han court, lay primarily in the fact that the former, and only the former, could politically fit the various neighboring barbarians into the Chinese imperial order. Thus considered, the tributary system, as was applied to the barbarians in Han times, may be legitimately understood as no less than a logical extension of the Han imperial system to the realm of foreign relations.[14]

The costs to China of this tribute in reverse were substantial, calculated in 91 A.D. at an annual rate of more than 2,500 kilograms of gold.[15] Total payments to all barbarians during this same period were more than

---

13. Yu, "Han Foreign Relations," 396.
14. Yu, *Trade and Expansion in Han China*, 39.
15. Yu, "Han Foreign Relations," 401.

four times the amount to the Hsiung-nu alone.[16] However, Hsiung-nu autonomy was increasingly constricted by Han official supervision. The Southern Hsiung-nu gradually became economic as well as political dependents of China. Unsubmissive Hsiung-nu tribes were denied even trade privileges along the frontier until they submitted and joined the tributary system. Han economic subsidies gradually produced a migration of the Hsiung-nu from the steppe to the Chinese frontier. Tribes who came to the border to surrender during the Later Han (25-220 A.D.) were settled within the frontiers in ecologically marginal areas and required to protect the frontier against their kinsmen who remained on the steppe. At the same time, many Ch'iang were being resettled within the Han frontier to remove them from proximity to the unsubmitted Hsiung-nu or from lands the Han desired for agriculture. Under this policy, a large population of unassimilated barbarians accumulated within the Han frontier.

Barbarians Within the Frontier

Han expansion at the end of the second century B.C. was accompanied by the incorporation of many Ch'iang and Hsiung-nu tribes within the new frontiers.[17] Some Ch'iang were resettled within the Han frontier, but most of the tribes spoken of as having been "settled within the frontier" were actually indigenous tribes incorporated within the expanding frontiers of the Han. In addition, Ch'iang herdsmen inhabited the higher elevations of Kansu, but they were accustomed to bringing their herds and flocks down to lower altitudes in the winter. As the Han settled in Ch'iang winter pastures, conflict became inevitable. Chinese settlements were established as military agricultural colonies for protection against the raids of the Ch'iang. The Great Wall was constructed partly to deny the steppe nomads access to their usual winter pastures. The nomads were forced to retreat to the steppe or to attack the Han to regain their

---

16. Yu, *Trade and Expansion in Han China*, 61. The Han made enormous payments to the Hsien-pi of southern Manchuria, not because the Hsien-pi had replaced the Hsiung-nu as the greatest threat to China, but due to the Han policy of bribing the Hsien-pi to attack the Hsiung-nu. The Han paid a bounty to the Hsien-pi for Hsiung-nu heads. The Hsien-pi presented little threat to China due to their lack of unified political organization. Their fragmentation, on the other hand, necessitated greater payments because each tribe had to be bribed separately.

17. Rafe de Crespigny, *Northern Frontier: The Policies and Strategy of the Later Han Empire*, Faculty of Asian Studies Monographs, n.s., no. 4 (Canberra: Australian National University Faculty of Asian Studies, 1984), 61.

winter pastures. The nomads' need for grain in times of crisis was exploited by Han traders.[18]

During the Han expansion into tribal areas, submissive tribes were rewarded with lands within the frontier of the Han, or Han title to their own lands, and a feudatory political status. Resistant tribes were persecuted in campaigns of annihilation. In 94 A.D., the Ts'ang-i Ch'iang surrendered in Szechuan with more than half a million people; in 107 and 108, another fourteen Ch'iang tribes of more than fifty thousand people surrendered.[19] A major rebellion of the Ch'iang occurred in 107 A.D. and was not successfully suppressed until 118. In this conflict, the Ch'iang were said to have fought as mounted warriors.[20] Further rebellions occurred between 119 and 150. In 184, the Ch'iang of Kansu in alliance with Hsiung-nu and Yueh-chih peoples rebelled against the Han.[21]

While some of the Ch'iang tribes submitted to the Han, others fled to the heights of Tibet. In one punitive expedition of 160, a Han force pursued a group of the Ch'iang as far as the mountains of Amne Machin, where the Ch'iang were defeated and slaughtered.[22] During the Former Han, many Ch'iang tribes fled to the highlands to escape Han expansion into Kansu and Kokonor. One Ch'iang tribe, the Mi-tang Ch'iang, after having suffered a decisive defeat by the Chinese, was said to have "passed far beyond the headwaters of the Ssu-chih Ho (the upper Yellow River), and dwelt there in dependence upon the Fa Ch'iang."[23] Thomas writes that Han punitive expeditions were characterized by great brutality, "thousands of decapitations" and the capture of hundreds of thousands of the nomads' livestock.[24] The *Hou Han Shu* (Later Han Records) has a passage describing Han expeditions against the Ch'iang:

> When the tribes were somewhat weakened, the imperial forces attacked them, and, they being still more weakened by the numbers of dead and wounded, the imperial troops followed up the pursuit. . . . Skinless bones were strewn on the tops of the loftiest precipices, beyond expression or calculation. There were no more than one or two in a hundred of the Jung able

---

18. Lattimore, *Inner Asian Frontiers*, 347.

19. Yu, "Han Foreign Relations," 429.

20. De Crespigny, *Northern Frontier*, 108.

21. Yu, "Han Foreign Relations," 434.

22. De Crespigny, *Northern Frontier*, 128.

23. Christopher Beckwith, "A Study of the Early Medieval Chinese, Latin, and Tibetan Historical Sources on Pre-Imperial Tibet" (Ph.D. diss. Indiana University, 1977), 5. Beckwith speculates that the Chinese *Fa*, which was pronounced something like the Tibetan *Bod*, was in fact a Chinese translation of the Tibetan ethnonym. Ibid., 6.

24. F.W. Thomas, *Nam: An Ancient Language of the Sino-Tibetan Borderland*, Publications of the Philological Society, XIV (London: Oxford University Press, 1948), 50.

to skulk away among the grass and stones, and so evade the lances and arrows of the troops.[25]

[The Ch'iang tribes] dwindled away in numbers, till they were unable to maintain their integrity. They were divided and dispersed, attaching their settlements to other bodies. Some were utterly destroyed, leaving no posterity. Some were led away into distant lands.[26]

Punitive expeditions against the Ch'iang from 107 to 118 A.D. cost the Han the equivalent of 600,000 kilograms of gold, and from 136 to 145 an additional 200,000 kilograms of gold. During this period, the Han spent more than three times as much on suppressing the Ch'iang as on the tributary system with the steppe nomads.[27]

By the last half of the first century A.D., the defects of Han policy were beginning to be manifested. Constant warfare with the Ch'iang in Kansu created a migration of Han settlers to safer areas to the south. "Pacified" Ch'iang and other barbarians previously incorporated or resettled within the frontiers of China replaced the Hsiung-nu as the greatest threat to China during the Later Han. The submitted Ch'iang tribes had been intended to form a barrier, or "pacification zone" (*sui fu*), between the Han and the Hsiung-nu. They were charged with the defense of the frontier, but frontier defense duty required that they remain armed and in possession of sufficient horses to constitute a defense force. They remained a threat, therefore, because they could ally with the Hsiung-nu as easily as with the Han. The perpetuation of their frontier lifestyle also prevented their rapid assimilation to Han culture.

A characteristic of Han frontier policy was the corruption of Han officials and their exploitation of the tribespeople. The effects of this policy were spelled out in memorials of two Han officials, the first in 33 B.C. and the second in 33 A.D.:

The Western Ch'iang offered to guard our frontier. Thus, they were in daily intercourse with the Chinese. The Chinese frontier officials as well as powerful people, bent on gain, often robbed the Ch'iang of their cattle, women, and children. This incurred the hatred of the Ch'iang and consequently they revolted against China.

Now in Liang-chou there are surrendered Ch'iang peoples who still lead a barbarian way of life. Nevertheless, they are living together with the Chinese. Since the two peoples are different in social customs and cannot communicate in language, very often the Chinese petty officials and crafty

---

25. Ibid. The author uses the generic term Jung to refer to the western barbarians.
26. Ibid., 51.
27. Yu, *Trade and Expansion in Han China*, 61.

people take the advantage to rob the Ch'iang of their belongings. Extremely enraged and yet helpless, they thus rise in revolt. We can almost say that this is the cause of all barbarian rebellions.[28]

Frontier Feudalism

The administration of submitted frontier barbarians fell within the feudalistic pattern previously established for internal barbarians. This pattern first fit the barbarians within the Chinese political framework and then, by increasing their economic dependence and constantly circumscribing their political autonomy, slowly assimilated them to Chinese culture. However, the new frontier feudalism, which Lattimore calls a "second stage" of feudalism, hindered barbarian assimilation.[29]

Submitted Ch'iang, as well as Hsiung-nu and other barbarians, were organized as dependent states (*shu-kuo*).[30] The *shu-kuo* were established in *wai-chun*, or "outer provinces," which had resulted from Han frontier expansion. The act of surrendering was termed *nei-shu*, or "to become inner subjects." Barbarian feudatories were usually confined to a set territory, forcing them to adopt a sedentary lifestyle. Surrender of their lands was a normal component of barbarian submission, as is indicated by the common term of submission, *chu-chung nei-shu*, "surrender as inner subjects together with land."[31] *Shu-kuo* were ruled by native chieftains, known as *Tu-shi*, or "administrators of native peoples." The *Tu-shi* supported themselves by their native resources; they were required to submit symbolic tribute. *Shu-kuo* retained some of the characteristics of dependent or federated states; the *Tu-shi* were hereditary and, theoretically, personally responsible to the emperor rather than to any lesser or provincial officials.

As Lattimore has indicated, the institution of this type of indirect, feudalistic rule had important social and political consequences:

> The new character of [feudatory] authority seems to be directly related to the function of the chief as representative of his tribe, recognized by the Chinese in order to provide institutions and conventions for the coexistence of the Chinese community and the tribal communities. The fact that the Chinese make him their go-between reinforces the power of the chief over his own people. In this way the hereditary principle is strengthened and a family of chiefs may come to have a vested interest in perpetuating the sub-

28. Yu, "Han Foreign Relations," 425.
29. Owen Lattimore, "Frontier Feudalism," in *Studies in Frontier History*, 528.
30. Yu, "Han Foreign Relations," 428.
31. Yu, *Trade and Expansion in Han China*, 71.

ordination of the people as a whole, in order to sustain its own authority. ... Frontier phenomena of this kind are probably one of the origins of feudalism. They are notable in the history of Tibet.[32]

Another characteristic of the frontier feudalistic system, as well as of the tributary system, was the award of official titles and seals of office to the indigenous rulers. These titles and seals were often employed by native rulers to legitimate their rule over their own people. Native rulers thus became dependent upon Chinese patronage. Although initially allowing a great deal of autonomy, the *Tu-shi* institution aimed at the political and eventually cultural assimilation of barbarians through their elites:

> The *Tu si* [*Tu-shi*] and their entourages adopted Chinese customs ... and became sedentarized; schools were opened by the Hans for the children of the local aristocracy, with the Imperial Treasury taking over responsibility for paying the costs of schooling. To oblige these children to attend these schools, it was laid down that the post of *Tu si* could only be inherited by someone, male or female, educated in the Chinese school; the brightest children of the aristocracy were called to pursue their studies in the provincial capitals, or even the Capital itself.[33]

Shu-kuo barbarians were often treated very leniently when they surrendered, given lavish gifts and provided with all of their economic necessities. However, this gradually led to their economic and political dependency. The *shu-kuo Tu-shi* were required to submit a census, since, as subjects of the Han empire, they were responsible for military service, corvee and taxation. Frontier *shu-kuo* were especially subject to Han military levies of men, animals, food and transport. When submitted tribes were required to fight against unsubmitted barbarians, they were forced to put their wives and children under the custody of Chinese officials as hostages in order to guarantee their loyalty. The barbarians were eventually subject to the Han government for compulsory labor on construction projects as well as to individual Han officials and even private traders, serving in many cases as little more than slaves. Taxes were increased as the barbarians were pacified and incorporated within the Chinese administrative system.[34]

As the *shu-kuo* were assimilated, they found that their autonomy had been substantially circumscribed and that their dependence upon the

---

32. Lattimore, "Frontier in History," 476.
33. Thierry, "Empire and Minority," 81.
34. Yu, *Trade and Expansion in Han China*, 84.

Han and their exploitation by the Han had correspondingly increased. Assimilated barbarian *shu-kuo* were eventually incorporated within the Chinese *chun-hsien* (province-district) system of administration. As Yu Ying-shih observed:

> The ultimate goal of the Han government was to gradually embrace all the barbarians within the empire into the arms of Chinese civilization so that they could be eventually treated just as the Chinese under the *chun-hsien* system. The *nei-shu* type of barbarian surrender, coupled with the incorporation of the newly-acquired lands into the *chun-hsien* administrative system, was used as a normal method of expansion in Han China.[35]

The significance of this fact for our study is that this method of expansion was later applied to territories beyond the Great Wall boundary, to Mongolia, East Turkestan (Sinkiang) and Tibet.

The attempt to assimilate frontier barbarians, who were more ethnically and culturally foreign to the Chinese than the "internal barbarians" of the past, sowed the seeds of later disasters for the Chinese. The frontier, instead of being civilized, was barbarized by inclusion of the Ch'iang and the Hsiung-nu. Ch'iang settled within the borders rebelled against the Han, especially during the second century, with increasing success. An essential element of the Han assimilation strategy—the assumption that the barbarians would be outnumbered by Han within the Han frontier—was negated by a Ch'iang population increase and Han migration to the south.

Han policy for dealing with Ch'iang within the frontier was to force them to become agriculturalists. However, Ch'iang methods of mixed agriculture and animal husbandry actually proved more adaptable to the conditions of northwest China than Chinese style intensive agriculture. Contrary to Han expectations, their policy resulted in a Ch'iang population explosion within the Han frontiers that came to constitute a grave threat to the Chinese. In addition, Han colonies in the Ch'iang territories were unsuccessful, due to pressure from the Hsiung-nu all along the northwestern border, continuing conflicts with the Ch'iang, and the unsuitability of Chinese methods of agriculture in the marginal territory between the Chinese plains and the steppe.

A Chinese official, in a memorial of the year 299, summed up the results of the Han Dynasty's policy:

> In the Jianwu period of Han [25-55 A.D.] Ma Yuan . . . attacked the rebel

---

35. Ibid., 77.

Qiang [Ch'iang] and shifted the survivors to the land within the passes, where they occupied the empty country, and lived mingled with the Chinese. . . .

Now the Land Within the Passes is well-watered, and all things grow in abundance. . . . It is in this region that emperors and kings have set their capitals, and I have never heard it said that the western or northern barbarians should possess this territory. They are no people of our race, and their hearts are surely alien to us. The barbarians have fierce ambitions, nothing in common with the Chinese. Yet when they were in a time of weakness and disorder, we brought them into the inmost territory of our nation. The gentry and common people of China paid them no respect, but despised them as unimportant and weak. This caused the spirit of anger to rise in them, until it spread its poison into the very marrow of their bones. When they became stronger and more numerous, it was only natural that they should wish to revolt.

With a nature that is greedy and cruel, and a spirit fierce and quick to anger, they waited for their chance and then took the opportunity to cause trouble and rebellion. Now they occupy the lands within the borders of our state, so we have no frontier defense against them.[36]

Conflict along the expansive Han frontier played a significant role in the decline and fall of the Later Han. The Han had considered the Ch'iang a lesser threat than the Hsiung-nu, but in the end they probably played a more significant role in the decline and fall of the Han dynasty. The Han dynasty fell primarily due to the loss of control of the northern frontier. With the collapse of centralized Chinese political power after the end of the second century, the steppe barbarians, allied with their affiliates already within the borders of China, attained political dominance in North China, eventually establishing their own petty states.

Three groups of barbarians were primarily responsible for this first barbarian conquest of northern China: Hsiung-nu, Hsien-pi and Ch'iang. Chi Li dates the periods of barbarian political ascendance as follows: Hsiung-nu, 304-439 in the central region; Ch'iang, 351-403 in the northwest; and Hsien-pi, 349-580 in the northeast.[37] Between 301 and 439, there were established in northern China sixteen "dynasties," four of which can be identified with the Hsiung-nu, five with the Hsien-pi, and four with the Ch'iang.[38] Northern China was again ruled by dynasties of non-Chinese origin in the tenth, eleventh and twelfth centuries, and finally, all

---

36. De Crespigny, *Northern Frontier*, 170.

37. Chi Li, *The Formation of the Chinese People* (Cambridge: Cambridge University Press, 1928), 267.

38. Luc Kwanten, *Imperial Nomads: A History of Central Asia, 500-1500* (Philadelphia: University of Pennsylvania Press, 1979), 292.

of China was ruled by dynasties of steppe or Manchurian origin in the thirteenth and fourteenth centuries and again in the seventeenth, eighteenth and nineteenth centuries.

Han dynasty frontier policies were to have several impacts upon the history of Tibet and Sino-Tibetan relations. The most immediate effect was, of course, that Han persecution of the Ch'iang caused many of them to migrate to the higher reaches of the Tibetan plateau, where they had an important impact upon Tibetan ethnic identity and the creation of the Tibetan state. Secondly, Han dynasty policies established the pattern for Chinese Inner Asian frontier relations into which Chinese or conquest dynasties attempted to place Tibet. Chinese policies intended to prevent alliance between non-Chinese peoples of the steppe and the Tibetan plateau were also to reappear in later Sino-Tibetan relations.

3

Foundations of the Tibetan State

Mythology of Origins

The mythological histories of the earliest local or petty states (*yul* or *lung*) of central Tibet were assimilated to and preserved in the mythology of the later Yarlung state, which achieved a confederation of the local states in the early 7th century. Previous local states' myths and even lineages were incorporated into the mythology of Yarlung in order to lengthen it or to provide the legitimation of antiquity. The mythology of Yarlung tends to confirm some of our earlier assumptions about Tibetan ethnic origins and reveals the beginnings of an alliance between religion and politics that was to become a defining characteristic of the Tibetan state.

Tibetan texts give widely varying dates for the beginning of the Yarlung dynasty (95, 125, 173, 252, 447 and 794 B.C.). But, according to Eric Haarh's study of Yarlung, "these chronological datings are late inventions, probably connected with the beginning of Buddhist historiography."[1] The Yarlung tradition counts 42 kings from the foundation of the dynasty until its fall in 842 A.D.[2] The first nine kings are, according to Haarh "clearly mythic," but, this does not mean that they can be dismissed as fictive: "some of the individual kings, viz. gNa'-khri-btsan-po, Gri-gum-bstan-po, and sPu-de-gun-rgyal may have some background in reality."[3] The next 14 kings Haarh believes were actually kings of the predecessor states to Yarlung.

The beginning of the prehistoric, "but real," line may be found with the 24th king in the lineage, Gyalthori Lontsan. The probable dawn of historical time in Tibet arrives with the 28th king in the lineage, Lhathothori

---

1. Erik Haarh, *The Yar-Lun Dynasty* (Copenhagen: G.E.C. GAD's FORLAG, 1969), 131.
2. Ibid., 33.
3. Ibid., 128.

Nantsan, "or his immediate successors."[4] The indisputable division between the prehistoric and the historic periods occurs at the 32nd in the lineage, Namri Lontsan, who united the Tibetan tribes and local states in the early seventh century A.D.

Many of the texts Haarh consulted agree that the time span from Lhathothori Nantsan to Srongtsan Gampo, the son and successor of Namri Lontsan (Namri died in 629), was one hundred and fifty years (although it is unclear if this figure includes the reign of Lhathothori Nantsan himself).[5] This would place Lhathothori Nantsan sometime in the middle of the fifth century. The date of Gyalthori Lontsan, the fourth predecessor of Lhathothori and the first "real" king, and the actual founding of the Yarlung dynasty may therefore be tentatively identified as sometime in the late fourth or early fifth century. The predecessor states to Yarlung then date to before the fifth century, but how much before is impossible to say. A third or fourth century origin of the first Tibetan local states correlates well with the known migration of Ch'iang tribes to the plateau during the second century.

The prominent kings of the early mythic period may or may not have been actual historical figures, but they definitely represent important transitions in the development of Tibetan culture and the Tibetan state. In the oldest mythology, the progenitor of the Tibetans is Olde Purgyal; later versions name Nakhri Tsanpo. That these two were regarded as identical is indicated by many Tibetan historians, including the Fifth Dalai Lama.[6] Nakhri Tsanpo's successor, Grigum Tsanpo, represents an important change in Tibetan culture and politics; his reign marks the introduction of the Bon religion. His son and successor, Pude Gungyal, is identified as the actual progenitor ancestor of Yarlung and the developer of the arts of Tibetan civilization.

This trinity of founders, Nakhri Tsanpo, Grigum Tsanpo and Pude Gungyal, possibly represents an amalgamation of the progenitors of different clans, regions or local states that were assimilated to Yarlung.[7] In the earliest myths, Olde Purgyal is an ancestor and local ruler, not the unifier of all the Tibetan tribes. This may indicate that the mythology of Olde Purgyal was incorporated with that of Nakhri as both local founder and sovereign of all Tibetans.[8] Haarh believes the name *Olde* derives from the *De* (deity) of O Yul (Olkha, the western district of Kongpo, in east-central Tibet) and associates the name with the mountain, Olde Gungyal, the

---

4. Ibid., 128.
5. Ibid., 130.
6. Ibid., 229, 234, 243.
7. Ibid., 161.
8. Ibid., 250.

Yul Lha (country god) of O Yul.[9] Olde Gungyal is regarded as the father of all the *Yul Lha* of Tibet, perhaps indicating that Olkha is the origin of the founding ancestor of the local state, or *yul*, whose mythology became that of the later Tibetan state.[10]

Nakhri Tsanpo is a further elaboration of the myth of Olde Purgyal:

> The study of the motive for the appearance of the ancestor gNa'-khri-btsan-po actually leads us to two different kinds of motives, one being mythic-religious, the other realistic or quasi-historical, and to three different concepts of the ancestor himself, viz. the ancestor of a small local dynasty, the primary common ancestor of more local dynasties, and the primary ancestor of the Tibetan kings, in the capacity of an All-Tibetan Sovereign.[11]

Grigum Tsanpo appears in the Tibetan legends as a transitional figure between mythic and actual historical periods. The mythic kings were said to have descended from the *Mu* deities and to have physically descended from the heavenly realms by the *Mu* rope or cord; at death, they ascended by the same means, leaving no physical corpse. The primary elements of the Grigum myth are his severing of the *Mu* cord and his physical death for which a funeral ritual had to be invented. Pude Gungyal, son and successor to Grigum, is an essential part of the myth in that he completes the transition from the mythic to the historical period, establishing the Yarlung dynasty and founding Tibetan civilization.

The myth of Grigum's severing of the *Mu* cord can be interpreted in several ways. The simplest interpretation is that the myth is essential to explaining why, despite the myth of the ancestral kings' descent from heaven and return there after death, actual kings die and leave corpses.[12] The myth may also have a more practical meaning in regard to the political status of Tibetan kings. A recurring story in Tibetan legends is of the ritual death of the Tibetan kings when their sons reached the age of thirteen, or when the king's son was capable of mounting a horse, that is, capable of ruling. There are many indications that this ritual regicide was an actual practice that, if true, would allow the king only a symbolic role representing the sacred nature of the lineage and the spiritual authority

---

9. Ibid., 268.

10. Rene de Nebesky-Wojkowitz, *Oracles and Demons of Tibet* (The Netherlands: Mouton and Company, 1956), 208; Haarh, 221.

11. Haarh, 239. Nakhri is also depicted as a foreign prince who was able to subdue and unite the Tibetans because of their disunion, or who was invited by the Tibetans to unite and rule them for the same reason or because they feared external threats. The characterization of Nakhri as foreign may derive from later Buddhist attempts to establish an Indian lineage for the Tibetan royalty. The pre-Buddhist legends have Olde Purgyal descending from an ancestral mountain with no reference to any foreign origin. Ibid., 234.

12. R.A. Stein, *Tibetan Civilization* (London: Faber and Faber, 1972), 221.

of the dynasty. The king was thought to embody the *bLa*, or the soul, of the state. As the physical embodiment of the collective soul, the king was required to maintain the *bLa* in perfect condition, free from any defect, even that of old age:

> It is, in fact, a very common belief in the inferior [primitive] societies that the soul participates actively in the life of the body. If the body is wounded, it is wounded itself and in a corresponding place. Then it should grow old along with the body. In fact, there are peoples who do not render funeral honors to men arrived at senility; they are treated as if their souls also had become senile. It also happens that they regularly put to death, before they arrive at old age, certain privileged persons, such as kings or priests, who are supposed to be the possessors of a powerful spirit whose protection the community wishes to keep. They thus seek to keep the spirit from being affected by the physical decadence of its momentary keepers; with this end in view, they take it from the organism where it resides before age can have weakened it, and they transport it, while it has as yet lost nothing of its vigor, into a younger body where it will be able to keep its vigor intact.[13]

The actual historical kings would have had a natural incentive to try to alter this practice, both for their physical survival and in order to increase their personal political power. In order for the king to assume a more dominant role, it was necessary to sever the connection of the sovereign with the soul of the ancestor. This was accomplished by means of the myth of Grigum Tsanpo cutting the *Mu* cord. The significance of this event is that the Tibetan kings were able to transcend their symbolic role and become actual ruling sovereigns. The myth of Grigum also signifies an important shift in Tibetan religious and cultural concepts. Because Grigum severed the *Mu* cord, the means by which he should return to the heavens at death, he was unable to ascend to heaven and left a corpse that had to be disposed of in a way befitting the king. The Tibetans therefore evolved a burial ritual and method of burial in a tomb, together known as *Dur Bon*, or Ritual of Tombs.[14]

Grigum Tsanpo has been identified as a local ruler in Kongpo, although much of the later mythology associates him with Yarlung.[15] After the death of Grigum Tsanpo, when he severed his *Mu* cord in a fight, the sons of Grigum fled to the east to Kongpo, Pobo and Nyang,

---

13. Emile Durkheim, *The Elementary Forms of the Religious Life*, trans. Joseph Ward Swain (New York: George Allen and Unwin, Inc., 1915; New York: Free Press, 1965), 78.

14. The myths of Grigum's funeral refer to the rites as having been introduced from Kashmir, Brusha (Gilgit) or Zhangzhung. Haarh, *Yar-Lun Dynasty*, 113.

15. H.E. Richardson, "The rKong-po Inscription," *Journal of Royal Asiatic Society*, 1972, 37.

where they became local rulers.[16] These three may have been local rulers whose lineages were assimilated into the mythology of the Yarlung state that incorporated their former territories. In the myth, one son is said to have gone west and founded Yarlung and to have thereafter been known as Pude Gungyal. The chronicles attribute to Pude Gungyal achievements that are characteristic of the founder of a nation: discovery of principal metals, introduction of agriculture and irrigation, building of the great castle of Yarlung, and introduction of the Bon religion.[17]

The mythology of Grigum Tsanpo's three sons, each of whom ruled one of the kingdoms of Kongpo, Pobo and Nyang, indicates that these states preceded Yarlung. That one of these kings, Pude Gungyal, then became king of Yarlung indicates a kinship relation between Kongpo and Yarlung, or simply the desire on the part of Yarlung to assimilate the mythology of an earlier center of Tibetan culture. The significance of the myth seems to be that Yarlung is the successor of three previous kingdoms to the east: Kongpo, Pobo and Nyang. Kongpo is known to Tibetan historians as an area originally of Mon habitation; the myth may therefore reflect the assimilation of the indigenous Mon population of the plateau along with their mythology.

Religious Foundations

The pre-Buddhist religion of Tibet is generally known as Bon. Bon actually means "invocation," in the sense of invoking a deity. Bon is usually divided into three stages: *Jol* Bon, *Dur* Bon and *Yungdrung* Bon.[18] *Jol* Bon is actually pre-Bon, the indigenous religion of Tibet. *Yungdrung* Bon appears to be a further and more complete version of the *Dur* Bon introduced during the time of Grigum Tsanpo. *Yungdrung* Bon may represent an early version of Buddhism. Its founder, Shenrab, "excellent shaman," may refer to the historical Buddha.[19]

Jol Bon was animistic in beliefs and shamanistic in its ritual aspects. Animism is an early and universal cosmological idea characterized, according to Paul Radin, by "a kind of undifferentiated monism."[20] The phenomena of life and nature tend to be understood as related in the

---

16. Haarh, *Yar-Lun Dynasty*, 152.

17. Ibid., 122, 328.

18. Ibid., 106.

19. David Snellgrove, *Indo-Tibetan Buddhism* (Boston: Shambhala, 1987), 390. Yundrung means swastika. The Bon swastika was left-handed. The right-handed swastika is a symbol of Buddhism.

20. Paul Radin, *Primitive Religion* (Viking Press, 1937; New York: Dover Publications, Inc., 1957), 273.

sense that both are animated by life-force or spirit. Both are thought to be connected; humans may believe that their actions are reflected in nature or vice-versa. This is described by Radin as "extreme subjectivism" or as a "tropism" between the ego and the external world.[21] Animism is actually a pre-religious form of human philosophical speculation: "Animism is not a religion at all; it is a philosophy. The belief in the general animation of nature has nothing to do with the supernatural."[22] At this early stage in the development of human religious and cosmological concepts, there is no heavenly realm of gods nor belief in the efficacy of appealing for heavenly assistance. There may be a primary conception of a distinction between Heaven and Earth, heaven being conceived of only in the sense of "Sky," but consciousness is primarily focused upon the realities of earthly existence. This undifferentiated monism becomes dualistic, or objectified, due not to cosmological distinctions between Heaven and Earth but to the essential distinction between Life and Death.

To the early Tibetans, death was thought to be a loss of the life-force but not an extinction of that force. The life-force was thought to continue to exist after death; it had obviously once existed, therefore, after its departure from the dead body, it must continue to exist in some other place. The conception that nature was animated by a force comparable with or even identical to that which animated humanity led to the belief that this force was transferrable. According to Tucci, "The *bLa* is a mobile soul which can take its residence anywhere, in a tree, a rock, an animal, but nevertheless remains most closely linked with the life of the person concerned."[23] Spirits of nature were thought tp have an essential connection with, and potential influence upon, human life. Such spirits could be benevolent but were also potentially malevolent because of their association with death, sickness and the fearsome powers of nature.

Human respect for the powers of nature is rooted both in a realistic appraisal of nature's powers, awesomely displayed in the environment of Tibet, and in a fear born of the primal awe of existence and the apprehension of death. Because the force of nature was thought to be identical with that which animated humanity, nature then had the potential to influence the life of humans; and because the environment was identified with the realm of the dead, through the population of nature with the souls of deceased humans, that influence had a potentially dangerous character. This conception led to an imaginary population of the natural environment with spirits and demons hungry for their former human

21. Ibid., 26, 7.
22. Ibid., 198.
23. Giuseppe Tucci, *The Religions of Tibet*, trans. Geoffrey Samuel (Berkeley: University of California Press, 1980), 192.

existence or nature spirits capable of meddling in the lives of humans. The Tibetans populated their cosmos with a multitude of spirits. The realm of the earth was thought to be inhabited by the *genii loci*, who fell into several main categories: the *Tsan*, "fierce ones" who inhabit the air; the *Nyan*, gods of stones, trees and mountains; *Sab Dag*, "earth owners," gods of the soil; *Zhi Dag*, "place owners;" and the *kLu*, serpent deities, who are associated with the underworld and with water in all its forms (springs, streams, lakes, rain).[24]

Because of the perception of the environment as inhabited by numerous, powerful and potentially malevolent deities upon whose domain humanity must inevitably transgress in the activities of life, Tibetans' relations with nature spirits were conducted as sensitive territorial negotiations with potentially hostile powers. Great efforts were made to avoid offense to the *genii loci* who inhabited the features of the environment, especially trees, stones, forests, springs, lakes and mountains. The dangers associated with offense to any of these spirits were those involving the human soul itself. Spirits of nature had the power to affect the health, prosperity and even the life of humans: "If, for instance, a man through his negligence causes the illness of a *klu*, then the offending man will meet the same fate himself."[25] Certain classes of spirits were associated with specific diseases, the *kLu* with leprosy and the *Nyan* with smallpox.[26]

Ekvall relates how in Amdo, eastern Tibet, leprosy is found almost exclusively among the agriculturalists and only rarely among the nomads, thus seemingly confirming the Tibetan belief that leprosy results from offense to the lords of the soil associated with plowing and planting. This example also indicates how such beliefs arose to explain the facts of life and the perils of existence within a hostile environment. Human encroachment on the rights of natural powers included pollution of springs or streams, disturbances of the soil or rock, and especially the insults to the gods of the soil inherent in the practice of agriculture:

Two of the many occasions which provoke the ill-humor and vengeance of particular powers (in this case the *klu* ruling the underground or the *sa bdag*) are the carrying away of stones and the digging of the earth. . . . These actions are dangerous in themselves and for those who perform them because they represent a damaging irruption into the domain of the powers of the underworld. Since the moment when the first king introduced agriculture this impurity has weighed upon man. The working of the earth

24. Robert B. Ekvall, *Religious Observances in Tibet* (Chicago: University of Chicago Press, 1964), 25, 78; Hoffman, 94.

25. Tucci, *Religions of Tibet*, 172.

26. Helmut Hoffman, "Early and Medieval Tibet," in *The Cambridge History of Early Inner Asia* (Cambridge: Cambridge University Press, 1990), 95.

by man signified the coming of a new order of things, upsetting the previous state. The *klu, gnyen, glud, lha, lha mo, sman* and all the other countless numina burned in anger at this and punished man's lack of consideration with all kinds of harm. Thus man was obliged to assure himself of the assistance of the seers, those first *institutores* of a civilized common life, who instructed him in the necessary rites of atonement and defence operations.[27]

The resèmblance of internal and external spirits opened up a field for professional specialization to shamans, sorcerers and medicine-men. These religious formulators or specialists were individuals who had some predilection toward speculation on the nature of existence, or they were those who were thought by others to have some insight, even connection, to the world of the dead because of their experience with near-death events, trance or epilepsy. The religious specialists' role usually began with a particular personal charisma and developed into a profession. Religious specialists had a personal interest in creating and magnifying the distinctions between the realms of life and death, objectifying and externalizing the conception of spirits, and proposing themselves as mediators between these realms. Subjective spiritual and religious impulses can be interpreted by anyone, but the externalized, personified spirits require the mediation of the specialist who has a technique or ritual for dealing with them. Because of the fearsome nature of the external spirits and their ability to affect humanity, both individually and collectively, in possibly negative and life-threatening ways, the religious specialist was able to accentuate his own role. This is not to say that religion is an invention of the religious specialists, but that they have a natural stake in the elaboration of religion:

> Who in primitive societies benefits most materially from the performance of magical rites? The answer is simple and decisive: the medicineman, the shaman, and the priest. He is paid doubly for his services, first by receiving gifts either in the form of money or its equivalent and, secondly, by acquiring power. It is to his interest to invest as much of the daily life of a group as he possibly can with magical implications and rites.[28]

Adept shamans were thought capable of both finding and concealing souls, or one of the multiplicity of souls, in external objects or animals. Much ritual was devoted to discovering the location of the these souls, either in order to benefit ailing humans or to ward off malevolent spirits or competitor shamans.[29] Each Bon practitioner, or Bonpo, had his own

27. Tucci, *Religions of Tibet*, 201.
28. Radin, *Primitive Religion*, 22.
29. Ibid., 25. See also Mircea Eliade, *Shamanism: Archaic Techniques of Ecstasy*, trans. Williard R. Trask (Princeton: Princeton University Press, 1972).

rituals in which he was proficient and his own specialities in terms of rituals, types of situations in which he was proficient, and panoply of spirits with whom he was supposedly familiar.

Besides being in a position of power himself, the religious formulator had a natural tendency to ally with political leaders. The two roles supported each other: the political leader authenticated the position of the religious specialist; the religious specialist provided religious legitimation to the political leaders. The Bonpo shamans were an integral element in the foundation and maintenance of the early Tibetan state: "The original (Bon) rituals had at their base the goal of assuring protection and assistance to the person of the king, the tribal chieftains and privileged families."[30] The royal authority or sovereign power of the Tibetan king was protected by Bon.[31] Bon was the protector of the sacred character of the king or of the king's *bLa*, or soul, in the sense that the king embodied the soul of the nation. Tucci describes the role of Bon as an essential element in the composition of the state:

> Bon dominates the community in general and its leaders in particular, above all the king. In this sense it is said in some chronicles that the Bon look after the life of the king or aid his ministers with word and deed, or that they keep in view the defense of the country's borders.[32]

The king had a natural tendency to ally with those of the religious class who favored the celestial over the animistic religion, thus freeing himself from his role as the purely symbolic soul of the ancestor on earth in favor of a more objective interpretation of his existence and function. As the Tibetan king began to free himself from the restrictions of religious conservatism, he was able to consolidate more power around himself and the institution of the Tibetan state. The Bonpo, in a symbiotic development, developed into a body of professionals whose role was the spiritual legitimation and protection of the state.

Epic Mythology

Many of the elements of Bon survived in Tibetan popular religion, known as *Mi-chos*, even after Buddhism became the predominant religion of Tibet. This popular religion has an unambiguous relation to Tibetan

---

30. Tucci, *Religions of Tibet*, 213.

31. Haarh, *Yar-Lun Dynasty*, 106.

32. Tucci, *Religions of Tibet*, 232. Bonpos, armed with clubs, led Tibetan troops into battle. Ren Shumin, "The Military Strength of the Tubo Kingdom," *Tibet Studies*, vol. 2, no. 1 (1991), 140.

cultural identity that Buddhism, as a foreign import, lacks. Some texts describe Tibetan political authority and legitimacy being protected and substantiated by the Bon, the *Grun* and the *De'u*.[33] The *Grun* are generally described as bards and the *De'u* are characterized as riddlers or diviners. The tales sung by the *Grun* were usually genealogies of families, myths of origin of the ancestors and histories of particular small areas: "These accounts give not merely genealogical outlines, but detailed histories of the origin of the family concerned, of the ancestor's descent from a mountain or from the sky, of struggles with hostile powers, the overcoming of demons and so forth."[34] The recitation by the *Grun* of these myths reminded the community of its origins and its past history.

The most popular myth of Tibet is that of Ling Gesar. This myth is of epic proportions and includes many of the elements of Tibetan mythology in popular form. Gesar was probably an actual historical king of Ling, or Lingtsang, in northern Kham, who reigned about 1050.[35] However, this historical king has been assimilated to a myth that vastly predates him. Gesar is also known as Gesar of Khrom, which Stein and Roerich believe derives from Caesar of Rome.[36] The name of the country of Ling may derive from the Sanskrit *Jambuling*, "Universe," therefore implying a universal, rather than exclusively local, character to the myth. Stein has shown that the local myth of Lingtsang may have an earlier version in that of the Lang tribe of Amdo, who were of the Don Sumpa tribal group.[37]

Gesar is worshiped by the nomads of Amdo as an *Amne*, or ancestor; the holy mountain of Amne Machin is known as the "Palace of Gesar."[38] In Ling, Gesar is said to have his *ku-lha*, or external soul, in the *Yul Lha* of Ling.[39] Gesar appears in the human realm to subdue the demons who make life difficult for humanity. In the epic, these demons appear mainly in the form of the kings of surrounding countries whom Gesar subdues. These demon-kings are identified as the kings of upper and lower Hor, Jang (Nanchao, in Yunnan), Mon and Tagzig (Persia), which indicates that the history of the expansion of the Tibetan empire has been incorporated into the myth.

The Gesar epic exists in nearly as many versions as there are reciters.

---

33. Haarh,*Yar-Lun Dynasty*, 106. Namkhai Norbu, *Drung, Deu and Bon: Narrations, Symbolic Languages and the Bon Tradition in Ancient Tibet* (Dharamsala: Library of Tibetan Works and Archives, 1995), xi.

34. Tucci, *Religions of Tibet*, 232.

35. R.A. Stein, "Introduction to the Gesar Epic," *Tibet Journal*, VI, no. 1 (1981), 11.

36. Ibid., 13; George N. Roerich, "The Epic of King Kesar of Ling," *Journal Royal Asiatic Society of Bengal*, VIII, 1942, 309.

37. Stein, "Gesar Epic," 12.

38. Roerich, "Kesar of Ling," 279.

39. Stein, "Gesar Epic," 6.

With the exception of the borrowed elements, the epic is a popularized version of Tibetan mythology and history, a never-ending saga to which the bards are constantly adding new material or reinterpreting the old. The bards are usually solitary individuals who wander and perform what they know of the epic from memory. They have all learned versions of the same general tale, and, even though they recite their versions differently and elaborate freely, they are recognized as performers of the same myth of Tibetan cultural origins. Shenrab, the founder of Bon, is often mentioned in the epic, confirming that the myth has origins that predate its Buddhist versions.[40] The narrative of the myth can be recited or sung, occasionally accompanied by dancers who act out the story. The bard often has a painting depicting the story he tells. The performance has a mystical and liturgical function of reviving of traditions and renewing the harmony of humanity and nature.

The *De'u* were in more modern times merely riddlers, but their art may have had an origin in *mantra* and their function may have previously had more ritualistic character and meaning. Both *Grun* and *De'u* clearly have their origins in Bon.[41] Their role in Tibetan culture and society is similar to that of the mountain cults. Both have a local particularist purpose, or are even a kind of regional religion, but because they contain so many universal elements they provide the basis for more unifying myths. The saga of Ling Gesar is popular in most areas of Tibet and has been transmitted to Mongolia where, as in Tibet, it became a local cultural myth despite its foreign origins.

Mountain Cults

Animistic beliefs were formulated by individuals and societies to facilitate human existence within a seemingly hostile world. Community beliefs and rituals in which most or all members of a group participate are both a manifestation of the need for group solidarity and a means to achieve that purpose. Societies evolve rules that serve collective needs for status, cohesion and social organization. Some degree of group conformity is usually required, due to the need for community solidarity in religious ritual and because the consequences of offences to the spirits were thought to accrue to the collective.

An example of communal ritual conformity in Tibet involves the spirits of springs, the *kLu*, who were thought to cause leprosy when offended by human conduct. Such offenses usually took the form of pollution of a spring in some manner such as bathing, washing clothes or defile-

---

40. Roerich, "Kesar of Ling," 284.
41. Tucci, *Religions of Tibet*, 232.

ment with human excrement. The prohibitions against such conduct serve as an aspect of community organization in that all must cooperate to avoid such pollution by any member of the community in order to avoid the wrath of the spirit against all. A beneficial ecological effect of this belief is that springs are kept pure for community water supply.

Perhaps the most significant sociological effect of the animistic belief system is the necessity of respect for and propitiation of the deceased ancestors. The cult of ancestors can be understood as humanity's attempt to orient itself psychologically within the physical environment. The conception that souls of the dead could inhabit features of the landscape naturally led to a sense of the environment, or salient aspects of the environment, as embodying the spirit of the ancestors. As each Tibetan valley became the territory of a clan or tribe, it was populated not only with Tibetans but with their "exterior souls" as well. Physical territory was psychologically secured by means of a population of the environment with the souls of the ancestors. Revered ancestors became embodied in the most awesome or unique features of the landscape and were considered in all of their roles—as ancestors, spirits and animated geography— to play a continuing part in the prosperity of the family, clan, tribe and region.

In Tibet, the majestic mountains became the natural locations for these ancestral spirits. In a study on mountain cults and state formation in Tibet, J. Russell Kirkland described the evolution of the connection between the ancestor and mountain cults:

> The original Kong-po tradition shows a mountain cult specifically adapted to respond to a group's need for externalized symbols of its shared ancestry and hence of its common identity. The mountain was first of all the focus of the land, of the territory which belongs to "us," embodying the homeland in a visible and concrete manner. Second, by the identification of the group's common ancestor with the spirit of the mountain, the mountain's presence served to recall the temporal "roots" of the group as well as to inspire a sense of solidity and endurance within the common fellowship. Descent from the common ancestor and proximity to the sacred mountain consequently worked together to provide the sense of common identity which permitted effective group action. The mountain cult and the ancestral tradition provided a combined effective conduit for translating spatial, temporal, and consanguinary data into a profound social reality.[42]

---

42. J. Russell Kirkland, "The Spirit of the Mountain: Myth and State in Pre-Buddhist Tibet," *History of Religions*, vol. 21, no. 3 (February 1982), 268. An example from a Tibetan border area illustrates the relations between a Tibetan community and its mountain deity

In Tibet, the names of some sacred mountains have the meaning of "forefathers" (A-myes or Amne, as in Amne Machin).[43] The progenitor ancestors with which Tibetan sacred mountains were identified were often great warriors who led the tribe or clan in taking possession of a particular territory:

> The sacred mountains are also warrior gods. They are denoted by terms meaning 'chief' or 'king' (*btsan*, like the ancient kings, or *rgyal*). They are regarded as mighty heroes who have died.[44]

> The 'gods of the country' (*yul-lha*) and the warrior gods are found as much in natural environments as in the human body. They are often regarded as kings, heroes and warriors of the past whose soul, exalted by their exploits, lives on and becomes a protecting deity.[45]

In the Bon tradition, the royal ancestor originates from the heavenly realm, the world of the *Lha*, and descends by means of the *Mu* chord onto the ancestral mountain. Both the *Mu* cord and the mountain appear as mythic connecting links between the cosmic worlds; both are characteristic of shamanistic mythologies. The first mythical king of Tibet, Olde Purgyal, descended onto a mountain to rule over Tibet. Seven of the kings of Tibet are said to have descended onto mountains, perhaps indicating that traditions of separate regions have been assimilated to one dynastic myth.[46] The names of the tombs of all the historical Tibetan kings contain the word *ri*, or mountain.[47]

A part of the Tibetan ritual cycle was the summer *sang* (incense) festival at the *Yul Lha* or holy mountain of each valley or region. This ritual, because it honored the ancestors and revived the sense of common ori-

---

(*Yul Lha*) in the ecological, spiritual and social sense. The Sherpa of Khumbu, now a part of Nepal, migrated to the Everest region only some 450 years ago. They established a prominent mountain, which is just above the main villages of Khumjung and Khunde, as their "country god," *Khumbu Yul Lha*. In fact, the area where the villages are situated was formed by a massive landslip from the front side of the mountain. The area of inhabitation is then an actual creation of the mountain itself. The village of Namche is located on the flank of the landslip, at the site of a perpetual spring, the home of a *kLu* deity. This example is perhaps extraordinary but not excessively so in the environment of the Himalaya and Tibetan plateau. Few sites for habitation are found except in similar geological circumstance. This example also demonstrates the mobility of the Yul Lha and the perseverance of the pre-Buddhist tradition within the Buddhist society of the Sherpa.

43. Stein, *Tibetan Civilization*, 207.
44. Ibid., 203.
45. Ibid., 228.
46. Tucci, *Religions of Tibet*, 218.
47. Haarh, *Yar-Lun Dynasty*, 392.

gins and collective destiny of the group, was an important aspect of the emerging sense of Tibetan collective identity. The manner in which this type of mountain cult was practiced varied from region to region, but the central idea remained the same everywhere. Samten Karmay describes the ritual, which has survived until the present time, as it was performed in the Ngaba area of eastern Tibet in 1985:

> On the first day, they (only men) gather together with their horses and tents on a plateau in front of the sacred mountain. . . . Each man must bring an arrow five or six meters long. . . . At the cairn (on top of the mountain) a fumigation offering takes place before the ritual of planting the arrows in the cairn; this is then followed by the scattering of "wind-horses" printed on small white printed squares launched by their thousands. . . . As the arrow is man's symbol, by planting it in the cairn, man, through this ritual gesture, places his person under the mountain divinity's protection. . . . Participation in such a ritual therefore implies being totally integrated into the community thereby inheriting social and political obligation, moral and individual responsibility, and affirming communal and national solidarity in face of external aggression. . . . The mountain cult in Tibetan culture therefore plays a very significant role in the build-up of national identity through each individual identifying himself as an active member of the community and as a patriot of the nation. . . . It is in fact a survival of the ancient tradition which the spread of Buddhism never totally effaced.[48]

These rituals accentuate local particularism but have universal aspects as well. Mountain rituals were universal in the Tibetan environment; the cult itself became a universal Tibetan tradition, conducted at the same time of the year in every area and employing similar ritual elements; mountain rituals were thus significant in terms of an emerging sense of a common Tibetan cultural identity.[49] The commonalty of these rituals provided some sense of common cultural identity even though the deities themselves were originally autonomous and even antagonistic. When the autonomous states, or *yul*, of central Tibet were politically unified, their mountain spirits, or *Yul Lha*, were united in a parallel political arrangement. Max Weber describes this as a universal process:

> Whenever a plurality of settled communities with established local gods

---

48. Samten Karmay, "The Question of National Identity in Tibet," paper presented at the Conference on Tibet, School of Oriental and African Studies, University of London, March 1990, 10.

49. Ibid., 12; Kirkland, "Spirit of the Mountain," 270. This is true even though mountain cults were not unique to Tibet but were prevalent in China and Mongolia as well, where they had similar effects.

expanded the area of the political association through conquest, the usual result was that various local gods of the newly amalgamated communities were thereupon associated into a religious totality.[50]

The Tibetan local states were first united in a confederate type of arrangement in which local autonomy was retained in exchange for recognition of some sort of dominance of the strongest. The local mountain gods were arranged in a similar fashion, in a kind of hierarchy in which the *Yul Lha* of the dominant area was considered to be in some sort of kinship relationship with the deities of the other local areas. The major mountain gods, including Nyenchenthangla, the *Yul Lha* of central Tibet; Yarla Shampo, the *Yul Lha* of Yarlung; and Amne Machen, the *Yul Lha* of Amdo, were considered sons of Olde Gungyal in Olkha, the most ancient of the mountain *Yul Lha*.[51]

The ancestor mountain cult formed the basis for the spiritual and political legitimation of the original small Tibetan states and later for the Yarlung dynasty. The Yarlung kings legitimated their rule by the mythology of the descent of the original kings from the heavenly realms, an elaboration of the original cult of the ancestor mountain. This descent from the gods was, according to Haarh, "the fundamental prerogative of the Tibetan kings, ultimately signifying the very foundation upon which the royalty had been instituted."[52] The ancestor mountain becomes the celestial deity descended upon earth to rule among men:

In descending from the mountain to rule his people, Nya-k'yi brought the ancestral divinity down with him. That is to say, the divinity of the ancestral mountain was no longer embodied in the mountain itself but rather in the person of the new king. Nya-k'yi assumed the kingship with its ancestral divinity and brought it down from above, into the world of men. His successors thus saw the source of their divine rule in him, Nya-k'yi, instead of in the old mountain spirit, 'O-lde gung-rgyal. Gradually the figure of Nya-k'yi developed from that of a mere historical ancestor into that of a heavenly being, who, at the beginning of time, descended upon the holy mountain to rule the world of men.[53]

50. Max Weber, *Economy and Society*, ed. Guenther Roth and Claus Wittich (Berkeley: University of California Press, 1968), 416.

51. Nebesky-Wojkowitz, *Oracles and Demons*, 208; Haarh, *Yar-Lun Dynasty*, 221.

52. Haarh, *Yar-Lun Dynasty*, 212.

53. Kirkland, "Spirit of the Mountain," 267.

Political Foundations of the Yarlung State

Tibetan mythic history reveals that the areas of earliest cultural and political origins in central Tibet were in the eastern districts centered around Kongpo. Olde Purgyal, the first Tibetan sovereign, is said to have descended upon the mountain Olde Gungyal in Olkha, in western Kongpo.[54] The first sovereign of Tibet, whether Olde Purgyal or Nakhri Tsanpo, was met upon his descent from the mountain by the chieftains of the local Tibetan *Yul*, the *Gyalphran*, who then united under his leadership. Some versions of the myth have Olde Purgyal being met by Bonpos, or *Gyalphran* and Bonpos. These Bonpos are described as the priests of the mountain cult.[55]

In a list of the countries of the *Gyalphran*, all that can be identified are located in contiguous areas of central Tibet. The mythology of this unification of the *Gyalphran* under the authority of a single ruler may reflect the actual historical unification achieved in the seventh century. Interestingly, all of the *Gyalphran* are listed with the names of their rulers, castles, ministers, chief shaman, and protecting *Lha*, *Yul Lha* and spirits of the place (*Zhidag*).[56]

Although there are varying lists of the *Gyalphran*, the tradition often refers to them, or their countries, as twelve in number. By a comparison of manuscripts, Haarh derived a list of twelve countries that are common to all manuscripts: (1) Nubs (*Nup*, "West") is associated with the Thangla pass in the Nyenchenthangla range to the northwest of Lhasa and may therefore be identified as Todlung, the region southeast of Nam Tso and northwest of Lhasa;[57] (2) Myan (Nyang) can be identified with the upper Nyang Chu, which enters the Tsangpo at Kongpo; not, as Tucci thought, the area of the same name near Gyantse;[58] (3) Kyiro is the valley of the Kyi Chu, the Lhasa valley;[59] (4) Naspo is the former name of Phenpo, the upper Kyi Chu valley north of Lhasa;[60] (5) Byero is unidentified); (6) O Yul may be Olkha; (7) Negs Yul is likely to have been within the Phenpo

---

54. Nebesky-Wojkowitz, *Oracles and Demons*, 221.

55. R.A. Stein, *Les Tribus Anciennes des Marches Sino-Tibetaines* (Paris: Imprimerie Nationale, 1959), 8.

56. Haarh,*Yar-Lun Dynasty*, 241.

57. F.W. Thomas, *Ancient Folk Literature from North-Eastern Tibet* (Berlin: Akademie Verlag, 1957), 10.

58. This identification has been convincingly argued by Beckwith and Richardson. Christopher Beckwith, "A Study of the Early Medieval Chinese, Latin, and Tibetan Historical Sources on Pre-Imperial Tibet," (Ph.D. diss., Indiana University, 1977), 224; Richardson, "The rKong-po Inscription," 37. The region known as Nyang adjacent to Kongpo is reputed to have been very populous in the ancient past and to have been the homeland of the Nyang clan. The confusion over this identification is somewhat explained by the fact that some texts mention two Nyang countries. Haarh, *Yar-Lun Dynasty*, 243.

59. Thomas, *Ancient Folk Literature*, 11.

60. Beckwith, "Pre-Imperial Tibet," 228; Thomas, *Ancient Folk Literature*, 10.

district, considering that it is later recorded as having been incorporated with Phenpo;[61] (8) Lumro is part of Phenpo;[62] (9) Sribs Yul is unidentified; (10) Kon Yul is Kongpo;[63] (11) Dags Yul is Dakpo;[64] (12) Chims Yul is the area near Samye and Tsetang on the Tsangpo to the north of Yarlung.[65]

Conspicuously absent from this list is Yarlung itself, but as the list derives from Yarlung dynasty mythology, it is to Yarlung that the *Gyalphran* submitted. Tibetan historical records discovered at Dunhuang describe the unification achieved under Yarlung in the early seventh century. Yarlung was actually the beneficiary of a revolt against the ruler of a predecessor state, Naspo, and its ruler, Zinpoje. The former vassals of Zinpoje submitted to the authority of the ruler of Yarlung, Tagbu Nyazig, swearing an oath of personal loyalty to him as ruler, or *Purgyal*. They swore to renounce Zinpoje forever, never be disloyal to *Purgyal*, never consider power themselves, and not obey anyone but *Purgyal*.[66] Tagbu Nyazig then acquired the appellation Namri, "Heavenly Mountain."[67]

The feudatory clan nobles who switched their allegiance from Zinpoje to Namri were nine in number: three from the Nyang clan, three from the Ba, one from the Mnon and two from the Tsepon.[68] The Nyang were probably the ruling clan of Nyang Yul, which borders on the valley of the Kyi Chu to the east. They were said to be "ministers of Lumro," which was allied to Zinpoje. The Ba were ministers of O Yul, which was also allied to Zinpoje. The Tsepon may be tentatively located in the area of a tributary of the Tsangpo to the east of Yarlung. They may have already been allied to Yarlung.[69] The location of the Mnon clan is unknown.[70] Each of these clans traced their origins to the "original" tribes of Tibet.[71]

As reward for their betrayal of Zinpoje, Nyang acquired Zinpoje's territory of Naspo, Ba acquired Maldro and the Tsepon acquired the valley of On, east of Yarlung, and Todlung to the northwest.[72] The name of Zinpoje's former domains were then changed from Naspo to Phen Yul or Phenpo.[73] Although Namri, by means of his deft alliance with the disaf-

61. Thomas, *Ancient Folk Literature*, 10.
62. Beckwith, "Pre-Imperial Tibet," 237; Thomas, *Ancient Folk Literature*, 10.
63. Thomas, *Ancient Folk Literature*, 9.
64. Ibid.
65. Ibid., 10.
66. Beckwith, "Pre-Imperial Tibet," 205.
67. H.E. Richardson, "Ministers of the Tibetan Kingdom," *Tibet Journal*, vol. II, no. 1 (1977), 13.
68. Beckwith, "Pre-Imperial Tibet," 224.
69. Richardson, "Ministers of the Tibetan Kingdom," 12.
70. Beckwith, "Pre-Imperial Tibet," 227.
71. Ibid., 210.
72. Richardson, "Ministers of the Tibetan Kingdom," 12.
73. Beckwith, "Pre-Imperial Tibet," 206.

fected vassals of Zinpoje, became the unifier of central Tibet, it is apparent that the honors more properly belong to Zinpoje, who apparently had established feudal relations with surrounding regions, including almost all of those that later became part of Yarlung's domains except Yarlung itself.

The territories of Yarlung were further expanded by the conquests of Tsang and Mon.[74] These campaigns were led by Kyungpo Zutse, of the Kyungpo clan and, presumably, of the Kyungpo region, the area between the Nag Chu and the Dza Chu to the northeast, indicating that Kyungpo was also part of the alliance. Namri finally subdued Dakpo to complete his consolidation of all the countries of central Tibet.[75] The headman of the Nyang clan, Nyang Zhangnang, is then said to have subdued the Sumpa on behalf of Yarlung.[76] Chinese chronicles state that Namri also subdued the tribes of Ch'iang on the Szechuan and Yunnan borders.[77]

In exchange for their loyalty to Yarlung, the clan nobles were awarded fiefdoms and subjects over whom they were to rule. These fiefdoms were generally their own home territories, with the territories formerly belonging to Zinpoje divided among them. Later, Kyungpo Zutse was awarded Tsang due to his having led the campaign that subdued Tsang on behalf of Namri, and Sengo Myichen, who subdued Dakpo, was awarded that land as his fiefdom. These fiefdoms would be inherited by the members of the feudal lord's clan should his actual male lineage be extinguished, rather than reverting to the state. The lord, for his part, pledged to abandon any members of his clan who were disloyal to the king.[78] These facts indicate that the feudatory nobles represented their clans; a feudal relationship was thus established with the clans, but the guarantee of this relationship was a personal oath of loyalty to the king taken by each of the clans' headmen.[79]

A member of each of the clans who submitted to Yarlung was appointed as a personal retainer (*ku gyal*) to the Yarlung king.[80] The *ku gyal* were more hostages than trusted courtiers or ministers.[81] The Tibetan system of

---

74. Ibid., 208. The conquest of the Mon reveals that the Mon were not yet completely assimilated. The Mon continue to exist as a separate ethnic group in Tibet to the present time.

75. Ibid., 209.

76. Richardson, "Ministers of the Tibetan Kingdom," 13.

77. Hoffman, "Early and medieval Tibet," 377.

78. A. Rona Tas, "Social Terms in the List of Grants of the Tibetan Tun-Huang Chronicle," *Acta Orientalia*, no. 1 (1972), 256.

79. Ibid.

80. Ibid., 267.

81. Beckwith, "Pre-Imperial Tibet," 231.

"same fate" is well known to have been applied during the historical dynasty, though we cannot know if it was established in conjunction with the unification under the reign of Namri. Under this system, at the birth of a future sovereign, several clan nobles were declared to be of his same fate. They would usually act as ministers to the king and share in his privileges, but they also had to share in his death, however that might occur. These "ministers" and their clans had a personal interest in preserving the life of the king as well as a strong disincentive against rebellion against the dynasty.[82] The *ku gyal* status was later decreed to be hereditary within clans, thus creating a feudal aristocracy based upon the clan, but also transcending the clan and creating a higher political structure based upon personal loyalty to the king.[83]

The Tibetan state under Yarlung owed its creation to the political machinations of the clans that defected from Zinpoje to Yarlung; these same clans continued to play a very large role in Tibetan politics, sometimes even overshadowing the authority of the sovereign. The defining characteristic of this system was the fact that the sovereign was more powerful than any of his vassals, but not as powerful as his vassals combined. The vassals retained much of the state-making power. This feudal system reflected the power structure of the transition between the clan system and the centralized state. The feudal clans were the creators of state power and they retained considerable autonomy, including control over territory and population within their fiefdoms, but the power of the state they created was increased by the transference of their personal loyalties from the clan to the sovereign.

The power of the Yarlung sovereign over his vassals was dependent upon their loyalty and their own political interest. The factor that allowed the sovereign to exercise actual authority over the clans was the creation of an administrative body, composed of retainers from each of the constituent clans, whose personal fate was tied to that of the king. The political system under Yarlung gradually developed from a relationship between clans, in which the clans held the actual power and retained autonomy, to a system of feudal privilege based upon personal and class relationships between the aristocracy and the ruling sovereign. Social classes also became more delimited and rigid, with less mobility between classes.[84]

The feudal system enabled the Yarlung sovereigns to establish military and administrative authority over territory far beyond the capability of Yarlung to directly administer, creating the political basis for the Tibetan state and, later, the Tibetan empire. Yarlung's political authority was

82. Haarh, *Yar-Lun Dynasty*, 346.
83. Rona Tas, "Social Terms," 269.
84. Ibid., 270.

enforced by the common interest of the clans as much as by the actual power of the ruling sovereign. The feudal system allowed the clan aristocracy to develop and increase its political power while the alliance between clans allowed them to project their combined power farther afield. Lattimore characterizes the pattern of formation of the early Tibetan state as inherently expansive:

> The moves that had made Lhasa [Yarlung] a capital had integrated the affairs of the most important Tibetan communities and had raised them from oasis-like isolation to at least a crude national level. The new state could not be stabilized at this level, however. Any attempt to stabilize without further development would necessarily have taken the form of internal conquest and the harsh domination of one region over others. The resentment arising out of this, working together with the obdurate geographical isolation of the various regions, would have resulted in breaking apart the new state and dislodging the king from his new position of superiority over the families that ruled the separate localities of the kingdom. It was necessary to compensate the interests that had been subordinated by extending the range and activity of conquest so that they too could benefit. . . . Only in this way, by making them participants in external conquests, was it possible to compensate those who had been subordinated to Lhasa.[85]

The nature of the political alliance established by Yarlung may best be described as a feudal confederation. The union of clans under Yarlung exhibited some of the characteristics of a confederation of the nomadic type in which tribes unite for the purpose of further conquests afield. Nomadic tribes usually unite only under the influence of some charismatic leader, often for the purpose of conquest of other nomads or of surrounding sedentary societies. The political union achieved by Yarlung, like nomadic confederations, was dependent upon rewards as a means of maintaining political unity. In some of its characteristics, the early Tibetan state fit the nomadic state pattern, but, in other aspects, it was significantly different.

The early Tibetan state was obviously not dependent upon exploiting surrounding sedentary societies, since central Tibet was an area of mixed economy and a sedentary style of life. In fact, the central Tibetan state expanded to include surrounding nomadic tribes, the reverse of the usual nomadic conquest of sedentary states. The political state that coalesced around the central agricultural base eventually united both the sedentary and nomadic populations of the plateau and combined the material

---

85. Owen Lattimore, *Inner Asian Frontiers of China* (Oxford: Oxford University Press, 1988), 221.

strengths of both economies. Within a period of little over a decade, the Yarlung confederation expanded to include all the peoples of the Tibetan plateau, creating in the process a centralized Tibetan state.

4

The Tibetan Empire

Consolidation of the Tibetan Empire

Namri died in 629. Kongpo, Nyang, Dakpo and Sumpa all revolted against Yarlung.[1] They were quickly subdued by Namri's son and successor, Srongtsan Gampo.[2] Srongtsan Gampo rapidly reconsolidated the Yarlung Tibetan state, moved the capital to Lhasa and resumed the process of territorial expansion. The first moves were toward the nomadic confederation to the immediate north of central Tibet, the Sumpa, and to the west toward central Tibet's cultural predecessor and rival, Zhangzhung. Sumpa was relatively easily subdued (a portion of the western Sumpa had already been subjugated by Zhangzhung). Zhangzhung, with its ancient culture and diverse economy, was more difficult to conquer. Zhangzhung was not finally overcome until 653.

The alliance with Sumpa facilitated further Tibetan expansion into the rich grasslands of the northeastern plateau, the territory of the Pailan and Tanghsiang, both in the area of the upper Yellow River (Ma Chu). Although the central Tibetans imposed their will upon the northeastern tribes by military force, their relations had much of a confederative character. Many of the nomadic tribes resisted Tibetan domination; on the other hand, many of the tribes of the northeast were apparently not too reluctant to unite with their distant kinsmen in order to oppose their traditional enemies, the Chinese. Some of the large tribal confederations, such as the Sumpa and Tanghsiang, may have bargained their military strength for a degree of equal treatment by the Tibetans and for a share in further territorial conquest.

In addition to the material and political resources of the sedentary population of the central Tibetan valleys, nomadic economy, especially wealth of mounted manpower, played a large role in Tibetan state formation. The nomadic tribes of the plateau were weak in political organi-

---

1. Helmut Hoffman, "Early and Medieval Tibet," in The Cambridge History of Early Inner Asia (Cambridge: Cambridge University Press, 1984), 377.

2. H.E. Richardson, "The rKong-po Inscription," *Journal of Royal Asiatic Society* (1972), 38.

zation but strong in terms of resources of men and animal power. All of these resources shared the characteristics of nomadic mobility and were therefore ideal for military campaigning. The nomadic tribes of the plateau provided mounted warriors, porterage by means of man and animal, and food on the hoof. Tibetan military strength was greatly increased by the addition of the horses they acquired by the conquest of the northeastern tribes.[3] The Tibetan style of warfare employed mounted and highly mobile cavalry, and typical nomadic weapons, the bow, short sword, lance and the shepherds' sling.[4] However, Tibetan armies could also adopt dismounted infantry tactics. Chinese sources describe the Tibetans' tactics as always putting their tribal allies in the forefront in battle. Only when these tribal auxiliaries were completely annihilated would the central Tibetan troops engage the enemy.[5]

Tibetan campaigns in the east were carried out under the leadership of the minister Gar Tongstan. The T'ang Annals state that it was chiefly due to Minister Gar that the Tibetans (Tu'fan) absorbed the Ch'iang tribes and "became preeminent in their native land."[6] Tibetan expansion to the northeast was facilitated by the weakness of the previously most dominant power of the area, the Tu-yu-hun. The Tu-yu-hun were a threat to Chinese control of the Kansu corridor leading to east Turkestan. The Chinese, in alliance with the Turks, attacked the Tu-yu-hun in 634 and 635 and forced their chief to seek safety among the Tanghsiang.[7]

The defeat of the Tu-yu-hun by the Chinese was convenient for the Tibetans, but it brought the Tibetans into conflict with the Chinese for influence in the Kokonor area. In 634 the Tibetans sent a mission to the T'ang court, a mission that the T'ang Annals describe as "tribute."[8] A Chinese ambassador was sent in reply. A Tibetan request for a marriage

---

3. The Kokonor area was famous for its horses. The Chinese traditionally sought Kokonor horses for their own armies. The Chinese bought these horses at a high price from all the frontier tribes as a means to weaken the Tibetans. Ren Shumin, "The Military Strength of the Tubo Kingdom," *Tibet Studies* (1991), 144.

4. Ibid., 140.

5. Ibid., 143. Khazanov mentions that nomadic confederations often put submitted tribes into the forefront in battle. A. M. Khazanov, *Nomads and the Outside World* (Cambridge: Cambridge University Press, 1984), 254.

6. F.W. Thomas, *Ancient Folk-Literature from North-Eastern Tibet* (Berlin: Akademie Verlag, 1957), 8. The T'ang dynasty (618-907) was virtually contemporaneous with the Tibetan empire (630-842).

7. Louis M. J. Schram, "The Mongours of the Kansu-Tibetan Frontier," *Transactions of the American Philosophical Society*, n.s., 51 (1961), 10.

8. F.W. Bushell, "The Early History of Tibet from Chinese Sources," *Journal of the Royal Asiatic Society* (1980), 443. This is Bushell's translation of the chapters relating to Tibet in the official *T'ang Dynasty Annals*.

alliance with the T'ang was refused.[9] In 637 or 638 the Tibetans attacked and defeated the Tanghsiang, Pailan and "other Ch'iang tribes," who then "formed the vanguard of the invading Tibetan armies."[10] The Tibetans also secured control of the former Tu-yu-hun territory. In 638 the Tibetans were encamped on the western border of China with an army reportedly of 200,000 men.[11]

The Tibetans sent envoys to the Chinese, bringing a suit of gold armour as "tribute." The Chinese responded by attacking the Tibetans. The T'ang Annals state that the Tibetans were defeated, waited several years and then apologized and again begged for an alliance, whereupon it was finally granted.[12] This version of events may reflect nothing more than the inability of the Chinese to admit their own weakness against the "barbarian" Tibetans. In any event, it was only in 640 that the Tibetan minister, Gar Tongtsan, by his personal eloquence, and, according to the Chinese version of events, a gift of 5,000 ounces of gold, persuaded the emperor to grant a princess in marriage to the Tibetan king.[13]

The Tibetans also made a marriage alliance with Nepal, apparently predating that with the Chinese, since the Nepalese princess, Belsa (Brikuti in Nepali), was considered by the Tibetans to be senior to the Chinese princess, Gyalsa (Wencheng in Chinese).[14] The Licchavi king of Nepal, Narendradeva, was exiled in Tibet from about 624 until 641. The marriage to Belsa may have taken place between 632 and 634.[15] The exile of the Licchavi king in Tibet, the marriage alliance and the fact that the Tibetans assisted in the restoration of Narendradeva in 641 are all evidence of a strong Tibetan influence in Nepal.[16] Srongtsan Gampo also married women of several prominent Tibetan clans as well as daughters of the kings of Zhangzhung and Minyak (Tanghsiang).[17]

---

9. Beckwith suggests that the T'ang ambassador may have suggested to the Tibetans that they seek a marriage alliance in order to establish good relations. Christopher Beckwith, The *Tibetan Empire in Central Asia* (Princeton: Princeton University Press, 1987), 22.

10. F.W. Thomas, *Nam: An Ancient Language of the Sino-Tibetan Borderland* (London: Oxford University Press, 1948), 31.

11. Bushell, "Early History of Tibet," 444. The number is probably an exaggeration. Chinese annals tended to inflate the numbers of "barbarian" armies as an explanation for why Chinese armies were defeated.

12. Ibid.

13. Beckwith, *Tibetan Empire*, 22.

14. Tsepon W.D. Shakabpa, *Tibet: A Political History* (New Haven: Yale University Press, 1967; New York: Potala Publications, 1984), 25.

15. Roberto Vitali, *Early Temples of Central Tibet* (London: Serindia, 1989), 114.

16. Ibid.

17. R.A. Stein, *Tibetan Civilization* (London: Faber and Faber, 1972), 62.

Srongtsan Gampo's marriage alliances with Nepal and China were important cultural influences on Tibet. Both the Nepalese and Chinese princesses were Buddhist; both brought large entourages of attendants and artisans. Each of Srongtsan Gampo's queens brought images of Sakyamuni Buddha to Lhasa; to house them, Brikuti founded the Jokhang, or Tsuglag Khang, and Wencheng founded the Ramoche.[18] The Jokhang was built over the site of a small pond that was reputed to be the home of a *naga* serpent spirit, the *Zhidag*, or *genii loci* of Lhasa. The Jokhang is therefore a symbol of the dominance of Buddhism over the indigenous spirits of Tibet. The Ramoche temple holds much lesser status in Lhasa and in Tibetan Buddhism, but the Buddha image brought by Wencheng and originally housed in the Ramoche was later exchanged with the Nepalese image in the Jokhang.[19]

The Chinese princess is said to have determined by means of Chinese divination (*feng shui*) that Tibet was like a demoness who must be subdued with Buddhist temples constructed on the various parts of her body. Buddhist temples were constructed for this purpose in a scheme of concentric circles from the center at Lhasa.[20] The temples of the inner circle are located at Yarlung, Lhasa, and in eastern and western Tsang. The middle circle is defined by temples at Kongpo, Lhotrak, Bhutan, and Saka Dzong in western Tsang. The outer zone is defined by temples in eastern Kham, Bhutan and Kyirong (near the Nepalese border). The location of the fourth temple of the outer circle is uncertain.[21] The building of these temples served not only to establish the Buddhist religion but also to define the territory of Tibet.[22]

---

18. Physical evidence of this identification is found in the orientation of the two temples: the Jokhang faces Nepal (or the route to Nepal), while the Ramoche faces directly to the east, toward China. Other temples and monasteries in Tibet almost invariably face to the south. Namkhai Norbu says that Tsuglag Khang means place, khang, containing the sacred scriptures, tsuglag. Tsuglag may be either Buddhist or Bon scriptures. Namkhai Norbu, *Drung, Deu and Bon* (Dharamsala: Library of Tibetan Works and Archives, 1995), 159.

19. This famous switch is the subject of several contradictory legends. The most likely explanation is that the switch was made because of rumors of a Chinese invasion. The Tibetans supposedly put the Chinese image in the Jokhang, assuming that an invading Chinese army would attempt to steal or destroy the Nepalese image. By switching the images, they hoped to dupe the invaders into stealing or destroying the wrong image.

20. Michael Aris, *Bhutan* (London: Aris and Phillips, 1979), 18.

21. Ibid., 23.

22. Ibid., 15. While the scheme for the construction of these temples is credited to the Chinese princess and to Chinese divinatory arts, Nepalese influence may have also played a part. Two elements of the legend in particular have counterparts in the mythology of Nepal. The location of the Jokhang over the home of a serpent spirit, and a story about how Nepalese masons building the Jokhang copied the outline of a stupa that had appeared by itself, recall the essential elements of the mythology of Svayambhu, the "self arisen" temple. Svayambhu arose out of the lake occupying the valley of Nepal in ancient times, the home

After the departure of Narendradeva and the arrival of Wencheng, both in 641, Chinese cultural influence apparently predominated over that of Nepal.[23] According to the T'ang Annals, Srongtsan Gampo "praised the costume of the great empire, and the perfection of their manners, and was ashamed of the barbarism of his own people." He reportedly "discarded his felt and skins, put on brocade and silk, and gradually copied Chinese civilization."[24] Chinese influence in Tibet was probably not as great as the Chinese claimed, but Srongtsan Gampo's loyalty to China after the marriage alliance was indicated by his dispatch of 7,000 Tibetan cavalry plus 5,000 men levied from Nepal to avenge the murder of a Chinese envoy to India.[25] Later Chinese governments would claim that Wenchung's arrival in Tibet began the process of civilization of the Tibetans and their cultural and political assimilation to China.

Among the entourage of Wencheng were scholars and scribes, who taught the Tibetans the bureaucratic and literary arts. However, at about the time of Wenchung's arrival, the Tibetans adopted a script for the writing of the Tibetan language from India. Srongtsan Gampo sent his minister, Thonmi Sambhota, to India to find an alphabet which could be adapted to the Tibetan spoken language. The alphabet chosen was an Indian Gupta script. The very rapid development of this script in Tibet has led many scholars to believe that prototype forms must have been introduced earlier. Zhangzhung may have already developed the basic elements of a written language before Thonmi Sambhota's journey. Both Zhangzhung's spoken and written languages may have been assimilated to Tibetan.[26]

The Tibetans' adoption of an Indian script reflects the predominance of their cultural ties with India and Inner Asia over those with China:

In Kushana times there had been chains of transmission all the way from India to China with the northwest Indian dialect of Gandhara and the Kharosthi script, which was favored by the Kushana, serving as the chief

---

of the Naga serpent spirits. The nagas had to be propitiated by a succession of Buddhas and Buddhist rites before the valley was fit for human habitation. The Nepal Valley was finally drained and the Naga spirits were compensated with temples built all over the Nepal (Kathmandu) valley. This legend of the creation of Nepal is found in written form as early as the third century; therefore, Brikuti and her entourage were surely familiar with this type of geomantic scheme. Manabajra Bajracharya and Warren W. Smith, *Mythological History of the Nepal Valley from Svayambhu Purana* (Kathmandu: Avalok Publishers, 1978).

23. Vitali, Early Temples, 114.

24. Bushell, "Early History of Tibet," 445.

25. Shakabpa, *Tibet: A Political History*, 28. Some of these Tibetan cavalry remained in Nepal as the Tamang (Tib. *Ta*, "horse," *mag* "soldier").

26. David Snellgrove, *Indo-Tibetan Buddhism* (Boston: Shambhala, 1987), 392.

literary media. But from the second century A.D. onward the use of Sanskrit greatly increased and the script in which the manuscripts that reached Central Asia were written was the typically Indian script known as Brahmi; its origin is obscure, but it develops from the third century B.C. onward as a peculiarly Indian script specially adapted to the sounds of the Sanskrit syllabary. This script prevails in Central Asia from perhaps the fourth century onward, and it was a form of this script that was adapted by the Tibetans in the early seventh century, if not before, for the writing of their own very different language.[27]

Thonmi Sambhota also produced a grammar and a standardized Tibetan spelling. Snellgrove regards this as evidence that earlier forms of spelling were in existence and had already begun the process of divergence; Tibetan writing of the seventh century shows a regularity that would be highly unlikely unless the grammar of Thonmi merely standardized a system of writing already in use for some time.[28] The Tibetan written language was acquired not for translating Buddhist texts, as later Buddhist historians would have it, but for the purposes of political administration. The ability to issue commands and to receive reports in a uniform written language facilitated the administration of the empire. An effect of the empire was that the Tibetan spoken language was standardized at least to the extent that people in outlying areas could understand the central Tibetan dialect sufficiently to follow orders and instructions.

Zhangzhung's role in the development of the Tibetan spoken and written languages are indicative of Zhangzhung's cultural influence on the development of central Tibetan civilization. The territory of Zhangzhung (Guge, Purang, western Chang Thang, Lahul, Spiti and Ladakh) supported a diverse economy based upon animal husbandry, agriculture and trade. Zhangzhung had contacts with the upper Indus valley and the civilizations of Kashmir, Baltistan and Gilgit, all of which had been greatly influenced by Gandharan culture. Further to the west, along routes that were certainly in use at the time, were the cultures of Bactria, Sogdiana and Persia. The center of Zhangzhung, the holy mountain of Kailash, was the center of the Indian cosmos as well; it was an ancient site of pilgrimage for Indians. Zhangzhung in the seventh century was an important cultural crossroads that undoubtedly had a significant influence upon the early stages of Tibetan civilization. That influence undoubtedly increased when Zhangzhung became a part of the Tibetan empire, even though Zhangzhung ceased to exist as an independent state.

Srongtsan Gampo was said to have spent the last years of his life con-

---

27. Ibid., 332.
28. Ibid., 387.

solidating his conquests, especially the difficult conquest of Zhangzhung.[29] A marriage alliance, of uncertain date, was made between Srongtsan Gampo's sister and Ligmi, the king of Zhangzhung. In 644 Ligmi's queen arranged an ambush of the king while he was on a tour of inspection of the western Sumpa; the Zhangzhung king was killed by central Tibetans led by Kyungpo Zutse, who was then made administrator of Zhangzhung. The Zhangzhung dynasty was subsequently abolished by the Tibetans in 653.[30]

Srongtsan Gampo died in 649 and was succeeded by his grandson, Mangsong Mantsen, who was still a child. The Gar family at this time gained dominance in the affairs of the Tibetan state.[31] In 654 Gar Tongtsan, in the name of the Tibetan Tsanpo (emperor), composed the first Tibetan legal code, established military administrative divisions, *ru*, or "horns," and watch posts on the frontiers, and prepared a census of Tibetan subjects and a measurement of agricultural fields for purposes of taxation. Tibetan ministers and governors were required to meet annually to decide upon military campaigns and administration of conquered territories.[32]

Administrative divisions were based upon the territorial power of the prominent clans or "shares of power of the regions," perhaps reflecting divisions of territory and power between the predominant clans of central Tibet.[33] This system of horns was originally composed of three districts: Central Horn in the Kyi Chu valley, Lhasa and Phenpo; Right Horn in southern central Tibet, eastern Tsang, centered around the Yarlung valley and perhaps including Dakpo; Left Horn in Nyang, Kongpo and perhaps Pobo. A fourth horn in Tsang was later added to these, and a fifth horn in the territory of Sumpa.[34] Insignia of rank, seals, "symbols of the heroes" and the flags of the horns were all designated.[35] Zhangzhung was not included in the Tibetan military system of horns, although it is described in other records as a "military district."[36] Each of the horns theoretically consisted of eight *tonde*, or "thousand-district," a district that

---

29. Beckwith, *Tibetan Empire*, 25; Hoffman, "Early and Medieval Tibet," 380.

30. Beckwith, *Tibetan Empire*, 20; G. Uray, "The Narrative of Legislation and Organization, *Acta Orientalia Hungarica*, XXVI (1972), 33. Ligmi's inspection tour of the Sumpa indicates that Zhangzhung, as late as 644, had some authority over parts of Sumpa.

31. Shakabpa, *Tibet: A Political History*, 29; Beckwith, *Tibetan Empire*, 26.

32. Uray, "Narrative of Legislation and Organization," 26.

33. Ibid., 18.

34. G. Uray, "The Four Horns of Tibet According to the Royal Annals," Acta Orientalia Hungarica, X (1960), 32.

35. Uray, "Narrative of Legislation and Organization," 21.

36. Snellgrove, *Indo-Tibetan Buddhism*, 388.

could field a thousand warriors.[37] Although some of these numbers may have been hypothetical, the figures provide some conception of the military capabilities of the Tibetans at the time. If all five horns and the royal bodyguards were included, the Tibetans theoretically could have fielded a force of over 40,000 troops. In addition, the nomadic tribes and frontier "savages" were divided into 60 tonde, potentially providing another 60,000 troops or porters.[38]

Sino-Tibetan Conflict

The territorial division of 654 reveals the extent of the Tibetan empire at the time. Sumpa was firmly under Tibetan control, but Zhangzhung was apparently still resistant. Even the Tu-yu-hun retained sufficient strength to require Gar Tongtsan to conduct campaigns there for eight years from 655.[39] In the northeast, the T'ang maintained their defenses at Sining and a strong presence east of Kokonor, preventing the Tibetans from gaining complete dominance in the Kokonor area.[40] Stalemated by the Chinese in the northeast, the Tibetans moved into the western Tarim via Zhangzhung, Great and Little Balur (Baltistan and Gilgit), and the passes of the Karakoram, making use of Zhangzhung for manpower, food and transportation.[41] In 659 the Tibetans, in alliance with two tribes of the Western Turks, captured Kashgar from the Chinese.[42] In 670 the four Chinese military garrisons of Anshi ("pacified west") in the Tarim (Kashgar, Khotan, Kucha and Karashar) were all given up to the Tibetans.[43] The T'ang sent an army of 100,000 men from the east to regain the Tarim, but they were defeated with great losses by a Tibetan army said (by the defeated Chinese) to number 200,000.[44]

In 667 Mangsong Mantsen died. Zhangzhung again revolted. In 678 the T'ang, taking advantage of the death of the Tibetan emperor and the revolt of Zhangzhung, attacked in the Kokonor with a large army but were defeated. The Chinese built a fortified city on the border of Tibet, at Sungpan, which they named Anjung Cheng, "Fortress for Pacification of Tibetans." This fortress was said to have been built "in order to cut off

---

37. Uray, "Four Horns," 31.
38. Uray, "Narrative of Legislation and Organization," 18.
39. Shakabpa, *Tibet: A Political History*, 29.
40. F.W. Thomas, *Ancient Folk-Literature*, 8.
41. Ibid., 30.
42. Ibid., 28.
43. Bushell, "Early History of Tibet," 448.
44. Ibid.

contact between the Tibetans and the Man."[45] The fortress was captured by the Tibetans, with Ch'iang assistance, the following year, after which many Man tribes are said to have submitted to the Tibetans.[46] The T'ang conceded that Tibetan territory "extended over more than ten thousand *li*, and from the Han and Wei dynasties downwards there had been no people among the nations of the west so powerful."[47]

In 692, due to Tibetan internal conflicts, the T'ang were able to regain their Tarim fortresses. The Gar clan, which had dominated Tibetan politics for some forty years, was challenged by a strong Tibetan Tsanpo, Khri Dusong Mangje. The Tibetans attempted to retake the Tarim in 693-94 but were defeated by the Chinese. Denied access to the Tarim, the Tibetans renewed their efforts in the northeast in Kokonor. After winning a decisive victory over a Chinese army in the Kokonor region in 695, and threatening Liangchou with an army of 40,000 in 696, the Tibetans sent an embassy to the Chinese proposing peace. The Tibetans proposed an alliance with the Chinese against the Turks, who were menacing both Chinese and Tibetans in the Tarim. The Tibetans offered to withdraw from the Tarim in exchange for the Kokonor territory. The T'ang, aware of Tibetan internal conflicts, countered that they, too, would withdraw from the Tarim in exchange for the Kokonor.

In 701 the Tibetans joined with the Turks in a raid on Liangchou. In the winter of 702 the Tibetans held a great levy of the Sumpa and then raided Maochou. Dusong died in 704 while leading an expedition against Nanchao.[48] Dusong's successor, Tride Tsugtsen, was a minor; therefore, his mother, Trimalo, served as regent. Trimalo, a devout Buddhist, took the initiative to arrange peace with the Chinese by means of another marriage alliance. The death of Tride Tsugtsen delayed the alliance until Trimalo was able to revive it on behalf of Tride's son, her grandson, Megasthom. The T'ang emperor, who was dominated by the empress dowager, a devout Buddhist, granted the request in 707, and the princess, Jincheng, was sent to Tibet. The official T'ang records described the marriage alliance as submission by the Tibetans:

45. Charles Backus, *The Nan-chao Kingdom and T'ang China's Southwestern Frontier* (Cambridge: Cambridge University Press, 1981), 26. The Tibetans are here referred to as "Jung," a generic term for the western barbarians. (Anjung means "pacification of Jung.") The peoples of the Min Shan south of Anjung and northwest of Chengdu, the Ch'iang of Gyalmorong, were still known as Man (Mon) to the Chinese. The peoples of the Anjung area were reputedly a mixture of Man and Ch'iang.

46. Ibid., 28.

47. Bushell, "Early History of Tibet," 450.

48. Shakabpa, *Tibet: A Political History*, 32.

As regards the Tu-fan, their abode is in the west country, from which, soon after the rise of our imperial house, they came early with tribute. . . . . Since this time, when the Princess Wencheng went and civilized this country, many of their customs have been changed. But our borders have been constantly full of troops. Now however the tsanp'u, and the k'otun his grandmother, and the chiefs have for several years shown true submission, and with a view to cement the ancient bonds of kinship they now ask to renew friendship.[49]

The Tibetans demanded and received, as part of the "dowry" of Jincheng, territory in the upper Yellow River valley known as the "Nine Bends West of the Yellow River." In the words of the T'ang Annals, the Tibetans thereby gained a "fertile and rich territory, where they could encamp troops and pasture their herds, which was also close to the T'ang border, and from this time they again revolted and began to lead warriors to invade and plunder."[50] The Tibetans proposed a boundary treaty in the upper Yellow River area in 714, but, when it was not agreed to by the T'ang, they plundered Chinese cities of Kansu, including Lanchou, and invaded areas as far east as the T'ao River and the headwaters of the Wei. The Tibetans also built a bridge across the Yellow River at Ragya to facilitate their campaigns east of river and stationed two armies and constructed fortifications along their frontier.

After being repulsed in areas around the T'ao, the Tibetans again proposed peace, claiming that their armies and defenses east of the Yellow River were there solely to protect their own territory against aggressive actions on the part of the Chinese. The Tsanpo's proposal for peace was accompanied by an appeal from Jincheng, but both were refused by the T'ang court because the Tibetans refused to "submit." The T'ang Annals state that "the Tu'fan, exulting in the strength of their warriors, whenever they sent despatches to court, asked for the ceremonies of equal nations, and used rude and disrespectful language, so that the Emperor was very angry."[51]

A coup at the T'ang court in 712 brought to power a new emperor, Hsuang-tsung, and spelled the end to any Sino-Tibetan peace for the immediate future. Hsuang-tsung was supported by a militaristic, empire-building faction at the T'ang court. The T'ang dynasty, now at its height, continued to campaign aggressively against the Tibetans in Central Asia and in the Kokonor. In 717 the T'ang defeated the Tibetans at the "Bends

---

49. Bushell, "Early History of Tibet," 457.

50. This is apparently the eastward course of the river from below Sining to Lanchou. Ibid, 458.

51. Ibid., 460.

of the Yellow River." In 722 they responded to an appeal from the king of Balur (Baltistan) and defeated the Tibetans there. Several of the states of Central Asia sent missions to the T'ang capital at Changan (the modern Xian). There was unrest even in Zhangzhung.[52] Faced with these T'ang successes, the Tibetans repeatedly requested peace in 716, 718 and 719.[53]

The Tibetans continued their attacks against the Chinese in Kansu. By 729 the Tibetans were again involved in Western Central Asia, this time allied with the Turgis Turks against the Umayyad Arabs. In 745 they regained control of Gilgit. In 727 the Tibetans attacked the Chinese in the Kanchou area, but were repulsed with great losses. The Tibetans retook the offensive at Kuachou (Anhsi, near Dunhuang) in the Tarim, where they captured, among other things, so much silk that even ordinary Tibetans were reportedly wearing Chinese silks. In 728 another raid on Kuachou failed and the defeated Tibetans were pursued and routed in Kokonor. The returning T'ang army also burned the Tibetan bridge at Ragya.[54]

In 729 the Tibetans sent missions to the T'ang to arrange for peace. This time, the Tibetan mission adhered to Chinese protocol, speaking of their relationship as of nephew to uncle. The Tibetans asked that the T'ang send a mission to visit Jincheng and renew the alliance with Tibet, a proposal to which the T'ang agreed. A Tibetan mission to the T'ang court in 730 advanced friendly relations by requesting copies of the Chinese classics. This request was granted despite objections that the Tibetans would learn the arts of statecraft and warfare from the Chinese books: "When versed in the odes they will know the use of armies for defence; by study of the Rites they will know the times of disbanding and enlisting troops; the records will teach them that in war there are measures of deceit and treachery; while by the Essays they will learn about letters of reprimand in mutual intercourse."[55] The Tibetan envoy at the peace negotiations wisely declined to accept symbolic gifts from the T'ang that would have implied Chinese sovereignty over Tibet. Boundary monuments were erected (at Ch'ihling) and both parties agreed never to encroach upon the other.[56]

The Tibetans were by this time sufficiently experienced in Chinese protocol that were able to employ the vanity of the Chinese as a diplomatic stratagem. The Chinese emperor was unable to resist the request of the "Tu-fan barbarians" to acquire Chinese culture. To the Chinese, the

---

52. Hoffman, "Early and Medieval Tibet," 381.

53. Beckwith, *Tibetan Empire*, 91.

54. Ibid., 101.

55. Bushell, "Early History of Tibet," 467.

56. Ch'ihling is said to be 320 li (100 miles) east of Sining, near Shihp'u. Ibid., 466.

request of the Tibetans to come to the T'ang court implied their submission and their recognition of Chinese political and cultural supremacy. In fact, the Tibetans had used the negotiations with the Chinese to secure their position in Central Asia. While Sino-Tibetan negotiations were proceeding, the Tibetans and the Turks had concluded an alliance in Western Turkestan and defeated the Arabs, gaining control of Central Asia, all unbeknownst to the T'ang. When the T'ang discovered the duplicity of the Tibetans, they immediately broke the treaty in the east, first by campaigning against the Turks and then by an invasion of Kokonor in 737. In 741 Jincheng died; the Tibetan mission sent to Changan to announce her death once again proposed peace, but this time the T'ang refused.

In 741 the Tibetans raided the Chinese military colonies and fortresses in Kansu. In 742 and 743 the T'ang replied with expeditions that defeated Tibetan armies and captured several fortified camps in the Kokonor region. In these engagements the Chinese would raid during the summer months when they could penetrate the highlands; the Tibetans would raid Chinese settlements in the harvest season when they could steal Chinese crops.[57] In 747 in a daring expedition, the Chinese retook Kashgar and Gilgit. However, the Chinese were defeated by the Arabs in Western Turkestan in 751 at the battle of Talas, northwest of Kokhand, when the Turgis allies of the Chinese switched sides and joined the Arabs. The Eastern Turkic allies of the T'ang were meanwhile responsible for some successes against the Tibetans in the Kokonor.

In 751, the Tibetans gained the peaceful submission of the Tibeto-Burman Nanchao kingdom of Yunnan. The six tribes (*chao*) of Yunnan had united in the 730s to create the Nanchao kingdom. Nanchao had maintained relations with the T'ang while expanding and becoming the dominant power in Yunnan and much of southwest China. The first Tibetan military expedition into the Nanchao area seems to have been that led by Dusong in 704. The Tibetans constructed an iron suspension bridge over the Yangtze river along the route of their advance into Yunnan.[58] Nanchao allied with the Tibetans in response to T'ang threats to attack Nanchao from Szechuan. Tibet awarded titles and seals of office to the Nanchao ruler and his ministers and referred to the Nanchao ruler as younger brother to the Tibetan Tsanpo. Nanchao adopted the Tibetan calendar and a new era beginning in the year 752.[59]

In 755 Megasthom died and was succeeded by his son Trisong Detsen. The T'ang court sent a mission "to renew friendship," but the Annals

57. Beckwith, *Tibetan Empire*, 128.
58. Backus, *Nan-chao Kingdom*, 36.
59. Ibid., 71.

complained that the Tibetans, "taking advantage of our difficulties, daily encroached on the borders."[60] In 756 the Tibetans proposed peace to the T'ang, who accepted. The agreement recognized the Tibetans' territorial gains north of the Kokonor.[61] In 756 the T'ang emperor was forced to flee Changan because of the An Lu-shan rebellion. Meanwhile, the Tibetans occupied all China's fortified camps in the Kokonor. In 757 the Tibetans, along with "Tanghsiang, Tu-yu-hun, etc.," captured the city of Sining and continued to advance into Kansu.[62] T'ang China was so weakened by the An Lu-shan rebellion that by 765 the Tibetans were able to briefly occupy the T'ang capital at Changan. They set up a new dynasty under the brother of Jincheng, but it lasted for only fifteen days.[63] The Tibetans simultaneously reentered the Tarim, this time from Kansu, and by 790 had reestablished their control over the Tarim cities.

For the next eighteen years the T'ang Annals speak of almost constant Tibetan attacks, often with "T'uchueh (Turk), T'uhun (Tu-yu-hun), Ti, Man, Ch'iang and Tanghsiang" auxiliaries.[64] The Tibetans took over Lanchou, Kanchou, Suchou and Kuachou between 764 and 766. Tibetan possession of virtually all the cities of the Kansu Corridor effectively cut the T'ang off from the Tarim. In 779 the Tibetans, "at the head of an army of 200,000 of the Southern Man," attacked Maochou and Szechuan.[65] The "Southern Man" were probably the Nanchao, who had simultaneously attacked Szechuan from the south.[66] The Nanchao armies were eventually driven from Szechuan. The Tibetans blamed Nanchao for this failure and punished them severely, alienating Nanchao from Tibet. The Tibetans had, during this period, also taken heavy levies of Nanchao troops for their campaigns in other areas.

In 783 the T'ang made an agreement to settle the border with the Tibetans, confirming the Tibetans' recent gains in Kokonor and Kansu and promising further concessions in exchange for the Tibetans' aid in defeating a challenger to the T'ang. The Tibetans actually fought alongside the T'ang and defeated the rebel and his Uighur allies, helping to save the T'ang dynasty. The T'ang subsequently failed to honor an agreement to turn over their remaining garrisons in the eastern Tarim.[67] The Tibetans responded by attacking Chinese cities all along the frontier.

---

60. Bushell, "Early History of Tibet," 475.
61. Ibid.
62. Beckwith, *Tibetan Empire*, 146.
63. Bushell, "Early History of Tibet," 476.
64. Ibid., 484.
65. Ibid., 484.
66. Backus, *Nan-chao Kingdom*, 84.
67. Beckwith, *Tibetan Empire*, 149.

Severely pressed by the Tibetan advances, the T'ang devised a strategy to turn the tables by making peace and alliances with all of the Tibetans' actual or potential enemies, including Nanchao, Uighur Turks, Arabs, and even Hindustan.[68] The T'ang already had relations with the Uighurs, who were eager to ally against the Tibetans, their rivals in the Tarim. The Tibetans and Arabs were at odds at this time, and the Arabs had already established relations with the Chinese. Perhaps worst for the Tibetans, Nanchao was feeling hard-pressed by its alliance with Tibet and was anxious to renew its "traditional" relations with China.[69] In 786 war broke out between the Tibetans and the Arabs, although whether due to T'ang influence or not is uncertain. In 787 the Tibetans retook Dunhuang, the last city in the eastern Tarim to hold out against them. In 791 or 792 the Tibetans took Khotan and thus established their control over the southern Tarim and its trade route. They were unable to take the northern Tarim from the Uighur, who remained allied with the Chinese.

In 788 the Tibetans, who were again trying to levy Nanchao troops for another attack on Szechuan, became aware of secret negotiations between Nanchao and the T'ang.[70] Finally, in 794 Nanchao went over to the T'ang, claiming that they had wanted to be loyal all along but had been forced into an alliance with the Tibetans. Nanchao, pretending to send troops requested for the Tibetans' campaigns, simultaneously attacked Tibet. The Tibetans were surprised and routed; Nanchao completed the break by destroying the iron suspension bridge over the Yangtze. A request for peace from the Tibetans in 797 was refused by the T'ang, who now held the advantage.[71]

The defection of Nanchao was not enough to stop the Tibetans' advances, however. In 813 a reported 50,000 Tibetan cavalrymen penetrated Inner Mongolia at the northwestern bend of the Yellow River to raid a Uighur mission returning from the T'ang capital at Changan. In the same year the Tibetans constructed a bridge over the Yellow River sixty miles north of Lanchou. The Tibetans continued to compete with the Uighurs in the Tarim, while their control of Kansu prevented any real alliance between the Uighurs and the Chinese. Diplomatic missions traveled back and forth between Changan and Lhasa while military campaigns on the frontier continued. The T'ang were anxious to make peace, even on less than desirable terms, due to the Tibetans' constant menacing of the T'ang frontiers. The T'ang attempted to salvage   their respect by

68. Ibid., 152.
69. Backus, *Nan-chao Kingdom*, 88.
70. Ibid., 91.
71. Ibid., 98.

describing Tibetan diplomatic missions as "submission" and "tribute."[72] Even while engaged in negotiations, the Tibetans were attacking all along the borders. The T'ang Annals report that it was as if "a swarm of ants had invaded our borders."[73]

In 822 the Chinese and Tibetans finally concluded a peace treaty. Although the Tibetans had suffered some reverses, they remained in control of the Kansu Corridor, the eastern and southern Tarim, and positions on the frontier in Kansu from which they could constantly threaten Chinese cities. The treaty confirmed Tibetan territorial gains all along the frontier with China; the border agreed upon was essentially the same as that of the treaty of 783.[74] The treaty of 822 acknowledged the military stalemate between Tibet and China. The treaty of 822, which was the culmination of 200 years of Sino-Tibetan conflict, was inscribed on a stone pillar placed in front of the Jokhang in Lhasa and reads as follows:

The Sovereign of Tibet, the Divine King of Miracles, and the great King of China, Hwang Te, the Nephew and the Maternal Uncle, have agreed to unite their kingdoms . . . . [75]

Tibet and China shall guard the land and frontier, of which they have hitherto held possession. All to the east of the frontier is the country of Great China. All to the west is certainly the country of Great Tibet.

Henceforth there shall be no fighting as between enemies, and neither side will carry war into the other's country. Should there be any suspected person, he can be arrested, questioned, and sent back. Thus the great Agreement has been made for uniting the kingdoms, and the Nephew and Uncle have become happy. In gratitude for this happiness it is necessary that travellers with good messages should go backwards and forwards. The messengers from both sides will also travel by the old road as before. According to the former custom ponies shall be exchanged at Chang-kun-yok, on the frontier between Tibet and China. At Che-shung-shek Chinese territory is met; below this China will show respect. At Tsen-shu-hwan Tibetan territory is met; above this Tibet will show respect.

The Nephew and Uncle, having become intimate, will respect each other according to custom. . . .

This Agreement, that the Tibetans shall be happy in Tibet and the Chinese happy in China and the great kingdoms united, shall never be changed.

---

72. Bushell, "Early History of Tibet," 513.
73. Ibid., 514.
74. Shakabpa, *Tibet: A Political History*, 49.
75. The "uniting" of China and Tibet is in the sense of a union in agreement or treaty.

The Three Precious Ones,[76] the Exalted Ones,[77] the Sun and Moon, the Planets and Stars have been invoked to bear witness. Solemn words were also uttered. Animals were sacrificed and oaths taken, and the Agreement was made.

Is this Agreement held to be binding? If this Agreement be violated, whether Tibet or China violates it first, that one has committed the sin. Whatever revenge is taken in retaliation shall not be considered a breach of the Agreement. In this way, the Kings and Ministers of Tibet and China took oath and wrote this inscription of the Agreement in detail. The two great Kings affixed their seals. The Ministers, considered as holding the Agreement, wrote with their hands. This Agreement shall be observed by both sides.[78]

In the treaty of 822 the Chinese were forced to treat with the Tibetans as equals, recognizing Tibet as a separate state with its own inviolable territory. The terminology of "Nephew and Maternal Uncle" was common diplomatic phraseology implying amicable relations as close as family relations, which, while according the Chinese symbolic superiority as "Uncle," did not imply any political dominance of China over Tibet. However, to assuage Chinese sensibilities the official T'ang court account of the treaty added a preamble absent in the Tibetan version: "The T'ang have received from Heaven rule over the eight points of the compass, and wherever their wise commands penetrate, all come to their court, and with awe and reverence, fearful of punishment for their misdeeds."[79]

The treaty of 822 proved to be the high point of the Tibetan empire. Peace, for an empire founded upon military expansionism, soon resulted in decline. The Tibetan Tsanpo who had begun his reign in 817, Ralpacan, was a Buddhist devotee and a sickly and weak ruler who neglected state affairs. As the T'ang Annals relate:

The *tsanp'u*, during his reign of about thirty years, was sick and unable to attend to business, and the government was in the hands of the chief ministers: consequently they were unable to rival China, and the frontier guards were left at peace. After his death, his younger brother, Tamo [Darma] succeeded to the throne. Tamo was fond of wine, a lover of field sports, and devoted to women, and, besides, cruel, tyrannical, and ungracious, so that the troubles of the state increased.[80]

---

76. The Buddhist Trinity of Buddha, Dharma and Sangha.
77. The Buddhist divinities, Bodhisattvas, etc.
78. Sir Charles Bell, *Tibet Past and Present* (Oxford: Clarendon Press, 1924), 271.
79. Bushell, "Early History of Tibet," 517.
80. Ibid., 522.

The events that brought Ralpacan's brother, Langdarma, to power in 839 also resulted in the downfall of the Tibetan dynasty. In contrast to Ralpacan, Langdarma persecuted Buddhism and the clans that support-ed Buddhism in favor of Bon and its proponents. Langdarma was assas-sinated by a Buddhist monk in 842, after which the succession was dis-puted. The Tibetan confederation quickly disintegrated into those petty states and tribes of which it had been composed, not to be united again for four hundred years. The T'ang dynasty fell shortly after, in 907, the last native dynasty to rule all of China until the fourteenth century.

Cultural and Political Effects of the Empire

Within a brief span of a little more that 200 years, a Tibetan political entity evolved from the previously autonomous clans and petty states of central Tibet into a confederative empire encompassing the entire Tibetan plateau and able to project its power into China and Inner Asia. A nation-al cultural and political identity corresponding to the territorial extent of the Tibetan plateau was created by the empire and survived the empire's collapse. It was in creating this sense of national identity that the Tibetan empire was most significant.

The characteristics which define Tibet as a nation—shared ethnicity, territory, culture, language and religion—were all consolidated by the shared historical experiences of the empire period.[81] The subjective sense of common ethnicity of already affiliated tribes was strengthened by their association for collective political and military purposes during the expansion of the Tibetan empire and in its conflicts with China. A Tibetan sense of collective identity was developed through encounters with the distinctly foreign cultures of Central Asia, the Tarim and China. The propagation of a standardized Tibetan spoken and written language did much to consolidate Tibetan cultural and national identity. Tibetan cul-tural territory was politically delimited by the conquest of the plateau and the institution of a centralized political administration, and thus became a national territory.

---

81. Robert B. Ekvall, *Religious Observances in Tibet* (Chicago: University of Chicago Press, 1964), 93. These characteristics, as enunciated by Tibetans themselves, were reported by Ekvall as:

CHos Lugs gCig, "religion-system one," Religion
KHa Lugs gCig, "mouth-or part-system one," Culture
sKad Lugs gCig, "speech-system one," Language
Mi Rigs gCig, "man-lineage one," Ethnicity
Sa CHa gCig, "soil-extent one," Territory

The political unification of Tibet and the rapid expansion of the Tibetan empire had much to do with the unique cultural ecology and economy of the plateau. The high Tibetan plateau physically delimits Tibet as a culture and as a nation. Tibet can be said to be a culture physically determined and defined by altitude. Common ecological adaptation to the conditions of high altitude, whether as pastoralists or agriculturalists, has been one of the most fundamental cohesive factors of Tibetan national identity.

Tibet undoubtedly possessed a high level of human and material culture in the early seventh century, certainly a higher level than is revealed by the very scant historical records of the era. Tibet during the empire period actively acquired intellectual and material culture from its neighbors, often by transporting artisans and craftsmen to Tibet. Central Tibet's early association with and later incorporation of Zhangzhung exposed Tibet to its culture as well as to all the cultural influences upon Zhangzhung from India, Gandhara, Persia and Central Asia. Tibetan contacts with Nepal were important in the development of Buddhism in Tibet as well as in the fields of arts and handicrafts. Tibetan contact with the Tarim states, though brief, was more important that is usually realized; Tibetan civilization was greatly influenced by the Buddhist cultures of Khotan and Dunhuang. The Tibetan association with China was not as important in cultural influence, later Chinese claims to the contrary notwithstanding, as in the influence that military and political competition with China had upon the development of a Tibetan sense of national identity and statehood.

Tibetan military successes were due not only to human and ecological resources but to technological innovation and adaptation. Tibetan body armour was reportedly of the finest workmanship in Asia at that time. According to the T'ang Annals, "The armour and helmet are very strong and cover the whole body, with holes for the eyes only, so that the strongest bow and sharpest sword can hardly do them much harm."[82] Another source states that both men and horses wore chain mail armour.[83] The Tibetans' capacity to manufacture armour of such quality, and in such large quantities, is one of the mysteries of their extraordinary rise to power.[84]

---

82. Bushell, "Early History of Tibet," 442.

83. Beckwith, *Tibetan Empire*, 110.

84. Stein, *Tibetan Civilization*, 62. This armour was said to have been produced in Markham, but there is some question about whether this reference was actually to Mar Yul (Zhangzhung). Yul and Kham in Tibetan both mean "country." Zhangzhung was exposed to the technological developments of India and Persia; Tibetan armour reputedly had Persian prototypes. Beckwith, *Tibetan Empire*, 110. On the other hand, the area of Yunnan

The two centuries of Tibetan imperial adventure had great implications for Tibetan ethnic identity, primarily in that the tribes of the plateau
were mixed to an extent that a new collective identity, "Tibetan," was created. The Tibetans employed their subject or allied troops all over the
plateau and beyond. Levies from Zhangzhung and Sumpa are often mentioned in campaigns against other tribes or against the Chinese. Tibetan
troops stationed along the frontier in Kansu became permanent settlers, a
strategy familiar from Chinese frontier policy in the same area. Many
tribes there trace their lineage to these frontier garrisons, known as *kha ma
lok*, from their instructions "not to return without orders."[85] The Sumpa
are said to have been sent to garrison the northeastern border in
Minyak.[86] The tribes of Ngolok, Ngawa and Tebo in the Amne Machen
area and south and east of the first bends of the Yellow River claim that
their ancestors came from Ngari (Zhangzhung) during the period of the
empire.[87] The effect of this military garrisoning was to establish an ethnic
border with China that has remained until the present.

Religion, both Bon and Buddhism, also played an important role in the
creation of a Tibetan cultural and national identity. The majority of the
Tibetan population, and especially the regional aristocracy, continued to
practice the familiar Bon rites and ceremonies. Bon remained the spiritual foundation and protector of the Tibetan state. Bonpos, not Buddhists,
led Tibetan troops into battle.[88] T'ang dynasty records state time and
again that their treaties with the Tibetans were solemnized by the
Tibetans with non-Buddhist rites of animal sacrifice.[89] This was true even
as late as the treaty of 822, during the reign of Ralpacan, one of the most
devoutly Buddhist of the Tibetan kings. At this treaty signing, the Tibetan
minister solemnized the agreement with Buddhist rites, as did the T'ang

---

in which the Tibetans were involved in their campaigns against, and later alliance with, the
Nanchao kingdom was known to be a source of iron ore. The Tibetan iron suspension bridge
built over the Yangtze in the early eighth century indicates that there was some metallurgy
in this area at the time. The first iron suspension bridges in human history were built in
southwest China at the end of the sixth century. Backus, *Nan-chao Kingdom*, 173. Some of the
nomadic tribes, especially the Sumpa, are associated with iron metallurgy. The Sumpa, and
perhaps the Ch'iang in general, were known as producers of excellent iron swords and iron
and leather breastplates. Stein, *Tibetan Civilization*, 62. An additional possibility is that Nepal
served as one area of production for the Tibetans' armour, as it did in later years for metal
statuary and coins.

85. Shakabpa, *Tibet: A Political History*, 43.
86. R.A. Stein, *Les Tribus Anciennes des Marches Sino-Tibetaines* (Paris: Imprimerie
Nationale, 1959), 43.
87. Tashi Tsering, personal communication, 1990.
88. Ren Shumin, "The Military Strength of the Tubo Kingdom," 140.
89. Bushell, "Early History of Tibet," 475.

ambassador, whereas the more than one hundred Tibetan chiefs accompanying the minister smeared their lips with blood according to the pre-Buddhist ritual.[90]

Buddhism remained, even during the periods of greatest royal patronage of the empire period, a court and upper class religion that apparently did not penetrate very deeply into Tibetan society.[91] Buddhism was preferred by the newly developing Tibetan intelligentsia because it represented a higher literary and philosophical tradition than the old Bon religion. Buddhism was also associated with the cultured societies with which the Tibetans were at this time coming into contact: India, Nepal, the Tarim city-states and China. The competition between Buddhism and Bon in the early Tibetan state represented a struggle between the regional clan aristocracy and the sovereign for political power. Geoffrey Samuel has described Tibetan religious history in the empire period as a transition from the individualistic shamanic Bon to the clerical religion of Buddhism. He describes shamanic religions as typical of unorganized, uncentralized preliterate societies, whereas clerical religions are more characteristic of centralized states. Although, as Samuel states, the shamanic and clerical forms coexisted in Tibetan religion, the clerical form was preferred by those attempting to establish centralized political authority.[92]

Tibetan Buddhist tradition identifies three kings as the primary promoters of Buddhism: Srongtsan Gampo (ruled 629-649), Trisong Detsen (754-797), and Ralpacan (815-838). In addition, the father of Trisong Detsen, Megasthom (704-754), and the father of Ralpacan, Sadnaleg (804-815), were known to have favored and promoted Buddhism. The firm establishment of Buddhism ascribed to Srongtsan Gampo by later Buddhist historians must be regarded as exaggerated. Srongtsan Gampo favored Buddhism and allowed its practice mainly due to the influence of his queens. Even the construction of Buddhist temples in all the regions and on the frontiers of Tibet may be more legitimately credited to Trisong Detsen.[93]

Tibetan conquests in the Tarim from 670 had an important effect on the propagation of Buddhism in Tibet. Tibetan armies are known to have destroyed Buddhist monasteries in the Tarim during their early campaigns. However, some of the displaced monks fled to Tibet because of the patronage of the Chinese queen of Srongtsan Gampo, Wencheng, who

90. Snellgrove, *Indo-Tibetan Buddhism*, 409.
91. Ibid., 401.
92. Geoffrey Samuel, "Early Buddhism in Tibet," in *Soundings in Tibetan Civilization*, ed. Aziz and Kapstein (New Delhi: Manohar Publications, 1985), 389.
93. Snellgrove, *Indo-Tibetan Buddhism*, 415.

lived until 683. The Chinese princess, Jincheng, who became the queen of Megasthom in 710, continued the practice of offering refuge to Buddhist monks. Later, as the Tibetans themselves adopted a more benign, even interested, attitude toward Buddhism, monks from Kashgar, Khotan and Dunhuang sought refuge in Tibet. Buddhist monks from the Tarim cities may have been of a wide variety of ethnic identities: Indo-European (Tocharians or Sogdians), Turks or Chinese.[94]

Trisong Detsen established Buddhism as the state religion in 762.[95] The monastery of Samye, the first Buddhist monastery of Tibet, was founded in 767. The founding of this monastery by the Indian Buddhist saint, Padmasambhava, and his subjugation of all of the pre-Buddhism deities and spirits of Tibet, is regarded in Tibetan history as the symbolic victory of Buddhism in Tibet.[96] However, the actual ambivalence of the king, and the continuing conflict between Buddhism and Bon, was revealed in Trisong Detsen's edict at Samye:

> I have wanted to establish these Tibetan lands in religion and much has been achieved in the way of images and temples, but as for obtaining scriptures and translators of religious works, although I have found them and sent the wise and intelligent ones to India where they find excellent scriptures, the ministers who are well disposed to Bon are jealous of this religion. They refuse it their approval and so I have had to dismiss it.
>
> Whether one may consider Bon religion or not, I have thought that [it] should be translated. I have summoned a sage (gShen-bon) from the land of Zhang-zhung. . . . They have translated the four volume Klu-'bum in the Avalokitesvara Temple. So now it is said that I am propagating Bon teachings. It is said that my tomb should be built at Mu-ri of Don-khar since such tombs are a Bon custom, so I have ordered my Bon ministers to build this tomb. It is said that I should build a stupa on the hill . . . since such stupas are a [Buddhist] religious custom, so I have ordered my religious ministers to build one.[97]

Buddhism played a somewhat contradictory role in the history of the empire, foreshadowing its role in later Tibetan history. Buddhism was both a pillar of the state and, at the same time, a weakness that contributed to the state's downfall. The career of Ralpacan demonstrates this thesis. Ralpacan became immersed in otherworldly affairs and neglected the mundane affairs of state. Ralpacan initiated the practice of having

---

94. Ibid., 418.

95. H.E. Richardson, "Ministers of the Tibetan Kingdom," *Tibet Journal* (1977), 20.

96. Guiseppi Tucci, *The Religions of Tibet* (Berkeley: University of California Press, 1980), 168.

97. Snellgrove, *Indo-Tibetan Buddhism*, 403.

monks as ministers of state.[98] His excessive patronage of Buddhism and the arrogance of the monks he favored led to his assassination in 838, the end of his lineage and the fall of the empire.

---

98. Ibid., 422.

5

The Emergence of the Tibetan Buddhist State

Post-Empire Interregnum

Upon the fall of the Yarlung dynasty, the clans, tribes and regions of the plateau reverted to their former fractious independence. For a period of some four hundred years, from 842 until Tibet came under the dominance of the Mongols in 1247, Tibet knew no central authority. The fall of Yarlung in Tibet and the T'ang in China allowed small states to emerge in frontier territories that had previously been under the domination of China or Tibet. The foremost of these in the Sino-Tibetan frontier area was the Tangut state (990-1227) in the region north of Kokonor and the Kansu corridor. The Tangut state was composed of remnants of the northeastern Tibetan plateau tribes, including Tanghsiang (Minyak) and Tu-yu-hun, as well as Uighur Turks of Kanchou, which the Tangut state absorbed in 1028.

A smaller state, Tsonkha, located in the region to the east of Kokonor, included Tibetans and Tanghsiang. Tsonkha rivaled the Tangut from the early eleventh century until it was taken over by the Sung in the early twelfth century. Tsonkha was finally included in the domains of the Jurchen Chin dynasty (1115-1234) of northern China in 1182. In the period of its independence Tsonkha used its good relations with the Sung to carry on trade in tea and horses; Tsonkha also benefitted as an alternative trade route to the Tarim and Central Asia, the usual route through the Kansu Corridor often being blocked by conflicts between the Tangut and the Sung.

After the fall of Yarlung, some of the Yarlung lineage established small states in Purang, Guge and Maryul (the former territories of Zhangzhung, now collectively known as Ngari).[1] These states preserved Buddhism and fostered its revival in the eleventh century by inviting the Indian Buddhist scholar, Atisha Dipankara (986-1054), to teach in Tibet.

---

1. Guiseppi Tucci, *Tibetan Painted Scrolls* (Rome: La Libreria dello Stato, 1949), 3.

Atisha arrived in Tibet in 1042 and remained there until his death. He founded many monasteries in western and central Tibet; his disciple Bromton (1008-1064) was responsible for founding, at Reting, the first Tibetan religious order, the Kadampa.[2] Tibetan religious orders grew up around lineages of teachers and disciples. Besides the Kadampa, the Sakyapa and Kagyudpa orders were founded by Tibetan disciples of Indian masters. The Sakyapa order derived from Brogmi (992-1072), who had traveled to India in search of the Buddhist doctrines. Brogmi's disciple Konchok Gyalpo founded the Sakya monastery in 1073. The Kagyudpa derived from the Indian master Naropa (956-1040) via his Tibetan disciples Marpa (1012-1096) and Milarepa (1040-1123). The disciples of Gampopa (1079-1153) founded six sub-orders of the Kagyudpa, the most important of which were the Phagmogrupa, founded by the lama of the same name (1110-1170) in the valley of the Tsangpo near Tsetang; the Karmapa, founded at Tsurpu in 1185; and the Brigungpa of the monastery of that name in Phenpo.

As Tibetan Buddhist sects founded monasteries throughout the country, their temporal as well as spiritual power increased. The religious sects also inherited the factionalism of the clans and regions; their rivalries increased as their own property, power and influence increased. Rivalries between monasteries often assumed the form of open battles; at the end of the twelfth century many monasteries were in ruins due to internecine warfare.[3] At the beginning of the thirteenth century Buddhist sects had become the dominant economic, political and spiritual authorities in Tibet, but Tibet remained disunited because no one sect was powerful enough to dominate the others. This situation was transformed with the rise of the Mongol empire, under whose patronage one sect achieved predominance and Tibet achieved political unity.

Tibetan Relations with the Mongols

The Mongols under Chingghis Khan attacked the Tangut in 1227.[4]

---

2. David Snellgrove, *Indo-Tibetan Buddhism* (Boston: Shambhala, 1987), 473.

3. Luc Kwanten, "Tibetan-Mongol Relations During the Yuan Dynasty, 1207-1368" (Ph.D. diss., University of South Carolina, 1972), 30.

4. Accounts of Chingghis Khan's having demanded and received the submission of Tibet in 1207 have been demonstrated to be mistaken references to Chingghis' later attack on the Tangut in 1227. Luciano Petech, "Tibetan Relations with Sung China and with the Mongols," in *China Among Equals*, ed. Morris Rossabi (Berkeley: University of California Press, 1983), 179; Jiunn Yih Chang, "A Study of the Relationship Between the Mongol Yuan Dynasty and the Tibetan Sa-skya Sect" (Ph.D. diss., Indiana University, 1984), 8; Kwanten, "Tibetan-Mongol Relations," 27.

Chingghis was killed during the campaign, in retaliation for which the Tangut state was almost completely destroyed. Some of the Tangut fled to Tibet. Chingghis was succeeded as Great Khan of all the Mongols, or *khaghan*, by his son, Ogadai. By 1234 the Mongols had conquered all of northern China. In 1236 Godan, the son of Ogodai, led a campaign against Szechuan and Yunnan.[5] Godan was subsequently awarded the appanage, or fief, of Liangchou, in the former Tangut territory.

In 1240 Godan sent an expeditionary force into Tibet under Dorta.[6] The nature of Dorta's expedition into Tibet is incongruous; the Mongols' usual policy was to demand submission from any state before attacking. Invasions of major territories were usually led by a Mongol prince rather than his subordinates; the incursion under Dorta may have been a reconnaissance to determine the nature of political authority in Tibet. Dorta burned several monasteries north of Lhasa, including Gyal Lhakhang and Reting, but Taglung and Brigung were spared. According to the Tibetan version, Taglung was obscured by a fog so that the Mongols could not see it and Brigung was saved by a miraculous shower of stones.[7] Dorta was reportedly so impressed by the powers of the Brigung Lama that he wanted to take the lama back with him to Godan's camp. The Brigung Lama avoided that honor by suggesting that the abbot of Sakya, being more learned, would be much the better choice.[8]

Dorta withdrew from Tibet in 1241. All Mongol activities from China to Europe were suspended in that year due to the death of Ogodai. A *kuriltai* of Mongol princes named Guyuk as the new *khaghan*.[9] In 1244 Godan summoned Sakya Pandita, abbot of Sakya monastery, to his camp in Liangchou. Sakya Pandita left Sakya accompanied by his nephews, Phagspa (age nine) and Phagna Dorje (age seven). He delayed for several months in Lhasa, where he apparently had to justify his response to Godan's summons. As Petech comments, the Sakya Lama had not been chosen by Tibetans to represent Tibet at the court of the Mongols.[10]

---

5. Petech, "Tibetan Relations," 181.

6. Shakabpa states that this force numbered thirty thousand, though this may be an exaggeration. W.D. Shakabpa, *Tibet: A Political History* (New York: Potala, 1984), 61.

7. Chang suggests that this may have been a meteor shower. Jiunn Yih Chang, "Yuan Dynasty and Sa-kya Sect," 26.

8. Petech, "Tibetan Relations," 181. Luc Kwanten suggests that, as was usual in later Buddhist historiography, the power of Buddhist lamas in pacifying and converting the Mongols has been exaggerated. Kwanten, "Tibetan-Mongol Relations," 75.

9. Ogodai's wife Toregene ignored his wishes for his successor and had herself named regent until her son, Guyuk, could return from campaigning in the west. Guyuk was not made *khaghan* until 1246. Jiunn Yih Chang, "Yuan Dynasty and Sa-kya Sect," 24.

10. Petech, "Tibetan Relations," 181.

Sakya Pandita arrived at the Mongol camp in 1245, but apparently met Godan only in 1247. Sakya Pandita then made his submission to Godan, and agreed to become the representative, or *darugachi*, of Mongol authority in Tibet. Knowing that submission to the Mongols would be resisted in Tibet, Sakya Pandita sent a letter to the ecclesiastical and lay notables in Tibet arguing for compliance with the Mongols' demands:

Having in mind the Buddha's teachings in general and (the good of) all created beings, and particularly what may be to the advantage of the Tibetan speaking populations, I have gone to the Hor.[11] The great patron was much pleased with me, whom he had invited. I had thought that aP'ags pa who had taken with him his so small brother and his retinue would be enough. But he said to me: "among my subjects, I consider you as the head, the others the feet. You have been called by me, the others will come through fear. ... I, protecting (the world) with the law of men, you protecting it with the law of the gods, will the Buddha's teachings not spread over all the world as far as the ocean which is the earth's external boundary?"

This king is a bodhisattva, who has the greatest faith in the Buddhist teachings generally, and in the three gems in particular. He protects the universe by good laws, and particularly he has a great attachment for me, far above the others. He said (to me): "Preach religion with a tranquil mind, I will give you what you wish. I know that you do good, heaven knows if I do so also." Above all he has a great attachment for aP'ags pa and his brother. Knowing how to govern freely, he has the good intention of being useful to all peoples.

By the way, the armies of this Hor king are numberless. I think that all the aDsam bu glin [Jambuling, the world] has submitted to him. Those who agree with him take part in his adversity and prosperity. If one does not listen sincerely to what the king says, he cannot be called his vassal. And in the end the king will cause his downfall. ... In the past for some years, no (Hor) soldiers came to upper Tibet. ... (This happened because I) did homage as a vassal. As this vassalage was successful, the upper mNa'ris [Ngari], dBus [U] and gTsan [Tsang] did homage as vassals. ...

Now hear what he says: "(In) your country, (in the) lay communities of your districts, whoever the various officers may be upon whom (office) has been conferred, let him (continue as before to) occupy it. I have called the Sa skya pa, who have the golden letters and the silver letters, and I have conferred the office of *da ra k'a c'e* [darugachi] upon them; this is just.

On the base of this recognition many useful messengers who come and go have been established: therefore let three (copies of the) list of the census officials' names, of the number of laymen, and of the tributes be made; let

---

11. Hor is the Tibetan name for the Mongols.

one be brought to me, one taken to the Sa skya and another kept by the various officials, and let it be clearly distinguished: this one is a vassal, this one is not a vassal. . . .

He who is in possession of the Sa skya pa golden letter, let him consult the officers of each country, and let him do what is good for all created beings, without any thought of increasing his own authority; and also the officers of the various countries, let them never act on their own initiative, without consulting him who is in possession of the Sa skya pa golden letter. . . . If you follow the Hor laws, good will result; go to meet those who are in possession of golden letters and serve them. . . ."

Generally speaking, do not say: "it does not profit me that the Sa skya have entered the Mongol confederation." I have entered the Mongol confederation with thoughts of love towards others, for the advantage of those who speak Tibetan. If you listen to what I say, it will be to your advantage. . . . Therefore it seems to me that now this is profitable: we have long enjoyed (earthly) happiness, (now) suddenly gloom and depression have set in, as when one is trampled upon. It is necessary that the people of dBus and gTsan should enter the Mongol confederation. I, whatever happens, good or evil, will not repent. It is possible that all may go well, through the blessings and the grace of the Masters and of the Three Gems: let all of you pray to the Three Gems. The king is bound to me as he is to no one else. For this reason, great men, spiritual preceptors of China, Tibet, Yu gur [Uighur], Mi nag [Minyak] or of other countries, listen to the Law with great wonder and feel great devotion.

I need not trouble concerning what the Hor will do to those who will come here [with tribute]; I wish all to feel confidence. As far as I am concerned, let all be tranquil. Concerning the tributes: gold, silver, ivory, large pearls, carmine and ruddle, bezoars, tiger, leopard, wild cat, otter skins, Tibetan wool, fine dBus wool, here these things are right. Generally speaking, concerning the property (to be brought as tribute) when one's riches be scanty, one is allowed to pay with those articles that are the best in one's country. If there is gold, think that there may be as much as you wish of it.

Let the Buddha's teachings be diffused over all the Mongol regions. May all receive good.[12]

Sakya Pandita's letter reveals much about his, and Tibet's, submission to Godan. Sakya Pandita made it clear that the power of the Mongols was overwhelming and submission to them was inevitable. Sakya Pandita did not attempt to present his status, or that of Tibet, as anything but a vassal of Godan. Sakya Pandita's statement that he had hoped that his nephews

---

12. Tucci, *Tibetan Painted Scrolls*, 10.

Phagspa and Phagna Dorje "would be enough" tends to confirm that the two were essentially hostages at the Mongols' camp.[13] Sakya Pandita appears as the Mongols' agent in achieving the submission of Tibet, not as a vassal ruler of Tibet. The Tibetan chiefs were directed to personally and individually offer submission to the Mongols, not to Sakya Pandita or to representatives of the Sakya monastery except as they functioned as the Mongols' intermediaries. Tibetan sources say nothing about whether any other Tibetans submitted to Godan or paid tribute to him, though it appears from Sakya Pandita's letter that some did while others were reluctant to do so. Godan did not treat Sakya Pandita as an official representative of Tibet, but as one whose authority would prove sufficient to gain the submission of all the rest.

Guyuk Khaghan died in 1247. Mongke, of the lineage of Tolui, was proclaimed *khaghan* in 1251, though not without opposition from the houses of Chagatai and Ogodai.[14] Khubilai was given responsibility for Mongol territories in northern China and for the conquest of the southern Sung dynasty. The shift in fortunes from the descendants of Ogodai to those of Tolui left Godan, the son of Ogodai, in a precarious position. Although he retained his appanage at Liangchou, Khubilai was given part of his domain in Kansu; Godan was no longer responsible for Tibet.

Sakya Pandita died in 1251. Mongke Khaghan ordered an invasion of Tibet in 1252, but his commanders stopped short of central Tibet; this may or may not indicate that Mongke acknowledged and intended to continue the special relationship established by Godan with the Sakyapas.

---

13. Turrell V. Wylie, "The First Mongol Conquest of Tibet Reinterpreted," *Harvard Journal of Asiatic Studies* (1977), 114. Wylie points out that the two nephews of Sakya Pandita were heirs to the temporal and spiritual lineages of Sakya. Hostage arrangements were usual in the submission of one tribe or state to another in Inner Asia. Hostages were usually treated as members of the sovereign's extended family and were acculturated to the customs of the foreign court, with the ultimate goal that they might become agents of foreign rule in their own countries. In this case, both Phagspa and Phagna Dorje were to become very significantly "Mongolized," and both were eventually employed as agents in the Mongols' scheme for ruling Tibet.

14. Chingghis' four sons were Jochi, Chagatai, Ogadai and Tolui. The house of Tolui, represented by Tolui's widow, Sorghaghtani Beki, had gained ascendancy over that of Ogodai. Sorghaghtani Beki's sons were Mongke, Khubilai, Hulegu and Ariq Boke. Sorghaghtani Beki received an appanage from Ogodai in northern China, and, as ruler of that territory, was one of the first Mongols to govern a non-nomadic territory. She ruled this Chinese territory with an understanding of the differences between China and the steppes; she was known for governing in a way beneficial to both Mongol overlords and Chinese peasants. Khubilai also received an appanage in northern China and adopted his mother's example. Hulegu was given the task of conquering the Islamic kingdoms; he was later to become the first of the Il-khans of Persia. Ariq Boke, as the youngest, was given the traditional responsibility for the Mongol homelands.

Whether the Mongols' subsequent peaceful policy toward Tibet was due to the influence of the lamas or only indifference is unknown. As Wylie said: "Tibet, whose formidable terrain was politically fragmented by local lords and lamas, posed no military threat to the Mongols, and it was all but ignored by them."[15] Petech suggests that Mongke intended to establish the appanage system in Tibet.[16] Mongol princes were awarded appanages in Kansu, Kokonor and the Sino-Tibetan borderlands. During this period Mongol princes of the house of Tolui became patrons of various Tibetan Buddhist sects. Mongol princes wanted Tibetan lamas at their courts because of the lamas' reputed spiritual powers, while the lamas needed Mongol patrons for protection against other Mongols and to further themselves in competition with rival Tibetan monasteries and sects. Mongke established a relationship as patron to the Brigungpa; Khubilai sponsored the Tsalpa; Hulegu was patron to the Phagmogrupa; and Ariq Boke had connections to the Taglungpa.[17]

In 1253 Khubilai summoned Phagspa from Godan's camp.[18] Shortly thereafter, Khubilai departed on a campaign against Szechuan and Yunnan (1253-1254). Upon his return Khubilai also invited Karma Pakshi, the head of the Karmapa sect.[19] Karma Pakshi was known as a famous miracle-worker, and was reported to have astonished Khubilai by performing innumerable miracles. Khubilai is said to have entertained doubts that the Sakyapas, represented by Phagspa, were as powerful as the Karmapa.[20] The biography of Phagspa claims that Phagspa also performed an impressive miracle:

> Phags-pa asked for a sword and said, `I shall transform my limbs into the five classes of Buddhas, and you, Khan and ministers will get your request to be reborn in whichever of the five Buddha fields you desire. If you do not so believe, visit where my limbless body rests on my bed!' So saying, he cut off his various limbs. He made the head Vairocana. The four limbs he trans-

15. Wylie, "Mongol Conquest," 122.

16. Petech, "Tibetan Relations," 183.

17. Ibid., 182; Jiunn Yih Chang, "Yuan Dynasty and Sa-kya Sect," 48.

18. Wylie suggests that Khubilai actually summoned Sakya Pandita, not being aware that he had died in 1251, and was disappointed to receive the young Phagspa instead. Wylie, "Mongol Conquest," 117.

19. Karma Pakshi later departed Khubilai's camp to seek his fortunes at the court of Mongke. This undiplomatic move was later to cost the Karmapas the patronage of Khubilai when he became *khaghan*. Karma Pakshi was the first Tibetan lama whose reincarnation was found in a child after his death, initiating the Tibetan Buddhist system of succession by reincarnation. Shakabpa, *Tibet: A Political History*, 65.

20. Jiunn Yih Chang, "Yuan Dynasty and Sa-kya Sect," 78.

formed into the four other classes, and thus emerged the five classes of Buddhas.[21]

In 1254 (or shortly thereafter), Phagspa conferred upon Khubilai initiations into the rites of Buddhism. Khubilai accepted Phagspa as his *guru*, or teacher in religious matters. This relationship required Khubilai, as the neophyte in religious matters, to accept the superiority of his teacher:

> The Khan [Prince Khubilai] asked, "What precepts must be observed?" [Phags-pa] replied, "Having requested initiation, the Lama takes the highest seat. (The devotee) physically prostrates (himself to his teacher) and heeds whatever he says; and (the devotee) must not act contrary to the thoughts (of the teacher)." The Khan said "I would not be able to observe such precepts."[22]

Although the rules of the traditional relationship between master and disciple were well established in Buddhism, Phagspa's demand that the khan physically prostrate himself and assume a lower seat in their dialogues required some audacity. At first, Khubilai was irritated by Phagspa's demands and accused him of being arrogant. The dispute was mediated by Chabi, Khubilai's favorite wife. Chabi had already been initiated by Phagspa; she had become a Buddhist and a strong supporter of Phagspa. Khubilai was known to have listened to Chabi's advice on many matters and to have moderated his behavior on many occasions due to her influence. In this case she proposed:

> There is a solution to that. The teacher shall occupy the higher seat when giving teachings and when (only) a few people are present. The Khan shall take the higher seat when there are large assemblies of men such as vassal rulers and lords. The affairs concerning Tibetan regions shall be done according to the words (of the teacher). The Khan shall not give orders without consulting the Lama. Apart from that, in all other affairs big or small the Lama need not be consulted.[23]

The complimentary roles of Phagspa, religious teacher, and Khubilai, religious patron, established a format for relations between Tibetan lamas and their Mongol patrons and overlords known in Tibetan as *Cho-Yon*, in which *Cho*, religion, was in an equal relation to *Yon*, the secular patron.

---

21. Ibid. The miracle performed by Phagspa has many of the essential elements of the famous Indian "rope trick" in which a fakir dismembers his assistant only to put him back together again, all accomplished by "projected visualization," a technique well developed in Indian mysticism.

22. Ibid., 77.

23. Ibid.

The *Cho-Yon* relationship established between Phagspa and Khubilai was later to become the idealized form of Mongol-Tibetan relations and of Sino-Tibetan relations. Khubilai made a "donation" to Phagspa of the thirteen myriarchies of western and central Tibet. As a second offering, Phagspa was given the three districts of Tibet: U-Tsang (central and western Tibet), Dotoh (Kham) and Domei (Amdo).[24]

When Mongke died in 1259, the succession was contested between Khubilai and his younger brother Ariq Boke, who was khan of the Mongol homelands. Khubilai was supported by Hulegu, who, like Khubilai, was lord of a sedentary domain (Persia). Khubilai had himself proclaimed *khaghan* and adopted a personal reign title (though not a dynastic title), in the Chinese style, in 1260.[25] Ariq Boke was simultaneously proclaimed *khaghan* by his allies, mainly the Ogodais and Chagatais. Ariq Boke retained control of the nomadic Mongols, but Khubilai controlled the settled areas from which the nomads had to obtain food and military supplies. Khubilai finally defeated Ariq Boke in battle near the Chinese border, when the Chagatai Khan went over to Khubilai. Ariq Boke was forced to surrender in 1264; he died as Khubilai's captive in 1266. Opposition to Khubilai and the house of Tolui was carried on by Khaidu Khan, a grandson of Ogodai, who had established a khanate in Transoxiana and who had himself proclaimed *khaghan* there in 1268.

The elevation of Khubilai to *khaghan* was significant for Phagspa, who had tied his fate to Khubilai. In 1260 Khubilai named Phagspa "National Preceptor" (*kuo-shih*).[26] Phagspa gained this position on his own merits, no doubt, but also due to his loyalty, his long presence at the Mongol court, and his acculturation to Mongol customs and his ability to speak their language. Phagspa must also have been by this time, like Khubilai

---

24. This donation is interpreted by Shakabpa as conferring "supreme authority" in Tibet to Phagspa. Shakabpa, *Tibet: A Political History*, 65. However, this donation has to be interpreted within the overall framework of Mongol authority; Tibet was a feudatory realm within the Mongol empire. As Tucci has written, "this was not a real donation, as Tibetan sources would have us believe; it was rather a nominal viceregency, over Tibetan territory, on the Mongol emperors' account; the abbots, in a word, were not sovereigns and lords, but officials, elected and confirmed every time by a seal and a decree of the Court." Tucci, *Tibetan Painted Scrolls*, 14.

25. Morris Rossabi, *Khubilai Khan: His Life and Times* (Berkeley: University of California Press, 1988), 56. Khubilai was at this time *khaghan* of the Mongol empire, not emperor of China. Khubilai declared a new Chinese dynasty and had himself proclaimed emperor of China only in 1270.

26. Petech, "Tibetan Relations," 184. The "nation" (*kuo*) of which Phagspa was "National Preceptor" was the Mongol empire, not China. This date has in modern times been cited by the Chinese as the time when Tibet became "part of China."

himself, quite familiar with Chinese customs.[27] Phagspa's role as *Kuo-shih* was to be the head of the Buddhist religion and of Buddhists within Khubilai's realm. This primarily involved organizing Buddhist rituals at court, providing initiations for Khubilai and his family, and making prayers for the long life of the *khaghan*. In 1264 the Office for Buddhist Affairs, the *Hsuan-cheng-yuan*, was established, and Phagspa was named as its head.

In that same year, 1264, Phagspa, along with Phagna Dorje, was sent back to Tibet, the first time that Phagspa had been in central Tibet since 1244. Phagspa's return to Tibet may have had something to do with Khubilai's rivalry with Ariq Boke and, later, with Khaidu. Tibet lay between Khubilai's domains and those of Khaidu. The Ogodais and their allies, the Chagatais, were also patrons of Tibetan Buddhist sects.[28] The Tibetan Taglungpa sect had been patronized by Ariq Boke; in addition, the Brigungpa had made the unfortunate decision to favor Ariq Boke in the dispute over the Mongol succession.[29] The Brigung alliance with Khubilai's rivals may be attributed to Brigung opposition to the Sakyapa (Khubilai had at one time been a patron of the Brigungpa). Khubilai also harbored suspicions that Karma Pakshi had secretly favored Ariq Boke.[30]

Phagspa's return to Tibet signified a shift in Mongol policy. Wylie interprets Phagspa's return to Tibet as Khubilai's first attempt to impose direct Mongol authority in Tibet: "In 1265 Khubilai Khaghan sent Phagspa Lama and his younger brother, Phyag-na rdo-rje, accompanied by a legion of Mongol cavalry, into Tibet to force the local lords and lamas there to acquiesce in the formation of a centralized political administration."[31] Petech speculates that "Khubilai may have intended to establish a lay principality in central Tibet, under Mongol suzerainty, and propped up by the spiritual authority of the Sa-skya-pa abbot."[32]

Phagspa and Phagna Dorje were ideally suited to Khubilai's purpose; they were, respectively, heir to the religious mantle of Sakya and the head of the Sakya Khon family. Phagna Dorje would function as head of the Khon family and administrator of Tibet, while Phagspa would be Tibetan intermediary with the Mongols. Phagna Dorje was appointed "head of all Tibet" in 1265, but died in 1267, at the age of twenty-nine,

---

27. It is uncertain how much Chinese Phagspa was able to speak. He did participate in the Buddhist-Taoist debates of 1258 with Chinese Taoists and Buddhists, and was to become an important official responsible for Chinese as well as Tibetan Buddhists, but he might have employed interpreters.

28. Jiunn Yih Chang, "Yuan Dynasty and Sa-kya Sect," 48.

29. Petech, "Tibetan Relations," 184.

30. Wylie, "Mongol Conquest," 124.

31. Ibid., 122.

32. Petech, "Tibetan Relations," 186.

probably by poison. Phagna Dorje's death, and subsequent events, reveal that there was considerable opposition to Phagspa and Phagna Dorje at Sakya, and perhaps to Sakya as representative of the Mongols in Tibet. Phagspa and his brother were accused of being more Mongol that Tibetan, even dressing in the Mongol style.[33] Opposition to Phagspa at Sakya was such that he had to remove himself in 1267 to Dam. In 1267 the Brigungpa allied with Du'a, khan of the Chagatais, an ally of Khaidu.[34]

Mongol troops were dispatched to Tibet in 1268 to put down the opposition to Sakya led by the Brigungpa.[35] Khubilai thereafter established in Tibet the administrative apparatus typical of Mongol rule in conquered territories. The office of *ponchen*, head of Sakya and Tibetan administration, was established under the supervision of Phagspa. In 1267 the Mongols conducted a census of central Tibet (excluding Kham and Amdo). A census of subjects for the purpose of taxation was the Mongols' typical first step in imposing their rule on any territory.[36] The census revealed that the population of central Tibet was 36,453 families (15,690 for Ngari and Tsang and 20,763 for U). Each family was assumed to average six persons, giving approximately 220,000 as the total population.[37]

Central Tibet was divided into thirteen administrative districts, or myriarchies (*khri-skor*), usually headed by monasteries.[38] Each of the myriarchies was responsible to the *ponchen* of Sakya. The Mongols instituted taxes according to property; some families were responsible for military service and others were delegated to provide services (*ulag*) for the relay or postal system. The post system was an essential part of Mongol administration of Tibet. The *ulag* obligation, though not onerous at first, became more so as increasing numbers of officials, both Mongol and Tibetan, were granted *ulag* privileges.

At the same time that Khubilai sent Phagspa to Tibet and reorganized its administration, he sent expeditions into eastern Kham and Amdo and established administrative districts there. Despite the formality of Khubilai's previous "donation" of the three regions of Tibet to Phagspa, after 1264 Kham and Amdo were separated from the administration of central Tibet. The Mongols adopted the Chinese terminology for the geographical regions of Tibet: *T'u-fan*, *Hsi-fan* and *Wu-ssu-tsang*. *T'u-fan*, the T'ang dynasty name for the Tibetan empire, now referred only to Amdo.

---

33. Wylie, "Mongol Conquest," 123.

34. Ibid., 124; Petech, "Tibetan Relations," 189.

35. Petech, "Tibetan Relations," 186.

36. Janos Szerb, "Glosses on the Oeuvre of Bla-ma Phags-pa: On the Activity of Sa-skya Pandita," in *Tibetan Studies in Honour of Hugh Richardson*, ed. Michael Aris and Aung San Suu Kyi (Warminster England: Aris and Phillips Ltd., 1979), 293.

37. Petech, "Mongol Census of Tibet," 234.

38. Wylie, "Mongol Conquest," 126.

Hsi-fan referred to the tribes of the southern Sino-Tibetan marches in Kham. *Wu-ssu-tsang* was a transliteration of U-Tsang (*dBus-gTsang*), or central Tibet. In 1264 Mongol troops pacified *T'u-fan*.[39] Mongol forces pacified *Hsi-fan* from 1264 to 1268.[40]

In theory, the Office for Buddhist Affairs (*Hsuan-cheng-yuan*) was responsible for all Tibetan affairs. However, in Hsi-fan and T'u-fan, the Pacification Bureau (*Hsuan-wei-shih*), which belonged to the regular military border administration, was more often employed.[41] Between 1256 and 1355 the Yuan had to send troops to Hsi-fan and T'u-fan 21 times.[42] In 1268 after defeating the revolt of Brigung, the Mongols also established a permanent military administration for central Tibet. The Sakya *ponchen* was placed under the authority of the Pacification Bureau.[43] The Mongols thereby achieved more direct control of central Tibet by applying the methods already practiced in Kham and Amdo and further circumscribed the already limited autonomy of the Sakyapa.

The Mongol administration of Tibet, though exhibiting characteristics typical of Mongol administration of other conquered territories, was somewhat unique. Tibet was treated as a special case due to the nature of Mongol khans' personal relations with Tibetan lamas. Tibet was allowed, at least under Khubilai, a great degree of autonomy due to the influence of Tibetan lamas, especially Phagspa, at the Mongol court. Tibet was integrated into the administration of the Mongol empire, but not into the administration of China: "The Yuan administrative structure in Tibet and the *de facto* military occupation of Tibet by Mongol troops made that country in reality, an integral part of the Mongol Empire. It was, however, not treated as a Chinese province but as a separate subjugated country."[44]

In 1269 Phagspa returned to China, where he devised the script for the Mongol language that bears his name. In 1270 Khubilai proclaimed a new Chinese dynasty, the *Yuan*, and made Phagspa imperial preceptor (*Ti-shih*).[45] In 1276 Phagspa returned to Tibet, accompanied by a Mongol army, perhaps because of the death (or murder) of the Sakya Ponchen.[46] Phagspa died at Sakya soon after his return in 1280, at the age of forty-

39. Petech, "Tibetan Relations," 185.

40. Wylie, "Mongol Conquest," 125; Chang, "Yuan Dynasty and Sa-kya Sect," 52.

41. Kwanten, "Tibetan-Mongol Relations," 153.

42. Jiunn Yih Chang, "Yuan Dynasty and Sa-kya Sect," 139.

43. Tucci, *Tibetan Painted Scrolls*, 33.

44. Kwanten, "Tibetan-Mongol Relations," 169.

45. Petech, "Tibetan Relations," 187. The Yuan dynasty thus began in 1270, though the Mongols had been in control of North China since 1234 and did not finally defeat the Southern Sung until 1276.

46. Wylie, "Mongol Conquest," 128.

five; poison was suspected. The new *ponchen* of Sakya was accused of poisoning Phagspa and was executed by a force of Mongols sent to investigate. In 1285 the Brigungpa, supported by "Tod Hor" allies, again attacked monasteries of the Sakyapa.[47] The Brigungpa were defeated by the Sakyapas and their Mongol auxiliaries, who then went on to destroy the monastery of Brigung.[48]

After the defeat of the Brigungpa, and Khubilai's defeat of Khaidu at Karakoram, there was a long period of peace in Tibet. Khubilai died in 1294, after which Yuan relations with Tibet lost the intimacy that had characterized the period of Khubilai and Phagspa. Tibetan Buddhism, however, continued to play a large role at the Yuan court:

> Although the Yuan court was no longer interested in Tibet as a political entity, it was still deeply involved with Lamas, especially Tantricists, and still bestowing enormous gifts on the Tibetan Buddhists, a practice that, according to the contemporary Chinese historians, placed a nearly unbearable burden on their own people. The Mongol emperors, however, were no longer interested in the teachings of Buddhism itself, but more in the practices of a degenerated form of Tantricism. They were interested in obtaining longevity and immortality and for this they turned to certain Tibetan Lamas, who taught them the so-called "secret doctrine."[49]

Cho-Yon

The idealized *Cho-Yon* relationship of Buddhist lama to Mongol khan, established by Sakya Pandita and Phagspa, became the pattern for Tibet's foreign relations, especially its relations with China. As Wylie commented, despite the significance of this relationship (or perhaps because of it), "perhaps no other development in Tibetan history has been recorded in such an anachronistic and obfuscated fashion."[50]

The tone of Sakya Pandita's letter was one of resignation to the inevitability of submission to the Mongols, but, at the same time, of an optimism that his own influence at the Mongol court could lead to a conversion of the Mongols and all their subjects to Buddhism. Sakya Pandita repeatedly mentioned in his letter that he and his nephews were the favorites of Godan. However, the Mongols were extraordinarily eclectic in their religious preferences and patronage. The Mongols were typically

---

47. The "Tod Hor" (Western Mongol) troops were sent by Du'a, chieftain of the Chagatais, who was an ally of Khaidu. Petech, "Tibetan Relations," 189.
48. Wylie, "Mongol Conquest," 132.
49. Kwanten, "Tibetan-Mongol Relations," 137.
50. Wylie, "Mongol Conquest," 103.

very respectful of religious practitioners of all types, especially if they could perform some visible manifestation of their spiritual powers. Almost all accounts of Tibetan lamas' audiences with Mongol Khans were accompanied by descriptions of the spiritual manifestations, magic or healing that the lamas performed. The Tibetan lamas had an elaborate mystical tradition of ancient origins and awesome reputation, which was in some ways similar to Mongol shamanism, and therefore familiar to the Mongols. The lamas also had an impressive formalized doctrine and philosophy, also of ancient origins. The Mongols therefore favored Tibetan Buddhism, but, because the Mongol religion was shamanistic, or non-clerical, they did not commit themselves to any one religious doctrine:

> The Mongols believed in Shamanism, which has many aspects that overlap with animism. Its highest god is "Mongke Tenggeri." The Teb-Tenggeri, people who have the ability to communicate with heaven (Tenggeri), get respect from the khan. Despite the Mongol shamans, even the priests of Buddhism and Taoism in China . . . were highly honored by the khans because they were qualified to be the Teb-Tenggeri. Therefore, the position of Sa-skya Pandita was only one of the Teb-Tenggeris.[51]

The Mongols favored religious practitioners of all types in all the countries they conquered, granting them immunity from taxation and judicial prosecution. This was due not only to their interest in all manifestations of religion, and, no doubt, to their fear of the supernatural, but also to a policy of using local religious authorities to impose and legitimate Mongol rule. Patronage of religious authorities could be manipulated to defuse discontent among subjugated populations while at the same time preventing the rise of any secular authority around which resistance might coalesce. This policy on the part of the Mongols may explain why a Tibetan lama was chosen to effect the submission of Tibet:

> The exploitation of religious leaders at the expense of secular lords in order to subjugate foreign populations was a sociological pattern not unknown to the Mongols. Therefore, given the fragmented and dichotomous nature of Tibetan society at the time, it was logical that Prince Koden would select a lama rather than a layman to surrender Tibet.[52]

Besides the significance of his act of submission to Godan Khan, there is no evidence that Sakya Pandita formulated or contributed to the theory of dual rule of the spiritual and temporal realms, the *Cho-Yon*. The

---

51. Jiunn Yih Chang, "Yuan Dynasty and Sa-kya Sect," 31.
52. Wylie, "Mongol Conquest," 112.

elaboration of this theory was the work of his nephew Phagspa. Phagspa's theory provided religious legitimation for Khubilai and subsequent Mongol rulers, as *chakravartins*, or universal Buddhist kings. Khubilai was glorified as an incarnation of the Buddhist deity Manjushri.[53] The Mongol rulers were thus legitimized as universal rulers, not just Mongol *khaghans* or emperors of China:

> In the religious sphere, the impact of Pags-pa can be seen chiefly in two achievements. He provided the Mongol emperors with a pseudo-historical theory which incorporated them into the line of succession of Buddhist universal emperors, and he developed a theory of theocratic rule for Khubilai and his successors. . . . Because of its inherent supranational character, Buddhist sacralization was acceptable to the Mongols. It provided them with a sacral kingship that legitimated their domination over China and the world.[54]

The *Cho-Yon*, as elaborated by Phagspa, was a theory of universal empire of both secular and spiritual realms. The secular and the spiritual were regarded as equal in importance; the secular ruler was required to guarantee peace to his subjects so that they might be able to devote themselves to religion. As the secular and spiritual realms were equal, so were the rulers of each. The head of state and the head of religion were equally necessary for the ultimate salvation of humanity. Without peace provided by the secular ruler, humanity would have no opportunity to seek religion; without the leader of religion, there would be no path to salvation.

Phagspa's theory of *Cho-Yon* was dependent upon extraordinary personal relationships. The *Cho-Yon* relationship was personal, between equal representatives of complimentary realms, or as the Mongols are more likely to have interpreted it, between lord and distinguished subject. It was a social and political relationship typical in many respects of the feudalistic character of the early period of the Mongol empire. It was not a theory, or a practice at this time, of state to state relations between the Mongols and Tibetans, despite later Tibetan attempts to interpret it as such.

Phagspa was one of many foreign administrators in Yuan China, dis-

---

53. Phagspa initiated Khubilai in the rites of the Sakya tutelary deity Gepa Dorje, the Sanskrit Hevajra, and of Mahakala. Rites of Hevajra and Mahakala thereafter became customary for the enthronement of Yuan emperors. Mahakala became the national protector of the Mongols; Mahakala in his fierce aspect being invoked when Mongol armies went into battle. Herbert Franke, "Tibetans in Yuan China," in *China Under Mongol Rule*, ed. John D. Langlois, Jr. (Princeton: Princeton University Press, 1981), 308.

54. Ibid., 306.

tinguished only by his religious role and his close personal relations with Khubilai and his family.[55] Franke questions whether it is appropriate to speak of Tibetans in Yuan China as if their nationality is relevant: "It would perhaps make more sense to speak of Buddhist clerics who happen to be Tibetans. The influence of the lamas in China rested solely on their religious position and not on their nationality."[56] Phagspa spent most of his career in Yuan China; he devoted much less of his life to administration of Tibet, and with less success, than to administration of Buddhism for the Yuan. Phagspa's interest was universal; he demonstrated little national or even sectarian interest. Phagspa refused the offer of Khubilai to prohibit all Tibetan Buddhist sects except the Sakyapa.[57] His political role in relation to Tibet was, in Petech's words, an invention of Khubilai:

> [Khubilai's choice of Phagspa] . . . could not have been dictated by any Sa-skya-pa preeminent position or influence in Tibetan society before the rise of the Mongols. Phags-pa as the political leader of Tibet was simply "invented" by Khubilai because he was the religious chief who offered the best guarantees of intelligent subservience to the aims of the new ruler of China.[58]

During the era of Phagspa and Khubilai, the idealized *Cho-Yon* relationship may have been realized, but, dependent as it was upon personalities and personal relationships, the *Cho-Yon* lasted only so long as did Phagspa and Khubilai themselves. Phagspa's theory of his personal relationship with Khubilai, and that of the Tibetan Buddhist church with the Mongol empire, was extremely sophisticated in its understanding of the cultural and political needs of the Mongols, but extremely naive in anticipating political implications for Tibet.

Khubilai's Yuan dynasty was rapidly Sinicized. After 1329, Yuan succession was a matter determined by Chinese political considerations alone. The steppe ceased to be a factor in Yuan politics; the Yuan emperor was by this time primarily emperor of China rather than Mongol

---

55. The Mongols employed many administrators of Inner Asian and Central Asian origins, as well as Tanguts, Jurchens and Khitans. Yuan society was divided into four classes. First were the Mongols themselves, next were the foreign administrators, then came the Northern Chinese, and last were the Southern Chinese. Only the first two classes could hold the highest positions. The Tibetans, unlike any other nationality in Yuan society, were confined primarily to a single role: Buddhist practitioners and officials of the *Hsuan-cheng-yuan*. Franke, "Tibetans in Yuan China," 297.

56. Ibid., 298.

57. Kwanten, "Tibetan-Mongol Relations," 110.

58. Petech, "Tibetan Relations," 185.

khaghan.[59] Tibetan clerics were seemingly unperturbed by this turn of events as hundreds of Tibetan Buddhist monks served long periods as religious officials in Yuan China. Most of the officials of the *Hsuan-cheng-yuan* within China were Tibetan monks; Tibetans were in charge of Buddhist affairs all over China.[60] The role played by Tibetan monks in Yuan administration aroused considerable resentment among Chinese Confucian officials and among the Chinese population. With the exception of Phagspa, who seems to have been generally revered by Mongols and Chinese alike, most Tibetan monks were regarded as arrogant and opportunistic, and as exploiting the high status and privilege that they were accorded.[61] Franke writes that "Lamaism and the actions of Tibetan lamas in China were antagonistic and even provoked proto-nationalist, anti-foreign feelings, not only among non-Buddhist intellectuals but even among Chinese monks."[62]

Fortunately for the historical legacy of Phagspa, neither his *Cho-Yon* ideology nor the actual function of Tibetans within the administration of China can be interpreted as the equivalent of Chinese sovereignty over Tibet, Chinese claims to the contrary notwithstanding. Phagspa's role was defined by Mongol-Tibetan relations, not Sino-Tibetan relations, despite the fact that the Mongols became emperors of China. The relationship remained primarily personal, even though both Sakya Pandita and Phagspa were agents for and represented Tibet's submission to the Mongols, because the Mongols were unable to transform their relationship between patron and church into relations between patron and state. The Mongols managed to transform the Tibetan lamas into administrators only within China; they never succeeded in making them actual administrators of Tibet. Khubilai's attempt to make Phagspa and Phagna

---

59. John W. Dardess, *Conquerors and Confucians* (New York: Columbia University Press, 1973), 7.

60. Franke, "Tibetans in Yuan China," 313.

61. In 1282 Khubilai had to issue a decree forbidding Tibetan monks' abuse of *ulag* privileges while traveling between Tibet and China. Jiunn Yih Chang, "Yuan Dynasty and Sakya Sect," 158. This edict had to be renewed in 1306 and 1311. Tibetan monks were apparently making unauthorized use of their free transport privileges for private, or monastic, commerce. Franke, "Tibetans in Yuan China," 315. Tibetan lamas and monks in Yuan China were accorded high status and great privilege, including almost complete judicial immunity: "An edict by Qubilai's successor specifically stated that no one, not even the regular officials, was allowed to touch the Lamas or force them to do something. The edict, after reviewing a minor incident, specified that when a layman touched a lama criminally with his hands, the hands were to be cut off; if he slandered or accused him, the tongue of the accuser was to be torn out. The edict contained instructions for its enforcement and authorized every fully ordained monk to make the accusations." Kwanten, "Tibetan-Mongol Relations," 161.

62. Franke, "Tibetans in Yuan China," 315.

Dorje administrators of Tibet encountered intense opposition, after which Khubilai instituted direct Mongol control in Tibet. Tibetans' involvement as Yuan officials might be interpreted as Tibetan political assimilation to Chinese administration had not the employment of foreign administrators been a Yuan characteristic, without evident political implications for the native states of those foreign officials.

Mongolia and Tibet were the only non-Chinese remnants of the Mongol empire left to the Yuan after 1260. Mongolia and Tibet therefore acquired a similar status as territories of Khubilai's realm as Mongol *khaghan*, pre-existing and separate from the realm he acquired as Chinese emperor. Mongol conquest and administration of Tibet, then, does not have any implication of Chinese sovereignty over Tibet, even though the Mongols became a Chinese dynasty and they administered Tibet from China. Their administration of Tibet remained separate from that of China, or of any province of China.

Although the *Cho-Yon* relationship did not survive the era of Phagspa and Khubilai except in theory, its effects on Tibetan domestic politics were more permanent. Mongol patronage, not only of the Sakyapas, but of all the Buddhist sects, was instrumental in establishing the political dominance of the Buddhist church in Tibet. Their role as agents for Tibetan submission to the Mongols allowed Tibetan lamas to play a political role not only in the Mongol empire but within Tibet as well. The sect that achieved the closest relations with the most powerful of the Mongols, in this case the Sakyapa with Khubilai Khan, was also able to achieve political dominance within Tibet.

Because the church was universalist, Tibetan Buddhist sects had less reluctance than the aristocracy to accept foreign patronage. Sakya Pandita and Phagspa were more pragmatic than the secular aristocracy in regard to Tibet's submission to the Mongols; their primary interest was not the political status of Tibet but the propagation of Buddhism. Sakya Pandita argued that his submission had prevented a Mongol invasion of Tibet and had opened up vast realms for the propagation of the Buddhist doctrine. Phagspa's elaborate theories of the equality of spiritual and temporal realms obscured the Sakyapas' political dependence upon foreign patrons and the implications of that dependence on Tibet's political status. As Lattimore has written: "Politically, the supreme pontiffs of Tibet have from the beginning acted as the agents of one or another alien overlord. . . . The supreme pontiff, in other words, is to be understood as the symbol of stagnation within Tibet and of alien imperial power over Tibet."[63]

---

63. Owen Lattimore, *Inner Asian Frontiers of China* (Oxford: Oxford University Press, 1988), 227.

Tibetan Buddhism at this stage in Tibetan history displays many of the sociological characteristics of religions of the type Weber characterized as "hierocratic."[64] Religious organizations of this type have typical sociological patterns that they pursue, consciously or unconsciously, in relation to secular authority. In general, they compete with the secular for political dominance with varying degrees of success:

> Wherever hierocracy in this sense occurred . . . it had far-reaching effects on the administrative structure. Hierocracy must forestall the rise of secular powers capable of emancipating themselves. . . . Hierocracy seeks to prevent the king from securing independent resources; it impedes the accumulation of the *thesaurus* which was indispensable to all kings of early history. . . . Hierocracy checks as much as possible the rise of an autonomous and secular military nobility. . . . This opposition to [secular] political charisma has everywhere recommended hierocracy to conquerors as a means of domesticating a subject population. Thus, the Tibetan, the Jewish and the late Egyptian hierocracy were in part supported, and in part directly created, by foreign rulers.[65]

The *Cho-Yon* relationship fulfilled the needs not only of the Tibetan Buddhist church but of the Mongols as well. The Mongols recognized the universalist nature of religion and favored religious practitioners over the more nationalist feudal nobility in every country that they conquered. As Weber wrote, "If the political ruler wants to create an apparatus of officials and a counterweight against the nobility. . . he cannot wish for a more reliable support than the influence of the monks on the masses."[66] As Weber recognized, however, an ecclesiastical organization is typically far from powerless in relation to its patron despite its total dependence in the political and military sense.[67] Religious leaders were armed with spiritual authority and charisma, magnified in this case by the Tibetan lamas' reputation for possessing magical powers. Tibetan lamas were not unwitting tools of the Mongol khans; they established a power position for themselves and for their doctrine far out of proportion to the actual or potential political power of Tibet at the time. Phagspa's influence at the

---

64. Weber defines a "hierocratic organization" as "an organization which enforces its order through psychic coercion by distributing or denying religious benefits." As examples of hierocracy Weber lists 1) a ruler who is legitimated by priests, either as an incarnation or in the name of God, and 2) a high priest who is also king. The second example Weber classes as the only true theocracy. Max Weber, *Economy and Society* (Berkeley: University of California Press, 1968), 54.

65. Ibid., 1160.

66. Ibid., 1171.

67. Ibid.

Mongol court was based upon the charisma of his religion, not on the political power or significance of Tibet to the Mongols.

Phagspa achieved the potential of the relationship with the Mongols envisioned by Sakya Pandita. As Sakya Pandita predicted, his submission to the Mongols forestalled their invasion of Tibet, while Mongol patronage allowed the Tibetan Buddhist church to vastly expand its influence. The compromise with the Mongols also created political unity in Tibet, at least in central Tibet. However, a political administration was created for Kham and Amdo separate from that of central Tibet that set the precedent for later Chinese administrative divisions of Tibet along the same lines. A more fatal flaw of the Tibetan relationship with the Mongols was that it established the Buddhist church, with its inherent dependence upon foreign patronage, as the dominant political authority in Tibet.

Later Yuan Dynasty

Mongol interest in Tibet declined after the death of Khubilai. The Sakyapa, fractured by succession disputes and no longer supported by the Mongols, were also in decline. In 1331 the Third Karmapa Lama, Ranjung Dorje, was invited to China; in 1332 he presided at the coronation of the last Mongol emperor, Togon Temur (reigned 1332-1370). The Fourth Karmapa, Rolpai Dorje, visited Togon Temur's court in 1360-62.[68] The decline of the Sakyapa revived sectarian and regional competition for power in Tibet. The predominant Tibetan clans usually had sectarian affiliations, or they had, like the Sakyapa Khon clan, both secular and sectarian lineages. Despite their religious affiliations, the aristocracy was uncomfortable with the political domination of Buddhist sects, or at least that of the Sakyapa, based as it was upon foreign patronage. The aristocracy opposed to the Sakyapa were, of course, closely connected with other sects who had also sought Mongol patrons.

The Sakyapa were finally succeeded in political paramountcy in central Tibet by another sect, the Phagmogrupa, which also combined religious and secular lineages. The Phagmogrupa sect derived some of its spiritual and political legitimacy from the Brigungpa; the Brigung were founded by a disciple of Dorje Gyalpo, the founder of the Phagmogrupa sub-sect of the Kagyudpa, so that the Brigung were actually part of the lineage of Phagmogrupa. A Phagmogrupa lama, Changchub Gyaltsan, overcame the Sakyapa by exploiting Sakya factionalism; by 1358 the defeat of Sakya was complete. The Yuan, by now powerless to intervene,

---

68. Elliot Sperling, "Early Ming Policy Toward Tibet" (Ph.D. diss., Indiana University, 1983), 49.

confirmed Phagmogrupa hegemony by awarding Changchub Gyaltsan the Mongol title *Darugachi* and a new Chinese title, *Tai Situ*. Having ascertained that the Yuan were now unlikely to interfere in Tibetan affairs, Changchub Gyaltsan reorganized the administration of Tibet. The Yuan myriarchies were abolished and a system of regional fortresses (*dzong*) was established. Yuan law codes were abolished and the law of the *chogyal*, the religious kings of Tibet of the imperial period, was reestablished. Sakyapa vassalage to the Mongols was condemned.

Tibet of the Phagmogrupa harkened back to the era of Tibet's imperial glory for its inspiration. Even the dress of the imperial period was revived and worn by Tibetan ministers during the New Year celebrations. Historical studies of the imperial period were inaugurated and a new class of "rediscovered" religious texts (*terma*), mainly of the teachings of Padmasambhava, was produced. The *terma* literature was primarily religious but included some secular history of the glories of the Tibetan empire. Although Buddhist, the *terma* had a nationalist and anti-clerical content. The exploits of individual saints were recounted, not the spiritual lineage of sects.

Phagmogrupa political dominance did not long outlast Changchub Gyaltsan, who died in 1364. Once again, regionalism and sectarianism fractured political unity. In 1434, when the succession was disputed between Phagmogrupa claimants, the Phagmogrupa were succeeded by the Rinpung family. The Rinpung, originally from the town of Rinpung in Tsang, were patrons of the *Zamar* "Red Hat" Karmapa sect; they soon relocated to Shigatse and made that town their center.

In 1372 Tsonkhapa, the founder of the reformed Gelugpa sect, came to central Tibet from Amdo. In 1409 he founded Ganden monastery near Lhasa. In 1416 he founded Drepung and in 1419 Sera, both in Lhasa. The Gelugpa rapidly became the dominant political power in Lhasa. In 1447 they founded Tashilhunpo in the Karmapa stronghold of Shigatse. In 1479 the Gelugpa refused a request by the Rinpung Karmapa of Tsang to build a Karmapa monastery in Lhasa, thus igniting a regional/sectarian conflict that was to continue for more than a century.

Tibetan Relations with the Ming

The Mongol Yuan dynasty fell in 1368 and was succeeded by the Ming (1368-1644), the first native Chinese dynasty to control all of China since the T'ang (618-907). The Ming took the T'ang as their model in both domestic and foreign policy. The early Ming emperors are said to have recognized the threat that Tibet posed to the T'ang and to have adopted the successful Yuan policy as the best method of dealing with Tibet.[69] The greatest threat to the early Ming, however, remained the Mongols, who had retired from China in a strategic retreat, but who retained both the intention and the capability to reimpose their rule upon China. The Ming were interested in avoiding any threat from Tibet, or from a Tibetan alliance with the Mongols, and in using Tibetan lamas' influence with the Mongols, but not in controlling Tibet directly.

The first Ming emperor, T'ai-tsu (reigned 1368-1392), was favorably disposed toward Buddhism, having been a monk himself from 1344 to 1368. He is said to have been especially impressed by those "who were thought able to perform acts of wizardry or seemingly supernatural feats."[70] Ming T'ai-tsu's first communication with Tibet was a proclamation in 1369 informing the Tibetans that the Ming had succeeded the Yuan. A subsequent mission confirmed Tibetan officials in the posts they had held under the Yuan, ignoring the fact that the Yuan offices had been abolished by Changchub Gyaltsan. The Ming also sent messages to Tibetan frontier chiefs and to lamas of the Phagmogrupa, Sakyapa and Brigungpa sects.[71]

Ming T'ai-tsu's successor, Ming Ch'eng-tsu (reigned 1402-1418), invited the Fifth Karmapa, Dezin Shekpa, to his court in 1403 to perform the Buddhist death and rebirth ritual for T'ai-tsu. The probable reason that the Karmapa Lama was chosen over other Tibetan lamas was that the Chinese, and Ch'eng-tsu personally, were familiar with the Karmapa sect from the visit of the Fourth Karmapa to Peking in 1260.[72] After a second invitation, the Karmapa Lama set out for China in 1406; he arrived at the Ming court at Nanking in 1407.

The Karmapa's stay at the Ming capital was marked by lavish celebrations, with honors and awards to the lama and his entourage. The Karmapa performed the death ritual for Ming T'ai-tsu and initiated Ch'eng-tsu and his consort into several of the Buddhist rituals of the Karmapa sect. During his visit, many miracles were said to have occurred, including clouds in auspicious shapes, rains of flowers, and radiant lights and sounds from the heavens.[73] The Karmapa was awarded a lavish and lengthy title, the essential part of which was *ta-pao fa-wang*, "Great Precious King of Dharma," one of the titles that Phagspa had held under the Yuan. Ming Ch'eng-tsu and the Empress Hsu (who,

69. Ibid., 38.
70. Ibid., 46.
71. Elliot Sperling, "The 5th Karma-pa and Some Aspects of the Relationship between Tibet and the Early Ming," in Aris and Suu Kyi, *Tibetan Studies* 280.
72. Sperling, "Early Ming Policy," 78.
73. Ibid., 84.

as a devout Buddhist, is said to have been an important influence on Ch'eng-tsu) were described in later Tibetan sources as incarnations of Manjushri and Tara, respectively (it is not stated specifically if these titles were bestowed by the Karmapa).[74]

Ch'eng-tsu offered to send the Karmapa back to Tibet with titles and military escorts sufficient to establish the predominance of his sect over others in Tibet. The Karmapa refused this offer, as well as a political relationship of the *Cho-Yon* type between himself and Ch'eng-tsu.[75] The Karmapa's refusal was no doubt influenced by Tibetan criticism of Yuan patronage of the Sakyapas, of which the Karmapa must have been aware, but was undoubtedly also based upon the calculation that the Ming had neither the interest nor the capability to establish the same sort of relationship with Tibet that had existed during the Yuan.

Lacking the will or the need to impose the type of dependent relationship upon Tibet that had existed under the Yuan, the Ming contented themselves with the superficial aspects of that relationship. The Ming continued to confirmed Tibetan officials' titles that had existed under the Yuan as if the Ming had inherited the Yuan relationship with Tibet. They continued to patronize, with lavish gifts and honorific titles, any lamas willing to travel to China, or failing that, sent missions to Tibet to bestow gifts upon Tibetan clerics.

During the time of Ch'eng-tsu the Ming patronized lamas from most of the sects of Tibetan Buddhism. The two most important of these lamas, both of whom visited the Ming court, were the Sakyapa Kunga Tashi, who was awarded the title *Ta-ch'eng fa-wang* (Great Vehicle King of the Dharma), and the Gelugpa Shakya Yeshe, who received the title *Ta-tz'u fa-wang* (Great Compassionate King of the Dharma). In his invitation to Kunga Tashi, the Ming emperor is said to have referred to himself as a *chakravartin*, clearly a reference to the *Cho-Yon* relationship.[76] Shakya Yeshe was a substitute for his teacher, Tsonkhapa, founder of the Gelugpa. The fact that Tsonkhapa dared to refuse the emperor's invitation is another indication of the lack of Ming political influence in Tibet. Ming records make no mention of the great founder of the Gelugpa or his refusal of the Ming invitation. Another five lamas received lesser titles without actually travelling to the Ming court.[77]

---

74. Ibid., 119.

75. Ibid., 89. The Karmapa's refusal of this offer was reminiscent of Phagspa's refusal of Khubilai's offer to prohibit other sects in Tibet.

76. Ibid., 140.

77. Three of these were of the Sakyapa sect, one of the Phagmogrupa, and one of the Brigungpa. The predominance of the Sakyapa may indicate that lamas of this sect may have had visions of renewed patronage for their sect similar to that bestowed by the Yuan. Two of these lamas were heads of Sakya estates in Kham, Lingtsang and Gonjo, and another was head of the Tagtsang sub-sect of the Sakyapa. Ibid., 137.

Tibetan lamas, with only a few exceptions, displayed little reluctance to accept Ming titles and gifts. In addition to the lamas who are known by name to have had contacts with the Ming, there were certainly many more. The *Ming Shih* states that the lamas came to China in an endless procession, "the feet of those who came touched those of another."[78] Tucci states that so many Tibetan clerics went to China, ostensibly to present tribute and receive titles, but actually "aspiring to imperial gifts and trading to enrich themselves," that the Ming had to limit the number of Tibetan missions, the time they could spend in China (at the court's expense) and the frequency of such missions to not more than once every three years. These visits diminished after the reign of Ch'eng-tsu. None of the later Ming emperors had the same interest in Buddhism, nor did the later Ming have much interest in Tibet.[79]

Tibet of the Ming period was no threat to China nor, in the later Ming period, were the lamas much needed for their influence on the Mongols. The Mongols had been weakened by energetic military campaigning by T'ai-tsu and Ch'eng-tsu. As the Mongol threat diminished, so did Ming interest in Tibet. Sonam Gyatso, the Third Dalai Lama, refused an invitation to visit the Ming capital at Peking in 1580, even though he was at Khoto Khotan (Hohhot, the modern Huhehaote, capital of Inner Mongolia), only a short distance from Peking, at the time, busily re-establishing the *Cho-Yon* relationship with the Mongols.[80] In 1615 the Fourth Dalai Lama also refused an invitation to visit the Ming, citing illness as an excuse; indeed, this was only one year before his death.[81]

The differences in Yuan and Ming policy in relation to Tibet are characteristic of the differences in frontier policies of conquest and native dynasties. The Mongols needed Tibetan spiritual legitimation within their Inner Asian empire; they also had the ability, as a steppe empire, to impose direct control over Tibet. The Ming, as a native Chinese dynasty, were more interested in domestic politics than in creating an empire beyond China. Ming Ch'eng-tsu mounted six expeditions against the Mongols, five of which he led personally, but he did not try to maintain control over territory beyond the Great Wall. After the offensive campaigns of Ch'eng-tsu eliminated the Mongol threat, the Ming did not have to face either a united steppe empire or a unified Tibet; their frontier policy thereafter was primarily defensive.

The early Ming emperors may have hoped that their patronage of Tibetan lamas could be transformed into political influence in Tibet

---

78. Ibid., 154.
79. Tucci, *Tibetan Painted Scrolls*, 25.
80. Shakabpa, *Tibet: A Political History*, 96.
81. Ibid., 99.

along the lines of that enjoyed by the Mongol Yuan dynasty. However, the Ming had no real interest in Tibet beyond Tibet's role in Ming relations with the Mongols. Once the Mongol threat passed, the Ming were no longer concerned with Tibet and did little to substantiate their claim to authority there. Despite later Chinese claims, Ming patronage of Tibetan lamas and their award of meaningless titles and non-existent official positions can hardly be said to be the equivalent of actual Ming authority over Tibet or evidence that Tibet was a "part of China" during the Ming.

Revival of the Cho-Yon Relationship with the Mongols[82]

Sectarian and regional rivalries continued in central Tibet during the period of Ming dynasty China. The Rinpung sect of Shigatse attacked Lhasa in 1480 and again in 1498, securing control there from 1498 to 1517. The Gelugpa were attacked by the Brigungpa in 1537 and lost eighteen monasteries in Olkha to them. Perhaps the most significant event of the Ming period for later Tibetan politics, however, was the migration of Mongol tribes to northern Tibet. Mongol tribes had begun migrating to the Kokonor area during the Yuan; this migration greatly increased after the fall of the Yuan.

During the Ming, the Mongols of the steppe were divided into eastern and western tribal alliances. The Western Mongols, the Oirat, controlled all the territory from Lake Balkash to Lake Baikal and dominated the Khalkha tribes of the Mongol homeland (centered in what is now Outer Mongolia). The most powerful of the Oirat confederation were the Dzungar, or "left wing," who inhabited the area north of the Tian Shan known as Dzungaria. The Eastern Mongols were weakened by attacks of the early Ming, but they experienced a resurgence under Dayan Khan (1473-1543). The Ming policy of denying trade relations with the Mongols kept the northern Chinese frontier in a state of conflict.[83]

Dayan's successor as leader of the Eastern Mongols, Altan Khan (1543-1582), of the Tumed tribe, regained control of the Khalkha territory from the Dzungar. Secen Khungtaiji, Altan's grand-nephew, invaded the Sining valley near Kokonor in 1566 and informed the Tibetans of that area that he would accept their religion if they submitted, but would conquer

---

82. This section, unless otherwise noted, relies primarily upon Shakabpa, *Tibet: A Political History*.

83. Nomads on the northern frontier of China usually preferred trade to raid. Often, raid was employed to force the Chinese to permit trade. The early Ming chose military action and denial of trade relations to the Mongols due to their fear of a Mongol resurgence from the steppe. Thomas Barfield, *The Perilous Frontier: Nomadic Empires and China* (Cambridge: Basil Blackwell, 1989).

them if they did not. The Tibetans submitted and sent a number of their lamas to Secen Khungtaiji's camp; some lamas were also sent to Altan Khan at Khoto Khotan.

In 1570 the Ming, in a shift in frontier policy, granted tribute and trade privileges to Altan Khan. This shift represented an abandonment of the Ming policy of active frontier defense in favor of the more passive policy of appeasement, and a victory for Altan, whose control of access to the wealth of China allowed him to create patronage relations among all Eastern Mongol tribes. In 1577 Altan invited Sonam Gyatso, the third incarnation of the Gelugpa abbot of Drepung, to his camp at Kokonor. Altan was reportedly encouraged to invite the lama by the suggestion that he should "follow the example of Phagspa and Khubilai."[84]

Sonam Gyatso met Altan Khan at Kokonor in 1578 and traveled with him from there to Altan's capital at Hohhot (Khoto Khotan). In an exchange of political and spiritual legitimations, Sonam Gyatso identified himself as an incarnation of Phagspa and Altan as an incarnation of Khubilai, thus providing Altan with a spiritual claim to the Chingghisid lineage, and securing Altan's political patronage for himself.[85] Sonam Gyatso acquired the name "Dalai," a Mongol translation of his name, thereafter becoming known as the Dalai Lama.[86] Altan prohibited worship of the Mongols' shamanistic deities and proclaimed that all his subjects must accept Buddhism; Mongol law was reformed to accord with the Buddhist laws of Tibet. From this time, Tibetan Buddhism spread rapidly among the Mongols.

Sonam Gyatso died in 1588; his reincarnation was discovered in Mongolia in the great-grandson of Altan Khan. The discovery of the Fourth Dalai Lama (two abbots of Drepung were counted as the first and second incarnations) among the Mongols established the *Cho-Yon* relationship on a new and more intimate basis. Mongol patronage of the Gelugpa strengthened the Gelugpa position in Tibet but aroused opposition from the Gelukpas' rivals. One source of conflict was the Mongol entourage of the Fourth Dalai Lama, who were zealous proponents of the Gelugpa sect.

Mongol migrations to the Kokonor continued and now included tribes of the Dzungar Oirat, who were in conflict among themselves and with

---

84. Zahiruddin Ahmad, *Sino-Tibetan Relations in the Seventeenth Century*, Serie Orientale Roma, XL (Roma: Istituto Italiano Per Il Medio Ed Estremo Oriente, 1970), 88.

85. Ibid., 90. Altan was not an actual descendant of Chingghis, therefore his recognition as an incarnation of Chingghis by Sonam Gyatso was potentially an important element in his attempt to achieve political legitimacy among the Mongols.

86. Sonam Gyatso means "oceanic virtue" in Tibetan; Dalai, "ocean" in Mongol, is a translation of Gyatso.

the Khalkha. Altan's death in 1583 led to a revival of conflicts among the Mongols of Kokonor. In 1590, 165 Tibetan tribes numbering 74,710 persons reportedly submitted to the Ming in order to avoid the depredations of the Kokonor Mongols.[87]

The rivalry between the Lhasa Gelugpa and the Tsang Karmapa continued. The death of the Fourth Dalai Lama in 1617 led to open conflict. In 1618 Tsang attacked Lhasa to avenge insults suffered at the hands of the Mongol attendants of the Fourth Dalai Lama. This provoked the Gelugpa to seek more Mongol patrons and more military assistance. The Gelugpa under the new Fifth Dalai Lama found a new patron in Gushri Khan of the Khoshot, who had recently migrated from Dzungaria. Gushri Khan attacked the Karmapas' patron, Chogtu Taiji of the Khalkha, in Kokonor and eliminated them as a threat to the Gelugpa. In 1638 Gushri Khan came to Lhasa and was awarded with the title of *Tenzin Choskyi Gyalpo*, or King of the Dharma.

In 1640 Gushri Khan attacked the Bonpo chief of Beri, in western Kham, who had conspired with the Tsang Karmapas. Gushri Khan's army then entered central Tibet and captured the Karmapa stronghold at Shigatse. In 1642 Gushri Khan conferred on the Fifth Dalai Lama temporal authority over all of Tibet, the first time that a Dalai Lama had attained both temporal and spiritual rule. Gushri Khan received the title of King of Tibet, but retired to the Kokonor with his armies. The effect of Gushri Khan's intervention on behalf of the Gelugpa was that regional and sectarian conflicts were finally eliminated and Tibet was politically unified, but once again this was accomplished only by means of Mongol political patronage and reliance upon Mongol military force.

In addition to their powerful Mongol patrons, the Gelugpas were more organized than other sects and practiced a stricter monasticism than the older unreformed sects. Although all sects sought Mongol patrons, the Gelugpa were particularly dependant on foreign patrons because they were a relatively new sect without an established network of Tibetan clan patronage. The Gelugpa adopted succession by incarnation, unlike the older sects that were ruled by hierarchical succession (uncle to nephew), which combined spiritual and secular lineages. Succession by incarnation was relatively autonomous of clan influence; clans had less incentive to patronize the Gelugpa because they could not thereby gain any hereditary influence.

The older sects tended to find more in common with each other than with the Gelugpa and therefore allied against them. Unlike Phagspa and

---

87. Louis M.J. Schram, "The Mongours of the Kansu-Tibetan Frontier," *Transactions of the American Philosophical Society* (1961), 48.

the Fifth Karmapa, who declined to suppress other sects, the Fifth Dalai Lama acquiesced in the forcible conversion to the Gelugpa sect of many monasteries of the older sects. The final triumph of the Gelugpa also signified the victory of monastic Buddhism over individual shamanic traditions and the more individualistic traditions within Buddhism. These traditions did not disappear but were increasingly marginalized.[88]

The hegemony achieved by the Gelugpa did have some positive political effects. Tibet was politically unified for the first time since the collapse of the empire some eight centuries previously. Lhasa emerged as the undisputed center of Tibetan culture and political administration; the districts of central Tibet were placed firmly under Lhasa's authority. A census was conducted in 1643 of Toh (Ngari) for the purposes of taxation and administration. In 1648, a similar census was conducted by Tibetan officials of all of the districts of Kham.[89] Kham was thus integrated into the Tibetan polity for the first time since the Tibetan empire. Amdo, however, was under the control of Gushri Khan, who ruled Amdo separately from the rest of Tibet, creating the political precedent for the later separation of Amdo from central Tibet. Gushri Khan also created a new nonsectarian regional rivalry between Lhasa and Shigatse by patronizing the Panchen Lama, of Shigatse's Tashilhunpo monastery, independently of Lhasa.[90]

Tibetan Relations with the Manchu

The Manchu were a people of mixed agricultural and forest nomadic economy inhabiting the rich territories that still retain their name, Manchuria. The Manchu were descendants of the Jurchen, who had formed the Chin dynasty in northern China (1115-1234). The Jurchen had been substantially Sinicized during their dynastic period and had

88. Tucci, *Tibetan Painted Scrolls*, 62.

89. Shakabpa, *Tibet: A Political History*, 113.

90. According to Uradyn Erden Bulag, Mongol patronage for the Panchen Lama was part of a conscious design to divide Tibet and Tibetans, a design to be followed by later patrons and conquerors of Tibet. Uradyn Erden Bulag, personal communication, December 1995. The Panchen Lama lineage derives from the Fifth Dalai Lama's tutor, who was given the Tashilhunpo monastery in Shigatse as a token of the Dalai Lama's respect. Panchen means "Great Pandit," and refers to the original Panchen's role as tutor of the Fifth Dalai Lama. The Panchen was also declared to be an incarnation of Amitabha, in the Buddhist pantheon the teacher and superior of Avalokiteshvara, of whom the Dalai Lama is considered to be the incarnation. Despite the relationship between the original Panchen and the Fifth Dalai Lama, and the fact that they were both of the Gelugpa sect, the Panchen's feudal authority in Tsang gradually came to be regarded as a temporal realm semi-independent of Lhasa.

retained some of this legacy even during their four hundred year retreat in Manchuria. The Manchu had some cultural affinities with the Mongols, but, unlike the Mongols, they were easily assimilable to Chinese culture due to their semi-agricultural economy and their previous history. The name Manchu derives from the Buddhist deity Manjushri; Nurachi (1559-1626), the unifier of the Manchu tribes, was given the title Manjushri by the Fourth Dalai Lama in 1615, signifying that the Manchu emperor was considered an incarnation of the deity.[91] The award of this title to the Manchu, who were not Buddhist, may represent a Tibetan attempt to create a *Cho-Yon* relationship with the Manchu.[92]

The Mongols also established political relations with the Manchu; five tribes of the Khalkha submitted to Nurachi in 1619. The Manchu alliance with the Eastern Mongols was instrumental in the Manchu conquest of China. In 1636 the Manchu Ch'ing dynasty was proclaimed, and in 1644 the Manchu conquest of China was completed. As early as 1637 Mongol envoys to the Manchu are reported to have encouraged the Manchu Emperor Ch'ung Te (reigned 1636-1644) to invite the Fifth Dalai Lama to visit the Manchu court.[93] Ch'ung Te died in 1644 and was succeeded by his son, who became the Shun Chih Emperor (reigned 1644-1662).

In 1645 Manchu forces penetrated as far as Sining, near Kokonor.[94] In 1647 the Oirat and Khoshot of Kokonor submitted to the Manchu and sent tribute. In 1647 the Manchu put down a revolt of the Chinese, Hui (Chinese Muslims) and Tibetans of Kansu-Sining.[95] In 1648 an invitation was sent to the Dalai Lama to visit the Manchu court at Peking.[96] An alliance was in the interest of both parties: the Tibetan Gelugpa wished to revive *Cho-Yon* relations with the dominant power in China and Inner Asia and the Manchu needed Tibetan influence in their relations with the Mongols.

The Dalai Lama began his journey to Peking in 1652. From Kokonor, the Dalai Lama sent a message to the Manchu emperor suggesting that the emperor meet him at Khoto Khotan, or at Taika Lake, near Tatung, outside the Great Wall. This request caused a certain amount of consternation among the emperor's advisors, especially his Chinese advisors.

---

91. The Yuan emperors had also been considered incarnations of Manjushri. Dawa Norbu, "An Analysis of Sino-Tibetan Relationships, 1245-1911," in *Soundings in Tibetan Civilization,* ed. Aziz and Kapstein (New Delhi: Manohar Publications, 1985), 185.

92. David M. Farquhar, "Emperor as Bodhisattva," *Harvard Journal of Asiatic Studies,* 1963, 15.

93. Ahmad, *Sino-Tibetan Relations,* 156.

94. Ibid., 163.

95. Ibid., 165.

96. Ibid., 166.

The request that an emperor should go out from his throne and his capital to meet a barbarian ruler outside the frontiers of China was unprecedented in Chinese protocol. The emperor therefore addressed a letter to the Manchu princes in which he sought their opinions about the protocol of the Dalai Lama's visit:

> During the reign of T'ai-tsung (1626-43) because We had not conquered one corner [of the earth], Khalka, and because the Mongols of our outer frontiers obeyed only the words of Lamas, messengers were sent to summon the Dalai Lama. Before his envoy arrived, Emperor T'ai-tsung died.
>
> After We took the rein of state, We summoned him; whereupon the Dalai Lama immediately departed from Tibet with a suite of 3000 men to come to Us. At present We would like to welcome him in person outside the Great Wall, so as to keep the Lama outside China Proper. We, therefore, order the Mongol princes of our outer frontier who desire to see the Lama to visit him there. If We allow the Lama to enter the Interior when the harvest of this year is poor and the followers of the Lama are so numerous, perhaps it will not benefit Us. If We do not welcome him, We fear that the Lama may be offended since We have invited him to come. Then he would have to return home having only come half way. Thus the Khalkas also will not submit to Us. As to whether We should welcome him in person, you, the ministers, should report to Us your opinions.[97]

The Manchu ministers reportedly recommended that the emperor should meet the Dalai Lama outside the frontiers, while the Chinese ministers opposed it for reasons of important symbolic protocol. The Dalai Lama's visit to Peking signified submission, at least in a nominal sense, within the protocol of China and Inner Asia. The Manchu emperor's power to summon the Dalai Lama to his court was symbolic of his authority over the Dalai Lama. As an unidentified Chinese emperor is quoted on this subject:

> Even if a monarch of a hostile country were to praise my righteousness, I would not send tribute to his court. Even if a feudal prince inside the frontier passes were to reproach my deeds, I would make him send birds as tribute to my court. Thus the more powerful can force others to come to their courts while the less powerful are forced by others to come to their court.[98]

---

97. Lo-shu Fu, *A Documentary Chronicle of Sino-Western Relations: 1644-1820* (Tucson: University of Arizona Press, 1966), 10.

98. Chusei Suzuki, "China's Relations with Inner Asia," in *The Chinese World Order*, ed. J. K. Fairbank (Cambridge: Harvard University Press, 1968), 184.

The Tibetans requested a meeting outside the Great Wall because the symbolism of the emperor travelling some distance to meet the Dalai Lama would signify a relationship of equality of the *Cho-Yon* type. The Tibetans, like the Chinese advisors to the Manchu emperor, were well aware of the diplomatic symbolism involved. Their ability to summon the emperor to meet with the Dalai Lama would imply that the meeting was something less than submission of the Dalai Lama to the Manchu. Even the distance that each party had to travel to meet the other was symbolic of their relative power. A meeting outside the Great Wall of China would signify an alliance between Inner Asian powers, rather than the submission of a barbarian chieftain to a Chinese emperor, as would be the case should the meeting take place in Peking.

After receiving the opinions of his ministers, the emperor decided to meet the Dalai Lama at Taika Lake; he conveyed this intention to the Dalai Lama in a letter dated 13 October 1652.[99] However, on 31 October the emperor received a memorial from his Chinese Grand Secretaries, in which they warned that certain astronomical calculations revealed that there were dangers in the emperor's traveling at that time:

> The Dalai Lama is coming from a distant country. To send a high official to receive him will be enough to show him our intention of according him good treatment. Moreover, that will make it possible to subdue the hearts of the Mongols. Why should the Emperor trouble himself to go to meet the Dalai Lama personally? The ways of Heaven are profound and remote— certainly they are not such as we can fathom. Nevertheless, (the fact that just at the time when) the Emperor is about to mount his chariot, the stars have suddenly changed, makes evident that this, indeed, is a manifestation of God's love towards the Emperor. We cannot but deeply ponder over and examine it.[100]

The emperor subsequently decided that, because the astronomical calculations were undoubtedly correct, "Our Imperial Progress will stop."[101] The emperor dispatched Manchu princes to the Dalai Lama at Taika Lake

---

99. Ahmad, *Sino-Tibetan Relations*, 170.

100. Ibid., 171. The astronomical calculations upon which the Grand Secretaries recommendations were based were performed by the Director of the Imperial Board of Astronomy and Sub-Director of the Court of Sacrificial Worship, T'ang Jo-wang. "T'ang Jo-wang" was the Chinese name of the German Jesuit, Johann Adam Schall, who had been appointed to this post in 1644 after successfully reorganizing the Chinese calendar. Lo-shu Fu, *Sino-Western Relations*, 10, 421. It is perhaps not too far-fetched to speculate that the Chinese Confucian ministers and the Jesuit missionary, Schall, conspired to oppose diplomatic concessions to the head of the Tibetan Buddhist church.

101. Ahmad, *Sino-Tibetan Relations*, 169. The wording may imply that the emperor had already begun his journey.

with his apologies for not travelling there himself, citing bandits and "affairs of State," as his excuses.[102] The Fifth Dalai Lama in his memoirs does not reveal any disappointment that the emperor had not come out to meet him personally; instead, he claims that the rank of the envoys and the ceremony of the meeting at Taika were recognition that he, the Dalai Lama, was the "legal King (of Tibet), of whom there was not the like in Tibet."[103]

The Dalai Lama proceeded to Peking, where he arrived and had audience with the emperor on 15 January 1653. The emperor descended from his throne upon the arrival of the Dalai Lama, advanced for a distance of approximately 30 feet and grasped the Dalai Lama by the hand. The Tibetans' hopes for a symbolic meeting between the Dalai Lama and the Manchu emperor of at some location between the two countries thus transpired 30 feet short of the emperor's throne; a concession by the emperor to the Dalai Lama, no doubt, but not of the magnitude that the Tibetans had desired. The Dalai Lama was not required to perform the kowtow (the "three kneelings and nine head knockings" required of all barbarian envoys). In other ceremony, the Dalai Lama was treated with extraordinary respect, the emperor and the Dalai Lama taking their tea simultaneously, etc., but the emperor's throne was slightly higher than the seat of the Dalai Lama.[104] Significantly, the Dalai Lama in his own memoirs states that he was presented with gifts "fit for an Imperial Preceptor (*Ti-shih*, the title that Phagspa had held)."[105]

The Dalai Lama was awarded the title "Great, Good, Self-Existent Buddha of the Western Heaven, He who rules over the Buddhist Faith in the Empire, the All-Pervading Vajradhara Dalai Lama." The Dalai Lama in his memoirs translates this title as "The Buddha who lives in the Great Virtue and Happiness of the Western Heaven, whose words and Injunctions have become the only Teaching of all the peoples of the Empire, the unchanging Vajradhara Dalai Lama." The Fifth Dalai Lama's title "He who rules over the Buddhist Faith in the Empire" is essentially the same title and position that Phagspa held. The Dalai Lama also states in his memoirs that he received other Edicts and Titles on golden tablets that invested him with "all the lands of the direction in which the sun sets."[106] The emperor also sent letters and awarded a title to Gushri Khan.[107]

102. Ibid., 173.
103. Ibid., 175.
104. Ibid., 176.
105. Ibid., 177.
106. Ibid., 186.
107. Ibid., 185.

The relationship established by the Dalai Lama's visit to Peking had some of the style and format of the *Cho-Yon*; however, the Manchu, like the Ming, desired relations with the Tibetans primarily because the Tibetans had extraordinary influence in Mongol affairs. The letters of the emperor make it clear that the purpose of Manchu relations with the Dalai Lama was to achieve the submission of the Khalkha Mongols. The Manchu emperor did not accept the Tibetan Buddhist faith, and he was not reported to have received any initiations from the Dalai Lama. At one point in the debate over the Dalai Lama's visit, the intentions of the emperor to remain outside the Buddhist church were clearly revealed in his statement: "What objection can there be to Our reverencing the Lama, without [Our] entering the Lama sect?"[108]

The Dalai Lama's visit to Peking has to be interpreted as having had the character of nominal political submission. The extraordinary respect shown to the Dalai Lama, including his exemption from the requirement to perform the kowtow, was not the equivalent of recognition of him as the head of an independent state. Independent heads of state did not travel to meet each other at this period of Inner Asian history; instead, they sent envoys. The significance of an emperor being able to summon another political potentate to his court was unmistakably one of nominal submission of the latter. Although the victory of the Gelugpa sect within Tibet and their alleged establishment of *Cho-Yon* relations with the Manchu have been interpreted by Tibetan Buddhist historians as the beginning of an era of independent rule of the Dalai Lamas, the same events may be seen as the beginning of Tibet's subservience to China.

---

108. Ibid., 169.

6

Tibet Under the Ch'ing

The Fifth Dalai Lama[1]

Tibet's importance in Inner Asian politics in the mid-seventeenth century, at the beginning of the Ch'ing dynasty, was almost entirely due to the Dalai Lama's influence with the Mongols. The Manchu Ch'ing dynasty maintained peaceful relations with the Eastern Mongols by allowing frontier trade, but the Western Mongols were independent of Manchu influence, and their potential to recreate the Mongol steppe empire still posed a threat to the Manchu. The Western Mongol's stronghold was in Dzungaria, a valley north of the Tian Shan and west of the Altai, a traditional locus of independent nomadic tribes. Dzungaria was also economically independent since it possessed some agricultural potential of its own and was situated near the oasis cities and trade routes of eastern and western Turkestan.

Dzungaria was the territory of the Oirat confederation, composed of the Choros, Dorbet, Khoshot and Torghut tribes. At the end of the sixteenth and beginning of the seventeenth centuries, these tribes came under pressure from the Khalkha (in what is now Outer Mongolia) to the east and Kazakh and Uzbeks to the west. In 1623 the Oirat defeated the Khalkha. In 1627 due to internal conflict among the Oirat, the Torgut migrated to the Volga in Russia (becoming known as the Kalmuks). In 1637 many Khoshots migrated to the Tsaidam and Kokonor for the same reason.

The Oirat tribes were finally reunited under Ba'atur, who promoted trade and agriculture, established diplomatic relations with the Russian empire, patronized Tibetan Buddhism and aided Gushri Khan in his campaigns in support of the Fifth Dalai Lama. In 1640 Ba'atur summoned a conference of all Mongol tribes that remained independent of the Manchus,

---

1. This and the next section, unless otherwise noted, rely primarily upon Zahiruddin Ahmad, *Sino-Tibetan Relations in the Seventeenth Century* (Roma: Instituto Italiano Per Il Medio Ed Estremo Oriente, 1970).

including the Khalkha. He succeeded in forming an alliance under Oirat, or Dzungar, leadership, which adopted Tibetan Buddhism as its religion. However this confederation fell far short of Ba'atur's goal of a new Mongol empire. The eastern Mongols were by this time too dependent upon the Ch'ing to contribute to Mongol power, while the Khalkha were unwilling to accept the leadership of the Dzungar.[2]

Ba'atur died in 1653 and was succeeded by his son, Galdan, who had been a monk in Lhasa. Galdan was assisted in the succession struggle with his brothers by the Fifth Dalai Lama and the Khoshot tribes of Kokonor. Galdan avoided offending the Ch'ing, who were occupied by revolt in southern China, by maintaining trade relations, which the Ch'ing, of course, interpreted as tribute. Between 1665 and 1685 Dzungar Mongol tribes continued to migrate to the Kokonor and Kansu because of factional conflicts taking place within Dzungaria. These tribes would typically request that the Dalai Lama assign them new territories in Kokonor, which the Dalai Lama did in cooperation with K'ang Hsi, the Ch'ing emperor. The Dalai Lama's role as mediator in Mongol affairs was more direct than that of K'ang Hsi, who merely confirmed the Dalai Lama's decisions. Despite the apparent cooperation between the Dalai Lama and the Ch'ing, the close relations between Tibet and the Mongols were a threat to the Ch'ing. An alliance between the Dzungar and the Tibetans had the potential to evoke support from other Mongols, including those who had submitted to the Ch'ing.

The Tibetan connection was also important to the Mongols in order to establish their own political legitimacy. In a 1674 meeting at Lhasa between some of the Khalkha and Oirat chieftains and the Dalai Lama, the Oirat evoked their predominance in Tibet to counter the Khalkhas' Chingghisid lineage. The Khalkhas claimed the traditional authority among Mongols due to their Chingghisid lineage, while the Oirat claimed the prestige of the Tibetan royal lineage, which they had acquired as *Choskyi Gyalpo*, or "Kings of the Faith."[3] The Oirat attempt to succeed to the lineage of the Tibetan kings, the Dharmarajas, indicates not only the assimilation taking place in northern Tibet between Tibetans and Mongols but also the revival of the *Cho-Yon* tradition as political legitimation among the Mongols.

In 1674 the Ch'ing sent envoys to Lhasa requesting the assistance of the Dalai Lama in quelling rebellion in Yunnan. The Dalai Lama agreed to send Mongol troops, but offended the Ch'ing emperor by his advice

---

2. Thomas Barfield, *The Perilous Frontier: Nomadic Empires and China* (Cambridge: Basil Blackwell, 1989), 279.

3. Ahmad, *Sino-Tibetan Relations*, 261.

that the Ch'ing should discontinue military operations against the rebels and allot them territorial fiefs. The Dalai Lama also received three separate envoys from the rebels, but refused to intervene on their behalf. The independent influence that the Dalai Lama exercised during the rebellion was irritating to the Ch'ing. K'ang Hsi attempted to eliminate the Dalai Lama's role as intermediary between the Ch'ing and Mongol tribes. He ordered, in an edict to the Board of Dependencies, that, thereafter, tribute would be accepted from Mongol tribes without reference to any credentials issued by the Dalai Lama.[4] The Ch'ing also began recognizing religious reincarnations and political successions among the Mongols rather than merely confirming the Dalai Lama's recognition as was the previous practice.

In 1674 the Dalai Lama had Mongol troops occupy Dartsendo (Tachienlu). This occupation, from 1687 to 1691, evoked a protest from the Ch'ing, who maintained that no frontier fortifications were necessary between the "Inner Territory" and Tibet because both were peaceful and under the overall authority of the Ch'ing.[5] During this period the Fifth Dalai Lama was at the height of his independent power in Tibet and his influence among the Mongols. The Dalai Lama apparently felt confident enough of his spiritual authority to conduct a foreign policy more or less independently of the Ch'ing. The Ch'ing remained suspicions about Tibetan relations with the Dzungar. The Tibetans were useful in Ch'ing policy toward the Dzungars, but only if the Tibetans remained loyal and refrained from conspiring with the Dzungar against the Ch'ing.

Death of the Fifth Dalai Lama and Rule of the *Desi*

In 1682 the Fifth Dalai Lama died. His death was concealed by the regent *(Desi)*, Sangye Gyatso (reputed to have been the actual son of the Dalai Lama). At the same time the Ch'ing, finally freed of domestic rebellions, was able to turn its attention to Inner Asian affairs. In Dzungaria, Galdan continued to gather his strength and to exhort his Mongol allies to retake China from the Ch'ing, pointing out that the Ch'ing were, after all, the descendants of the Jurchen, whom the Mongols had conquered in establishing the Yuan Dynasty.

Galdan's plan was based upon an alliance with, or domination of, the Khalkha. Galdan attacked the Khalkha in 1686 with an army reportedly numbering 30,000. The *Desi* sent an envoy with letters, in the Dalai

---

4. Ibid., 257.
5. Ibid., 220-227. The implication being that no "frontier" actually existed since all territory, Chinese and Tibetan, was under Ch'ing authority.

Lama's name, ordering the Dzungar and the Khalkhas to "be at peace." K'ang Hsi also ordered Galdan to cease military operations and, further, requested that the Dalai Lama order them to cease fighting. Galdan ignored the orders of the emperor and the Dalai Lama (Galdan was presumably unaware that the Fifth Dalai Lama was deceased) and continued his attacks upon the Khalkha, defeating them in August 1688. Galdan thus secured control of all of what is now Outer Mongolia. The defeat of the Khalkha was significant in that it marked the end of joint Ch'ing-Tibetan diplomacy in Mongol affairs and brought the Dzungar into direct confrontation with the Ch'ing. In 1690 Galdan advanced to the Ch'ing frontier and defeated a force sent to oppose him.

The Dzungar threat to the Ch'ing was complicated by the possibility that they might ally with the Russians. In the end, in 1689 their common fear of the Dzungar, and other mutual interests, led the Russians and the Chinese to reach an agreement, the Treaty of Nerchinsk, which was negotiated with the assistance of European Jesuits (who translated from Manchu and Chinese to Latin). Both parties agreed upon their respective spheres of influence, if not actual territorial borders, and to the establishment of trade relations, which were not to be interpreted by either side as tribute. Although its effects were not finally manifested until the early or mid-eighteenth century, the Treaty of Nerchinsk marked the beginning of the end of the era of the great steppe empires. The Inner Asian nomads were now squeezed between the expanding empires of Russia and China and were becoming increasingly sedentarized. The introduction of firearms during the same era spelled the end to the nomads' former military dominance. Tibetan influence in Inner Asia and Tibetan autonomy of the Ch'ing also decreased along with the strength of the Mongols.

At the end of 1690 a large Ch'ing army inflicted a defeat upon Galdan near Jehol; Galdan subsequently retired from the Ch'ing frontier and promised to respect the will of the Ch'ing emperor and refrain from further attacks upon the Khalkha. However, K'ang Hsi was now determined to extirpate Galdan and his followers "root and branch."[6] In 1691 several of the Khalkha khans submitted to the Ch'ing, performing the ceremony of "three kneelings and nine head-knockings, and were incorporated into the Manchu Imperial Banner system."[7] An imperial edict was sent to the Dalai Lama informing him that the affairs of these Mongols "need not be discussed again," that is, that the Ch'ing would no longer solicit the Dalai Lama's opinion or his mediation in the affairs of these Mongol tribes.[8] In

---

6. Ibid., 286.
7. Ibid., 287.
8. Ibid.

1692 a Ch'ing envoy to Galdan was intercepted and murdered by some of Galdan's tribesmen. The emperor then accused Galdan of breaches of diplomatic protocol and of disobeying the Dalai Lama: "Seeing this, it is clear that, (although) openly you honor the Dalai Lama's words, secretly you disobey the Dalai Lama's orders."[9] As Ahmad observes, the Dalai Lama's influence had been reduced to a moral principle "adherence to which each of the two contestants claims for himself, and deviation from which he accuses the other."[10]

In 1693 the *Desi* complained to the Ch'ing throne that Tibet was unable to control the Mongols of Kokonor, after which the Ch'ing annexed the Kokonor territory, giving the lake and the territory the name "Ch'ing-hai."[11] In addition, the Ch'ing annexed the Tibetan border district of Dartsendo (Tachienlu), in eastern Kham. Meanwhile, the *Desi* sent the seal that the Ming had bestowed upon the Phagmogrupa and requested that it be renewed by the Ch'ing as a title for himself, informing the Ch'ing that, the Dalai Lama being old, he (the *Desi*) was managing Tibetan affairs. The Ch'ing complied, thus legitimizing the *Desi*'s role, but only as agent for the Fifth Dalai Lama who, it was assumed, was still alive. The *Desi* almost immediately exceeded his authority, at least as interpreted by the emperor, by requesting that Galdan not be deprived of his titles awarded by the Ch'ing and that Ch'ing troops be withdrawn from Kokonor. The emperor refused, assuming that the *Desi* was acting as agent for Galdan.[12]

The K'ang Hsi Emperor finally destroyed Galdan by luring him into a trap. Galdan heard a prophecy from two Tibetan lamas, supposedly made by the Dalai Lama, that a move to the east would be propitious. Galdan then demanded the submission of the Korchins to his east, but they informed the Ch'ing, who met Galdan on his way to accept the submission of the Korchins in 1696 with three Ch'ing armies and totally defeated him. Ch'ing artillery and muskets played a significant role in the Mongols' defeat.[13] Galdan, who survived with a few followers, blamed his defeat upon the Dalai Lama, saying, "At first, I did not wish to come to the territory of the Kerulen river, but because the Dalai Lama misled

9. Ibid, 290, quoting a letter from the Ch'ing emperor to Galdan, in *Ch'ing Dynasty Annals*.

10. Ibid.

11. *Ch'ing* means "blue" (this is not the *Ch'ing* of the Ch'ing dynasty) while *hai* means sea. The name is a translation of the Mongol Kokonor and the Tibetan *Tsongon*, both of which mean "blue sea."

12. Ahmad, *Sino-Tibetan Relations*, 296.

13. Rene Grousset, *The Empire of the Steppes: A History of Central Asia* (New Brunswick: Rutgers University Press, 1970), 530.

me, therefore, I came here. Hence, the Dalai Lama ruined me, and I have ruined you [the Dzungar]."[14]

In an attempt to capture some of Galdan's family, who had escaped to the Kokonor, the emperor commanded the Mongols of Ch'ing-hai to send them under escort to Peking. The Dalai Lama's representative in Amdo (Kokonor) refused to comply with this order without receiving instructions from Lhasa, to which the K'ang Hsi Emperor acceded.[15] However, K'ang Hsi suspected that Galdan himself had fled to Tibet and that the *Desi* had all along been secretly allied with him. Some of the Dzungar captured by the Ch'ing had revealed that the Dalai Lama was actually dead. The emperor therefore accused the *Desi*, Sangye Gyatso, of conspiring with Galdan. An edict of the emperor ordered the *Desi* to hand over all of the followers of Galdan who had fled to Tibet and to explain why he had not reported the death of the Dalai Lama:

> If you do these things, We shall, as usual, treat you according to the custom of enriching you with Our bounty. If you do not do these things, if of those things which have been enumerated, even one is not done, We shall certainly enquire into your lies and falsehoods, your crimes of deceiving the Dalai Lama and the Pan-chen Khutugtu, and of aiding dGa'-ldan. We shall send out a large army from Yun-nan, Ssu-ch'uan, Shen-si and other places. According to the precedent set by the destruction of dGa'-ldan, either We shall go personally to punish you, or We shall send the Princes and high officials to punish you. Formerly, you said to Our envoy that the Four Oirad were the lords who protected your faith; therefore, you could summon the Four Oirad to help you. We shall see how they will help you.[16]

Ch'ing envoys were dispatched to determine if the Fifth Dalai Lama had truly died or had been in meditation for the past fourteen years as the *Desi* had claimed. The *Desi* welcomed the envoys of the Ch'ing with the announcement that the Dalai Lama had "emerged from his meditation." The *Desi* cleverly presented the envoys with the young Sixth Dalai Lama and invited them to ascertain whether or not he was the true incarnation of the Fifth, as if the issue were the authenticity of the reincarnation, not whether the *Desi* had concealed the death of the Fifth and ruled in his stead. The *Desi* thus posed as a regent ruling during the absence of the Fifth and minority of the Sixth Dalai Lamas, not an usurper of the authority of the Fifth. The *Desi* attempted to flatter the emperor:

---

14. Ahmad, *Sino-Tibetan Relations*, 300, quoting *Ch'ing Dynasty Annals*.

15. Ibid., 303. This instance demonstrates that, despite the Ch'ing "annexation" of the Kokonor territory, Tibetan officials appointed by Lhasa retained authority there.

16. Ibid., 309, quoting *Ch'ing Dynasty Annals*.

"The Emperor is divinely perspicacious. He has known in advance that the Dalai Lama will emerge from his meditation [i.e. be reborn as the Sixth] next year."[17] The emperor decided to diplomatically acquiesce in the *Desi's* clever deception, at least for the time. On 8 December 1697, with Ch'ing approval, the Sixth Dalai Lama was formally enthroned.

Lhazang Khan[18]

In 1697 Galdan Khan committed suicide; Tsewang Rapten, now leader of the Dzungar, acceded to the Ch'ing demand that Galdan's bones and all his surviving family be sent to China. In that same year the Mongol khans of Kokonor were invited by the emperor to come to Peking to receive honorific titles. They went only after receiving the consent of the Dalai Lama. In 1700 Tsewang Rapten sent emissaries to the Mongols of Kokonor. In 1703, to counter Dzungar influence, the Ch'ing once again summoned the khans of Kokonor. In 1702 the Ch'ing accepted the submission of the chiefs of Nyarong, exchanging their Ming titles and seals for those of the Ch'ing.

In 1703 Lhazang Khan, the grandson of Gushri Khan, succeeded to the title of *Chosgyal*, or Dharmaraja, of Tibet, after murdering his brother who was the legitimate heir. Lhazang, unlike his predecessors, who had been "Kings of Tibet" in name only, took an activist attitude toward his role. Lhazang was opposed to the *Desi's* assumption of power, his concealment of the death of the Fifth Dalai Lama, and his selection of the Sixth Dalai Lama. Lhazang was supported by the K'ang Hsi Emperor. The *Desi* reputedly attempted to have Lhazang poisoned.[19] In 1702 the Sixth Dalai Lama, who had turned out to be a respectable poet but an unfortunate choice as the spiritual ruler of Tibet, refused to take his vows as a Buddhist monk. The *Desi*, faced with opposition from the emperor and Lhazang Khan, and growing dissatisfaction with the Dalai Lama, was finally forced to resign in 1703.

In 1705 a meeting of Mongol princes and Tibetan lamas was convened in Lhasa to determine what to do about the Sixth Dalai Lama. Lhazang Khan strongly favored the Dalai Lama's abdication; the Tibetans suggested that Lhazang should retire to Kokonor and leave Lhasa politics to the Tibetans. Lhazang Khan retired but only to gather his armies. Later that same year, he invaded Lhasa, executed the *Desi*, and assumed polit-

---

17. Ibid.
18. This and the next three sections, unless otherwise noted, rely primarily upon Luciano Petech, *China and Tibet in the Early XVIIIth Century* (Leiden: E.J. Brill, 1972).
19. Guiseppi Tucci, *Tibetan Painted Scrolls* (Rome: La Libreria dello Stato, 1949), 77.

ical control of Tibet. In 1706 Lhazang Khan, with the compliance of the K'ang Hsi Emperor, deposed the Sixth Dalai Lama.

Lhazang's interference in Tibetan political and spiritual affairs was opposed by most Tibetans, who still supported the Dalai Lama despite his behavior. The deposed Sixth Dalai Lama was being taken to China to appear before the emperor when he died near Kokonor. Lhazang subsequently installed his own candidate (rumored to be his son) as the "real" Sixth Dalai Lama, but this choice was not accepted by Tibetans. Lhazang's actions were also opposed by his Khoshot rivals, who resented both his usurpation of the Khoshot leadership and his actions in Tibet. The Ch'ing emperor therefore intervened, sending an emissary to Tibet to ascertain the situation and approve or disapprove of Lhazang's actions. The Ch'ing emissary traveled to Lhasa with many of the Kokonor Mongol khans; they also traveled to Tashilhunpo to ascertain the Panchen Lama's opinion. The Panchen supported Lhazang's Dalai Lama, whom he had initiated, but the emperor still refrained from recognizing Lhazang's choice because of opposition from the Kokonor Mongols.[20]

In 1709 a Ch'ing representative, Ho-shou, was dispatched to Tibet "to support Lajang [Lhazang] Khan against the disaffected and to finish restoring order among the lamas partisans of the *sde-srid* [*Desi*]." Ho-shou was the first Ch'ing official sent to Tibet to supervise the Tibetan administration.[21] Ho-shou was accompanied by several specialized personnel, some of whom were instructed to prepare maps of "all the countries immediately subject to the Dalai Lama." In 1711 Ho-shou returned to China, presenting to Father Regis, the Jesuit in charge of the mapping project, sketches of Tibet that were the basis of the four maps of Tibet in the Jesuit atlas of China, of 28 sheets, presented to K'ang Hsi in 1718.[22]

In 1715-1717 the Jesuits dispatched two lamas, who they had trained in geometry and arithmetic, to Tibet to supplement the original survey. These measurements were incorporated in the second woodblock edition, in 32 sheets, of the atlas, which was published in 1721.[23] The incorporation of Tibet in the Jesuit atlas indicates that the Ch'ing definitely considered Tibet a part of their empire. The Ch'ing maps of Tibet, though usually neglected in studies of Sino-Tibetan relations, was an important

---

20. Petech, *China and Tibet*, 18.

21. Ibid., 19. The records do not state whether Ho-shou was Manchu or Chinese, but, given the usual policy of the early Ch'ing to employ only Manchu, or Mongols, in Inner Asia, he is likely to have been non-Chinese.

22. K'ang Hsi had commissioned European Jesuits to draw a map of all the Ch'ing domains. Tibet was not included in the portion to be surveyed by the Jesuits themselves, but was to be included as a "supplement." Petech, *China and Tibet*, 19-20.

23. Ibid., 25.

practical and symbolic substantiation of the Ch'ing claim to authority and control over Tibet. The Ch'ing, even though they were a conquest dynasty, were particularly intent upon discovering and claiming as Ch'ing territory the sources of China's two major rivers, the Yellow and Yangtze, both of which lay in Tibet.

In 1710 K'ang Hsi finally recognized Lhazang's choice as Dalai Lama. In 1710 or 1711, however, a child was discovered in Lithang who possessed signs of being the reincarnation of the deceased Sixth Dalai Lama, who had hinted in a poem that he would be reborn in Lithang. Lhazang's Mongol rivals took the child to Kokonor where he was installed in Kumbum monastery. The child was subsequently recognized as the reincarnation by some of the Kokonor princes. The Ch'ing, realizing that Lhazang's candidate, and Lhazang himself, were not accepted by the Tibetans, agreed to protect the child at Kumbum in case Lhazang and his new Sixth Dalai Lama should be overthrown. Lhazang Khan had by then thoroughly alienated the Tibetan clergy and aristocracy, who resented his foreign rule under the protection of the Ch'ing and his deposing the Sixth Dalai Lama.

The Dzungar Invasion

After the defeat of Galdan, the Dzungar reconsolidated under the leadership of Tsewang Rapten. The Ch'ing did not oppose Tsewang Rapten or try to impose their control over him because they mistakenly thought that he was loyal to the Ch'ing. Tsewang Rapten had assisted the Ch'ing in their defeat of Galdan by remaining uninvolved in the conflict, but this was because he wished the Ch'ing to destroy Galdan, not because he intended to become a vassal of the Ch'ing. By 1715 he had reconsolidated Dzungar power; he then turned toward Tibet in order to acquire Tibetan spiritual legitimation. In 1714 Tsewang Rapten proposed a marriage alliance between his daughter and the son of Lhazang Khan. This alliance was not unprecedented (Tsewang Rapten had married Lhazang's sister); nevertheless, Lhazang had reason to be suspicious of the Dzungar. Lhazang knew that the Dzungar wished to reestablish their former relationship with Tibet, to avenge the murder of their ally, the Desi, and to enthrone the Tibetan choice as Seventh Dalai Lama. Nevertheless, the marriage was concluded in 1714.

The Dzungar's already established relations with Tibet enabled them to conspire with Tibetan lamas for the overthrow of Lhazang. The lamas of the Lhasa monasteries were enthusiastic supporters of the Dzungar conspiracy; they sent strong young monks to Dzungaria to assist in a planned Dzungar expedition to Tibet.[24] In the winter of 1717 the Dzungar sent an army of 6000 men under Tsering Dhondup, a cousin of Tsewang Rapten, into Tibet through the uninhabited northwestern Chang Thang. The Dzungar concealed their intent to any Tibetans they encountered by explaining that they were escorting Lhazang's son back to Tibet after his marriage. Lhazang Khan had some warning of the Dzungar advance from the governor of Ngari and nomads of Nagtsang, but was reluctant to believe the deceit of Tsewang Rapten.

Lhazang was unprepared and only halfheartedly supported by his Tibetan auxiliaries. Nevertheless, he held the Dzungar at Dam for two months, due mainly to the valor of his Tibetan lieutenant, Polhanas. However, the dissatisfaction of other Tibetans in Lhazang's army was exacerbated by the information that the Dzungar were bringing the rightful Dalai Lama from Kokonor to Lhasa. In fact, the Dzungar force (consisting of only 300 men) sent to obtain the Dalai Lama from Kumbum had been defeated by Ch'ing defenders. Nevertheless, uncertain of the loyalty of his Tibetan troops, Lhazang withdrew to Lhasa, the defenses of which Lhazang had strengthened with a strong wall. The Dzungar encamped around the walls of the city, where they were encouraged and supplied by the monks of Drepung and Sera.

When the Dzungar attacked the walls of Lhasa on 30 November 1717, Tibetan sympathizers threw down ladders and opened the gates. The Dzungar found themselves in control of Lhasa, but without the legitimacy that the presence of the Seventh Dalai Lama would have provided them. In addition, they looted Lhasa and abused the citizens, destroying overnight the support they had previously enjoyed among Tibetans. The Dzungar, patrons of the Gelugpa sect, began persecuting the Nyingmapa sect, destroying several of their monasteries.

In response to Lhazang Khan's appeal for assistance against the Dzungar, the Ch'ing Emperor K'ang Hsi dispatched armies from Sining and Szechuan. However, in the meantime, Lhasa had fallen and Lhazang had been killed. The mission of the Ch'ing armies therefore became the conquest of the Dzungar in Tibet. Realizing that their resources were insufficient for this, the Ch'ing commanders temporarily withdrew to muster their forces. In preparation for an expedition from Szechuan, the Ch'ing established control of Tachienlu (Dartsendo), Lithang and Ba along the southern route into Tibet. The Ch'ing Szechuan army invaded over this route in 1720, entering Lhasa without opposition on 24 September. The Dzungar concentrated their forces at Dam in the north against an expected Ch'ing army coming from Kokonor. After the fall of

---

24. Ibid., 34.

Lhasa, the Dzungar fled back along the route that they had originally taken into Tibet. A Ch'ing army from Sining arrived in Lhasa in mid-October, bringing with them the young Dalai Lama. Tibetan forces under the Tibetan leaders Kanchenas and Polhanas had meanwhile regained the territory of Tsang from the Dzungar.[25] The Ch'ing entered Tibet as the patrons of the Kokonor Mongols, the liberator of Tibet from the Dzungar, and the supporters of the Seventh Dalai Lama.

Although the Mongols of Kokonor had joined with the Ch'ing in driving the Dzungar out of Tibet and restoring the rightful Dalai Lama, they harbored resentment because the Ch'ing had replaced them as lords of Kokonor and of Tibet. An immediate cause of resentment was a perceived lack of respect accorded to the Kokonor Mongols at the installation of the Dalai Lama in Lhasa. Once back in Kokonor, the Mongols began fomenting revolt, led by a grandson of Gushri Khan, Lobsang Danjin, who wished to restore the privileges due his clan as "Kings of Tibet." The Mongol revolt was joined by most of the Tibetans of Kokonor, led by the lamas of Kumbum. The lamas, particularly those of Kumbum and of all its affiliates, were intense in their opposition to the Ch'ing; they reportedly provoked their Tibetan and Mongol adherents into a state of frenzy. In late 1723 a reported 200,000 Tibetans and Mongols attacked Sining.[26] The Ch'ing summoned troops from Szechuan and suppressed the rebellion with thoroughness and brutality. The revolt was quelled by 1724, but the Kokonor region suffered great destruction:

> The revolt, quelled with draconian severity in less than a year, had been the ruin of Huangchung [the Sining River valley]. Not a single valley in the country was encountered through which the troops did not pass, fighting or pursuing the enemy. The number of villages destroyed and burned, and the number of stolen cattle were countless. The number of Tibetans, Mongols and lamas killed rates terribly high. The war was one of the bloodiest. All who made a stand were killed. All the provisions and property of the people had disappeared. All the lamaseries were destroyed or burned down. The depredation of the country was wicked and ruthless, the destitution of the people tragic. Huangchung, which during the previous centuries had so many times suffered from wars and revolts, never had suffered as much as in 1723-1724.[27]

---

25. Shakabpa states that the Dzungar fled Lhasa due to the advance of these Tibetan forces, but Petech maintains that Kanchenas and Polhanas did little more than hold Tsang and Ngari while the Ch'ing armies advanced. Ibid., 65; W.D. Shakabpa, *Tibet: A Political History* (New York: Potala, 1984), 139.

26. Louis M.J. Schram, "The Mongours of the Kansu-Tibetan Frontier," *Transactions of the American Philosophical Society* (1961), 58.

27. Ibid., 59.

The revolt of 1723 in Kokonor had its roots in Mongol and Tibetan resistance to increased Ch'ing control. Ch'ing control was perhaps more immediately felt in Kokonor, where Ch'ing presence had existed since an earlier time and with a greater intimacy than in central Tibet. The lamas of Amdo were intensely opposed to Ch'ing control, despite the role of the Ch'ing in restoring the Dalai Lama. The central Tibetans not only did not assist the Kokonor Mongols and Tibetans against the Ch'ing, but provided a force under Polhanas that prevented the Mongol and Tibetan tribes' escape from Ch'ing suppression.

The Ch'ing subsequently reorganized the administration of Kokonor and made clear their intention to exercise more direct control there. The Tibetan and Mongol tribes previously dependent upon the Khoshot Khan were reorganized into units responsible only to the Ch'ing administration. Both the Mongol and Tibetan tribes were allotted fixed territories and were forbidden to infringe upon the territories of others. Lama monasteries had their lands and properties confiscated. Those who had paid taxes to the monasteries or to Mongol overlords now paid directly to Ch'ing officials. Kokonor was thus effectively incorporated into the Ch'ing empire. In 1725 a census was taken that revealed that there were 50,020 persons in the territory.[28] The boundaries between Amdo and Kham were subsequently demarcated, following along the lines established by the Yuan dynasty.[29]

Ch'ing Protectorate Over Tibet

Upon their entry into Lhasa in 1720, the Ch'ing established a provisional government composed of two Khalkha princes, two Khoshot princes and two Tibetans, headed by the Ch'ing commander. This provisional government ruled until the spring of 1721 when a government was established under a council, *Kashag*, of three Tibetan ministers, *kalon*, headed by Kanchenas. In 1721 one of the Khalkhas of the provisional council was named as the official Ch'ing representative in Tibet, or *amban*.[30] The other Khalkha was put in charge of military affairs. The position of the Dalai Lama in the Ch'ing imposed government was purely symbolic, though that symbolism remained of great importance; the Dalai Lama continued to exercise great influence with the Ch'ing due, as usual, to the reverence he received from the Mongols. The Tibetan coun-

---

28. William Woodville Rockhill, *The Land of the Lamas* (London: Longmans, Greek and Co., 1891; New Delhi: Asian Educational Services, 1988), 82.

29. Schram, "Kansu-Tibetan Frontier," 58.

30. Petech points out that the title "*amban*" was an honorific, which could be applied to any of the many envoys of the Ch'ing. Petech, *China and Tibet*, 87.

cil of ministers remained under the close supervision of the commander of the Ch'ing garrison of 3,000 men. The walls of Lhasa were demolished. The main body of the Ch'ing army marched back to China via the southern route, leaving detachments at Ba, Lithang and Chamdo. Kham was placed temporarily under the administration of Szechuan. In 1722 the Lhasa garrison was reduced to 1,900 men in order to alleviate the economic burden on Tibetans of maintaining the garrison.[31] A system of 65 postal stations was established on the southern route between China and Tibet, to be manned by members of the Ch'ing garrison.

In 1722 the K'ang Hsi Emperor died after a rule of sixty years (1662-1722). K'ang Hsi's successor usurped the throne from an older brother to become the Yung-cheng Emperor.[32] Yung-cheng initially reduced the Ch'ing presence in Tibet. In 1723 the new emperor ordered a withdrawal of the garrison and the Ch'ing officials from Lhasa. A force of 1,000 men was to be retained at Chamdo and 6,000 at Sining. Kanchenas, who was dependent upon the Ch'ing for political support, requested that the Ch'ing not withdraw, but to no avail. The Ch'ing maintained their supervision of Tibetan affairs through a semi-permanent *amban*. In 1724 this official was transferred from Lhasa to Sining, leaving Tibetan affairs in the hands of Kanchenas.

Late in 1725, however, the administration of Tibet and the border areas of Kham was reorganized and strengthened. Tibet west of the watershed between the Jinsa Jiang (Yangtze) and the Mekong was to be administered by Lhasa officials supervised by an *amban* in Lhasa; the territory to the east of that line would be administered by native chiefs under the supervision of the governor of Szechuan. A boundary stone dividing the administrative areas was erected at the Bum La, the pass between the Yangtze and Mekong.[33] A Manchu *amban*, with a Mongol lama as assistant, or junior *amban*, were stationed as permanent residents at Lhasa; Kanchenas was formally given the title of Prime Minister.

In 1725 the Ch'ing sent to Lhasa the recently completed Peking edition of the Tibetan Buddhist *Tengyur* and the complete works of Tsonkhapa, indicating that patronage of Buddhism was still a part of Ch'ing policy. In 1726, however, Ch'ing patronage of Tibetan Buddhism took an ominous turn when Yung-cheng sent an edict ordering the proscription of the Nyingmapa sect and the conversion of their monasteries to the Gelugpa. Petech suggests that this step was taken on the advice of Mongol lamas at Peking, who were more zealous in their sectarianism than the Tibetans

---

31. Ibid., 86.

32. Barfield, *Perilous Frontier*, 291.

33. Eric Teichman, *Travels of a Consular Officer in Eastern Tibet* (Cambridge: Cambridge University Press, 1922), 2.

themselves. Although sectarianism was not unknown in Tibet, religious eclecticism had always been strong in Tibetan Buddhist tradition. In addition, the Gelugpa were now completely dominant and had little need for the complete prohibition of all other teachings.[34]

Tibetan administrative officials under the Ch'ing were predominantly secular; with the exception of the Dalai and Panchen Lamas, the clergy played little role. This was primarily due to the Ch'ing's mistrust of Tibetan lamas and monks after their conspiracies with the Dzungar. Tibetan officials were riven by personal feuds, however, and by political and regional factions. Kanchenas and Polhanas, representatives of the nobility who had been loyal to Lhazang Khan and to the Ch'ing, were of western Tibetan origin (Tsang and Ngari). They saw Tibet's (and their own) best interest as lying in the protection afforded by the Ch'ing. They were opposed by the Lhasa nobility, many of whom had been supporters of the Dzungar and opponents of Lhazang Khan and Ch'ing interference in Tibet. Polhanas attempted to reconcile the various factions, pointing out the benefit of unified Tibetan administration. However, Polhanas and Kanchenas soon fell out over the issue of the persecution of the Nyingmapa.

These internal disputes finally came to a head in 1727. The news reached Tibet that the emperor was dispatching new *ambans*, who would more closely superintend Tibetan affairs under the administration of Kanchenas. The anti-Ch'ing faction decided to act before the new *ambans* arrived. On 5 August 1727 they murdered Kanchenas in the council chambers in the Lhasa Jokhang and took over control of Lhasa. Polhanas was at his estate at Polha and, having been warned in advance, was able to escape. He retired to Ngari, securing the support of Kanchenas' brother, who was governor there. Polhanas gathered his supporters in Ngari and Tsang; he sent messages to the Ch'ing informing them of events and requesting Ch'ing assistance.

By September, only a month after the assassination of Kanchenas, Polhanas, by an impressive feat of political and logistical organization was able to start on a reconquest of Tsang with the troops he had gathered in Ngari. The Lhasa officials who had revolted against Kanchenas summoned troops from Kongpo, Dakpo and various Mongol tribes. The factional struggle then took on characteristics typical of past regional conflicts between U and Tsang. Polhanas brought up his forces and con-

---

34. Petech, *China and Tibet*, 107. Polhanas, who had been a Nyingmapa monk, had campaigned for the restoration of the Nyingmapa monasteries pillaged or destroyed by the Dzungar (a reported 550 monasteries or temples), but this was opposed by the Mongol princes and the Dalai Lama. Until the edict of 1726, however, the Nyingmapa had been permitted to restore their monasteries with their own resources. Ibid., 83.

fronted the Lhasa army between Gyantse and Shigatse. After three days of fighting, Polhanas was forced to retreat back to the west to Sakya. The Lhasa ministers then disbanded their army, only garrisoning the *dzongs* (forts) of Tsang, thinking that the fighting was over for the winter. Polhanas managed to retain his army and retook the offensive, taking the Lhasa garrisons by surprise and regaining control of Tsang.

At this point, a truce was agreed upon, each side having appealed to the Ch'ing emperor for assistance. Polhanas, who may have been fairly assured that he would be supported by the Ch'ing, soon broke the truce due to his desire to gain control of the situation before the Ch'ing mission could arrive. After garrisoning his strongholds in Tsang, Polhanas sent his forces by various routes toward Lhasa. Polhanas himself proceeded with a small force by the northern route to Yangbaijan, northwest of Lhasa. From there, after gaining the allegiance of some of the Mongols of Dam, Polhanas approached Lhasa. Polhanas now held the advantage; the army of the Lhasa ministers melted away, allowing Polhanas to enter Lhasa in July 1728, virtually without opposition.

The Rule of Polhanas and the Ch'ing Ambans

A Ch'ing military expedition to Tibet was organized in 1727 but was postponed until 1728 after the emperor learned that the conflict in Tibet did not involve the Dzungar. The Ch'ing army finally left Sining in June 1728 and reached Lhasa on 4 September. Considering that Polhanas had already brought the civil war to a close, the main purpose of the expedition was to administer justice to the rebels, a right of the emperor that Polhanas was careful not to usurp. The ministers and their followers, a total of eighteen men, were found guilty of rebellion and were ceremoniously executed by the "slicing process." Ch'ing justice required that the immediate relatives of the eighteen men, including women and children, also be executed, which was done. The populace of Lhasa was effectively cowed by this display of the justice and retribution of the Ch'ing.

The young Seventh Dalai Lama, or rather his father, was identified as an organizer of anti-Ch'ing resistance and both were exiled from Lhasa. The Ch'ing *ambans*, in an audience with the Dalai Lama, invited him to travel to Peking and reside there for one year. However, the Ch'ing *ambans* apparently used the ruse of the invitation, which the Dalai Lama could scarcely refuse, to remove him and his father to another location in Tibet.[35] The Dalai Lama and his father departed Lhasa on 23 December

---

35. Ibid., 152.

1728, along with the main body of the Ch'ing expeditionary force, on the southern route through Kham, and were deposited at Gatar Gompa in eastern Kham near Dartsendo.

In the Dalai Lama's absence, the Ch'ing *ambans* cultivated the Panchen Lama, who had remained nonpartisan in the civil war (except to attempt numerous mediations), as a political figurehead. He was summoned to Lhasa, where he was presented with an imperial edict granting him temporal authority over Tsang and Ngari, a move clearly intended to limit the temporal authority of the Dalai Lama. The territorial and political division between the Dalai and Panchen Lamas thus created was to become a feature of Chinese policy in Tibet. Polhanas is not recorded as having opposed this measure, although he had bravely opposed many Ch'ing decrees in the past. The award of temporal authority to the Panchen Lama may be interpreted as a reward to Polhanas and the Tsang Tibetans for their loyalty to the Ch'ing.[36]

Two permanent Ch'ing *ambans* remained in Lhasa. The senior *amban* was to supervise Lhasa and U, while the junior *amban* was responsible for Tsang and Ngari. The ambans' authority was bolstered by a garrison of 2,000 men in Lhasa; another 1,000 were at Chamdo and 1,000 at Lithang. All firearms were confiscated from Tibetans, with the exception of some of the veterans of Polhanas' army, who were commissioned as a permanent military force intended to eventually replace the Ch'ing garrison. However, the Tibetan troops were not allowed to remain in Lhasa; they were sent to the north to Dam for training.

Actual administration in Tibet was in the hands of Polhanas, who reestablished order, commerce, the postal system and taxation. He also revived religious ceremonies, improved relations between the lamas and the government, and restored monasteries. In 1731 the Ch'ing emperor granted Polhanas a seal of office and judicial powers in Tibet. In 1733 Polhanas petitioned for a reduction of the Lhasa garrison to 500 men; this was granted because the situation in Tibet was considered stable. The garrison was also moved to the north of Lhasa, near Sera monastery. The Chamdo garrison was also reduced, to 500 men. In the next year, the Chamdo garrison was completely eliminated and that at Lithang reduced to 600 men.

In 1735 the Dalai Lama was permitted to return to Lhasa. While at Gatar, he had been highly restricted in his activities, especially his audiences, and this regime was continued at Lhasa. Also in 1735 Yung-cheng died and was succeeded by his son, who became the Ch'ien-lung Emperor. In 1736 the Dalai Lama made a state visit to Tsang; the Panchen

---

36. Ibid., 154.

Lama, who was aged and infirm, excused himself from meeting the Dalai Lama. Petech interprets the Dalai Lama's state visit to Tsang as an assertion of his sovereignty there, and a refutation of the 1728 Ch'ing award of temporal sovereignty to the Panchen; he interprets the Panchen's failure to meet the Dalai Lama as a refusal to accept the Dalai Lama's authority in Tsang.[37] In 1738 the Tibetans petitioned for a return of Ba and Lithang in southern Kham to Tibetan administration, but this was refused. Because Tibet was now peaceful under Polhanas' rule, Polhanas was awarded another title, *Chun Wang*, or prince of the second class. Polhanas' position was dependent upon the Ch'ing; nevertheless, Ch'ing supervision was nominal; Polhanas at the end of his career was undisputed master within Tibet, dominant even over the Dalai Lama.

Polhanas died in 1747 and was succeeded by his youngest son Gyurmey Namgyal, who soon demonstrated that he was not of the same loyal and submissive nature as his father. Gyurmey Namgyal attempted to reduce the *ambans'* influence in Tibet by requesting a reduction in the now very small Ch'ing garrison in Lhasa. The emperor agreed to this request, perhaps in the spirit of good relations with the new Tibetan administrator, and reduced the garrison to 100 men. The Ch'ing were now confident of their position in Tibet, despite a rather serious revolt in Kham from 1747 to 1749. Gyurmey Namgyal first raised the suspicions of the Ch'ing by a request to send Gelugpa lamas to the monasteries of the unreformed sects (Nyingmapa, Sakyapa and Karmapa) in Kham and Amdo. His purpose was to gain Gelugpa control, and therefore the political control of Lhasa, over Tibetan territories of Kham and Amdo, which the Ch'ing had separated from Lhasa's administration. To this the emperor did not agree.

The *ambans* in Lhasa became alarmed when Gyurmey Namgyal began assembling an army. They suspected that he might be conspiring with the Dzungar against the Ch'ing. Ch'ien-lung displayed an uncharacteristic naivete in dealing with the situation, refusing to believe the reports of the *ambans* that Gyurmey Namgyal might be planning a revolt against the Ch'ing. The emperor, uncertain about what to do in the situation, delegated authority to the *ambans* in Lhasa. In 1750 the *ambans*, convinced that Gyurmey Namgyal was intent upon rebellion, and knowing that he was regarded as a tyrant by many Tibetans, decided to take steps to eliminate him. The *ambans* lured Gyurmey Namgyal to their residence and murdered him by their own hands.

Gyurmey Namgyal's attendant escaped the *ambans'* residence and gathered a crowd to avenge the death of his master. Although the Dalai

---

37. Ibid., 177.

Lama and the abbot of Reting tried to calm the crowd, claiming that Gyurmey Namgyal had received what he deserved, the mob attacked the *ambans'* residence, killing the two *ambans* and most of their escort. The Dalai Lama quickly assumed authority in Lhasa. The Tibetans then awaited the arrival of the Ch'ing army, which they knew would be dispatched to administer justice. By the time the Ch'ing had assembled their expeditionary force, the situation in Lhasa had stabilized. The emperor therefore dispatched only 800 men to Lhasa. The leader of the mob and six others were publicly executed by the slicing process. The family of Gyurmey Namgyal was also executed when evidence was produced that he had been conspiring with the Dzungar. The political authority of the *ambans* was increased, and it was decided that they should more closely supervise the Tibetan administration than before. The emperor also resolved to regain complete control of the mail stages to Tibet and to never again allow the Ch'ing garrison at Lhasa to fall below 1,500 men.

The Tibetan government was once again reorganized, this time with a *Kashag* of four members, one of whom was to be a lama, all under the authority of the Dalai Lama. The Dalai Lama had stabilized the situation in Lhasa and had demonstrated loyalty to the Ch'ing during the crisis. The Dalai Lama was therefore reinvested with spiritual and temporal rule; this was announced as a restoration of the system that had existed under the Fifth Dalai Lama. The Ch'ing may have decided to restore the traditional ecclesiastical system of rule out of exasperation with the factional conflicts of the Tibetan aristocracy. The decision may also reflect Ch'ing political conservatism; the Ch'ing court was always concerned with political precedents; they therefore chose the system originally established between the Ch'ing and the Fifth Dalai Lama. The Dalai Lama's temporal authority, however, was in name only; the Ch'ing emperor through the *ambans* was now more than ever in actual control of Tibetan affairs.

After the events of 1750, the Ch'ing finally accepted a modified *Cho-Yon* system of rule for Tibet. From 1652 to 1720 the Ch'ing had employed Tibetan influence in Inner Asian affairs without any need to impose direct rule over Tibet. However, when the Tibetans conspired with the Dzungar, the Ch'ing were forced to institute a more direct supervision over Tibetan affairs. After experimenting with secular rule in Tibet, an experiment that was successful only under Polhanas, the Ch'ing reverted to the format established by the Fifth Dalai Lama's "submission" in 1652. Polhanas had been successful only because he combined roles as a regional rival to the Lhasa nobility, a lay rival to the Buddhist church and the Dalai Lama, and a loyal servant to the Ch'ing. However, with the exception of Polhanas, most of the secular aristocracy were too nationalistic to loyally serve a foreign master. The Ch'ing reversion to the political elements of the *Cho-Yon* relationship was based upon their recognition of the anti-nationalist nature of ecclesiastical rule and its need for foreign political patronage.

In addition, the Ch'ing no longer had any fear of conspiracies between Tibetan lamas and the Mongols. The Dzungar had been in decline for some time. The death of Galdan Tsering in 1745 led to a succession dispute that allowed the Ch'ing to play one side against the other. Ch'ing expeditions in 1755, 1756 and 1757, coinciding with a smallpox epidemic in Dzungaria, virtually exterminated the Dzungar. The survivors were deported to Manchuria, while the Dzungar territory was repopulated with Kirghiz, Kazakhs, Kashgar and Kansu Muslims, Khalkha Mongols, and finally in 1771, by Torgut Mongols returning from the Volga.[38] The Dzungar territory was directly annexed by the Ch'ing and even the name Dzungar was proscribed.

Zenith of Ch'ing Authority in Tibet[39]

The political administration established after 1750, of joint rule by the Dalai Lama (or his regent) and the Ch'ing *ambans*, might have sufficed for dealing with Tibetan domestic politics for some time had not foreign relations become a factor. The Seventh Dalai Lama died in 1757. The Eighth Dalai Lama was born in Tsang in 1758 and was discovered and brought to Lhasa in 1762. In 1774 the Panchen Lama wrote to the British viceroy of India, Warren Hastings, in an attempt to mediate in a dispute between Bhutan and India. The British, who were interested in establishing trade relations with Tibet, replied by sending an envoy, George Bogle, to Shigatse.[40] In 1779 the Ch'ien-lung Emperor invited the Panchen Lama to visit Peking. The Panchen traveled to Jehol (north of Peking, where the Ch'ing were constructing a "New Lhasa," intended to replace Lhasa as a pilgrimage site for Mongols) and then to Peking. According to a Chinese account, the Panchen Lama performed the kowtow to the Ch'ien-lung Emperor, the first time a Tibetan Lama is alleged to have done so.[41] The

---

38. Grousset, *Empire of the Steppes*, 538.

39. This section and the next section, unless otherwise noted, rely primarily upon Shakabpa, *Tibet: A Political History*.

40. The British were also animated by legends of gold to be found in Tibet. Alastair Lamb, *British India and Tibet: 1766-1910*, 2nd ed., rev. (London: Routledge and Kegan Paul, 1960, 1986), 12, 28.

41. Tieh-tseng Li, *Tibet: Today and Yesterday* (New York: Bookman Associates, 1960), 51. Traditionally, Tibetan lamas had not been required to kowtow to Mongol Khans or Yuan or Ming emperors. That the Panchen was required to do so indicates that the Cho-Yon had become a purely political relationship, despite the Manchu emperors continuing patronage of Tibetan Buddhism.

Panchen Lama died of smallpox in Peking in 1780. In 1781 the Eighth Dalai Lama assumed political authority. At that time, a dispute was brewing between Tibet and Nepal. Tibet had an arrangement with Newari silversmiths of Kathmandu for the minting of coins with silver supplied by Tibet, but the silversmiths had gradually begun to debase the coins by adding copper. After the Gurkha conquest of Kathmandu in 1769, the Gurkhas arranged to mint pure coins for the Tibetans but required that the previously minted impure coins be devalued. The Tibetans could not agree to this proposal since a devaluation of the old coins would unfairly discriminate against all who held the coins in Tibet. The Gurkhas became increasingly annoyed at Tibet after the Tibetans intervened against a Gurkha attack on Sikkim in 1775. The Gurkhas then used the Tibetans' refusal to devalue their coins as an excuse to invade Tibet.

The Gurkhas entered Tibetan territory at Nyalam and advanced as far as Shekar Dzong in the summer of 1788. The Tibetans and the *ambans* appealed to the Ch'ing emperor for assistance. An advance Ch'ing army was sent, but its commander negotiated a truce agreement that required Tibet to make a tribute payment to Nepal in return for the withdrawal of the Gurkhas. After Tibetan delays in paying tribute, the Gurkhas invaded Tibet again in 1791, capturing Shigatse and looting the Tashilhunpo monastery. The Tibetans responded by surrounding the Gurkhas at Shigatse and Shekar Dzong; in the spring of 1792 they forced their withdrawal to the border districts.

At this point, another Ch'ing army, composed mainly of Tibetans (only 3,000 of the 13,000 troops were non-Tibetan), arrived, drove the Gurkhas out of Tibet and continued into Nepal via Nyalam and Kyirong. The Tibetan-Ch'ing army had advanced to the approaches to the Kathmandu valley when a truce was reached. The Gurkhas had to agree to return the treasures they had looted from Tashilhunpo and to send tribute to Peking every five years. The successful Ch'ing invasion of Nepal became the basis for a later Chinese claim to sovereignty over Nepal, but, more importantly, for a further strengthening of Ch'ing control over Tibet. The Ch'ing regarded the rise of foreign powers capable of threatening Tibet as a reason for strengthening their control of Tibet's domestic as well as foreign affairs. Not only were the Gurkhas a threat, but the British, whom the Ch'ing apparently regarded as another barbarian tribe, had been appealed to by the Gurkhas during the Ch'ing invasion.

The Ch'ien-lung Emperor took the occasion of the presence of the Ch'ing army in Tibet to effect a more extensive, and final, restructuring of the Ch'ing protectorate over Tibet. The *ambans* were elevated above the *Kashag* and the Dalai Lama in responsibility for Tibetan affairs. The Dalai and Panchen Lamas were no longer allowed to petition the Ch'ing emperor directly but could only do so through the *ambans*. The *ambans* took control of Tibetan frontier defense and foreign affairs. Tibetan authorities' foreign correspondence, even with the Mongols of Kokonor, had to be approved by the *ambans*. The *ambans* were put in command of the Ch'ing garrison and the Tibetan army (whose strength was set at 3,000 men). Trade was also restricted and travel could be undertaken only with documents issued by the *ambans*. The *ambans* were to review all judicial decisions. The Tibetan currency, which had been the source of trouble with Nepal, was also taken under Ch'ing supervision.

The Ch'ing also required that the incarnations of the Panchen and Dalai Lamas and other high lamas be chosen under the supervision of the *ambans*. The Ch'ing instituted a system of "choosing of lots from the golden urn," whereby the names of the final candidates for any incarnation, usually three in number, were rolled into dough balls, placed in the golden urn and one was picked out of the urn by the *amban*. The symbolism of this procedure was that the final authority over the selection of reincarnations, and thus over political succession in the Tibetan system of combined spiritual and temporal rule, belonged to the Ch'ing; the Ch'ing was therefore the sovereign power in Tibet. This measure was also intended to prevent any high incarnations being found among the aristocracy, separating the aristocracy from the Buddhist church and preventing any of the aristocracy from gaining both secular and religious power.[42]

The Ch'ing also began the first attempts to "civilize," or Sinicize, Tibetan customs. The practice of "sky burial" was prohibited. Offenders, or even those who watched a sky burial, were to be executed by the slicing process.[43] However, these reforms were without lasting effect. Despite the claims of later Chinese regimes that the reforms of 1793 established full Chinese sovereignty and administrative authority over Tibet, their nebulous nature was revealed by a recorded statement by the commander of the Manchu army in Tibet, General Fu K'ang-an, to the Eighth Dalai Lama:

---

42. The discovery of incarnations among the aristocracy was not specifically prohibited but was clearly intended to be limited. Ch'ing intentions in this regard are revealed in the even more restrictive measure they introduced at about this time among their Mongol subjects, prohibiting the selection of any lama incarnations from among the Mongol aristocracy. Owen Lattimore, *Inner Asian Frontiers of China* (Oxford: Oxford University Press, 1988), 89.

43. Qu Qingshan, "On the Funeral Reform in Tibet in 1793," in *Tibet Studies*, vol. 2, no. 2 (1990), 158. "Sky Burial" is the Tibetan practice for disposing of the dead by dissecting the body and pounding of the bones (mixed with barley flour) into small pieces, which are then consumed by vultures. The modern prevalence of sky burial in Tibet is evidence that this

The emperor issued detailed instructions to me, the Great General, to discuss all the points, one by one, in great length. This demonstrates the
emperor's concern that Tibetans come to no harm and that their welfare be
ensured in perpetuity. There is no doubt that the Dalai Lama, acknowledging his gratitude to the emperor, will accept these suggestions once all the
points are discussed and agreed upon. However, if Tibetans insist on cling-
ing to their age-old habits, the emperor will withdraw the Ambans and the
garrison after the troops have been pulled out. Moreover, if similar inci-
dents occur in the future the emperor will have nothing to do with them.
The Tibetans may therefore, decide for themselves as to what is in their
favor and what is not or what is heavy and what is light, and make a choice
of their own.[44]

The tone of the General's statement indicates that the Ch'ing were
somewhat weary of the repeated need to send armies to save Tibet from
foreign threats or their own internal conflicts. Far from claiming actual
ruling authority in Tibet, the Ch'ing would seem to have been content
with a symbolic role in Tibet in the absence of any foreign threat to Tibet
or any threat to Tibet's status as a dependency of the Ch'ing. Tibet's
dependency status under the Ch'ing was of greater advantage to Tibet
than to the Ch'ing on occasions such as the Gurkha invasion. Tibet was
able to call on the Ch'ing for protection, while for the Ch'ing, the necessity of sending expeditions to Tibet was a considerable and constantly
recurring expense. The General's statement seems to imply that the
advantage in the relationship lay with the Tibetans; therefore, they
should decide for themselves whether they wished to accept Ch'ing
authority that went along with Ch'ing protection.

The Ch'ing, unlike typical native Chinese dynasties, had a realistic
appraisal of the limits of its territorial influence. This is evident from an
edict of Ch'ien-lung in 1771 (in regard to Ch'ing possessions in Sinkiang):

We do not disturb those tribes of the farthest regions because We understand well the theory that only when you know how to be contented, will
you not be humiliated; only when you know how to stop conquering will
you not be exhausted. Why should We cherish the ambition to conquer all
regions which Heaven covers, even to the uttermost corners of the oceans,

---

attempt failed to alter Tibetan customs. That the punishment for watching a sky burial, execution by slicing, was considerably more barbaric than the practice of sky burial itself was
seemingly lost on the Ch'ing administrators in their zeal to impose cultural conformity on
the Tibetans.
44. Quoted from Ya Han Chang, "Biography of the 8th Dalai Lama," in *Bhod ki LorGyus
Rags Rims gYu Prengba*, vol II (Lhasa: Tibet Institute of Social Sciences, 1991), 316.

compelling their rulers and their subjects to become our servants and subjects?[45]

Most of the reforms of 1792 were never fully implemented or quickly fell into disuse. The most significant reform in terms of implications for Tibet's sovereignty, the right to approve reincarnations, became essentially symbolic or was ignored altogether. The nature of the Ch'ing relationship with Tibet remained one between states, or an empire and a semi-autonomous peripheral state, not a relationship between a central government and an outlying part of that same state. The reforms of 1792 fell far short of establishing Chinese sovereignty over Tibet.

Decline of the Ch'ing

The measures undertaken in 1792 represent the height of Ch'ing influence in Tibet. From this time the Ch'ing dynasty began to decline and, with it, Ch'ing control in Tibet. Chusei Suzuki dates the Ch'ing decline from the White Lotus rebellion of 1796-1804 and the death of Ch'ien-lung in 1799.[46] Others date it from the Opium War of 1840. A succession of corrupt or incompetent *ambans* after 1792 contributed to the decline of Ch'ing authority in Tibet.

The Eighth Dalai Lama died in 1804, having taken little part in Tibetan political affairs, preferring to leave politics to the regents and the *ambans*. The Ninth Dalai Lama was discovered in 1806 and confirmed by the traditional process, without recourse to the Ch'ing golden urn lottery system, possibly due to the outbreak of demonstrations in Lhasa against Ch'ing interference in the selection.[47] A revolt in 1807 of the Golok of Amdo was put down by armies dispatched from China and from Lhasa.[48] In 1814 British India went to war with Nepal over Sikkim; although the Nepalese appealed to China for assistance, the Ch'ing refused to respond, revealing that they regarded Nepal as only a tributary state, not a part of

---

45. "The Emperor Commands Submission of the Turgots, October 15 1771," in *A Documentary Chronicle of Sino-Western Relations: 1644-1820*, ed. Lo-shu Fu (Tucson: University of Arizona Press, 1966), 262.

46. Chusei Suzuki, "China's Relations with Inner Asia," in John K. Fairbank, ed., *The Chinese World Order* (Cambridge: Harvard University Press, 1968), 193.

47. Shakabpa, *Tibet: A Political History*, 172.

48. Joseph Fletcher, "Ch'ing Inner Asia," in *The Cambridge History of China: Late Ch'ing, 1800-1911*, vol. 10, ed. John K. Fairbank (Cambridge: Cambridge University Press, 1978), 94. This event can be interpreted either as evidence of Lhasa's continuing authority in eastern Tibet or as an example of the feudatory duties of Lhasa to assist its suzerain when ordered or requested.

the Ch'ing empire. British influence in Sikkim and their capture of the territories of Kumaun and Garwal to the west of Nepal from the Nepalese brought them into territorial contact with Tibet, and by extension, with a part of the Chinese (Ch'ing) empire.[49]

The Ninth Dalai Lama died in 1815. His reincarnation was found in Lithang in 1817 but was not confirmed until 1822. The Tenth incarnation was determined by traditional Tibetan methods; however, the *ambans* insisted that, for the benefit of Peking and themselves, it should be announced that the lottery had been conducted. The Tibetan regent, Tengyeling, therefore announced that the lottery system had been employed.[50] The Ch'ing were thus able to claim authority over the selection of the Dalai Lama while the Tibetan populace was satisfied that the incarnation had actually been chosen by traditional methods.

In 1822 Tibetans of Kokonor revolted against Mongol tribes who, they claimed, had received the best lands in a territorial redistribution after the revolts of 1724. The Ch'ing were unable to intervene, being preoccupied with a revival of the White Lotus rebellion in eastern Kansu (1822 to 1831). Lhasa sent soldiers in an attempt to restore order. The Kokonor revolt was not finally quelled until 1854. The Tibetans of Kokonor regained some of their territories from the Mongols.[51] In 1835 Lhasa also sent an army to restore its authority in Pobo (east of Kongpo), whose ruler had refused to pay taxes to Lhasa.[52]

The Tenth Dalai Lama also died at an early age in 1837; his reincarnation was found in Gatar in 1841 and confirmed, this time apparently by the use of the Ch'ing lottery.[53] The regent, Tshomoling, who was accused by the Panchen Lama and others of having had a hand in the untimely death of the Tenth Dalai Lama, was deposed by the Ch'ing emperor in 1843 and exiled to Manchuria.[54] In 1841 western Tibet was invaded by the Dogra rulers of Jammu and Kashmir in an attempt to capture the lucrative *pashim* wool trade, which originated in the Chang Thang of western Tibet and Ladakh. The Dogras were repulsed by the Tibetans without assistance from the Ch'ing.[55] The Ch'ing garrison in Lhasa deteriorated due to the failure to rotate or reinforce the troops stationed in Tibet.

---

49. Lamb, *British India and Tibet*, 43.

50. Shakabpa, *Tibet: A Political History*, 175.

51. Schram, "Kansu-Tibetan Frontier," 65.

52. Joseph Fletcher, "The Heyday of the Ch'ing Order in Mongolia, Sinkiang and Tibet," in *The Cambridge History of China: Late Ch'ing, 1800-1911*, vol. 10, ed. John K. Fairbank (Cambridge: Cambridge University Press, 1978), 402.

53. Shakabpa, *Tibet: A Political History*, 176.

54. William Woodville Rockhill, "Dalai Lamas of Lhasa and Their Relations with the Manchu Emperors of China: 1644-1908," *Toung Pao*, XI (1910), 67.

55. Shakabpa states that the Ch'ing were too busy with the Opium War to help the Tibetans (which may imply that the Tibetans appealed to the Ch'ing for assistance). British

In 1847 the Lhasa *amban*, Ch'i-shan, abandoned military and financial powers to Tibetan administration, presumably because of Ch'ing difficulties in the Opium War and thereafter.[56] In 1842 the Panchen Lama died; in 1856 his successor was chosen by means of the Ch'ing lottery.[57] The Eleventh Dalai Lama assumed temporal power in 1855 but died less than a year later.

In 1855 the Gurkhas of Nepal, now under Jang Bahadur Rana, again attacked Tibet, supposedly over a trade dispute, but actually because the Gurkhas, knowing that the Ch'ing were now unlikely to intervene in Tibet, hoped to avenge their defeat of 1792.[58] The Gurkhas occupied Nyanang, Rongshar, Dzongka and Purang. The Ch'ing were unable to respond to the Tibetans' requests for assistance, this time due to the Taiping Rebellion. Tibet was forced to pay tribute to Nepal and grant judicial extraterritoriality to Nepalese subjects in Tibet. In 1858 the

---

Indian records assume that the Tibetan troops were part of the Ch'ing garrison and therefore "Chinese." The Ch'ing emperor is credited with being a party to the treaty which settled the conflict. C.U. Aitchison, *A Collection of Treaties, Engagements and Sanads Relating to India and Neighboring Countries* (Calcutta: Government of India, 1929), 15. Lamb admits that British sources at this point do not always distinguish between "Chinese" and "Tibetan." Lamb, *British India and Tibet*, 67. Shakabpa claims that the treaty was concluded between Tibetan ministers and the Dogra without any Ch'ing representative. Shakabpa, *Tibet: A Political History*, 179. In 1959, when India brought up this treaty as evidence that China had recognized the border between Tibet and Ladakh, Chou En-lai denied that Chinese representatives had participated in the 1842 Treaty. Letter from Chou En-lai to Prime Minister Nehru, 8 September 1959, in Chanakya Sen, *Tibet Disappears: A Documentary History of Tibet's International Status, the Great Rebellion and Its Aftermath* (New Delhi: Asia Publishing House, 1960), 448

56. Tieh-tseng Li, *Tibet: Today and Yesterday*, 59; S.A.M. Adshead, *Province and Politics in Late Imperial China: Viceregional Government in Szechuan, 1898-1911* (London: Curzon Press, 1984), 57.

57. Rockhill, "Dalai Lamas of Lhasa," 68.

58. The Gurkhas had requested Ch'ing assistance against the British in 1814, and again in 1840, 1842 and 1846, but each time they had been refused. Although Nepal's tributary status in relation to the Ch'ing had proven to be of no practical consequence in terms of Ch'ing assistance against the British, the Gurkhas continued to send tribute missions to Peking. These missions proved to be immensely valuable as trade privileges. The mission of 1852 returned in 1854 with the news that the Taiping Rebellion had broken out in China, convincing the Gurkha that the Ch'ing would be powerless to intervene in Tibet. The Gurkha mission of 1852, sent out by Jang Bahadur, carried opium worth 300,000 rupees, duty free under diplomatic privilege. Nepalese missions often took several years in transit, due not only to the distances involved, but to the fact that the Nepalese mission, like all such "tribute" missions to China, was entertained during its entire travel and stay in China at Chinese expense. Fletcher, "Heyday of the Ch'ing," 405.

Twelfth Dalai Lama was selected by the Tibetan method but was confirmed by means of the lottery.[59]

The regent during the minority of the Twelfth Dalai Lama, Reting
Rimpoche, precipitated an evolution in the Tibetan political system by his
abuse of authority. Among other things, Reting was accused of having
employed the lottery for the selection of the Twelfth Dalai Lama only in
order to win favor for himself with the Ch'ing. Reting was attacked by
Ganden and Drepung monks and forced to flee to China. Reting attempted to gain Ch'ing support for a return to power, but the Ch'ing were occupied with their own problems and were unable to assist the regent, who
finally died in China.

The alliance of monks and secular officials that had opposed Reting,
known as the *Gandre Drungche*, or "Assembly of monks of Ganden and
Drepung," ruled Tibet from 1862 to 1871. In 1872 this body was dissolved
and the *Tsongdu*, or national assembly, which included representatives of
all the Lhasa monasteries as well as secular officials, was created. By the
late nineteenth century the Tibetans were beginning to evolve a political
system that was a combination of ecclesiastical and secular interests and
thus had the potential to resolve the faults of Tibet's exclusively ecclesiastical method of rule.

The Twelfth Dalai Lama assumed temporal power in 1873 but died in
1875. By this time the Ch'ing garrison in Tibet consisted almost entirely
of sons of Manchu or Mongol soldiers and Tibetan mothers. Most of the
soldiers spoke only Tibetan and identified themselves as Tibetan rather
than as representatives of the Ch'ing. The Ch'ing were unable to pay the
garrison on several occasions, forcing the soldiers to seek menial employment and placing the *ambans* in the humiliating position of having to borrow money from the Lhasa government.

The decline of Ch'ing ability to intervene in Tibet, and the Tibetan
recovery of their own political administration, is demonstrated by events
in eastern Tibet. In the early 1860s Gonpo Namgyal, a chieftain of
Nyarong in eastern Kham, had seized control of all of Nyarong, the Hor
states to the north, Derge and Lingtsang to the northwest, and was threatening Lithang and Ba to the southwest.[60] His campaigns produced thousands of refugees who fled to Lhasa, demanding that the Tibetan
Government put a stop to the depredations of Gonpo Namgyal. The

---

59. Shakabpa, *Tibet: A Political History*, 183. What this implies is that the name of the same
boy was on all three slips of paper put into the golden urn.

60. Tashi Tsering, "Nag-ron mGon-po rNam-gyal: A 19th Century Khams-pa Warrior,"
in *Soundings in Tibetan Civilization*, ed. Aziz and Kapstein (New Delhi: Manohar
Publications, 1985), 200.

chieftains of the conquered states appealed to both the Ch'ing governor of Szechuan and the Tibetan Government at Lhasa for assistance. The governor of Szechuan, unable to respond due to the spread of the Taiping Rebellion to his province, was forced to approve a Tibetan expedition to subdue Gonpo Namgyal.

The Tibetan Government sent an army into Kham in 1863 and defeated the Nyarong chieftain, taking Nyarong under the administration of Lhasa. The Tibetans offered to withdraw in exchange for payment for the costs of their expedition, but the Ch'ing, being unable to pay or to administer Nyarong themselves, permitted Nyarong to remain under Lhasa. This agreement was respected by the Ch'ing until the early twentieth century.[61] Lhasa also took over effective control of Derge and the Hor states. The administrative division established by the Yuan and confirmed by the Ch'ing that had confined Lhasa's administration to the area west of the Yangtze-Mekong watershed was thus altered.

In 1883 the Tibetan tribes of Nangchen asked the Sining *amban* to take them under his administration. They claimed to be oppressed by the raids of the Golok, the territorial ambitions of Derge and the taxes of Lhasa. Nangchen was then brought under the authority of the Sining *amban*.[62] In 1894 the Tibetans of Nyarong again rose in revolt; they were subdued by the viceroy of Szechuan, who was not, however, allowed by Peking to annex Nyarong. A Chinese army marched from Nyarong to Derge, where they gained control of that state by intervening in a dispute over the chieftainship. Once again, the viceroy of Szechuan was not allowed to take over the administration of that state. At the end of the century the states of northern Kham were still under the authority of Lhasa while those of southern Kham (Lithang and Ba) were under the loose supervision of the Ch'ing viceroy of Szechuan.

By the second half of the nineteenth century Ch'ing *ambans* still exercised some, primarily symbolic, authority. Their lack of actual administrative functions is revealed by a memorial to Peking from the governor of Szechuan during the period 1876-1885, in which the governor complained that the Tibetan administration was no longer subordinate to the Ch'ing.[63] The *ambans* of Lhasa still exercised some functions, such as confirming Tibetan official appointments (the source of enormous bribes from Tibetan aspirants to official posts), and inspecting defenses on the frontier with Nepal. The nature and extent of the *ambans'* authority in Tibet, and therefore of Ch'ing control in Tibet, at the end of the nineteenth

61. Teichman, *Travels of a Consular Officer,* 5.
62. Rockhill, *The Land of the Lamas,* 185.
63. Tieh-tseng Li, *Tibet: Today and Yesterday,* 63.

century, are revealed in the accounts of two knowledgeable foreigners: Sarat Chandra Das, an Indian Tibetologist (and secret agent for the Government of India), who travelled to Shigatse and Lhasa in 1879 and 1881-82, and William Woodville Rockhill, secretary of the United States Legation in Peking from 1884 to 1888, who travelled in Amdo and Kham in 1889.

Sarat Chandra Das was in Shigatse in 1881 and observed the annual visit of the *amban* to inspect the border defenses against Nepal.[64] Das reports that it was the custom for the two *ambans* to draw lots each year to determine which of them would undertake the journey; in 1881 the task fell to the junior *amban*. Das was informed that, in addition to providing *ulag* (transportation services) for the amban and his entourage, it was a "pre-established custom" for the Tibetan Government to pay the *amban* a daily travelling allowance of four *dotse*,[65] which, like the *ulag*, would be extracted from the Tibetans along the route of travel. In this instance, the junior *amban* demanded, instead of the usual four *dotse*, a daily allowance of six *dotse*, which the local Tibetans refused to pay. The *amban's* Chinese escort attempted to extort the sum and then sold the animals that the Tibetans had provided for the *amban's* transport.

In Shigatse, the *amban* precipitated a revolt of the local officials and populace by his uncompromising extortionist demands. The Shigatse officials refused the *amban's* demands; the *amban* then ordered them flogged. The Tibetan officials were rescued from this fate by an angry crowd who stoned the soldiers and the *amban*. The dispute was finally settled by Lhasa officials and the senior *amban*, who determined that the junior *amban* had exceeded his authority. However, the Tibetan officials who had refused the *amban's* demands were subjected to humiliating and, in two cases, fatal punishments. Two Shigatse officials were demoted, flogged two hundred blows with the bamboo and had the skin stripped off their hands. Six village headmen who had resisted were ordered flogged four hundred blows and imprisoned for two months. Eight village elders were ordered flogged fifty blows and required to wear the *cangue* for six months. Two of the headmen later died from their injuries.[66]

At Shigatse, the Chinese *ambans* celebrated the anniversary of the emperor's accession to power, a celebration that reveals much about the

---

64. Sarat Chandra Das, *Journey to Lhasa and Central Tibet* (Delhi: Cosmo Publications, 1902, 1988), 50. The responsibility of the *ambans* to inspect the border with Nepal dates from the war of 1792. Das' information in 1881 that the tour was performed every year would indicate that the *ambans* still regularly exercised this authority.

65. A *dotse* was an ingot of silver of fifty Chinese ounces (taels), equivalent at that time to 160 Indian rupees. Ibid., 51.

66. Ibid., 52.

style of Chinese authority in Tibet. Das states that all Chinese and "subjects of the Ch'ing empire" were required to celebrate this anniversary annually, but he supposed that the Tibetans of Shigatse did not normally do so with such pageantry as was displayed on this occasion. The *ambans* organized a grand procession consisting of themselves, their entourages and Tibetan officials, accompanied by as much pageantry as could be mustered. Each of the *ambans* was carried in a sedan chair bourne by eight Chinese soldiers; to each chair were attached cords that were pulled by some fifty Tibetan soldiers, symbolizing their duty to the *amban*. The senior *amban* was preceded by several men carrying tablets on which were written, in Chinese and Tibetan, the *amban's* titles and his "commission to supreme authority over the whole of Tibet." In addition, Das comments, "throughout the march the Tibetans occupied a subordinate position, and the Chinese displayed their superiority in every possible way."[67]

Das' account reveals that the ambans' power was mainly extortionist and abusive, primarily intended to maintain the symbol of Ch'ing Chinese authority over Tibet. However, the *ambans'* ability to exploit the Tibetans for *ulag* and "allowances," and their capability to punish any resistance to their demands, even if unjust and unprecedented, reveals that they retained a large measure of dominance over the Tibetans. In addition, the fact that the *ambans* still conducted a yearly inspection of the border reveals that the Ch'ing still took responsibility for Tibet's frontier.

Rockhill reported that the Sining *amban*, who was responsible for Ch'ing-hai, had a staff of thirty-two agents, or *t'ung-shih*, who "carry the orders of their head to the different chieftains, arbitrate quarrels between tribes, collect the money tribute, and are practically the only representatives of the Chinese government known among the remoter tribes."[68] These agents of the *amban*, like the Lhasa *ambans*, made their fortunes by exploiting the *ulag* privilege. The *t'ung-shih*, when sent out on an official mission, would requisition transport far in excess of his actual needs, which the local people would be required to pay for in cash or local produce. A *t'ung-shih* might also use *ulag* privileges for his private business or sell the privilege to private, usually Chinese, traders.

The Mongol chieftains of Kokonor were required to visit the Sining *amban* once each year to receive presents and to kowtow in the direction of Peking. Every three years, the Mongol chieftains were required to travel to Peking to "carry tribute to the emperor and to renew their oaths of allegiance."[69] The Tibetans of Kokonor were also nominally under the

---

67. Ibid., 61.
68. Rockhill, *Land of the Lamas*, 52.
69. Ibid., 54.

authority of the Sining *amban*, but apparently were not required to visit the *amban* or travel to Peking. Some of the Tibetans, the Panaka south of Kokonor in particular, were, according to Rockhill, "practically independent of the Chinese, not even supplying the few *t'ung-shih* who venture into his country with any *ula* [*ulag*] unless paid in full for it."[70]

According to Rockhill, there were no Chinese military posts in Amdo, while in Kham there were six: at Nyachuka, Lithang and Ba on the southern route, and at Gatar Gompa, Dawo and Kanze on the northern route. The officers of these posts had no authority over the local Tibetans but were responsible for Chinese trade and *ulag* for Chinese officials. The Tibetans of Kham were also visited by *t'ung-shih* (from both Sining and Chengtu, Rockhill reports), who collected a nominal tax. The chieftains of Kham were required to send tribute missions to Chengtu once every five years and to Peking once every ten years, but these missions were usually headed by stewards rather than the chieftains themselves.

Rockhill's account reveals that the *amban's* authority in Kokonor was similar to that of the Lhasa *ambans*, consisting of a nominal right of territorial jurisdiction and rights to transport. The situation was similar in Kham, although here there was no *amban*, the area, with the exception of Nyarong, being under the loose authority of the governor of Szechuan. The "tribute" required of Mongols of Kokonor and some Tibetan chieftains of Kham was more a valuable trade privilege than a political act of submission. Ch'ing authority was an overlay above local Tibetan authority, rarely felt by ordinary Tibetans except those required to provide *ulag* (and they had to provide the same services for Tibetan officials).[71]

As Rockhill's and Das' accounts reveal, the Ch'ing still played a role in Tibet at the end of the nineteenth century, but that role was primarily symbolic. The extent of Ch'ing authority at the end of the nineteenth century in any part of Tibet was considerably less than at the end of the eighteenth century. The reforms of 1792 might have provided the basis for a Ch'ing, and later Chinese, claim to have exercised actual administrative authority over Tibet had those reforms actually been implemented and perpetuated. However, it is doubtful that any of the reforms of 1792 were

---

70. Ibid., 74.

71. Tibetan Government influence in Kham was hampered by the lack of Gelugpa ecclesiastical authority there. Kham had become the refuge of the unreformed sects of Tibetan Buddhism since the time of the Fifth Dalai Lama. The early Ch'ing territorial divisions put Kham further beyond the reach of Lhasa. The monasteries of Kham retained their connections with the central monasteries of their sects in central Tibet, Sakya and Tsurpu, but were beyond the temporal authority of the Gelugpa. See C.W. Cassinelli and Robert B. Ekvall, *A Tibetan Principality: The Political System of Sa sKya* (Ithaca, New York: Cornell University Press, 1969), 406.

long-lasting or of permanent significance. The most significant provision—that the Ch'ing should have final authority over the selection of high reincarnations—was adhered to only sporadically. By 1847 the Ch'ing *amban* had formally abandoned his most significant functions to the Tibetan Government. By the end of the century, the *ambans* in central Tibet had little more than their powers of extortion and abuse left as symbols of Tibet's subservience to the Ch'ing empire.

Political Status of Tibet Under the Ch'ing

The Ch'ing dynasty, like the previous conquest dynasty, the Yuan, distinguished Inner Asia from China in both political status and administrative divisions. China, the "interior empire" for the Ch'ing, was regarded as a subjugated state; Inner Asian tribes and states, or the "exterior empire," were treated as dependent allies during the early Ch'ing.[72] The Ch'ing established a special board to deal with Inner Asian affairs, the *Lifan Yuan*, which "allowed the Manchus to continue their relations with Mongolia, Tibet, and Xinjiang [Sinkiang] along the same lines they had followed before the conquest, without the interference of the traditional Chinese agency for foreign affairs, the Board of Rites."[73]

Tibet was part of the "exterior" Ch'ing empire, which included Manchuria, Mongolia, the Tarim states and Dzungaria. In an edict of Ch'ien-lung in 1787 the emperor reprimanded an official for referring to an envoy of the Dalai Lama as a "barbarian" envoy. As Ch'ien-lung said: "The Interior and the Exterior of our Empire are one family. Moreover, Tibet has long been incorporated into Our territory and should not be compared with Russia which is still savage and to be tamed and therefore, rightly called `barbarian.'"[74] The exterior empire was also distinguished from mere tributary states on the periphery of the empire, such as Nepal. In 1816 the Ch'ing refused to go to the aid of Nepal against the British, while demanding that Nepal continue to send tribute, making

---

72. Perhaps the most visible symbol of this distinction was that the Tibetans, along with the Mongols and the Turks, were not required to wear the Manchu queue. The "typically Chinese" queue, or pigtail, accompanied by a shaved forehead, was imposed upon the Chinese by the Manchu as a sign of submission. Chinese rebels against the Manchu would usually announce their defiance by allowing the hair in front to grow and by cutting the queue.

73. Shelley Rigger, "Voices of Manchu Identity, 1635-1935," in *Studies on Ethnic Groups in China*, ed. Stevan Harrell (Seattle: University of Washington Press, 1995), 192.

74. "Tibetans Are Not Barbarians, December 17 1787," in Lo-shu Fu, *Sino-Western Relations*, 302. This edict reveals that the Tibetans enjoyed a status as a protectorate of the Ch'ing but were far from being regarded as the same as Chinese if the emperor had to remind his officials not to call them barbarians.

this territorial distinction: "If your tribe resided within the boundary of Tangut [Tibet], then the grand army would naturally guard you."[75] Tibet was allowed an unique autonomous status even within the exterior empire. Tibet's inaccessibility and the difficulties involved in imposing direct administration contributed to the Ch'ing preference to maintain Tibet's semi-autonomous status within the empire.

Ch'ing policy in Inner Asia may be divided into three periods. From 1644 to 1683 the Ch'ing were occupied with domestic disorders and were unable to intervene in Inner Asian affairs. From 1683 until the beginning of the dynasty's decline in the early nineteenth century the Ch'ing were able to project their power externally and to play a large role in Inner Asia. During the nineteenth century, the Ch'ing were preoccupied with foreign imperialism and were unable to pay much attention to Inner Asia.[76]

The first period of Ch'ing-Tibetan relations was one of virtual Tibetan independence, compromised only by the nominal submission of the Dalai Lama to the Ch'ing and by the role of the Kokonor Mongol khans as "kings" of Tibet. As long as the Mongols regarded their role as purely symbolic (until Lhazang Khan) and Tibetan spiritual influence was useful to the Ch'ing in their relations with the Mongols (up to 1720), Tibet played an important and largely autonomous role in Inner Asian politics. The fact that the *Desi* was able to conceal the fact of the Fifth Dalai Lama's death for some fifteen years is an indication of the autonomy Tibet enjoyed and the lack of Ch'ing supervision of Tibetan affairs.

With the consolidation of Ch'ing control in China, and the decline of Mongol power, the Ch'ing were enabled to intervene in Tibet without regard for Tibet's role in Inner Asian affairs. From 1720 to 1792 the Ch'ing gradually increased their control in Tibet, intervening in the case of third party invasions of Tibet (1720 and 1792) and internal disorders (1750). Each intervention resulted in an increase in Ch'ing administrative control over Tibetan affairs until in 1792 the Ch'ing significantly restricted Tibetan autonomy, at least temporarily, in both domestic and foreign affairs.

The nineteenth century saw the decline of Ch'ing ability to intervene in Tibet. The voluntary abandonment of financial and military powers to the Tibetan Government by the *amban* in 1847 represents the effective end of direct Ch'ing administration in Tibet. By the late nineteenth century Tibetans had created autonomous governmental institutions that combined secular and ecclesiastical interests but avoided the foreign depen-

---

75. "China Will Not Aid Ghorkhas Against Bengal, February 20 1816," in Ibid., 401.
76. Chusei Suzuki, "China's Relations with Inner Asia," 196.

dence that had characterized the Tibetan ecclesiastical system in the past. The creation of the *Kashag* and the *Tsongdu* as actual governing bodies in Tibet formed the political and administrative basis for an independent Tibetan polity.

The history of the Ch'ing protectorate in Tibet follows not only the pattern of Ch'ing history, but was partly determined by the inherent weakness of the Tibetan political system. The system of ecclesiastical rule in Tibet, while creating internal cultural and political unity and preserving Tibetan autonomy by an astute use of Tibetan influence in Inner Asian politics, also perpetuated the fatal dependence upon foreign political patrons. Tibet enjoyed autonomy only when its political patron was disinterested in Tibetan domestic affairs, as were Gushri Khan and his descendants up to Lhazang Khan. In the case of a politically involved patron, whether Lhazang Khan, the Dzungar or the Ch'ing, Tibetan sovereignty was effectively in foreign hands. The Tibetan ecclesiastical establishment idealized the *Cho-Yon* as a personal and equal relationship between the Dalai Lama and the Manchu emperor. However, the Ch'ing employed the Tibetan lamas' influence for their own political purposes; after 1720 they disposed of Dalai Lamas or prevented their exercise of political power when it suited their political purposes, without regard to any responsibility as religious patrons of the Tibetan Buddhist church.

The Ch'ing protectorate over Tibet was supported by some of the Tibetan secular aristocracy, Polhanas being the most obvious example. The Ch'ing displayed no great eagerness to intervene in Tibet when there was internal stability and no third party interference. Indirect rule in Tibet was advantageous to the Ch'ing because of the difficulty involved in attempting to impose direct rule, and advantageous to the Tibetan political system because the Ch'ing reinforced both secular and ecclesiastic authorities in Tibet without threatening Tibetan cultural and domestic political autonomy:

> In Inner Asia, as in China proper, Ch'ing authority was an overlay, far above the emperor's subjects in periods of peace, pressing down upon them only in times of rebellion. The Ch'ing superstructure rarely interfered in the affairs of ordinary men, but, by its presence, held indigenous hierarchies in their positions of power and preserved, even rigidified, local institutions.[77]

Ch'ing policies in Inner Asia shifted as the last of the independent steppe Mongols were eliminated and the Manchu were assimilated to Chinese political culture. After the final elimination of the Dzungar threat

---

77. Fletcher, "Ch'ing Inner Asia," 105.

in the mid-eighteenth century, Inner Asia no longer occupied the attention of the Ch'ing. By the nineteenth century, Ch'ing conceptions of Inner Asian relations had become typical of traditional Chinese frontier policies. The Manchu were eventually thoroughly assimilated, losing their ethnic identity and language. The exterior empire was eventually regarded not as territory of the Manchu Ch'ing empire but as Chinese territory. The Ch'ing relationship with Tibet, begun as nominal submission, evolved to became Ch'ing suzerainty and then Chinese suzerainty.

As the Ch'ing dynasty's political prerogatives changed, it adopted a more typically Chinese conception of frontier relations. Inner Asia was no longer regarded as an exterior empire, separate from China, but simply as frontier feudatory tribes and states surrounding China. Chinese frontier feudalism on the Tibetan frontier was facilitated by Ch'ing administrative divisions separating Kham and Amdo from central Tibet. Kham and Amdo were thereafter separated politically and conceptually from what the Chinese thought of as "Tibet." The system of indirect rule by *tu-shi*, or vassal princes and chieftains, was instituted for the tribes of Amdo and petty states of Kham. All three provinces of Tibet—central Tibet, Kham and Amdo—were administered by frontier feudatory type arrangements; only central Tibet remained a single administrative territory while Kham and Amdo were administered as autonomous tribes and states. All of Tibet was regarded as having begun the process of assimilation to Chinese political administration, a process beginning in the most accessible areas of the northeast in Amdo and gradually proceeding westward to the more inaccessible central Tibet.

Although Tibet was placed, in the Chinese mind, in the category of "Chinese territory," Tibetan cultural, ethnic and national identity was essentially unaffected by Tibetan relations with China during the Ch'ing. Despite later Chinese claims, Tibet did not become an "integral part of China" during the Ch'ing dynasty (nor previously, during the Yuan). Tibet's political status was not permanently determined by its relationship with the Ch'ing empire. Although Tibet was a dependent state of the Ch'ing empire, and the Ch'ing empire was transformed into a Chinese ruling dynasty, Tibet did not thereby become a part of China. Tibet remained a distinct nation.

Some Tibetan opposition to foreign control arose during the Ch'ing among the Lhasa aristocracy, in Amdo in the revolt of 1723, and in Kham in several revolts in 1747-49, 1844 and 1860-63. At the end of the nineteenth century Tibetan nationalism was in a rudimentary stage of development. This is in part at least a reflection of the nature of feudal political relationships. The feudal type of political dependency was usually advantageous to the dependent state and posed little threat to either the internal political autonomy or cultural identity of the dependent state. Ch'ing domination of Tibet had only a small effect on the Tibetan sense of national identity and it did little to arouse Tibetan nationalism. However, when the Ch'ing protectorate over Tibet was later interpreted by the Chinese as the equivalent of Chinese sovereignty over Tibet, Tibetan nationalism was aroused in response.

7

The Thirteenth Dalai Lama and the Quest for Independence

The end of the Ch'ing dynasty was contemporaneous with the end of the feudal age and the beginning of the age of modern nationalism in China, Inner Asia and Tibet. Nationalism as a political ideology led to attempts by both China and Tibet to alter the nature of their relationship. In recognition of the changed international situation in the early twentieth century, especially the British threat to China's role in Tibet, the late Ch'ing attempted to impose a more direct control upon Tibet consistent with its claim to sovereignty. At the same time Tibet, aware of the threat that the suzerain authority of the Ch'ing over Tibet might be transformed into Chinese sovereignty, attempted to achieve independence.

The British and the Great Game

The Thirteenth Dalai Lama was born at Dakpo, in southern central Tibet, in 1876 and was confirmed as the reincarnation in 1879 without the use of the Ch'ing lottery system.[1] He was invested with temporal authority in 1895, becoming the first Dalai Lama to actually rule Tibet since the Great Fifth.[2] The Thirteenth Dalai Lama entered a world significantly different from that of his predecessors. In 1895 China suffered defeat in war with Japan, beginning the final decline of the Ch'ing. The late Ch'ing was beset by Chinese nationalism, aroused as a reaction both to foreign imperialism and to the foreign rule of the Manchu. Competition between the British and Russian empires over influence in Inner Asia, known to its British participants as the Great Game, began to transform Tibet from a remote dependency of the Ch'ing into an object of international interest.

---

1. Bell states that the Tibetans waited for the emperor's approval before confirming the reincarnation. Sir Charles Bell, *Portrait of a Dalai Lama: The Life and Times of the Great Thirteenth* (London: William Collins, 1946; London: Wisdom Publications, 1987), 47.

2. Others, notably the Seventh and Eighth Dalai Lamas, had reached maturity and had been invested with temporal power, but none since the Great Fifth had effectively exercised that power.

In the 18th century the Russians had consolidated their position in Siberia as far as the Pacific and expanded rapidly into Central Asia. This brought them into contact with Persia, where the British had interests, and Afghanistan, control of which the British considered necessary for the protection of the northwestern frontier of India. Russia's presence in Central Asia and their influence in Mongolia and Sinkiang placed them close to the borders of Tibet, which the British thought, by a rather unrealistic leap of the imagination, to be a potential invasion route to India. British fears were heightened by their knowledge that many Russians thought Russia the natural heir to the former Mongol empire (because Russia had once been part of that empire). The Russian empire already included Buryat Mongols, religious subjects of the Dalai Lama, who might conceivably act as agents for the Russians in Lhasa.

The British empire was dependent upon constantly expanding economic influence. Defense of the British position in India did not in itself require further expansionism, but the maintenance of a sphere of political and economic influence was thought necessary. The British did not attempt to impose their control directly upon territories on the frontiers of India, since the potential political and economic benefits usually did not justify the great difficulties involved, as they had learned in Afghanistan. Instead, they created an outer zone of indirect rule, a system whose similarity to Chinese frontier policy, especially Ch'ing policy in Tibet, was recognized by Lattimore:

> In conquering and occupying it [India] the British moved stage by stage up to an arc of natural inland frontiers. Until they reached these limits every political and territorial acquisition was a profitable accretion, enlarging an empire with a natural center of gravity of its own. Beyond these limits it was unprofitable to expand because expansion became converted into a drag away from the center. The inland frontier of India is to this extent analogous to the Great Wall Frontier of China.[3]

Other factors of a more subtle nature were also involved. In the maintenance of foreign rule, the ability to overawe natives with cultural or technological superiority was essential for any colonial power. British interests on the frontiers of India were not only political and commercial, but were intended to prevent any other power from establishing imperial "prestige" within the orbit of cognizance of British subjects in India. As Lattimore wrote, "The prestige indispensable to the rule of the British over India demands that their subjects shall not be allowed to see on any

---

3. Owen Lattimore, *Inner Asian Frontiers of China* (Oxford: Oxford University Press, 1988), 234.

horizon the rise of a power even remotely comparable to that of the British."[4] The British foreign secretary claimed this sort of influence in Tibet: "It seemed to me that in cases of this kind where an uncivilized country adjoined the possessions of a civilized Power, it was inevitable that the latter should exercise a certain amount of local predominance. Such a predominance, as I had before explained to him, belonged to us in Tibet."[5]

The British attempted to extend their influence to Tibet in 1876, when, in a "Separate Article" to the Chefoo Convention, they secured permission from the Chinese to send a "mission of exploration" from Peking to India via Tibet, or directly from India to Tibet.[6] In 1885, in preparation for sending a mission from India to Tibet, the British secured Chinese permits in Peking, but were then informed that the Tibetans had refused to permit the mission to enter Tibet.[7] According to Shakabpa, the Tibetan *Tsongdu* refused to permit the mission, and the Chinese were powerless to force their compliance. The *Tsongdu* further swore to never allow the British to enter Tibet.[8] In compensation for their inability to secure Tibetan compliance, the Chinese had to recognize British India's annexation of Burma.[9]

The Tibetans, anxious about British interest in penetrating Tibet, intervened in a civil dispute in Bhutan in 1883 and fortified their border with Sikkim in 1885. The British disputed the Tibetans' demarcation of the Sikkim frontier, claiming that they had occupied Sikkimese territory, and again protested to the Chinese, who were once again proven powerless to force the Tibetans to comply. The British subsequently attacked the Tibetan frontier post and defeated the Tibetans. At this point, the Lhasa *amban* attempted to salvage the situation, and China's role in Tibet, by proceeding to the Sikkim border, where he negotiated directly with the Indian foreign secretary.[10] The Chinese, like the Tibetans, claimed author-

---

4. Ibid., 236.

5. Despatch from the Marquess of Landsdowne to Sir C. Scott, 18 April 1903, *British Parliamentary Papers: Papers Relating to Tibet*, Cd. 1920 (1904), vol. 67, (London: His Majesty's Stationery Office, 1904), 187.

6. The Chefoo Convention provided for reparations from China to Britain for the murder of a British official in Yunnan. Separate Article to Chefoo Convention, in Hugh E. Richardson, *Tibet and Its History*, rev. 2nd ed. (Boston and London: Shambhala, 1984), 264.

7. Alastair Lamb, *Tibet, China and India 1914-1950* (Hertingfordbury: Roxford Books, 1989), 3.

8. W.D. Shakabpa, *Tibet: A Political History* (New York: Potala Publications, 1984), 198.

9. Lamb, *Tibet, China and India*, 4, 127. The Chinese had their own reasons for opposing British intrusions into Tibet and may have used Tibetan opposition as an excuse. Ibid., 130.

10. Ibid., 5; Premen Addy, *Tibet on the Imperial Chessboard* (New Delhi: Academic Publishers, 1984), 48.

ity over Sikkim, but were forced to recognize the actuality of British control of Sikkim in the Treaty of 1890.[11] An appendix to the treaty granted the British the right to establish a trade mart within Tibet at Yatung.[12] The Tibetans subsequently refused to grant the British permission to set up the trade mart, contending that they had not been a party to the treaty and that China had no authority to negotiate on their behalf. British complaints via Peking to the Lhasa *amban* produced no results with the Tibetans.[13]

British frustration in dealing with the Chinese over Tibet finally led some Government of India (GOI) officials to the opinion that they must deal directly with the Tibetans. Lord Curzon, who became viceroy of India in 1899, initiated a more active British policy toward opening Tibet. Curzon, who had travelled in Russia and written a book on Russia's ambitions in Central Asia, believed that Russia was a threat to British possessions in Asia. Russia's ultimate ambition, he wrote, was, "the domination of Asia. . . . Each morsel but whets the appetite for more, and inflames the passion for pan-Asiatic dominion. If Russia is entitled to these ambitions, still more is Britain entitled, nay compelled, to defend that which she has won."[14]

Curzon let it be known to the Tibetans, through Sikkimese intermediaries, that the GOI was ready to deal directly with Tibet. The Tibetans, reluctant to abandon Ch'ing protection for the unknown benefits of a relationship with the British, were unwilling to establish direct communication. But in order to alleviate the fears of the British in regard to Russia, the Tibetans let it be known through a Nepalese intermediary that the same policy of exclusion applied to the Russians.[15] While this may have been true in theory, the Buryat Mongols, who were Russian subjects, travelled freely to Lhasa. One such Buryat Mongol, Agvan Dorjiev, was to play a large role in Tibetan politics. Dorjiev was a monk at Drepung in Lhasa since 1880 and a tutor and confidant of the young Dalai Lama since 1888. Dorjiev was reputed to have contacted the Russian czar on behalf of the Dalai Lama in 1900 and again in 1901. The British were considerably

11. "Convention of March 17th 1890 between Great Britain and China relating to Sikkim and Tibet," in Richardson, *Tibet and Its History*, 265. The British, by negotiating directly with China over territory claimed by Tibet, indirectly recognized China's authority over Tibet.

12. Regulations regarding Trade, Communication, and Pasturage, to be appended to the Convention between Great Britain and China of March 17, 1890, relative to Sikkim and Tibet. 5 December 1893, in Ibid., 266.

13. Lamb, *Tibet, China and India*, 6; Addy, *Tibet on the Imperial Chessboard*, 49.

14. "Minute by Lord Curzon on Russian Ambitions in Eastern Persia," 28 October 1901, in Addy, *Tibet on the Imperial Chessboard*, 60.

15. Addy, *Tibet on the Imperial Chessboard*, 72.

upset at this news, the validity of which they were unable to confirm due to their lack of established communications with the Tibetans.[16]

In fact, Agvan Dorjiev had met with Czar Nicholas in 1898, 1900 and 1901, each time having been sent by the Dalai Lama to establish closer relations with Russia.[17] Dorjiev had convinced the Dalai Lama that the Russian czar was sympathetic to Buddhism.[18] The Tibetans thought of Russia as an imperial power capable of protecting Tibet against both the Chinese and the British but too far away to be a threat to Tibet itself.[19] According to Dorjiev's account, Tibetan opinion was split into three factions. One was the pro-Manchu ecclesiastical faction, whose opinion, as summarized by Dorjiev was: "Since the kindness of the Manchu Emperor is so great, even now his compassion will not fail us; so we must not separate ourselves from China." The second, primarily secular faction argued that the British were Tibet's best protection against the Chinese. The third faction argued that the Russians were the best choice to protect Tibet against both the Chinese and the British.[20] The only consideration all three factions had in common was the belief that Tibet could not survive without a powerful political patron.

Dorjiev's missions to Russia raised British suspicions that, despite Russian denials, some sort of secret agreement had been reached for Russian protection of Tibet against the British. Curzon proposed direct relations with Tibet, disregarding China's supposed authority there, or its suzerainty over Tibet, which he characterized as "a constitutional fiction—a political affectation which has only been maintained because of

---

16. Ibid., 69.

17. John Snelling, *Buddhism in Russia: The Story of Agvan Dorzhiev, Lhasa's Emissary to the Tsar* (Rockport, Massachusetts: Element, 1993), 54, 72, 83. Dorjiev said, in his last will and testament in 1936, that the "Tibetan Government and the Supreme Ruler of Tibet, the Dalai Lama, in 1901 officially appointed me, Khambo Agvan Dorzhiev, to serve as the Plenipotentiary Representative of Tibet at the Government of Great Russia." Ibid., 245. On the third mission, in 1901, Dorjiev was accompanied by three official Tibetan representatives. Ibid., 74.

18. As early as 1891, Dorjiev had argued that Tibet should seek the protection of the Russian Empire. In that year, the Tibetans had been favorably impressed by a visit of the Russian Hier Apparent, Nicholas, to Buryatia and his respectful treatment of the Buryat Mongols. Ibid., 38. Dorjiev in his arguments may have evoked Tibetan mythology in which the paradise of Shambhala was supposed to lie to the north. Dorjiev called the plan for a political union of Inner Asian Buddhist states his "Shambhala Project." Ibid., 77.

19. The proponent of Russian influence in Tibet was another Buryat Mongol, Dr. P.A. Badmayev, who served as an expert on Mongol affairs in the Russian Foreign Ministry from 1875 to 1893. Czars Alexander and Nicholas reputedly dreamed of attaining influence in Inner Asia by posing as the patrons of the Dalai Lama. Alastair Lamb, *British India and Tibet: 1766-1910* (London: Routledge and Kegan Paul, 1960), 251.

20. Snelling, *Buddhism in Russia*, 64.

its convenience to both parties." Curzon maintained that relations should be established directly with the Dalai Lama:

> There are, in the present circumstances of Tibet, special reasons for insisting that Tibet herself shall be a prominent party to any new Agreement. For the first time for nearly a century that country is under the rule of a Dalai Lama, who is neither an infant or a puppet, but a young man, some twenty-eight years of age, who, having survived the vicissitudes of childhood, is believed to exercise a greater personal authority that any of his predecessors, and to be *de facto* as well as *de jure* sovereign of the country. In other words, there is for the first time in modern history a ruler in Tibet with whom it is possible to deal instead of an obscure junta masked by the Chinese Amban.[21]

The opportunity Curzon was seeking to initiate a more activist policy in Tibet came in April 1903. The Ch'ing *amban* in Lhasa finally responded to repeated British requests to renegotiate the 1893 trade mart provisions of the 1890 Sikkim treaty, offering to send his own representative and an official of the Tibetan Government to a site of British choosing. Curzon specified Khampa Dzong, in Tibetan territory, since this would provide him with an excuse to enter Tibet. A British party of 200 men under the command of Colonel Francis Younghusband proceeded to Khampa Dzong in July 1903. The Tibetan *Tsongdu* was adamant in refusing to authorize negotiations unless the British expedition withdrew to the frontier.[22] British representations to Peking to force the Tibetans to negotiate produced no results. Meanwhile, the *amban* was unable to meet the British at Khampa Dzong because he was refused transport by the Tibetans.[23]

In October, in the absence of any Tibetan willingness to negotiate, Curzon determined to press on to Gyantse. Withdrawal without having achieved the objective of negotiations was thought to be potentially harmful to British prestige. In addition, Gyantse was suitable for winter quarters should the expedition be forced to remain in Tibet. Curzon maintained that only the lamas and the Chinese, who wished to preserve their privileged positions in Tibet, were opposed to trade and intercourse with the outside world:

---

21. "Letter of Curzon to Lord Hamilton, Secretary of State for India," 8 January 1903, as quoted in Addy, *Tibet on the Imperial Chessboard*, 91.

22. However, some ministers of the *Kashag*, who had a better appraisal of the military capabilities of the British and who saw no harm in commercial relations, preferred negotiations. Shakabpa, *Tibet: A Political History*, 208.

23. Viceroy to the Secretary of State for India, 19 March 1904, *British Parliamentary Papers: Further Papers Relating to Tibet*, Cd. 2054 (1904), vol. 67, 3.

They [the Tibetans] are ruled by an ignorant hierarchy of monks, whose continued monopoly of all power and substance in the country depends upon the exclusion of any alien influence. China endows the principal monasteries and thereby keeps a hold on the ruling clique. But she is absolutely without power or authority in Tibet, and she is equally afraid of any outside shock that might expose the hollowness of her alleged suzerainty.[24]

The advance to Gyantse was sanctioned by the British Foreign Office, which was reluctant either to withdraw or advance and was therefore dependent upon its officers in the field to salvage the situation. The situation had developed exactly as Curzon had hoped when he suggested Khampa Dzong as the negotiation site. However, opposition to the expedition within the British Government delayed the British advance until March. The Tibetans had meanwhile fortified a position at Guru, blocking further advance in the direction of Gyantse.

Younghusband made his move on 31 March 1904, after receiving reinforcements of 3,000 men from India. At Guru, the British and Indian troops attempted to disarm the Tibetans, who had positioned themselves behind a stone wall. A situation that some of the British officers described as "absurd" ensued, in which the Indian troops—with somewhat good humor—wrestled with the Tibetans for their antiquated weapons. A shot was fired, then a volley and another. The final result was 600 to 700 Tibetans killed or wounded out of a total of 1500. The British and Indians suffered only a dozen casualties.[25]

The British force thereafter proceeded to Gyantse, where it waited for three months, receiving several high-level Tibetan officials but no Chinese, since the Tibetans still refused to provide transport for the *amban* or any of his representatives to meet with the British. None of the Tibetans were willing to negotiate until the British force withdrew to the frontier.[26] On 14 July Younghusband continued the advance to Lhasa, fighting an engagement at the Karo La pass between Gyantse and Nangkartse where another 300 Tibetans were killed. On 3 August,

---

24. "Letter of Curzon to Brodrick, Secretary of State for India," 2 October 1903, as quoted in Addy, *Tibet on the Imperial Chessboard*, 107.

25. Addy, *Tibet on the Imperial Chessboard*, 116; Peter Fleming, *Bayonets to Lhasa* (Oxford: Oxford University Press, 1961, 1986), 148.

26. Francis Younghusband, *India and Tibet: A History of the Relations between the Two Countries from the Time of Warren Hastings to 1910; with a Particular Account of the Mission to Lhasa of 1904* (Hong Kong: Oxford University Press, 1985), 182, 264, 291.

Younghusband and his army arrived at Lhasa to find that the Dalai Lama, along with his adviser Dorjiev, had fled.[27]

The Ch'ing *amban*, whose involvement in the affair to that point had been effectively prevented by the Tibetans, denounced the Dalai Lama for fleeing and issued an imperial decree on 26 August that "temporarily confiscated" the appointment of the Dalai Lama and appointed the Panchen Lama in his place. The *amban's* decree was posted around the streets of Lhasa but was pulled down by the Tibetans. On 10 September, the *amban* issued a proclamation that "the Dalai Lama will hereafter be responsible for religious matters and shall only be concerned slightly in the official matters, while the Amban will conduct all Tibetan affairs with the Tibetan officials, and all important affairs will be referred to the Emperor."[28] These measures represented an attempt to restore Ch'ing authority over Tibetan affairs, including a presumed authority to "appoint" the head of Tibetan Buddhism and the Tibetan Government.

Younghusband demanded negotiations with the responsible authorities in Lhasa, which brought up the question of who was authorized to enter into an international treaty on behalf of Tibet. If the answer was the Tibetans, then who were the Tibetan authorities capable of negotiating in the Dalai Lama's absence? Younghusband eventually negotiated exclusively with Tibetan representatives, the *amban* having admitted to Younghusband his powerlessness to negotiate on the Tibetans' behalf. However, Younghusband's account reveals that he allowed the *amban* to assume a role of authority in Tibetan affairs previously denied him by the Tibetans themselves.[29] Younghusband intentionally elevated the *amban's* stature and his authority over Tibetan affairs, presumably because the only British justifications for the expedition were that the Tibetans had failed to live up to a treaty made on their behalf by the Chinese.[30] Younghusband even lectured the Tibetans that, had they followed the *amban's* advice and negotiated at Khampa Dzong or Gyantse, the British would not have been compelled to advance upon Lhasa.[31]

---

27. Far from encouraging the Tibetans against negotiations with the British, Dorjiev reportedly counseled moderation because Tibet had no power to resist the British. Dorjiev was reported to the British to have been engaged in managing the Tibetan arsenal during the British invasion, but his occupation seems to have been mainly with the Tibetan mint. Snelling, *Buddhism in Russia*, 112.

28. W.W. Rockhill, "Dalai Lamas of Lhasa and Their Relations with The Manchu Emperors of China: 1644-1908," *Toung Pao*, XI (1910), 90.

29. Younghusband, *India and Tibet*, 263, 286, 305, 306, 420.

30. Ibid., 270.

31. Letter from Colonel F.E. Younghusband to the Secretary to the Government of India, 2 September 1904, *British Parliamentary Papers: Further Papers Relating to Tibet*, Cd. 2370 (1905), vol. 58, 261; Younghusband, *India and Tibet*, 300.

While turning up no evidence of Russian arms or influence in Lhasa, Younghusband claimed to have uncovered evidence that the reason for the Tibetans' defiant attitude toward both British and Chinese imperial representatives was that they thought they had acquired a new and more powerful protector in the Russian czar.[32] Younghusband managed to conclude an agreement with the Tibetan authorities on 7 September; the *amban* was credited with having assisted in the procedures but, on the instructions of Peking, did not sign the agreement. The *amban's* appointee to replace the Dalai Lama, the Panchen Lama, neither took part in the negotiations nor signed the treaty. The Tibetans who affixed their seals to the treaty were the abbots of Ganden, Drepung, and Sera, the Ganden *Tri Rimpoche* on behalf of the Dalai Lama, and the leaders of the *Kashag* and *Tsongdu*.[33] Younghusband treated the Tibetans in a high-handed, though formally respectful manner, allowing no deviation in the terms or conditions for a settlement, all for the purpose of establishing British prestige and impressing the Tibetans with the consequences of defying the British empire.

By the terms of the 1904 Lhasa Convention, the British secured the trade privileges that had been their ostensible reason for invading Tibet, with trade marts to be established at Gyantse, Yatung and Gartok. According to further articles, the Russians were to be excluded from Tibet; no territory was allowed to be ceded or sold to any foreign power; no concessions for railways, roads, telegraphs or mines could be granted; no representatives of any foreign power were to be admitted to Tibet; and no foreign power was permitted to intervene in Tibetan affairs. The British imposed an indemnity of 75 *lakh* rupees on the Tibetans, by which the Tibetans were to compensate the British for the expenses of their expedition. This indemnity was to be paid in 75 annual installments; until the payment was complete, the British would occupy the Chumbi valley, on the main route into Tibet from India, as security.[34]

The indemnity, the occupation of Tibetan territory, the granting of exclusive trading rights and the stationing of a British resident at Gyantse established the essentials of a British protectorate over Tibet, without any of the responsibilities usually associated with such an arrangement.

---

32. Younghusband, *India and Tibet*, 320. Dorjiev's account tends to confirm this impression. Snelling, *Buddhism in Russia*, 74.

33. Letter from Colonel F.E. Younghusband to the Secretary to the Government of India, 9 September 1904, *Parliamentary Papers*, Cd. 2370 (1905), vol. 58, 265; Younghusband, *India and Tibet*, 305.

34. Text of "Convention between Great Britain and Tibet," 1904, in C.U. Aitchison, *A Collection of Treaties, Engagements and Sanads Relating to India and Neighboring Countries*, vol. XIV (Calcutta: Government of India, 1929), 23. A lakh is 100,000 rupees.

However, some of the provisions of the treaty were later repudiated by the British Government, which was less enthusiastic than was the GOI for imperial adventures on the Indian frontier and for the imperial responsibilities that were sure to follow. Russia's defeat by Japan in 1905 had greatly reduced Russia's prestige in Asia and the perceived threat of Russian intrigues in Tibet.

The 1904 British expedition to Tibet ended Tibet's international isolation and exposed the myth of China's claimed authority in Tibet. The opening of Tibet also began to break the hold of the lamas over every aspect of Tibetan culture and consciousness, gradually giving Tibetans an awareness of the outside world and of changing world politics. However, the expedition also resulted in the flight of the Dalai Lama and an inevitable Chinese attempt to recover their position at Lhasa.

Treaties of 1906 and 1907

The 1904 Lhasa Convention did not address the issue of Chinese adhesion. China's right to participation in any treaty regarding Tibet could not be denied, at least by the British, since Britain continued to recognize Chinese "suzerainty" over Tibet. The Chinese were able to exploit this fact in order to salvage their legal position in Tibet. The Chinese Government agreed to negotiations at Calcutta in the hope of winning international recognition of their claims upon Tibet. The Chinese were willing to recognize some, if not all, of the provisions of the Lhasa Convention, but were intent that Tibet's right to independently conclude international agreements should be denied. China therefore moved to assume the obligations of the Convention and convert what had been an agreement between Britain and Tibet into one between Britain and China.

Negotiations with Britain over Tibet required China to define its role in Tibet within the terms of international law and to substantiate its claim to actual governing authority in Tibet. Until that time, the Ch'ing dynasty had placed Tibet within a category of frontier dependencies of the external empire, but, unlike Eastern Turkestan and Mongolia, which were under direct Ch'ing administration, Tibet had remained an autonomous dependent state. When the British inquired of the Chinese foreign office what claim China had on Tibet, this distinction was evident: "The Tsungli Yamen [Chinese Foreign Office] makes a point of Tibet's condition and says that it is not the same as the Turkestan frontier, Manchuria, or Mongolia which belong to China, but is to be dealt with by China as having something of the simple tributary state in it still."[35]

---

35. "Letter of Curzon to Brodrick," 10 July 1905, as quoted in Addy, *Tibet on the Imperial Chessboard*, 159.

Despite the nebulous nature of China's relationship with Tibet, the Chinese took the opportunity offered by negotiations with Britain to claim full sovereignty over Tibet. The Chinese were aware that the term the British favored to define China's authority over Tibet, "suzerainty," was interpreted as a limited supervisory role for China in Tibet. The Chinese negotiator at Calcutta, T'ang Shao-yi, was Western educated and familiar with concepts of international law. He refused to ratify the Lhasa Convention and insisted that all further negotiations in regard to Tibet be conducted directly between China and Britain. He also insisted that China was not a "foreign power" in relation to Tibet, but that Britain definitely was, and Britain should therefore disclaim any intention to interfere in Tibet. T'ang also insisted that China would pay the indemnity required by the Lhasa treaty. The British refused these conditions, stating that they recognized China's suzerainty in Tibet, the precise definition of which they would leave to be sorted out between the Chinese and the Tibetans, but that Britain claimed a "special interest" in Tibetan affairs and would deal with Tibet as an autonomous country capable of independently entering into international agreements.[36]

The British began negotiations at Calcutta by submitting a draft agreement accepting China's suzerainty in Tibet. However, the Chinese continued to claim sovereign status, which the British were unwilling to recognize. The British regarded the Chinese claim as an attempt to gain international recognition of a status for China in Tibet that did not exist in reality. The expedition of 1904 had produced ample evidence that Chinese authority in Tibet was virtually nonexistent. The Chinese subsequently suggested that Britain should merely accept the "existing authority of China over Tibet." However, the British regarded this as equivalent to recognizing Chinese sovereignty. The British countered that the matter need not be addressed at all; Chinese acceptance of the Lhasa Convention was all that was required. The negotiations thus reached an impasse and were temporarily abandoned; the Chinese insisted on recognition of their sovereignty over Tibet, and British exclusion from Tibet, while the British were unwilling to abandon the gains of their 1904 expedition.[37]

Negotiations were reopened in 1906 at Peking. The British Government was now interested in an alliance with Russia. A first step in that direction would be to alleviate Russian fears concerning British designs upon Tibet. An agreement was therefore quickly concluded. The Chinese agreed to accept the Lhasa Convention of 1904; the British agreed

---

36. Addy, *Tibet on the Imperial Chessboard*, 158.
37. Alastair Lamb, *The McMahon Line: A Study in the Relations between India, China and Tibet, 1904 to 1914* (London: Routledge and Kegan Paul, 1966), 67.

not to interfere in China's administration of Tibet if the Chinese would exclude all other foreign powers. China was defined as not a foreign power in relation to Tibet, which implicitly recognized Chinese sovereignty over Tibet.[38]

The Lhasa Convention had established direct relations between the British and the Tibetans, upon which Tibet might theoretically have built a case for international recognition as an independent state. The Peking agreement relegated Tibetan affairs once again to a concern of China, with whom all foreign parties, including Britain, had to deal in regard to Tibet. The Tibetan indemnity, reduced to 25 lakh rupees, was paid by the Chinese out of the Szechuan treasury, legally requiring the British to withdraw from the Chumbi valley. The Chinese considered the Adhesion Treaty of 1906 not as a recognition of the Lhasa Convention of 1904, but as a repudiation of the Lhasa Convention and a recognition of their "traditional authority" in Tibet.[39]

The 1904 Younghusband expedition to Tibet ultimately gained nothing for Britain; Indian security was theoretically improved by the elimination of Russia as a threat, but that threat had hardly existed in reality. As Hugh Richardson summed up the results of the expedition:

> By the treaty of 1904 we established direct and friendly intercourse with Tibet and terms which, if they had been carried out, would have led to the opening of trade; but the Convention with China in 1906 had the unfortunate result of nullifying the advantages we had gained at Lhasa. China was given the opportunity of reaffirming her influence which had almost reached the vanishing point.
>
> We had broken down Tibetan exclusion and stubbornness and had encouraged the deposition of the Dalai Lama by the Chinese, only to withdraw from Lhasa and later, without consulting the Tibetans, to sign terms which acknowledged China's right to preserve the integrity of Tibet, without seeking to limit Chinese interference in Tibetan internal affairs to the suzerainty she had enjoyed before 1904.[40]

In 1907 Britain and Russia reduced the tensions of the Great Game by concluding a treaty addressing their relative spheres of influence in Inner Asia. The agreement covered Persia, Afghanistan and Tibet. Persia was divided between British and Russian influence; Russia recognized Britain's pre-

---

38. Addy, *Tibet on the Imperial Chessboard*, 172. Text of "Convention between Great Britain and China," 1906, in Aitchison, *Treaties, Engagements and Sanads*, 27.

39. Ibid.

40. Hugh Richardson, *Tibetan Precis* (Calcutta: Government of India, 1945), 9.

dominant interests in Afghanistan; Russia also recognized that Britain had a "special interest in the maintenance of the status quo in the external relations of Tibet." Both parties recognized China's "suzerainty" in Tibet. Each side agreed not to interfere in the internal administration of Tibet nor to enter into negotiations with Tibet except through the intermediary of the Chinese Government. Buddhist subjects of either party were allowed to have direct relations with Tibet as long as they were of a purely religious character. Tibet was not informed of the negotiations between Britain and Russia, nor of any of the provisions of the Treaty of 1907.[41] Mongolia, though not mentioned in the agreement, was left by default to the Russians.[42] By the 1907 Treaty the British accorded the Russians a free hand in Mongolia in exchange for the same privilege for themselves in Afghanistan and a guarantee of Russian non-interference in Tibet.[43]

The treaties of 1906 and 1907 prevented Russian interference in Tibet but also limited the British role. British strategy assumed an impotent China unable to control its own internal territory, much less Tibet. China, however, bolstered by international recognition of its rights in Tibet, however loosely defined, and fearful of losing Tibet altogether, began to take steps to reassert its authority. The British soon found their trade privileges, won at such high cost, restricted to almost nothing by the interference of the Chinese representative in Tibet, Chang Yin-t'ang.[44] Chang made it clear that he interpreted the 1906 Convention as superseding the 1904 Convention between Britain and Tibet and as equivalent to a recognition of Chinese sovereignty over Tibet.[45] Negotiations between Britain

41. "Convention between Great Britain and Russia relating to Persia, Afghanistan and Tibet," 31 August 1907, in Richardson, *Tibet and Its History*, 273.

42. In July 1907, Russia had concluded a similar sphere of influence treaty with Japan, in which Japan recognized Russia's influence in Mongolia in return for Russian respect for Japan's influence in Korea and Manchuria. Britain was informed of this agreement, therefore Russia did not require British recognition of its role in Mongolia. Gerard M. Friters, *Outer Mongolia and Its International Position* (Baltimore: Johns Hopkins University Press, 1949), 217.

43. The Anglo-Russian Treaty of 1907 related Russian and British privileges in Persia, Afghanistan and Tibet, rather than in the more comparable situations of Mongolia and Tibet. Lamb suggests that, had the British not invaded Tibet in 1904, the Russians might have been willing to relate their privileges in Mongolia to those of the British in Tibet (while still conceding to the British exclusive influence in Afghanistan). Lamb, *British India and Tibet*, 284.

44. Chang had been assistant to T'ang Shao-yi at the negotiations in 1906. He was posted to Lhasa as Chinese Government representative in Tibet, not as *amban* (an *amban*, Lien Yu, remained in Lhasa at the same time). Chang was a new kind of Chinese official (Han rather than Manchu), representative of a new Chinese policy toward Tibet. Lamb, *British India and Tibet*, 268.

45. Richardson, *Tibetan Precis*, 9.

and Tibet in regard to the development of trade, provided for in the 1904 treaty, were held in India, at Simla, in 1908, where the Chinese managed to exclude the Tibetans except as observers.[46] The resulting agreements allowed the Chinese such authority to regulate trade in Tibet that the trade marts were effectively obstructed.[47] By 1908 the Chinese, through skillful diplomacy, had restored their position in Tibet.

Exile of the Dalai Lama

After fleeing Lhasa on 30 July 1904, the Dalai Lama, accompanied by Dorjiev, travelled to Outer Mongolia, where he stayed for over a year. The Dalai Lama met with the Russian consul at Urga and the Russian minister to China, who travelled from Peking for the purpose.[48] Dorjiev was once again dispatched to St. Petersburg for an audience with the Russian Emperor.[49] The Russians offered to facilitate the Dalai Lama's return to Lhasa by means of a Buryat Mongol escort, a prospect the British objected to as tantamount to a Russian expedition to Tibet.[50] The Dalai Lama's contacts with the Russians also alarmed the Chinese, who sent a mission to Mongolia to warn the Dalai Lama that if he intrigued with the Russians he would be permanently deposed.[51]

Neither the British nor the Chinese wanted the Dalai Lama to remain at Urga but they did not want him back in Lhasa either. The Chinese were busily consolidating their hold in Lhasa, a process facilitated by the Dalai Lama's absence. The British, who blamed the Dalai Lama's "hostility" for provoking their interference in the first place, were now opposed to his return, preferring to cultivate relations with the Panchen instead.[52] The Chinese finally achieved a compromise by securing the Dalai Lama's

---

46. China was represented by Chang Yin-t'ang. The Tibetan observer at the 1908 negotiations, Tsarong Shape, was described by the British as acting "under the directions" of the Chinese representative. Aitchison, *Treaties, Engagements and Sanads*, 29.

47. Text of "Tibet Trade Regulations," 1908, in *Ibid.*, 28.

48. Lamb, *McMahon Line*, 20. Snelling believes that the Dalai Lama went to Outer Mongolia for the specific purpose of contacting the Russians, or even for the purpose of seeking exile in Russian territory, probably in Buryatia. Snelling, *Buddhism in Russia*, 119. The Dalai Lama's exile facilitated his contacts with the Russians, seemingly defeating the British attempt to isolate Tibet from Russian influence.

49. Snelling, *Buddhism in Russia*, 119.

50. Lamb, *McMahon Line*, 84. The Russians may have hoped that their good relations with the Dalai Lama could be used to improve their position in Mongolia, much as the Ch'ing had used the Dalai Lama in their relations with the Mongols.

51. Snelling, *Buddhism in Russia*, 121.

52. Parshotam Mehra, *Tibetan Polity, 1904-37: The Conflict Between the 13th Dalai Lama and the 9th Panchen* (Wiesbaden: Otto Harrassowitz, 1976), 14.

return to Kumbum Monastery, near Sining, where he would be isolated from the Russians and the Mongols.[53]

Meanwhile, the British had promised the Panchen Lama protection from Lhasa's political authority, in exchange for a trade mart at Shigatse and an increased British presence in Tsang and southern Tibet. The British trade agent at Gyantse proposed to open a trade mart at Shigatse under the terms of the Lhasa Convention and "to let it be clearly understood that any intrigues of other Powers at Lhasa would be met with a corresponding extension of our influence in the province of Tsang and southern Tibet; and all this might be done without openly impugning or infringing Chinese suzerainty."[54] The Panchen Lama attended ceremonies in India in honor of a visit of the Prince of Wales in the winter of 1905-06. The British were eventually unable to commit themselves to the Panchen Lama, since providing him protection against both the Chinese and the Dalai Lama would have required the establishment of a British protectorate in southern Tibet, a step the British Government was not prepared to take.[55]

By 1908 the Chinese had sufficiently consolidated their position in Tibet that they favored a return of the Dalai Lama to Lhasa in order to legitimate their control. The Dalai Lama had been unsuccessful in securing international support, even though he had contacted not only the Russians from Urga but the British and Americans from his exile at Kumbum, and therefore had to contemplate the necessity of submission to Chinese authority in order to return to Lhasa.[56] At the end of 1907 the Dalai Lama travelled from Kumbum to Wu-tai Shan, the Buddhist sacred mountain near Peking. At Wu-tai Shan, the Dalai Lama met William Woodville Rockhill, the American consul in China. According to Rockhill, the Dalai Lama said that he had received several "pressing invitations" from the Chinese to come to Peking. He said that he was desirous of returning to Tibet, but would select his own time, and would not submit to Chinese dictation in the matter.[57]

At Wu-tai Shan, the Dalai Lama received an official summons to an audience with the emperor, complete with the ceremony and protocol

---

53. Lamb, *McMahon Line*, 20.

54. "Letter of O'Connor to White," 23 November 1905, as quoted in Lamb, *McMahon Line*, 24.

55. The Chinese responded to the Panchen's visit to India by informing the GOI that he had no temporal authority and was not empowered to negotiate any Tibetan foreign affairs. Addy, *Tibet on the Imperial Chessboard*, 167.

56. Lamb, *McMahon Line*, 173.

57. *India Office Library and Records*, no. 29341, 19 July 1908, as quoted in Mehra, *Tibetan Polity*, 19.

that would be observed during the visit. The Dalai Lama was informed that he would be received in audience by the empress dowager and the emperor on 6 October, at which time he would be required to perform the kowtow. Upon hearing this, the Dalai Lama protested that this was in violation of all previous tradition and refused to attend the audience under those conditions. The Dalai Lama reached Peking on 27 September 1908 and was installed at the Yung-ho Kung, the Yellow Temple. The imperial court yielded to the Lama's objections and altered the protocol, requiring only that the Dalai Lama kneel on one knee. This was accepted and the audience took place on 14 October.[58]

The empress dowager requested that the Dalai Lama perform a "long-life" ritual for her on the occasion of her birthday on 3 November. On 2 November, the ceremony was performed; the Dalai Lama was reported to have kneeled three times and kowtowed twice, but, given his previous objections, it is unlikely that this is what actually took place. On the day of the empress dowager's birthday, all the court, including the emperor and the Dalai Lama reportedly kowtowed to the empress dowager. Rockhill states that this actually took place, but his only source for this information was the imperial court records.[59] The empress dowager issued an edict to the Dalai Lama on the day of her birthday ceremony, conferring upon him a new title and imperial instructions. The Dalai Lama's previous title of "Great, Good, Self-existent Buddha of Heaven" was altered to "Loyally Submissive Vice-gerent, the Great, Good, Self-existent Buddha of Heaven." The Dalai Lama was henceforward to be provided with a Chinese government stipend out of the Szechuan treasury. The edict set out the format expected to regulate future relations with Tibet:

> When he has arrived in Tibet, he must carefully obey the laws and Ordinances of the Sovereign State, and make known to all the goodwill of the Chinese Court; and he must admonish the Tibetans respectfully to observe the laws and learn the ways of rectitude. In all matters he shall follow the established law of reporting to the Imperial Resident in Tibet for transmission by Memorial to us, as occasion arises; and he shall respectfully await our decision. We hope that the frontier regions may thus ever be preserved in peace; that the line of cleavage between the priests and people

---

58. Rockhill, "Dalai Lamas of Lhasa," 79. The Fifth Dalai Lama, the only previous Dalai Lama to visit Peking, had not been required to prostrate or to kneel during his audience in 1652.

59. Ibid., 84. Considering that this ceremony was primarily a personal one without the usual political significance—even the emperor performed the kowtow to the empress dowager—the Dalai Lama may have had less reason for objection than on the earlier occasions.

may be completely effaced; and that our fervent desire to protect and uphold the Yellow Church in peace upon the borders of the Empire may not be disregarded.[60]

The Dalai Lama made a special request to be allowed to petition the emperor directly, since his inability to do so would reduce his power in relation to the Lhasa *amban*. However, his request could not be acted upon, nor the investiture of his new title performed, due to the deaths of the emperor on 14 November and the empress dowager on the following day. The Dalai Lama performed the death ritual for both at the Yung-ho kung and was present at the enthronement of the last Ch'ing emperor. In his meetings with the Chinese Foreign Office, Chinese officials reportedly "referred to the 1906 Agreement between China and Great Britain and requested the Dalai Lama to see that the terms of that agreement were carried out."[61] The Dalai Lama complained of Chinese interference in eastern Tibet (Kham), and the Chinese agreed to curb the excesses of Chinese troops and officials there.

While in Peking the Dalai Lama was allowed to meet with representatives of European countries, including the British ambassador, but only in the presence of Chinese officials.[62] The Chinese strictly limited these meetings, turning them into little more than courtesy calls. The Tibetans complained to the Russian ambassador that the behavior of Chinese officials was both "insolent and insulting." The meeting with the British ambassador lasted only eight minutes, during which the Dalai Lama disclaimed any responsibility for the events leading up to the British expedition of 1904. After the audience, the Dalai Lama's attendants asked for, and later received, the texts, in English, of the 1907 Anglo-Russian Convention relating to Tibet and the 1908 trade regulations.[63]

The Dalai Lama departed Peking on 21 December, reaching Kumbum on 26 February 1909. At Kumbum, he received the investiture of his title

---

60. Extract from the Peking Gazette of 3rd November, 1908, Imperial Decree issued in the name of the Empress-Dowager (Translation), *British Parliamentary Papers: Further Papers Relating to Tibet*, Cd. 5240 (1910), vol. 68, 170.

61. Shakabpa, *Tibet: A Political History*, 222.

62. Eric Teichman, *Travels of a Consular Officer in Eastern Tibet* (Cambridge: Cambridge University Press, 1922), 14.

63. Lamb, *McMahon Line*, 178. Lamb states that these diplomatic contacts had been initiated on behalf of the Dalai Lama by Dorjiev, who had rejoined the Lama at Peking, who hoped that international support would bolster the Dalai Lama's position with the Chinese. Dorjiev found, however, that Britain and Russia had, by agreement among themselves, decided against interference in Tibetan affairs. The British found Dorjiev to be a simple and honest monk, devoted not to international scheming on behalf of the Russian czar, as the British had imagined, but to assisting the Dalai Lama in the preservation of Tibetan autonomy, now greatly threatened by Chinese advances in Tibet. Ibid.

from the Sining *amban*. The Dalai Lama's new title of "Loyally
Submissive Vice-gerent," and China's title of "Sovereign State" in Tibet,
clearly stated China's claim to full sovereignty over Tibet. The Dalai
Lama's humiliating treatment in Peking made it apparent that the nature
of Tibet's relationship with China had been altered and Tibet's precarious
autonomy was no longer guaranteed. The traditional relationship of
patron and priest, to which the Dalai Lama repeatedly referred in meetings with the Chinese and with foreign representatives, obviously no
longer existed. Tibetan autonomy had suffered from the absence of the
Dalai Lama from Lhasa, during which time the Chinese had increased
their political control in central Tibet and had made advances into Kham
from Szechuan. Tibet was faced with effective incorporation within the
Chinese state.

Chinese Incursions in Eastern Tibet

The 1904 British expedition to Lhasa stimulated China to restore its
position in Lhasa and to advance the Chinese frontier from Szechuan.
Kham had theoretically been under the supervision of Szechuan since
K'ang-hsi's 1725 territorial division of Tibet. However, Chinese authority
in Kham consisted of little more than military posts that provided for the
post system and transport of Chinese officials from Szechuan to Lhasa.
Lhasa regained control of part of eastern Kham by intervening in the 1860
revolt in Nyarong. Chinese control over the southern route through
Lithang and Batang was weakened by a revolt of Lithang monastery in
1894.[64]

In 1900 the Szechuan governor-general, Lu Ch'uan-lin, submitted a
memorial containing his arguments in favor of the imposition of direct
Chinese rule in Nyarong and eastern Kham. Lu remained at the Ch'ing
court until his death in 1910 and no doubt had an influence in favor of a
forward policy on the Tibetan frontier. Lu was replaced as Szechuan governor-general in 1900 by Hsi-liang, a Mongol, who in mid-1903 received
a proposal from the Grand Council in Peking to establish a special commissionership to promote Chinese colonization, commerce and mining in
Kham.[65] In March 1904 Hsi-liang approved a proposal of the senior *amban*

---

64. S.A.M. Adshead, *Province and Politics in Late Imperial China: Viceregional Government in
Szechuan, 1898-1911* (London: Curzon Press, 1984), 57.

65. Ibid., 58. This proposal was contemporaneous with the shift in Ch'ing policy on
Chinese colonization. Ch'ing Dynasty policy had prohibited Chinese colonization beyond
the Great Wall. But, by the end of the nineteenth century the Manchu had adopted more
typically Han Chinese attitudes and policies. In addition, many more Han officials had
assumed official positions and, fearing the loss of control over frontier territories, had
adopted traditional Chinese frontier assimilationist policies. Peter S.H. Tang, *Russian and
Soviet Policy in Manchuria and Outer Mongolia, 1911-1931* (Durham: Duke University Press,
1959), 294.

at Lhasa that the junior *amban* be transferred from Lhasa to Chamdo with a garrison of 500 men.[66] In October an edict, which began by referring to the British expedition, called upon all Chinese officials to exhibit an energetic response and made the Chamdo *amban* responsible for Kham.[67] In June Feng Ch'uang, a former police chief of Chengdu, was appointed *amban* for Chamdo. In September Hsi-liang proposed the establishment of a military-agricultural colony at Hor Drango, the most centrally situated of the five Hor states on the north road. At the end of October an edict from Peking directed that, in view of the British expedition to Lhasa, the Tibetan protectorate in Nyarong should be abolished and direct Chinese rule established there.[68]

Feng Ch'uang arrived at Batang enroute to Chamdo at the end of 1904. Batang, which lay in the valley of the upper Yangtze at a relatively low altitude, was suitable for Chinese colonization; Feng therefore remained at Batang to establish the first colony. Batang was already the site of a French Catholic missionary station; the French had themselves promoted Chinese colonization due to their lack of success in making Tibetan converts. Feng, who regarded lamas as parasites, was particularly undiplomatic in his treatment of them. Feng attempted to limit the power of the monasteries by prohibiting them from accepting recruits for a period of twenty years. Resentment against Feng escalated until in March 1905 the Batang Tibetans revolted, killing Feng, the Chinese colonists and two French Catholic priests. The revolt spread to Chamdo, Lithang and Nyarong. Chinese control was temporarily lost all along the south road; Tibetan cavalry were reportedly threatening Tachienlu.[69]

Despite the Batang Tibetans' protestations that the revolt had been caused by the arrogance of Feng, Szechuan officials mounted a punitive expedition intended to reaffirm Chinese authority.[70] A force of 2,000 men was dispatched from Szechuan, led by Ma Wei-ch'i, the Szechuan military commander, and a Manchu magistrate of Szechuan, Chao Erh-feng. Ma arrived in Batang in mid-summer; he executed local Tibetan officials and exiled their families to China. Chao, who had been left at Lithang to secure the supply route, did the same with officials of Lithang who resist-

66. Adshead, *Province and Politics*, 58.

67. Ibid., 61.

68. Ibid., 62. Chinese administration was not established in Nyarong until 1911.

69. Teichman, *Travels of a Consular Officer*, 20; Elliot Sperling, "The Chinese Venture in Kham, 1904-11, and the Role of Chao Erh-feng," *Tibet Journal*, vol. 1, no. 2 (1976), 13.

70. A Chinese historian claimed that the Tibetans were not rebelling against Chinese administration but against what they thought were "foreigners," presumably British, since "Feng's bodyguard had adopted the foreign style of uniform and had a foreign band; the natives supposed that they were officered by foreigners." Adshead, *Province and Politics*, 66.

ed his demands for transport. After Chao arrived in Batang, the abbots of the local monastery were executed and the monastery was burned. In September Ma returned to a hero's welcome in Chengdu, leaving Chao Erh-feng in command in Batang. In Chengdu, a temple was erected to the spirit of Feng, who had given his life for the "advance of civilization."[71]

In April 1906 in Batang Chao announced: "The head T'u Ssu (native chieftain) and the assistant T'u Ssu having been beheaded, the office of T'u Ssu is hereby abolished for ever. Both the Chinese and the tribesmen of Batang are henceforth subjects of the Emperor of China, and subject to the jurisdiction of Chinese officials."[72] Chao Erh-feng put down a revolt of a monastery to the south on the Yunnan border, Chantreng Gompa. Chao mounted a siege of the strongly defended monastery that lasted several months, finally overcoming the monks by deceit. All of the monks who surrendered were executed.[73] Chao returned to Chengdu in November 1906 and was rewarded by being named frontier commissioner, a post created by the Ch'ing court as part of a new forward policy in Kham.[74] The frontier commissionship, which was created for the limited purpose of "reclaiming waste lands and settling them with troops," became under Chao Erh-feng the means for abolishing the old system of native rule in favor of direct Chinese administration and colonization.

Chao initiated a series of reforms in the areas of Kham under his control. Tibetans were thenceforth required to pay taxes to Chinese officials and were to cease observing any obligations, including taxes, to native officials or monasteries. Chinese temples were to replace Tibetan monasteries; Tibetan monasteries could continue to exist but were limited to a maximum of 300 monks. Lamas were not allowed to interfere in any way with Chinese administration. Chinese schools were to be established. The "barbarous methods of burial" practiced by the Tibetans were to be abolished. Tibetans were required to adopt Chinese surnames. Every man was required to shave his forehead in the Manchu style and wear the queue: "No one will be permitted to have his hair in the dishevelled state hitherto the custom, which makes men resemble living demons." Nomadic and semi-nomadic Tibetans were to be sedentarized and forced to adopt agriculture, from which it was presumed that culture and civilization would naturally evolve.[75]

---

71. Ibid.; Sperling, "Chinese Venture in Kham," 15.

72. Despatch from the Acting Consul-General, Cheng-tu, to Sir J. Jordan, 29 December 1906: Regulations for the future Administration of Batang, *Parliamentary Papers:* Cd. 5240 (1910), 98.

73. Adshead, *Province and Politics*, 68; Sperling, "Chinese Venture in Kham," 18.

74. Adshead, *Province and Politics*, 72.

75. Ibid., 99. Neither the queue nor any of the other requirements for Chinese acculturation were adopted by the Tibetans of Kham.

Chao's program for the repression of monastic influence represented a departure from the traditional Yuan, Ming and Ch'ing policy of maintaining influence in Tibet through patronage of Buddhism. Chao, like many Chinese before him and after, thought that he could break the spiritual and economic hold of the monasteries by publicly revealing their economic exploitation and by disproving the reputed spiritual powers of the lamas. An essential element of Chao's program was colonization. Chinese settlers were to be provided with travel expenses, food and free land. Colonists were intended to establish a core population loyal to China and provide an example of civilized ways for the natives to emulate. In a proclamation to potential colonists, Chao promised that local bandits and thieves had been suppressed, Chinese officials installed and Chinese justice instituted, so that settlers need fear no harm from the natives:

> Formerly in the districts beyond Ta Chien Lu [Dartsendo] the Grain Commissaries there established concerned themselves solely with the providing of transport and the forwarding of supplies, and Chinese subjects who were oppressed by the natives or involved in land disputes had no official to whom they could appeal. The troops stationed beyond the frontier were formerly so few in numbers that they only sufficed to fulfill the functions of couriers, and were totally inadequate to protect the people who lived in constant fear of violence from the mountain robbers. . . . All anxiety from these causes is now at an end. The native Rulers have been abolished for ever and their families deported to China. Who will now prevent you from going there?
>
> . . . Emigrants who bring up their families will find that they can live much more economically than in China. The unmarried man, on the other hand, will find the women more numerous than the men among the border tribes. The females, moreover, are industrious, and the males lazy. A native girl taken as wife will prove of great assistance in the work, for these women perform all the carrying of water, cooking of food, hoeing of the ground, and cutting of firewood. Nor is any dowry necessary, for all that is needed are garments in which to clothe her.[76]

Hsi-liang was transferred from Szechuan in March 1907 and Chao Erh-feng was appointed as interim governor-general. In March 1908 Chao Erh-feng's brother, Chao Erh-hsun, was appointed governor-general of Szechuan; Chao Erh-feng was appointed *amban* at Chamdo

---

76. Proclamation issued by his Excellency Chao Erh Feng, Commissioner in charge of the Yunnan-Szechuan Frontier, calling for settlers for the new District of Batang, 7 February 1907, *Parliamentary Papers*, Cd. 5240 (1910), 109.

and retained his position as frontier commissioner. The Ch'ing court, in an edict of 9 March 1908, shortly before the Dalai Lama was summoned to Peking, announced an ambitious program of military advances, administrative reorganization, colonization and civilization of the natives of the Tibetan frontier to be implemented by the Chao brothers and the Lhasa *amban*, Lien-yu.[77] Peking would contribute some of the necessary financing but substantial contributions would also be required of Szechuan.[78]

With political and financial backing assured, Chao Erh-feng was prepared to implement his plans for the colonization of Kham. In 1908 Chao returned to Kham along with 2,000 troops he was to send to Lhasa to be placed under the command of the Lhasa *amban*. While in Tachienlu, Chao received news of trouble in Derge and immediately requested permission to proceed there. The troops intended for Lhasa continued along the southern route under the command of Chung Ying. Chao arrived in Derge, where he intervened in a succession dispute and installed the candidate of his choice (much as Lu Ch'uan-lin had done in 1895). Chao thus gained control (although resistance was not finally crushed until May 1909) of one of the most important and previously most independent districts of Kham.[79]

The new prince of Derge was induced to "request" that Derge be taken under direct Chinese administration and that Chao's program for Kham, including Chinese colonization, be implemented. Peking responded on 25 January 1910, approving Chao's recommendation that "the native state of Derge should be allowed to adopt our civilization and come under our direct rule."[80] Chao justified the imposition of Chinese administration as a natural and inevitable process:

> When the wild tribes submitted to China, native states were created in various provinces, and on account of the customs of these tribes differing from China official rank and authority were given to the chiefs in the hope of keeping the districts quiet. As regards the administration of these states, the Viceroys and Governors were to investigate, and degrade and promote when necessary. Moreover, it is laid down in the imperial institutes of the reigning dynasty, that native chiefs who do not govern properly must be

77. Adshead, *Province and Politics*, 78; Sperling, "Chinese Venture in Kham," 24.

78. Adshead, *Province and Politics*, 82.

79. Ibid., 87.

80. Memorial by the Reform Council in reply to a Memorial from Chao Erh Feng, Warden of the Tibetan Marches, proposing that the Native State of Derge should be brought under direct Chinese rule, Extract from "Gazette" of the 27th January, 1910 (translation), *Parliamentary Papers*, Cd. 5240 (1910), 192.

denounced and punished, either by the substitution of other chiefs or by their territory reverting to China. Accordingly, whenever a case occurred of disturbance in a native state, we have, after careful consideration, established a prefecture or magistracy in its place.[81]

A similar proposal by Chao to take over direct administration of Nyarong was refused by Peking out of concern for upsetting the agreement it had made with the Dalai Lama at Peking in 1908.[82] In the spring of 1909 Chao resigned as junior *amban*, a move that reflected his primary interest in establishing Chinese administration in Kham. Chao's frontier commissionership, however, was expanded to include Chamdo, Dragyab and Markham in western Kham, beyond the previous border at the Yangtze-Mekong divide.[83]

By August 1909 the troops under Chung Ying had reached Markham, which, unlike some of the other small states of western Kham such as Chamdo and Dragyab, was directly administered by Lhasa.[84] Here the Chinese encountered opposition from local Tibetans organized by Tibetan Government officials (demonstrating that the Ch'ing *amban* had little control over the Tibetan Government). The expedition attempted to deviate to the northern route via Chamdo but was again stopped by Tibetan resistance. The Tibetans simultaneously advanced upon Batang. Chao Erh-feng dispatched troops to assist the expedition in its attempt to reach Lhasa. Chao proceeded with his troops to Chamdo, which he had to take by force. Some of Chao's troops were dispatched to the south to retake Markham; the rest accompanied the Lhasa expedition through Shobando, fighting several engagements with the Tibetans, to Giamda, where they stopped, leaving the original expedition to proceed alone to Lhasa.

In February 1910 Chinese troops were at Giamda, prepared to march on Lhasa. Tibetans assumed that the Chinese troops advancing to Lhasa were being led by Chao, by now known to Tibetans as "Butcher Chao."

---

81. Ibid. "Submission" of tribes or states was inevitably interpreted by the Chinese as the acceptance of Chinese rule in principle and as justification for its eventual imposition in fact.

82. Adshead, *Province and Politics*, 86. Presumably, part of the agreement at Peking was that China would respect Lhasa's authority in Nyarong.

83. Ibid., 87.

84. Teichman, *Travels of a Consular Officer*, 130. Chamdo and Dragyab were indirectly administered by Lhasa through local monastic authorities. Riwoche and Pagsho "states" were actually estates of the Taglung Kagyudpa sect and the Kundeling Gelugpa monasteries, respectively. Gonjo was indirectly administered through local authorities of Markham. Geoffrey Samuel, *Civilized Shamans: Buddhism in Tibetan Societies* (Washington: Smithsonian Institution Press, 1994), 76.

The Dalai Lama, who had arrived in Lhasa in late December 1909, appealed to foreign countries to request the Ch'ing emperor to cease the invasion of Tibet. Another appeal was sent to the emperor (the child Pu-yi) asking that he restrain his officials in Kham; since the Dalai Lama had been promised in 1908 that the excesses of Chinese officials in Kham, Chao in particular, would be curbed, the Dalai Lama diplomatically assumed that the emperor did not know what his subordinates were doing.[85] On 12 February when the Chinese advance force entered Lhasa, firing on Tibetans in the streets, the Dalai Lama and his government officials fled. The Chinese, not knowing if he had fled north to seek assistance from the Russians or south to the British, sent out troops in both directions to bring him back.

In the meantime, Chao, who had returned to Kham from Giamda, was busily consolidating Chinese control in Kham, instituting direct Chinese administration in the Hor states, Nyarong, Chamdo and Markham. By late 1911 all of Kham was under Chinese control. However, although achieving initial success, Chinese advances into Kham and central Tibet resulted in several negative consequences for Chinese policy. The flight of the Dalai Lama only shortly after his return to Lhasa was embarrassing; not only was the legitimating authority of the Dalai Lama lost to the Chinese, but his response to the introduction of Chinese troops into Lhasa was identical to his response to the British invasion in 1904, revealing that Tibetans regarded both the Chinese and the British as foreign invaders. The Chinese had miscalculated in assuming that the Dalai Lama was prepared to be truly loyal and submissive and that the actual imposition of Chinese administration into Kham and the introduction of Chinese troops into central Tibet would be accepted by the Tibetans. In addition, the expenditures incurred by the Szechuan treasury in supporting the advance of Chinese troops into Tibet were one of the factors contributing to a financial collapse in Szechuan in 1911, leading to a revolt against the Ch'ing authorities in Szechuan and to the revolution of 1911, the fall of the Ch'ing dynasty and the subsequent loss of the Chinese position in Tibet.[86]

---

85. Letter from the Political Officer, Sikkim, to the Secretary to the Government of India, Foreign Department, 21 December 1909: Telegram from the Dalai Lama and Council of Tibet to Great Britain and all the Ministers of Europe, *Parliamentary Papers*, Cd. 5240 (1910), 187.

86. In Adshead's opinion, "Without its new imperial role [in Tibet], Chengdu might have avoided the crisis of 1911, and the empire might have escaped the revolution." Adshead, *Province and Politics*, 85.

The Dalai Lama in India

The Dalai Lama and his party evaded a Chinese pursuit and crossed into Sikkim on 21 February 1910. The Chinese Government issued a proclamation on 25 February deposing him and directing that a new incarnation be found. This proclamation reveals much about the late Ch'ing's interpretation of its relation with Tibet:

> The Dalai Lama of Tibet has received abundant favors from the hands of Our Imperial predecessors. He should have devoutly cultivated the precepts of religion in accordance with established precedent in order to propagate the doctrines of the Yellow Church. But, ever since he assumed control of the administration, he has shown himself proud, extravagant, lewd, slothful, vicious, and perverse without parallel, violent and disorderly, disobedient to the Imperial Commands, and oppressive towards the Tibetans.

> In July, 1904, he fled during the troubles, and was denounced by the Imperial Amban to Us as lacking in reliability. A Decree was then issued depriving him temporarily of his Titles. He proceeded to Urga, whence he returned again to Sining. We, mindful of his distant flight, and hoping that he would repent and reform his evil ways, ordered the local officials to pay him due attention. The year before last he came to Peking, was received in Audience, granted new Titles, and presented with gifts. On his way back to Tibet he loitered and caused trouble; yet every indulgence was shown to him in order to manifest Our compassion. In Our generosity we forgave the past.

> Szechuan troops have now been sent into Tibet for the special purpose of preserving order and protecting the Trade Marts. There was no reason for the Tibetans to be suspicious of their intentions. But the Dalai Lama spread rumours, became rebellious, defamed the Amban, refused supplies, and would not listen to reason. When the Amban telegraphed that the Dalai Lama had fled during the night of February 12 on the arrival of the Szechuan troops, We commanded that steps be taken to bring him back. At present, however, his whereabouts are unknown. He has been guilty of treachery, and has placed himself beyond the pale of Our Imperial favor. He has shown base ingratitude toward his superiors, and has failed to carry out his duty towards his inferiors. He is not fit to be a Reincarnation of Buddha. Let him therefore be deprived of his Titles and of his position as Dalai Lama as a punishment. Henceforth, no matter where he may go, no matter where he may reside, whether in Tibet or elsewhere, let him be treated as an ordinary individual. Let the Imperial Amban at once cause a search to be made for male children bearing the miraculous signs and let him inscribe their names on tablets and place them in the Golden Urn, so that one may be drawn out as the true Reincarnation of previous Dalai Lamas. Let the matter be reported to Us, so that Our Imperial favor may be

bestowed upon the selected child, who will thus continue the propagation of the doctrine and glorification of the Church.

We reward Virtue that Vice may suffer. You, lamas and laymen of Tibet, are Our children. Let all obey the laws and preserve the Peace. Let none disregard Our desire to support the Yellow Church and maintain the tranquility of Our frontier territories.[87]

The Chinese Government maintained that their deposition of the Dalai Lama "merely personally concerns the Dalai Lama as a man." The Chinese Foreign Ministry claimed that the Dalai Lama, because of his numerous faults, was "extremely detested by the people." Precedents for China's deposing of Tibetan high lamas were cited, including the example of the Sixth Dalai Lama. China claimed to the British that troops had been sent to Tibet only to police the trade marts and to meet Tibet's obligations toward neighboring states, as required by Chinese agreements with the British.[88] The Chinese also requested the British to ignore "false reports spread by lamaists as to outrages and burning of monasteries."[89]

The Dalai Lama remained in India, at Darjeeling, from 1910 to 1912. His requests for assistance were refused by the Government of India, despite his warnings that Chinese imperial ambitions were not confined to Tibet but extended to Nepal, Sikkim, Bhutan and even India. The Dalai Lama claimed that past difficulties between Tibet and the British were all the fault of the Chinese; he had been prohibited by the Chinese, he said, from responding to letters from Curzon and Younghusband.[90] The Dalai Lama also stated that Tibet could not recognize the treaties of 1890 and 1906 made by China on Tibet's behalf.[91]

In March 1912 a Tibetan official, Lonchen Shatra, requested that the Indian foreign secretary, Sir Henry McMahon, escort the Dalai Lama back to Lhasa and that Britain become Tibet's temporal patron. Shatra report-

---

87. "Imperial Decree of February 25, 1910 (Translated from the *Government Gazette*)," as quoted in Teichman, *Travels of a Consular Officer*, 16. Perhaps the most striking thing about the imperial decree is that the Chinese Government presumed to treat the Dalai Lama as just another appointed official whose position could be revoked at will. This presumption depends upon the authority that the Ch'ing had claimed since 1793 to confirm the Dalai Lama's reincarnation.

88. Despatch from Mr. Max Muller to Sir Edward Grey, (Peking), 14 March 1910: Note from the Wai-wu Pu to Sir J. Jordan, 9 March 1910, *Parliamentary Papers*, Cd. 5240 (1910), 211.

89. Mr. Max Muller to Sir Edward Grey, (Peking), 26 February 1910, *Parliamentary Papers*, Cd. 5240 (1910), 196.

90. Viceroy to Secretary of State for India, 3 March 1910, *Parliamentary Papers*, Cd. 5240 (1910), 200.

91. Viceroy to Secretary of State for India, 17 March 1910, *Parliamentary Papers*, Cd. 5240 (1910), 206.

edly said that Tibet, being a religious country, could not exist without another country to help and support it.[92] The British explained that they could not assist Tibet because Britain was bound by the 1907 Anglo-Russian Treaty. The Dalai Lama was greatly disappointed by the lack of British support; nevertheless, a relationship was established between the Dalai Lama and British Indian officials that was to play a significant role in future Tibetan relations with British India.

The British Government's rationale for imperial adventures on the Indian frontier had faded since the rapprochement with Russia. The British were prepared to be content with the new Chinese position in Tibet, as well as with the continuing exile of the Dalai Lama in India, if the Chinese would respect their treaty obligations to facilitate trade between Tibet and India. At the same time, however, they had to be concerned by the increase in Chinese troops in Tibet. The British felt obliged to warn the Chinese of the "inadvisability of locating troops upon or in the neighborhood of the frontiers of India and the adjoining States in such numbers as would necessitate corresponding movements on the part of the Government of India and the rulers of the States concerned."[93]

In the Dalai Lama's absence from Lhasa, the Chinese attempted to set up the Panchen Lama in his place (the idea of selecting another incarnation of the Dalai Lama having proved utterly unacceptable to Tibetans). The Panchen went along with this scheme to the extent of occupying the Dalai Lama's Norbulinka quarters and participating in official ceremonies with the *amban*, but the Panchen stopped short of assuming the Dalai Lama's temporal authority. The Chinese had by this time realized the difficulties in ruling Tibet without the Dalai Lama (or in appointing a new incarnation while the present one was still alive). At the same time, they were very anxious about allowing the Dalai Lama to return to Lhasa. The British ambassador in Peking, Max Muller, reported that the Chinese were contemplating inviting the Dalai Lama to Peking, where he would be set up as "head of the Lamaist church in some temple in the neighbourhood." Veneration of the Lama would be permitted, but not "political agitation."[94]

---

92. Lamb, *McMahon Line*, 415. The Dalai Lama made essentially the same offer—to put Tibet under the protection of the British—in his communications with Charles Bell. "The Thirteenth Dalai Lama's rebuttal of Chinese charges," 2 May 1910, quoted in Parshotam Mehra, *The Northeastern Frontier: A Documentary Study of the Internecine Rivalry between India, Tibet and China* (Delhi: Oxford University Press, 1979), vol. 1, 25.

93. Letter from the Under-Secretary of State, India Office, to the Under-Secretary of State, Foreign Office, 31 March 1910, *Parliamentary Papers*, Cd. 5240 (1910), 213.

94. Mehra, *Tibetan Polity*, 23.

Finally, in September 1910 the *amban* invited the Dalai Lama to return to Lhasa, offering to rescind the deposition order. The offer stated that the Dalai Lama could reside in the Potala and resume his religious functions but would be allowed no political role. The Panchen Lama also wrote to the Dalai Lama inviting him to return, but the Panchen also conveyed a secret message explaining that his letter was written under orders from the *amban* and warning the Dalai Lama not to return unless his safety was guaranteed by the British.[95] The Chinese were able to contemplate a return of the Dalai Lama to Tibet because of the military and administrative control they had achieved in the two years of his absence. Between 1910 and 1912 the Chinese increased their military control of Lhasa and central Tibet, building a barracks for their troops in Lhasa at Drapchi capable of housing 1,200 men and opening a Chinese school.[96] Another 500 troops were reportedly at Giamda and 500 at Larigo, both on the border between western Kham and central Tibet.[97]

In a long letter of reply to the Chinese Government, the Dalai Lama refused to return to Tibet under the current conditions. The Dalai Lama complained of the invasion of eastern Tibet and the complicity of the *amban* in the advance of Chinese troops to Lhasa. He revealed that he had restrained Tibetan officials from forcibly resisting the Chinese troops; had he not done so, "it would not have been impossible for us to defeat your army, owing to our knowledge of the terrain."[98] He stated that he had fled Tibet to avoid "a situation similar to the Muslim invasion of India," and that, upon arrival in India, he had found that he had been deposed by the Chinese Government:

> Since the Emperor has done everything on the recommendation of the Manchu Amban in Lhasa, without considering the independence [*rang wang*] of Tibet and the religious relationship between our two countries, I feel there is no further use in my negotiating directly with China. I have lost confidence in China and in finding any solution in consultation with the Chinese.
>
> I have contacted the British because the 1904 Convention permits us to deal directly with them. The Chinese are responsible for this action of mine. . . .

---

95. Ibid., 24.

96. Lamb, *McMahon Line*, 273.

97. From Viceroy to Secretary of State for India, 11 April 1910, *Parliamentary Papers*, Cd. 5240 (1910), 215.

98. "Letter of 13th Dalai Lama to Lo T'i-t'ai, Chinese representative in India," as quoted in Shakabpa, *Tibet: A Political History*, 234. The Dalai Lama complained that the *amban* had broken the promise made to him by the Chinese Government in Peking in 1908 that the Dalai Lama would have the same powers as before in governing Tibet. Viceroy to Secretary of State for India, 2 March 1910, *Parliamentary Papers*, Cd. 5240 (1910), 199.

Because of the above, it is not possible for China and Tibet to have the same relationship as before. In order for us to negotiate, a third party is necessary; therefore we would both request the British Government to act as an intermediary. Our future policy will be based on the outcome of discussions between ourselves, the Chinese and the British.[99]

In January 1911 Chao Erh-feng was appointed governor-general of Szechuan and was replaced as frontier commissioner by General Fu Sung-mu. (Shortly thereafter, Chao Erh-feng was murdered by anti-Ch'ing revolutionaries.) Fu submitted a memorial in August 1911 proposing that Kham be converted into a new province to be known as Sikang, "West-Kham." The 1911 revolution against the Ch'ing precluded action on this proposal; however, Fu's memorial, and a later pamphlet on the subject, reveal that the stimuli to Chinese advances into Tibet were both political and cultural:

The frontier territory lies between Szechuan in the east and Tibet in the west and is bounded by the Kokonor Territory in the north and Yunnan Province in the south. It was formerly divided up into more than twenty Native states and Tribes, the inhabitants of which, while paying tribute to the Emperor, were not actually Chinese subjects. The time has now come when this whole region should be converted into a regular province, which should be named Hsikang. The frontier regions in question march with Tibet and beyond Tibet lies the territory of a mighty Power. This Power is closely watching Tibet, which it no longer regards as a dependency of China. By converting the frontier regions of Kam into a Chinese province we shall secure ourselves against territorial aggression.[100]

Kham was formerly quite distinct from Tibet, and the original boundary between the two should be restored. The creation of Kham as a province will thus secure territorial annexation as well as supplying a distinguishing name. ... As Mencius says, the savages have been converted into Chinese. Today, mighty cities of China were once the haunt of barbarians, even as the tribes of Kham before their acquisition of Chinese citizenship. On the creation of a province out of Kham, it too becomes a part of the glorious empire, and in its turn Kham has savage tribes [central Tibetans] on its frontier.[101]

---

99. "Letter of 13th Dalai Lama to Lo T'i-t'ai," as quoted in Shakabpa, *Tibet: A Political History*, 236.

100. Fu Sung-mu, as quoted in Teichman, *Travels of a Consular Officer*, 33.

101. "From the `History of the Creation of Hsi-Kang Province,' by General Fu Sung-mu," in Mehra, *Northeastern Frontier*, vol. 1, 189. The need to "supply a distinguishing name" for Kham—to distinguish Kham from Tibet—reveals the artificial nature of "Sikang" and the incremental nature of Chinese territorial encroachment on Tibet. Presumably, the time when Kham was "quite distinct from Tibet," to which Fu referred, was the 1725 administrative division by the Ch'ing.

The "province of Sikang" was to include 33 districts (*hsien*), 27 already established by Chao east of the Salween as well as six districts yet to be established west of the Salween in Shobando, Sangachu Dzong, Zayul, Lari (Larigo), Pomed (Powo) and Giamda.[102] Chao Erh-feng had in 1910 announced a plan for Chinese colonization in Zayul, which, due to its relatively low altitude, was thought to be suitable for rice cultivation. Zayul bordered the tribal area of Assam, which was claimed but not administered by British India; Chao's move thus brought the Chinese frontier and Chinese colonists into proximity to Indian territory for the first time.

Chinese penetration into areas bordering upon unadministered territories claimed by India alarmed the GOI, which, for the first time, began to contemplate the implications of a direct frontier with China. The British were particularly concerned about the Tibetan district of Tawang, to the east of Bhutan, which formed a salient penetrating almost to the plains of the Brahmaputra valley in Assam. Tawang's conversion into Chinese territory could pose a significant threat to India. The Chinese presence in Tibet also raised the possibility that the Chinese would attempt to convert their vague claims to suzerainty over Nepal, Bhutan and Sikkim into something more substantial.[103] British fears of a drastic alteration in the status of their northern Indian frontier were expressed in a *London Morning Post* article of 1910:

> A great Empire, the future military strength of which no man can foresee, has suddenly appeared on the North-East Frontier of India. . . . The men who advocated the retention of Lhasa, have proved not so far wrong. . . . China, in a word, has come to the gates of India, and the fact has to be reckoned with.[104]

British policy in regard to China and Tibet had greatly underestimated the capability of the declining Ch'ing to take action in its Inner Asian interior. The Ch'ing still had interests and capabilities in frontier areas unique to conquest dynasties. The Ch'ing Empire had been constructed in Inner Asia; these territories therefore had special significance for Ch'ing legitimacy. As Premen Addy has pointed out, the Ch'ing were also sensitive to their Inner Asian possessions because this was an area of their greatest weakness in terms of ethnic unity:

---

102. Fu Sung-mu, in Teichman, *Travels of a Consular Officer*, 35.

103. The Nepalese sent their last tributary mission to Peking in 1908. In 1911 the British declared China's suzerainty over Nepal at an end; Britain's authority to do so was challenged by neither Nepal nor China. Lamb, *McMahon Line*, 281.

104. "China as India's Neighbor," excerpts from the *Morning Post*, 28 February 1910, in Mehra, *Northeastern Frontier*, vol. 1, 15.

It was in China's outlying dependencies, sparsely populated and inhabited largely by non-Chinese subjects, where her authority was most vulnerable. It was here, therefore, that she faced the greatest need to assert her sovereign rights and have them recognized by the international community, even if the administrative control normally associated with such claims had to await a more favorable hour. In China proper the strong bond of national identity compensated for the weakness of the Central Government.[105]

By 1911 the Ch'ing had restored its lapsed authority in Tibet to an extent that, had the Ch'ing dynasty not soon fallen, Tibet would very likely have been incorporated within the Chinese state and would have ceased to exist as a separate political entity. Instead, Tibet was granted a temporary reprieve. However, China, though temporarily impotent, had been sufficiently aroused by Britain's forcible entrance into Tibetan affairs that it was now determined to impose direct Chinese control upon Tibet at the first opportunity.

In October 1911 the revolution against the Ch'ing began; on 12 February 1912 the last Ch'ing emperor abdicated, and, on the 15th Yuan Shih-k'ai was elected president of the new Chinese Republic. Chinese troops in Tibet mutinied and looted Lhasa. In April the Chinese garrison in Lhasa surrendered to the Tibetans but refused to be repatriated to China in the hopes that an expedition from the east would come to their rescue. The Chinese Republican government attempted to make the Chinese garrison commander in Lhasa their representative, but this move was resisted by the Tibetans, who demanded the evacuation of all Chinese soldiers and officials from Tibet. Chinese troops were finally removed from Tibet, via India, at the end of 1912.

The Dalai Lama reentered Tibet in July 1912, taking up residence at Samding Monastery near the lake Yamdrok Yumtso until the last of the Chinese garrison could be removed. There he was again joined by Dorjiev, travelling overland from Russia, where he had been engaged in the establishment of a Buddhist temple in St. Petersburg. Dorjiev's presence in Tibet was now uncomfortable for the Dalai Lama, who wished to rely upon British patronage and eliminate any suspicion of Tibetan intrigues with the Russians. Dorjiev was therefore entrusted by the Dalai Lama with powers to establish Tibetan relations with newly independent Outer Mongolia.[106] In January 1913 the Dalai Lama finally returned to Lhasa. Tibet was free of the Chinese for the first time since 1720.

---

105. Addy, *Tibet on the Imperial Chessboard*, 208.
106. Snelling, *Buddhism in Russia*, 148.

The Tibetan Declaration of Independence and the Tibet-Mongolia Treaty

The new Chinese Republic quickly moved to salvage at least the appearance of Chinese authority in Tibet. In a presidential mandate of 28 October 1912, Yuan Shih-k'ai restored the rank and title of the Dalai Lama:

> Now that the Republic has been firmly established and the Five Races united into one family, the Dalai Lama is naturally moved with a feeling of deep attachment to the mother country. Under the circumstances his former errors should be overlooked, and his Title of Loyal and Submissive Vice-Gerent, Great, Good and Self Existent Buddha is hereby restored to him, in the hope that he may prove a support to the Yellow Church and a help to the Republic.[107]

The Dalai Lama replied, according to Charles Bell, who was present in Lhasa, "that he was not asking the Chinese Government for any rank, as he intended to exercise both temporal and spiritual rule."[108] The Dalai Lama issued a proclamation to Tibetans describing the history of Tibet's *Cho-Yon* relationship with China and the course of recent events:

> During the time of Genghis Khan of the Mongols, the Ming dynasty of the Chinese, and the Ch'ing dynasty of the Manchus, Tibet and China co-operated on the basis of benefactor and priest relationship. A few years ago, the Chinese authorities in Szechuan and Yunnan endeavored to colonize our territory. They brought large numbers of troops into central Tibet on the pretext of policing the trade marts. I, therefore, left Lhasa with my ministers for the Indo-Tibetan border, hoping to clarify to the Manchu Emperor by wire that the existing relationship between Tibet and China had been that of patron and priest and had not been based on the subordination of one to the other.[109]

The Dalai Lama's proclamation to the Tibetan people, along with his refusal of rank from the Chinese Republic, are regarded by Tibetans as a Tibetan declaration of independence from China.[110]

The Republican regime at first blamed the former Manchu regime and the Lhasa *amban* for the actions of Chinese troops that had led to the flight of the Dalai Lama. The Tibetans generally agreed that the *amban*, along

---

107. "Presidential Mandate of 28 October 1912," *Government Gazette*, as quoted in Teichman, Travels of a Consular Officer, 17.

108. Bell, *Portrait of a Dalai Lama*, 155.

109. "Dalai Lama's Proclamation," as quoted in Shakabpa, *Tibet: A Political History*, 246.

110. Shakabpa, *Tibet: A Political History*, 246.

with Chao Erh-feng, had been responsible, but they were no longer prepared to trust any Chinese promises or accept Chinese authority over Tibet. The *amban*, Lien Yu, who had been particularly despised by the Lhasa Tibetans for his arrogance and deceitfulness, returned to Peking, where he laid all blame for the fiasco in Tibet on the military commander, Chung Ying. Chung Ying was executed while Lien Yu went free, and the news of the execution of Chung Ying was conveyed to Lhasa as an example of Chinese justice.[111] This did little to mollify the Tibetans, whose dissatisfaction with Chinese rule was not confined to individual officials. The episode illustrates the inability of the Chinese to comprehend the reasons for Tibetan rejection of Chinese rule.

By the summer of 1912 the Chinese garrisons in Kham had been withdraw or had deserted after being attacked by the Tibetans. The Republican authorities of Szechuan attempted to salvage the situation by dispatching 5,000 troops under Yin Ch'ang-heng, a leader of the revolution in Szechuan (and the murderer of Chao Erh-feng). Yin regained control of most of Kham by the end of 1914, but at the cost of further Tibetan animosity. The Dalai Lama now realized that Tibet needed to be able to militarily protect itself; the Tibetan Army was reorganized on British principles and sent out to oppose the Chinese in Kham. The Tibetan Army repelled the Chinese from Shobando, Lho Dzong and Khyungpo, and established a line of Tibetan Government control along the watershed between the Salween and Mekong.[112]

The new Chinese Republic was meanwhile attempting to transform the Inner Asian dependencies of the Ch'ing into integral parts of the Chinese state. The Republican Government was propagating a doctrine of equality among the "Five Races" of China—the Chinese, Manchu, Mongols, Tibetans and Tatars (Turks: Uighurs, Kazakhs, Kirghiz)—the component parts of the former Ch'ing empire. The five races doctrine was premised upon the belief that frontier peoples wanted only equality of treatment under Chinese administration, not freedom from Chinese control altogether. The "five races" should "voluntarily unite" as integral parts of the new Chinese Republic in a new era of harmony and equality devoid of the feudal exploitation of the past:

> Now that the Five Races are joined in democratic union, the lands comprised within the confines of Mongolia, Tibet and Turkestan all become a part of the territory of the Republic of China, and the races inhabiting these lands are all equally citizens of the Republic of China. The term *dependencies*, as used under the Monarchy, must therefore cease to be used, and

---

111. Teichman, *Travels of a Consular Officer*, 40.
112. Ibid., 42.

henceforth, as regards Mongolia, Turkestan and Tibet a complete scheme must be devised to arrive at a unified system of administration, and so promote unity in general among all races of the Republic. The reason why the Republican Government did not create a special Ministry to deal with dependencies was that Mongolia, Turkestan and Tibet are regarded on an equal footing with the provinces of China proper. For the future all administrative matters in connection with these territories will come within the sphere of internal administration.[113]

Despite its pretensions to authority over the colonial possessions of the Ch'ing, the new Chinese government found itself in a weak position in Inner Asia. China now had little physical presence in Inner Asia, especially in Tibet or Outer Mongolia. Britain, Russia, France and Japan were attempting to secure spheres of influence in China's peripheral areas. Japan was interested in Manchuria and Inner Mongolia; Russia in Outer Mongolia and Sinkiang; France in Yunnan; and Britain in Tibet. The new Chinese government, furthermore, was in greater need of foreign support and recognition than the imperial powers were in need of good relations with China.

The Republican government's propaganda failed to convince the Tibetans or the Mongols to join the Chinese state. In 1911, Mongolia declared its independence.[114] A delegation of Mongol princes travelled to St. Petersburg in August 1911 and offered Russia a protectorate over Mongolia in exchange for support for Mongolia's independence of China.[115] The Russians encouraged the Mongols in their attempts to gain autonomy from China, but not independence. They provided 15,000 rifles and an equal number of sabres as assistance.[116]

Russia's ambitions in Mongolia were similar to those of Britain in Tibet: to gain exclusive trading and mineral exploration rights while avoiding having to undertake Mongolia's defense (which support for full independence would require). Russia was also inhibited by mutual agreement among the European powers to respect China's territorial integrity (a position favored by the United States). If Mongolia were independent, other imperial powers would be able to establish diplomatic

---

113. Lamb, *McMahon Line*, 391.

114. The Mongolian revolution was of a nationalist character, led by the feudal nobility. Chinese economic exploitation of the Mongols had resulted in much of the Mongol population being hopelessly indebted to Chinese merchants and much of Mongolia's production going just to pay interest on debts. C.R. Bawden, *The Modern History of Mongolia* (London: Kegan Paul, 1968; 1989), 189.

115. Bawden, 194. This was just a few months before the Tibetans made a similar offer to the British, in March 1912.

116. Friters, *Outer Mongolia*, 61.

and commercial relations there; the same would be the case should Mongolia remain a part of China, subject to the most-favored nation principle whereby all imperialist powers shared the privileges gained by any. Mongolian autonomy in foreign affairs and trade relations was the only solution that would secure exclusive rights and privileges for Russia, and could be rationalized as consistent with Russia's treaty relations. Russia feared that, if they did not support the Mongols, Japan might do so. Russia therefore attempted to secure by treaty with China a degree of autonomy for Mongolia sufficient for their own interests, much as Britain was attempting in Tibet.

China refused to negotiate the issue with the Mongols or the Russians, hoping to unilaterally reimpose Chinese control over Mongolia at some time in the future more to their advantage. Russia therefore concluded on 3 November 1912 a bipartite agreement with Mongolia, the Russo-Mongolian Treaty, by which Russia recognized Outer Mongolian autonomy. Russia refused to recognize the inclusion in the autonomous Mongolian state of Mongol areas in Manchuria (Barga), China (Inner Mongolia, Dzungaria and Altai) or Russia (Buryat and Urianghai (Tannu-Tuva). Russia did not establish formal diplomatic relations with Mongolia nor allow Mongol diplomatic or commercial relations with third states.[117]

In January 1913, Mongolia also concluded a treaty of mutual recognition of independence with Tibet.[118] The treaty was signed in Urga between the new Mongolian government and a representative of the Dalai Lama (the ubiquitous Dorjiev). The essential provisions of the treaty were as follows:

Whereas Mongolia and Tibet, having freed themselves from the Manchu dynasty and separated themselves from China, have become independent States, and whereas the two States have always professed one and the same religion, and to the end that their ancient mutual friendships may be strengthened. . . .

The Dalai Lama, Sovereign of Tibet, approves of and acknowledges the formation of an independent Mongolian State, and the proclamation . . . of the master of the Yellow Faith Je-tsun Dampa Lama as the Sovereign of the land.

The Sovereign of the Mongolian people Je-tsun Dampa Lama approves and acknowledges the formation of an independent State and the proclamation of the Dalai Lama as Sovereign of Tibet. . . .

---

117. Ibid., 84. "Text of Russo-Mongol Treaty," in Lamb, *McMahon Line*, 606.
118. Friters, *Outer Mongolia*, 72.

Both States, the Mongolian and the Tibetan, shall henceforth, for all time, afford each other aid against dangers from without and from within.[119]

The validity of this treaty is often questioned, mainly on grounds of the authority of Dorjiev to negotiate on behalf of Tibet and the later somewhat equivocating endorsement of the treaty by Tibet.[120] The fact that Dorjiev was a Russian citizen somewhat compromises his role; the treaty had obvious advantages to Russia in that it could be interpreted as extending Russia's protectorate over Mongolia to encompass Tibet. Neither Britain nor Russia recognized the treaty as valid. The Russians were interested in improving relations with the British at the time and did not want to arouse British suspicions in regard to Russian interest in Tibet. The British did not want to see Tibet linked with Outer Mongolia because of Russia's influence there. The treaty nevertheless exists; Dorjiev undoubtedly had the Dalai Lama's authority to negotiate with Mongolia, and the treaty represented the interests of both parties involved.[121]

Dorjiev was also entrusted by the Dalai Lama with a letter for the Russian Czar and instructions to ascertain whether Russia might be interested in, according to Snelling's account, "re-negotiating the 1907 convention with a view to becoming, with the British, joint protectors of a fully autonomous Tibet."[122] Dorjiev revealed the details of this proposed joint protectorate to I.Y. Korostovets, the Russian diplomat who had negotiated the Russo-Mongolia Treaty, whom Dorjiev met in Urga. As related by Korostovets after his meeting with Dorjiev, Tibet wanted to enter into a pact with Russia similar to the Russian pact with Mongolia:

> The Dalai Lama wanted to break with China. He had already been proclaimed secular ruler, had appointed new ministers and wanted to enter into a new pact with Russia similar to the Russo-Mongolian one. The basis for this pact or treaty could be a mutual Russo-English protectorate over Tibet and the elimination of Chinese sovereignty. The conditions of the treaty would be as follows: Russia and England to get freedom of entry to

---

119. Richardson, *Tibet and Its History*, 280; Snelling, *Buddhism in Russia*, 150.

120. The Tibetans were equivocal in explaining this treaty to the British; however, this may be due to their fear of arousing British suspicions of Tibetan connivance with the Russians. The Dalai Lama denied, according to Richardson's account, that the Mongolia-Tibet Treaty was a "regular treaty," rather, it was merely an "exchange of friendly assurances." Richardson, *Tibetan Precis*, 14.

121. Snelling believes that "the Dalai Lama invested Dorzhiev with plenipotentiary powers to negotiate and finalize a rapprochement between Mongolia and Tibet as sovereign states." Snelling, *Buddhism in Russia*, 150. Dorjiev was undoubtedly an active player in the attempt to establish an alliance between Tibet and Mongolia. The scheme bears the marks of Dorjiev's "Shambhala Project." Ibid., 151.

122. Ibid., 148.

Tibet; the Tibetan Government to consult Russian and English advisers and instructors on the organization of its financial and military systems. Russia to get the right of duty-free trade and a concession for exploiting the natural resources of the land. In exchange Russia to grant Tibet a financial loan, with its gold deposits as surety. Russia and England to provide arms for Tibet.[123]

Dorjiev travelled to St. Petersburg, where his proposals were received by the Russian Foreign Ministry without favor. Dorjiev was informed that Russia was bound by the terms of the 1907 Convention with Great Britain.[124] In fact, Russia was quite satisfied with its new position in Mongolia, a situation that the 1907 convention had permitted, and was loath to upset that arrangement even in order to achieve an opening of Tibet to Russian influence. The Russians were undoubtedly aware that a joint protectorate over Tibet would be dominated by the British from their stronghold in India, while Russia had no common border with Tibet. The Russians may also have feared that such a move might stimulate the Chinese to try to regain their position in both Tibet and Mongolia.

After the conclusion of the Russo-Mongolian Treaty of 1912, Russia attempted to secure the acceptance of its provisions by China. China was confronted with Russia's recognition of *de facto* Mongolian "autonomy," the possibility that Mongolian autonomy might increase under Russian influence, the threat that other Mongol areas might also be included in autonomous Mongolia and the prospect that Mongolian autonomy might be defended by Russia with force.[125] By accepting Mongolian "autonomy," China could secure Russia's recognition of Chinese "suzerainty" there, a term that the Chinese could interpret to mean that Mongolia remained a part of Chinese territory. Chinese nationalists, however, were aroused in indignant opposition to the loss of "Chinese" territory and dispatched missions to Urga to explain to the Mongol "rebels" the "five races" policy of the Republic and to offer bribes in return for renunciation of the Mongolian declaration of independence.

China finally signed a Sino-Russian agreement on 5 November 1913, but only after the resignation of the Chinese foreign minister and Yuan Shih-k'ai's liquidation of the KMT, primary opponents of the treaty in the Chinese parliament. China recognized the autonomy of Mongolia and agreed not to send troops or colonists there; Russia then recognized

---

123. Korostovets, as quoted in Ibid., 150. Dorjiev argued that Tibet had as much right to declare its independence and deal directly with other states as did Mongolia, whose ability to do so was recognized only by Russia. Ibid.

124. Ibid., 153.

125. Friters, *Outer Mongolia*, 170.

Chinese suzerainty over Mongolia. In a separate exchange of notes, Chinese suzerainty was interpreted to mean that Mongolia remained a part of Chinese territory; this provision was emphasized within China to mollify Chinese nationalists.[126]

The Simla Convention

In August 1912 while Russia was negotiating with Mongolia, Britain embarked upon a more aggressive policy toward China over Tibet. The British presented the Chinese Foreign Office with a series of conditions:

1. His Majesty's Government, while they have formally recognized the `suzerain rights' of China in Thibet, have never recognized, and are not prepared to recognize, the right of China to intervene actively in the internal administration of Thibet, which should remain, as contemplated by the treaties, in the hands of the Thibetan authorities. . . .

2. On these grounds His Majesty's Government must demur altogether to the conduct of the Chinese officers in Thibet during the last two years in assuming all administrative power in the country, and to the doctrine propounded in Yuan Shi-kai's presidential order of the 21st April 1912, that Thibet is to be `regarded as on an equal footing with the provinces of China proper,' and that `all administrative matters' connected with that country `will come within the sphere of internal administration.' His Majesty's Government formally decline to accept such a definition of the political status of Thibet. . . .

3. While the right of China to station a representative, with a suitable escort, at Lhassa, with authority to advise the Thibetans as to their foreign relations, is not disputed, His Majesty's Government are not prepared to acquiesce in the maintenance of an unlimited number of Chinese troops either in Lhassa or in Thibet generally.

4. His Majesty's Government must press for the conclusion of a written agreement on the foregoing lines as a condition precedent to extending their recognition of the Chinese Republic. . . .[127]

The British may have been trying to steal a march on the Russians by submitting their demands to the Chinese before the conclusion of the Russian treaty with Mongolia (November 1912). Considering the change in Russia's role in Mongolia, the British thought a corresponding increase

---

126. Ibid., 173. Text of Russo-Chinese Treaty in Lamb, *McMahon Line*, 615.
127. Memorandum to Wai-chiao Pu, 17 August 1912, in Dorothy Woodman, *Himalayan Frontiers* (New York: Praeger, 1969), 382.

of their own role in Tibet appropriate and consistent with the 1907 Treaty.[128] The British also feared that, if Britain failed to support Tibet, the Tibetans might approach the Russians. The British were also, of course, anxious to secure India's northern border. One means of doing so would be to establish Tibet as an autonomous state. British intentions in Tibet were frankly stated in a Foreign Office memorandum:

> Tibet, while nominally retaining her position as an autonomous State under the suzerainty of China, should in reality be placed in a position of absolute dependence on the Indian Government . . . there should be set up an effective machinery for keeping out the Chinese on the one hand and the Russians on the other. . . . What is essential at present is that we should obtain a completely free hand both by an agreement with Russia and by an agreement with China.[129]

The first step, the Foreign Office memorandum proposed, was to "inform Russia of our desire to reverse the 1907 Agreement and thereby obtain a free hand in Tibet, and then ask what her price is to be."[130] However, the Russians were not willing to relate their privileges in Mongolia to those of the British in Tibet since they had not been related in 1907. In exchange for an increase in the British presence in Tibet, Russia thought it appropriate to demand some compensation in Afghanistan or Persia. The solution for the British was to create an autonomous Tibet under Chinese suzerainty, but to do so in a tripartite agreement between China, Britain and Tibet that would not violate the 1907 agreement in which Britain had agreed to not directly negotiate with Tibet. The British hoped to define Tibet's border with China and counter the Russian threat to Tibet via Mongolia by imitating the division of Mongolia into Inner and Outer zones (relative to China). An autonomous Outer Tibet, under Chinese suzerainty, would achieve the British goal of an Indian frontier with Tibet rather than with China, while still recognizing some degree of Chinese authority over Tibet. An Inner Tibet under Chinese sovereignty would satisfy China's claims to eastern Tibet and reduce the threat of Russian influence in Tibet via Mongolia by interposing Chinese territory (Inner Mongolia and Inner Tibet) between Tibet and Mongolia.

---

128. The British India Office in 1912 outlined a proposed convention with Russia, giving Russia a free hand in Outer Mongolia and Sinkiang in exchange for similar privileges for Britain in Tibet, and providing for the "protection of Russian and British interests respectively should either Power eventually assume complete control of the districts in question." Woodman, *Himalayan Frontiers*, 106.
129. Foreign Office Memorandum, 1 September 1912, in Ibid., 149.
130. Ibid., 150.

The British proposed that a tripartite conference on Tibet's status be held in India at Simla, the summer headquarters of the GOI. The British moved the Chinese to negotiate by the threat to withhold British recognition of the Chinese Republic and by the implied threat to negotiate directly with Tibet, as Russia had negotiated with Mongolia. The renewed British interest in Tibet may have convinced the Chinese that they stood to lose Tibet to British influence, much as Mongolia had been lost to Russia, if China did not exercise at least her recognized rights as suzerain to negotiate over Tibet. China finally agreed to attend the negotiations, even though they protested Tibetan representation as an equal party.

The conference was convened in October 1913 (while the Chinese were still agonizing over the Sino-Russian Treaty).[131] Both China and Tibet began with statements of their positions. The Tibetan statement clearly expressed, for the first time, the Tibetan claim to independence:

Firstly, the relations between the Manchu Emperor and the Protector, Dalai Lama the fifth, became like that of the disciple towards the teacher. The sole aim of the then Government of China being to earn merit for this and for the next life, they helped and honoured the successive Dalai Lamas and treated the monks of all the monasteries with respect. Thus friendship united the two countries like the members of the same family. The Tibetans took no notice of their boundary with China for they thought that the actions of the latter were all meant for the good of Tibet. Gradually the Chinese Emperor lost all faith in the Buddhist religion, and he treated the precious Protector, the Dalai Lama, with less respect. The Chinese Amban in Tibet and his subordinate officials and troops entertained very little respect, later on, for the precious Protector, the Dalai Lama, although they knew him to be the owner and Ruler of Tibet both in religious and secular affairs, while they treated the people of Tibet, both laymen and monks, most disrespectfully and meanly as if they were pigs, asses and cattle. They oppressed the Tibetans and treated them with partiality, thus driving them to grief and desperation. . . . [A long discourse on the deterioration of relations and the events of the Chinese invasion of Tibet follows.]

Tibet and China have never been under each other and will never associate with each other in future. It is decided that Tibet is an independent state and that the precious Protector, the Dalai Lama, is the ruler of Tibet, in all temporal as well as spiritual affairs. Tibet repudiates the Anglo-Chinese

---

131. The Tibetans reportedly wanted to include Russia as a fourth party to the negotiations in order to increase international guarantees for their status, but this was vetoed by the British. Richardson, *Tibetan Precis*, 15. The Tibetan Government also reportedly wanted Dorjiev to participate at the conference, presumably as an advisor to the Tibetan Government. Snelling, *Buddhism in Russia*, 154.

Convention concluded at Pekin on the 27th April 1906, . . . as she did not send a representative for this Convention nor did she affix her seal on it. . . . [Tibet's territorial claim follows, listing the names of the places through which the traditional Sino-Tibetan border ran.]

After all this trouble, great enmity has been generated between the Chinese and the Tibetans. It will therefore be only a source of constant friction if they were to live together in one country in future. It has already caused great trouble to the people of Tibet owing to the oppressive ways of the Chinese officials and troops. In future no Chinese officials and troops will be allowed to stay in Tibet. . . . In order therefore to insure peace between the two countries in future no Chinese Amban or other officials and no Chinese soldiers or colonists will be permitted to enter or reside in Tibet . . . [A claim to the right to approve incarnations of Mongolian lamas and for compensation for taxes for Tibetan districts occupied by the Chinese and for damage done by Chinese troops follows].[132]

The Tibetan claims came as something of a surprise to the British, who had previously negotiated with China over Tibet on the assumption that China actually exercised substantial authority over Tibet, an assumption that the Tibetan claims refuted. Britain had been prepared to recognize a boundary of Chinese control "far in excess of that which the Tibetans were willing to accept, whilst our existing treaties with China in regard to Tibet were based on a recognition of, and a reliance on, an extended and substantial suzerainty."[133]

The Chinese, who came to the conference prepared to negotiate with the British, not the Tibetans, were equally surprised at the Tibetans' ability to negotiate on their own behalf and the strong presentation and documentation of their case. The Chinese were relatively unprepared to substantiate their claim either to central Tibet or to those areas of eastern Tibet ostensibly under Chinese jurisdiction; they therefore submitted a dissembling statement of their claim to overall sovereignty over Tibet:

Since the commencement of intercourse between China and Tibet there have been many occasions on which the latter has received much needed assistance and protection from the former. A Chinese expedition first entered Lhasa in the seventh century, and in 1206 Tibet was again subdued

---

132. *The Boundary Question between China and Tibet: A Valuable Record of the Tripartite Conference between China, Britain and Tibet, Held in India*, 1913-1914 (Peking, 1940), 1. Lamb states that this work, which is attributed only to "a Pekinese," "contains genuine documents from the British archives, marred only by occasional typographical errors. I have compared all its contents with the versions in the India Office and Foreign Office archives." Lamb, *McMahon Line*, 478.

133. Political and Secret Files, 1913, in Woodman, *Himalayan Frontiers*, 162.

by Genghis Khan, who incorporated it into his wide-spread Empire. Tibet remained in this relation to China during the time of the Ming Dynasty. In 1650, the fifth Dalai Lama came to China to pay respects to the Emperor Shen Chih, who confirmed him in that title by issuing to him a warrant and a seal. In 1717 the Zungarians invaded Tibet and overran the whole country, and with the assistance of the Chinese the Tibetans afterwards succeeded in driving out their enemies. In response to a request proffered by the Tibetans, who were grateful to the Chinese, the Emperor Kang Hsi appointed an Amban to reside in order that the Tibetans could be better looked after. In the reign of Yung Cheng, two Ambans were appointed instead of one.

From thenceforward Tibet was twice invaded by the Gurkhas. . . . So powerless and helpless were the Tibetans that they again went to China for assistance. To their supplication China responded at once by sending over 50,000 soldiers to Tibet; and accordingly the Gurkhas were driven out of the country. Tibet was then definitely placed under the sovereignty of China.

What sacrifices China has made in money and lives for the sake of protecting the Tibetans and their territory!

Not only are these events recorded in Chinese history, but they are also referred to in English records and books, both official and private.

As regards the recent events between China and Tibet which have resulted in such a misunderstanding as now exists between the two peoples, it is not China that can be blamed, but it is entirely due to the conduct of His Holiness the Dalai Lama himself. . . .

With regard to the action which China has taken within recent years on her frontier, it is because the Chinese and local inhabitants in that quarter have been frequently treated with injustice by the Lama authorities and they have appealed to the Chinese authorities for protection. Their appeal was immediately responded to, but the Tibetans aggravated the situation by their brutal murder of Amban Fung and many Chinese officials, who were skinned to death.

From what has been related it is evident that the claims presented in the Tibetan statement are inadmissible, and in answer to them the following demands are made as the only basis for the negotiation of the Tibetan question:

It is hereby agreed that Tibet forms an integral part of the territory of the Republic of China, that no attempts shall be made by Tibet or by Great Britain to interrupt the continuity of this territorial integrity, and that China's rights of every description which have existed in consequence of this territorial integrity shall be respected by Tibet and recognized by Great Britain.

The Republic of China engages not to convert Tibet into a Chinese province, and Great Britain engages not to annex Tibet or any portion of it. . . .

Tibet undertakes to be guided by China in her foreign and military affairs and not to enter into negotiation with any foreign Powers except through the intermediary of the Chinese Government.[134]

At the next session of the conference in December 1913, discussions on the boundary between Chinese administered eastern Tibet and autonomous central Tibet were initiated. This session of the conference was described by Sir Henry McMahon, the British negotiator:

The Lonchen [Shatra], whilst expressing his interest in the opinions expressed by the [foreign] authors, refused to accept as conclusive any statements which lacked the weight of an official seal. In support of the Tibetan claim he produced a large number of original archives from Lhasa, tomes of delicate manuscripts bound in richly embroidered covers, he confronted his opponent also with the official history of Tibet, compiled by the 5th Dalai Lama . . . a work of great scope and colossal dimensions.

The Lonchen claimed recognition for the Chinese-Tibetan Treaty of 822 A.D., which was recorded on three identical pillars. . . . He announced moreover that he would lay on the table the original records of each Tibetan State as far east as Tachienlu, proving that the lamaseries and tribal chiefs had exercised a continuing administrative control over the country for many centuries, and that they held their lands, collected their taxes and received their subsidies by virtue of their association with the Government at Lhasa.[135]

For some days Mr. Chen showed evident signs of panic; he protested that his Government would never consent to the production of evidence in regard to the country east of Batang or the discussion of Kokonor; he telegraphed for an official copy of the "Institute of the Manchu Dynasty;" and he stated that he relied on China's position in international law, by which Chao Erh-feng's effective occupation of the country cancelled any earlier Tibetan claim.[136]

---

134. *Boundary Question*, 7. China also claimed Tibet on the rather tenuous basis that "The Republic has no right to alienate any part of the territory which she has inherited from the Manchu dynasty, and she must maintain the extent of her territory the same as before." "Statement by Mr. Ivan Chen," in Mehra, *Northeastern Frontier*, vol. 1, 75.

135. The Tibetan tax records, in 56 volumes, went back as far as the 1648 census conducted by the Fifth Dalai Lama's *Desi*, Sonam Chosphel. Shakabpa, *Tibet: A Political History*, 113.

136. McMahon's Final Memorandum, *India Office Records*, enclosure 1, 5. Peking telegraphed to Ivan Chen suggesting that he not resort to the 822 treaty between Tibet and China to substantiate China's claim to overall authority in Tibet, since "the Chang Ching

The Chinese negotiator, Chen I-fan (anglicized as Ivan Chen) attempted to substantiate Chinese claims to Kham by referring to a pamphlet
compiled by General Fu Sung-mu, the successor to Chao Erh-feng in
Kham, which recorded the frontier campaigns of Chao. Fu, who had
urged the creation of Sikang province, argued that China should for the
time being concentrate on the Chinese position in Kham rather than upon
the status of central Tibet. An advance of the frontier would constitute a
permanent territorial gain, while the status of Outer Tibet was always
subject to alteration sometime in the future when China had regained the
advantage. Fu's strategy was to claim as much of Kham as possible as a
defense against the potential loss of Outer Tibet to the British. As Fu
wrote: "The sequel to the Anglo-Tibetan treaty may well be an Anglo-
Kham treaty following hard upon it unless Kham be separated from
Tibet."[137]

Chen also telegraphed to Lu Hsing-chi, who had been appointed
Chinese administrator of Tibet, but who was residing in Calcutta since
the Tibetans refused to permit him entry into Tibet, requesting that he
secure any available maps of Tibet that would support the Chinese
case.[138] Lu sent for the maps of Fu Sung-mu emphasizing that "if we can
use as proof the map prepared by Fu Sung-mu, former Warden of the
Marches, which shows Chiang-ta [Giamda] as the frontier, not only shall
we be able to include several thousand *li* extra but every important strate-

---

(821-825) epoch of the Tang dynasty was that in which the Tu-fan [Tibetan] power was at its
greatest height and then not only included the Szechuan marches and Kokonor but also . .
. 80 percent of modern Kansu province. The inscription on this monument should therefore
on no account be referred to as an authority." Mehra, Northeastern Frontier, vol. 1, 162.

137. "From the `History of the Creation of Hsi-Kang Province,' by General Fu Sung-mu,"
in Mehra, *Northeastern Frontier*, vol. 1, 189.

138. Lu sent his credentials to Lhasa from Kalimpong in May 1913, along with a message
from Yuan Shih-k'ai: "Recent disorders in Tibet were due to the maladministration of Lien
Yu and Chung Ying; these officers have now been recalled and I have appointed Lu Hsing-
chi, Administrator in Tibet." Lu demanded that the Tibetan Government send a delegation
to escort him to Lhasa. Mehra, *Northeastern Frontier*, vol. 1, 146. However, Lu had to admit
that he had "sent numerous letters and telegrams to the Dalai Lama, hoping to draw him
into closer communication with us; to not a single one have I received an answer." Ibid., 152.
Lu then proposed to bribe his way into Tibet and requested 500,000 Chinese dollars to do
so. Ibid., 147. Lu Hsing-chi remained at Calcutta during the Simla negotiations, attempting
to influence their outcome by a variety of means. He admitted to having bribed some of
Lonchen Shatra's assistants. Ibid., 156. He also conspired with the Panchen Lama, who,
unlike the Tibetan Government, recognized Lu's appointment and accepted a title sent by
Lu, "Most Loyal Exponent of Transmigration." Ibid., 148. The Panchen Lama, who hoped to
preserve his feudal autonomy relative to Lhasa by means of Chinese patronage, asked Lu
to obtain representation for Tashilhunpo at Simla. Ibid., 151.

gical point will come into our possession."[139] In regard to the status of Outer Tibet, Lu emphasized that "the Dalai Lama has not hitherto categorically disclaimed allegiance to the Central Government; the British also continue to regard Tibet as a dependency of China; we must cling to these threads of opportunity."[140]

Each side at Simla was allowed time to prepare its border claims. When the next session opened in January 1914, the Chinese claimed as under direct Chinese administration all territory to the east of Giamda, only a few hundred miles east of Lhasa, based upon the "historic connections of all those places with China" and the conquests of Chao Erhfeng, or "what is called in International Law 'effective occupation.'" The Chinese claimed that the border between Ch'ing-hai and Tibet ran along the line of the Nyenchentangla range, a claim that would have included in Ch'ing-hai the valley of the upper Salween and the districts of Nagchukha and Khyungpo, which were under Lhasa's administration.[141]

The Chinese went on to claim all of Tibet as Chinese territory, since these territorial boundaries were "the demarcation of the boundaries between China and Tibet for that time only, for after the death of Emperor Yung Cheng, the Emperor Kien Lung (Ch'ien Lung), successor of Yung Cheng, formally annexed Tibet in 1720 and since then Tibet has been under Chinese sovereignty and the whole of Tibet cannot be otherwise considered than Chinese territory."[142] As substantiation for their claims to eastern Tibet, the Chinese submitted a list of places in Kham, along with altered Chinese names, that had been made districts of Szechuan in 1912.

The Chinese Government replied that "the representatives sent by Tibet were recommended by Great Britain; they were neither nominated nor sent by China. It would appear better not to cavil at distinctions between Anterior and Ulterior Tibet [U and Tsang], since both China and Great Britain have accepted the said representatives it follows that they represent the whole of Tibet." Ibid., 159.

139. Ibid., 160.

140. Ibid., 147.

141. The Chinese claimed that all the territories east of the Mekong-Yangtze watershed had been under the administration of Szechuan "since the early period of the reign of Emperor Yung Cheng." "Chinese Statement on Limits of Tibet, January 12, 1914," in *Boundary Question*, 14.

142. Ibid. The Ch'ing expedition to Lhasa took place in 1720 under K'ang Hsi (1662-1722), not Yung-cheng (1722-1735), and it was therefore K'ang Hsi, not Yung-cheng or Ch'ien-lung (1735-1799), who, in 1720, "formally annexed Tibet." The administrative division along the line of the Mekong-Yangtze watershed took place in 1725, under Yung-cheng. The Chinese also claimed as "directly under Chinese control" Tashilhunpo and Sakya (presumably based upon Sakya's former loyalty to the Yuan and the Panchen's acceptance of title from Lu). Ibid., 19.

Kokonor was claimed since its conquest, again by Yung Cheng, "in about 1700."[143]

The Tibetans reiterated their claim to the territory established by treaty in 822 and marked at that time by stone pillars at the border points (Merugang, north of Sining; the bend of the Ma Chu, Yellow River; and Chortenkarpo, "white stupa," near Ya-chao in Szechuan), all the inhabitants of which were "Tibetans by race, manners, customs, language and Buddhist by religion."[144] Furthermore, they pointed out in regard to Kham that all of Kham had been conquered by Gushri Khan, who had presented it and Amdo to the Fifth Dalai Lama. A census had been conducted in Kham, the 56 volumes of which the Tibetans presented as evidence. The Tibetans admitted that Lhasa exercised its authority in eastern Tibet only indirectly through local princes, chieftains, monasteries or monastic sects, but this did not negate the fact that Kham and Amdo remained "unquestionably Tibetan territory."[145]

The Tibetans claimed that the imposition of Manchu authority over Tibet in 1720 and the territorial division of 1725 did not affect Tibetan sovereignty in central Tibet or in Kham and Amdo.[146] Tibetan authority in Kham had been reaffirmed in 1863-64 when the Tibetan Government suppressed Gompo Namgyal, after which direct control was instituted in Nyarong, somewhat less direct control in Derge, and all the other states of Kham were restored to their hereditary chieftains "on condition of rendering special services on extraordinary occasions of necessity and of

---

143. Ibid., 20.

144. "Tibetan Statement on Limits of Tibet, January 12, 1914," in *Boundary Question*, 25.

145. Ibid., 27. The political authority of the Tibetan Government was generally delegated to estate holders in central Tibet and to native chieftains, hereditary officials or monasteries in Kham and Amdo. Monastic sects exercised authority over estates that were in some cases essentially petty states. However, monastic officials of the Gelugpa sect were appointed or confirmed by Lhasa (either by the Dalai Lama or the parent monastery, Drepung, Sera or Ganden) and monks were trained in Lhasa. Monasteries of the other sects were under a similar type of relationship to parent monasteries located in central Tibet. Furthermore, as Lonchen Shatra said, "the monastic rules and regulations as well as the laws which govern the people are framed and passed by the Tibetan Government in common with those which are in force in all the Tibetan territories." Ibid., 45. In all areas of Tibet, the administration of justice and collection of taxes was delegated, but "in serious and important cases the Tibetan Government sends down special officers to inquire and try the cases." Ibid., 32. Ivan Chen accused the Dalai Lama of confusing spiritual influence with temporal authority in Kham and Amdo, and maintained that local taxes paid to monasteries were charity, not evidence of delegated political authority. Tibetan Government appointment of officers was said to be invalid unless signed and sealed by the Lhasa *amban*, therefore Lhasa's appointment of officials in Kham did not have the political significance claimed by the Tibetan Government. "Statement by Mr. Ivan Chen," in Mehra, *Northeastern Frontier*, vol. 1, 78.

146. *Boundary Question*, 29.

complying with the usual orders and customary duties." This was done even though "the Tibetan Government would have been quite justified if they had kept the whole under its direct control and administration." The heads of all these states had sworn written oaths of allegiance to Lhasa, which were submitted as evidence.[147]

The Tibetans rejected Chinese claims to Kham by right of conquest by Chao Erh-feng, stating that "unlawful encroachment, like a large insect swallowing up a small one, or in other words asserting 'might is right'— an uncivilized method—it is hoped, will not be permitted, and that lawful right will be respected and the lawful owner will allowed to enjoy peaceful possession."[148] They challenged the Chinese claim to actual administration in the area of Chao's conquests west of the Yangtze, citing Lhasa's appointment of officials and tax records for those territories, direct administration by Lhasa of Markham and Powo, and supervision by Lhasa monasteries of the monastic estates of Chamdo, Pagsho and Dragyab. The Tibetans rejected the Chinese claim to a southern border of Ch'ing-hai territory at the Nyenchentangla range, on the basis that administration over the Mongol and Tibetan tribes of Nagchukha and Khyungpo (Gyade) was entirely Tibetan.[149]

At this point McMahon intervened to propose the British plan for an Inner and Outer Tibet under different degrees of Chinese and Tibetan control. Inner Tibet (eastern Kham and Amdo) would come under Chinese control, allowing the Chinese to "restore and safeguard their historic position there." Outer Tibet (western Kham, central and western Tibet) would have its "established autonomy" recognized. In Inner Tibet, Lhasa would be allowed control over monastic affairs and the right "to issue appointment orders to chiefs and local officers and to collect all customary rents and taxes." All of Tibet, Inner and Outer, would be recognized as a "State under the suzerainty, but not the sovereignty, of China."

---

147. These included the Hor states, Drango and Derge. Ibid., 39, 76. Derge was under its own chieftains who, however, had to "voluntarily submit the entire lands, both State and monastery, to the Tibetan Government's direct control and swear allegiance to the Government promising to lay down life and property at the Government's bidding." Ibid., 40. Local authority was also restored in Chagla, Lithang, Batang, Lingtsang and Golok, but the leaders of those states are not recorded as having sworn oaths of allegiance. Ibid., 36.

148. Ibid., 30.

149. Ibid., 43. The Chinese claimed Gyade based on its name; Gyade means "Chinese settlement," which the Chinese took to mean that the population were Chinese. The name, however, refers to the fact that taxes of these districts had been allotted for the expenses of the Manchu *ambans* at Lhasa, thus they were the *amban's* tax estates, but the population was Tibetan and Tibetanized Mongols and the area was administered by the Tibetan Government, not by the *amban*. Pedro Carrasco, *Land and Polity in Tibet* (Seattle: University of Washington Press, 1959), 106.

The plan would theoretically be implemented "without in any way infringing the integrity of Tibet as a geographical and political entity." Both China and Britain would abstain from interference in the administration of Outer Tibet. McMahon proposed a boundary between Inner and Outer Tibet following the Ch'ing division of 1725, along the watershed between the Yangtze (Dri Chu) and Mekong (Dza Chu) in Kham and along the Tangula range between Outer Tibet and Ch'ing-hai (not the Nyenchentangla range further to the south). The boundary of Inner Tibet with China would essentially follow the line claimed by Tibet as the border between Tibet and China.[150]

The Tibetan side protested this plan, reiterating their ethnic nationalist appeal that the peoples who would come under the Chinese in Inner Tibet were Tibetans, who should for that reason be under Tibetan government. The Tibetans made the case that to put Tibetans already in revolt against Chinese rule under Chinese control was a solution likely to increase rather than lessen political strife in eastern Tibet.[151] The Chinese, for their part, protested the qualification that China had suzerainty but not sovereignty over Tibet. They demanded that Tibet should be defined as a part of Chinese territory, that the Chinese Government should have authority to invest the Dalai Lama, that the *amban* should guide the Tibetans in their foreign policy and that Tibet should be represented in the Chinese Parliament.[152] The Chinese side also expressed a dislike for the whole idea of Inner and Outer zones.[153]

The British then produced a draft treaty, which read: "The Governments of Great Britain and China recognizing that Tibet is under the suzerainty of China, and recognizing also the autonomy of Outer

---

150. "The British Plenipotentiary Proposes Solution of the Problem, February 17, 1914," in *Boundary Question*, 90. McMahon's statement that this solution would not compromise the "integrity of Tibet as a geographical and political entity" may be regarded as an attempt to convince the Tibetans to accept the division of their country. In 1921 Charles Bell, McMahon's assistant at Simla, explained the British strategy to the Dalai Lama as a means to retain a Tibetan claim to all of Tibet: "The Chinese wanted to give the parts of Tibet near China Chinese names, and treat them as provinces of China. We arranged for them to be called Inner Tibet, thus keeping Tibet's name on them. Later on, if your army grows strong enough to ensure that Tibet's rights are respected, you may regain the rightful possession of this part of your country. But not if the name be lost." Bell, *Portrait of a Dalai Lama*, 232.

151. "The Tibetan Plenipotentiary Protests to the British Proposal, March 6, 1914," in *Boundary Question*, 98.

152. "Interview between the Chinese Plenipotentiary and the Assistant to the British Plenipotentiary, April 15, 1914," in *Boundary Question*, 101.

153. Ibid., 109. The Chinese, especially the Szechuanese, claimed all of the conquests of Chao Erh-feng as integral parts of China, and therefore objected to the terminology of Inner Tibet, since that implied that Kham was still Tibetan.

Tibet, engage to respect the territorial integrity of the country, and to abstain from interference in the administration of Outer Tibet (including the selection and installation of the Dalai Lama), which shall remain in the hands of the Tibetan Government at Lhasa."[154] China was not to station troops or officials in Outer Tibet, with the exception of an *amban* with no more than 300 soldiers. An appendix stated: "It is understood by the High Contracting Parties that Tibet forms part of Chinese territory." The Dalai Lama would be selected by the Tibetan Government, which would inform the Chinese Government, which would then award "titles consistent with his dignity which have been conferred by the Chinese Government." The Tibetan Government retained the right to appoint all officers in Outer Tibet and monastic officials in Inner Tibet. Tibet was not to be represented in the Chinese Parliament.[155]

The Tibetans tentatively agreed to the draft treaty, protesting only that Nyarong and Derge should be in Outer Tibet. The Chinese delayed due to instructions to the Chinese delegation from Peking regarding Inner Tibet.[156] On 27 April 1914 the Tibetans agreed to the revised document; the Chinese delegate was convinced to "initial" the document, contingent upon his government's final approval.[157] However, on 29 April 1914 the Convention was repudiated by the Chinese Government.[158]

McMahon's strategy to force the Chinese to negotiate by the threat to conclude a bilateral treaty with Tibet had succeeded in resolving all issues except the border, but McMahon apparently thought he could secure Chinese ratification of the concluded treaty by the same tactic.

---

154. "Convention between Great Britain, China and Tibet (Revised Bill)," in *Boundary Question*, 133.

155. Ibid., 138.

156. Peking proposed to eliminate Inner Tibet; Kokonor (Ch'ing-hai) and southern Kham would be regarded as under direct Chinese administration; northern Kham (Nyarong, Derge) and western Kham up to the Salween would be a "special zone" where "the Central Government shall have the right of doing whatever they think necessary for the consolidation of their position in that country"; the boundary with Outer Tibet in Kham would be along the Salween. "Telegram from the Wai Chiao Pu to Ivan Chen, April 20, 1914," in *Boundary Question*, 131.

157. Since the Chinese written language is not alphabetic, the Chinese delegate could not, of course, "initial" the document, but had to sign using the full characters of his name. In McMahon's opinion, Chen initialed the agreement only to prevent Britain signing a bipartite treaty with Tibet. Sir Henry McMahon's Final Memorandum on the Tibet Conference, 23 July 1914, *India Office Records*, L/PS/10/344, 3160, 4.

158. "Proceedings of the 8th Meeting Held at Simla, July 3, 1914," in *Boundary Question*, 146. The Tibetan reaction to the Chinese Government's repudiation of the treaty was, "If they disavowed the action of their Plenipotentiary now, how could they be trusted to respect the Convention even after it was formally signed and sealed?" Lonchen Shatra remarked that he had also been instructed by his government not to sign the agreement if

McMahon expected that the Chinese would finally ratify the treaty rather than lose British recognition of Chinese suzerainty over Tibet and China's position as arbiter of Tibetan affairs.[159] The Chinese, however, seemed to think that the scenario of 1906 would be repeated, with negotiations being transferred to Peking (or London), resulting in an bilateral agreement between China and Britain, excluding the Tibetans.[160] Both Britain and China miscalculated, and the result was that no agreement on Tibet's status was reached.

After the close of the Simla Convention, the Chinese Foreign Ministry sent numerous communications to Simla, London and the British ambassador in Peking protesting that they had made significant concessions in regard to the frontier, none of which had been appreciated or reciprocated by the Tibetan or British. The Foreign Ministry indicated that the frontier remained the only issue to which China objected: "As regards the present Draft Agreement, apart from the boundary question dealt with in Article 9, the ideas of both parties are generally speaking in agreement as to the remaining, and it will not be a difficult matter to reach an agreement by mutual consultation."[161]

China's emphasis upon boundary issues and the status of Inner Tibet created the impression among British observers that the status of Outer Tibet was less an issue than that of Chinese control of as much territory as possible up to the border of Outer Tibet, as if China anticipated the possibility that Outer Tibet would be lost, at least temporarily, to Chinese control. As Louis King, a member of the British Peking Legation, commented, "the establishment of the province of Hsi K'ang [Sikang] is a move on China's part to secure as large a buffer territory as possible on her western frontier in case of some such eventuality as a foreign protectorate over Tibet."[162]

Despite the failure of the Simla Convention, the British did not fail to secure their own interests in regard to the Indo-Tibetan border. In a confidential "Exchange of notes between the British and Tibetan

---

Nyarong and Derge were not included as part of Outer Tibet, but that he had done so for the sake of the rest of the agreement and expected that his government would not repudiate his actions. "Tibetan reaction to Chinese disavowal of Ivan Chen," 8 May 1914, in Mehra, *Northeastern Frontier*, vol. 1, 83.

159. McMahon's Final Memorandum, *India Office Records*, 1.

160. "China wants negotiations in London or Peking," 10 May 1914, in Mehra, *Northeastern Frontier*, vol. 1, 90.

161. "Memorandum to Sir John Jordan by Wellington Ku," 25 April 1914, in Mehra, *Northeastern Frontier*, vol. 1, 87. In this memorandum, the Chinese stated that "Tibet should be Chinese territory, on the same footing as Outer Mongolia." Ibid.

162. "Excerpts from Louis King's report," in Mehra, *Northeastern Frontier*, vol 1, 184.

Plenipotentiaries," India and Tibet agreed to a Indo-Tibetan border from Bhutan to Burma, which was thereafter known as the McMahon Line.[163] The border was delimited on a detailed map, which was signed by McMahon and Lonchen Shatra.[164] By this agreement Tibet gave up its claim to the Tawang tract, an area under the administration of Lhasa's Drepung monastery.[165] The Tibetan understanding of this agreement was that it was contingent upon the British finally securing Chinese recognition of Tibetan autonomy and a definite Tibetan frontier with China in eastern Tibet.[166] A joint declaration recognizing the validity of the Simla Convention was initialed on 3 July 1914 by McMahon and Lonchen Shatra:

> We, the Plenipotentiaries of Great Britain and Tibet, hereby record the following Declaration to the effect that we acknowledge the annexed Convention as initialled to be binding on the Governments of Great Britain and Tibet, and we agree that so long as the Government of China withholds signature to the aforesaid Convention, she will be debarred from the enjoyment of all privileges accruing therefrom.[167]

163. Text of "India-Tibet Frontier," 1914, in Aitchison, *Treaties, Engagements and Sanads*, 34. The McMahon Line accorded to India territories north of that actually administered by India, including some administered by Tibet (Tawang), thus setting the stage for later Sino-Indian border disputes. The Simla Convention and its appended Indo-Tibetan agreement did not appear in Aitchison's *Treaties* (the official GOI record), including the final 1929 edition, since the unratified Simla Convention was not a valid international treaty and the Indo-Tibetan agreement was secret. The 1929 edition was withdrawn by a British Indian official, Olaf Caroe, in 1938, and a new edition was issued that included the Simla Convention and the McMahon-Shatra notes (but not the Anglo-Tibetan agreement or the *McMahon Line* map). Lamb, McMahon Line, 546. Even though the McMahon line maps were not included in the reissued Aitchison's *Treaties*, the McMahon Line boundary was subsequently indicated on Survey of India maps and regarded by India as the officially delimited border. Lamb, *Tibet, China and India*, 280, 428.

164. The map is reproduced in *Premier Chou En-lai's Letter to the Leaders of Asian and African Countries on the Sino-Indian Boundary Question (November 15, 1962)* (Peking: Foreign Languages Press, 1973) and in Woodman, *Himalayan Frontiers*. The map bears the signature of McMahon and the signature and seal of Lonchen Shatra. The map is quite detailed for both southern Tibet and what is now Assam; the Tibetan names for all towns, districts and geographical features on both sides of the frontier are written in, indicating a comprehensive Tibetan knowledge of their geography and territorial claims.

165. Tawang continued to be under Tibetan administration until 1951. Lamb, *McMahon Line*, 580.

166. Ibid., 547.

167. "Declaration appended to the 3 July 1914 text of the Simla Convention," Lamb, *McMahon Line*, 625. The fact that the declaration was only initialled made ratification contingent upon either Chinese agreement to the Simla Convention or British Government approval for a British-Tibetan treaty. The latter would have been an obvious violation of the

McMahon subsequently attempted to secure China's agreement to the Simla Convention by the threat that China would lose the recognition of its suzerainty by failure to ratify the Convention.[168] The argument has since been made that China's failure to ratify resulted in the loss of China's suzerainty over Tibet.[169] This argument, which assumes that China's status in Tibet depended upon international recognition, is refuted by Alfred P. Rubin:

> Since, in the actual case, the Chinese rights in Tibet were never thought by any of the parties, with the possible exception of the British (who had more political than legal reason for seeming to incline to this position), to depend to any degree on British recognition, it is difficult to see any substance to this argument. The facts upon which the recognition of "suzerainty" depended did not change because express recognition of that "suzerainty" was withheld. . . .
>
> In any event, the British, regardless of their unwillingness to "recognize" it, continued to assert that China had in fact an undefined "suzerainty" over Tibet.[170]

In the end, British efforts to achieve a trilateral agreement on Tibet's status at Simla yielded satisfactory results only for themselves, and those were of a temporary nature. Their bilateral border treaty with Tibet sufficed only so long as the Chinese were unable to make good on their claim to sovereignty over Tibet. Ultimately, they failed to achieve any security for Tibet or for their own border agreements with Tibet. Tibet in the following years was restrained in claiming full independence, even when independence existed in fact, out of fear of losing the British guarantee for Tibetan autonomy and their commitment to secure China's ratification of the Simla Convention. The British were similarly restrained in recognition of Tibet's *de facto* independence since they continued to rec-

---

1907 Anglo-Russian Treaty and was rejected by the British Government in 1914. The McMahon Line map, on the other hand, was signed by both parties, thus making it, theoretically, a legal document, contingent only upon Tibet's legal standing as a polity able to make international treaties. Ibid., 519. The Chinese delegate specifically stated that his government would not recognize any agreement between Britain and Tibet. *Boundary Question*, 147.

168. McMahon's Final Memorandum, *India Office Records*, enclosure 1, 12; enclosure 4, 3.

169. Shakabpa, *Tibet: A Political History*, 256; Michael C. van Walt van Praag, *The Status of Tibet* (Boulder: Westview Press, 1987), 138.

170. Alfred P. Rubin, "The Position of Tibet in International Law," *The China Quarterly* (July-September 1968), 125. However, Tibetan acceptance of Chinese suzerainty was contingent upon Chinese ratification; therefore China's failure to ratify may be held to constitute Tibetan repudiation of China's suzerainty over Tibet.

ognize Chinese suzerainty *de jure*. However, despite Tibet's reluctant acknowledgement of Chinese suzerainty (in exchange for a guarantee of autonomy), the position taken by the Tibetans at Simla was the clearest statement to date of Tibet's claim to independence of China. Simla also thrust the issue of Tibet's status into the international arena. As Dawa Norbu has written, "the dialectics of Anglo-Chinese negotiations on Tibet provided not only the catalyst but the crucible within which the further international status of Tibet was shaped."[171]

Shortly after the end of the Simla Convention, in September 1914, the delayed tripartite convention between Russia, China and Mongolia convened at Kiakhta, Outer Mongolia, near the frontier with the Buryat region of Russia.[172] A treaty was concluded in June 1915 that confirmed the provisions of the Sino-Russian agreement of 1913; China had to recognize Mongolian autonomy, but Russia and Mongolia confirmed Chinese suzerainty over Mongolia. No mention was made of the 1912 Russo-Mongolian Treaty, thus China was not required to admit Mongolia's right to independently conclude international treaties.[173] China immediately published an internal decree that the independence of Mongolia was abolished and that Mongolia remained Chinese territory. China dispatched a mission to Mongolia to confirm and elevate the titles of Mongol lamas and princes, including the Jebtsundampa Lama, the Mongolian head of state.[174]

Alastair Lamb makes the case that Simla might have been concluded successfully had McMahon followed more closely Russia's tactics with China over Mongolia. The Mongolian agreements left the border undefined; Lamb suggests that the British might also have "concentrated on the political objectives and left the question of geography until later."[175] However, on the Sino-Tibetan border, geography was the most important issue. The Sino-Mongolian border was the virtually uninhabited Gobi desert; the Sino-Tibetan border in Kham was the most populated area of Tibet and had been the scene of recent conflict; the Sino-Tibetan border issue was therefore much more complicated than that between China and Outer Mongolia. Mongolia's frontier with China was not in fact resolved

---

171. Dawa Norbu, "The Europeanization of Sino-Tibetan Relations, 1775-1907: The Genesis of Chinese `Suzerainty' and Tibetan `Autonomy,'" *Tibet Journal*, vol. XV, no. 4 (1990), 29.

172. The delay had been caused, according to Friters, by the Mongols, who were disconcerted by Russia's negotiating with China without Mongolian participation and Russian recognition of China's suzerainty over Mongolia. Friters, *Outer Mongolia*, 174.

173. Ibid., 180.

174. Ibid., 182.

175. Lamb, *McMahon Line*, 527.

at the tripartite convention; it was not finally delimited until after Chinese recognition of Mongolian independence in 1945.[176]

In addition, Russia was able to deal with Mongolia and China separately, only bringing the two together when the essentials of agreement had been reached with each independently. In contrast, Britain was forced, due to the intricacies of its 1907 obligations to Russia, to initiate a tripartite conference, a situation fraught with difficulties, including the initial requirement that each party recognize the others' right to negotiate the issue in question. China agreed to negotiate Tibet's status at Simla but never accepted Tibet's right to equal representation. There were also fundamental differences between the two situations. Russia was an expanding land empire with perpetual interests along its frontier with China. Britain was an overseas empire, already in the process of contraction, with no permanent interests in Tibet and no permanent frontiers with China. The British were unwilling and unable to establish a protectorate over Tibet; therefore, they attempted to craft legalistic guarantees of Tibet's autonomy sufficient for their own limited purposes. The Russians never relied on treaties alone; the Soviet Government concluded entirely contradictory treaties in 1924, simultaneously recognizing Mongolian independence and Chinese sovereignty over Mongolia. Mongolia's status was ultimately determined by Russia establishing a protectorate over Mongolia and committing itself to Mongolia's defense.

The timing of the Simla Conference was ultimately unfortunate; the Sino-Mongolian Treaty was concluded in November 1913, accompanied by much Chinese nationalist resistance, at a time when the Simla negotiations had only begun (October 1913). Another such concession on the part of the Republican Government may have been impossible. Even if an agreement could have been reached at Simla, China could later have denied its validity, as it did the agreement over Mongolia. Subsequent events reveal that Chinese strategy, or that of the nationalist faction in Chinese politics, was to resolve its relations with the former territories of the Ch'ing empire unilaterally, rather than respect "unequal" treaties concluded with imperialist powers. However, even though China repudiated the Simla Convention, China was unable to exercise actual control over Tibet and therefore remained in need of international recognition of her claim to sovereignty over Tibet. China was concerned by rumors of a secret accord between the Tibetans and the British, and therefore did not completely abandon the search for a negotiated solution to the Tibetan issue.

---

176. Friters, *Outer Mongolia*, 292.

Tibetan Advances in Kham and Post-Simla Negotiations

In Kham, the Chinese continued to hold all the territory east of the Mekong, plus part of Chamdo district to the west. In the summer of 1915, Yuan Shih-k'ai abolished the position of Sining *amban* and transferred the administration of Ch'ing-hai Territory to the Hui (Chinese Muslims) of Sining. Unlike the *amban*, whose authority in the Kokonor region had been nominal, the Hui were determined to more directly impose their authority. They sent troops and officials to all the tribes of Kokonor as far as the borders of central Tibet and Szechuan-administered Kham. They were especially intent on controlling Nangchen, formerly an autonomous nomadic region under the nominal authority of the Sining *amban*, due to competition from the Chinese garrison commander at Chamdo, who attempted to impose his authority there.[177]

The Chinese Republic remained in need of some means to reestablish its position in Tibet. The apparent success of the 1915 Kiakhta agreement with Russia in negating Mongolia's declaration of independence and in securing the reentry of Chinese officials to Mongolia encouraged China to reopen negotiations with Britain over Tibet. The Chinese expressed a willingness to concede Chamdo to Outer Tibet in exchange for a Kokonor border at the Nyenchentangla Range; Tibet was to be clearly indicated as Chinese territory; Tibet would expressly acknowledge Chinese suzerainty; Chinese as well as British trade agents would be allowed in central Tibet.[178] However, Britain was at this time opposed to any agreement that would upset its wartime relations with Russia; the GOI opposed any change in the *status quo*, especially the reintroduction of Chinese officials to Tibet or any agreement with China that might jeopardize its secret border agreement with Tibet. The GOI had adopted a policy of assisting the Tibetans in the preservation of their *de facto* independence by the provision of arms and ammunition.[179]

The proposals of 1915 were China's last attempt to reach an agreement with the British over Tibet. Yuan's attempt to name himself emperor shortly thereafter created rebellion in the provinces. Both Yunnan and Szechuan declared their independence of Peking in 1916. The death of Yuan in 1916 further accelerated the process of disintegration. War ensued between Yunnan and Szechuan. The Chinese garrisons in Kham degenerated.

---

177. Teichman, *Travels of a Consular Officer*, 49.

178. Lamb, *Tibet, China and India*, 34.

179. This was in keeping with McMahon's promise to Shatra at Simla that Britain would provide Tibet with arms. McMahon's Final Memorandum, *India Office Records*, 11. The British sold to the Tibetans 5,000 Lee-Enfield rifles and 500,000 rounds of ammunition.

In September 1916 the British Peking Legation, realizing that a Chinese ratification of Simla was now probably an impossibility, undertook a reappraisal of the Tibetan situation. Chinese objections to an agreement over Tibet were primarily involved with the issue of boundaries in eastern Tibet. Some form of "autonomy" for central Tibet appeared more acceptable than any concession on the boundaries or political status of Chinese claims in eastern Tibet. The Moslem regime in Ch'ing-hai and the regional warlords in Szechuan and Yunnan were even more adamant about territorial claims in eastern Tibet than was Peking. The lack of any Chinese central control raised the possibility that one of the Chinese warlords would unilaterally undertake to impose Chinese control over all of Tibet in imitation of Chao Erh-feng's campaigns of 1905-1910.

The British Foreign Office therefore attempted to secure some guarantee of Tibetan autonomy while such a possibility still existed. The British proposed to concede Chinese territorial ambitions in eastern Tibet, eliminating the special status of Inner Tibet, in order to secure Chinese agreement to the remainder of the Simla provisions. China would be permitted to reestablish its presence, still defined as suzerainty, in Outer Tibet, in return for a formal guarantee of Outer Tibetan autonomy. Since the Tibetan Government was not likely to agree to these terms, it was proposed that negotiations should be bilateral between Britain and China, excluding Tibet. However, these proposals of the British Peking Legation were never presented to the Chinese since they were opposed by British Indian officials for the same reasons as in 1915.[180]

Conflict on the Tibetan border was renewed in 1917 by the Chinese commander of the garrison at Chamdo, General P'eng Jih-sheng, who, apparently on his own authority and in pursuit of his own ambition, broke the existing truce and announced his intention to advance upon Lhasa.[181] The Tibetan commander, Kalon Chamba Tendar (referred to as the Kalon Lama), sent letters to P'eng requesting that he respect the truce, to which P'eng replied:

I have received your letters. You must be aware that Tibet, which was formerly subject to the Emperor of China, is now subject to the President of the

---

Lamb thinks that these were actually the earlier model Lee-Metfords, from which the Lee-Enfield evolved. The Tibetans were later supplied with Lee-Enfields, distinguished from the Lee-Metfords by their shorter barrels. Lamb, *Tibet, China and India*, 19.

180. Lamb, *Tibet, China and India*, 39. The terms of the British proposal were so similar to those of Kiakhta, allowing the Chinese to reestablish their presence in return for an entirely formal guarantee of autonomy, that it may be presumed that they were modeled on that agreement.

181.Ibid, 57.

Chinese Republic. You Tibetans have rebelled, as servants revolting against their masters. Evil thoughts have entered your hearts and your lips have uttered falsehoods. The Chinese Emperor can protect his own dominions and has no need of British mediation. The Chinese soldiers who have advanced from Riwoche [west of Chamdo] are travelling in their own country and can go where they please. The Chinese forces are now about to advance on Lhasa, and you are ordered to make all the necessary preparations for their march.[182]

Unfortunately for P'eng, the Tibetans were now better armed and trained than P'eng's Chinese soldiers, and were not overawed by P'eng's imperious manner. The Tibetans had received another 500,000 rounds of rifle ammunition at the end of 1917.[183] The Tibetans repulsed the Chinese advance and drove the Chinese back to their garrison at Chamdo. The Tibetans also advanced into Dragyab and Markham. The Chinese garrison at Chamdo was surrounded and, by the end of April 1918, forced to surrender.[184] The fall of Chamdo precipitated a general uprising of the Tibetan states of Kham. The Tibetan Army, assisted by local recruits, advanced to retake Gonjo and Derge to the east of the Mekong. The Chinese frontier commissioner at Tachienlu had to divert his attention from rivals in Szechuan in order to prevent the Tibetans from advancing into Kanze and Nyarong. The Chinese managed to stop the Tibetans short of Kanze, at Rongbatsa, but the Tibetans were also advancing south from Derge toward both Nyarong and Batang. The Tibetans were effectively resisted only at Kanze, and nominally at Batang, but were advancing in all other directions and would soon have cut off the Chinese at Kanze.

The Tibetans were prepared to retake all of Kham when the British consular agent stationed at Tachienlu, Eric Teichman, stepped in and negotiated a truce.[185] The Tibetans, still anxious to achieve Chinese acceptance of the Simla accords, were forced to accept British mediation even

---

182. Teichman, *Travels of a Consular Officer*, 53, quoting Letter from General P'eng to the Kalon Lama.

183. Lamb, *Tibet, China and India*, 56.

184. General P'eng at first blamed the fighting on his subordinates, whom he claimed had forced him to initiate action; then, astoundingly, he begged for a position with the Lhasa government. General P'eng and his troops were well-treated by the Tibetans; P'eng remained, with his Tibetan wife, in Tibet on a Tibetan Government pension, while his troops were repatriated to China via India. Ibid., 58.

185. Teichman claimed that his mediation was requested by "local Chinese leaders on the frontier." Teichman, *Travels of a Consular Officer*, 58. Lamb, however, thinks that Teichman acted on his own initiative. Lamb, *Tibet, China and India*, 53. Teichman was formerly of the Peking Legation and was probably one of the authors of the Legation's 1916 proposals on Tibet. Ibid., 39.

though it meant that the Chinese would remain in some parts of Kham that the Tibetans might have retaken had they been allowed to continue their advance. Teichman acknowledged that the Tibetans would have soon recovered all of Kham but he believed that Tibetan control of Kham would not provide as permanent a resolution of the situation as would some compromise with Chinese territorial demands:

> The purpose of our mission is to stop the advancing Tibetan wave, which threatens to submerge all the country up to Tachienlu. If we are unsuccessful in doing so, years of bitter border warfare will ensue; for the Chinese will never agree to surrender their claims to these districts, which they profess to regard as part of Szechuan; while the Lhasa Tibetans, once they have seized all the country up to Tachienlu, will never retire willingly from regions which they hold to be part of Tibet. The best course would appear to be to endeavor to stop the fighting on, or as near as possible to, the old historical frontier line between the Yangtze and the Mekong; in which case there might be a reasonable chance of inducing both sides to accept the situation.[186]

While negotiating a cease-fire, Teichman managed to exert pressure on the Tibetans to accept a settlement by recommending to his government that Tibetan requests to British India for more arms and ammunition be refused.[187] The truce reached in 1918 established a border along the line between the Yangtze and Mekong, with the exception that Gonjo and Derge to the east of the Yangtze remained in Tibetan hands. The Chinese retained control of the Hor states (Kanze, etc.), plus Nyarong, Lithang and Batang. Since the Chinese commander in the field was unable to communicate with his government, the cease-fire was provisional on final ratification by Peking. That ratification was not forthcoming; the British ambassador at Peking confessed that his meetings with the Chinese foreign minister were futile, the minister, like his predecessors, being "obsessed with his country's sovereign rights in Tibet."[188]

The British sought to reopen negotiations in 1919 after the end of the war in Europe. Ch'en Lu, the acting Chinese foreign minister, who had been involved in negotiations with Russia over Mongolia, thought that the Mongolian agreement might serve as a model for a Tibetan settlement since, "In the past the Chinese Government have treated Mongolia and

---

186. Teichman, *Travels of a Consular Officer*, 73. Teichman unwittingly accepted China's claim that the administrative division made by the Ch'ing between central and eastern Tibet actually constituted a "historical frontier" between China and Tibet.

187. Addy, *Tibet on the Imperial Chessboard*, 312, 327. The Tibetans' request for a million rounds of ammunition was turned down during the conflict.

188. Ibid., 328.

Tibet in the same manner. Outer Mongolia having already been permitted to enjoy autonomy, it follows that no opposition will be placed in the way of Tibetan autonomy."[189] On 30 May 1919 Ch'en proposed a settlement based upon revision of four points: a statement that Tibet was a part of China; Outer Tibet must recognize Chinese suzerainty; the frontier between Inner and Outer Tibet would be renegotiated; and Chinese agents would be stationed at Tibetan trade marts.

Negotiations actually began in August 1919 in Peking. Tibet was not represented, since a Tibetan presence was thought to be a potential hindrance, especially if territorial concessions to China were to be contemplated.[190] The Chinese suggested that all of Kokonor up to the Nyenchentangla Range should be in Inner Tibet, or Ch'ing-hai, but that Derge and Nyarong might be part of Outer Tibet. At this point, the Chinese broke off negotiations, citing domestic opposition.[191] The 4 May 1919 protests against the post-War award of German rights in Shantung to Japan had just occurred (making, perhaps for the first time, Chinese public opinion a significant factor in Chinese politics) and Chinese anti-foreign nationalism was at a high pitch, making any concessions to Britain in Tibet, or even negotiating with Britain over "Chinese" territory, a political impossibility. The warlords of Yunnan, Szechuan and Ch'ing-hai had also voiced vigorous opposition to giving away any of what they regarded as provincial territory and threatened noncompliance with any agreement made by Peking, a real possibility considering their virtual autonomy.[192] Another factor may have been that, by the summer of 1919, China had virtually regained its position in Mongolia; the prevalent mood in China was that, given time, the Chinese position in Tibet might be similarly recovered.[193]

Teichman, now at the British Foreign Office, suggested in a memorandum in early 1920 that, since China was no longer likely to negotiate with Britain over Tibet, and because the Russian Revolution could be argued

---

189. Lamb, *Tibet, China and India*, 86. The Chinese, of course, had interpreted the Kiakhta Treaty as an abrogation of Mongol independence and, since 1917 when Russia was removed from the scene, had been actively reestablishing Chinese influence there. At the end of 1918, Chinese troops were increased and the Chinese foreign minister announced China's intention to cancel the previous treaties in regard to Mongol autonomy. Friters, *Outer Mongolia*, 185.

190. Tibetan representation was considered undesirable since Tibet had recently successfully defended itself against the Chinese in eastern Tibet, even regaining territory, and was in no mood to make territorial concessions. Lamb, *Tibet, China and India*, 90.

191. Addy, *Tibet on the Imperial Chessboard*, 328; Lamb, *Tibet, China and India*, 88.

192. The Szechuan Provincial Assembly, in particular, was willing to accept nothing short of Chao Erh-feng's border at Giamda. Lamb, *Tibet, China and India*, 94.

193. Ibid., 91.

to have eliminated the restrictions of the 1907 Anglo-Russian Treaty, Britain could and should establish closer bilateral relations with Tibet. As Teichman said, "It is immoral to continue a policy which has for its object the checking of all progress in Tibet, when the Tibetans themselves are waking up and looking to us for assistance in their development."[194] Teichman suggested that Tibet should no longer be intentionally isolated by British policy, but that it should be opened to the outside world, via India, and thus, by modernization and economic development, be strengthened in its ability to resist Chinese ambitions.

Teichman felt that only British protection of Tibet could ultimately prevent a reimposition of control by China. He suggested that, should Tibet be established as a self-governing dominion with a relationship to Britain similar to the states members of the British Commonwealth, Tibet's case might then be taken up before an international tribunal such as the League of Nations: "If a British Dominion can join the League and sign the Arms Convention, while remaining a part of the British Empire, why should not Tibet do the same, without prejudice to Chinese suzerainty?"[195] However, in order to preserve British relations with China and Britain's exclusive rights in Tibet, Tibet could not be encouraged or supported in its aspirations for independence. British policy would be to continue to press China to agree to a Simla type solution, but, in the meantime, it would be assumed that all parties accepted the Simla Convention in principle, with the exception of the disagreement over the border.[196]

In November 1919 China abrogated Mongol autonomy, ostensibly in response to a petition signed by Mongol leaders. The Chinese did little to endear themselves after their reimposition of rule, and were overthrown in October 1920 by a White Russian refugee, Baron Ungern Sternberg, known as the "Mad Baron," who had visions of a pan-Mongol Buddhist empire. He managed to gather Mongol, Russian and even a few Tibetan troops, armed and supported by the Japanese, who eliminated the Chinese in Outer Mongolia.[197] Sternberg was overthrown by Mongol revolutionaries supported by the Soviet Red Army in July 1921. The Soviet Government recognized Mongolia as an independent state in 1921, making no mention of any Chinese rights.[198]

---

194. "Memorandum by E. Teichman," 29 February 1920, in Mehra, *Northeastern Frontier*, vol. 2, 22.

195. Ibid., 21.

196. Lamb, *Tibet, China and India*, 98.

197. Seventy Tibetan troops were reportedly sent by the Thirteenth Dalai Lama to support Mongol Buddhist aspirations. Peter Hopkirk, *Setting the East Ablaze: Lenin's Dream of an Empire in Asia* (New York: Norton, 1984), 127.

198. Friters, *Outer Mongolia*, 121. In 1924 in a draft treaty with the Peking government,

China attempted to reestablish its influence in Tibet in 1920 by means of mission sent by the provincial authorities of Kansu, whose purpose was reported to have been to persuade Tibet to make an accommodation with China and exclude British influence. The Dalai Lama instead sent a message to the British suggesting that a British representative, preferably Charles Bell, should be sent to Lhasa for consultations. This was approved, since the British foreign secretary agreed that the 1907 Anglo-Russian Convention, which had previously prohibited the British having a representative at Lhasa, could be regarded as no longer valid.[199]

Bell's visit to Lhasa in 1920-21 renewed Anglo-Tibetan relations but also evoked a conservative reaction, led by the monks of Drepung, against British influence. Tibetan conservatives were opposed to British modernization and education schemes; some favored an accommodation with China in order to salvage Tibet's traditional autonomous status and, hopefully, Chinese patronage of Buddhism.[200] Many in the monastic community thought that the only good reason for establishing relations with the British was if the British would take over the role of patron of Tibetan Buddhism in place of the Chinese, a role which the British neither understood nor were willing to play. Upon his return to India, Bell pointed out that Britain's policy of excluding everyone, including themselves, from Tibet had strengthened the Chinese position; he recommended that Britain revive the Tibetans' trust by an increase in military aid. As Bell reported to the GOI:

> We should recognize that Tibet, a well-governed country, does not wish her internal administration should come again under the misgovernment and oppression of China. We should recognize that she has for ten years maintained troops at great sacrifice on her eastern frontier to keep out the Chinese invaders. Finally, we should recognize India's vital interests in this problem and the dangers that threaten her in our present policy of inaction.[201]

---

the Soviet Union agreed to recognize Chinese sovereignty in Outer Mongolia, on the understanding that China would not press its claim. The Mongolian People's Republic was formally established in 1924 and was immediately recognized by the Soviet Union. Ibid., 195.

199. Addy, *Tibet on the Imperial Chessboard*, 333.

200. Dawa Norbu claims, based upon interviews with former Tibetan aristocrats, that "Nationalist China bribed and instigated the abbots in Lhasa" to oppose British and Tibetan Government modernization efforts. Dawa Norbu, "Changes in Tibetan Economy, 1959-76," *China Report*, 24:3 (1988), 222.

201. "Bell to India," 19 January 1921, as quoted in Lamb, *Tibet, China and India*, 116. Bell also emphasized Tibet's role as a "barrier against Bolshevism." Richardson, *Tibetan Precis*, 26.

The Indian Government accepted Bell's argument that Tibetan autonomy was precarious and should be supported against Chinese ambitions; a more forceful Indian policy was essential or India would soon find an expansive and belligerent China on its northern border. Recent Tibetan military successes in Kham provided hope that the Tibetan situation could be salvaged by the Tibetans themselves, with judicious British assistance. In addition, the British were coming under pressure from the Americans, who tended to regard British support for Tibetan autonomy as an unsavory remnant of British colonialism, to abandon their colonialist policy in Tibet in favor of the American Open Door policy on China, which was opposed to exclusive areas of influence of the European imperial powers.[202]

In August 1921 the British again approached the Chinese to negotiate, threatening that if they did not do so, Britain would deal with Tibet bilaterally, recognize Tibetan autonomy, and supply Tibet with arms. On 26 August 1921 a memorandum was presented to the Chinese ambassador in London, inviting China to resume negotiations without delay in London or Peking:

> In view of commitments of His Majesty's Government to the Tibetan Government arising out of the tripartite negotiations of 1914 and in view of the fact that, with the exception of the boundary clause, the draft Convention of 1914 providing for Tibetan autonomy under Chinese suzerainty was accepted by the Chinese Government who in their offer of 1919 formally reaffirmed their attitude in this, His Majesty's Government, failing a resumption of negotiations in the immediate future, do not feel justified in withholding any longer their recognition of the status of Tibet as an autonomous state under the suzerainty of China and intend dealing with Tibet in future on this basis.[203]

The Chinese Foreign Minister replied that he was preoccupied with

---

202. Addy, *Tibet on the Imperial Chessboard*, 338. On the Open Door policy, see Shutaro Tomimas, *The Open-Door Policy and The Territorial Integrity of China* (Arlington, Virginia: University Publications of America, 1919, 1976).

203. Richardson, *Tibetan Precis*, 27. Britain had not previously withheld recognition of Tibetan autonomy, or Chinese suzerainty, thus the distinction here is easily lost. The essential element was that Tibet was to be regarded as an autonomous state with the ability to conduct independent foreign relations. This status would allow Britain to sell arms to Tibet as a state separate from China without violating an international arms control agreement of 1919. Britain was to regard Tibetan autonomy, which was to extend to foreign as well as domestic affairs, as equivalent in practice to independence; Chinese "suzerainty" would be entirely symbolic. Britain thus hoped to have it both ways, to treat Tibet as independent in practice without abandoning its recognition of Chinese "suzerainty" over Tibet and without violating its commitment with other nations to respect Chinese territorial integrity.

preparations for the upcoming post-war Washington Conference, and made "contemptuous enquiries whether we [the British] really thought that Tibet was capable of self-government."[204] The Foreign Minister threatened to denounce British policy in Tibet at the Washington Conference as a violation of the Open Door policy.[205] The 1922 Washington Conference was convened to deal with post-war armaments issues, but also dealt with issues of the Far East, including the American-sponsored Open Door policy. The Nine Power Treaty signed at the Conference confirmed the Open Door policy and committed the contracting parties to respect the "sovereignty, the independence, and the territorial and administrative integrity of China."[206]

The territorial limits of the Chinese state whose territorial integrity was to be respected was the subject of some debate. The French delegate questioned the territorial definition of China.[207] The American delegate proposed to distinguish between "China proper and the territories over which China exercised suzerainty." He suggested taking China proper, for "if the committee had to deal with outlying districts at the same time, it would only lead to confusion; it would be possible to deal with the outlying districts later; it was impossible to do both at once."[208]

The Chinese delegate, Wellington Koo, objected that, since he represented the Republic of China, he would not discuss anything less than the territory claimed by the Republic.[209] The Chinese delegation maintained that the resolution should call for respect for the territorial integrity of the Chinese Republic.[210] The American delegate compromised by avoiding the term "China proper," but did not adopt the term "Chinese Republic." Instead, the treaty left vague the definition of the territories under Chinese sovereignty by referring to the territorial integrity of "China." As the American delegate explained this compromise, "It was, on the whole, desirable to adhere to the use of terms already frequently employed in various treaties and declarations, without variation. Such agreements have uniformly used the expression China. He did not think any attempt should be made to define or expand terms and therefore used the expression China."[211]

---

204. Ibid., 28.

205. Addy, *Tibet on the Imperial Chessboard*, 339.

206. Nine Power Treaty, 6 February 1922, in *Treaties and Other International Agreements of the United States of America*, vol 2 (1918-1930), 377.

207. Washington Conference, Minutes of Committee on Pacific and Far Eastern Questions, in *Senate Documents, 67th Congress, 2nd Session, 1921-1922* (Washington: Government Printing Office, 1922), 448.

208. Ibid., 451.

209. Ibid.

210. Ibid., 444.

211. Ibid., 454.

The resulting language did not recognize all the territories claimed by the Chinese Republic, but neither was the territorial integrity of "China" limited to "China proper." Therefore, China did not achieve specific recognition that Tibet was a part of the territory of China. However, US officials at the Washington Conference, in the first official US reference to Tibet, orally assured the Chinese that the United States recognized Chinese sovereignty over Tibet.[212] The Nine Power Treaty also upheld the Open Door, which was opposed in principle to exclusive spheres of influence such as the British claimed in Tibet.

Britain thereafter dealt with Tibet as a *de facto* autonomous state but ceased efforts to achieve Chinese recognition of that fact. Instead, Britain proposed to "regard the problem as settled by China's acceptance of the 1914 Convention, except for the boundary clause, and her reaffirmation of that attitude in 1991." Sales of military equipment to Tibet were increased. In addition, Tibetans were given military training at Gyantse and some were brought to India for the same purpose. Assistance was provided for the construction of a telegraph line from Lhasa to Gyantse and for a small hydroelectric unit for Lhasa. A geological survey was conducted and an English school was opened at Gyantse.[213]

In addition, Britain informed the Tibetans that, given the state of disunity in China and the lack of British leverage, the Chinese could not be brought to accept or to renegotiate the Simla Convention. The British advised the Tibetans to protect their border as it existed at the time and refrain from further advances in Kham (even though at that time the Chinese presence in Kham was virtually nonexistent) in order to avoid provoking a Chinese response. The Tibetans were disappointed at Britain's inability to achieve any confirmation from China of Tibet's autonomous status; they requested that the British continue their

---

212. I have been unable to find any reference to this assurance in the voluminous documents of the Washington Conference. This reference is from a 1950 State Department analysis of Tibet's status, which added: "Probably in the use of the word `sovereignty' nothing more was meant than that the United States recognized that China retained some undefined rights over Tibet analogous to what the British meant in the term `suzerainty.'" "Legal Status of Tibet," State Department Memorandum, 5 December 1950, National Archives, 793B.00/11-2250.

213. Richardson, *Tibetan Precis*, 29. Military supplies amounted to 10 2.75-inch mountain guns with ammunition, 20 machine guns, 10,000 Lee-Enfield rifles and a million rounds of .303 ammunition (for both rifles and machine guns). In fact, Tibet did not take delivery of the full component of arms due to difficulties in making payment, and, according to Lamb, sold some of the ammunition to Bhutan. Lamb, *Tibet, China and India*, 179. The practical, if not quite legal, implications of British supply of arms to Tibet on a government-to-government basis were that Britain recognized Tibet as an autonomous state. Ibid., 136.

attempts to force the Chinese to negotiate.[214] The Dalai Lama also continued his contacts with the Russians through Dorjiev, empowering Dorjiev to represent Tibet to the Soviet Union.[215] The Dalai Lama also reportedly expressed fears that the Chinese would attempt to divide Tibet by means of intrigues with the Panchen Lama.[216]

Flight of the Panchen Lama

The Dalai Lama's apprehensions in regard to the Panchen Lama proved to be well founded. The reforms initiated by the Thirteenth Dalai Lama had aroused resentment among the most conservative elements in Tibet. Not only were the reforms themselves perceived as a threat, but the expenses involved, the most significant of which were for arms, had to be bourne in part by the monasteries and the aristocracy. The Tibetan Government had few sources of cash revenue; the expenses of maintaining an army required that the government find new sources of revenue or acquire revenue producing estates from the aristocracy or monasteries.

Tibetan attempts to impose taxes on trade with India were vetoed by the GOI, which had acquired duty-free trade privileges with Tibet by the terms of the Simla Convention. The only other way to raise revenue was for the Lhasa government to impose itself between estate holders and their taxpayers.[217] Several semi-autonomous estates had previously paid

---

214. Tibet also held the British to their promise to secure Chinese ratification of the Simla Convention as a condition for the agreement over the border with India by which Tibet had ceded territory (Tawang) to India. Lamb, *Tibet, China and India*, 124.

215. Dorjiev had continued his activities in favor of Buryatia and Tibet as a member of the Soviet Nationalities Commission. He attempted to draw parallels between Buddhism and Communism in order to preserve Buddhism in the Soviet Union. He argued that the good treatment of Buddhists in the Soviet Union was the best foundation for promoting Soviet influence in Outer Mongolia and Tibet. Dorjiev was associated with two missions of Buryat pilgrims to Lhasa in 1922 and 1927, both intended to cultivate Soviet relations with Tibet and to impress the Tibetans with the treatment of Buddhists in the Soviet Union. By the time of the latter mission, however, Dorjiev had become so disillusioned with Soviet practice toward religion that he sent a secret message to the Dalai Lama with the latter group advising the Dalai Lama to have nothing to do with them. Snelling, *Buddhism in Russia*, 212, 220.

216. Richardson, *Tibetan Precis*, 30.

217. The estate system was essentially one of indirect administration and indirect taxation; rights to taxation were awarded to aristocratic families who, in return, provided officials to the state, or to monasteries for their own maintenance. The Tibetan Government also possessed some estates that paid their taxes directly, but these were mainly in the form of goods and services. Estate holders in central Tibet had some delegated authority (taxation, juridical), but this authority was delegated to them in their capacity as bureaucratic officers

some taxes to Lhasa and had contributed both men and money to the Tibetan army in times of crisis. The post-1912 demands of the Dalai Lama were much greater and more permanent, however, and were an increase in Lhasa's centralized control that several semi-autonomous estates, both secular and monastic, thought an infringement of their traditional autonomy. The Tibetan Government also tried to raise revenue by means of a poll tax, a one-time tax on individuals, known as the "ear tax" because the Dalai Lama stated that everyone who had ears had to pay.[218]

The Tibetan ecclesiastical establishment was also resistant to paying taxes to support the Tibetan Army, not only because violence was against Buddhist principles, but because the army threatened to rival the Buddhist Church's traditional power. The political role played by the monasteries' corps of "fighting monks" was also threatened by the creation of a secular army and police force. The young Tibetan army officers were also a new factor in Tibetan politics; they were relatively modern, usually pro-British and often supporters of Tibetan nationalism and independence. Some of the army officers were aware that it was the church's dependence upon foreign patrons that had compromised Tibet's independence in the past and were therefore in favor of a more secular administration in Tibet.

Relations between the Dalai and Panchen Lamas, already strained by the Panchen's actions during both of the Dalai Lama's exiles, were further exacerbated by the requirement placed on Tashilhunpo to bear a quarter of the total financial burden of the army.[219] This precipitated a conflict between Lhasa and Tashilhunpo in regard to the traditional relations between the Dalai and Panchen Lamas and between U and Tsang. As Richardson describes it, the conflict was "between the determination of Lhasa to reduce Tashilhunpo to the status—on which there was fair reason to insist—of an honoured vassal, and the reluctance of Tashilhunpo to give up any of the privileges which it had acquired in the past century

---

of the state; estate holders were not semi-independent "vassals" with only a personal relationship to the sovereign. All land was the property of the state, or the Dalai Lama, who could award or confiscate estates at will. The Tibetan estate system was more a means of indirect taxation than of feudal indirect rule. Tibetan administration was more akin to what Weber termed "praebendal feudalism," under which fiefs are awarded according to the income they yield in exchange for services to the state. Max Weber, *Economy and Society* (Berkeley: University of California Press, 1968), 260.

218. This tax was later denounced by the Chinese Communists, who claimed that the tax was known as the ear tax because those who refused or could not pay had their ears cut off.

219. The precedent for a one-quarter share to be bourne by Tashilhunpo was their contribution of one fourth of the expenses to expel the Gurkhas in 1791. Melvyn Goldstein, A *History of Modern Tibet*, 1913-1951 (Berkeley: University of California Press, 1989), 110.

or more."[220] The Panchen's traditional temporal powers were, in Richardson's words, "never more than those which the Tibetan feudal nobility and the great monasteries exercised over their large estates."[221] On the other hand, the Panchen Lamas had exercised more spiritual influence than Dalai Lamas during the previous century due to the failure of the Dalai Lamas of that era to reach maturity. This had led to "a growth in their [the Panchen Lamas'] prestige and authority and to an air of independence in the administration of their fief."[222]

In 1922 Tashilhunpo's assessed contribution being in arrears, some of the monastery's representatives in Lhasa were imprisoned. The Panchen Lama asked the British to mediate in the dispute, but this they refused to do on the grounds that it would have "constituted interference in Tibetan internal affairs."[223] In December 1923 the Panchen Lama, accompanied by most of his retinue, departed Tashilhunpo for an unspecified destination to the north. Troops were dispatched from Lhasa to bring the Panchen back but they failed to apprehend him. The Panchen later announced that because of the unreasonable demands of the Lhasa officials, not the Dalai Lama himself, he had been forced to flee. The purpose of his journey, he said, was to seek mediation and to raise funds from disciples.[224]

The Panchen travelled first to Mongolia and then in February 1924 turned up in Peking. His Chinese hosts, delighted to have gained this wedge into Tibetan politics, showered him with honors. The Dalai Lama was greatly distressed at this turn of events, realizing that the revival of Tibetan regional rivalries would play into the hands of the Chinese. He accused the Panchen of selfishness in putting his own welfare above that of Tibet and appointed an administrator to take over Tashilhunpo in the Panchen Lama's absence.[225] The Chinese, occupied with their own civil

---

220. Richardson, *Tibet and Its History*, 126.

221. Ibid., 53. The Sakya estate, also in Tsang, was traditionally more autonomous than Tashilhunpo. Only Sakya shared with Lhasa the designation as *shung*, "government," due to Sakya's role as government of Tibet under the Yuan. Both Lhasa and Sakya officials wore their hair in topknots as insignia of office. This privilege was traditionally denied to Tashilhunpo officials; a request from the Panchen Lama that it be granted was denied by Lhasa (no date is given). C.W. Cassinelli and Robert B. Ekvall, *A Tibetan Principality: The Political System of Sakya* (Ithaca: Cornell University Press, 1969), 46, 50.

222. Richardson, *Tibet and Its History*, 126.

223. Ibid., 127.

224. The Panchen construed his flight as within Tibetan traditional religious and political traditions, a fact that only seems to have increased the Dalai Lama's irritation. The Panchen departed because of "foreign" political interference, as had the Dalai Lama, and he traveled to Mongolia and China in search of patrons, as had Sakya Pandita, the Third Dalai Lama, the Fifth Dalai Lama, and the Thirteenth Dalai Lama. The Panchen himself had previously travelled to India and had there sought support for his independent political rights.

225. Mehra, *Tibetan Polity*, 46.

war, found no immediate way to capitalize upon the Panchen's presence in China, except to constantly threaten to restore him by force. The Panchen's exile was an embarrassment to the Dalai Lama, not least of all because the Panchen's access to the international press promoted his version of the dispute. The Panchen was portrayed as the innocent victim of a power-hungry and intolerant Dalai Lama. The Chinese did not fail to point to the affair as evidence that Tibet was not a unitary state but merely an assortment of feudal dependencies of China.

It was in Tibet that the most serious effects were felt. The Panchen Lama's flight hampered the Dalai Lama's attempts to create Tibetan political unity and centralize Tibetan administration. The Panchen was highly revered for his gentle nature and great learning not only in Tsang but throughout Tibet, and his exile was generally taken as an ill omen. Animosity arose against the officials of Lhasa, and even against the Dalai Lama himself, as well as against taxation, the creation of an army and modernization in general. Regional rivalries were exacerbated and Lhasa's predominance was resented not only in Tsang but in other regions of Tibet. A revolt against Lhasa's centralization policies, especially taxation, occurred in Powo (Pobo), in eastern central Tibet. Lhasa's authority was affirmed but not without some difficulty; the ruler of Powo, the Kanam Depa, sought refuge in Assam.[226]

The Panchen's flight strengthened the hand of conservatives, who blamed the Dalai Lama's reforms for the difficulties between Lhasa and Tashilhunpo. The reaction to the Dalai Lama's reforms included criticism of British influence, and all that was identified with that influence, including the army and modernization in general. The British were also blamed for pursuing their own imperialist interests in relation to Tibet rather than Tibet's interest, a charge that had some validity. In particular, the British were faulted for their failure to secure Chinese recognition of Tibetan autonomy. The British-trained Tibetan Army was thereafter allowed to deteriorate, and other British innovations, such as the English school at Gyantse, were cancelled. British efforts to mediate the dispute with the Panchen were turned down by the Dalai Lama due to his unwillingness to appear too dependent upon the British.[227]

The decline of British influence in Lhasa encouraged the Chinese, who were convinced that anti-Chinese sentiments in Tibet were solely due to British influence. In 1928 China came under the more unified administration of the Kuomintang. An anti-British "Save Tibet" campaign

226. Shakabpa, *Tibet: A Political History*, 264.

227. Mehra, *Tibetan Polity*, 48. Apparently, the British volunteered to mediate when the dispute became an international affair.

emerged in Szechuan. The plan to make Sikang a province was revived by the KMT in 1928, and Liu Wen-hui, the warlord of western Szechuan, announced his intention to make it a reality.[228] In 1928 Ch'ing-hai was made a province. The Panchen Lama and his entourage actively cultivated Chinese support. According to Tieh-tseng Li: "In 1928, a year after the establishment of the Nationalist Government in Nanking, the Panch'en sent delegates to express his respects to the new regime, and at the same time put forward a request that the Chinese Government assume full charge of affairs in Tibet in order to save it from becoming a `second India.'"[229] In 1928 the KMT also established a "Mongolian and Tibetan Affairs Commission," which was ostensibly responsible for the administration of Mongolia and Tibet but whose actual purpose was to convince Mongolians and Tibetans to return to the Chinese fold. The Commission recommended that both the Dalai and Panchen Lamas should be made members of the Nationalist Government.[230]

Last Years of the Dalai Lama

In 1929 the Chinese Government sent Liu Man-ch'ing, a woman interpreter at the Mongolian and Tibetan Affairs Commission, to Lhasa "for the purpose of conveying to the Tibetan Government and people its good will and friendship and to make a report on conditions in that region."[231] Liu had been born in Lhasa of a Chinese father and Tibetan mother and spoke Tibetan. She explained the change of government in China to the Tibetans and conveyed the wish of Chiang Kai-shek that Tibetans should "rejoin the family of the Republic as brothers." In Tieh-tseng Li's account of Liu Man-ch'ing's conversation with the Dalai Lama, the Dalai Lama reportedly said that he expected from China "unity and peace," a statement that Li interpreted to mean that the Dalai Lama favored Tibetan unity with China, rather than the more logical and likely interpretation

---

228. Liu was unable to make good on his promise at the time. The idea was revived again in 1935, when the KMT issued an ordinance to make Sikang a province, to take effect on 1 January 1939. Borders were to extend to Giamda, as had been claimed by Chao Erh-feng. However, the Szechuan warlord, Liu Wen-hui, was again unable to extend his control over Sikang because of his involvement in rivalries with other Szechuan warlords. The presence of a semi-autonomous Chinese warlord in western Szechuan posed a constant threat to central Tibet but, along with Ma Pu-feng's regime in Ch'ing-hai, may actually have hampered any KMT move toward reestablishing its control in Tibet. Lamb, *Tibet, China and India*, 303.

229. Tieh-tseng Li, *Tibet: Today and Yesterday* (New York: Bookman Associates, 1960), 150.

230. Lamb, *Tibet, China and India*, 177.

231. Tieh-tseng Li, *Tibet: Today and Yesterday*, 149.

that he hoped that China would achieve internal unity after a period of civil war.[232]

A separate official communication from Peking was dispatched to Lhasa via the Yungon Dzasa, the Tibetan abbot of the Lama Temple (Yung-ho Kung) at Peking, who had been appointed to this post by the Dalai Lama in 1922.[233] The Chinese attempted to initiate a dialogue on Tibet's status by means of written questions that were to be posed to the Dalai Lama. These questions reveal much about Chinese negotiating tactics and their assumptions about Tibet's status; the replies of the Dalai Lama (as recorded by the Yungon Dzasa and reported by Li) correspondingly reveal much about the Tibetans' views on their traditional and contemporary relationship with China. The question and answer method employed by the Chinese allowed them to frame and limit the dialogue to their own advantage. Each of the questions presupposes that a certain relation already exists between China and Tibet; the progression of questions tends to confirm what that relationship will be regardless of the Dalai Lama's answers:

Q. How might relations between Tibet and the Central Government be restored?

A. If the Central Government would treat the patronage relationship between China and Tibet with sincerity and good faith as it previously did, Tibet on its part, having always shown sincerity in its dealings in the past, would from now on make an even greater effort to give full support to the Central Government.

Q. How shall the Central Government exercise administrative control over Tibet?

A. It would be advisable to work out a written understanding on the measures to be taken for securing a fundamental stabilization both in the political and the religious affairs of Tibet.

Q. How shall the autonomy of Tibet and its scope be defined?

A. As from now on, the patronage relationship between the Central Government and Tibet is going to be faithfully observed and the Central Government is to show sincerity to make Tibet feel safe and secure; the area over which autonomy is to be exercised should naturally be the same as before. It is expected that the Central Government will return to Tibet those districts which originally belonged to it but which are now not under its control so that a perpetual peace and harmony will surely be the result.

---

232. Ibid., 151.
233. Ibid., 152.

Q. Shall the Dalai and Panch'en Lamas join the Kuomintang?

A. On account of his advanced age and the tremendous burden in managing temporal and religious affairs, and also considering the fact that he is not able to proceed to the capital until the consent of the three leading monasteries and of the members of the National Assembly is obtained, the Dalai Lama is not at the present time in a position to join the Kuomintang. As the Panch'en Lama is now residing in China Proper and his duty has always been confined to the religious affairs of Tashilhunpo, for he has no political affairs to attend to, he should be available for membership of the Kuomintang. It must be understood, however, that he has never had any say in the settlement of Tibetan affairs.

Q. Shall the relative position of the Dalai and the Panch'en Lama and their respective jurisdiction in political as well as religious affairs be maintained as before or new provisions be made?

A. Political and religious affairs have always been administered by the Tibetan Government at Lhasa. The Panch'en Lama has had only the Tashilhunpo monastery in his control. Actually the Tashilhunpo monastery was built by the first Dalai Lama. It was the second Dalai Lama who entrusted the administration to a fellow monk and conferred upon the latter the honorary title of Panch'en, when he moved his seat to Lhasa. Later, in view of the tutor-disciple relationship existing in turn through generations between the Dalai and the Panch'en, the fifth Dalai Lama awarded this monastery to the fourth Panch'en Lama. If this age-old practice were to be continuously observed, all Tibetans would be only too pleased.

Q. How shall the Dalai welcome the Panch'en back to Tibet and how shall the Central Government escort him?

A. Among the Panch'en's retinue, many employed the terms "Anterior" and "Ulterior" Tibet with intend to sow discord.[234] They disobeyed orders of the Tibetan Government and acted frequently against their superiors. Both their thought and conduct are corrupt. In the year 1904, the Panch'en went to India and conspired with the British, but all his efforts were of no avail. In the year 1911 he intrigued with the Resident Lien-yu and made an attempt to seize the reins of government and control of the church during the absence of the Dalai Lama. But his efforts were thwarted by the opposition of the people and especially of the clergymen of the three leading monasteries. According to established practice, the Panch'en should contribute one quarter of the provisions for the Army. Not only did he fail to make such contributions, but he also committed acts in violation of law. Had the offenders been punished strictly in accordance with the letter of the law, there would have been no such state of affairs as now exists. It is only in consideration of the long-standing and close tutor-disciple relation-

---

234. "Anterior," meaning U, and "Ulterior," meaning Tsang; the implication was that the two were separate political entities.

ship between the Dalai and the Panch'en through generations that a policy of tolerance and forgiveness has been followed. Yet these people not only remained unrepentant, but further advised and urged the Panch'en to flee away from Tashilhunpo. A dispatch inviting him back was soon sent to the Panch'en but he refused to accept. He then fled to Urga and had secret dealings with the communists. Only upon the death of the Chief Lama of Mongolia, Cheputsuntanpa [Jebtsundampa], was he obliged to come to China Proper. Consequently, the Tibetan Government dispatched officials to Tashilhunpo to take proper care of the monastery. Now, these offenders are still conspiring and making trouble. As the matter stands, Tibet would find it very difficult to welcome them unless they can give a satisfactory explanation as to their reason for taking to flight.

Q. Has the Dalai Lama the intention of setting up in the Capital an office for the convenience of keeping closer contact? As to its expenses, the Central Government is prepared to grant the necessary funds.

A. At first, offices are to be set up in Nanking, Peiping, and Sikang.[235] If and when such offices are required for other places, applications will be filed accordingly.

Q. Is there anything else that Tibet expects of the Central Government?

A. For the purpose of protecting itself against aggression, Tibet's hope for the present is only that the Central Government will supply it with arms. In case any other help may be needed in the future for strengthening its security, it will make requests to the Central Government.[236]

The progression from the first question, "How might relations be restored?" to the second, "How shall the Central Government exercise administrative control over Tibet?" is an example of how the questions themselves attempt to define Sino-Tibetan relations. The use of the term "Central Government," instead of "Chinese Government," implies a relationship of Tibet to a Chinese center of authority. The questions assume that the "Central Government" will administer Tibet; Tibet will have some vague "autonomy." The inquiry whether the Lamas would join the Kuomintang implies that Tibetan officials, in particular the Dalai and Panchen Lamas, were in some sense "Chinese" officials. The division of political authority between the Dalai and Panchen Lamas was to be determined by the Central Government. The questions assume that the

---

235. The Dalai Lama was unlikely to have used the term "Sikang." Chinese from the early twentieth century referred to Kham as Sikang, with the result that foreign diplomats and journalists thought that Sikang was the proper name for Kham and that it was a part of China.
236. Tieh-tseng Li, *Tibet: Today and Yesterday*, 153.

Panchen will return with a Chinese escort. In every "question," an administrative role for the Chinese Government is insinuated, the overall implication being that China had some authority over Tibet. The Dalai Lama admitted to a relationship with China, which he interpreted within the traditional framework of the *Cho-Yon*. However, his demand for the return of Kham indicates that his interpretation was that the relationship would be essentially the same as that which existed during the Ch'ing, with the exception that Tibet would now provide for its own defense. His reply to the suggestion that he and the Panchen join the KMT was in the form of a denigration of the Panchen just for being in China and an emphasis that the Panchen had no temporal role. Tibet had no political parties at the time; it is uncertain whether the Dalai Lama understood the implications of his or the Panchen's membership in the KMT. The Dalai Lama succumbed to Chinese "suggestions," combined with offers to pay all expenses, to upgrade Tibetan contacts with China by means of setting up "offices" in the Chinese capital; however, his idea that this would require Chinese permits leads to the interpretation that he thought of the offices as similar to consulates. The Dalai Lama requested arms from China, a request that must have astounded the Chinese, with whom the Tibetans had recently been at war. His request implied state-to-state relations between Tibet and China and indicated that he intended to continue to defend Tibetan independence.

The "dialogue" reveals the extent to which the Panchen's flight had compromised the Dalai Lama's attempts to achieve national unity and independence. Because of the affair, the Chinese were afforded a role as paternalistic mediator between the feuding Lamas. The Chinese suggestion that new provisions be made (by themselves) concerning the political jurisdiction of the Panchen demonstrates the damage to Tibetan unity that the Panchen's actions caused. The Chinese were now in a position to mediate in this dispute and thus to perpetuate this political and territorial division of Tibet.

From 1918 until 1931 the Tibetans continued to respect the 1918 ceasefire line in Kham in the hope that a final settlement with China might be reached. In 1931 a dispute broke out in Kham when the chief of Beri, one of the Hor states, seized the estates of Nyarong monastery. The Nyarong Lama sought refuge at Dargay monastery in Nyarong and requested the assistance of Tibetan Army troops at Derge. The dispute involved, or was suspected by Lhasa to involve, the Panchen Lama's followers on the side of the chief of Beri. Tibetan troops at Derge intervened on the side of Dargay; Chinese troops of the Szechuan warlord Liu Wen-hui intervened on the side of the chief of Beri.

The Tibetans quickly drove the Chinese almost all the way back to Tachienlu. A cease-fire was negotiated that left Derge in Tibetan hands and Nyarong and Kanze under divided control. This settlement aroused protest among the Szechuanese, who still considered all of Kham up to Giamda to be Chinese territory. The Chinese suspected British intrigues: "The Nationalist press, although far from the scene of action and from any reliable sources of information, at once launched out into the frantic anti-British propaganda which was almost automatic whenever the Tibetans got the better of the Chinese. British-trained troops with British officers were alleged to have established themselves in Chamdo; and charges of British instigation of the Tibetans were hurled about."[237]

In April 1932 Liu Wen-hui's troops counterattacked and forced the Tibetans out of Nyarong, Kanze and Derge, at which point the Tibetan commanders agreed to a truce. While this conflict was taking place in Kham, another monastic dispute erupted in Nangchen, near Jyekundo. Tibetan troops were dispatched from Chamdo to Nangchen, provoking a response from the Hui governor of Sining, Ma Pu-feng. Here again, involvement on the part of the Panchen Lama's followers was suspected (the Panchen Lama was reportedly in Kokonor at the time). The troops of Ma Pu-feng pushed the Tibetans back to Chamdo and re-established Chinese control over Nangchen. An agreement was finally concluded between both sides to respect the previous borders.[238]

The Tibetan Government, indicating a willingness to negotiate the border in Kham, requested British intervention. British representations to the Chinese produced the response that relations between China and Tibet were an internal affair of China in which Britain had no right to be involved. This response on the part of the Chinese essentially ended the era of British mediation with China in regard to Tibet.[239] The Nationalist government finally managed to produce a cease-fire in Kham, due less to its authority in Szechuan than to the outbreak of civil war between the Szechuan warlords.[240] As a result of the agreement, a frontier was established along the Yangtze, with the Tibetans losing Derge. Tieh-tseng Li reports that a proposal from Liu Wen-hui to the Nationalist government to "settle the Tibetan issue by force" by mobilizing troops from Yunnan, Szechuan and Ch'ing-hai was rejected by the Chinese Government due to its policy of "equality of nations" within the Republic, internal disunity, fears of British counteraction on the coast, and preoccupation with the Japanese occupation of Manchuria.[241]

---

237. Richardson, *Tibet and Its History*, 134.
238. Shakabpa, Tibet: A Political History, 254.
239. Lamb, *Tibet, China and India*, 207.
240. Richardson, *Tibet and Its History*, 137.
241. Tieh-tseng Li, *Tibet: Today and Yesterday*, 159.

Regardless of whether the Panchen Lama's followers were behind the conflicts in Kham and Nangchen, his continuing exile and his increasingly close relations with the KMT government remained a threat to Lhasa. Even the British abandoned their efforts to resolve the conflict because the Panchen was now perceived to be an agent of the Chinese; his return to Tibet might be accompanied by unwelcome Chinese influence. In a press interview in December 1932, the Panchen was reported to have stated that he "had been in China for ten years, during which he had visited many parts of Mongolia and the interior of China for the purpose of winning over his followers to Nanking. . . . He only hoped that the Tibetans would return to the fold of the Central Government so that the Government would be relieved of its anxiety regarding the western frontier."[242]

On 17 December 1933 the Thirteenth Dalai Lama died. During the lifetime of the Thirteenth Dalai Lama, Tibet's status evolved from a dependency of the Ch'ing Empire to a *de facto* independent state. The Dalai Lama attempted to achieve political unity and independence for Tibet by modernizing and centralizing a medieval internal administration; he attempted to transcend Tibet's feudal relationship with China by acquiring a new political patron capable of protecting Tibet against the ambition of China to transform its suzerain authority over Tibet into full sovereignty. Events temporarily favored the Tibetan effort, and Tibet achieved political autonomy equivalent to independence.

The Tibetan claim to independence was based upon the principles of national self-determination, even though Tibetans did not articulate their claim in those words. Tibet's territorial and political claim at Simla was based on national criteria of ethnicity and culture. The historical basis for the Tibetan claim was the Treaty of 822, by which China and Tibet recognized each other's territorial boundaries according to what then reflected both political control and ethnic identity. The Lonchen Shatra cited the 822 Treaty from the inscription on the pillar at Lhasa as, "downward from the place where Chinese are met will be China and upward from the place where Tibetans are met will be Tibet."[243] The Tibetan Government at Lhasa had since lost political control over some of what it claimed as its national territory, but claimed the right to national self-determination of all Tibetan cultural territory at Simla.

Tibet's claim to Kham and Amdo was hampered, however, as was Tibet's overall sovereignty, by the legacy of Tibet's relationships with the

242. Mehra, *Tibetan Polity*, 54.
243. "Tibetan Statement on Limits of Tibet," *Boundary Question*, 25.

Mongol and Manchu empires. Tibet in the 20th century could still claim to exercise some indirect control and a large degree of spiritual influence over eastern Tibet, but Tibetan claims were now compromised by Yuan and Ch'ing administrative divisions of Tibet. Tibet was able to achieve tentative recognition at Simla of its right to autonomy in central Tibet, but only the most illusory rights to a Greater Tibet. Beyond the realm of its actual control, the Tibetan Government was unable to substantiate its ethnic nationalist claims to all Tibetan inhabited areas. The weakness of the system of indirect political authority became painfully obvious in the Tibetan Government's inability to refute the claims of China in eastern Tibet without the substance of actual political control.

Nevertheless, Tibet under the Thirteenth Dalai Lama achieved an unprecedented degree of national unity within central Tibet (with the exception of the affair of the Panchen Lama), presented its case for independence and for inclusion of all Tibetan cultural areas within a Tibetan polity, and maintained a military and diplomatic defense against the encroachments of the Chinese. Tibetan ethnic and cultural identity and integrity, upon which a continuing claim to national self-determination could be based, was preserved in almost all Tibetan inhabited areas. The Tibetan plateau remained Tibetan in cultural identity, even after Chao's conquest of Kham and the creation of an illusory "Sikang Province" there. According to Louis King, the last British consul stationed at Dartsendo, Chao's attempt at cultural assimilation and colonization in Kham was by 1914 a total failure:

> The various reforms initiated by Chao Erh-feng have all fallen into desuetude. Chao's schools are attended by Chinese and half-breeds only. ... The Chinese laws forbidding polyandry and other native practices—notably concerning the disposal of the dead—are ignored. The tribesmen have not adopted the Chinese calendar nor the Chinese designations of the various places. Nor have they taken the least notice of the proclamation calling upon them to take Chinese surnames. In no way have they responded to the efforts of the Chinese to impose Chinese laws and customs and language on them, and the magistrates have not felt themselves strong enough to attempt coercion.[244]

By 1931 only nine of the thirty-one magistracies set up by Chao Erh-feng still existed. Perhaps most telling of the actual state of affairs in Kham was that Chinese currency was not generally accepted by Tibetans.[245] Chinese Moslem (Hui) control in Amdo was more firmly

---

244. "Excerpts from Louis King's report, Louis King to Jordan," 18 January 1914, in Mehra, *Northeastern Frontier*, vol. 1, 185.
245. Samuel, *Civilized Shamans*, 69.

established but was perhaps even more superficial; the only requirements upon Tibetans were for taxes, nominal allegiance and occasional *ulag*.

In contrast to the Tibetan claim to territorial sovereignty based on the right to national self-determination, the Chinese claim to sovereignty over Tibet was based upon imperialist rights of conquest, whether by the Mongols, the Manchu or, in Kham, by Chao Erh-feng. For the Chinese, Tibet's ethnic nationalist claims were irrelevant. Tibetan ethnic and cultural identity was not thought of as any basis or justification for political independence. Tibetan nationalism was equated with barbaric resistance to the advance of civilization or credited to foreign imperialist inspiration. The Chinese regarded the expansion of Chinese culture as a natural and inevitable process of civilization replacing barbarism. Tibetan "culture" was hardly regarded as such by the culturally chauvinistic Chinese; Tibetans were regarded as barbarians who could be civilized only by acculturation and assimilation.

China's territorial expansionism was revealed at Simla by the defense of territorial advances in eastern Tibet as integral parts of China, while central Tibet was allowed a nebulous "not yet assimilated" status. The same feelings were held even more adamantly in Szechuan, where it was thought that Tibet might have some autonomous status, but that Kham was entirely Chinese due to the fact of conquest and superficial administration, without regard to the fact that the territory was entirely Tibetan in population. The Chinese questioned whether the Khampas (people of Kham) were even Tibetans, claiming that the inhabitants of "Sikang" were of a different race than the central Tibetans.[246]

All educated Chinese had been taught that Tibet was Chinese territory and accepted this as fact despite the degree of wishful thinking that this entailed. Some Chinese diplomats during the period from 1914 to 1919 may have been willing to contemplate the loss of Tibet, at least temporarily, to British influence; however, with the rise of Chinese nationalism after 1919, the advocacy of the alienation of any "Chinese" territory was considered treasonous. The Chinese position after 1919 was that no concessions in regard to Tibet were possible since any compromise of

---

246. Chen submitted that the inhabitants of Kham were known as *Kang Bawa* (Kham Popa) while those of Central Tibet were Tsang Bawa (Tsang Popa), perhaps unaware that the ethnonym in question is Popa, which is common to both names. (Central Tibetans called themselves Tsang Tibetans, or U-Tsang Tibetans, while Khampas called themselves Kham Tibetans.) Chen makes the further interesting, and typically imperialistic statement that Chao Erh-feng invaded Eastern Tibet "in response to the supplication made to China by the inhabitants of that place." In any case, "as Tibet is a dependency of China, we have a perfect right to settle the matter between Sikang and Tibet." "Statement by Mr. Ivan Chen," in Mehra, *Northeastern Frontier*, vol. 1, 78.

Chinese sovereignty over Tibet was unacceptable to the Chinese people. Chinese negotiations over Tibet up to that time had revealed, however, that they regarded Tibet not as an "integral part of China," but as a dependency potentially lost to a foreign imperial rival.

The rise of Chinese nationalism, and the formation of the KMT Government in 1928, ended the era of tripartite negotiations over the status of Tibet. The KMT refused to accept British mediation in China's relations with Tibet or that Britain had any legitimate interests in Tibet at all. The era of imperialist competition over Tibet, and that of the possibility of an international agreement over Tibet's status, thus came to an end. The Tibetan Government retained hope for an international or bilateral settlement, and therefore maintained an equivocal position on whether Tibet demanded independence or would accept some form of autonomy. This equivocation only served to confuse international opinion as to what was Tibet's actual, or even desired, political status. Chinese propaganda did not fail to exploit this ambiguity. China's constantly reiterated claim that Tibet was part of Chinese territory, even when Chinese authority had ceased to exist in virtually all of Tibet except Amdo, was effectively contradicted neither by Britain nor by Tibet and was therefore accepted as fact by the international community.

The lesson for the British in Tibet, and for Tibet itself, was that only a permanent commitment to military defense was likely to secure Tibetan independence. The British were unwilling and unable to undertake Tibet's defense against China, but they did convince the Dalai Lama to strengthen Tibet's defenses and provided him with the military arms and training to do so. The Thirteenth Dalai Lama's attempt to create the means by which Tibet might defend itself militarily was obstructed by Tibetan conservatism and regionalism, but Tibetan military successes in Kham in 1918 and again in 1931 revealed a potential for Tibetan self-defense.

British involvement in Tibetan affairs introduced Tibetans to the outside world and had some positive effects in arousing and supporting Tibetan nationalism and Tibet's attempts to preserve its independence of China, but the British attempt to define Tibet's status to Britain's advantage had an ultimately negative effect. Britain's role as mediator of Tibet's status and excluder of other foreign influence from Tibet was dependent upon Tibetan "autonomy" under Chinese "suzerainty." British support for Tibetan autonomy was helpful to the Tibetans in maintaining that autonomy, but Britain's continuing recognition of China's "suzerainty" over Tibet allowed the Chinese to maintain their claims even when their actual authority was nonexistent. British patronage for Tibet also allowed the Chinese to characterize Tibetan nationalism and Tibetan desires for independence as machinations of the British.

Britain's definition of China's role in Tibet as "suzerain" gave a name to a status previously undefined and, therefore, to some extent served to perpetuate that status. Recognition of China's "suzerainty' necessarily implied that Tibet was to some undefined degree less than independent. This was accurate in terms of Tibet's relation to the Manchu Ch'ing, and the British did no more than define that which already existed, but their continuing recognition of China's suzerain status in Tibet, for reasons of their own self-interest, when that relationship had disappeared in fact, served to confirm and perpetuate China's claim to sovereignty over Tibet. Other countries followed the lead of Britain because Britain was the international power most interested in and familiar with Tibet's status. The United States, at that time ignorant of Tibet's actual situation, also weighed in on the side of China.

British imperialism may be said to have stimulated Tibetan and Chinese nationalism to opposite purposes, one to achieve Tibetan independence, the other to deny it. Tibetan nationalism, born of Tibetan aspirations and stimulated by British influence, experienced a rapid and significant growth during the time of the Thirteenth Dalai Lama. Under British tutelage and with British assistance, the Dalai Lama attempted to create some of the institutions of a modern state, in particular an army, in order to preserve Tibet's *de facto* independence of China. Ultimately, the Thirteenth Dalai Lama fought a losing battle with both internal and external systems of dependency relationships, and with social and religious conservatism. However, his adamant stand on Tibetan independence and his refusal to allow a reintroduction of Chinese influence into Tibet became the legacy to which Tibet attempted to adhere during the subsequent period of his absence. The Thirteenth Dalai Lama prepared Tibet as well as possible for the coming trial. However, as the Dalai Lama's political testament reveals, he thought that trial would be a test of Tibetan civilization:

> In particular, we must guard ourselves against the barbaric red communists, who carry terror and destruction with them wherever they go. They are the worst of the worst. Already they have consumed much of Mongolia, where they have outlawed the search for the reincarnation of Jetsun Dampa, the incarnate head of the country. They have robbed and destroyed the monasteries, forcing the monks to join their armies, or else killing them outright. They have destroyed religion wherever they have encountered it, and not even the name of the Buddha Dharma is allowed to remain in their wake. I am sure you have heard the reports coming out of Urga and other such places.

> It will not be long before we find the red onslaught at our own front door. It is only a matter of time before we come into a direct confrontation with it, either from within our own ranks or else as a threat from an external nation.

And when that happens we must be ready to defend ourselves. Otherwise our spiritual and cultural traditions will be completely eradicated. Even the names of the Dalai and Panchen Lamas will be erased, as will those of the other lamas, lineage-holders and holy beings. The monasteries will be looted and destroyed, and the monks and nuns killed or chased away. The great works of the noble Dharma kings of old will be undone, and all of our cultural and spiritual institutions persecuted, destroyed and forgotten. The birthright and property of the people will be stolen; we will become like slaves to our conquerors, and will be made to wander helplessly like beggars. Everyone will be forced to live in misery, and the days and nights will pass slowly and with great suffering and terror.

Therefore, now, when the strength of peace and happiness is with us, while the power to do something about the situation is still in our hands, we should make every effort to safeguard ourselves against this impending disaster. Use peaceful means where they are appropriate; but where they are not appropriate, do not hesitate to resort to more forceful means. Work diligently now, while there is still time. Then there will be no regrets.[247]

---

247. Thirteenth Dalai Lama, "The Last Political Testament," Glenn H. Mullin, trans., in *Lungta*, no. 7, August 1993, 9.

8

Interregnum

Death of the Thirteenth Dalai Lama

After the death of the Thirteenth Dalai Lama, lay officials of the *Tsongdu* suggested a Council of Regents of two or three members, both lay and monastic, as interim head of government rather than a monastic regent as was the traditional practice. The system of monastic regents had been proven to have its faults; past regents were either excessively other-worldly or so enamored of power that their involvement in the prema-ture deaths of several Dalai Lamas was suspected. However, the abbots of the great monasteries insisted that Tibet must have a lama as regent.[1] The 24 year old abbot of Reting monastery was subsequently selected. However, the role of the *Kashag* and *Tsongdu* in Tibetan administration was increased due to the absence of the Dalai Lama and the youth of the regent.[2]

The Nationalist Government of China was informed of the Dalai Lama's death and warned that China should not consider the absence of the Dalai Lama an opportunity to interfere in the affairs of Tibet. The Chinese Government replied with a request to send a mission of condo-lence. The *Kashag* preferred to refuse, but this was opposed by the major monasteries, which imagined that the mission would be purely reli-

---

1. Melvyn Goldstein, *A History of Modern Tibet*, 1913-1951 (Berkeley: University of California Press, 1989), 186.
2. The *Kashag*, created by the Ch'ing in 1720, was, in the 1930s, composed of four *Shapes*, three lay and one monastic. The *Tsongdu* was created in 1872 to replace the *Gandre Drungche*, "Assembly of monks of Ganden and Drepung," which had been formed in 1862. The *Tsongdu*, from its creation, included both monastic and lay officials. The *Tsongdu* was a lower and more popular body than the *Kashag* and could be convened on its own or by the *Kashag*; it was composed of representatives of most of the important monasteries of central Tibet and of all government departments. In the 1930s, there were also Tibetan Army representa-tives. The *Tsongdu* was dominated by monastic officials, but its broad base of representation ensured that it reflected popular concerns.

gious.[3] In April 1934 a Chinese mission under General Huang Mu-sung, Chiang Kai-shek's vice chief of general staff, arrived in Lhasa, along with "technical experts" and a radio set. Huang at first confined himself to the religious aspects of his mission, "visiting the great monasteries with lavish presents, making a great show of reverence in the holy places, and chanting prayers in a doleful voice."[4] His first political move was to offer a seal and a memorial tablet to the deceased Dalai Lama; this the Tibetans examined closely and accepted only after finding no language implying Tibetan subordination to China.[5]

Huang initiated political negotiations by presenting to the Tibetans the KMT's "five races" policy, and explaining the concept of the Chinese Republic, which the Tibetans were invited to join as equals (i.e., as one of the five races).[6] The only non-Chinese account of the Tibetan Government's replies to any of Huang's proposals is from a representative of the Government of India, a Sikkimese, Rai Bahadur Norbu Dhondup, who had been sent to Lhasa to observe Huang's mission. The Tibetans, according to Norbu Dhondup's account, replied to Huang that the republican form of government was incompatible with Tibet's traditional dual lay-monastic system; in addition, because Tibet was an independent country, none of the other Chinese proposals was thought appropriate. Huang, imagining that the Tibetans' objections were not to union with China, but only to the form of the Chinese government, reiterated that Tibet would not have to change its system of government but would simply become one of the "five races" of the Chinese republic. Huang presented this arrangement as entirely advantageous to Tibet without defining the political implications of Tibet's "union" with China. Huang also reportedly hinted that, since the Panchen Lama had joined the republic, he might be returned to Tibet by force.[7]

The Tibetan *Tsongdu* remained hostile to any negotiations with Huang; however, the *Kashag*, anxious to obtain some guarantees from China in regard to Tibet's autonomy, asked that Huang submit a detailed proposal defining Tibet's relations with China. Huang then submitted the fol-

---

3. Goldstein, *History of Modern Tibet*, 144.

4. Hugh Richardson, *Tibetan Precis* (Calcutta: Government of India, 1945), 50. Goldstein reports that Huang was supplied with 400,000 silver dollars to be dispensed as "gifts," including two silver dollars for each of the monks at the three great monasteries of Lhasa. Goldstein, *History of Modern Tibet*, 224.

5. Richardson, *Tibetan Precis*, 50.

6. Huang also arranged a public display of placards explaining the "five races" ideology. Alastair Lamb, *Tibet, China and India 1914-1950* (Hertingfordburg: Roxford Books, 1989), 234.

7. Richardson, *Tibetan Precis*, 50.

lowing proposal (according to his own report to the Chinese Government, as related by Tieh-tseng Li):

A. Two fundamental points that Tibet is asked to observe: (1) Tibet must be an integral part of the territory of China; (2) Tibet must obey the Chinese Government.

B. Declarations in regard to the political system in Tibet: (1) Buddhism shall be respected by all and given protection and its propagation encouraged; (2) In the preservation of the traditional political system, Tibet shall be granted autonomy. Any administrative measures within the authority of the autonomy of Tibet, the Central Government will not interfere with. On foreign affairs, there must be unitary action. All administrative matters which are nation-wide in character shall be administered by the Central Government, such as: (a) Foreign affairs shall be directed by the Central Government; (b) National Defense shall be planned by the Central Government; (c) Communications shall be managed by the Central Government; (d) The names of important officials of Tibet, after they have been elected by the autonomous government of Tibet, shall be submitted to the Central Government for their respective appointments.

C. The Central Government shall grant Tibet autonomy, but for the purpose of exercising full sovereignty in an integral part of its territory, the Central Government shall appoint a high commissioner to be stationed in Tibet as the representative of the Central Government, on the one hand to carry out national administrative measures, and on the other to guide the regional autonomy.[8]

To these proposals the Tibetan Government responded, as reported by Li, again from Huang's report to the Chinese Government:

1. In dealing with external affairs, Tibet shall remain an integral part of the territory of China. But the Chinese Government must promise that Tibet will not be reorganized into a province.

2. Tibetan authorities, big or small, external or internal, and Tibetan laws, regulations, etc., may be subjected to the orders of the Chinese Government provided such orders are not, either religiously or politically, harmful to Tibet.

3. Traditional laws and regulations dealing with the internal affairs of Tibet shall remain independent as at present, and the Chinese Government will not interfere with Tibetan civil and military authorities. On this matter it

---

8. Tieh-tseng Li, *Tibet: Today and Yesterday* (New York: Bookman Associates, 1960), 168. Li cited Huang's "Report to the Central Committee of the National Government" in the archives of the Mongolian and Tibetan Affairs Commission.

shall be in accordance with the oral promises made at different times in the past.

4. To maintain the present peaceful condition of Tibet, there shall be friendly relations with all its neighboring states and all the peoples believing in Buddhism. In the future, any important treaty between Tibet and any foreign country shall be made by joint decisions with the Chinese Government.

5. One representative of the Chinese Government may be stationed in Tibet, but his retinue shall not exceed twenty-five. There shall be no other representative either civil or military. This representative must be a true believer in Buddhism. When a new representative is appointed to replace the old, the route he and his retinue take to and fro must be by sea [via India] and not through Sikang.

6. Before the recognition of the reincarnation of the Dalai Lama and before his taking over the reins of government, the inauguration of the regency and the appointments of officials from the bKa'-blon up shall be conducted or made by the Tibetan Government as at present. Of such inauguration and appointments, the representative of the Chinese Government in Tibet shall be notified soon after they have taken place.

7. Those Chinese people who have long resided in Tibet and have been under the jurisdiction and protection of the Agricultural Bureau since the Chinese-Tibetan War of the year jen-tzu (1912) shall remain under the control of the Tibetan Government and abide by the local laws and regulations. The representative of the Chinese Government shall exercise no control over them.

8. Military forces to be stationed on the borders of Tibet for defense purpose shall be dispatched by the Government of Tibet as at present. If and when there should be foreign invasion, the Chinese Government shall be consulted on military measures to be taken.

9. For permanent harmony and friendship, to avoid any possible disputes, and to maintain peace on the borders, the northeastern boundary between Kokonor and Tibet should be maintained as proposed during the negotiations of the year before last, with O-lo [Golok?] which has long been under Tibet to be included on the Tibetan side. As for the boundary between Tibet and Szechuan, the territory and people, together with the administration of De-ge [Derge], Nyarong, Ta-chieh Ssu [Dargay Monastery], should be turned over to the Tibetan Government at the earliest possible date.

10. The Chinese Government should not give asylum to or acknowledge as representative, any Tibetan, ecclesiastical or secular, who has rebelled against the Tibetan Government and escaped to China Proper.[9]

---

9. Ibid., 169.

Li commented that the "Tibetan counterproposal," as he has recorded it, "shows clearly that the Lhasa authorities were not yet ready to place their trust and reliance on the Chinese Government of the day. . . . However, they went a considerable way to meet the Chinese wishes."[10] Li's version has the Tibetans accepting, in principle, Chinese sovereignty over Tibet, being concerned mainly with minor points of local autonomy.

Norbu Dhondup reported a considerably different version of the Tibetan response to Huang's proposals, one that reveals a far more uncompromising Tibetan stance on independence. Norbu obtained a complete transcription of Huang's proposals, submitted in writing, and the *Kashag* and *Tsongdu* replies, which differ substantially and significantly from the Chinese version. Huang's proposals as reported by Norbu are given first, and then the replies of the *Kashag* and *Tsongdu*:

1. The relations between the Central Government and the Tibetan Government should be those of benefactor and lama.

The Kashag accepted, provided "Chinese Government" was substituted for "Central Government" which was a new term.[11] The Assembly [Tsongdu] agreed.

2. The Chinese Government should always consider Tibet a holy and religious country.

[Kashag and Tsongdu] Agreed.

3. Tibet has religion, men, and complete administrative arrangements. Therefore China should consider Tibet to be independent (?autonomous) and should not interfere in its internal administration.

Agreed.

4. No Chinese troops should be kept on any of the frontiers of Tibet.

Agreed.

5. Five thousand troops should be selected from the Tibetan army and called Frontier Guards. They should be posted on the various frontiers. China should pay, arm, equip, and train the troops.

The Kashag said that troops might be posted on the frontiers but there was no need to call them by any special name.[12] They did not want pay or arms from the Chinese. The Assembly added that it was not necessary to post troops on the frontiers until an emergency arose.

---

10. Ibid., 170.
11. Clearly the Tibetans had by now realized the implications of this terminology.
12. "Frontier" would require a definition of whose frontier, Tibet's or China's.

6. A Chinese Officer should be posted at Lhasa to advise the Tibetan Government. He should be given an escort out of the Frontier Guards and should control the movements of the whole force.

The Kashag said they would prefer no Chinese officer to be posted at Lhasa. If one were appointed he should have nothing to do with the Tibetan army, but he might have a small Chinese escort. The Simla Treaty had said 300. The Assembly said that 25 servants would do as an escort, and that the Chinese officer should strictly observe the provision for non-interference in Tibetan internal affairs.

7. The Tibetan Government should consult the Chinese Government before corresponding with other nations about external affairs.

The Kashag said that Tibet is independent and would deal with external affairs without consulting the Chinese. The Assembly agreed and added that the Tibetan Government would correspond with all nations "headed by the British Government" whenever they wished.

8. The Chinese Government should be consulted about the appointment of officers of the rank of Shape and above.

The Kashag refused, but offered to inform the Chinese Government after the appointments had been made. The Assembly agreed [with the Kashag].

9. China should recognize the boundary existing at the time of the Emperor Kuang Hsu [K'ang Hsi].

This was considered favorable; but demands were made for additional territory including Nyarong, Batang, Lithang, and the Golok country.

10. China should fight with or mediate with any nations who try to invade Tibet.

The Kashag and Assembly both said that as Tibet is a religious country no one is likely to attack her. If they do she will deal with them herself without Chinese help. The question of mutual help could be considered if it arose.

11. China should be informed when the incarnation of the Dalai Lama is discovered so that she can offer him a seal and title.

The Kashag agreed. The National Assembly said that China should be informed only after the installation had taken place to avoid trouble such as was created in the case of the sixth and seventh Dalai Lamas.

12. The Tibetan Government should invite the Tashi Lama [Panchen Lama] to return at once, should restore to him his former powers, estates and property, and should guarantee that no harm should befall him or his followers. If this were done the Chinese Government would take away his munitions.

The Kashag and Assembly replied that the Tashi Lama being a religious person required no arms and ammunition; they would welcome him back and guarantee his personal safety if the Chinese took away his arms. They added that he should be asked to return via India in accordance with the wishes of the late Dalai Lama.

13. All Tibetan officers in China should receive salaries from the Chinese Government.

The Kashag agreed. The Assembly said that it was a matter of indifference to them but only officials appointed by the Tibetan Government should attend meetings.[13]

14. All half-Chinese in Tibet should be under the sole jurisdiction of the Chinese officer at Lhasa.

The Kashag and Assembly replied that when the Chinese were turned out of Tibet in 1912 the Tibetan Government asked all Chinese to return to China. Those born in Tibet asked permission to remain, and signed an agreement to pay taxes and submit to Tibetan jurisdiction. This article was therefore inacceptable.[14]

According to Norbu, as reported by Richardson, Huang received these replies and then once again petitioned the *Kashag* to accept three essential principles:

That Tibet should admit subordination to China; that all direct correspondence with outside nations should cease, or failing that, China should be consulted before the Tibetan Government replied to any communication with outside nations; that China should be consulted before appointments were made to the post of Shape or higher officers.

The Tsongdu decided, after long deliberations:

Tibet might be considered subordinate to China to the extent laid down in the Simla Treaty; that Tibet would correspond with all nations direct "headed by the British," and would not consult China on the subject; in view of religious ties, Tibet would inform China after the appointment of all officers above the rank of Shape. The Assembly also desired that the British Government should be a party to any agreement reached between Tibet and China.[15]

---

13. This was in order to avoid unauthorized representatives, like the Panchen Lama, at Chinese government functions.

14. Richardson, *Tibetan Precis*, 51.

15. Ibid., 52. It is uncertain whether this language implied that Tibet would consult China on contacts with countries not "headed by the British."

Norbu's version of the negotiations appears significantly different from the version Huang reported to the Chinese Government. Some of Huang's articles, particularly the first two, are altogether missing in the Norbu version. In particular, the Tibetans admitted no Chinese right to make laws or give orders to Tibet. Tibet admitted Chinese "suzerainty" over Tibet to the extent specified at Simla, apparently in the continuing hope that the Chinese might finally be persuaded to accept the Simla Convention, but not that Tibet should "remain an integral part of the territory of China." Norbu's version also has the Tibetans claiming authority to conduct their own foreign affairs (Article 7), to take care of Tibet's defense (Article 10), to install incarnations of the Dalai Lama without any authorization from China (Article 11), to appoint officials to represent Tibet in China (Article 13) and to impose jurisdiction over Chinese in Tibet.

Based upon Norbu's version of events, the Tibetan *Tsongdu* displayed a remarkable consistency in maintaining Tibet's claim to continuing autonomy of China, an autonomy interpreted as essentially equivalent to independence. Huang emphasized in his report that the Tibetans had accepted, in principle, China's "suzerainty" over Tibet, but as Richardson commented, "the make-believe was not carried too far."[16] Huang's mission achieved little success except that the Chinese did succeed in negotiating directly with Tibet, without the mediation of the British, for the first time since Simla. The radio and its operator, which the Chinese contrived to leave behind "until such time as they would be turned over to the Tibetan Government, upon the conclusion of an agreement between Tibet and China," was portrayed within China and to the outside world as a Chinese Resident in Tibet.[17] The Chinese publicized the mission as evidence of China's continuing authority over Tibet. As a reward for his efforts, Huang was made Chairman of the Mongolian and Tibetan Affairs Commission.[18]

The British responded to the Huang mission by sending a mission of their own in 1936, under Basil Gould, political officer in Sikkim. The mission brought a radio in response to the one left by the Chinese; a member of Gould's party, Hugh Richardson, was left in Lhasa to counteract the influence of the Chinese representative. This was the first time a British representative was permanently established in Lhasa. Richardson remained there, with a break during the Second World War, until 1950. The good relations established by the 1936 British mission were marred

---

16. Ibid., 53.
17. Goldstein, *History of Modern Tibet*, 245.
18. Lamb, *Tibet, China and India*, 237.

by Gould's bringing up the issue of Tawang before the Tibetan *Kashag*. Gould informed the Tibetans that British India considered the Simla agreements between Tibet and India in regard to the border valid. The *Kashag* reportedly replied that:

> Up to 1914 Tawang had undoubtedly been Tibetan. They regarded the adjustment of the Tibet-India boundary as part and parcel of the general adjustment and determination of boundaries contemplated in the 1914 Convention. If they could, with our help, secure a definite Sino-Tibetan boundary they would of course be glad to observe the Indo-Tibetan border as defined in 1914. They had been encouraged in thinking that His Majesty's Government and the Government of India sympathized with this way of regarding the matter owing to the fact that at no time since the Convention and Declaration of 1914 had the Indian Government taken steps to question Tibetan, or to assert British, authority in the Tawang area.[19]

In February 1934 the Panchen Lama was made a member of the Supreme Council of the Nationalist Government; in February 1935 he was appointed "Special Cultural Commissioner for the Western Regions," with headquarters at Sining and an escort of 500 soldiers. One of the Panchen's entourage was put in charge of Tibetan affairs on the Mongolian and Tibetan Affairs Commission. The death of the Dalai Lama and renewed bilateral relations between Tibet and China revived the hopes of the Panchen Lama and his followers that their return to Tibet might finally become a reality. The Panchen's demands thereafter increased to include the right to independent military control in Tsang and political authority over Shigatse, Nangartse, Namling and Penam Districts.[20]

The Tibetan Government agreed to restore the Panchen Lama's property, but continually refused him temporal authority over any territory or control over an independent military force. In addition, far from forgiving his refusal to pay taxes, Lhasa demanded the payment of taxes going back to 1924. The Tibetan Government informed the Chinese Government in 1936 that the Panchen would not be permitted to enter Tibet with a Chinese escort.[21] Nevertheless, the Panchen proceeded from Sining to Jyekundo with a small Chinese escort.[22] In the summer of 1937

---

19. Dorothy Woodman, *Himalayan Frontiers* (New York: Praeger, 1969), 203.

20. Tieh-tseng Li, *Tibet: Today and Yesterday*, 173.

21. Parshotam Mehra, *Tibetan Polity, 1904-37: The Conflict Between the 13th Dalai Lama and the 9th Panchen* (Wiesbaden: Otto Harrassowitz, 1976), 63.

22. Ibid., 71.

the Panchen informed the authorities of Tashilhunpo that he would depart Jyekundo for Tibet with an escort of 20 Chinese officials and 500 soldiers. The *Tsongdu,* offended that the Panchen announced his return without informing the Tibetan Government, as if there were no government in Tibet to whom he was responsible, announced that they would resist his entry and mobilized troops to do so.

The Chinese complained that the British were behind Lhasa's resistance to the Panchen Lama's return. A Chinese newspaper recommended that force be used to secure the return of the Panchen and China's position in Tibet:

> The relation of Tibet to the Central Government is but superficial and nominal but the Central Government has been exceedingly generous and gracious to the Panchen Lama with the hope of utilizing the religious position of the Panchen Lama to form a link between the Central Government and the Tibetan Local Government. . . . Since the Central Government now has so many troops, why not send a portion of them westwards to Tibet? If this is not done, Tibet will sooner or later be wiped out of the map of China.[23]

Lhasa's resistance to the Panchen's return was now primarily because the Panchen had become a tool of the Chinese; his return was certain to facilitate the revival of Chinese influence in Tibet. In November 1937 the Panchen Lama died at Jyekundo, "to the mingled sorrow and relief of the Tibetan people."[24] The sad affair of the Ninth Panchen Lama was finally over; the Chinese had been unable to restore the Panchen, thus the full negative potential of the situation was not (yet) realized.

The Reting Regency

In contrast to the responsible role played by the *Tsongdu* during the absence of the Dalai Lama, the Reting Regent requested confirmation of his position and accepted presents of money from the Chinese Government.[25] As Li comments, "This was the first time since the Chinese Revolution of 1911 that an appointment in Tibet was ever referred to the Chinese authority. Without the least delay the Chinese Government

---

23. Parshotam Mehra, *The Northeastern Frontier: A Documentary Study of the Internecine Rivalry between India, Tibet and China* (Delhi: Oxford University Press, 1979), 75, quoting Yung Pao, 27 March, 1937.

24. Hugh Richardson, *Tibet and Its History* (Boston: Shambhala, 1984), 146.

25. Ibid., 143; Tieh-tseng Li, *Tibet: Today and Yesterday,* 166.

granted its confirmation." Li mentions that Reting, whom he characterized as pro-Chinese, also disbanded a large portion of the Tibetan Army
and restricted arms purchases from India.[26]

Reting's first responsibility was to find the reincarnation of the Dalai
Lama. A likely candidate was discovered in Amdo at Takse village in
1937. In order to secure his release from the Moslem governor of Sining,
Ma Pu-fang, the Tibetan Government had to pay a ransom of 400,000 silver dollars.[27] These negotiations took almost two years; the young candidate was unable to depart for Lhasa until the summer of 1939. The
Tibetan Government was forced, for reasons of traditional Sino-Tibetan
diplomatic protocol, to allow a Chinese representative to attend the
enthronement ceremony, but agreed to do so only if the Chinese official
would travel to Tibet via India. The invitation to the Chairman of the
Mongolian and Tibetan Affairs Commission, Wu Chung-hsin, to attend
the installation ceremonies was construed by the Chinese as a Tibetan
request for confirmation and officiation at the enthronement by a representative of the Chinese Government. Upon arrival in Lhasa, Wu
demanded that he meet the young Dalai Lama in a private interview to
ascertain whether he was the true incarnation. This was agreed to by
Reting. Wu then demanded that the regent request confirmation of the
Dalai Lama by the Chinese Government, which Reting did. Wu then submitted to the Chinese Government that the boy be confirmed as the
Fourteenth Dalai Lama.[28]

The Reting Regent acquiesced in these diplomatic maneuvers in order
to improve his personal relations with the Chinese, allowing the Chinese
to perpetuate the illusion that they had chosen and installed the Dalai
Lama. Wu also awarded a title, a golden patent and a golden seal to the
regent, and similar titles of Chinese administrative status to Tibetan
kalons.[29] The regent did object to the setting up of a Chinese High
Commissioner for Tibet, but neither he nor the *Kashag* or *Tsongdu* objected when Wu declared the abandoned office of the wireless operators
reconstituted as an office of the Mongolian and Tibetan Affairs
Commission.[30]

In the wake of the Chinese Communists' Long March of 1934-35, the

---

26. Tieh-tseng Li, *Tibet: Today and Yesterday*, 166.
27. Goldstein, *History of Modern Tibet*, 321; Lamb, *Tibet, China and India*, 284.
28. Tieh-tseng Li, *Tibet: Today and Yesterday*, 183.
29. Ibid., 184.
30. Goldstein, *History of Modern Tibet*, 330; Lamb, *Tibet, China and India*, 286.

Nationalist government established more direct control over Szechuan.[31] At the end of 1937 the Nationalist Government was removed to Chunking in Szechuan; after this time the Nationalists became more interested in their western frontier. A "Preparatory Commission to Create the Province of Sikang" had been set up in 1935. In July 1938 Sikang Province was formally created, at least in theory, over the opposition of some Szechuanese who preferred that Sikang be made a part of Szechuan. In January 1939 a provincial government was installed at Tachienlu (Dartsendo, now Kangding), the only place in "Sikang Province" actually under Chinese control. Despite its almost entirely imaginary nature, the Chinese announced to the world the creation of this new province. The boundary of Sikang and Tibet was to be at the Yangtze, although Li reports a movement in Szechuan to extend the frontier to that claimed by Chao Erh-feng at Giamda.[32]

In April 1939 Reting consolidated his personal power by threatening to resign, complaining of lack of undisputed authority in governing. The *Kashag* and *Tsongdu* then conferred upon Reting the authority he desired. In October 1939 Reting demanded enormous awards to the Reting estate (*labrang*) as reward for his discovery of the Dalai Lama. Reting's venality and the sharp dealing of his *labrang* in trade activities aroused increasing opposition. Reting's undoing came about due to another of his personal failings. Reting, as regent, was responsible for administering the vows of monkhood to the young Dalai Lama, including the vow of celibacy. However, Reting himself was not celibate, having had several affairs that were sufficiently well known to be undeniable. Such behavior was forgivable for an incarnation, whose purposes were generally believed to be incomprehensible to ordinary people, but not acceptable for the monk who would administer vows to the Dalai Lama. If that person did not adhere to the vows, their transmission to the Dalai Lama was considered ineffective. Reting contrived, therefore, to "retire" for a period, supposedly due to a predicted danger to his health, and named Taktra Rimpoche, a lama as unambitious and ethical as Reting was the opposite,

---

31. The Red Army moved into Kham in June 1935. One group, under Mao, moved into Shensi in late 1935. Another group of 10,000 led by Chang Kuo-t'ao fell out with Mao and remained in Tibet at Ngaba and then moved to Kanze after being attacked by Nationalist forces and established a "Tibetan People's Government" in the Kanze area. In May 1936 this group was attacked by Nationalist troops and withdrew to the north, where many were wiped out by attacks by Ma Pu-feng's Hui troops. *Tibet 1950-67* (Hong Kong: Union Research Institute, 1967), 761.

32. Tieh-tseng Li, *Tibet: Today and Yesterday*, 187, 281, fn. 176.

as regent on the private understanding that Taktra would return the regency to Reting at a future date.[33]

The Taktra Regency

Taktra became regent in February 1941. The retirement of the pro-Chinese Reting signaled a shift to a more nationalist and anti-Chinese policy. The Tibetans had enjoyed a period of relative peace due to Chinese preoccupation with the Japanese invasion, but it was generally believed that once the Chinese had their own situation in order they would turn to Tibet. In 1942 the Tibetan Government established a Foreign Affairs Bureau. The British readily agreed to deal with this new bureau; the Nepalese asked that their relations be continued through the special office established for that purpose, which was agreed; the Chinese refused to deal with the new office, as that would imply that China was a foreign country in relation to Tibet. China's refusal to deal with the new Tibetan Foreign Affairs Bureau virtually eliminated official Chinese contact with the Tibetan Government.

The absence of any Chinese control over Tibet, or even any official Chinese representation at Lhasa, was revealed shortly thereafter by an American plan to transport war supplies from India to China via Tibet. This scheme had the approval of the Chinese, but the Tibetans refused permission, since they regarded themselves as a neutral country. The British, now allies of China in the war, attempted to put pressure on the Tibetans, but also took the opportunity to suggest to China that a guarantee on their part of Tibetan autonomy might do much to alleviate Tibetan resistance. The Tibetans tentatively agreed to the transport of non-military supplies by traditional means along established trade routes.[34]

The Chinese attempted to use the war supplies transport plan to improve their position in Tibet; they announced that they would dispatch agents to supervise the transport of supplies all along the Tibetan trade routes. The Tibetans refused to allow this, even threatening to use force to prevent the entry of Chinese officials to Tibet. The Tibetans refused even to arrange transport through Chinese agents and in March 1943 curtailed all transport to China.[35] This Tibetan insubordination infuriated

---

33. Goldstein, *History of Modern Tibet*, 355.

34. Richardson states that this action was taken by the regent and the *Kashag* without consulting the *Tsongdu*, which would undoubtedly have opposed it. Richardson, *Tibetan Precis*, 72.

35. Ibid., 73.

Chiang Kai-shek, who ordered Yunnan, Szechuan and Chinghai to move troops to the Tibetan border. The governors of Yunnan and Szechuan (Liu Wen-hui) ignored the government's orders, while Ma Pu-fang moved troops to Jyekundo after extorting military supplies from the Chinese central government. Chinese pressure on Tibet was reduced after their British and American allies inquired about why so much energy was expended in attempting to discipline Tibet and so little against the Japanese.[36]

A British request to the US to put pressure on China to provide a guarantee of Tibetan autonomy, as a condition for transport of supplies, produced the first American statement on Tibet's status. Secretary of State Cordell Hull made a noncommittal reply to the British request:

> As you are aware, the Chinese Government has long claimed suzerainty over Tibet, the Chinese constitution lists Tibet among areas constituting the territory of the Republic of China, and this Government has at no time raised question regarding either of these claims.[37]

The United States brought up the matter with the Chinese foreign affairs minister, who maintained that "Tibet was considered a part of the Republic of China; but that China had no intention of altering the situation whereby internal administration in Tibet is in fact autonomous."[38]

In order to get Tibetan agreement for the transport of allied war materials through Tibetan territory, the United States, aware that China had no authority over Tibet, initiated the first official US-Tibetan contacts. In July 1942 President Franklin Roosevelt made a personal request to the Dalai Lama for permission for two Americans of the Office of Strategic Services (OSS, the precursor to the Central Intelligence Agency), Ilya Tolstoy and Brooke Dolan, to visit Tibet. Neither the purpose of the visit nor the affiliation of the visitors was revealed to the Tibetans; the request was therefore logically interpreted by the Tibetans as the establishment of diplomatic relations.[39] The actual purpose of the mission was to survey a pos-

---

36. Ibid., 74; Lamb, *Tibet, China and India*, 344.

37. Secretary of State to the Ambassador in China, 3 July 1942, *Foreign Relations of the United States (FRUS), 1942, China* (Washington: Government Printing Office, 1956), 626.

38. The Ambassador in China to the Secretary of State, (Chungking), 13 July 1942, *FRUS, 1942, China*, 627. One KMT official opined that "Chinese relations with Tibet [should] be put on a realistic footing and that Tibet be recognized for what it is—a `self-governing dominion.'" Memorandum by the Counselor of Embassy in China to the Ambassador in China, (Chungking), 30 July 1942, *FRUS, 1942, China*, 629.

39. President Roosevelt to the Dalai Lama of Tibet, 3 July 1942, *FRUS, 1942*, China, 625. The request, as proposed by William J. Donovan, OSS Director, via the Secretary of State,

sible route, by road or otherwise, for transport of war supplies from India to China via Tibet.

The two Americans travelled from India and reached Lhasa on 12 December 1942. In Lhasa they expressed some sympathy for the Tibetans' desire for independence and suggested ways in which Tibet might achieve international recognition of its independent status. Tolstoy suggested that Tibet might be invited to a post-war peace conference, a suggestion that the Tibetans naturally took as an indication of American support. Support from the British representative in Lhasa for the Americans' proposals inflated the hopes of the Tibetan Foreign Office that the Americans and British would together secure Tibet's independence by means of some sort of international declaration at a post-war peace conference. Tolstoy passed on a Tibetan request for radios, a request to which the US Government reluctantly agreed, over the opposition of the State Department.[40]

While the American mission was in Lhasa, the Regent Taktra and the young Dalai Lama sent letters to President Roosevelt reiterating Tibet's claim to independence, which, as the Dalai Lama said, had been enjoyed by Tibet "from time immemorial."[41] The Tibetan Foreign Office acceded to Tolstoy's request that he and Dolan be allowed to continue their journey to Kansu via Jyekundo, in view of the fact that this was the "first time that friendly relations were established between Tibet and the USA," even though one of the original conditions of their permission to enter Tibet had been that they would enter and exit via India[42] The results of the war supplies transport issue were that Tibet established relations with

---

was to be addressed to the Dalai Lama "in his capacity as religious leader of Tibet, rather than in his capacity as secular leader of Tibet, thus avoiding giving offense to the Chinese Government." Secretary of State to President Roosevelt, 3 July 1942, *FRUS, 1942,* China, 625. In fact, the letter addressed the Dalai Lama as "Your Holiness," and in no way distinguished between the Dalai Lama's secular and religious capacities. The Tibetans were therefore justified in thinking that this was an official communication between heads of state. The letter was delivered through the Consulate of the Indian Government in Lhasa, the Tibetans having refused a previous request delivered by the Chinese representative in Lhasa. Richardson, *Tibetan Precis,* 75.

40. Memorandum by the Assistant Chief of the Division of Far Eastern Affairs, 30 March 1943, *FRUS, 1943, China* (Washington: Government Printing Office, 1957), 624.

41. The Dalai Lama of Tibet to President Roosevelt, 24 February 1943, *FRUS, 1943, China,* 623.

42. The Tibetan Foreign Office to Captain Ilya Tolstoy and Lieutenant Brooke Dolan, February 1943, *FRUS, 1943, China,* 622. Goldstein suggests that Tolstoy was aware that he had promised more support than his government was likely to approve, even that he may have overemphasized the potential for American support in order to secure permission to travel through northern Tibet to China. Goldstein, *History of Modern Tibet,* 395.

the United States and Tibet's *de facto* independence and its desire for independence *de jure* were made known to the outside world.

In 1943 the British Foreign Office again contemplated withdrawing recognition of Chinese suzerainty over Tibet if the Chinese continued to withhold guarantees of Tibetan autonomy:

> If the Chinese Government contemplate the withdrawal of Tibetan autonomy, His Majesty's Government and the Government of India must ask themselves whether in the changed circumstances of today it would be right for them to continue to recognize even a theoretical status of subservience for a people who desire to be free and have, in fact, maintained their freedom for more than thirty years.[43]

The British were soon to depart India; they realized that their definition of China's authority over Tibet as suzerainty was a term with no legal or practical definition. After the departure of the British, the Chinese would be left to define the term to suit themselves. Tibet had been provided with no *de jure* status, despite its *de facto* independence, and India would be left with an undefined and insecure northern border. Also, unstated in British reasoning, was the realization that British recognition of Chinese suzerainty over Tibet had allowed the Chinese to maintain their claim over Tibet in the absence of any actual authority there.[44]

In the end, Britain refrained from withdrawing its recognition of Chinese suzerainty over Tibet. The British decided that any foreign attempt to alter Tibet's status would only increase China's determination to settle the issue unilaterally.[45] The Chinese response to both British and American representations in regard to Tibetan autonomy was consistently that all Chinese regarded Tibet as an integral part of China and Chinese relations with Tibet as an internal issue. As Chinese Foreign Minister T.V. Soong told the Americans: "In their study of geography the Chinese have

---

43. British Embassy to the Department of State, 14 September 1943, *FRUS, 1943, China,* 634.

44. Hugh Richardson, in his 1945 report to the GOI, defined suzerainty as "nominal sovereignty over a semi-independent or internally autonomous state." However, he added that, in practice, the term had "never been defined and, indeed, appears incapable of definition." Richardson, *Tibetan Precis,* 97. Richardson revealed that the Tibetans had inquired of the GOI in 1943 about the legal definition of suzerainty, to which the British had no reply except that "suzerainty is a term used to describe the relations, frequently ill-defined and vague, existing between one state and a second which, to a greater or less degree is dependent on the first, or better 'owes some degree of allegiance to the first.'" Ibid., 102.

45. Goldstein, *History of Modern Tibet,* 399; Lamb, *Tibet, China and India,* 326.

long been taught that Tibet is a part of China and they have no thought whatever that this is open to question."[46]

In 1945, after the end of the war, Britain, anxious about the possibility that post-war China, under either the KMT or the Chinese Communists, would attempt to reimpose Chinese control in Tibet, reviewed its policy once again. The GOI suggested bringing Tibet's case before the United Nations. However, the policy review produced the same conclusions as in 1943, that neither Britain nor India had any power to prevent a unilateral reimposition of Chinese control over Tibet by force, but that their intervention in any form might provoke China take action in Tibet, while, in the absence of any foreign threat to China's authority in Tibet, the Chinese might be content to allow Tibet its traditional autonomy.[47] The British nevertheless intensified their attempt to legitimize India's northern frontier by having Tibet recognize the validity of the Simla agreements regarding Tawang and the McMahon Line; they simultaneously increased their administrative control over Tawang and other previously unadministered areas in northeastern India up to the McMahon Line.[48] The British continued arms sales to Tibet, in increased quantities, in 1943 and again in 1947. The interim Indian Government also agreed to continue arms sales after the 1947 transfer of power, which they did, supplying Tibet with arms as late as 1950.[49]

In the 1945 Soviet-Chinese Treaty of Friendship and Alliance, China was forced to recognize the independence of Mongolia.[50] Perhaps hoping to avoid having to do the same for Tibet, while at the same time appearing to be acting in accord with the post-war anti-colonialist spirit, the KMT adopted what appeared to be a major concession in Chinese policy toward Tibet. Chiang Kai-shek made a statement that Tibet would be accorded a high degree of autonomy, or even independence, if that was what the Tibetans themselves wanted and if they could demonstrate that they were economically viable and capable of defending their territory:

The aim of our National Revolution is two-fold. In our relations with other

46. Acting Secretary of State to the Ambassador in China, 29 September 1943, *FRUS, 1943, China,* 641.

47. Goldstein, *History of Modern Tibet,* 547.

48. Lamb, *Tibet, China and India,* 478, 487.

49. Ibid., 505, 519, 530.

50. China was forced to recognize Mongolian independence as part of the Yalta agreements (at which China was not represented), which secured the entry of the Soviet Union into the war against Japan. At Yalta, the Soviet Union secured secret agreements as to the Kurile Islands, Outer Mongolia, and special privileges in Manchuria, while Soviet claims to privileges in Sinkiang were abandoned. Gerard M. Friters, *Outer Mongolia and Its International Position* (Baltimore: Johns Hopkins University Press, 1949), 209.

nations we seek national independence and freedom. Within the nation we seek equality for all racial groups. . . .

Upon the basis of Dr. Sun Yat-sen's teachings, I shall now state, as a representative of the Kuomintang, our policy toward carrying out the Principle of Nationalism. . . . I shall first take up the racial questions in Outer Mongolia and Tibet. Outer Mongolia and Tibet both have a long history. The racial groups in these two areas have always lived by themselves and are totally different from the racial groups inhabiting the border provinces which mix freely with other groups.[51]

Following the Kuomintang reorganization in 1924, Outer Mongolia sent representatives to extend greetings and felicitations to our Party. Dr. Sun Yat-sen was at that time already treating them as members of a friendly neighboring country and as honored guests. . . . We have never regarded the people of Outer Mongolia as colonials or oppressed them as the Peking [Republican] Government did.[52] Ever since the inauguration of the National Government [1928] we have maintained friendly relations not only with the Outer Mongolians but also with the Tibetans. Our people should realize that if we ignore the aspirations of these racial groups for freedom and restrain their urge for independence and self-government, it will not only be contrary to our National Revolution but will also tend to increase friction between the racial groups and jeopardize our entire program of national reconstruction. This in turn will adversely affect world peace and security.

The racial group in Outer Mongolia had, in effect, declared its independence from the mother country as early as 1922 when the Peking Government was in existence.[53] . . . We should, in accordance with our revolutionary principles and the Kuomintang's consistent policy, recognize, with bold determination and through legal procedure, the independence of Outer Mongolia and establish friendly relations with it.

---

51. What Chiang apparently meant was that the Mongols and Tibetans remained ethnically distinct in contrast to the frontier tribes (the peoples of Szechuan, Yunnan and Kansu) who were substantially mixed with the Han Chinese.

52. On the contrary, the KMT demanded Russian recognition of Chinese sovereignty over Outer Mongolia in 1924; the Mongolian and Tibetan Affairs Commission was established to regain Chinese control in those two areas; China protested the 1936 Soviet-Mongolian Protocol of Mutual Assistance (against Japan) as a violation of Chinese sovereignty in Mongolia; the 1941 Soviet-Japanese neutrality pact, which recognized Japan's rights in Manchuria and the Soviet Union's rights in Mongolia, was also protested by China. The KMT never abandoned its claim to sovereignty over Outer Mongolia until forced to do so by the post-war agreements. Friters, *Outer Mongolia*, 195. The KMT government in Taiwan later revived the claim to China's sovereignty over the Mongolian People's Republic and maintains that claim to this day.

53. The position that Mongolia declared its independence only in 1922 denies the legitimacy of the 1911 Mongolian declaration of independence.

We should honestly aid all racial groups which have given evidence of their capacity for self-government and shown spirit of independence. We should help them achieve national independence through self-determination.[54]

If frontier racial groups situated in regions outside the provinces[55] have the capacity for self-government and a strong determination to attain independence, and are politically and economically ready for both, our Government should, in a friendly spirit, voluntarily help them to realize their freedom and forever treat them as brotherly nations, and as equals of China. We should entertain no ill-will or prejudice against them because of their choice to leave the mother country.

Our frontier racial groups should, in a friendly spirit and through legal channels, make known their wishes to the Government of their mother country. In this way they may be able to realize their aspirations. They should not defy the mother country and stir up mutual hatred.[56]

We should accord the large and small racial groups inside the provinces legal and political equality, and unhindered economic and religious freedom, so that a warm community spirit and friendly collaboration may develop among all the groups.

As regards the political status of Tibet, the Sixth Kuomintang Congress decided to grant it a very high degree of autonomy, to aid its political advancement and to improve the living conditions of the Tibetans. I solemnly declare that if the Tibetans should at this time express a wish for self-government, our Government would, in conformity with our sincere tradition, accord it a very high degree of autonomy. If in the future they fulfill the economic requirement for independence, the National Government will, as in the case of Outer Mongolia, help them to attain that status. But Tibet must give proof that it can consolidate its independent position and protect its continuity [territorial integrity?] so as not to become another Korea.[57]

Finding a solution for the racial problems of Outer Mongolia and Tibet is a very great task of our National Revolution. It will be a touchstone of the

---

54. The KMT did in 1923 recognize a right of China's "races" to "self-determination," the first time that principle had been invoked, but self-determination was interpreted as the right to "equality" within the Chinese state, not the right to secession. Walker Connor, *The National Question in Marxist-Leninist Theory and Strategy* (Princeton: Princeton University Press, 1984), 67.

55. This stipulation would obviously exclude the Tibetans of Kansu, Chinghai, Yunnan and "Sikang."

56. The characterization of China as the "mother country" in relation to Mongolia and Tibet is equivalent to a Chinese claim to be the legitimate arbiter of Mongolia's and Tibet's future.

57. Chiang was undoubtedly referring to imperialist (Japanese and Russian) attempts to control and divide Korea.

success of our Principle of Nationalism. . . . I hope that all the Chinese people, in accordance with our revolutionary principles and spirit of national independence, [will] assist the Government in finding an answer to these questions. For world peace and security as well as for the solidarity and reconstruction of our own nation, we must deal with the world's racial questions in conformity wit'ı the spirit of the Atlantic Charter and the Three Principles of the People.[58]

Chiang's statement undoubtedly reflects the Western Allies' influence on China during the world war and immediately after. His statement raises the interesting question of whether a partial or tentative Chinese recognition of Tibetan autonomy, if not independence, might have been obtained by Britain and the United States at the time if only they had pursued the issue. However, Chiang may only have hoped to entice the Tibetans back into the Chinese fold with this offer; China's recognition of Outer Mongolian independence may have been calculated to put pressure on the Soviet Union to abandon its influence in Sinkiang and Manchuria. China was threatened by the possibility that Tibet might be brought up by Britain or the United States at a post-war peace conference (even though it had not arisen at Yalta). Hugh Richardson, who was in Lhasa at the time, suspected such motives in Chinese attempts to win the Tibetans' friendship:

> The matter that is agitating Chinese minds most is clearly anxiety to avoid having the status of Tibet examined by any international body. . . . It would be most inconvenient if the rest of the world were to realize that Tibet has been independent since 1912 and that, so far from living up to the Atlantic Charter by allowing Tibet the government of her choice, China wants to reduce the degree of freedom already enjoyed by Tibet, and to extend the Chinese Empire.[59]

As part of China's conciliatory policy toward Tibet, Chiang appointed a Chinese Buddhist, Shen Tsung-lien, as Chinese representative in Lhasa (representing the Mongolian and Tibetan Affairs Commission). Shen Tsung-lien arrived in Lhasa in August 1944 and immediately set about cultivating goodwill with the Tibetans. Shen was an astute diplomat and apparently a sincere Buddhist; he treated Tibetans with respect and

---

58. Chiang Kai-shek, "National Independence and Racial Equality," *The Collected Wartime Messages of Generalissimo Chiang Kai-shek: 1937-1945*, comp. Chinese Ministry of Information (New York: John Day Company, 1946), 854.

59. Hugh Richardson, as quoted in Goldstein, *History of Modern Tibet*, 530.

undertook the usual amount of bribery to lamas and monks.[60] Shen tried to convince the Tibetans that the postwar atmosphere in China was very conducive to a resolution of Sino-Tibetan relations, a resolution that would accord Tibet a degree of autonomy practically equivalent to independence. He implied that even the border issue could be resolved to Tibet's satisfaction. Shen emphasized that Tibet should begin negotiations with China while the Chinese Government was formulating its postwar policies. He suggested that a Tibetan delegation attend the Chinese National Constitutional Assembly, where such issues as the autonomy or independence of Tibet could be discussed.[61]

The Tibetans, aware of the imminent departure of the British from India, were anxious to secure a guarantee of their autonomy before the Chinese could regain their ability to intervene in Tibet. Given Chiang Kai-shek's seeming offer of independence to Tibet, and Shen's assurances that all was possible under the new political conditions in China, the Tibetans decided to send a delegation to negotiate with the Chinese Government. Uncertain, however, about the nature of the meeting that Shen suggested they attend, and anxious to be noncommittal in their approach to the Chinese as well as to not alienate the British, the Tibetans construed their mission as a Victory Congratulations Mission to India, China, Britain and the United States as allies and victors in the World War. However, in a separate communication, forwarded through Kham so that it would not come to the notice of the British in India, the Tibetan *Tsongdu* set out the conditions for peace with China. The Tibetan letter referred to traditional relations between China and Tibet as within the *Cho-Yon* format:

> On the occasion of the great victory achieved this year by the Chinese Government over Japan, after many years of war between the two countries, and upon the termination of war and establishment of world peace and security for mankind, the Government of Tibet is sending a special delegation to China and the Allied Governments of the United States and Great Britain to offer congratulations on the victory. . . .
>
> His Holiness Taktra Pandita, the Regent, advised the National Assembly through the Kashag to discuss how the delegation might explore the ways

---

60. Goldstein, *History of Modern Tibet*, 530. By making offerings to monks, the very essence of the religious patron's responsibility, the Chinese, in contrast to the British who refused to participate in this game, were considered to be fulfilling their responsibilities as patrons of Tibet, and were therefore favored by the monks in competition with the British.

61. Shen also reportedly played upon Tibetan anti-British feelings over the Tawang issue. Ibid., 531, 534. It may not be too cynical to suggest that Chiang's liberal offers to Tibet may also have been partly calculated to entice Tibet to send representatives to the Chinese National Assembly.

of improving the patron-preceptor relationship—which has been good—between China and Tibet. . . .

We urge the Government of China to seek an unstrained relationship which has its precedent in the patron-preceptor relationship. The Tibetan Government, for its part, shall endeavor to maintain such a relationship with China, as clearly intended by the religious and secular communities of Tibet.

Tibet remains the special fountainhead of the precious teachings of Buddha. China and all those who share this sacred tradition and who value it more than life itself should endeavor to promote and expand it. As an independent nation with a dual system of temporal and spiritual rule, Tibet will continue to function independently, maintaining and protecting (this system) and not introducing any new systems which would be harmful.

Tibet and Greater Tibet—consisting of the Western Highlands (Toh), i.e., the three provinces of three subdivisions each, the four central provinces in U and Tsang, and the Lower Regions of Kham, the Land of the Four Rivers and Six Ranges—has been a territory unmistakably under the control and protection of the Dalai Lama, the living Bodhisattva of Compassion. There is plenty of evidence to support this fact.

We shall continue to maintain the independence of Tibet as a nation ruled by the successive Dalai Lamas through an authentic religious-political rule.

The peace and security of the borders rests on the stable and unstrained relations between China and Tibet. At various times Chinese leaders in the border provinces have seized by force territories which were definitely Tibetan, both linguistically and culturally. . . .

Moreover, the annexation by force of small nations and territories by big ones is against well-known international rules. We urge you to instruct the individual (leaders) to reinstate these territories to us. . . .

Tibet, for its part, will devote itself to religious endeavors and services aimed at assuring the prosperity and stability of the Chinese system of government as well.

Tibet has been an independent state, managing its own domestic and foreign, civil and military affairs. It continues to maintain its political and spiritual authority in its own way. Following the tradition established by previous incarnations, the present Dalai Lama as supreme master of the complete Buddhist tradition will exercise his power over the recognition of reincarnate lamas of high and low ranks belonging to the great and small monasteries of the various orders, over the appointment of the functionaries, and over the reformation of traditions. Neither the Chinese nor any other government should interfere in this. . . . [62]

---

62. Ibid., 538. Full text in Goldstein. The context of the last paragraph quoted makes it

In addition, the *Tsongdu* demanded that Chinese in Tibet should be subject to the laws of Tibet, and that they should apply for entry visas for Tibet; the Chinese Government should conduct its diplomatic correspondence with Tibet through the Tibetan mission at Nanking; Tibetan representatives to China would carry Tibetan Government credentials, and no others should be accepted by China as official representatives of Tibet. The *Tsongdu* promised to maintain friendly relations with China but reserved the right to conduct relations with other countries and to negotiate and protect Tibet's frontier. If any country should attack Tibet, however, Tibet should be able to call upon China under the terms of the *Cho-Yon* relationship to come to Tibet's assistance. The Tibetan message concluded by inviting China to make an agreement with Tibet in accordance with the Tibetan proposals.[63]

The Tibetan proposal would have reduced China's "suzerainty" to little more than a polite acknowledgement of China's security interests. The Tibetan letter reflects an awareness of the necessity of establishing between Tibet and China some of the format of contemporary international relations between independent states. Chiang perhaps invited such an assertive Tibetan response by his extravagant promises of respect for Tibet's right to self-determination. However, while in India the Tibetan delegation was warned by British officials, who had become aware that the delegation intended to attend the Chinese Constitutional Assembly, that their attendance could be construed as implying that Lhasa accepted Chinese sovereignty over Tibet. Nevertheless, the delegation continued to China, where they presented their letter and awaited a reply. The delegation had instructions to attend the assembly only as observers, if at all, but the Chinese were determined to achieve the full propaganda value of the delegation's presence. The Chinese convinced the Tibetans that the Constitutional Assembly would discuss Tibet's situation; therefore, the Tibetans agreed to participate in order to put forward Tibet's case.[64]

In the event, the Chinese Constitutional Assembly did not address the Tibetan issue except to assert that "all the people of the countries whose delegates are present in this Assembly are subjects of the Chinese Kuomintang Government."[65] The Tibetan delegation found that it had been tricked into participating in an entirely Chinese governmental affair as representatives of Tibet. The Chinese never mentioned the Tibetans'

---

clear that the Dalai Lama was claiming religious authority over all Tibetan monasteries, including those in areas under Chinese rule.

63. Ibid., 543.

64. W.D. Shakabpa, *Tibet: A Political History* (New York: Potala Publications, 1984), 290; Lamb, *Tibet, China and India*, 496.

65. Goldstein, *History of Modern Tibet*, 556.

letter nor their request to negotiate Tibet's status, nor did they ever reply to the letter nor agree to any negotiations. However, the Chinese press fully publicized the presence of the Tibetan delegation, conveying the impression of official Tibetan participation in the Chinese Constitutional Assembly.

In March 1946 the Tibetan Victory Congratulations Mission met with the British viceroy and with the American ambassador to India in Delhi. The delegation presented gifts and letters from the regent and the Dalai Lama to President Truman; these occasioned an American debate concerning the appropriate response, as well as a reappraisal of US policy toward Tibet. The possibility of a communist victory in the civil war in China gave Tibet a new strategic significance. Tibet was thought to form a potential bulwark, both geographically and ideologically, to the spread of communism in Asia:

> In a central position in a continent threatened by Soviet expansionism and torn by internal strife in its two most populous countries, China and India, the people of Tibet will probably resist Soviet influence and other disruptive forces longer than any other Asiatic people. The conservative and religious nature of the Tibetan people and the relatively firm control exercised by their government combine to produce comparatively stable conditions in a vast area completely surrounded by territories seriously affected by political upheavals or Soviet schemes of aggrandizement.
>
> Tibetans' seeming aversion to Communist doctrines may tend to counteract the effect of Communist activities in many parts of Asia, for the Dalai Lama's influence extends to followers far beyond the borders of Tibet.
>
> Tibet may therefore be regarded as a bulwark against the spread of Communism throughout Asia, or at least as an island of conservatism in a sea of political turmoil, and a gesture of friendship from the United States might go a long way toward encouraging the Tibetans to resist possible Soviet or Communist infiltration into the Tibetan Plateau which, in an age of rocket warfare, might prove the most important territory in all Asia.[66]

The American Embassy in India proposed to send a response to the Tibetans via an American mission to Lhasa and to ignore Chinese considerations, since "it is far more important for our Government to take advantage of its present opportunity to offer Tibet concrete evidence of its friendship than to be unduly concerned over any objections which the

---

66. Chargé in India to the Secretary of State, 13 January 1947, *FRUS, 1947, vol. VII: The Far East: China* (Washington: Government Printing Office, 1972), 589.

present Chinese Government might offer."[67] The US Government had previously considered British support for Tibetan autonomy a somewhat repugnant remnant of British imperialism; however, with Soviet communism replacing Russian imperialism as a threat to what the US perceived as its interests in Asia, the US contemplated taking over Britain's role as patron and defender of Tibet against Soviet expansionism (the Chinese Communists were considered little more than proxies of the Soviets). The New Delhi Embassy's suggestion thus formed the basis for an almost seamless transformation of the Great Game into the Cold War in Asia. However, the State Department preferred to make no official change in US policy on Tibet for the time being, replying to the Embassy that "no useful purpose would be served at the present time by action likely to raise the question of our official attitude with respect to the status of Tibet." A letter of reply was sent to the Dalai Lama and the possibility of future "unobtrusive and unofficial" missions to Tibet was left open.[68]

In March 1947 Tibet was invited by the Indian Council of World Affairs, a non-governmental body, to attend an Asian Relations Conference in India. The conference participants included academic and government representatives from thirty-two Asian countries. The Chinese Government attempted to have the invitation to Tibet withdrawn on the grounds that China could represent and make any decisions on Tibet's behalf, but India refused to withdraw the invitation. In New Delhi, the Chinese representative tried to convince the Tibetans to be represented by China; he also offered each delegate 10,000 rupees "spending money."[69] The Tibetans resisted all Chinese blandishments, insisting that they could adequately represent themselves. The Chinese did manage to have a map that showed Tibet separate from China withdrawn and the Tibetan flag removed. The conference did not address any of the political issues between Tibet and China nor the border disputes between Tibet and India.[70]

The Asian Relations Conference was organized during the transition period to Indian independence and perhaps reflected the vestiges of British support for Tibet. Independent India was much less willing to mediate between China and Tibet than Imperial Britain had been, as was revealed in the first Indian position paper on Tibet:

---

67. Ibid.
68. Acting Secretary of State to the Chargé in India, 14 April 1947, *FRUS, 1947, vol. VII*, 594.
69. Goldstein, *History of Modern Tibet*, 563.
70. Lamb, *Tibet, China and India*, 498.

The conditions in which India's well-being may be assured and the full evolution be achieved of her inherent capacity to emerge as a potent but benevolent force in world affairs—particularly in Asia—demand not merely the
development of internal unity and strength but also the maintenance of
friendly relations with her neighbors. To prejudice her relations with so
important a power as China by aggressive support of unqualified Tibetan
independence is therefore a policy with few attractions. It follows that,
while the Government of India are glad to recognize and wish to see
Tibetan autonomy maintained, they are not prepared to do more than
encourage this in a friendly manner and are certainly not disposed to take
any initiative which might bring India into conflict with China on this issue.
The attitude which they propose to adopt may be best described as that of
a benevolent spectator, ready at all times—should opportunity occur—to
use their good offices to further a mutually satisfactory settlement between
China and Tibet.[71]

At the very time when Tibet was most in need of internal unity in
order to confront the threat of a unified China, the failures of the Tibetan
political system were most manifest. The Dalai Lama had not yet attained
maturity and the country was still ruled by Regent Taktra. Taktra's high
ethical standards had slipped, but he was still far superior in that regard
to Reting. Taktra, unlike Reting, remained strongly anti-Chinese.
Unfortunately, Reting chose this time to attempt to regain the regency.

Reting had come to Lhasa at the end of 1944 amid great pomp and ceremony, but Taktra had not been impressed and had not offered to step
down. Shortly thereafter, Taktra subdued a revolt of the monks of Sera
Che, Reting's college. Reting's supporters made a clumsy attempt to
assassinate Taktra in early 1947. Reting also maintained secret relations
with Chinese agents, whom he tried to convince that Taktra was an obstacle to friendly relations with China. Reting dispatched two of his representatives from Kanze to attend the Chinese Constitutional Assembly.[72]
Reting had also conveyed a message through the two Kanze men requesting Chinese military assistance in his return to power in exchange for
acknowledgement of Chinese authority over Tibet.[73]

The Tibetan Government was informed of Reting's communications

71. Goldstein, *History of Modern Tibet*, 564, citing *Foreign Office Confidential Prints*,
371/63943, 7 November 1947.

72. The Chinese used the presence of the Kanze Tibetans to convince the Tibetan
Government representatives to attend the assembly in order to counter their influence.

73. Goldstein, *History of Modern Tibet*, 473. Later Chinese Communist propaganda invari-
ably describes Reting as "patriotic" (in relation to China), and Taktra and those who purged
Reting as "tools of foreign imperialism." Ngawang Jaltso (Ngawang Gyatso) "'Protection of
Religion' and Other Conditions in Tibet," *New China News Agency*, Peking, 22 April 1959, in

with the Chinese by their representatives in Nanking. Reting was arrested at his monastery in April 1947 and brought to Lhasa for trial. Reting was convicted of having tried to assassinate Taktra and of having conspired with the Chinese to regain power. Before the Tibetan Government could decide on his punishment, Reting died in prison, probably by poison. The elimination of Reting removed the danger that the Chinese might intervene on his behalf.

The Tibetan Trade Mission

While Tibet was engaged in a mini-civil war between the supporters of Taktra and Reting, the actual civil war in China was reaching a conclusion that posed a new threat to Tibet. Tibetans feared the Communists more than the Nationalists for several reasons. Communists were atheists; their policy toward religion was well known from the fate of Mongolia; the Thirteenth Dalai Lama had predicted that the "Red menace" was a particular threat to Tibet. In anticipation of a Communist victory in China, Tibet intensified its efforts to achieve international recognition and support. The Tibetan Finance Ministry originated the idea for a trade mission to India, Britain and the United States, whose purpose would be to improve trade relations and to purchase gold to back up the Tibetan currency. The proposed mission, led by W.D. Shakabpa, had other important goals, including international recognition of Tibetan official passports.[74]

The trade mission travelled to India, where the first difficulties were encountered. Tibet had not yet recognized the transition from British to Indian government, due to Tibetan uncertainties as to future relations with both Britain and India and Tibet's claim to Tawang. The Indian Government refused to release US dollars, which Tibet had earned through its exports to the United States and which the mission hoped to use to purchase gold.[75] The mission travelled to Hong Kong, on British

Current Background, no. 563 (Hong Kong: United States Consulate, 1959), 11. Ngawang Gyatso was an abbot of Sera and supporter of Reting who was forced to flee Tibet for China after the Reting incident. He became an important collaborator after 1950.

74. Shakabpa was aware that gold sales were made only between sovereign states (having been informed of that fact by Sudyam Cutting, an American who visited Lhasa in 1935) and was intent upon purchasing gold from the US even though gold from Mexico was available at a lower price, since that would imply that the US recognized that Tibet was independent. Goldstein, *History of Modern Tibet*, 596. Shakabpa himself stated that the purpose of the mission was to "open formal relations with other nations of the world," and to "demonstrate Tibet's independent and sovereign status." Shakabpa, *Tibet: A Political History*, 295.

75. India paid Tibet in Indian rupees for Tibetan exports to other countries through

visas issued on their Tibetan passports, but was required by the Chinese to accept "Chinese papers" to enter China.[76] The delegation refused to attend the Chinese National Assembly, and $50,000 offered on the condition that the delegation travel on Chinese passports.

The US Embassy in Nanking agreed to issue visas to the United States on the Tibetans' passports, but told them they would have to first obtain exit visas from China. Since Chinese exit visas would only be issued on their Chinese papers, the mission traveled to Hong Kong, where they received US visas on their Tibetan passports.[77] Upon arrival in the United States, the mission occasioned an immediate protest from the Chinese Embassy in Washington to the effect that:

1. The Tibetan authorities have no authority to deal with other nations as an independent country.

2. The Tibetan Trade Mission is in possession of Tibetan travel documents rather than Chinese passports, which they should bear. The Chairman of the Mission, Shakabpa, has no authority to negotiate directly with the United States Government.

3. The United States Consul at Hong Kong in issuing visas to the Mission did not notify the Chinese Special Commissioner at Hong Kong.

4. The United States Government has always recognized Chinese sovereignty over Tibet and the Chinese Government is amazed at the acceptance by the American Consul General at Hong Kong of Tibetan travel documents. The Chinese Government wishes to know whether the American Consul General at Hong Kong issued the visas on his own initiative or whether he was authorized to do so by the United States Government. If he was authorized by the United States Government to issue these visas, the Chinese Government would wish to be informed whether the United States Government has changed its "usual attitude toward Tibet."[78]

The mission requested a meeting with the US President in order to

---

Calcutta and kept the foreign exchange earned for its own use. This was one of the problems that the mission had hoped to resolve. Memorandum by the Second Secretary of Embassy in India, 30 December 1947, *FRUS, 1947, vol. VII*, 607.

76. Shakabpa claimed that these papers were in the form of a "letter of invitation" from China, not Chinese passports. Goldstein, *History of Modern Tibet*, 579.

77. The State Department had previously decided that the mission would be issued US visas not on their passports but on Form-257 (for persons from countries the US did not recognize). Secretary of State to the Ambassador in India, 28 October 1947, *FRUS, 1947, vol. VII*, 601. This message was communicated to India, before it was known where the mission would apply for their American visas, but was apparently not received or was misinterpreted by the US Consulate in Hong Kong.

78. Memorandum by Chief of the Division of Chinese Affairs, 12 July 1948, *FRUS, 1948*,

deliver letters and gifts from the Dalai Lama. The Chinese protested this unless the mission were accompanied by the Chinese ambassador, which the Tibetans refused.[79] The mission did meet with Secretary of State George Marshall. Marshall was careful to reiterate US recognition of "China's *de jure* sovereignty over Tibet," but pointed out that "the fact that it exerts no *de facto* authority over Tibet is root cause of [the] situation." Marshall went on to state that President Truman had "expressed personal interest in greeting Tibetans," and that "if it should become known that their intended call on President was frustrated by ChiGovt [Chinese Government], believe press would make the most of situation to China's disadvantage. Such story might also be raised in light of self-determination which is popular concept among American people."[80] Marshall recommended that the Tibetans be allowed to purchase gold from the US Treasury since that would not "constitute an impairment of United States recognition of China's *de jure* sovereignty over Tibet, since the Department does not intend that such a sale would affect the continuation of this Government's recognition of China's *de jure* sovereignty over Tibet."[81] The Tibetan mission also met with General Eisenhower, then president of Columbia University.[82]

---

vol. VII, 759. The Chinese Embassy went on to offer to facilitate the mission under China's auspices but requested that it not be dealt with as "representative of an independent state." The US State Department informed the Chinese Embassy that, as per its instructions, the visas had not been issued on the Tibetans' passports but on Form-257. Memorandum by the Chief of the Division of Chinese Affairs, 16 July 1948, *FRUS, 1948, vol. VII,* 763. This, however, is clearly not the case, as the photocopy of Shakabpa's passport reveals. Shakabpa, *Tibet: A Political History,* 370.

79. Shakabpa pointed out that, in 1943, the US contacted Tibet (Tolstoy and Dolan mission) without consulting with the Chinese. Memorandum by Division of Chinese Affairs, 2 August 1948, *FRUS, 1948, vol. VII,* 771.

80. Secretary of State to the Ambassador in China, 28 July 1948, *FRUS, 1948, vol. VII,* 767. The meeting with Secretary Marshall was entirely innocuous in a political sense, since the Tibetans confined themselves to trade issues. Memorandum of Conversation by the Secretary of State, 6 August 1948, *FRUS, 1948, vol. VII,* 775. Shakabpa's strategy seems to have been to achieve recognition of Tibet's political status informally, by implication, through trade agreements, rather than by open recognition, which was hardly likely in any case.

81. Secretary of State to the Secretary of the Treasury, 27 August 1948, *FRUS, 1948, vol. VII,* 780. In other words, that whatever the usual legal implications of such a sale, this was an exception not intended to affect US policy toward China or Tibet. The US refused to grant a loan to Tibet to be used to purchase the gold (to be repaid when India released Tibetan foreign exchange). Secretary of State to the Leader of the Tibetan Trade Mission (Shakabpa), 27 September 1948, *FRUS, 1948, vol. VII,* 785.

82. The purpose of this meeting, arranged by Ilya Tolstoy, was so that Eisenhower could thank the Tibetans for their assistance in recovering the crew of a American transport plane that crashed in Tibet during the war. Shakabpa, *Tibet: A Political History,* 297.

The trade mission next travelled to Great Britain, on visas issued on their Tibetan passports in China (which the British attempted to refuse, stating that the issuance in China had been a "technical error"), where they were treated as a strictly trade mission and isolated from public notice. After returning to India, the mission managed to secure the release of $250,000 from the Indian Government and finally purchased gold worth $425,800 from the US Government.[83] The US ambassador in India informed the trade mission that, as it was the policy of the US to recognize Chinese suzerainty over Tibet, "for the present relations between Tibet and the United States would have to be strengthened by indirect means."[84]

The Tibetan trade mission was only a limited success; Tibetan passports were accepted by Britain and the United States, but both disavowed any intent to recognize Tibet as an independent country. The US State Department specified that it "does not consider that any of the courtesies extended to the Tibetan Trade Mission while in the United States have the effect of altering the status quo among China, Tibet, and the United States. In particular, the willingness of the US to sell gold to the Tibetan authorities does not constitute recognition of the Tibetan administration as a sovereign government."[85]

Perhaps the greatest success of the mission was in demonstrating Tibet's intention to conduct its affairs independently; this was especially important for the Americans, who had little previous awareness of Tibet's desire for independence of China. As a State Department observer commented, "Tibet, according to the leader of the Tibetan Trade mission, is completely independent and the Chinese Government has no control whatsoever over the internal or external affairs of the country."[86] This realization moved the State Department to undertake a reappraisal of US policy toward Tibet. The State Department thought Tibet worthy of support if China should fall to the Communists; in that case it was thought

---

83. India remained unconvinced that the gold was not intended for private use, to be smuggled into India where the price was much higher than official rates. Ambassador in India to the Secretary of State, 31 May 1949, *FRUS, 1949, vol. IX*, 1075.

84. Memorandum of Office of Far Eastern Affairs to the Division of Chinese Affairs, 12 April, *FRUS, 1949, vol. IX*, 1065. What these "indirect means" would entail was not specified. The author of the memorandum pointed out the vagueness of the terminology of "suzerainty," noting that it was difficult to draw a precise line of demarcation between suzerainty and sovereignty. It was suggested desirable "to avoid a possible controversy over `sovereignty' versus `suzerainty' by referring in future to Chinese *de jure* authority over Tibet or some similar comprehensive term." Ibid., 1069.

85. Secretary of State to the Ambassador in India, 2 July 1949, *FRUS, 1949, vol. IX*, 1078.

86. Memorandum by Miss Ruth E. Bacon of the Office of Far Eastern Affairs to the Chief of the Division of Chinese Affairs, 12 April 1949, *FRUS, 1949, vol. IX*, 1067.

better to treat Tibet as independent rather than as a part of Communist China. On the negative side, however, was the long-standing policy of the United States to respect the territorial integrity of China, and US opposition to Soviet influence in Mongolia. (The US did not recognize the Mongolian Peoples' Republic at that time and opposed Mongolia's admission to the UN.)[87]

The US realized that it could do little to support Tibet politically or militarily, especially without the cooperation of India, which seemed disinclined to become involved, while moral support alone might achieve results opposite to those intended: "By recognizing Tibet as independent while we are not in position to give Tibet the necessary practical support, because of its remoteness, we may in fact be pointing the way for Communist absorption of the area."[88] The State Department finally recommended a position that in its halfhearted support for Tibet was reminiscent of former British policies: "We should accordingly maintain a friendly attitude toward Tibet in ways short of giving China cause for offense."[89]

However, the US Embassy in India, always more ready to support Tibet than the State Department, pointed out that the US recognized Chinese sovereignty over Tibet only because of the US policy of supporting the KMT; a Communist victory in China would remove the logic from that position:

> The extension of Communist control over Tibet would adversely affect the overall position of the United States versus world Communism. United States policy toward Tibet is defined as the recognition by the United States of Chinese sovereignty over the country. Undoubtedly, one of the reasons for the adoption of this policy was our desire to strengthen the [Nationalist] Chinese Government, in view of the strong ties of friendship between the United States and China, and forestall in so far as it would be possible for us to do so the fragmentation of greater China which would result if Sinkiang and Tibet were to be recognized or treated as independent political units. I am not certain that the foregoing policy is best adapted to further American interests if the Communists are successful in their efforts to obtain control of the Chinese Government.[90]

---

87. Ibid., 1066.

88. Ibid.

89. Ibid., 1070. The US did think that Tibet had a legitimate cause for complaint against India in regard to the foreign exchange issue. Since Tibet was a landlocked country with possibilities of trade and transit only through China, India or Soviet territory, India's policy was thought likely to drive Tibet into the arms of the Soviets or Chinese, as well as being "contrary to the principles of freedom of international trade and intercourse which we are espousing." Ibid., 1068.

90. Ambassador in India (Henderson) to the Secretary of State, 12 April 1949, *FRUS,*

Despite last-minute Tibetan efforts to achieve some international recognition of Tibet's actual independence of China, and last-minute United States interest in making a stand against international Communism in Tibet, the period of the Reting and Taktra regencies ended with Tibet little prepared to withstand the Chinese diplomatically or militarily. Some efforts were made, especially by the *Tsongdu*, to heed the advice of the Thirteenth Dalai Lama, but the weakness of the Tibetan political system in the absence of a ruling Dalai Lama was apparent. The British policy of recognizing Tibetan "autonomy" under Chinese "suzerainty" left Tibet in 1950 with no international recognition of its *de facto* independence of China, while China retained international recognition of its authority over Tibet.

However, the evolution of Tibetan national consciousness and the Tibetan desire for independence are evident in Tibet's most significant political statements of this period. The 1934 Tibetan response to the mission of Huang Mu-sung expressed Tibet's rejection of any compromising relationship with China. Tibet continued to hope for a Chinese recognition of the Simla Convention, and therefore spoke of a continuation of a *Cho-Yon* relationship, but almost all of the aspects of Chinese "suzerainty" were denied. The Tibetans repeatedly spoke of Tibet as an independent country, albeit one with some traditional relations of a special character with China. The stationing of a Chinese representative in Lhasa was opposed unless he were to function exclusively as an ambassador of China in Tibet, without any role in Tibetan foreign or domestic affairs. The *Tsongdu's* positions are evidence that a Tibetan nationalist consciousness and desire for national independence permeated the Tibetan leadership.

In the Tibetan Government's 1946 letter to Chiang Kai-shek, Tibet continued to acknowledge a special relationship with China. However, the political relationship was to be circumscribed to the extent that the Tibetans suggested that China and Tibet establish the format for diplomatic relations between independent states, including exchange of representatives and a system for diplomatic correspondence, jurisdiction over nationals, and visa formalities.

The Tibetan statements of 1934 and 1946, along with Tibet's position presented at the 1914 Simla Convention, constituted a Tibetan declaration

---

1949, *vol. IX*, 1071. The ambassador suggested that contacts with Tibet should be immediately improved since, "If we make no effort to demonstrate a friendly interest in Tibet until a Communist dominated regime consolidates its hold on China, the impression will be created among the Tibetans that we were moved only by a desire to contain Communism and not to develop cordial relations with the Tibetan people." Ibid., 1073.

of independence of China. The Tibetan refusal to transmit Allied supplies for China during the war is further evidence of the Tibetan intention to exercise full sovereignty. The Tibetan declaration was sometimes equivocal, because Tibet continued to hope that China might guarantee Tibetan autonomy equivalent to independence, but Tibetans admitted to no more than a traditional patronage relationship with China. Tibet declared, and maintained, actual, or *de facto* independence of China during the 1912-1950 period.

The paradox of the Tibetan situation was that Tibet, having achieved a temporary release from its feudal relations with China, having attained all the requirements of *de facto* and *de jure* political independence except international recognition, was finally to fall victim to Chinese imperialism disguised as "national liberation." Furthermore, this happened at a time of international condemnation of colonialism and international resolutions on the right of all peoples to self-determination.

9

The Chinese Invasion of Tibet

Prelude to Invasion

In July 1949 the Chinese Communist People's Liberation Army (PLA) took Peking. Fearful of Communist spies in Lhasa and the possibility that the KMT mission might be transformed into a Communist presence, the Tibetan Government expelled all Chinese from central Tibet. This action produced a response from the Communists in the *New China Daily* (the forerunner of the *People's Daily*), which blamed the Tibetan action on foreign imperialists, both British and Indian:

> The affair of expelling the Han Chinese and Kuomintang officials at Lhasa was a plot undertaken by the local Tibetan authorities through the instigation of the British imperialists and their lackey—the Nehru Administration of India. The purpose of this "anti-Chinese affair" is to prevent the people in Tibet from being liberated by the Chinese People's Liberation Army.[1]

The PLA entered Tibetan areas of Kansu and Chinghai (Ch'ing-hai) in September 1949, precipitating Tibetan resistance in the Kokonor area and Tibetan areas east of the Yellow River (Choni, Nangra and Trika).[2] On 1 October 1949 the People's Republic of China (PRC) was formally proclaimed in Peking. In early November the Tibetan Foreign Bureau sent Depon Surkang, one of the members of the 1947 trade mission, to India

---

1. "No Foreign Aggressors Will be Allowed to Annex China's Territory," *New China Daily*, 2 September 1949, as quoted in Lee Fu-hsiang, "The Turkic-Moslem Problem in Sinkiang: A Case Study of the Chinese Communists' Nationality Policy," (Ph.D. diss., Rutgers University, 1973), 131.

2. Amdo Rigchok, Tsayul Tulku, personal interviews, Dharamsala, 1989; *Tibet Under Chinese Communist Rule: A Compilation of Refugee Statements: 1958-1975* (Dharamsala: Information and Publicity Office of His Holiness the Dalai Lama, 1976), 14. Some KMT and Ma Pu-feng's Hui troops also resisted the PLA's advance into Chinghai. Some of these anti-communist Chinese troops held out in Amdo until 1953, occasionally being supplied by air from Taiwan after the Nationalists retired there. George Patterson, *Tibet in Revolt* (London: Faber and Faber, 1960), 92.

with an appeal to the United States, Britain and India for assistance in the event that Mao Tse-tung should "take an aggressive attitude, sending his troops toward Tibet." Surkang said that Chinese troops had moved into Lanchou, Chinghai and Sinkiang, all on the Tibetan border, and "therefore Tibetan Government has written Mao Tse-tung asking him to respect Tibet's territorial integrity."[3]

On 24 November *Radio Peking* announced that the Panchen Lama (twelve years old at the time) had appealed to Mao to "liberate" Tibet.[4] On 1 January 1950 the new Chinese government promised to liberate Taiwan and Tibet.[5] This message was broadcast to Tibet, to which the Tibetans responded that they had no wish to be "liberated."[6]

The prevailing opinion of the Government of India (GOI) was that Tibet must be "written off," since India could not afford to become involved in military adventures in Tibet.[7] The British held out hope that an immediate Chinese takeover in Tibet might be prevented by financial, logistical and political difficulties, or that China might even leave Tibet alone, or take over slowly "by infiltration" rather than by military means, "unless questions of face [are] raised by Tibetan assertions of formal independence." Therefore, their opinion was that the Tibetans should be "dissuaded from provocative action such as proclaiming independence."[8]

Having received noncommittal replies to their appeals for assistance,

---

3. Chargé in India to the Secretary of State, 21 November 1949, *Foreign Relations of the United States (FRUS), 1949, vol. IX: The Far East: China* (Washington: Government Printing Office, 1974), 1081.

4. The reincarnation of the Ninth Panchen Lama, who had died in exile in 1937, had been discovered by the Panchen's entourage in Sining, but had not been confirmed by Lhasa, which had another candidate. Shakabpa claims that the Panchen's followers surrendered to the Chinese Communists, sending congratulations to Mao and requesting that Tibet be liberated, in exchange for the recognition by the Chinese of their candidate as the actual incarnation. "Memorandum submitted to the International Commission of Jurists by Mr. T. Shakabpa," in *Tibet and the Chinese People's Republic: A Report to the International Commission of Jurists by its Legal Inquiry Committee on Tibet* (Geneva: International Commission of Jurists, 1960), 316.

5. Robert Ford, *Wind Between the Worlds* (New York: David McKay, 1957; Berkeley: Snow Lion Graphics, 1987), 3. Ford was a radio operator for the Tibetan Government at Chamdo.

6. W.D. Shakabpa, *Tibet: A Political History* (New York: Potala Publications, 1984), 299.

7. Chargé in India to Secretary of State, 21 November 1949, *FRUS, 1949, vol. IX*, 1082.

8. Chargé in India to Secretary of State, 23 November 1949, *FRUS, 1949, vol. IX*, 1084. British Foreign Office officials even suggested that publicity about Tibet's potential or actual incorporation by China should be discouraged since "Tibetan collapse would have more serious effect in neighboring countries if issue were played up in advance." Ambassador in the United Kingdom to the Secretary of State, 20 June 1950, *FRUS, 1950, vol. VI: East Asia and the Pacific* (Washington: Government Printing Office, 1976), 365.

the Lhasa authorities decided to send official missions to India, Nepal, Britain and the United States. The mission delegated to the United States was also to approach the United Nations. In a message sent by wire from Gyantse, this mission asked for US support for Tibet's appeal to the UN:

> As Tibet being an independent state, we have no dangers from other foreign countries but in view of the spread of Communism and their success in China, there is now imminent danger of Communist aggression towards Tibet.

> As all the world knows that Tibet and Communist China cannot have any common sympathy by reasons of religion and principles of life which are just the opposite, therefore in order to defend our country against impending threat of Communist invasion and also to preserve our future independence and freedom, we consider it most essential for Tibet to secure admission of her membership in the United Nations General Assembly.

> We are sending a special mission to the United States in this connection but, in the meantime, we shall be most grateful to you and your Government if you would kindly help us and place our humble appeal to the United Nations immediately through your good office so that Tibet could take her place in the United Nations as a member state.[9]

Peking Radio promptly condemned the Tibetan missions and the very concept of Tibetan independence:

> Tibet is the territory of the Chinese People's Republic. This is known to everyone in the world and is a fact which has never previously been denied. Since this is so the Lhasa authorities have no right arbitrarily to despatch any "mission" even less have they the right to show what they call their "independence." The fact that Tibetan "independence" is to be proclaimed to the Governments of U.S.A., Britain, India and Nepal and that it has been announced by the American United Press makes it easy for people to see that, if this news was not manufactured by the United Press, it is nothing but a puppet show played by American Imperialism and its conspirators in the invasion of Tibet. The demand of the Tibetan people is to become a member of the great democratic family of the Chinese People's Republic, is to exercise appropriate regional autonomy under the unified leadership of the Chinese Central People's Government and this has already been provided for in the common program of the Chinese Peoples' Political Consultative Conference. If the Lhasa authorities send representatives to Peking to discuss the peaceful liberation of Tibet on this basis then

---

9. Tibetan Cabinet Ministers to the Secretary of State, (Gyantse), 3 December 1949, *FRUS, 1949, vol. IX*, 1087. Tibet approached the US and Britain in regard to a UN appeal but apparently did not request Indian assistance.

such representatives will naturally be received. Otherwise if the Lhasa authorities go against the will of the Tibetan people and accept the orders of the imperialist aggressors and send illegal "missions" to engage in splitting the motherland and traitorous activities then the Chinese Peoples' Government will be unable to pardon such activity on the part of the Lhasa authorities and any state which receives such an illegal mission will be considered as harboring hostile intentions towards the Chinese Peoples' Republic.[10]

The Tibetan intention to appeal to the UN set off a flurry of consultations between Britain, the US and India. Britain advised India that Tibet's admission to the UN was hopeless since any Tibetan application was sure to be vetoed by the USSR.[11] British policy was that while Britain was "still interested in Tibet maintaining its autonomy, Tibetan problem is almost exclusively of concern to India."[12] India agreed that Tibet's admission to the UN was hopeless, and felt that even to bring Tibet's case up at the UN "would unduly agitate Tibetan question and might provoke earlier action by Chinese Communists."[13]

Britain and the US asked India to convey to Tibet, through its representative at Lhasa (Richardson), the request that the proposed missions be suspended or, if they had already departed, as seemed to be the case, that they meet with UK and US representatives at their respective embassies in New Delhi.[14] On 21 December, the US Secretary of State sent a reply to the Tibetan mission's letter from Gyantse informing the Tibetans that their request was being given sympathetic consideration, but advising them to avoid provoking the Chinese:

Tibetan effort to obtain UN membership this time would be unsuccessful in view certain opposition USSR and [Nationalist] Chinese delegations, both of whom have veto power in Security Council. Tibetan plan despatch special mission obtain UN membership may at this time serve to precipitate Chinese Communist action to gain control Tibet. . . . Tibet now appears [to] enjoy de facto freedom [from] Chinese control . . . any obvious move this time complete separation from China in form as well as substance would

---

10. *Peking Radio,* 20 January 1950, New Delhi to Department of State, 15 June 1950, National Archives, 793B.00/6-1550.

11. Chargé in the United Kingdom to the Secretary of State, 9 December 1949, *FRUS, 1949, vol. IX,* 1090.

12. Chargé in the United Kingdom to the Secretary of State, 12 December 1949, *FRUS, 1949, vol. IX,* 1091.

13. Ambassador in India to the Secretary of State, 14 December 1949, *FRUS, 1949, vol. IX,* 1091.

14. Ibid.

probably hasten Chinese Commie efforts thereby jeopardizing present status.[15]

India expressed reservations about having the Tibetan delegations meet with British and American representatives in New Delhi, since China would make propaganda about India being the center of a conspiracy to separate Tibet from China. In view of the reluctance of India, Britain and the US to even receive Tibetan missions, Tibet abandoned the plan to send international missions; the Tibetans expressed "considerable disappointment that no aid would be forthcoming."[16]

The US Embassy in Delhi, which had at one time entertained the thought of sending an official mission to Tibet, now felt that this too would be inadvisable for the reasons that "it might cause Communists expedite execution their program for conquest Tibet," or "official visit might mislead Tibetans into believing we [are] prepared aid them resist incursion Chinese Communist troops. . . . It would be unfair for US take any action which might encourage them to resist because of mistaken idea of help from US."[17] In an informal position paper on Tibet, the US State Department concurred with these views, but thought that some covert military assistance to Tibet by India might increase Tibet's ability to resist:

Comparatively little assistance in the form of specialized military instruction and supplies might stiffen Tibetan resistance and make a Chinese Communist military expedition so costly that it would not be undertaken, particularly in the absence of a manifestation by the Western States of extraordinary interest in Tibet or an attempt to alter its international status. . . . Owing to its geographic position and special trade and other relationships with Tibet, India is perhaps the only country which could undertake this task. Furthermore, Indian interests are most immediately and directly concerned. The Government of India is believed to have taken an increasing interest in this problem and is understood to be providing the Tibetans with some military supplies.[18]

American policy toward Tibet was limited by that of India and Britain.

---

15. Secretary of State to the Ambassador in India, 21 December 1949, *FRUS, 1949, vol. IX*, 1096.

16. Ambassador in India to the Secretary of State, 20 January 1950, *FRUS, 1950, vol. VI*, 283.

17. Ambassador in India to the Secretary of State, 15 December 1949, *FRUS, 1949, vol. IX*, 1092. The ambassador did hold out the possibility of an unofficial or covert US mission.

18. "Informal Outline of Present Thinking Respecting Tibet," Memorandum of Conversation, Department of State, 16 June 1950, National Archives, 793B.00/6-1650.

The US looked to Britain to sponsor Tibet's case at the UN, but Britain felt that its responsibilities in regard to Tibet had devolved upon India. Indian Foreign Secretary Krishna Menon informed the American ambassador that "India had no intention of assuming all British responsibilities in regard to Tibet."[19] On the last day of 1949, India recognized the Chinese Communist government. India seemed to hope that Tibet's autonomous status might be respected by China out of regard for good relations with India. But, as the US ambassador to India pointed out, "India is not requesting Chinese Communists to respect Tibetan autonomy, or even to recognize previous treaties between China and pre-Independence Indian government dealing with Tibet, as prerequisite to establishment [of] relations."[20]

Indian policy was predicated upon the belief, shared by the British, that an immediate Chinese invasion of Tibet was not likely, given the logistical difficulties involved. The Chinese Communists were thought to be faced with such domestic difficulties involved with the consolidation of their regime that they would be able to exercise only a superficial and symbolic degree of authority over Tibet. India had concluded that Tibet's only chance to preserve any measure of autonomy was by means of an entirely non-confrontational policy. India suggested that neither the Tibetans nor any interested foreign parties should actively challenge China's claims over Tibet. India discouraged the Tibetans from declarations of independence and the US from considering open diplomatic assistance to Tibet. India was reluctant to cooperate with Britain or the US in regard to Tibet, since that might be seen by the Chinese as evidence of India's collusion with imperialists' attempts to detach Tibet from China. India also reportedly advised the Nepalese Government to be "extremely cautious" in offering any expression of support for Tibet.[21] Despite its

---

19. Ambassador in India to the Secretary of State, 10 January 1950, *FRUS, 1950, vol. VI,* 273.

20. Ambassador in India to the Secretary of State, 30 December 1949, *FRUS, 1949, vol. IX,* 1097. Indian Prime Minister Jawaharlal Nehru did not wish to allow the Tibetan issue to upset India's relations with China. However, his ambassador to China, K.M. Pannikar, pointed out in a 1948 study of Indian policy toward Tibet that Indian recognition of Chinese sovereignty over Tibet would invalidate the 1914 Indo-Tibetan border agreement (McMahon Line) and change the status of India's northern border from demarcated by treaty with Tibet (actually only delimited) to undemarcated. K.M. Pannikar, as quoted in Alastair Lamb, *Tibet, China and India 1914-1950* (Hertingfordburg: Roxford Books, 1989), 518.

21. In March 1950 the American ambassador in New Delhi was told by an official of the Nepalese Government that Nepal would like to extend what aid it could to Tibet but had been advised by the GOI to be extremely cautious in this regard. "It was evidently the view of the GOI that obvious and direct assistance by Nepal to Tibet, whether under the

policy of non-interference in Tibet, however, India felt itself able to accede to Tibet's request for arms as a continuation of British policy, although this was done discretely. In March 1950, India made its last delivery of arms to Tibet.[22]

Early in 1950, in response to the Communists' announced threats to "liberate" Tibet, the Tibetan Government sent a mission led by Shakabpa to inform the Chinese of Tibet's intention to maintain its independence.[23] The Chinese had invited Tibet to send a delegation to Peking, but the Shakabpa delegation preferred Hong Kong as a more neutral ground and because they hoped for British Government support.[24] The mission traveled through India, where they attempted to secure travel documents from the Indian and British governments to proceed to Hong Kong. However, the GOI refused to honor the Tibetans' passports and the British refused them visas to Hong Kong, both out of concern for their relations with China.[25] Shakabpa later expressed relief that his mission had been prevented from leaving India, since he feared that from Hong Kong he would have been pressured by China, and perhaps even by Britain, to proceed to Peking.[26]

On 18 January 1950 the Chinese Communists convened a "Forum on the Tibetan Issue" for Tibetans in Peking, at which they expressed their intention to "liberate" Tibet.[27] A Communist delegation was sent to Tibet, arriving in Lhasa in May, which invited the Tibetan Government to send

---

Nepalese-Tibetan treaty of 1856 or not, might provoke earlier Chinese Communist reactions. However, the Nepalese Government has received a couple of Tibetan officers in Katmandu where they are understood to be serving in a liaison capacity with the Nepalese Army." New Delhi Embassy to Department of State, 30 March 1950, National Archives, 793B.00/3-3050.

22. India also agreed to train some Tibetans at Gyantse. In order to do this, they quietly replaced some ordinary soldiers at Gyantse with qualified instructors. Britain was reportedly instrumental in persuading India to supply these arms to Tibet. Ambassador in India to the Secretary of State, 8 March 1950, *FRUS, 1950, vol. VI*, 317.

23. Shakabpa, *Tibet: A Political History*, 300. Indian Ministry of External Affairs (MEA) officials told the American ambassador that they thought Shakabpa was "hoping to persuade Chinese Communists that if they will accord Tibet autonomy and not interfere in Tibet's internal affairs Tibet will not associate itself with powers opposed to international Communism." Ambassador in India to the Secretary of State, 24 April 1950, *FRUS, 1950, vol. VI*, 333.

24. Ford, *Wind Between the Worlds*, 28.

25. Ambassador in the United Kingdom to the Secretary of State, 20 June 1950, *FRUS, 1950, vol. VI*, 366. The British were uncomfortable about the choice of Hong Kong for negotiations since the status of Hong Kong itself was in question.

26. Ambassador in India to the Secretary of State, 7 August 1950, *FRUS, 1950, vol. VI*, 426.

27. Shih Hung-lin, "Peking's `Peaceful Liberation' of Tibet in Retrospect," in *Issues and Studies* (Taiwan), vol 25, no. 5, 113.

a delegation to Peking to negotiate.[28] *Radio Peking* reiterated in its May Day message (1 May 1950) that the tasks for the PLA in 1950 were to liberate Taiwan and Tibet. Tibet was offered regional autonomy and religious freedom and invited to send representatives with full powers to negotiate its "peaceful liberation," with the warning that it was "certain to be liberated in any event." Tibet was also warned not to count on geographical factors or British or American assistance.[29] On 9 May Sherab Gyatso, vice-chairman of the Chinghai People's Government, broadcast on *Radio Sian* a message to the Dalai Lama stating that the PLA would soon set out to liberate Tibet and inviting him to send delegates to Peking to negotiate.[30]

The first outline of a proposed political program for Tibet was formulated by Liu Po-ch'eng, who, as commander of the Southwestern Military Region, was responsible for the liberation of Tibet. The provisions of this "Political Program for Tibet" were:

(1) Carry out regional autonomy for the nationalities; (2) Allow the people to enjoy freedom of religion, with the Communist forces assuring protection of the Lama temples from damage or destruction; (3) Promote education in the Tibetan language and afford protection to the agricultural, pastoral, industrial and commercial production so as to improve the people's living standard; (4) Maintain the status quo of Tibet's political system; (5) Officials at all levels may remain at their posts; (6) Incorporate the Tibetan army as part of the PLA; (7) All the reform measures concerning Tibet are to be made in accordance with the will of the Tibetans, and all questions involved should be settled through negotiations between the Tibetan people and their leaders.[31]

In the meantime, the PLA moved troops into position in Chinghai, "Sikang" (Kham), Yunnan and Sinkiang in preparation for the invasion of Tibet. The main thrust of the invasion was to be by the PLA 18th Army from Szechuan. On 23 March 1950 the PLA moved into Kangding (Dartsendo) on the ethnic border with Tibet. In the middle of April an advance unit of the 18th Army numbering 30,000 troops entered Kham from Dartsendo, reaching Kanze on the 28th. In the beginning, logistics for the Chinese invasion force were so tenuous that supplies had to be air-

---

28. The Tibetan Government reportedly refused the Chinese Communist delegation's offer of negotiations and placed the delegation members under surveillance while they were in Lhasa. The delegation remained in Lhasa until 25 June 1950 (at the time of the outbreak of the Korean War). Ibid.

29. Ford, *Wind Between the Worlds*, 46.

30. *Tibet 1950-67* (Hong Kong: Union Research Institute, 1967), 765.

31. Shih Hung-lin, "Peking's `Peaceful Liberation' of Tibet," 114.

dropped to Chinese troops. However, according to a foreign missionary observer in Dartsendo, the PLA soon began a buildup of troops and supplies, including bridge-building equipment and girders in long columns of American and Russian trucks.[32]

A motorable road was completed from Dartsendo to Kanze in August 1950. PLA units simultaneously entered Chinghai and established a base at Yushu (Jyekundo), on the border of territory administered by the Tibetan Government, and began constructing a road to the south toward Chamdo. The forces entering Kham incorporated some of the troops of the Szechuan warlord Liu Wen-hui; those entering Amdo incorporated the Hui troops of Ma Pu-feng. Each of the PLA armies recruited as many Tibetans or other "border nationalities" as possible as guides, interpreters, etc., and styled themselves the "Tibetan People's Liberation Army."[33] PLA troops paid for all their transportation and food requirements, "taking not even a single needle and thread from the people."[34] The first priority was to construct a road from Dartsendo to Kanze and an airport at Kanze, for both of which Tibetans were forcibly conscripted for labor, although they were adequately compensated.[35]

Some of the PLA units sent into Kham were of the "vanguard" type, trained in the theory and implementation of the Party's nationalities policies and instructed to treat the local inhabitants with deference and respect. The role of the PLA vanguard troops was to "make friends and do good deeds," while propagandizing the unity of nationalities against upper class exploiters and foreign imperialists. The PLA employed mass meetings, film, drama, and loudspeakers to convey their message. Money was lavishly distributed to Tibetans; local Tibetan officials were awarded new titles and official positions with large salaries.

Tibetans from all areas reported the same version of Chinese justifications for having entered Tibet: they had come to Tibet to help the Tibetans and they would leave when Tibet had been "improved" and Tibet was

---

32. "Invasion of Tibet by Chinese People's Liberation Army," Hong Kong to Department of State, 21 August 1950, National Archives, 793B.00/8-2150. The Scottish missionary, Beatty, said that a PLA officer had told him that large numbers of yak, wild and domesticated, would be needed to feed the PLA troops. The PLA officers and men talked of going on to India once Tibet was in their hands. Ibid.

33. Shih Hung-lin, "Peking's `Peaceful Liberation' of Tibet," 115.

34. A Tibetan informant from Kanze, Ama Adi, reports that airdrops included silver *dayan* (Yuan Shih-k'ai silver dollars), with which the Chinese ingratiated themselves and paid for their transport and provisions, leading to the Tibetan saying that the Chinese were accompanied in their entry into Tibet by a "rain of *dayans*." Ama Adi, personal interview, Dharamsala, January 1990.

35. Jamyang Norbu, *Warriors of Tibet* (London: Wisdom Publications, 1986), 82.

capable of self-rule.[36] As the Chinese commander at Kanze reportedly said, "In a year or two we will leave, and you will have to manage on your own. Even if you ask us to stay then, we will not do so."[37]

These tactics, and the Khampas' traditional animosities towards the Lhasa government, secured some Khampa collaborators for the PLA. Khampas were traditionally jealous of their independence, having been little controlled by any central government. Some Khampa opponents of Lhasa's control had established contacts with the Chinese before 1950; some acquired "progressive" ideas under KMT or Communist influence. During the passage of the Red Army through Kanze in 1935, a few Tibetans were recruited; they were later trained at the CCP's Minority Nationalities Institute at Yenan.[38]

Khampas often differed in regard to whether they preferred to reform the Tibetan government or to form an independent polity in eastern Tibet; some naively thought that the Chinese would assist in those goals, but few if any were proponents of Chinese control over Tibet. In 1949 the Chinese Communists' offered to support the Khampas' ambitions against Lhasa but only if Kham were constituted as an East Tibet Autonomous Region and the Khampa movement became part of the Communist liberation of Tibet, which Khampa leaders refused.[39] Khampa leaders hurriedly attempted to restore relations with Lhasa for a united resistance after the PLA entered Kham in 1950, but they were no longer trusted by Lhasa since their collaboration with the Chinese was well known. The final result of Khampa political maneuvering was that not only was Tibet not united against the Chinese but there was no unified resistance among the Khampas themselves. Many Khampas opportunistically collaborated with the PLA, acting as guides and interpreters. Perhaps the most damaging effect of some Khampas' collaboration was that the Chinese were able to propagandize about their acceptance by the Khampas and thus obscure the actual nature of their entrance into Tibet.

In late May or early June the PLA reached the Yangtze to the north of Chamdo where, at Dengo, site of a Tibetan Army outpost and radio transmitter, the first clash took place.[40] In July the Chinese sent Geda Lama, of

36. Abu Chonga, Abu Gonkar, Nyima Assam, Ani Gonjo Pachim Dolma, Rinzin Paljor, personal interviews, Dharamsala, 1989-1990.

37. Jamyang Norbu, *Warriors of Tibet*, 81.

38. Very few were recruited, apparently, if a photograph of Tibetans at Yenan in 1937, five in number, is indicative. Israel Epstein, *Tibet Transformed* (Beijing: New World Press, 1983), 126.

39. According to George Patterson, a missionary in Kham at the time, the Khampas were told that Tibet was to be liberated within a year, followed by Nepal, Sikkim and Bhutan in three years and India within five years. Patterson, *Tibet in Revolt*, 63.

40. Ford, *Wind Between the Worlds*, 54.

Kanze monastery, then vice-chairman of the "Sikang Provincial People's Government," to Lhasa to "arrange for the peaceful unification of Tibet with the Motherland."[41] Geda Lama was halted at Chamdo by Lhalu, the Tibetan governor of Chamdo district; Geda died shortly thereafter at Chamdo under mysterious circumstances (poison was suspected), an event that apparently convinced the Chinese that the Tibetans would have to be forced to negotiate.[42] By August the PLA had moved into position all along the Yangtze in Kham and into Nangchen and Jyekundo in Chinghai, and were thus poised all along the *de facto* political border of Tibet.[43]

While the PLA was advancing into eastern Tibet, the Shakabpa delegation remained in India; on 9 June they met with US officials in New Delhi. Shakabpa expressed the opinion that India "seemed prepared to hand Tibet over to the Chinese." US officials pointed out that recognition of Chinese "suzerainty" over Tibet, by India or anyone else, did not mean agreement to "loss by Tibet of its autonomy and of Tibet being incorporated into a centralized Communist Chinese state." Shakabpa replied that Tibetans "hoped through negotiations with Chinese Communists to maintain their freedom but if negotiations failed they expected invasion and without foreign help saw little chance of preserving their freedom."[44]

In May 1950 the US resumed aid to the KMT on Taiwan (discontinued since August 1948) and undertook support for Nationalist covert actions on the mainland. This policy reflected the American strategic decision to contain Communism, whether Soviet or Chinese. On 25 June North

---

41. Ibid., 236.

42. Geda Lama had cooperated with the Red Army during its penetration into Tibet in 1935 and had been made a vice-chairman of the "Tibetan People's Government" in Kanze at that time. Robert Ford, the British radio operator in the employ of the Tibetan Government at Chamdo, was captured and spent three years in Chinese prisons for the murder of Geda. Ford maintained throughout that he had nothing to do with Geda's murder and refused to confess. Ford was finally released after confessing to the lesser crime of "illegally entering China." Ibid., 94. After the invasion of Chamdo, the Chinese entrusted the captured Tibetan commander, Ngawang Jigme Ngapo, to make an investigation of the circumstances of Geda's death. Ngapo concluded that Geda had died of an adverse reaction to medicine, but this conclusion was rejected by the Chinese, who wished to blame foreign imperialist intrigues for Geda's death. Jigme Ngapo (son of Ngawang Jigme Ngapo), personal communication, February 1995, Washington D.C. On the other hand, Ford said in his book that he "had good reasons for believing that Geda was murdered, and I think I know who killed him. I hope he will never be found out." Ford, *Wind Between the Worlds*, 98.

43. Shakabpa reported that Chinese troops were in Jyekundo, Nangchen, Batang and Derge and that PLA units in Sinkiang were also preparing to move into western Tibet. Ambassador in India to the Secretary of State, 10 September 1950, *FRUS, 1950, vol. VI*, 494.

44. Ambassador in India to the Secretary of State, 9 June 1950, *FRUS, 1950, vol. VI*, 361.

Korea attacked the South; the US moved the Seventh Fleet into the Taiwan Straits and committed itself to the defense of Taiwan. The US also became more interested in assistance to Tibet as a part of its policy to contain the spread of Communism. On 11 July the State Department solicited the opinion of the Embassy in New Delhi in regard to the advisability of offering military assistance to the Tibetans. The Embassy replied that such assistance might be acceptable to India if it were first requested from India by Tibet, assuming that India would be unable to provide further assistance itself but would not object to procurement by Tibet of military equipment by means of "purchases from abroad."[45]

On 22 July the State Department informed the New Delhi Embassy that military assistance to Tibet had been approved, contingent upon Indian cooperation.[46] On 4 August Shakabpa was informed that "if Tibet intended to resist Communist aggression and needed help US Government was prepared to assist in procuring material and would finance such aid." The US advised that it "considered it important that prompt steps be taken now as it would be extremely difficult [to] make aid available in time if Tibet were to wait until invasion had started." Shakabpa inquired whether US assistance meant that troops and planes would be sent to Tibet's aid. Shakabpa was pessimistic about Tibet's ability to resist a Chinese invasion and feared that "India might come to some understanding with Chinese Communists at Tibet's expense."[47]

India had meanwhile informed China of its hope that the Tibetan issue could be peacefully resolved. The Indian ambassador was authorized to state that India would regard China's application to the UN in a different light should China invade Tibet.[48] Peking's reply was that it "maintained its sovereignty over Tibet; that it did not however wish to have armed conflict; that it therefore had instructed its ambassador to India to enter into tentative conversations with Tibetan representatives shortly after the ambassador's arrival in Delhi with the understanding [that] final conversations would take place in Peking."[49]

On 6 September the Shakabpa delegation met with the Chinese charge

---

45. India was, however, not thought to be more amenable to assisting Tibet because of Korea since India was attempting to play a role as mediator in that conflict and wished to avoid any exacerbation of the Tibetan issue that might distract from those efforts. Ambassador in India to the Secretary of State, 15 July 1950, *FRUS, 1950, vol. VI*, 377.

46. Secretary of State to the Embassy in India, 22 July 1950, *FRUS, 1950, vol. VI*, 386.

47. Ambassador in India to the Secretary of State, 7 August 1950, *FRUS, 1950, vol. VI*, 424.

48. The US ambassador to India thought it unlikely that K.M. Pannikar, the Indian ambassador to China, had in fact been so forceful. Ambassador in India to the Secretary of State, 14 August 1950, *FRUS, 1950, vol. VI*, 441.

49. Ambassador in India to the Secretary of State, 25 August 1950, *FRUS, 1950, vol. VI*, 449.

at Delhi for the purpose of informing him that they would meet with the Chinese ambassador when he arrived. They also protested the presence of a reported 20,000 PLA troops in Kham poised to strike against central Tibet. The delegation was given a pamphlet describing the Chinese Communists' nationalities policies and informed that the PLA would "go to Tibet to liberate it but when they reach Tibet they will not change anything in Tibetan culture and religion."[50] The charge informed them that any negotiations in regard to Tibet's status must take place in Peking.[51] On 16 September the Shakabpa delegation met with the new Chinese ambassador to India, who invited them to proceed to Peking for "peace negotiations."[52]

The Shakabpa delegation also met with Indian Foreign Minister Krishna Menon and Prime Minister Nehru. The delegation requested that India mediate between Tibet and China as Britain had at Simla, but Nehru promised only that India would adhere to British India's policy of recognizing Tibet as an autonomous part of China.[53] In the meantime, another Tibetan delegation was sent to negotiate with the Americans and Indians about military assistance. This mission met with Indian officials but was apparently so discouraged with India's attitude and so threatened by the imminent Chinese invasion that it never raised the issue of arms purchases from third parties. The American opinion of these events was that the Tibetans "completely lost heart from attitude of Government of India."[54]

The Invasion of Tibet

Tibetan attempts to secure foreign assistance were brought to an end on 7 October 1950 by the advance of PLA troops across the Yangtze from Kham, south from Jyekundo in Chinghai and north from Yunnan. The Chinese invaded central Tibet almost simultaneously with their massive introduction of troops into the Korean conflict; Chinese troops crossed

50. Shakabpa, cited in Melvyn Goldstein, *A History of Modern Tibet*, 1913-1951 (Berkeley: University of California Press, 1989), 672.

51. Ambassador in India to the Secretary of State, 10 September 1950, *FRUS, 1950, vol. VI*, 494.

52. "Exchange of Notes between the Governments of India and of the People's Republic of China concerning the advance of the Chinese army units into Tibet," in *The Question of Tibet and the Rule of Law* (Geneva: International Commission of Jurists, 1959), 136.

53. Goldstein, *History of Modern Tibet*, 674.

54. Ambassador in India to the Secretary of State, 26 October 1950, *FRUS, 1950, vol. VI*, 541.

the Yalu one week later, on 14 October.[55] United Nations involvement in Korea, led by the United States, was undoubtedly regarded by China as evidence of renewed imperialist attempts to impose domination on Asia and to reverse the Chinese revolution. Tibet, which the Chinese still imagined to be under foreign imperialist domination, or potentially so, was thought to be particularly vulnerable to imperialist attacks via India.[56]

The intention of the Chinese Communists to "liberate Tibet from foreign imperialism" has to be understood within the context of the CCP's anti-imperialist ideology and the previous one hundred years of Chinese history, a period to which the Chinese refer as the "hundred years of imperialist domination." To the Chinese Communists, the actual numbers of foreigners in Tibet was not as relevant as the history of foreign involvement since the early part of the twentieth century, a history thought to be the sole reason for Tibet's estrangement from China and the sole source of Tibetan anti-Chinese nationalism.[57] To the Chinese

---

55. China's entry into the Korean conflict was precipitated by the American Inchon landing of 15 September and the subsequent advance across the 38th parallel. Gordon Chang, *Friends and Enemies: The United States, China and the Soviet Union, 1948-1972* (Stanford: Stanford University Press, 1990), 77. The invasion was late in the season, when cold would add to other natural difficulties for Chinese troops. The timing of the invasion was undoubtedly due to the Korean conflict.

56. Robert Ford reported that after his capture he saw posters in Chamdo announcing the liberation of Tibet in which the date was written as 195_, perhaps indicating that the Chinese had been uncertain of the timetable for their invasion of Tibet until forced to take action by events in Korea. Ford, *Wind Between the Worlds*, 188. Ford reported that the theme of Chinese propaganda to Tibetans was: "Tibet has been kept apart from the Motherland by the imperialists. We have come to free you from them." Ibid., 180.

57. Prior to the Chinese invasion, there were only seven Europeans in Tibet. There were the two British radio operators hired by the Tibetan Government, Robert Ford and Reginald Fox; two Austrian mountaineers who had escaped from British internment camps in India, Heinrich Harrer and Peter Aufschnaiter; a White Russian, Nedbailof, who had been hired to work with Aufschnaiter on a hydroelectric project; and an English missionary, Geoffrey Bull, in Markham at the time of the invasion. Richardson and Fox departed before the invasion, Harrer and Aufschnaiter escaped to India, and Ford and Bull were captured by the Chinese. Harrer, Ford and Bull wrote books based upon their experiences in Tibet: Heinrich Harrer, *Seven Years in Tibet* (London: Rupert Hart-Davis, 1953); Robert Ford, *Wind Between the Worlds* (first published as *Captured in Tibet*); Geoffrey Bull, *When Iron Gates Yield* (London: Hodder and Stoughton, 1955) and *Tibetan Tales* (London, 1966). In addition, for a short time in the summer of 1950, an American, Frank Bessac, was in Tibet. Bessac was recruited by the OSS to go to China in 1944 and was in 1949-50 connected with the CIA. Bessac had been in East Turkestan (Sinkiang) along with Douglas MacKiernan, vice consul at the American Consulate at Tihwa, who was also CIA and had been engaged in organizing resistance to the Communists. In late 1949 when the Communists began entering Sinkiang, Bessac and MacKiernan, along with several White Russians and a few Kazakhs, fled toward Tibet. On 29 April 1950 MacKiernan was accidently killed by Tibetan border guards north of Nagchukha. Bessac arrived in Lhasa on 11

Communists, Tibet was a part of China in need of liberation from both foreign imperialism and its own exploiting classes.

Tibetan resistance to the PLA advance was quickly overwhelmed. The Tibetan governor general who had recently replaced Lhalu at Chamdo, Ngawang Jigme Ngapo, fled and was captured by the advancing PLA. After taking Chamdo, the PLA advanced, taking Lho Dzong on 22 October and Shopando on 27 October. The PLA halted at Giamda at the line claimed (at Simla) as the border of the "province" of Sikang. On 18 October the Shakabpa delegation, still in New Delhi, met with the Chinese ambassador to protest the invasion of Tibet, accusing China of violating international law by attacking Tibet and of doing so while negotiations were in process. The ambassador informed Shakabpa that Tibet would be "liberated," but that if the Shakabpa delegation would proceed to Peking for negotiations on Tibet's "peaceful liberation," there would be no further military action.[58]

In a note of 26 October 1950 the Government of India protested that the unprovoked invasion of Tibet could hardly be reconciled with China's previously stated intentions to settle the issue peacefully:

> We have been repeatedly assured of a desire by the Chinese Government to settle the Tibetan problem by peaceful means and negotiations. ... Now that the invasion of Tibet has been ordered by the Chinese Government, peaceful negotiation can hardly be synchronized with it and there naturally will be fear on the part of Tibetans that negotiations will be held under duress. In the present context of world events, invasion by Chinese troops of Tibet cannot but be regarded as deplorable.[59]

The Chinese replied on 30 October:

> Tibet is an integral part of Chinese territory. The problem of Tibet is entirely the domestic problem of China. The Chinese People's Liberation Army

---

June and remained there for some time, finally crossing the Indo-Tibetan border on 21 August 1950. Bessac was reportedly the conduit, by radio, for American messages to the Tibetan Government that they should officially request American military assistance. The Chinese Communists were well aware of MacKiernan's activities in Sinkiang and presumably suspected that Bessac was also connected with the CIA. Ambassador in India to the Secretary of State, 3 June 1950, FRUS, 1950. vol VI, 358. The information in regard to Bessac's affiliations and the messages he passed was supplied by Thomas Laird, who interviewed Bessac in 1994.

58. Goldstein, *History of Modern Tibet*, 699.

59. "Exchange of Notes between the Governments of India and of the People's Republic of China concerning the advance of the Chinese army units into Tibet," in *Question of Tibet and the Rule of Law*, 132.

must enter Tibet, liberate the Tibetan people and defend the frontiers of China. This is the resolved policy of the Central People's Government. . . . Therefore with regard to the viewpoint of the Government of India on what it regards as deplorable, the Central People's Government of the People's Republic of China cannot but consider it as having been affected by foreign influences hostile to China in Tibet.[60]

India responded on 31 October:

The Government of India have read with amazement the statement in the last paragraph of the Chinese Government's reply that the Government of India's representation to them was affected by foreign influences hostile to China and categorically repudiates it. . . . It is with no desire to interfere or gain advantage that the Government of India have sought earnestly that a settlement of the Tibetan problem should be effected by peaceful negotiations adjusting the legitimate Tibetan claim to autonomy within the framework of Chinese Suzerainty.[61]

The Chinese replied on 16 November, reminding the Indians that they had recognized Chinese sovereignty over Tibet:

According to the provisions of the Common Program adopted by the Chinese People's Political Consultative Conference, the relative autonomy granted by the Chinese Government to national minorities inside the country is an autonomy within the confines of Chinese sovereignty.

This point was recognized by the Indian Government in its aide memoire to the Chinese Government dated August 28 this year.[62] However, when the

---

60. Ibid., 133.

61. Ibid.

62. Richardson believes that the claim that the Indian ambassador to China, K.M. Pannikar, recognized Chinese sovereignty, not suzerainty in this *aide memoire* of 28 August is a Chinese fabrication, since India was at this time very careful in its policy to recognize only Chinese suzerainty over Tibet. Hugh Richardson, *Tibet and Its History* (Boston: Shambhala, 1984), 181. However, Pannikar states in his memoirs that India recognized Chinese sovereignty: "Our rejoinder, though couched in equally strong words, recognized Chinese sovereignty over Tibet and disclaimed all desire to intervene in its affairs and emphasized once again our desire that the issue between the Tibetans and the Chinese should be decided peacefully and not by use of force." K.M. Pannikar, *In Two Chinas*, 112. Nehru's admission that there was little distinction between the terms is perhaps the crux of the matter. Nehru stated in a speech to Parliament at the time (7 December 1950) that India did not challenge Chinese suzerainty over Tibet, adding, "Please note, that I use the word suzerainty, not sovereignty. There is a slight difference—though not much." "Prime Minister Nehru's Speech in Parliament," 7 December 1950, in Chanakya Sen, comp. and ed., *Tibet Disappears: A Documentary History of Tibet's International Status, the Great Rebellion and Its Aftermath* (New Delhi: Asia Publishing House, 1960), 119.

Chinese Government actually exercised its sovereign rights, and began to liberate the Tibetan people and drive out foreign forces and influences to ensure that the Tibetan people will be free from aggression and will realize regional autonomy and religious freedom the Indian Government attempted to influence and obstruct the exercise of its sovereign rights in Tibet by the Chinese Government. This cannot but make the Chinese Government greatly surprised.

The Central People's Government of the People's Republic of China sincerely hopes that the Chinese People's Liberation Army may enter Tibet peacefully to perform the sacred task of liberating the Tibetan People and defending the frontiers of China. It has therefore long since welcomed the delegation of the local authorities of Tibet which has remained in India to come to Peking at an early date to proceed with peace negotiations. Yet the said delegation, obviously as a result of continued outside obstruction, has delayed its departure for Peking. Further, taking advantage of the delay of negotiations, the local authorities of Tibet have deployed strong armed forces at Changtu [Chamdo], in Sikiang [Sikang] Province, in the interior of China, in an attempt to prevent the Chinese People's Liberation Army from liberating Tibet.

On August 31, 1950, the Chinese Ministry of Foreign Affairs informed the Indian Government through Ambassador Pannikar that the Chinese People's Liberation Army was going to take action soon in West Sikang according to set plans, and expressed the hope that the Indian Government would assist the delegation of the local authorities of Tibet so that it might arrive in Peking in mid-September to begin peace negotiations. In early and middle September, the Chinese Charge d'Affairs, Shen Chien, and later Ambassador Yuan Chung-Hsien, both in person, told the said delegation that it was imperative that it should hasten before the end of September, otherwise the said delegation should bear the responsibilities and be responsible for all the consequences resulting from the delay.[63]

In mid-October, Chinese Ambassador Yuan again informed the Indian Government of this. Yet still owing to outside instigation, the delegation of the local authorities of Tibet fabricated various pretexts and remained in India.

Although the Chinese Government has not given up its desire of settling

---

63. This would imply that the decision to invade had been taken at the end of August and that the invasion was to be confined to "West Sikang," that is, up to the claimed border of Sikang at Giamda. The Chinese would thus be able to claim that they had not invaded "Tibet" at all, only that they had re-established control over the "province" of Sikang. Therefore, by means of subsequent negotiations, the liberation of what they referred to as "Tibet" (central Tibet) would be "peaceful." The reference to Chamdo, "in the interior of China," reflects the Chinese pretension that eastern Tibet was no longer "Tibet."

the problem of Tibet peacefully, it can no longer continue to put off the set plan of the Chinese People's Liberation Army to proceed to Tibet. And the liberation of Changtu further proved that through the instrument of Tibetan troops, foreign forces and influences were obstructing the peaceful settlement of the problem of Tibet. But regardless of whether the local authorities of Tibet wish to proceed with peace negotiations no foreign intervention will be permitted. The entry into Tibet of the Chinese People's Liberation Army and the liberation of the Tibetan people are also decided. . . .

What the Chinese Government cannot but deeply regret is that the Indian Government, in disregard of the facts, has regarded a domestic problem of the Chinese Government—the exercise of its sovereign rights in Tibet—as an international dispute calculated to increase the present deplorable tensions in the world.

The Government of the Republic of India has repeatedly expressed its desire of developing Sino-Indian friendship on the basis of mutual respect for territory, sovereignty, equality and mutual benefit, and of preventing the world from going to war. The entry into Tibet of the Chinese People's Liberation Army is exactly aimed at the protection of the integrity of the territory and the sovereignty of China. And it is on these questions that all those countries who desire to respect the territory and the sovereignty of China should first of all indicate their real attitude towards China.

We consider that what is now threatening the independence of nations and world peace is precisely the forces of those imperialist aggressors. For the sake of the maintenance of national independence and the defence of world peace it is necessary to resist the forces of those imperialist aggressors. The entry into Tibet of the Chinese People's Liberation Army is thus an important measure to maintain Chinese independence, to prevent the imperialist aggressors from dragging the world towards war, and to defend world peace.[64]

Shortly after the invasion and the fall of Chamdo, the Tibetan Government appealed to India for assistance and the Shakabpa delegation, now at Kalimpong, sent an appeal on behalf of the *Kashag* to the United Nations.[65] The Tibetan appeal to the UN, dated 11 November 1950, began by comparing international opposition to aggression in

---

64. "Exchange of Notes between the Governments of India and of the People's Republic of China concerning the advance of the Chinese army units into Tibet," in *Question of Tibet and the Rule of Law*, 135. That China herself might be regarded as an "imperialist aggressor" by the Tibetans was disregarded because the Chinese thought of Tibet as already "part of China."

65. Shakabpa, *Tibet: A Political History*, 302.

Korea with the lack of international attention to similar events in Tibet, which were "passing without notice." The appeal described Tibet's historical relations with China as entirely personal and spiritual relations that "had no political implications." Nevertheless, the Chinese,

In their natural urge for expansion, have wholly misconstrued the significance of the time of friendship and interdependence that existed between China and Tibet as between neighbors. To them China was suzerain and Tibet a vassal State. It is this which first aroused legitimate apprehension in the mind of Tibet regarding China's designs on its independent status. . . .

In 1911-1912 Tibet, under the Thirteenth Dalai Lama, declared its complete independence . . . while the Chinese revolution of 1911, which dethroned the Manchurian Emperor, snapped the last of the sentimental and religious bonds that Tibet had with China. Tibet thereafter depended entirely on its isolation, its faith in the wisdom of the Lord Buddha, and occasionally on the support of the British in India for its protection. No doubt in these circumstances the latter could also claim suzerainty over Tibet. . . .

The slender tie that Tibet maintained with China after the 1911 revolution became less justifiable when China underwent a further revolution and turned into a full-fledged Communist State. There can be no kinship or sympathy between such divergent creeds as those espoused by China and Tibet. . . [Tibet] desires to live apart uncontaminated by the germ of a highly materialistic creed, but China is bent on not allowing Tibet to live in peace. Since the establishment of the People's Republic of China, the Chinese have hurled threats of liberating Tibet and have used devious methods to intimidate and undermine the Government of Tibet. . . .

The armed invasion of Tibet for the incorporation of Tibet in Communist China through sheer physical force is a clear case of aggression. As long as the people of Tibet are compelled by force to become a part of China against their will and consent, the present invasion of Tibet will be the grossest instance of the violation of the weak by the strong. We therefore appeal through you to the Nations of the world to intercede on our behalf and restrain Chinese aggression.

The problem is simple. The Chinese claim Tibet as a part of China. Tibetans feel that racially, culturally and geographically, they are far apart from the Chinese. If the Chinese find the reactions of the Tibetans to their unnatural claim not acceptable, there are other civilized methods by which they could ascertain the views of the people of Tibet, or should the issue be purely juridical, they are open to seek redress in an international Court of Law. The conquest of Tibet by China will only enlarge the area of conflict and increase the threat to the independence and stability of other Asian countries.[66]

---

66. "Text of the Cablegram from Kashag (Cabinet)," (Kalimpong), 11 November 1950, UN Doc. A/1549, in *Tibet in the United Nations* (New Delhi: Bureau of His Holiness the Dalai Lama), 3.

Tibet's case was brought up at the UN, on 14 November, by the El Salvador delegation.[67] Both Britain and the US deferred to India as the party most concerned with the situation.[68] The British maintained that Tibet was a state entitled to bring its case before the United Nations, based upon the Simla Convention and the fact that Tibet had accepted Chinese suzerainty only on the condition that China recognize Tibetan autonomy. Britain had accepted Tibet's right to enter into direct relations with other states since 1914, thus Britain's position was that Tibet had external as well as internal autonomy. However, the British UN delegate thought that this position was likely to contradict that of India, which had accepted that Chinese suzerainty was equivalent to sovereignty. The British thought that UN characterization or condemnation of China's actions in Tibet as aggression was also likely to involve the UN in further unsupportable resolutions; therefore, British officials decided not to maintain that Tibet was fully independent and to otherwise follow the lead of India.[69]

The US State Department instructed its UN delegation to support the inclusion of the resolution on Tibet but not to sponsor the resolution or lead UN discussion on the issue:

> You should support El Salvadorian request as item of important and urgent character. . . . US would of course vote in favor its inclusion in line with our historical policy of not objecting to free discussion of controversial questions. . . . We do not, however, wish to take initiative on this question. We doubt UN can bring effective pressure upon Chi Commie Govt to withdraw or agree to respect Tibet's autonomy. Nevertheless, we think that GA [General Assembly] consideration of the problem may be of some value as

67. "Request for the inclusion of an additional item in the agenda of the Fifth Session: Letter from the Chairman of the delegation of El Salvador," UN Doc. A/1534, 18 November 1950, in *Tibet in the United Nations*, 4.

68. On 2 November Nehru advised the US ambassador to India that the "US could be most helpful by doing nothing and saying little just now. A series of announcements by US Government condemning China or supporting Tibet might lend a certain amount of credence to Peking's chargés that great powers had been intriguing in Tibet and had been exercising influence over India's Tibet policies." Ambassador in India to the Secretary of State, 3 November 1950, *FRUS, 1950, vol. VI*, 551. The US State Department recommended that the US should not embarrass India over the Tibet issue: "In view of the delicacy of India's position and of the personal nature of the Indian policy-making process, there should at the present time be no public discussion in Washington of the Tibetan matter by Departmental representatives in order that there be no compromise or adverse influence of the Indian position by reason of statements which might be made in Washington." Office Memorandum, Office of Chinese Affairs, 1 November 1950, National Archives, 793.B.00/11-150.

69. Goldstein, *History of Modern Tibet*, 717.

propaganda in exposing Chi Commie actions. . . . Dept feels question is one of concern primarily to India and that any leadership given to its management in GA should come from India.[70]

India was reluctant to allow Tibet to influence larger issues, one of which was India's ambition to play a role as mediator in Cold War conflicts. India thought itself suited to this role due to its supposed moral authority and India's non-aligned position in the East-West conflict. The Korean conflict was regarded as a suitable case for India to play this role because of India's "special relations" with China, one aspect of which was India's sponsorship of Communist Chinese membership at the UN. The Tibetan issue threatened to upset the two primary principles of India's foreign policy: friendly relations with China and a role for India as a mediator in international conflicts.[71]

A fundamental premiss of Indian policy was that peaceful relations among the major powers of Asia were possible in the post-colonialist period. The only legal interests or obligations that India had in Tibet were the legacy of British imperialism, a legacy which India was determined to disavow. By not claiming any of the rights or privileges inherited from the British or any special interest in the maintenance of Tibetan autonomy, India hoped to allay Chinese fears that India intended to inherit British imperial ambitions toward Tibet. India thought that if China were thus disabused of the idea that Tibet was threatened by imperialism, or the legacy of imperialism, it might foresee less need to forcibly impose direct Chinese control upon Tibet.[72]

India was apparently reluctant to "let Tibet down" at the UN, but had hoped that another country, preferably a member of the Security Council, would co-sponsor the resolution with El Salvador. India also contemplated seconding the El Salvador resolution, but abandoned this plan after receiving the 16 November Chinese message, which India interpreted as

---

70. Secretary of State to the United States Mission to the United Nations, 16 November 1950, *FRUS, 1950, vol. VI,* 577.

71. Lowell Thomas Jr. maintains that Indian acquiescence in Chinese actions in Tibet allowed India to play its role as mediator in the Korean conflict. Lowell Thomas, Jr. *The Silent War in Tibet* (New York: Doubleday, 1959), 97.

72. Mullik states that Nehru was under no illusions as to Chinese intentions toward Tibet: "Pandit Nehru was never blind to China's imperialist ambitions. . . In various talks he had stressed that the Chinese leaders were goaded by their extremely nationalistic and imperialist tendencies and Communism was only a cloak under cover of which they were trying to further their nationalistic ambitions." B.N. Mullik, *My Years with Nehru: The Chinese Betrayal* (New Delhi: Allied Publishers, 1971), 84.

indicating a willingness to negotiate.[73] India thus declined, at the UN, to protest China's actions. As the Indian delegate explained:

> The Peking Government had declared that it had not abandoned its intention to settle those difficulties by peaceful means. It would seem that the Chinese forces had ceased to advance after the fall of Chamdo, a town some 480 kilometers from Lhasa. The Indian Government was certain that the Tibetan question could still be settled by peaceful means, and that such a settlement could safeguard the autonomy which Tibet had enjoyed for several decades while maintaining its historical association with China. His delegation considered that the best way of obtaining that objective was to abandon, for the time being, the idea of including that question in the agenda of the General Assembly."[74]

Based upon India's position, other interested parties also thought a "peaceful" solution was still possible. The British UN delegate stated that the General Committee of the General Assembly "did not know exactly what was happening in Tibet nor was the legal position of the country very clear. Moreover, it could still be hoped that the existing difficulties in Tibet could be settled amicably by agreement between the parties concerned." The US voted for the adjournment "in view of the fact that the Government of India, whose territory bordered on Tibet and which was therefore an interested party, had told the General Committee that it hoped that the Tibetan question would be peacefully and honourably settled." On 24 November the United Nations General Committee voted unanimously to postpone consideration of the Tibet issue. Britain, the US and India each expressed hope that some semblance of Tibet's past autonomy could still be preserved and China's imposition of control over Tibet could remain "peaceful" if negotiations were to take place.[75] China's tac-

---

73. As an Indian Foreign Ministry official told the American ambassador: "Their advance has not been beyond boundaries [between] China and Tibet, as CCP understands them . . . this situation will most effectively be negotiated on bilateral [China-Tibet] basis outside UN." Ambassador in India to the Secretary of State, 20 November 1950, *FRUS, 1950, vol. VI*, 578.

74. "United Nations General Assembly Fifth Session, General Committee 73rd Meeting," 24 November 1950, in *Tibet in the United Nations*, 11. The Indian Foreign Office, however, told the American ambassador in India that "GOI had suggested that Tibet order its mission not to proceed Peiping since in light new developments such mission would clearly be working under duress." Ambassador in India to the Secretary of State, 31 October 1950, *FRUS, 1950, vol. VI*, 546.

75. "United Nations General Assembly Fifth Session," 24 November 1950, in *Tibet in the United Nations*, 14. The USSR and the Socialist Bloc countries accused the United States of being the actual instigator of the El Salvador resolution. Ibid., 8. The USSR held that "Tibet was an inalienable part of China and its affairs were the exclusive concern of the

tic of halting the advance of the PLA at what they defined as the border of "Tibet" and calling on the Tibetans to "negotiate" was thus successful in defusing much international criticism of China's actions.

The Tibetan Government could do little but express "grave concern and dismay" at UN inaction on Tibet's behalf.[76] On 17 November 1950, after consulting the State oracles, the officials of the Tibetan Government and the Regent Taktra conferred temporal power upon the 16 year-old Dalai Lama (two years before the normal time). After the failure of Tibet's appeal to the UN and the arrival in Lhasa of the Dalai Lama's elder brother, Taktser Rimpoche, abbot of Kumbum monastery near Sining, with news of actual conditions in Amdo under Chinese control, the decision was made to remove the Dalai Lama from Lhasa.[77] Meanwhile, a message was received from Ngapo, still held at Chamdo, containing Chinese conditions for Tibet's "peaceful liberation":

> With serious concern for the people of Tibet, who have suffered long years of oppression under American and British imperialists and Chiang Kai-shek's reactionary Government, Chairman Mao Tse-tung of the Central People's Government and Commander in Chief Chu Te of the People's Liberation Army ordered the People's Liberation Army troops to enter Tibet for the purpose of assisting the Tibetan people to free themselves from oppression forever.
>
> All the Tibetan people, including all lamas, should now create a solid unity to give the People's Liberation Army adequate assistance in ridding Tibet

---

Chinese Government." Ibid., 12. The Nationalist Chinese delegate said that "Tibet had been part of China for 700 years and all Chinese, whatever their party or religion, regarded it as such," but condemned the Communist incursion into Tibet since it would lead to a "heritage of hatred between the Tibetan branch and the other branches of the Chinese family." Ibid., 12.

76. "Text of Cablegram dated 8 December 1950 received from the Tibetan delegation [Kalimpong]," UN Doc. A/1658, 11 December 1950, in *Tibet in the United Nations*, 15.

77. Thupten Jigme Norbu, *Tibet is My Country* (London: Wisdom Publications, 1986), 232. Taktser Rimpoche had been hounded for months at Kumbum by Chinese cadres who attempted to "reform his thinking." He was approached to become the agent by which the Tibetan Government would be convinced to accept Chinese rule. If successful in persuading the Tibetan Government to "welcome the entry of Chinese Communist troops into Tibet as liberators," he was to be made Governor-General of Tibet. He was further advised that, in pursuit of this lofty goal of "progress" and "socialist construction," nothing should be allowed to stand in his way, even his own brother, the Dalai Lama. It was implied that ways and means could be found for the Dalai Lama's departure from the scene: "They even let me see quite clearly that if necessary they would regard fratricide as justifiable in the circumstances if there remained no other way of advancing the cause of communism. They even pointed out occasions on which people had actually committed such crimes `in the interests of the cause' and had subsequently been rewarded with high office." Ibid., 222.

of imperialist influence and in establishing a regional self-government for the Tibetan people. They should at the same time build fraternal relations, on the basis of friendship and mutual help, with other nationalities within the country and together construct a new Tibet within new China

With the entry of the People's Liberation Army into Tibet, life and property of the Tibetan lamas and people will be protected. Assistance will be rendered to the Tibetan people in the direction of developing their educational, agricultural, pastoral, industrial, and commercial enterprises, and their living conditions will be improved.

No change will be made in the existing administrative and military system of Tibet. Existing Tibetan troops will become a part of the National Defense Forces of the People's Republic of China. All lamas, officials and chieftains may remain at their posts. Matters relating to reforms in Tibet will be handled completely in accordance with the will of the Tibetan people and by means of consultations between the Tibetan people and Tibetan leaders.[78]

Ngapo and the other Tibetans captured at Chamdo had undergone "reeducation" on Chinese Communist Party (CCP) policies on minority nationalities and lenient treatment for collaborators, the results of which, as described in Chinese propaganda, were that the captured Tibetans were completely convinced:

The officers and men of the Tibetan army agreed that life during the period of study was the most pleasant of their lives. . . . At group meetings, they spoke in earnest and took part in discussions. During the day and even at night they could be heard singing happily or chanting litanies. At the conclusion of the course of study, many of the officers and men said that they had been like blind men in the past and that their eyes were now opened, and that they now realized that the Tibetan people must drive away the imperialists and return to the big family of the motherland if they wanted to be liberated. Having received their travelling allowances and travel permits, they respectfully bowed to the pictures of Chairman Mao and Commander in Chief Chu before returning to their homes with their horses. They hoped that the radiance of Chairman Mao would soon be shed over Lhasa and all Tibet.[79]

Ngapo offered his services as negotiator with the Chinese should the *Kashag* depute him to do so. The Tibetan Government accepted Ngapo's offer, appointing him and sending two officials from Lhasa to assist him.

---

78. "Memorandum from Office of China Affairs to Office of Far Eastern Affairs," 22 November 1950, National Archives, 693B.00/11-2250.

79. "The Graces of Mao are Higher Than Heaven," in *Tibet 1950-67*, 731.

The Tibetan negotiators were instructed to deny any imperialist influence in Tibet, to demand the return of Tibetan territories in Kham and Amdo, to promise to seek assistance from China, as in the past, in case of any foreign attack upon Tibet, and to demand the withdrawal of the PLA from Tibetan territory.[80]

Despite agreeing to negotiate, the Tibetan Government did not abandon its plan to remove the Dalai Lama from Lhasa. On 20 December 1950 the Dalai Lama departed for Yatung on the Indian border. On 8 December the Shakabpa delegation in India again appealed to the UN. The Tibetan message invited the UN to send a fact-finding mission to Tibet and proposed to present Tibet's case before the UN. In addition, the delegation sent further appeals to the US, Britain and Canada. The renewed Tibetan appeal moved the US State Department to suggest that a joint US-UK-India initiative on Tibet at the UN might be organized; the State Department also instructed the ambassador in India to ascertain the "possibility of getting active Indian support of Tibetan case at UN" and the "probable reaction of GOI to a proposal for quiet US support of more positive measures designed to stiffen Tibetan resistance."[81]

Bajpai, secretary-general of the Indian Ministry of External Affairs (MEA), informed the US ambassador that the GOI was "at present so immersed in problem maintaining world peace it was giving little thought to Tibet."[82] Bajpai expressed the opinion that "militarily Tibet was in hopeless position and there was little likelihood of any foreign power being able to lend it assistance which would enable it to halt Chinese Communist invasion."[83] Britain opted to continue to follow India's lead, being reluctant to take any initiative, especially in cooperation with the US, that could be regarded by India or China as interference.[84]

The US ambassador in India advised the State Department that, despite much Indian sympathy for Tibet and a strong sentiment in favor of some action on Tibet's behalf, those in charge of Indian foreign policy, including Nehru, Foreign Minister Krishna Menon, Ambassador

---

80. In addition, the Chinese were requested to ignore the trouble-making activities engaged in by the late Panchen Lama and Reting Rimpoche and their entourages. Goldstein, *History of Modern Tibet*, 745.

81. Secretary of State to the Embassy in India, 14 December 1950, *FRUS, 1950, vol. VI*, 602.

82. Ambassador in India to the Secretary of State, 25 January 1951, *FRUS, 1951, vol. VII*, 1529.

83. Ambassador in India to the Secretary of State, 18 December 1950, *FRUS, 1950, vol. VI*, 603.

84. Britain was reluctant to offend China due to the precarious situation of Hong Kong. Gordon Chang, *United States, China and the Soviet Union*, 48.

Pannikar, and UN Representative B.N. Rau, were opposed to any action likely to upset India's relations with China. Britain would follow India's lead. The US would have to contemplate support for Tibet in the absence of those two countries most interested in and most knowledgeable about Tibetan affairs:

> We have been giving considerable thought this end to problem Tibetan case before UN. Thus far seemed preferable India take lead this matter UN. Representatives GOI had repeatedly assured us it intended to do so. Now appears views B.N. Rau and other Indian officials who do not wish India make any move in present world context which might offend Communist China have prevailed and GOI continues postpone taking initiative re [in regard to] Tibet in UN. Seems likely Communist China will have taken over Lhasa and have fastened firmly its grip on Tibet before GOI prepared take lead in UN. We seem faced with choice supporting some power other than India taking initiative or of continuing postpone hearing Tibetan pleas until autonomous Tibet ceases exist. We are wondering whether this would be to credit [of] UN. . . . We suggest Tibetan question be reviewed before substantive reply is made to letter from Tibetan delegation.[85]

The US State Department undertook a study to determine if the US might be legally justified in supporting Tibetan independence or Tibet's case before the UN. The study of Tibet's legal status determined that there were no legal obstacles to American support for Tibetan independence, though there were political obstacles, and there were certainly no obstacles to American support for the Tibetan issue being brought up at the UN:

> This Office [State Department Legal Adviser] does not believe that as of today Tibet can be classified as a fully sovereign and independent member of the family of nations. This is not to say that Tibet is not a "state" within the meaning of international law, for complete independence is not a prerequisite of international personality. It does not appear that any country with the possible exception of Nepal has unqualifiedly recognized Tibet as a sovereign independent Government. . . .

> If this Government is satisfied that Tibet possesses the machinery of a state, administers the government with the consent of the people and is able to fulfill its international obligations, the only legal bar to recognition of Tibet on our part might be Article I, Paragraph I of the Nine Power Treaty of 1922 in which the contracting powers agreed "to respect the sovereignty, the independence, and the territorial and administrative integrity of China."

---

85. Ambassador in India to the Secretary of State, 30 December 1950, *FRUS, 1950, vol. VI*, 612.

The embarrassing factor here is that US Government officials assured the Chinese orally that the United States recognized Chinese "sovereignty" over Tibet. . . . Probably in the use of the word "sovereignty" nothing more was meant than that the United States recognized that China retained some undefined rights over Tibet analogous to what the British meant in the term "suzerainty." As a matter of fact, this Office believes that China does not have and has not had "sovereignty" over Tibet. . . .

It is not believed that there is anything in the treaty structure relating to Tibet which would preclude the United States from recognizing Tibetan independence. . . . If it should be decided to recognize Tibet, it must be bourne in mind that the Chinese Nationalists will undoubtedly claim that this is an unfriendly act. . . .

It is difficult to place a categorical label on the nature of Tibet's "dependence." However, since Tibet appears legally entitled at the least to control over its domestic affairs, this Office considers that its invasion by the Chinese Communists is not a purely internal matter but that in view of the situation which has in fact obtained in Tibet since 1912 China is estopped from denying that armed invasion of Tibet is a question of international concern.[86]

Based upon this analysis, the US formulated a tentative position on Tibet that would justify US support for bringing up the Tibetan issue at the UN:

The United States, which was one of the early supporters of the principle of self-determination of peoples, believes that the Tibetan people has the same inherent right as any other to have the determining voice in its political destiny. It is believed further that, should developments warrant, consideration could be given to recognition of Tibet as an independent State. The Department of State would not at this time desire to formulate a definitive legal position to be taken by the United States Government relative to Tibet. It would appear adequate for present purposes to state that the United States Government recognizes the de facto autonomy that Tibet has exercised since the fall of the Manchu Dynasty, and particularly since the Simla Conference. It is believed that, should the Tibetan case be introduced into the United Nations, there would be ample basis for international concern regarding Chinese Communist intentions toward Tibet, to justify under the United Nations Charter a hearing of Tibet's case in either the UN Security Council or the UN General Assembly.[87]

---

86. "Memorandum on the Legal Status of Tibet," 5 December 1950, National Archives, 793B.00/11-2250.

87. Department of State to the British Embassy, 30 December 1950, *FRUS, 1950, vol. VI,* 612. On the other hand, the United States UN mission expressed opposition to approaching friendly UN delegations in regard to Tibet since "the position of the United States in

The State Department instructed the Embassy in New Delhi to inform the Tibetan delegation at Kalimpong that its 21 December appeal was "noted" and that the US remained "interested in continuance Tibetan autonomy and views sympathetically Tibetan appeal to UN." The Tibetans were informed that the State Department considered that, despite the lateness, the matter "should not be permitted go by default, particularly in light UN action re Korea and also need for checking Chi Commie advances where feasible. . . every feasible effort should be made to hinder Commie occupation and give case appropriate hearing in UN. The US still stands ready [to] extend some material assistance if appropriate means can be found for expression Tibetan resistance to aggression."[88] These messages were communicated to Tibetan representatives at Kalimpong in early January and, receiving no reply, again on 4 April 1951.[89]

In the meantime, the US ambassador in India reported that the GOI "appears to have abandoned hope, and in view this fact and its anxiety not to offend Peking it would not be easy to prevail on it to extend further assistance or to permit armed shipments through India for Tibet."[90] American analysis of the situation finally came to the conclusion that, despite American interest in assisting Tibet, at the moment neither material nor political assistance was feasible. Material assistance was impossible without Indian cooperation. Neither the UN nor the US had the ability to actually affect the situation in Tibet. Although US sponsorship of Tibet at the UN might have encouraged the Tibetans to resist, the US remained reluctant to do so without Indian and British support. US sponsorship of the Tibet issue at the UN would have at best only propaganda value. In addition, Tibetan failure to reply to American communications created uncertainty as to what course of action Tibet intended to take and therefore what assistance might be offered by the United States.

The Tibetans had not replied to American communications because the Tibetan Government was in the process of debating what course of action Tibet should take. The Dalai Lama had arrived at Yatung on 7 January 1951 and had summoned the Shakabpa delegation from Kalimpong.

the UN regarding China is so suspect that any moves regarding Tibet might further injure our chances of getting what we need in connection with Korea." Memorandum by Robert C. Strong of the Office of Chinese Affairs to the Director of that Office, 24 January 1951, *FRUS, 1951, vol. VII*, 1528.

88. Secretary of State to the Embassy in India, 6 January 1951, *FRUS, 1950, vol. VI*, 618.

89. New Delhi Embassy to Department of State, 28 June 1951, National Archives, 793B.00/6-2851.

90. Ambassador in India (Henderson) to the Secretary of State, 12 January 1951, *FRUS, 1951, vol. VII: Korea and China* (Washington: Government Printing Office, 1983), 1506.

Shakabpa reported that American interest and offers of support were, as the Americans themselves repeatedly said, dependent upon Indian cooperation, which did not appear likely to be forthcoming. The Tibetans did not consider the US offer of visas if the Tibetans wished to attend the UN an "invitation" to that body; the Tibetans were apparently not aware that they could send a delegation to the UN without an invitation.[91]

Meanwhile, the abbots of Sera, Drepung and Ganden sent a delegation to Yatung to implore the Dalai Lama to return to Lhasa. Representatives of the people of Lhasa also sent a letter to the Dalai Lama at Yatung imploring him to return.[92] Citing Chinese terms relayed by Ngapo from Chamdo that promised that the Tibetan political and religious systems would remain unchanged, ecclesiastical and popular representatives argued that, if the Dalai Lama went into exile, the Chinese would be less likely to honor those terms and Tibet would have no governmental authority to ensure that they did so.

The opinion that Tibet should seek the best arrangement possible in negotiation with China eventually prevailed; a delegation was sent to New Delhi to meet with the Chinese ambassador. In a meeting on 24 March, the Chinese ambassador informed them that, if Tibet negotiated its "peaceful liberation," China would honor its pledge not to alter the Tibetan political or religious systems.[93] This delegation reported back to Yatung, after which the decision was made to send a delegation to Peking to negotiate; two more officials, plus the Dalai Lama's brother-in-law, P.T. Takla, acting as interpreter, were sent to Peking (via India) to join Ngapo's three man party, which was now directed to proceed to Peking from Chamdo. The delegation from Yatung had instructions to accept

---

91. The State Department had informed the Embassy in New Delhi on 3 January 1951 that the Tibetan delegation at Kalimpong should be advised that they could make application for visas at the US Consulate in Calcutta, which had instructions to approve. The Tibetan delegation was informed to that effect on 5 January. Ibid., 1508. The delegation and the Tibetan Government seemed to think that an invitation to present its case was a necessity. Realistically, the active support of a UN member was a necessity.

92. Rinchen Paljor, personal interview, Dharamsala, November 1989.

93. Goldstein, *History of Modern Tibet*, 758. The Tibetan delegation also met with Indian Foreign Minister Krishna Menon on 26 March and with Nehru on 27 March, from both of whom they requested Indian diplomatic support in the forthcoming negotiations in Peking. Menon and Nehru suggested that Tibet would have to admit Chinese claims to sovereignty over Tibet, but when informed that the Chinese were demanding control over Tibet's foreign affairs and border defense, they expressed the opinion that Tibet should reject the latter as unnecessary since Tibetan frontiers were with India and Nepal, both of which were countries "friendly to both Tibet and China." If the negotiations in Peking should break down, the Tibetans were advised that India then might agree that the issue be dealt with at the UN. Ambassador in India to the Secretary of State, 27 March 1951, *FRUS, 1951, vol. VII*, 1609.

that Tibet was part of China only in a token sense; they were to confer with the Tibetan Government by wireless and were not to conclude any agreement with China without Tibetan Government approval.[94]

The 17-Point Agreement

The Chinese were obviously pleased to have convinced the Tibetans to negotiate at Peking, as was evident by the fact that the Ngapo group was met on 22 or 23 April at the Peking railway station by Chou En-lai, and the group from Yatung was met on 26 April by Chu Teh. The chief Chinese negotiator was Li Wei-han, chairman of the National Minorities Commission of the National People's Congress and chairman of the United Front Work Department. The interpreter for the Chinese side was Phuntsok Wangyal, a Batang Tibetan who had been recruited by the Red Army during its passage through Kham in 1935. The Tibetan Government interpreter was the Dalai Lama's brother-in-law, P.T. Takla.[95]

The first issue with which the Tibetan Government delegation was confronted was the status of the Panchen Lama. The Chinese demanded that the Panchen, who had not been accepted by Lhasa as the true incarnation, be officially accepted before negotiations could begin.[96] The Tibetan delegates were puzzled by the emphasis that the Chinese placed

---

94. This was confirmed by Shakabpa in a meeting with the US ambassador in which he stated that the "Tibetan delegation did not have full powers and was required under its instructions to refer all important points to Yatung." Ambassador in India to the Secretary of State, 11 June 1951, FRUS, 1951, vol, VII, 1707. Heinrich Harrer conveyed a similar message, also in a meeting with the American ambassador: "With great reluctance the Dalai Lama is sending the present mission to Peking. He has not given this mission any plenipotentiary powers since he fears that even though his brother-in-law is a member of the mission that it might yield to pressure. The Dalai Lama has doubts about returning to Lhasa. Some of the monks about him, however, insist that he should come to terms with Peking and do so." Ambassador in India to the Director of the Office of South Asian Affairs, 29 March 1951, *FRUS, 1951, vol, VII,* 1611.

95. Takla probably did not share Phuntsok Wangyal's proficiency in Chinese and was certainly not as familiar with Chinese Communist political and administrative terminology; thus, the Tibetans were at a considerable disadvantage in their understanding of much of the Chinese version of the terms under negotiation. The Tibetans had to rely on the Tibetan version, which did not always accurately convey the meaning of the Chinese terminology. The Chinese used this advantage to secure Tibetan compliance to many vague terms.

96. Goldstein, *History of Modern Tibet,* 683; Lamb, *Tibet, China and India,* 494; Parshotam Mehra, *Tibetan Polity, 1904-37: The Conflict Between the 13th Dalai Lama and the 9th Panchen* (Wiesbaden: Otto Harrassowitz, 1976), 29; Shakabpa, *Tibet: A Political History,* 306. The Chinese would thus fulfill their obligation to secure the recognition of the Panchen by Lhasa.

on the status of the Panchen Lama; for the Chinese, however, the rivalry between the Dalai and Panchen Lamas symbolized the disunity of Tibet, a disunity which they were determined to exploit to the fullest extent. The negotiations focused on this issue for the first six or seven days and were deadlocked, since the Tibetan delegation did not have the authority to recognize the incarnation of the Panchen. The Chinese described the issue as one of "face"; Mao had recognized the Panchen as the true incarnation, thus the dignity of Mao, the Chinese government and the Chinese nation was at stake.

Finally, the Tibetan delegation had to secure the recognition of the Panchen Lama from the Tibetan Government at Yatung, which, having already decided to negotiate, could hardly allow this issue to abort an agreement. The Tibetans found the Panchen and his entourage accredited by the Chinese with diplomatic status equivalent to that of the delegation from the Tibetan Government, as if the Panchen represented a separate Tibetan government. A third Tibetan delegation, representing the "Chamdo Liberation Committee," the "government" of Chinese-occupied western Kham, was also accorded a high status but appeared to play no other role than to create the appearance of a variety of political entities claiming authority in Tibet.[97]

The issue of the Panchen Lama's recognition was one of the last about which the Tibetan delegation was able to consult with the Tibetan Government at Yatung. The Tibetans initially communicated with Yatung by means of a telegraphic code, which, they believed, the Chinese were unable to decipher. This appears to have been the case, since the delegates reported that the Chinese asked them what was in their telegrams and, after the Tibetans refused to tell them, prohibited any further communication. The delegation members were closely guarded at their hotel and at the old Japanese Embassy, where the talks took place, and their contacts were restricted.[98]

The Tibetans were told that they were free to discuss any of the points of the proposed agreement, but whenever they attempted to do so the Chinese would get annoyed and threaten: "Do you want a peaceful lib-

---

97. Neither the Panchen nor any of his entourage are, however, listed as delegates to the negotiations, presumably because the Panchen had already pledged his loyalty to the new Chinese government. The Panchen was, however, credited with "assisting" in the negotiations. "Li Wei-han's Speech on Peaceful Liberation of Tibet," *New China News Agency (NCNA)* (Peking), 27 May 1951, in *Survey of China Mainland Press* (Hong Kong: United States Consulate).

98. "Conversation with Yapshi Sey, Phuntsok Tashi, Brother-in-Law of the Dalai Lama," American Consul, Calcutta to the Department of State, 18 August 1951, National Archives, 793B.00/8-1851.

eration or a liberation by force?" According to P.T. Takla, "The Chinese were polite when the Tibetans were not saying anything; when the Tibetans tried to say anything, the Chinese got very angry." On the basic issue of whether they were prepared to admit that Tibet was a part of China, the Tibetans requested permission to communicate with their government at Yatung, but were told that that would not be necessary since "other nations also regarded Tibet as a part of China."[99] The Chinese held the ultimate advantage during the negotiations by threatening to have their way in Tibet whether the representatives of the Lhasa government agreed or not. China's preponderance of force constituted a final argument in any instance of Tibetan disagreement.

The Dalai Lama later described the process by which the "agreement" was achieved:

> As soon as the first meeting began, the chief Chinese representative produced a draft agreement containing ten articles ready-made. This was discussed for several days. Our delegation argued that Tibet was an independent state, and produced all the evidence to support their argument, but the Chinese would not accept it. Ultimately, the Chinese drafted a revised agreement, with seventeen articles. This was presented as an ultimatum. Our delegates were not allowed to make any alterations or suggestions. They were insulted and abused and threatened with personal violence, and with further military action against the people of Tibet, and they were not allowed to refer to me or my government for further instructions.[100]

The Tibetans were eventually forced to accept the Chinese draft of an agreement with only a few alterations of minor points. The Tibetan delegates undoubtedly felt a responsibility to reach an agreement in order to prevent renewed Chinese hostilities against Tibet. Rather than reject an ambiguous agreement, some of whose points seemed to promise substantial and essential Tibetan autonomy while others seemed to eliminate any semblance of autonomy, the delegates left that choice to the Tibetan Government.

When the agreement was completed, the Chinese insisted that the Tibetan delegation sign on behalf of the Tibetan Government. The Tibetan delegates informed the Chinese that they did not have the power to approve the agreement without consulting their government; nevertheless, the Chinese insisted on announcing the agreement as completed and approved. The Tibetan delegates signed, but because they had not secured the approval of the Tibetan Government for the agreement, they

99. Ibid.
100. Dalai Lama, *My Land and My People* (New York: Potala Press, 1983), 87.

did not use the Tibetan Government seal. Instead, they affixed their names to the agreement using their personal seals. The Tibetans were told that they could inform their government by telegram that the agreement had been concluded; they were also told to ask the Dalai Lama to send a congratulatory message to Mao Tse-tung. Instead, the delegates informed their government that they had been forced to sign the agreement and that they would discuss the terms upon their return, after which the Tibetan Government could decide to accept or reject the agreement.[101]

The agreement, concluded on 23 May 1951, was entitled "Agreement of the Central People's Government and the Local Government of Tibet on Measures for the Peaceful Liberation of Tibet":

> The Tibetan nationality is one of the nationalities with a long history within the boundaries of China and, like many other nationalities, it has performed its glorious duty in the course of the creation and development of our great Motherland. But over the last one hundred years or more, imperialist forces penetrated into China, and in consequence also penetrated into the Tibetan region and carried out all kinds of deceptions and provocations. Like previous reactionary governments, the Kuomintang reactionary government continued to carry out a policy of oppression and sowing dissension among the nationalities, causing division and disunity among the Tibetan people. And the local government of Tibet did not oppose the imperialist deceptions and provocations, and adopted an unpatriotic attitude toward our great Motherland. Under such conditions, the Tibetan nationality and people were plunged into the depths of enslavement and suffering.
>
> In 1949, basic victory was achieved on a nationwide scale, . . . In accordance with the Common Program passed by the Chinese People's Political Consultative Conference, the Central People's Government declared that all nationalities within the boundaries of the People's Republic of China are equal, and that they shall establish unity and mutual aid and oppose imperialism and their own public enemies, so that the People's Republic of China will become a big fraternal and cooperative family, composed of all its nationalities, that within the big family of nationalities of the People's Republic of China, national regional autonomy shall be exercised in areas where national minorities are concentrated, and all national minorities shall have freedom to develop their own spoken and written languages and to

---

101. "Conversation with Yapshi Sey," National Archives, 793B.00/8-1851. According to Takla, the Tibetan seals appearing on the 17-Point Agreement are in Tibetan script—evidence that these are the delegates' personal seals, since the official seal of the Tibetan Government is in three scripts: Tibetan, Lantsa script and Phagspa script (the script formulated by Phagspa for Khubilai). P.T. Takla, personal communication, 4 October 1992. See Shakabpa, *Tibet: A Political History*, frontispiece, for an example of this seal.

preserve or reform their customs, habits, and religious beliefs, while the Central People's Government shall assist all national minorities to develop their political, economic, cultural and educational construction work. Since then, all nationalities within the country, with the exception of those within the areas of Tibet and Taiwan, have gained liberation. Under the unified leadership of the Central People's Government and the direct leadership of higher levels of People's Government, all national minorities are fully enjoying the right of national equality and have established, or are establishing, national regional autonomy.[102]

In order that the influences of aggressive imperialist forces in Tibet might be successfully eliminated, the unification of the territory and sovereignty of the People's Republic of China accomplished, and national defence safeguarded; in order that the Tibetan nationality and people might be freed and return to the big family of the People's Republic of China to enjoy the same rights of national equality as all other nationalities in the country and develop their political, economic, cultural and educational work, the Central People's Government, when it ordered the People's Liberation Army to march into Tibet, notified the local government of Tibet to send delegates to the central authorities to conduct talks for the conclusion of an agreement on measures for the peaceful liberation of Tibet.

In the latter part of April 1951, the delegates with full powers of the local government of Tibet arrived in Peking. The Central People's Government appointed representatives with full powers to conduct talks on a friendly basis with the delegates with full powers of the local government of Tibet. As a result of these talks, both parties agreed to conclude this agreement and guarantee that it will be carried into effect.[103]

1. The Tibetan people shall unite and drive out imperialist aggressive forces from Tibet: the Tibet people shall return to the big family of the Motherland—the People's Republic of China.

2. The local government of Tibet shall actively assist the People's Liberation Army to enter Tibet and consolidate the national defense.

---

102. The preamble repeated virtually verbatim the language regarding nationalities in the Common Program of the Chinese People's Political Consultative Conference (1949); therefore, reference to that document would have provided the Tibetans with no additional information as to what the Chinese meant by "national regional autonomy."

103. The Tibetan delegates are repeatedly and invariably referred to as "delegates with full powers," implying that they had the power to conclude an agreement without the approval of their government, which they did not. By the use of this terminology, Peking was setting the stage to ignore a possible rejection of the agreement by the Tibetan Government. Reference to the Tibetan Government as "local government of Tibet" implies that the Tibetan Government was merely the local government of a region of China, a characterization that the necessity of concluding a treaty with Tibet would seem to contradict.

3. In accordance with the policy toward nationalities laid down in the Common Program of the Chinese People's Political Consultative Conference, the Tibetan people have the right of exercising national regional autonomy under the leadership of the Central People's Government.[104]

4. The Central Authorities will not alter the existing political system in Tibet. The Central Authorities also will not alter the established status, functions, and powers of the Dalai Lama. Officials of various ranks will hold office as usual.

5. The established status, functions, and powers of the Dalai Lama and of the Panchen Ngoerhtehni shall be maintained.

6. By the established status, functions, and powers of the Dalai Lama and of the Panchen Ngoerhtehni are meant the status, functions and powers of the Thirteenth Dalai Lama and of the Ninth Panchen Ngoerhtehni when they were in friendly and amicable relations with each other.[105]

7. The policy of freedom of religious belief laid down in the Common Program of the Chinese People's Political Consultative Conference shall be carried out. The religious beliefs, customs, and habits of the Tibetan people shall be respected, and lama monasteries shall be protected. The central authorities will not effect a change in the income of the monasteries.[106]

8. Tibetan troops shall be reorganized by stages into the People's Liberation Army, and become a part of the national defense forces of the People's Republic of China.[107]

9. The spoken and written language and school education of the Tibetan nationality shall be developed step by step in accordance with the actual conditions in Tibet.

10. Tibetan agriculture, livestock raising, industry, and commerce shall be

---

104. According to Goldstein, the Tibetans were deceived by the term used for "Central People's Government." The term employed in Tibetan was not U Shung, "Central Government," but a Chinese word taken by the Tibetans to mean "China," as if the Chinese and Tibetan governments were to remain separate. Goldstein, *History of Modern Tibet,* 766.

105. The Tibetans objected to specific mention of the Panchen Lama and his implied political functions, but they were told that, if the Panchen were not mentioned by name, then the Dalai Lama would also not be mentioned. Ibid., 766.

106. This article reportedly secured the support of the two monk officials, who ascertained that "income" meant that the monasteries could continue to be supported by their estates. Ibid., 767.

107. The Tibetans managed to secure a secret agreement that some Tibetan army regiments would be retained. The Chinese insisted that this agreement be secret so as not to reveal that a supposedly Chinese territory would possess an independent military force. Jigme Ngapo, personal interview, Washington D.C., February 1995.

developed step by step, and the people's livelihood shall be improved step by step in accordance with the actual conditions in Tibet.

11. In matters related to various reforms in Tibet, there will be no compulsion on the part of the central authorities. The local government of Tibet should carry out reforms of its own accord, and when the people raise demands for reform, they shall be settled by means of consultation with the leading personnel of Tibet.[108]

12. In so far as former pro-imperialist and pro-KMT officials resolutely sever relations with imperialism and the KMT and do not engage in sabotage or resistance, they may continue to hold office irrespective of their past.

13. The People's Liberation Army entering Tibet shall abide by all the above-mentioned policies and shall also be fair in buying and selling and shall not arbitrarily take a single needle or thread from the people.

14. The Central People's Government shall conduct the centralized handling of all external affairs of the area of Tibet; and there will be peaceful coexistence with neighboring countries and establishment and development of fair commercial and trading relations with them on the basis of equality, mutual benefit, and mutual respect for territory and sovereignty.

15. In order to ensure the implementation of this agreement, the Central People's Government shall set up a military and administrative committee and a military area headquarters in Tibet, and apart from the personnel sent there by the Central People's Government, shall absorb as many local Tibetan personnel as possible to take part in the work. Local Tibetan personnel taking part in the military and administrative committee may include patriotic elements from the local government of Tibet, various districts, and leading monasteries; the name list shall be drawn up after consultation between the representatives designated by the Central People's Government and the various quarters concerned, and shall be submitted to the Central People's Government for appointment.[109]

16. Funds needed by the military and administrative committee, the military area headquarters, and the People's Liberation Army entering Tibet

---

108. The Tibetans reportedly assumed that this article assured the continuation of traditional Tibetan culture and religion since the Tibetan people would never demand that they be changed. Goldstein, *History of Modern Tibet*, 768. The Tibetans were undoubtedly unaware of Marxist-Leninist definitions of who were "the people," by what means "the people" would "raise demands" for reform or what the Chinese Communists meant by reform.

109. The Tibetans objected to this article because it obviously contradicted their understanding that the Tibetan administrative system would not be altered, that is, that it would remain in the hands of Tibetans. At this point, the Chinese reportedly threatened to impose their will by force if the Tibetans refused to accept. Ibid., 769.

shall be provided by the Central People's Government. The local government of Tibet will assist the People's Liberation Army in the purchase and transport of food, fodder, and other daily necessities.

17. This agreement shall come into force immediately after signature and seals are affixed to it.[110]

The Chinese Government announced the 17-Point Agreement and the "peaceful liberation of Tibet" on 26 May, as if the Agreement were conclusive. This confused the Tibetan Government at Yatung, which knew that it had not agreed to any treaty, and many other interested international parties. Nevertheless, legal ratification still depended upon the Tibetan Government. The agreement could be held to be void *ab initio*, considering the lack of plenipotentiary powers of the Tibetan negotiators, and, of course, the fact that the agreement was secured only by the use and threat of further use of force against Tibet. The Tibetan Government's acceptance would conclusively legitimate the agreement, whereas its rejection would deny the agreement that legitimation and create a major embarrassment for China. However, the Chinese had achieved the appearance of having negotiated a peaceful solution to Tibet's status, an appearance that deflected international criticism.

Li Wei-han, the chief Chinese negotiator, Chu Teh, Ngawang Jigme Ngapo, the Panchen Lama and Mao all made speeches praising the agreement. The *New China News Agency* described the process of events whereby military invasion was transformed into "peaceful liberation":

When the Central People's Government ordered the People's Liberation Army to march to Tibet, it notified the local government of Tibet to send its delegates to negotiate with the Central Authorities for the peaceful liberation of Tibet. Responding to the Central People's Government principle of peaceful liberation of Tibet and its policy of national equality, the local government of Tibet sent to Peking its delegates with full powers.[111]

---

110. "Text of Agreement on Measures for Peaceful Liberation of Tibet," NCNA, 27 May 1951, in Survey of *China Mainland Press*. The stratagem of the last article was to construe the agreement as binding without the approval of the Tibetan government.

111. "Agreement on Peaceful Liberation of Tibet Signed in Peking," *NCNA*, 27 May 1951, in *Survey of China Mainland Press*. The Chinese never refer to Tibet's "liberation" except as the "peaceful liberation." Tibet's "liberation" was "peaceful" if by "Tibet" one means that part of central Tibet west of Giamda where the PLA had stopped its advance before calling on the Tibetan Government to "negotiate." In the Chinese point of view, the PLA's advance up to Giamda was not an "invasion of Tibet," but simply the imposition of Communist control over Chinese provincial territory.

Chinese propaganda portrayed the "liberation" of Tibet as part of China's anti-imperialist struggle:

In the last one hundred years and more, imperialism penetrated into China and at the same time also into Tibet. As early as the latter half of the 18th century, British imperialists began to penetrate into this part of our country; and after the 2nd World War, American imperialism also barged in. Following the victorious development of the great revolution of the Chinese people and the people's liberation war, the imperialists and their lackeys became still more frantic like mad dogs, and hastily manufactured the so-called "Tibetan independence" and various "anti-communist" plots in an attempt to make the Tibetan people to be completely cut off from their motherland, to lose their independence and freedom completely and become their complete slaves.[112]

Considering their almost total lack of knowledge of conditions in Tibet (none of the Chinese Communists had so much as set foot in central Tibet), it is possible that many Chinese believed their own propaganda that the Tibetans had fallen into "the depths of enslavement and suffering" and that the Chinese conquest of Tibet actually represented liberation for the Tibetan people. The *New China News Agency*, in a "background information" article, took this line:

China's close relations with Tibet date back to the 8th century. Since 1794, Tibet has become a constituent part of China. The People's Liberation Army began the big drive into Tibet on October 7, 1950, to liberate it from imperialism. The news of the People's Liberation Army's march into Tibet was enthusiastically supported by all sections of the population. In particular Tibetans in all parts of China jubilantly celebrated the news and demanded their return to the motherland.[113]

Ngawang Jigme Ngapo also read a statement, reportedly prepared for him by the Chinese,[114] that echoed the Chinese Communist Party's version of events:

We, the delegates of the local Government of Tibet, whole-heartedly express our gratitude to the leaders of the Central People's Government for their concern and guidance during the period of the month or more of our stay in Peking, especially to the delegates of the Central People's

---

112. "Support Agreement on Measures for Peaceful Liberation of Tibet," *NCNA*, 28 May 1951, in *Survey of China Mainland Press*.

113. "NCNA Background Information on Tibet," *NCNA*, 27 May 1951, in *Survey of China Mainland Press*. Interestingly, 1794 is cited as the date that Tibet "became a part of China."

114. "Conversation with Yapshi Sey," National Archives, 793B.00/8-1851.

Government, headed by Li Wei-han, Chairman of the Commission of Nationalities Affairs. Their sincere and patient explanation have helped us to become more fully aware that the imperialist aggressors are the greatest enemy of our motherland, especially of us Tibetans; and that the disunity created by the imperialists and their reactionary governments of the past must be eliminated from among the Tibetan people.

Under the great inspiration of Chairman Mao Tse-tung's national policy, the disharmony that has existed for a long time among the Tibetan people since the late 13th Dalai and 9th Panchen has been fairly settled.

Today we fully recognize that only with the leadership of the Central People's Government and Chairman Mao Tse-tung and the unity and coop-eration of all fraternal nationalities throughout the country can we drive out our common enemy, the aggressive imperialist forces, consolidate national defence in the Southwest, and build up the prosperous and happy big family of our motherland.[115]

The Panchen Lama, credited with "rendering kind assistance through his representatives" to the successful conclusion of the negotiations, said:

A problem concerning nationalities within China, the Tibetan problem, which had not been settled for many years has now been successfully set-tled under the leadership of Chairman Mao Tse-tung, the brilliant leader of people of all nationalities in China. The peaceful liberation of Tibet is a most joyous event in the big family of all nationalities in China. The unity of the Central People's Government, the Dalai Lama and the Panchen Lama can only be achieved under the leadership of the Communist Party of China and the People's Government.[116]

Despite the Chinese Communists' attempt to construe the 17-Point Agreement as an internal affair, the 17-Point Agreement has some of the characteristics of an international treaty. The very necessity of a treaty between Tibet and China is indicative of their separate political status. No other region of the PRC required such an instrument of incorporation. China's language on Tibet's "return to the Motherland" is an admission that Tibet was separate from the Chinese state.

The 17-Point Agreement was a contradictory document, guaranteeing

---

115. "Head of Tibetan Delegation on Peaceful Liberation of Tibet," *NCNA*, 27 May 1951, in *Survey of China Mainland Press*.

116. Obviously, these words were put into the mouth of the 13 year old Panchen. Li Wei-han referred to the reconciliation between the Dalai and Panchen Lamas as the agreement's most important achievement after that of the "return of Tibet to the Motherland." "Chairman Mao on Signing of Agreement," *NCNA*, 27 May 1951, in *Survey of China Mainland Press*.

on the one hand no alteration of Tibetan political and religious systems (Article 4), while on the other hand providing for Tibet to be governed by the system of "national regional autonomy" (Article 3) under a "Military Area Headquarters" and "Military and Administrative Committee" (Article 15). The Tibetan delegation was astute enough to realize that Article 15 seemed to contradict Article 4, but the meaning of "national regional autonomy" was apparently a mystery that they chose to ignore. The system of national regional autonomy, while promising much in generalities, was vague as to specifics, and was entirely dependent upon Chinese interpretation and implementation. The same may be said for all the guarantees that Tibet was allowed in the agreement. While the Tibetans took solace in guarantees that nothing would change, the Chinese intended that everything would eventually change in accordance with the Chinese Communist Party's program for "socialist transformation."

The key to Chinese intentions was Article 11, which provided for "various reforms" to be undertaken by the "Tibetan local government" if the Tibetan people themselves should "raise demands for reforms." The key to Article 11, and to the 17-Point Agreement as a whole, was Chinese political control in Tibet. Under Chinese control, "demands" for reforms could be raised by a variety of persuasive and coercive methods; the nature of those reforms would be whatever the Chinese, not the majority of Tibetans, desired. Every aspect of Tibetan "autonomy" within the Chinese state and Tibet's future would be determined by the Chinese rather than Tibetans. Further, Tibetans would find that, by the Chinese interpretation of Tibet's "return to the Motherland," Tibetans had not only lost their independence, but their very identity; Tibetans were no longer just Tibetans, but were now to be defined as Chinese of the "Tibetan minority nationality."

The Dalai Lama's Return to Lhasa

After the signing of the 17-Point Agreement in Peking at the end of May, the Tibetan Government began an intense debate about whether or not to accept the agreement. At the same time, American diplomatic activity was aimed at persuading the Dalai Lama and the Tibetan Government to reject it. The American diplomatic initiative was undertaken by the US ambassador in New Delhi, Loy Henderson, at the end of March (before the conclusion of the 17-Point Agreement, but in anticipation of that agreement), after a conversation with Heinrich Harrer, who informed the ambassador that the Dalai Lama was "very much in need of advice" about his option to accept or to reject an agreement with China. Harrer reported that the Dalai Lama was uncertain whether India would give him asylum, no offer to that effect having been communicated to him in Yatung.[117]

The US ambassador therefore drafted a message on the US position to be sent to the Dalai Lama at Yatung:

A high foreign official who has recently visited Asia and who has sympathy for Tibet and deep concern for the welfare of His Holiness and His people sends the following earnest suggestions to His Holiness:

1. The Peiping Communist Regime is determined to obtain complete control through trickery rather than through force. They are anxious to persuade His Holiness to make an agreement which would allow them to establish a representative in Lhasa.

2. The establishment of a representative of the Peiping Communist regime in Lhasa would serve only to speed up the seizing of all of Tibet by the Chinese Communists.

3. Until changes in the world situation would make it difficult for the Chinese Communists to take over Tibet, His Holiness should in no circumstances return to Lhasa or send his own treasures or those of Tibet back to Lhasa. . . . [118]

4. His Holiness should not return to Lhasa while the danger exists that by force or trickery the Chinese Communists might seize Lhasa. He should leave Yatung for some foreign country if it should look like the Chinese Communists might try to prevent his escape.

---

117. The US had received information that Chou En-lai had told the Indian Ambassador, Pannikar, that the Tibetan question had been "settled" before the Tibetan delegates had even arrived in Peking. Chou reportedly believed that 80 percent of Tibetan monks had accepted the Chinese formula for settlement since they were "convinced that neither their religion nor their property was endangered." Ambassador in the United Kingdom to the Secretary of State, 27 March 1951, *FRUS, 1951, vol. VII*, 1610. The Tibetans thought it appropriate for India to make some indication of its attitude in regard to asylum and regarded the lack of any Indian communication with the Dalai Lama at Yatung as evidence of a lack of Indian support. Ambassador in India to the Secretary of State, 29 March 1951, FRUS, vol. VII, 1611.

118. What "changes in the world situation" the ambassador contemplated are not known. The advice concerning the Dalai Lama's "treasures" refers to the gold that was brought to India at the time and left there to keep it out of the hands of the Chinese. This treasure was generally exaggerated, as had been rumors of Tibetan gold in the past; it consisted of gold worth some five million US dollars. The American belief that Tibet possessed vast resources in gold was later to hamper efforts to assist the Tibetans, since the US assumed that the Dalai Lama had ample resources for himself and a considerable entourage.

5. It is suggested that His Holiness send representatives at once to Ceylon. . . .

6. If His Holiness and His Household could not find safe asylum in Ceylon he could be certain of finding a place of refuge in one of the friendly countries, including the United States, in the Western Hemisphere.

7. It might also be useful for His Holiness immediately to send a mission to the United States where it would be prepared to make a direct appeal to the United Nations. It is understood that His Holiness is already aware that favorable consideration will be granted to the applications made by members of a Tibetan mission to the United Nations for United States visas.[119]

Henderson's message was approved by the State Department on 6 April, with the exception of paragraph 7, which the State Department requested to be deleted because "in a recent survey of other countries, the Department has found little support for United Nations action."[120] This message (presumably, without paragraph 7) was delivered to Tibetan officials at Kalimpong on 13 May to be conveyed to the Dalai Lama at Yatung. The message was unsigned and written on paper purchased in India that bore no indication of its origin.[121]

On 21 May the Dalai Lama personally replied to the ambassador's letter, expressing appreciation for US interest in Tibetan affairs. The Dalai Lama mentioned that "peace negotiations" were proceeding at Peking at that time, but he hoped that, should he have to approach the US Government for assistance, the US would be able to help Tibet. An American Embassy officer at Kalimpong remarked that he had been told by Dzaza Liushar, Tibetan foreign minister, that, "because Tibet had received no response from the United Nations and some of its member states with respect to its appeal regarding Communist China's invasion of Tibet in October 1950, the Tibetan authorities had fallen into a dejected and fatalistic frame of mind and appeared to be convinced that they would have to accede to the demands of Communist China."[122]

119. Ambassador in India to the Secretary of State, 29 March 1951, *FRUS, 1951, vol. VII,* 1612.

120. Ambassador in India to the Secretary of State, 4 April 1951, *FRUS, 1951, vol. VII,* 1619. American support for a Tibetan appeal to the UN was reinstated in a personal message from Secretary of State Dean Acheson to the ambassador on 22 June. Secretary of State to the Embassy in India, 22 June 1951, *FRUS, 1951, vol. VII,* 1715.

121. Ambassador in India to the Secretary of State, 29 March 1951, *FRUS, 1951, vol. VII,* 1611.

122. "Translation of the Tibetan letter from His Holiness the Dalai Lama to His Excellency Loy W. Henderson the American Ambassador in New Delhi, India," New Delhi Embassy to Department of State, 20 June 1951, National Archives, 793B.00/6-2851.

On 29 May Shakabpa and Jigme Taring met with US Embassy officers at Calcutta. Shakabpa inquired whether, assuming Tibet rejected the agreement with China, Tibet should then report that fact to the United Nations, and if the Dalai Lama chose to go into exile, would the US grant asylum, treat the Dalai Lama as head of state and provide military assistance for Tibetan resistance?[123] Shakabpa said that the Tibetan Government intended to repudiate the agreement but was waiting for its delegates to arrive from China before doing so out of concern for their personal safety. Shakabpa indicated that the extent of US assistance would be an important factor in the Tibetan decision.[124]

Shakabpa was informed that Tibet might reiterate its appeal to the UN at any time and might want to dispatch a delegation to Lake Success (UN temporary headquarters) without waiting for an invitation. The US preferred the Dalai Lama seek asylum in an Asian Buddhist country, but would be willing to grant US asylum to the Dalai Lama and approximately 100 followers; the Dalai Lama would be received as an "eminent religious dignitary and head [of] autonomous state of Tibet." The US was "still prepared provide military assistance providing practicable ship [to] Tibet without violating laws or regulations of India." The Embassy advised the State Department that "US should demonstrate interest in Tibet in every practical political and economic way; otherwise there is little doubt Tibet will fall under complete Communist Chinese control."[125]

In an interview with Bajpai shortly after news of the 17-Point Agreement was received, the US Embassy was given the impression that "GOI [was] taken by surprise at extent [of] Tibetan capitulation." Indian officials were reportedly disappointed at the failure of the Tibetans to secure better terms. Bajpai seemed surprised at the suggestion that Tibet might refuse to ratify the agreement, and was uncertain what attitude India might take to a Tibetan rejection of the agreement.[126] On 5 June Bajpai stated that India was still taking it for granted that Tibet would accept the agreement as the best terms obtainable, but, should they reject it, he thought India would "find it difficult to regard the treaty as a legal document" and, in that case, "could not well refuse" asylum to the Dalai Lama.[127]

The State Department responded to Embassy suggestions that urgent action was necessary if Tibet were not to be subsumed "by default" with-

---

123. Chargé in India to the Secretary of State, 29 May 1951, *FRUS, 1951, vol. VII*, 1687.

124. Ambassador in India to the Secretary of State, 11 June 1951, *FRUS, 1951, vol. VII*, 1707.

125. Ibid.

126. Ambassador in India to the Secretary of State, 31 May 1951, *FRUS, 1951, vol. VII*, 1691.

127. Ambassador in India to the Secretary of State, 5 June 1951, *FRUS, 1951, vol. VII*, 1702.

in the Chinese state: "Dept believes Tibet should not be compelled by duress accept violation its autonomy and that Tibetan people should enjoy certain rights self-determination, commensurate with autonomy Tibet has maintained since Chinese revolution [1911]. Dept believes further that cause world peace would be served if general support could be mustered for this point of view, and agrees with Embassy that US itself should demonstrate interest in case in every practical political and economic way."[128]

The State Department agreed to provide assistance to Tibet, assuming the Tibetan Government rejected the agreement with China, with the qualification that "US is not assuming responsibility guidance Tibetan Government." The US would support another Tibetan UN appeal but felt that Tibetan efforts were necessary to "mobilize some influential world opinion in support of its case," which a "strong stand by Tibetan Government against any clear aggression" would further. The US reiterated its offer of "limited assistance in terms light arms," depending upon the attitude and cooperation of the GOI. The US was willing to support Tibetan resistance only so long as military and political resistance continued inside Tibet. The Department agreed to previous Embassy proposals in regard to asylum for the Dalai Lama in Ceylon or the US, but declined to promise any financial assistance, since "Tibetan Govt by all reports possesses much treasure in gold and silver." The Embassy was directed to reiterate American interest to Tibetans but also the "ineluctable fact [that] India by reasons of traditional relationships and geographic position plays very important role. Tibetans should be under no illusions likewise that military assistance can be obtained for them through UN action." The US would assist Tibet "as far as practicable," but only if the Dalai Lama "not let himself come under control [of] Peiping," and "Tibetans themselves make real effort and take firm stand."[129]

The US was unable to make any moves in regard to assistance for Tibet, however, until Tibet formally and publicly repudiated the 17-Point Agreement:

It looks like Peiping exerted pressure on members of Tibetan delegation to obtain agreement and is now trying through pressure to prevail on Dalai Lama to accept. So long as Tibetan Government remains silent it is difficult for US to denounce agreement as effort to deprive Tibet of its autonomy by pressure and threat of force. In case Tibetan Government should announce

---

128. Secretary of State to the Embassy in India, 2 June 1951, *FRUS, 1951, vol. VII*, 1693.
129. Ibid.

refusal to accept the agreement we believe US should be prepared to issue sharp statement denouncing Peiping machinations to force Tibetans under duress to abandon their long established rights to autonomy. Such announcement should, of course, be couched in such terms as not to give offense to non-Communist [Nationalist] China by questioning Chinese sovereignty over Tibet.[130]

On 15 June the Embassy in India was informed that the new Chinese representative to Tibet, Chang Ching-wu, would depart Hong Kong for Calcutta about 20 June. The Embassy informed Shakabpa and suggested that if the Tibetan Government were going to repudiate the Sino-Tibetan agreement it would want to do so before the Chinese representative arrived in Yatung. The New Delhi Embassy provided a draft of a US public statement intended to follow Tibet's announcement of its rejection of the 17-Point Agreement, which expressed US sympathy for the plight of the government and people of Tibet and the hope that Tibet would bring its case before the UN, and promised US support for Tibet at the UN if it did so.[131]

On 25 June the consular officer at Calcutta met with Taktser Rimpoche, who was in Calcutta awaiting his departure to the US. Taktser reiterated his understanding that the Dalai Lama was in favor of repudiating the agreement and would soon do so.[132] The Dalai Lama's concerns in regard to the possibility of exile were conveyed to US officials by Shakabpa on 26 June. Shakabpa had received five questions from the Tibetan Government:

(1) Whether GOI would allow Dalai Lama to transit India "en route to USA." (2) Whether US aid would be restricted to "assisting Dalai Lama's flight" or whether aid might be forthcoming for resistance. (3) Whether US aid would be given "openly or surreptitiously." (4) Whether US Govt would give any assistance if Tibetan Govt should announce its acceptance

---

130. Ambassador in India to the Secretary of State, 3 June 1951, *FRUS, 1951, vol. VII,* 1694.

131. Chargé in India to the Secretary of State, 15 June 1951, *FRUS, 1951, vol. VII,* 1710. The UK High Commissioner in India was informed of the American intention to make the foregoing statement, to which he replied that the proposed US policy might be embarrassing to India. The UK intended to keep step with India in regard to Tibet and would likely support the Indian position even if that differed from the US position. The American reply was that US policy was only intended to uphold Tibetan autonomy, a position that India and the UK had also recognized. Chargé in India to the Secretary of State, 27 June 1951, *FRUS, 1951, vol. VII,* 1719.

132. Consul General at Calcutta to the Secretary of State, 26 June 1951, *FRUS, 1951, vol. VII,* 1718.

Sino-Tibetan Agreement. (5) If Dalai Lama should go to USA, how would he be received?[133]

The Embassy found the implications of the fourth item "extremely disturbing." This question, which had not been previously raised, indicates that the Tibetan Government did not realize the full implications of the 17-Point Agreement. Shakabpa said that he feared that "not over 50 percent of Tibetan Government officials had clear understanding of implications of present situation faced by Tibetan Government." Shakabpa also raised an objection to US Government statements in support of Tibetan autonomy rather than independence and requested that, since Tibet had never accepted Chinese suzerainty, the US in its statements "please not mention suzerainty or autonomy."[134]

On 1 July Chang Ching-wu, along with the members of the Tibetan delegation (Ngapo excluded),[135] arrived at Calcutta, where Chang issued a statement announcing the "peaceful liberation of Tibet":

Tibet is an inseparable part of China's territory and the Tibetan nationality is one of the nationalities in China that have a long and enduring history. Upon his assuming administration, Dalai Lama sent a delegation of the local Government of Tibet to discuss with the Central People's Government measures for peaceful liberation of Tibet. As a result, an agreement on measures for the peaceful liberation of Tibet was signed on May 23, 1951. By this agreement, the Tibetan nationality has now attained liberation and returned to the great family of the People's Republic of China. From now on, under the leadership of the Central People's Government and Chairman Mao Tse-tung, the Tibetan nationality will ever march along the path of brightness and happiness. The peaceful liberation of Tibet and the great solidarity of all nationalities in China will benefit the lasting peace in Asia and in the world. Now that Tibet has been peacefully liberated, the People's Republic of China is ready, on the basis of equality, mutual benefit and mutual respect for territory and sovereignty, to live peacefully together with all her neighboring countries, and to establish and develop fair relations of trade and commerce with them.[136]

---

133. Consul General at Calcutta to the Secretary of State, 2 July 1951, *FRUS, 1951, vol. VII*, 1726.

134. The State Department replied to Shakabpa's request: "Dept does not wish to commit itself on what it may or may not say re legal status Tibet. If Shakabpa should press suzerainty point, he could be merely told that his views had been made known to this Govt." Ibid.

135. Ngapo was returned overland, presumably because the Chinese were unwilling to risk the defection of the leader of the Tibetan delegation.

136. New Delhi to Department of State, 9 July 1951, National Archives, 793.B00/7-951.

Taktser Rimpoche met with the Tibetan delegates in Calcutta and reported to US officials the delegates' version of events in Peking. They reported that they had been forced to sign the agreement on Chinese terms and had been denied the opportunity to refer to Yatung for instructions. They had been told to sign or "there would be war." They had felt while in China "as in an iron box," and had been constantly watched and followed. They were very anxious about the Tibetan Government's reaction to the results of their negotiations.[137] Shakabpa met with the delegates at Kalimpong and reported a similar version of events. The Tibetan delegates all reportedly expressed animosity toward the Chinese for their treatment in Peking, where they felt that they had been coerced into signing the 17-Point Agreement. All emphasized that they had signed only on behalf of the delegation, not the Tibetan Government. Shakabpa asked for the views of each member separately on whether the Dalai Lama should return to Lhasa. Each thought it would be unwise for the Dalai Lama to do so. They reported that Ngapo had said that the Dalai Lama and the Tibetan Government should "not worry about him" in making their decision, which the delegates took to imply that Ngapo also was not in favor of accepting the agreement.[138]

Shakabpa predicted that the Dalai Lama and the Tibetan Government would discuss the agreement with Chang Ching-wu at Yatung, but that they would not accept the agreement without significant alterations regarding Tibetan autonomy. Since the Chinese were thought unlikely to make any concessions, he predicted that the Dalai Lama would reject the agreement and then seek exile in India. Shakabpa reported that the Dalai Lama was opposed to eight of the clauses of the agreement, particularly article two, which allowed the Chinese to station troops in Tibet. Shakabpa said that he had received a telegram on 4 July in which the Dalai Lama said that he planned to leave Tibet in about a week for India. However, Shakabpa also expressed the fear that "Tibetan officials around the Dalai Lama might be able to keep him from leaving." He reported that the Dalai Lama's message had said that he was still interested in

---

137. Taktser Rimpoche departed on 5 July for the United States even though he was requested by the Dalai Lama to delay. Taktser believed that the decision to receive the Chinese delegation at Yatung implied Tibetan capitulation, and therefore it was important for him to reach the United States, where he would represent an independent Tibetan voice. Consul General at Calcutta to the Secretary of State, 3 July 1951, *FRUS, 1951, vol. VII*, 1728.

138. Shakabpa also reported that PLA units from Sinkiang had moved into western Tibet and established a garrison at Rutok. "Experiences of Tibetan Delegates in China as Related by Tsepon Shakabpa," American Consul Calcutta to Department of State, 9 July 1951, National Archives, 793B.00/7-951.

coming to India but that those surrounding him were placing him under the strongest pressure to remain in Tibet. The Dalai Lama also expressed continuing uncertainty as to India's attitude toward granting him asylum.[139]

The Chinese and Tibetan delegations flew to Kalimpong on the 6th; the Tibetans proceeded to Yatung, while the Chinese waited in Kalimpong.[140] In the meantime, the US Embassy, uncertain whether the Dalai Lama or the Tibetan Government had received a clear indication of US offers of support (although Shakabpa had told them that the Tibetan Government had received all US communications), sent another letter (again, on plain paper, unsigned and containing no reference to the United States) "toward the end of June" reiterating the offer of US support for Tibet should the Dalai Lama repudiate the 17-Point Agreement. This letter was thought to have been received by the Dalai Lama "about July 6":

> We sent you a letter two months ago about the dangers of the Chinese Communists. Some of your advisers probably think that they understand the Chinese Communists and can make a bargain with them. We do not think they understand Communism or the record of its leaders. . . . Your Holiness is the chief hope of Tibet. If the Chinese Communists seize control of Tibet, you will be of greater help to Tibet outside Tibet where you will be the recognized leader and will symbolize the hopes of the Tibetans for the recovery of Tibet's freedom.

> Since sending the previous letter we have read in the newspapers your delegation to Peiping signed an agreement with the Chinese Communists. We do not believe they signed it with your permission but were forced to do so. However, the world is beginning to think that you do not object to the agreement because you have made no statement about it. We think you should make this statement soon because the Chinese Communists are sending a delegation to Yatung through India. If you make your statement before they reach India, it should make it difficult for the Chinese delegation to come to Tibet. If you do not make such a statement, we think that Tibetan autonomy is gone forever.

> The only access we have to Tibet is through the country of India. It is therefore important that Tibet tell India what you now want to do and persuade India to help you or permit other countries to help you. We don't know for

---

139. Shakabpa revealed that he had advised the Dalai Lama to wait in Yatung to talk to the Chinese, because he was confident that the Tibetans could achieve some alteration in the terms, or if not that the Dalai Lama could still escape to India. The American consul remarked that this advice was probably a mistake. American Consul at Calcutta to Department of State, 21 July 1951, National Archives, 793B.00/7-2151.

140. George Patterson, *Requiem for Tibet* (London: Aurum Press, 1990), 128.

sure but think it possible India will permit help because although India now seems friendly with the Chinese Communists we know many Indians are fearful of the Communists near India.

We ourselves are willing to help Tibet now and we will do the following things at this time:

1. After you issue the statement disavowing the agreement which your delegation signed with the Chinese Communists in Peiping, we will issue a public statement of our own supporting your stand.

2. If you decide to send a new appeal to the United Nations, we will support your case in the United Nations.

3. If you leave Tibet, we think you should seek asylum in India, Thailand or Ceylon in that order of priority because then you will be closer to Tibet and will be able to organize its resistance to the Chinese Communists. . . .

4. If you leave Tibet and if you organize resistance to the Chinese Communists, we are prepared to send you light arms through India. We think, however, that you should first ask India for arms and, if they cannot give them to you, ask India for permission for other countries to send them through India. If you are able to organize resistance within Tibet, we will also give consideration to supplying you with loans of money to keep up the resistance, spirit and morale of the Tibetan people. . . .

5. We have already told your brother, Taktse Rimpochi, that he can go to our country and we are making arrangements for his departure.

We are willing to do all these things. We have sent you many messages to this effect. We do not know if you have received them. Therefore we ask you to write us whether you have received this letter. We ask you also to send us a personal representative, or write to us which Tibetan representatives in India have your confidence.[141]

Tibetan Government officials assembled at Yatung from 7 to 10 July after the arrival of the Tibetan delegates. Their debate revolved around whether Tibet could preserve more of its cultural and political identity by accepting China's demands or by refusing them. The latter option required that the Dalai Lama seek asylum outside Tibet; the main objections to this option were the lack of demonstrated foreign support, especially that of India, and the fact that, unlike the Dalai Lama, the Tibetan nation and its institutions could not escape into exile or be preserved there. Neither option was attractive, but there was little choice.

---

141. This last sentence reflects American uncertainty about whether Shakabpa had the Dalai Lama's confidence. Chargé in India to the Department of State, 11 July 1951, *FRUS, 1951, vol. VII,* 1743.

To many Tibetans, repudiation of the agreement and exile seemed to be more capitulatory than acceptance, since, in the former case, the Chinese would gain total control over Tibet, whereas, in the latter, the institutions capable of resisting complete Chinese control would remain; cooperation with the Chinese offered at least some chance to preserve Tibetan institutions and Tibet's political and cultural identity. Chinese promises to leave Tibetan institutions unchanged, including the estate system upon which many of them depended, convinced much of the clergy as well as some of the aristocracy that acceptance of China's terms was Tibet's best option. Many thought China more likely to impose strict control on Tibet if the Dalai Lama angered them by repudiating the agreement, whereas Tibetan acquiescence to the Chinese conditions, and the Dalai Lama's continuing influence, might ameliorate conditions of the Chinese occupation of Tibet. The argument that the Chinese could and probably would renege on all their promises once they gained complete control of Tibet was countered by the point that the only Tibetan institution capable of holding the Chinese to their promises was the Dalai Lama; if the Dalai Lama went into exile, Tibet would have no protection against whatever the Chinese chose to do.

The faction that preferred repudiation was unable to demonstrate what benefit the Dalai Lama would be to Tibet from exile; the US had offered support, but their offers were contingent upon Indian cooperation, which seemed unlikely to be forthcoming. Despite the contention of some members of the Dalai Lama's own family and some of his most experienced advisers that the Tibetan cause for independence would be forever lost by accepting the agreement, the conservative faction finally predominated. Few clerical officials, ignorant of communist ideology, could comprehend why, if unprovoked, the Chinese would want to destroy the Tibetan Buddhist church, the example of Mongolia notwithstanding. Despite the Tibetans' knowledge of what had happened in Mongolia, few Tibetans, either secular or religious, had any real awareness of conditions under Communist regimes. Tibetans sought hope in those clauses of the 17-Point Agreement that seemed to indicate that Chinese control over Tibet would be nominal, as it had been in the past; China would be allowed the formality of sovereignty over Tibet while Tibet would continue to govern itself. The conservatism and lack of political sophistication of most Tibetan officials, as well as their confidence that they could deal with the Chinese within Tibet better than they could deal with the unknown outside world, were also important factors.

On or about 10 July the decision was made to return to Lhasa.[142]

---

142. The final decision was accompanied by oracle consultations and an appeal to a lottery process: "According to several sources, this was done by writing `Go to India' and

Shakabpa received a message in Kalimpong on 12 July that the Dalai Lama would return to Lhasa in ten days.[143] The Dalai Lama met with Chang Ching-wu on 16 July. The Dalai Lama telegraphed Mao on 20 July that he would return to Lhasa and would discuss the terms of the 17-Point Agreement there. The Dalai Lama rejected Chang Ching-wu's request that he accept the 17-Point Agreement in this telegraph message on the grounds that the *Tsongdu* in Lhasa had to confirm the decision. On 21 July the Dalai Lama left Yatung for Lhasa.[144] The Dalai Lama and the Tibetan Government had not yet officially accepted the terms of the 17-Point Agreement, but their decision to return to Lhasa was equivalent to acceptance of coexistence with the Chinese on those or some other terms.

Before the Dalai Lama's departure, US officials, aware only of assurances from Shakabpa, Taktser Rimpoche and others that the Dalai Lama had favored rejection of Chinese conditions and had intended to seek exile, convinced themselves that either their offers had not been adequately conveyed or comprehended or that the Dalai Lama was "no longer a free agent."[145] They also imagined, based upon the information

---

`Go to Lhasa' on two bits of paper, each of which was rolled into a ball of dough. The balls were then placed in a bowl and rotated in front of an image of Buddha, and the ball saying `Go to Lhasa' had come out first." "Conversation with Yapshi Sey," National Archives, 793B.00/8-1851. George Patterson, who was in Kalimpong at the time, reports a somewhat different version. Patterson received a letter from the Dalai Lama explaining how the decision to return had been made: "The three abbots of the three great monasteries in Lhasa, Sera, Drepung and Ganden, had arrived in Yatung from Lhasa, and suspecting that the Dalai Lama might be contemplating leaving for India, they had insisted that he consult the State Oracle. The Dalai Lama had submitted to this and the State Oracle, under possession, had advised him to return to Lhasa. The Dalai Lama had been unwilling to accept this, and had defied precedent by demanding a second possession. Again the State Oracle had decreed that he should return to Lhasa. When the Dalai Lama had been going to refuse this direction as well, the three abbots had said: `If you do not accept the direction of the gods on high, how can you expect to be accepted as their representative on earth?' and he had to submit." Patterson, *Tibet in Revolt*, 84.

143. Consul General at Calcutta to the Secretary of State, 12 July 1951, *FRUS, 1951, vol. VII*, 1747.

144. "Conversation with Yapshi Sey," National Archives, 793B.00/8-1851.

145. Secretary of State to the Embassy in India, 13 July 1951, *FRUS, 1951, vol. VII*, 1749. The consular official at Kalimpong, who had been in contact with Shakabpa and others during the final weeks before the decision, had a more accurate appraisal: "During this critical week he was convinced, after talking to numerous persons, that most of the Tibetan officials with any knowledge of outside affairs are anxious for the Dalai Lama to leave Tibet. Apparently, however, they are unable to counterbalance the tremendous weight of superstition and selfish officialdom including delegations from monasteries, oracles of incredible influence, and the misguided wish of the Lhasa Government itself to preserve, within Tibet, the religious integrity of Tibetan life as personified and symbolized in the Dalai Lama." American Consul, Calcutta, to Department of State, 21 July 1951, National Archives, 793B.00/7-2151.

that a final Tibetan acceptance had not been made at Yatung, that the Dalai Lama might still reject the agreement. The US therefore continued to try to convey their assurances to the Dalai Lama and to remove obstacles to his asylum in India or another country, including the US.

On 16 July Shakabpa was given a message from the US State Department containing "a paraphrase of the information conveyed by the Department to Taktser Rimpoche in Washington on July 12, 1951." The only additional assurances provided to Taktser by the State Department were that the Dalai Lama would be treated as "head of an autonomous Tibet" and "US similarly will endeavor persuade other nations take no action adverse DL's position as head autonomous Tibet."[146] Shakabpa, who was leaving Kalimpong for Yatung on the 17th, was requested to convey this message to the Dalai Lama at Yatung. Shakabpa was also asked to meet with Dayal, the Indian political agent at Gangtok, Sikkim, in order to receive assurances that India would grant asylum to the Dalai Lama, the US having persuaded the Indian Ministry of External Affairs to convey such information to Dayal. When Shakabpa arrived in Gangtok, however, Dayal had not yet received any information from New Delhi and was thus unable to offer any such assurances.[147]

US officials, assuming that the Dalai Lama might still seek asylum in India if given the opportunity, devised several plans to bring the Dalai Lama from Yatung before his scheduled departure for Lhasa on 22 July. Informed by Shakabpa that the Dalai Lama "had made decision under compulsion," US officials thought that the "Dalai Lama may be persuad-

---

146. Consul General at Calcutta to the Department of State, 16 July 1951, *FRUS, 1951, vol. VII*, 1753. As had been the case with previous messages, all references to the United States were deleted. Secretary of State to the Embassy in India, 12 July 1951, FRUS, 1951, vol. VII, 1748. The Consul at Calcutta remarked that "In preparing this message we repeated the references to Tibetan autonomy which are contained in the Department's telegram, though it may be difficult to convey to the Tibetans exactly what the Department has in mind, in view of the fact that the Tibetan language does not differentiate between the concepts of autonomy and complete independence." Consul General at Calcutta to the Department of State, 16 July 1951, FRUS, 1951, vol. VII, 1753. The problem was not with the Tibetan language but with the concepts themselves. In the English language, autonomy and independence are synonymous; Webster's definition of autonomy is "independent in government; having the right of self-government."

147. Chargé in India to the Secretary of State, 19 July 1951, *FRUS, 1951, vol. VII*, 1757. The Indian MEA assured American officials that India's offer would be passed along by other means before the Dalai Lama left Yatung, but it is uncertain if this ever happened. Ambassador in India to the Secretary of State, 21 July 1951, *FRUS, 1951, vol. VII*, 1759. Information from Tibetan contacts indicated that "no word had been received from GOI in regard to asylum" prior to the Dalai Lama's departure. Consul General at Calcutta to the Secretary of State, 16 August 1951, *FRUS, 1951, vol. VII*, 1791.

ed reverse decision when presented with definite plans for escape."[148] These plans were coordinated between sympathetic Tibetans, including members of the Dalai Lama's family, and US officials; one plan involved Heinrich Harrer and George Patterson, who, along with a group of Khampas, would kidnap the Dalai Lama (with his cooperation) and smuggle him to Bhutan and then to India.[149] However, all such schemes were terminated by the Dalai Lama's departure for Lhasa.

American analyses of their failure to persuade the Dalai Lama to leave Tibet blamed "unreliable intermediaries" or the failure of Tibetan officials to understand American offers.[150] However, US officials were subsequently informed that Tibetan officials had been unimpressed by unsigned American messages, assuming that anonymous offers of support were hardly credible. Nevertheless, the US was still reluctant to send a signed letter, since it might fall into Chinese hands and be used to demonstrate American interference in Chinese affairs.[151] The US was also concerned that, "if Tibs were hard pressed in further negotiations with Commie China, that Tibs might use such document to reinforce their position."[152] However, the US sought to increase the credibility of its offers, since it was thought that the "Dalai Lama still desires come India and Tibs may disavow agreement following discussions in Lhasa. In such circumstances, formal statement our attitude might be deciding factor." This view was bolstered by information that the numbers of Chinese troops to enter Tibet remained an issue which might lead to Tibetan rejection of the agreement.[153]

---

148. Consul General at Calcutta to the Secretary of State, 17 July 1951, *FRUS, 1951, vol. VII*, 1754. The US consistently misunderstood the nature of this "compulsion," assuming that it involved communist sympathizers, whereas Shakabpa was undoubtedly referring more to the fact that the Dalai Lama had to respect the opinions of Tibetan monastic and lay officials.

149. Ibid.; Patterson, *Requiem for Tibet*, 130.

150. Secretary of State to the Embassy in India, 4 August 1951, *FRUS, 1951, vol. VII*, 1769; Consul General at Calcutta to the Secretary of State, 13 August 1951, *FRUS, 1951, vol. VII*, 1776. In fact, all American communications had been conveyed to the Dalai Lama and were apparently understood by the Dalai Lama and his officials. Intermediaries in this exchange were Taktser Rimpoche, Shakabpa, P.T. Takla, Yutok Dzaza, Kukula (daughter of the Maharaja Kumar of Sikkim), Ragashar Shape, and Trijang Rimpoche. Jamyang Norbu, personal communication, Washington, June 1995.

151. Consul General at Calcutta to the Secretary of State, 13 August 1951, *FRUS, 1951, vol. VII*, 1777.

152. Chargé in India to the Secretary of State, 14 August 1951, *FRUS, 1951, vol. VII*, 1786.

153. Consul General at Calcutta to the Secretary of State, 13 August 1951, *FRUS, 1951, vol. VII*, 1778. The US thought that Tibet would "continue to temporize in their dealings with Commie Chinese in hope developments in Korea will make it difficult for Commie Chinese implement such provisions Sino-Tib agreement as stationing Commie Chinese troops in Tibet." Ambassador in India to the Secretary of State, 1 September 1951, *FRUS, 1951, vol. VII*, 1795.

The Calcutta Consulate therefore conveyed to the Dalai Lama a message received from the State Department on 4 August indicating continuing US interest in Tibet (again with references to the US deleted):

> We understand and sympathize with the reasons there exist which might lead to your remaining in Tibet at this time. However, we desire to repeat our belief that you can best serve your people and country by evading Communist control at earliest opportunity and by denouncing agreement with Communist China after you will have reached safe asylum in India or Ceylon. Taktser is well and safe in our country and hopes that you will consider favorably our pledge of assistance previously made [to] you and your entourage in asylum.[154]

A final attempt to transcend the limitations of US policy in regard to sending an official letter to the Dalai Lama was suggested by Heinrich Harrer in a conversation with US consular officers in Calcutta on 10 September. It involved having a Tibetan official read an official letter in New Delhi, the contents of which he would convey to Lhasa and which he would swear had borne the US ambassador's signature.[155] This was done, the contents of the letter being conveyed to Lhasa by Yutok Dzaza.[156] The ambassador's letter, in part, read as follows:

> It is the opinion of the United States Government that if you could arrange to leave Tibet and seek asylum in some country such as Ceylon, you might be able to continue your struggle to preserve the autonomy of Tibet and the liberty of the Tibetan people. . . . The United States . . . is prepared to support resistance now and in the future against Communist aggression in Tibet, and to provide such material aid as may be feasible. . . . The readiness of the United States to render you the assistance and support outlined above is conditional upon your departure from Tibet, upon your public disavowal of agreements concluded under duress between the representatives of Tibet and those of the Chinese Communists, and upon your continued willingness to cooperate in opposing Communist aggression. An essential part of our cooperation would be a public announcement by the United States that it supports the position of Your Holiness as the head of an autonomous Tibet. The United States would also support your return to Tibet at the earliest practicable moment as the head of an autonomous and

154. American Consul at Calcutta to Department of State, 18 August 1951, National Archives, 793B.00/8-1851.

155. "Plan Suggested by Henrig Harrer to Show Signed United States Letter to Tibetan Official," American Consul at Calcutta to Department of State, 12 September 1951, National Archives, 793B.00/9-1251.

156. "United States Policy Concerning the Legal Status of Tibet," November 1957, National Archives, 793B.00/11-157.

non-Communist country. The position of the United States in this regard is fundamental and will not be affected by developments in Korea.[157]

On 6 September State Department officials met in Washington to decide on US policy toward Tibet in the event that Tibet either "does not repudiate or affirms the agreement through obvious Chinese pressure." The most probable development was thought to be "involuntary Tibetan acquiescence in the Agreement." In that case, the US considered making a unilateral statement "setting forth the decision of the US not to take cognizance of the Sino-Tibetan Agreement."[158] Legal and political options were obviously few and ineffectual, but there was a reluctance to allow "the Chinese Communists to consolidate their position inside Tibet without receiving any public condemnation from any non-Communist country. If Tibet's *de facto* autonomy is lost, the US should not let this Communist success be classified as a victory through diplomatic default." At the very least, the US should "endeavor to use Tibet as a weapon for alerting GOI to the danger of attempting to appease any Communist Government and, specifically, for maneuvering GOI into a position where it will voluntarily adopt a policy of firmly resisting Chinese Communist pressure in south and east Asia."[159]

On 28 September 1951 the Tibetan *Kashag* and *Tsongdu* at Lhasa formally accepted the 17-Point Agreement, on the majority opinion that it promised the continuation of Tibet's religious government and monastic system together with the estate system on which it was based.[160] Information received by the US indicated that Ngapo reported that he had been given verbal assurances in Peking that the Chinese would not interfere in Tibetan internal affairs; the Chinese military and administrative offices in Lhasa would only exercise control over Chinese troops and supervise Chinese interests. The Tibetan Government therefore decided, rather than attempt to reopen negotiations, to request official assurances that the Chinese understanding of what had been agreed upon corresponded to Ngapo's understanding. Apparently some such assurance was received and the Tibetans therefore accepted the Agreement.[161]

---

157. American Embassy New Delhi to Department of State, 18 September 1951, National Archives, 793B.00/9-1851.

158. Memorandum by the Deputy Director of the Office of Chinese Affairs to the Deputy Assistant of State for Far Eastern Affairs, 6 September 1951, *FRUS, 1951, vol. VII*, 1799.

159. Ibid., 1801.

160. Goldstein, *History of Modern Tibet*, 812.

161. "Report from Lhasa, September 16-October 15, 1951," American Embassy London to Department of State, 25 January 1952, National Archives, 793B.00/1-2552.

On 25 October the Dalai Lama sent a letter to Mao Tse-tung formally accepting the 17-Point Agreement.[162] In a message to the US via Taktser Rimpoche in early 1952 the Dalai Lama expressed his hope that the US would not abandon its interest in Tibet because the Tibetans had been forced to capitulate to Chinese demands. He indicated that he and Tibetans had some hope that their situation might be altered in the future; in the meantime, however, the Chinese were being very careful in their own policy, therefore it seemed appropriate for Tibet also to avoid exacerbating the situation. Taktser was instructed to suggest to the Americans that they not bring too much attention to the situation.[163]

The period of Tibetan *de facto* independence thus ended. During its period of independence, Tibet found sympathy for its cause but no new patron capable of opposing the ambition of China to substantiate its claim to sovereignty over Tibet. Britain played that role until Indian independence in 1947, but the British policy of recognizing Tibetan "autonomy" under Chinese "suzerainty" was equivalent to an acknowledgement of Chinese sovereignty. After 1947 Indian Prime Minister Nehru admitted that there was very little difference in the meaning of the two terms, and, while publicly recognizing only Chinese suzerainty over Tibet, India privately conceded that this was equivalent to sovereignty. Having conceded that Chinese suzerainty was functionally and legally equivalent to sovereignty, neither India nor any other interested party was able to put much political or legal substance into Tibetan autonomy.

Independent Indian policy was pragmatic, and moral in its repudiation of the legacy of British imperialism, but excessively idealistic in its hope that the Chinese would preserve Tibet's traditional autonomy and that Tibet would remain a buffer state between China and India. In pursuit of its idealistic but ambitious goal to play a role as a nonaligned peacemaker in international politics, India did a disservice to Tibet by its lack of support for Tibet at the UN. India and Britain may be held to have had a moral obligation to at least make the facts of Tibet's case known to

---

162. Chargé in India to the Secretary of State, 30 October 1951, FRUS, 1951, vol. VII, 1839.

163. Memorandum of the Substance of a Conversation, by William O. Anderson of the Office of Chinese Affairs, 13 February 1952, FRUS, 1952-1954, vol. XIV: China and Japan (Washington: Government Printing Office, 1985), 9. The Americans agreed, expressing the opinion that the situation was developing to their advantage in that Tibetan resistance was growing without outside instigation and Indian opinions were shifting against China due to their actions in Tibet and pressures on the Indian border. Memorandum by the Acting Director of the Office of Chinese Affairs to the Assistant Secretary of State for Far Eastern Affairs, 14 May 1952, FRUS, 1952-1954, vol. XIV, China and Japan, 51.

the world, by reason of their familiarity with Tibet's situation, if not because of their role in creating or perpetuating that situation.

American patronage briefly appeared to offer some hope to the Tibetans. The US was as interested in opposing Soviet and Chinese Communism as the British had been in opposing Russian imperial expansionism. The US, however, had accepted Chinese sovereignty over Tibet in the past, and was reluctant to support Tibetan independence against the Chinese Communists because of US relations with the Nationalist Chinese Government on Taiwan, who continued to claim sovereignty over Tibet. The US therefore carefully expressed its support for Tibetan autonomy, not independence, clearly revealing to Tibetans the limits of American support. The Dalai Lama later remarked in his autobiography that the US was not interested in Tibetan independence, only in Tibetan resistance to Communism, a statement which reveals that he had made an accurate appraisal of US policy.[164]

Tibetan independence ultimately remained hostage to the legacy of Tibet's historical relations with China. Those countries that sympathized with Tibet's desire for independence in 1950 were constrained from recognition of such by their past acceptance of Chinese authority over Tibet and their current relations with China (Nationalist or Communist). Countries sympathetic to Tibet recognized the political and logistical difficulties of coming to Tibet's aid against a China determined to impose its control. United Nations action in Korea gave Tibet some hope for assistance from that body, but the illusion that the UN was capable of acting purely on principle was soon dispelled by UN inaction on the Tibetan issue.

The Dalai Lama and Tibetan Government officials made the decision to return to Lhasa and to accept the terms of the 17-Point Agreement in the hope that the influence of the Dalai Lama could ameliorate the conditions of Tibetans' existence under the Chinese. Tibet's decision to compromise with the Chinese was rational, realistic and, within Tibetan tradition, comparable to compromises Tibet had made in the past. The Dalai Lama was the symbol of Tibetan national identity; his departure from Tibet would have meant that Tibet as Tibetans knew it would have ceased to exist; his continued presence offered at least the hope that Tibet might survive.

However, after attempting to coexist with the Chinese for the next seven and a half years, the Tibetans were finally forced to choose the other alternative. Little was gained by returning to Tibet, but much was lost. Tibet's legal and even moral case for political independence was

---

164. Dalai Lama, *Freedom in Exile* (New York: Harper Collins, 1990), 122.

compromised and obscured by the formality of Tibetan acceptance of Chinese sovereignty. Even though Tibetan agreement to the 17-Point Agreement was coerced, and thus could be held to be in violation of international law, Tibet's formal acceptance of the agreement, and thus of Chinese sovereignty over Tibet, essentially eliminated Tibet's claim to independent statehood within international law. Tibet's ultimate rejection (in 1959) of Chinese sovereignty could not regain what was lost in 1951.

Mural in the Potala showing, in the upper left, Brikuti arriving in Tibet with the *Jowo* image from Nepal and, in the upper right, Wencheng arriving with the Jowo from China. In the center left, the Jokhang is being constructed over the *naga* pool in Lhasa. In the center right is the completed Jokhang. 1982.

Statues of Brikuti, left, and Wencheng, right, in the Potala. To Brikuti's right in the shadow is Strongtsan Gampo. Brikuti is placed closest to Srongtsan Gampo because she was the first of his queens. 1982.

The new deity. Mao's image in the place of the *Jowo* in the Ramoche Jokhang. 1982. The Ramoche was used for political meetings and *Thamzing* until 1979.

Mao leading the minority nationality peoples into the new socialist paradise. Painting in Sining railway station. 1982.

Destruction at Shide Monastery, Lhasa. 1982.

Ganden Monastery, 1985. The few standing buildings in the center have been reconstructed since 1980. For the *Serthang* ceremony, the golden *thanka* is hung from the large building in the center.

Defaced murals at Chamdo Monastery. 1982.

Destroyed statue at Dau Monastery, eastern Kham. 1982.

Tibetan girl doing prostrations in front of the Jokhang. 1982. This practice was allowed in 1981 after being banned since 1959.

View from the entrance to the Jokhang, 1982. Tibetans are gathered for the return of the Panchen Lama for the first time since 1964. The Panchen Lama is on the roof. The dead tree in the background is supposedly a descendent of a willow planted by the Wencheng and represents Sino-Tibetan friendship. The tree mysteriously died in 1959. The buildings in the background have since been removed to make a plaza in front of the Jokhang.

View toward the entrance to the Jokhang. Tibetans prostrating. 1982. This area was blocked by an iron fence until 1981.

Derge monastery, northern Kham. 1982. Derge, famous for its edition of the Buddhist *Tengyur* and *Kangyur,* is the only place in Tibet where the blocks for printing those texts survived. Derge monastery began printing again in 1981.

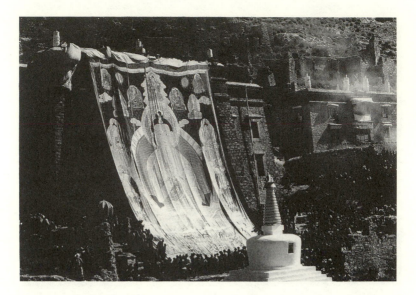

Serthang ceremony at Ganden. 1985. The *chorten* in the foreground contains the remains of Tsongkhapa, the founder of Ganden and the Gelupa sect of Tibetan Buddhism.

Return of the *Jowo* image to the reconstructed Ramoche Jokhang in Lhasa. 1985.

Restoring murals at Ganden. 1982.

Reconstruction of a *chorten* near Drigung. 1985.

Reconstruction of a large image at Drepung. 1982.

School at Tingri, with posters of Marx, Engels, Lenin and Mao. 1995.
Photo by Nancy Jo Johnson.

Chinese posing on Mig-19 in front of Potala. 1993. Photo by Nancy Jo
Johnson.

Tibetan holding image of Dalai Lama. 1993. All Dalai Lama images and photos have since been banned. Photo by Nancy Jo Johnson.

10

Chinese Nationality Policy and the Occupation of Tibet

Without the Chinese Communist Party there would have been no New China—no prosperous and happy mother country; without a socialist mother country there would not be a prosperous and happy new Tibet.[1]

Upon Tibetan acceptance of the terms of the 17-Point Agreement, Tibet came under the domination of an alien nation and political regime. Armed with Marxist-Leninist nationalities doctrine, the Chinese Communists entered Tibet with the certainty that they were the liberators of Tibet from feudalism and imperialism and that they could transform Tibetan "local nationalism" into proletarian internationalism and patriotism to the Chinese state. The Chinese may have assumed that their "liberation" of Tibet and Tibet's "return to the Motherland" would be popularly received by Tibetans, or at least that any resistance could be resolved by Chinese Communist Party (CCP) nationalities policies. However, Tibetans were unreconciled to the loss of their independence; the entry of the Chinese into Tibet aroused resistance that grew with every step the Chinese took to increase their control over Tibetans' lives.

Chinese Nationalism and Nationality Policies

Chinese nationalism arose in opposition to both the alien Manchu and European imperialists who dominated China after the Opium War of 1840. Chinese nationalists were determined to preserve China's territorial integrity against the encroachments of European imperialists both on the seacoast and in Inner Asia.

Imperialist threats to China's possessions in Inner Asia stimulated China to transform its vague authority in Inner Asia into more definite terms compatible with modern Western concepts of international law:

---

1. "Report of the Work Committee on Problems Relating to the Nationalities Policy," *Tibet Daily* (Lhasa), 15 October 1957, in *Tibet: 1950-67* (Hong Kong: Union Research Institute, 1967), 222.

The pattern at work as the Chinese modernized their conduct of foreign relations under the pressures of having western concepts of sovereignty and international law imposed upon them ironically enough can be interpreted as favoring the Chinese in several ways. . . . The imposed definitions of sovereignty and of international law as the norm for interstate relations drew firm boundaries of political right enclosing the territory of China, where the Chinese themselves had been content with more ambiguous demarcations that were no longer enforceable; moreover, the new boundaries by and large secured an empire for China at a time when the builders of that empire were no longer capable of maintaining it. . . . Despite the west's assault on China's territorial integrity in the nineteenth century, western concepts of sovereignty which then prevailed internationally served to acknowledge and guarantee China's Inner Asian empire as a continuing part of the Chinese state.[2]

In addition, Lattimore speaks of a phenomenon of "secondary imperialism," which had the effect of increasing Chinese control of the Inner Asian frontier. Chinese business interests attempted to compensate for their loss of control over commerce on the seacoast and in the interior by participating in Chinese commercial expansion into Sinkiang and Mongolia, facilitated by railroad construction:

There was an attempt, under an alliance of the new (Western model) industrialists and bankers and the old landlords, to anticipate the wider spread of foreign control over China by subjugating the whole interior and hinterland under a Chinese conquest, led and controlled by the most highly organized Chinese groups. In Frontier questions this meant treating all non-Chinese peoples beyond the Great Wall as conquered subjects in order to provide China with a margin of imperial expansion compensating for the privileges surrendered, in the coastal provinces, to foreign imperialism.[3]

The revolution of 1911 did not produce any movement toward abandoning the conquests of the Ch'ing. The Republic justified its existence as a nation, not as a multinational state; the territorial boundaries inherited by the Chinese Republic were not those of the Chinese nation; nevertheless, there is little evidence that Chinese nationalists thought of Ch'ing imperial possessions in Inner Asia as anything but Chinese. The Chinese Republic's attempt to create a Chinese nation-state that included all the territory of the former Ch'ing empire required that inhabitants of the Ch'ing possessions in Inner Asia be transformed into members of a

---

2. Gilbert Rozman, ed., *The Modernization of China* (New York: The Free Press, 1981), 59.
3. Owen Lattimore, *Inner Asian Frontiers of China* (Oxford: Oxford University Press, 1988), 193.

Chinese national polity. The non-Chinese peoples of Inner Asia had therefore to be defined as somehow "Chinese." This was accomplished by defining the Chinese state as one nation and the non-Chinese minorities as sharing "Chinese" origins. Only by this semantic sleight of hand could the Republic claim sovereignty over the territory of the Ch'ing empire without admitting to imperialism in relation to the non-Chinese.

The founder of the Chinese Republic, Sun Yat-sen, spoke of China as being composed of "one race." Sun acknowledged that there were non-Chinese peoples in China, but their numbers were insignificant in relation to those of the Han; China was therefore essentially one nationality:

> Although there are a little over ten millions of non-Chinese in China, including Mongols, Manchus, Tibetans, and Tartars [Tatar], their number is small compared with the purely Chinese population, four hundred million in number, which has a common racial heredity, common religion, and common traditions and customs. It is one nationality.[4]

The nationalities doctrine of the Chinese Republic was founded on the "five races" ideology, derived from the national components of the Manchu empire (Manchu, Chinese, Mongol, Tatar and Tibetan), and was symbolized by the five stripes of the flag of the Chinese Republic.[5] The doctrine of the equality of the "five races" within the Chinese state was employed to convince the Tibetans, Mongols and others to "return" to the Chinese fold. The Republican and, later, the Nationalist Government (1928-1949) promoted the use of the term *chung-kuo-jen* (central kingdom people) to refer to all of the peoples of the Chinese state, Han and national minorities alike, to inculcate a sense of Chinese patriotism regardless of nationality.[6] The Manchu prohibition against marriage between the Chinese and the other constituent nationalities of the Ch'ing empire was

---

4. Sun Yat-sen, "Race and Population," in Leonard S. Hsu, *Sun Yat-sen: His Political and Social Ideals* (Los Angeles: University of Southern California Press, 1933), 168. Sun's inclusion of the Tatars as one of the four "clans," who, along with the Han, compose the Chinese state, is interpreted by many later commentators as having been a reference to the Hui (Chinese Muslims). Sun, however, did not consider the Hui as a separate ethnic group but as Han of the Muslim religion. The Tatars were the Turks (Uighurs, Kazakhs, Kirghiz, etc.) of East Turkestan, or Sinkiang, who, along with Manchu, Mongols, Tibetans and the Chinese, were the major national components of the Manchu empire.

5. Usually translated as "races," but also as five nations, nationalities, or even clans. The terminological confusion was introduced by Sun, who had determined that China was of only one race and that, in China, nation and nationality were synonymous. What is actually meant by the term (*min-tsu*), translated as race, is ethnic group. The "five races" then are "one race composed of five ethnic groups."

6. George Moseley, *The Consolidation of the South China Frontier* (Berkeley: University of California Press, 1973), 7.

lifted, and the "five races" were exhorted to intermarry freely in order to "cultivate affection."[7]

The Chinese nationalists, like the Communists, were influenced by self-determination doctrines of both Wilsonian and Leninist forms; however, they interpreted self-determination only in the context of China's right to freedom from foreign imperialist interference, not as a right of any of China's nationalities to independence. Sun first used the term "self-determination" in regard to the "five races" of China in 1924, in the declaration of the Kuomintang (KMT) platform, but this was interpreted only as their right to "free alliance" in a "free united Republic of China":

> The second aspect of the Doctrine of Nationalism is racial equality. . . . Unfortunately, the present government of China is controlled by the surviving elements of old officialdom who know nothing of racial equality and freedom; and consequently the other races in China are discontented with the present state of affairs. . . . We have over and over insisted upon the common interest of all peoples within China and the necessity of their consolidation in the people's revolution and in solving all interracial problems. We hereby repeat solemnly that we recognize the right of self-determination for all peoples in China, and that a free united Republic of China based upon the principles of free alliance of the different peoples will be established after the downfall of imperialism and militarism.[8]

Sun's policy of racial, or national, equality within a Han Chinese state derived from a typical Chinese conception that the only reason frontier peoples were reluctant to be civilized by assimilation to Chinese culture was their past or present mistreatment by the Han Chinese. That any uncivilized peoples should chose to remain unassimilated to Chinese culture was credited to their barbarism and ignorance, which had to be overcome by patient education in order to bestow upon them the enlightenment and benefits of Chinese civilization. Resistance to the civilizing efforts of the Chinese was also believed to have been encouraged, even created, where no native resistance actually existed, as in Tibet, by the intrigues of foreign imperialists.

Neither Sun nor any of the Chinese nationalists regarded Tibet or Mongolia as nations deserving of the right of independence, but only as not yet assimilated frontier territories of China. Sun specified that China, including Ch'ing imperial possessions in Inner Asia, was an indivisible unitary state:

---

7. Alastair Lamb, *The McMahon Line: A Study in the Relations between India, China and Tibet, 1904 to 1914* (Toronto: University of Toronto Press, 1966), 390.

8. Sun, "Manifesto of the First Kuomintang National Convention," in Hsu, *Sun Yat-sen*, 128.

In Chinese history, unification of the country has been regarded as the normal phenomenon, and the separation of the country as an abnormal phenomenon. The country is composed of eighteen provinces known as China Proper and the Three Eastern Provinces [of Manchuria]; Sinkiang; many special districts, such as Jehol, Suiyan [Inner Mongolia], and Chinghai; and the territories of Mongolia and Tibet. Although some of these regions were added to China after the Han dynasty, throughout the Han, the T'ang, the Sung, the Yuan, the Ming, and the Tsing [Ch'ing] dynasties, China has been a united nation, not a federated state.[9]

Sun Yat-sen's nationalities policy was continued under the KMT regime by Chiang Kai-shek. Chiang simplified the nationality issue and idealized China's benevolence toward other nations in the past. Chiang, unlike Sun, admitted no imperialism on China's part:

Because it would not encroach upon and humiliate other clans, the Chinese nation, in the process of eliminating the sufferings and misfortunes of internal conflict, was able by virtue of its great and enduring civilization to blend these neighboring clans into the nation. In short, our Chinese nation has resisted the armed might of alien clans, but has not resorted to armed might against others. Instead, it has accepted and absorbed their civilizations while at the same time imparting to them on a wide scale the civilization of China. This has been the outstanding characteristic of the survival and expansion of our Chinese nation. . . .

The common historical destiny of the various clans is due to China's ancient virtues that enabled her to bind them in friendship toward her, and also to convert their original characteristics. In return for the tribute offered by her neighbors, China responded with luxurious gifts and favors, and never harbored designs of economic exploitation. In the conflicts among her neighbors, China always adhered to the principle of "re-establishing interrupted dynasties and reviving dismembered states," and never adopted the policy of taking advantage of the precarious position of other countries to seize their territory. . . . Those clans that lived in peace with China evolved from the status of tribute bearers to feudatories, and from feudatories to self-governing units.[10]

Chiang, like Sun, conceived of a natural territorial unity of China:

---

9. Sun, "Democracy at Work," in Hsu, *Sun Yat-sen*, 325.

10. Chiang Kai-shek, *China's Destiny* (New York: Roy Publishers, 1947), 34. Chiang thus claimed that China never pursued a policy of "using barbarians against barbarians," or "divide and rule," both of which were fundamental Chinese policies. Chiang's claim that feudatories evolved to self-governing units can hardly be supported by the historical record; the pattern of Chinese history is, in fact, the opposite.

With regard to her geographical configuration, China's mountain ranges and river basins form a self-contained unit. Taking a birds-eye view from west to east, starting from the Pamir plateau on the "roof of Asia," we have in the north the Tian Shan and the Altai mountain ranges leading to the Three Northeastern Provinces [Manchuria]; in the center, the K'un-lun Mountains extending down to the plains of southeastern China; and in the south the Himalayas extending down to the Mid-South Peninsula [Indo-China]. Within these three great mountain chains lie the Heilungkiang, Yellow, Huai, Yangtze, and Pearl river basins. The Chinese nation has lived and developed within these river basins, and there is no area that can be split up or separated from the rest, and therefore, no areas that can become an independent unit.

As regards national defense, if any region within this geographical system is occupied by an alien nation, then the whole nation and state lose the natural bulwark that protects them. There are no natural frontiers in the areas of the Yellow, Huai, Yangtze, and Han rivers where a strong defense line can be prepared. Therefore, Formosa, the Pescadores, the Four [?] Northeastern Provinces, Inner and Outer Mongolia, Sinkiang, and Tibet are each a fortress essential for the nation's defense and security.[11]

Chiang adhered to the belief that Tibet had immediately begun a process of assimilation to China as soon as Sino-Tibetan relations were initiated:

Following the conversion of the Tufans in Tibet to Buddhism, the orientation of Tibet's development was toward China. Under the Sui and T'ang dynasties, Tibet looked to China for direction. During the Yuan dynasty, Tibet was under the jurisdiction of the Hsuan Cheng Yuan, and during the Ch'ing dynasty, it was under the Li Fan Yuan. Thus, Tibet's period of assimilation has lasted over thirteen hundred years.[12]

Chiang proclaimed that all of China's peoples had common ancestry: "It is revealed [from Chinese history] that Huang Ti [the legendary first Chinese emperor] was the forefather of both the Manchus and Tibetans of today."[13] The distinctions between the peoples of China, he claimed, were only regional and religious:

That there are five peoples designated in China is not due to difference in

11. Ibid., 35. Within two-thirds of the territory described, there were historically few if any Chinese, therefore Chiang's justification for the inseparability of all this territory is far-fetched.

12. Ibid., 38. In fact, Tibet had no relations with the Sui and fought the T'ang to a standstill.

13. Ibid., 39.

race or blood, but to religion and geographic environment. In short, the differentiation among China's five peoples is due to regional and religious factors, and not to race or blood. This fact must be thoroughly understood by all our fellow countrymen.[14]

Chiang, as Sun before him, interpreted self-determination as equal access for the frontier peoples to the benefits of Chinese civilization within a unitary Chinese state:

> Sun Yat-sen enunciated the great principle of "A Republic of Five Peoples" in order to eliminate the friction among the clans within the state and bring them to a status of unity and equality. . . These [policies of the KMT] call for . . . establishing complete equality among all clans within the state. They also call for rendering positive assistance to develop the ability of self-government and to improve the status of the border clans, granting them religious, cultural, and economic opportunities for a balanced development, so that all of them will love, cherish and support the whole state and the central government through harmonious endeavor and mutual concern. . . . This is the underlying spirit of the Revolution of the Kuomintang of China and the one and only mission of its domestic policy.[15]

Chiang's book, *China's Destiny*, was printed in massive quantities and sold at a price subsidized by the state. It was required reading in Chinese schools and in the army; civil servants were required to pass examinations upon its contents. Chiang's simplistic, indeed, false, version of China's relations with other peoples thus became part of the consciousness of most Chinese.

Leninist Nationality Theory and Policy

The Chinese Communists considered themselves the heirs to Sun Yat-sen's nationalist doctrines. Marxism provided the Chinese Communists with a sophisticated theory of the interrelationship between nationalism and imperialism, as well as a theory and policy on nationality relations, all of which were fundamentally compatible with Chinese political culture. The Marxist critique of nationalism and imperialism gave the Chinese Communists a doctrine that purported to explain the sources of all of China's problems and also provided the solution for those problems, a solution that included a vision of a socialist paradise reminiscent of the *Da Tung*, "Great Harmony," doctrine of ancient Chinese culture and of the early Chinese nationalists.

---

14. Ibid., 40.
15. Ibid., 50.

The driving force of human history was, according to Marx, not nationalism but the conflict between socioeconomic classes. Nationalism is a political doctrine of a subjective nature, in contrast to Marxism, which supposes that objective material conditions determine politics. Marx's attitude toward nationalism was conditioned by his belief that economic factors determine human behavior. According to Marx, the ideology of any stage of political development is the ideology of the ruling class of that stage. Nationalism, as the ideology of the bourgeoisie, would naturally pass with the downfall of the bourgeoisie itself. Marxism was not a reaction to nationalism *per se*, but an alternative form of social organization that Marx thought would supersede nationalism.

Marx identified conflict among nations as the origin of nationalism and assumed that the elimination of such conflict would be the end of nationalism itself. Marx underestimated nationalism due to the very method of his analysis; class analysis, as an intellectual tool, is incapable of comprehending a subjective phenomenon of the complexity of nationalism. Essential to Marxist theory is the identity of class rather than national interests with the "self" that seeks liberation, or self-determination. As Marx and Engels said in the *Communist Manifesto*: "In proportion as the exploitation of one individual by another is put an end to, the exploitation of one nation by another will also be put an end to. In proportion as the antagonism between classes within the nation vanishes, the hostility of one nation to another will come to an end."

Essential to an understanding of Marxist nationalities policies is an understanding of the role that Marx predicted for nations and nationalism in the transition to socialism. Marx recognized that the struggle between the proletariat and the bourgeoisie must take place within the political organization of bourgeois capitalism; the proletarian movement must therefore develop within national boundaries. As Marx said, again from the *Manifesto*: "Though not in substance, yet in form, the struggle of the proletariat with the bourgeoisie is at first a national struggle. Since the proletariat must first of all acquire political supremacy, must rise to be the leading class of the nation, must constitute itself the nation, it is, so far, itself national, though not in the bourgeois sense of the word."

In the Marxist dialectical view, nationalism might be a progressive or reactionary force, depending upon the economic stage of development. In general, the national political format was considered to be progressive in the bourgeois-democratic period of socioeconomic development because national organization allowed the growth of capitalism (also considered progressive for that period). The survival of the nation into the socialist period would be judged on an individual basis according to the usual dialectical criteria. Nationalism was considered to be a progressive force in the transition from feudalism, during the establishment of an independent state and up until the stage of developed capitalism, at which point it became reactionary. Colonialism was usually reactionary, but it could be a progressive force in the transformation from feudalism of stagnant and backward countries.

Marx and Engels did not favor independence for every nation; they took a "situationalist" approach to the question. In general, nations large enough to be economically viable were thought deserving of political independence. Nations too small for economic viability, "nationalities" in Marxist terminology, were thought best assimilated to larger units.[16] Nationalities were those "relics of peoples" who did not constitute sufficiently large or important groups to have maintained their own independent state in the past and therefore probably did not deserve independent statehood in the future. Even "progressive" nations might be denied the right to independence if the broader strategic requirements of the advance of the world socialist cause dictated it, and reactionary nations might be awarded the right for similar reasons. Marxist criteria for national independence were not abstract, or concerned with the "inherent rights" of nations, but were determined by the overall effects that nationalist movements would have upon the overall international progress toward socialism.

Lenin adapted Marx's national policy to the conditions of pre-revolutionary Russia. Because of the growth of nationalism in the early twentieth century (rather than the decline, as Marx had predicted), and the exacerbation of nationalism during the 1914 War, Lenin was forced to recognize the continuing strength of nationalism and the necessity of a doctrine to combat and manipulate it in the interests of socialism. Lenin had expected that war in Europe would create the conditions for socialist revolution. He had assumed that the proletariat, because of its natural internationalist sentiments, would unite in opposition to national-imperialist wars. The failure of the European proletariat to do so, plus the nationalist attitudes adopted by the European socialist parties, were a great disappointment to Lenin and had a profound effect upon the evolution of his doctrine. Contrary to his theories, nationalism had proven a more powerful force than class consciousness. Lenin therefore developed his theory of imperialism as the "highest" or "final" stage of capitalism in order to explain the unexpected vitality of the capitalist system.

---

16. Only in Marxist terminology is nationality used to mean "a small nation." In general usage, "nationality" is equivalent to nation, or implies national quality or character. To complicate the matter, Marxist writers are inconsistent in their usage, often employing the term in both Marxist and non-Marxist meanings.

Lenin's theory of imperialism, while explaining how capitalism had gained a new lease on life through colonial expansion, recognized that socialist revolution in Europe was unlikely until colonial exploitation had ceased. Lenin's emphasis on the significance of colonialism and anti-colonial nationalism shifted the focus of socialist revolution to the backward and colonial countries and created the alliance of socialism with anti-colonial nationalism. Because anti-colonialist movements were predominantly bourgeois, this policy necessitated an alliance with the bourgeoisie in the colonial countries. Lenin's thesis on imperialism emphasized the division of the world into oppressed and oppressor *nations*, rather than classes within nations. This was necessary because the colonial countries were at the stage of the bourgeois-democratic rather than socialist revolution; in order to defeat the European capitalists, alliance had to be made with anti-colonial bourgeois revolutionaries. Specific to the argument, of course, was the theory that imperialism was exclusively a phenomenon of capitalism.

A theory and policy on self-determination was the obvious key for socialist alliance with the nationalist anti-imperialist struggle in the colonies. This policy was also extremely efficacious in regard to the colonies of Czarist Russia itself. Lenin regarded the right to secession as the ideological and tactical key to his self-determination policy. He thought that the theoretical right of secession would satisfy a nationality's need for freedom of choice; given that freedom, any nationality would naturally opt for the most beneficial economic arrangement, which would mean union with larger economic units. Lenin expected that the freedom to secede would defuse the force of nationalist separatism; it would be a freedom in abeyance, so to speak, which, because of its availability, would not need to be exercised. As Stalin paraphrased Lenin's formula:

> Lenin sometimes expressed the thesis of national self-determination in the form of a simple formula, "disunion for the purpose of union." . . . It even smacks of the paradoxical. And yet this "self-contradictory" formula reflects the living truth of Marxian dialectics which enabled the Bolsheviks to capture the most impregnable fortresses in the sphere of the nationality question.[17]

Lenin distinguished between what he called the two nations within each nation: the *bourgeois* nation and the *proletarian* nation. The right of self-determination was a right of the *proletariat* of each nation. Writing in 1903, in *The National Question in Our Program*, Lenin stated:

---

17. Stalin, as quoted in Xenia Joukoff Eudin and Robert C. North, *Soviet Russia and the East*, 1920-1927 (Palo Alto: Stanford University Press, 1964), 19.

Our unreserved recognition of the struggle for freedom of self-determination does not in any way commit us to supporting every demand for national self-determination. As the party of the proletariat, the Social-Democratic Party considers it to be its positive and principal task to further the self-determination of the proletariat in each nationality rather than that of peoples or nations.[18]

By replacing an ethnic definition of nation with one based on class, Lenin essentially defined nationalism out of existence. Lenin's definition of the rights of nations as inherent exclusively in the proletariat of that nation eliminated all national rights. Proletarian consciousness was universalist; the proletariat, once its proletarian consciousness was raised, would voluntarily abandon separate national identities and interests. In a socialist state, the question of nationalism would hardly arise because exploitation would not exist. With the elimination of class exploitation, the right of nationalities to self-determination would disappear because the need would disappear. National oppression, and nationalism itself, was a creation of bourgeois rule, and thus a phenomenon exclusively of capitalism; socialism, or rule of the proletariat, would correspondingly create proletarian internationalism free of nationalism and nationalist oppression. Stalin, in his simplified but succinct style, paraphrased the doctrine in 1921:

Whereas private property and capital inevitably disunite people, foment national strife and intensify national oppression, collective property and labour just as inevitably unite people, strike at the root of national strife and abolish national oppression. The existence of capitalism without national oppression is just as inconceivable as the existence of socialism without the liberation of the oppressed nations, without national freedom.[19]

Contrary to Lenin's expectations, many nationalities declared their independence from the new Soviet state, exercising their theoretical right to national self-determination. To combat this tendency, Lenin and Stalin (Stalin, as the "expert" on the nationality question) resorted to a semantic subterfuge. Because the proletariat of any nationality would "naturally" prefer union with the Soviet state, a separatist movement could only be dominated by bourgeois "reactionary" elements, and therefore must be denied. In the absence of any proletariat in the nationality concerned,

---

18. Vladimir Ilyich Lenin, "The National Question in Our Program," 1903, in *On Proletarian Internationalism* (Moscow: Progress Publishers, 1967), 17.

19. Joseph Stalin, "The Immediate Tasks of the Party in the National Question," 1921, in *Marxism and the National-Colonial Question* (Moscow: Proletarian Publishers, 1975), 140.

or, in the inconceivable event that an existing proletariat should opt for separation, then the "proletariat" of the larger state was authorized to make the choice for the non-existent or misguided nationality proletariat.

The theory of accelerated revolution, or the skipping of stages of socioeconomic development based upon the role of the "revolutionary activists" of the Communist Party, could also be applied to nationalities within a socialist state. Nationalities in the pre-capitalist stage of development could accelerate or entirely skip the capitalist stage, transitioning directly to socialism, with the assistance of the majority nation proletariat or its Communist Party playing the role of the absent nationality proletariat. This introduced a national contradiction into Leninist theory: the nationality in question would be led into socialism by activists of a foreign "fraternal socialist" nationality representing the nonexistent nationality proletariat. Trotsky articulated this doctrine quite frankly:

> We do not only recognize, but we also give full support to the principle of national self-determination, wherever it is directed against feudal, capitalist, and imperialist states. But whenever the fiction of national self-determination, in the hands of the bourgeoisie, becomes a weapon directed against the proletarian revolution, we have no occasion to treat this fiction differently from the other "principles" of democracy perverted by capitalism.[20]

Because the Soviet state was confronted by separatist movements and was in a generally precarious situation, Lenin agreed, despite his previous opposition, to establish the Soviet Union on a federal basis. The potentially fragmentary effects of the federal system were to be negated by a highly centralized Communist Party organization. Lenin considered federalism to be a temporary expedient, necessary only until nationalities could be convinced of the non-chauvinist nature of the Soviet regime. The federal system also provided the potential for other nations to federate with the Soviet Union (not considered unlikely in the general euphoria after the success of the Bolshevik Revolution).

Post-revolutionary minority nationalism would be combatted by means of "nationalities work," whose goal was the simultaneous "flourishing" and "coming together" of minority nationalities' cultures. Nationalities work meant convincing minority peoples that nationality consciousness was in fact misplaced class consciousness, the result of economic class exploitation by ruling classes of the dominant nationality in collusion with members of the same class within the minority nationali-

---

20. Leon Trotsky, *Between Red and White* (London: Communist Party of Great Britain, 1922), as quoted in Peter Zwick, *National Communism* (Boulder: Westview Press, 1983), 47.

ty. As socialism eliminated class exploitation, the justification for local nationalism would also be eliminated; any remnants of local nationalism must therefore be the acts of reactionaries or agents of imperialism and must be vigorously opposed. Lenin reasoned that after class oppression, and thus national oppression, had been eliminated, nationalities would experience a period of cultural flourishing. On the other hand, the elimination of oppression and mistrust of one nationality by another would lead to their "coming together" within a multinational culture and state. The term assimilation was avoided because it was supposedly applicable only to capitalist countries where absorption of minority nationalities by the dominant majority was practiced. In socialist countries, no nationality would predominate (nationalism itself having been eliminated); instead, a completely new form of being, a "new Soviet man," would be created.

This process of creation would be facilitated by a strategy employing "national forms," or national language and traditions, to propagate the socialist message. This strategy derived from the *Communist Manifesto* wherein Marx and Engels decreed: "though not in content, yet in form, the socialist struggle remains a national struggle." The idea was that minority nationals would accept the socialist message if it came wrapped in familiar language and cultural attire—national in form, socialist in content. The contradictions inherent in attempting to achieve cultural homogeneity by fostering minority cultures, as well as in Leninist nationalities doctrine in general, was characterized by Stalin as the essence of Marxist dialectics:

> It may seem strange that we, who are in favor of the fusion of national cultures in the future into one common culture (both in form and content), with a single, common language, are at the same time in favor of the blossoming of national cultures at the present time, in the period of the dictatorship of the proletariat. ... It may be said that, presented in this way, the question is "self-contradictory." But is there not the same sort of "self-contradiction" in our treatment of the question of the state? We are in favor of the withering away of the state, yet we are at the same time in favor of strengthening the dictatorship of the proletariat, which represents the most powerful and mighty of all state power that have hitherto existed. ... Is that "self-contradictory?" Yes, it is "self-contradictory." But this contradiction is a living thing, and it is a complete reflection of Marxian dialectics. The same must be said of the formula of national culture: the blossoming of national cultures (and languages) in the period of the dictatorship of the proletariat in one country, with the object of preparing the way for their dying away, and fusion into a single, common, socialist culture (and a single common language) in the period of victory of socialism all over the world. Whoever has failed to understand this peculiarity and this "self-con-

tradictory" nature of our transitional times, whoever has failed to understand this dialectical character of historical process, is lost to Marxism.[21]

If the dialectical approach is required anywhere it is required here, in the national question.[22]

Marxist-Leninist nationalities doctrine was, in practice, a cynical exploitation of a supposed right to national self-determination in order to achieve assimilation of minorities to a majority nationality within a unified socialist state. By means of Marxist dialectics, Communists were able to support national self-determination in theory while opposing it in practice, except against capitalist states. The same right against socialist states disappeared, or was theoretically achieved by the magic of the dialectical argument. The whole process was, furthermore, theoretically voluntary since the "real" interests of all nations, or of their proletariat, were, by definition, best served by their inclusion within socialist states. Convincing nationalities of this fact, or forcing them to remain within socialist states until the process of "nationalities work" could alter their attitudes, however, might involve some political, ideological or even physical coercion, all of which were considered justified in pursuit of the socialist goal.

Chinese Communist Party Nationalities Policy to 1949

Chinese Communist Party (CCP) doctrine on minority nationalism reflects both Marxist-Leninist nationalities doctrine and traditional Chinese frontier assimilationist ideology, all under the Maoist formula "combining the universal truths of Marxism-Leninism with the concrete conditions of China." The Chinese Communists, like the Nationalists before them, assumed that equality within a Chinese state was the equivalent of self-determination for minorities; to remain separate meant to remain in barbarian darkness or to be exploited by imperialism. Leninist nationalities theory and policy furthered the goals of traditional Chinese assimilationism and provided an ideological justification for assimilation as equivalent to nationalities' self-determination. Both Leninist dialectical self-determination and traditional Chinese assimilationism are evident in the assumption that these nations would voluntarily choose to unite with

---

21. Stalin, "Deviations on the National Question: Extract from a Report Delivered at the Sixteenth Congress of the C.P.S.U., June 27, 1930," in *Marxism and the National-Colonial Question*, 393.

22. Stalin, "Marxism and the National Question," 1913, in *Marxism and the National-Colonial Question*, 40.

China because they would realize that their cultural and economic interest lay in union with the more advanced state.

The earliest CCP resolutions on nationality policy reflect the influence of Marxist-Leninist doctrine and Comintern (Communist International) agents. The 1922 Manifesto of the Second Congress of the CCP proposed that China proper (including Manchuria) should be a democratic republic; Mongolia, Turkestan and Tibet would be autonomous, self-governing regions in a Chinese federated republic.[23] The Third Congress of the CCP (1923) adopted a resolution that "the territories of Tibet, Mongolia, Sinkiang and Tsinghai [Chinghai] shall be continually affiliated with China proper, but they may exercise the right of national self-determination."[24]

After the break with the KMT in 1928, the CCP temporarily adhered more closely to Leninist policy, including supporting the right to secession. In 1930, at a meeting in Shanghai of "delegates from various soviets," the right of minorities to secede was recognized. The 1931 Constitutional Conference was dominated by Comintern agents and a group of young Chinese who had been trained in the Soviet Union, collectively known as the "28 Bolsheviks," whom the Comintern manipulated into positions of power in the CCP. The 1931 Conference adopted a resolution recognizing national minorities' right to self-determination, including the right to secede and form independent states:

> The Soviet Government of China recognizes the right of self-determination of the national minorities in China, right to complete separation from China, and to the formation of an independent state for each national minority. All Mongolians, Tibetans, Miao, Yao, Koreans and others living on the territory of China shall enjoy the full right to self-determination, i.e., they may either join the Union of Chinese Soviets or secede from it and form their own state as they may prefer. The Soviet regime of China will do its utmost to assist the national minorities in liberating themselves from the yoke of imperialists, the KMT militarists, t'u-ssu [Tu-shi], the princes, lamas and others, and in achieving complete freedom and autonomy.[25]

This resolution, Article 14 of the 1931 Constitution, was limited by a separate document, "Resolution of the First All-China Congress of Soviets on the Question of National Minorities in China," which more accurately and in greater detail expressed CCP policy on minorities. The promised rights were here addressed to the "toiling masses of the nation-

---

23. Conrad Brandt, Benjamin Schwartz and John Fairbank, *A Documentary History of Chinese Communism* (London: Allen and Unwin, 1952), 64.

24. Ibid., 71.

25. Ibid., 219.

al minorities" (the phrase "toiling masses" was repeated ten times), a well known code phrase employed by the Soviet Union to deny the right of self-determination to any but the proletariat (most often non-existent) of the nationality in question.[26] After accusing the KMT of deception, oppression, exploitation and persecution in its own nationalities policy, the resolution restated CCP policy in words that differ somewhat from the Draft Constitution:

> The First All-China Congress of Soviets of Workers', Peasants', and Soldiers' Deputies declares that the Chinese Soviet Republic categorically and unconditionally recognizes the right of national minorities to self-determination. This means that in districts like Mongolia, Tibet, Sinkiang, Yunnan, Kweichow, and others, where the majority of the population belongs to non-Chinese nationalities, the toiling masses of these nationalities shall have the right to determine for themselves whether they wish to leave the Chinese Soviet Republic and create their own independent state, or whether they wish to join the Union of Soviet Republics [USSR], or form an autonomous area inside the Chinese Republic. The Chinese Soviet Republic shall do its utmost to assist and encourage all the struggles of the national minorities against imperialism, against the Chinese militarists, landlords, government officials, and merchants and usurers' capital. The Chinese Soviet Republic shall also support the national-revolutionary movement and the struggle waged against the attacks and threats of the imperialists and the Kuomintang militarists by these national minorities that have already won their independence as, for example, the Outer Mongolian National Republic. ... In the Fundamental Law of the Chinese Soviet Republic it shall be clearly stated that all national minorities within the confines of China shall have the right to national self-determination, including secession from China and the formation of independent states, and that the Chinese Soviet Republic fully and unconditionally recognizes the independence of the Outer Mongolian People's Republic.[27]

The influence of the Comintern is strongly at evidence here, especially in the repeated recognition of the independence of Outer Mongolia and the extraordinary suggestion that any of China's minorities might have the choice of union with the USSR rather than with China. Although the

---

26. Walker Connor, *The National Question* in Marxist-Leninist Theory and Strategy (Princeton: Princeton University Press, 1984), 74.

27. Chang Chih-i, "Resolution of the First All-China Congress of Soviets on the Question of National Minorities in China, in George Moseley, *The Party and the National Question in China* (Cambridge: Massachusetts Institute of Technology Press, 1966), 164. Moseley's book is a translation, with commentary, of Chang Chih-i's 1956 essay, "A Discussion of the National Question in the Chinese Revolution and of Actual Nationalities Policy." Moseley describes Chang's treatise as "the only systematic analysis of the CCP's theoretical approach to the national minority question."

Chinese national minorities were promised the right of secession, they and their territories were obviously thought of as part of China at the time.

While proffering the right to secession and independence, the resolution makes a case for the nationalities remaining within the "Chinese Republic," pointing out that exploiters were within their own nationality as well as among the Chinese and foreign imperialists:

> The toiling masses of the national minorities are oppressed and exploited not only by the imperialists and Chinese militarists, landlords and bourgeois but also by their own ruling classes: in Mongolia, by the princes and "Living Buddhas"; in Tibet, by the lamas; in Korea, by the gentry; while the Miao, the Yao, and other nationalities are exploited by their own t'u-ssu and so on. . . . Consequently the First All-China Congress . . . calls upon the toiling masses of the national minorities to unite with the Chinese masses of workers and peasants in a joint struggle against their common oppressors and exploiters.[28]

Mao later criticized the 1931 Constitution for its theoretical position on the minority question that failed to consider the "concrete conditions" of China. After Mao's rise to power in 1935 the right to secession or even federation was no longer emphasized, although it remained official CCP policy. During the Long March, the Chinese Communist encountered their first actual national minorities; their experience was far from pleasant, despite later propaganda claims to the contrary. CCP propaganda on self-determination for nationalities was employed to some effect among the tribes of Yunnan but was of little use among the Tibetans of eastern Kham, most of whom simply fled at the approach of the Red Army. Those same areas of eastern Tibet had only recently been the scene (1905-1917 and 1930) of Sino-Tibetan conflict and Chinese attempts at military conquest. By their own account, the Red Army abandoned its nationalities policies and resorted to force to get supplies, capturing Tibetan livestock, harvesting Tibetan crops and taking grain supplies from monasteries.[29] In conversation with Edgar Snow, Mao described the Red Army's forcible confiscation of supplies as "our only foreign debt . . . some day we must pay the Mantzu and the Tibetans for the provisions we were obliged to take from them."[30] The experience of the Communists on the Long March convinced them that their nationalities policies would be insufficient to convince most minorities, especially the Tibetans, to voluntarily join the Chinese state.

---

28. Ibid., 165.
29. *Tibet 1950-67*, 761.
30. Edgar Snow, *Red Star Over China* (New York: Grove Press, 1973), 203.

At the end of the Long March, the Communists found themselves at Yenan, near the border with Inner Mongolia, which lay between them and the Soviet Union, their source of supply and possible line of retreat. To gain local support, the CCP made promises of self-determination and independence to the Inner Mongolians and the Hui of Kansu. The CCP also emphasized its minorities policies after the creation of the KMT-CCP United Front against the Japanese in 1937, in order to contrast CCP policy with the assimilationism of the KMT. The CCP promised minority nationalities either federation or independence: "National self-determination means that an oppressed minority people have the right to arrange their own political life as they see fit and the right to either join other nationalities in a federated state or keep separate from them."[31]

Mao's statements during the same period never went so far as to promise independence. In a talk with Edgar Snow in 1936, Mao promised federative status to Tibet and Sinkiang and assumed that Outer Mongolia would also become part of a Chinese federation: "When the people's revolution has been victorious in China, the Outer Mongolian Republic will automatically become a part of the Chinese federation, at their own will. The Mohammedan and Tibetan peoples likewise will form autonomous republics attached to the China federation."[32] Mao's statement that Mongolia would "automatically" return to Chinese sovereignty is perhaps based upon an unrealistic assumption that relations between fraternal socialist states would transcend Soviet strategic interests. Mao's chauvinism is evident in his belief that the MPR, Tibet and Turkestan would federate with China "at their own will."[33]

In 1938 Mao reiterated his conception of the CCP's minority nationality policy and its anticipated alleviation of nationalities' traditional fears of Han control and assimilation: "The Meng, Hui, Tsang, Miao, Yao, I and Fan minorities must be allowed to have equal rights with the Han people.

---

31. "The Nationality Problem in China During the Anti-Japanese War," as quoted in Lee Fu-hsiang, "The Turkic-Moslem Problem in Sinkiang: A Case Study of the Chinese Communists' Nationality Policy." (Ph.D. diss. Rutgers University, 1973), 93. Lee makes much of the wording of this statement, which seems to define self-determination as a right only of oppressed minorities; the right would theoretically disappear if a minority were not oppressed; a socialist state was by definition incapable of oppression, therefore the right to self-determination could only be claimed against the KMT. Ibid. Liu Shao-ch'i was in charge of propaganda on the policy on self-determination. For some of the statements he made at the time, Liu was charged by Red Guards in 1967 with advocating the heresy of "national separatism." Connor, *National Question*, 81.

32. Snow, *Red Star Over China*, 96.

33. Lee Fu-hsiang suggests that Mao proffered federative status to Tibet, Turkestan and Mongolia only as a strategy to induce Mongolia to return to the Chinese fold. Lee Fu-hsiang, "Turkic-Moslem Problem in Sinkiang," 95.

Under the principle of common struggle against Japan, they have the right to control their own affairs, and, at the same time, unite with the Han people to establish a unified country."[34] Under Mao, CCP minority nationalities policy reverted to the traditionalist Han assimilationist doctrine that the only thing minority nationalities wanted was equal treatment within a Chinese state. In 1945 Mao contrasted CCP policy on minorities with that of the KMT, claiming that, while the KMT had abandoned Sun Yat-sen's doctrine on self-determination, the CCP still upheld it:

In 1924, Dr. Sun Yat-sen wrote in his Manifesto of the First National Congress of the Kuomintang that "the Principle of Nationalism of the Kuomintang has a twofold meaning, first, the self-liberation of the Chinese nation, and second, the equality of all nationalities of China" and that "the Kuomintang solemnly declares that it recognizes the right to self-determination of all nationalities in China and that a free and united republic of China (a republic of China based on the free union of all nationalities) will be established after the victory of the anti-imperialist and anti-warlord revolution."

The Chinese Communist Party fully agrees with Dr. Sun's policy on nationalities as stated above.[35]

Both Nationalist and Communist Chinese promised equality to all nationalities, but only to be equally Chinese. In the final analysis, CCP policy on nationalities was little different from typical Chinese frontier assimilationist policies. Imperial China, Republican China and Communist China all had a common policy toward minority nationalities, derived from Chinese ideologies of cultural supremacy and frontier assimilationism.

Post-Revolutionary CCP Nationality Policy

With the victory over the KMT in 1949, the CCP claimed that the self-determination of nationalities was achieved along with the liberation of all the "Chinese" people. The "leading revolutionary task" of the Chinese revolution had been to liberate "the great mass of the Chinese people"

---

34. Mao Tse-tung, as quoted in Connor, *National Question*, 82. Meng are Mongols; Tsang must be Tibetans (from Wu-ssu-tsang, the Yuan transliteration of U-Tsang); I and Fan are traditional Chinese names for barbarians in general, in this case apparently referring to the minorities of Yunnan and Szechuan whom the Red Army encountered during the Long March.

35. Mao Tse-tung, "On Coalition Government," 24 April 1945, in *Selected Works of Mao Tse-tung*, vol III (Peking: Foreign Languages Press, 1965), 305.

from foreign imperialism; the great historical contradiction to overcome had been that between the Chinese people, including the minorities, and the imperialists, not that between the Chinese and the minority nationalities.[36] The fate of China's minority nationalities was "historically determined" by both Chinese cultural ideology and by Marxist-Leninist doctrine to be assimilation within the Chinese "multinational state."

The CCP also denied minority nationalities the political status of federation, citing the particular "concrete conditions" of China. No nationality of the People's Republic of China (PRC) was comparable in population, or, it was implied, in culture, to the Han. Therefore, unlike the Soviet Union, the PRC could not logically be organized as a federation of equal national states. Russia had been an imperialist state and therefore had to recognize the formerly independent status of its colonies. China had not only not been imperialist, but was itself a nation oppressed by imperialism; the task of the Chinese revolution was therefore to liberate the Chinese, along with their "national minorities," from imperialism. This doctrine was elaborated with the theory that China had been in the precapitalist stage of development and thus, according to Marxist ideology, could not have been in an imperialistic relationship with its minorities.

The federal system was also considered impractical because national territorial boundaries in most cases could not be drawn. This conclusion was made more apparently logical by making no distinction between China's internal and external nationalities. The Chinese did not wish to emphasize that the frontier nations were in any way different from the internal minorities; federation would seemingly accord recognition to the frontier nations' political as well as territorial and cultural uniqueness and thus possibly perpetuate those characteristics. None of China's minorities, it was claimed, were in exclusive possession of contiguous territories free of other minorities or Han Chinese, and were therefore considered undeserving of federal status. These circumstances were characterized as typical of China's minority nationalities, thus denying any separate or unique status to the frontier nations. The frontier nations were admittedly of a distinctly different national, territorial and political status, but they could be equated in terms of smallness of population and lack of cultural development (as seen by the Chinese) with the internal minorities. The CCP's decision to accord minority nationality status to many small internal nationalities, some of whom differed from the Han only in superficial aspects, or who were in fact descendants of Han who had migrated to minority areas and adopted minority customs, served to

---

36. Chang Chih-i, in Moseley, *Party and National Question*, 56.

further trivialize the definition of nationality in the PRC to the detriment of the frontier nations.[37]

The populations of the Inner Asian nations were almost insignificant in relation to the Han Chinese, but their territories and resources were very significant. China had substantial security considerations in the frontier territories. The frontier nations involved China in international issues, including trans-border populations (Thai, Tibetan, Kazakh, Mongol), pan-nationalism (Turkic or Mongol), and international religious ties (Buddhism and Islam). Chinese history was full of instances of invasion from the Inner Asian frontiers, and, while the Inner Asians themselves might no longer pose a threat, their territories were open to imperialist intrigues or territorial encroachment of states, including fraternal socialist states, bordering Inner Asia.[38] China's security interests demanded that no frontier nationality be given the choice of secession; the Chinese realized that, if given that choice, Tibet would certainly seek independence, as would the Uighur of Sinkiang, while the Inner Mongols would undoubtedly seek to join the MPR.

Instead of self-determination (in its secessionist meaning) or federation, the CCP adopted a system of "national regional autonomy," which was said to be in accord with Marxist-Leninist principles as well as the "concrete conditions" of China. National minority areas would be divided into counties, districts and regions, all of which would be "autonomous," but which would be integral parts of a unitary Chinese state. The CCP considered the system of regional autonomy to be much more flexible and practical under Chinese conditions where minorities were all assumed to be mixed with other minorities or the Han Chinese; meaningful territorial boundaries would not have to be drawn and the PRC's political system of "democratic centralism" could function more efficiently.

The People's Republic of China was established in 1949 by convening a Chinese People's Political Consultative Conference (CPPCC). The CPPCC evolved out of the CCP's anti-Japanese United Front and the 1945 Political Consultative Conference, which had attempted to form a coali-

---

37. June Dreyer, *China's Forty Millions: Minority Nationalities and National Integration in the People's Republic of China* (Cambridge: Harvard University Press, 1976), 143.

38. The US received information about Mao's meeting with Stalin in Moscow (December 1949-February 1950) indicating that negotiations were hung up over Soviet demands for special economic and political privileges in Manchuria and Sinkiang and a "buffer" status for Sinkiang, Chinghai and Tibet. Peiping Embassy to Secretary of State, 13 February 1950, National Archives, 793B.00/2-1350. The Soviet Union was reportedly allowed some economic privileges in Manchuria and Sinkiang until the mid-1950s, in exchange for Soviet assistance to the PRC.

tion government with the KMT. The CPPCC was composed of representatives of China's non-communist political parties and the minority nationalities, with the CCP dominating in representation and actual decision making power.[39] On 29 September 1949 the CPPCC adopted a Common Program, on whose principles the PRC was established two days later, on 1 October. The Common Program's provisions regarding nationalities were as follows:

> Article 9. All nationalities within the boundaries of the People's Republic of China shall have equal rights and duties.

> Article 50. All nationalities within the boundaries of the People's Republic of China are equal. They shall establish unity and mutual aid among themselves, and shall oppose imperialism and their own public enemies, so that the People's Republic of China will become a big fraternal and cooperative family composed of all its nationalities. Nationalism and chauvinism shall be opposed. Acts involving discrimination, oppression, and disrupting the unity of the various nationalities shall be prohibited.

> Article 51. Regional autonomy shall be exercised in areas where national minorities are concentrated, and various kinds of autonomous organizations for the different nationalities shall be set up according to the size of the respective peoples and regions. In places where different nationalities live together and in the autonomous areas of the national minorities, the different nationalities shall each have an appropriate number of representatives in the local organs of state power.

> Article 52. All national minorities within the boundaries of the People's Republic of China shall have the right to join the People's Liberation Army and to organize local people's public security forces in accordance with the unified military system of the state.

> Article 53. All national minorities shall have freedom to develop their spoken and written languages, to preserve or reform their traditions, customs, and religious beliefs. The people's government shall assist the masses of all national minorities in their political, economic, cultural, and educational development.[40]

Gone were any references to self-determination, even in principle. All of China's national minority territories were now integral parts of the PRC; any acts that undermined their unity within China, presumably including any mention of the previously promised right to self-determi-

---

39. Representatives of national minorities constituted 2.2 percent of the membership of the CPPCC. Lee Fu-hsiang, "Turkic-Moslem Problem in Sinkiang," 103.

40. Common Program of the Chinese People's Political Consultative Conference, 29 September 1949, in Theodore H.E. Chen, ed., *The Chinese Communist Regime: Documents and Commentary* (New York: Praeger, 1967), 34.

nation, were prohibited. The system of national regional autonomy was said to have been decided upon by nationalities' representatives at the CPPCC. In fact, the system of national regional autonomy had already been implemented on 1 May 1947 by the creation of the Inner Mongolian Autonomous Region (IMAR). CCP control had been established in the Inner Mongolian region well in advance of the final victory over the KMT, thus allowing the Chinese Communists to create a model for political organization of nationalities in an area where the CCP had full military control, amongst a nationality already substantially assimilated, and where previous political preparations had been made by the cultivation of numerous Mongol cadres.

In the 1952 General Program for the Implementation of Regional Autonomy for Minorities, nationalities' autonomy was further circumscribed. According to the General Program: "Each autonomous area is an integral part of the territory of the People's Republic of China. The autonomous organ of each autonomous area is a local government led by the government of the next higher level, under the unified leadership of the central government." The duty of each autonomous organ of an autonomous area was described as to "educate and guide the people living in the area towards unity and mutual assistance between all nationalities of the country, and towards love for the People's Republic of China in which all nationalities live together in a spirit of fraternity and cooperation like one big family."[41]

Nationalities' autonomy was not to include economic control, which was "subject to the unified financial control of the state." Autonomous areas were to undergo "reforms," led by "local leaders who are associated with the people" and cadres who "have a highly developed sense of patriotism." The people of autonomous areas were guaranteed the rights of "freedom of thought, speech, publication, assembly, association, correspondence, person, domicile, change of domicile, religious belief, and the freedom to hold processions and demonstrations." The final article allocated the interpretation or amendment of these rights and all other provisions of the General Program exclusively to the Central Government.[42]

Similar provisions were repeated in the 1954 Constitution, which stated, in Article 3:

> The People's Republic of China is a unified state of many nationalities. All the nationalities are equal. Discrimination against or oppression of any

---

41. General Program of the People's Republic of China for the Implementation of Regional Autonomy for Minorities, 9 August 1952, in *Policy Towards Nationalities of the People's Republic of China* (Peking: Foreign Languages Press, 1953), 1.

42. Ibid.

nationality, or any act that undermines the unity of the nationalities, is prohibited. All the nationalities have freedom to use and foster the growth of their spoken and written languages, and to preserve or reform their own customs or ways. Regional autonomy shall be exercised in areas entirely or largely inhabited by minorities. Such autonomous areas are inalienable parts of the People's Republic of China.[43]

The 1954 Constitution specified that national minority autonomous areas might be established at the *ch'u* (region, equivalent to provincial status), *chou* (prefecture, within an autonomous region or province) or *hsien* (county, within another nationality district or a Han district) levels. The CCP justified its system of national regional autonomy on the basis that it allowed for the exercise of autonomy by scattered nationality populations wherever they were found, rather than only in a single region (as would be the case under a federal system) or as individual members of a minority nationality (as would be the case in a system of national autonomy).[44] National *regional* autonomy was purportedly the most appropriate for the situation of China's minorities because it allowed for the exercise of collective autonomy by minorities in their scattered areas of concentration:

This national regional autonomy is a correct combination of national autonomy and regional autonomy, a correct combination of economic and political factors; this not only makes it possible for a nationality living in a compact community to enjoy the right to autonomy, but also enables nationalities which live together to enjoy the right of autonomy. Thus, practically all nationalities—those with large populations as well as those with small ones, those which live in big compact communities as well as those which live in small ones—have founded autonomous units commensurate with their size, fully enjoying the right of national autonomy. Such a system is a creation hitherto unknown in history.[45]

---

43. The Constitution of the People's Republic of China, 20 September 1954, in Henry Schwartz, comp., *Chinese Policies Towards Minorities: An Essay and Documents*, (Bellingham, Washington: Western Washington State College, 1971), 82. The same policy was reiterated in the 1975 Constitution and in the 1978 Constitution, which added that "any acts that undermine the unity of nationalities or instigate their secession are prohibited." Connor, National Question, 88.

44. National autonomy, or "extraterritorial national cultural autonomy," was a system proposed by Austrian Social Democrats in the early twentieth century. Under this system, members of minorities would exercise individual autonomous rights independent of their territorial location within the state.

45. Zhou Enlai (Chou En-lai), "Some Questions on Policy Towards Nationalities," *Beijing Review*, 3 March 1980, 22. Chou's speech was originally delivered at the meeting on nationalities policy at Tsingtao in 1957 but was not published at the time because it was considered too "liberal" for the rapidly leftist-shifting policy of the time.

The national regional autonomy system divided the frontier nations into numerous separate territorial political units, which prevented any from having a unified territory or united political representation. This allowed for the exercise of the principle of democratic centralism, or central rule from Peking, and thus was "appropriate" not for China's minorities but for China's security needs. Although organs of government within autonomous regions were theoretically to be determined "in accordance with the wishes of the majority of the people of the nationality or nationalities enjoying regional autonomy in a given area," in fact, nationality areas were organized in political units having the same function and same relation to the central government as local governmental organization in Han areas. The only right specifically granted to minorities was the right to use their own languages; all other special regulations regarding nationalities were subject to central government approval.[46] Governance of nationality areas was left up to the interpretation of the CCP and the Han Chinese; national regional autonomy would therefore have as much or as little actual meaning as the CCP decided.

The Chinese Communists could claim to have chosen a logical and practical system of political organization of China's minority nationalities, and one in accordance with the principles and goals of Marxism-Leninism; nevertheless, they had to explain why earlier promises of self-determination and federation had been abandoned, and demonstrate that the system adopted had, in fact, been a voluntary choice of the nationalities concerned. Elaborate evidence was evoked to demonstrate the voluntary nature of the nationalities' common revolutionary struggle along with the Han, and the nationalities' voluntary choice both for inclusion within the Chinese state and for the Chinese socialist path. Chang Chih-i, deputy director of the United Front Work Department, writing in 1956, repeated the CCP's position that China's minority nationalities had achieved liberation in 1949 along with the Han Chinese:

As the Chinese revolution has evolved, so has the national question; the tasks imposed by the national question vary according to the way the revolution develops. . . . With each nationality in the country having achieved liberation, with the system of nationalities oppression basically abolished, and with the nationalities of our country having already entered the era of nationalities equality, can "national liberation" still be regarded as the task

---

46. The Constitution of China on National Autonomous Areas, in Wang Ke, "Regional Autonomy for National Minorities," *Peking Review*, 6 May 1958, 9. Only the right to use their own languages was specified; all other autonomous rights remained unspecified and limited by laws regarding local organs of state (Article 69), state law (Article 70), the military system of the state (Article 70), the Standing Committee of the National People's Congress (Article 70) and the system of "democratic centralism."

of each national minority? Of course, it cannot. Since the system of nationalities oppression no longer exists, the aim of national liberation has
already been achieved. If it is said that people of certain nationalities still
suffer from oppression and slavery and still have the task of "liberation,"
that does not imply the oppression of small and weak nationalities by a
large one; rather, it has to do with the continuing existence of the system of
oppression—of the slave system and the feudal system—within certain
nationalities. If the people of each national minority seek complete liberation, they do so in order to eliminate their internal systems of oppression
and to develop their government, economy, and culture; there is no other
question involved. This concept must be made absolutely clear, for otherwise individual reactionary elements within certain nationalities might
take advantage of it.[47]

According to Chang Chih-i, common revolutionary struggle had so
united China's nationalities that the former issues of self-determination
or federation had been resolved by the nationalities' voluntary choice for
union within the "great family of the Motherland:

> Why does the Chinese Communist Party, with respect to the tasks concern-
> ing the national question in the transition period, give prominence to safe-
> guarding the unity of the motherland and nationalities solidarity rather
> than the principle constantly emphasized by Lenin—that of "national self-
> determination"? . . . Led and instructed by the Chinese Communist Party,
> the people of each nationality had already heightened their internationalist
> and patriotic consciousness, greatly changed and transcended their original
> situation of mutual antagonism, and gradually formed bonds of equality,
> unity, mutual help and cooperation as a basis for realizing common politi-
> cal aims and interests. Therefore it was in accord with this noble wish of the
> people of all nationalities that the Chinese Communist Party advocated the
> principles of nationalities equality and national regional autonomy within
> the unity of the great family of the motherland and discontinued the slogan
> of national self-determination and federalism. Consequently, the question
> of national division or national separation does not even arise in present-
> day circumstances: such schemes would inevitably meet with the violent
> opposition of the broad masses of all nationalities.[48]

Self-determination, Chang explained, was in any case not "an invari-
able thing," but a principle employed by Marxists "for the purpose of uti-
lizing the struggle against national oppression for the higher purpose of
an anti-imperial war." With the defeat of imperialism, national oppression would automatically disappear, and with it the need for national

---

47. Chang Chih-i, in Moseley, *Party and National Question*, 57.
48. Ibid., 68.

self-determination, at least in its separatist meaning. As Chang explained the dialectical view of self-determination, there were two ways to understand self-determination—either as "freedom to separate or as freedom to unite."[49]

The system of national regional autonomy was based upon the theory that China was a "unitary multinational state." As Chou En-lai explained, the Chinese nationalities had opted for union within China's "big family of nationalities" as part of a natural historical process; in pre-liberation times, they were already integrated to such an extent that none occupied a distinct territory free of Han or other minority nationalities:

> China has a large number of nationalities, and they live together with such a distribution of nationalities, we could not conceivably adopt the Soviet pattern of forming national republics. This is because a national republic so formed must be an independent economic unit with the overwhelming majority of the people of one nationality living there in compact community. . . . Historically the situation in China was entirely different from that in tsarist Russia. In China the nationalities developed in such a way that the areas they inhabited became interlocked. . . . This resulted in the phenomenon of various nationalities living together in the same area, with relatively few or even very few examples of a nationality living in a compact community by itself.[50]

The threat of international imperialism and the inability of any of "China's minorities" to exist or to develop independently of China was cited by Chang Chih-i as sufficient reason why no nationality could be allowed to separate from the Chinese state:

> Only in the case of the national minorities of Sinkiang and Tibet was there a high, virtually complete degree of concentration. But in political, social, economic, cultural, and other respects, these peoples, like the other national minorities, were ill prepared for separation; all the national minorities (including those of Sinkiang and Tibet), because of cultural and historical conditions, and especially because of close economic relations, formed with the Han a single, unbreakable unit. In recent history, certain national minorities in our country have experienced independence movements. Not only did these meet with complete failure, but before one foot could get picked up to walk away from the motherland, the other foot had already sunk in the trap set by the imperialists. This historical lesson has served as a warning for the leading personalities of China's comparatively large

---

49. Ibid., 69.
50. Chou En-lai, "Some Questions on Policy Towards Nationalities," *Beijing Review*, 3 March 1980, 20.

national minorities. Assuming that they did become separate without falling into the arms of the imperialists and that their "independence" followed its own course, the situation of such national minorities would simply have been that, having missed the benefits of the victory of China's revolution, including the fraternal, progressive help of the Han people, their difficulties and suffering would only have been made more acute.[51]

In fact, it was Chinese interests, not those of the minority nationalities, that determined that frontier territories should not be allowed to separate from China. Their separation would not be in the interests of the Chinese for strategic defense reasons and because the frontier territories were thought to be rich in the natural resources necessary for China's economic development. These territories were also regarded as virtually empty space into which the Chinese population could expand; in doing so, they would, of course, assist in the development of the minority peoples, and also, though this was unstated, finally resolve the nationalities issue in China. China would "liberate" the nationalities in question, help alleviate their labor shortages by means of an influx of Han "advisors," and allow them to participate in China's march to socialism, in exchange for their territories and resources. As Mao wrote in 1956:

> The population of the minority nationalities in our country is small, but the area they inhabit is large. The Han people comprise 94 per cent of the population, an overwhelming majority. If they practised Han chauvinism and discriminated against the minority peoples, that would be very bad. And who has more land? The minority nationalities, who occupy 50 to 60 per cent of the territory. We say China is a country vast in territory, rich in resources and large in population; as a matter of fact it is the Han nationality whose population is large and the minority nationalities whose territory is vast and whose resources are rich, or at least in all probability their resources under the soil are rich.[52]

As Moseley has commented on Mao's statement,

> Mao's is a typically Han Chinese approach to the matter. The corollary of his lack of concern about the national minorities as such is his very deep concern about the adhesion to China of the vast territories inhabited by them. For Mao, the inhabitants were but one of the given characteristics of the frontier regions, and one that was not unalterable.[53]

The CCP achieved a semantic resolution to China's nationalities ques-

51. Chang Chih-i, in Moseley, *Party and National Question*, 73.

52. Mao Tse-tung, *On the Ten Major Relationships* (Peking: Foreign Languages Press, 1977), 17.

53. Moseley, *Party and National Question*, 19.

tion by defining the Han Chinese as but another nationality comparable to all the others. The "broad masses of all nationalities" who had voluntarily and collectively opted for political union included the majority nationality, the Han, who were defined as just one of the nationalities of "multinational China."[54] The overwhelming predominance of the population of the "Han nationality" in relation to any other nationality or to all other nationalities combined in the Chinese "multinational state" assured that the will of the Han majority would predominate. The "noble wish of the people of all nationalities" was thus in fact the will of the Han majority, since 95 percent of the "people of all nationalities" were Han. Majority nationality (Han) determinism was thus substituted for national self-determination. As Dawa Norbu has pointed out,

> In general it is true that the principle of self-determination does not have any practical meaning in any socialist country, and China is no exception to this. But in China the will of the dominant nation is openly imposed upon the national minorities as if it were the will of all nationalities.[55]

For most Chinese, there was literally no question of Tibet (or Mongolia or Turkestan) as an independent state; in the Chinese mentality, these were territories of China (based upon unilateral claims of China) and had been so for centuries. The Chinese had great difficulty in comprehending that any of these "barbarian" nations would actually want to be independent of China when that independence meant either perpetuation of barbarism or domination by foreign imperialism. However, Tibet was clearly an exception to CCP rationalizations for its national regional autonomy system. Tibet clearly satisfied Chou's criteria for federative status, "an independent economic unit with the overwhelming majority of the people of one nationality living there in compact community," and therefore should have been allowed federative, if not independent, status. The PRC's justifications for its national regional autonomy system obscured Tibet's national territorial integrity and identity, its formerly autonomous or *de facto* independent political status and its legitimate right to national self-determination.

---

54. "Han" thus became an ethnonym, like Tibetan or Mongol, no longer equivalent to "Chinese." "Chinese" (*Zhong Guo Ren*) became a political terminology defining all inhabitants of the PRC. Thus, Mongols and Tibetans were Mongol Chinese or Tibetan Chinese just as the Han were Han Chinese. It was no longer permissible, therefore, to distinguish between Tibetans and Han as Tibetan and Chinese.

55. Dawa Norbu, "Marxism, Nationalism and Revolution: The Rise of Neo-Nationalism in Communist Countries" (Ph.D. diss., University of California, 1982), 605.

Implementation of Nationality Policy

Chinese physical control in frontier territories was secured by the entry, by force in the case of Tibet, of the Chinese People's Liberation Army. PLA vanguard units were trained in nationalities policy and instructed to treat local peoples well, to pay for all supplies and to cultivate good will by helpful assistance whenever possible. Once entry was achieved, the PLA repressed open resistance and began a campaign of repression of anti-Chinese nationalists as "counterrevolutionaries." Physical control was not finally secured in frontier areas of Sinkiang and Tibet until a transportation infrastructure linking those areas with China was completed. In Sinkiang, this took the form of the Lanchou to Urumchi railroad, and, in Tibet, the Szechuan-Tibet and Chinghai-Tibet motor roads. Once these transportation links were opened, Chinese personnel could be supplied and additional military forces dispatched in case of rebellion. The completion of these essential links allowed the Chinese to begin the alteration of local political institutions and the physical and political integration of these territories into the Chinese state.

The territorial format for Chinese political control was the system of "national regional autonomy." The majority nationality of Sinkiang, the Uighur, were wherever possible divided into districts containing a collective majority of other nationalities, including Kazakhs, Kirghiz and Mongols. The Uighurs' predominance over other nationalities and their leadership of Turkic nationalism was diluted by emphasis upon other nationalities' autonomous rights in relation to the Uighur.[56] The already small proportion of Mongols in Inner Mongolia was further reduced by inclusion of several predominantly Chinese districts. Tibetan nationality territories were divided among one Tibetan autonomous region and ten Tibetan autonomous *chou* in Chinghai, Kansu, Szechuan and Yunnan.

Once physical control over frontier territories was secured, large-scale Chinese colonization was initiated in all frontier nationality areas, with the exception of that portion of Tibet intended to become the Tibet Autonomous Region. Colonization was an essential element of CCP frontier policy as it had been in past Chinese history. Only colonization could secure China's borders and permanently resolve the "nationalities question." The Chinese mistrusted the loyalty of frontier nationalities, with good reason, and were willing to entrust the defense of China's frontiers only to Han Chinese. Colonization was begun in earnest in Inner Mongolia, where the Mongols were already a minority in relation to the Chinese, and in Sinkiang, where there were few Chinese (the 1949 population of Chinese in Sinkiang was estimated at only 200,000).[57] By 1949

---

56. Lee Fu-hsiang, "Turkic-Moslem Problem in Sinkiang," 173.
57. Ibid., 313.

Chinese outnumbered Mongols in Inner Mongolia by a ratio of 5 to 1. This proportion was increased by the colonization program of the PRC until in 1962 the ratio of Chinese to Mongols reached 7 to 1.[58]

Colonization of Sinkiang was initiated by the Chinese Production and Construction Corps (PCC), which was composed of PLA units, decommissioned PLA soldiers and civilian colonists. Colonization by means of the PCC, a system derived from the military-agricultural colonies of China's traditional frontier policy, was intended to solve the problems of national integration, development and defense. These units engaged in land reclamation, water conservancy and agricultural, industrial, transportation and mining enterprises. Their military and collectivist organization was intended as a model for the socialist transformation of China's frontier areas. After completion of the Lanchou to Urumchi railroad in 1954, recruitment of civilian colonists began; by 1957 the PCC in Sinkiang had some 300,000 members, almost all of whom were Han Chinese.[59] By 1964 the Han in Sinkiang numbered 3,500,000 out of a total population of eight million.[60]

Tibet, or at least that part of central Tibet scheduled to become the Tibet Autonomous Region (TAR), was immune, at least temporarily, from the colonization program, although many of the PLA and Chinese cadres initially sent to Tibet eventually became permanent residents. Tibetan areas of Amdo and Kham remained relatively free from large-scale colonization, at least in higher altitude semi-nomadic and nomadic areas due to their unsuitability for agriculture. Low altitude areas were more immediately subjected to colonization. However, systematic Chinese colonization began in many areas of Chinghai, even high altitude areas, by means of the prison and labor camp system.

Although the PRC's prison and labor camps were organized by province, and prisoners usually remained within the province of their arrest, many of the worst common criminals and those convicted of counterrevolutionary crimes were sent to Sinkiang and Chinghai, where they constructed roads and highways and engaged in large-scale land reclamation and mining projects. Most of these prisoners were serving long terms and were usually required to remain in the same camp after release as low paid labor, and were thus essentially colonists. Local nationality prisoners also filled these camps.

Implementation of regional autonomy was delayed in some areas until

---

58. Asia Watch Report, *Crackdown in Inner Mongolia* (Washington: Human Rights Watch, 1991), 18.

59. Donald H. McMillen, *Chinese Communist Power and Policy in Xinjiang, 1949-1977* (Boulder: Westview Press, 1979), 65.

60. Lee Fu-hsiang, "Turkic-Moslem Problem in Sinkiang," 313.

political control was firmly secured and sufficient nationality cadres were recruited to create a facade of local administration; Sinkiang achieved autonomous status in 1955 and the TAR only in 1965. Membership in the CCP was purported to be the means by which nationalities would exercise local autonomy, but, in fact, nationality cadres often became agents of the Chinese for the subjugation of their own people. Local governmental institutions were altered by the institution of collaborative committees and political organs preparatory to granting "regional autonomy." These included social organizations, which gradually took on more political functions, as well as "preparatory committees" established to plan the transition to national regional autonomy. The preparatory committees, composed of collaborative local officials overseen by Chinese cadres, gained for the Chinese a role in local governmental functions, leading inevitably to Chinese usurpation of local political authority.

According to provisions of the national regional autonomy system, heads of local governmental organs should be of the local nationality. As the system actually operated, however, nationality cadres in positions of symbolic authority were always seconded by a Chinese vice-chairman, who retained all actual authority.[61] In any case, the ultimate ruling authority in nationality areas resided not with governmental organs but with PLA and CCP "work committees." Such was the monopoly of power in the hands of Chinese cadres that Chinese officials in some nationality areas eventually became semi-independent potentates similar to the warlords of past Chinese history. This phenomenon was exacerbated by central government ignorance of actual conditions in minority areas and local Chinese cadres' monopoly on information provided to the center.

The CCP furthered its goal of attaining political control in nationality regions by creating social divisions and class conflict, while at the same time cultivating collaborators among all classes under the "United Front." The United Front policy was intended to smooth the transition to Chinese control by retaining some of the former ruling class in symbolic positions of authority. The United Front policy derived from CCP collaboration with the KMT against the Japanese; it was later applied to noncommunist political parties and interest groups, including national minorities. The United Front was described by Mao as a policy of the "new democratic" phase of political alliance, during which all patriotic elements would unite under the leadership of the Communist Party to

---

61. This was actually provided for by the Standing Committee of the National People's Congress in 1955, which decreed that vice-chairmen of people's councils in minority nationality regions did not have to be of the local nationality. Ibid., 224.

oppose imperialism.[62] The United Front was a tactic for consolidating CCP predominance under an ostensible coalition of political power. In national minority areas, the United Front was an alliance with former traditional leaders and "progressive" members of the lower classes. The ultimate goal of United Front policy in interior China was to circumscribe and then liquidate the power of the capitalist and gentry class; in minority areas, the goal was to eliminate the power of the traditional ruling class.

The United Front policy was described as working "from above and from below," with both upper class collaborators and lower class sympathizers. As Chang Chih-i described it, the united front of nationalities, "with the Han nationality as its core," consisted of two alliances: "The first alliance is that between the Chinese working class and the laboring people of each national minority. This alliance is the foundation of China's revolutionary united front of all nationalities; on this foundation there exists the alliance between the laboring people of all China's nationalities and the non-laboring people among the national minorities." The second alliance, that between the "laboring people of all nationalities" and the minority upper class, or "non-laboring people," was necessary because the Party recognized that the upper classes still exercised considerable influence:

> Every aspect of development in the national minority regions is, generally speaking, different from that among the Han people: the consciousness of the masses is lower, resulting in a comparatively slow expansion of revolutionary strength among the great mass of the people; as already described, the alienation among China's nationalities and especially between the Han nationality and the minorities, still persists; and the influence of religion among the masses of the national minorities is vastly deeper and more widespread than it is within the Han nationality. For these reasons, within each national minority the upper-level personages have definite connections—based on nationality and, in some cases, on religion as well—with the laboring people. They have long been the public leaders of their respective nationalities. In certain national minorities, people of this type have a great deal of influence and authority. The Chinese Communist Party has made a correct estimate of the influence and usefulness these upper-level personages can contribute to the resolution of the national question and the safeguarding of nationalities unity; it recognizes, moreover, that these cir-

---

62. The "new democratic" phase was equated with the bourgeois-democratic revolution. Moseley, *Party and National Question*, 103. The chief Chinese negotiator at the conclusion of the 17-Point Agreement, Liu Wei-han, was director of the United Front Work Department. Chang Chih-i specifically credited the success of those negotiations and Tibet's "peaceful liberation" to the United Front policy of uniting with the former ruling class. Ibid., 133.

cumstances are the product of a long history of national and religious oppression.[63]

Upper class secular and religious leaders were co-opted by honorific social and political positions and stipends from the Chinese government. The United Front policy of the Chinese Communists was thus somewhat like the *T'u-ssu* system of the past; however, under the regional autonomy system, local officials were closely supervised and eventually deprived of all but symbolic authority.[64]

The United Front alliance with the lower classes was based upon the theory of proletarian class unity against upper class oppression and exploitation. Members of the lower class were recruited by release from indenture or debt, elevation to symbolic social or political positions, economic support and the offer of education in China. Lower class collaborators were often recruited from the very lowest levels of society: social outcasts, criminals or outlaws, or the disgruntled of all sorts. These included any who were demonstratively sufferers of class oppression, such as indentured servants or "serfs"; outcasts such as butchers, blacksmiths and those who disposed of the dead; or beggars, prostitutes and thieves. Those of the most oppressed classes or outcastes were considered to be the most receptive to communist propaganda, since they had the most to gain from an overturning of society.

The United Front policy involved the creation of a variety of social organizations, led by members of the upper class but open to all classes. These included youth, women's, and religious organizations. United Front organizations were employed to propagate a "progressive" message and to initiate political campaigns. They were also involved in the organization of secular education and the recruitment of children for schooling in China. A primary means of cultivating activists among both upper and lower classes was by offering scholarships for education in China. Nationalities Institutes were established to train minority children; an institute was created at Hsienyang near Sian (modern Xian) in

---

63. As Moseley points out, the united front policy is an implicit admission that national unity—at least at this stage—is in fact more prevalent than class unity. Chang Chih-i rationalized this admission by the argument that failure to unite with the upper class among the national minorities might jeopardize the "security and unity of the motherland." Therefore, "uniting with the upper-level elements among the national minorities who have definite connections with the masses has no objective other than that of serving the interests of the laboring people of each nationality." Ibid., 131.

64. Local nationality officials were presented with new seals of office by the Communists, in imitation of the traditional practice whenever a new dynasty had come to power in the past. George Moseley, *The Consolidation of the South China Frontier* (Berkeley: University of California Press, 1973), 114.

Shansi specifically for Tibetans of the lower class; upper class Tibetan children were sent to the Central Nationalities Institute in Peking. Nationalities Institutes were located in interior China rather than in the nationality areas in order to remove children from local cultural and political influences and to initiate assimilation to Chinese culture.[65]

All classes among the national minorities were subjected to propaganda campaigns intended to create proletarian class consciousness and to effect an ideological transformation of "local nationalist" sentiments into loyalty to the Chinese state. All available media were employed, including newspapers, magazines and books, public meetings and speeches, loudspeakers, radio (broadcast via loudspeakers), song, dance, drama and film. Minority populations, even in the most remote areas, were soon saturated with endless and inescapable propaganda, especially from loudspeakers, which were an ubiquitous aspect of life in Communist China. Themes concentrated on anti-imperialism, anti-exploitation and patriotism to China. The equal treatment to be accorded to nationalities under the CCP's nationalities policy was emphasized; anti-Han sentiments were diffused by contrasting the imperialist and exploitative policies of previous Chinese governments with the non-imperialist socialist internationalism of the "new Chinese."

CCP nationality policy was generally successful in defusing nationalities' resistance until Chinese control could be secured. The United Front policy effectively co-opted and divided classes within nationalities, preventing unified resistance. Much of the Party's propaganda on equality of treatment and nationality autonomy was effective in defusing nationalities' apprehensions, at least temporarily. CCP nationalities policies and the system of national regional autonomy were intermediate solutions to the national question; having achieved its primary purpose of preserving the territorial integrity of the Chinese state, the Party could implement the more coercive measures of "democratic reforms and socialist transformation."

Party propaganda of the early 1950s portrayed the task of national unification as having been basically achieved, thanks to the efficacy of CCP nationalities policies. The Party was convinced that the application of Leninist nationalities doctrines had not only eliminated minorities' mistrust of the Han but had created a new type of Han cadre who refrained from mistreating minorities. While admitting some mistakes on the part of Han cadres (but not in nationalities policy itself), the Party blamed any and all actual resistance to the imposition of its control in minority areas on foreign rather than indigenous factors:

---

65. Israel Epstein, *Tibet Transformed* (Beijing: New World Press, 1983), 357.

Many instances have been exposed where imperialism and its lackey, the Chiang Kai-shek remnant bandits, have incited the minority nationalities to riot. Ample proof has been found of such criminal acts showing that almost every rebellion in the minority nationalities region has been instigated by secret agents and counter-revolutionaries and has resulted from senior individuals of the minority nationality being first duped by the enemy plots.[66]

While warning against local nationalism and pan-nationalism (pan-Turkic, Mongol and Tibetan nationalism were implied), the CCP magnanimously admitted in the early 1950s that "great Hanism poses the principle threat in present national relationships."[67] However, all such chauvinistic sins, both local nationalism and great Hanism, could be dissolved by the application of the principles of Marxism-Leninism:

> The effective method of overcoming the trend towards pan-nationalism and the trend toward local nationalism is for all minorities to follow the principle of Marxism-Leninism, to strengthen education concerning patriotism and internationalism and educational policy, and to practice self-criticism. At the moment, it is most essential to educate the Han nationality cadres and people and lead them to carry out self-criticisms in order to overcome great Hanism and the remaining influences of great Hanism. Great Hanism, in essence, is an expression of the bourgeois thought of nationality relations. The bourgeois thought, particularly great Hanism, must first be overcome in our nationalities work before equality among nationalities can be truly realized and the various minorities effectively helped to overcome all sorts of local nationalism.[68]

In a September 1956 directive of the State Council, Liu Shao-ch'i said that the main problem in nationality relations remained Han chauvinism, which it was essential to overcome because the nationalities (or rather their territories and their resources) had a large role to play in China's socialist construction:

> To overlook the important part played by the national minorities in the socialist construction of our country is another manifestation of great-Hanism. Although the minority peoples constitute only 6% of the country's total population, the areas inhabited by them roughly amount to 60% of the

---

66. "Great Success in the Suppression of Counter-Revolutionaries During Past 3 Years," *New China News Agency (NCNA)*, 27 September 1952, in *Survey of China Mainland Press* (Hong Kong: United States Consulate), 31.

67. "Summary of Basic Experiences in Promoting Regional Autonomy," 9 September 1953, in *Tibet 1950-67*, 28.

68. Ibid.

country's total area. Many of these areas are rich in various kinds of industrial resources. It is clearly wrong to think that our country can be built into
a great socialist country through the efforts of the Han people alone, without the concerted efforts and active participation of the national minorities.[69]

Gaps in the perceptions of both sides—minorities and Han Chinese—
were evident; many minorities actually thought that autonomy meant
that the Chinese would leave them alone: "In certain districts, some of the
minority nationalities thought that after the realization of regional autonomy, they could live separately from the Hans and get along without the
Han people."[70] In a speech on nationality relations in 1952, Ulanfu dispelled the illusion that autonomy meant that minorities would not have
to implement "democracy" ("democratic reforms") or that minorities
could hope to be left alone:

> Some tend to think that regional autonomy means independence and self-
> government without leadership by the people's government of a higher
> level. Some regard regional autonomy as mere autonomy without any
> democracy. Others believe that, with regional autonomy, they have nothing
> more to do with the Han people. Still others are afraid that, when regional
> autonomy is established, the Han cadres who have been helping them in
> their work whole-heartedly might leave them. We have given explanations
> and carried out an educational campaign to dispel such doubts, misgivings
> and misunderstandings.[71]

The Chinese Communists countered the misconception that autonomy
meant that minorities would exist apart from the Han Chinese with the
assertion that the nationalities could not develop culturally or economically without the assistance of the "advanced nationality," the Han:

> As the Han nationality is the bulwark of the revolution . . . and represents
> the pivot of solidarity among the various nationalities in our country, the
> strengthening of the solidarity centered on the Han nationality . . . [is] the
> basic task concerning the settlement of the question of nationalities. . . .

---

69. Liu Shao-ch'i, "Political Report of the Central Committee of the Communist Party of
China," 15 September 1956, in Robert R. Bowie and John K. Fairbank, eds., *Communist China
1955-1959: Policy Documents and Analysis* (Cambridge: Harvard University Press, 1962), 191.
70. "Great Success in the Suppression of Counter-Revolutionaries," 27 September 1952,
in *Survey of China Mainland Press*, 29.
71. Ulanfu, "Report on the General Programme for the Implementation of Regional
Autonomy for Nationalities," 8 August 1952, in *Policy Towards Nationalities of the People's
Republic of China*, 53.

For the sake of development and progress of the various national minorities and for the sake of building socialism . . . the national minorities should strive to learn from the Han nationality and welcome the help given by the Han nationality . . . the question of whether or not to seek help from the Han nationality and learn from the Han nationality is . . . the question of having or not having socialism and seeking or not seeking to develop and prosper the nationalities. Any thinking against learning from the Han nationality and against welcoming the help given by the Han nationality is completely wrong. Any conduct against the Han nationality is contradictory to the basic interests of the people of the national minorities and therefore must be resolutely opposed.[72]

Nationalities' "autonomy" in local political and cultural affairs was not to mean that they would be allowed to remain immune from the socialist transformation taking place in the PRC; the economic and cultural development of the minorities was regarded as inseparable from their political and social reform.[73] Despite guarantees of cultural and political autonomy, or promises that existing political institutions would be preserved (as in the case of Tibet), nationalities were required to undergo "democratic reforms" and "socialist transformation" along with the Han Chinese.

The Occupation of Tibet: 1951-1954

The first period of the Chinese occupation of Tibet was devoted to consolidation of Chinese physical control in preparation for Tibet's later political and social transformation. For the first four years, before the completion of motorable roads, Chinese control in Tibet was exceedingly tenuous. Preliminary Chinese strategy in Tibet was to adhere to the provisions of the 17-Point Agreement and CCP nationalities policies until control could be secured. At the same time, however, every effort was made to undermine the authority and functions of the "Tibet local government." Despite the promises of the 17-Point Agreement, the Chinese were not willing to tolerate for long the existence of a competing political authority. The Tibetan polity was to be circumscribed and then transformed into an "autonomous" nationality administration within the PRC's system of "national regional autonomy."

Tibet was unique among the frontier territories the CCP attempted to

72. Hsieh Fu-min, "Carry Through the Socialist Education Movement Opposing Local Nationalism," *Nationalities Unity*, no. 6 (March 1956), in Tibet 1950-1967, 271.

73. "Summary of Basic Experiences in Promoting Regional Autonomy," 9 September 1953, in *Tibet 1950-1967*, 37.

integrate into the Chinese state. Tibet had much greater geographic, cultural and political distinctiveness than any other "national minority" area, including Inner Mongolia and East Turkestan (Sinkiang). Tibetans were united by cultural and religious identity and a primarily latent but autochthonous nationalist consciousness. Tibet was the only formerly *de facto* independent state incorporated within the PRC; only Tibet had required an invasion and a negotiated agreement similar to an international treaty to do so. Tibet's national, political and territorial characteristics contradicted the CCP's justifications for the national regional autonomy system.

The 17-Point Agreement did not address the issue of Tibetan territorial boundaries.[74] Many Tibetans apparently assumed that all Tibetan cultural areas were to be treated alike under the provisions of the 17-Point Agreement. Ordinary Tibetans never made the distinction that eastern Tibet was not "Tibet" because it was not administered by the Tibetan Government at Lhasa. The Chinese, however, defined "Tibet" as only that territory of central Tibet under the direct authority of the Dalai Lama's government and decreed that the 17-Point Agreement should apply only to that area. Central Tibet (U-Tsang) was to be constituted as the Tibet Autonomous Region (TAR) while Kham and Amdo were to be divided into several autonomous districts within Chinghai, Szechuan, Kansu and Yunnan.

The Chinese justified these administrative divisions on historical and practical grounds. Amdo and Kham had been administratively separated from central Tibet since 1725; Amdo was in 1950 under the jurisdiction of Chinghai and Kham was theoretically under "Sikang." However, these political divisions were the legacy of the historical territorial encroachment of China upon Tibet and of unilateral Chinese political divisions of Tibetan territory. They were in any case political rather than national or cultural divisions; they were neither the boundaries of the Tibetan nation

---

74. The issue did, however, come up during the negotiations and were the subject of an "understanding" between the Tibetan delegates and Chou En-lai. Chou proposed that the territorial issue should not be regarded as of the same importance as before, since all of Tibet was now a part of the Chinese state. The more important issue now, he maintained, was economic; eastern Tibetan areas already under Chinese administration were at a stage of economic development similar to the Chinese landlord system, whereas central Tibet was still at the more primitive stage of feudal serfdom. Therefore, for reasons of economic development, eastern Tibet should be administered separately from central Tibet. Chou held out the possibility that Tibetan areas might be reunited within one administrative region once economic and political issues had been resolved. There was also an understanding that the area under the "Chamdo Liberation Committee" would be returned to the autonomous region of Tibet "at an appropriate time." Jigme Ngapo, personal communication, Washington, February 1995.

nor of the Tibetan nationality within the Chinese state. The divisions reflected Chinese strategic interests; China was, as in 1914 at Simla, intent upon placing as much territory as possible within Chinese provincial administration.

CCP nationalities doctrine prescribed that autonomous territorial units (autonomous regions, districts or counties) should correspond to areas where nationalities were in compact and contiguous occupation. Autonomous nationality units should not include significant numbers of Han, but might be composed of more than one minority nationality. Autonomous territorial status was theoretically granted to nationalities according to their current patterns of settlement, not according to former political divisions. All Tibetan nationality territory, including Amdo, where Tibetans were mixed with Mongols, should therefore have constituted a single autonomous region. CCP nationality policy nowhere states that a nationality cannot be divided between several autonomous units, but any contiguous territory where a single nationality is in the majority would logically constitute a nationality district. By the CCP's own criteria, the Tibetans deserved a single autonomous territory.

The fact that the divisions of Tibetan nationality territory were an exception to the CCP's criteria for its regional autonomy system was admitted by Chou En-lai in a speech in 1957, but the fact was obscured by reference to past political divisions perpetuated by the PRC:

> We often say that Xinjiang [Sinkiang] is a place where minority people are concentrated, but Xinjiang has 13 nationalities, not one. Tibet is comparatively unmixed, but this is only in the area under the jurisdiction of the Preparatory Committee for the Tibet Autonomous Region, whereas in other places the Tibetans also live among other nationalities. . . . There are only over one million Tibetans living in places under the jurisdiction of the Preparatory Committee for the Tibet Autonomous Region; another million or so live in the Tibetan autonomous prefectures and autonomous counties in Qinghai [Chinghai], Gansu [Kansu], Sichuan [Szechuan] and Yunnan Provinces. It is more convenient for these autonomous prefectures and counties to co-operate with the provinces in which they are located because of their closer economic ties.[75]

---

75. Zhou Enlai (Chou En-lai), "Some Questions on Policy Towards Nationalities," *Beijing Review*, 3 March 1980, 20. In his original speech, Chou reportedly used the terms "Outer Tibet" and "Inner Tibet" to refer to the area under the PCTAR and Tibetan areas in other provinces, respectively. This wording was changed to "area under the jurisdiction of the Preparatory Committee for the Tibet Autonomous Region" and "Tibetan autonomous prefectures and autonomous counties in Qinghai, Gansu, Sichuan and Yunnan" in the 1980 version. Jigme Ngapo, personal communication, Washington, February 1995. "Outer Tibet and Inner Tibet" no doubt brought up too many reminders of the Simla Conference, where this terminology was first proposed, and parallels with Inner and Outer Mongolia.

This argument was further elaborated by Party ideologists:

Fairly large numbers of Tibetans live in compact communities in Tibet. However, if the Tibetans who live in Szechuan, Chinghai, Kansu and Yunnan Provinces are taken into account, it is true to say that the Tibetans, like the other minority people of China, are dispersed in different areas of the country and do not live in compact communities in a single area.[76]

By this circular argument, the political divisions made by the Chinese Communists were justified not by the CCP's criteria for national regional autonomy, but by the political divisions made by the Ch'ing. Tibetans were only "dispersed in different areas" by the arbitrary political divisions created by the Chinese themselves. Only by means of arbitrary political divisions were Tibetans of Amdo and Kham defined as minorities within Chinese provinces. Chinese rationalizations denied the reality that all Tibetan cultural areas were contiguous and did in fact form a single nationality territory. It was "more convenient" to divide Tibetans among Chinese provinces not for economic reasons, but for the political reason that a unified Tibetan nationality area (or even the limited area of the TAR) could not justifiably be included within the PRC's system of national regional autonomy at all, but should more legitimately have formed a federative or even an independent state.

The CCP decision to make Chinghai a provincial unit, rather than including its minority districts within the TAR or creating a multinational autonomous region, was based upon historical precedent as well as political expediency. Under its previous Hui administration, Chinghai had been made a province by the KMT in 1928. However, Chinghai was a predominantly minority nationality province; the only significant Chinese population in Chinghai was in the provincial capital of Sining, a city with a population of several million Chinese. Six autonomous districts were created in Chinghai, of which five were Tibetan and one was combined Kazakh-Mongol-Tibetan.[77] Virtually all of the territory of

---

76. Wang Ke, "Regional Autonomy for National Minorities," *Peking Review*, 6 May 1958, 8.

77. These were Haipei (Tib. Tshochang, "north of Kokonor"), Hainan (Tib. Tsholho, "south of Kokonor"), Huangnan (Malho, "south of the Ma Chu," Yushu (Tib. Jyekundo) and Kuolo (Tib. Golok) Tibetan Autonomous Districts and Haisi (Tib. Tshonub, "west of Kokonor") Mongol-Tibetan-Kazakh Autonomous District. There is one Mongol autonomous prefecture within Huangnan Autonomous District and one Hui autonomous prefecture (contiguous to Kansu) within Haipei (Haibei) Autonomous District. The designation Kazakh has since been dropped from the Haisi (Haixi) Autonomous District, indicating that there are now few, if any, Kazakhs there. Haisi is divided into two areas separated by a portion of Yushu District.

Chinghai Province, with the exception of the city of Sining and the Sining valley (which is contiguous to Chinese inhabited areas of Kansu), was made up of autonomous districts of a majority Tibetan population, contiguous to the TAR and thus logically part of the TAR.

The two Tibetan autonomous districts of Kansu are also contiguous to Tibetan territory of Chinghai; the Tibetans of those districts were made a minority in a majority Han province only by being included in Kansu Province. Eastern Amdo became Kanlho (Southern Kansu) Autonomous District in Kansu. The Ngaba area of southeastern Amdo became Apa (Ngaba) Autonomous District of Szechuan. Ngaba is contiguous to Tibetan areas of Kham and Amdo; it was formerly a part of Kham. Ngaba Autonomous District has since been expanded to include the Ch'iang population to the east and is now designated Aba (Ngaba) Tibetan-Qiang (Ch'iang) Autonomous District.

Kham is contiguous to central Tibet; it should logically have been made part of the TAR. Instead, "Sikang" was made a separate Sikang Autonomous Region until 1956, when western Kham was incorporated within the TAR and eastern Kham was included within Szechuan as Kanze Autonomous District.[78] A portion of southern Kham was made Dechen Autonomous District of Yunnan.

Only Muli Tibetan Autonomous Prefecture, within the Yi Autonomous District of Yunnan, is not contiguous to other Tibetan occupied areas. The only other significant nationality within Tibetan autonomous districts of Chinghai, Kansu, Szechuan and Yunnan are Mongols, most of whom are now indistinguishable from Tibetans, and whose situation could most logically have been addressed by providing them with autonomous district status within an overall Tibetan autonomous region.

Within what was to become the Tibet Autonomous Region, further territorial divisions were created. The Panchen Lama's domains in Tsang were constituted as a separate area of administration as if deriving from a previously separate "local government" (with the implication that even central Tibet had not been a unified state in the past). The Panchen Lama was returned to Tibet in 1952 and installed in Shigatse, his prestige and authority being construed as equal to that of the Dalai Lama. The Chinese created political institutions for the Panchen Lama equivalent to those of the Dalai Lama. In this they were assisted by the embittered entourage of

---

78. Had "Sikang" remained separate, China would have found itself with three Tibetan provincial-size territorial units (TAR, Chinghai and Sikang), duplicating the three provinces claimed by Tibet itself, a situation calling attention to Tibet's size and territorial distinctiveness. Szechuan's regional interests, represented within the CCP by Teng Hsiao-p'ing, reportedly predominated in the decision to include "Sikang" in Szechuan. Jigme Ngapo, personal communication, Washington, February 1995.

the Panchen, who had been exiled from Tibet since 1924 and were now determined to create for themselves a political domain independent of Lhasa (if not of China). Tibetans of Tsang report that the Panchen Lama's legitimacy as the rightful reincarnation and his political authority were accepted only by his own entourage.[79] While the Panchen's administration was ostensibly in charge in Shigatse, all actual political power lay in the hands of the Chinese.

The Chamdo region of Kham, from the Yangtze to Giamda (the western border of "Sikang"), was constituted as a separate territory of indefinite status until 1956. The Chamdo district was within Sikang until 1956 and within the TAR after that date. Until 1956 Chamdo was theoretically under the authority of the "Chamdo Liberation Committee," established in January 1951, but was actually administered by the PLA directly under the authority of the State Council in Peking. Western Tibet, or Ngari, was put under the control of the PLA of the Sinkiang Military District, and was thus effectively removed from Tibetan Government authority. The Chamdo district, the Panchen's domain and Ngari were reintegrated into the TAR in 1956 after their exclusion from the Tibetan Government's domains had been made unnecessary by the elimination of most of that government's authority.

By excluding eastern Kham and all of Amdo from the Chinese territorial definition of "Tibet," more than half of Tibetan nationality territory (by far the richest half in physical resources) and two-thirds of its population were excluded from the TAR and from the provisions of the 17-Point Agreement. Within what remained of the TAR, the Tibetan Government's authority was circumscribed by the exclusion of Tsang, Ngari and Chamdo. The Chinese nevertheless claimed that they had not in any way altered the political system in "Tibet" nor the authority of the Tibetan Government. The PRC's policy of treating Tibetan nationality areas of eastern Tibet as parts of Chinese provinces, where the restrictions of the 17-Point Agreement would not apply, was to be a significant factor in the eventual Tibetan revolt against Chinese rule.

After the signing of the 17-Point Agreement, PLA advance units marched from Chamdo to Lhasa. The first PLA units to enter Lhasa, on 9 September 1950, were from the Southeastern Military Command, headquartered in Szechuan; PLA units of the Northwest Military Command headquartered in Sinkiang arrived via Kansu and Chinghai on the first of

---

79. Tseten Namgyal, personal interview, Dharamsala, January 1990. Tseten Namgyal reports that Tibetans referred to the Panchen as "Mao's Panchen" or the "son of Mao," and some actually believed that he was Mao's son. Some of the Panchen Lama's officials reportedly imagined that they would independently rule a territorial domain that included all of Tsang. Ibid.

December.[80] Western Tibet was placed under the authority of the Northwest Military District, since it was more accessible from Sinkiang than Szechuan (or even from Lhasa). These two PLA commands were later to form the basis of a factional rivalry among the military and civilian Chinese administrators of Tibet. Many Chinese PLA soldiers and CCP cadres went to Tibet under the illusion that they were the liberators of the Tibetans and would be welcomed as such. This assumption soon turned to disillusionment and defensiveness as the Chinese found that they were regarded not as liberators but as alien conquerors.

Despite their prohibitions against "taking a single needle and thread from the people," the first PLA units to enter Tibet were forced to rely upon local resources for food and transport. All available transport animals were requisitioned and, although compensation was provided, many Tibetans claimed that only half the usual rates were paid and that many animals were driven to exhaustion and death by mistreatment.[81] The Chinese established rates for food, fodder and transport in accordance with local rates, but then continued to pay the same rates even after their needs had inflated costs as much as ten times. Tibetans report that quotas for transport were established by district; animals were often driven to exhaustion and death, after which human transport was required to fulfill the quota. Fodder for animals, as well as food for themselves, had to be provided by the Tibetans. Tibetans were also fined for damaged goods.[82] The priority for transport of military supplies and money in the form of silver *yuan* meant that little food could be transported. PLA logistical supply units were sent into all areas of Tibet from

---

80. Chinese troops are often said to have entered Tibet from Sinkiang via the Aksai Chin, the territory later to be disputed between India and China. The only evidence of this, however, is a statement by Chou En-lai to that effect, which is disputed by the then Director of Indian Intelligence, B.N. Mullik. Mullik claims that the PLA did not enter western Tibet until June 1951, and even then not by the Aksai Chin. According to Mullik, the Chinese began construction of a route through the Aksai Chin only in late 1952. Mullik thinks Chou made the claim in order to establish the priority of Chinese territorial claims to Aksai Chin. B.N. Mullik, *My Years with Nehru: The Chinese Betrayal* (New Delhi: Allied Publishers, 1971), 196.

81. *Tibet Under Chinese Communist Rule: A Compilation of Refugee Statements* (Dharamsala: Information and Publicity Office of His Holiness the Dalai Lama, 1976), 4.

82. "Statements made by Tibetan refugees," in *Tibet and the Chinese People's Republic: A Report to the International Commission of Jurists by its Legal Inquiry Committee on Tibet* (Geneva: International Commission of Jurists, 1960), 224, 226, 246, 253, 254, 255, 260, 284. Abuse of animal transport was inadvertently confirmed by the Chinese press in 1989, when, in an article on development of transportation in Tibet, it was revealed that the Northwest Military District units proceeding via Kansu had requisitioned 20,000 camels, three-fourths of which had been worked to death. "Golmud—A New Plateau Town," *Peking Review*, 20-26 November 1989, 25.

which food could be procured, especially the agricultural districts of Dakpo and Kongpo.[83]

The Tibetan economy was almost immediately disrupted by the presence of a large Chinese garrison dependent upon local provisions, a situation similar to that encountered during the Ch'ing dynasty whenever the garrison at Lhasa had been increased. The Chinese were forced to "borrow" the grain reserves of the Tibetan Government and monasteries; they requested "loans" of the gold and silver reserves of the Tibetan Government in order to acquire more provisions. In addition, "one time contributions" in grain or money were requested from estate owners and monasteries. These became annual demands or, in effect, a tax against landowners. The Chinese presence caused immediate and long lasting food shortages and inflation of food prices, creating hardship for Tibetans, especially for the lower classes whose favor the Chinese had hoped to cultivate.

Land for PLA camps was acquired, often without any compensation, as well as housing for PLA officers and civilian Chinese officials. As Tibetan leaders later complained:

> Gardens and public parks, owned by private persons and by the government at places like Lhasa and other towns, are gradually being taken over by the Chinese without compensation. Trespassing the enclosures in the beginning as if ignorant of their owners, they finally filled them with tents and human dwellings, and feigned surprise when asked to vacate the areas and 'innocently' said that the dwellers were 'liberators' who should be assisted. In their intrusion into private lives, the Chinese have actually laid hands on hundreds of private houses and other landed property in all the big towns.[84]

In other instances, especially involving cooperative members of the upper class, high rents or purchase prices were paid for residences and food supplies. As in Kham, where the PLA paid generously in silver for provisions when they were dependent upon local cooperation, the "rain of *dayans*" was repeated in Lhasa because the Chinese were dependent upon Tibetan provisions, especially at the end of 1951, when they were unprepared for winter. The Chinese sought to ingratiate themselves in other ways as well; for example, by opening free medical clinics staffed by very ostentatiously courteous personnel.

---

83. Drakton, personal interview, Dharamsala, 1989. Kongpo and Dakpo are the only Tibetan districts in which pigs are commonly raised.

84. "Memorandum by Tibetan Leaders," in *The Question of Tibet and the Rule of Law* (Geneva: International Commission of Jurists, 1959), 155.

China's position in Tibet at this time was very precarious, as was admitted by Mao in a directive of the CCP Central Committee on Tibet policy:

> We depend solely on two basic policies to win over the masses and put ourselves in an invulnerable position. The first is strict budgeting coupled with production for the army's own needs, and thus the exertion of influence on the masses; this is the key link. Even when highways are built we cannot count on moving large quantities of grain over them. India will probably agree to send grain and other goods to Tibet on the basis of exchange, but the stand we must take is that our army should be able to carry on even if India stops sending them some day. We must do our best and take the proper steps to win over the Dalai and the majority of his top echelon and to isolate the handful of bad elements in order to achieve a gradual, bloodless transformation of the Tibetan economic and political system over a number of years; on the other hand we must be prepared for the eventuality of the bad elements leading the Tibetan troops in rebellion and attacking us, so that in this contingency our army could still carry on and hold out in Tibet. It all depends on strict budgeting and production for the army's own needs. Only with this fundamental policy as the cornerstone of our work can we achieve our aim. . . .
>
> As yet we don't have a material base for fully implementing the Agreement, nor do we have a base for this purpose in terms of support among the masses or in the upper stratum. To force its implementation will do more harm than good. Since they are unwilling to put the Agreement into effect, well then we can leave it for the time being and wait.[85]

As in eastern Tibet, the Chinese said that they had come only to help improve Tibet and they would leave as soon as Tibetans were able to take care of themselves. The Dalai Lama was told by the Chinese that they had come to Tibet to help Tibet develop her resources and protect her against imperialist domination; they would go back to China as soon as Tibet was able to administer her own affairs and protect her own frontiers. He

---

85. Mao Tse-tung, "On the Policies of Our Work in Tibet," *Selected Works*, vol. 5 (Peking: Foreign Languages Press, 1977), 74. What Mao meant by the phrase "fully implementing the Agreement" was apparently the "reform" of Tibet's social and political system. Mao admitted that Tibetans were "unwilling to put the Agreement into effect," which leads to the suspicion that the Tibetans had not understood or had been deceived about the provisions of the Agreement in regard to reforms. The latter is hardly unlikely considering that reforms were mentioned in the 17-Point Agreement only in the context that Tibetans might voluntarily choose to "preserve or reform" their customs, habits and religious beliefs, without any explication of what the Chinese meant by reforms. Mao predicted that either scenario, a gradual Tibetan acceptance of Chinese reforms or a Tibetan rebellion, "will be favorable to us." Ibid.

quotes the Chinese PLA commander in Lhasa as saying that "When you can stand on your feet, we will not stay here even if you ask us to."[86] However, In October 1952, on the occasion of the Chinese National Day (anniversary of the 1949 victory), in an address to a group of Tibetan delegates in Peking, Mao indicated that the Party intended to proceed slowly in the political reorganization in Tibet, but he also made a rather cryptic statement on China's plans for population increases in Tibet:

> Tibet covers a large area but is thinly populated. Its population should be increased from the present two or three million to five or six million, and then to over ten million. Then economy and culture should also be developed. ... The Chinese Communists, standing for national equality, do not want to oppress and exploit you, we want to help you achieve development in population, economy and culture. The entry of the People's Liberation Army into Tibet is aimed at giving you such assistance. Not much assistance can be expected in the beginning but in three years, much help can be given to you; if not, the Chinese Communist Party will be of no use.[87]

Mao's plan to increase Tibet's population is usually interpreted as implying Chinese colonization; however, Mao's actual intentions remain unclear considering that he gave no time frame. A natural increase of the Tibetan population to the levels Mao indicated was feasible, given sufficient time. Considering that the Chinese position in Tibet at the end of 1952 was precarious, it may seem unlikely that Mao would openly announce to Tibetans an intention to colonize Tibet. On the other hand, the CCP thought that its nationality doctrine and policy would eliminate all animosities between nationalities; Mao may have thought that colonization by the "fraternal Han nationality" would be palatable to Tibetans once they were educated in "proletarian internationalism." The Chinese were at that time practicing a policy of colonization in Inner Mongolia and Sinkiang, as well as in eastern Tibet, especially Amdo. The Dalai Lama is on record (in a statement made after his flight in 1959) as having understood that Mao intended Chinese colonization: "It was clearly stated to me while I was in Peking in 1955 that Tibet was a vast country with scarce population and China has a large population with insufficient land, so land and people should be exchanged."[88]

---

86. Dalai Lama, *My Land and My People* (New York: Potala Press, 1983), 92.

87. Mao, as quoted in "Radio Address of Leosha Thuptentarpa to the Religious and Secular Officials of the Tibet Local Government and the Entire Tibetan People," *People's Daily* (Peking), 22 November 1952, in *Tibet 1950-67*, 43.

88. "Statement of the Dalai Lama to the Legal Inquiry Committee at Mussoorie, India," 14 November 1959, in *Tibet and the Chinese People's Republic*, 311. The Dalai Lama also mentioned a statement made to the Panchen Lama: "In 1955, just before returning to Lhasa we

China's strategy in that part of Tibet that was to become the TAR was characterized by cautiousness, diplomacy and adherence to the provisions (as they interpreted them) of the 17-Point Agreement and the CCP's nationalities policy. Chinese tactics were pragmatic, avoiding offense while their position was weak, but constantly probing for weaknesses in Tibetan society that could be exploited to create disunity among Tibetans in favor of unity with the Han. In general, before 1954, the Chinese confined themselves to activities that might be characterized as within the realm of foreign aid rather than foreign conquest, aimed at impressing Tibetans with the benevolent assistance China could provide without affecting Tibetan autonomy or altering Tibetan society. The Chinese substantially adhered to those provisions of the Agreement promising no change in Tibet's government or social and religious systems. Less publicized activities were aimed at undermining that autonomy in favor of dependence upon China. Since the Tibetan Government had officially accepted the 17-Point Agreement and was bound by its provisions, Tibetans were unable to challenge the authority of the Chinese or to refuse their ostensibly benevolent assistance. The Chinese concentrated in the early years on road building to link Tibet with China, securing control of Tibetan commerce, and creating the basis for later class divisions by means of propaganda and the United Front.

Chinese propaganda was directed at exposing the intrigues of foreign imperialism, creating trust in the "new Chinese" and educating Tibetans in socialism and patriotism to the Chinese state. Public discussions, led by Tibetans coached by the Chinese, were organized to "speak bitterness" against the old pre-liberation society. A primary theme of such meetings was the overwhelming significance of Tibet's "return to the Motherland," compared to the insignificance of Tibet's former religious and cultural relations with India. A poster campaign of 1951-52 was intended to depict the might of China, the solidarity of China and the USSR, and the need for Tibetans and Chinese to unite against Anglo-American imperialism. These posters were so often defaced that the Chinese had to resort to portable billboards, which were hung up only during the day and were closely guarded. By April 1952 the situation in Lhasa had deteriorated to such an extent that the Chinese had reversed their policy on PLA fraternization with the Tibetan population and had instructed their troops to avoid personal contact with Tibetans.[89]

---

had been to see Liu Shao-ch'i. He mentioned to the Panchen Lama that Tibet was a big country and unoccupied and that China had a big population which can be settled there." "Statements to the legal inquiry committee by the Dalai Lama and officials," in Ibid., 289.

89. American Consulate, Calcutta to Department of State, 8 July 1952, National Archives, 793B.00/7-852.

The United Front, which purported to create a "democratic" alliance of political parties and classes, was in fact a means to co-opt all political and social groups. The primary target of the United Front was the Tibetan Government. Because the Tibetan Government was required to cooperate with the Chinese by the terms of the 17-Point Agreement, even the most patriotic Tibetan officials were required to become collaborators. The United Front strategy diffused the resistance of the upper classes by maintaining their privileges, political positions and social status. The lowest classes, those the Chinese characterized as serfs or slaves in traditional Tibetan society, as well as beggars, thieves and social outcasts, were cultivated by elevating them to symbolic positions of authority.

Several United Front organizations were established, including a Patriotic Women's Association, and a Cultural Association of Patriotic Youth.[90] These groups, which included members of all classes, served not only to convey the impression of local autonomous political authority but as mediums for the propagation of Chinese campaigns and ideological indoctrination. United Front organizations were also employed for gathering information and for cultivating sympathizers and participants in other "progressive" programs. Both lower and upper class collaborators were favored with tours of China and opportunities for education in minority nationalities institutes. A program for sending Tibetan children to China for education was also begun (primarily in eastern Tibet before 1955).[91] Many Tibetans bitterly resisted this program but quotas were established with which they had to comply. Some children and some families participated in Chinese programs because they represented the only opportunity for secular education or social modernization available in traditionally conservative Tibet. "Education" offered to Tibetan students in China, however, often turned out to be far different from what was expected. As one Tibetan who was sent to China to study medicine relates:

We soon found that science and medicine were not in the curriculum. The school taught only political theories with the main emphasis on Marxism. The Chinese brand of Marxism was contrasted with Tibet's 'Backward Society.' We were taught Chinese, the history of mankind, and the history of China, in which Tibet was always referred to as an integral part of the Chinese motherland. . . . In the beginning, we studied Tibetan for one hour

---

90. George Ginsburgs and Michael Mathos, *Communist China and Tibet: The First Dozen Years* (The Hague: Martinus Nijhoff, 1964), 57.

91. From Amdo, there are also numerous reports of babies having been taken by force. "Statements made by Tibetan refugees," in *Tibet and the Chinese People's Republic*, 222, 224, 229, 242, 250, 259, 264, 273.

once a week. Later, this was completely suspended. In fact, we were told that Tibetan would not be of use and that we should devote more time to Chinese. . . . From time to time we were made to write to our parents, relatives and friends. The letter was more or less dictated and contained inducements to accept Communism as well as criticism of the Tibetan way of life. . . . Frequent debates and discussions on political issues were held and all were encouraged to speak in Chinese. During self-criticism sessions, one student would accuse another in an effort to prove his own ideological convictions. The slightest indication of Tibetan patriotism meant that the student was branded as nationalistic, backward and reactionary, with the result that he would be subjected to severe criticism and humiliation. Spying was common and mutual suspicion extreme.[92]

Despite the promise of the 17-Point Agreement to make "no change in the status and functions of the Dalai Lama," the powers and political functions of the Tibetan Government had to be acquired by the Chinese in order to implement their plans for the transformation of Tibetan society. This was facilitated by means of the United Front policy on the official or governmental level between the Chinese Government and the "Tibetan local government." The 17-Point Agreement in Article 15 had provided for the establishment of a "military and administrative committee," which theoretically would coordinate between the PLA and the Tibetan Government. However, Chinese attempts to establish the committee were resisted by the Tibetans on the grounds that this would constitute a violation of the Agreement's promises regarding autonomy and preservation of the "status, functions, and powers," of the existing Tibetan Government. The effort to establish the committee was not vigorously pursued by the Chinese; in 1954 the military and administrative committee system was abandoned for all nationality areas because the CCP had decided to transition directly to national regional autonomy.[93]

Constant attempts were made to reduce the status of the Dalai Lama by the institution of reforms that could be portrayed as democratic and that were likely to meet with Tibetan popular approval. One of these measures was to make the Dalai Lama more accessible to ordinary Tibetans by encouraging him to appear in public and to assume a more direct administrative role. The Chinese also took every opportunity to reduce the role of religion and its exponents in Tibetan social, cultural

92. Tsundu Gyatso, in *Facts About Tibet: 1961-1965* (New Delhi: Bureau of His Holiness the Dalai Lama, 1966), 20.

93. Ginsburgs and Mathos, *Communist China and Tibet*, 56. The system of military-administrative committees was eliminated for all areas of the PRC at the time of the adoption of the 1954 Constitution. Lyman P. Van Slyke, *Enemies and Friends: The United Front in Chinese Communist History* (Stanford: Stanford University Press, 1967), 237.

and political life. In an effort to institute its own reforms, the Tibetan Government created an Advisory Council to assist the Dalai Lama in proposing reforms; it proposed reforms in interest on loans, abuses on use of *ulag* privileges, landholdings of Tibetan Government officials and landholdings of aristocratic families who no longer contributed government officials, monastic landholdings in excess of actual needs of monasteries and the holding of government estates by monk officials. The Dalai Lama claims that all these reforms were opposed by the Chinese, since they wished that all reforms be seen as having been instituted by themselves. The Chinese opposed any Tibetan initiatives that preserved Tibetan institutions or perpetuated a role for the Tibetan Government.[94]

Tibetan popular opposition to the Chinese presence was expressed by the formation, in March 1952, of a loose organization of Lhasa residents and nearby villagers known as *Mimang Tsongdu*, or People's Assembly. The *Mimang Tsongdu* presented a petition to the *Kashag* that complained of price rises and food shortages and requested that Chinese civilian and military personnel be reduced since there was no foreign threat to Tibet and their presence was creating great hardship for the Tibetans.[95] The Chinese responded by demanding the arrest of the petitioners and by banning of public assembly and all criticism of themselves, especially criticism expressed through popular songs. The petitioners were later condemned as unrepresentative of the majority of Tibetans and as agents of foreign imperialism; their demands were characterized as unlawful and without merit; the Chinese threatened to arrest any who repeated such demands. In February 1952, the Chinese took steps to limit the celebration of the *Monlam Chenmo*, or "Lama Raj," during which the lamas of the Lhasa monasteries traditionally took over civil administration, out of fear of public demonstrations.

The Chinese attempted to alleviate the food shortage crisis by importing rice via India, offering loans to Tibetan villagers to be repaid in grain, and prohibiting the making of Tibetan barley beer.[96] The Chinese

---

94. Dalai Lama, *Freedom in Exile* (New York: Harper Collins, 1990), 80.

95. *Tibet Under Chinese Communist Rule*, 4. The Dalai Lama later said that the *Mimang Tsongdu* was assembled by the people of Lhasa since the *Tsongdu*, or National Assembly, had been rendered powerless to do anything more than ratify decisions already taken by the Chinese. "Statement of the Dalai Lama to the Legal Inquiry Committee at Mussoorie, India, on November 14, 1959," in *Tibet and the Chinese People's Republic*, 312. According to Chinese sources, the *Mimang Tsongdu* and elements of the Tibetan Army surrounded the residence of Chang Ching-wu to present these demands and, furthermore, "agitated for a revolt." *Tibet 1950-67*, 736.

96. India allowed China to transport goods via India to Tibet. China sold 6,000 tons of rice to India, despite reported shortages in China, on the condition that 1,000 tons be transported to Tibet. Eventually, as much as 3,500 tons were shipped to Tibet. "Prime Minister

blamed the Tibetan Prime Minister, Lukhangwa, for allowing Tibetan resistance and demanded that the Dalai Lama dismiss him, which he did. The Dalai Lama describes these events as "distressingly familiar in any country which has been the victim of invasion."

> The invaders had arrived believing—with how much sincerity one cannot tell—that they had come as benefactors. They seemed to be surprised to find that the invaded people did not want their benefactors in the least. As popular resentment grew against them, they did not try to allay it by withdrawing, or even by making concessions to the people's wishes. They tried to repress it by ever increasing force, and rather than blame themselves, they searched for scapegoats.[97]

In Kham and Amdo (now part of Chinese provinces and thus considered immune from the restrictions of the 17-Point Agreement), experiments with agricultural and pastoral reorganization were conducted beginning in the early 1950s. The Chinese attempted to introduce "democratic reforms" in some agricultural areas of Amdo as early as 1952. Property of some members of the upper classes, primarily those not collaborating with the United Front, was confiscated, often based upon charges of collaboration with the KMT or the former government of Ma Pu-fang. The CCP also attempted to organize mutual aid teams in areas where conditions permitted.[98]

In pastoral areas, the Chinese experimented with the development of animal husbandry and fixed settlements. They refrained, however, from making class divisions or initiating "democratic reforms" in pastoral areas due to their dependence upon the role and expertise of the former upper classes. In 1953, the Party announced: "The policy of 'no struggle, no division, and no class distinction' and of 'benefits to both pastoral workers and pastoral lords' has been put into effect in the pastoral areas."[99] The CCP had to confess to some failures due to their inexperi-

---

Nehru's Press Conference," *Times of India*, 5 April 1959, in Indian Committee for Cultural Freedom, *Tibet Fights for Freedom* (New Delhi: Orient Longmans, 1960), 138; American Consulate Calcutta to Department of State, 29 July 1952, National Archives, 793.B00/7-2952.

97. Dalai Lama, *My Land and My People: Memoirs of the Dalai Lama of Tibet* (New York: Potala, 1977), 94.

98. This seems to have been the case in agricultural areas contiguous to areas of Chinese settlement; democratic reforms for all areas did not begin until 1956. "Statements made by Tibetan refugees," in *Tibet and the Chinese People's Republic*, 229, 233, 266, 268, 275, 276, 286.

99. "Basic Summing Up of Animal Husbandry in the several Pastoral Areas of the Inner Mongolia Autonomous Region, Suiyuan, Tsinghai, and Sinkiang, as Made at 3rd (Enlarged) Session of the Central Nationalities Affairs Commission," *Ta-Kung Pao* (Tientsin), 9 September 1953, in *Tibet 1950-67*, 78.

ence in pastoral economies and the tendency of Han personnel to dictate policy without consulting with the local people:

> Animal husbandry is new to many of our cadres, and these cadres do not know or do not fully know the laws governing its development. . . . The work of developing animal husbandry must be carried out in close conjunction with the work of including the people of all nationalities and all strata in the united front. . . . In a few areas in the past, such directives were not properly observed and some deviations occurred with huge adverse effects on the development of animal husbandry, even resulting in losses, so that animal husbandry was not again normalized until things had been set right. . . . There were several causes for these mistakes. In the first place, some people mechanically thought that historically the transformation from a nomadic economy into an agricultural economy was the normal way of progress, and therefore there was no future for animal husbandry today unless it was transformed into agriculture.[100]

Usurpation of Tibetan Governmental Authority

By the end of 1954 China's strategic hold over Tibet had tightened. In April 1954 China concluded an agreement with India regarding Tibet's political status in which India recognized China's sovereignty over Tibet. At the end of 1954 two motorable roads, one from Szechuan via Kham and another from Kansu and Chinghai via northern Tibet, were completed. These two events marked a shift in Chinese policy in Tibet. The roads allowed for the supply of Chinese forces in Tibet from China or the introduction of more forces in the case of rebellion. The political agreement with India eliminated Indian political interests in Tibet and guaranteed that neither India nor any third country in collaboration with India could affect China's future course of action in Tibet. Chinese physical and political control over Tibet was now secure, enabling the Chinese to accelerate reforms with less concern about Tibetan resistance.

The treaty with India, entitled "Agreement between the Republic of India and the People's Republic of China on Trade and Intercourse between Tibet Region of China and India," was a major international achievement for the PRC. The treaty secured Indian recognition of China's full sovereignty in Tibet and established the doctrine of peaceful coexistence as China's policy on relations with other Asian states.[101] The treaty is generally known by its India title, *Panchshila*, or "five principles

---

100. Ibid.
101. "Agreement between the Republic of India and the People's Republic of China on Trade and Intercourse between Tibet Region of China and India," *People's Daily* (Peking), 29 April 1954, in *Tibet 1950-67*, 66.

of peaceful coexistence." The five principles were: mutual respect for each other's territorial integrity and sovereignty, mutual non-aggression, mutual non-interference in each other's internal affairs, equality and mutual benefit, and peaceful co-existence. India and China thus claimed to have initiated a new era in their relations, but this had been achieved at the expense of Tibet, whose independence may be held to have been violated in the specifics of each of the five principles.

Although presented by both India and China as an example of the possibility of peaceful relations between Asian countries, the treaty actually signified India's acquiescence to China's conquest of Tibet. By the terms of this treaty, India gave up all the special privileges in Tibet it had inherited from the British and agreed that Tibet was exclusively an internal affair of China. Shortly afterward, the PRC concluded a similar treaty with Nepal by which Nepal relinquished its extraterritorial rights over Nepalese citizens in Tibet.[102]

In an address to the Indian Parliament, Prime Minister Nehru pointed out that India had accepted the fact of China's sovereignty in Tibet in 1950, or even earlier:

> So far as Tibet is concerned, it is a recognition of the existing situation there. In fact, that situation had been recognized by us two or three years ago. Some criticism has been made that this is a recognition of Chinese sovereignty over Tibet. . . . I am not aware of any time during the last few hundred years when Chinese sovereignty, or if you like suzerainty, was challenged by any outside country and all during this period whether China was weak or strong and whatever the Government of China was, China always maintained this claim to the sovereignty over Tibet. It is true that occasionally when China was weak, this sovereignty was not exercised in any large measure. When China was strong, it was exercised. Always there was a large measure of autonomy of Tibet, so that there was no great change in the theoretical approach to the Tibetan problem from the Chinese side. It has been throughout the last 200 or 300 years the same. The only country that had more intimate relations with Tibet was India, that is to say, British India in those days. Even then, when it was British policy to have some measure of influence over Tibet, even then they never denied the fact of Chinese sovereignty over Tibet, although in practice it was hardly exercised and they laid stress on Tibetan autonomy. So what we have done in this agreement is not to recognize any new thing, but merely to repeat what we have said previously, and what, in fact, inevitably follows from the circumstances, both historical and practical, today.[103]

---

102. According to Mullik, India exerted pressure on Nepal to conclude this treaty. Mullik, *My Years with Nehru*, 625.

103. Nehru's Statement in Parliament regarding the Sino-Indian Agreement on Tibet, in Chanakya Sen, comp. and ed., *Tibet Disappears: A Documentary History of Tibet's International Status, the Great Rebellion and Its Aftermath* (New Delhi: Asia Publishing House, 1960), 120.

Nehru's explanation was not accepted in India without protest. A member of the Indian Parliament, Acharya Kripalani, exposed the duplicity of Nehru's argument and that of the Chinese in regard to the legitimacy of a modern claim to sovereignty based upon archaic and inherently colonialist suzerain rights:

> The plea is that China had the ancient right of suzerainty. This right was out of date, old and antiquated. It was theoretical; it was never exercised and even then theoretically. It has lapsed by the flux of time. . . . It is not right in these days of democracy by which our Communist friends swear, by which the Chinese swear, to talk of this ancient suzerainty and exercise it in a new shape in a country which has and had nothing to do with China. . . . I consider this as much a colonial aggression on the part of China as any colonial aggression indulged in by Western nations. The definition of colonialism is this, that one nation by force of arms or fraud occupies the territory of another nation. In this age of democracy when we hold that all people should be free and equal, I say that China's occupation of Tibet is a deliberate act of aggression.[104]

Shortly after the *Panchshila* agreement, China completed motorable roads from the interior to Tibet. On 29 November 1954 the *New China News Agency* reported that the 2,255 kilometer "Sikang-Tibet Highway," with an average altitude of 12,000 feet, had been completed. Twenty thousand Tibetans were reported to have engaged in the construction.[105] The road took the northern route from Dartsendo (Tachienlu, now Kangding) through Kanze, Derge and Chamdo, to Kongpo and Lhasa. (A southern route in Kham, via Lithang and Batang, was added later.) On 19 December the Chinghai-Tibet highway, of "over 2,000 kilometers," was completed.[106] Although unpaved, these roads represented major engi-

---

104. Ibid., 121.

105. "The Sikang-Tibet Highway," *NCNA* (Lhasa), 29 November 1954, in *Tibet 1950-67*, 54. Tibetans were required to work on these roads by an order secured by the Chinese from the Tibetan Government. Compensation was reportedly inadequate, since Tibetans had to provide their own provisions, including tents; this became more expensive as the work took them farther from their homes. "Statements made by Tibetan refugees," in *Tibet and the Chinese People's Republic*, 231, 282.

106. "The Tsinghai-Tibet Highway," *China News Service* (Lhasa), 19 December 1954, in *Tibet 1950-67*, 55. The majority of these roads remain unpaved but are well-maintained by Chinese personnel stationed at road stations approximately every 20 kilometers. The hastiness with which all roads to Tibet were constructed is apparent to anyone who has travelled them, especially in the shifting alignments and the sloppy construction of roadbeds. Many sections of the roads had to be realigned or rebuilt almost immediately after opening and have required enormous efforts to keep them open ever since. The Golmud to Lhasa section of the Chinghai-Tibet highway was finally paved in 1985, making this the only paved road

neering achievements; they effectively established China's logistical capability to maintain its hold over Tibet in any eventuality. A western route from Sinkiang via Gartok and Shigatse was completed in 1957.[107]

The Chinese claimed that the construction of these roads indicated the "concern and care" that the Chinese Communist Party and Chairman Mao had for the Tibetan people. Their real purpose was to consolidate China's physical control over Tibet so that the political and social transformation of Tibet could proceed, a fact revealed by Chinese statements at the time that the completion of the roads was "conducive to the early establishment of a Preparatory Committee for the Tibet Autonomous Region as well as the consolidation and integration of efforts in undertaking various construction projects in Tibet towards the realization, in gradual stages, of regional autonomy in Tibet."[108] The roads were also reported to have facilitated the travel of Tibetan "officials and youths" to various parts of China to "watch and study," and the transfer of several hundred "specialist cadres" from China to Tibet. The roads also allowed the Chinese to shift Tibetan trade from India to China, despite the much greater expense of doing so (and despite China's claims to be developing trade with India), and to reap a propaganda benefit by reducing the cost of Szechuan tea on the Tibetan market.

At the same time, independent Tibetan trade was being restricted by exorbitant taxes on Tibetan traders (especially monastic agents). At Dartsendo, Tibetan traders were charged 100 percent duty on all items; local Chinese and Tibetans were instructed not to pay any debts to Tibetan traders.[109] By late 1954, China had a virtual monopoly on Tibetan commerce, transportation and communications. In addition to road construction, the Chinese were busily establishing military installations, including numerous military airfields and communications facilities. Consolidation of China's political position and logistical infrastructure in Tibet permitted an acceleration of the pace of Tibet's political integration into the Chinese state, including the transition from indirect political control through the Tibetan Government to direct Chinese administration.

---

into Tibet. A survey for a railroad along this route was undertaken as early as 1957 but encountered the problem of permanently frozen ground, or permafrost, which has prevented the Chinese from realizing their dream of a railway to Tibet.

107. "Sinkiang-Tibet Highway Completed," *Kuang-ming Jih-pao*, 6 October 1957, in *Tibet 1950-67*, 263. The Sinkiang road was the subject of conflict with India in 1962 because the road passed through the (uninhabited) Aksai Chin, which India claimed as its territory.

108. Fan Ming (Deputy Secretary, Tibet Work Committee), "Another Major Accomplishment in the Reconstruction of Tibet," NCNA (Lhasa), 20 October 1955, in *Tibet 1950-67*, 55.

109. "Memorandum by Tibetan Leaders," in *Question of Tibet and the Rule of Law*, 156.

In late 1954 the Dalai Lama was persuaded to attend, along with the Panchen, the inaugural meeting of the National People's Congress (NPC) in Peking, at which the Constitution of the PRC was to be approved. Tibetan leaders later claimed that the Dalai Lama was convinced to attend under false pretenses: "The Chinese so arranged this visit in 1954 as to give the Tibetans, including the Dalai Lama, the impression that in so doing they were conferring something of an equality of status on Tibet. They had even given hopes that the visit was in the nature of a political step towards giving complete independence to Tibet."[110] The CCP thus achieved what the KMT, by similar methods, had attempted to achieve in 1945: the participation of Tibetan representatives at a Chinese state constitutional convention. The implication was that Tibet was a willing participant in the formation of the new Chinese state.

Tibet (TAR) was represented at the NPC by nine delegates, three of whom represented the Panchen Lama, while the still-autonomous (in relation to the administration of Lhasa) "Chamdo Liberation Committee" was represented by an additional three delegates. As Ginsburgs and Mathos remarked:

> The fact that the Dalai Lama condescended to attend that well-publicized forum without known protest in a capacity of less than sole spokesman for all Tibet also played directly into Chinese hands. Indeed, though the Tibetan monarch tried throughout to act as the only figure legitimately representing the whole Tibetan people, and the Chinese could not in many respects avoid acknowledging the preeminence of his authority at home, formally things had been so arranged in advance as to convey in the course of the proceedings the impression that he stood, at best, as a primus inter pares on the overall Tibetan political scene: i.e., to picture him on the secular plane as merely a local potentate, albeit the foremost prince in the constellation of the local nobility, vested with circumscribed territorial jurisdiction and sharing the governance of the country with like independent polities adjacent to his private domain.[111]

In a repetition of the 1945 KMT convention, where Tibetans were treated as "subjects of China," the Dalai Lama and other Tibetan representatives found themselves participating in a political event intended to define the relationship of minorities in general to the Chinese state, or, more accurately, to glorify the system of "national regional autonomy." The Tibetan Government representatives were treated as but one of a myriad of minority nationalities with equal status and equal rights with-

---

110. Ibid., 153. This statement was made by the former Prime Minister Lukhangwa, Shakabpa, and the Dalai Lama's elder brother, Gyalo Thondup.

111. Ginsburgs and Mathos, *Communist China and Tibet*, 79.

in the framework of the Chinese state. Although the 17-Point Agreement was theoretically to remain in effect, the Chinese considered it to have been transcended by the new constitution. The TAR thus lost some of its special status. Tibet was now governed by Chinese domestic law rather than by a bilateral agreement between China and Tibet. Tibetans could no longer claim a unique status for Tibet within the PRC nor that Tibet was anything less than an integral part of the Chinese state.

Both the Dalai and Panchen Lamas remained in Peking after the NPC meeting. In January 1955 an official agreement was reached concerning "historic and unsettled problems" between the two lamas. The problems resolved were "labor service, annual military expenditures, lawsuits and fines, the gold tax, and other such problems."[112] These were indeed historic problems, all deriving from disputes dating from 1924, none of which had the slightest significance in the present circumstances, except to convey the impression that the Panchen's former independence had been violated by Lhasa in the past, that the Tibetan Government in Lhasa did not represent all Tibetans even within the TAR, and that China was the legitimate, disinterested and beneficent mediator between the feuding feudatories of Tibet.

The Panchen Lama announced, after an obligatory testimony that his and the Dalai Lama's visit to Peking had "enabled us to realize all the better the greatness of the Motherland and love her all the more deeply," that "the problem of the future unification of Tibet has been solved smoothly after 40 days' consultations and deliberations, as a decision to set up a Preparatory Committee for the Tibetan Autonomous Region has been reached."[113] The Panchen Lama, 18 years of age at the time, was pleased to make this announcement since his "government" was to be included in the forthcoming Preparatory Committee as a political entity equal to the Tibetan Government. This event was propagandized as an historic "unification of Tibet," and the Chinese posed as mediators between two ostensibly previously autonomous political entities. The Chamdo Liberation Committee was also incorporated within the TAR (or what

---

112. "Report of Director Changtang Ji Jigme on Work of Panchen Kanpo Lija Committee," *NCNA*, 12 March 1955, in *Survey of China Mainland Press*. This "historic agreement" was preceded by repeated demands from the Panchen Lama's entourage for an administration independent of Lhasa, accompanied by suggestions that the Chinese should mediate a compromise. American Embassy, London to Department of State, 12 August 1953, National Archives, 793B.00/8-1253.

113. "Panchen Ngoertheni's Speech at the 7th Meeting of the State Council," *NCNA*, 12 March 1955, in *Survey of China Mainland Press*.

was to become the TAR), but remained under direct Chinese administration.[114]

On his return to Tibet from Peking in 1955 the Dalai Lama passed through Amdo. Tibetan leaders of Amdo gathered at Kumbum monastery to present a petition to the Dalai Lama requesting that they be put under the authority of Lhasa, and, consequently, under the restrictions of the 17-Point Agreement, in order to avoid the "reforms" being propagated by the Chinese in Amdo. After the Dalai Lama departed for Lhasa, the signers of this petition were arrested and subjected to public criticism and "struggle" sessions.[115] The Dalai Lama also passed through Chamdo and dispatched representatives to other parts of Kham in order to ascertain conditions there; the Chinese later claimed that the Dalai Lama and his representatives used this opportunity to stir up resistance.[116] The Dalai Lama stated in his autobiography that he had found Chinese officials in Amdo to be "rude and unsympathetic," and that in all of eastern Tibet he found "the same heavy air of foreboding":

> They simply meant to ignore the people's feelings. One Chinese general even went so far as to tell me they were bringing extra troops into the district in order to enforce their reforms, no matter what the people wanted. . . .
>
> Among the Tibetans, I saw mounting bitterness and hatred of Chinese; and among the Chinese, I saw the mounting ruthlessness and resolution which is born of fear and lack of understanding.[117]

Upon his return to Lhasa, the Dalai Lama found the Chinese there busily making preparations for the establishment of the Preparatory

---

114. Tibetan representatives of Chamdo, no doubt reflecting the interests of the Chinese officials in charge of the Chamdo region, reportedly opposed the reintegration of the Chamdo region with the TAR. Jigme Ngapo, personal communication, Washington, February 1995.

115. The Amdo leaders sought to "take refuge" with the Dalai Lama. They stated that they had formerly given allegiance to the Panchen Lama, since the Thirteenth Dalai Lama had not granted them audience (during his exile after 1904); they were more familiar with the Panchen who had spent several of his years of exile (after 1924) in Amdo. Now, however, since the present Dalai Lama was born in Amdo and had offered them audience (1954), they were willing to give their allegiance to Lhasa. Amdo Rigchok, personal interview, Dharamsala, January 1990. This event illustrates the inseparability of religion and politics in traditional Tibet.

116. Dalai Lama, *My Land*, 128. At least one of these representatives, Trijang Rimpoche, is indeed rumored to have stirred up resistance to the Chinese in Kham. Jamyang Norbu, personal communication, Washington, D.C., June 1995.

117. Dalai Lama, *My Land*, 128.

Committee for the Tibet Autonomous Region (PCTAR), which, unbeknownst to the Dalai Lama and the Tibetan Government, who had gone to Peking expecting an increase in Tibetan autonomy, the Chinese intended as a major alteration in the Tibetan political system, transferring effective governing authority to themselves and allowing them to implement their plans for the transformation of Tibetan society. The official announcement of the decision to create the PCTAR reveals that the Chinese regarded this transition as consistent with the provisions of the 17-Point Agreement and the new Chinese constitution. The Chinese had decided to abandon their previous intention to set up a supervisory military and political committee (in fact, PLA and Han civilian officials already performed this function); instead, the TAR was to prepare for the transition to national regional autonomy:

> According to the "Agreement between the Central People's Government and the Tibetan Local Government on Measures for Peaceful Liberation of Tibet," signed on May 23, 1951, a military and political committee should have been set up. However, since the Constitution has been adopted, the military and political committees in all regions have been abolished and, especially, as marked success has been registered in all fields since the peaceful liberation of Tibet for over three years, conditions have changed, which makes the establishing of the military and political committee unnecessary. Therefore, it entirely conforms with the spirit of the Constitution and the concrete conditions of Tibet at present to set up a Preparatory Committee for the Tibetan Autonomous Region. A group to undertake preparations for the Committee has recently been set up, comprising representatives of the Central People's Government in Tibet, representatives of the Tibetan Local Government, representatives of the Panchen Kanpo Lija Committee and representatives of the People's Liberation Committee of the Chengtu [Chamdo] area. ... The Preparatory Committee for the Tibetan Autonomous Region will have the nature of a state organ, charged with responsibility of making preparations to establish the Tibet Autonomous Region, and will be directly under the State Council.[118]

The Chinese thus bypassed previous Tibetan opposition to the plans for a "military and political committee" by setting up a new political body, which, while purporting to guarantee Tibetan representation, actually secured Chinese control over all governing institutions in Tibet. This change was presented not as an alteration of the existing Tibetan Government, but as a concession to Tibetans' opposition to the previous

---

118. "Decision of the State Council Concerning the Setting Up of a Preparatory Committee for the Tibetan Autonomous Region," NCNA, 12 March 1955, in *Current Background* (Hong Kong: United States Consulate), no. 332.

plan. At this time, only a "preparatory committee" for Tibetan regional autonomy was established, signifying that Tibet retained some of its unique political status, if only because Tibetans were considered unprepared for full "autonomy," but the PCTAR was presented as an accelerated "grant" of "national regional autonomy." The PCTAR was also presented as a unification of previously separate Tibetan political entities (Tsang, Chamdo, and Ngari were to be reunited within the TAR), which would expand the territory within which Tibetans would (theoretically) exercise self-rule.

The PCTAR was required to function under the PRC State Council, a provision that effectively abrogated the autonomy promised to the Tibetan Government under the provisions of the 17-Point Agreement (still, theoretically, in effect) as well as the autonomy of the PCTAR itself. The Preparatory Committee had to secure approval for all its actions and to refer to the State Council any administrative question upon which it was unable to render a unanimous decision, a provision that allowed the Chinese members or their collaborators to withdraw any measure from the deliberation of the Committee in favor of its resolution by Peking. All appointments to the Committee, and to any subsidiary bodies that the Committee created, were to be referred to the State Council for approval. The Committee was also charged to "cooperate closely" with the PLA headquarters in Tibet.[119]

The Preparatory Committee was originally set up with 51 members: 15 from the Dalai Lama's government, ten from the Panchen's entourage, ten from the "Chamdo Liberation Committee," 11 representatives of "major monasteries, religious sects, social dignitaries and public bodies" and five Chinese cadres. The Dalai Lama was made chairman, while the Panchen Lama and Chang Kuo-hua, PLA Commander in Tibet, were made vice-chairmen. However, when the Committee began to function in 1956, the numbers of its representatives had been arbitrarily changed; the "Tibetan Local Government" was reduced from 15 to only ten members, in parity with the Panchen and Chamdo, and representatives from religious and "popular" organizations were increased to 17.[120]

The PCTAR, despite being completely under Chinese control, was composed almost entirely of Tibetans (only five Chinese members); it was therefore presented as representing an autonomous Tibetan administration. The Dalai Lama agreed to the establishment of the PCTAR, apparently hoping that it might be able to function as an actual autonomous governing body, since it was composed primarily of Tibetans (as indeed it might had the Chinese intended that it should). The fact that the true

119. Ibid.
120. Ibid.

nature of the Preparatory Committee was not lost on Tibetans was revealed a few years later by Chang Kuo-hua, who mentioned that Tibetans had criticized the Preparatory Committee as a surreptitious means of altering Tibet's formal governmental structure.[121] The plan to establish the PCTAR revived Tibetan opposition in Lhasa, a fact that may explain why the PCTAR was not formally inaugurated until 22 April 1956.

On the occasion of the inauguration of the PCTAR, Chen Yi, who led the central government delegation "composed of 17 nationalities," praised Tibetans' "love for the motherland, and their zeal for unity with the various nationalities in the great family of the motherland." Chen mentioned that reforms like those planned for the TAR had already been initiated in eastern Tibet, where they had created some resistance, but that this was no cause for alarm in the TAR, since no reforms would be undertaken without Tibetans' consent:

> The reports and statements made by representatives at the [PCTAR] meeting all touched upon the question of the enforcement of democratic reform in the Tibet region [TAR]. Before the meeting was held, news had reached Tibet of the reforms in progress or about to be introduced in the neighboring provinces. Counterrevolutionary elements had in the meantime spread rumors, so that some representatives at the meeting had anxieties over certain concrete policies connected with the reform. ... After enthusiastic and serious discussions, the representatives at the meeting unanimously considered that the Tibetan nationality must, in common with the other nationalities, pursue the road to Socialism. ... As to when reform should be introduced, and how should there be implemented the method of reform through peaceful consultation in accordance with the special characteristics of the Tibetan nationality full discussions must first be undertaken by the autonomy organs of Tibet, and the agreement must be obtained of the public leaders of Tibet before a decision may be reached. This has been provided for in principle in the Constitution of our country and in the Agreement on the Peaceful Liberation of Tibet. For this reason there must be earnest and repeated consultations with the public leaders of all sides, and only with their agreement may reform be undertaken. Otherwise it should be postponed.[122]

Chen Yi went on to promise that the political status and living standard of the aristocracy and lamas would be protected during

---

121. "Chang Kuo-hua Address at Lhasa Gathering," NCNA (Lhasa), 22 April 1958, in *Current Background*, no. 505.

122. Chen Yi, "Summary Report of the Central Government Delegation to Tibet," *People's Daily* (Peking), 15 September 1956, in *Current Background*, no. 409.

reforms, that reforms would not be monopolized by the Han but would be carried out by Tibetans themselves, and that the livelihood of the monasteries would be guaranteed by the state. He also promised that there would be no interference in the affairs of religion, and that "necessary reforms in internal organization of religion" would be carried out "by those in the internal ranks of religion itself."[123]

In his report at the inaugural meeting of the PCTAR, the Dalai Lama expressed the hope that the "reforms" promised by the Chinese would only be carried out, as Mao had promised, at the wish of the Tibetans themselves: "The reform will be done through consultation by the leaders of Tibet and the broad masses of the people themselves, and not by others on their behalf." The Dalai Lama reported that Mao had "clearly told us that reform was aimed at improving the people's livelihood, and was not intended to degrade it. Therefore, there is no need to be apprehensive or fear reform or to worry too much."[124] However, after his departure from Tibet in 1959, the Dalai Lama revealed that he was soon disillusioned that the Committee was actually intended to function as an autonomous government of Tibet:

> Twenty of the members, although they were Tibetans, were representing the Chamdo Liberation Committee and the committee set up in the Panchen Lama's western district. These were both purely Chinese creations. Their representatives owed their positions mainly to Chinese support, and in return they had to support any Chinese proposition; although the Chamdo representatives did behave more reasonably than the Panchen Lama's. With this solid block of controlled votes, in addition to those of the five Chinese members, the Committee was powerless—a mere facade of Tibetan representation behind which all the effective power was exercised by the Chinese. In fact, all basic policy was decided by another body called the Committee of the Chinese Communist Party in Tibet, which had no Tibetan members. We were allowed to discuss the minor points, but we could never make any major changes. Although I was nominally chairman, there was nothing much I could do. Sometimes it was almost laughable to see how the proceedings were controlled and regulated, so that plans already completed in the other committee received a pointless and empty discussion and then were passed. But often I felt embarrassed at these meetings. I saw that the Chinese had only made me chairman in order to give an added appearance of Tibetan authority to their schemes.[125]

123. Ibid.

124. "The Dalai Lama's Report at the Inaugural Meeting of the Preparatory Committee for the Autonomous Region of Tibet," *People's Daily* (Peking), 25 April 1956, in *Tibet 1950-67*, 144.

125. Dalai Lama, *My Land*, 133.

The establishment of the PCTAR set the stage for the "enforcement of democratic reforms" alluded to by Chen Yi. Despite the fact that these reforms, already implemented in eastern Tibet in early 1956, had led to opposition there, the Chinese had decided to accelerate the socialist transformation of all minority nationalities, Tibetans of the TAR no longer excluded. This intention was clearly indicated in Chen's phrase "the Tibetan nationality must, in common with the other nationalities, pursue the road to Socialism." That the delegates to the PCTAR enthusiastically agreed to this plan as Chen claimed is doubtful, even if their unanimous consent was secured; certainly, they could not have comprehended its implications. Tibetans continued to cling to the promise that reforms would be undertaken only with the agreement of the "public leaders of Tibet," presumably the Dalai Lama and his government. However, Tibetans had little idea of what the Chinese meant by "democratic reforms" and could not anticipate the methods of coercion and deceit by which the Chinese would implement their "reforms."

11

The Revolt in Tibet

Until 1955 most minority nationalities in the PRC were relatively immune from what the Chinese called "democratic reforms and socialist transformation." In 1955-56, however, Mao initiated a rapid acceleration of the socialist transition process, known as the "High Tide of Socialist Transformation." Because the CCP imagined that Chinese control was now secure in all minority nationality areas and that the nationalities were reconciled to Chinese rule, minority nationalities were also included in the "High Tide." Only Tibetans within the TAR remained immune, due to lingering Chinese respect for the promises of the 17-Point Agreement and the fact that the remnants of the Tibetan Government, to whom those promises had been made, still existed. However, Tibetan areas of Kham and Amdo, which, in the Chinese conception, were not part of "Tibet," were included in the socialist transition process. Despite the CCP's expectations that minority nationalities' opposition had already been substantially defused by the Party's "correct" nationalities policies, such was not the case in eastern Tibet. When the Chinese attempted to introduce "democratic reforms" in Kham and Amdo, both areas erupted in revolt.

Democratic Reforms and Socialist Transformation

The transition to socialism in Chinese practice was intended to be implemented in two stages: democratic reforms and socialist transformation. Democratic reforms consisted of redistribution of land, suppression of landlords and "counterrevolutionaries" and initiation of class divisions and class struggle. Democratic reforms lasted from 1950 to 1953 in Han areas but were implemented in few minority nationality areas until 1954 or 1955. The CCP regarded democratic reforms, along with coalition government under the United Front, as a pre-socialist (bourgeois-democratic) stage preliminary to socialist transformation.

Socialist transformation, or collectivization, was also divided into two stages: a preliminary stage, cooperativization, followed by full collectivization. Cooperativization involved the establishment of mutual aid teams and agricultural producers cooperatives; collectivization involved advanced cooperatives, collectives and amalgamated collectives, or communes. Cooperativization and collectivization are usually subsumed under the general heading of collectivization, but differ in that the first stage, cooperativization, left private property intact while the second, collectivization, eliminated private landholdings (in collectives) and then all private property (in communes). The CCP equated collectivization with the transition to socialism, and often referred to it as socialist transformation.

The first stage of collectivization in Han areas was initiated by the Five Year Plan that began in 1954. Until that time the CCP had pursued a relatively cautious policy in the socialist transformation of Chinese society, trying to adhere to the Marxist-Leninist criteria that social reforms should be voluntary and produce actual economic and social benefits. Lenin had recognized that coercion was anathema to true socialist democracy: "Cooperatives must be organized as to gain the confidence of the peasants . . . coercion would ruin the whole cause. Nothing is more stupid than the very idea of applying coercion in economic relations with the middle peasants."[1] The dangers of forced collectivization were apparent in Stalin's attempt to employ "socialist accumulation" in order to achieve industrialization in the Soviet Union in the early 1930s. By means of the collectivization of agriculture, the state acquired "surplus" agricultural products, which were then sold, often on the foreign market, to finance industrialization. Rather than the "forces of production," or industrialization, producing "socialist relations of production," or collectivization, as Marxist theory required, Stalin reversed the process by employing collectivization to produce industrialization. Stalin achieved collectivization in the Soviet Union, but only by force.

The Chinese Communists were initially intent upon avoiding the coercion and disruptions of agriculture that had accompanied forced collectivization in the Soviet Union. The primary obstacle to overcome was Chinese peasants' strong preference for private landownership. Collectivization would have to proceed by slow and careful stages, initiated only when peasants themselves were convinced that collectives would out-perform individual farming both in production and in a more equitable distribution of agricultural products. Democratic reforms, particularly land redistribution and the founding of mutual aid teams, had been accomplished in the early 1950s, substantially by the initiative of the

---

1. V.I. Lenin, *Alliance of the Working Class and the Peasantry*, 283, as quoted in Mark Selden, "Cooperation and Conflict: Cooperative and Collective Formation in China's Countryside," in Mark Selden and Victor Lippit, eds., *The Transition to Socialism in China* (Armonk, New York: M.E. Sharpe, Inc., 1982), 78.

peasants themselves; in some cases, the Party even had to restrain the enthusiasm of the poorest peasants. Democratic reforms had resulted, according to Mao's calculation, in the public executions of some 700,000 landlords.[2]

Bolstered by the success of the "democratic revolution" in the Chinese countryside, the CCP planned to initiate cooperatives and advanced cooperatives, or collectives.[3] However, in 1955, Mao decided that the rate of collectivization had to be accelerated. Mao criticized the gradual course of collectivization for allowing a continuous re-polarization of wealth and a "spontaneous regeneration of capitalism." The best guarantee against capitalist restoration, Mao felt, was to achieve full collectivization rapidly rather than to progress slowly through transitional stages. Mao was convinced that the poor peasants were ready for, even demanding, higher stages of collectivization. This may have been the case for some of the poorest peasants, who had been the beneficiaries of land redistribution and whose fortunes could only improve with each subsequent leveling of peasant property, but most peasants remained reluctant to give up their private plots even for a further redistribution of land and property.[4]

Mao adopted a strategy of mass mobilization to achieve rapid socialist transformation; Chinese agriculture would provide the basis for industrialization, which would then make mechanization of agriculture possible. Mao's strategy for simultaneous agricultural collectivization and industrialization employed Stalin's theory of socialist accumulation, by which agricultural surpluses are employed to finance industrialization. Mao, like Stalin, was aware that the "surplus" of agriculture could more easily be extracted from collectivized peasants because of the greater degree of state control that collectivization achieved. While aware of Stalin's failures, Mao repeatedly stated that China must follow the pattern of the Soviet Union.[5]

Mao shared with Stalin a belief in the ability of mass action to overcome material conditions, or in Marxist terms, in the ability of socialist relations of production (collectivization) to produce the necessary forces of production (industrialization). Mao believed in the efficacy of class

---

2. Mao Tse-tung, "Contradictions Among the People " (Speaking Notes), in Roderick MacFarquhar, Timothy Cheek and Eugene Wu, eds., *The Secret Speeches of Chairman Mao* (Cambridge: Harvard University Press, 1989), 142.

3. Selden and Lippit, *Transition to Socialism in China*, 67.

4. Maurice Meisner, *Mao's China and After: A History of the People's Republic* (New York: The Free Press, 1986), 146.

5. Mao Tse-tung, "The Question of Agricultural Cooperation," 31 July 1955, in Robert R. Bowie and John K. Fairbank, eds., *Communist China 1955-1959: Policy Documents and Analysis* (Cambridge: Harvard University Press, 1962), 101.

struggle as a catharsis for social transformation; in this he adhered to Stalin's doctrinal innovation that the transition to socialism would exacerbate rather than reduce class conflict. In 1955 Mao managed to have a program for accelerated cooperativization adopted, over the objections of the CCP Central Committee, most of whom preferred a more cautious course.[6]

In the late 1955-early 1956 "High Tide" of collectivization, 88 percent of China's peasants entered advanced Agricultural Producers Cooperatives (APC), or collectives, which abolished private landownership. Mao had actually planned to create only elementary APCs, which preserved private landownership, but the movement once launched had been overcome by cadres' zeal to achieve impressive results. The call from Mao to the Party to "lead the movement forward boldly and according to plan, not timidly" and his equation of cautious collectivization with "rightist opportunism" gave cadres tremendous incentive to produce results and good reason to fear going too slowly.[7]

Mao was able to claim that the transition to socialism had been achieved in the Chinese countryside without the resistance or agricultural crisis that had accompanied the same process in the Soviet Union, but the principle of voluntarism was generally violated; peasants were coerced into collectives by a variety of means.[8] Many middle peasants experienced the transition as a loss of personal property and personal freedoms to increased state control. Another source of peasant discontent was the very high "rate of socialist accumulation"; agricultural "surplus" was very liberally defined and agricultural products were priced low in relation to manufactured products. As Lucien Bianco observed, the revolution in China was not a peasant revolution except to the extent that peasants were expected to finance it:

> The policy the Chinese Communists have followed since coming to power confirms their Marxist faith; they have used the peasants to force the progress of history, without wasting much time on the narrow-minded aspirations of the rural masses. This course of action implies not a change of heart but a remarkable consistency. The Chinese Communists did not transform themselves into peasants. They simply recognized and exploited two things the peasants had to offer: a reservoir of discontent great enough to overthrow the old regime, and a reservoir of labor great enough to make possible the primitive accumulation of capital.[9]

6. Selden and Lippit, *Transition to Socialism in China*, 60.
7. "Decisions on Agricultural Cooperation," 31 July 1955, in Bowie and Fairbank, 106.
8. Meisner, *Mao's China*, 209.
9. Lucien Bianco, *Origins of the Chinese Revolution, 1915-1949* (Stanford: Stanford University Press, 1971), 77

"High Tide" and Socialist Transformation Among Nationalities

Socialist transformation was delayed for minority nationalities until Chinese control could be firmly established and, theoretically, until the minorities could be convinced to voluntarily request, or at least to accept, social and economic reforms. Before 1956 the previously most unassimilated nationalities in the PRC—Tibetans, Mongols and the various Turkic nationalities of Sinkiang—were exposed to only the most superficial aspects of Chinese administration and none of the processes of socialist transformation. However, in 1956 the Party made a review of its nationalities work, which determined that minorities' opposition to central Chinese state control had been essentially eliminated; therefore, the national minorities, with the exception of Tibetans within the TAR, were ready for the implementation of "national regional autonomy." A seemingly contradictory element of "autonomy" was that minority nationalities would henceforth be subjected to socialist transformation.[10] Anthropological studies of all the national minorities were undertaken to determine the level of social development of each minority, according to Marxist criteria, thus providing information for their subsequent transformation.[11]

The decision that minority nationalities were ready for socialist transformation coincided with Mao's 1956 acceleration of the socialist transition process; both decisions reflected a radical or leftist line in Chinese politics. Mao personally decided not only upon the course of accelerated transformation but also that minority nationalities should be included, or rather that they should not be excluded from the expected benefits of collectivization:

> Some people say that among the minority nationalities cooperativization cannot be carried out. This is incorrect. We have already come upon many cooperatives run by people of Mongol, Hui, Uighur, Miao and Chuang nationalities, and they have registered very good achievements. These refute the mistaken viewpoint of those who adopt an attitude of looking down on the minority nationalities.[12]

---

10. This decision was announced at the Eighth National Congress in Peking in September 1956. George Moseley, *The Consolidation of the South China Frontier* (Berkeley: University of California Press, 1973), 97.

11. June Dreyer, *China's Forty Millions: Minority Nationalities and National Integration in the People's Republic of China* (Cambridge: Harvard University Press, 1976), 142.

12. Mao Tse-tung, as quoted in T'ang Hsien-chih, "Upsurge of Socialism in China's Countryside," February 1956, in *Current Background* (Hong Kong: United States Consulate), no. 388. Mao's opinion set the stage for later criticisms of nationality autonomy, especially the preservation of minority cultures and traditions, as "rightist" and not in the best interest of the minorities themselves.

The subsequent 1955-56 High Tide proved to be the turning point in nationality relations in the PRC. Socialist transformation among minority nationalities had nationalist implications absent in Han areas. Socialist transformation among minority nationalities had the effect of replacing local nationality administration with Chinese administration. While Mao may have been able to claim that the socialist transition was successful in Han areas, the same campaigns in nationality areas produced widespread resistance and rebellion.

In October 1955 the CCP Central Committee called for greatly accelerated cooperativization of Chinese peasants, including most minority nationalities, but warned against precipitous action in nationality areas.[13] The Party already had some experience in nationality areas where democratic reforms had been attempted before 1956: many peoples of the minority nationalities had regarded the process as a Han Chinese intrusion into their affairs, an intrusion incompatible with the promises of "national regional autonomy." This was admitted in a 1953 report on the progress of regional autonomy:

> Due to the lack of sufficient knowledge about the social characteristics of the minorities and the erroneous application of the measures adopted for land reform in the Chinese areas, dissatisfaction was caused among certain minorities, resulting in confusion for a while and damage to the work of regional autonomy. At present, conditions show that disregard for the special characteristics and concrete conditions of the minorities and the mechanical application of the experience and methods gained and employed in Han nationality areas is a sign not just limited to a few minority districts but is rather widespread.[14]

Based upon this experience, the Party had determined that reforms in minority areas must be undertaken with caution. Liu Shao-ch'i, leader of the pragmatic wing of the CCP, stated that those nationality areas that had not yet undergone democratic reforms or socialist transformation would do so, but unhurriedly and voluntarily:

> In the future, in regions which still await democratic reforms and socialist transformation, we must continue to pursue the prudent policy we have been pursuing all along. That is to say, all reforms must be deliberated in an unhurried manner and settled through consultation by the people and the public leaders of the nationality concerned, the settlement being in accord

---

13. "Decisions on Agricultural Cooperation," 11 October 1955, in Bowie and Fairbank, *Communist China 1955-1959*, 115.

14. "Summary of Basic Experiences in Promoting Regional Autonomy," 9 September 1953, in *Tibet 1950-67* (Hong Kong: Union Research Institute, 1967), 27.

with the wishes of the nationality itself. In carrying out reform, peaceful means must be persisted in, and no violent struggle should be resorted to. In regard to the members of the upper strata of the minorities, after they have given up exploiting and oppressing the working people, the state will take appropriate measures to see that they do not suffer as regards political treatment or in their standards of living, and will convince the people of the need for co-operation with them for a long time to come. In regard to religious beliefs in the areas of the minorities, we must continuously and persistently adhere to the policy of freedom of religious belief and must never interfere in that connection during social reform.[15]

A further directive of the Central Committee and State Council reiterated the "principle of self-willingness," and reminded cadres that the characteristics of each nationality were to be taken into consideration. Single-nationality cooperatives were to be the norm; multi-nationality cooperatives were to be established only where it was absolutely necessary. The abrupt merging of cooperatives so as to form joint cooperatives was "not permissible." Pastoral cooperatives were to be established only on a trial basis, and "any haste in carrying this out should be completely eliminated."[16]

Nevertheless, despite warnings against haste in nationality areas, democratic reforms of all minority areas, with the sole exception of the TAR, and collectivization of some areas proceeded at a rapid rate. A 20 June 1956 report on implementation of nationalities policies by Ulanfu, the Chairman of the CCP Nationalities Affairs Commission, revealed that most minorities areas were fully involved in the High Tide:

Since the 2nd session of the 1st NPC, the people of all nationalities in our country have brought about a high tide of socialist construction and socialist transformation all over the country. Along with the development of the socialist cause throughout the country, the construction work has also gained a considerable development in the minority areas. The inner solidarity of all nationalities has been strengthened further and the socialist consciousness and activity of all nationalities have been heightened as never before. Where conditions are present, socialist construction and socialist transformation are actively going on in the minority areas; where

---

15. Liu Shao-ch'i, "Political Report of the Central Committee of the Communist Party of China," 15 September 1956, in Bowie and Fairbank, *Communist China 1955-1959*, 190.

16. "Consolidate Guidance Over Agricultural Producer Cooperatives in Minority Areas," *New China News Agency* (NCNA), 12 September 1956, in Henry Schwartz, comp., *Chinese Policies Towards Minorities: An Essay and Documents*, (Bellingham, Washington: Western Washington State College, 1971), 91.

conditions are not present, conditions are being actively created to pursue the socialist path.[17]

The means for "creating the conditions" to pursue the socialist path were the introduction of "democratic reforms." Some nationality districts underwent almost simultaneous democratic reforms and collectivization. Ulanfu reported that agricultural areas of Inner Mongolia and Tsinghai (Chinghai) achieved "semi-socialist and fully socialist cooperation" by June 1956; 70 to 90 percent of the peasant households of those areas had joined "higher agricultural producers cooperatives" (collectives).[18] The Sinkiang Uighur Autonomous Region was expected to achieve fully socialist cooperation (advanced APCs) by 1957. Some Tibetan areas of Szechuan were also reported to have undergone democratic reforms and socialist transformation in rapid succession:

> The method of peaceful consultation was adopted to carry out democratic reform in some minority areas where no democratic reform had been carried out. . . . Agrarian reform was basically completed in some hsien of agricultural areas in the Ahpa [Ngaba] Tibet autonomous chou in Szechuan, Kantza [Kanze] Tibet autonomous chou and Liangshan Yi autonomous chou. Agricultural producers cooperatives began to be built in these areas after completion of agrarian reform. All peasants of the minority areas, like the peasants of Han Chinese areas, are now throwing themselves in the high tide of agricultural production designed to increase production and peasants' income.[19]

In September 1956 Liu Shao-ch'i reported to the Eighth Party Congress that socialist transformation, meaning the introduction of higher cooperatives or collectives, had been completed in the majority of nationality areas:

> Of the more than 35 million people of the national minorities in China, 28 million inhabit areas where socialist transformation has been basically completed; 2.2 million inhabit areas where socialist transformation is being carried out; and nearly 2 million inhabit areas which are undertaking democratic reforms; thus only some 3 million still inhabit areas which have not yet carried out democratic reforms.[20]

---

17. Ulanfu, "Success in Nationalities Work and Questions of Policy," NCNA, 20 June 1956, in *Current Background*, no. 402. Ulanfu, a highly Sinocized Mongol who did not speak Mongolian, was the CCP's most prominent nationality cadre.

18. Ibid.

19. Ibid.

20. Liu, "Political Report," in Bowie and Fairbank, *Communist China 1955-1959*, 190.

Liu's statistics reveal that socialist transformation of most minority areas had been carried out at the same rapid pace as in Han areas, despite a generally lower level of preparation and warnings against precipitous action. Only some remote pastoral areas, many in eastern Tibet, and the territory of the TAR remained free of democratic reforms. Despite claims that reforms were carried out by "peaceful means" and with the "enthusiastic support of the people of the minority nationalities," democratic reforms and collectivization did not proceed without resistance. As Ulanfu pointed out: "social reform is after all going to change the old system in the minority areas. . . . It is impossible not to encounter any obstacle and not to wage the necessary struggle. There have been cases in minority areas where a small number of ignorant elements, instigated by counter-revolutionaries, committed acts against the will of the majority of their nationality."[21] Chang Chih-i, deputy director of the CCP United Front Work Department, revealed that democratic reforms and socialist transformation in minority areas had aroused resistance of a mass character in some areas, although he maintained that such resistance had class rather than nationalist origins:

> At present, democratic reforms and socialist transformation have already attained a decisive victory in most national minority regions. . . . It must be pointed out, however, that it is difficult to imagine socialist reform being realized without encountering any obstacles or any need to struggle. In individual national minority areas, it has happened that some ignorant people, under the instigation of counterrevolutionary elements, have adopted a course of action contrary to the will of the great majority of the people of the nationality in question and have opposed democratic reform and socialist transformation. The actual nature of this opposition is class struggle, not national struggle. . . . A great number of laboring people of the national minorities have taken part in this struggle, in which the land has been distributed to the numerous persons who were either landless or possessed very little land and to the slaves and serfs. In the present struggle, people of the Han nationality are not as they were in the national struggles of former periods of reactionary rule, when they plundered and seized land; now, on the contrary, they give every kind of support to the people of the national minorities. But the problem is not as simple as this, for this small number of blind, reactionary figures of the upper classes is making use of national and religious banners; posing as guardians of the nation and the religion, they have tricked a part of the masses. This activity, which is opposed to reform, has thus, to a certain extent, taken on a mass nature in some areas.[22]

---

21. Ulanfu, "Success in Nationalities Work," in *Current Background*, no. 402.

22. Chang Chih-i, in George Moseley, *The Party and the National Question in China* (Cambridge: Massachusetts Institute of Technology Press, 1966), 127.

Democratic reforms were usually initiated through public meetings at which landlords or members of the former ruling classes—excluding those who were cooperating with the United Front—were subjected to public accusation and "struggle." Struggle between classes, or class conflict, was the Marxist method for "resolving class contradictions." Struggle often lasted for several days until the victim was exhausted. Those subjected to the most severe struggle were sometimes permanently disabled or even killed by their tormenters. Others were sentenced to public execution. Most who survived were arrested and disappeared into prison or labor camps. Public struggle was intended not only to raise the class consciousness of the lower classes but to intimidate the upper classes and the population in general. Struggle, as described by Bao Ruowang, left the accused no defense and was intended to reform and intimidate not only the accused but all those participating in the struggle:

[Struggle] is a peculiarly Chinese invention combining intimidation, humiliation and sheer exhaustion. Briefly described, it is an intellectual gang-beating of one man by many, sometimes even thousands, in which the victim has no defense, even the truth. . . . The technique was a thing of utter simplicity: a fierce and pitiless crescendo of screams demanding that the victim confess, followed by raucous hoots of dissatisfaction with any answer he gave them. . . . The Struggle was born in the thirties, when the Communists first began making headway in the great rural stretches of China. Developed over the years by trial and error, it became the standard technique for interrogating the landlords and other enemies who fell into the hands of the rebellious peasants. There is a system and a real rationale behind it all. The Communists were and remain very formalistic: A man must be made to confess before he is punished, even if his punishment has been decided beforehand. The captured landlord was pushed, shoved or carried to a handy open area and forced to kneel and bow his head as dozens or hundreds or thousands of peasants began surrounding him. Screamed at, insulted, slapped, spat upon, sometimes beaten, hopelessly confused and terrorized, no victim could hold out for long. . . . There is never any time limit to a Struggle. It can go on indefinitely if the leaders of the game feel that not enough contrition has developed . . . a Struggle is rarely resolved quickly; that would be too easy. At the beginning, even if the victim tells the truth or grovellingly admits to any accusation hurled at him, his every word will be greeted with insults and shrieks of contradiction. . . . After three or four days the victim begins inventing sins he has never committed, hoping that an admission monstrous enough might win him a reprieve. After a week of Struggling he is prepared to go to any lengths.[23]

---

23. Bao Ruo-wang (Jean Pasgualini), *Prisoner of Mao* (New York: Penguin Books, 1976), 59. Bao was a French citizen of mixed French and Chinese descent who was arrested as a

"Democratic reforms," or the suppression of "class enemies" and "counterrevolutionaries" was a primary means of imposition of CCP rule in China and of Chinese control over minority nationalities:

Relations between various nationalities have also gained improvement as a result of the victory of the campaign for suppression of counterrevolutionaries. During the early period of liberation of certain national minority districts, counterrevolutionaries exploited the historical differences between nationalities, fabricated many rumors to undermine the nationality policy of the People's Government and attempted to excite national minorities to take part in revolt. But the People's Government correctly carried out the nationality policy, led the national minorities to wage appropriate but firm struggle against counterrevolutionaries, and dealt blows to those heinous counterrevolutionaries hated by the majority of the people of national minorities, thereby furthering the unity of all nationalities.[24]

Many minority nationalities experienced the "High Tide" as a rapid and unprecedented imposition of Chinese control. Democratic reforms were accompanied by rhetoric on the United Front, regional autonomy, freedom from class oppression, and the elimination of oppression of one nationality by another in a socialist state. Accompanying the suppression of traditional leaders was the elevation of lower class collaborators to symbolic positions of authority. However, the elimination of indigenous administration could not be disguised by the role of Chinese-controlled collaborators and activists. "Democratic reforms" were often perceived by nationalities not as relief from class exploitation, as the Chinese intended, but as the imposition of foreign domination. To nationality peoples, collectivization represented state control identified not with the "autonomous" nationality administration but with the Chinese.

As the Chinese Communists were well aware, nationalist consciousness among the minorities resided predominantly in the ruling classes; therefore, nationality resistance could be virtually eliminated by the repression or co-option of a single class, under the guise of liberation from upper class exploitation. However, the imposition of Chinese rule over peoples previously ruled only loosely even by indigenous authorities aroused a popular nationalist opposition in response. Although most of the former ruling class were co-opted or repressed, and many of the

---

counterrevolutionary in 1957. As Bao realized after participating in the struggle of another prisoner, "we had been Struggling ourselves at the same time, mentally preparing to accept the government's position with passionate assent, whatever the merits of the man we were facing." Ibid., 82.

24. "Great Success in the Suppression of Counter-Revolutionaries," 27 September 1952, *Survey of China Mainland Press* (Hong Kong: United States Consulate), 31.

lower class were induced to collaborate by a variety of means, many others of all classes experienced an arousal of nationalist consciousness.

Nationalist consciousness, previously confined to a small segment of the educated upper class, was spread among the population in general by the very fact of foreign conquest and rule. In addition, the repression of local leaders under the guise of "democratic reforms" was more successful in creating resistance to the Chinese than it was in creating "proletarian class consciousness." Many local social, political and religious leaders subjected to humiliation and suppression during democratic reforms were not regarded as class exploiters, but as respected, even revered, figures who represented that nationality's cultural, religious or national identity. While the CCP astutely co-opted those of the upper classes who were willing to cooperate in the United Front, it miscalculated in thinking that it could repress uncooperative members of the upper classes without arousing national resistance.

The arousal of what the Chinese called "local nationalism" was in fact a result of many of the Party's nationalities policies, all of which were intended to produce the opposite result. Propaganda against local nationalism often had the contradictory effect of stimulating national identity and nationalist consciousness. Education of minority nationality students and cadres in the ideology of nationality autonomy increased their awareness of nationality identity and led to demands that autonomy should actually be respected. In addition, increased facilities for local intercommunication helped transcend regional identities within each nationality. These included transportation, which increased physical contact and lessened regionalist identification; political participation, which increased awareness of common identity within a nationality; and programs for education of minorities in China, which increased awareness of national identity in contrast to the Chinese.

The 1955-56 High Tide was a turning point in both the course of Chinese politics and in nationality relations. The High Tide set the pattern for future Chinese politics. Mao's leftist enthusiasm for a rapid transition to socialism in the PRC produced repeated campaigns of precipitous collectivization, with consequent social and economic disruptions, leading inevitably to periods of more gradual socialization and attempts to repair the damage of rampant leftism. The High Tide produced active resistance and opposition, even open revolt in nationalities areas, and led to a fatal deterioration in nationality relations.[25] Subsequent leftist peri-

---

25. Revolts occurred in eastern Tibet, among the Tibeto-Burman Lolo (Yi) of Yunnan and in Sinkiang. Jamyang Norbu, *Warriors of Tibet* (London: Wisdom Publications, 1986), 97; Donald H. McMillen, *Chinese Communist Power and Policy in Sinkiang, 1949-1977* (Boulder: Westview Press, 1979), 117.

ods saw campaigns for the socialist transformation of nationalities, and disregard for their special characteristics, cultural preservation, or political autonomy. Leftist policies reflected the view that nationalities' best interests lay in abandonment of their backward cultures in favor of socialist progress and development along with the Han.

Revolt in Tibet: 1956

After the creation of the Preparatory Committee for the Tibet Autonomous Region, the Chinese moved quickly to institute campaigns on many fronts, all intended to further consolidate power in their own hands. The PCTAR spawned numerous subcommittees intended to take over the affairs of administration from the Tibetan Government. The PCTAR gradually assumed most of the territorial administrative functions of the Tibetan Government by setting up district and regional branches, staffed by Tibetans in symbolic positions of authority, but with Chinese personnel actually in charge.[26]

Once this political infrastructure was established, the Chinese moved to implement development projects, which, although small in scale, entailed a significant increase in the number of Chinese personnel in Tibet and in Chinese involvement in Tibetan affairs. Development was planned in agriculture, animal husbandry, mining and industry, exploitation of forest resources, and small hydroelectric projects. Social development projects in health and education were begun, the latter arousing resistance from the ecclesiastical class. The Chinese initiated a campaign to establish secular education in May of 1955.[27] Primary and secondary schools were created with a curriculum including Tibetan and Chinese languages and the history of China and the Chinese revolution. Education was conducted in the Tibetan language but, in accordance with the formula "national in form, socialist in content," was laden with Marxist and Chinese Communist ideology. Minority Nationalities Institutes specialized in training students of Tibetan nationality were established at Hsianyang, Sining and Chengdu (in addition to the Central Nationalities Institute in Peking) and Tibetan children were recruited to attend them.

Additional United Front organizations were created, including a

---

26. One Tibetan reported that in response to Tibetan objections to the PCTAR, the Chinese said that if the Tibetans didn't want to participate in the PCTAR, then the Chinese would administer it without them. Rinzin Paljor, personal interview, Dharamsala, November 1989.

27. George Ginsburgs and Michael Mathos, *Communist China and Tibet: The First Dozen Years* (The Hague: Martinus Nijhoff, 1964), 96.

Tibetan Youth Conference, Association of Patriotic Youth of Tibet, Young
Pioneers, a Tibetan branch of the Chinese Buddhist Association, and a
Tibet Committee of the Chinese People's Political Consultative
Conference that included representatives of Tibet's traditional ruling
class and the major monasteries. The first Tibetan members of the CCP
(from the TAR) were admitted in July 1956.[28]

All of these activities required an increase in the numbers of Chinese
administrators in Tibet and caused increased friction with the Tibetan
population. Private trade was circumscribed and, even though Chinese
state trading organizations paid high prices for Tibetan agricultural and
pastoral products and imported many manufactured products from
China at subsidized prices, Tibetans experienced inflation in prices for
essential food items because of Chinese requirements. Tibetan discontent
was also aroused due to the alteration in the functions of the Tibetan
Government, the introduction of Chinese influence into many aspects of
Tibetan political and social life and Chinese repressive measures against
dissent.

Tibetan discontent was manifested by a revival of the informal people's assembly, *Mimang Tsongdu*, which, although of only rudimentary
organization and effectiveness, seems to have been regarded by the
Chinese as a major threat. They quickly moved to force the Tibetan
Government to repress this organization and to characterize it as a false
representative of the popular will, that role being exclusively reserved for
the Chinese Communist Party. The *Mimang Tsongdu* was therefore
banned in 1955 and its leaders arrested as "agents of foreign imperialists."[29]

Chinese activities within the TAR remained relatively benign compared to what was simultaneously taking place in eastern Tibet. The TAR
was still considered immune from the High Tide and socialist transformation, but Tibetan autonomous districts of Chinghai, Kansu and
Szechuan had already "achieved regional autonomous status," and were
therefore considered ready for the implementation of "democratic
reforms" and "socialist transformation."[30]

---

28. Ibid., 93.

29. *Tibet Under Chinese Communist Rule: A Compilation of Refugee Statements* (Dharamsala:
Information and Publicity Office of His Holiness the Dalai Lama, 1976), 5.

30. The majority of the Tibetan autonomous districts in eastern Tibet were established at
the end of 1953 and early 1954. Exceptions were those established earlier: Kanze
Autonomous Prefecture in Szechuan (24 November 1950); Yushu (Jyekundo) Autonomous
Prefecture in Chinghai (25 December 1951); and Apa (Ngaba) Autonomous Prefecture in
Szechuan (1 January 1953). Dechen Autonomous Prefecture in Yunnan was the last to be
established (13 September 1957). Ma Yin, ed., *China's Minority Nationalities* (Beijing: Foreign
Languages Press, 1989), 434.

The first step in preparation for implementation of reforms was the cultivation of lower class collaborators and activists, who were promised an overturning of society in which they would become the new ruling class. Collaborators were rewarded with material goods, including outright bribes. Coercion also played a role in gaining collaborators; reluctant members of the lower classes were threatened with denunciation as reactionaries if they refused to cooperate. Lower class collaborators assisted the Chinese in gathering data upon which class divisions would be based. Tibetans were generally unaware of the purposes behind Chinese interest in their family economy, and willingly revealed information that would be used to impose class divisions and confiscate wealth:

> The Chinese visited all homes and surreptitiously noted the state of the family and the amount of gold, silver and grain it possessed. They gave presents to members of the household and made conversation. Direct questions about wealth and status were not asked. Instead, innocent inquiries were made about neighbors and the leading notables of the locality. The villagers were naive and thought themselves clever for getting free food and clothing from the Chinese in exchange for some common information that was no real secret. In this manner the Chinese managed to get an accurate and complete list of all the prominent people in the district and the amount of wealth in every household. They were very thorough. They gave candies to small children and asked them questions about their parents and elders.[31]

"Democratic reforms" were initiated by making class divisions and stimulating conflict between what were often artificially created classes. Tibetans were divided into three primary classes, determined by property ownership: *Jorden*, property owners (literally, "holders of wealth"); *Jording*, middle class ("middle wealth'); *Jormei*, those with no property ("without wealth").[32] The upper class was singled out for immediate confiscation of property and public criticism (with the exception of those cooperating with the United Front). The middle class was also subjected to scrutiny for any exploitative practices or politically "reactionary" attitudes. Only the lowest classes were considered free of any inherent guilt. Democratic reforms were implemented in eastern Tibet by Chinese PLA

31. Jamyang Norbu, *Warriors of Tibet*, 86.
32. These three primary classes were also occasionally divided into five: (1) *Sabdak* (landlord); (2) *Chudak* (wealthy); (3) *Jording* (considerable property); (4) *Jorchung* (small property); and (4) *Jormei* (no property). The first two classes were subsumed under the *Jorden* category, while the last two were considered to be *Jormei*. Amdo Some (Tenzin Palgye), personal interview, Dharamsala, December 1989.

troops accompanied by Chinese and Tibetan officials and Tibetan activists, who travelled from village to village and nomadic camp redistributing property and holding struggle sessions of those of the upper class accused of exploiting the people. Tibetans report that property of the upper classes was confiscated with much propaganda and fanfare, but when redistribution took place they found that the Chinese had taken the best of everything for themselves, including land and livestock.[33]

Class divisions and land and property redistribution was accompanied by "struggle" of upper class "exploiters" and uncooperative traditional leaders. Struggle (*thamzing* in Tibetan) was the CCP's primary tool for social transformation. By this violent method the CCP hoped to induce "democratic" participation and class awareness, as well as an atmosphere of fear and conformity in order to ensure that further social transformations would proceed without resistance. The Chinese may have expected that Tibetans, once convinced of the truth of their exploitation by the upper classes and the lamas, would engage in a voluntary process of public and violent denunciation of the members of that class, as had occurred within China. Struggle, within Chinese psychology, exploited the power of ages of repressed animosities and the latent violence and aggression of Chinese society. Buddhist Tibetans, however, imbued with the ideology of non-violence, were appalled by the violence and brutality against so-called exploiters, reactionaries or counterrevolutionaries, who were often highly regarded traditional leaders or revered lamas. The violence and brutality of Chinese methods of social reform served to intimidate Tibetans of all classes, but was not a "democratic catharsis," as the Chinese intended, but a psychological trauma for Tibetans, often leading to suicides, despair and hatred of what the Chinese had brought upon Tibetan society. As Jamyang Norbu has written,

> These "struggles" were diabolically cruel criticism meetings where children were made to accuse their parents of imaginary crimes; where farmers were made to denounce and beat up landlords; where pupils were made to degrade their teachers; where every shred of dignity in a person was torn to pieces by his people, his children and his loved ones. Old lamas were made to have sex with prostitutes in public. And often the accused was beaten, spat and urinated upon. Every act of degradation was heaped upon him—and it killed him in more ways than one. When someone was

---

33. "Statements made by Tibetan refugees," in *Tibet and the Chinese People's Republic: A Report to the International Commission of Jurists by its Legal Inquiry Committee on Tibet* (Geneva: International Commission of Jurists, 1960), 252, 265.

through in a thamzing session, no one ever spoke of him again. He was no martyr for the people, because the people had killed him. His death lay in the hands of those who should have honoured and remembered him; but in their guilt, the people tried to forget him and the shameful part they had played in his degradation.[34]

The process of accusation began with the most easily identifiable of the upper classes: the hereditary aristocracy and upper class lamas (those not cooperating with the United Front). Other opponents of the Chinese were accused as "enemies of the people." An essential element of the Chinese Communist class categorization was that political criteria were also applied; thus, a person of any economic category could be classified as an "enemy of the people" because of a "reactionary" attitude, evidence of which, in Tibet, was any opposition to Chinese rule. Many traditional leaders were subjected to "struggle" as exploiters, even if they had not been large property owners, in order to eliminate any potential leaders of resistance. This purpose was reportedly admitted by a Chinese cadre in eastern Kham:

> It is of paramount importance to recognize the people who have the ability to affect public opinion, and who are acknowledged by the masses as reliable men and leaders. Without such vital knowledge, we will never be able to introduce democratic reforms into the country. The first and quintessential step is to sever the bond between the masses and their traditional leaders, or the people they normally look to for guidance. Further steps are impossible without first accomplishing this. It can only be achieved in the guise of elevating the economic plight of the masses.[35]

> We have to watch those people who have qualities of leadership, or those that the masses look to for guidance. This is Party policy. In order to disillusion the people about their reactionary leaders, we expose them as serf-owners, thus revealing their true and ugly faces behind the masks. Of course, not all these people are really serf-owners. Some of them might be as poor as the rest of the people. But that is only a technicality as the thoughts of all these people are reactionary and feudal. If they had the opportunity they would undoubtedly become serf-owners.[36]

Religion was ostensibly protected during democratic reforms: "The Government on the basis of the aspirations of the people and religious leaders enforced the Party and Government policy on freedom of religious belief and protection of religion on the one hand and gave the nec-

34. Jamyang Norbu, *Warriors of Tibet*, 133.
35. Ibid., 85.
36. Ibid., 111.

essary and proper solution to the economic relations between the temples and the masses on the other."[37] However, the "necessary and proper solution," was that the masses should realize their exploitation by the monks and cease to support them. Monasteries were deprived of their estates during land reforms, thus depriving them of their subsistence, forcing a general depopulation of monasteries and, consequently, a reduction in the social and political influence of organized religion. Religion was especially attacked because the church was considered one of the main institutional obstacles to Chinese control and socialist revolution and Buddhism was regarded as the primary ideological competitor to communism. In eastern Tibet, monastic authorities often administered large areas and were large landowners. Lamas were therefore attacked both as landlords and as political leaders.

The struggle process was initiated among a reluctant Tibetan populace by lower class activists, who were instructed by the Chinese; the activists were always the first to accuse and the first to initiate violence against those being struggled. Tibetans learned that unenthusiastic participation in criticism of the accused was grounds for being characterized as lacking in revolutionary fervor or for being labeled as reactionary and subjected to struggle themselves. Due to this pressure on all the participants to demonstrate their activist zeal, struggle sessions were characterized by demands for ever more severe or horrible forms of punishment (often suggested by the Chinese). Mandatory popular participation in the denunciation of the upper classes and lamas was intended as a lesson in "people's democracy."

High lamas were often publicly humiliated, beaten and even tortured to death. Lamas were tormented and tortured (usually by the Chinese, since even Tibetan collaborators refused to participate) as a demonstration of their inability to summon divine assistance and therefore evidence of the falsity of their religion and the powerlessness of their gods. Many high lamas were killed during their public tortures; other lamas were imprisoned or sent to "reform through labor" camps. Lower status monks were considered less guilty and generally reformable; they were often released, but were required to marry and to become economically productive.

Sangye Yeshe (Tien Pao), one of the Tibetans recruited by the Red Army during the Long March through eastern Tibet and now vice-chairman of the Kanze Autonomous District and chairman of the Nationalities Affairs Commission of the Szechuan Provincial Government, instructed

---

37. "Conditions in the Tibetan Autonomous Chou of Szechuan," *NCNA*, 25 June 1956, in *Current Background*, no. 409.

the Kham Tibetans that democratic reforms were an essential step on the road to socialism, one that required a radical and violent restructuring of Tibetan society:

> Democratic reform is the process through which the people of various nationalities in the preliminary stage of capitalist development must pass in order to attain socialism. Without the abolition of capitalism, socialism cannot be established; socialism cannot possibly be built on the foundation of the old social system. Without reform a clear class distinction cannot be drawn between the slave owners and feudal lords on the one hand and the labouring masses on the other; the broad masses of the labouring people cannot be mobilized and organized; cadres of various nationalities cannot receive their due training; and it will be impossible to discover and cultivate large numbers of activists and basic level cadres or to establish a solid political power at the basic level. The principal task of democratic reform is to crush the old and corrupt social system restricting the development of society and nationalities and to set up the people's own political regime. . . . The reform must necessarily be a violent, sharp and most complicated class struggle.[38]

The CCP did not regard Tibetans' unpreparedness for democratic reforms and socialist transformation as a reason to proceed slowly, but as a justification for "jumping stages of history." The CCP thought Tibetans and other "backward" nationalities potentially capable of an accelerated rate of development, due to their very backwardness: "After the completion of democratic reform, they can fully accomplish socialist reform at a comparatively high speed, surpassing one or even several stages of historical development and jumping from a slave society directly to a socialist society."[39] Marx, Lenin and Mao had all stated that "great leaps" over stages of economic development were possible beginning from the most primitive conditions: "Under the influence of the victory in socialist revolution and the leap forward in construction throughout the whole country today, under the leadership of the Party and the direct assistance of the advanced Han nationality . . . one step to heaven is completely possible and necessary."[40]

Democratic reforms began early in 1956 in Ngaba and Kanze Autonomous Districts of Szechuan; by September democratic reforms

---

38. Sangye Yeshe (Tien Pao), "Plant Red Flags in Every Corner of the Tibetan and Yi Regions of Szechuan," *Nationalities Unity*, no. 9 (Peking), 6 September 1958, in *Tibet 1950-67*, 323.

39. Ibid.

40. "Pastoral Areas of Tsinghai Province in the Great Revolutionary High Tide," in *Survey of China Mainland Magazines* (Hong Kong: United States Consulate), no. 155, 35.

were reported to have been completed for 95 percent of the Tibetan population in those areas. Six hundred thousand "slaves and semi-slaves" and four hundred thousand "serfs" were reportedly liberated. 2.17 million *mou* of land was confiscated from "slave owners and feudal landlords" and redistributed. The usual Chinese practice was to redistribute some portion of confiscated lands for the support of PLA troops, Han officials and Chinese colonists. Agricultural Producers Cooperatives, including some higher APCs, or collectives, were introduced in the Apa (Ngaba) Autonomous District as early as June 1956.[41]

Democratic reforms were implemented more rapidly in agricultural than in pastoral areas, but the Chinese simultaneously began to propagandize the advantages of fixed settlements to the nomads. Sedentarization was the first step to collectivization: "Fixed abode and nomadic herd-raising has one important significance at present, namely, the promotion of the mutual-aid and cooperation movement."[42] The goal of socialist transformation in pastoral areas was said to be to replace private ownership with joint state-private ownership and then by "ownership by the whole people." By this means it was hoped to "eliminate the system of exploitation and ultimately to wipe out the class of livestock owners."[43] "Experimental" lower stage cooperatives were set up in the nomadic district of Yushu (Jyekundo):

> During the past years, in conjunction with carrying out the central tasks, patriotism has been continuously propagandized among the masses in all tribes. In the spring of this year [1956], the policy of mutual aid and cooperation was propagandized. In this way, the broad masses of the herdsmen began to understand the preparations that were being made for the socialist transformation of the pastoral areas. At the voluntary request of the masses, four pastoral producers cooperatives and agricultural-pastoral producers cooperatives were set up by way of experiment, as well as 80 permanent and 82 temporary mutual-aid teams.[44]

Democratic reforms were begun in early 1956 not only in Tibetan areas of Szechuan, Chinghai and Kansu, but in western Kham (Kham west of

---

41. Ibid., 321; "Conditions in the Tibetan Autonomous Chou of Szechuan," in *Current Background*, no. 409.

42. Li Tsung-hai, "Positively Promote Fixed Abodes and Nomadic Herd-Raising," 14 March 1958, in *Tibet 1950-67*, 296.

43. "Pastoral Areas of Tsinghai Province in the Great Revolutionary High Tide," 1 October 1958, in *Survey of China Mainland Magazines*, no. 155, 33. Most Tibetan pastoralists owned some livestock even though they might also work for others.

44. Chao K'un-yuan, "Further Manifest the Effect of Nationalities Regional Autonomous Power," *Tsinghai Daily*, 24 November 1956, in *Tibet 1950-67*, 191.

the Yangtze), the area formerly under the "Chamdo Liberation Committee," even though those territories had been "returned" to the TAR and therefore should have been immune. This was done by attempting to coerce local leaders to "request" that reforms be instituted.[45] The Chinese attempted to bypass these restrictions by securing a "voluntary request" for reforms from the leaders of western Kham.

In April 1956, shortly after the ceremonies in Lhasa inaugurating the PCTAR, Tibetan leaders of western Kham were summoned to Chamdo, where they were propagandized to "request" that reforms be introduced. According to the Dalai Lama's account of this event, the Khampa leaders were told that the Dalai Lama preferred to delay the introduction of reforms until Tibetans were ready, whereas the Panchen had demanded that they be immediately introduced; they were asked to express their own preference. About a hundred voted to go along with whatever the Dalai Lama agreed to, forty voted to have the reforms immediately and about 200 voted never to have reforms under any circumstances. The leaders were then dismissed with gifts of picture books, pens and toilet articles.[46]

A month later (May or June 1956), the same leaders were summoned to Jomda (within the Chamdo district, northeast of Chamdo, on the road to Derge) where they were surrounded by PLA troops and informed that reforms would be introduced immediately. The Khampas pretended to agree with the plans of the Chinese, after which the Chinese guards relaxed and the Tibetans were able to escape. Thereafter, they had no choice but to take to the mountains in rebellion.[47] The attempt to force the introduction of democratic reforms in the Chamdo district was the beginning of the Tibetan revolt in western Kham.

Eastern Kham also erupted in revolt when democratic reforms were introduced. One reason for this was that "reforms" included confiscation of weapons from the Khampas, for whom weapons were regarded as part of their normal accoutrement. The revolt began in Nyarong, led by Dorje Yudon, the wife of Gyari Nyima, chieftain of the area, who was in Dartsendo at the time attending a meeting at which the Chinese announced their reforms. The actual spark for revolt was the murder of the women and children of another official, who was also at Dartsendo, who refused to surrender their family's weapons. Dorje Yudon gathered the men of the Gyari clan and others of Nyarong and attacked Chinese outposts in Nyarong. She also sent emissaries to other areas of Kham,

45. Nyima Assam, Kalsang Wangdu, personal interviews, Dharamsala, January 1990.

46. Dalai Lama, *My Land and My People: Memoirs of the Dalai Lama of Tibet* (New York: Potala, 1977), 136.

47. Nyima Assam, Kalsang Wangdu, personal interviews, Dharamsala, January 1990.

urging them to rise against the Chinese. Revolt soon became general in Kham due to Khampas' resistance to "democratic reforms." Tibetan attacks on the Chinese were initially successful due to the Khampas familiarity with the terrain and their martial skills, but the Chinese held out in their fortresses and began a massive introduction of troops to quell the rebellion. Soon, many of the Kham Tibetans were forced to leave their villages and take to the hills from where they waged a guerilla campaign.[48]

By the end of 1956, all Tibetan cultural areas outside the TAR, and western Kham, within the TAR, had been subjected to "democratic reforms." "Socialist transformation," or collectivization, had been propagandized in all areas and initiated in some, mostly agricultural areas, although some pastoral areas had also undergone initial stages of collectivization. The Chinese did not decrease the pace of socialist transformation in the face of rebellion but quickened it in order to suppress the rebellion. Democratic reforms were an effective means of eliminating Tibetan leadership, while collectivization increased Chinese control over the Tibetan population. However, the CCP had to admit that its reforms had produced violent resistance:

> The democratic reform movement was not without its problems. It should be noted that although reform was based on the aspirations of the laboring people and public figures of all nationalities, was discussed and approved at the representative conference and was carried out in moderate ways, a small number of feudal lords would not give up too unreasonable exploitation and would not quit the political position of feudal lords or else they looked at their post-reform life and political position with anxiety. Instigated by the remnant gangs of the Kuomintang, they engineered national antagonism by enlarging on certain defects in our work, and consequently revolts broke out in some areas. . . . The Government adopted a lenient policy of pardoning, educating and winning over those taking part in the revolts.[49]

The imposition of democratic reforms also led to rebellion in pastoral areas, as an article from Chinghai revealed:

> When the socialist great revolution in the pastoral areas of our province was still in its primary stage, the die-hards among livestock owners and counterrevolutionaries in religious circles staged an armed revolt against

---

48. Jamyang Norbu, *Warriors of Tibet*, 106.
49. "Conditions in the Tibetan Autonomous Chou of Szechuan," 25 June 1956, in *Current Background*, no. 409.

socialism, the people, and the Communist Party in an attempt to fight the masses of the people and to stop the huge wheel of history. The result was their utter defeat. The religious and feudal power was completely burned away by the flames of revolution.[50]

Sangye Yeshe ascribed the rebellion to "reactionary slave owners and feudal lords representing the old system." He warned against the "dangerous trend of local nationalism," supported by the former ruling classes who were ever ready to "take advantage of certain defects in our work to spread their nationalistic poison under the banner of nationality and religion."[51] Liu Ke-ping, the Chairman of the Nationalities Affairs Committee of the National People's Congress, admitted in an interview with a foreign journalist that there had been revolts, but denied that they had "the least nationalist content." He claimed that the revolts had not been in "Tibet" (TAR), but "in Western Szechuan, in the Kanze Autonomous Chou, on the border of Tibet." Liu reportedly stated that the rebellion "started around the end of February," was "limited to the area of Batang and Lithang," and was "instigated by remnant Kuomintang agents, and launched by a few feudal landlords hostile to the introduction of even the most elementary reforms in the backward social structure of that region." Liu stated that the rebellion had been "mainly settled and its leaders were being treated leniently," and that "the principle in the Chinese Constitution for reforms in the areas of national minorities was being strictly carried out—through peaceful negotiations, with the local people and leaders making their own decisions."[52]

The revolt in eastern Tibet involved not only Lithang and Batang but virtually all of eastern Kham, including Changtreng, Minyak, Dau, Nyarong and Kanze, as well as Chamdo, in western Kham, and Golok, in Chinghai.[53] The Chinese, far from treating the leaders of the revolt leniently, had instituted repressive measures, leading many Tibetans to seek refuge in the mountains where they formed groups organized for resistance. Chinese repression in Lithang, particularly an attempt to arrest local lay and religious leaders during the *Monlam* ceremonies in the spring of 1956, led to two or three thousand Tibetans being surrounded in the large Lithang monastery by PLA troops. The Chinese

---

50. "Pastoral Areas of Tsinghai Province in the Great Revolutionary High Tide," 1 October 1958, in *Survey of China Mainland Magazines*, no. 155, 31.

51. Sangye Yeshe, in *Tibet 1950-67*, 324.

52. "Liu Ke-ping Denies Rumored Tibet Rebellion," *NCNA*, 7 August 1956, in *Current Background*, no. 409.

53. Gompo Tashi Andrugtsang, *Four Rivers, Six Ranges: A True Account of Khampa Resistance to Chinese in Tibet*, (Dharamsala: Information and Publicity Office of H.H. The Dalai Lama, 1973), 47.

bombarded the monastery with mortars, but, unable to persuade the Tibetans to surrender, summoned the Chinese Air Force. Lithang monastery was then bombed by Iluyshin Il-28 twin-engine jet aircraft that the Chinese had recently received from the Soviet Union. Hundreds of the Tibetans within the monastery grounds were killed or wounded; others were killed by PLA troops who stormed the monastery after its walls had been pierced; a few escaped to join the Tibetan resistance.[54] Dzachukha monastery in Golok as well as several other places were also bombed.[55]

Despite Chinese attempts to deny or obscure the nature of the revolt in Tibet, the revolt was not unknown to official circles in the outside world, as is evidenced by a letter, dated 20 July 1956, from Thupten Nyenjik (Thupten Nyingje), the former abbot of Gyantse monastery and governor of Gyantse district (in the TAR), who fled Tibet in 1956. This letter, describing the events in eastern Tibet as well as the situation within the TAR, was sent via the Dalai Lama's brother, Gyalo Thondup, to the *Statesman* newspaper in New Delhi, to the Indian and Pakistan premiers, and to President Eisenhower and Secretary of State Dulles in the United States. The letter accused the Chinese of imperialism, colonialism and oppression of the Tibetan people:

> To us Tibetans the phrase the "liberation of Tibet," in its moral and spiritual implications, is viewed as a deadly mockery. The country of a free people was invaded and occupied under the pretext of Liberation. Liberation from whom and what? Ours was a happy country with a solvent government and a contented people till the Chinese invasion in 1950 since when we have been so exploited that we have been reduced to a state of intellectual, spiritual and economic bankruptcy. Are the ruthless attacks by land and air, the indiscriminate and cold-blooded bombing of Dzachukha in Gelek [Golok] and of Lithang proof of the Chinese concern for our progress and welfare? In Lithang alone, over four thousand men, women and children have been killed and the capital razed to the ground. The survivors have taken to the hills and are now waging a desperate guerilla warfare with the Chinese. The ferocity with which this campaign is being carried out may be judged by the words of General Chang Kua Hwa [Chang Kuohua] in his speech in Lhasa on April 26 1956 on the occasion of the inauguration of the Preparatory Committee for the Regional Autonomy of Tibet, in which he declared, "We have bombed Lithang and shall wipe out all such revolts in the same manner." . . .

---

54. Ibid.

55. American Embassy, Karachi to Department of State, 6 September 1956, National Archives, 793B.00/9-656.

It is here, in Outer Tibet [eastern Tibet], an area about one million square miles, where the Chinese for the past 42 years and more, ever since the days of the Manchus, have been doing their utmost to colonize the country and have imported large numbers of Chinese settlers, that the trouble has first broken out—ample testimony to the failure of an alien government to subjugate and absorb the Tibetans who believe in their own national integrity. . . .

Viewed in its historical perspective, the so-called "Liberation" of Tibet is the latest and most formidable attempt of the Chinese, prompted by the greed of an over-populated country for the vast area which comprises Tibet and her wealth in natural resources . . . to colonize Tibet in a struggle that has persevered through the centuries. For let there be no mistake about it, the "Liberation" of Tibet is nothing but a newer form of brutal, ruthless colonialism to be more dreaded than the old because here, the aim is not only exploitation but the complete absorption of a people—absorption or extermination are the only two alternatives offered to the people of Tibet by the Chinese. That they are committed despite all their talk of autonomy, to the obliteration of the religion, culture and tradition of a non-Chinese people is all too clear, for as General Chang Kua Hwa himself in his speech in Lhasa on April 26, 1956 . . . quoting Mao Tse Tung, said, "In a few years the population of Tibet must be raised from two-three million to over ten million." This can only mean the genocide, the complete disappearance of an ancient culture and people through the importation of Chinese on a gigantic scale. Such is the meaning of Chinese autonomy for Tibet.

It was a blot on the conscience of the world when not a single finger was lifted by any country to prevent the forcible occupation of a free people; it should now be a matter of the deepest shame that not one country raises its voice against the butchery of that people.[56]

The letter from the Gyantse abbot and governor was not publicized by the Indian, Pakistan or US governments (and was not, apparently, printed by the *Statesman*).[57] The truth about the Tibetan revolt therefore

---

56. The letter also complained of the "disappearance" of Tibetans for the "casual expression of anti-Chinese sentiments," the adverse economic effects of the Chinese occupation, the elevation of the Panchen Lama to an undeserved and unprecedented political status, and violations of the 17-Point Agreement, including attempts to undermine the "spiritual and temporal sovereignty of His Holiness the Dalai Lama" by every means. The letter warned of Chinese attempts to "mislead the world" by means of "Chinese prepared speeches in praise of the fictitious benefits of the regime," which the Dalai Lama was forced to read by pressure brought upon him by Chinese threats. Ibid.

57. The letter in the National Archives bears marks indicating that it was distributed to US Embassies and Consulates in London, New Delhi, Calcutta, Hong Kong and Taipei. It was also distributed within the State Department, to the CIA, USIA, and Army, Navy and Air Force. Ibid.

remained unknown in the outside world except to a few world leaders who chose to keep the information confidential. However, despite their denials, the Chinese were aware that they had aroused major resistance in eastern Tibet. Large numbers of Chinese troops were introduced into Kham to suppress the revolt and to prevent its spreading to the TAR.

Retrenchment Policy in the TAR: 1957

In early 1956 the Maharaj Kumar of Sikkim, president of the Buddhist Mahabodhi Society, invited the Dalai Lama to India at the end of the year to attend the Buddha Jayanti, the 2500th anniversary of the birth of Lord Buddha. The Maharaj Kumar may have hoped that the Dalai Lama would take the opportunity of a visit to India to seek exile there. The Maharaj Kumar contacted the American Consul at Calcutta on 28 June 1956 to inquire whether the Americans would support the Dalai Lama if he should choose to seek exile. In response, the Americans repeated their offers of 1950-51.[58] Tibetans were anxious that the Dalai Lama should go to India in order to reestablish relations with India as a counter to Chinese influence; the Chinese, for the same reasons, were equally anxious that he should not go.[59]

The Maharaj's personal invitation was soon followed by an official invitation from the Government of India to both the Dalai and Panchen Lamas. The Chinese, having only recently (1954) established relations of "peaceful coexistence" with India, could not prohibit the Dalai Lama's acceptance of the invitation without international embarrassment. The Chinese finally agreed to the visit, but took the precaution of briefing the Dalai Lama on what he should say in India. They also insisted on equal status for the Panchen at all occasions. Chinese officials specifically

---

58. The Maharaj's daughter, Kukula, was married to a Tibetan aristocrat of the Phunkang family (another daughter, Kula, was married to a Tibetan of the Yutok family) and had been a go-between and informant to the Americans during the 1950-51 period. "United States Policy Concerning the Legal Status of Tibet," November 1957, National Archives, 793.B00/11-157.

59. In fact, Mao may have favored allowing the visit, against the advice of the CCP Central Committee, since he, in his ignorance of conditions in other countries, imagined that the Dalai Lama would be unfavorably impressed by capitalist India in comparison to socialist China. Mao was reportedly not greatly fearful that the Dalai Lama might defect, since he believed that the Dalai Lama was not only not essential but was even an impediment to Chinese plans in Tibet, implying that he thought the Dalai Lama would eventually have to be eliminated, or his influence reduced to insignificance, if China's plans in Tibet were to be achieved. Mao reportedly compared the Dalai Lama's potential defection with that of Chang Kuo-t'ao, who had split off from the Red Army in Tibet during the Long March, saying that the Party had survived Chang's defection and it could survive that of the Dalai Lama. Jigme Ngapo, personal communication, Washington D.C., February 1995.

warned the Dalai Lama about the recent events in Hungary (November 1956), pointing out that socialist countries had united to resist the Hungarian "counterrevolution," a warning the Dalai Lama took to mean that he could expect no international support for any similar "counter-revolution" in Tibet.[60]

The Dalai Lama, along with the Panchen and Ngawang Jigme Ngapo, arrived in Delhi on 26 November 1956. The ceremonies in honor of the Dalai Lama's visit were marked by great respect for the Dalai Lama, considerably less for the Panchen, and a conscious ignoring of the symbols of Tibet's subservience to China. As an American observer remarked on the visit:

> It was interesting to observe how the Indians treated their distinguished guests as Tibetans rather than as subjects of Communist China. On most public occasions, Chinese Communist officials were kept well in the background, and Prime Minister Nehru and other officials of the Indian Government, using their own interpreters, held several private conversations with the Dalai Lama. The planes flying the Dalai and Panchen Lamas to New Delhi carried only the flags of India and the respective personal flags of the Lamas—a fact which drew protests from Chinese Communist officials. At public functions the Lamas were usually surrounded by their own officials and presented a spectacle uniquely Tibetan in character.[61]

The treatment accorded to the Panchen failed to meet the standard demanded by the Chinese, and was also the subject of Chinese protests:

> It is generally accepted that the Tibetans look on the Dalai Lama as the symbol of their culture and independence and tend to regard the Panchen Lama as an imposter and stooge of the Chinese Communists. Apart from questions of protocol, it was therefore quite in line with Indian objectives to give the Dalai Lama precedence over the Panchen Lama on all occasions, despite reported requests from Chinese Communists that the two Lamas be treated separately and as equals. An incident at Bagdora airport in West Bengal illustrates the conflict between the Chinese Communists and Indians on this point. Here at a public gathering, two thrones were set up for the Lamas, the one for the Dalai Lama being raised a little higher than the one intended for the Panchen. Chinese Communist officials objected to this form of discrimination and attempted by placing stones and logs under the Panchen Lama's throne to raise it to the same level as the Dalai's.[62]

---

60. Dalai Lama, *My Land*, 141.

61. American Consulate Calcutta to Department of State, 1 February 1957, National Archives, 793B.11/2-157.

62. Ibid. The Dalai Lama also related an incident that occurred at the beginning of his visit in Sikkim: "The Maharaja of Sikkim and his ministers joined us and I changed from the

In his meeting with Indian Prime Minister Nehru, the Dalai Lama indicated that he was considering seeking asylum in India because of the hopelessness of the situation in Tibet. Nehru, emphasizing that the Tibetans could not expect help from India, suggested that the Dalai Lama try to resolve his differences with Chou En-lai, who was due to arrive in Delhi at the end of January. Nehru reminded him that no country had recognized Tibetan independence; Tibet had no choice but to try to live within the provisions of the 17-Point Agreement. The Dalai Lama met with Chou, who, when informed that reforms were being imposed against the will of the Tibetans, seemed surprised and replied that local Chinese officials must be making mistakes (i.e., that involuntary imposition of reforms was not CCP policy). Chou also met separately with the Dalai Lama's brothers, Gyalo Thondup and Thupten Norbu, who told Chou about the problems caused by the Chinese presence in Tibet.[63] Chou responded by promising to alleviate food shortages in Tibet by withdrawing some PLA troops, and he promised to convey the Tibetans' complaints to Mao. He warned the Dalai Lama against staying in India, on the grounds that to do so would be "harmful to the Tibetan people."[64]

While in India the Dalai Lama received a message from the Chinese commander at Lhasa asking him to return because the situation within the TAR had deteriorated and revolt was feared imminent. When Chou returned to India from his European tour he met again with the Dalai Lama. Chou confirmed that the situation in Tibet had worsened and that the PLA was prepared to put down the revolt with force. The Dalai Lama remarked that Chou "spoke as though he still could not understand why Tibetans did not welcome the Chinese."[65] Chou informed the Dalai Lama that the Chinese Government had decided to postpone reforms in Tibet for six years (the period of the next five-year plan) and, "if after that we were still not ready, they could be postponed for fifty years if necessary."[66] The Dalai Lama speculated whether this decision was "a result of my protests to Chou En-lai in Delhi; whether it was or not, it came too late to have much effect on the people's hostility."[67]

---

jeep to his car. . . . It was flying a Sikkimese flag on one side and a Tibetan flag on the other. . . . I was surprised to see a solitary Chinese gentleman, who turned out to be the Ambassador's interpreter, furtively removing the Tibetan flag and tying on a Chinese flag instead." Dalai Lama, *My Land*, 145.

63. Dalai Lama, *My Land*, 148.

64. Dalai Lama, *Freedom in Exile* (New York: Harper Collins, 1990), 119.

65. Dalai Lama, *My Land*, 151.

66. Dalai Lama, *Freedom in Exile*, 119. Chou apparently did not specify what was meant by "Tibet," although Chinese practice was to use the name "Tibet" (*Xizang*) to refer only to the TAR.

67. Dalai Lama, *My Land*, 157.

Chou's promises convinced the Dalai Lama to return to Tibet, "to give the Chinese one last try, in accordance both with the advice of Nehru and the assurances of Chou En-lai."[68] Nehru had also advised the Dalai Lama to return, based upon the assurances he had received from Chou. Chou (as related by the Dalai Lama) had assured Nehru that Tibet was to remain essentially a buffer state between Indian and China:

> While Tibet had long been a part of the Chinese state, they [the CCP] did not consider Tibet as a province of China. The people were different from the people of China proper, just as in other autonomous regions of the Chinese state the people were different, even though they formed part of that state. Therefore, they considered Tibet an autonomous region which would enjoy autonomy. He [Chou] told me [Nehru] further that it was absurd for anyone to imagine that China was going to force communism on Tibet.[69]

The Chinese intention to delay reforms in Tibet was confirmed by Mao in his 27 February 1957 "On Contradictions Among the People" speech in which Mao promised that Tibet would be exempted from reforms for the period of the next five-year plan (1957-1961) and for the subsequent plan as well if the Tibetans themselves were not ready to accept reforms:

> As a result of the efforts of the people of all nationalities over the past few years, democratic reforms and socialist transformation have in the main been completed in most of the national minority areas. Because conditions in Tibet are not ripe, democratic reforms have not yet been carried out there. . . . It has now been decided not to proceed with democratic reform in Tibet during the period of the Second Five-Year Plan.[70]

An oral transcript of Mao's speech reveals that he spoke at greater length about Tibet and in a manner not revealed in the official version:

---

68. Dalai Lama, *Freedom in Exile*, 122. George Patterson indicates that Chou's assurances included a substantial withdrawal of Chinese personnel from Tibet, which Nehru would authenticate by visiting Tibet in 1957. George Patterson, *Tibet in Revolt* (London: Faber and Faber, 1960), 139. In 1958 Nehru expressed an intention to honor his promise to the Dalai Lama to visit Tibet, but the visit was vetoed by the Chinese because Tibet was by then embroiled in revolt. Ibid., 161.

69. Dalai Lama, *My Land*, 152. Nehru reportedly imagined that the subsequent retrenchment policy in Tibet was a concession that he had won for the Dalai Lama from the Chinese. Dorothy Woodman, *Himalayan Frontiers* (New York: Praeger, 1969), 229.

70. Mao Tse-tung, "On the Correct Handling of Contradictions Among the People," in Bowie and Fairbank, *Communist China 1955-1959*, 287. Mao's speech was not published at the time (February 1957), due to Mao's conflicts with the majority on the CCP Central Committee. It was published only in June 1957 in a sanitized and altered version.

There's a group in Tibet who want to set up an independent kingdom. Currently this organization is a bit shaky; this time India asked us to let them return.[?] We permitted the Dalai to go to India; he has already gone to India. Now he has already returned to Tibet. [The Dalai Lama was still in Kalimpong at the time.] America does its work [i.e., against China]. There is a place in India called Kalimpong, where they specialize in sabotaging Tibet. Nehru himself told the Premier [Chou] that this place is a center of espionage, primarily American and British. If Tibet wants to be independent our position is this: you want to agitate for independence, then agitate; you want independence, I don't want independence. We have a seventeen point agreement. We advised the Dalai that he'd be better off coming back: If you stay in India, then go to America, it might not be advantageous [?]. Chou has spoken with him several times. Also with other independence movement people, a group of those residing in Kalimpong, Chou has also talked with them, saying they'd do better to return. As for reform, the seventeen points stipulate that reforms be made; but the reforms need your agreement. You don't want reform, then we won't have any. If in the next few years you don't want reforms, then we won't have any. This is the way we have spoken to them just now. There will be no reform under the second FYP, in the third FYP we will see what you think; if you say reform, then reform; if you say no reform, then we'll continue not to reform. Why such a hurry?[71]

The Chinese leadership apparently took several factors into account in deciding upon a retrenchment in Tibet. The CCP feared the spread of the revolt in eastern Tibet to the TAR. An immediate reason was the need to lure the Dalai Lama back from India and to silence criticism from Tibetan exiles in India or Indian supporters of Tibet. An additional consideration may have been the fact that the Americans were once again evidencing interest in Tibetan affairs. Chou En-lai's personal intervention in the issue may also have been a factor. Chou usually favored a pragmatic approach in foreign and domestic affairs and may have argued that open revolt in Tibet was potentially harmful to China's international reputation. Chou was more cosmopolitan and less chauvinistic than Mao or most of the CCP leadership and usually favored a more liberal approach to nationality affairs. His personal involvement in the Tibetan issue at this time in favor of the retrenchment policy may be assumed, particularly since he had given the Dalai Lama his personal assurances.

After meeting with Chou En-lai in India, the Dalai Lama traveled to Kalimpong, where he met with the former Prime Minister Lukhangwa, Thupten Norbu and Gyalo Thondup, all of whom were opposed to his return to Lhasa. His brothers had received expressions of support from

---

71. Mao, in MacFarquhar, Cheek and Wu, *Secret Speeches of Chairman Mao*, 184.

an Indian politician (Jaya Prakash Narayan) and from the American CIA (this fact, however, according to the Dalai Lama's later account, was not revealed to him at the time).[72] A delegation from Lhasa sent to escort the Dalai Lama back to Tibet also suggested that he should stay in India, "because the situation in Tibet had become so desperate and dangerous." Even Ngapo reportedly thought that "if it were possible to come up with a definite plan, then it might be worthwhile to consider staying."[73] Faced with this opposition, the Dalai Lama decided to consult the Nechung and Gadong oracles. Both said that he should return to Tibet, but some suspicion of deception was present. The Dalai Lama described the scene during the consultation of the oracle:

> Lukhangwa [the prime minister deposed by the Chinese] came in during one of these consultations, at which the oracle grew angry, telling him to remain outside. It was as if the oracle knew that Lukhangwa had made up his mind. But Lukhangwa ignored him and sat down all the same. Afterwards, he came up to me and said, 'When men become desperate they consult the gods. And when the gods become desperate, they tell lies.'[74]

Once again, for similar reasons as in 1951, and due to Chou En-lai's assurances, the Dalai Lama returned to Tibet. He departed India in mid-March and arrived in Lhasa on 1 April. Upon his return, the Dalai Lama sought to act "strictly in accordance with the 17-Point Agreement, and by pressing in every way I could toward autonomy." This did not, however, produce any change in the attitude of the Chinese in Tibet: "At first, I could see no reaction from the Chinese, but slowly I began to understand that they simply thought that I was acting under foreign influence."[75]

Chinese authorities in Lhasa informed the Dalai Lama that the

---

72. Dalai Lama, *Freedom in Exile*, 121. The Dalai Lama said that the CIA, through his brothers, had agreed to supply some limited assistance to the Tibetan freedom fighters, "not because they cared about Tibetan independence, but as part of their worldwide efforts to destabilize all Communist governments. To this end they undertook to supply a limited amount of simple weaponry to the freedom fighters by airdrop. They also made plans for the CIA to train some of them in techniques of guerrilla warfare and then parachute them back into Tibet. Naturally, my brothers judged it wise to keep this information from me." Ibid., 122.

73. Ibid., 121.

74. Ibid. Lukhangwa's allegation was apparently that the ecclesiastical establishment had once again, as in 1951, influenced the decision concerning the Dalai Lama's return to Tibet.

75. Dalai Lama, *My Land*, 156. The Dalai Lama's threat to remain in India was reportedly a turning point in the minds of many Chinese officials in Tibet, who thereafter thought that the Dalai Lama could not be trusted. Jigme Ngapo, personal communication, Washington D.C., February 1995.

promised delay in reforms applied only to the TAR, but they admitted that the decision to postpone reform in the TAR was made because of the disturbances that reforms had caused in eastern Tibet. In June, the Chinese made further moves to reduce Tibetan discontent in the TAR; in addition to the policy of delaying reforms, it was announced that there would be a substantial reduction in the number of Chinese cadres in Tibet and a nationalization (Tibetanization) of the administration of the TAR. A large number of Han administrators were said to be no longer needed in Tibet as reforms were not to be introduced:

> In view of the concrete situation in Tibet, the Central Government has reached a decision on the policy of not carrying out reforms in Tibet within the next six years. Stemming from the policy, the present set-up and staff, especially the Han cadres, of the PCTAR were found to be too big. These Han cadres have cooperated well with the Tibetan cadres and their work has brought about definite achievements. Since reforms will not be carried out in Tibet during the next 6 years, most of the Han cadres will find no work to do there at present.[76]

The proclamation maintained that many Tibetans wanted "democratic reforms," but the Party had decided to delay their implementation because the majority of the upper strata were not yet prepared to accept them. Tibetans may have hoped for a permanent relief from the "socialist transformation" of Tibet, but the Chinese made it clear that the delay was a temporary measure: "To be able to live happily, the Tibetan people must take the road of socialism; and to enforce democratic reform is the unavoidable path the Tibetan people have to follow in gradually passing into a socialist society." Warnings were also issued to Tibetans that the retrenchment policy did not mean a victory for their opposition to Chinese control; opposition would continue to be vigorously suppressed:

> We must continue to struggle resolutely against counterrevolutionary organizations sabotaging the motherland's unity and manufacturing disuniting activities, and severely punish them according to the law of the state. Members of these reactionary organizations may have their past crimes pardoned as long as they can genuinely correct their mistakes and stop engaging in any more counterrevolutionary activities from now on. . . . If any imperialist element or any separatist takes the opportunity of our reduction of our establishment, or under any pretext in the future, to try to conduct sabotaging activities and incite revolts, then we will give him this

---

76. "20th Meeting of Standing Committee of Preparatory Committee for Tibet Autonomous Region Adopts Resolution on Retrenchment and Reduction of Han Cadres," *Tibet Daily* (Lhasa), 18 June 1957, in *Current Background*, no. 490.

solemn warning: We are determined to implement the agreement on the peaceful liberation of Tibet; but if someone dares violate any one of the seventeen articles of the agreement and incite revolts, then the PLA has the responsibility to suppress revolt; by that time the PLA will certainly join hands with all patriotic citizens in dealing firm and telling blows to the rebellious elements.[77]

These warnings reveal that opposition to the Chinese in Tibet was assuming threatening proportions. For the first time, counterrevolutionary and reactionary "organizations" were mentioned. Chinese awareness of American CIA involvement with Tibetan exiles in India was specifically mentioned in a speech by the PLA Commander in Tibet:

The American imperialists are engaged in carrying out subversive activities through some escapees from Tibet. Judging from the reactionary leaflets handed out by the escapees and the series of events which occurred during the past few months [the Dalai Lama's threat to remain in India], it is apparent that these were political activities in line with the subversion policy of the American imperialists. We must, therefore, greatly heighten our vigilance. If these escapees continue to serve the American imperialists and dare to continue to engage themselves in subversive acts of provocation, our PLA units stationed in Tibet will deal a counter-blow in accordance with the 17 article agreement on peaceful liberation of Tibet for the purpose of safeguarding the fatherland's unification, protecting the interest of the fatherland's Tibetan people and uniting more closely with the masses of the people in Tibet.[78]

Despite the decision for retrenchment in the TAR, the Chinese stubbornly held on to the "advances" they had made in the institution of reforms in Tibetan areas outside the TAR.[79] Conditions in Tibetan areas "within Chinese provinces" were said to be entirely different and irrelevant to conditions within the TAR. Eastern Tibetans were not to think that the concessions granted to the TAR could be applied in other Tibetan

---

77. "Outline of Propaganda for CCP Tibetan Working Committee Concerning the Policy of Not Implementing Democratic Reforms in Tibet Within Six Years," *Tibet Daily* (Lhasa), 2 August 1957, in *Current Background*, no. 490.

78. "Struggle for the Sacred Task of National Defense, Internal Security and Consolidation of the Fatherland's Unification," *Tibet Daily* (Lhasa), August 1, 1957, in *Current Background*, no. 490.

79. Teng Hsiao-p'ing reportedly played a role in the decision to continue reforms in eastern Tibet, possibly against the opinion of Mao and others. Teng was not in charge of Tibet policy at the time but, as a native of Szechuan, he was considered a representative of Szechuanese opinion about eastern Tibetan areas now part of Szechuan. Jigme Ngapo, personal communication, Washington, February 1995.

areas, nor should Tibetans within the TAR think that they were forever immune from reforms:

> The reason for the continuation until fulfillment of the democratic reform in Tibetan nationality areas in Szechuan and Yunnan provinces should be solemnly pointed out. The continuation of reforms in those areas is a good thing determined by the local people and upper strata personages. It conforms to actual conditions and is closely in line with the policy of peaceful [voluntary] reform. Meanwhile, it should also be pointed out that regional autonomy will eventually be realized in Tibet [TAR] according to the stipulations of our Constitution, that based upon historical conditions in Tibet the State Council has already set up a preparatory committee for introducing autonomy into Tibet including the adjacent Chamdo area, and that within this region the Tibetan people have the right to manage their affairs of a local nature. Historical conditions in Tibetan nationality areas in other provinces are different from those in Tibet. These Tibetan nationality areas belong to other provinces, and autonomy has long been given to those areas where internal affairs local in nature should be handled by the local people themselves.

> The democratic reform in Tibetan nationality areas in Szechuan province has been conducted according to actual conditions there as well as the wish of the local people. People in various circles in Tibet should sympathize with the reform undertaken by people in those areas, and should neither take conditions in Tibet as basis nor take the case of Tibet as a precedent in interfering with the democratic reform of the Tibetan nationality areas in Szechuan. Anybody who has opinions may forward them to the Central Government. But there are some people who are ignorant of their . . . duty, and who secretly support and even direct the rebellious elements in Kiangtang [Kangding, referring to southern Kham] to continue to incite revolts and oppose reform. This is not right and is not permissible, and will not lead to good results.[80]

The message was that the Chinese would slow down the process of socialist transformation within the TAR, but that eastern Tibetans should not look to the TAR in hopes of being granted a similar reprieve. While the TAR retained some special status, all other portions of Tibet now "belong to other provinces," where "autonomy has long been given," that is, where the system of national regional autonomy, along with socialist transformation, was already instituted and would not be revoked. The mention of the Chamdo region as "adjacent to Tibet" apparently indicated that Chamdo's former special status continued, at least in the minds of the Chinese, despite its having been included in the TAR in

---

80. "Struggle for the Sacred Task of National Defense," in *Current Background*, no. 490.

1956. Democratic reforms might be "voluntarily" introduced there despite the restrictions of the retrenchment policy (or to justify having prematurely attempted to introduce them in 1956). The phrase, "within this region [Chamdo] the Tibetan people have the right to manage their internal affairs of a local nature," refers not to the theoretical autonomous rights of Tibetans within the TAR, but of the "right" of Chamdo to go against the policy of no reforms in the TAR if the local people "requested" or "demanded" that reforms be bestowed upon them. The "no reform" policy was announced in Chamdo in August 1957, but revolt was already general in this area since the attempt to institute reforms by force in early 1956.[81]

By the middle of 1956 revolt in Kham had already assumed a permanent character. The Tibetans had the upper hand for a short while, until the Chinese were able to introduce large PLA forces, after which the Tibetans were unable to maintain large concentrated resistance forces. Many Tibetans of Kham and Amdo then had no alternative but to flee to central Tibet. The Dalai Lama observed that there were already thousands of refugees from Kham and Amdo in Lhasa when he returned in April 1957.[82] The Dalai Lama stated that, shortly after his return to Lhasa, the Chinese admitted that they were facing a major revolt in the east, and, according to refugees in Lhasa, harsh methods of repression had been adopted:

> There, in the district which had been entirely under Chinese rule since the invasion began, the number of Khampas who had taken to the mountains as guerrillas had grown from hundreds to tens of thousands. They had already fought some considerable battles with the Chinese army. The Chinese were using artillery and bomber aircraft, not only against the guerrillas when they could find them, but also against the villages and monasteries whose people they suspected, rightly or wrongly, of having helped them. Thus villages and monasteries were being totally destroyed. Lamas and lay leaders of the people were being humiliated, imprisoned, killed, and even tortured. Land was confiscated. Sacred images, books of scriptures, and other things of holy significance to us were broken up, derided, or simply stolen.[83]

The proportions of the revolt, threatening the highways which passed through Kham, was hinted at in the *Lhasa Daily* in August:

---

81. "People of Upper Strata and Government Cadres of Chamdo Area Hold Forum on Policy of 'No-Reform in Six Years.'" *Tibet Daily*, 29 August 1957, in *Current Background*, no. 409.

82. Dalai Lama, *My Land*, 156.

83. Ibid., 158.

Tibet is an inseparable part of our motherland; the Tibetan people have the extremely glorious duty of consolidating the unity of the motherland and reinforcing the country's national defense. Therefore, we must obey the 17 articles of the Agreement and continue to enforce the regulation that all affairs involving foreign relations should be handled by the Central Government in a unified manner. At the same time, Tibetan people should positively protect highways essential to national defense, and help support the People's Liberation Army to strengthen the national defense of the motherland.[84]

The Chinese retrenchment forestalled immediate revolt within the TAR, but tensions continued to mount due to the constant influx of refugees from Kham and Amdo carrying tales of Chinese brutality, including the humiliation, arrest and public execution of lamas and the looting and destruction of monasteries. There was no lessening of conflict in the east: "Within a short time after my return to Lhasa, people were taking up arms throughout the east, northeast and southeast of Tibet. It was only the western and central parts of the country which were still in comparative peace."[85] The Dalai Lama's personal conception of the "no reforms" policy was apparently that eastern Tibet should also have been exempted from reforms:

Every time I met them [the Chinese commanders in Lhasa], they repeated the assurances that Chou En-lai had given me in India: no drastic changes would be made in Tibet for at least six years, and even after that they would not be enforced against the wishes of the people. Yet they were already enforcing them, against the very emphatic wishes of the people, in the eastern districts. Perhaps they were able to persuade themselves that these districts were part of China itself, not of Tibet.[86]

Contradictions Among the People

Despite considerable resistance in nationality areas and some economic disruption in Han areas, the CCP considered the High Tide a successful first step toward collectivization. The Party bureaucracy remained

---

84. "Outline of Propaganda," 2 August 1957, in *Current Background*, no. 490. The reference to foreign relations was apparently intended to curtail individual Tibetans' appeals to India, the United Nations, or the United States for assistance. The threat to the road from Szechuan through Kham was apparently the reason that the Chinese began in March 1956 constructing the road from Sinkiang, completed in October 1957. Woodman, *Himalayan Frontiers*, 64.

85. Dalai Lama, *My Land*, 159.

86. Ibid., 161. The Chinese indeed regarded Tibetan areas of Kham and Amdo as integral parts of Chinese provinces and only the TAR as "Tibet."

conservative, however, and remained in favor of a gradual course of socialization. In the meantime, Mao's ability to take further initiatives was diminished by international events. In February 1956 Khrushchev had denounced Stalin and the "cult of personality." In October Hungary revolted against communism and Soviet domination. Mao's ability to take unilateral action was diminished by criticism of the "cult of personality," while fears of a Hungarian-style revolution led the CCP to attempt to broaden its base of support.[87]

Khrushchev's denunciation of Stalin led Mao to formulate a theory explaining how "contradictions" could exist in a socialist society and a strategy to alleviate such contradictions. Mao theorized that the Communist Party of the Soviet Union had become alienated from the people; his solution for that potential problem in China was for the CCP to build bridges with non-Party intellectuals and political figures. The cooperation of intellectuals and technicians was regarded as a necessity for "socialist construction." In the spring of 1956 a campaign to improve relations with the intellectuals and the democratic parties was initiated, under the slogan of "Let a hundred flowers bloom, let a hundred schools of thought contend." The campaign was launched to elicit criticism and dialogue, intended to alleviate contradictions between the Party and the people.

In February 1957, in his speech "On the Correct Handling of Contradictions Among the People," Mao invited the political participation of intellectuals, with the promise that criticism of CCP policies was necessary and permissible. Even Marxist ideology, he said, could be criticized: "Since Marxism is accepted by the majority of the people in our country as the guiding ideology, can it be criticized? Certainly it can. As a scientific truth, Marxism fears no criticism. If it did, and could be defeated in argument, it would be worthless."[88]

The ideological basis for the theory on contradictions and the Hundred Flowers campaign was Mao's dialectical theory, which he first explicated in a 1937 essay, *On Contradiction*: "The law of contradiction in things, that is, the law of the unity of opposites, is the fundamental law of nature and of society and therefore also of thought."[89] The opposites within every

---

87. Roderick MacFarquhar, *The Origins of the Cultural Revolution: Contradictions Among the People 1956-1957* (New York: Columbia University Press, 1974), 47.

88. Mao Tse-tung, "Contradictions Among the People," in Bowie and Fairbank, *Communist China 1955-1959*, 289. This was the same speech in which Mao announced the "no-reforms" policy in the TAR.

89. Mao Tse-tung, "On Contradiction," in *Selected Readings from the Works of Chairman Mao* (Peking: Foreign Languages Press, 1971), 128. This is also the fundamental thesis of Chinese Taoism and the *I Ching*, or Book of Changes.

phenomenon were regarded as their dynamic aspect, capable of creating change, and thus causing contradictions to emerge. But opposites were also capable of resolving contradictions because of the essential interplay of opposites within any phenomenon. This process could be employed to create change by stimulating a dialogue, or struggle, between opposites, with the ultimate purpose of achieving a resolution, or unity of opposites. This dialectical approach was already employed in the theory of class struggle and in the "struggle" of landlords and counterrevolutionaries in "democratic reforms." As Mao said in his February 1957 speech: "In 1942 we worked out the formula `unity-criticism-unity' to describe this demo-cratic method of resolving contradictions among the people. To elaborate, this means to start off with a desire for unity and resolve contradictions through criticism or struggle so as to achieve a new unity on a new basis."[90]

Mao distinguished between antagonistic contradictions, or those between the people and their enemies, and non-antagonistic contradic-tions, or those "within the people." Antagonistic contradictions were thought to have already been substantially resolved; therefore, it was thought possible, and safe, to stimulate a struggle of non-antagonistic contradictions, or those "within the people," in order to further the socialist transformation process. Mao believed that class conflict still existed in the PRC but was primarily reflected in ideological struggles that socialism could easily resolve:

> Contradictions in a socialist society are fundamentally different from con-tradictions in old societies, such as capitalist society. Contradictions in cap-italist society find expression in acute antagonisms and conflicts, in sharp class struggle, which cannot be resolved by the capitalist system itself and can only be resolved by socialist revolution. Contradictions in socialist soci-ety are, on the contrary, not antagonistic and can be resolved one after the other by the socialist system itself.[91]

Mao specified several political and social contradictions that remained in Chinese society: those between the Party and the United Front demo-cratic parties, between the Party and the intellectuals, and between the Han and the minority nationalities. All of these contradictions were assumed to be non-antagonistic; the democratic parties, the intellectuals and the minority nationalities were assumed to have accepted rule by the CCP, or in the case of nationalities, their inclusion within the Chinese

---

90. Mao Tse-tung, "Contradictions Among the People," 27 February 1957, in Bowie and Fairbank, *Communist China 1955-1959*, 273.
91. Ibid., 280.

state. As Mao's introduction to the 1957 "Contradictions" speech reveals, remaining contradictions were thought to be about the mechanics of the socialist system, not about the legitimacy of socialism or the rule of the CCP:

> Never has our country been as united as it is today. The victories of the bourgeois-democratic revolution and the socialist revolution, coupled with our achievements in socialist construction, have rapidly changed the face of old China. ... Led by the working class and the Communist Party, and united as one, our six hundred million people are engaged in the great work of building socialism. Unification of the country, unity of the people and unity among our various nationalities—these are the basic guarantees for the sure triumph of our cause.[92]

The Hundred Flowers campaign was slow to elicit any real dialogue or criticism since most Chinese, especially the intellectuals who were the main target of the campaign, were wary of CCP promises. Criticisms finally began to emerge in the spring of 1957, after Mao's "Contradictions" speech (unpublished at the time, but delivered to a large audience of Party and non-Party people). Some of these criticisms surprised the Party by their fundamental and very antagonistic rejection of communist ideology, the CCP's methods, and even its legitimacy to rule. The CCP responded by publishing, on 18 June, Mao's February "Contradictions" speech, to which was added a list of the means by which it was to be determined whether criticisms were "flowers" or "poisonous weeds":

> In the political life of our country, how are our people to determine what is right and what is wrong in our words and actions? Basing ourselves on the principles of our Constitution, the will of the overwhelming majority of our people and the political programmes jointly proclaimed on various occasions by our political parties and groups, we believe that, broadly speaking, words and actions can be judged right if they:
> (1) Help to unite the people of our various nationalities, and do not divide them;
> (2) Are beneficial, not harmful, to socialist transformation and socialist construction;
> (3) Help to consolidate, not undermine or weaken, the people's democratic dictatorship;
> (4) Help to consolidate, not undermine or weaken, democratic centralism;
> (5) Tend to strengthen, not to cast off or weaken, the leadership of the Communist Party;

---

92. Ibid., 275.

(6) Are beneficial, not harmful, to international socialist solidarity and the solidarity of the peace-loving peoples of the world.[93]

Had this list been issued in February along with Mao's "On Contradiction" speech, it is likely that little criticism would have emerged, as almost all criticism was subsequently defined as anti-Party and anti-socialist. Non-antagonistic contradictions "among the people" were transformed into antagonistic contradictions with "enemies of the people," contradictions that necessitated repression rather than peaceful resolution. When "flowers" turned into "poisonous weeds," the Hundred Flowers campaign was transformed into an anti-rightist purge of the Party's critics and of "rightists within the Party."

Nationality Contradictions

Mao's belief, expressed in his "On Contradictions" speech and in the Hundred Flowers policy, that contradictions between nationalities and the Han were no longer antagonistic—that minority nationalities had fully accepted Han rule—was a serious miscalculation of the actual state of affairs. Nationality cadres responded during the Hundred Flowers period with fundamental criticisms of Chinese rule over non-Chinese peoples, revealing a non-acceptance of the unification of China that Mao thought firmly achieved, once again arousing primal fears in the CCP of territorial dismemberment of China and imperialist exploitation of national separatist movements.

During democratic reforms, the CCP had denied that the opposition it had encountered among nationalities had represented more than a small minority of "reactionaries," "serf-owners," or "tools of foreign imperialism." However, in retrospect, and in the light of nationalities' criticisms during the Hundred Flowers, it had to admit that nationalities' opposition had been more popular and widespread. Wang Feng, Deputy-Director of the Nationalities Affairs Commission of the State Council, revealed that the Party had encountered serious and troubling opposition among nationalities:

> On the road of the victorious march of the people of all nationalities, we cannot say that no difficulties have been encountered, but we must rather say that there have been numerous difficulties. It is worth pointing out that after the basic realization of the socialist transformation of the system of

---

93. Ibid., 290. The priority, number (1) on the list, of the prohibition of criticisms that went against the "unity of nationalities" in China is surely not without significance.

ownership of the means of production in the absolute majority of minority areas, local nationalism has seen a new growth. From data exposed during the current rectification campaign, such ideology has found growth not only among a few minorities, but rather among many minorities. It is not only reflected clearly among certain people outside the Party, but also seriously reflected within the Party. Some high ranking cadres among certain minorities also have such ideological trends. Among certain people, local nationalism has even developed to a very serious and alarming stage.[94]

The survival of local nationalism "within the Party" was particularly threatening since it contradicted the ideological and tactical premises of nationalities policies, which assumed that local nationalism could be defeated by educating minority nationalities cadres in Marxist-Leninist nationality theory and policy. Education in Marxism-Leninism was intended to reveal the class basis of "local nationalism" and transfer nationality cadres' loyalty to the Chinese multinational state. Instead, nationality cadres demanded that socialism be built within their own nationalities, and cited Marxist-Leninist theory as well as CCP nationalities policies to make their case. Some of these "bourgeois nationalist" demands of minority nationality cadres were enumerated by Wang Feng:

Local nationalism is sharply projected in the following three ways: Over the issue of regional autonomy for minorities, it finds expression in the disregard for historical development and actual conditions, and the unprincipled demand by leaders of autonomous areas for larger administrative areas and higher administrative positions. In certain areas, there even exists to a grave extent separatist tendencies, the tendency toward secession from the big family of the motherland. Over the issue of relations among the nationalities, it finds expression in the reservedness toward other nationalities, the opposition to unity and cooperation among the nationalities, the ousting of Chinese cadres and people, the rejection of the Chinese people's help, and the refusal to learn from the advanced nationalities. Over the issue of Communist Party construction, it finds expression in the opposition to Party unity and solidarity, the contravention of Party principles, the attempt to split the Party with bourgeois nationalist principles, the idea that no Party members other than those of one's own nationality can seek happiness for this minority, the demand to divide Party organizations according to their component ratios of nationalities, the attitude of rejection toward the participation in local Party organizations by Party members of other nationalities from other areas, and especially the opposition to the

---

94. Wang Feng, "On the Rectification Campaign and Socialist Education Among Minorities," *NCNA*, 28 February 1958, in Schwartz, *Chinese Politics Towards Minorities*, 108.

assumption of leading posts in local Party organizations by Party members of other nationalities from other areas.[95]

Minority nationalities afflicted with the sin of local nationalism obviously included the Tibetans of Kham and Amdo, who had openly resisted democratic reforms and collectivization campaigns in 1956, but also the Inner Mongols and the Uighur, the predominant Turkish nationality of Sinkiang. Unlike the Tibetans, Inner Mongols and Uighurs were well represented within the CCP and were often versed in Marxism and Leninist nationalities doctrines. Some had been educated in the Soviet Union and were familiar with nationalities policies as practiced there. Local nationalism, "seriously reflected within the Party," refers primarily to criticisms the CCP received during the Hundred Flowers period from Uighur cadres and from a variety of nationalities students at the Central Nationalities Institute in Peking.[96]

Uighur grievances were enumerated in a study by Lee Fu-hsiang:

(1) secession from China through the process of national self-determination;

(2) creation of a body politic in Sinkiang under the name of Eastern Turkistan or Uighurstan and comparable in status to a union republic or autonomous republic of the Soviet Union;

(3) "nativization" of the cadres and Party organizations;

(4) suspension of the migration and colonization program;

(5) postponement of the socialist transformation program.[97]

The Uighur were obviously familiar with Leninist self-determination doctrines and the fact that the Soviet Union had been formed on a federal basis, unlike the system of "regional autonomy" in the PRC. They also

---

95. Ibid. "Historical development" undoubtedly means the "historical and natural merging of nationalities," while "actual conditions" refers to the supposedly advanced state of that process in China. The last paragraph refers to the Uighurs' demand for their own nationality communist party, dismissed here as "bourgeois nationalism." George Moseley, *A Sino-Soviet Cultural Frontier: The Ili Kazakh Autonomous Chou* (Cambridge: Harvard University Press, 1966), 72. A consequence of the Marxist definition of all of China's minorities as nationalities rather than nations was that they were not allowed to create their own nationality communist parties, should that thought have arisen, since Marxist dogma held that nations could have communist parties but that nationalities could not. The interests of all nationalities were theoretically equally represented within a multinational socialist state. Moseley, *Party and National Question*, 7.

96. Lee Fu-hsiang, "The Turkic-Moslem Problem in Sinkiang: A Case Study of the Chinese Communists' Nationality Policy." (Ph.D. diss. Rutgers University, 1973), 352; Moseley, *Ili Kazakh Autonomous Chou*, 59.

97. Lee Fu-hsiang, "Turkic-Moslem Problem in Sinkiang," 337.

emphasized that, since there were many Communist Party members of Uighur nationality or of the other nationalities of Sinkiang, there was no reason that Han cadres had to be in charge there. The reference to the migration and colonization program reflects their opposition to the policy that the Chinese had adopted in Sinkiang of overwhelming local minorities with an influx of Chinese.

Minority nationalities' criticisms of CCP policies focused on the abrogation of promises regarding local autonomy, the forcible implementation of democratic reforms and socialist transformation accompanied by the repression of all resistance, and colonization. Nationality students at the Peking Central Institute of Nationalities were offended by constant denigration of all their customs and traditions, denial of their previous political independence or autonomy, and the chauvinistic doctrine that their nationalities could only develop with Chinese assistance, an assistance that illogically was dependent upon their nationality being an integral part of the Chinese state. Constant criticism of all aspects of nationalities' identity increased rather than diminished "local nationalist" sentiments among many national minority students.[98]

"Local nationalism" in all its forms was particularly threatening to the Chinese state and infuriating to most CCP cadres, who imagined that their policy had been vastly superior in its treatment of minorities compared to that of Chinese governments of the past. The CCP had devoted great efforts to "helping" the minorities in achieving "democratic reforms" and "socialist transformation," none of which seemed to have been appreciated by the minorities themselves. The Party attempted to rectify the particularly troubling criticisms from nationality cadres at a meeting on nationalities policy in August 1957 at Tsingtao, which was attended by nationality minority delegates to the NPC, along with heads of the various nationalities affairs committees, and was presided over by Ulanfu, Chou En-lai and Mao.

---

98. Tsering Dorje Gashi, a Tibetan student at the Central Nationalities Institute in Peking from 1956 to 1960, reports that many Tibetans at the Nationalities Institute had become more rather than less nationalistic as a result of their isolation as a group at the Institute and their experience of Chinese chauvinism and propaganda against minority nationalism. Their education in Marxist-Leninist nationalities theory increased the students' nationalist sentiments and their awareness of the nature of Chinese imperialism. Tibetan students organized secret pro-independence groups during the anti-local nationalism campaigns of 1957-58. This "local nationalism" of the nationalities students was considered a serious threat to CCP nationalities policies and was severely repressed by numerous and violent struggle sessions and the arrest and disappearance of many nationalist students. Tsering Dorje Gashi, *New Tibet: Memoirs of a Graduate of the Peking Institute of National Minorities* (Dharamsala: Information Office of His Holiness the Dalai Lama, 1980), 33.

In a report on local nationalism at the conference, Wang Feng asked, "How is it, that, while most minority areas in China have virtually realized socialist transformation in the system of ownership of the means of production, local nationalism has grown instead of diminished?" The answer, he said, was that although socialist transformation had solved the problems in the socialist revolution on the economic front, it had not and could not solve all problems on the political and ideological fronts. Local nationalism, by definition, had to be a reflection of the interests of the bourgeois class; the growth of local nationalism therefore "reflects the antagonism and opposition to socialism by the bourgeois elements and elements of other exploiting classes among the minorities who do not accept transformation."[99]

Wang Feng characterized local nationalism, indeed nationalism in general, including "great-Hanism," as an aspect of capitalism, and thus the antithesis of socialism. Wang explained the basic differences between socialism and nationalism:

> First of all, with respect to the attitude toward the big united family of the motherland and the relations among the various nationalities of China, the socialist stand supports the unity of the motherland and the solidarity among nationalities, while the nationalist stand impairs or even splits the unity of the motherland and the solidarity among nationalities. . . . Second, unification of the motherland and unity among the various nationalities are fundamental for the protection of the people of all nationalities against imperialist aggression. . . . Third, the unity of the motherland and the solidarity among nationalities are the basic requirements of the historical development of our country. . . . Another basic difference between the socialist stand and the nationalist stand is that, while the former supports the leadership of the Party, the latter opposes it.[100]

At the Tsingtao conference nationality cadres expressed some of their grievances, which greatly offended Mao and led to the inclusion of anti-local nationalism into the ongoing anti-rightist rectification campaign.[101] In a "Report on the Rectification Campaign," delivered at the Central Committee meeting at Tsingtao, Teng Hsiao-p'ing, head of the anti-right-

---

99. Wang Feng, "On the Rectification Campaign," in Schwartz, *Chinese Policies Towards Minorities*, 109. Wang's attempt to explain the rise of local nationalism by means of Marxist theory did not adequately explain its presence, and even increase, among CCP nationality cadres and nationality institute students, all of whom had been exposed to Marxist-Leninist nationalities ideology and CCP nationalities policies aimed at the diminution of local nationalist ideology.

100. Ibid., 113.

101. Lee Fu-hsiang, "Turkic-Moslem Problem in Sinkiang," 354.

ist campaign, stated that the campaign had been expanded from educational institutions and the Party to the general society, including the PLA and the national minorities. While most contradictions within China's socialist society remained "within the people," some elements, including some of those who had expressed the rightist and reactionary ideology of local nationalism, had been exposed as enemies of the people and had to be repressed. While Han chauvinism remained the greatest acknowledged problem in nationalities relations, some manifestations of "local nationalism" had clearly become "antagonistic" and were even threatening the territorial integrity of the Chinese state:

> Socialist education and anti-rightist struggles among the national minorities have the same content as in the Han areas, but stress should also be laid on opposition to nationalist tendencies. . . . It should be pointed out to the officials and members of the upper strata of the national minorities that the tendencies of local nationalism and Han chauvinism are both bourgeois, anti-socialist tendencies and a danger to the solidarity and unity of the various nationalities of the socialist motherland. . . . As regards those extremely bad elements who openly instigate national divisions, they should be resolutely exposed and repudiated . . . . It should be clearly recognized that all those who make use of local nationalist sentiments and the estrangement between nationalities left over from the past in order to divide national unity and undermine the unification of the motherland act contrary to China's Constitution and jeopardize the socialist cause of our country. They are all anti-socialist rightists.[102]

Teng went on to recommend that nationalities should be reminded of the differences between the new society and the old, as well as "the benefits and necessity of national solidarity and unity within the big family of nationalities under the leadership of the Chinese Communist Party." Nationalism should be exposed as a bourgeois ideology "opposed to Marxism-Leninism and Communism." He further recommended that minority nationality schools should stress "class education and education in the Marxist-Leninist position on the nation."[103]

What made the rise of "local nationalism" so threatening to the Chinese state was that it revealed that Marxist-Leninist ideology and the CCP's nationality policy were not an automatic solution to the national question, as previously thought, but that they had in fact aroused anti-Chinese nationalism among the nationalities. Nationality cadres' had been subjected to a great amount of consciousness raising on the subject

---

102. Teng Hsiao-p'ing, "Report on the Rectification Campaign," 23 September 1957, in Bowie and Fairbank, *Communist China 1955-1959*, 356.
103. Ibid.

of patriotism to China, and their nationalist consciousness had indeed been raised, but it had coalesced around the more personal and natural level of loyalty to their own nationality rather than to the Chinese state.

After the Tsingtao conference, a "Socialist Education Movement Opposing Local Nationalism" was launched, which was intended to combat local nationalism with education on "socialism and patriotism."[104] Han chauvinism, though still characterized as "bourgeois," was thereafter ignored in favor of a campaign against local nationalism. Not surprisingly, local nationalism was attacked with much more vigor than had ever been displayed in opposition to Han chauvinism. The rise of "local nationalism" was so threatening to China's political legitimacy and territorial integrity that all of the resources of the state were brought to bear against it. Because bourgeois nationalism reflected the struggle between socialism and capitalism, local nationalism, in some of its manifestations, was characterized as an antagonistic contradiction and local nationalists were condemned as enemies of the people:

> Since the opposition to local nationalism is a component part of the struggle between the two roads, the contradictions in this connection must necessarily be classified as contradictions between the enemy and ourselves in certain respects and as contradictions within the ranks of the people in all other respects. Local nationalists are bourgeois rightists wearing a nationalist overcoat. They are reactionaries who oppose socialism and the Communist Party leadership and sabotage the unity of the motherland and the solidarity among the various nationalities. They are remnants of the feudal society who do not accept transformation. They are mostly part of the bourgeoisie, bourgeois intellectuals and elements of other exploiting classes. They form only a very small portion either in their minorities or in their classes. The contradictions between them and ourselves are contradictions between the enemy and ourselves. We must thoroughly expose and criticize them and completely isolate them.[105]

The aim of CCP nationalities policies was not to eliminate nationalism, but to shift its focus onto the multinational Chinese state. Bourgeois local nationalism was to be transformed into patriotism to the Chinese state, which, by definition, was not bourgeois, or even nationalist, because the PRC was a socialist state that had theoretically transcended the bourgeois stage and nationalism.[106] This sort of sophistry might have been reassur-

---

104. Hsien Fu-min, "Socialist Education Movement Opposing Local Nationalism," March 1958, in *Tibet 1950-67*, 271.

105. Ibid., 110.

106. Patriotism to the Chinese state is not, strictly speaking, nationalism, but "stateism," or "multinational stateism"; however, since the Chinese state is predominantly one nation-

ing to Chinese cadres, but it failed to alleviate the phenomenon of local nationalism among nationality cadres. The CCP attempted to defeat each of the local nationalists' arguments with reasoning having as its common denominator the political and strategic interests of China. Local nationalism in its separatist manifestation was characterized as contrary to the "long historical trend" of union of nationalities and its "basic requirement" for economic cooperation and development and united resistance against imperialism. No individual nationality was considered capable of independent political existence or of resisting imperialism without the assistance of China's united nationalities, centered on the Han nationality:

> Any nationality, if it succeeds in secession, will not only lose for certain the great achievements of liberation and equality which have already been effected, but will also fall for certain under the yoke of imperialism once more. . . . Only by uniting themselves in the big united family of the motherland can the various nationalities of China construct socialism and resist imperialism. Any nationality, if it attempts to secede from the big family of the motherland, is bound to leave the socialist road and follow the imperialist and colonial road. Either it follows the socialist road which is a road to prosperity, or it follows the imperialist road and colonial road, which is a road to extinction. There is no middle course. . . separation, or the so-called independent construction of nationalities, can be only of advantage to imperialism, not to the people of the various nationalities. Under many circumstances, this separation is like a stick, one end of which is found in the country while the other end is found outside the country. The "independence" movement of Tibet is a good illustration of this point.[107]

Nationality cadres' calls for increased autonomy, including federative status, were rejected with the argument that "historical development" had not provided any conditions for the setting up of federal republics: "How can the Chinese who account for 94 percent of the country's population and the people of several dozen minorities who account for only 6 percent, set up separate federal republics . . . . How are we to lay the boundary lines separating these minority republics from one another?"[108] Demands for increased autonomy, for nationality communist parties or for separate national socialist development were rejected because of the

---

ality, and that nationality exercises almost total political dominance, patriotism to the Chinese state is essentially equivalent to Chinese nationalism, a fact evident to minority nationalities if not to the majority Chinese.

107. Wang Feng, "On the Rectification Campaign," 115.

108. Ibid., 120.

impossibility of minority nationalities building socialism without Han cadres and the help of the CCP:

> It is absolutely impossible for the various minorities to build socialism without the leadership of the Communist Party. For reasons of historical development, the minorities in China are not advanced politically, economically or culturally. Some were still at the stage of a slave-owning and serf systems even in the early years after liberation. If the Chinese Communist Party did not lead the country along the socialist road, how could all the minorities register within the short period of eight years what is universally recognized as marked growth politically, economically and culturally? And how could the minorities in their various stages of development come to build socialism, bypassing one or several stages of social development? All this would be obviously impossible.[109]

Minorities' opposition to Chinese colonization was refuted with similar arguments: the minorities could not possibly develop or achieve socialism without the fraternal assistance of the Han. They were not, however, to confuse this "natural fusion" with assimilationism:

> It must be understood that the question of wanting or not wanting Han cadres and resettlers is, in a large measure, the question of wanting or not wanting socialism and prosperity for the minorities. . . . The opposition to all anti-Chinese tendencies constitutes an important facet of the struggle against local nationalism. In ousting the Chinese, certain people do so under the pretext of the so-called assimilation problem. They describe the efforts exerted by Chinese cadres and people to help the fraternal minorities construct socialism as efforts to "assimilate the minorities." This, of course, is absurd. The gradual fusion of the various nationalities on the basis of equality is the natural law governing social development. . . . We have all along opposed the assimilation of the minorities by force, because that is oppression. But we will never oppose the natural fusion among the nationalities, because this is the progressive trend of historical development.[110]

The Chinese, like other majority nations, disregarded the fact that assimilation usually seems more natural and just to the majority than to the minority being assimilated. Wang, in arguing the advantages of "unity of the motherland" and "solidarity among nationalities," repeated Mao's unwitting admission that it was not so much the nationalities themselves as their territories and natural resources with which the Chinese wished union. The bargain proffered to nationalities was that

109. Ibid.
110. Ibid., 118.

they were to be provided the economic benefits of socialism and cultural benefits of inclusion within the Chinese state in exchange for their "virtually unpopulated" territories and their resources:

> The unity of the motherland and the solidarity among nationalities are the basic guarantee to socialist construction. Among China's population of over 600 million people, the Chinese account for more than 94 percent. ... Though the minorities account for only six percent of the country's population and are less developed politically, economically and culturally, yet they are scattered over places with a total area more than one-half of the country's area. These places are also rich in natural resources.[111]

The phenomenon of local nationalism was accurately identified by the Chinese as a rejection of Chinese culture and Chinese "assistance," and, despite Party warnings, it aroused the most chauvinistic and nationalistic reaction among Han cadres. This was apparently true even at the highest level; Mao himself was offended during the Hundred Flowers by the ingratitude of the minority nationalities. The survival and even exacerbation of anti-Chinese nationalism among minority nationality cadres trained in Marxist-Leninist and CCP nationalities policies exposed the failure of those policies to "solve the national question." The campaign against local nationalism thereafter was effectively unrestrained; many Chinese cadres called for the elimination of the United Front policy, the system of national regional autonomy, the policy of preserving minority nationalities' cultures and nationalities' freedom of religious belief. The campaign led to an exacerbation of Chinese chauvinism and nationalism toward minority nationalities that Marxist-Leninist semantics was unable to overcome or obscure.

The Great Leap Forward

Although Mao had miscalculated by letting loose the Hundred Flowers campaign, he was able to transform the anti-rightist campaign that followed into a nationwide purge of his enemies both within the CCP and in society at large. This purge paved the way for the next collectivization campaign, the Great Leap of 1958, a campaign that not only furthered China's socialist transformation but, because of the increased political control inherent in collectivization, provided another means for the suppression of anti-socialist rightists and local nationalists. The atmosphere of fear already engendered by the anti-rightist campaign

---

111. Ibid., 113.

added a new level of coercion to collectivization; now, any opposition to collectivization was characterized as rightist, anti-Party and anti-socialist.

The Great Leap Forward was designed to alleviate the stagnation and confusion in agriculture caused by partial collectivization, to recreate the Maoist program for simultaneous transformation of agriculture and industry, and to achieve the transition from socialism to communism. Since Mao had adopted the Stalinist strategy of employing "relations of production," meaning collectivization, to transform the "means of production," or actual increases in agricultural and industrial production, the transition to "socialist relations" received the main emphasis during the Great Leap. Collectivization and the socialist consciousness that would theoretically be stimulated by collectivization was presumed capable of producing a "great leap" in agricultural and industrial output; this, of course, was totally contradictory to Marx's fundamental doctrine that economic factors determine consciousness, not the other way around.

The Great Leap began with a water conservation campaign in the winter of 1957-58; labor was organized for irrigation and afforestation projects on such a large scale that a labor shortage occurred when the time came for spring planting. Women were mobilized for agriculture, necessitating child care facilities and common kitchens. The movement was expanded in the summer of 1958 by amalgamating APCs into communes in order to mobilize labor for ever larger projects. By the end of 1958, 99.1 percent of Chinese peasants were in communes.[112]

This rate of collectivization was unintended even by Mao, who thought that an accelerated course would still take decades to achieve full communization. The zeal of cadres to achieve results and their desire to avoid criticism as anti-socialists if they did not push for higher levels of communization were large factors in the actual course of events. Cadres were tempted to jump directly to communization partly because of the complexity of administrative forms required by each of the intermediate stages of collectivization. However, the simplicity of administration under full communization did not take into account the complexity of the agricultural economy or the myriad handicraft and sideline occupations that accompanied agriculture.

---

112. Franz Schurman, *Ideology and Organization in Communist China* (Berkeley: University of California Press, 1968), 493. The seemingly inevitable progression from social mobilization for water conservancy to increased political centralization seems to confirm Wittfogel's thesis on the origins of "oriental despotism." Karl A. Wittfogel, *Oriental Despotism: A Comparative Study of Total Power* (New Haven: Yale University Press, 1957; New York: Vintage Books, 1981).

During the Great Leap, the lowest level of government administration was shifted from traditional village authorities to the Party commune organization. Private plots were amalgamated and private property was collectivized. Restrictions on private enterprise and personal mobility reduced the production of private plots, sideline occupations and individual trading activities. Peasants were organized into People's Militia, intended to repel imperialist aggression, which facilitated their mobilization for large scale land reclamation and water works projects. A slogan of the time reveals the regimentation and militarist frenzy that characterized this period: "Militarize Organization, Turn Action into Struggle, Collectivize Life!"[113]

The Great Leap greatly exacerbated all of the problems in nationality relations already created by the High Tide. Nevertheless, Mao's decision not to deny the nationalities the "benefits" of rapid socialist transformation was not altered during the Great Leap. At the height of the Great Leap, in August 1958, many nationality areas were precipitously communized, without regard to their previous level of "socialist transformation." The collectivization campaign was pushed because of the greater degree of Party control that collectivization facilitated, and, in areas still unsettled by revolt, as a means of suppression of revolt. In addition, previous restrictions on alteration of traditional minority cultures were loosened during the Great Leap and nationalities' autonomy was less respected. Because local nationalism had been declared "rightist" and "antisocialist," the preservation of local nationalist cultures and traditions was also denounced as rightist.

During the Great Leap, nationalities were pressured to adopt Chinese culture (because Chinese culture was considered equivalent to "socialism") and to drop those of their traditions considered to be impediments to socialist development. The CCP declared itself judge of which aspects of minority nationalities' traditional cultures were innocuous, and would be allowed to survive, and which were incompatible with socialism, and would therefore be repressed: "We feel that the customs and practices of each nationality consist partly of factors favorable to socialism and helpful to the nationality concerned, and partly of factors unfavorable to socialism and prejudicious (*sic*) to the development of the nationality concerned."[114]

Those minority customs and habits considered "favorable to socialism" were, as listed by Chang Chih-i: "for instance, boldness, martial

---

113. Schurman, *Ideology and Organization in Communist China*, 479.

114. Hsien Fu-min, "Socialist Education Movement Opposing Local Nationalism," in *Tibet 1950-67*, 281

spirit, fondness for work, sincerity, love of singing and dancing, free choice in marital matters, and so forth."[115] Language and religion were conspicuously absent from this list. Han cadres had been singularly remiss at learning nationality languages, but not at pushing minorities to learn Chinese. Much of the terminology of Chinese socialism was dependent upon unique meanings and usages of the Chinese language. Religion was declared to be among those nationality customs unfavorable to socialism:

> Since religion is harmful to the socialist construction of the mother country, it will inevitably prove harmful to the progress and development of the minority nationalities. Religion is not a condition for the formation of a nationality, still less is it a condition for the development and advance of a nationality. All national characteristics unfavorable to socialist construction and national progress can and should be reformed.[116]

Beginning in the spring of 1958, nomadic pastoralists were urged to adopt "fixed abode and nomadic herd-raising"; only those actually needed for livestock production would remain nomadic, and all herdsmen would be settled in the winter season.[117] The emphasis on sedentarization of nomads reflected the traditional Chinese equation of nomadism with barbarism.[118] The primary purpose of sedentarization of nomads was to facilitate collectivization and control, as was revealed by Chu Teh's statement that "all nomadic herdsmen should settle in order to facilitate socialist transformation and socialist construction."[119] In August 1958 many minority nationality areas, agricultural and pastoral, were collectivized or communized.[120] In the spring of 1959, the CCP issued instructions that the two million herdsmen of Sinkiang, Kansu and Chinghai would no longer be permitted to be nomadic.[121]

---

115. Chang Chih-i, in Moseley, *Party and National Question*, 117.

116. "Communists are Complete Atheists," *Nationalities Unity*, no. 18 (Peking), March 1959, in *Tibet 1950-1967*, 246.

117. The nomads were said to have had "no plan at all for the use of pastures." The nomadic life was denigrated as "neither beneficial to the development of animal husbandry nor to the prosperity of the human population." "Positively Promote Fixed Abodes and Nomadic Herd-Raising," *Nationalities Unity*, no. 3 (Peking), 14 March 1958, in *Tibet 1950-67*, 294.

118. "Pastoral Areas of Tsinghai Province in the Great Revolutionary High Tide," *Tsinghai Red and Expert*, no. 4 (1 October 1958), in *Survey of China Mainland Magazines*, no. 155, 31.

119. Chu Teh, as quoted in "Positively Promote Fixed Abodes and Nomadic Herd-Raising," in *Tibet 1950-67*, 294.

120. "Communization in a Single Stride," 6 November 1958, in *Tibet 1950-67*, 330.

121. McMillen, *Chinese Communist Power and Policy in Sinkiang*, 158.

Collectivization crystalized nationalities' resistance, already aroused by democratic reforms and the anti-local nationalist campaign. The policies of the Great Leap transformed localized revolt in eastern Tibet into a general uprising in eastern Tibet, which soon spread to the TAR. Open resistance also erupted in Sinkiang, but a popular uprising was prevented by the preponderance of force available to the Chinese and the already large number of Han settlers there. An exodus to the Soviet Union of Sinkiang's nomadic populations, primarily Kazakhs living near the border, began at this time, culminating in the flight of some 60,000 in the summer of 1962.[122] A revolt of the Yi (Lolo) of Yunnan and an exodus of the Thai of Yunnan into Burma also took place from 1956 to 1959.[123]

The failure of nationalities policy to resolve the issue of local nationalism led the CCP to rely on more open coercion and to accelerate the process of assimilation. The Great Leap saw a greater emphasis upon class struggle and assimilation in nationality policy, corresponding to the "coming together" element of communist theory on nationality relations at the expense of the "flourishing of nationality culture" aspect of that theory. The CCP justified socialist assimilation as entirely different from capitalist assimilation. Socialist assimilation was defined as natural and voluntary. Chou En-lai defined socialist assimilation in a speech on nationalities policy in 1958: "Assimilation is a reactionary thing if it means one nation destroying another by force. It is a progressive act if it means natural merger of nations advancing toward prosperity. Assimilation as such has the significance of promoting progress."[124] Assimilation was considered progressive, historically determined and just, based upon the Marxist doctrine that national identities and national interests were only misplaced or misconstrued class identity and class interests. Mao's formula that "the national question is in essence a class question," epitomized this doctrine.[125]

---

122. Moseley, *Ili Kazakh Autonomous Chou*, 109.

123. Ma Yin, *China's Minority Nationalities*, 30; Moseley, *South China Frontier*, 120.

124. Chou En-lai, "Some Questions on Policy Towards Nationalities," *Beijing Review*, 3 March 1980, 19. Chou's speech, repressed until 1980, apparently erred in describing Han chauvinism and local nationalism as equal problems, while Party policy had shifted to repression of local nationalism. Chou's opinion reflected the more liberal wing of the Party on nationalities policy, but even Chou considered assimilation the ultimate goal.

125. This slogan, which, incidentally, invalidated the United Front approach to nationalities policy, was first formulated by Mao in 1956 and it "began to appear and prevail in the Chinese press in the early 1960s." The origin of this slogan is the Marxist-Leninist theory that class interests are more fundamental than nationalism, and, specifically, Lenin's class-based definition of nation. "Is the National Question Essentially a Class Question?" *Beijing Review*, 25 August 1980, 17. Interestingly, Mao first expressed the relation between class and nationality during the Chinese national struggle against the Japanese in the 1930s in the

The CCP is generally credited with having achieved the socialist transition, or collectivization, in China without the resistance that accompanied that process in other communist countries. While this is essentially true for Han areas, there was violent and sustained resistance in nationality areas, especially in Tibet. The failure of CCP nationalities policies to transform the nationalist consciousness of minority nationalities finally led to an abandonment of the myth of the voluntary nature of reforms and of Han-minority cooperation, in favor of physical coercion and repression and a reversion to the traditional and proven method of resolution of frontier nationalities questions by means of political, cultural and physical assimilation.

Revolt in Central Tibet

The decisions taken at the Tsingtao Conference in August 1957 led to an increased pace of "democratic reforms" and collectivization in eastern Tibet, despite already open revolt there.[126] "Democratic reforms" were employed to eliminate the leadership, or potential leadership, of the Tibetan resistance. Collectivization was undertaken not only despite the revolt, but as a means of quelling the revolt. Collectivization, which was equivalent to forced detention in a circumscribed area, was employed to concentrate and control Tibetans and to prevent their contact with the resistance. However, the pursuit of "democratic reforms" in late 1957 and the initiation of collectivization and communization in 1958 only intensified revolt in Amdo and Kham.

Tibetan areas outside the TAR, including pastoral areas, were precipitously communized in August 1958:

---

opposite manner: "In a struggle that is national in character, the class struggle takes the form of national struggle." Mao Tse-tung, "The Question of Independence and Initiative within the United Front," *Selected Works*, II, 215, as cited in Lyman P. Van Slyke, *Enemies and Friends: The United Front in Chinese Communist History* (Stanford: Stanford University Press, 1967), 99.

126. Such was the shift in the attitude toward nationalities at the Tsingtao conference that the negotiator of the 1951 17-Point Agreement with Tibet, Li Wei-han, was criticized for the "internationalist" characteristics of that agreement. Phuntsok Dekyi, paper delivered at Conference on Sino-Tibetan Dialogue, 5 October 1992, Washington, D.C. At Tsingtao, Ngawang Jigme Ngapo reportedly asked Chou for the return of eastern Tibetan areas to the TAR, a subject that had been broached in 1951. Ngapo suggested that at least the Derge region, part of which was already within the TAR (Derge district west of the Yangtze), should be returned to the TAR. Chou reportedly replied that the opposite logic might also apply: since most of Derge was in Szechuan, those areas west of the Yangtze should also be included in Szechuan. Rather than raise this issue, and confront Szechuanese territorial interests, Chou suggested that it was better to leave the situation as it was. Jigme Ngapo, personal communication, Washington D.C., February 1995.

On September 15 [1958], the entire Kan-nan Chou [Southern Kansu Tibetan Autonomous District] was completely communalized. Altogether there are 67 people's communes; 90.1% of the households, or 93.58% of the herdsmen have joined the communes. The 46,000 Tibetan herdsmen, who only a short time ago still basically lived in a feudalistic society, have now, on the basis of having scored victories in the suppression of counter-revolutionaries and carried out a social reform, flown over several ages in the short period of a fortnight, and, singing and dancing, have now reached heaven in one stride, taking them into People's Communes in which are carried the seeds of communism.[127]

The Great Leap in nationality areas included Chinese efforts to repress all aspects of nationalities cultures. Religion in particular was declared "harmful to socialist progress." In Tibet, where religion remained the primary institutional and ideological obstacle to Chinese socialist ideology, the campaign against religion was intensified. Tibetans of Chinghai and Kham were coerced into denunciations of lamas and religion; Party propaganda claimed that the Tibetan masses had realized the falsity and exploitative nature of religion:

In this violent class struggle, after a campaign of propaganda and education was deeply carried out and after contrasting the old and new societies, the class consciousness of the vast labouring herdsmen was rapidly promoted. After they perceived the reactionary essence of the feudalistic exploiting class, they were all greatly surprised; and rose up with set teeth to accuse the exploiting class of their heinous crimes; and they voluntarily bound the counterrevolutionary elements and bad elements and handed them over to the government, asking for them to be punished. After stripping off the religious cloak of the counterrevolutionary elements in religious circles, they exposed their fraud; and the masses say: "We shall never permit these man-eating wolves to do evil things while riding on the neck of the people waving religious banners." At the debate meetings, the masses were so excited that they shouted continuously: Long Live Chairman Mao! Long Live the Communist Party! We Are Liberated![128]

In the latter stages of the Great Leap, labor shortages appeared in the Chinese countryside due to massive irrigation projects and rural steel production campaigns. Food shortages appeared in cities due to the neglect of agriculture. The Party responded to these difficulties with a

---

127. Hsien Chan-ju, "Communization in a Single Stride," *Nationalities Unity*, 6 November 1958, in *Tibet 1950-67*, 330.

128. Liu Tse-hsi, "Herdsmen on the Tsinghai Pastures Advance Bravely with Flying Red Flags," *Nationalities Unity*, no. 11 (6 November 1958), in *Tibet 1950-67*, 325.

campaign to "send down" city dwellers to the countryside or to sparsely populated national minority areas. This campaign included an intensification of colonization efforts in Tibetan areas, particularly in Chinghai. An article entitled "The Rich Frontier Regions Await the Exploration of Our Youth" revealed that 40,000 Chinese youths had been resettled in Chinghai in 1956, "on the grassland left uninhabited for several thousand years." The article called on Chinese youth to "go to the frontier regions" and "turn the frontier regions into the fatherland's beautiful garden."

> The fatherland is calling you. The people of our brother nationalities of the frontiers are calling you. An unlimited wealth of resources is awaiting you. Youth, go to the frontiers! Go there and show what you can do! For the happiness of the next generation, for the happiness of our brother nationalities, for the brilliant page of history of socialist and communist construction.[129]

The precipitous communization of the summer of 1958 exacerbated the ongoing revolt in Kham and revived it in Amdo. Agricultural areas of Amdo had undergone democratic reforms in 1956, but many nomadic areas experienced the full impact of Chinese control and reform only in 1958. At that time, with the simultaneous imposition of democratic reforms and collectivization, or "communization in a single stride," many of the nomads of Amdo revolted. Revolts were reported in the nomadic areas of southern Kansu: Amchok, Zayul and Bora. Some nomadic areas of Amdo were reported to have been virtually emptied of men, all having fled or been killed or imprisoned.[130] Most of the population of the Sokpo (Mongol) area east of the Ma Chu were reportedly massacred.[131]

Labrang Tashikyil monastery, the largest in Amdo with 3,000 monks, was forcibly emptied, even though the monastery had not participated in the revolt. Two thousand of the Labrang monks were arrested, of whom 600 were deported to labor camps in Sinkiang. Many Amdo Tibetans were sent to the Sinkiang camps, where two-thirds of them reportedly

---

129. The Chinese colonists were resettled in the Hainan (south of Kokonor) and Haihsi (west of Kokonor) Tibetan Autonomous Districts, both primarily pastoral areas. The 40,000 Chinese youth were reported to have "reclaimed" 330,000 mou of land (or to have converted pastoral land to agriculture). "The Rich Frontier Regions Await the Exploration of Our Youth," *Chinese Agriculture and Reclamation*, 20 February 1959, in *Survey of China Mainland Magazines*. The arrests of rightists in 1957 and after also increased Chinese populations in the prison camps in Chinghai, all of whom were essentially colonists during their imprisonment and the majority of whom were required to remain in Chinghai even after their release.

130. Tsayul Tulku, personal interview, Dharamsala, 1989.

131. Amdo Rigchok, personal interview, Dharamsala, 1990.

died. The remainder of the Labrang monks were placed in "reform through labor" camps in Amdo. Most of the monasteries of Amdo were depopulated and looted of their valuable metals and artifacts, and then physically destroyed, their timbers and stones often being used to construct barracks for Chinese PLA troops or Chinese settlers.[132] More than 1,000 monks of Trakar Gompa, in Shangke Dzong near Kokonor, who had not participated in the revolt, were gathered in the monastery's courtyard and killed by machine guns mounted on the courtyard's walls.[133]

The revolt in Amdo, although involving a large proportion of the Tibetan population, was suppressed within six months due to the preponderance of force available to the Chinese. Few Amdo Tibetans were able to escape to central Tibet. A particular aspect of the suppression of the revolt in Amdo was the use by the Chinese of Hui (Chinese Moslem) cavalry, formerly the troops of Ma Pu-fang, and Inner Mongolian cavalry, who, unlike the PLA, were adept at operations on the grasslands.[134] Whole nomadic encampments were reportedly massacred by these or other PLA troops; in one case, an encampment of some 400 people in the nomadic country between Amdo and Kham (Dzachukha) was reportedly massacred.[135]

In Amdo Ngaba (Apa Autonomous Chou of Szechuan), Tibetan leaders were systematically eliminated between 1956 and 1958. Revolt in Ngaba began in 1958 when the Chinese attempted to remove Tibetans from their homes and place them in collectives. In all, 500 to 600 people were reportedly arrested, only 20 percent of whom ever reappeared in Ngaba.[136] After the suppression of the revolt, those Tibetans remaining, both nomads and villagers, were removed from their homes and placed in detention camps, called communes, where their "socialist transformation" could proceed.[137]

In Kham, revolt was continuous from 1956, with only a brief lessening due to a liberalization of Chinese policies in early 1957. Tibetans from southern and western Kham gathered in Markham in 1956 and formed a Tibetan Resistance Army (*Pokyi Tensum Tanglang Mag*), which had a triangular flag, outlined in blue with a snow lion against a mountain in the center. By the end of 1957 the Chinese had committed eight PLA divisions and at least 150,000 men to the suppression of the revolt in eastern

132. Tsayul Tulku, personal interview.
133. Amdo Rigchok, personal interview.
134. Uradyn Erden Bulag, personal communication, November 1995.
135. Jamyang Norbu, *Warriors of Tibet*, 140.
136. Amdo Some, personal interview.
137. Amdo Rigchok, personal interview.

Tibet.[138] Hui cavalry, *Siling Magmi* (Sining Army), were also employed in southern Kham.[139] By the end of 1958 the PLA had begun to contain the revolt in eastern Tibet; many Khampas and Amdowas who had already left their homes to fight the Chinese now began to move toward Lhasa. PLA tactics were to confine refugees in the east; relatively few Tibetans from the east (more from Kham than Amdo) were able to reach Lhasa without being killed or detained.

In Lhasa, tensions had also reached a critical point. Early in 1958 Chinese authorities had expelled some 1,500 Chinese from Lhasa, most of whom had fled to Tibet during the 1950s to escape the communists. They were returned to China to an unknown fate.[140] In May 1958 the Chinese began a census of the several thousand refugees from Kham and Amdo in Lhasa or encamped in the vicinity. Refugees were told that no one would be allowed to remain without an identity card signed by a Chinese official.[141] Since few of the easterners could return to their homes, this step precipitated an exodus of the easterners to the guerrilla camps now in central Tibet. By the middle of 1958, despite the efforts of the Lhasa government to dissuade Tibetans from rising in revolt against the Chinese, the revolt had substantially shifted to central Tibet. Lhasa government officials were unresponsive to Chinese demands that they put down the resistance; instead, some began surreptitiously offering sympathy and covert support for the resistance, and allowing regional armories to fall into their hands.

The Tibetan resistance, now mostly under a unified command known as *Chushi Gangdruk*, "Four Rivers, Six Ranges," consisted of some 5,000 men in the southern Tibetan district of Lhoka.[142] This force fought a series of running battles with the Chinese over the next nine months, inflicting numerous casualties but always being ultimately overpowered by Chinese superiority in numbers, armaments and mobility. They were also powerless against the Chinese use of aircraft for surveillance and attack. The *Chushi Gangdruk*, as well as numerous other bands of Tibetan resisters, continued to harass the Chinese until April 1959.[143]

Until the final crisis in Lhasa, the Dalai Lama attempted to prevent vio-

---

138. Dalai Lama, *Freedom in Exile*, 125.

139. Nyima Assam, personal interview.

140. Andrugtsang, *Four Rivers, Six Ranges*, 55. These Chinese, most of whom had good relations with the Tibetans, were no doubt the "Kuomintang agents" often blamed for inciting the Tibetans to resist the "new Chinese," the Chinese Communists.

141. Dalai Lama, *My Land*, 159; Andrugtsang, *Four Rivers, Six Ranges*, 58.

142. Andrugtsang, *Four Rivers, Six Ranges*, 63. "Four Rivers, Six Ranges" was the traditional name for Kham.

143. Ibid., 95.

lence by mediating with the Chinese, even requesting those in the resistance to lay down their arms. He protested to the Chinese against the methods of suppression they were employing. At the same time, the Chinese accused the Dalai Lama and his government of sympathizing with the resisters and of supplying them with arms. As the Dalai Lama later wrote in his autobiography:

> The revolt had broken out in the district they themselves had controlled for seven years; yet now they furiously blamed our government for it. Their complaints and accusations were endless, day after day: the Cabinet was not trying to suppress the "reactionaries," it was leaving Tibetan armories unguarded, so that "reactionaries" could steal arms and ammunition. Consequently, hundreds of Chinese were losing their lives, and the Chinese would take vengeance in blood for them. Like all invaders, they had totally lost sight of the sole cause of the revolt against them: that our people did not want them in our country, and were ready to give up their lives to be rid of them.[144]

The situation finally reached a climax with an invitation from the Chinese commander in Lhasa to the Dalai Lama to attend a theater performance in the Chinese military camp on 10 March 1959. The Dalai Lama was instructed to bring none of his attendants or bodyguards, an extraordinary request that led Tibetans to believe that he was to be kidnapped.[145] The Dalai Lama had been invited to attend the Chinese National People's Congress the next month, which he had refused; however, Chinese cadres in Tibet had promised Peking that he would attend, leading to the suspicion that they hoped to isolate him from his advisors in order to apply persuasion to convince him to attend the NPC or simply to transport him to Peking against his will.[146]

On 10 March a crowd of Tibetans surrounded the Norbulinka to prevent the Dalai Lama from leaving to attend the theater. The Dalai Lama announced that he would not attend and, fearing Chinese reprisals

---

144. Dalai Lama, *My Land*, 162.

145. There were good reasons for such suspicions; on four recent occasions, high lamas of eastern Tibet had been abducted after accepting invitations from the Chinese to social functions; three had been killed, one arrested. Ibid., 169. The Dalai Lama later said that, although he doubted that the Chinese really intended to kidnap him, they handled the situation in a peremptory manner guaranteed to arouse suspicion. Ibid., 168.

146. Ibid., 168. One can easily imagine that the Chinese authorities in Lhasa were placed in an untenable position, since they had promised Peking that the Dalai Lama would attend the NPC, but were then unable to convince him to do so. After the revolt, and the flight of the Dalai Lama, the Chinese flew the Panchen Lama to Peking to represent Tibet at the NPC meeting.

against the crowd, requested that the crowd disperse. Instead, they took matters into their own hands, organizing a permanent guard at the Norbulinka and then, in a hastily assembled *Mimang Tsongdu* convened at the foot of the Potala, declaring Tibet's independence. On the 12th an assembly of the women of Lhasa demanded the withdrawal of the Chinese from Tibet and the restoration of Tibetan independence. The women's leaders also presented an appeal for assistance to the Indian Consulate in Lhasa.[147]

During the following days most Tibetan Government officials declared their support for independence; an official resolution to that effect was passed in a meeting with leaders of the *Mimang Tsongdu*. The three great Lhasa monasteries, Sera, Drepung and Ganden, also declared their support for independence.[148] By 17 March a confrontation with the Chinese authorities and troops in Lhasa was imminent. Two mortar shells exploding within the walls of the Norbulinka convinced the Dalai Lama's advisers that he must escape.

On the evening of the 17th the Dalai Lama escaped with the aid of his bodyguard and his closest advisers. On the far side of the Kyichu his party was met by members of the *Chushi Gangdruk* who remained with him as escort until he reached India. The Chinese were unaware of the escape until two days later. The Dalai Lama and his party took a route through Lhoka, territory controlled by the *Chushi Gangdruk*, a route far to the east of the usual route to India, reaching the Indian border at a point near Tawang.[149] At Lhuntse Dzong, before crossing the Indian border, the

---

147. Peissel reports that news of the revolt in Lhasa and of the Tibetans' appeal to India was transmitted by telegraph to New Delhi, but was suppressed by Indian authorities. Michel Peissel, *Cavaliers of Kham: The Secret War in Tibet* (London: Heineman, 1972), 139.

148. The Chinese later published these documents in an attempt to prove that the Dalai Lama had been opposed to the "rebels." The Dalai Lama had indeed, according to Tibetan documents, been opposed to a confrontation with the Chinese, and had refused to allow the meeting of the *Mimang Tsongdu* within the Norbulinka (therefore, they had retired to the Tibetan Government Mint in front of the Potala). "Documents Captured in Rebel Headquarters Further Prove that the Dalai Lama is being Held under Duress and Contact between Rebels and Indian Expansionists," *NCNA* (Lhasa), 27 April 1959, in *Tibet 1950-67*, 362.

149. Tawang is east of Bhutan, whereas the usual route to India is via the Chumbi valley (Yatung), entering India between Bhutan and Sikkim. It is undoubtedly the unusual route that the Dalai Lama's party took, plus the fact that the territory through which he travelled was controlled by the Tibetan resistance, that allowed him to escape Chinese detection or pursuit. There are no indications that the CIA played any role in the departure of the Dalai Lama or his successful evasion of pursuit. Two CIA-trained Tibetans who had parachuted into Tibet met in Lhasa with one of the Dalai Lama's officials, Phala, shortly before the revolt. They conveyed a message that the US was willing to provide assistance, but wanted an official request from the Tibetan Government before doing so. The circumstances of this

Dalai Lama and his government formally repudiated the 17-Point Agreement and established a temporary government.[150] On 31 March the Dalai Lama and his party entered India. In Lhasa on the 20th the Chinese began a bombardment of the Norbulinka, still thinking the Dalai Lama was inside, and an attack on all the Tibetans' fortified positions. Within three days the fighting in Lhasa was over, Chinese superiority in organization and weaponry having enabled them to crush Tibetan resistance.

The Tibetan revolt that culminated in Lhasa in March 1959 was only the climax of a process set in motion by the forcible incorporation of Tibet within the Chinese state. China's attempt to treat Kham and Amdo as if they were not part of a Tibetan national entity precipitated revolt in eastern Tibet, ultimately leading to revolt in central Tibet, despite the "no reform" policy in the TAR. The Tibetan revolt was a national uprising against the Chinese invasion and occupation of Tibet and Chinese policies of "democratic reforms" and "socialist transformation," not, as the Chinese claimed, a revolt of "serf-owners and reactionaries" determined to preserve their personal power and privileges. Although many minority nationalities resisted Chinese political control, only in Tibet did resistance amount to a national uprising.

The period from the 1951 17-Point Agreement to the revolt in 1959 was one of transition for Tibet from a *de facto* independent state to a part of the People's Republic of China. During this period the Chinese became the masters of Tibet, but saw their role transformed from "liberators" into colonialist oppressors. Many Chinese who were sent to Tibet may have thought that they were truly liberators and would be welcomed by Tibetans as such, but, by the end, most knew that their presence was opposed by the majority of Tibetans. Chinese administrators and soldiers in Tibet gradually responded by adopting the typically defensive attitudes of colonialists. While many Chinese in Tibet may have attempted to apply minority nationalities policies conscientiously in the beginning, few did so by the end.

The Chinese reacted to Tibetan opposition and resistance with increasing oppression and brutality. China finally achieved the political integra-

---

message make it clear that the Americans neither planned nor anticipated the revolt; the message asking for an official request for US assistance makes it apparent that the US thought that the Dalai Lama and the Tibetan Government would remain in Tibet. Jamyang Norbu, personal communication, Washington, D.C., June 1995. These two CIA-trained Tibetans, one of whom was equipped with a radio that enabled him to maintain contact with CIA agents in India, joined the Dalai Lama's party in Lhoka. The Dalai Lama was aware of this person and the fact that he "apparently was in touch with his headquarters throughout the journey." *Dalai Lama, Freedom in Exile*, 140.

150. Dalai Lama, *Freedom in Exile*, 141.

tion of Tibet within the Chinese state, not by the successful employment of Marxist-Leninist and CCP nationalities theory and policies (except in that deceit was successfully employed), but by a relentless imposition of force and usurpation of political authority in Tibet, which culminated, like it began, in violence. The Tibetan revolt ultimately refuted China's claim that Tibet constituted an integral part of China or that it was "peacefully liberated."

Tibetan nationalism, a previously unfocused or localized ideology among most Tibetans, was aroused by the Chinese invasion of Tibet. However, effective resistance against the Chinese was precluded by the Tibetan Government's acceptance of the terms of the 17-Point Agreement. In addition, Chinese policies of friendly and respectful treatment of Tibetans in general and the employment of the former ruling class within the United Front were initially very effective. The upper classes were prevented from playing their natural role as leaders of resistance to the Chinese, while the under classes were cultivated as activists, or, if they attempted to resist, found no support from their traditional leaders.[151] CCP nationalities policies were effective in creating social divisions and in cultivating collaborators, but were ultimately counterproductive in that they stimulated the very nationalist consciousness they were intended to suppress.

CCP nationalities policies were unable to transform ethnic nationalism into state patriotism, to create a "union of nationalities" in a Chinese multinational state, or to convince minority nationalities of the benevolent intentions of the Chinese or of the benefits of Chinese socialism. Propaganda and education campaigns on anti-imperialism, anti-local nationalism and Chinese patriotism consolidated rather than reduced Tibetan nationalist consciousness. The initiation of "class conflict," which for the Chinese had no nationalist content, was for the Tibetans almost entirely of nationalist significance, a fact that Chinese propaganda was unable to obscure. For most Tibetans, the initiation of "democratic reforms" produced not an upsurge of class anger against class oppression, but a national uprising against national oppression. The true significance of democratic reforms, obvious to all Tibetans, was the replacement of Tibetan leadership and political authority by Chinese colonial rule.

---

151. The traditional hierarchical nature of Tibetan society has been faulted by many Tibetans for providing little basis for united national resistance and much potential for divisive Chinese tactics based upon class. The hierarchical nature of Tibetan society fostered a culture of subservience among the lower classes that was not conducive to a sense of popular or democratic responsibility for the functioning of the political system or the fate of the nation.

The perseverance and resurgence of "local nationalism" in Tibet was something of a surprise for CCP ideologues, who imagined that the issue of Tibetan national identity had been settled in 1951 by Tibet's "peaceful" incorporation within the PRC. However, the failure of nationalities policies to defuse Tibetan nationalism could be credited to "feudal reactionaries" or imperialist influences rather than to an error in Marxist-Leninist ideology. Marxist-Leninist and CCP nationality theory and policy was, in any case, primarily a tactic for defusing opposition until military and political control could be secured and the possibility of a successful revolt eliminated; in this purpose it was successful.

The inevitable upsurge of Tibetan resistance was delayed until the imposition of "democratic reforms" and "socialist transformation," which, for most Tibetans, actually constituted a greater intrusion upon their lives than had the original entry of the Chinese into Tibet. The immediate cause of revolt in Tibet was the precipitous implementation of "national regional autonomy" and the accompanying democratic reforms and socialist transformation in eastern Tibet. Chinese policies in the TAR were successful in preventing revolt there until the revolt spread from eastern Tibet. In the end, the Dalai Lama was still attempting to mediate when his own government and the majority of his people were at the last stage of exasperation and about to embark upon violent resistance, a resistance that the Dalai Lama could not support because of his commitment to cooperate with the Chinese and his adherence to the Buddhist doctrine of non-violence. Tibetan nationalist resistance was no doubt inevitable, but the Dalai Lama's influence could perhaps have prevented open revolt for an indefinite time, even in the east, had the Chinese not treated the east as if it were not part of Tibet.[152]

---

152. A related issue is whether Tibetan armed resistance might have been more effective had it had the benefit of the Dalai Lama's leadership. The people of Lhasa finally had to take matters into their own hands by preventing the Dalai Lama going to the Chinese camp and their declaration of independence. Ginsburgs and Mathos have suggested that Tibetans may have surrounded the Norbulinka not only because of their fear that the Dalai Lama was about to be kidnapped, but because of the fear that he would make more concessions to Chinese demands. Ginsburgs and Mathos, Communist China and Tibet, 122. The question of the Dalai Lama's role takes us back to the time of the debate over whether to accept or reject the 17-Point Agreement. At that time, the Dalai Lama's leadership was considered necessary to mediate with the Chinese. Once that decision was made, armed resistance was no longer feasible since the Dalai Lama and the Tibetan Government were resigned to cooperation with the Chinese. By 1959 a Tibetan revolt had little chance of success, with or without the Dalai Lama's leadership. Had the Dalai Lama called for national resistance to the Chinese in 1959, a position impossible for him to take consistent with his religious role, the final revolt might have been more dramatic, but would undoubtedly been put down by an even greater use of force.

By 1959 the Chinese were not entirely adverse to a final showdown with the Tibetan "government of serf-owners," since they were secure in the knowledge that they had attained a preponderance of force and that they could not be dislodged from Tibet. The Tibetan revolt was not without advantage for the Chinese. Mao had previously said that the particular policies applied to Tibet would either be successful in preventing revolt or that "bad elements" would lead a rebellion; either scenario, he said, "will be favorable to us."[153] In 1956 Mao expressed little concern about the possibility that the Dalai Lama might seek exile in India, an attitude that might indicate that Mao considered the Dalai Lama an impediment to Chinese plans for Tibet and would ultimately have to be removed in one way or another. Although the revolt and the exile of the Dalai Lama were an international embarrassment for the Chinese, they were also undoubtedly relieved to finally have a completely free hand in Tibet.

In the final analysis, the Chinese Communist program for Tibet's incorporation differed little from traditional Chinese frontier assimilationist policies. CCP nationalities policies promised to provide the benefits of Chinese socialist culture in exchange for minority nationalities' territories and resources, a bargain calculated to benefit the Chinese, not the people whose territory was incorporated. Modern ideological rationalizations were incapable of disguising this reality. Mao and the Chinese leadership unintentionally exposed their real concerns toward Tibet and other frontier territories by repeatedly expressing the rationale that good treatment of minority nationalities was necessary because their territories and resources were essential for the strategic security and economic development of China. Presumably, once those territories were firmly secured, the rationale for good treatment of minority nationalities would disappear.

---

153. Mao Tse-tung, "On the Policies of Our Work in Tibet," *Selected Works*, vol. 5, 74.

12

Tibet Transformed

The Chinese National Flag, symbol of light and happiness, flutters in the breeze over Lhasa, greeting the re-birth of this ancient city.[1]

Aftermath of the Revolt

The Lhasa revolt was a national uprising against the Chinese presence in Tibet. The PLA finally put down the revolt after it had assumed an undeniably popular pro-independence character. Many thousands were reportedly killed in the process; the streets of Lhasa and the Norbulinka were littered with bodies, whose disposal took several days.[2] Many Tibetans, both active resistance fighters and ordinary villagers, attempted to escape to India, but apparently only a small proportion were successful.[3]

---

1. "Order Restored in Lhasa," *New China News Agency (NCNA)* (Lhasa), 30 March 1959, in *Current Background* (Hong Kong: United States Consulate), no. 553.

2. *Tibet Under Chinese Communist Rule: A Compilation of Refugee Statements: 1958-1975* (Dharamsala: Information and Publicity Office of His Holiness the Dalai Lama, 1976), 32, 33. Tibetan estimates of the number killed in the Lhasa revolt vary from 5000 to 10,000, with as many as 20,000 arrested after the revolt. Chinese statistics provide some estimate of the numbers of Tibetans "eliminated" by the PLA in the TAR during and after the revolt. A document captured by the Tibetan Resistance in 1966, entitled "Political Situation in Tibet and Basic Education Document, People's Liberation Army Political Bureau, 10 January 1960," reads "People's Liberation Army activists under Party control with local resident Tibetan population eliminated 87,000 enemies in the rebellion from March 1959 to the beginning of October 1960." *Tibet: The Facts: A Report by the Scientific Buddhist Association for the United Nations Commission on Human Rights* (Dharamsala: Tibetan Young Buddhist Association, 1990), 356. "Eliminated" does not necessarily mean killed; those imprisoned may, or may not, have been included in this figure.

3. Escape was particularly difficult from Amdo since PLA tactics were to confine refugees within that region. More escaped from Kham since many Khampas were resistance fighters and had already reached Central Tibet before 1959. Many Tibetans report attacks by Chinese military aircraft and massacres of whole groups attempting to escape. "Statements by Tibetan refugees," in *Tibet and the Chinese People's Republic: A Report to the International Commission of Jurists by its Legal Inquiry Committee on Tibet* (Geneva: International Commission of Jurists, 1960), 227. Tibetans from Kham and Amdo report that less than 10% of those who fled reached India. Ibid., 266; *Tibet Under Chinese Communist Rule*, 81; Abu

Most of the men of Lhasa, and those women who had participated in anti-Chinese demonstrations, were detained at a variety of sites in Lhasa until their "crimes" could be determined. Former government leaders, secular and ecclesiastic, were arrested and detained at the Chinese military camp. Monasteries, government buildings, large houses of the aristocracy and the Norbulinka were turned into temporary prisons.[4] Some Tibetans, especially women, were released if there was no evidence of their actual participation in or support for the revolt; however, most of the Lhasa population was recruited for forced labor projects, particularly the hydroelectric project at Nachen Trang east of the city. Most men were deported to labor camps; for several years, Lhasa was a city virtually without Tibetan men.[5]

Organized Tibetan resistance continued for only another month. The *Chushi Gangdruk* suffered several losses in late March and early April. On 20 April Gompo Tashi Andrugtsang, the *Chushi Gangdruk* leader, and many of the resistance fighters crossed the border into India.[6] Disorganized resistance continued somewhat longer, even until early 1960 in some areas.

The flight of the Dalai Lama eliminated the last obstacle to Chinese control of Tibet. The "Tibetan local government" was dissolved by order of the State Council, announced by Chou En-lai on 28 March. The Preparatory Committee (PCTAR) took over the functions of the "former Tibetan local government." The Dalai Lama's position as chairman of the PCTAR was preserved, based upon the belief that he was being held under duress. In the absence of the Dalai Lama, the Panchen Lama was to function as acting chairman of the Preparatory Committee.[7] In fact, Tibet was now under the control of the People's Liberation Army (PLA). Military Control Commissions were established in all districts of Tibet except in Shigatse, where there was said to be "no need" to do so.[8] The

---

Chonga, Abu Gongkar, Nyima Assam, Ani Pachim Dolma, personal interviews, Dharamsala, 1989-1990.

4. Tsayul Tulku, personal interview, Dharamsala, December 1989; *Tibet Under Chinese Communist Rule*, 88; John Avedon, *In Exile from the Land of Snows* (New York: Vintage Books, 1986), 247.

5. Sonam Dolkar, personal communication, Lhasa, 1982.

6. Gompo Tashi Andrugtsang, *Four Rivers, Six Ranges: A True Account of Khampa Resistance to Chinese in Tibet* (Dharamsala: Information and Publicity Office of H.H. the Dalai Lama, 1973), 105.

7. "Order of the State Council of the People's Republic of China," *Peking Review*, 31 March 1959, 6.

8. Chou revealed that four of the six *Kalons* of the Tibetan *Kashag*, as well as eighteen members of the Preparatory Committee, had joined the rebellion. "Communique on Rebellion in Tibet," *NCNA*, 28 March 1959, *Peking Review*, 31 March 1959, 8. Chou did not reveal how many were arrested and how many escaped to India.

PCTAR issued a communique ordering all administrative personnel of the "defunct Tibet local government" to register with local military control commissions.[9] Tibetan students at the Minority Nationalities Institutes in Peking and Hsienyang were returned to Tibet shortly after the revolt to take over administrative positions, but they were not trusted with positions of any real authority.[10]

The Chinese seemed both surprised and relieved at the violent culmination of their "peaceful liberation" of Tibet. The peaceful nature of Tibet's incorporation within the PRC now appeared a hollow claim; nevertheless, complete control had finally been secured. The Chinese engaged in considerable taunting about their military victory, which became a standard theme of lectures in prisons and in community meetings. Reported statements included: "Your precious Potala is now ours"; "You people have opposed us a great deal though we have come here to liberate you. . . you stand as much chance of getting your independence as you do of seeing the sun rise from the west"; and "We are here to rule you, and that is a fact."[11]

The Chinese expected their revolution to lead to the conquest of Nepal and India: "There is nobody to equal our strength. We shall gradually conquer all the other countries of the world. India, where all the reactionaries are hoping to escape, will be taken just as a matter of course."[12] Tibetans were exhorted to complete roads to the Indian border because the Indians were "suffering under the imperial yoke and are anxiously awaiting democratic reforms." The Chinese also proclaimed their intention to "spread democratic reforms throughout the world in the next five years."[13]

Although the revolt eliminated organized Tibetan resistance, the revolt and the flight of the Dalai Lama were an international embarrassment for the Chinese. The Chinese were surprised by the escape of the Dalai Lama, having mistaken his acquiescence for approval of their policies. His escape also posed a challenge to their claim that he and the Tibetan peo-

---

9. "Resolution of Tibetan Committee on Implementation of State Council Order," *NCNA* (Lhasa), 10 April 1959, in *Current Background*, no. 555.

10. Returned Tibetan students of the former upper classes were reportedly given jobs, usually as translators, in finance, agriculture, etc., whereas those of lower class background were employed in intelligence and police work. Trinley Phuntsok, personal interview, Dharamsala, January 1990. Tsering Dorje Gashi, *New Tibet: Memoirs of a Graduate of the Peking Institute of National Minorities* (Dharamsala: Information Office of His Holiness the Dalai Lama, 1980), 33, 63.

11. *Tibet Under Chinese Communist Rule*, 33, 34, 75.

12. Ibid., 75. The communist conquest of India was expected to be by means of the popular revolt of their own people, supported by China.

13. Ibid., 104.

ple had voluntarily accepted Chinese rule. The CCP counterattacked with a barrage of propaganda claiming that the revolt had been led by a handful of serf-owners and that its suppression represented a popular overthrow of the "reactionary serf-owner government."

The themes of Chinese propaganda were the "undeniable fact" that Tibet was an "integral part of China" and the class basis of the revolt. The rebels were depicted as an "upper strata serf-owning reactionary clique," who, under the guise of defending the Tibetan nation and religion, were actually intent only upon preserving their own class privileges, and who had been in league with reactionaries and imperialists of all types, domestic and foreign. The Tibetan "masses" were claimed to have been patriotic to China and unsupportive of the rebels; they had begged the PLA to intervene and supported it when it did so. Peace had been quickly restored because neither the revolt nor the very idea of Tibetan independence had any support among Tibetans. The Dalai Lama had also opposed the revolt, it was claimed; therefore, he must have been kidnapped and was still being held under duress in India.

The Chinese attempted to obscure the issue of Tibetan independence by constant reference to the 17-Point Agreement, which had theoretically forever resolved that issue. Furthermore, it was claimed, the "reactionary Tibetan local government," not the Chinese People's Government, had violated the provisions of the agreement. In an attempt to remove the issue of Tibetan independence from contemporary or even historical relevance, and thus to lay to rest any issue of a Chinese "invasion" of Tibet, evidence was presented that Tibet had been "an integral part of China," at least since the 13th century. According to Chinese propaganda, Tibet had begun the "natural process" of union of nationalities during the T'ang dynasty of the seventh century. The almost continuous warfare between China and Tibet of the T'ang was described as "an era which saw the great development of friendly contact between the Tibetan and Han peoples. This laid a foundation for the unity between the Tibetan peoples and the other nationalities of China, first of all, between the Tibetan and Han peoples, and for the Tibetan people to join the great family of the motherland and work together with the other nationalities to build a unified country."[14]

Chinese propaganda attempted to push as far back into history as possible the date when Tibet became an "integral part of China," and thus to minimize any history of Tibet as a country separate from China.

---

14. "Tibet: An Integral Part of China," *Peking Review*, 5 May 1959, 13. The article stops short of claiming that Tibet became part of China during the T'ang, only that a foundation for the inevitable merging of nationalities was laid. No mention was made of the fact that Tibet, if not a part of China at that time, must have been a separate country.

Tibet became an integral part of China, it was claimed, in 1253, when Mongko (Mongke), "Emperor Hsien Tsung of the Yuan dynasty," sent an army to Tibet. Tibet was then incorporated into the Yuan empire and "has been a part of the territory of China ever since."[15] Since the time of the Yuan, Tibet's "political and religious systems were gradually defined by the successive central governments of China." "Friendly relations" continued during the Ming; Ming Tai Tsu supposedly made the Fifth Karmapa "ruler of Tibet." Furthermore, the Manchu Emperor Shun Chih "officially established" the title of Dalai Lama in 1653.[16]

The Chinese were intent upon regarding the issue of Tibet's political status as settled, and therefore constantly referred to political resolutions and institutions of their own making, such as the 17-Point Agreement and the Preparatory Committee of the TAR, as the defining articles of Tibet's political status. In this way, they hoped to confine the issue of Tibet to the process of its integration within the Chinese state, to the exclusion of any remaining "separatist" issues. The Chinese emphasized those provisions of the 17-Point Agreement calling for Tibet's integration within China rather than those guaranteeing Tibetan autonomy.

The Chinese also emphasized their own patience in implementing reforms; the Tibetans were supposed to have understood that reforms were an essential part of what they had agreed to in 1951. That social reforms would eventually be carried out was said to have been "unequivocally stated in the agreement on measures for the peaceful liberation of Tibet." The CCP had "consistently adhered" to the provisions of that agreement and had provided many "fine things, all beneficial to the Tibetan people," such as the United Front and the PCTAR, all initiated only after full consultation with "persons of the upper social strata." Nevertheless, the Chinese spokesman complained, "the clique of reactionaries in Tibet do not want regional autonomy at all. What they are after is the so-called `independence of Tibet' plotted by the imperialist aggressors for many years. . . . They organized the illegal `people's conference' and prepared, once they had mustered considerable forces, to tear up right away the Agreement on Measures for the Peaceful Liberation of Tibet and abolish the Preparatory Committee for the Autonomous Region of Tibet." The problem, the Chinese complained,

---

15. Ibid., 14. Mongke was posthumously made the first emperor of the Yuan, but the Yuan was not proclaimed until 1260, by Khubilai. How the fact that Tibet became a part of the Yuan empire made it a part of China, also a part of the Yuan empire, was not explained.

16. Ibid. This version of history was reconciled with the fact that the Dalai Lama whom the Shun Chih Emperor met in 1652 was the Fifth, the title having been given by Altan Khan to the Third Dalai Lama in 1579, by the theory that titles of "frontier barbarians" attained legitimacy only by Chinese recognition.

was that some Tibetans had never actually been reconciled to their "peaceful liberation" and had not accepted the socialist road as the "inevitable trend of the development of history and the common desire of the people of all nationalities."[17]

Repeated mention of the "illegal people's conference," the *Mimang Tsongdu*, makes it apparent that this popular movement was particularly threatening to the Chinese Communists since it challenged the CCP's claim to be the sole legitimate representantive of the people's interests. Rather than admit the popular nature of the revolt, the Chinese attempted to place blame upon the "former Tibetan local government," despite the fact that the Dalai Lama and the Tibetan Government had attempted to persuade Tibetans against violent resistance. The Tibetan Government was accused of having "torn up the 17-articles on the Measures for the Peaceful Liberation of Tibet."[18]

Pains were taken to put the revolt within the correct Marxist framework. The idea of Tibetan independence was portrayed as a subterfuge of the exploiting classes, who were using nationalism for their own selfish purposes:

> This reactionary clique had hoped to stage their rebellion under the cloak of nationalism; they wanted to conceal the true nature of their aim which was to preserve the interests of the reactionary serf-owning class. Events have shown that this rebellion and its quelling was definitely not a "national war" but a class war, a war instigated by a handful of arch-reactionary feudal serf-owners to oppose the Communist Party's leading the broad masses of the serfs to stand up; it was an uncompromising class war.[19]

The "reactionary clique of the upper social strata," in its attempt to eternally maintain the rule of feudal serfdom, had "plotted to separate Tibet from the motherland." They had, however, "lifted a stone only to crush their own feet," resulting in "their own destruction at an early date, the further consolidation of the unity of the motherland, the democratization of Tibet and a new life for the Tibetan people":

> The act of a small handful of traitors who carry out counterrevolutionary rebellion in Tibet in collaboration with the imperialists and the bandits has aroused the great indignation of the people. These traitors try to prevent the Tibetan people from realizing their own true wishes, and to lead the Tibetan

---

17. "Put Down the Rebellion in Tibet Thoroughly!" *Peking Review*, 7 April 1959, 7.
18. Ibid., 6.
19. Chang Ching-wu, "The Victory of Democratic Reforms in Tibet," *Peking Review*, 29 March 1959, 13.

people away from the leadership of Chairman Mao and stop them from
receiving the attention and assistance of the people of the great Han nationality.[20]

The rebels were said to have enjoyed no actual support among the
Tibetan "masses," with the exception of those they had duped into believing that this was a struggle in defense not of their own class interests but
of the Tibetan religion and nation. The rebels were characterized as isolated from the "broad masses" of the Tibetan people, who "hated and
opposed" them. In contrast, the Tibetan people supported the PLA:
"Large crowds of jubilant Tibetans cheered and waved greetings at road-
sides or on hills wherever the units of the People's Liberation Army
passed on their march to mop up the rebels. . . . Wherever the PLA
troops went, the Tibetans treated them like kinsmen returned home from
after a long absence. They tearfully told the PLA of the monstrous crimes
committed by the rebels."[21]

To counteract the effect of popular demonstrations in Lhasa accompanying the revolt, the Chinese organized "spontaneous" demonstrations
to condemn the revolt and support the "people's government." Rallies
were organized in Shigatse on 30 March, addressed by the Panchen
Lama, and in Lhasa on 31 March. Rallies "spontaneously" occurred in
many localities in Tibet at the same time; the unanimous themes of condemnation of the rebels and support for the PLA were expressed.
"Patriotic and progressive" Tibetans parroted CCP slogans emphasizing
the class rather than national nature of the revolt and the interests of
Tibetans in preserving their "national unity" within China. Also praised
were the forbearance of the people's government in tolerating, against
the actual wishes of the people, the upper strata's opposition to social
reforms, and the PLA's restraint in quelling the revolt.[22] On 15 April the

---

20. Ibid.

21. "Tibetans Support PLA in Mopping Up Remnant Rebels," *NCNA* (Lhasa), 24 April
1959, in *Current Background*, no. 567, 4. Abuses of the Tibetan population by the Khampa
resistance had been a major theme of Chinese propaganda, playing upon central Tibetans'
fears of the Khampas. In fact, the Chinese had perpetrated most of these atrocities themselves by using Tibetan collaborators or even Chinese dressed up as Khampas to abuse the
Tibetan population. This tactic fooled some Tibetans and forced the Resistance to issue identification for their own men. Andrugtsang, *Four Rivers, Six Ranges*, 66.

22. "Lhasa People Warmly Support State Council Order," *NCNA* (Lhasa), 30 March 1959,
in *Current Background*, no. 553, 19; "Nationwide Support for Building a New Tibet," *Peking
Review*, 7 April 1959, 9; "Panchen Erdeni Cables Chairman Mao and Premier Chou
Supporting Decisions on Tibet," *NCNA* (Lhasa), 30 March 1959, in *Current Background*, no.
553, 12; "Ngawang Jigme's Report to 1st Session of Tibetan Committee," *NCNA* (Lhasa), 10
April 1959, in *Current Background*, no. 553; "Chinese Buddhist Leader Shirob Jaltso on
Tibetan Question," *NCNA*, 29 March 1959, in *Current Background*, no. 553, 22; "Tsinghai

remaining citizens of Lhasa, mostly women and children, plus "more than 2,000 monks," were again turned out "to demonstrate their support for the Central People's Government in quelling the rebellion in Tibet."[23]

At the end of March the *NCNA* published the Dalai Lama's letters to the acting Chinese commander at Lhasa, T'an Kuan-san, in which the Dalai Lama had referred to the rebels as "evil reactionaries" and their resistance to the Chinese as "unlawful actions of the reactionary clique." These were submitted as evidence that the Dalai Lama had not supported the rebellion. His letter of 16 March, the day before he fled, in which he said that he would proceed to the Chinese military camp when able, was submitted as evidence that he must have been abducted.[24] The Dalai Lama later explained that his letters had been intended to reassure the Chinese, and to "disguise my true intentions," but also that they reflected his belief that violence was no solution. As he said after reaching India, "Until the last day, I tried to bring about a peaceful settlement, the failure of which resulted in the armed uprising of my people who were compelled to fight for their freedom."[25]

On 18 April in Tezpur the Dalai Lama issued a statement refuting the Chinese contention that he had been abducted and accusing the Chinese of having violated their promise to respect Tibet's autonomy:

People Support State Council Order," *NCNA* (Sining), 29 March 1959, in *Current Background*, no. 553, 26; "Tibetans in Szechuan Province Support State Council Order," *NCNA* (Chengtu [Chamdo]), 30 March 1959, in *Current Background*, no. 553, 29; "Tibetans Throughout China Support State Council Order," *NCNA*, 31 March 1959, in *Current Background*, no. 553, 34.

23. "The Rebirth of Tibet," *Peking Review*, 14 April 1959, 8. This was described as the "biggest demonstration ever held in Tibetan history," and was clearly intended to counteract the effect of the well-known women's march during the Lhasa revolt.

24. "Letters Exchanged between the Dalai Lama and General T'an Kuan-san," *NCNA*, 29 March 1959, in *Tibet 1950-67* (Hong Kong: Union Research Institute, 1967), 369. The Dalai Lama was, no doubt, not in control of events leading up to his flight. Leaders of the opposition to the Chinese, especially certain aristocrats in his administration, were instrumental in precipitating the final crisis and in convincing the Dalai Lama that he had no choice but to flee; however, their role can hardly be described as "kidnapping."

25. "News Conference Held by the Dalai Lama on June 20, 1959, at Mussoorie, India," in *The Question of Tibet and the Rule of Law* (Geneva: International Commission of Jurists, 1959), 201. As to the use of terminology about "reactionaries," the Dalai Lama explained: "The Chinese . . . insisted that the word `reactionaries' should always be used to describe the Khampas who had taken arms against them. The word has a special significance for Communists, but of course it had none for us. Everybody, in the government and out, began to use it as a synonym for guerillas. To Communists, no doubt, it implied the height of wickedness, but we used it, on the whole, in admiration. It did not seem to matter to us, or to the Khampas, what their fellow-Tibetans called them; but later, when I innocently used the word in writing, it did cause confusion among our friends abroad." Dalai Lama, *My Land and My People: Memoirs of the Dalai Lama of Tibet* (New York: McGraw Hill, 1962; New York: Potala, 1977), 161, 189.

In 1951 under pressure from the Chinese Government a 17-point agreement was made between China and Tibet. In that agreement the suzerainty of China was accepted as there was no alternative left to the Tibetans. But even in the agreement it was stated that Tibet would enjoy full autonomy. Though the control of external affairs was to be in the hands of the Chinese Government it was agreed that there would be no interference by the Chinese Government in the Tibetan religion and customs and in her internal administration. In fact, after the occupation of Tibet by Chinese armies, the Tibetan Government did not enjoy any measure of autonomy, even in internal matters; the Chinese Government exercised full powers in Tibetan affairs.

In 1956 a Preparatory Committee was set up for Tibet with the Dalai Lama as the Chairman and the Panchen Lama as Vice-Chairman and General Chang Kuo-hua as the representative of the Chinese Government. In practice, even this body has little power and decisions on all important matters were taken by the Chinese authorities. The Dalai Lama and his government tried their best to adhere to the 17-point agreement but interference by the Chinese authorities persisted. By the end of 1955 a struggle had started in Kham Province and this assumed serious proportions in 1956. In the consequential struggle, Chinese armed forces destroyed a large number of monasteries. Many lamas were killed and a large number of monks and officials were taken and employed on the construction of roads in China and interference in the exercise of religious freedom increased. . . .

[The next section describes the circumstances of the theater invitation and the surrounding of the Norbulinka to prevent the Dalai Lama from attending.]

Large crowds of Tibetans went about the streets of Lhasa demonstrating against Chinese rule in Tibet. Two days later thousands of Tibetan women held demonstrations protesting against the Chinese authorities. In spite of this demonstration by the people, the Dalai Lama and his government endeavoured to maintain friendly relations with the Chinese and tried to carry out negotiations with the Chinese representatives as how best to bring about peace in Tibet and assuage the people's anxiety. . . .

The Dalai Lama would like to state categorically that he left Lhasa and Tibet and came to India of his own free will and not under duress. . . . [26]

An American CIA report illuminates the circumstances of the Dalai Lama's statement at Tezpur, including not only the GOI role in that statement but Tibetan dissatisfaction with Nehru's role in 1956 in convincing the Dalai Lama to return to Lhasa and to accept a status of autonomy within the PRC:

---

26. "The Dalai Lama Issues Statement in Tezpur, India," *NCNA*, 20 April 1959, in *Tibet 1950-67*, 375.

The Dalai Lama at his first meeting with the Government of India (GOI) political officer at Tawang requested that a telegram be sent to Nehru thanking him for granting asylum and asking that Gyalo Thondup be allowed to see him immediately to discuss political matters with him. The Dalai Lama added that he was now in the same refugee status as Gyalo Thondup and that therefore there was no need to restrict their meetings as had been done during his (the Dalai Lama's) previous visit to India in 1956.[27] The Ministry of External Affairs (MEA) kept a reply pending until the MEA representative, P.N. Menon, met the Dalai Lama at Bomdila.

Menon told the Dalai Lama that Nehru would arrange for Gyalo Thondup to meet the Dalai Lama at Khelong, between Bomdila and Tezpur. Menon stated that Nehru was very sorry about the developments in Tibet, most sympathetic concerning the Dalai Lama's escape and the plight of the Tibetans, and was looking forward to seeing the Dalai Lama in person. Menon gave Nehru's opinion that internal autonomy, not independence, should be Tibet's goal. Menon recommended that the Dalai Lama make only a very brief press statement merely giving thanks for asylum in India.

The last point provoked the Dalai Lama who stated that he returned to Tibet in 1957 on Nehru's advice to work peacefully for wider autonomy. The Chinese Communists had ignored this approach, continually pressured him to denounce the resistance movement and to go to Peiping and finally endangered his life forcing him to escape to India. He and all Tibetans were now convinced that attempts to obtain autonomy were useless, that Tibetans were fighting and dying for complete freedom and independence, and that he was determined to struggle for this goal no matter how long it took regardless of the GOI attitude. The Dalai Lama said that his press statement had already been drafted before he crossed into India and pointed out the spontaneity of the uprising in Lhasa, the Tibetan denouncement of the 17 Point Agreement, the Tibetans' peaceful approach to the Chinese Communists over past years, the escape from Lhasa, the establishment of a Free Tibetan Government at Lhuntse Dzong, the fact that he was now in India to fight the Chinese Communists and to appeal to the free countries of the world for support and recognition of a Free Tibetan Government.

Menon urged the Dalai Lama not to make such a statement.

The Dalai Lama then replied that he hoped the GOI was not thinking along the same 1956 line of autonomy but that the GOI would give him and his

---

27. This is the first indication that the GOI had limited the Dalai Lama's contacts with his brother Gyalo Thondup during the 1956 visit to India. Presumably, the Dalai Lama was referring to some restrictions placed upon his meeting with Gyalo Thondup while both were in Delhi, since the Dalai Lama later had apparently unrestricted meetings with both his brothers and the former prime minister Lukhangwa in Kalimpong. Gyalo Thondup was known to be in contact with the CIA, a fact that may have inspired the Indians to attempt to limit his influence.

people active support. If, however, his stay in India were an inconvenience which might embarrass the GOI and if the GOI were unwilling to reconsider its policy of only autonomy, then he and his cabinet felt that they should not accept Indian asylum but persist in a goal of complete independence and find asylum elsewhere.

Menon cabled the above information to the MEA. The MEA suggested that Menon relax his stand on only a brief press statement but that in the first statement no mention should be made concerning the establishment of a Free Tibetan Government, the letters exchanged between the Dalai Lama and the Chinese Communists, or of Tibetan termination of the 17 Point Agreement. The MEA cabled a draft of the actual press statement which was written in the third person for softer effect.

The Tibetan cabinet members had urged that the statement be in the first person but Menon preferred the MEA draft explaining that it was only an initial statement which could be clarified later. The Dalai Lama thus was planning to make an explicit statement on his exchange of letters with the Chinese Communists, the Free Tibetan Government and a goal of independence. [The next sentence has been omitted by CIA censors.][28]

The Dalai Lama felt that at a personal meeting with Nehru on 24 April he (the Dalai Lama) should follow up on the stand taken with Menon at Bomdila concerning the struggle for independence and recognition of a free Tibetan Government. The Dalai Lama felt that twice he had made a mistake concerning autonomy, once on 1951 and again on Nehru's advice in 1957, so that he was unwilling to betray his people a third time. The Dalai Lama also planned to appeal to Nehru to grant asylum to an unlimited number of refugees.[29]

The *NCNA* responded to the Dalai Lama's Tezpur statement on the 20th, claiming that it was "a crude document, lame in reasoning, full of lies and loop-holes." The authenticity of the Dalai Lama's Tezpur statement was challenged by the Chinese, who pointed out that the entire statement was in the third person, a "European style," and that such terms as "suzerainty" were used, further pointing to a "European, probably British, influence." Aspersions were placed on the Indian Government as well: "Is this not an attempt to place the Dalai Lama in a

---

28. Considering the discrepancy between the Dalai Lama's intended statement (as indicated in this document) and the statement actually released by the Indian MEA, the MEA may have altered the Dalai Lama's statement. This may be what was referred to in the excised sentence. The statement as released makes no mention of Tibetan repudiation of the 17-Point Agreement, the establishment of a Free Tibetan Government or letters between the Dalai Lama and the Chinese military commander at Lhasa.

29. "Desire of Dalai Lama to Continue Struggle for Freedom and Independence of Tibet," Central Intelligence Agency, Teletyped Information Report, E79-0129, 23 April 1959.

position of hostility to his motherland, thus blocking the road for him to return to it? Is this not an attempt to create a situation for compelling the Indian Government to permit the Tibetan rebels to engage in anti-Chinese political activities in India?"[30]

Much was made in Chinese propaganda of the "preposterous notion" that, because the Tibetans were of a different nationality from the Hans, they were therefore deserving of a separate country; the Chinese pointed out that China, like many if not most countries, was a "multinational state," none of whose nationalities, with the exception of the Tibetans, "asks for independence."[31] The Dalai Lama was accused of "disregarding the fact that China is a unified country made up of dozens of nationalities," and of "beating the drum" for the "so-called independence of the Tibetans." All of Tibet's political institutions were said to have been "laid down by the Central Government in Peking over the hundreds of years between the 13th and 18th centuries"; not even the position and powers of the Dalai Lama, it was said, were the creation of the Tibetans themselves.[32] The NCNA denied that the 1951 agreement was concluded under pressure by referring to the "friendly basis" of the negotiations; it also denied the charge that Tibetan autonomy was violated in any way: "In a word, in the past eight years, the political, social and religious systems in Tibet remained as they were before the peaceful liberation. There was hardly any item in Tibetan internal affairs for which the former Tibetan local government was not responsible."[33]

The Dalai Lama made a short statement to the press a few days later, saying that he had indeed been responsible for the first statement and stood by it. In his autobiography (published in 1962) he expressed his "astonishment to see how the Chinese blamed everyone they could think of for the revolt—like an injured dog which snaps at everybody. They could not allow themselves to recognize the truth: that it was the people themselves, whom the Chinese had claimed to be liberating, who had revolted spontaneously against their liberation, and that the ruling class of Tibet had been far more willing than the people to come to agreement."[34]

---

30. "Commentary on the So-called Statement of the Dalai Lama," NCNA, 20 April 1959, in Tibet 1950-67, 379. The Dalai Lama's statement was translated and distributed by a representative of the Indian Ministry of External Affairs (MEA), accounting for the usage of the third person and the English terminology. The statement's distribution by the Indian MEA was taken by the Chinese as evidence of Indian "complicity."

31. Ibid., 384. Much is made of the "multinational" characteristic of China in later propaganda; in fact, China is one of the world's most ethnically homogeneous states; 95% of the population is Han Chinese. The domination of a single nationality in China is virtually total, a fact that propaganda on China's multinational character attempts to obscure.

32. Ibid., 379.

33. Ibid., 381.

34. Dalai Lama, My Land, 218.

On 27 April the Chinese Government published captured documents of the "rebel clique," which "reveals their opposition to nationalities regional autonomy and their mad plot for `independence'" and purportedly proved that they had surrounded and detained the Dalai Lama from 10 March.[35] In an article on the origins of the revolt in Kham, the "Tibetan local government" was accused of having sabotaged the agreement and of having initiated and directed the revolt in Kham:

> The "rebellion" was staged by a very few reactionary slave owners and feudal lords in this area ["Sikang"] to retain their dark regime by intimidating some of the people into becoming their followers. They committed arson, murder, pillage and every kind of atrocity and brought serious damage to the lives and property of local Tibetans. These inhuman rebellious activities were under the command of the upper strata reactionary clique in Tibet.[36]

The Dalai Lama's complaints about Chinese policies in eastern Tibet were rejected because "the whole world knows that the Sikang area was not even part of Tibet at all." The article went on to deny that any loss of life or destruction occurred, except as a consequence of the repression of the rebellion: "In the battles to quell the rebellion, of course, some lives were lost and some buildings damaged—for this the rebels and, first of all those who directed the rebellion, must be held responsible. Aside from this, there was no such thing as large numbers of lamas being killed or many monasteries destroyed as is alleged."[37]

At the meeting of the National People's Congress (NPC) in Peking on 23 April (the meeting that the Chinese had hoped the Dalai Lama would attend), the most prominent Tibetan collaborators—the Panchen Lama, Ngawang Jigme Ngapo, Geshe Sherab Gyatso and Ngawang Gyatso—echoed the Chinese version of Tibetan history and recent events.[38] In a

---

35. "Documents Captured in Rebel Headquarters Further Prove that the Dalai Lama is being Held under Duress and Contact between Rebels and Indian Expansionists," *NCNA* (Lhasa), 27 April 1959, in *Tibet 1950-67*, 362.

36. "Facts on the `Khamba Rebellion,'" *NCNA*, 26 April 1959, in *Tibet 1950-67*, 359.

37. Ibid. The Chinese maintained that "Sikang" was not part of Tibet but admitted that the Tibetan Government had considerable influence there, a contradiction that illustrates the fallacy of their policy of treating eastern Tibet as not part of Tibet.

38. Ngawang Jigme Ngapo had been made Vice-Chairman and Secretary General of the PCTAR after the rebellion. Geshe Sherab Gyatso, a lama from Amdo who received his Geshe degree at Drepung, had been a Chinese sympathizer since the 1930s; he was a member of the KMT's Association for the Promotion of Tibetan Culture and the China Association for the Promotion of Border Culture. At this time, he was Chairman of the Chinese Buddhist Association. Ngawang Gyatso was a former abbot of Sera Monastery in Lhasa who had been a supporter of Reting Rimpoche and had been forced to flee to China at the time of Reting's downfall. He was, at this time, a Vice-Chairman of the Chinese Buddhist Association and "Vice-Head" of the Kanze Autonomous District. All were deputies to the NPC.

historical analysis aimed at demonstrating that "Tibet has always been an inseparable part of China's territory, historically and at present," Sherab Gyatso said that "The 5th Dalai Lama, the first ever to appear in the political arena, was appointed by the Central Government in Peking during the reign of Emperor K'ang Hsi of the Ching Dynasty (1662-1723), who conferred on him the title of `Dalai.'"[39] Sherab Gyatso heaped scorn on those who said that the CCP did not protect religion; he went so far as to elevate Mao to the status of a *Dharmaraja*, stating that even the Indian Emperor Ashoka could not compare to Mao.[40] Ngawang Gyatso cited the murder of the "patriotic" Reting by the "upper strata reactionary clique in collusion with imperialists" as evidence that the "Tibetan traitors" were no protectors of religion.[41]

The Panchen Lama was "greatly incensed," he said, at the Dalai Lama's statement, which was obviously "imposed on him by foreigners." Tibet was an "inalienable part of Chinese territory," he held, "which nobody can deny." Tibetans were different in nationality from the Han, no doubt, but "difference in nationality cannot in any way be used as a pretext to split the motherland." That Tibetans had any "strong desire for independence," as the Dalai Lama had claimed, was "completely fabrications [*sic*]." As the Panchen said, "The Tibetan people know from their own experience that the inevitable outcome of the separating from the motherland would not be so-called independence, but to turn Tibet into a colony and protectorate of a foreign country."[42]

Ngapo refuted the Dalai Lama's statement that the 1951 agreement had been concluded under duress. Ngapo said that he, the leader of the Tibetan delegation in 1951, could testify to the fact that the agreement was concluded after "detailed discussions on an intimate and friendly basis which arrived at unanimous opinions satisfactory to everybody." After the signing of the Agreement, the Central People's Government had "never used any compulsion with regard to the political prerogatives and work of the former Tibet local government." After the usual litany on

---

39. "Leading Tibetans Give Lie to So-Called `Dalai Lama's Statement,'" *NCNA*, 23 April 1959, in *Current Background*, no. 564, 10. The Fifth Dalai Lama, who was neither appointed nor given his title by the Chinese Government, went to Peking in 1651, long before the reign of K'ang Hsi.

40. Shirob Jaltso (Sherab Gyatso), "Tibet is an Inalienable Part of China," *NCNA*, 24 April 1959, in *Current Background*, no. 567, 18.

41. Ngawang Jaltso (Ngawang Gyatso), "`Protection of Religion' and Other Conditions in Tibet," *NCNA*, 22 April 1959, in *Current Background*, no. 563, 11.

42. Panchen Erdeni, "The Rebellion in Tibet and the So-Called Statement by Dalai Lama," *NCNA*, 22 April 1959, in *Current Background*, no. 563. In fact, it is the Tibetan collaborators whose public statements were reputedly "imposed on them by foreigners," that is, by the Chinese. Jigme Ngapo, personal communication, Washington, February 1995.

how the policy of the "Central People's Government" had been invariably correct, but had been obstructed in its goal of helping the Tibetan people by the reactionary "Tibet local government," Ngapo stated that, as an intimate of the Dalai Lama, he could testify to the Dalai Lama's real feelings and intentions:

> In the past eight years, neither from his public statements, nor from his intimate talks with us government officials, did we ever hear anything about "the independence of Tibet" or the sundering of the unity of the motherland. What we heard was that he cared deeply not only for the happiness of the Tibetan people, but also for the consolidation and strengthening of the unity of the motherland. Therefore we can categorically affirm that the statement issued in India in the name of the Dalai Lama definitely does not conform to the will of the Dalai lama himself. It is absolutely clear that this statement was not written in the style of the Dalai Lama himself, nor does it look like writing by Tibetans in the Tibetan language. It looks very much like a piece written by foreigners and imposed on the Dalai Lama.[43]

To some extent, no doubt, the Dalai Lama's compliance had deceived the Chinese as to his real sentiments; as a Buddhist he was opposed to the use of force, which may have been interpreted by the Chinese as opposition to the Tibetan resistance rather than opposition to violence. It is difficult to comprehend how the Chinese thought to maintain their version of events, given that the Dalai Lama was free to contradict it, unless they actually believed their claims or intended them only for domestic consumption. The Chinese may have thought that "peaceful coexistence" with India meant that they could demand the Dalai Lama's return. On the other hand, this may be an example of the dynamics of Chinese propaganda formulas whereby a line is maintained even in the face of reality until compliance with that version—at least domestic compliance—creates a new "reality."

The Dalai Lama's statement had come at the time of the meeting of the National People's Congress, which was intended as a celebration of the "correct policy in Tibet." His contradiction of the Chinese version of events was therefore a considerable embarrassment. Delegates to the NPC complained that the Indian Government had allowed the Dalai Lama to release a statement, "which openly attacks our government." Much was made of the fact that the Dalai Lama's statement had been released by an official of the Indian Ministry of External Affairs.[44] The

---

43. Ngapo Ngawang Jigme, "Conditions in Tibet and the Tezpur Statement of the Dalai Lama," NCNA, 22 April 1959, in *Current Background*, no. 563.

44. Nehru later explained the statement as necessary because of the extraordinary num-

respectful and sympathetic welcome that the Dalai Lama had received in India was regarded as an "unfriendly act" and a violation of the spirit of the "Five Principles of Peaceful Co-existence." The Chinese complained that Nehru had even gone so far as to meet the Dalai Lama in person (at Mussoorie). The Chinese also protested the criticism in the Indian and international press of their handling of the Tibetan crisis, and especially the suggestions that the Dalai Lama should take Tibet's case to the United Nations or that a tripartite conference should be convened between China, Tibet and India to discuss the issue. A demonstration before the Chinese Consulate in Bombay, during which Mao's portrait was defaced, was regarded as an intolerable insult to China.[45]

It was apparent from Indian reaction to the Tibetan revolt that many in India, like the Tibetans themselves, had imagined that China's role in Tibet would remain that of a distant suzerain and Tibet would remain a "buffer zone" between India and China. India regarded the 1951 17-Point Agreement and the 1954 Panchshila Agreement, as well as Chou En-lai's assurances to Nehru in 1956-1957, as confirmation that China would not eliminate Tibet's traditional autonomy. This, of course, aroused the Chinese to challenge India's denial of China's full sovereignty (past and present) over Tibet and to make comparisons between the Indians and their former masters, the British imperialists.

NPC delegates wondered aloud if Indian sympathy for the Tibetans did not imply that India had been behind the revolt: "If their rebellion has no connections with Indian expansionists, why are certain Indian political figures so sympathetic with the traitorous crimes of the Tibetan reactionary clique?"[46] The delegates to the NPC expressed the hope that, in keeping with the policy on friendly relations, the Indian Government would adhere to Nehru's promise that no political activities harmful to China would be permitted in India, "nor will open-minded Indian people tolerate for long the criminal anti-Chinese activities carried out by the Tibetan traitors in India in collusion with the Indian expan-

---

ber of foreign newsmen who were demanding access to, or some statement from, the Dalai Lama. The official from the Ministry of External Affairs was sent because he was the former Indian Consul-General in Lhasa and was therefore known to the Dalai Lama and his officials. "Statement by Mr. Nehru in the Indian Parliament," 27 April 1959, in *Question of Tibet and the Rule of Law*, 171.

45. "Deputies to the Second National People's Congress Condemn the Imperialists and Indian Expansionists Who Openly Support the Rebellion in Tibet," in *Concerning the Question of Tibet* (Peking: Foreign Languages Press, 1960), 88. The Chinese may have imagined that "peaceful coexistence" meant that India should not only have not distributed the Dalai Lama's statement, but perhaps should have prevented him making any statements "unfriendly to China" at all.

46. Ibid., 85.

sionists."[47] An article in *Peking Review* warned that the people of China were "enraged by the provocations of the Indian expansionists," and would tolerate no "outside interference against the unity of their motherland."[48] Furthermore, the article said that India should return the Dalai Lama to China, unless India chose to conspire in his abduction.[49]

Nehru's reply to Chinese accusations, made in a report to the Indian Parliament on 27 April, was remarkably restrained:

> When the news of these unhappy developments [the revolt in Lhasa and the flight of the Dalai Lama] came to India, there was immediately a strong and widespread reaction. The government did not bring about this reaction. Nor was this reaction essentially political. It was largely one of sympathy based on sentiment and humanitarian reasons, also on a certain feeling of kinship with the Tibetan people derived from long-established religious and cultural contacts. . . . We have no desire whatever to interfere in Tibet; we have every desire to maintain the friendship between India and China; but at the same time we have every sympathy for the people of Tibet, and we are greatly distressed at their hapless plight.[50]

Nehru criticized the Panchen Lama's "provocative references to India" as not doing justice to "India or China or Tibet or even to himself," and invited the Panchen to come to India to meet the Dalai Lama and ascertain for himself whether the Dalai Lama was being held under duress.[51] The Panchen declined the invitation offered by Nehru to meet the Dalai Lama in India:

> Prime Minister Nehru said in his speech that he would welcome my going to India to see the Dalai Lama or any person I wanted to meet. . . . But it is reported that this invitation has been extended to me with the view of having me verify that the Dalai Lama was not abducted to India. Since Prime Minister Nehru has also said that the Dalai Lama admitted the authenticity of his three letters to General Tan Kuan-san, I think this fact alone gives convincing proof that the Dalai Lama was abducted. In these

---

47. Ibid., 95.

48. "Warning to all Expansionists: Chinese People Will Not Tolerate Foreign Intervention in Tibet," *Peking Review*, 29 April 1959, 8.

49. "On Prime Minister Nehru's Statements," *Peking Review*, 29 April 1959, 16.

50. Nehru's Statement in Lok Sabha on developments in Tibet, 27 April 1959, in *Prime Minister on Sino-Indian Relations, vol. I: In Parliament* (New Delhi: Ministry of External Affairs Government of India), 39. Nehru's report was published in the Chinese press and the Chinese populace was directed to study it in discussion groups. "Nationwide Discussion of Nehru's Statement on Tibet Begins," *Peking Review*, 5 May 1959, 5.

51. "Panchen Lama Can Visit India—Nehru's Offer to Peking," (Mussoorie) *Hindu*, Madras, 24 April 1959, in *Tibet Fights for Freedom* (New Delhi: Orient Longmans, 1960), 143.

circumstances, I see no point of my visiting India. If Prime Minister Nehru meant that he hoped I would go to India to enter into talks on the so-called Tibet question, then I must solemnly declare that the Tibet question can be solved only in Tibet; it can be solved only in China, and definitely not in any foreign country.[52]

China responded to Nehru's statement, and to Indian criticism in general, with an article by the editorial staff of the *People's Daily* on 6 May. The editorial considered India's "humanitarian sympathy" as misplaced, since those with whom they sympathized were responsible for a "reactionary, dark, cruel and barbarous serf-system." The Indian opinion that Tibet had been given no autonomy was challenged on the grounds that the Tibetan "former local government" had been allowed to continue to exist. In addition, democratic reforms had not been instituted even though they were urgently demanded by the Tibetan masses: "If the Central People's Government had not given the former local government of Tibet any right of autonomy . . . then those reactionaries, whose treason had been established, would have been arrested and punished long ago and the democratic reforms in Tibet would not have been put off up to the present."[53]

The editorial went on to lecture Nehru on the subject of the resolution of nationality problems achieved by socialism and the inevitably interventionist policy of a bourgeois state such as India:

Here in the relations between nationalities, the fundamental keypoint is still the method of class analysis. . . . Only the revolutionary proletariat can find a thorough and correct solution to historical national problems. Disputes and barriers between nationalities are in the main created by the exploiting classes and can never be eliminated by them. . . . The Indian big bourgeoisie maintains manifold links with imperialism and is, to a certain extent, dependent on foreign capital. Moreover, by its class nature, the big bourgeoisie has a certain urge for outward expansion. This is why, while it [India] opposes the imperialist policy of intervention, it more or less reflects consciously or unconsciously, certain influences of the imperialist policy of intervention.[54]

---

52. Panchen Erdeni, "The Tibet Question Can Be Settled Only in China," *Peking Review*, 5 May 1959, 12. The Chinese were unlikely to allow the Panchen to go to India; the Panchen was apparently loyal to the "motherland," but, if the Dalai Lama had concealed his true sentiments from them, then so could the Panchen. The Chinese were intent upon maintaining for as long as possible the fiction that the Dalai Lama was acting under duress. They also wished to avoid any internationalization of the Tibet issue, especially mediation by India.

53. "The Revolution in Tibet and Nehru's Philosophy," 6 May 1959, quoting Nehru's speech of 27 April, *Peking Review*, 12 May 1959, 8.

54. Ibid., 10.

The editorial denied that there were ever any "assurances" given to India that China would not exercise full sovereignty in Tibet. Indian ideas about Tibetan autonomy were characterized as "suzerainty," not sovereignty, and were said to be similar to, if not inspired by, British imperialism in Tibet in the past, as well as India's contemporary relationships with Sikkim and Bhutan. What the Indians imagined as autonomy was definitely not what the Chinese meant by "national regional autonomy." Chinese rule over Tibet was said to be preferable to Tibetan independence since, "Any status of semi-independence for Tibet would be detrimental to the Tibetan people, to the Chinese people, to the Indian people, to Sino-Indian friendship and to Asian peace."[55] Indian proposals for a tripartite conference on Tibet were described as suspiciously akin to the abortive British attempt to detach Tibet from China at Simla in 1914. The proposal to raise the Tibet issue at the United Nations was rejected as an interference in the exercise of China's sovereignty over Tibet: "No interference by any foreign country or by the United Nations under whatever pretext or in whatever form will be tolerated. ... Any question concerning Tibet can only be settled by China and in China, and not in any foreign country."[56]

On 20 June the Dalai Lama issued another press statement in which he repudiated the 17-Point Agreement, describing it as having been forced upon Tibet by invasion, threats and deceit:

The very structure, terms and conditions of the so-called Agreement of 1951 conclusively show that it was an agreement between two independent and sovereign States. It follows, therefore, that when the Chinese armies violated the territorial integrity of Tibet they committed a flagrant act of aggression. The Agreement which followed the invasion of Tibet was also thrust upon its people and government by the threat of arms. It was never accepted by them of their own free will. The consent of the government was secured under duress and at the point of the bayonet. My representatives were compelled to sign the Agreement under threat of further military operations against Tibet by the invading armies of China leading to utter ravage and ruin of the country. Even the Tibetan seal which was affixed to the Agreement was not the seal of my representatives but a seal copied and fabricated by the Chinese authorities in Peking, and kept in their possession ever since.[57]

55. Ibid., 14.

56. Ibid.

57. "Indictment of China: Dalai Lama," (Mussoorie), in *Tibet Fights for Freedom*, 100. In testimony to the International Commission of Jurists Legal Inquiry Committee on Tibet, Dzasak Khemey Sonam Wangdu, one of the signers of the 17-Point Agreement, testified: "Although the official seal of the Commissioner of Eastern Tibet [Ngapo] and the seals of

With the publication of the Dalai Lama's 20 July statement, the propaganda battle temporarily came to an end. Perhaps the Chinese did not want to open the issue of the legitimacy of the 17-Point Agreement. In the meantime, the real battle was taking place within Tibet, where the Chinese were "honoring" the Tibetans' ostensible "demands" for the quelling of the revolt and the simultaneous "granting" of democratic reforms.

"Democratic Reforms"

Since the "government of the serf-owners" in Tibet was dissolved, there was now no longer any need to delay the "democratic reforms" that the Tibetan "serfs" had supposedly been demanding. Tibetans were said to have complained: "We are not completely liberated even after the arrival of the People's Liberation Army in Tibet, and we shall never be emancipated completely without carrying out the democratic reforms."[58] The "broad masses" were said to have been clamoring for the Chinese to bestow reforms upon them since the early days of the "liberation," but reforms had long been delayed due to the Party's policy on seeking the voluntary acceptance of reforms by all classes, even the exploiters:

> In the days immediately following the peaceful liberation of Tibet and the entry of the People's Liberation Army, the working people of Tibet, unknown to the serf-owners, approached the People's Liberation Army and comrades working in the local Party organizations and denounced the evils of the serf system and expressed their desperate need of change. They submitted appeals wrapped in hata (khata) demanding reforms and inquired about the policy and date of such reforms. But due to obstruction by the former local government of Tibet and the reactionary clique of the upper social strata, this justified urgent demand of the working people to put an end to the miserable lot of the serfs could not be realized. It was, therefore, only natural that when the reactionary clique of the upper social strata in Tibet staged open armed rebellion in the vain hope of perpetuating the serf system, the Tibetan people were eager to thoroughly suppress the rebellion

the delegation were with us, the Chief Delegate Minister Ngabo could not risk using the seal, as it was a forced agreement, and so concealed the fact that they had seals with them. The Chinese however, made us use the seals they had made specially for the purpose and they were later returned to them (Chinese)." *Tibet and the Chinese People's Republic*, 163. In a 1991 article Ngawang Jigme Ngapo revealed that the seals used to sign the 17-Point Agreement were the personal seals of the Tibetan representatives and that "there was no seal of the local government of Tibet on the agreement." "Ngapo Ngawang Jigme on Tibetan Issues," *Beijing Review*, 25 March 1991, 20.

58. "Tibetan Peasants Demand End of Serfdom," *NCNA* (Lhasa), 7 May 1959, in *Current Background*, no. 571.

and immediately enforce democratic reforms. At mass meetings for quelling the rebellion held in various places, the people, while accusing the rebel clique of its crimes, advanced one demand after the other for democratic reforms and the abolition of the serf system.[59]

From the Chinese point of view, the rebellion hastened Tibet's "rebirth" via "democratic reforms." The format of reforms was announced by Chang Kuo-hua, Ngapo Ngawang Jigme and the Panchen Lama at a meeting of the PCTAR in July. Chang characterized the rebellion as a bad thing that had changed into a good thing since it had allowed the Tibetans to "speed up the period of conducting the democratic reforms so as to march forward on the road of socialism." He announced that the reforms would be carried out in two stages simultaneously: "The first stage will consist of mobilizing the masses, through suppression of the rebellion and the campaign to oppose the rebellion, and the conducting of the `Three Anti's and Two Reductions' movements. The second stage will be the redistribution of land."

The repressive function of reforms is indicated by the fact that repression and "reform" could be carried out simultaneously; in fact, the first priority of "democratic reforms" was the suppression of rebellion. The "three anti's" were anti-rebellion, anti-*ulag*, and anti-slavery (house servants had been characterized as slaves); the "two reductions" were in interest on loans and in rents paid to landlords. Land reform, or redistribution of land, was to be carried out based upon a policy of confiscating land and property of families any member of which had supported the revolt (even by innocently selling supplies or offering lodging to the rebels).[60] Land and material possessions were confiscated from the former Tibetan Government, former government officials, most of the aristocracy, and monasteries. A policy of "redemption" was adopted for those landholders against whom there was no evidence that they had supported the revolt.[61] Those landholders who had neither participated in the revolt nor were accused of having sympathized with the rebels were to have 80 percent of their crop confiscated and redistributed. They would later be "bought out" by the state, whereby a small percentage of

---

59. "Tibetans Support PLA in Mopping Up Remnant Rebels," *NCNA* (Lhasa), 24 April 1959, in *Current Background*, no. 567, 15.

60. One informant claims that the majority of the population of Lhoka, where the Chushi Gangdruk had been located, were classified as "reactionaries," had their property confiscated and were arrested because of suspicions that most had aided or supported the resistance. Drakton, personal interview, Dharamsala, December 1989.

61. "Chang Kuo-hua's Speech at the 2nd Plenary Session of Preparatory Committee for Tibet Autonomous Region," *NCNA* (Lhasa), 2 July 1959, in *Current Background*, no. 571.

their property value was paid to accounts in the "People's Bank" (to which they had no access).

Confiscated land was redistributed to the former "serfs" or tenants. Tibetans were gathered for meetings at which land deeds and loan papers were burned. Former tenants were given title to lands, but only temporarily; that same land would soon be confiscated by the state as communal property. Confiscated personal property was also redistributed. Valuable items became the property of the state; Tibetans report that the Chinese kept the best of everything.[62] In pastoral areas, the property of rebels was confiscated, but other stockholders were not bought out, nor were class divisions made nor nomads subjected to class struggle until 1962.

All Tibetans were required to exchange their Tibetan money for Chinese *yuan* at a rate only 50 percent of that before the revolt. Chinese silver dollars, *dayan*, were exchanged one for one for paper *yuan*. Many Tibetans kept their Tibetan money because they hoped that the Dalai Lama would return and Tibet would recover its independence; many also kept the silver *dayan* because they trusted the worth of silver more than that of Chinese paper money. After a short (7 to 10 day) exchange period, both Tibetan money and the silver *dayan* were declared worthless.[63] The houses of Tibetans who had fled or been arrested were sealed and their contents were carried off. Eventually, all of the citizens of Lhasa, and, presumably, of other places as well, were required to bring their valuables, including all religious objects, to a collection point where they were confiscated. Many Lhasans preferred to throw their possessions, especially religious objects, into the Kyichu river rather than give them up to the Chinese.[64]

The first stage of agricultural collectivization was initiated by the formation of Mutual Aid Teams (MAT) in the summer of 1959. Tibetans were organized into MATs and required to work on irrigation, water conservation, land reclamation and afforestation projects.[65] "Mutual aid" was intended to collectivize labor; landholdings and agricultural production theoretically remained individual with the harvest going to individual landholders. For the Chinese, however, the primary purpose of MATs was to gain control over Tibetan agricultural production and distribution.

---

62. Rinchen Paljor, personal communication, Lhasa, October 1982; Avedon, *In Exile from the Land of Snows*, 226.

63. Rinchen Paljor, Jampa Gyaltsen, personal interviews, Dharamsala, 1989.

64. Rinchen Paljor, personal communication, Lhasa, October 1982.

65. Between 1959 and 1966 the total acreage under irrigation reportedly increased by 30 percent. Dawa Norbu, "Changes in Tibetan Economy, 1959-76," in *China Report* 24:3 (1988), 229.

Tibetans report that the majority of the harvest was confiscated under the name of a variety of "voluntary" taxes, or "bought" without actual compensation. Tibetans received only a ration, much as was the case in higher stage collectives in the Chinese interior. Despite claimed increases in production, Tibetans received less since the majority of agricultural produce was confiscated by the Chinese.[66]

"Mutual aid" in Tibet achieved governmental control over labor and production virtually equivalent to collectivization. The facade of voluntarism was preserved in the formation of MATs, in which membership was theoretically voluntary. However, MATs were given the best land to work as well as all agricultural implements and animals; those refusing or not allowed to join MATs were allotted only the worst land. Membership in MATs was therefore virtually essential for survival. Tibetans tagged with a reactionary label—either as sympathizers with the revolt or for having formerly employed labor, making them "exploiters"—were not allowed to join MATs.

Private trade, handicrafts and industry were also restricted. The lack of freedom of movement restricted private commerce, while the Chinese monopoly on transportation eliminated that formerly lucrative field of employment. Trade, industrial and commercial functions were taken over by state enterprises.[67] Private traders had their capital confiscated and "deposited" in the "People's Bank."

Tibetans were subjected to and required to repeat propaganda about how everything now belonged to "the people," who were to exercise the "people's democratic dictatorship." The Chinese explained the confiscation of Tibetans' wealth and produce with the rationalization that the Han in Tibet were also "the people"; the Tibetans must support Han "working personnel" who had sacrificed so much for the liberation of Tibet. Tibetans were also told that they must help alleviate famine (caused by the Great Leap) in interior China.

The Tibetan religious establishment was also subjected to "democratic reforms." The Chinese were suspicious of the loyalty of all lamas and monks and intended to sort out the "loyal and patriotic" from the disloyal and rebellious by the same means as within Tibetan lay society. Monks were confined in monasteries until their participation in or sympathies toward the revolt could be determined. Lamas and monks who had sympathized with the revolt were accused, "struggled," and beaten by other monks.[68] High lamas, especially *tulkus* (reincarnate lamas), and

---

66. Dawa Norbu, *Red Star Over Tibet*, 203.

67. "The Network of a Socialist Commerce in the Entire Region of Tibet Has Been Basically Formed," *NCNA*, 18 August 1965, in *Tibet 1950-67*, 580.

68. Monks were subjected to the usual Chinese Communist indoctrination during their confinement, an interesting element of which was instruction, conducted by Chinese

monastic officials were arrested and deported to labor camps. Monastic estates were confiscated, the payment of taxes to monasteries was prohibited and any monks remaining in the monasteries were required to be supported by their own labor.

Many Lhasa monks were employed in forced labor at the Nachen Trang hydroelectric project a few miles east of Lhasa. Some of the monks who labored at Nachen Trang report that they were taken to Lhasa to participate in a Chinese film intended to demonstrate that monks had fought in the revolt.[69] This was apparently intended as further justification for the repression of Tibetan religious institutions. Many Tibetan monasteries had participated in the revolt by supplying the rebels with arms or food stored in monasteries. If any of a monastery's monks had fled, this was taken as evidence of the whole monastery's sympathy with the revolt. Only those few monasteries that had no role in the revolt whatsoever were spared "democratic reforms;" however, most of those soon fell victim as their anti-Chinese sentiments were revealed. Chinese policy was to spare "patriotic" monks and monasteries, but almost all monasteries opposed the Chinese and were depopulated within the next two years (1959-1960).

The clerical population of the TAR, estimated in a Chinese census of 1958 at 114,100 (9.5 percent of the total population of the TAR), had dropped to 18,104 (1.44 percent of the population) in 1960. The number of "functioning monasteries and temples" in the TAR dropped from 2,711 in 1958 to 370 in 1960.[70] Beginning in 1959 and proceeding through the period of the Cultural Revolution, depopulated monasteries were systematically looted of their treasures, which were trucked to China.[71] Tibetans

women, in songs of praise of Mao and his life, as if to transfer Tibetan religious sentiments onto a new deity. "Statements made by Tibetan refugees," in *Tibet and the Chinese People's Republic*, 262.

69. *Tibet Under Chinese Communist Rule*, 36.

70. Jing Jun, "Socioeconomic Changes and Riots in Lhasa," (unpublished paper), 1990, citing Zhang Yianlu, *Population Change in Tibet* (Beijing: Tibetan Studies Publishing House of China, 1989), 28. Jing Jun was a member of a Chinese Academy of Science census team sent to Tibet in the late 1980s.

71. *Tibet Under Chinese Communist Rule*, 58, 62, 80, 87, 94, 105; Dawa Norbu, *Red Star Over Tibet* (New York: Envoy Press, 1987), 199. This process had already been going on in Amdo and Kham since 1956. "Statements made by Tibetan refugees," in *Tibet and the Chinese People's Republic*, 240, 242. Ama Adi reports seeing convoy after convoy of trucks loaded with Tibetan Buddhist statues headed to China near Dartsendo (Kangding). This reportedly went on for years, as more and more monasteries were revealed to harbor anti-Chinese sentiments and were then depopulated and looted. Adi reports that, in the beginning, the trucks contained small, precious statues of gold and silver; later, the larger and less valuable statues were cut up and transported to China to be melted for the metal. "Ama Adhe's Story," in David Patt, *A Strange Liberation: Tibetan Lives in Chinese Hands* (Ithaca: Snow Lion,

were told that the confiscation of the wealth of monasteries was for "all the people," that is, for all the Chinese people. At the same time, the Chinese were promising that the religious establishment would be preserved; the state, under its policy of freedom of religion, would "protect patriotic and law-abiding lamaseries and cultural relics in the monasteries."[72]

An inevitable aspect of democratic reforms was the initiation of class divisions and class struggle. As had been the case in eastern Tibet, Tibetans of central Tibet were divided into three primary classes: *Jording* (large property holders), *Jorchung* (small property holders), and *Jormei* (no property). In Lhasa, two upper class categories were added: aristocracy and representatives of the aristocracy. The primary divisions in Tibetan society between the aristocracy and the lower classes were obvious, but differentiations among the lower class were not so apparent. In the absence of other indicators, such as obvious wealth, divisions were made according to percentages of hired labor.[73] These distinctions were important because only the lowest class was considered free of all implications of exploitation and thus was not subject to criticism, struggle or arrest unless charged as politically "reactionary." The process of class division and class struggle continued by further class divisions within the middle class and by constant campaigns with various individuals, institutions or ideologies as targets. Class conflict, considered essential to socialist transformation, was thus extended to all Tibetans.

1992), 72, 99. Tibetans report that the process of looting the wealth of the Tibetan monasteries and people went on until the end of the Cultural Revolution in 1976. Tsering Wangchuk, personal interview, Dharamsala, February 1990. In 1983 a team of Tibetans led by Rinbur Tulku was allowed to try to recover Tibetan artworks still in China. More than 30 tons of statues and ritual objects were found and returned to Tibet. 13,537 statues of brass and copper were recovered, but almost all statues made of gold or silver had disappeared. Although many were recovered, many more statues of brass and copper had been melted; one foundry near Peking, only one of many melting Tibetan statues, had melted 600 tons of Tibetan statues by the time the process was stopped in 1973. Rinbur Tulku, *The Search for Jowo Mikyoe Dorje* (Dharamsala: Office of Information and International Relations, Central Tibetan Secretariat, 1988). Perhaps not coincidentally, the PRC paid off its considerable debt to the Soviet Union in 1962, even though China was suffering the disastrous economic consequences of the Great Leap. At least one Tibetan reports the rumor that the Russians accepted Tibetan artworks as payment. *Tibet Under Chinese Communist Rule*, 87.

72. "Report by Ngapo Ngawang Jigme at the 2nd Plenary Session of Preparatory Committee for Tibet Autonomous Region," *NCNA* (Lhasa), 7 July 1959, in *Current Background*, no. 571.

73. At Sakya, according to Dawa Norbu, "If 40-50 per cent of the total annual labour was hired, a family was classified as rich farmer, or upper middle class; with 30-40 per cent hired labour, it was lower middle class; and with 30 per cent and below, it was poor farmer, or proletariat." Dawa Norbu, *Red Star Over Tibet*, 188.

Tibetans were also divided into "study groups," the "small groups (*hsiao tsu*) of Chinese Communist practice within which socialist transformation was intended to take place by means of study and mutual criticism. These artificial social groups were intended to transcend traditional primary groups, such as family or religious associations, since traditional groups were considered too conservative and mutually supportive to allow socialist transformation to take place. The requirement within the small groups to inform upon and to criticize others led to conformity, outwardly at least, to the required political line. Lack of participation was considered equivalent to opposition; even refuge in silence was therefore not available. The study group broke the bonds of trust within traditional groups such as family and peer groups because pressures to reveal any deviation were so intense that even trusted individuals were forced to inform on others; the usual security within traditional groups was thus destroyed.[74]

Study groups might include several members of a family, but the family was not the basis for division. Study groups were often identical with work units, mutual aid teams or neighborhood committees, or sections thereof. Study groups were usually composed of 12-15 people, but larger gatherings were also held for instructions from Chinese or Tibetan cadres or for criticism and struggle sessions of notable people. Within study groups, which met after work each day, often until late hours, policies presented via cadres' speeches or newspaper articles were studied and discussed. Personal attitudes were examined by requiring each individual to review his or her life history, especially examining one's background for evidence of having exploited others; these personal histories were then subjected to self-criticism and mutual criticism for any deviance from the approved Party line. Groups were judged upon their ability to create conflict and struggle, upon which transformation was considered to be dependent, a process initiated by activists but in which everyone was required to participate:

> During this study activity group members are expected to engage in regular mutual criticism and self-criticism. Each person is supposed to analyze his thoughts and actions, comparing them critically with the standards set in assigned study materials. He is expected to criticize his own shortcomings, to accept the criticism of the rest of the group, and in turn to point out the failings of others. In this manner group social pressure is mobilized to

---

74. "Small groups" had their origins in the Soviet practice of study and criticism within cadres' cells (not applied by the Soviets to society in general) and the Ch'ing pao-chia system of social control by mutual responsibility. Martin King Whyte, *Small Groups and Political Rituals in China* (Berkeley: University of California Press, 1974), 19

encourage individuals to change their attitudes and conduct in order to conform more closely to the demands of higher authorities.[75]

Individuals within groups were encouraged, by means of a system of rewards and punishments, to support official policies and to oppose others who were reluctant to do so.

> Within these groups individuals who can be expected to support official demands are placed in leadership positions and encouraged to find other group members who will support them. Through political study and mutual criticism, group leaders and their supporters organize pressure on other group members to join them in enthusiastically supporting official policies. At least in theory, then, social groupings are provided for individuals, groupings with built-in obligations to develop support for organizational and national goals.[76]

Study groups were employed to propagate the party line from the center and to initiate the myriad political campaigns characteristic of Chinese Communist society. Tibetans were subjected to all Chinese political campaigns in addition to campaigns particularly targeted to Tibet, such as attacks on former local or national leaders or the "three pillars of Tibetan feudalism" (Tibetan Government, the monastic system and the aristocracy). Tibetans were often required to express agreement with positions intended to test their loyalty, such as that Tibet had always been part of China or that the Dalai Lama had personally engaged in particularly exploitative or licentious activities; their reluctance to agree with these allegations would brand them as insufficiently loyal to the new order.

A noteworthy campaign of the early 1960s was known as "speaking bitterness" against the old society, intended in the Chinese interior to remind the Chinese people that their sufferings in the famine of 1959-62 could not compare to what they had suffered before liberation. This campaign was also considered particularly applicable to national minorities since they had only recently been liberated from feudal backwardness and exploitation, for which, it was thought, they should be profoundly grateful. The Chinese, who were convinced that Tibetans had been horribly oppressed in the past, intended the campaign in Tibet to remind Tibetans of what they had suffered under their former class oppressors; for most Tibetans, however, what they were currently suffering was much worse than anything in the past.[77]

---

75. Ibid., 3.
76. Ibid., 10.
77. As Dawa Norbu commented: "Anybody who did not shed tears and cry aloud

A similar tactic to elicit criticism, stimulate class conflict and cultivate collaborators was the posting of boxes into which Tibetans could drop anonymous criticisms of others. This campaign often backfired; the notes were anonymous, therefore Tibetans often took the opportunity to criticize the Chinese.[78] Another campaign applied with particular intensity in Tibet was "Destroy the Four Pests," which was intended to eliminate parasites: rats, mice, flies and sparrows. This campaign had the added advantage of requiring Tibetans to violate their religious beliefs by killing "pests." Old people were set to work killing mice and flies, while the young killed sparrows, dogs (including pets) and small wild animals.[79]

Tibetans, like the Chinese, were subjected to a constant barrage of propaganda. All media were put to the task of propagandizing socialism and the Party's policies, in keeping with Mao's dictum that all art and literature must serve the cause of socialism. Newspapers, magazines and books were extensively employed in group study; all, of course, supported the Party line. Posters were also used to elicit the participation of the masses and to propagate slogans.[80] Propaganda was broadcast by local radio connected to loudspeakers on streets and in all places of work, both urban and rural. From the loudspeakers blared a constant stream of exhortations to increase production, maintain the proper ideological attitudes, or support particular policies or campaigns. "Cultural" programs were also broadcast, all with a socialist content.[81] Most programing

[about] his injuries and sorrows was suspect, for it was presumed that the people (excluding the rulers) had a life of continual oppression and suffering; thus any commoner who did not shed crocodile tears while pouring out past sorrows was not of the people." Dawa Norbu, *Red Star Over Tibet*, 186.

78. During the UN debates on Tibet in 1961, the Nationalist Chinese delegate described one such note that read: "During the old government there was a word called hell, and no one knew what it really meant. But now we know what hell is, and we know that the old government was heaven." This message was disclosed and propagated among Tibetan indoctrination groups by the Chinese themselves in their attempt to discover who had written the note. General Assembly Sixteenth Session, 19 December 1961, in *Tibet in the United Nations: 1950-1961* (New Delhi: Bureau of His Holiness the Dalai Lama), 284.

79. Tsering Dolkar, personal communication, Lhasa, October 1982.

80. In Tibet, the poster format took the unique form of white stones arranged on hillsides to spell out various slogans. The use of "big character posters" had obvious dangers, since constant control was not possible; dissidents could, and did, use posters to criticize state policies. Personal observations and personal communications, Lhasa, July-November 1982.

81. The system of "line broadcasts" (programming from Peking broadcast via local stations) and loudspeakers was begun as soon as the Communists took over, but did not reach a level of near total saturation until the early 1960s. In 1962, there were a total of 6,700,000 loudspeakers in Chinese cities and towns. Frederick T.C. Yu, *Mass Persuasion in Communist China* (New York: Praeger, 1964), 127. The blaring noise of these loudspeakers was, until recent times, one of the most ubiquitous and irritating intrusions encountered in the PRC.

emanated from Peking, insuring ideological conformity throughout the PRC. Film and dramatic media were put to the same task; traditional Tibetan opera was adapted to Chinese political purposes.

Policies were constantly elaborated or refined and new campaigns initiated, facilitating a continual process of identifying "progressives" and "reactionaries," those who supported official policies and those who were resistant or who harbored reactionary or "green" minds.[82] In each new campaign, quotas were established of a certain percentage of the population who were to be classified as reactionaries and subjected to criticism or struggle.[83] Tibetans were repeatedly required to give oral and written reports on their life histories, indicating their connections to individuals or institutions identified as opponents of the Chinese regime. Each individual's report was criticized by others, with rewards for accusations and punishment for refusing to accuse others.

Those identified as reactionaries, exploiters or lackluster supporters of the Chinese regime were subjected to "struggle." Struggle could take place within the study group, or larger meetings could be summoned for more serious or symbolic cases. Tibetans accused of sympathizing with the revolt or opposing the Chinese were denounced by the Chinese and their Tibetan activists for "treason against the motherland." Struggle of former landlords (those not cooperating with the United Front) was often accompanied by a symbolic burning of land deeds or records of debts and labor obligations. The Tibetan audience was required to add their accusations, with the incentive that lack of display of a "revolutionary consciousness" would reveal their own reactionary minds and possibly make them subject to the same process. The Party applied a policy of lenience for the conformist or the repentant and strict punishment for the non-conformist or non-repentant. As one Tibetan relates, the struggle process separated the "reactionary supporters of feudalism" from the "progressive supporters of socialism": "Either you stand for socialism or for feudalism. There is no other way. If you don't participate in *thamzing* (struggle) then you're for feudalism; if you're for socialism then you must pursue criticism until a person confesses. If you're not for socialism then you yourself must have *thamzing*."[84]

---

82. Both the characterization of old Tibetan society as "barbaric" and of Tibetans as "green brains" or "uncooked brains" were traditional pre-Communist Chinese terms for unacculturated barbarians.

83. Harry Wu, *Bitter Winds: A Memoir of My Years in China's Gulag* (New York: John Wiley and Sons, 1994), 31. Quotas often derived from Mao's estimates of what percentage of the population did not support the Party at any time. Tibetans report that in campaigns in Tibet this quota was usually 3 to 5 percent; campaigns took place approximately twice each year. Amdo Some, Amdo Rigchok, personal interviews, Dharamsala, February 1990.

84. Abu Chonga, personal interview.

Tibetans were instructed that by accusing their former exploiters they were to learn to be their own masters. By this process the Tibetans learned what the Chinese meant by "mobilizing the masses" to exercise the "people's democratic dictatorship." Tibetans were cowed by the endless campaigns and pressures for conformity; mutual distrust and incrimination became the predominant atmosphere and conformity in all outward manifestations, if not in thought, became the norm. Some Tibetans, especially the young and the opportunistic of all ages, became enthusiastic converts to the Chinese cause. After 1959 political activism in support of the Chinese policies was the most obvious and practically the only route to advancement for Tibetans. Most Tibetans, however, became adept at outward conformity to required political rituals while sublimating and concealing their actual beliefs. Tibetan cadres became particularly adept at conformity to required jargon and political formulae while hiding their true feelings. This produced a situation where, not only could Tibetans not trust each other, but the Chinese could not trust the loyalty of any Tibetans, even their most ardent collaborators.[85]

Prisons and Labor Camps

After the suppression of the revolt, Tibetan Government and monastic leaders were initially detained at the Chinese Military Headquarters at Silingbuk. The Chinese placed all upper class officials and high lamas in the "historical counterrevolutionary" category.[86] Most were deported to labor on railroad construction in Kansu.[87] Other Tibetans were impris-

---

85. Lack of a true perspective on public opinion seems to be an aspect of all totalitarian systems, which are able to enforce conformity in practice but cannot be certain to what extent conformity exists in actual belief. The Chinese Communists had experienced this phenomenon once before, during the Hundred Flowers campaign, when a small liberalization had led to a surprising outpouring of anti-Party sentiments.

86. "Historical counterrevolutionary" status referred to those of the former ruling class, who were dispossessed of power and privilege by the socialist revolution and who were therefore its natural opponents. Officials of the former Tibetan Government were historical counterrevolutionaries—regardless of whether or not they had supported the revolt—even though the policy of the Chinese Government until 1959 had been to cooperate with those same officials. However, collaborators were characterized as "upper class progressives."

87. This was apparently the Lanqing Railway Project (Lanchou to Sining) or the Lanchou to Sinkiang route, or both. Out of 600 deported, only 27 returned. *Tibet: The Facts*, 30. Some former Tibetan Government officials were held at Drapchi. Tsipon Shuguba was at Drapchi and Sangyip for the entire nineteen years of his imprisonment. Out of eighty former officials in his group at Drapchi, sixty died in the first three years, primarily due to overwork and starvation. Sumner Carnahan and Lama Kunga Rinpoche, eds., *In the Presence of My Enemies: Memoirs of Tibetan Nobleman Tsipon Shuguba* (Santa Fe: Clear Light Publishers, 1995), 170.

oned in Lhasa at Drapchi,[88] the former Tibetan Army barracks, or sent to the prison complex at Po Tramo in Kongpo,[89] or the labor camps at Tsalo Karpo in the Chang Thang.[90] Others, especially women of the upper classes and monks, were subjected to forced labor at the hydroelectric project at Nachen Trang.[91] Tibetans at Nachen Trang were told: "From now on you are not mere prisoners, but workers for the *Tang* [the Communist Party]. So you will have to bathe in the water of liberty and offer your heart to the Tang!" After this, a ceremony called "Offering Your Heart to the Tang" was held. *Thamzing* was held for those resisting this indoctrination.[92]

Tibetans of the Chamdo district of the TAR were held at Markham Gartok, Chamdo Monastery, Tsa Pomda and Po Tramo.[93] Tibetans of Kham east of the Yangtze were sent to a lead mine east of Dartsendo and

---

88. Drapchi reportedly held 800 prisoners in 1959. Shuguba, 169. The Lhasa prison complex was later expanded to include an interrogation prison (Gurtsa) and a prison for former Tibetan leaders (Sangyip), plus two labor camps (Yititu, First Labor Reform Camp and Wutitu, Fifth Labor Reform Camp); Drapchi was expanded to six units each holding 200-300 prisoners. All are in the plains in the northern part of the Lhasa valley. The total number of prisoners in all Lhasa prisons by the mid-1970s was estimated at 7,000. Abu Gongkar, Abu Chonga, Nyima Assam, personal interviews.

89. Po Tramo (also known as Nyingtri) was a complex of 7 camps (Dongchu, Dzongna, Talung, Chundo, Nangdep, Goshang, Damchu) in Kongpo, holding approximately 7,000 prisoners (in 13 units, each with approximately 400-500 prisoners). The dead from these camps were buried at a place called Tolang Gu, where in 1961 a flood revealed many bodies; prisoners were sent out to collect the bones, which filled thousands of sacks. Abu Gongkar, Abu Chonga, personal interviews.

90. Tsala Karpo was near Nag Tsang, to the west of Nam Tsho in the western Chang Thang. Nyima Assam estimates that there were 20,000 Tibetans at Tsala Karpo, of whom only one in a hundred survived. *Tsala Karpo*, "white earth," refers to borax in Tibetan, but the place itself was also known by this name; Tibetans were told by the Chinese that *tsala karpo* was worth more by weight than gold. Other Tibetans report that *tsala karpo* was in fact chromium ore and was being shipped to the Soviet Union. Soviet engineers were also reported to have been at Tsala Karpo (1960). *Tibet Under Chinese Communist Rule*, 46; Nyima Assam, personal interview. Recently, in 1996, it was reported that *tsala karpo* is boron, used in the manufacture of glass, steel and in the nuclear industry. "The Last Caravan," *Far Eastern Economic Review*, 18 April 1996, 67.

91. There were a reported 3,700 prisoners working at Nachen Trang in 1959.

92. *Tibet Under Chinese Communist Rule*, 35.

93. The were 5,000 prisoners at Markham Gartok. Chamdo Monastery reportedly held 3,000 prisoners, while there were some 8,000 at Tsa Pomda. Both were scenes of mass starvation; only a small percentage reportedly survived at either place (700 out of 8,000 at Tsa Pomda, according to Abu Gongkar, and 500 out of 5,000 at Chamdo, according to Nyima Assam). The dead at Chamdo were buried at the foot of the mountain behind the monastery. Abu Gongkar, Nyima Assam, Gonjo Pachim Dolma, Kalsang Wangdu, personal interviews.

to a labor camp complex in the Minyak area west of Dartsendo.[94] Tibetans of Amdo were sent to prisons in Sining or Lanchou or to labor camps in Sinkiang (Ansi) or to the complex of prison and labor camps established for both Chinese and Tibetans in Chinghai.[95]

The Chinese Communist penal system consisted of prisons and forced labor camps. Imprisonment, or Convicted Labor Reform, entailed fixed sentences and deprivation of the rights of citizenship; forced labor, or Reeducation Through Labor, did not have fixed sentences or deprivation of rights. One could be placed in a forced labor camp for an indefinite period without trial or conviction. Those arrested were held in detention centers without charges, often for several years, until a confession could be elicited, after which they were either convicted and sentenced to prison, or sent to a labor camp without sentencing.[96]

According to Hongda Harry Wu, most crimes in the PRC for which prison sentences were received were political, or "counterrevolutionary," crimes.[97] Counterrevolutionary crimes were of three types. First were the "historical counterrevolutionaries." These were former KMT officials, bourgeoisie or landlords. This category was mostly eliminated in the late 1950s (except in Tibet) and was superseded by "active counterrevolu-

94. Ama Adi reports that at the Kotok Gyapo lead mine, where both Tibetans and Chinese were engaged in forced labor, 11,219 (out of an estimated 20,000-30,000) died during the years 1960, 1961 and 1962, according to official statistics to which she gained access. The Minyak complex, the main prison complex for the Kanze Autonomous District, was composed of 21 camps, of which 5 were prisons and 16 were labor camps, each holding from 400 to more than 1,000 prisoners. Most of the camps were devoted to farming and forestry. Ama Adi, personal interview, Dharamsala, January 1990.

95. Tsayul Tulku reports that of the 3,500 monks of Labrang Tashikyil, 2,000 were arrested; 800 were sent to prisons and 1,200 to "reform through labor" camps. Those sent to prison were mainly lamas, *tulkus*, monastic administrators or monks of the upper class. Of the group of 600 sent to prisons in Sinkiang, only 200 survived, even though their imprisonment there was only for a period of three years. Of those sent to labor at a marble quarry near Labrang (no doubt quarrying marble for statues of Mao), the majority were thought to have perished. Monks were told that they were "rocks on the road to socialism" and that they must be eliminated even if they had to be killed. Tsayul Tulku, personal interview.

96. Hongda Harry Wu states that, "according to internal Communist documents, 13 percent of criminals are confined to prisons, 87 percent to labor reform disciplinary production camps." This was dependent not only upon the severity of the crime, or the nature of the counterrevolutionary activity, but upon one's class status as well. Wu estimates that some 50 million people have been confined within the Chinese prison or labor camp system in the 40 years from 1950 to 1990. Hongda Harry Wu, *Laogai—The Chinese Gulag* (Boulder: Westview Press, 1992), 8, 15.

97. Wu estimates that 90 percent of the crimes for which persons were sentenced to prison or labor reform in the 1950s were political. Ibid., 19. By making counterrevolution a crime (an innovation of the Soviet system), the CCP was (and is) able to claim that it has no "political" prisoners.

tionaries," or those who opposed any of the Communists' campaigns or programs. The first two types of offenders were usually sentenced to prison terms. The third category, "anti-socialist elements," was invented by Mao in 1957 to define those who expressed "contradictions among the people." These people were not active counterrevolutionaries (enemies of the people), but were in need of education in proletarian consciousness. For this category, the system of "reeducation through labor" was created. No trial or sentence was required; terms were determined by progress in reform. This category of prisoners often remained in forced job placement upon release from labor reform.

Those sentenced to Convicted Labor Reform received one of several sentences: execution; suspended execution; life imprisonment; or prison terms of 20, 18, 15, 12 or 10 years. Sentences were often extended for uncooperative behavior. Capital sentences were for active opposition to Communist rule, although executions were often suspended pending the possible reform of those charged. Reeducation Through Labor was of no fixed sentence and could be and often was extended indefinitely. Upon "release" from prison, prisoners were usually assigned to forced job placement. Those Tibetans eventually released (few were released until 1979) were almost invariably put into forced labor at the same or some other site.[98]

The prison and forced labor system was closely integrated within the Chinese economy; the economic importance of forced labor became such that the economy became dependent upon it; this factor determined that released prisoners be retained within the forced labor production system.[99] Official Chinese policy was to reform prisoners, while exploiting their labor, rather than to exterminate opponents. In this way it differed from the Soviet system. However, the lives of those who refused to cooperate were in greater jeopardy than those who did. Cooperative prisoners received better labor assignments, food rations and treatment from the

---

98. Tseten Namgyal, Ama Adi, Nyima Assam, Gonjo Pachim Dolma, personal interviews.

99. According to Wu, 95 percent of released prisoners during the 1950s and 1960s were retained in forced job placement. Those in the counterrevolutionary category were usually considered to be "accustomed to crime," therefore justifying their retention in forced job placement. Those who had reformed, or who were of the lower class or were common criminals were released. Those "whose homes lie in border areas" were included among those who should be detained. Wu, *Laogai*, 111. Chinese imprisoned in remote areas such as Chinghai or Sinkiang often were required to remain there after release. Ibid., 113. Another aspect of forced job placement was that families who had urban residence registrations were allowed to join released prisoners in order to remove population from cities; in remote areas in need of population, such as Chinghai, even relatives with rural registrations were allowed to join released prisoners. Ibid., 115.

guards; those who refused to reform or attempted to escape were starved, beaten or even executed as an example to others. While Chinese policy may not have been to exterminate prisoners, survival rates in Chinese prisons were probably no better than in the Soviet gulag. From the prisoners' point of view, the Soviet system might be preferable, since Soviet prisoners were not subjected to the mental pressures of Chinese thought reform.

All prisoners in Chinese prisons (even foreigners) were subjected to thought reform, which had three components: acknowledgement of crime, submission to the law, and submission to thought reform. Since the Communist Party was considered infallible, there was no use in denying guilt once one had been arrested; to do so was considered evidence that one was "resisting reform." One must therefore confess completely and reveal all of one's crimes including "thought crimes." This process began with a written analysis of one's life from age seven, and criticism and self-criticism based upon that analysis. Only after one had fully submitted to the fact of one's crimes might reform occur.

Those who refused to submit were subjected to struggle, sometimes for days or weeks on end. Struggle was conducted within the cell by one's cellmates or in larger gatherings. The most recalcitrant were sometimes subjected to continuous struggle in one cell after another. Within the cell, the atmosphere was of constant mutual recriminations as each prisoner tried to gain reform points by informing on others and inventing false criticisms of each other. Finally, the pressures to confess were such that prisoners admitted to the most fantastic and impossible crimes; this the Party considered a sign that the prisoner was now open to indoctrination in a new reality. However, even acceptance was not sufficient to avoid criticism, because the Party instituted constant rectification campaigns and thought examinations to root out reactionary attitudes. Prisoners were constantly scrutinized for evidence of violation of prison rules or resistance to reform in thought or action.[100]

Prisoners found no support within the group for resistance against the government, and an atmosphere of mutual dishonesty and suspicion was created, as was the case in society at large:

---

100. For an excellent account of the Chinese prison system, see Robert Ford, *Wind Between the Worlds* (Berkeley: Snow Lion Graphics, 1987) and Geoffrey T. Bull, *When Iron Gates Yield* (London: Hodder and Stoughton, 1955). Ford was the British radio operator for the Tibetan Government who was captured at Chamdo. Bull was a British missionary captured at Markham. Ford and Bull's experiences in Chinese prisons were similar to that of Tibetans not only because both were captured in Tibet and were accused of trying to separate Tibet from China but because they, like Tibetans, were foreigners to both Chinese political culture and Chinese communism but were subjected to pressures to conform to both. Also see Bao Ruo-wang (Jean Pasqualini), *Prisoner of Mao* (New York: Penguin Books, 1976).

Government policies encourage informing and betrayal. Even if the evidence brought against a person proves to be totally false, the accuser is nonetheless praised by public security cadres. The reason for this lies in the fact that the authorities view the ultimate truth or falsity of an accusation as secondary in importance; most important is the allegiance to the government shown by the act of accusation. The encouragement of blind accusation and "ratting" not only changes convicts' political ideology but alters their sense of conscience and moral character. This phenomenon is frequently seen in general society as well; in this sense, the LRC [labor reform camp] system is a microcosm of mainland Chinese society as a whole under Communist rule.[101]

Geoffrey Bull, a British missionary captured in Tibet and imprisoned by the Chinese as an imperialist spy, was subjected to the same pressures to conform to the communist system as Chinese prisoners. Bull describes the combination of factors of prison life as an almost unbearable physical and mental strain:

Firstly, there was the maintained suspense of the threat of execution or life imprisonment. This was made the more excruciating by tantalizing the prisoner with promises of pardon, if only he would reform himself more wholeheartedly and acknowledge his "crimes" more deeply. This state of tension was aggravated by almost incessant provocation and baiting, by attacks on his integrity and self-respect in regard to his political default, and by investigations into his daily thought, conduct and observance of the regulations. From morning to night, day after day, month after month and year after year, it was "learning," mutual haranguing, criticism and struggle meetings, in one form or another. Every physical and mental movement was maintained under vigilant scrutiny by official, warder or fellow prisoner, all of whom, for fear of their own future would not dare to relent. By the system of reciprocal spying and reporting all ideas of friendship or exchange of confidences were excluded. Living constantly in this atmosphere of conflict, distrust and lack of love from any quarter, life for many became unbearable. In this unthinkable environment, interrogation often continued unabated, together with searching interviews as to the prisoner's reaction and attitude, and with exacting demands to remember the minutest details of actions and events that happened years previously. These sufferings were in addition to the usual heartbreak of being shut within four walls, kept under strict discipline and feeding on a diet which was too deficient in vitamins to maintain full vitality. All of course was designed with one end in view, to bring the mind into absolute submission to the will and indoctrination of the Marxist way of life.[102]

---

101. Wu, *Laogai*, 32.
102. Bull, *When Iron Gates Yield*, 236.

As Robert Ford wrote, there was no mental escape from the Chinese Communists' thought reform:

> The diabolical cleverness of thought reform—or brain-cleansing, to translate literally from the Chinese—is that the victim is made to want to believe. Unless he is exceptionally intelligent and a brilliant actor he has no hope of release until he does. If he merely had to listen to propaganda, or even repeat it parrot-fashion himself, he might be able to emerge mentally unscathed. But he has to create and deliver the propaganda himself.[103]

In prisons and labor camps in Tibet (as well as among the population in general), political indoctrination went along with forced labor. Tibetans in prison were subjected to all the same campaigns and political rituals as were Tibetans on the outside, with the promise that repentance for past crimes, active learning of Communist ideology and support for the Party's policies could alleviate prison conditions or secure an early release. In contrast, nonrepentance and nonconformity would elicit harsh treatment and an indefinite extension of one's sentence. Political study sessions were held every evening for two or more hours, or all day for a month or more during winter months. During these study sessions prisoners were required to examine their former lives or to study and discuss CCP policies or articles in Chinese newspapers.

The primary themes of political reeducation for Tibetans were patriotism, socialism and internationalism. The patriotism theme included China's power and leading role in the world liberation movement, Tibet as a historical part of China, and the impossibility of Tibetan independence. The socialism theme concentrated on identification of the three feudal exploiters of the former Tibetan society: aristocracy, religion and government. Internationalism included the duty to spread socialism worldwide and the inevitability of that spread, especially to India, where Tibetans therefore had no hope of permanent refuge. Much propaganda was mounted against imperialism in general and America in particular and included the inevitability of the eventual spread of socialism even to the most capitalist countries and, thus, the futility of Tibetans' hope for assistance from America or any other source.[104] Tibetans were offered

---

103. Ford, *Wind Between the Worlds*, 307.

104. "Any other source" included any transcendental source. The Chinese attempted to discredit Tibetans' hopes for divine intervention by anti-religious propaganda and by repeated demonstration of lamas' powerlessness to summon assistance. Tibetans were instructed to instead hope for assistance from the thoughts of Chairman Mao, leading one Tibetan lama to wonder aloud what was the difference between the Tibetan Buddhist deities and those of the Communist Chinese (for which he received three years of continuous *thamzing*). Tsayul Tulku, personal interview, Dharamsala, November 1989. Many Tibetans

only two paths: the path of light, socialism and eventual release; or the path of darkness, feudalism and death.[105]

Tsayul Tulku, imprisoned in Ansi in Sinkiang, reports that prisoners were worked from early morning until night and then subjected to lectures, criticisms and struggles until late in the evening. They were fed two *ti momo* (steamed dumplings) per day unless they were sick, and then the ration was only one. Prisoners received an extra *ti momo* for informing on others. During the famine years, the *ti momo* were made of kaoling mixed with grass and sand. Later, in a "political reeducation center" in Kansu, he and other Tibetan prisoners were subjected to beatings and torture.[106] Tseten Namgyal, imprisoned at Po Tramo, says that many Tibetans were given *thamzing* or even executed for plotting to escape, for practicing religion or for uncooperative attitudes. Informers were required to report on anyone reciting prayers. He also reports a story of a Tibetan arrested for killing an animal called *gya*; the Chinese thought he had killed a Chinese (*gyami*). He was unable to explain to the Chinese, since they accused him of not truthfully confessing, and he spent 20 years in prison for a nonexistent crime.[107]

The nature of the Chinese prison system was such that only by conformity to the regime was survival possible. Resistance resulted only in death from execution, torture or overwork and starvation. Ama Adi reports that most of the active resisters to the Chinese did not survive imprisonment; in particular, most intellectuals were eliminated.[108] By 1962 Tibetan social, political and religious leaders had been co-opted, eliminated or forced into exile. By "democratic reforms" and the purge of "reactionaries" and "counterrevolutionaries" the Chinese eliminated the leadership of the Tibetan nation and any who opposed Chinese rule and imposed strict conformity on all the rest.

The revolt in Tibet occurred at the end of the Great Leap and the beginning of the three years of famine (1959-61) that the Great Leap policies produced. Between 1959 and 1961 some 10-20 million Chinese perished.[109] In Tibet starvation conditions prevailed, not because harvests

---

report that the Chinese emphasis upon anti-American propaganda gave them hope that, if America were such an enemy of China, then there was some hope of assistance from the Americans.

105. Tsayul Tulku, Ama Adi, Abu Gonkar, Abu Chonga, Nyima Assam, Lobsang Wangyal, personal interviews.

106. Tsayul Tulku, personal interview.

107. Tseten Namgyal, personal interview.

108. Ama Adi, personal interview.

109. Maurice Meisner, *Mao's China and After: A History of the People's Republic* (New York: The Free Press, 1986), 250. During this time, the Chinese PLA in Tibet subsisted partly by hunting Tibetan wildlife, some species of which were virtually eliminated.

were poor, but because virtually all agricultural and pastoral production was confiscated by the Chinese. Tibetans report that food was trucked from Tibetan areas to adjacent Chinese provinces (Szechuan and Kansu were among the worst famine areas); this was justified as Tibetans' duty to "pay back" the motherland for its assistance, including "liberation," economic improvements, health care and road building.[110] Imprisoned Tibetans suffered the worst during the famine; as "enemies of the people," they were regarded as hardly worth feeding in any case.[111] Tibetans in prisons and labor camps were subjected to demands for intensive labor while denied sufficient food for subsistence. Tibetans who survived imprisonment report massive numbers of deaths in the early 1960s, mainly from overwork and starvation.[112]

In 1984 the Tibetan Government in Exile estimated that 173,221 Tibetans had died in prisons and labor camps. The total number of Tibetans who lost their lives as a result of the Chinese invasion and occupation of Tibet was estimated as 1,207,387 (the majority between 1950-65). In addition to the deaths in prisons and labor camps, there were an estimated 156,758 by execution, 342,970 by starvation, 432,705 in battles and uprisings, 92,731 by torture, and 9,002 by suicide.[113]

Sino-Indian Border Dispute

The Sino-Indian border dispute began with the Indians' discovery that the Sinkiang-Tibet highway, completed in late 1957, passed through terri-

---

110. Tsayul Tulku, personal interview.

111. Wu, *Laogai*, 60. Some imprisoned Tibetans report that their Chinese captors told them that "reactionaries must die;" therefore, they were not provided medical care even though Chinese doctors were available. The Chinese were reportedly happy when Tibetans died since, the Chinese said, they didn't want the people of Tibet, only the land. This statement was reportedly made by a Chinese prison camp commander at Samye to the assembled prisoners: "You are reactionaries; we don't want you; we want land; you should die." Amchi (Doctor) Lobsang Wangyal, personal interview, Dharamsala, February 1990.

112. Ama Adi, Abu Gonkar, Abu Chonga, Nyima Assam, Lobsang Wangyal, personal interviews.

113. *Tibet: The Facts*, 297. The Tibetan Government in Exile's figures were obtained by interviews with Tibetan refugees in India. The Chinese response to the Tibetan Government in Exile's claim that more than a million Tibetans had died was that this was preposterous, since "Tibet" had a population of only a little more than a million at the time. The tactic of referring to the TAR as Tibet conceals the actual number of Tibetans in the PRC—3.87 million by Chinese statistics in 1982 and 2.77 million in 1953—and therefore obscures the issue of how many deaths might actually have occurred. "Tibetan-Inhabited Areas: Demographic Changes," *Beijing Review*, 4 April 1988.

tory, the Aksai Chin, that India claimed.[114] Nehru had inquired of Chou En-lai in 1954 and again in 1956 about Chinese maps that showed not only the Aksai Chin but the area east of Bhutan, India's Northeast Frontier Agency (NEFA), as part of China. Chou had assured Nehru that the PRC was still using old KMT maps, not yet having had time to prepare their own. In order to ascertain the layout of the Sinkiang-Tibet road, the Indians sent out a patrol in July 1958, which was detained by the Chinese. On 8 October 1958 the Indians protested to China that the road traversed Indian territory, to which the PRC replied that the territory in question was Chinese.

On 14 December 1958 Nehru wrote a friendly letter to Chou En-lai, reminding him of their previous conversations in regard to the border issue and reiterating the Indian understanding that China, although not approving of the 1914 McMahon Line because of its imperialist origins, was nevertheless prepared to accept the McMahon alignment in practice for the sake of good relations with India. Nehru was therefore "puzzled," he said, about a recent *China Pictorial* article in which China continued to claim both NEFA and Aksai Chin. The article in question was the one announcing the opening of the Sinkiang-Tibet highway, though Nehru did not mention the road or the fact that it traversed the Aksai Chin.[115]

Chou replied on 23 January 1959 that the Chinese position was that the border had "never been formally delimited." He reminded Nehru that no treaty regarding the border had been concluded between the "Chinese Central Government and the Indian Government," in other words, that India could not base its claims on the McMahon Line. Furthermore, he indicated that there were some outstanding differences in regard to the border alignment. Chou specifically claimed that the Aksai Chin area had "always been under Chinese jurisdiction." Chou nevertheless felt that a friendly and "realistic" settlement could be reached by accurate surveys and by negotiations.[116]

---

114. Neville Maxwell says that the Indians discovered the existence of this road only through the Chinese announcement of its completion, on 6 October 1957. Neville Maxwell, *India's China War* (New York: Anchor Books, 1972), 83. B.N. Mullik, then director of Indian Intelligence, says that India was well aware of the construction of the road but was uncertain of its exact alignment until a patrol party confirmed that the road transgressed Indian territory in the Aksai Chin. B.N. Mullik, *My Years with Nehru: The Chinese Betrayal* (New Delhi: Allied Publishers, 1971), 198.

115. Letter from the Prime Minister of India to the Prime Minister of China, 14 December 1958, in Chanakya Sen, ed., *Tibet Disappears: A Documentary History of Tibet's International Status, the Great Rebellion and Its Aftermath* (New Delhi: Asia Publishing House, 1960), 441.

116. Letter from the Prime Minister of China to the Prime Minister of India, 23 January 1959, in Sen, *Tibet Disappears*, 445. The legality of the McMahon alignment could not be accepted by China since the agreement had been negotiated between the British and the Tibetans at Simla (in an additional agreement not involving the Chinese representative). For the Chinese to recognize the legality of the line would be the same as recognizing the Tibetans' right to independently negotiate international agreements.

Nehru wrote again on 22 March, expressing his surprise that China did not accept the McMahon Line, since his understanding had been that China would do so, if not in principle, at least in practice. Nehru also claimed that the border was "traditional," followed the "geographical principle of watershed on the crest of the High Himalayan Range," and had the sanction of international agreements between the Indian Government and the central government of China. Nehru cited the 1890 and 1895 treaties on the border of Sikkim, the 1842 treaty between Kashmir and the "Emperor of China and the Lama Guru of Lhasa," and the Simla Convention (considering that China's objections at Simla had been in regard to the border between China and Tibet, not Tibet and India).[117]

Chou En-lai did not reply until 8 September 1959, by which time relations had significantly deteriorated. Chou now held the position that there were "fundamental differences" between the two governments on the boundary question. Chou expressed surprise that India, which like China had suffered under imperialism, could base her claim upon imperialist treaties. Chou proposed that both sides accept the *status quo* as a provisional measure to avoid further clashes, which would have effectively recognized Chinese control over the Aksai Chin and Indian control in NEFA. Rather than allowing India to assume that this was the final Chinese position, however, Chou continued to describe the McMahon Line as illegal, and the border as undelimited, and to demand eventual negotiations on the border alignment.[118]

The Indian Government had, in the meantime, decided that the McMahon Line was India's northern border, an issue not subject to negotiation, a position to which India would adhere as a point of national honor.[119] The dispute over the Aksai Chin was obviously the crux of the matter, since the Chinese were prepared to be reasonable in regard to the larger (90,000 square kilometers) and more important NEFA territory, but would not deviate on the issue of the Aksai Chin (33,000 square kilometers), an uninhabited salt plain, but essential to Chinese communications between Sinkiang and Tibet. India might have been prepared to compro-

---

117. Letter from the Prime Minister of India to the Prime Minister of China, 22 March 1959, in Sen, *Tibet Disappears*, 448. Nehru of course did not mention the fact that the McMahon Line had been secretly negotiated at Simla between McMahon and the Lonchen Shatra.

118. Letter from Premier Chou En-lai to Prime Minister Nehru, 8 September 1959, in Sen, *Tibet Disappears*, 452. Chou incidentally denied that any Chinese representative had participated in the 1842 treaty between Kashmir and Tibet, thus correcting the British Indian assumption that it was Chinese, not Tibetan representatives, who had signed that treaty.

119. Maxwell, *India's China War*, 96.

mise on the issue of the Aksai Chin, since it was hardly comparable to NEFA, had the Indian Government not made it an issue of national honor not to negotiate the border alignment, and had the revolt in Tibet not been a factor. The Indians also substantially misunderstood the Chinese position, mistaking the Chinese refusal to accept the McMahon Line in principle for a refusal to accept it in fact. Chinese maps showing NEFA as part of Tibet, and now of China, were interpreted to mean that China claimed NEFA (which it did, in principle, but was prepared to abandon in exchange for the Aksai Chin).[120]

Chou En-lai came to New Delhi in April 1960, at Nehru's invitation, in an attempt to resolve the border dispute. Enroute to India, Chou stopped in Burma and Nepal, where he concluded border treaties with both states, recognizing the actual McMahon alignment in both cases, without recognizing the legitimacy of the way in which the McMahon Line had come about. This only served to increase Indian suspicions that Chou was trying to isolate India by appearing to be flexible in compromising with Burma and Nepal, thus portraying India as the unreasonable party in the Sino-Indian dispute. The attempt at reconciliation foundered over the Chinese contention that the border was undemarcated and thus had to be negotiated (by which China could supposedly bargain NEFA for Aksai Chin, though India could not be sure that this was the position the Chinese would actually take). India maintained its stand that the McMahon Line was India's border, about which there could be no negotiation.[121]

The Tibetan revolt and the influx of Tibetan refugees to India finally hardened the Indian attitude toward China to such an extent that negoti-

---

120. China's willingness to abandon part of NEFA, the Tawang district, may not have been obvious to India, since the Chinese maintained a claim to Tawang in principle, pointing out that the "local government of Tibet" had, after the independence of India, demanded the return of Tawang to Tibet. "The Truth of the Matter," *Peking Review*, 15 September 1959, 9. Chou En-lai later (15 November 1962) stated that China "took the position that an amicable settlement of the Sino-Indian boundary question should be sought through peaceful negotiations, and that, pending a settlement, the status quo of the boundary should be maintained." *Premier Chou's Letter to the Leaders of Asian and African Countries on the Sino-Indian Boundary Question* (November 15, 1962) (Peking: Foreign Languages Press, 1973), 8.

121. In a press conference in New Delhi, Chou repeated the traditional Chinese belief in China's nonaggression against its neighbors and its victimization by invaders: "China has never committed aggression against the territory of any country. Moreover, China in its history has always suffered from aggression by others." Chou En-lai's Press Conference, 30 April 1960, in Dorothy Woodman, *Himalayan Frontiers* (New York: Praeger, 1969), 398. Chou also repeated the accusation that the Dalai Lama had been taken from Lhasa under duress and that "The persons surrounding the Dalai Lama have made him go farther and farther, pushing him into betrayal of the Motherland and trying their utmost to prevent his return to the fold of the Motherland." Ibid., 402.

ations, had they ever been a possibility, were now out of the question. India regarded the imposition of direct Chinese control over Tibet as a betrayal of its understanding with China about Tibet's status. China's military presence in Tibet and the Tibetan revolt had converted India's peaceful border with Tibet into a hostile frontier with China. China wished to deal with the issue as if a Chinese frontier with India in Tibet had existed since ancient times, if undemarcated; however, the elimination of Tibet as a buffer state and the reality of a direct Sino-Indian territorial frontier was not yet psychologically accepted in India. The PLA's movement up to the border brought them into close proximity to Indian outposts, and convinced the Indian public that further Chinese advances into areas claimed by China, such as Tawang, were imminent. On 25 August 1959 an armed clash occurred between Chinese and Indian border guards at the Tawang border.

Tibet at the United Nations

In a speech to the Indian Council on World Affairs on 7 September 1959, the Dalai Lama announced his intention to appeal Tibet's case to the United Nations. In addition to laying out the basis for Tibet's appeal, the Dalai Lama commented on India's position on its border with Tibet and the nature of China's "suzerainty" over Tibet. The Dalai Lama pointed out that India's position on the legality of the McMahon Line depended upon its recognition of Tibet as an state capable of entering into international agreements. As the Dalai Lama said, "If Tibet did not enjoy international status at the time of the conclusion of the [Simla] convention, it had no authority to enter into such an agreement. Therefore, if you deny sovereign status to Tibet you deny the validity of the Simla Convention and therefore you deny the validity of the McMahon Line." In regard to suzerainty, the Dalai Lama pointed out that "suzerainty does not imply loss of international personality."[122] On the next day, 8 September, the GOI officially rejected the contention that the McMahon Line was dependent upon Tibet's juridical status.[123]

The Dalai Lama's appeal to the United Nations, dated 9 September

---

122. "Dalai Lama Pleads for Support," (New Delhi), *Hindustan Times*, Delhi, 7 September 1959, in *Tibet Fights for Freedom*, 226.

123. US Embassy, New Delhi to Secretary of State, 9 September 1959, National Archives, 793B.00/9-959. The legality of the McMahon Line did, of course, depend upon Tibet's ability to conclude international agreements, a fact that India chose to ignore. No doubt, few Indian officials remembered that the McMahon Line had been agreed upon in a secret bilateral agreement between British India and Tibet or that the Simla agreement itself had never been ratified by China.

1959, referred to Tibet's 1950 appeal, which had been shelved contingent upon the possibility of a peaceful resolution of Sino-Tibetan differences. The Dalai Lama informed the UN that no peaceful resolution had been achieved; instead, Chinese aggression had continued. The appeal reiterated Tibet's status as a sovereign state, based upon the Thirteenth Dalai Lama's declaration of independence in 1912, the 1914 Simla Convention, Tibet's World War II neutrality, and the recognition of Tibetan passports used by Shakabpa's 1946 Tibetan Trade Delegation. The majority of the Tibetan argument was based upon Tibet's political status, with a secondary appeal based upon humanitarian grounds, including dispossession of Tibetans' property, forced labor, mass murder and persecution of religion.[124]

China protested the Dalai Lama's appeal to the UN as a violation of India's responsibilities to China under the principles of mutual non-interference and Nehru's assurances that India would neither recognize a Tibetan exile government nor allow any Tibetan political activities in India. China complained that "the Dalai Lama has all along been engaged in political activities against China and has submitted the so-called Tibet question to the United Nations in the name of the so-called government of Tibet, thus exceeding by far what is permissible under the international practice of asylum."[125]

On 25 July 1959 the International Commission of Jurists (ICJ) published a preliminary report on Tibet, entitled *The Question of Tibet and the Rule of Law*, which influenced several countries' decision to support Tibet's appeal to the UN. The report, prepared by the Indian international lawyer, Purshottam Trikamdas, examined the issues of China's obligation to abide by its own system of national regional autonomy, to allow freedom of religious belief and protection of religious institutions, to permit free trade and to respect the property of the Tibetan people. The report examined the issue of violations of human rights, based upon the 1948 Universal Declaration of Human Rights, and the question of genocide, based upon the 1948 Genocide Convention.

The ICJ report included an analysis by Trikamdas of Tibet's legal sta-

---

124. "Message from His Holiness the Dalai Lama to the Secretary-General Dag Hammarskjold dated 9th September 1959," in *Tibet in the United Nations*, 17. The Dalai Lama acknowledged US advice that his appeal should be confined to human rights issues, but stated that he intended to present his appeal as a continuation of the 1950 Tibetan appeal to the UN: "The Dalai replied that the 1950 case had been a case of invasion of an independent country and that by basing his appeal to the UN on the continuance of the previous case he was thereby reasserting the independence of invaded Tibet." Embassy, New Delhi to Department of State, 10 September 1959, National Archives, 793B.11/9-1059.

125. "Vice-Premier Chen Yi's Speech," *Peking Review*, 15 September 1959, 14.

tus, entitled "The Position of Tibet in International Law," documentation on international agreements regarding Tibet, and official statements of the Chinese Government, the Dalai Lama and Indian Prime Minister Nehru. The Secretary-General of the ICJ concluded, on the basis of Trikamdas' analysis, that Tibet's legal status "was not easy to appraise," and that it "cannot be fitted into a logical category." Nevertheless, "Tibet has been to all intents and purposes an independent country and has enjoyed a large degree of sovereignty," therefore it would be "difficult" for the PRC to claim domestic jurisdiction in regard to Tibet. The report reached the tentative conclusion that:

> The events in Tibet constitute prima facie a threat to and a breach of the fundamental legal principles which the International Commission of Jurists stands for and endeavours to promote and protect. From the present report there emerges also, it is submitted, a prima facie case of the worst type of imperialism and colonialism, coming precisely from the very people who claim to fight against it.[126]

Despite the fact that the Dalai Lama's appeal had been based upon a violation of Tibet's sovereignty, and the ICJ report had also addressed the political issue, international support for Tibet's case at the UN was confined to human rights violations to the exclusion of the political issues of Tibetan independence or China's violation thereof. The US, which took the lead in arousing support for Tibet at the UN, recommended this position, not only for reasons of its relations with Taiwan, but because of the fact that few countries, particularly Asian countries, were willing to challenge China's claim to sovereignty over Tibet. Even though Tibet's political status remained the issue in theory, in practice even countries sympathetic to Tibet could raise only humanitarian or human rights issues, since they recognized Chinese sovereignty over Tibet.

The US advised the Dalai Lama in August that "the UN is limited in its ability in a practical way to alleviate the plight of the Tibetan people. On the other hand, it can generate considerable moral support for the Tibetan cause by dramatizing the Chinese Communists' perfidy and brutality." The Dalai Lama was advised that "to achieve maximum world impact, it [the appeal] should focus on the outrages and atrocities committed against the Tibetan people and the denial of human rights resulting from the actions of the Chinese Communists. For technical reasons, it would not be desirable to include charges of aggression in the appeal."

---

126. *Question of Tibet and the Rule of Law*, iv. The ICJ described itself in the preface to the preliminary report as a "non-governmental and non-political organization." The ICJ has consultative status with the United Nations Economic and Social Council.

The "technical reasons" included the inability to achieve support from a sufficient number of countries at the UN for a resolution based upon political grounds and the US desire to avoid embarrassing India. Indian support, or at least an absence of Indian opposition, was essential to the success of any appeal to the UN. In addition, the Dalai Lama, as a refugee in India, was dependent upon Indian good will, which it was thought would probably not be jeopardized by the Dalai Lama's appeal "so long as he avoided insisting on the concept of Tibetan independence."[127]

The US sent instructions to its UN delegation to consult with the delegations of governments thought likely to support the inclusion of a resolution on Tibet on the UN agenda. In particular, the USUN delegation was instructed to approach the UN representatives of UK, France, Burma, Cambodia, Ceylon, Indonesia, Iran, Japan, Malaya, Nepal, Pakistan, Philippines, Thailand, El Salvador and Ireland. Those countries were informed that the US did not wish to be the primary sponsor of a resolution on Tibet but would be prepared to cosponsor.[128] The Federation of Malaya and Ireland expressed an interest in sponsoring the resolution. However, their efforts and those of the US were countered by the reluctance of Asian countries, Malaya excepted, to confront China, and Indian and even British lack of enthusiasm. Britain took the position that the Chinese invasion of Tibet had turned many Asian countries against China and against Communism; however, if the Tibet issue at the UN were to turn into a predominantly Western-sponsored affair or a Cold War issue, Asian opinion might shift to an attitude of greater solidarity with China. The US concurred but thought that many nations, Asian nations included, were "willing to support an item on Tibet limited to violations of human rights," but "would not support Tibetan claims of independence and charges of [Chinese] aggression."[129]

To represent Tibet at the UN, the Dalai Lama sent his brother, Gyalo Thondup, accompanied by Shakabpa, Rinchen Sandutsang as interpreter, and Hugh Richardson as advisor. Thondup immediately encountered the

---

127. State Department Memorandum, National Archives, 793B.00/8-559.

128. Department of State to USUN, 12 September 1959, National Archives, 793B.00/9-1259. The US preferred to play a secondary role in the Tibet resolution in order to minimize the inevitable charge by the Soviet bloc that the US was pushing Tibet as a Cold War issue. For the same reason, the US wished to confine the resolution to human rights rather than political issues.

129. State Department Memorandum of Conversation, 2 October 1959, National Archives, 793B.00/10-259. In addition to the "technical reasons" for limiting the Tibetan appeal to human rights violations, the US, and no doubt many other countries, felt that the legal question on Tibet was enormously compounded by the Sino-Tibetan Agreement of 1951 and its subsequent implementation and the Sino-Indian Agreement of 1954. London Embassy to Secretary of State, 6 October 1959, National Archives, 793B.00/10-659.

insistence of the Irish and Malayan delegations that the issue be confined to human rights violations in order to gain sufficient support to be heard at the UN; Thondup was advised to cease making public statements demanding UN consideration of Chinese aggression against Tibet and the issue of Tibetan independence. Thondup was reportedly "distressed" at the lack of Asian support for Tibet and the "political facts of life at the UN," which prevented the political issue of Tibet being discussed, but finally was "reconciled to the importance of Tibetans avoiding any action which might jeopardize the Irish-Malaysian initiative."[130]

While agreeing to downplay all but the human rights aspects of the Tibetan appeal, Thondup repeatedly questioned US representatives, including Henry Cabot Lodge, head of the US mission, whether "action on human rights basis would in some way affect adversely cause of Tibetan independence." Thondup was assured that only on those grounds would the Tibetan issue be considered at all, but that even a resolution so moderately worded could be used by the Tibetans as "evidence of UN interest and support for people of Tibet" and as an entrance for the Tibetan issue into the UN, which could conceivably be expanded at some later date. Tibetan insistence that the UN consider the issue of Tibet's international political status, on the other hand, might close the door to any UN consideration of the Tibet issue at all.[131]

The "Tibet Question" was proposed for inclusion on the General Assembly's agenda on 28 September by Ireland and the Federation of Malaya.[132] Preliminary debate in the agenda committee began on 9 October. The item raised the question of the relationship between United Nations human rights resolutions, in particular the Universal Declaration of Human Rights, and article 2, paragraph 7, of the United Nations Charter, which prohibits any interference in the domestic affairs of states. During the debate on Tibet, only El Salvador, the sponsor of Tibet's 1950 appeal, brought up the question of Tibet's political status as an issue deserving of special consideration by the United Nations. El Salvador proposed that a United Nations commission be appointed to ascertain the wishes of the Tibetans in regard to their political allegiance.[133]

The Soviet Union and the Communist bloc vehemently opposed any

---

130. USUN to Secretary of State, 6 October 1959, National Archives, 793B.00/10-659.

131. USUN to Secretary of State, 8 October 1959, National Archives, 793B.00/10-859.

132. "Request for the Inclusion of an Additional Item in the Agenda of the Fourteenth Regular Session: Item Proposed by the Federation of Malaya and Ireland. The Question of Tibet. Letter dated 28th September 1959 from the Permanent Representatives of the Federation of Malaya and Ireland to the United Nations, addressed to the Secretary General." UNGA Doc. A/4234, 29 September 1959, in *Tibet in the United Nations*, 19.

133. Ibid., 21.

inclusion on the UN agenda of the "so-called Tibet question," claiming that Tibet was an integral part of China and therefore beyond the juris-diction of the United Nations, and, in any case, there was no "question of Tibet," the issue having been contrived by the United States to oppose the "peace policy" of the Soviet Union and to revive the Cold War. The Soviet Union and its allies repeated, often nearly verbatim, China's rhetoric on Tibet's former barbaric feudalism, its liberation by China and the enthu-siastic acceptance by Tibetans of Chinese sovereignty and Chinese reforms. The Socialist bloc accused Ireland and Malaya and all other sup-porters of the issue of being little more than tools of the United States.

For many countries, however, the issue of Tibet raised fundamental questions of justice and human rights as well as the role of the United Nations in such questions. Many states demurred for reasons of uncer-tainty about Tibet's political status or for fear of violating the UN's pro-vision against interference in the internal affairs of states, since Tibet's status seemed to be something less than full independence. Others felt that consideration by the United Nations was legally possible without violation of Article 2(7) because Tibet's status was sufficiently established as a separate national entity in some autonomous relationship to China. Many states (outside the Communist bloc) felt that human rights were a legitimate international issue, in some instances overriding states' rights to non-interference. In the end, a majority of states voted for inclusion of the Tibet question as an item for General Assembly debate.[134]

In General Assembly debate, Malaya and Ireland refuted charges that they were acting at the behest of other states. Malaya confined its argu-ment to human rights issues, maintaining that "any problem which involves a violation of the principles enshrined in the Charter of the United Nations and the Universal Declaration of Human Rights and which might have far reaching effects of increasing international tension cannot be regarded as exclusively an internal problem."[135]

Ireland responded to Soviet allegations that support for Tibet was equivalent to support for a feudalistic system and American imperialist schemes by pointing out the incongruity between the Soviet Union's call for peaceful coexistence and China's use of force in Tibet. The UN's func-

---

134. The vote in the preliminary committee considering the issue was 11 in favor, 5 against and 4 abstaining. General Assembly Fourteenth Session, 9 October 1959, UN Doc. A/4234, in *Tibet in the United Nations*, 60. In the General Committee, the vote was 43 in favor, 11 against and 25 abstaining. India neither participated in the debate nor voted on the issue. General Assembly Fourteenth Session, 12 October 1959, UN Doc. A/4237, in *Tibet in the United Nations*, 82.

135. General Assembly Fourteenth Session, 20 October 1959, UN Doc. A/4237, in *Tibet in the United Nations*, 90.

tion was to oppose colonialism worldwide, while China was perpetrating an act with all the features of "old-fashioned imperialism" against Tibet. China's "civilizing mission" in Tibet was compared with the usual justification employed by nineteenth century imperialism. The Irish delegate wondered whether the delegations of former colonies now represented at the United Nations would "put to themselves the question whether if they ignore or brush aside the questions of what is happening in Tibet they would not be condoning in the case of that hapless people precisely the same type of action against which they have so often vigorously protested here in this Assembly and elsewhere."[136]

Ireland refuted the contention that Tibet was an issue entirely within the domestic jurisdiction of China such that its discussion by the United Nations was prohibited. Ireland did not propose to debate the legal status of Tibet, conceding that it was entirely within China's power to do whatever it wished in regard to Tibet since the United Nations was not likely to intervene, but thought that Tibetans were "a distinct people by race, by language, by culture and by religious organization," and that their welfare was a legitimate issue for United Nations debate. As the Irish representative said:

> I cannot conceive how any nation which has undergone foreign rule, whether for long or short periods, can regard the past period of Chinese imperial hegemony over Tibet as depriving Tibet of a claim on our attention now. . . .

> We repudiate the contention advanced by the Soviet representative that, as the people of Tibet have not always since the beginning of time been able to resist being treated as subjects by a stronger Power, the case of Tibet is dead, never to be revived. Indeed to admit that contention would be to destroy the basis upon which most of our Member nations have established the right to live in freedom and to govern themselves in accordance with the wishes of their own peoples.[137]

Several countries, including Great Britain, Turkey and New Zealand, felt that Tibet's national identity or traditional autonomy was sufficiently well established to transcend the UN prohibition on interference in a state's internal affairs.[138] Others, including Cuba, the Netherlands, Ecuador and Venezuela, held that the United Nations had the duty to

---

136. General Assembly Fourteenth Session, 13 October 1959, UN Doc. A/4237, in *Tibet in the United Nations*, 56.

137. General Assembly Fourteenth Session, 20 October 1959, UN Doc. A/4237, in *Tibet in the United Nations*, 96, 100, 101.

138. Ibid., 38, 49, 64, 226.

concern itself with violations of human rights regardless of Article 2(7).[139] Some, including Belgium, France and Spain, while expressing sympathy with Tibet, upheld the principle of noninterference.[140] The Republic of China (Taiwan held the UN seat for China at the time) voted to examine the "Tibet Question," while emphasizing that Tibet was an integral part of China.[141] El Salvador echoed the Dalai Lama's point that a less than totally independent state, under some form of suzerainty or protection by another state, was still a state under international law.[142] Britain made an important but often ignored point that "allegations of serfdom and feudalism which we have heard during this debate are . . . beside the point, even if any part of them could be substantiated."[143]

Malaya pointed out that small states were dependent upon the United Nations for support against large states and therefore they should support the principle of United Nations intervention on behalf of the rights of a small nation such as Tibet, since "once the barrier of world public opinion, freely expressed in this Assembly, is down, it will only make future violations very much easier."[144] This advice might have been taken by Nepal, but was not; Nepal submitted an opinion that avoided any challenge to China's status or its actions in Tibet, echoing Chinese propaganda: "If we speak of human rights and their suppression in Tibet, we should first try to find out what human rights the Tibetan people have enjoyed through the centuries and which of these human rights have been denied to the people of Tibet today. Even Tibet has to be viewed in the context of the new, changing, revolutionary Asia." Nepal voted against the inclusion of the Tibet issue.[145]

After abstaining on the question of inclusion of the Tibet question for United Nations debate, India entered the debate in the General Assembly. The Indian delegate pointed out that the Dalai Lama's letter to the Secretary General "seeks to establish the Tibetans' status and seeks recognition of their sovereignty as a result of our discussion," whereas the draft resolution of Malaya and Ireland dealt only with the human rights issue: "Therefore, in what the Assembly is seized of now there are no political issues, therefore it is unnecessary for my Government to argue

---

139. Ibid., 114, 157, 200, 218. This was obviously before Cuba became a client state of the Soviet Union.

140. Ibid., 128, 141, 173. These countries all had colonialist problems of their own, which may have influenced their opinions.

141. Ibid., 164.

142. Ibid., 153.

143. Ibid., 193.

144. Ibid., 93.

145. Ibid., 103.

this question at all."[146] Acknowledging that many countries looked to India for leadership on the issue, India nevertheless emphasized that its abstention was due not to any fear of displeasing China, but "in the interest of reconciliation in the future, because it [the resolution] does not promote any constructive step at all."[147] India maintained that discussion of Tibet in the United Nations would serve no purpose, since "nobody is going to send an army to Tibet," except to further annoy China and possibly produce "reactions on the Chinese Government which are more adverse to Tibet and the Tibetan people than even now."[148]

The Federation of Malaya and Ireland closed the debate with forceful statements on an issue that obviously aroused the concern of many. Malaya reiterated the fundamental considerations of national and human rights which were evoked by the Tibetan issue:

> I may point out that the violations of human rights and fundamental freedoms may appear in different forms and different guises in different parts of the world, some of which are being justified by their perpetrators and their apologists as progressive reforms. In the view of my delegation, any action which by the use of brutal force seeks to deny individuals their right to freedom of worship and religion and to enjoy their own inherent culture and traditional way of life certainly constitutes a violation of human rights and fundamental freedoms.[149]

Ireland warned that the issue of Tibet was symbolic of fundamental issues of international law and self-determination:

> Those also who have struggled here in the cause of any oppressed people or victimized minority should think very carefully before they decide . . . to ignore the call of the Tibetan people. By ignoring that call they would be weakening the very source to which they look for redress—the moral force

---

146. Fourteenth Session General Assembly, Provisional Verbatim Record of the Eight Hundred and Thirty-fourth Plenary Meeting, 21 October 1959, UN Doc. A/PV.834, in *Tibet in the United Nations*, 201. India (represented by Krishna Menon) further argued that "India inherited the British position in Tibet in 1947—that is to say, that Tibet was under Chinese suzerainty. In 1954 we entered into an agreement which was not a political agreement in regard to the political status of Tibet as such, but was an agreement relating to trade matters." Ibid., 201. Despite this contention, Menon cited the 1954 Treaty as indicative of India's position on the political status of Tibet. Ibid., 205. Menon also repeated Chinese propaganda that the Tibetan revolt was begun by Khampas who "are not in Tibet proper; they are in the Chinese province. They are Chinese themselves. However, the Tibetans joined them, and a very considerable revolt appears to have taken place." Ibid., 202.

147. Ibid., 208.
148. Ibid., 206.
149. Ibid., 221.

of this Assembly—and weakening also the moral force of their own appeals. . . .

The question of Tibet is a test case, a challenge to this Assembly. If, despite our Charter, a powerful country may force its will, with impunity and without protest, upon a distinctive people one-hundredth part its size, by what principle could it be denied the right to impose its will by force upon a nation one-tenth or one-half its size?[150]

The Tibet Resolution was finally adopted on 21 October by a vote of 46 in favor, 9 against and 26 abstaining.[151] The final form of the Resolution on the Question of Tibet was as follows:

The General Assembly, recalling the principles regarding fundamental human rights and freedoms set out in the Charter of the United Nations and in the Universal Declaration of Human Rights adopted by the General Assembly on 10 December 1948,

Considering that the fundamental human rights and freedoms to which the Tibetan people, like all others, are entitled include the right to civil and religious liberty for all without distinction,

Mindful also of the distinctive cultural and religious heritage of the people of Tibet and of the autonomy which they have traditionally enjoyed,

Gravely concerned at reports, including the official statements of his Holiness the Dalai Lama, to the effect that the fundamental human rights and freedoms of the people of Tibet have been forcibly denied them,

Deploring the effect of these events in increasing international tension and in embittering the relations between peoples at a time when earnest and positive efforts are being made by responsible leaders to reduce tension and improve international relations,

1. Affirms its belief that respect for the principles of the Charter of the

---

150. Ibid., 223.

151. Those states voting for the Resolution were: Argentina, Australia, Austria, Bolivia, Brazil, Canada, Chile, China, Colombia, Costa Rica, Cuba, Denmark, Ecuador, El Salvador, Malaya, Greece, Guatemala, Haiti, Honduras, Iceland, Iran, Ireland, Israel, Italy, Japan, Jordan, Laos, Liberia, Luxembourg, Mexico, Netherlands, New Zealand, Nicaragua, Norway, Pakistan, Panama, Paraguay, Peru, Philippines, Sweden, Thailand, Tunisia, Turkey, United States, Uruguay, Venezuela.

Those against were: Albania, Bulgaria, Byelorussia, Czechoslovakia, Hungary, Poland, Romania, Ukraine, Soviet Union.

Those abstaining were: Afghanistan, Belgium, Burma, Cambodia, Ceylon, Dominican Republic, Ethiopia, Finland, France, Ghana, India, Indonesia, Iraq, Lebanon, Libya, Morocco, Nepal, Portugal, Saudi Arabia, Spain, Sudan, South Africa, United Arab Republic, United Kingdom, Yemen, Yugoslavia. Ibid., 224.

United Nations and of the Universal Declaration of Human Rights is essential for the evolution of a peaceful world order based on the rule of law;

2. Calls for respect for the fundamental human rights of the Tibetan people and for their distinctive cultural and religious life.[152]

After the conclusion of the UN session, the Tibetan delegation went to Washington, where they had a series of meetings with State Department officials. At the first of these meetings, the Tibetans expressed their thanks for US assistance at the UN and elsewhere, but complained that the UN resolution did not provide "any effective means of achieving the object which His Holiness and his people have in view."[153] The Tibetans were informed that the US stood for the principle of self-determination and intended to make an official statement to that effect at some time in the near future.[154]

The Tibetans did not fail to realize the significance of this promise and, at a subsequent meeting, requested a clarification of the US position. The Assistant Secretary of State for Far Eastern Affairs, Graham Parsons, then informed the Tibetans that:

> The historical position of the United States hitherto has been to consider Tibet an autonomous country under the suzerainty of China. However, it was also the traditional policy of the American people to support the principle of self-determination for all peoples. This was why the United States believed the Tibetans entitled to have the controlling voice in their own affairs and felt that it could at an appropriate time make a public declaration of its support for the self-determination of the Tibetan people.[155]

The Tibetans were told that the US intended to inform the Republic of China, India and Britain before making this statement public; the Tibetans were requested to keep this information confidential until that time. In conversations with the ambassador of the Republic of China, the

---

152. "Text of Resolution adopted by The General Assembly at the 14th Session on the Question of Tibet," in *Tibet in the United Nations*, 230.

153. Gyalo Thondup to Robert D. Murphy, Under Secretary of State, 2 November 1959, National Archives, 793B.00/11-259. The US was at the same time increasing its clandestine assistance to the Tibetan resistance.

154. State Department Memorandum of Conversation, 29 October 1959, National Archives, 793B.00/10-2959.

155. State Department Memorandum of Conversation, 31 October 1959, National Archives, 793B.00/10-3159. In response to an American question about the territorial extent and divisions of Tibet, the Tibetans replied that Tibet was traditionally composed of three provinces, U-Tsang, Kham and Amdo, and they remarked that the Tibetans present were from each of the three provinces (Thondup from Amdo, Sandutsang from Kham and Shakabpa from U-Tsang). Ibid.

State Department indicated that it had "made a decision to go somewhat beyond its previous position with regard to Tibet, namely, that it is an autonomous country under the suzerainty of China." This decision, it was said, was "mindful of the statement on Tibetan self-determination made by President Chiang on March 26."[156] Chiang's statement, made to express Nationalist support for the Tibetans' revolt against the Chinese Communists, was as follows:

> In connection to the future political status and institutions of Tibet, as soon as the puppet Communist regime on the mainland is overthrown and the people of Tibet are once again free to express their will, the Government will assist Tibetan people to realize their own aspirations in accordance with the principle of self-determination.[157]

The State Department indicated in a telegram to US Embassies in New Delhi, London and Taipei that "in supporting self-determination for Tibet we are not necessarily committing the US to ultimate recognition of Tibetan independence, but only to the concept that Tibetans have the right to choose whether or not Tibet is to be independent." In addition, the US "does not recognize Chinese Communist sovereignty over any part of China including Tibet and never recognized the validity of the 1951 agreement between Tibet and Peiping."[158]

US Secretary of State Christian Herter made an official statement on the US position on Tibet's right to self-determination on 20 February 1960:

---

156. State Department Memorandum of Conversation, 3 November 1959, National Archives, 793B.00/11-359.

157. Department of State Outgoing Telegram, 6 November 1959, National Archives, 793B.00/11-659.

158. Ibid. While the US did not recognize Chinese Communist sovereignty over Tibet, it continued to recognize Nationalist Chinese "suzerainty"; therefore, its refusal to recognize the PRC's sovereignty over Tibet was not equivalent to a recognition of Tibet's right to independence. "United States Policy Concerning the Legal Status of Tibet," November 1957, National Archives, 793.B00/11-157. The Nationalist Chinese Government took exception to the use by the US of the term "suzerainty" to describe China's relationship with Tibet and to the reference to Tibet as an autonomous "country." Both expressions, it was said, were "clearly at variance with the legal status of Tibet as provided in the Constitution of the Republic of China. . . That in the Constitution of the Republic of China Tibet is designated an autonomous area does not confer upon Tibet the status of an independent or autonomous `country.'" The Nationalist Chinese Government suggested that, in any US statement regarding the legal status of Tibet, it would be "judicious and desirable" to refer to Chiang's 26 March 1959 statement (in other words, that Tibet's legal status was a prerogative of the Nationalist Chinese Government). State Department Aide-Memoire, 28 February 1960, National Archives, 793B.00/2-2860.

While it has been the historical position of the United States to consider Tibet an autonomous country under the suzerainty of China, the American people have also traditionally stood for the principle of self-determination. It is the belief of the United States Government that this principle should apply to the people of Tibet and that they should have the determining voice in their own political destiny.[159]

Meanwhile, the PRC condemned the UN Tibet Resolution as a "fantastic farce" and a "cold war farce directed by the United States from first to last." Ireland and Malaya were characterized as "imperialist lackeys" of the US.[160] China's position was that "the quelling of the rebellion of the reactionary clique of the upper social strata in Tibet and the democratic reforms there are solely China's business and no foreign country or international organization has any right whatsoever to interfere."[161] China attempted to put the most favorable interpretation on the fact that a majority of countries, including many Asian countries, had supported the Tibet Resolution: "The final vote at the UN General Assembly on the US designed Irish-Malayan resolution shows that the United States, after putting the dollar squeeze on others, could only gain a bare simple majority while most of the Asian and African countries abstained."[162]

China echoed the Soviet claim that the United States had employed the "so-called Tibet question" simply for the purpose of sabotaging the Soviet peace offensive, pointing out that the US had demanded of the Soviet Union that it "share the responsibility" for China's actions against Taiwan and Tibet. This strategy would never succeed, it claimed, because relations between fraternal socialist countries were not like those between the US and its satellites: "The great alliance between China and the Soviet Union is based on internationalism, on the pursuit of a common objective; it represents the fraternal relations of equals, relations of mutual respect, mutual encouragement and mutual assistance; and it is everlasting and indestructible."[163]

The Chinese also employed their most important Tibetan collaborators, the Panchen Lama and Ngawang Jigme Ngapo, to refute the claims of the Dalai Lama about the circumstances of the revolt and actual conditions in Tibet. Both claimed that Tibet had "scored tremendous successes in consolidating the unification of the motherland and in

159. *Tibet in the United Nations*, 277.

160. "'Cold War' Ballyhoo in the UN," *Peking Review*, 20 October 1959, 2.

161. "Oppose US Aggravation of the 'Cold War'," *Peking Review*, 27 October 1959.

162. Ibid.

163. Ibid. In fact, the "everlasting and indestructible alliance" with the Soviet Union came apart within a year.

strengthening the unity of all the nationalities and has won great victories in people's democratic revolution, socialist revolution and socialist construction." This had been made possible because of "the revolutionary enthusiasm of the masses of the Tibetan people, which had long been held back by the reactionaries." Tibet's "one million serfs" had "stood up and with their own hands they want to abolish completely the cruel, backward, dark and reactionary feudal serfdom."[164]

The Panchen described how "democratic reforms" had improved Tibetan class consciousness and Han-Tibetan relations: "They are deeply aware that the Communist Party alone is their saviour and that only by firmly trusting the Communist Party and firmly following the leadership of Chairman Mao Tse-tung can they achieve real emancipation and happiness." The emancipated Tibetan "serfs" were said to praise Mao as "the sun, the lode star and a real Buddha." Chinese cadres in Tibet were said to "have the same hearts as we do though they do not speak Tibetan, while the reactionary upper social strata of Tibet have hearts different from ours even though they speak Tibetan."[165]

In regard to the contention that Tibetans were being denied their human rights, the Panchen claimed that they were only now achieving human rights after having been denied fundamental human rights and civil liberties by the former feudal serf system:

> The United Nations has absolutely no right to interfere in the internal affairs of our country. . . . The Tibetan people will absolutely not alter the direction of their advance because of the clamour of the imperialists. Countless facts have shown that what the imperialists malign us for are precisely the things we should do and have done right. We must, under the leadership of the Central People's Government, completely destroy feudal serfdom, which is cruel, savage, reactionary and backward, and continue to weed out the remnant rebels who carry on their activities clandestinely. Only by doing so will the Tibetan people be able to have genuine fundamental human rights, genuine civil liberties and freedom of religion. Only by so doing can the Tibetan nationality advance and prosper.[166]

Subsequent Chinese propaganda concentrated on the human rights issue rather than Tibet's political status, since China's sovereignty over Tibet was internationally unchallenged. The Chinese excoriated Tibet's international supporters for their lack of concern about human rights violations perpetrated by Tibet's former "reactionary, backward, barbarous

---

164. Panchen Erdeni, "Implementing Democratic Reform in Tibet," *Peking Review*, 20 October 1959, 6.

165. Ibid., 8.

166. Ibid., 9.

and cruel serf-system." It was entirely incongruous, the Chinese said, that they should be concerned about Tibetans' "fundamental human rights" when Tibetans were "enjoying for the first time in history human rights, civil liberties, and religious freedom."[167] The Chinese attempted to shift the debate from the issue of Tibetan national self-determination to Marxist class self-determination, and in this they were largely successful, given the international community's reluctance to address the fundamental political issue.

Rather than focusing on Tibet's political status, the legitimacy of the Chinese invasion and occupation of Tibet, or Tibetans' right to national self-determination, the subsequent debate over Tibet became mired in contradictory claims about the nature of Tibet's former social system compared to the supposed improvements made by the Chinese. Despite attempts by the Dalai Lama to return the debate to Tibet's right to independence, the issue thereafter was primarily confined to whether or not the Tibetans were better off under Chinese rule than they had been under their own supposedly mis-rule. Because the Chinese had an almost total monopoly on information, the reality of what was happening within Tibet became ever more obscure. Refugees continued to flee Tibet, but their accounts of atrocities were dismissed as exaggerated by a world reluctant to believe that the Chinese could actually behave so brutally when their own propaganda so skillfully portrayed them as concerned only with social reform and modernization.

Tibetan Resistance and the CIA

American interest in supporting Tibetan resistance to the Chinese Communists had declined after 1951, but was revived in early 1956 when Chinese policies began to produce revolt in eastern Tibet. The American dialogue with the Dalai Lama in 1950-51 had been conducted by the US State Department through the US Embassy in New Delhi and the Calcutta Consulate; however, after 1951, US interests in Tibet had to be conducted clandestinely since Tibet was now a part of the PRC—to which the US had not accorded diplomatic recognition but which was nevertheless a sovereign state. US involvement in the Tibetan situation was thereafter conducted by the Central Intelligence Agency. Unlike the American dialogue with the Tibetans in 1950-51, which appears in official US State Department records (most, but not all, of which are now declassified), the history of later American involvement remains classified.

---

167. "No UN Interference in China! " *Peking Review*, 27 October 1959, 9.

Nevertheless, the majority of the story can be pieced together from information available in the Tibetan exile community.

Early CIA contacts were with the Dalai Lama's two elder brothers, Thupten Norbu (Takser Rimpoche), who had been brought to the US in 1950 with CIA funds, and Gyalo Thondup, who in 1956 was resident in Kalimpong. In 1956 Thupten Norbu returned to India where, along with Gyalo Thondup and the Maharaj Kumar of Sikkim, he attempted to convince the Dalai Lama, then visiting India, to seek asylum.[168] In his autobiography, the Dalai Lama remarked that his brothers revealed to him at that time that the Americans had repeated their offers of political support and also that they "undertook to supply a limited amount of simple weaponry to the freedom fighters by airdrop. They also made plans for the CIA to train some of them in techniques of guerrilla warfare and then parachute them back into Tibet."[169]

The CIA began recruiting Tibetans in Darjeeling and Kalimpong in late 1955 or early 1956. Tibetan recruits were taken to East Pakistan (now Bangladesh) for transfer to training camps. India at that time had good relations with China and was not cooperative in assisting Tibetan resistance. The first batches of Tibetan recruits were flown in CIA aircraft to the American-administered Pacific island of Saipan, where they were given training in guerilla warfare, weapons handling, parachuting and communications.

Five of the first trainees were parachuted into Tibet in 1957; three were dropped near Lithang in southern Kham and two near Samye in central Tibet. Two of the three dropped at Lithang were killed; the two dropped at Samye reached Lhasa where they contacted one of the Dalai Lama's ministers, Phala, and conveyed to him a US offer to supply clandestine assistance to Tibet if it received a request from the Tibetan Government to do so. They also accompanied the Dalai Lama on his escape in 1959. Two additional supply drops were made before March 1959, but this was the only assistance the US supplied before the Lhasa revolt. Training of more Tibetans continued, however, and at some point moved to Camp Hale, a former US Army ski mountaineering training site in Colorado.

The March 1959 revolt encouraged the CIA to mount an increased effort, based upon the assumption that organized resistance could continue within Tibet. No assistance was forthcoming while organized resistance continued in Lhoka; the CIA operation did not begin delivering men and supplies until long after the *Chushi Gangdruk* had crossed over

---

168. "United States Policy Concerning the Legal Status of Tibet," November 1957, National Archives, 793.B00/11-157.

169. Dalai Lama, *Freedom in Exile*, 121.

into India (end of April). The CIA airdrops began only in the summer of 1959, continuing through the early fall months. The drops were concentrated on areas where resistance was thought to continue, particularly Shotalhosum and Markham, the westernmost districts of Kham (within the TAR).

Several drops of men and supplies were made, each consisting of small arms, grenades, mortars and radios. Each CIA-trained Tibetan was supplied with a watch containing a cyanide pill, which he was instructed to swallow rather than being captured. Resistance leaders were informed that they would be assisted with arms supplies as long as they could hold their area. Organized resistance continued in some areas of Tibet until early 1960, reportedly even until April 1961 in one area (Markham),[170] but was finally overcome by massive numbers of PLA troops, including some Hui troops, assisted by aerial reconnaissance and bombing. Most of the resisters were killed or captured: few were able to escape to India. Some individuals continued to resist until 1961 or even 1962.[171] In the meantime, efforts were being undertaken to organize external resistance.

Shortly after the collapse of organized resistance within Tibet, survivors began filtering into the Mustang (Lho Mantang) area of northern Nepal. Most travelled overland from Darjeeling and Kalimpong, but some arrived directly from Tibet. The decision to relocate in Mustang and to continue the resistance from there was made in coordination with the CIA, which presumably secured a secret agreement from Nepal to tolerate an anti-Chinese resistance on Nepal's territory.[172] Soon after their arrival in Mustang, the Tibetans began receiving airdrops of supplies and arms.[173] After the 1962 Sino-Indian border war, India allowed the Tibetans in Mustang to be supplied via India. After this time, all supplies came overland from India via Pokhara in Nepal). At about this time, India also

---

170. Nyima Assam, personal interview.

171. Drakton, Abu Chonga, Abu Gonkar, Nyima Assam, personal interviews.

172. Despite the fact that Nepal had signed a border treaty with the PRC in 1960, had friendly relations with China and had accepted Chinese aid for road building projects in Nepal, Nepal's complicity in the Mustang operation is apparent. The Mustang operation was accompanied by a considerable increase in USAID assistance to Nepal.

173. These flights may have originated in Thailand, crossed Burma, Bhutan and Sikkim and proceeded along the Nepal-Tibet border to a point north of Mustang; or, more likely, given East Pakistan's cooperation in the project from the beginning, flights may have originated in Pakistan, crossed the narrow strip of Indian territory (eliciting Indian complaints) into Nepal and continued along the Himalaya to Mustang. Airdrops were made inside Tibet north of the border with Mustang, not within Mustang itself, indicating that some restrictions were placed on the operation by the Government of Nepal. There are also indications that the US wanted the resistance to operate within Tibet and was only willing to supply the Tibetans if they could continue operations inside Tibet.

organized a Tibetan unit, "Unit 22," within the Indian Army. Unit 22 was organized by the Indian Intelligence Research and Analysis Wing and also received CIA organizational and training assistance; Unit 22 thereafter became the main focus of Indian and US efforts to the neglect of the Mustang operation.[174]

The Mustang operation was never very effective in harassing the Chinese in Tibet. Mustang bordered on a sparsely populated and strategically unimportant area of Tibet. The Tibetans in Mustang were able to harass Chinese road communications along the original Tibet to Sinkiang route, which passed just north of Mustang, only until the mid-1960s, when the Chinese constructed a new route that passed further to the north.[175] Supplies also diminished as the CIA realized the limited value of the operation. CIA assistance was terminated in 1972 when the US sought rapprochement with China.

The Tibetan resistance was finally eliminated in the winter of 1974-75 after the Chinese demanded of King Birendra of Nepal that he suppress the Tibetan operation in Mustang in exchange for good relations with China and Chinese economic assistance. The Dalai Lama sent a message to the remaining Tibetans in Mustang requesting that they peacefully surrender to the Nepalese; most honored the Dalai Lama's request, with the exception of a few who attempted to escape to India but were ambushed and killed or captured by Nepalese troops in far western Nepal near the Indian border.[176]

The CIA-supported Tibetan resistance in Mustang, like the CIA operation within Tibet, was insignificant in its effects upon Chinese political and military control within Tibet. Had American assistance to the Tibetan resistance begun on a large scale in 1956 or 1957, the story might have been different. The offers of American political, diplomatic and even mil-

---

174. Unit 22, which attained a strength of 10,000 men, and some women, was an entirely Tibetan unit, officered by Tibetans under Indian Army and Indian Intelligence supervision. The unit still exists at this time (1996).

175. The new route departs from the old at Lhatze Dzong, where it crosses to the north of the Tsangpo, joining with the old route at Dzongpa. A road was later completed via the northern Chang Thang, avoiding Dzongpa and the route along the Tsangpo altogether; this route travels north from Saka Dzong and then west to Gartok.

176. Several British helicopter pilots employed by the Nepalese Army, who ferried Nepalese troops to the ambush site, were awarded honors by the Nepalese for their role in the operation. American-made weapons recovered by the Nepalese Army in Mustang were displayed in Kathmandu in February 1975 as part of the ceremonies accompanying the coronation of King Birendra. The Nepalese attempted to obscure the well-known fact that the US had been supporting the Tibetans in Mustang, and Nepalese complicity in the operation, by explaining that even though all the captured weapons were American-made they could have been acquired by the Tibetans on the international arms market. Personal observation, Kathmandu, February 1975.

itary support in 1950-51 and again in 1956 were potentially significant factors in Tibetan political events, had the Tibetans accepted them, whereas the later clandestine operations were not.

ICJ Report and Second United Nations Resolution

On the recommendation of its 1959 preliminary report, the International Commission of Jurists constituted a Legal Inquiry Committee on Tibet, which was instructed to "examine all such evidence obtained by this Committee and from other sources and to take appropriate action thereon and in particular to determine whether the crime of Genocide—of which there is *prima facie* evidence—is established and, in that case, to initiate such action as is envisaged by the Genocide Convention of 1948 and by the Charter of the United Nations." The ICJ Legal Inquiry Committee on Tibet was composed of eleven international lawyers, headed by Purshottam Trikamdas and including two additional members from India and one each from Ceylon, the Philippines, Ghana, Norway, Burma, Malaya, Thailand and the United Kingdom.[177]

In August 1960 the ICJ published the findings of its Legal Inquiry Committee, entitled *Tibet and the Chinese People's Republic*. The Committee examined the issues of Tibet's legal status, human rights and the question of genocide. The Committee published further documentation, including interviews with the Dalai Lama and transcripts of the oral statements of 55 Tibetan refugees in India. The Committee found from the evidence it examined that Tibetan human rights had been violated in respect to the following:

> The right to life, liberty and security of person was violated by acts of murder, rape and arbitrary imprisonment; torture and cruel, inhuman and degrading treatment were inflicted on the Tibetans on a large scale; arbitrary arrests and detention were carried out; rights of privacy, of home and family life were persistently violated by the forcible transfer of members of the family and by indoctrination turning children against their parents; children from infancy upwards were removed contrary to the wishes of their parents; freedom of movement within, to and from Tibet was denied by large-scale deportations; the voluntary nature of marriage was denied by forcing monks and lamas to marry; the right not to be arbitrarily deprived of private property was violated by the confiscation and compulsory acquisition of private property otherwise than on payment of just compensation and in accordance with the freely expressed wish of the Tibetan people; freedom of thought, conscience and religion were denied by acts of

---

177. *Tibet and the Chinese People's Republic*, 7.

genocide against Buddhists in Tibet and by other systematic acts designed to eradicate religious belief in Tibet; freedom of expression and opinion was denied by the destruction of scriptures, the imprisonment of members of the Mimang group and the cruel punishments inflicted on critics of the regime; the right of free assembly and association was violated by the suppression of the Mimang movement and the prohibition of meetings other than those called by the Chinese; the right to democratic government was denied by the imposition from outside of rule by and under the Chinese Communist Party; the economic, social and cultural rights indispensable for the dignity and free development of the personality of man were denied; the economic resources of Tibet were used to meet the needs of the Chinese; social changes were adverse to the interests of the majority of the Tibetan people; the old culture of Tibet, including its religion, was attacked in an attempt to eradicate it; the right to reasonable working conditions was violated by the exaction of labour under harsh and ill-paid conditions; a reasonable standard of living was denied by the use of the Tibetan economy to meet the needs of the Chinese settling in Tibet; the right to liberal education primarily in accordance with the choice of parents was denied by compulsory indoctrination, sometimes after deportation, in communist philosophy; the Tibetans were not allowed to participate in the cultural life of their own community, a culture which the Chinese have set out to destroy.

Chinese allegations that the Tibetans enjoyed no human rights before the entry of the Chinese were found to be based on distorted and exaggerated accounts of life in Tibet. Accusations against the Tibetan "rebels" of rape, plunder and torture were found in cases of plunder to have been deliberately fabricated and in other cases unworthy of belief for this and other reasons.[178]

In regard to the question of genocide, the Committee concluded that there was sufficient evidence to accuse China of the attempt to destroy Tibetans as a religious group, but insufficient evidence to conclude that China intended to destroy Tibetans as a national or ethnic group. According to the definition of the Genocide Convention, the attempt to destroy a religious community falls under the definition of genocide prohibited by the Convention:

According to the Convention for the Prevention and Punishment of Genocide, which was adopted by the General Assembly of the United Nations in December, 1948, human groups against which genocide is recognized as a crime in international law are national, racial, ethnical (sic)

---

178. Ibid., 4.

and religious. The Committee found that acts of genocide had been committed in Tibet in an attempt to destroy the Tibetans as a religious group, and that such acts are acts of genocide independently of any conventional obligation.[179] The Committee did not find that there was sufficient proof of the destruction of Tibetans as a race, nation or ethnical group as such by methods that can be regarded as genocide in international law. The evidence established four principle facts in relation to genocide: (a) that the Chinese will not permit adherence to and practice of Buddhism in Tibet; (b) that they have systematically set out to eradicate this religious belief in Tibet; (c) that in pursuit of this design they have killed religious figures because their religious belief and practice was an encouragement and example to others; (d) that they have forcibly transferred large numbers of Tibetan children to a Chinese materialist environment in order to prevent them from having a religious upbringing.[180]

In regard to the question of Tibet's legal status, the Committee concluded that:

Tibet was at the very least a de facto independent State when the Agreement on Peaceful Measures in Tibet was signed in 1951, and the repudiation of this agreement by the Tibetan Government in 1959 was found to be fully justified. . . . Tibet demonstrated from 1913 to 1950 the conditions of statehood as generally accepted under international law. In 1950 there was a people and a territory, and a government which functioned in that territory, conducting its own domestic affairs free from any outside authority. From 1913-1950 foreign relations of Tibet were conducted exclusively by the Government of Tibet and countries with whom Tibet had foreign relations are shown by official documents to have treated Tibet in practice as an independent State.

Tibet surrendered her independence by signing in 1951 the Agreement on Peaceful Measures for the Liberation of Tibet. Under that Agreement the Central People's Government of the Chinese People's Republic gave a number of undertakings, among them: promises to maintain the existing political system of Tibet, to maintain the status and functions of the Dalai Lama and the Panchen Lama, to protect freedom of religion and the monas-

---

179. The meaning of this phrase was later expanded by quoting the opinion of the International Court of Justice that "the principles underlying the [Genocide] Convention are principles which are recognized by civilized nations as binding on States, even without any conventional obligations." "Advisory Opinion on Reservations to the Convention on Genocide, *International Court of Justice Reports,* (1951), 15, in Ibid., 12. The meaning of "without any conventional obligations" was that genocide was a crime in international law without regard to any internal or international obligations, or lack of same, undertaken by the offending state.

180. *Tibet and the Chinese People's Republic,* 3.

teries and to refrain from compulsion in the matter of reforms in Tibet. The Committee found that these and other undertakings had been violated by the Chinese People's Republic and that the Government of Tibet was entitled to repudiate the Agreement as it did on March 11, 1959.[181]

The ICJ's purpose was not "to attempt a definitive analysis in terms of modern international law of the exact juridical status of Tibet," but to determine whether the question of Tibet was entirely within the domestic jurisdiction of China or was of legitimate concern to the United Nations. The Committee determined that "Tibet's status was such as to make the Tibetan question one for the legitimate concern of the United Nations even on the restrictive interpretation of matters `essentially within the domestic jurisdiction' of a State."[182]

The ICJ report was regarded by those countries who had sponsored the 1959 United Nations resolution on Tibet as sufficient evidence that China had not, as the UN had demanded, begun to respect the fundamental human rights of the Tibetan people and their distinctive cultural and religious life. On 19 August 1960, shortly after the publication of the ICJ report, Malaya and Thailand requested that "The Question of Tibet" once again be considered by the United Nations General Assembly in its 15th (1960) Session, considering that:

> The fundamental human rights of the Tibetan people continue to be systematically disregarded. The report by the International Commission of Jurists by its Legal Inquiry Committee on Tibet, published on 8 August 1960, gives clear confirmation of a continuing attempt to destroy the traditional and distinctive way of life of the Tibetan people and her religious and cultural autonomy."[183]

The request was accompanied by another letter from the Dalai Lama reiterating Tibet's claim to independence based upon the Thirteenth Dalai Lama's declaration, the 1913 treaty of mutual recognition with Mongolia, the Simla Convention, and Tibet's *de facto* independence between 1912 and 1950. As had been the case with the previous appeal, the Dalai Lama requested UN assistance in the restoration of Tibetan independence. However, the draft resolution submitted by Malaya and Thailand spoke only of Tibetan religious and cultural autonomy, although it did, for the first time, mention the "principle of self-determination of peoples and nations."[184]

---

181. Ibid., 6
182. Ibid.
183. General Assembly Fifteenth Session, 19 August 1960, UN Doc. A/4444, in *Tibet in the United Nations*, 231.
184. Ibid., 232.

In accordance with UN rules, the debate on the item, "The Question of Tibet," was initiated by three countries speaking in favor of inclusion and three against. This debate took place on 10 October 1960. New Zealand, El Salvador and Ireland spoke in favor and Indonesia, the Soviet Union and Romania spoke against. Despite the burgeoning Sino-Soviet split, the Soviet Union maintained socialist solidarity with the PRC, reiterating the Chinese position that Tibet was an internal affair of the PRC and that the "so-called Tibet question" was nothing more than an attempt to poison the international atmosphere by the revival of Cold War issues. The Soviet Union denied that there were any violations of human rights in Tibet; only the ambitions of capitalist imperialism in relation to Tibet were being denied (socialist states being incapable of imperialism), while in reality Tibet had achieved genuine human rights under Chinese rule. This line was repeated almost verbatim by Romania.[185]

The position of those countries in favor of UN debate on the Tibet issue was that the denial of fundamental human rights transcended the prohibition against violation of a state's territorial integrity and its rights of domestic jurisdiction. El Salvador spoke forcefully in favor, reminding other countries that it had been the only country to take up the Tibetan appeal in 1950, but, "unfortunately, it was the view of the United Kingdom and India that prevailed."[186] El Salvador reminded the General Assembly members that discussion of an issue in the UN was not equivalent to actual intervention in the domestic affairs of any state and that the General Assembly had already, in 1959, "pronounced itself to the effect that it was competent to discuss the question of Tibet."

El Salvador further refuted the contention of the Soviet Union that discussion of Tibet at the UN was intended to fan the flames of the Cold War; on the contrary, the El Salvador delegate said, only the Soviet Union and its satellite states had spoken in antagonistic terms against other states in the General Assembly. Chinese actions against Tibet and Soviet support for those actions, not UN debate on the issue, were the cause of increased world tension. Furthermore, El Salvador held that the question of Tibet had not ceased just because China had succeeded in imposing its rule upon Tibet: "The question of Tibet has not finally been settled simply because Communist China has succeeded in achieving domination over the small country of Tibet, nor has the question of Hungary been concluded because of the circumstances that prevail in that country."[187]

Ireland also refuted the contention of the Soviet Union and the PRC that Tibet was entirely an internal affair of China, maintaining that this was,

---

185. Ibid., 242, 247.
186. Ibid., 244.
187. Ibid., 247.

A line of argument that all of us who have lived under foreign rule have rejected in relation to ourselves; a line of argument that would have kept half the nations in this Assembly in servitude forever and prevented the world from ever discussing our condition. Looking around this Assembly, and looking at my own delegation, I think how many benches would be empty here in this hall if it had always been agreed that when a small nation or a small people fell into the grip of a major Power, no one could ever raise their case here; that once they were a subject nation, they must always remain a subject nation.

Tibet has fallen into the hands of the Chinese People's Republic for the last few years. For thousands of years, or for a couple of thousand of years at any rate, it was as free and as fully in control of its own affairs as any nation in this Assembly, and a thousand times more free to look after its own affairs than many of the nations here.[188]

The vote on the inclusion of the item, "The Question of Tibet," was 49 in favor, 13 opposed and 35 abstaining. Asian states voting in favor included Japan, New Zealand, Australia, Philippines, Pakistan, Thailand, Nationalist China and the Federation of Malaya. Those states voting against were exclusively members of the Soviet bloc, with the addition of Indonesia, Mali and Guinea. Abstentions among Asian states included India, Nepal, Afghanistan, Laos, Burma, and Ceylon; all but Ceylon shared borders with the PRC. Eventually, the Tibet issue was not discussed in the General Assembly 15th Session (1960) due to time constraints.[189]

At the General Assembly's 16th Session (1961) on 18 August 1961, Malaya and Thailand again brought up the Tibet issue, and were joined by Ireland and El Salvador in submitting a draft resolution on Tibet. The item was brought up for discussion on 26 September 1961. Indonesia and the Soviet Union again spoke against inclusion, while Japan and Malaya spoke in favor. Malaya reiterated its position that Tibet should be discussed despite the contention that to do so would inflame Cold War tensions:

It has been alleged that Tibet is a dead issue. I see no logic in this. To some nations, perhaps, the initial shock of the outrage perpetrated against the Tibetan people may have worn off, but this does not make Tibet a dead issue. The outrage still continues and the people of Tibet are still deprived of their fundamental human rights and freedoms, and, so long as this state of affairs continues, the General Assembly has as much right to deal with the issue now as it had to deal with the issue in 1959.[190]

---

188. Ibid ., 251.
189. Ibid., 252.
190. General Assembly Sixteenth Session, 26 September 1961, in *Tibet in the United Nations*, 256.

The item, "Question of Tibet," as well as the draft resolution submitted by Malaya, Thailand, Ireland and El Salvador, was placed on the agenda of the General Assembly by a vote of 48 in favor, 14 opposed and 35 abstaining. Once again, those opposed were confined to the Soviet bloc (Cuba now included), with the addition of Indonesia and Guinea. Those Asian states abstaining were the same as before with the exceptions that Laos was now in favor while Afghanistan and Burma did not vote.

The Tibet issue came up for discussion on the General Assembly's agenda on 19 December 1961. The representative of Malaya, responding to allegations that his delegation was "aggravating the cold war," or was "acting at the instigation of others," replied that "ironically enough, these criticisms . . . came from those very quarters who made loud protestations about keeping cold war bitterness out of the Assembly." As to the charge of outside instigation, he stated that it had been one of the cornerstones of the policy of his government "to give its full and unstinted support to the struggle of subject peoples for freedom from colonialism in all its forms and manifestations."[191] The Malayan delegate made a further appeal for consideration of the Tibetan issue:

> Ever since the occupation of Tibet in 1950 by the armed forces of the People's Republic of China, an occupation ironically described by the Chinese authorities as a "peaceful liberation," Tibet has known no peace and the Tibetan people no freedom. Their religion and culture, which for centuries have identified them as a distinctive people with a character and personality of their own, were forcibly and systematically uprooted. Thousands of Tibetans who had the courage to resist the conquerors in defence of their liberty and freedom were mercilessly liquidated. Thousands more, many of whom were Buddhist priests, were conscripted for forced labor. And innocent Tibetan children were separated from their families and deported to China on a massive scale. All these measures were part of a grand policy of the People's Republic of China designed to destroy the Tibetan people as a religious community with a distinct cultural identity of their own and to incorporate Tibet with China.[192]

These sentiments, and the draft resolution on Tibet, were seconded by El Salvador, Ireland, Thailand, New Zealand (speaking also for Australia), the United Kingdom, Nationalist China and the United States. All those in favor quoted evidence from the two ICJ reports. Britain, having abstained in 1959, now supported the resolution on Tibet, but main-

---

191. General Assembly Sixteenth Session, 19 December 1961, in Ibid., 261.
192. Ibid.

tained its traditional (but by now archaic and unrealistic) policy of support for Tibetan autonomy under Chinese suzerainty.[193]

Those states speaking in opposition were the Soviet Union, Albania and Czechoslovakia. The Soviet Union and its allies made the accusation that the International Commission of Jurists was funded by "influential reactionary circles in the United States" and the US Central Intelligence Agency, who were also the instigators of all other criticism of Chinese actions in Tibet. The Soviet Union also accused the CIA of supporting Tibetan resistance against China and of operating a special training center for Tibetans in the US. In addition, the USSR accused Malaya of "assuming the role of an attorney for the United States State Department."[194]

The resolution on Tibet was adopted by a vote of 56 in favor, 11 opposed and 29 abstaining. Those in favor included most of the new members of the UN. Asian states in favor were Malaya, Laos, Nationalist China, Australia, New Zealand, Thailand and Japan. Those states opposed were confined to the Soviet Union, its two internal republics, Byelorussia and Ukraine, and its satellites, now including Cuba and Mongolia. Those Asian states abstaining once again included China's neighbors, India, Nepal, Pakistan, Afghanistan, Burma and Cambodia, as well as Ceylon. Indonesia was now abstaining. The resolution as adopted was as follows:

> Recalling its resolution 1353 (XIV) of 21 October 1959 on the question of Tibet,
>
> Gravely concerned at the continuation of events in Tibet including the violation of fundamental human rights of the Tibetan people, suppression of their distinctive cultural and religious life which they have traditionally enjoyed,
>
> Noting with deep anxiety the severe hardships which these events have inflicted on the Tibetan people as evidenced by the large-scale exodus of Tibetan refugees to the neighbouring countries,
>
> Considering that these events violate fundamental human rights and freedoms set out in the Charter of the United Nations and the Universal Declaration of Human Rights, including the principle of self-determination of the peoples and nations, and have the deplorable effect of increasing international tension and embittering relations between peoples,

---

193. Ibid., 307.

194. Ibid., 293, 301. The US delegate replied that the members of the ICJ Legal Inquiry Committee were "eleven independent, fair-minded jurists of unimpeachable integrity and impartiality." Ibid., 273.

1. Reaffirms its conviction that respect for the principles of the Charter and of the Universal Declaration of Human Rights is essential for the evolution of a peaceful world order based on the rule of law;

2. Solemnly renews its call for the cessation of practices which deprive the Tibetan people of their fundamental human rights and freedoms including their right to self-determination;

3. Expresses the hope that member states will make all possible efforts as appropriate toward achieving the purpose of the present resolution.[195]

Despite having, for the first time, been accused of violating Tibetans' right to self-determination, China did not react to the 1960-61 UN debate on Tibet with a flurry of propaganda as had been the case in late 1959. In fact, Chinese propaganda on Tibet virtually ceased after the end of 1959, with the exception of two reports by the Panchen Lama, one in January 1961 and one in October 1961. B.N. Mullik, the then head of Indian Intelligence, suggests that the PRC at that time adopted a semi-isolationist policy, considering its disputes with both the US and the Soviet Union, its bad relations with India and many Asian states, and its failure to gain admission to the UN.[196]

Despite its international isolation, the PRC found that American and UN opposition to its role in Tibet was ineffective as long as China was not a member of the UN and did not have to defend itself there. The PRC had gained total and undisputed control over Tibet. International criticism of China's role in Tibet was primarily confined to questions of human rights, not the issue of the legitimacy of Chinese sovereignty over Tibet. The PRC may therefore have decided that its best policy was to consolidate its control quietly and implement its changes in Tibet with as little publicity as possible. Even many Chinese must have realized that the "liberation" of Tibet had not turned out as expected; the best policy from now on might be to remove the Tibet issue from international scrutiny. In addition, China's attention was now occupied by an escalation of the border dispute with India, an issue that obviously resulted from the Chinese occupation of Tibet, but one which China wished to disassociate from Tibet.

---

195. Question of Tibet, Resolution of the General Assembly Sixteenth Session (1961), 20 December 1961, in Ibid., 311.
196. Mullik, *My Years with Nehru*, 290.

Sino-Indian Border War[197]

The PRC construed the border issue as exclusively a Sino-Indian affair, having nothing to do with the Chinese occupation of Tibet. China attempted to characterize the issue as one of a historic, if undemarcated, "traditional customary boundary line" that had "taken shape on the basis of the extent of each side's administrative jurisdiction in the long course of time during which the two peoples lived together in peace." According to the PRC, this peace had been disturbed only by the intrigues of British imperialism.[198] The Chinese argument attempted to obscure the fact that there was no "traditional" border between the Indian and Chinese peoples before the Chinese conquest of Tibet in 1950. Both China and India were well aware that it was the imposition of Chinese control over Tibet after 1950 that had created for the first time a frontier between directly administered Chinese territory and that of India. The source of Indian apprehension was the transformation of India's formerly peaceful border with Tibet into a border with a revolutionary Chinese state apparently intent upon exporting its form of "liberation."

In his 1962 letter to leaders of Asian and African countries, Chou En-lai accused India of having inherited the British imperialists' "covetous desires" towards the "Tibet region of China" and of having "persisted in regarding Tibet as India's sphere of influence, or sought at least to transform it into a buffer zone between China and India." He accused India of having attempted to prevent Chinese control in Tibet and of initiating the current border conflict: "The Indian Government tried its best to obstruct the peaceful liberation of Tibet in 1950. When these attempts proved of no avail, India pressed forward in an all-out advance on the illegal McMahon Line in the eastern sector of the border and completely occupied China's territory south of the illegal line and north of the traditional customary line."[199] Chou also accused India of having had a hand in the 1959 revolt: "In March 1959 a rebellion of serf-owners broke out in the Tibet region of China. The Indian Government not only aided and abetted this rebellion, but gave refuge to the remnant rebels after the rebellion had been put down, and connived in their anti-Chinese political activities in India."[200]

Indian public opinion was by this time convinced that the uninhabited Aksai Chin was indisputably Indian territory; India was therefore

---

197. Unless otherwise noted, the account of the Sino-Indian border war is taken from B.N. Mullik, *My Years with Nehru: The Chinese Betrayal*, and Neville Maxwell, *India's China War*.

198. *Premier Chou En-lai's Letter on the Sino-Indian Boundary Question*, 3.

199. Ibid., 7.

200. Ibid., 9.

unprepared to make the otherwise reasonable compromise of an exchange of the Aksai Chin for NEFA. India refused to accept Chinese proposals for negotiations until Chinese forces had withdrawn from all "Indian" territory in the Aksai Chin. China attempted to bring India to negotiate by unilaterally abandoning patrolling (but not its numerous outposts) in the Aksai Chin area. In late 1961, in response to China's halting of border patrols, India adopted a "forward policy" of penetrating into the Aksai Chin area, intended to establish an Indian presence there. India established posts within sight of Chinese posts or in positions intended to cut Chinese posts off from their lines of supply. Indian and Chinese troops were thereafter involved in numerous clashes. In addition, India refused to renew the 1954 Sino-Indian Panchshila agreement, which was due to expire on 29 April 1962, despite Chinese proposals for renewal, because Indian trade with Tibet, the ostensible subject of the agreement, had virtually ceased due to Chinese restrictions.

In the east, in NEFA, India also pursued its "forward policy," moving military posts up to the actual border. In one area, at the point of conjunction of the Bhutanese, Indian and Tibetan borders, the Indian Army had already in 1959 crossed the McMahon Line in order to create a more defensible frontier along a ridge line. Indian rationalizations for this move were that McMahon had no doubt intended to draw his line along the ridge. This move resulted in a clash with the Chinese at the time. When in June 1962 Indian troops again moved into positions in this area, the Chinese immediately reacted. On 8 September Chinese troops took up positions surrounding the Indian post, a move interpreted in India as a Chinese violation of India's frontier. India then made the decision to expel the Chinese forces, a move dictated largely by Indian public opinion rather than Indian military capabilities. Chinese forces were within three hours of a roadhead on the Tibetan side and were well-positioned and supplied, while Indian troops were several days trek from the nearest Indian roadhead and their overall logistical supply situation was extremely tenuous.

Despite India's military disadvantage, political considerations dictated that India must "expel" the Chinese troops from what the Indian public had been led to believe was Indian territory. Indian troops therefore attacked the Chinese post on 10 October. China responded on 20 October with an attack in force all along the frontier in the east as well as in the west in the Aksai Chin, quickly overrunning Indian positions on all fronts. Within the next month Chinese forces expelled the Indians from the Aksai Chin and moved south in NEFA to the line they had claimed as the border, the former "inner line" of British Indian administration. On 21 November China announced a unilateral cease-fire and withdrawal to the McMahon Line in the east (retaining their positions in the Aksai Chin) and renewed its call for negotiations.

The Sino-Indian border war was a military humiliation for India; China gained possession of the Aksai Chin and a propaganda victory due to the magnanimous return of the NEFA territory to India.[201] China was nevertheless portrayed as the aggressor in the conflict as far as international opinion was concerned. Western media had all along characterized China as the aggressor and India as the innocent victim because of China's confrontational international politics. International unease about Chinese domestic policies, including its policy in Tibet, may also have played a role. China was unable to disguise the fact that its aggression against Tibet was the ultimate source of its conflict with India.

During the course of the conflict, while Chinese forces were rapidly moving south without opposition from the Indian Army, India panicked and requested immediate military assistance from Britain and the United States. Both responded with alacrity, the Americans in particular initiating a massive airlift of military equipment to India. The results of the conflict were that China was branded the aggressor and further isolated internationally, the Sino-Soviet split was widened due to a lack of Soviet diplomatic support for China, India moved into closer relations with China's most adamant foe, the United States, and the era of *Hindi Chini Bhai Bhai* ("India and China are brothers") was ended. The needs of the PLA during the conflict further exacerbated Tibetan food shortages and increased forced labor requirements. Tibetans were conscripted to carry supplies to PLA units on the border. The border war also revealed to the Chinese that they could not trust the Tibetans to support China in a conflict with India.[202]

Purge of the Panchen Lama

The Chinese program for gaining the allegiance of Tibetans, or at least of the Tibetan "serfs and slaves," was dependent upon increases in production and more equal distribution of production in order to demonstrate the superiority of the socialist system. The coincidence of democ-

---

201. Nevertheless, China continues to indicate the NEFA area as Chinese territory on all maps published in China. India has, similarly, continued to claim the Aksai Chin and indicate it as Indian territory on maps published in India and has even gone to the extent of altering borders with watercolors on maps published in other countries and distributed in India.

202. B.N. Mullik reports that Indian Intelligence was in possession of a PLA document on the tactics of warfare on the Tibetan plateau, which revealed that the Chinese regarded Tibetans as potential enemies in any conflict with India. Mullik, *My Years with Nehru*, 294.

ratic reforms in Tibet with the post-Great Leap famine, however, meant that even those favored by the communist system had the greatest portion of their food production confiscated in order to feed the Chinese. By 1961 the last year of the Chinese famine, even the most collaborationist Tibetans could not ignore the fact that Chinese rule in Tibet had produced not a socialist paradise but only oppression and suffering. Even those Tibetans most dependent upon or supportive of Chinese ideologies and policies were disillusioned by the abrogation of the promise of self-rule for Tibetans and the lack of correspondence between Chinese promises and the reality in Tibet.

Tibetans continued to be arrested and imprisoned for the slightest expression of discontent with Chinese rule. "Democratic reforms" and a process of "re-checking of democratic reforms" constantly revealed more Tibetan "reactionaries" and "counterrevolutionaries." Other Tibetans were determined by forever more precise and artificial class divisions to have somehow been "exploiters." By the end of 1961 even the Panchen Lama, previously the most sycophantic loyalist (if his public statements are to be believed), was expressing discontent with the results of Chinese policies.

The turning point in the Panchen Lama's sympathies can be dated to 1961 when he returned to Tibet after delivering his report, "Tibet in 1960," to the National People's Congress in Peking. In this report, which summed up the results of the year, the Panchen reported that Tibet, "under the brilliant and correct leadership of the Central Committee of the Chinese Communist Party and Chairman Mao Tse-tung," had continued to advance in the movement to "build socialism, the big leap forward and people's communes." The Panchen Lama described "democratic reforms" in monasteries as the achievement of "genuine freedom of religious belief," in which "the political rights of the broad masses of lamas and nuns and their right to freedom of religious belief have been safeguarded." The patriotism and the political understanding of "patriotic and law-abiding people in religious circles" had also been enhanced, he said, and they "warmly support the Party's policy on freedom of religious belief and are grateful for the concern and care the Party and the People's Government have shown to them."[203]

The Panchen revealed the existence of "a handful of the most reactionary serf-owners and their agents who are not reconciled to the elimination of feudal serfdom," and that the "sabotaging activities of counterrevolutionary elements are also rather wild." Nevertheless, he said, these reactionaries and counterrevolutionaries were being opposed by the

---

203. Panchen Erdeni, "Tibet in 1960," *Peking Review*, 13 January 1961, 16.

broad masses of the labouring people whose class consciousness had been enhanced by democratic reforms.[204] The Panchen also announced a campaign to scrutinize Tibetan cadres in regard to their ideological stand.[205]

The Panchen reported that 15,000 mutual aid teams, "embracing more than 100,000 peasant households," had been organized in agricultural areas in the winter of 1959 and spring of 1960, and that 10,400 irrigation ditches and 1,500 reservoirs and ponds were constructed, resulting in a 15 percent increase in the harvest over that of 1959. The Panchen credited this increase to "the inevitable result of the heightened class consciousness and enthusiasm for production among the broad masses of peasants who have become masters of their land and the new society after the implementation of democratic reform."[206] The Panchen's report cited numerous instances of the irrational Tibetan way of doing things that had been vastly improved with the fraternal assistance of their "big brothers," the Han, whose continual assistance was essential if Tibet were to progress.[207]

The Panchen concluded by stating that, while Tibetans had politically and economically benefitted from democratic reforms, they remained in need of a similar "turning over" in the cultural field. This would soon be accomplished by means of schools devoted to the principle of "education serving proletarian politics" and by opera and dance troupes whose programs would "expose and accuse the feudal serf system and the crimes committed by the three types of feudal owners, praise the great Communist Party of China and Chairman Mao, our great leader, and sing of the new life." As the Panchen commented, "The groans of misery can no longer be heard today in the wide countryside and the towns of Tibet; everywhere there is song and a joyful new atmosphere."[208]

However, when the Panchen Lama returned to Tibet, he found that in his absence his own monastery, Tashilhunpo, had undergone "democratic reforms," during which, "through voluntary withdrawal, under the

---

204. Ibid., 17.

205. Obviously, the Party was having a problem with the ideological indoctrination of Tibetan cadres. The Panchen reported that 3,000 young Tibetans sent in 1957 to the Hsienyang Tibetan Nationalities Institute near Sian had been returned in 1959 and 1960. Ibid., 20. In 1962 many of the returned Tibetan students were transferred to lower level rural positions or directly to agricultural production, ostensibly as part of a program to alleviate food shortages all over China by transferring cadres to agricultural production. However, Tibetan cadres regard this move as due to Chinese mistrust of Tibetan cadres and as serving their goal of retaining all power in their own hands. Gashi, *New Tibet*, 89.

206. Panchen Erdeni, "Tibet in 1960," 17.

207. Ibid., 20.

208. Ibid., 21.

policy of religious freedom," the monk population had been cut in half, from approximately 4,000 monks to 1,980.[209] After this time, the Panchen Lama began to devote himself to the preservation of Tibet's religious heritage, now undeniably under assault; he took measures to repair Lhasa's temples and monasteries and save their treasures, moving many artifacts from the now depopulated Drepung, Sera and Ganden to the Lhasa Jokhang. He also began a series of public religious sermons, attended sometimes by several thousand people, during which he instructed Tibetans to cooperate with the Chinese and accept their assistance, but emphasized that, as Mao himself had instructed, Tibetans had to develop and govern Tibet themselves. He assured Tibetans that CCP nationalities policy allowed religious freedom and encouraged them to practice their religion. He also offered prayers for the health of the Dalai Lama and for his eventual return to Tibet.[210] On 9 July 1961 the Panchen's "government," the Panchen Kanpo Lija Committee, was dissolved by the Chinese State Council because it had "fulfilled its historical purpose."[211]

The Panchen travelled to Peking again at the end of 1961 for the annual meeting of the National People's Congress. There, despite his growing disillusionment with Chinese policies in Tibet, he delivered a speech on 17 October in which he reported "tremendous achievements of the past year." The major accomplishment was that "over 90 per cent of the peasant households in Tibet's rural areas are now organized on a voluntary basis according to the principle of mutual benefit." Schools had been established to "do more than give the people a general education; they also help to explain the Communist Party's policies and enhance the people's political consciousness." Monks and nuns were reported to have "enhanced their political understanding as a result of the democratic reforms." The Panchen also reported that "democratic elections" for local people's congresses had been held in the past year. These were intended to "create conditions for the convening of the regional people's congress-

---

209. Israel Epstein, *Tibet Transformed* (Beijing: New World Press, 1983), 428. According to information received by the Tibetan Government in Exile in India, Tashilhunpo's monks were accused of keeping the portrait of the Dalai Lama and praying for his long life, praying for the extermination of the Chinese Communists, disfiguring the portraits of Mao Tsetung, abusing those Tibetans serving the Chinese, and making statements harmful to the Chinese. *Facts About Tibet, 1961-1965* (New Delhi: Bureau of His Holiness the Dalai Lama, 1966), 9.

210. Gashi, *New Tibet*, 84; Kunsang Paljor, *Tibet: The Undying Flame* (Dharamsala: Information and Publicity Office of His Holiness the Dalai Lama, 1977), 25.

211. Peter Cheng, *A Chronology of the People's Republic of China* (Totowa, New Jersey: Littlefield, Adams, 1972), 133. Presumably, its "historical purpose" was to create exploitable regional and political divisions within Tibet, and, having fulfilled this, it was no longer needed.

es and the formal establishment of the Tibet Autonomous Region in the future."[212]

However, in contrast to his public report to the NPC, the Panchen Lama revealed his apprehensions about the course of Chinese policies in Tibet in a written report to Mao. The Panchen's report, thereafter referred to as the "70,000 character report,"[213] has never been publicly released, but something of its content was revealed much later, in 1987, by the Panchen himself.[214] The Panchen stated that he had complained to Mao that, after the Lhasa revolt, "The authorities did not make any distinction between those guilty and not guilty of participation in the disturbances. People were arrested and jailed indiscriminately." He also complained that loyal aristocrats had been arrested and imprisoned just for the crime of upper class status; others of all classes had been persecuted for having innocently offered hospitality to those later accused of having been rebels or to the Dalai Lama during his flight. Tibetan lamas and monks, he said, had experienced "untold sufferings." The Panchen revealed that his own family members had been subjected to *thamzing*. He mentioned that a large number of Chinese cadres had been sent to Tibet in 1959, after which, "the leftist influence became firmly rooted in Tibet. Those cadres immediately started the commune system, long before the democratic reforms were completed."[215]

The Panchen also revealed some estimates on the numbers of Tibetans imprisoned and killed:

In my 70,000 character petition, I mentioned that about five per cent of the population had been imprisoned. According to my information at the time, it was between 10 to 15 per cent. But I did not have the courage to state such a huge figure. I would have died under Thamzing if I had stated the real figure... In Qinghai [Chinghai], for example, there are between one to three or four thousand villages and towns, each having between three to four thousand families with four to five thousand people. From each town and village, about 800 to 1000 people were imprisoned. Out of this, at least 300 to 400 of them died in prison. This means almost half the prison population perished.[216]

---

212. Panchen Erdeni, "Tibet Forges Ahead," *Peking Review*, 27 October 1961, 9.

213. The report was originally in Tibetan, its informal title, "70,000 character report," refers to its length in Chinese translation. Jigme Ngapo, personal communication, Washington, April 1996.

214. *The Panchen Lama Speaks: Text of the Panchen Lama's Address to the TAR Standing Committee Meeting of the National People's Congress held in Peking on 28 March 1987* (Dharamsala: Department of Information and International Relations, Central Tibetan Administration of His Holiness the Dalai Lama, 1991).

215. Ibid., 9.

216. Ibid., 14. The Panchen's estimate corresponds, at least in magnitude, to the Tibetan Government in Exile's estimate of 173,000 deaths in prisons and labor camps.

In response to the Panchen's criticisms (even though they were not publicly revealed), the Chinese mounted a propaganda campaign to discredit him; the Panchen was thereafter characterized as a "rock on the road to socialism." After his return to Lhasa in early 1962, the Chinese demanded that the Panchen denounce the Dalai Lama and assume the Dalai Lama's place as head of the PCTAR. The Panchen refused, after which his public appearances ceased and his public role was diminished. The Panchen was not yet removed from his political position, but his disaffection revealed to the Chinese that they could not trust any Tibetan collaborators. As Chinese hopes to win the genuine loyalty of Tibetans faded, they gradually abandoned the pretense that Tibet would now or in the future exercise autonomy under a Tibetan administration. The disaffection of the Panchen and many Tibetan cadres during this time served to convince the Chinese that Tibet would remain securely within the Chinese state only under direct Chinese military control and political administration.

The Dalai Lama's activities in India tended to confirm the Chinese in this opinion. In his 10 March 1963 speech in Dharamsala commemorating the 1959 revolt, the Dalai Lama announced the promulgation of a Tibetan democratic constitution applicable to Tibetans in exile, and potentially to those within Tibet as well, once Tibet was freed from Chinese oppression.[217] The Dalai Lama's proclamation became known within Tibet, encouraging Tibetans that the Dalai Lama was working on their behalf. China accused India of a "serious provocation" in allowing the publication of this statement; India was also accused of having "never been reconciled to China's exercise of sovereignty in China's own territory Tibet."[218]

---

217. "Statement of His Holiness the Dalai Lama on the 4th Anniversary of the Tibetan People's National Uprising Day of 10th March 1959," 10 March 1963, in *The Collected Statements, Articles, and Interviews of His Holiness the Dalai Lama* (Dharamsala: Information Office of His Holiness the Dalai Lama, 1982), 10. The Tibetan Constitution specified that the Tibetan Government would continue to be headed by the Dalai Lama, assisted by a *Kashag*, or council of ministers, appointed by the Dalai Lama. Legislative functions would be carried out by a National Assembly, 75 percent of whose members would be directly elected, 10 percent elected by monasteries, 10 percent elected by regional or district councils, and 5 percent appointed by the Dalai Lama. The Constitution provided for an independent judiciary and the right to trial by law. A Council of Regency composed of three members, one of whom was to be a monastic representative, was to be elected by the National Assembly during the absence or minority of a Dalai Lama. Tibetans were guaranteed all rights consistent with the Universal Declaration of Human Rights. All land was to be the property of the state, which the state would make available on the payment of rent. Tibet also renounced war as an instrument of policy. "Constitution of Tibet," in *Tibet 1950-67*, 532.

218. "Chinese Foreign Ministry Note Protests Against Use of Tibetan Rebel Bandits by Indian Government for Interfering China's Internal Affairs," *NCNA*, 29 March 1963, in *Tibet 1950-67*, 560.

In 1964 the Chinese again protested to the Indian Government for allowing the publication of the Dalai Lama's 10 March 1964 statement and, further, for allowing him to send representatives to other countries (such as Switzerland, where some 300 Tibetans had been resettled) and allowing him to make his first trip outside India (a tour of Asian Buddhist countries). China once again accused India of having "engineered and supported" the 1959 revolt and, now, of "openly instigating the Dalai Lama to operate outside India." China warned India to "fulfill its past promise [to not allow the Dalai Lama to engage in any political activities], observe the minimum principles guiding international relations and immediately stop all interference in China's internal affairs."[219]

In 1964 at the August meeting of the PCTAR the Panchen was finally purged as an "obstacle to socialism." Acting on Chinese instructions, several Tibetan activists criticized the Panchen Lama, after which the Chinese suggested that the Panchen should be subjected to *thamzing* to ascertain the extent of his "crimes." He was subjected to 17 days of struggle sessions in Lhasa, during which Tibetan activists were manipulated to criticize the Panchen on cue. The Panchen was accused of being a "reactionary enemy of the State" and a secret supporter of the Dalai Lama. The Panchen was finally accused of crimes that included "attempted restoration of serfdom," murder, planning to launch a guerilla war against the State, illicitly cohabiting with women, "criticizing and opposing China in a 70,000 character document," "declaring open support for the Dalai Lama and misleading the masses," and "theft and plunder of images and other property from monasteries."[220]

The Panchen Lama was arrested and taken to Peking, where he was subjected to further struggle sessions by Tibetan students at the Minority Nationalities Institute. The Panchen was imprisoned in Peking for the next nine years and eight months, during which time he was tortured and subjected to solitary confinement. He was released from prison in 1974 and confined under house arrest until his rehabilitation in 1978. The Panchen was allowed to return to Lhasa only in July 1982, still partially paralyzed on one side of his body from having been forced to lie continually on one side, facing his prison cell door (a common regimen in PRC prisons). In 1987 the Panchen revealed that he was accused by "some leaders" in 1964 of "turning against the motherland" and "trying to start

---

219. Ibid., 561; "Another Revelation of Indian Expansionism," *Peking Review,* 3 April 1964, in *Tibet 1950-67,* 562.

220. Paljor, *Tibet: The Undying Flame,* 29. The basis for the last charge was apparently the Panchen's attempts to save some of the treasures of Ganden, Sera and Drepung by moving them to the Jokhang.

a secessionist rebellion." These leaders (presumably Mao) warned: "Even if the whole of the Tibetan population is armed, it will only make over 3 million people. We are not scared of this." The Panchen Lama said that "On hearing this, I felt very sad and realized how it is to be without freedom."[221]

Tibet's Final Appeal to the United Nations

In late 1964 the International Commission of Jurists conducted interviews in India with recently arrived refugees and published a report that revealed that systematic abuse of Tibetans' fundamental human rights continued unabated.[222] In response to the ICJ report and another appeal from the Dalai Lama, the issue of Tibet was reintroduced at the United Nations. El Salvador, Ireland, Malaysia, Malta, Nicaragua, Philippines and Thailand introduced a draft resolution in August 1965, essentially repeating the language of the previous (1959 and 1961) resolutions on Tibet.

The debate was, as usual, characterized by an ideological split along Cold War lines. Although the sponsors attempted to disassociate the Tibetan situation from Cold War issues, that proved impossible since the Socialist bloc again accused "United States imperialism" of raising the "nonexistent issue of Tibet." The Philippines, India, Ireland, Nationalist China, New Zealand, El Salvador, Malta, Guatemala, United States, Nicaragua, Australia, Costa Rica, Malaysia and Norway spoke in favor of the resolution. Albania, Romania, Soviet Union, Hungary, Algeria, Poland, Czechoslovakia, Congo, Cuba, Guinea and Bulgaria spoke against.[223]

Although most of the sponsors stated that they did not wish to raise ideological or political issues, and intended to confine themselves to the question of fundamental human rights, the Philippines representative made a forceful statement challenging both China's claim to rule over Tibet and the nature of communist "national liberation" movements. The Philippines representative cited recent testimony from refugees collected by the ICJ as evidence that "the Chinese Communist plan to destroy the distinctive character of the Tibetan nation is nearing completion." China's claim to have liberated Tibet from imperialism was also challenged:

---

221. *The Panchen Lama Speaks*, 1, 14.

222. *Bulletin of the International Commission of Jurists*, no. 21, (December 1964), 42-48.

223. United Nations General Assembly, Twentieth Session, 14 December 1965, (A/PV/1394), in GAOR, Twentieth Session (New York: United Nations, 1967), 1.

To this day, the Chinese Communists have not identified the "aggressive imperialist forces" in Tibet. Is it any wonder that people of many emerging countries of Asia, Africa and Latin America have come to look with deep suspicion on what have been euphemistically described as "movements of national liberation"? The phrase, sacred in the memory of freedom fighters everywhere, has been abused for selfish ideological reasons. The record of the Chinese Communist occupation of Tibet conforms to the worst type of imperialism and colonialism, past or present.[224]

The Philippines representative maintained that the political and human rights aspects of the Tibetan question were linked, and that "unless the political problem is solved, the human situation will be extremely difficult to alleviate." Because Tibetans were a separate people having their own distinct culture, language and religion, as well as a recent history of independence of China, political factors reinforced human rights considerations: "If the people of Tibet are entitled as members of the human family to the protection of the Charter and the Universal Declaration of Human Rights, then they are doubly entitled to such protection by reason of their status as an independent nation."[225]

India for the first time spoke in favor of a UN resolution on Tibet, a shift in position clearly due to the 1962 border war. India explained that its former opposition to discussion of Tibet at the UN in 1950 was due to its "hope for a peaceful solution," and in 1959 due to its "hope against hope that wiser counsel would prevail among the Chinese"; however, "the passage of time has completely belied our hopes." India now supported "fully and wholeheartedly, the cause of the people of Tibet."[226]

India claimed that China had violated its guarantee to allow Tibetan autonomy and had turned Tibet into a base for aggression against the northern frontiers of India. The Indian representative revealed that India was receiving considerable information about conditions in Tibet from refugees, some 50,000 of whom were said to have reached India. In particular, it was claimed that the Chinese had gained control of the Tibetan food supply, which was diverted to feed their own army and administrators while Tibetans had to subsist on what little remained. India also denounced "the campaign to dispossess Tibetan peasants of their land and to distribute their property [which] is also being accelerated with the definition of what precisely constitutes feudal elements being expanded, from time to time, to cover a wider and wider range of peasants. In fact, these so-called land reforms are being used by the Chinese Government

---

224. Ibid., 3.
225. Ibid., 4.
226. Ibid., 6.

to advance its own political purpose and to turn the Tibetan peasants into slaves of its system."[227]

Ireland also brought up the issue of Tibet's political status, stating that Tibet could rightly claim to have been an independent country in the past. The periods during which Tibet acknowledged Chinese suzerainty could not be held to constitute a denial of its right to independence, since to do so would be to deny the claim to independence of many members of the United Nations who had been, at one time or another, under foreign domination. Ireland also belittled those who denied that Tibetans were suffering any violations of their human rights and who had offered the Panchen Lama's testimony to bolster their claim in the past, but who were now silent on the status of the Panchen and had ceased to quote his testimony.[228]

The Nationalist Chinese delegate did not question Tibet's status as part of China but claimed that the issue was "the result of the fact that an inhuman, oppressive and tyrannical communist regime has been imposed on the mainland of China." The Nationalist government had also received information on the food situation in Tibet, and described shortages as due to "large scale confiscation of food and livestock . . . to feed the army of occupation and the large volume of civilian Chinese who have settled in Tibet, and also to send to China to meet shortages there." The Nationalists also revealed that they were providing support for Tibetan resistance and refugees, some of whom had settled in Taiwan, and would continue to do so.[229]

The remaining delegations supporting the Tibet resolution confined their remarks to the human rights issue. Malaysia once again spoke forcefully and eloquently in support, refuting the charge that it was acting on any but humanitarian interests, and making the case that human rights violations were a legitimate issue for UN discussion. The Malaysian representative pointed out that all people everywhere were under the domestic jurisdiction of some country; thus, if domestic jurisdiction were to be invoked in every case, then UN human rights resolutions would be meaningless. The Malaysian delegate, describing the Chinese system in Tibet as a "new serfdom," had little hope that a UN resolution would move the Chinese to alleviate conditions for Tibetans, but thought it the moral duty of the international community to "lift the pall of darkness" over Tibet, even if ever so little, in order to "bring some comfort to an

---

227. Ibid.
228. Ibid., 9.
229. Ibid., 11.

ancient people" whose rights were being "systematically, almost scientifically, suppressed and crushed."[230]

The Soviet Union and its satellites once again accused the United States of drumming up the Tibet issue for Cold War purposes and, now, of attempting to divert attention from its role in Vietnam. Violations of human rights in Tibet were denied by recitation of Chinese claims of having brought freedom and progress to Tibetans.[231]

The final vote on the resolution, of which the first four paragraphs "follow in substance the pattern of previous resolutions" and the fifth appeals to all states to "use their best endeavors to achieve the purposes of the present resolution," was approved by a vote of 43 in favor, 26 opposed, and 22 abstaining. Joining the Soviet bloc in opposition were Nepal, Pakistan, Sudan, Syria, United Arab Republic, Tanzania, Congo, Ethiopia, Guinea, Iraq and Mali.[232]

United Nations' action on the Tibet issue ended as it had begun, in inaction. Although many countries were sympathetic to the Tibetans' plight, there was little they could do beyond expressing those sympathies. Support for Tibet was necessarily confined to human rights issues; the fundamental issue of the legality of China's claim to sovereignty over Tibet could not be discussed because no country had recognized Tibetan sovereignty in the past and none wished to challenge Chinese sovereignty in the present. Tibet's acceptance of the 17-Point Agreement had essentially eliminated the issue of Tibet's political status.

In the end, India was right in its opinion that discussion of Tibet at the UN would serve no purpose since "nobody was going to send an army to Tibet." Even the United States, which supported Tibetan self-determination and might have opposed communism in Tibet as in Korea, found that it was politically, legally and logistically impossible to come to Tibet's aid, especially without the cooperation of India. No country, the US included, was willing to support more than a moral condemnation of China in the UN; but, even if they had been willing to approve some action, the Soviet Union retained its power to veto. The Soviets had learned the lesson of Korea and would not be absent for another UN vote on an anti-communist police action; the Soviet Union and the entire socialist bloc therefore vigorously opposed the discussion of Tibet at the UN.

---

230. United Nations General Assembly, Twentieth Session, 18 December 1965, (A/PV/1403), in GAOR, Twentieth Session (New York: United Nations, 1967), 9.

231. Ibid., 3, 5; United Nations General Assembly, Twentieth Session, 17 December 1965, (A/PV/1401), in GAOR, Twentieth Session (New York: United Nations, 1967), 1, 8, 12, 13, 14, 15, 16, 17.

232. United Nations General Assembly, Twentieth Session, 18 December, (A/PV/1403), in GAOR, Twentieth Session (New York: United Nations, 1967), 10.

The UN finally voted to condemn China for human rights violations in Tibet, but even this moral victory was diminished by the fact that the PRC was not a member of the UN and therefore could ignore its resolutions. Tibet's potential patrons all eventually had to face the fact that there was little they could do to oppose Chinese control over Tibet. United Nations debate on Tibet did reveal, however, that Chinese and Communist bloc propaganda on Tibet had failed to obscure the facts of what many countries considered a fundamental issue of territorial aggression of one nation against another.

Inauguration of the Tibet Autonomous Region

The purge of the Panchen Lama in 1964 indeed removed another "rock in the road" toward Tibet's socialist transformation. Secure and uncontested control in Tibet allowed the Chinese to finally institute "national regional autonomy" and to formally establish the Tibet Autonomous Region.[233] This process was initiated by "elections" to "people's congresses," at the local *hsien* (county) level. Regulations governing elections in Tibet were announced by Liu Shao-ch'i on 30 March 1963. The rules provided for "general suffrage" with the exception of "rebels, counter-revolutionaries and others who have been deprived of political rights according to law."[234]

The electoral regulations provide an insight into Chinese Communist style "elections." Elections at the local level were organized by committees appointed by the "People's Government" at the Autonomous Region level, the PCTAR. The PCTAR Election Committee consisted of "representatives of the Chinese Communist Party and the people's organizations and other patriots." The PCTAR Election Committee chose lower level committees, which in turn chose appropriate local candidates (one for each position).[235] The format of choosing candidates was described by *Radio Peking*: "Before the elections, candidates were compared by the people during discussions, ensuring that only those noted for their firm stands, their obedience to the party and their determination to follow the

233. Tibet lagged 10 years behind all other Autonomous Regions in achieving Autonomous Region status and "national regional autonomy."

234. "Electoral Regulations for Tibet Made Public," *NCNA*, 30 March 1963, in *Tibet 1950-67*, 503. This last category included many of the upper class and those who had served prison or labor reform terms and had been released but were still deprived of rights. These individuals were labeled or characterizes as having a "hat" that signified that they had been deprived of rights. Those having "hats" could not speak to other people, visit others, or go anywhere without permission from the local neighborhood committee.

235. Ibid.

road to socialism would be elected."[236] These candidates were then unanimously approved by the people and thus "elected." Those chosen at the county level then elected representatives to the district level.

The process of local "elections" in Tibet continued until 1965, when all 70 counties of the TAR had finally organized "people's congresses." People's congresses at the county level then chose a total of 301 delegates (226 Tibetan, 59 Han and 16 of other nationalities, mainly Monpa, Lhopa, Ladakhi Muslim and Chinese Muslim) to the Tibet Autonomous Region People's Congress, which convened on 1 September 1965 to formally establish the Tibet Autonomous Region.[237] The length of time required to complete this process, even when choices were dictated by the Chinese through Tibetan cadres or activists, is perhaps indicative of Chinese mistrust of Tibetan cadres and their difficulty in organizing sufficient numbers of loyal Tibetan representatives to achieve a semblance of Tibetan political participation. Although the formal establishment of the TAR was accompanied by much fanfare and propaganda in regard to its significance in the achievement of Tibetan self-rule, it had little meaning for Tibetans since all political authority remained firmly in the hands of the CCP Tibet Regional Committee and the PLA Tibet Military Region Command, virtually all of whose members were Han Chinese.

The convening of the First People's Congress of the Tibet Autonomous Region was accompanied by great pageantry and ceremony. A delegation from the central government attended, led by Vice-Premier Hsieh Fu-chih, who described the event as a "congress of victors in the great revolution of the Tibetan people." Hsieh, along with Chang Kou-hua, Chang Ching-wu and Ngawang Jigme Ngapo, made speeches summarizing the process by which the Tibetan people had "risen in revolution to emancipate themselves," from a pre-liberation Tibet described as "a blood-soaked world of darkness under the diabolical serf system and the monastic-aristocratic dictatorship." The theme of Tibetan participation in all stages of Tibet's socialist revolution was diligently pursued, including the claim that Tibetans themselves had begun the process by demanding the setting up of the Preparatory Committee in 1956.[238]

---

236. *Radio Peking*, August 1965, as quoted by the US Ambassador to the United Nations, in United Nations General Assembly Twentieth Session, 17 December 1965 (A/PV/1401), in GAOR, Twentieth Session (New York: United Nations, 1967), 11.

237. The "working committee" of the People's Congress was a "People's Council" composed of 37 members, of whom only 14 were Tibetans; 10 were Han and the rest were of "other nationalities." "Work Report of 1965 Administrative Year in Tibet," *NCNA*, 31 December 1965, in *Tibet 1950-67*, 497.

238. "Speech Delivered by Hsieh Fu-chih, Head of Delegation from Peking, Member of CCP Central Committee and Vice Premier at First Session of First People's Congress of Tibet Autonomous Region," *NCNA*, 1 September 1965, in *Current Background*, no. 771, 1.

The PCTAR had, it was said, created the "antithesis of two regimes, the regime of the people's democracy [the PCTAR] and the regime of the reactionary serf-owners [the Tibetan Government]."[239] This "antithesis of two regimes" had supposedly raised the class consciousness of the Tibetan masses until, in 1959, they "urgently called for the overthrow of the diabolical system of feudal serfdom." This was resisted by the feudal serf-owners, who initiated a rebellion; therefore, "in order to liberate themselves and to establish their own regime, the working people had no alternative but to adopt the method of armed struggle and quell the rebellion."[240] The Party "firmly supported the demand of the masses for quelling the rebellion and carrying out democratic reforms and led the masses to a great victory."[241]

The establishment of the "Tibetan People's Congress" and the Tibetan Autonomous Region ostensibly marked the culmination of the Tibetan people's revolutionary struggle against imperialism and its own exploiting classes, a struggle described as a "class war carried out by the million serfs against the extremely reactionary serf-owning class."[242] The Tibetan people's struggles had supposedly proven the truth that "class interests of the working people of the various nationalities are the same and the interests of the nationalities are identical."[243] The Tibetan People's Congress concluded by sending a message to Chairman Mao: "Respected and beloved Chairman Mao, it is with boundless gratitude and unsurpassed excitement that we now report to you that the Tibet Autonomous Region has now been founded and that the wish of the Tibetan people has been realized."[244]

The creation of the TAR in September 1965 marked not only the establishment of the permanent system of Chinese control in Tibet, but also an acceleration in the pace of ideological indoctrination, collectivization and Sinocization. The Chinese central government representative to the cere-

---

239. Chang Kuo-hua, "Hold High the Great Red Banner of the Thought of Mao Tse-tung, Strive for a Great Victory in Socialist Revolution and Building a Socialist New Tibet," NCNA, 14 September 1965, in *Current Background*, no. 771, 13. Chang was apparently oblivious to the implication of his statement in regard to the provisions of the 17-Point Agreement that had promised no changes in the Tibetan system of government.

240. Ngawang Jigme Ngapo, "Report on Work of Preparatory Committee for Tibet Autonomous Region at People's Congress of Tibet Autonomous Region," 7 September 1965, in *Current Background*, no. 771, 21.

241. Chang Kuo-hua, "Hold High the Great Red Banner," 14.

242. Hsieh Fu-chih, "Speech Delivered by Hsieh Fu-chih," 5.

243. Ibid., 6.

244. "Message of Respect to Chairman Mao from the First Session of First People's Congress of Tibet Autonomous Region," 10 September 1965, in *Current Background*, no. 771, 31.

monies marking the establishment of the TAR, Hsieh Fu-chih, was a member of the leftist Maoist clique; his visit to Lhasa was accompanied by an increase of the pace of collectivization and a renewed emphasis on class struggle. Hsieh called for "class education, socialist education and education in patriotism, with class struggle as the central theme," and recited Mao's leftist slogan, "the national question is essentially a class question." As Hsieh said, "The history of Tibet's liberation, and of the 15 years since, is one of sharp class struggle. . . . The armed struggle that quelled the rebellion in Tibet was in essence a class war fought by the million serfs against the extremely reactionary serf-owning class."[245]

In 1964-1965, after the PRC had recovered from the Great Leap, Mao was once again propagating the line that the defects of partial collectivization could be solved not by a slower pace but by complete collectivization, which would eliminate the evils of private property and achieve the full potential of socialist cooperation. The pace of collectivization in the PRC had slowed in the fall of 1960 due to the famine. In the TAR, this meant that collectivization remained at the level of the MAT, or, in communist jargon, that the democratic revolution was not yet turned into the socialist revolution. The delay in socialist transformation in Tibet was justified because "the masses still do not have a completely clear understanding of socialism," although the poor laboring people were said to be "demanding cooperatives and demanding to go the socialist road." By 1964 Tibetans of the TAR were supposedly asking why Tibetan areas of Szechuan and Chinghai already had socialism while they in the TAR did not.[246] CCP leftists preferred a more rapid pace of collectivization in the TAR in order to bring Tibet up to the same level of collectivization as other nationality regions and the Han Chinese; in addition, collectivization would facilitate more immediate Chinese control over both population and production.

At the end of 1964 the Party answered the "plea" of the Tibetan peasants for higher stages of collectivization. The *NCNA* reported that Tibetan peasants had organized 22,000 mutual aid teams (MATs), embracing nine out of every ten peasant households; 4,000 of these were said to be permanent rather than merely seasonal.[247] MATs were organized in pastoral

---

245. "Great Revolutionary Changes in Tibet," *Peking Review*, 10 September 1965, in *Tibet 1950-67*, 468.

246. US Consulate, Hong Kong to Department of State, 6 February 1961, National Archives, 793B.00/2-661.

247. Permanent mutual aid teams, unlike the seasonal ones, held reclaimed land in common, plus livestock and tools purchased by the team (but not private land, livestock or tools). Private property was retained, at least in theory. The 10 percent of Tibetans who had not joined MATs were those not allowed to do so because of an upper class or reactionary

areas beginning in 1962; by 1965 there were 4,500 of these, 1,580 of which were permanent.[248] Class divisions were made among pastoralists simultaneously with their organization into MATs.[249] Class divisions were made based upon the percentage of a pastoralist's income that had been derived from "exploitation," which was defined to include even hired labor. Those who had 75 percent or more of their income from "exploitation" were classed as herdowners; their animals were confiscated except for a number equivalent to the average holding of a poor herdsman. Those who derived 20 to 75 percent of their income from exploitation were defined as rich herdsmen; their animals were "bought out" and they could repurchase the average holding of a middle herdsman. If income from exploitation was under 30 percent, pastoralists were classed as middle herdsmen and their herds were not confiscated. Poor herdsmen were those whose income derived entirely from their own labor.[250] Tibetans report that the best animals were confiscated by the Chinese; only the worst animals were distributed to the poor Tibetan herdsmen.[251]

Tibetan peasants, who had earlier "demanded" the overthrow of the former "serf-system" and the establishment of mutual aid teams, were now said to be dissatisfied with the semi-socialist nature of mutual aid, which retained private property intact and thus allowed for the regeneration of capitalism and a repolarization of economic classes, and were writing letters to the local and regional CCP headquarters demanding the immediate benefits of communization.[252] In September 1964 the first Agricultural Producer's Cooperative (APC) in the TAR was organized. In July 1965 the first experimental communes were established; these retained private property at least in theory, but the transition to fully collectivized property was intended to take place within the commune framework.[253]

Higher collectivization in Tibet, as in China, involved the amalgamation of political functions within the collectives until, at the commune level, the commune was equivalent to and took over all the political administrative functions of the *hsien*, or county. In addition, the transition from MATs to APCs involved the collectivization of land; lower level col-

---

background. These Tibetans were forced to subsist on a small portion of their former lands and with a few of their former animals and tools after the rest had been confiscated. "Mutual-aid Teams Develop in Tibet," *NCNA*, 23 December 1964, in *Tibet 1950-67*, 576.

248. Epstein, *Tibet Transformed*, 79.
249. Paljor, *Tibet: The Undying Flame*, 8.
250. Epstein, 325.
251. Abu Chonga, personal interview.
252. Epstein, *Tibet Transformed*, 85.
253. Ibid., 76, 80.

lectives paid wages and dividends according to the amount of land an individual contributed, while higher level collectives paid only wages according to labor.[254] The transition to communes also involved the collectivization of all private property. In Tibet, the transition was primarily one of size; MATs had already collectivized labor and had effectively eliminated the "evil of private property." Property had remained private in theory but this distinction was meaningless for many because much of their personal property had been confiscated in "democratic reforms"; for the remainder, property in land was only theoretical, since the produce of the land was confiscated by the state.[255]

The first experimental collectives were actually models, supplied with livestock, seed and agricultural implements, and intended to convince Tibetans to "demand" the benefits to be found within collectives. A propaganda campaign to convince Tibetans to join collectives followed. Tibetans were coerced by Chinese cadres and Tibetan activists to demand that they be "allowed" to set up collectives. Since the methodology of coercion was by now known to all, Tibetans "demanded" collectivization as instructed.[256] An increased wave of collectivization ensued at the end of 1965 and early 1966, during which some 130 "people's communes" were established.[257]

With the inauguration of the TAR the pattern of political administration in Tibet was established. Institutions of Tibetan political "autonomy" formed a facade of Tibetan leadership and popular political participation behind which the Chinese continued to exercise all real political power. The political format of "national regional autonomy" allowed a small degree of cultural autonomy, but any and every manifestation of political resistance would be repressed. The Tibetan state had ceased to exist. Public and private wealth of Tibetans had been confiscated; monasteries and temples, the great repositories of Tibetan wealth and culture, had been depopulated and stripped of articles of value; however, most monasteries, with some exceptions, continued to physically exist.[258] CCP policy on religion allowed individual religious belief and practice; in addition, non-belief, which had allegedly been prevented by the religious

---

254. Ibid., 314.

255. Dawa Norbu, *Red Star Over Tibet*, 210.

256. Ibid.

257. "Upsurge in Socialist Transformation of Agriculture and Livestock Breeding on Tibetan Plateau," *Peking Review*, 31 July 1970.

258. Drepung, for example, in 1965 had only 715 monks (out of a previous population estimated at 10,000 to 12,000 monks). Epstein, *Tibet Transformed*, 422. A few remote monasteries and shrines (in the TAR) seem to have survived relatively intact until this time, with reduced monk populations. Rinchen Paljor, personal communication, Lhasa, October 1982.

state in the past, was now protected; Tibetans were said to now enjoy "true religious freedom."

Tens of thousands of Tibetans still languished in prisons and labor camps. Some who had not been active participants in the revolt had been released, contingent upon their having confessed to their crimes and "reformed their way of thinking." The fundamental requirement was that Tibetans should admit that Tibet was, had always been and would forever be a part of China. All Tibetans were by now aware of the CCP's policy of leniency for confession and conformity in contrast to merciless repression for any opposition or resistance. Tibetans had the choice of either cooperation, repression or flight. Many chose the latter, including an estimated 50-70,000 who, between 1959 and 1965, escaped into exile in India, Nepal or Bhutan.[259]

The problem of escaped Tibetans—who could convey to the outside world an impression of actual events and conditions in Tibet—was considered serious enough that in 1964 the Chinese mounted a campaign to entice refugees to "return to the motherland," to "abandon darkness to come to light." Returnees were promised rewards for the surrender of any weapons or documents; those who convinced others to return were to be substantially rewarded. Tibetan refugees were promised that they would not be punished; they would be provided with livelihood "according to their wishes"; their confiscated property would be returned; and they would be allowed freedom of religion, all without regard to their former position or participation in the revolt.[260] The few who returned

259. On 17 October 1959 the GOI announced that 15,000 Tibetan refugees had reached India. *Tibet 1950-67*, 797. In December 1960 Nepal reported 20,000 Tibetan refugees in Nepal. Ibid., 801. In the same month India reported 17,000 in India. Ibid., 802. In August 1961 the GOI reported 33,000 Tibetan refugees in India. Ibid., 804. In March 1964 there were 37,500 in India. Ibid., 811. In April 1967 the GOI reported 50,000 Tibetan refugees in India. Ibid., 823. Some 36 Chinese, most of them PLA soldiers, also sought refuge in India after the Tibetan revolt. *Tibet Fights for Freedom*, 216.

260. "The Preparatory Committee of Tibet Autonomous Region and the People's Liberation Army Tibet Military Region Formulated Regulations Rewarding Surrendering Tibetan Compatriots Who Fled After Participation in the Rebellion," Lhasa, 5 August 1964, in *Tibet 1950-67*, 528. Tibetans whose relatives were in exile were forced to write letters—checked and approved by the Chinese—or to make radio broadcasts urging their relatives to return. However, some Tibetans managed to smuggle letters from Tibet warning Tibetans in exile not to believe the promises. Radio broadcasts also claimed that there was an abundance of food in Tibet and an inadequate food supply for Tibetans in India. Tibetans in India, it was said, would be used as soldiers by the Indians and would inevitably be killed by the Chinese in combat. Chinese officials reportedly blamed their past mistakes in Tibet on Soviet influence, "which led to public trials, torture, imprisonment, confiscation of properties, murder, deportation, etc. We have now realized our mistakes and are sending the old officials to China to be re-educated. From now on, we shall abandon the bad Soviet system and follow the good Chinese system." *Facts About Tibet*, 18.

were well treated, though the campaign failed to produce any significant number of returnees, partly because refugees were continuing to flee Tibet with stories of actual conditions under Chinese rule.

At the end of 1965 most Tibetans were still reeling from the loss of their freedom and independence, the death and imprisonment of family members and the exile to India of others, including the Dalai Lama, and the destruction and repression visited upon them by the Chinese. No doubt, many thought that the hells so vividly depicted in the Buddhist Wheel of Life paintings had come to life. Many may have imagined that their earthly and transcendental protectors had abandoned them and that life on this earth could get no worse. As the Dalai Lama said at the time:

> Tibet had always enjoyed a free and independent existence, living in friendship with her neighbors, until the Chinese, in the name of liberation, invaded our peaceful and beloved country and enslaved us. The Chinese announced that Tibet was to be freed from imperialists, but imperialists had never existed in Tibet. Now, however, Tibet for the first time in its history is under the yoke of the most ruthless imperialists, who strive to own a man, body and soul, and then destroy them both. Before China's invasion, Tibet knew no famine. Every Tibetan had enough food and the kind of clothing and shelter required by the climate. Today, Tibetans live near starvation. Their only dwelling place is work camps where they die like flies from exhaustion and cold. Even the grace of Lord Buddha is no longer permitted to them because, the Chinese say, to believe in religion is equivalent to being a traitor.[261]

Having suffered so much already, Tibetans were undoubtedly unprepared for what was to come. As Tibetans said, they could understand foreign conquest; what they could not understand was why the Chinese should feel the need to eradicate all aspects of Tibetan culture and religion. Why were the Chinese not satisfied, having taken over physical control of Tibet; why would they not rest until they had taken over Tibetans' minds as well?[262] Perhaps the answer was that the evidence of Chinese imperialism in Tibet would not be eradicated until the ethnic, cultural and national category "Tibetan" ceased to exist and Tibetans became indistinguishable from the Chinese.

---

261. "Statement of His Holiness the Dalai Lama," New Delhi, 26 October 1965, in *Facts About Tibet*, 3.
262. Personal communication with various Tibetans, Lhasa, 1982.

13

The Great Proletarian Cultural Revolution in Tibet

The Great Proletarian Cultural Revolution began as an attempt by Mao to overcome revisionism and bureaucratism in the CCP by means of a revival of the forms, spirit and consciousness of collectivism. Mao preferred to create the new by first destroying the old, rather than building the new on the foundation of the old. This method, Mao said, was like "writing on a clean slate." As the Cultural Revolution was to demonstrate, however, destruction was much easier to accomplish than creation. Mao unleashed the Red Guards to destroy the "four olds," (old ideas, old culture, old tradition, old customs). The cultures and traditions of minorities epitomized the "four olds" and were thus a particular target.

In 1965, at the time of the inauguration of the Tibet Autonomous Region, the CCP was still basically adhering to its nationality policy. However, nationality policies had come under attack before, during the anti-rightist campaign of late 1957 and the subsequent Great Leap of 1958-61. Local nationalism had been branded counterrevolutionary; nationality cultures and religions had been excoriated as a hindrance to socialism, and their preservation condemned as anti-socialist rightism. In 1965 the leftists were once again on the rise, as was indicated by the revival of collectivization campaigns in that year. The rise of Mao and the leftist wing of the CCP signaled renewed attacks on nationality policies and nationality cultures, a portent of which was revealed in late 1964 in an article calling for a "cultural revolution" among national minorities:

> Reactionary culture and art are tools used by our class enemies at home and abroad to poison the people of the national minorities, split the unity of the motherland, undermine national unity, sabotage the socialist revolution and socialist construction and restore the feudal system and even the system of slavery in the minority areas. Therefore, a cultural revolutionary movement of the national minorities must also be developed energetically as part of the great nationwide cultural revolution. ... This demands that all cultural and artistic activities in the minority areas, including spare-time cultural activities, have a revolutionary ideological content. ... The peo-

ple of the national minorities urgently need a revolutionary culture and art with new ideas and new content. . . . The revolutionary culture and art of the national minorities should pay attention to using national forms, so that they can be more easily accepted by the minority peoples. The culture and arts of all the nationalities must be revolutionary in content and conform to the interests of socialism. There must be unity and only unity is allowed in this matter.[1]

Mao began his counterattack against the right wing of the Party led by Liu Shao-ch'i, whose pragmatic economic policies had rescued the Chinese economy after the folly of Mao's Great Leap, with the Socialist Education Campaign of May 1963. However, Mao found his efforts resisted by a Party bureaucracy that he no longer directly controlled. Mao then directed his campaign against the Party itself, or, "those within the Party taking the capitalist road." At a meeting of the Party Central Committee in January 1965 Mao called for a "cultural revolution" to combat bureaucratism and restore collectivism and the collectivist spirit. Again countered by the Party bureaucracy, Mao undertook a provincial tour from the end of 1965 to early 1966 to drum up support for his program.

In the spring of 1966 Mao created the Cultural Revolution Group, headed by his wife, Chiang Ch'ing, to organize and guide the Cultural Revolution. Mao was supported by the PLA under the leadership of Lin Piao, a Mao loyalist and proponent of the Maoist cult. Mao, the Cultural Revolution Group and Lin Piao initiated the Cultural Revolution at the end of May 1966 by inviting students to attack Party bureaucrats, especially those suspected of resisting Maoist policies. By mid-June the Cultural Revolution was in full swing; on 18 June university exams were postponed so that students, now designated as "Red Guards," could have free time for political action. The speed and organization of the Cultural Revolution is indicated by the fact that Red Guards appeared almost immediately in every major city in China. Red Guard groups from Peking arrived in Tibet as early as the beginning of July.[2]

The first Red Guard groups sent to Tibet were organized in Peking educational institutions by the Cultural Revolution Group. One of the first of these groups included a contingent of Tibetan students from the Peking Minority Nationalities Institute, led by Chinese instructors. The number of Red Guards from Peking institutions sent to Tibet totaled more than 3,000, including 400 from the Nationalities Institute. These

1. Lu Ting-yi, "Cultural Revolution of China's National Minorities," *Peking Review*, 4 December 1964, 23.

2. Kunsang Paljor, *Tibet: The Undying Flame* (Dharamsala: Information and Publicity Office of His Holiness the Dalai Lama, 1977), 50.

were soon joined by 4,000 Tibetan students from the Hsienyang Tibet Minorities School, some 700 from the Southwest Minority Nationalities School in Chengdu, and 80 from Lhasa Middle School.[3] At the same time, Red Guard groups were sent to Sinkiang and Inner Mongolia.[4]

The Cultural Revolution was officially launched in Tibet on 25 August. Acting on the suggestion of the Red Guards, "revolutionary masses of various nationalities" invaded the Tsuglhakhang, or Jokhang, Lhasa's Central Cathedral. Relics from Sera, Drepung and Ganden previously stored in the Jokhang on the Panchen Lama's orders were removed and trucked to China before the destruction began. Frescoes and scriptures were destroyed on the spot. The Ramoche, Norbulinka and other Lhasa monasteries and shrines were also attacked; in each case, Chinese and Tibetan Red Guards were led by Chinese cadres. Tibetan Red Guards were encouraged by the Chinese to engage in the actual destruction. Tibetans report that Chinese residents in Lhasa joined in the vandalism and looting.[5]

By mid-September every doorway, house or wall in Lhasa was festooned with portraits of Chairman Mao, some 40,000 of which were distributed, and posters "singing the praises of the great Chinese Communist Party and the great teacher, great leader, great supreme commander and great helmsman, Chairman Mao, and acclaiming the great Chinese people and their great army, the PLA."[6] Lhasa's streets were "freshened" by the removal of all "superstitious and feudal" Tibetan names, which were replaced by new revolutionary Chinese names. Prayer flags were removed from roofs and replaced by the Chinese five-star red flag. Other "vestiges of the old society, odious of feudal superstition," such as *mani* stones, *chortens* and *mani* walls, were destroyed,

---

3. Ibid.

4. Many of the Red Guards in Sinkiang were recruited from the members of the Production and Construction Corps units already in Sinkiang. Donald H. McMillen, *Chinese Communist Power and Policy in Xinjiang, 1949-1977* (Boulder: Westview Press, 1979), 182. Many Red Guards were sent from Peking and other northern Chinese cities to Inner Mongolia, the PRC's "model autonomous region." In 1968, the CCP launched a campaign to unearth a non-existent "New Inner Mongolian People's Revolutionary Party." Between the end of 1968 and May 1969 thousands of Mongols were arrested and tortured to reveal the names of anti-Chinese nationalists. According to official figures released in 1981, more than half a million people were incarcerated, more than 16,000 died, and tens of thousands were injured and crippled. Unofficial statistics claim that as many as 50,000 people may have died (out of a Mongol population in Inner Mongolia of two million). "Crackdown in Inner Mongolia," Asia Watch Report, July 1991, 19.

5. Paljor, *Tibet: The Undying Flame*, 56.

6. "Lhasa Takes on New Look," *New China News Agency* (*NCNA*), 15 September 1966, in *Tibet 1950-67* (Hong Kong: Union Research Institute, 1967), 606.

except "those that the State has decided to preserve as ancient relics of culture." Former aristocrats and high lamas were paraded through the streets in duncecaps and required to confess their "crimes."

Tibetans were said to be eagerly studying the little red book, *Quotations from Chairman Mao*, 28,000 copies of which in Tibetan had been distributed, "in response to Tibetans' requests to study Mao's works." Mao's "Thought," once grasped, was said to be capable of "changing the spiritual appearance of a society as a whole."[7] The cult of Mao, fostered from 1964 by Lin Piao and the PLA, was a predominant characteristic of the Cultural Revolution. "Mao's Thought" was accredited with mystical powers, supposedly capable of transforming individual and social consciousness and was regarded as a requirement for socialist transformation for Han and minority nationalities alike. Minority nationalities' backward cultures were regarded as an obstacle to the propagation of "Mao's Thought." Red Guards took up Mao's iconoclasm with enthusiasm; a Red Guard slogan, "destruction before construction," was indicative of the course the Cultural Revolution was to take in Tibet.

Every aspect of Tibetan culture came under attack during the Cultural Revolution. The most distinguishing characteristics of Tibetan culture, especially Tibetan religion, were targeted for systematic destruction. The number of "functioning monasteries," according to a Chinese estimate, had dropped from 2,711 in 1958 to 370 in 1960, while the number of monks had been reduced from an estimated 114,000 to 18,104 (both figures refer only to the TAR).[8] By the beginning of the Cultural Revolution an additional unknown number of monasteries were depopulated and looted; nevertheless, most monasteries and religious monuments had so far escaped physical destruction. During the Cultural Revolution, these most distinguishing symbols of Tibetan culture and national identity were to be eradicated.

Religious repression in Tibet now entered its final stage with the desecration and destruction of all Tibetan religious monuments. Local Tibetan youths, usually members of the Communist Youth League, were designated as Red Guards and sent out to all religious structures to perform the supposedly politically and psychologically cathartic act of vandalism

---

7. "The Sunlight of Mao Tse-tung's Thought Shines Over New Lhasa," *China News Service*, October 1966, in *Tibet 1950-67*, 608.

8. Jing Jun, "Socioeconomic Changes and Riots in Lhasa" (unpublished paper), 1990, 1, citing Zhang Tianlu, *Population Change in Tibet* (Beijing: Tibetan Studies Publishing House of China, 1989), 28. These figures refute the common Chinese contention that the destruction of Tibetan religion took place during the Cultural Revolution and was exclusively the fault of the "gang of four." Only the final physical destruction took place during the Cultural Revolution.

and destruction. Tibetan "Red Guards," or, often, all villagers in a particular area, were coerced by Chinese and Tibetan cadres into the final
destruction of religious monuments. The Chinese removed all portable
valuables from temples and monasteries in advance. Tibetans report that
Chinese in Lhasa and other towns were allowed to retain Tibetan religious relics looted from temples and monasteries, such as paintings, car-
pets and statues.[9] Irremovable religious artifacts such as frescoes were
defaced and large clay statues smashed. Buddhist scriptures were burned
or used by the Chinese to line the inner soles of their shoes or for toilet
paper; wood printing blocks were turned into floorboards or furniture or
other objects degrading to religious sentiments.

The orgy of destruction thereafter became more systematic; Tibetans
were required to dismantle temples and monasteries for their timber and
stone, which was then used to construct Chinese offices, housing or PLA
barracks. The destruction was sometimes so complete that all trace of
some monasteries disappeared. Other religious monuments, such as
small roadside shrines, chortens, *mani* stones (stones on which the
Buddhist mantra *Om Mani Padme Hum* were carved) or *mani* walls (walls
constructed of *mani* stones), were all destroyed. *Mani* stones were often
employed in walkways or flooring, so that Tibetans would have to dese-
crate their religion by walking upon them, or used to construct public toi-
lets. Private religious shrines were also desecrated; Tibetans were
required to surrender all personal religious objects of value to the
Chinese authorities. Virtually all physical evidence of Tibet's previously
pervasive Buddhist culture was eradicated within a few months at the
end of 1966 by the Red Guards' rampage, although the seemingly chaot-
ic destruction was obviously planned and systematically pursued.

All "reactionary" Tibetan customs, traditions, songs and dance, even
language were to be replaced by "progressive, socialist" Chinese styles.
Tibetans were required to dress like Chinese, cut their long hair short in
the Chinese style, sing songs in praise of Mao in Chinese, and replace traditional Tibetan "feudal" religious holidays and secular festivals with
Chinese revolutionary holidays and ceremonies. Chinese propaganda
claimed that this was all done voluntarily by the "emancipated Tibetan
serfs":

> We emancipated serfs have today thrown to the very bottom of the Tsangpo
> River all the old wicked songs, dances and dramas that prettify the
> serfowners and spread superstition about gods and supernatural beings. . . .

---

9. The Chinese often made table lamps out of Tibetan Buddhist statues. Tsering
Wangchuk, personal interview, Dharamsala, February 1990.

> Revolutionary music, dances and dramas prevail in Tibet, in praise of Chairman Mao, the great leader, supreme commander and helmsman; in praise of the all-conquering thought of Mao Tse-tung and of heroes nurtured by his thought; in praise of the great, glorious and correct Chinese Communist Party; the Great People's Liberation Army, and the Great Proletarian Cultural Revolution. . . . Emancipated peasants and herdsmen write the stories of their sufferings and of emancipation as plays; stage them in village clubs and in theatres in the cities.[10]

All aspects of the colorful Tibetan artistic sense in personal and household decoration were replaced with Chinese proletarian green or blue. Tibetans had to paint over their decorative woodwork and painted window borders in dull proletarian colors. Even the large brass cooking pots, utensils and water containers, so conspicuous a decoration in almost every Tibetan household, were confiscated on the pretext that they represented the old society. The campaigns against the "four pests" were continued and political indoctrination in neighbor committees was intensified. *Thamzing* was often employed against those identified as reactionary, indifferent or merely non-participatory. Suicide, anathema to Tibetans as Buddhists, was an often reported response, especially to the trauma of *thamzing*.

Tibetan language, already subjected to the "national in form, socialist in content" requirement, which established Marxist terminology as the content of discourse, was also subjected to alterations in form. This movement was partly driven by the difficulty in translating the concepts of Chinese communism, highly loaded with subjective cultural and ideological meaning, into nationality languages. All minority languages were characterized as archaic in relation to the "advanced" Chinese language.[11] Many "archaic" forms of language, such as the honorifics and all of the corresponding grammar in Tibetan, were prohibited. The Chinese attempted a radical amalgamation of the Tibetan language with Chinese by adding Chinese vocabulary, intended to produce a "Sino-Tibetan Friendship Language," which would have meant the effective demise of spoken Tibetan.

During the Cultural Revolution, Red Guards were charged by Mao to not only destroy the "four olds" but also to "bombard the headquarters," that is, to criticize those in the Party bureaucracy "taking the capitalist road," a euphemism for bureaucrats less leftist than the Maoists. In Tibet,

---

10. "Emancipated Tibetan People Build New Socialist Culture," Lhasa, 20 October 1966, in *Tibet 1950-67*, 727.

11. In fact, Tibetan and other alphabetic nationality languages are much less archaic than the ideographic Chinese.

two Chinese officials, Chang Kuo-hua and Wang Ch'i-mei, came under criticism, Chang for "occupying the Tibet highland and treating it as his independent kingdom," and Wang for defending the "special characteristics" of Tibet and the "problems of nationalities, religion and the united front." The Red Guards accused the Party bureaucracy of using the excuse of Tibet's "special characteristics" to "restrict and strangle" the Cultural Revolution. Red Guards complained that the excuse of "special characteristics" was used to "provide the reactionary line with a theoretical basis." They argued that "Mao Tse-tung's thought is our uniform thought," which superseded all special characteristics, "so long as we are in the territory of China."[12]

By the end of 1966 the "little Red Guard generals" (as they were called by Chiang Ch'ing) had created so much havoc in China that to restore order Mao had to establish a "triple alliance" of Party cadres, the PLA, and "mass revolutionary organizations." In practice, the triple alliance meant political control by the Party and the PLA and repression of the more radical Red Guards. In Tibet the Red Guards succeeded in taking over the Tibet Daily on 10 January; at the end of the month Chang Kou-hua was removed from his position in the TAR and transferred to Szechuan. In February the Party, now led by Ren Rong, counterattacked with the formation of a rival Red Guard organization, the Great Alliance (Tib. *Namdrel*), which attempted to divert criticism away from the Party bureaucracy to more traditional targets—class enemies and intellectuals—and attacked the more radical Red Guard groups, primarily those from Peking, now collectively known as Revolutionary Rebels (Tib. *Gyenlok*).

The period of repression of Red Guard excesses by the Party and PLA (later known all over China as the "February adverse current") was reversed in the spring by the Cultural Revolution Group after it threatened to restore the Party bureaucracy and provide the means by which rightists within the Party might regain control. Red Guards were once again let loose; some Red Guards who had departed Tibet for Peking returned with reinforcements. By the first of June the Revolutionary Rebels were once again established with official support in Lhasa. Conflicts between rival Red Guard groups, reflecting the struggle

---

12. "Comment on the Region Party Committee's Stand, Viewpoint and Attitude on the Struggle Between the Two Lines in the Great Proletarian Cultural Revolution," 3 December 1966, in *Tibet 1950-67*, 613. "Special characteristics," are the code words for the cultural traditions of minorities that justify their right to autonomy. Tibet also had some "special characteristics" of its own due to its past history and the delays in its socialist transformation to that point. What the Red Guards were criticizing was the very concept of minority autonomy.

between leftists and rightists in the Party, now began to turn more violent in Lhasa, as was the case all over China.

By August factional violence had created such chaos in the Chinese interior that Mao had to order the PLA to assume control. Even this did not halt the violence, however, since by now the PLA was also riven by factionalism. The PLA had by that time provided arms to all Red Guard factions; armed clashes between Red Guard factions and between the Red Guards and the PLA ensued, resulting in great loss of life. Order was finally restored only by the creation of a "Cultural Revolutionary Committee" in each province, incorporating the triple alliance of Party cadres, the PLA and mass revolutionary organizations; actual control was exercised by the PLA. Only in September 1968 was a "Revolutionary Committee" established in the TAR, making it, along with Sinkiang, one of the last two areas in the PRC to finally achieve the "overthrow" of the Party bureaucracy.

Until this time the Cultural Revolution in Tibet was primarily a Chinese affair; although Tibetans participated in the Cultural Revolution in Tibet, they did so primarily as tools of Chinese Red Guard leaders. In all of the arcane literature concerning disputes over the correct line to take in the Cultural Revolution within Tibet, Tibetan authors or names of Tibetan participants are conspicuously absent. Tibetan Red Guards were put in the forefront in the attacks on all manifestations of the "four olds" in Tibet, but Tibetans apparently had little to do with the ideological battles between factions. Some report that the attack on the "four olds" was virtually all that most Tibetans comprehended about the Cultural Revolution.[13]

The Nyemo Revolt

After the establishment of the Tibetan "Revolutionary Committee," factional conflict in Tibet continued, but took on a nationalist content previously absent. The two Red Guard factions polarized along ethnic lines until the *Gyenlok* faction was predominantly Tibetan while the *Namdrel* faction was mostly Chinese.[14] Participation in the Cultural Revolution had for some Tibetans a democratizing effect, which in turn increased their nationalist awareness. Solidarity among Tibetans increased because of their common experience of repression; the attack on all aspects of Tibetan culture produced an inevitable nationalist reaction in many Tibetans.

---

13. Tsering Wangchuk, personal interview.
14. Tsering Wangchuk, Lobsang Tenzin, personal interviews, Dharamsala, 1990.

Tibetans took the opportunity provided by Cultural Revolution campaigns to criticize Chinese and Tibetan CCP cadres, none of whom, except Mao and his wife, were immune from criticism. Tibetans exploited the opportunity to criticize Ngapo and other collaborationists; they demanded that Ngapo be struggled for his aristocratic background, forcing the Chinese to remove him to Peking. The chaos and relatively permissive atmosphere of the Cultural Revolution allowed Tibetans to pursue nationalist goals, first by criticism and then, later, as the level of violence increased, by more violent means. As the factional conflict increased in violence, Tibetans began to attack Chinese cadres on the pretext of factional disputes or Mao's call to "bombard the headquarters."

In 1968 the Chinese revived the communization campaign; this, along with compulsory grain requisitions by the PLA, resulted in food shortages and further Tibetan discontent. In addition, Tibetans report that war hysteria was prevalent among the Chinese who were convinced that the third world war would soon break out on the Indian border. The PLA therefore requisitioned and stored food, refusing to release food supplies to Tibetans.[15] Tibetans were told to work harder and to prepare for war, and that the advance of socialism to other countries was more important than their local difficulties. At the same time, Tibetans were forced to excavate bomb-proof shelters for the Chinese military and construct roads to the Indian border.[16]

By late 1968 food shortages and the chaos of the Cultural Revolution led to revolt in rural areas, beginning in the Nyemo area to the west of Lhasa. Revolt eventually spread to 20 of the 70 counties of the TAR, from Nyemo, Phenpo and Nagchu, near Lhasa, to Biru, Shotalhosum and Markham in the eastern TAR. The revolt actually began as an attempt by the PLA to suppress the *Gyenlok*. Nyemo and many other rural areas surrounding Lhasa were centers of *Gyenlok* factional strength. The revolt in Nyemo was led by a woman known as Nyemo Ani. The revolt became known among Tibetans as the Nyemo revolt or the "second Tibetan revolt."[17] The Chinese were said to have referred to the revolt as the "second reactionary revolt."[18]

The Nyemo revolt had undeniably nationalistic characteristics,

---

15. John Avedon, *In Exile from the Land of Snows* (New York: Vintage Books, 1986), 298, 300.

16. *Tibet Under Chinese Communist Rule: A Compilation of Refugee Statements: 1958-1975* (Dharamsala: Information and Publicity Office of His Holiness the Dalai Lama, 1976), 113, 118, 119, 124, 128, 138. Dhondub Choedon, *Life in the Red Flag People's Commune* (Dharamsala: Information Office of His Holiness the Dalai Lama, 1978), 27.

17. Tsering Wangchuk, personal interview.

18. Lobsang Tenzin, personal interview.

although some of its nationalist significance may have been exaggerated by the Chinese themselves as an excuse for repression.[19] Several Tibetans report that the Nyemo revolt became an independence movement.[20] The revolt involved the rural and nomadic population of a large part of central Tibet.[21] The revolt assumed such a magnitude by late 1969 that PLA units of the Northwestern (Sinkiang) Military District had to be called in to reinforce PLA units in Tibet (of the Southwestern Military District). The revolt was finally put down with great brutality; many of its leaders, including Nyemo Ani, were publicly executed in Lhasa.[22] At about the same time, Kundeling Kunsang, wife of Kundeling Dzaza, who had helped the Dalai Lama escape, and three other women, who had led the women's march in March 1959, were publicly executed.[23] An "anti-revolutionary group of adolescents," which Tibetans describe as a youth independence movement, was exposed and nine members were executed.[24]

The late Cultural Revolution was accompanied by an "anti-rightist rectification campaign," aimed at preventing those purged as "capitalist roaders" from creeping back into the Party. In Tibet, this campaign was manifested as yet another purge of Tibetan cadres, this time focusing on

---

19. During the Cultural Revolution the PLA often emphasized external or nationalist separatist threats to rally support against the more radical Red Guard factions. In Tibet the PLA used the nationalist nature of the Nyemo revolt as a justification for repression of the revolt and the *Gyenlok* faction with which it was identified. The war hysteria of the era may also have been substantially invented, or at least exacerbated, to provide an excuse for PLA control and repression.

20. Tsering Wangchuk, Lobsang Tenzin, Jampa Gyaltsen, personal interviews. One informant claims that the Tibetan flag was seen during the revolt. Other more mystical phenomena with nationalist significant were also reported, such as a rumor that Ling Gesar would return or had been sighted in the northern areas, a rumor that Tsongkhapa was alive in his burial *chorten* at Ganden, or that the image of the Dalai Lama had been seen in the sky or in the sun. Tsering Wangchuk, personal interview.

21. Tsering Wangchuk, personal interview.

22. Lobsang Tenzin, personal interview; Jigme Ngapo, "Behind the Unrest in Tibet," *China Spring*, vol. 2, no. 1 (January-February 1988), 24.

23. Ani Gonjo Pachim Dolma, personal interview, Dharamsala, 1989.

24. Ngapo, "Behind the Unrest in Tibet," 25. The Dalai Lama reported that, according to information received in India, 58 Tibetans had been publicly executed in February 1970; another 124 were executed shortly thereafter, after the revolt was finally crushed, along with nine members of a youth independence movement. He said that Tibetans reported that more than 1,000 Chinese were killed during the revolt. "Statement of His Holiness the Dalai Lama on the 12th Anniversary of the Tibetan People's National Uprising Day of 10th March 1959," 10 March 1971, in *Collected Statements of His Holiness the Dalai Lama*, 33. All of these executions followed the typical Chinese Communist ritual. Family members of those executed were not allowed to grieve, but were required to express gratitude to the state for eliminating such anti-social elements and to pay the state for the cost of the bullet used in the execution.

the Tibetan students who had been sent back to Tibet before the Cultural Revolution or those recruited as Red Guards within Tibet. This purge took place in 1969-1970, simultaneous with the repression of the Nyemo revolt. The violence, destruction and cultural iconoclasm of the Cultural Revolution associated with the rampage of the Red Guards continued for two years in China (mid-1966 to mid-1968) but for somewhat longer in Tibet; control was not finally restored by the PLA in some Tibetan areas until the spring of 1970.[25]

Communization During the Cultural Revolution

The campaign for communization, disrupted by the chaos of the early Cultural Revolution, was revived in 1968. Communes were forcibly established by the PLA as a part of the campaign to reestablish political control.[26] In Tibet, where only approximately 130 communes had been established before the Cultural Revolution, this meant in some cases transitioning directly from mutual aid teams to communes, or, as the Chinese said: "Tibet leapfrogged the stage of co-ops and moved directly from mutual-aid teams to people's communes."[27] By the end of July 1970, 666 communes were established; 34 percent of the counties of the TAR were undergoing communization with 13 counties fully communized.[28] Tibetan peasants were reportedly joyous at having finally been "allowed" to set up the communes that they supposedly had long desired but had been prevented from achieving by Liu Shao-ch'i's "counterrevolutionary revisionism."[29] By the summer of 1974 communes were reportedly established in 90 percent of Tibet's counties.

Chinese propaganda claimed that the communes were established by "adhering to the principle of voluntariness and mutual benefit."[30] By September 1975 the CCP was able to announce that 99 percent of the townships had set up communes and that "the socialist transformation of agriculture and animal husbandry has been basically completed." As *Peking Review* proclaimed:

---

25. Lobsang Tenzin, personal interview.

26. Tsering Wangchuk, personal interview.

27. "Tibet's Big Leap: Great Changes," *Peking Review*, 11 July 1975.

28. "Upsurge in Socialist Transformation of Agriculture and Livestock Breeding on Tibetan Plateau," *Peking Review*, 31 July 1970.

29. "Mao Tse-tung Thought Lights Up the Tibetan Plateau," *Peking Review*, 10 October 1969, 25.

30. "People's Communes Set Up in 90 Per Cent of Tibet's Townships," *Peking Review*, 19 July 1974, 9.

The emancipated serfs and other laboring people understand that the people's commune is the `golden bridge' leading to their complete liberation. . . . The million emancipated serfs, under the leadership of Chairman Mao and the Communist Party, are determined to take the socialist road. Because they suffered the heaviest oppression and exploitation under the feudal serf system, they cherish boundless love for Chairman Mao and socialism.[31]

Grain production was claimed to have soared after the introduction of communes; grain output, which was said to have increased in 1964 by 45 percent due to mutual aid, was reported to have increased by 150 percent in 1974 (over 1959) due to the introduction of communes.[32] However, Tibetans, who suffered starvation during the period 1959-1962, again report famine conditions during the period 1968-1973.[33] The 1968-73 famine seems to have been the result of the disruptions created by the introduction of communes (as was the case in the Chinese interior during the Great Leap); confiscation of grain for Chinese consumption and war preparation was also a factor.[34]

Communized Tibetans subsisted on a ration based upon work points, *karma*, according to the socialist principle "from each according to his ability, to each according to his work." Work points, which enabled Tibetans to buy their own grain from the Chinese, were awarded at the rate of 10 *karma* per day for officials and activists, 8 *karma* per day for the most diligent laborers, 5 to 7 for the less diligent, 4 *karma* for shepherds and 2 to 3 *karma* for old people who worked and children below age 14. Old people unable to work and children too young to work got no *karma* and no ration; they were expected to be supported by their families on their own inadequate ration. 10 *karma* per day enabled a worker to receive a ration of 15 kilograms of grain and half a kilo of butter or oil per month, barely a subsistence ration, but only officials, activists and a few "model workers" received this ration, while most Tibetans received less. The Chinese justified the sacrifice and hardship as necessary to reach the socialist paradise, an era that would bring unbounded happiness and prosperity. The socialist utopia would be attained, the Chinese explained,

---

31. "Tibet Advances Along the Socialist Road," *Peking Review*, 19 September 1975, 9. In rural areas of Tibet, the township was the administrative equivalent of the commune; therefore, the statement that communes were set up in 99 percent of the townships meant that 99 percent of Tibetan townships, agricultural and pastoral, were communized. Dawa Norbu, "Changes in Tibetan Economy, 1959-76," in *China Report*, 24:3 (1988), 227.

32. "Tibet's Big Leap: Great Changes," *Peking Review*, 18 July 1975, 23.

33. Avedon, *In Exile from the Land of Snows*, 299.

34. Dhondub Choedon reports that in the Red Flag commune more than 50 percent of the harvest was confiscated. Choedon, *Red Flag People's Commune*, 36.

as a matter of historical inevitability, after the Third World War when all the countries of the world would adopt socialism.[35]

Food shortages reportedly persisted in Tibet during the entire period of the 1970s due to communization, restrictions on subsidiary crops ("taking grain as the key link" campaign) and the disastrous results of an attempt to substitute the cultivation of wheat for Tibetan barley.[36] The Chinese introduced the cultivation of wheat along with communization; wheat was claimed to give much higher yields than barley (and was much more palatable to the Chinese); the substitution of wheat for barley had previously been impossible, it was said, "because of the limitations imposed by the individual economy."[37] Wheat cultivation seems to have begun in earnest in 1973-74 as the TAR approached full communization.[38] PLA and state farms, many of which were established on confiscated lands in the most fertile areas, began cultivating wheat and reported increased yields.[39] Wheat cultivation was soon introduced into marginal areas of low fertility or high altitude, including waterlogged grasslands converted to agriculture. In these areas, wheat was vulnerable to adverse conditions such as spring frosts or summer droughts. Wheat cultivation even in the best areas eventually led to soil depletion, greatly reduced yields, and, by the end of the decade, renewed food shortages.[40] Despite

---

35. Jamyang Norbu, *Warriors of Tibet* (London: Wisdom Publications, 1986), 101.

36. According to a study published by the International Center for Integrated Mountain Development (ICIMOD) in Nepal, based upon research by Academia Sinica from 1973 to 1979, "Sharp decreases in cultivated legumes, rape and jingke [barley], plus prolonged wheat growth, induced degradation of the soil capacity. As a result, the total amount of grain yield remained almost at the same level, as a whole, for ten years [1966-1976] in the Autonomous Region." Zhang Rongzu, *Nyemo County* (Kathmandu: ICIMOD, 1989), 6. At the same time, of course, population increased; therefore, per capita food production decreased.

37. "Tibet's Big Leap: Great Changes," *Peking Review*, 18 July 1975, 25. "After the people's communes were set up, a greater acreage was sown to winter wheat every year." "People's Communes Embrace 90 Percent of Tibetan Townships," *NCNA*, Lhasa, 27 September 1974, in *Survey of China Mainland Press* (Hong Kong: United States Consulate).

38. Winter wheat was said to have been sown on one third of the farmland in one county in 1973. "People's Communes Embrace 90 Percent of Tibetan Townships," *NCNA*, Lhasa, 27 September 1974, in *Survey of China Mainland Press*. Statistics from Nyemo County, west of Lhasa, reveal that in 1976 wheat was sown on 10 percent of farmland while barley was sown on 69 percent; in 1978, the percentages were 25 and 44, respectively; in 1980, 26 and 43 percent; while in 1982, the percentages had reverted to 5 percent for wheat and 64 for barley. Zhang Rongzu, *Nyemo County*, 7. This would seem to indicate that the greatest proportion of wheat was cultivated between the years 1978-80, while shortages due to the failure of wheat cultivation were manifested by 1981.

39. Dawa Norbu, "Changes in Tibetan Economy, 1959-76," 231.

40. Total yield of grain as well as grain per person show a precipitous drop (approximately 190,000 to 140,000 *jin* total yield and 900 to 650 *jin* per person) between 1980 and 1983. Zhang Rongzu, *Nyemo County*, 29.

these disasters, the Chinese continued to propagandize the alleged increases in grain production, due to communization and the introduction of wheat cultivation, as "improvements" that they had brought to Tibet.[41]

US-PRC Rapprochement

A shift in US policy on Tibet—from the 1960 stand on the Tibetan right to self-determination, and covert assistance to the Tibetan Resistance, to an unqualified recognition of Chinese sovereignty over Tibet—occurred in 1972, simultaneous with beginning of the US rapprochement with the PRC. There were no official statements on Tibet policy at the time, but it may be assumed that termination of US support for the Tibetan Mustang operation was a precondition for the 1972 summit meeting between Richard Nixon and Mao Tse-tung.

In his greeting to President Nixon in Peking, Chinese Premier Chou En-lai proposed "establishing normal state relations on the basis of the Five Principles of mutual respect for sovereignty and territorial integrity, mutual nonaggression, noninterference in each other's internal affairs, equality and mutual benefit, and peaceful coexistence."[42] The identical phrase appeared in the subsequent Shanghai Communique, which established the basis for US relations with the PRC.[43]

In the Shanghai Communique, the Chinese side made the following statement in regard to political rights:

------

41. The Chinese claimed to have provided 30 percent of the grain consumed in Tibet between 1970 and 1974, grain whose source is not mentioned, but would appear to have been taken from Tibetans as taxes in the first place. Dawa Norbu, "Changes in Tibetan Economy, 1959-76," 233. Ren Rong, the TAR Party chief during the 1970s, was later charged by Tibetans and others with having inflated his reports of production and conditions in general in Tibet. Ren's claims were reportedly refuted by Zhao Ziyang, CCP secretary in Szechuan at the time, who openly wondered why, if conditions were so good within the TAR, starving refugees were fleeing the TAR for western Szechuan (Kham). Tsering Wangchuk, personal interview.

42. "President Nixon's Visit to the People's Republic of China," *The Department of State Bulletin*, 20 March 1972, 420. The "Five Principles of Peaceful Coexistence" date from the 1954 "Agreement between the Republic of India and the People's Republic of China on Trade and Intercourse between Tibet Region of China and India," by which India recognized Chinese sovereignty over Tibet. The Chinese emphasis on these principles in 1972 clearly implied that the US should no longer meddle in the affairs of either Tibet or Taiwan. Kissinger was asked by an American reporter whether the US had ever before entered into an international agreement based upon the Five Principles of Peaceful Coexistence, to which he replied: "I have to say I am simply not sure." Ibid., 429.

43. "Text of Joint Communique, Issued at Shanghai, February 27," in Ibid., 437.

Wherever there is repression, there is resistance. Countries want independence, nations want liberation and the people want liberation—this has become the irresistible trend of history. All nations, big or small, should be equal; big nations should not bully the small and strong nations should not bully the weak. China will never be a superpower and it opposes hegemony and power politics of any kind. The Chinese side stated that it firmly supports the struggles of all the oppressed people and nations for freedom and liberation and that the people of all countries have the right to choose their social systems according to their own wishes and the right to safeguard the independence, sovereignty and territorial integrity of their own countries and oppose foreign aggression, interference, control and subversion. All foreign troops should be withdrawn to their own countries. [44]

US recognition of the PRC was formalized by the establishment of diplomatic relations, announced by President Carter on 15 December 1978, intended to take effect on 1 January 1979.[45] US diplomatic recognition of the PRC necessarily implied recognition of Chinese sovereignty over Tibet.[46]

End of the Cultural Revolution

Full communization increased Chinese control over all aspects of Tibetans' lives. While full communization was not reached until 1975, the post-Maoist liberalization did not occur in Tibet until 1979; thus the 1970s were for most Tibetans the high point of collectivist regimentation. A minor liberalization was initiated in 1972 with the rise of Chou En-lai and the rehabilitation of Teng Hsiao-p'ing. "Four Freedoms" were offered to Chinese citizens: freedom to worship, to buy and sell privately, to lend

---

44. Ibid. The Chinese statement did not use the words "self-determination," perhaps because they had ceased using that phrase in relation to their own "minority nationalities" after 1949. Nevertheless, the statement calls for the equivalent of self-determination for nations. However, the Chinese deny that any such principles should apply to Tibet because Tibet has "always" been a part of China, and is, in any case, not a nation or a "country" separate from China, but only one of many "minority nationalities" of the multinational Chinese state. The PRC stands for the principle of self-determination for other nations, but claims to have already provided self-determination to Tibetans by "liberating" them from their own legally constituted government.

45. "U.S. Normalizes Relations with the People's Republic of China," in *The Department of State Bulletin*, January 1979, 25.

46. In a 1987 US House of Representatives hearing on Human Rights in Tibet, the Deputy Assistant Secretary of State, Bureau of East Asian and Pacific Affairs, J. Stapleton Roy, was asked, "When did we first take the position that Tibet is a part of China?" He replied, "In 1978." "Hearing before the Subcommittees on Human Rights and International Organizations, and on Asian and Pacific Affairs of the Committee on Foreign Affairs, House of Representatives, 14 October 1987," 40.

and borrow with interest, and to hire laborers or servants. Restoration of a few religious monuments in Tibet, primarily the Jokhang and Potala, was initiated.[47]

Famine conditions eased somewhat after 1973, although food shortages continued; war hysteria, and war preparations in Tibet, ended after the death of Lin Piao and the rapprochement with the United States in 1972. However, political repression in Tibet continued during the campaigns of the early 1970s to criticize Mao's opponents or former opponents within the CCP. Campaigns were launched against Liu Shao-ch'i, Lin Piao (and Confucius) and Teng Hsiao-p'ing, little of which the Tibetans comprehended except as evidence of the Chinese Communists' fallibility and their factional conflicts. Perhaps the most galling aspect of the political campaigns of the 1970s was that Tibetans were required to sing praises of Mao and the fraternal Chinese for bringing freedom and prosperity to Tibet, and had to criticize the Dalai Lama, and now the Panchen Lama as well, and all aspects of Tibetan society before the Chinese liberation.

The Chinese attempted to disguise the lack of correspondence between their claims in Tibet and the reality by a new campaign intended to contrast present conditions with the supposed horrors of the past, similar to the "remembering bitterness" campaign of the early 1960s. Since there was little evidence that present conditions were favorable, the past was attacked with lurid descriptions of the "hell on earth" that Tibet had supposedly been before the Chinese liberation. Pre-1950 Tibetan society was described as "the most reactionary, dark, cruel and barbarous feudal serf system." Tibet's "million emancipated serfs," who had suffered oppression and exploitation under the feudal serf system, now cherished "boundless love for Chairman Mao, the Communist Party and socialism," and were determined to take the socialist road and to never permit the revival of the serf system. The people's communes, they said, were their "golden bridge leading to complete liberation."[48]

All the resources of Chinese propaganda were devoted to the demonization of pre-liberation Tibetan society. Individuals who had suffered oppression in the past were collected and, their stories suitably elaborated, required to recite their accounts for Tibetans and foreign visitors. In case this was less than convincing, an elaborate display was created in Lhasa, an exhibition of life-size clay sculptures entitled the "Wrath of the Serfs." Included were 106 life-size clay figures, "complete with decor,

47. *Forbidden Freedoms: Beijing's Control of Religion in Tibet* (Washington: International Campaign for Tibet, 1990), 13.
48. "Tibet Advances Along the Socialist Road," *Peking Review*, 19 September 1975, 10.

lighting, oral explanations and taped music to produce the optimum artistic effects." The exhibition was divided into four sections: "Feudal Estate Owners' Manors—Miserable Infernos on Earth; Lamaseries—Dark Man-Eating Dens; Local Reactionary Government of Tibet—An Apparatus of Reactionary Rule; and, Serfs Rise in Struggle and Yearn for Liberation."[49]

The sculptures were created by Chinese artists, who studied "again and again" Chairman Mao's *Talks at the Yenan Forum on Literature and Art*, in which Mao had dictated that all literature and art must serve socialist goals. The artists also interviewed Tibetans, who told them of their "past sufferings and present happy life." The "Wrath of the Serfs" became a required item on the itinerary of foreign visitors, who were told that the exhibition invoked in Tibetans memories of the "reactionary, dark, ruthless and savage hell on earth" that was old Tibet and made them determined "to educate their posterity never to forget the damnable dark days in old Tibet and to always remember the kindness and concern of Chairman Mao and the Communist Party, and to follow the Communist Party in carrying on the revolution from generation to generation."[50]

The campaign to criticize Lin Piao and Confucius in Tibet included the requirement to criticize the Dalai Lama and the Panchen, who were identified as examples of leaders whose legitimacy and authority derived from "mandate of heaven ideology and Confucian rites."[51] The Dalai Lama was attacked in fantastically invented propaganda, in which he was alleged to have regularly demanded human sacrifices in his religious practices. The Dalai Lama was said to have killed 21 serfs and slaves and to have used their hearts, livers, blood and flesh as sacrificial offerings in a religious ceremony to curse the PLA in 1949 in a "vain attempt to prevent the victorious advance of the Chinese People's Liberation Army." He was alleged to have used 30 human heads and 80 portions of human blood and flesh as sacrificial offerings every year in scripture reading ceremonies.[52]

---

49. "Wrath of the Serfs—A Tableau of Sculptures," *Peking Review*, 19 September 1975.

50. Ibid. This exhibition occupied a building at the foot of the Potala; it was closed after 1979, apparently after it was realized that such blatant propaganda was often ineffective, even counterproductive, when presented to foreign visitors. The "Wrath of the Serfs" was also produced as a book of photographs of the sculptures, which was widely distributed within China and Tibet and internationally.

51. "Tibet Advances Along the Socialist Road," *Peking Review*, 19 September 1975, 9.

52. "Visual Denunciation of Serf-Owners' Atrocities," *Peking Review*, 19 July 1974, 11. This image of the Dalai Lama remains in the minds of many Chinese to this day, as is evidenced by the statements of Chinese officials who, in response to questions about Tibet, describe in lurid detail the practice of making bowls from human heads and trumpets from the thigh bones of virgin girls who, it is implied, were sacrificed for the purpose. Beyond

In September 1975, on the tenth anniversary of the founding of the TAR, the Chinese Government celebrated the "resplendent socialist new Tibet, standing rock-firm on the southwestern frontiers of our mother-land." Hua Kou-feng, then the Minister of Public Security, informed Tibetans that the changes in Tibet since liberation were a "great victory for the Party's policies towards the nationalities and on regional autono-my and a great victory for Chairman Mao's proletarian revolutionary line."[53] The great advances in Tibet were said to have come about due to the CCP's adherence to the basic Marxist principle that conflicts between nations were due to class conflicts within nations and to Mao's dictum that national struggle was, in essence, class struggle. The Chinese "Central People's Government" was said to have achieved success in its nationality policies, achieving "national equality and national unity," by eliminating the system of exploitation upon which national oppression and national discrimination were based.[54]

Chinese propaganda campaigns of the 1970s had an effect on many Tibetans contradictory to that intended. The denigration of the Dalai Lama and traditional Tibetan society tended to increase Tibetans' soli-darity, reducing the ability of the Chinese to cultivate collaborators and informers.[55] In addition, Tibetans educated in Nationalities Institutes became adept at criticizing Chinese policies, while preserving an immu-nity for themselves, by conveying their criticisms in communist jargon. The Chinese were uncertain of the loyalty of any of their Tibetan collab-orators and frustrated in their attempt to create a core of loyal Tibetan cadres. The only solution was to continue colonialist rule by Chinese cadres in Tibet.

While propaganda contrasting Tibet's supposed social and economic development with the dark feudal past was unconvincing to Tibetans,

---

the political reasons for this demonization of Tibetan society may lie a psychological need to justify Chinese destruction of that society. Chinese propaganda about the evils of the for-mer Tibetan society also tended to reflect and reinforce chauvinistic Chinese attitudes about the backward and barbaric Tibetans.

53. "Tenth Anniversary of Founding of Tibet Autonomous Region Celebrated," *Peking Review*, 19 September 1975, 7. Hua reportedly visited a well-stocked shop in Lhasa, the "Anti-Imperialist Shop," and was fooled, or chose to be fooled, by the "Potemkin" display of goods which in fact were not for sale. Tsering Wangchuk, personal interview, Dharamsala, January 1990. This practice—common in communist countries—was contin-ued in Tibet at least until the early 1980s. Personal observation, 1982.

54. "Tibetans and Hans are Members of One Family," *Peking Review*, 19 September 1975, 14.

55. Amdo Some, personal interview, Dharamsala, February 1990. Collaboration was vir-tually essential for survival in Tibet; therefore, all "collaborators" cannot be condemned, unless one unreasonably wants to condemn all Tibetans who found themselves under Chinese rule.

who were aware of the disparity between Chinese claims and reality, Chinese propaganda was virtually the only source of information on conditions inside Tibet for the Chinese people or for the outside world. The Chinese populace accepted without question that China was engaged in a selfless civilizing mission in Tibet and that the Chinese sent to Tibet had sacrificed all of the comforts of civilization in order to assist the backward, barbaric Tibetans. International opinion was almost totally dependent upon the Chinese version of reality in Tibet, a version that was not effectively countered by the Tibetan Government in Exile, which was not yet sophisticated in the techniques of international opinion making.

A few selected foreign visitors, mainly journalists from fraternal socialist countries of Eastern Europe or Western communist sympathizers, were allowed to visit Tibet before the Cultural Revolution. In the 1970s foreign visitors were again permitted highly regimented tours of Tibet as part of the CCP's campaign to demonstrate its achievements. The accounts of these visitors carefully selected for their pro-Chinese or pro-communist viewpoints tended to uncritically repeat Chinese propaganda.[56]

The success of Chinese propaganda in obscuring the reality in Tibet was a frequently expressed source of frustration to Tibetans both within Tibet and in exile.[57] Much of this success was due to the general pro-

---

56. The most notoriously sycophantic accounts from the period before 1979 were: Anna Louise Strong, *When Serfs Stood Up in Tibet*; Stuart and Roma Gelder, *The Timely Rain: Travels in the New Tibet*; and Han Suyin, Lhasa: *The Open City*. Anna Louise Strong visited Lhasa in 1960 with a group of Eastern European journalists; the Gelders were in Lhasa in 1962; Han Suyin visited in 1975. All accepted the Chinese version of events without question. Two accounts from the subsequent period also fall into this category: Israel Epstein, *Tibet Transformed* and A. Tom Grunfeld, *The Making of Modern Tibet*. Israel Epstein, a naturalized Chinese citizen of Polish descent, was the editor of *China Reconstructs*; he visited Tibet in 1955, 1965 and 1976. Epstein is a professional apologist for the Chinese Communist regime. A. Tom Grunfeld's anachronistic account, published in 1987, echoes the Chinese viewpoint that the issue of Tibet is social, not political. Grunfeld's analysis is affected by his socialist bias and his lack of personal familiarity with Tibet. See also Paul Hollander, *Political Pilgrims: Travels of Western Intellectuals to the Soviet Union, China and Cuba* (New York: Harper Colophon, 1983).

57. As Kunsang Paljor expressed it, "China has today attained the dubious distinction of being the number one nation in the world in the production of lies, false claims, fabrications and deceptions." Paljor, *Tibet: The Undying Flame*, 70. Several Tibetans who escaped to India in the 1970s or 1980s spoke with bitterness of the "lying foreigners" who had perpetuated the Chinese version of conditions in Tibet. Ibid., 71; Choedon, *Red Flag People's Commune*, v. The Dalai Lama repeatedly spoke of his frustration in countering Chinese propaganda and the biased accounts of Chinese Communist sympathizers. "Statement of His Holiness the Dalai Lama on the 19th Anniversary of the Tibetan People's National Uprising Day of 10th March 1959," 10 March 1978, in *Collected Statements of His Holiness the Dalai Lama*, 51.

socialist bias of the era (1960s and 1970s) and the Chinese monopoly on information about events and conditions within both China and Tibet. Western Sinologists tended to uncritically accept Chinese claims in regard to the progress achieved in China and Tibet and to dismiss the accounts of Tibetan refugees (if they noticed them at all) as biased. Many Sinologists—then and now—were affected by their "secondary Sinocentrism." The Chinese successfully misrepresented the issue of Tibet as social rather than political and substantially misconstrued the nature of Tibet's social system both before and after "liberation." Only when a few non-communist Western visitors were allowed into Tibet did a different image of the Tibetan reality begin to emerge.[58]

After 1975 the Chinese sponsored colonization in Tibet by retired PLA veterans, those having served in Tibet and elsewhere, and by "educated youth" (graduated high school students) from China's eastern cities. The colonists were described as permanent settlers who had volunteered to dedicate their lives to socialist construction in Tibet and the defense of the southwest frontiers of the Motherland.[59] The Dalai Lama reported in March 1977 that he had received information that 6,600 Chinese, both retired PLA veterans and youth, had been dispatched to the TAR as colonists.[60] Tibetan women had long been pressured to marry Chinese men; marriages between Tibetan men and Chinese women, on the other hand, were prohibited; Tibetans, however, became increasingly resistant to intermarriage.[61]

The post-Maoist liberalization finally reached Tibet in 1979. Tibetans imprisoned since 1959 were released (many to forced job placement). Communes were abandoned. The Panchen Lama, imprisoned for eight years in Peking (1964-1972) and kept under house arrest thereafter, was rehabilitated early in 1978. The Panchen was exceedingly contrite, thanking the "wise leader," Chairman Hua, for allowing his release. He apolo-

---

58. The first group of Americans to visit Tibet, a group with former secretary of defense James Schlesinger in 1976, remarked on the obviously colonialist nature of the Chinese presence in Tibet, which was described as "peculiarly oppressive even by colonial standards, for it aims at a total domination." Edward N. Luttwak, "Tibetan Interlude," in *Glimpses of Tibet Today* (Dharamsala: Information Office of His Holiness the Dalai Lama, 1978), 1. Luttwak also described as "scandalous" the willingness of the Western press and academia to accept blatantly exaggerated or false Chinese propaganda claims without investigation. Edward N. Luttwak, "Seeing China Plain," in Ibid., 44.

59. "Peking Sends Chinese Immigrants to Tibet," in *Glimpses of Tibet Today*, 67. Very few Chinese went to Tibet voluntarily; Chinese colonists were, like the Tibetans, victims of the Chinese state.

60. "Statement of His Holiness the Dalai Lama on the 18th Anniversary of the Tibetan People's National Uprising Day of 10th March 1959," in Ibid., 49.

61. Paljor, *Tibet: The Undying Flame*, 44; Choedon, *Red Flag People's Commune*, 21.

gized for having followed his "original reactionary class stand," and for having "got the idea of committing treason and running away."[62] As the Panchen said, "the exposure and criticism of me conducted by the government and the people were entirely justified, in the interests of the country, in conformity with the will of the Tibetan people and designed to save me." The Panchen promised that he was "determined to follow the Communist Party steadfastly from now on," and that he would "devote my life to enhancing the great unity of all nationalities in China, building a new socialist Tibet and transforming our motherland into a great socialist country."[63]

At the end of the Cultural Revolution some 20 percent of the Tibetan population (Dharamsala's estimate) had been physically eliminated for the crime of resistance to the Chinese conquest. Tibetans had been subjected to endless propaganda on Marxist-Leninist and Chinese Communist nationalities ideology; Tibetan history and culture had been subjected to relentless denigration. The former Tibetan governmental structure and religious establishment, the infrastructure of Tibetan nationalism, had been totally eradicated. Less than 1,000 monks remained in the eight monasteries not destroyed during the Cultural Revolution.[64] The Tibetan political and cultural elite, upon which a cultural or political revival would ordinarily depend, had been co-opted, eliminated, or forced into exile. Even those aspects that distinguished Tibet physically or visually—architecture, especially monastic architecture and religious monuments of all types, and all forms of decoration in art, architecture and even dress styles—had been destroyed or homogenized to accord with Chinese Communist proletarian styles. All aspects of Tibetan cultural distinctiveness had been attacked during the Cultural Revolution; little remained to distinguish Tibetans from Chinese except ethnic identity, a memory of cultural distinctiveness, language, and a collective experience of foreign oppression.

Surprisingly, these few factors were sufficient for the survival and even the revival of Tibetan nationalism. By some accounts, after almost 30 years of Chinese rule, Tibetan nationalist consciousness was more evolved at the end of the Cultural Revolution than at any time in Tibetan history.[65] This fact was apparently little comprehended by the Chinese,

---

62. This is the first indication that the Panchen had contemplated defecting before his purge in 1964; this threat may have been part of the reason for his imprisonment.

63. "Panchen Erdeni Interviewed," *Peking Review*, 17 March 1978, 41.

64. Ch'ing Jun, "Socioeconomic Changes and Riots in Lhasa."

65. The Dalai Lama stated in his 10 March 1980 address that, "Never in the history of Tibet have the people been so united as they are today." "Statement of His Holiness the Dalai Lama on the 21st Anniversary of the Tibetan People's National Uprising Day of 10th March 1959," 10 March 1980, in *Collected Statements of His Holiness the Dalai Lama*, 57.

despite the phenomenon of anti-colonial nationalism being clearly predicted by Marxism, since the Chinese denied to themselves that their presence in Tibet was in any way colonialist. Most Chinese believed their own propaganda about the social and economic progress made in Tibet; they had little reason to believe otherwise, since Chinese cadres in Tibet sent to Peking exaggerated and optimistic reports about progress in Tibet and the loyalty and gratitude of Tibetans. In any case, given the prevailing atmosphere of repression of all manifestations of Tibetan nationalism, Tibetans provided the Chinese few clues that would reveal their actual sentiments. Tibetans had become adept at making false professions of undying loyalty to the Communist Party and the Chinese state—an essential requirement for survival in Tibet under Chinese rule.

In the post-Maoist period the Chinese tended to congratulate themselves on their newly liberalized policies rather than to dwell upon the mistakes of the past. The Chinese were apparently confident that their policies had been successful, if not in creating Tibetan loyalty to China, at least in the suppression of Tibetan nationalism. However, Tibetan discontent was greater than the Chinese imagined. Chinese rule in Tibet in its 30 years was responsible for destroying much, but its primary creation may have been Tibetan nationalism—that which it had devoted its most intense efforts to eradicate.

14

Revival of Tibetan Nationalism

In 1979 at the beginning of the post-Maoist liberalization in Tibet, Tibetan nationalism was apparently a dead issue. The most visibly distinguishing characteristics of Tibetan culture had been thoroughly eradicated. Even the Tibetan language had been altered by simplification, or "proletarianization," and the incorporation of Chinese words and Marxist terminology. Tibetan ethnic identity remained, but this could be expressed by Tibetans only to distinguish themselves as non-Han, not as non-Chinese. Tibetans shared a cultural and historical memory and an experience of foreign oppression, but these could not be openly expressed for fear of repression.

Assuming that the demise of Tibetan nationalism had been substantially achieved, post-Maoist liberalization aimed at improving Tibetan economic conditions and allowing some of the more innocuous expressions of Tibetan culture, including some Tibetan religious practices. This economic and cultural liberalization, it was anticipated, would defuse the remnants of Tibetan discontent with Chinese rule. Undoubtedly, few Chinese would have predicted that an improvement in Tibetan economic and political conditions would lead to a dramatic revival of Tibetan nationalism. For Tibetans, however, economic liberalization, accompanied by a slight political liberalization, allowed for the expression of shared identity and culture, including the common experience of oppression, for the first time since 1959.

Sino-Tibetan Dialogue

The deaths in 1976 of Zhou Enlai (Chou En-lai), Zhu De (Chu Teh) and Mao Zedong (Mao Tse-tung) began the period of liberalization in Chinese politics.[1] Little would change in Tibet until 1979, but many Tibetans interpreted the deaths of the three most prominent leaders of the Chinese rev-

---

1. The PRC began using the Pinyin system of transliteration in 1979. In keeping with this practice, Chinese names in this and in following chapters will appear in Pinyin with the previous transliterations given in parenthesis at the first usage.

olution, along with the Tangshan earthquake at the end of July 1976, as foretelling a disintegration of Communist China along with its control of Tibet.[2]

The CCP abandoned its ultra-Left line in nationalities policies, symbolized by the slogan, "the national question is essentially a class question." The nationality policy of the Maoist era was criticized for branding nationality contradictions as "antagonistic" or "contradictions between the enemy and ourselves." However, "democratic reforms" among nationalities were defended as "mainly class struggles . . . a matter of revolution within the various nationalities, not a matter of inter-relations between nationalities." The policy of characterizing the national question as "in essence a class question" had allowed "local nationalism" to be defined as a class issue and "local nationalists" as class enemies. Now, with the revival of the Party's original nationalities policy, nationalities' "special characteristics" would once again be respected; nationality issues would be handled as "non-antagonistic." However, the warning was added that these could become antagonistic "if not handled properly." Marxism-Leninism-Mao Zedong Thought was cited to demonstrate that it was well understood that nationalism would outlive classes and that there were still national questions in the PRC.[3]

On 4 November 1977 a group of 24 "officials of the former local government in Tibet, living Buddhas and former commanders of local rebel forces" was released from prison. Tien Pao (Sangye Yeshe) announced the release and called upon exiled Tibetans to "extricate themselves from their predicament of living on alms and suffering discrimination," to realize China's "excellent internal and international situation," and to "return home to participate in socialist construction."[4] This appeal to exiled Tibetans was repeated on 6 January 1979, at which time the Dalai Lama was specifically included among those invited to return.[5] On 17 March 1979, during rallies to celebrate the 20th anniversary of the "launching of democratic reforms" in 1959, 376 prisoners who had taken part in the 1959 rebellion were released. Reactionary labels, or "hats," were removed from some 6,000 who had "served their sentences and been assigned work [forced job placement] or had undergone reform through labor under surveillance in society."[6]

---

2. John Avedon, *In Exile from the Land of Snows* (New York: Vintage Books, 1986), 323.

3. "Is the National Question Essentially a Class Question?" *Beijing Review*, 25 August 1980, 17.

4. "Major Criminals in Tibet Released," *Beijing Review*, 24 November 1978, 3.

5. "Dalai and Other Tibetan Compatriots Welcome," *Beijing Review*, 19 January 1979.

6. "Last Group of Tibetan Prisoners Taking Part in Rebellion Released," *Beijing Review*, 30 March 1979, 6.

A key aspect of the post-Maoist reform policy was a revival of the United Front policy on nationalities and overseas Chinese, including the Taiwanese. The revival of the United Front was equivalent to an admission that the "transition to socialism" in China was still in its preliminary stage. The United Front policy was revived to achieve some of the most significant goals left unaccomplished by that policy in the past: the unification of Taiwan with the mainland and the return of Tibet's exiled Dalai Lama. The CCP hoped that the Dalai Lama's "return to the Motherland" could permanently resolve the issue of China's legitimacy in Tibet, while a favorable resolution of the Tibet issue would help convince Taiwan to accept a similar status of autonomy within the PRC.[7].

In December 1978 the Dalai Lama's elder brother, Gyalo Thondup, was invited to Beijing (Peking) to meet with Deng Xiaoping (Teng Hsiao-p'ing) to discuss the return of the Dalai Lama. Deng offered to hold discussions on the return of the Dalai Lama, with the caveat that Tibet's political status as an integral part of China was not open to discussion. Deng agreed to permit Tibetan exile representatives to visit Tibet to see for themselves how conditions had improved.[8] China's strategy was to deal personally with the Dalai Lama and to treat all Tibetan representatives as his personal emissaries. China had no intention of implying any recognition of the Tibetan Government in Exile by negotiating with its representatives.

Beijing's ignorance of actual conditions in Tibet, cultivated by glowing reports and wildly exaggerated claims conveyed to Beijing by Chinese cadres in Tibet, led to an overly optimistic view of the ease with which it would be possible to impress the Dalai Lama and other Tibetans in exile and to convince them to return. The Chinese tended to think only of the improvements that their new policy in Tibet would achieve rather than to dwell upon the mistakes of the past, all of which were blamed on the "Gang of Four." The Chinese believed much of their own propaganda about material progress, the achievement of "people's democracy" under socialism, and their characterization of pre-liberation Tibet as a "hell on earth."

A delegation from the Tibetan Government in Exile, led by the Dalai

---

7. Tseten Wangchuk Sharlho quotes an internal Chinese document entitled, "Henceforth, No Longer Refer to the `Dalai's Renegade Clique'": "To make the Dalai Clique return is very important. . . . It would greatly benefit . . . our efforts to make Taiwan reunite with the motherland, as well as the achievement of the grand unification of the motherland." Tseten Wangchuk Sharlho, "China's Reforms in Tibet: Issues and Dilemmas," *The Journal of Contemporary China*, vol. 1, no. 1 (Fall 1992), 38.

8. Dawa Norbu, "China's Dialogue with the Dalai Lama 1978-90: Prenegotiation Stage or Dead End?" *Pacific Affairs*, vol. 64, no. 3 (Fall 1991), 352.

Lama's younger brother, Lobsang Samten, arrived in China via Hong Kong at the beginning of August 1979. After two weeks in Beijing, the delegation entered Tibetan territory in Gansu (Kansu) at Labrang Tashikyil, formerly the largest monastery of eastern Amdo. The reception the delegation received here at the traditional border of Tibetan territory was a portent of things to come. The Tibetans of Amdo, desperate for any contact with representatives of the Dalai Lama, mobbed the delegation members, whom they greeted as potential deliverers from their torment. This reception considerably upset local Chinese cadres and those accompanying the delegation since it revealed how loyal Tibetans remained to the Dalai Lama and how ignorant the Chinese were about Tibetans' actual sentiments. If all means of propaganda and control were ineffective in preventing such an outburst of emotion, what would happen if the Dalai Lama himself were to return?[9]

Considering the reception the delegation received in Amdo and the inability of the Chinese to control Tibetans' spontaneous outbursts of emotion, Beijing had to consider the wisdom of allowing the delegation to continue to Lhasa. Chinese cadres in Lhasa were informed of the problem encountered in Amdo, but they, led by Ren Rong, maintained that the same thing could never happen in Lhasa since the Tibetans there had a much higher level of ideological education and class consciousness. Lhasa Tibetans were said to harbor great animosity toward the "reactionaries" of the former Tibetan Government and the Dalai Lama in particular, since many had been his actual slaves and serfs or had been exploited by the former serf system. Local Chinese cadres predicted that there would be no welcome offered to the representatives of the former serf system in Lhasa; in fact, Tibetans would have to be instructed to suppress their animosity toward the hated serf-owners. Beijing was reportedly relieved by this information and allowed the delegation to proceed.[10]

The Chinese administration in Lhasa proved to be as out of touch with Tibetans' sentiments as were Chinese cadres in Amdo. The strictly conformist regime imposed by the Chinese themselves isolated them from accurate information concerning the real feelings of Tibetans. The Chinese had convinced themselves that the slogans that Tibetans were required to repeat affirming their love for the CCP and the socialist system and their hatred for the old system represented their true feelings, or at least that any contrary expressions could be repressed. The people of Lhasa were instructed in advance in regard to every aspect of their expected behavior: they should be polite, but express no emotion either

---

9. Avedon, *In Exile from the Land of Snows*, 333.

10. Jigme Ngapo, "Behind the Unrest in Tibet," *China Spring*, vol. 2, no. 1 (January/February 1988), 25.

positive or negative in greeting the delegation members; they should reply to all questions with the standard Party line about their greatly improved conditions and happy life. Lhasa was given a face-lift and Tibetans who were to meet with the delegation were provided with new clothes and household utensils.[11]

Despite these preparations, the reception that the delegation received in Lhasa was even more tumultuous than that in Amdo. The delegation arrived in Lhasa (by air from Lanzhou) at the end of September. The people of Lhasa could not be restrained in greeting them; thousands gathered at the Jokhang and broke through the gate of the iron fence in front (placed there in the mid-1960s to prevent Tibetans from entering the Jokhang or prostrating in front of it) to reach the delegation members. A similar situation occurred at the guest house where the delegation was staying (the VIP quarters of Guest House No. 1, in the center of Lhasa) and at a picnic in the Norbulinka. Chinese cadres were shocked at the spontaneous outpouring of emotion Tibetans displayed in greeting the delegation, despite all their prohibitions.

The delegation also went to Shigatse, Sakya and Gyantse, but in each case most local Tibetans had been assigned rural labor for the duration of the visit. The delegation continued through Kham and returned to Beijing where, to the displeasure of Chinese officials, the delegation members informed the Chinese that they had been shocked to see Tibetans' poverty and desperation. After the delegation's return to India, the results of the visit were kept secret by the Dharamsala government not only from the international press but from Tibetans in India as well. The reason for this was an agreement with the Chinese that any negotiations would be kept secret. In addition, the Tibetan Government wanted to avoid offending the Chinese in the hope that Beijing would continue its contacts with Dharamsala. Beijing's demand that the negotiations be kept secret, and their condition that only the Dalai Lama's personal status could be discussed, were essential to their requirement that the Tibet issue should not be "internationalized," either by involving any other parties, including the Tibetan exile community, or by treating the Tibet issue as anything but an internal affair of China.[12]

The Chinese apparently were profoundly shocked by what the delegation's visit had revealed. Twenty years of repression of all aspects of Tibetan culture and nationalism and endless propaganda on the superiority of Chinese socialism had not eradicated Tibetans' faith in the Dalai Lama or their dissatisfaction with Chinese rule. Furthermore, these senti-

---

11. Avedon, *In Exile from the Land of Snows*, 338
12. Ibid., 343.

ments had been concealed from Chinese cadres, some of whom had been in daily contact with Tibetans for almost thirty years. In April 1980 the CCP convened its first Tibet Work Meeting, during which it was decided to send a high-level fact-finding mission to the TAR, to be led by CCP General Secretary Hu Yaobang. Hu was accompanied by Vice-Premier Wan Li, Yang Jingren, vice-chairman of the CPPCC and chairman of the Nationalities Affairs Committee of the NPC, and Ngawang Jigme Ngapo, then vice-chairman of the Standing Committee of the NPC. Hu's mission visited Tibet from 22 to 31 May 1980.[13] Hu was reportedly shocked by the poverty of Tibetans he observed, and is reported to have commented, in a closed meeting with Chinese cadres, that the apparent results of China's role in Tibet was reminiscent of colonialism.[14]

A transcript of Hu's speech reveals some contrition on his part at the Party's mishandling of the Tibetan situation, but no acknowledgement that Chinese rule was fundamentally at fault:

> Our present situation is less than wonderful because the Tibetan people's lives have not been much improved. There are some improvements in some parts, but in general, Tibetans still live in relative poverty. In some areas the living standards have even gone down. We comrades in the Central Committee, Chairman Hua as well as several vice-chairman, were very upset when we heard about this situation. We feel that our party has let the Tibetan people down. We feel very bad! The sole purpose of our Communist Party is to work for the happiness of the people, to do good things for them. We have worked nearly thirty years but the life of the Tibetan people has not been notably improved. Are we not to blame?[15]

Hu removed Ren Rong from his position as first secretary of the CCP in Tibet, personally taking him back to Beijing, presumably so that he could not sabotage the reform plans intended for Tibet.[16] Ren Rong was replaced by Yin Fatang, another former PLA man who had been in Tibet

---

13. Hu stayed only 11 days because he came down with altitude sickness, a common affliction of the Chinese in Tibet. Yang Jingren remained for approximately three months. At the time of Hu's visit, 28 percent of the rural population in Tibet were said to be living in "dire poverty, desperate for basic food and clothing." 320,000 Tibetans were reportedly "totally dependent on the government's emergency aid for survival." Jing Jun, "Socioeconomic Changes and Riots in Lhasa," unpublished paper, 1989, 2.

14. Jigme Ngapo, "Behind the Unrest in Tibet," 26. Hu undoubtedly meant this in the economic, not political, sense.

15. "Hu Yaobang's Statement in Lhasa," in Robert Barnett and Shirin Akiner, eds., *Resistance and Reform in Tibet* (Bloomington: Indiana University Press, 1994), 288.

16. Melvyn C. Goldstein and Cynthia M. Beall, "The Impact of China's Reform Policy on the Nomads of Western Tibet," *Asian Survey*, vol. XXIX, no. 6 (June 1989), 626. Chinese cadres in Tibet were reportedly resistant to any liberalization in policy there. Sharlho, "China's Reforms in Tibet," 35.

since 1951. Upon his return to Beijing Hu proposed a radical reform program for the TAR that included relief from taxation and uncompensated labor requirements and compulsory state purchase quotas for a period of three years; decollectivization of agricultural and pastoral production and further privatization of land and property; autonomy in application of policies in Tibet in recognition of Tibet's special circumstances; and a nativization of administration in Tibet in which it was intended that there be no more than "two or three" Hans in any district level administration and no more than 30 percent above district level. Han cadres in the TAR, with the exception of the PLA, were to be reduced by 85 percent. Those Han remaining in Tibet would be required to learn the Tibetan language. In addition, there would be a general liberalization of economic policies in Tibet aimed at a diversification of the Tibetan economy; Chinese subsidies to Tibet would be increased; Tibetan culture, including religion, would be revived, with the state financing the reconstruction of some religious monuments and monasteries.[17]

In addition, autonomous district governments in Tibetan areas of Qinghai (Chinghai), Gansu, Sichuan (Szechuan) and Yunnan were directed to study the directives of the Party Central Committee concerning Tibet with a view to taking "appropriate measures suited to their respective regions."[18] The new policy for the TAR was announced with the caveat that all affairs in Tibet would continue to be decided "under unified leadership" of Beijing and would be implemented only so long as Tibet's "socialist orientation" was upheld:

> Full play must be given to the right of regional autonomy of minority nationalities under the unified leadership of the Party Central Committee. . . . The right to decide for oneself under unified leadership should not be abolished. . . . The autonomous region should fully exercise its right to decide for itself under the unified leadership of the Party Central Committee, and it should lay down laws, rules and regulations according to its special characteristics to protect the right of national autonomy and its special national interests. . . . So long as the socialist orientation is upheld, vigorous efforts must be made to revive and develop Tibetan culture, education and science. . . . The Tibetan people's habits, customs, history and culture must be respected.[19]

---

17. Jigme Ngapo, "Behind the Unrest in Tibet," 26; "New Changes on the Plateau," *Beijing Review*, 25 May 1981, 21.

18. "New Economic Policy," *Beijing Review*, 16 June 1980, 4.

19. *Foreign Broadcast Information Service* (FBIS), 30 May 1980. The last item in this list represents a reversal of the Cultural Revolution campaign to attack the "four olds." Now, the four olds were to be revived.

After the implementation of Hu Yaobang's liberalized policies, conditions for Tibetans improved immediately, primarily because they were now allowed to consume what they produced. The elimination of grain taxes and compulsory sales to the state alleviated the food situation for Tibetans, but required a substantial increase in the import of foodstuffs for the Chinese in Tibet, even though their numbers were to be reduced.[20] Decollectivization removed previous restrictions on Tibetans' freedom of movement and reduced compulsory labor requirements. This, combined with increased economic power and the transfer of most Party officials to the district level, allowed Tibetans to take advantage of relaxed restrictions on religion to resume religious practices and privately begin the reconstruction of religious monuments. Beijing also granted funds to rebuild or restore a few major monasteries as cultural monuments and future tourist attractions.

In preparation for further scheduled Dharamsala delegation visits, CCP cadres warned Tibetans not to express any emotion upon meeting the delegation members nor offer them *khata* (greeting scarves) and especially not to shout any slogans, such as "Long live the Dalai Lama." Tibetans were told that if they ignored this advice they would suffer the same fate as Tsering Lhamo, a Lhasa woman who had shouted "Tibet is independent" during the first delegation's visit and who subsequently had been imprisoned and tortured.[21] Tibetans were told to refute any implied references to Tibetan independence past or present with the assertion that Tibet had always been a part of China.[22]

---

20. In a study of the Tibetan economy in 1984, Wang Xiaoqiang and Bai Nanfeng stated that grain imports into the region (presumably the TAR) had increased by an average of 12 percent every year between 1959 and 1983. The state transported 100 million kg. of grain to the TAR in 1983 and planned to increase that to 150 million kg. in 1984 and 200 million kg. in 1985. In addition, in 1983, 2.1 million kg. were imported from Nepal. One hundred million kg. had already taken up more than half of the freight capacity at the time (1983); it was pointed out that the Chinese state could not increase this to twice that figure with the existing freight capacity. The conclusion reached was that in order to support even a reduced number of Chinese in Tibet, the state would have to continue to depend upon local (voluntary) grain purchases, as well as the maximum feasible imports from the Chinese interior, and increase imports from Nepal. Wang Xiaoqiang and Bai Nanfeng, Angela Knox, trans., *The Poverty of Plenty* (New York: St. Martin's Press, 1991), 113. The Qinghai-Tibet railway was completed from Sining to Golmud in July 1979. "Qinghai-Tibet Railway," *Beijing Review*, 17 August 1979, 6. Of the 1,940 kilometers of the Qinghai-Tibet highway (Golmud to Lhasa), 1,205 kilometers were paved by early 1982. Seventy percent of all imports to the TAR were carried over this road. "Progress in Tibet," *Beijing Review*, 12 April 1982, 6.

21. Tsering Lhamo was thereafter popularly known as Rangzen Ama, "Mother of Independence."

22. Phuntsog Wangyal, "The Report from Tibet," in *From Liberation to Liberalization* (Dharamsala: Information Office of His Holiness the Dalai Lama, 1982), 153.

At the end of May 1980 two more delegations from Dharamsala entered Tibet, the second delegation led by Tenzin Namgyal Tethong and the third by Jetsun Pema Gyalpo, the younger sister of the Dalai Lama. The second delegation entered Kham from Sichuan, while the third followed the path of the first, travelling from Lanzhou in Gansu to Labrang Tashikyil. Both delegations evoked ecstatic receptions wherever they went, even though the Chinese invariably tried to prevent their meeting with local Tibetans. The third delegation discovered the lamentable absence of anything that could be described as education in Tibet. Jetsun Pema Gyalpo expressed her continual frustration at the "lies and deceptions" of the Chinese.[23]

The second delegation was in Lhasa at the end of July 1980. Like the first delegation, they were mobbed when they visited the Jokhang. On 27 July they visited Ganden, which Tibetans had recently begun to repair. For the first time since 1958 the summer festival of *Serthang* (Golden *Thanka*), which included the hanging of an enormous applique Buddha image, was held at Ganden. The delegation members' visit to Ganden for the *Serthang* festival was a cathartic event for themselves as well as for the thousands of Tibetans who made their way there from Lhasa. For the Lhasa Tibetans this was the first such gathering of Tibetans free of the usual supervision of Chinese cadres or Tibetan collaborators (except for the usual spies, informers and photographers) since the 1959 revolt. The gathering inevitably took on a political and nationalistic character, of which the Chinese of course became aware. However, there was little the Chinese could do except to retaliate against the truck drivers who transported Tibetans to Ganden by confiscating their driver's licenses.[24]

Upon the delegation's return to Lhasa, more Tibetans were gathered at the guest house. One delegation member addressed the crowd; this was observed by a group of foreign journalists, coincidentally in Lhasa at the time, who had been prevented from accompanying the delegation to Ganden. Two of the delegation members later met with a group of these journalists. The following day the delegation visited the Norbulinka and were again met on their return by a gathering of several thousand Tibetans and the foreign journalists. Two delegation members addressed the crowd, and, once again, some of the journalists attempted to question the delegation members but were prevented from doing so by the Chinese. These events, and the potential for an international incident

---

23. Jetsun Pema Gyalpo, "Three Months in Tibet: A Personal Viewpoint," in *Liberation to Liberalization*, 113.

24. Tenzin N. Tethong, "Report on the Second Delegation to Tibet," in *Liberation to Liberalization*, 103.

should the foreign press members become aware of what was happening, finally convinced the Chinese to cancel the rest of the delegation's tour and spirit them out of Lhasa as quickly as possible.[25]

Once they had returned to Beijing, the delegation refused a Chinese request that they tour Chinese provinces. They demanded to meet with high-level Tibetan cadres residing in Beijing, but were informed that they were all on rural tours. However, the delegation did meet with Yang Jingren, who had accompanied Hu Yaobang on his visit to Tibet. Yang blamed all that the Tibetans complained of concerning destruction of culture and religion and Tibetans' suffering under Chinese rule on the Cultural Revolution and the Gang of Four. He claimed that now, with the Party's new policy in Tibet, all the mistakes of the past would be corrected. In a warning similar to that given to those within Tibet whose hopes were raised by the delegations' visits, Yang advised the delegation members to be careful about what they said to the media upon their return to India. After they left, he said, the Chinese would still be in charge in Tibet and it was they, not the Tibetans in exile, (nor, it was implied, the Tibetans within Tibet) who would decide Chinese policy towards Tibet in the future.[26] In addition, after the fiasco of the second and third delegations, the Chinese cancelled a fourth scheduled delegation visit.

Despite the entirely unexpected and negative results of the Dharamsala delegations' visits, the Chinese continued their efforts to secure the return of the Dalai Lama. In July 1981 Hu Yaobang conveyed to Gyalo Thondup the CCP's policy on the Dalai Lama's return. First, the Dalai Lama was assured that a new era of political liberalization and stability, including economic prosperity and improved relations among nationalities, had dawned, a situation that, it was promised, would remain in effect for a long time to come.[27] Hu stated that China did not wish to argue over events of the past and would forgive all those who rebelled in 1959. The Dalai Lama was promised that his status and privileges would be the same as before 1959; he would also be appointed a vice-president of the NPC and vice-chairman of the CPPCC. Upon his return, a grand reception would be organized and he would be allowed to hold a press conference. As a final point, the Dalai Lama would be provided with a residence in Beijing, so that he could attend to his duties in

25. Phuntsog Wangyal, "The Report from Tibet," 157.

26. Ibid., 161.

27. The assurance that this new policy was permanent was a standard characteristic of previous negotiations with Tibet (in 1950 and 1957) and future negotiations with Taiwan and Hong Kong. Such assurances were necessary because CCP policies continually changed as factional power shifted.

the NPC and CPPCC, and would be allowed to visit Tibet "from time to time."[28]

Despite the transparency of China's intentions in confining negotiations to the personal status of the Dalai Lama, and China's unwillingness to negotiate with the Tibetan Government in Exile about any meaningful issues concerning Tibet's status or Chinese policy in Tibet, the Tibetans were anxious to continue the dialogue in the hope of a more realistic Chinese response. In April 1982 a delegation composed of three Government in Exile *Kalons*, Juchen Thupten Namgyal, Lodi Gyaltsen Gyari and P.T. Takla (interpreter for the Tibetan Government delegation at the 1951 signing of the 17-Point Agreement), arrived in Beijing for a meeting with Xi Zhongxun, Secretary of the CCP Central Committee, Ulanfu, head of the Nationalities Affairs Commission, and Yang Jingren.

At this meeting, the Tibetans proposed that all Tibetan cultural areas should be reunited into one autonomous region and that this unified TAR should be accorded a higher degree of autonomy than that currently being offered to Taiwan.[29] They insisted that Tibet was due a higher status of autonomy than Taiwan because Tibetans were a non-Chinese nationality. However, they were informed that the difference was that Tibet had already "returned to the Motherland" while Taiwan had not. Taiwan had to be offered concessions in order to secure its return, but the PRC had no reason to make any concessions to Tibet. As a *Beijing Review* editorial later explained:

> Tibet has been liberated for more than three decades. It has completed democratic reforms and socialist transformation, has abolished the feudal serfdom characterized by a combination of political and religious rule, and has long been an autonomous region under the leadership of the central government. The nine-point principle [offered to Taiwan], therefore, is not applicable to Tibet.[30]

The proposal to reunite Tibetan cultural areas in one autonomous region initially received some tepidly positive response, but the idea was ultimately rejected.[31] A reunification of Tibetan ethnic territories would

---

28. Dawa Norbu, "China's Dialogue with the Dalai Lama 1978-90," 353. The requirement that the Dalai Lama reside in Beijing was obviously made out of fear that his return to Tibet might create the same sort of uncontrollable Tibetan response as the delegations' visits had, only perhaps many times magnified.

29. Ibid., 357.

30. "Policy Towards Dalai Lama," *Beijing Review*, 15 November 1982.

31. Ulanfu reportedly supported this Tibetan demand, recalling that the late Zhou Enlai had promised Tibetan Government delegates at the signing of the 17-Point Agreement that the reunification of Kham and Amdo with the TAR could be "separately looked into."

undo the CCP's territorial dismemberment of Tibet and create a politically unified Tibet of enormous size, uncomfortably comparable in size to
interior China. A revival of Tibetan nationalism within that territory
could seriously threaten China's territorial integrity. Provincial authorities of Sichuan, Yunnan, Qinghai and Gansu would also, of course,
oppose the loss of Tibetan ethnic territories to the TAR. The CCP therefore invoked its version of the history of Tibet's territorial divisions, stating that the Tibetans had "for centuries lived in separate communities
within four other provinces as well as Tibet [TAR] itself." Therefore, it
was "not reasonable to change the historically determined administrative
divisions simply according to the distribution of nationalities."[32] The CCP
was intent that no issue of Tibet's territorial or political status should be
allowed to reappear and that Tibetans should in no way be distinguished
from China's other national minorities, all of whom had long been organized in their respective autonomous territorial units and had, in the
CCP's view, achieved the permanent status of "national regional autonomy."

The CCP also took the opportunity to squelch "critics abroad" who
were once again raising the issue of "so-called Tibetan independence."
Tibet became part of China's territory in the 13th century, it was said, and
the "so-called independence of Tibet in modern history has always been
a dirty allegation of imperialist aggression against China and has been
opposed by the Chinese people, and most strenuously by the Tibetan
people." Furthermore, they claimed that the recent "frenzied welcome"
accorded to representatives of the Dalai Lama in Tibet had no nationalist
or political significance at all, but was merely a remnant of Tibetans' religious devotion: "Tibetan Buddhists regard not only Dalai Lama, but all
others they call `Living Buddhas' as gods incarnate, and welcome them
accordingly."[33]

The same three Tibetan Government in Exile officials returned at the
end of October 1984 to continue the Sino-Tibetan dialogue. They met
again with Yang Jingren, now director of the United Front Work

---

Ngapo had brought the idea up again at the 1957 Tsingtao Conference. Hu Yaobang had
also reportedly told Gyalo Thondup in 1981 that "this [reunification] is a new idea which
needs to be considered." Dawa Norbu, "China's Dialogue with the Dalai Lama 1978-90,"
358.

32. "Policy Towards Dalai Lama," *Beijing Review*, 15 November 1982. In a 1994 White
Paper on Tibet, the Chinese Government explained the presence of so many Tibetans in
"Chinese" provinces: "As a result of long historical changes, ethnic Tibetans have settled
not only in Tibet but also in areas in Sichuan, Qinghai, Gansu and Yunnan provinces."
"Tibet—Its Ownership and Human Rights Situation, *Beijing Review*, 28 September 1992, 39.

33. "Policy Towards Dalai Lama," *Beijing Review*, 15 November 1982.

Department, to whom they complained about recent arrests of dissidents in Tibet (in conjunction with the Anti-Spiritual Pollution Campaign, instituted by the leftist faction in 1983) and the cancellation of further delegation visits. They informed the Chinese that the Dalai Lama rejected China's proposed conditions for his return and they reiterated their earlier demands for a reunification of all Tibetan territory and an enhanced autonomous status for all of Tibet.[34]

Yang suggested that they not "quibble over the events of 1959" and repeated the conditions for the Dalai Lama's return laid down by Hu Yaobang in his talks with Gyalo Thondup in 1981. The Dalai Lama, if he returned, would enjoy the "same political status and living conditions as he had before 1959." Yang complained that "while the Dalai Lama expresses his wish of improving relations with the central authorities, some of his followers carry out activities advocating Tibetan independence." He warned: "It will never do for anyone to play with the idea of an independent Tibet."[35]

The Chinese were apparently having second thoughts about the wisdom of reopening the Tibetan issue at all. The Chinese were increasingly uncertain about the potential effects of the Dalai Lama's return, even if he were to be confined to Beijing, since he was now a subject of international interest. The decision of CCP "liberals" to open dialogue with the Dalai Lama came under attack since it had revived seemingly forever buried issues, had exposed Tibetans' rejection of Chinese rule to the world, and had neither convinced the Dalai Lama to return nor proven effective in similar efforts directed at Taiwan. The Chinese were perturbed that the issue of Tibet's political status had been revived, whether in regard to independence, past or future, or some altered form of autonomy within the Chinese state. The Chinese had interpreted certain statements made by the Dalai Lama in 1978, 1979 and 1980, in which he had said that the "happiness" of the Tibetan people was the "core of the issue," as implying his abandonment of the demand for independence and his concession to Chinese preconditions for negotiation.[36] Despite this implied under-

---

34. Dawa Norbu, "China's Dialogue with the Dalai Lama 1978-90," 358.

35. "Beijing Receives Dalai Lama's Envoys," *Beijing Review*, 3 December 1984, 9.

36. *The Collected Statements, Articles and Interviews of His Holiness the Dalai Lama* (Dharamsala: Information Office of His Holiness the Dalai Lama, 1982), 51, 59, 114, 131. The Dalai Lama's statements were made in his belief that the issue was not his own status but the benefit of Tibetans, for whom "happiness" meant freedom, self-determination, and free choice of political system. Ibid., 102. In this context, he said, "Independence is in itself a means to gain happiness." Ibid., 114. Nevertheless, his statements seem to have been taken by the Chinese, as well as by many Tibetan exiles, as an abandonment of the demand for independence. Gyalo Thondup was also suspected by many Tibetans of having conveyed this impression to the Chinese leaders, since this was thought to be his personal position.

standing, the Tibetan delegations had instigated "separatist" disturbances in Lhasa and other places in Tibet and Tibetan exile organizations
and publications had continued to agitate for independence.[37]

The Chinese were adamant that the Tibetans abandon not only their
hopes for future Tibetan independence, or even any change of Tibet's status within China, but also their claim that Tibet had been anything but an
integral part of China in the past.[38] The implied consent of the Dalai Lama
to the reality that Tibet had been effectively a part of China since 1951 was
insufficient for Chinese hardliners. Unless Tibet was already a part of
China in 1950, China's "peaceful liberation" of Tibet could be characterized as imperialist aggression. Pragmatists within the CCP may have
been willing to ignore this issue since it was not likely to have any practical consequences, given China's predominance of force in the issue, but
conservative ideologues preferred to eradicate the very idea that Tibet
had ever been an independent state or a "country" separate from China.
Any retreat from the position that China's 1950 invasion was a peaceful
liberation of territory already part of China was adamantly resisted, since
it called into question the CCP's anti-imperialist ideology and the legitimacy of Chinese sovereignty over Tibet.

The CCP's "Tibet model" for the reintegration of Taiwan was not only
unsuccessful in improving relations with Taiwan but had encouraged the
Tibetans to demand a "Taiwan model" for Tibet. For the CCP, the salient
characteristic of the "Tibet model" was the successful and permanent resolution of the Tibet issue by means of the 17-Point Agreement in 1951, not
the later history of Chinese rule in Tibet. The Taiwanese, however, pointed out that the CCP had violated that agreement, had driven the Tibetans
to revolt and then had eliminated the Tibetan Government, whose continued existence had been guaranteed; they wondered how the
Communists could offer their record in Tibet as an example for a resolution to the problem of Taiwan. Taiwan published an analysis of the CCP
regime in Tibet that heaped scorn on the CCP's claims to have achieved
"people's democracy" there, and rejected any such arrangement for
Taiwan. The CCP's "Tibet model" was described as an "out and out political deception," which had "brought no happiness but unending disaster
to the Tibetan people." The PRC's "oppression and enslavement" of the
Tibetan people was, it was said, "more brutal than any Western colonialism or traditional feudalism."[39]

---

37. The Chinese seem to have imagined that the Dalai Lama could, if he wished, exercise the same sort of thought control over his people and public organs as the CCP exercised
over theirs.

38. Dawa Norbu, "China's Dialogue with the Dalai Lama 1978-90," 356.

39. Taiwan's statement stopped short of characterizing the PRC's invasion of Tibet as

After the impasse of the 1984 negotiations in Beijing, the Sino-Tibetan dialogue was virtually discontinued (except for a final delegation visit to Amdo in 1985). China achieved neither an end to the issue of Tibet's political status, the propaganda victory it expected for instituting a liberal policy in Tibet, nor the return of the Dalai Lama and the benefits expected to derive therefrom. Instead, liberalization in Tibet led to a revival of Tibetan nationalism, including a renewed faith in the Dalai Lama and Tibetan religion, and a revival of Tibetans' messianic hopes that the Dalai Lama or some outside force would be capable of delivering them from the oppression of Chinese rule.

Revival of Tibetan Religion, Culture and Nationalism

Contrary to Chinese expectations that economic and social liberalization would remove the basis for Tibetan discontent, the loosening of social restrictions led to a spontaneous revival of Tibetan civil and cultural life and a resurgence of Tibetan nationalism. The reconstruction of religious monuments and monasteries, to which Tibetans devoted a large portion of their newly recovered economic resources, was, at least in its beginning stages, free of Chinese control and interference. The revival of Tibetan Buddhism was for Tibetans a communal experience with inevitable political significance, given the traditional relationship between Tibetan religion and politics. The revival of religion and the restoration and reconstruction of religious monuments became a focus and center for the revival of autonomous Tibetan social and political life.

A few of the most famous monasteries were restored at government expense, but no reconstruction of destroyed monasteries was undertaken. In Lhasa the Jokhang, Drepung and Sera would be restored but Ganden would not be rebuilt. The other monasteries to be restored with state funds were Tashilhunpo, Sakya, Gyantse and Shalu in Tsang, Derge and Chamdo in Kham and Kumbum, and Labrang Tashikyil in Amdo. Restoration work on the Jokhang temple, Drepung, Sera and Tashilhunpo was begun in 1972 and completed in April 1980. Restoration of Sakya and the Gyantse Palkor Chode was reportedly under way in 1980.[40] In 1982 the Chinese Government announced plans to restore an additional 53

---

imperialist aggression against a separate country (since the KMT also maintained its claim to sovereignty over Tibet). The 1959 revolt was characterized as an "anti-communist uprising," not anti-Chinese. *The True Features of Chinese Communist "Tibet Model"* (Taipei: Asian People's Anti-Communist League, 1982), 2, 42.

40. "Tibet Renovates Temples and Monasteries," *Beijing Review*, 28 April 1980, 29.

large or historic monasteries, including the main temples of Tibet's four primary religious sects.[41]

The most superficial aspects of religious practice, such as circumambulation, prostration and the offering of butter lamps to deities were also allowed; a few monks would be allowed to attend the restored monasteries, but their numbers would be restricted and all would have to engage in productive labor. The premise of the new policy on religion was that the physical manifestations of Tibetan Buddhism would be restored as cultural museums, but institutional Buddhism would not be allowed to revive. In a document acquired by the second Dharamsala delegation in 1980, the CCP's policy on the restoration of religion was set out. The document (from Chamdo) reveals that the Party's policy on religion had not changed: religion was still condemned as a "tranquilizing poison," and "blind faith," and was still "against the law and counterrevolutionary." Tibetan cadres were prohibited from engaging in any religious practices, public or private. No one was allowed to contribute money to the revival of religion or to "try to revive the power of religion that has already been destroyed."[42]

The political threat that the revival of religion posed is evident in the document's warning: "Under the guise of religious practice, counterrevolutionaries may pass messages, conduct espionage, and urge people to destroy communism and organize themselves into organizations." CCP cadres' opposition to the religious revival and their attempts to limit its effects were apparent:

> Nowadays in the name of religious freedom people create ugly rumours. They say that the Dalai Lama is being invited back to Tibet, which is a sign of weakness of China and the victory of the Dalai Lama. They say that the Dalai Lama will come, the times will change, the people's communes will break up and the old Tibetan system of Chosi—government according to religion—will be restored. ... They dig up old prophecies. ... This is all wrong. Also people take youngsters to religious places and try to teach them religious ideas. Some schoolteachers even try to use their position to talk about religion. ... This is strictly against the Constitution, and, as it says in Article 165: "If anyone collects money or commodities in the name of God and in blind faith, he will incur a minimum punishment of two years imprisonment, or in some cases up to seven years."[43]

---

41. "Tibet: An Inside View (V)—Religious Freedom Returns," *Beijing Review*, 20 December 1982.

42. Phuntsog Wangyal, "The Report from Tibet," 144. In fact, cadres' fear of being seen at religious sites contributed to the autonomous character of the religious revival.

43. Ibid.

Despite the efforts of local cadres to restrict the religious revival, Tibetans took maximum advantage of religious freedoms promised by Beijing. Tibetans of all ages flocked to the newly reopened temples and monasteries and enthusiastically devoted their labor and economic resources to the restoration and rebuilding of religious monuments. The removal of Chinese cadres at the county level allowed Tibetans to reconstruct many *chortens, mani* walls and local monasteries without supervision. Pilgrims from rural areas of the TAR and from Kham and Amdo travelled to Lhasa with or without permission from local authorities. In Lhasa the iron fence blocking access to the Jokhang was removed and Tibetans visited this holiest of shrines in numbers reported at 90,000 per month.[44] Lhasa Tibetans and pilgrims, especially those from Amdo (birthplace of Tsongkhapa), began the reconstruction of Ganden, an important symbol of the Tibetan nation and state, having been the first of the three great state monasteries founded in the early 15th century by Tsongkhapa, the founder of the Gelugpa sect and Tibet's system of government.

The rebuilt monasteries attracted former and new monks, all of whom were supported by private donations. Many Tibetans, alienated by the continuing propaganda and denigration of Tibetan culture encountered in the Chinese schools, began to send their children to the monks for schooling. Monks, some of whom remembered what life in Tibet was like before the Chinese invasion, exposed young Tibetans to an entirely different picture of their own culture than that propagated by the Chinese. Monasteries became the locus of a Tibetan cultural and political revival even for Tibetans of little or no religious faith because of the symbolism of Buddhism and religious institutions in Tibetan national identity.

The Dharamsala delegations' visits also had a dramatic impact on the Tibetan nationalist revival in that the delegation visits provided the first evidence in 20 years that Tibet had not been completely abandoned to its fate under the Chinese. In addition, many exiles were allowed to visit Tibet and a few Tibetans were permitted to visit their relatives in India and Nepal (family members had to be left behind as security). This contact increased Tibetans' sense of communal solidarity by exposing them to a reality beyond that of Chinese propaganda, and emboldened them to challenge Chinese claims.[45] The Chinese attempted to respond by establishing "Reception Committees for Tibetan Returnees" in Lhasa and other

---

44. Sharlho, "China's Reforms in Tibet," 40.

45. Tibetans had been permitted no correspondence with the outside world for 20 years and thus knew no reality beyond what they were told by the Chinese. For example, Tibetans had been told that all exiles were living in poverty, since only China and the socialist countries had achieved economic prosperity. They were thus surprised when exiles returned well clothed, well fed and laden with cash and gifts. One Tibetan exile visiting from the

cities, which promised returning exiles a restitution of their former property, including assistance in repair of houses and in "solving their difficulties of living," if they would remain in Tibet.[46] However, returning exiles were less than impressed with Chinese "improvements" when they saw the impoverished conditions of relatives who often appeared aged beyond their years due to poor health conditions, inadequate diet, or prison or labor experience. Few chose to remain in Tibet, while quite a number Tibetans who were allowed to visit India remained there despite sanctions against their families.

Tibetans' exposure to an alternative reality was also increased by foreign visitors to Tibet. Highly restricted group tours were permitted in Tibet after 1979, but the first real contact Tibetans had with foreigners began with the initiation of individual tourism in the summer of 1982.[47] Contact with individual travelers, who were often appreciative of Tibetan culture or even sympathetic to the Tibetan political cause, helped to revive Tibetans' sense of self-respect.

Tibetans became more resistant to ideological coercion and indoctrination due to their increased sense of communal solidarity, and the awareness that they had some support in the outside world beyond the reach of the Chinese. As is usually the case with totalitarian systems, the efficacy of CCP indoctrination depended upon a total monopoly on information sources; when that monopoly was broken by exposure to contradictory information, the whole system tended to collapse due to its revealed lack of correspondence with reality. The removal of much of the former infrastructure of indoctrination and repression only hastened the collapse. Some Tibetans, especially those newly released from prisons or labor camps, were emboldened in their opposition to all aspects of Chinese rule in Tibet, saying that they had suffered so much under Chinese rule that they no longer feared repression or cared for their personal fate.[48]

United States was offered potatoes by her sister, whom she had not seen for twenty years, because the sister had heard that Americans were so poor that they didn't even have potatoes to eat. Dolma Tenpa, personal communication, Lhasa, October 1982.

46. *The True Features of Chinese Communist "Tibet Model,"* 29.

47. The first individual travel permits were given to foreigners on an experimental basis in the summer of 1982 (individual travel was not yet officially permitted in any part of the PRC). No announcement was made of this change in policy; permits to Lhasa were available in only three small cities in China; some 150-200 individual travellers reached Tibet that summer. Individual tourism in China and Tibet was officially permitted from 1984. Personal observation, Lhasa, 1982. Between 1980 and 1983 only 6,300 foreign tourists visited Tibet, mostly in group tours. In 1984 the number was 3,000, by now including a substantial number of individual tourists. In 1985 the number rose to 7,182; in 1986 to 30,711 and in 1987 to 43,000. Jing Jun, "Socioeconomic Changes and Riots in Lhasa," 3.

48. Personal communication with various Tibetans, Lhasa, 1982.

The Panchen Lama was returned to Tibet in July 1982 (for a visit only), the first time he had been in Tibet since 1964. Tibetans by the thousands sought the Panchen's blessing, which he gave at the Jokhang over a period of several days, and attended a speech he delivered at Sera. Although many Tibetans had been somewhat ambivalent about the Panchen Lama due to his past and present collaboration, his reputation considerably improved during his Lhasa visit. The Panchen spoke frankly about the past, including his imprisonment and his partial paralysis, which had resulted from having to lie on one side facing his cell door so that he could be continually observed, a common regimen in Chinese prisons. The Panchen was once again supportive of religious freedom in Tibet; his reappearance reminded Tibetans that he had confronted the Chinese over their policies in Tibet in 1964 and had suffered torture and imprisonment as a consequence. His reception could not, however, have led Party cadres to believe that the Panchen could provide an adequate substitute for the Dalai Lama; one Tibetan commented that the Panchen's return was a "small joy," while the joy of the Dalai Lama's return would be of a considerably greater magnitude.[49]

In August 1982 Tibetans again celebrated the *Serthang* festival at Ganden (in 1981 Tibetans were prevented from going to Ganden for this event by roadblocks at the Kyichu bridge). Work had continued at Ganden, despite cadres' attempts to intimidate workers and to stop their sources of funding; by the summer of 1982, the burial *chorten* of Tsongkhapa and three *lhakhangs* had been rebuilt. The Chinese suspected that Dharamsala was behind the reconstruction of Ganden, since it was still difficult for them to believe that Tibetans, whom they had instructed so well in anti-religious propaganda, were devoting so much of their still meagre economic resources to this endeavor.[50] The approximately 300 Tibetans working at Ganden were supported by private donations; cadres were unable to exercise economic or work unit control over them, nor were the workers intimidated by threats, since the reconstruction of Ganden had become such a symbol of the revival of Tibetan culture and religion.[51]

Chinese cadres in Tibet were surprised by the resurgence of religious belief, which they had thought substantially eradicated. Chinese cadres, along with many old Tibetan cadres, opposed Hu Yaobang's liberalization and obstructed its implementation as much as possible. The post-Maoist purge of leftist cadres was not carried out with persistence in

---

49. Ibid.
50. Ibid.
51. Personal observation, Lhasa, 1982.

Tibet, since many Chinese cadres had entrenched themselves in local positions of power and were difficult to dislodge, especially since they represented the CCP's body of expertise in regard to the Tibetan situation. Loyal Tibetan cadres, many of whom were as committed to leftist ideology and to their own positions of power as the Chinese, could not easily be removed since there were few young Tibetans whose loyalty the Chinese trusted.[52] Many of the leftist cadres of the old leadership in Tibet were quickly rehabilitated as soon as the political winds shifted in 1983-84. The Panchen Lama later complained that the leftist influence in Tibet was not sufficiently eradicated and that many leftists had been rehabilitated in a campaign known as "Repenting for the Past Mistakes and Willing to Change."[53] In 1983-1984 leftists in the CCP made a comeback with an "Anti-Spiritual Pollution Campaign," targeted at the bourgeois and capitalist effects of economic liberalization and the opening to the outside world.

By 1984 the program of repatriation of Chinese workers and cadres was discontinued.[54] The CCP rationalized its retreat from the promise to substantially reduce the number of Chinese cadres and workers in Tibet with the explanation that Tibetans were still not ready for self-rule: "The key to realizing real autonomy for minority nationalities is to let minority nationality cadres administer their own affairs. But as a result of centuries of serfdom, most Tibetan working people are not intellectual and so there is need for people of other nationalities to help in administration."[55]

Recognizing that the policy of allowing the unsupervised revival of religion had led to a revival of Tibetan nationalism, the CCP moved to restrict the reconstruction of monasteries, the number of monks being initiated and religious instruction by monks. Reconstruction at Ganden was

---

52. Sharlho, "China's Reforms in Tibet," 52.

53. *The Panchen Lama Speaks* (Dharamsala: Department of Information and International Relations, Central Tibetan Administration of HH the Dalai Lama, 1991), 9.

54. *Beijing Review* revealed in 1987 that the number of Han in Tibet (TAR) had been reduced from 92,000 in 1982 to 71,000 in 1985. "Tibet's Population Develops," *Beijing Review*, 17 August 1987, 20. This number, a reduction of only 21,000, or 23 percent, far less than the 85 percent promised in 1980, does not include the PLA in the TAR, nor any increases in the PLA, nor the large influx of workers and petty bourgeoisie who entered Tibet after 1984, all of whom were considered temporary residents. Tsering Wangchuk reports that many of the Chinese cadres repatriated from Tibet sought to take as many material goods with them as possible, in particular, gold, artworks and wooden furniture. Since wooden furniture had become rare and valuable in the Chinese interior, many of the Chinese departees had wood furniture made in enormous quantities, causing a wood shortage in Lhasa. Tsering Wangchuk, personal interview, Dharamsala, 1990.

55. "Tibet: Changes in a Quarter Century," *Beijing Review*, 9 April 1984, 6.

virtually halted in 1983 by the arrest of many of the workers there. Quotas for the number of monks were established at each restored monastery; an age limit of 18 years was set for initiation, a measure intended to eliminate the usual practice of educating monks from an early age. The age restriction guaranteed that children would receive "socialist education" (or none at all) until age 18. Furthermore, approval had to be obtained from local Party committees before any monk could be initiated. Monks were required to be "patriotic" and of a good class and political background.

The Party also attempted to control monasteries from within by instituting "democratic management committees" as a means of attaining political control over monasteries. Monks with anti-Chinese sentiments or nationalistic attitudes were to be reported to the authorities. Monastic education was limited to the most superficial aspects of Buddhist practice; monks were intended to be relegated to a role as caretakers of cultural monuments and as exhibits for foreign tourists. Controls over donations to religion were established, at least at the major sites in Lhasa, by the confiscation of monetary donations and even of butter offerings, which were taken for use in state bakeries. By 1984 the CCP had substantially reestablished political control over the religious revival, confining it primarily to individual expressions of faith and the most superficial aspects of religious practice, which were considered relatively innocuous and had the added benefit of creating the illusion of religious freedom for foreign visitors.

The resurgence of Tibetan culture and nationalism was an inevitable result of the liberalization of previously very repressive policies. The Chinese miscalculated in imagining that liberalization would alleviate Tibetans' remaining discontent with Chinese rule. As had been the case in 1957 during the Hundred Flowers liberalization, the CCP mistook Tibetans' fundamental rejection of Chinese rule for discontent with certain unpopular policies. The Chinese remained oblivious to the actual sentiments of Tibetans and the fact that the legitimacy of China's rule in Tibet was still an issue for Tibetans. There was also a tendency to ignore the mistakes of the past in the belief that all would be resolved by a new "correct policy." An additional factor may have been that conditions in China were little better than those in Tibet; the situation in Tibet was not as shocking to Chinese as it was to foreigners or to returning Tibetan exiles. The Chinese imagined that the exiles were living in poverty in India and would be impressed by "improvements" in Tibet. China had devoted large economic resources to Tibet, and, despite Hu Yaobang's comment that there was no obvious result to show for this, many Chinese no doubt believed that China had done much to help Tibet and that this in some way must be apparent.

1984 Law on National Regional Autonomy

In 1984 the CCP published a new Law on National Regional Autonomy. According to the provisions of the "new" law, autonomous regional governments were given the authority to "formulate regulations with respect to regional autonomy and other regulations in accordance with its own political, economic and cultural characteristics"; to "alter or cease to implement any laws or regulations issued by the Central Government if these laws and regulations do not suit the conditions of an autonomous area"; to "adopt special policies and flexible measures in accordance with local economic conditions," and "promulgate its own economic policies and plans in light of the local economic conditions"; and to "pursue foreign trade and open foreign trade ports." Autonomous regions were given authority over natural resource usage in their own areas and control over transient populations.[56] In the cultural and linguistic field, citizens of minority nationalities were to be allowed freedom of religious belief, but the central government retained the power "to restrict religious activities in the interest of public order, health, and education." Religious groups were prohibited from being "subject to any foreign domination." Nationalities had the right to "use and develop their own spoken and written languages and freedom to preserve their own customs," and to "set up its own education system and curricula." Elementary education was to be conducted in the nationality language, but, "senior students should learn Mandarin."[57]

All of these "autonomous rights" were subject to the guidelines and approval of the central government, the State Council, the NPC and the PRC Constitution. The head of the "people's government" of autonomous regions was required to be a member of the majority nationality in that region, but the head of the CCP in that region could be of any nationality. In practice, the head of the CCP in nationality regions was almost invariably Han; in the TAR, this had been the case since 1951. The CCP justified this policy, and the fact that no Tibetan had ever been the head of the CCP in the TAR, with the theory that Party organization was not nationality specific. Any Party member could rise to high levels without regard to nationality; therefore, "there is no direct link between whoever takes the post of first secretary of the regional Party committee and regional national autonomy."[58]

56. 1984 Law on Regional Autonomy, in *The Myth of Tibetan Autonomy: A Legal Analysis of the Status of Tibet* (Washington: International Campaign for Tibet and International Human Rights Law Group, 1994), 17.

57. Ibid., 41.

58. "A Dialogue on Tibet (III): Regional Autonomy and Special Policies," *Beijing Review*, 23 November 1987, 25.

Religious freedom was to encompass only the most superficial aspects of personal faith, while organized Buddhism was subjected to rigorous supervision and controls. Language policy was one of the most contentious issues, since lack of any higher educational facilities in Tibetan since 1959 had resulted in a deterioration of most Tibetans' spoken and written language. The provision that higher education would still be conducted in Chinese meant that, for any Tibetan to attain more than menial employment or to seek higher education, Chinese language skills had to be pursued rather than Tibetan. Hu Yaobang's 1980 promise that Chinese cadres in Tibet would be required to learn the Tibetan language had been quietly dropped since the Chinese in Tibet had made little effort to comply.

Economic policy was still dictated by Beijing. Foreign trade remained a monopoly of state trading companies; only Tibetans living within 30 miles of the Nepal, India and Bhutan frontiers were allowed to engage in border trade (and only by barter).[59] Despite the provision of the Law on National Regional Autonomy that autonomous regions should have authority over natural resource usage, Tibetans had little or no control over resource exploitation; in fact, the "bargain" Mao had offered western frontier regions—that they should supply natural resources while the interior would provide them with developmental assistance—was repeated almost verbatim in the article announcing the "new" law on national regional autonomy.[60] Tibet not only had no control over the transient Chinese population, as promised in the new law, but no control over Chinese colonization of Tibet.

The 1984 Law on National Regional Autonomy was more detailed (67 articles) than the 1952 General Program for National Regional Autonomy which it replaced, but its basic provisions were similar. The major addition to the "new" law consisted in the provision that minority nationalities law must adhere to Deng Xiaoping's "Four Fundamental Principles."[61] Autonomous regional governments were allowed no more autonomy, and, in the case of the TAR, perhaps less autonomy, than any provincial government in the PRC.[62] With the exception of the new provisions on economic autonomy, all of which were extremely circum-

---

59. *The Myth of Tibetan Autonomy*, 19.

60. "Regional Autonomy for Minorities," *Beijing Review*, 11 June 1984, 4.

61. The "Four Fundamental Principles" were that China must adhere to socialism, the people's democratic dictatorship, the leadership of the Communist Party, and Marxism-Leninism-Mao Tse-tung Thought. The Four Fundamental Principles were incorporated in the 1984 PRC Constitution.

62. Jigme Ngapo, "Behind the Unrest in Tibet," 27; Sharlho, "China's Reforms in Tibet," 53.

scribed by central government control, there was so little new in the 1984 law that the question is raised concerning the CCP's reasons for issuing a "new" law, unless the message intended was that the CCP's promises in regard to nationality autonomy would finally be respected.

1984 Tibet Work Meeting

The unexpected results of the post-Maoist liberalization in Tibet led the CCP to reappraise its policies. Dialogue with the Tibetan exiles was essentially abandoned, although the Chinese continued to maintain that they were willing to negotiate if the Dalai Lama would give up the idea of independence. Although social, especially religious, liberalization was more strictly circumscribed, liberalized economic policies were not abandoned. In fact, economic development intended to integrate the Tibetan economy into that of interior China, further making Tibet an integral and inseparable part of China, became the cornerstone of the CCP's policy in Tibet. A highly significant aspect of that policy was the abandonment of Hu Yaobang's commitment to allow Tibetan autonomy by restricting the number of Han Chinese in Tibet. Instead, Tibet was opened to a flood of Chinese administrators, "experts" and private entrepreneurs.

The CCP held a Tibet Work Meeting from 27 February to 6 March 1984, only the second time such a meeting was held (the first was in April 1980). Some 300 Tibetan and Chinese cadres working in the TAR were summoned to Beijing to attend. Hu Yaobang chaired each of the daily sessions. The meeting's primary focus was on economic issues; however, the political issue in Tibet was also addressed. The debate focused on finding the right combination of economic liberalization and political control to continue economic development while keeping the lid on the Tibetan religious and nationalist revival. The meeting was also intended to lay plans for the celebration in 1985 of the 20th anniversary of the founding of the TAR.

CCP policy at the time called for the development of a "socialist market economy," which included all of the aspects of capitalism (without calling it capitalism) except political freedom. Decollectivization had improved Tibetans' economic conditions somewhat, but Tibet lagged far behind interior provinces in the development of a market economy. As the CCP described the situation, "three years of natural calamities, plus the lack of sufficient measures to enliven the economy due to 'leftist' thinking among some people in the leading bodies of Tibet, have retarded the growth of agriculture and animal husbandry and since 1980 living standards have not improved much."[63]

---

63. "Tibet Carries Out New Policies," *Beijing Review*, 21 May 1984, 6. Part of the reason

The Tibet Work Meeting made several decisions. Tax relief, first implemented in 1980 for a period of three years, was extended until 1990. The central government would no longer issue directives for agricultural and pastoral production. Animal husbandry would be emphasized over agriculture; lands converted to grain production during the campaign for "taking grain as the key link" would be returned to pasturage. Land was redistributed to individual households and animals were divided equally among families. Stress was to be placed upon the development of free markets, a diversified economy and commodity production, including economic exchange with neighboring countries and interior Chinese provinces. Economic relations with interior provinces were intended to "strengthen economic exchanges and cooperation with other provinces and municipalities in the Chinese hinterland, including actively introducing advanced equipment, technology and scientific and technical personnel from the hinterland." Tibet was to be more fully opened to tourism. Tibetan culture, language, arts and religion would continue to be developed and the Party would "cooperate sincerely" with representatives of the upper social stratum in the revived United Front.[64]

The CCP also announced its intention to undertake 43 large construction projects in the TAR, at a total cost of 470 million *yuan*, all scheduled for completion in time for the 20th anniversary celebrations in 1985. The projects were to be financed by the central government as well as by interior provinces and cities. The projects included hydroelectric, geothermal, solar and wind power plants, hospital additions, cultural centers, tourist hotels, a gymnasium and a stadium. All aspects of construction, "including designing, building and interior decorating," were to be handled by "personnel supplied by the cooperating provinces and cities."[65]

The CCP's decisions on economic policy in Tibet were influenced by or reflected similar conclusions as a study on the economic situation in minority nationality areas published in 1984 by Wang Xiaoqiang and Bai Nanfeng.[66] Wang and Bai identified the lack of response to the new economic liberalization in "backward" national minority areas, despite a concentration of natural resources in nationality regions, as due to the "poor quality of human resources" among the national minority populations. As Wang and Bai phrased it, the problem was backwardness, the "reason for backwardness is backwardness," and "the intrinsic determi-

---

for Tibet's poor economic performance was that the negative effects of the wheat cultivation policy of the mid-1970s were felt in the 1980-82 period.

64. Ibid.

65. "Inland Helping Tibet," *Beijing Review*, 10 September 1984, 8.

66. Wang Xiaoqiang and Bai Nanfeng, *The Poverty of Plenty*. Both Wang and Bai were associated with the relatively liberal economic reformist school grouped around Zhao Ziyang.

nant of backwardness is the poor quality of human resources."[67] In the post-Maoist period of economic liberalization, many Chinese areas had quickly taken advantage of economic opportunities to develop a commodity economy; however, minorities had typically reverted to a natural economy. Minorities were criticized for a lack of initiative necessary to undertake the development of a commodity economy. As Wang and Bai wrote,

> The traditional way of life prolongs the traditional modes of production, and moreover sustains traditional concepts of value and leads to contentment with the traditional way. When people are satisfied with the traditional natural economy there is no demand for commodities that are solely available through exchange, and consequently the initiative engendered by exchange vanishes in backward regions . . . .
>
> People who live within the natural economy of the vast backward regions require neither commodities manufactured by modern industries nor the up-to-date culture and education brought in alongside those industries, but remain materially and spiritually content with their old way of life.[68]

As Wang and Bai observed, the problem was not in creating social wealth, which was possible within the natural economy, but in "reversing the attitude of the local inhabitants towards social wealth and changing their traditional ways of exploiting natural resources." This was necessary because "progress in a socioeconomic system is determined by the success of its restructuring and the upgrading of human resources, and the essence of this socioeconomic restructuring is the promotion of an all-embracing commodity economy."[69]

Tibetans were specifically cited for their tendency to adhere to traditional determinants of wealth, such as possession of large herds among pastoralists. Tibetans were not only content with the "vicious circle" of the natural economy, but they wasted their economic resources on the nonproductive support of religion and restoration of religious monuments. Religious superstitions were also criticized as inhibiting economic development.[70] Tibetans were so unsophisticated in their needs and habits that there was little incentive for commodity production. Tibetans, they said, "neither eat vegetables or fish or raise poultry"; they eat their meat raw, thus there was "absolutely no demand for pots or pans, bowls or utensils, or any condiments such as oil, salt, soy sauce or vinegar."

---

67. Ibid., 23.

68. Ibid., 146.

69. Ibid., 92.

70. Ibid., 34. Wang and Bai, like most Chinese, were particularly offended by the Tibetan practice of burning vast quantities of butter as offerings in monasteries and temples.

They had even refused the benefits of state plans for the cultivation of wheat instead of barley, even though wheat gave double the yield, because "they have neither the equipment for cooking wheat nor the culinary techniques other than roasting grain." Therefore, "even though the authorities ordered the wide-scale planting of wheat, which resulted in a tremendous leap in grain production, in the end they had no option but to allow a return to growing barley."[71]

Wang and Bai cited numerous instances of irrational economic planning and inefficiency and corruption in implementation. They admitted that central government policy shifts had "affected the sustained efforts to develop the region's infrastructure," and that "the turning point that marked the plunge into deficit was precisely the year 1960, when Tibetan enterprises which had been primarily regulated by the market were reformed and fully integrated into the `one big pot' system." Specifically implicated were the legacy of collectivization, which had inhibited the development of a market economy and stifled entrepreneurial initiative, and irrational policies such as the "taking grain as the key link," including conversion of pasture to agriculture and quotas for increases in livestock production, which had resulted in overgrazing and deterioration in animal husbandry.[72] The tremendous transportation costs involved in importing grain and other commodities to the TAR were implicated as one of the primary reasons for economic losses in the administration of Tibet, without any realization that it was the needs of the Chinese administration, not any fault of the Tibetan population, which was the source of unproductive costs and economic losses.[73] Apparently not comprehended or admitted was the fact that virtually all of the factors implicated as responsible for the lack of economic development in Tibet were the results of irrational Chinese state policies and maladministration or the effects of the Chinese occupation of Tibet, not the fault of Tibet's "quality of human resources."[74]

------

71. Ibid., 158. Despite Wang and Bai's misinformation, the cultivation of wheat, which the Chinese preferred and which was intended for their consumption, was abandoned due to its spectacular failure, not because of irrational Tibetan resistance.

72. Grass yields per area in Qinghai were said to have fallen by approximately 50 percent due to overgrazing, with the result that the livestock population was reduced to a state of "semi-starvation, with both a high mortality rate and a widespread drop in the numbers and quality of surviving animals." Ibid., 159.

73. Ibid., 122.

74. Any lack of the "quality of human resources" in Tibet necessary for economic development can be attributed to 30 years of repression rather than to Tibetans' "backwardness." Tibet's entrepreneurial class had been eliminated along with all Tibetan wealth or investment capital. Tibetans were hampered by their inability to speak Chinese and their lack of education. What education most Tibetans had was in a now discredited and useless ideology rather than in any useful skills.

As the Chinese economists' analysis reveals, even the most liberal Chinese reformers betrayed a cultural chauvinism in their ideas about Tibetans, as revealed by the ignorant comments about Tibetans' eating habits and their supposed lack of the most rudimentary cooking implements. They were ill-informed about many of the effects of Chinese policies applied to Tibet, the issue of wheat versus barley, and the grain issue in general, being a case in point. Their comment on grain shortages in Tibet, "If its people do not provide for themselves, then who will?" completely ignores the fact that the Tibetans were forced to feed the Chinese in Tibet, and in the past had been starved to do so; the problem of food supply in Tibet was due to the need to feed the Chinese, not the Tibetans themselves.

The Chinese economists also ignored their own evidence in regard to indigenous economic development in Tibet, in particular, commodity production stimulated by tourism. Tourism was the one sector they identified as a "favored choice for orientation in backward regions," since tourism was considered low in development costs and high in returns, with beneficial economic and cultural effects in exposing minorities to modern technology and material culture.[75] Tourism had already stimulated local handicraft production, they admit, but this was not regarded as commodity production because of the lack of any exchange with the Chinese economy.[76] Tibetans' ability to develop an indigenous natural economy, or even a commodity economy independent of the Chinese economy, was ignored in the quest to integrate Tibet within the Chinese economy, to resolve the problem of unproductive subsidies to Tibet and, finally, to pay for the Chinese occupation.

The Chinese economists associated with Hu Yaobang and Zhao Ziyang were liberal reformers, but their typical chauvinism affected their recommendations. Despite the evidence that Chinese rule, not Tibet's "low quality of human resources," was the ultimate reason for the lack of economic development in Tibet, Wang and Bai concluded that "imposed implants which transcend natural historical progression" were the solution for backward areas. As they said, in the past, "the influx of a large

---

75. Tourism was even thought to have some economic advantages over economic assistance from the interior since "information comes free with the tourists who at the same time are contributing enormous amounts to capital accumulation for the economic development of backward regions, while the personnel from developed regions [of China] are brought in at the cost of huge deficits in the backward region's finances." Ibid., 171.

76. Wang and Bai commented that representatives of Tibet's tourism departments often told them that "foreign tourists were prepared to change vast amounts of foreign currency into yuan in order to buy cheap, worthless local souvenirs." Ibid., 172.

body of `immigrants' has brought new learning and culture," and "this is precisely where hopes for the invigoration of the economies lie today."[77]

The 43 development projects announced at the Tibet Work Meeting were financed by Chinese provincial and municipal governments and contracted with provincial organizations and firms. Chinese workers of those provinces and cities were to complete the projects in Tibet, but they were intended to be in Tibet on limited contracts and then return to their home provinces when their projects were completed. Hu Yaobang, who chaired the Tibet Work Meeting, apparently accepted the abrogation of his promise to reduce the number of Chinese in Tibet, at least temporarily, as a necessity in order for Tibet to be developed. In addition, Hu had been under pressure from hardliners in Tibet and in Beijing to modify some of the policies announced in 1980, particularly the promise to reduce the number of Han in Tibet.[78] The decision to rely upon economic development and to allow Chinese cadres, workers and entrepreneurs into Tibet to pursue that development was a turning point in post-Maoist Chinese policy in Tibet.

The effects of the decisions taken at the 1984 Tibet Work Meeting were felt almost immediately in Tibet. In September 1984 Beijing announced that some 500 experts and 8,000 workers had been sent to Tibet to aid in the 43 development projects scheduled to be completed for the 20th anniversary celebrations in September.[79] In 1985 another 60,000 Chinese workers arrived in Tibet.[80] The Chinese workers were not only engineers and "experts"; many were low skilled or unskilled workers; Tibetans were employed for only the most menial tasks. All of the Chinese workers were on temporary contracts, but many eventually remained in Tibet to pursue other economic opportunities.

These development projects, plus continuing economic subsidies to Tibet, attracted individual Chinese traders and petty entrepreneurs from adjacent provinces, who were now for the first time able to travel freely to pursue economic opportunities. The opening of Tibet to individual

---

77. Ibid., 145-147. "Immigrants" was placed in quotes to indicate that the Chinese colonizing Tibet were not immigrants from another country but migrants within Chinese territory. Wang and Bai apparently retained the Maoist belief that Tibetans could be convinced to voluntarily accept Chinese colonization as a part of the "development" of Tibet.

78. Tseten Wangchuk Sharlho, personal communication, Washington, 1996.

79. "Inland Helping Tibet," *Beijing Review*, 10 September 1984, 8.

80. Sharlho, "China's Reforms in Tibet," 50. Sharlho lists the numbers of these workers as 28,650 from Sichuan, 4,410 from Gansu, 4,380 from Qinghai, 3,870 from Zhejiang, 2,470 from Anhui, 1,290 from Shanxi, 1,870 from Hunan, 1,860 from Ningxia, 1,850 from Jiangsu, 1,670 from Fujian, 1,540 from Henan, 810 from Hebei, 720 from Hubei, 663 from Shandong and 750 from other provinces or cities. Ibid.

entrepreneurs was apparently not part of the policy decided upon at the Tibet Work Meeting, but rather a result of the lifting of the prohibition on individual movement within the PRC.[81] These Chinese were welcomed by Chinese cadres and workers in Tibet, who provided them with the permits necessary to remain in Tibet and to do business. Chinese cadres in Tibet were paid up to three times the salary of a cadre in the interior and therefore had disposable income; since few products from the interior were available in state shops, the new arrivals had a ready market for whatever they could import.

At least 10,000 individual Chinese, mainly Sichuanese and Kansu Hui, came to the TAR, primarily to Lhasa, in 1984-85.[82] These Chinese immigrants soon monopolized business in Lhasa and other Tibetan towns. Lhasa also experienced an inflation of prices for basic commodities, which the Chinese could afford to pay but many Tibetans could not.[83] The influx of Chinese, especially the private entrepreneurs, who took Tibetans' jobs and business and who showed no signs of leaving, increased the discontent of Tibetans, who were well aware that a primary component of the post-Maoist reform policy had been the promise to reduce the number of Chinese in Tibet.

Before the 20th anniversary celebrations, Beijing replaced the CCP secretary in Tibet, Yin Fatang, with Wu Jinghua, a member of the Yi nationality of Sichuan.[84] Wu proved to be surprisingly respectful of Tibetan culture and religion and a proponent of full implementation of the CCP's policies on nationalities' autonomous rights, especially education in the Tibetan language and use of Tibetan as the administrative language for the TAR. Wu's liberalism earned him the respect of most Tibetans, but not that of the conservative cadres, Chinese or Tibetan. Wu's appointment satisfied neither the conservative Chinese, who mistrusted all minorities, nor the conservative Tibetan leadership, who felt insulted that a Yi

---

81. However, the Chinese Government resisted the movement of people into interior urban areas, particularly Beijing and Shanghai, in order to prevent social instability, and permitted, even encouraged their movement to Tibet and other frontier regions. *New Majority: Chinese Population Transfer into Tibet* (London: Tibet Support Group UK, 1995), 50.

82. Ibid., 50. By 1988 there were 11,884 Chinese entrepreneurial households established in the TAR. Ibid. This figure does not include those who were without official permits.

83. Jing Jun reports that the price of free market butter in 1988 was five times higher than the fixed state price of 1985. The price of yak meat increased nine times during the same period. Jing Jun, "Socioeconomic Changes and Riots in Lhasa," 4.

84. Sharlho describes the replacement of the hardline Yin Fatang as a concession on the part of Beijing to the Panchen Lama, who had considerable influence at the time. Tseten Wangchuk Sharlho, personal communication, Washington, 1996. The Yi are closely related to the Tibetans; the Yi language is considered Tibeto-Burman and the Yi are traditionally adherents to Bon or unreformed Buddhism.

nationality was more trusted in a leadership position in Tibet than were any of the Tibetan cadres, some of whom had been loyal to the Chinese since the early 1950s.[85]

Additional measures were taken to improve the political atmosphere in Tibet prior to the 20th anniversary celebrations. A fifth Dharamsala delegation (actually the fourth, the fourth scheduled delegation visit having been cancelled) was allowed to visit parts of Amdo in July 1985 but was not allowed into the TAR. In July 1985 a grand ceremony was held in Lhasa to return the Ramoche *Jowo* image to the restored Ramoche cathedral.[86] Tibetans were also allowed to continue the rebuilding of Ganden, and pilgrims were once again allowed to go there and donate funds to the restoration.[87] In late July the *Serthang* ceremony was held at Ganden for the first time since 1982; the same ceremony was held at Tashilhunpo for the first time since 1964 (the year the Panchen was removed to Beijing).[88] The Chinese attempted to take credit not only for restoring monasteries destroyed "during the Cultural Revolution," claiming to have devoted 35 million yuan (12 million US dollars) for repair, but for having helped save the few that survived, "thanks to the timely protection of the government and the People's Liberation Army troops."[89]

Despite these measures to alleviate Tibetans' discontent, the situation in Lhasa was still so tense that, in preparation for the 20th anniversary celebration on 1 September, the TAR government took the precaution of increasing security, including arresting known opponents of the regime and removing all of the several thousand tourists in the TAR for the duration of the celebrations. Most of the 43 development projects were completed on time by rushed efforts. Beijing dispatched convoys of trucks

---

85. Sharlho, "China's Reforms in Tibet," 54.

86. The Ramoche Jowo (historical Buddha) image was the one brought by the Nepalese princess, Brikuti, the images having been switched in the interim. The image had been discovered in two pieces in China and returned to the Lhasa Jokhang, where it was repaired. The image was returned to the Ramoche after the restoration of that temple. Personal observation, Lhasa, July 1985.

87. *Beijing Review* reported that "in addition to the Tibetan pilgrims, about 100,000 worshipers each year come to the temple from adjacent Sichuan, Qinghai and Gansu provinces on pilgrimages." "Ganden Monastery Renovated," *Beijing Review*, 26 August 1985, 18. The point of contrasting "Tibetan" pilgrims with pilgrims from the adjacent provinces is a bit of obscurantism intended to cultivate the habit of confining the usage of the nomenclature "Tibetan" to those Tibetans of "Tibet," or the TAR, whereas Tibetans of Kham and Amdo, now Sichuan, Gansu, Qinghai and Yunnan, would gradually lose that designation. 100,000 pilgrims a year, excluding "Tibetans," is obviously a huge number and is indicative of Ganden's significance in the Tibetan cultural and religious revival.

88. "Sunning-the-Buddha Festival," *Beijing Review*, 26 August 1985, 18.

89. 170 monasteries had reportedly been renovated or were in the process of repair and 50 had opened to the public. "Buddhism Permeates Tibetan Society," *Beijing Review*, 26 August 1985, 18.

festooned with celebratory bunting and laden with presents for the Tibetans (reportedly including 20,000 digital watches) over the Qinghai to Lhasa road (the paving of which was finally completed in the summer of 1985).

Hu Qili, member of the CCP Central Committee, and Vice-Premier Li Peng led the central government delegation to the anniversary celebration, attended by Wu Jinghua and the Panchen Lama. The central government delegation called on local officials to "follow the Party's policies of respect for the customs and religions of China's ethnic minorities. Tibet should fully exercise its right to local autonomy."[90] The Panchen Lama revived the suggestion that all cadres working in Tibet should have a "good command of the Tibetan language" and called for the restoration of more temples and monasteries, although he also criticized demonstrations for Tibetan independence by Tibetans in India as harmful to the basic interests of the Tibetan people and possibly detrimental to the "progress achieved so far."[91]

In February 1986 the Panchen Lama returned to Lhasa from Beijing to lead the *Monlam Chenmo*, or Great Prayer Ceremony, held, according to the Chinese media, for the first time since 1966, "the year the traumatic `cultural revolution' began."[92] The Panchen Lama bestowed blessings on 100,000 participants and took the opportunity to reiterate the invitation to the Dalai Lama to return, citing the revival of the *Monlam Chenmo*, which even Tibetan cadres attended, as evidence that religious freedom was permitted in Tibet.[93]

The Panchen repeated this offer to a group of journalists from Hong Kong and Macao in April 1986, but with the stipulation that the Dalai Lama "must abandon activities for an `independent Tibet.'" The Panchen offered no new conditions for the Dalai Lama's return, only that he would enjoy "the same political treatment and living conditions as he did before he fled to India in 1959." He could issue a "brief statement to the press, and it would be up to him to decide what he would say in the statement." No mention was made of the requirement that he must reside in Beijing, with only occasional visits to Tibet, although this regimen was

---

90. "Lhasa Celebrates as Region Turns 20," *Beijing Review*, 9 September 1985, 6.

91. Ibid., 7.

92. "Lhasa Celebrates Prayer Ceremony," *Beijing Review*, 10 March 1986, 7. The *Monlam Chenmo*, during which the monks of Lhasa's monasteries traditionally took over civil jurisdiction in Lhasa, could only have been held in a much altered and reduced form from 1959 to 1966, if at all. The point that Chinese propagandists wished to make in claiming that the ceremony was held until 1966 was that religious freedom in Tibet was preserved until the Cultural Revolution.

93. Ibid.

still applied to the Panchen himself. The Panchen said that the Dalai Lama must not continue his attempt to gain a status for Tibet similar to the "one country—two systems" formula being offered to Taiwan. These were two "entirely different issues that should not be mixed up," he said, recalling that there was "no such concept in 1951, when the central government signed an agreement on the liberation of Tibet."[94] The Panchen Lama's offer was, perhaps significantly, not repeated at the time by any Chinese leaders. The Panchen's efforts may have reflected his personal hopes more than a renewal of the PRC's efforts to negotiate with the Dalai Lama or any concessions on their part.

In fact, although both sides remained publicly willing to negotiate, the era of Sino-Tibetan dialogue was effectively at an end. The visits of the Dharamsala delegations had called into question the wisdom of allowing the Dalai Lama to return even if he should agree to do so. Dialogue with the Dalai Lama and the Tibetan exiles had exposed Tibet and China's policies in Tibet to international scrutiny, with adverse consequences to China's reputation. Cultural and religious liberalization had produced a revival of Tibetan nationalism that was threatening to China's territorial integrity and its political control in Tibet. In addition, the economic development strategy decided upon at the 1984 Tibet Work Meeting appeared to provide a solution to China's problems in Tibet, a solution not dependent upon the Dalai Lama.

The Tibetan Government in Exile was disappointed that nothing had come of China's purported willingness to negotiate. The Tibetan Government in Exile continued its efforts to dialogue with the Chinese, but decided to ignore the Chinese prohibition against the "internationalization" of the issue in order to put pressure on China to resume negotiations. The Tibetans thereafter concentrated on increasing their newly found international support.

---

94. "Dalai Welcome, Says Bainqen [Panchen]," *Beijing Review*, 21 April 1986, 9. The point of the latter statement was that Tibet's status had been settled once and for all in 1951 and was no longer open to discussion. The site of the Panchen's interview was not mentioned.

15

Internationalization of the Tibet Issue

International opinion on Tibet before 1980 was characterized by benign neglect or unquestioning acceptance of the Chinese version of reality about Tibet. With the opening of Tibet to the outside world, however, the climate of opinion began to shift in favor of the Tibetan exiles' claims that China's "peaceful liberation" of Tibet had been an armed conquest, and that Chinese rule in Tibet since that time had been colonialist, oppressive and destructive of Tibetan civilization. The opening of Tibet was accompanied by international tours by the Dalai Lama and activities by supporters of the Tibetan cause that contributed to an alteration of international opinion on the issue. The Dalai Lama's international travels began in earnest in 1979 and continued without interruption thereafter. The Dalai Lama confined himself in his early travels to purely personal or religious concerns, and was usually restricted to those issues by the terms of his invitations to most countries. The PRC protested every visit, pointing out that the Dalai Lama was "not just a religious figure but an exile engaged in political activities," and attempted to pressure foreign governments to deny him visas or prohibit his meeting with political leaders.

By 1987, since negotiations with China had been entirely stalemated since the last negotiating team's visit in 1984, the Tibetan Government in Exile's strategy had shifted to a campaign for international political support. In addition, the PRC's relatively liberal policies of 1985 and 1986 had given way by 1987 to a new "leftist wind," manifested by an "Anti-Bourgeois Liberalization Campaign." In January 1987 Hu Yaobang was purged from his position as CCP general secretary, partly, it was rumored, because of the conservatives' dissatisfaction with his Tibet policy.[1] Hu's ouster seemed to bode ill for Tibet; despite Party officials' assurances that CCP nationalities policies were unchangeable, all aspects of the

---

1. Tseten Wangchuk Sharlho, "China's Reforms in Tibet: Issues and Dilemmas," *The Journal of Contemporary China*, vol. 1, no. 1 (Fall 1992), 54.

reform policy were in jeopardy without Hu's support. In any case, even CCP "liberals," in the misguided belief that only the Chinese could develop Tibet, had reneged on their promise to restrict the number of Han Chinese in Tibet and had allowed a flood of Chinese to enter Tibet.

Despite Chinese prohibitions and protestations, the "internationalization" of the Tibet issue had been inevitable once Tibet was opened to the outside world. Tibet was inherently an international issue since it involved relations between two distinct nations, a fact that CCP definitions of Tibetans as a minority nationality within the Chinese multinational state could not disguise. Tibetans in exile and those within Tibet inevitably sought foreign support, a natural thing to do within their traditional political culture.[2] The opening of Tibet exposed the reality of Tibet to outside observers who did not accept Chinese characterizations of pre-1950 Tibet as a "hell on earth" and were not impressed with Chinese "improvements" in Tibet since that time. The most immediate impression gained by most foreign visitors to Tibet was the obvious destruction of Tibetan civilization and the colonialist nature of the Chinese occupation.

The first official international support for the Tibetan political cause came in 1987 when members of the US Congress attached a resolution to a State Department authorization bill deploring human rights violations in Tibet. The resolution was adopted by the House of Representatives on 18 June 1987. The resolution accused the Chinese Communists of having "invaded and occupied Tibet" in 1950 and, since that time, of having "exercised dominion over the Tibetan people, who had always considered themselves as independent, through the presence of a large occupation force." The resolution also repeated the Tibetan Government in Exile's claim that more than one million Tibetans had perished "as a direct result of the political instability, executions, imprisonment and wide scale famine engendered by the policies of the People's Republic of China in Tibet," and that over 6,000 monasteries had been destroyed and their "irreplaceable national legacy of art and literature either destroyed, stolen, or removed from Tibet."[3]

The resolution further accused the PRC of having exploited Tibet's

---

2. See P. Christiaan Kliegar, "Accomplishing Tibetan Identity: The Constitution of a National Consciousness," Ph.D. diss. University of Hawaii, 1989; *Tibetan Nationalism: The Role of Patronage in the Accomplishment of a National Identity* (Berkeley: Folklore Institute, 1992).

3. United States Foreign Relations Authorization Act Fiscal Years 1988 and 1989, Washington DC, in *Government Resolutions and International Documents on Tibet*, 2nd ed. (Dharamsala: Office of Information and International Relations, Central Tibetan Secretariat, December 1989), 23.

natural resources "with limited benefit to the Tibetan people," of having imprisoned many Tibetans for the nonviolent expression of their religious and political beliefs, and of having encouraged "a large influx of Han Chinese into Tibet, thereby undermining the political and cultural traditions of the Tibetan people." The resolution expressed the opinion of Congress that the US should "make the treatment of the Tibetan people an important factor in its conduct of relations" with the PRC and that the US Government should urge the PRC to "actively reciprocate the Dalai Lama's efforts to establish a constructive dialogue on the future of Tibet." The US Government was directed to link the transfer of defense articles to the PRC's treatment of Tibetans, to establish a program of assistance to displaced Tibetans and provide 15 scholarships for study in the US to Tibetans "who are outside Tibet."[4] This resolution was followed up by a letter from 91 members of the US Congress to the PRC, "expressing support for direct talks between Beijing and the representatives of His Holiness the Dalai Lama and the Tibetans in exile."[5]

The Chinese response was to protest that the US Congressional resolution "runs counter to the foreign policy of the US Government itself. The fact that Tibet is part of China is universally recognized by the world, including the governments of India and the United States." The Chinese Embassy in Washington wrote to members of Congress, informing them that the resolution contained "fabricated stories," and urging them to "take a fair and just position on the question."[6] Beijing was particularly upset because, not only had the Tibet issue achieved official support, but the US Congress had accepted the Tibetan Government in Exile's claim that one million Tibetans had perished due to the Chinese occupation. Chinese propaganda organs therefore mounted an attack on this "slander." In order to refute this charge, the Chinese published census data for Tibet for the first time. The figures for the first census in Tibet (TAR) in 1953 were given as 1,274,000. This number was described as an estimate arrived at by Tibet's "grass-roots units and upper circles." In the second census in 1964 the population of the TAR was 1,208,700 Tibetans and 42,000 Han or other nationalities (not counting PLA). By 1982 the population of the TAR had increased to 1,786,500 Tibetans and 105,500 Han or other nationalities, an average annual increase in the Tibetan population of 2.2 percent. In 1985 the population of the TAR was given as

---

4. Ibid.
5. Ibid., 25.
6. "China Objects to 2 US Amendments," *Beijing Review*, 6 July 1987, 7.

1,920,000 Tibetans and 70,000 Han or other nationalities, a decrease in the numbers of Chinese attributed to the reduction in cadres since 1980.[7]

The article glossed over the decline in population from 1953 to 1964, attributing it to exaggeration in the 1953 estimate, the departure of many Tibetans in 1959 and the "millennium old trend of population stagnation in Tibet." Instead, the growth of the Tibetan population since that time was emphasized, an increase, it was claimed, "due mainly to the Chinese government's policy of increasing the region's population and improving people's quality of life." By giving population statistics for only the TAR as the population of "Tibet" without mentioning the Tibetan population outside the TAR (greater than that inside the TAR), the Chinese attempted to create the impression that the Tibetan population was only some 1.2 million in the 1950s; therefore, it was preposterous for the Tibetan Government in Exile to claim that one million Tibetans had perished. As to the "slander" that the Chinese Government had practiced genocide against the Tibetans, the article said, "one need only look at Tibet's population figures since the peaceful liberation of the region in May 1951 to reach one's own conclusion."[8]

On 21 September 1987 the Dalai Lama addressed the US Congressional

---

7. "Tibet Population Develops," *Beijing Review*, 17 August 1987, 20. Chinese workers and entrepreneurs in Tibet were all considered temporary residents. A Tibetan official, Gyaincain Norbu, chairman of the People's Government of the TAR, compared Chinese in Tibet to foreign businessmen in China, neither of whom could be regarded as immigrants. "Tibetan Official Refutes Dalai Lama's Lies," *Beijing Review*, 14 June 1993, 4.

8. Ibid. Given the statistics provided, one may "reach one's own conclusion" that tends to support the Tibetan claim of massive numbers of deaths rather than the Chinese denial. Rounding the base population of the TAR in 1953 to 1.2 million (to account for exaggeration) and calculating a normal rate of increase of 2.2 percent, the Tibetan population of the TAR in 1964 should have been approximately 1,524,000. Subtracting 40,000 as an estimate of the number of the TAR population who escaped to India (assuming an additional 30,000 from Kham and Amdo), this still represents a shortfall of approximately 275,000 compared to the 1964 census figure of 1,208,700. Even assuming a pre-1964 rate of increase of 1.7 percent to account for the celibate monk population before 1959 (monks were 9.5 percent of the total TAR population in 1958, or 19 percent of the male population, and could therefore account for a 19 percent reduction in the birth rate), a 1.7 percent average annual population increase upon a 1953 base of 1.2 million would give a population of approximately 1,440,000 in 1964. The actual Tibetan population in the TAR in 1964 was only 1,208,700, a shortfall of approximately 235,000. Assuming that 40,000 from the TAR escaped to India, the number of "missing" Tibetans in the TAR alone is still approximately 195,000. In an article in October 1987 the Tibetan population of the TAR in November 1959 was given as 1.262 million. "A Dialogue on Tibet (II): Religion, Crime and Citizens' Rights," *Beijing Review*, 26 October 1987, 26. The means by which this number was derived were not specified. Taking this number and assuming a normal rate of population increase of 2.2 percent (the monk population had been substantially reduced by the end of 1959), the Tibetan population of the TAR in 1964 should have been approximately 1,407,000. Subtracting 40,000 escapees (from the TAR), this represents a shortfall of approximately 160,000 compared to the 1964

Human Rights Caucus, where he proposed a "five-point peace plan" for Tibet. The Dalai Lama criticized the Chinese Government for attempting to "reduce the question of Tibet to a discussion of my own personal status," rather than "addressing the real issues facing the six million Tibetan people." His peace plan was presented as an attempt to reopen the dialogue on a more realistic basis by proposing preliminary steps to reduce tensions. The five points of the Dalai Lama's peace plan did not attempt to define Tibet's political status, but to set the stage for negotiations on that status:

1. Transformation of the whole of Tibet into a zone of peace;

2. Abandonment of China's population transfer policy which threatens the very existence of the Tibetans as a people;

3. Respect for the Tibetan people's fundamental human rights and democratic freedoms;

4. Restoration and protection of Tibet's natural environment and the abandonment of China's use of Tibet for the production of nuclear weapons and dumping of nuclear waste;

5. Commencement of earnest negotiations on the future status of Tibet and on relations between the Tibetan and Chinese peoples.[9]

US Congressional resolutions in support of Tibet were not matched by similar support by the executive branch of the US Government. At a House of Representatives Committee on Foreign Affairs hearing on Human Rights in Tibet in October 1987, the Deputy Assistant Secretary of State for East Asian and Pacific Affairs, J. Stapleton Roy, complained that the Dalai Lama had violated the understanding upon which he had been granted a visa to the United States by engaging in "activities inconsistent with his status as a respected religious leader... He was granted a US visa solely in his capacity as a religious leader, since the US Government considers Tibet to be a part of China and does not in any way recognize the Tibetan Government in exile that the Dalai Lama claims to head." The United States was "unwavering" in its support for human rights," Secretary Roy said,

---

census figure of 1.208,700. Even a lower rate of increase of 2.0 percent would give a figure of approximately 144,000 Tibetans unaccounted for in the TAR alone.

9. Address to Members of the United States Congress: Five Point Peace Plan for Tibet, 21 September 1987, in *Government Resolutions on Tibet*, 6. The Dalai Lama warned that population transfer must stop or Tibetans "will soon be no more than a tourist attraction and relic of a noble past." Ibid., 8.

But when he [the Dalai Lama] assumes a political status and advances a political program for Tibet, which we consider to be part of China, the US Government cannot support him. This distinction is crucial to understanding why the administration disavows any support for the Dalai Lama's five-point program. Neither the United States nor any other member of the United Nations recognizes or has ever recognized Tibet as a sovereign state independent of China. We do not believe it is in the interest of the United States, or of the Tibetan people, to link the issue of human rights in Tibet to a political program that is contrary to US policy and that constitutes interference in the internal affairs of another country.[10]

The Chinese response to the Dalai Lama's five-point plan was that "the status of Tibet" was "a question which simply does not exist." His plan, they said, was nothing but the "continued preaching of `the independence of Tibet.'" The Tibetan people, "have never before enjoyed such full democracy and freedom as today, and these facts cannot be changed by lies or slander."[11] The Dalai Lama was denounced within China and Tibet as not representing the sentiments of the Tibetan people, who were said to be happy with conditions as they were.

Demonstrations in Lhasa

The Dalai Lama's visit to Washington and the Chinese denunciation of his five-point peace plan coincided with the public execution in Lhasa on 24 September of two Tibetans accused of being criminals, but whom many Tibetans maintained were political prisoners. On 27 September a group of 21 monks from Drepung, joined by five laymen, marched around the Barkhor (the circumambulation route around Lhasa's Jokhang temple) in support of the Dalai Lama. They were later accused of having carried the "snow mountains and lions" flag, the prohibited Tibetan national flag, and of having shouted Tibetan independence slogans.[12] They monks were beaten and arrested. The "Dalai Clique" and its

---

10. "Hearing before the Subcommittees on Human Rights and International Organizations, and on Asian and Pacific Affairs of the Committee on Foreign Affairs, House of Representatives, 14 October 1987," 24. Secretary Roy noted that "During many periods in history, the concept of legal independence such as we now have in mind was not terribly relevant to that part of the world." Ibid., 38. Representative Tom Lantos excoriated the State Department for its "spineless" policy on Tibet and commented in his questioning of Secretary Roy that he had been "irritated by your repeated attempt to establish this utterly phoney dichotomy between the role of the Dalai Lama as a religious leader and the role of the Dalai Lama as a political leader." Ibid., 47.

11. "China Opposes Dalai's Statements," *Beijing Review*, 5 October 1987, 6.

12. "Demonstrations Disrupt Peace in Lhasa," *Beijing Review*, 12 October 1987, 5.

supporters both in and outside Tibet were denounced by the Chinese in the harshest terms. This served only to arouse Tibetans' resentment and set the stage for further protests.[13]

Chinese claims that the monks arrested on the 27th had no support among the Tibetan people prompted other Tibetans to demonstrate their support. On 1 October, the PRC's National Day, monks from Sera, Jokhang and Nechung, along with lay Tibetans, circled the Barkhor shouting independence slogans. Some 60 were arrested and taken to a police station near the Jokhang, where a crowd gathered to demand their release. The crowd began throwing stones at the police station and at police videotaping the demonstration from nearby rooftops; soon they overturned and burned police vehicles and attempted to smash down the door of the police station in order to free those inside. Eventually, they tried to set fire to the station door; fire vehicles and police reinforcements were prevented from reaching the scene by the growing crowd of Tibetans. A few Tibetan monks stormed the building in an attempt to rescue their fellow monks, after which firing began both inside and outside the police station. Three monks were shot and killed inside the station; at least three other Tibetans were killed outside and several others were injured.[14]

The Dalai Lama's visit to Washington, his peace proposal and his denunciation by the Chinese were the sparks that ignited this outburst; however, tensions in Tibet were already high due to Tibetan resentment at the lack of any real autonomy and the recent influx of Chinese. As Tseten Wangchuk Sharlho has written, "The Dalai Lama's testimony and his subsequent denunciation by the Chinese authorities merely sparked the social, economic and political crisis that had become inevitable."[15] Beijing denied that there was any Tibetan discontent behind the riot that had "disrupted the peaceful atmosphere of Lhasa," claiming that the incident was "designed in faraway quarters as an echo to the Dalai Lama's separatist activities during his visits to the United States and Europe." They further claimed that the demonstrations had aroused strong opposition from most Tibetans, who had condemned demonstrators for carrying on "splittist" activities under the cover of monks' robes. Police were said to have strictly observed the orders of higher authorities not to open

---

13. Sharlho, "China's Reforms in Tibet," 55.

14. *Defying the Dragon: China and Human Rights in Tibet* (London: Tibet Information Network and Law Association for Asia and the Pacific Human Rights Standing Committee, 1991), 21.

15. Sharlho, "China's Reforms in Tibet," 56.

fire, but "some rioters went so far as to snatch away guns carried by the policemen and opened fire at the police and bystanders."[16]

On 6 October 90 Drepung monks went to the TAR government office where they demanded the release of their colleagues. 250 People's Armed Police arrived immediately, brutally assaulted the monks and arrested them all.[17] All of these monks were released within a few days. Thirteen of the Tibetans arrested in the 27 September and 1 October demonstrations were released on 28 October and 59 on 21 January 1988 at the instigation of the Panchen Lama.[18] Some 15 who had been found guilty of "criminal offenses" were not released.[19]

The riots in Lhasa stimulated the US Senate to pass the Tibet resolution attached to the Foreign Relations Authorization Act on 6 October (already passed by the House of Representatives on 18 June), to which they added language condemning the executions of two Tibetans on 24 September and the arrests and violent repression of the demonstrations of 27 September and 1 October.[20] Chinese media condemned the resolution as "another serious incident engineered by a small number of people in the US Congress." The NPC Foreign Affairs Commission issued a statement saying that interference in China's internal affairs had "badly hurt the feelings of the Chinese people" and had become a "negative factor detrimental to the further development of Sino-US relations." The Chinese also said that "a very small number of foreigners took part in the riot aimed at undermining the unity of China."[21] Further articles attempted to denigrate the arrested rioters by revealing that some were ex-prisoners or former inmates of "reform through labor." Tibetans were quoted as expressing indignation at the riots and commenting that the rioters (by acting on the command of foreign instigators) "ignored the rights of Tibetans to be masters of their own homeland." Others reportedly worried that separatist activities might affect the implementation of reform policies in Tibet.[22]

The Panchen Lama warned that activities by the "splittist clique" might "tempt the Party and government to abandon their policies on religious freedom." The Panchen claimed that the majority of Tibetans were supportive of the policies implemented in Tibet since 1979 and were

---

16. "The Tibet Myth Vs. Reality," *Beijing Review*, 12 October 1987, 4.

17. *Defying the Dragon*, 24. The People's Armed Police (PAP) was formed from the PLA and was used to maintain civil order.

18. "Police Free 59 Held Over Riots in Tibet," *Beijing Review*, 1 February 1988, 12.

19. "Tibetan Leaders Condemn Rioters," *Beijing Review*, 21 March 1988, 9.

20. *Government Resolutions on Tibet*, 24.

21. "China Rejects US Senate Move," *Beijing Review*, 19 October 1987, 5.

22. "Lhasa: Facts About Rioters Uncovered," *Beijing Review*, 26 October 1987, 11.

"opposed to splittism and want to safeguard the integrity of the mother-land and its stability and unity."[23] The Panchen was apparently warning that domestic and foreign opposition would only increase the strength of the hardliners within the CCP, perhaps jeopardizing the little cultural and religious freedom Tibetans had enjoyed since the reform began.

In response to the Dalai Lama's international campaign, the PRC reit-erated its position on negotiations (ostensibly in answer to foreign read-ers' questions in *Beijing Review*). Beijing's 1984 conditions were repeated without change: the Dalai Lama was urged to "let bygones be bygones" in regard to Tibet's historical status and to "forget what happened in 1959." In answer to a question about whether it would be considered a violation of the law to "raise a cry for Tibetan independence," the article stated: "Favoring separatism in Tibet is against the Constitution of our country, the common will and the fundamental interests of the people of Tibet and other nationalities." The Chinese spokesman reiterated the position that meetings between the officials of any country and the Dalai Lama or his representatives "would not be acceptable to the Chinese Government." The Dalai Lama's activities abroad were criticized as incompatible with his stated wish to improve relations with the Chinese Government. The proposals of the Tibetan Government in Exile to reuni-fy all Tibetan nationality areas into a greater Tibetan Autonomous Region was specifically refuted as "unrealistic and unattainable," since Tibetan areas, "though bordering one another on the map . . . have not been uni-fied in history because of separation by the mountainous terrain." Uneven economic and cultural development was said to have "stifled the possibility for a unified economic region." Lastly, the rights of minority nationalities should be safeguarded, but national unity and the regional administration and economic and cultural growth also had to be consid-ered. A greater Tibetan autonomous region would not benefit economic and cultural development, it was said, "on the contrary, it would exert an unfavorable influence on the region's autonomy."[24]

The CCP was adverse to any concession on Tibetan territorial reunifi-cation since a reunified Tibet would increase Tibet's political significance in relation to China and other minority nationality regions. The PRC had been considerably successful in dividing Tibet and obscuring the former territorial extent of Tibetan cultural areas by referring only to the TAR as "Tibet." In a contemporaneous article, China's territorial encroachment

---

23. "Panchen Lama Condemns Riot," *Beijing Review*, 19 October 1987, 5.

24. "Our Differences With the Dalai Lama," *Beijing Review*, 19 October 1987, 15. Presumably what was meant by this last statement was that linking eastern Tibetan areas with the backward economy of the TAR would be less economically advantageous than linking them with the more advanced economy of adjacent Chinese provinces.

upon and territorial redefinition of Tibet was employed in a specious argument to "prove" that Tibet was part of China:

> Of the present population of 6 million Tibetans, only 2 million are living in Tibet while the remaining 4 million are in other provinces of China. The distribution of these people indicates that the Tibetan nationality is an integral part of the Chinese nation. The Dalai Lama, born in Qinghai Province, is himself Chinese. His talk of splitting China would mean not only separating Tibet from China, but also dividing all the areas inhabited by Tibetans.[25]

In April 1988 the PRC published another article attempting to refute the Tibetan Government in Exile's claim that more than a million Tibetans had died as a result of the Chinese occupation and the Dalai Lama's claim that Tibetans were now outnumbered in Tibetan areas as a whole or within the TAR. Figures for the Tibetan population in 1953 were provided, and the means by which that census was conducted were further revealed:

> When the first national census was conducted in 1953, the Tibetan population in Tibet [TAR] and Qamdo Prefecture [Chamdo not then being a part of the TAR] could only be estimated. However, the census was conducted at the county level for other areas, so the figures were accurate. The total Tibetan population in the whole country was then 2.77 million strong, of whom about 1 million were in Tibet (not including the 274,000 Tibetans in Qamdo Prefecture). This figure was calculated on the basis of a report of the Tibet local government.[26]

The article gave the figures for the 1982 census of a total Tibetan population in the PRC of 3.87 million. Of these, 1,786,544 were within the TAR (leaving 2,083,000 as the 1982 Tibetan population outside the TAR). The increase in the Tibetan population in the TAR (from 1953 to 1982) was given as "more than 510,000 persons," while "the growth rate of the

---

25. "Sino-US Relations Over the Past Year," *Beijing Review*, 15 February 1988, 29. The meaning of the last sentence is that the Dalai Lama's efforts to separate "Tibet," the TAR, from China would mean the separation of other Tibetan areas from the TAR. This statement—reminiscent of the Chinese position at Simla—is obviously intended to define Tibetan areas outside the TAR as part of interior China and to confine any discussion of Tibet's status to the TAR. Chinese figures for the Tibetan population in this statement are greatly approximated; later Chinese figures gave the total Tibetan population in the PRC in 1982 as only 3.87 million.

26. "Tibetan-Inhabited Areas: Demographic Changes," *Beijing Review*, 4 April 1988. One million as the population of U-Tsang in 1953 was obviously an estimate on the part of Lhasa officials. The population of the TAR including Chamdo was 1,274,000. The Tibetan population of Kham and Amdo in 1953 was then 1,496,000 (2.77 million less 1.274 million).

Tibetan population in other areas was even higher with an increase of more than 580,000."[27] The number of Han Chinese in all Tibetan autonomous regions, prefectures and districts was given as 1.54 million, 26.9 percent of the total; 67.1 percent were Tibetans and 6 percent were of other nationalities.[28]

In an attempt to repair the damage caused by the October riot and to put Beijing's religious policy in Tibet back on track, the Panchen Lama was dispatched to Lhasa in January 1988 to prepare for the *Monlam Chenmo*, which many monks had threatened to boycott. He arranged for the release of most of those monks arrested in October who were still

---

27. Ibid., 27. The newly released figures for the Tibetan population in 1953 as well as information about how those numbers were derived provide another means for calculating the number of Tibetans unaccounted for, given normal rates of population increase. Taking the population for all of Tibet in 1953 (2.77 million) as the starting point and assuming a 1.7 percent annual rate of increase from 1953 to 1962 (to account for various "stagnating" factors) and 2.2 percent thereafter (the actual rate of increase from 1964 to 1982 according to Chinese statistics), the total Tibetan population in 1982 should have been some 4.87 million, one million more than the 1982 census number of 3.87 million. However, this does not imply a shortfall of one million, since the removal of some lesser number from the procreating population at an earlier date would have resulted in a larger number unaccounted for in later years. Arbitrarily reducing by 660,000 at the year 1962 results in the actual figure for 1982 of 3.87 million. We can therefore assume that, based upon these population statistics and our assumed rate of increase, some 660,000 people were removed from the procreating population by 1962. Subtracting the known number of refugees (70,000) from this figure gives a calculation of 590,000 Tibetans removed from the procreating population. This estimate may be corroborated by using figures for the Tibetan population outside the TAR in 1953 (1.496 million), said to have been an accurate census. Calculating with the same rates of increase, the Tibetan population outside the TAR should have been 2.632 million in 1982, compared to the actual census figure of 2.083 million. Reducing the calculation in the year 1962 by 363,000 results in the actual 1982 census number of 2.083 million. Subtracting 30,000 for the estimated numbers of refugees from Kham and Amdo gives 333,000 people removed from the procreating population of Kham and Amdo. Adding these numbers to the figures calculated for the TAR (145,000-195,000) gives a total of 478,000-528,000, within the range estimated above as missing from the total Tibetan population (590,000). The conclusions which may be derived from these calculations, based on the PRC's own statistics, are that some hundreds of thousands of Tibetans were removed from the procreating population by death or imprisonment (imprisonment would remove one from the procreating population, at least temporarily).

28. Ibid., 28. The number of Han in the TAR in 1982 were given as 92,000; in the six autonomous prefectures in Qinghai province there were 504,000 Han (more than 200,000 were in Haixi Autonomous Prefecture, which includes the Tsaidam Basin and the city of Golmud); in Tibetan autonomous areas in Sichuan there were 520,000 Han; in Gansu 375,000, and in Yunnan 50,000. Ibid., 26. In 1986 the number of Han in the TAR was claimed to have dropped to 73,534, accounting for only 3.6 percent of the population, most of whom were "sent to help develop the local economy and stimulate scientific, educational and cultural advancement." Ibid., 28; "The Tibet Myth Vs. Reality," *Beijing Review*, 12 October 1987, 4.

detained and announced that the Monlam would be held as scheduled.[29] The *Monlam* ceremony went off without incident until the last day, 5 March. During the concluding ceremonies, at which Tibetan government cadres were present, a large number of monks shouted demands for the release of a Tibet University teacher, Yulo Dawa Tsering, who had been arrested for speaking to a foreign journalist about Tibetans' animosities against the Chinese. The monks' protests led to an assault on Tibetan government officials and Chinese cameramen videotaping the event. One monk was shot dead by one of the officials' bodyguards, after which the *Monlam* ceremony degenerated into a full-scale riot both within the Jokhang and around the Barkhor outside. Violent confrontations with the People's Armed Police ensued; several Tibetans (most of them monks) and one Chinese PAP were killed, many were injured and as many as a thousand Tibetans were arrested, beaten and tortured.[30]

After a visit to Tibet to investigate the situation, the head of the PRC's Public Security Police, Qiao Shi, called for "merciless repression" of Tibetan separatists.[31] The Panchen Lama and Ngawang Jigme Ngapo also condemned the rioters and called for punishment "according to law." The previous policy had proven to be a mistake, the Panchen said, since the rioters regarded the government's leniency and forbearance as a sign of weakness, "assuming that the more violently they riot the more we will give in."[32] Ngapo claimed that Tibetan farmers and herdsmen, more than 95 percent of the population, were "against any move aimed at splitting the motherland and damaging national unity."[33]

The Dalai Lama's Strasbourg Proposal

In June 1988, in an address to the European Parliament at Strasbourg, France, the Dalai Lama attempted to revive negotiations with the PRC by formally accepting Deng Xiaoping's precondition that he "give up the

---

29. "Police Free 59 Held Over Riots in Tibet," *Beijing Review*, 1 February 1988, 12.

30. *Defying the Dragon*, 25.

31. "Beijing calls for `merciless repression' of Tibet protests," *South China Morning Post*, 20 July 1988, in *Tibet Press Watch*, November 1988, 21.

32. "Tibetan Leaders Condemn Rioters," *Beijing Review*, 21 March 1988, 9.

33. "Tibetan Leaders on the Tibet Situation," *Beijing Review*, 18 April 1988, 18. The Panchen Lama indicated, in reply to a journalist's question about whether the Dalai Lama would be allowed to live in Tibet, that the Dalai Lama would be allowed to live "anywhere in China." He would not, however, be allowed to continue any "separatist activities" within China. China's Constitution, he said, "stipulates that citizens have the freedom to live where they choose." Ibid., 20. Since Chinese citizens, the Panchen included, did not in fact have the right to live where they chose, the Panchen's statement may be regarded as propaganda for the journalists to whom he was speaking, not a new offer to the Dalai Lama.

idea of Tibetan independence." The Dalai Lama's proposal was the first acknowledgement that he and the Tibetan Government in Exile would accept the reality of Chinese sovereignty over Tibet in exchange for genuine and well-defined autonomous rights. The Dalai Lama also refined his proposal for Tibet's future status.

The "Strasbourg Proposal" elaborated some of the conditions first proposed by Tibetan negotiating teams in 1982 and 1984 in regard to Tibetan autonomous rights. The Tibetan proposals were again based upon the "one country two systems" formula the PRC had offered to Taiwan and Hong Kong. The Tibetans demanded more, not less, autonomy than Hong Kong or Taiwan, based upon Tibet's ethnic differences and history of independent statehood. The Strasbourg statement also attempted a legal definition of Tibet's proposed special status within China. The Dalai Lama's proposal defined Tibet's status in relation to China as one of political "association." Tibetan political autonomy would include all affairs concerning Tibetans except defense and foreign political (but not cultural) relations, and the Tibetan political system would be democratic:

> The whole of Tibet known as Cholka-Sum (U-Tsang, Kham and Amdo) should become a self-governing democratic political entity founded on law by agreement of the people for the common good and the protection of themselves and their environment, in association with the People's Republic of China.

> The Government of the People's Republic of China could be responsible for Tibet's foreign policy. The Government of Tibet should, however, develop and maintain relations, through its own Foreign Affairs Bureau, in the fields of religion, commerce, education, culture, tourism, science, sports and other non-political activities. Tibet should join international organizations concerned with such activities.

> The Government of Tibet should be founded on a constitution of basic law. The basic law should provide for a democratic system of government entrusted with the task of ensuring economic equality, social justice and protection of the environment. This means that the government of Tibet will have the right to decide on all affairs relating to Tibet and the Tibetans.[34]

The Dalai Lama maintained that Tibet had never given up its sovereignty in the past. There had been periods, he said, when Tibet had been

---

34. Address to Members of the European Parliament by His Holiness the Dalai Lama, 15 June 1988, in *Government Resolutions on Tibet*, 11. The Dalai Lama's desire for a "basic law" governing Tibet was modeled on the 1990 Basic Law that was to govern Hong Kong after 1997.

under the influence of "neighbors" (Mongols, Manchu, Chinese, British India and Gurkha Nepal), but, while Tibetans had accepted a certain degree of dominance, they had never accepted that this constituted a loss of Tibetan sovereignty. In the Strasbourg formula, Tibetan autonomy was to be subject to a nationwide referendum of the Tibetan people, thereby leaving open the final resolution of Tibet's political status.[35] The Dalai Lama's acceptance of China's sovereignty thus appeared to the Chinese as temporary and conditional. The Dalai Lama had not accepted the condition that he give up the demand for independence in the sense that the Chinese required—that Tibet had always been and always would be a part of China.

The Tibetan exile government may have thought that the combination of international pressure, trouble within Tibet, and Tibetan acceptance of Deng Xiaoping's primary condition for negotiations—abandonment of the demand for independence—might move the Chinese to reopen negotiations. However, while the Strasbourg Proposal was hailed in the West as a major concession, and condemned by many Tibetan exiles for the same reason, China condemned the Dalai Lama's proposal as an attempt to "tamper with history, distort reality, and deny Tibet's status as an inalienable part of China's territory under Chinese sovereignty." China expressed its intention to resist any attempts to internationalize the "so-called Tibet question," and make no concession on the question of sovereignty. The Dalai Lama's formula for a Tibetan "associative" status in relation to China was characterized as "semi-independence" or "disguised independence."[36]

The CCP's primary goal in opening dialogue with the Dalai Lama had been to secure his unconditional "return to the motherland" and thus achieve a final legitimation of China's rule in Tibet. The dialogue had, however, opened up all the political issues of Tibet, including the fundamental issue of the legitimacy of Chinese sovereignty over Tibet, and had exposed that issue to international scrutiny. The Chinese interpreted the Strasbourg statement not as a concession, but as perpetuating and elaborating the "idea of Tibetan independence." Even the characterization of Tibet as a dependency of China in the past, under Chinese "suzerainty," as the Tibetans were willing to admit, revived the issue of Tibet as a country separate from China and the legitimacy of China's "liberation" of Tibet in 1950.[37]

The special status demanded for Tibet, giving Tibet an international

---

35. Ibid., 14.
36. "The Dalai Lama's `New Proposal,'" *Beijing Review*, 1 August 1988.
37. "What Is Behind the Dalai Lama's `Plan,'" *Beijing Review*, 19 February 1990, 21.

legal identity and certain international rights, was rejected by China as perpetuating the separate identity of Tibet and threatening the future territorial integrity of the Chinese state. The Dalai Lama's demand for extensive autonomy and a democratic political system was regarded as an attempt to alter the PRC's semi-sacrosanct system of "national regional autonomy" and to "negate the superior socialist system established in Tibet." The Dalai Lama's intention, the Chinese said, was "to transform China's internal affairs into a question between two countries and thus to lay the groundwork for an attempt to separate Tibet from the rest of China."[38]

In contrast to the Chinese response, the international community and Tibetan exiles reacted to the Strasbourg proposal as a major concession. The international community generally applauded the Dalai Lama's diplomatic initiative as an important compromise with significant potential for resolution of the Tibetan issue, and as a potential example for the resolution of many difficult problems of the ethnic nationalist type. Many Tibetans, however, regarded the Dalai Lama's compromise on the issue of independence as an abandonment of the essence of the Tibetan political cause and a betrayal of all that for which so many Tibetans had fought, suffered and died. While popular opposition to an initiative of the Dalai Lama might be taken for a rather healthy sign of the growth of democracy in the previously autocratic Tibetan political system, the controversy over Strasbourg created damaging divisions in Tibetan society and doubt over the goals of the Tibetan struggle and the willingness of Tibetan exile leaders to persevere in that struggle.

In an article critical of the Strasbourg Proposal, Phuntsog Wangyal expressed the opinion that virtually all Tibetans were united in their desire for independence; the only difference in their opinions was that some saw that possibility as realistic while others thought it unrealistic. Comparing the quest for independence with the quest for Buddhist enlightenment, he commented that although both goals might be unrealistic, the attainment of independence was certainly more likely than the attainment of Buddhahood; however, the abandonment of either goal would have a negative psychological effect upon Tibetans as Tibetans and as Buddhists. Phuntsog Wangyal also commented that the opinion that the goal of Tibetan independence was unrealistic seemed more

---

38. Ibid. China's contention that Tibet had "always" been an "integral part of China" required that Tibet not be defined as a "country" at all (even, presumably, before the 13th century). The press counselor of the PRC's Washington embassy, Chen Defu, responded to an article by A.M. Rosenthal entitled "One Small Country" with the information that: "Tibet is not a country. It is recognized by governments all over the world that Tibet is an inalienable part of Chinese territory." Chen Defu, letter to *New York Times*, 22 March 1991.

prevalent among foreigners than among Tibetans themselves and that the Strasbourg statement seemed to have been influenced by foreigners' opinions or advice.[39] Phuntsog Wangyal's apprehension at the negative effect the Strasbourg statement would have on Tibetans' spirits was seconded by Jamyang Norbu, who agreed that Strasbourg had been influenced by foreign advisors and named those thought to be most involved.[40]

Another non-Tibetan whose role was criticized was the Dalai Lama's "legal adviser," Michael van Walt, who in his book *The Status of Tibet*, published in 1987, had proposed the legal concept of "association" to define Tibet's relations with China. Van Walt suggested three possible solutions to the Tibet situation based upon the 1960 UN Resolution 1514, "Declaration on the Granting of Independence to Colonial Countries and Peoples," and the accompanying Resolution 1541, which set out the means by which a "Non-Self-Governing Territory could be said to have reached a full measure of self-government."[41] These were: emergence as a sovereign state; free association with an independent state; or integration with an independent state.[42]

---

39. "Giving Up the Struggle," *Tibetan Review*, September 1988. Phuntsog Wangyal had been a member of the second delegation and was currently Tibetan representative in London.

40. Former British Prime Minister Edward Heath, British Parliamentarian Lord Ennals, and former American President Jimmy Carter had all made brief visits to Tibet, had been uncritical of Chinese rule there, had met personally with the Dalai Lama and had reportedly advised him to make some compromise with the Chinese on the issue of independence. Jamyang Norbu, *Illusion and Reality: Essays on the Tibetan and Chinese Political Scene from 1978 to 1989* (Dharamsala: Tibetan Youth Congress, 1989), 89. In the Strasbourg Proposal, the Dalai Lama specifically thanked "a growing number of governments and political leaders, including former president Jimmy Carter of the United States," for their "keen interest" in Tibet's situation. *Government Resolutions on Tibet*, 13.

41. United Nations General Assembly, 15th Session, Resolution 1514, "Declaration on the Granting of Independence to Colonial Countries and Peoples," 14 December 1960, (New York: United Nations, 1961), 66; United Nations General Assembly, 15th Session, Resolution 1541, "Principles which should guide Members in determining whether or not an obligation exists to transmit the information called for under Article 73e of the Charter (Annex)," 15 December 1960, in GAOR, 15th Session, Supp. No. 16 (A/4684), 29. These means by which a people might attain self-determination were reiterated in the 1970 "Declarations on Principles of International Law concerning Friendly Relations and Co-operation among States," UNGA, 25th Session, Res. 2625, in GAOR, Supp. No. 28 (A/8028), 1971.

42. Michael van Walt van Praag, *The Status of Tibet: History, Rights, and Prospects in International Law* (Boulder: Westview Press, 1987), 198. Van Walt proposed that these United Nations criteria were applicable to the "status and rights of the Tibetan people," despite the fact that Tibet had not been designated as a Non-Self-Governing Territory by the UN or by any of its member states, and would certainly not be so recognized by the PRC. The lack of any such international recognition would very likely have impeded the ability of the UN or

Van Walt suggested that independence would be the "most satisfactory resolution of the Sino-Tibetan question," but that the "free association" arrangement offered a solution far more satisfactory than full integration of Tibet with China. The status of free association, proposed for Tibet in the Dalai Lama's Strasbourg statement, was defined in Resolution 1541 as follows:

(a) Free association should be the result of a free and voluntary choice by the peoples of the territory concerned expressed through informed and democratic processes. It should be one which respects the individuality and the cultural characteristics of the territory and its peoples, and retains for the peoples of the territory which is associated with an independent State the freedom to modify the status of that territory through the expression of their will by democratic means and through constitutional processes.

(b) The associated territory should have the right to determine its internal constitution without outside interference, in accordance with due constitutional processes and the freely expressed wishes of the people. This does not preclude consultations as appropriate or necessary under the terms of the free association agreed upon.[43]

An associative international legal status for Tibet would theoretically satisfy China's primary interests in the fields of defense and foreign relations while guaranteeing for Tibet an international political identity and internationally sanctioned cultural and political autonomy. Van Walt cited associative status as "a consensual one between two sovereign States" and claimed that "Tibet would thereby resume the exercise of its sovereignty."[44] The free association status was identified by Van Walt as

---

its member states to support a settlement of the Tibetan issue based upon Resolutions 1514 and 1541.

43. "Annex to Resolution 1541," in GAOR, 15th Session, Supp. No. 16 (A/4684), 29. The "constitutional processes" referred to in both paragraphs presumably refer to the constitution of the independent state.

44. Van Walt, *The Status of Tibet*, 201, 202. Van Walt's contention that an associated state under the UN definition would attain sovereignty is not supported by the language of Resolution 1541, which refers to the associate as neither a state nor a sovereign state but only as a territory. The authorities cited by Van Walt to corroborate this assertion also do not go so far as to claim that associative status preserves the full sovereignty of the associate. Hannum and Lillich, cited by Van Walt, state that "In essence, associated states have all the powers and prerogatives of sovereign independent states, except for those powers they unilaterally choose to delegate to the principal government (typically foreign affairs and defense)." These authorities also state, however, that associative status "recognizes the political and economic dependence of one territory on another, although at the same time acknowledging the dependent territory's existence as a discrete entity with at least some degree of international personality," and that the associated state "retains the potential of achieving full sovereignty and independent statehood." Hurst Hannum and R.B. Lillich,

similar to the protectorate relationship, but different in that the associated state would have the unilateral power to alter the association arrangement according to its own freely expressed democratic choice. Associative status was therefore claimed to offer a pattern for the future for the transition to self-government of formerly dependent or colonial states.[45] Van Walt proposed that associative status was appropriate to Tibet's situation since it "bears significant similarities to the traditional *Cho-Yon* relationship."[46]

Van Walt's claims that associative status was equivalent to sovereignty and his comparison to the traditional *Cho-Yon* may be reasonably suspected of having contributed to China's rejection of the Dalai Lama's Strasbourg Proposal (if in fact China ever seriously considered it). The Chinese criticized the associative status proposal as an attempt by the Dalai Lama to turn the question of regional autonomy among China's national minorities into one of relations between a suzerain state and a dependency, a type of relationship "long cherished by imperialists," since it would "pose a direct challenge to Tibet's legal status as an inalienable part of China."[47] The proposed associative arrangement was seen by the Chinese as essentially a Tibetan attempt to undo the Chinese "liberation" of Tibet and the 17-Point Agreement. The Chinese regarded the Tibetan proposal as an attempt to negate one of the great achievements of the Chinese revolution, the "reunion" of Tibet with China and the final establishment of centralized Chinese control in Tibet.

The factors that the Tibetan Government in Exile had hoped would create both domestic and international pressure on China to reopen negotiations had only increased Chinese nationalist resistance to any discussion of the Tibet issue. CCP hardliners were once again in the ascendancy in 1987-1988. A primary consideration for Tibetans after 1985 had been

---

"The Concept of Autonomy in International Law," in *American Journal of International Law*, 74 (1980), 886, 888. In other words, the associated state or territory has given up some degree of sovereignty or has never attained full sovereignty and is thus not a fully sovereign state, unless it exercises its theoretical right to regain full sovereignty.

45. The examples offered of currently successful associative relationships were, however, few and substantially irrelevant to Tibet's situation. All were islands of small significance, usually considerably distant from the mainland protectorate or colonial state: Puerto Rico, Micronesia, Cook Islands and Western Samoa, none of which are relevant to Tibet's situation or lend much credence to the contention that associative status offers a solution for issues of self-government in the future. Van Walt, *The Status of Tibet*, 284.

46. Ibid., 202. The comparison to the *Cho-Yon* and protectorate relationships reveals an archaic aspect to the associative status proposal. Associative status does bear significant similarities to the *Cho-Yon* relationship and may be characterized as a Tibetan Government in Exile attempt to undo the 17-Point Agreement and return to its concept of Tibet's traditional relationship with China.

47. "What Is Behind the Dalai Lama's `Plan,'" *Beijing Review*, 19 February 1990, 21.

the extent of Chinese population transfer to all parts of Tibet, which the Dalai Lama said in his 1987 Five-Point Peace Proposal to have already made Tibetans a minority in their own country. This consideration, which had assumed "alarming proportions" by 1988, may have driven the Dalai Lama to offer up the one card he had to play: his recognition of Chinese sovereignty over Tibet.[48]

The Strasbourg Proposal did for a brief time put pressure on the Chinese to come up with an adequate response. However, this was finally dealt with by imposing impossible conditions for dialogue. On 23 September 1988 the Chinese Embassy in New Delhi delivered the Chinese response to the Dalai Lama's proposal. The Strasbourg Proposal was rejected as the basis for negotiations "because it has not at all relinquished the concept of the `independence of Tibet.'" The Chinese insisted upon a return to the original conditions for dialogue set out by Deng, with the addition that any actual talks would have to include personal participation by the Dalai Lama (so as to construe the issue as one of the Dalai Lama's personal status). The Chinese refused to negotiate with officials of the Tibetan Government in Exile, a Tibetan polity they did not recognize, or a foreign legal advisor on the Tibetan negotiation team (Van Walt). The message advised the Dalai Lama that if he were really sincere in improving relations with the "Central Government" and if he were really concerned for the happiness of the Tibetan people, he should "give up the `idea of independence.'"[49] As the Chinese media stated in 1990, "China's central government has made it clear that it cannot accept the so-called `new proposals' made by the Dalai Lama at Strasbourg, France, in June of 1988, let alone make them the basis of the dialogue, because the proposals were formed on the pretext that `Tibet used to be a country.'"[50]

The Dalai Lama's Strasbourg Proposal ultimately received a favorable response neither from the Chinese at whom it was directed nor from Tibetans in whose interest it was offered. The proposal impressed only the international community, for whom the fundamental issues of sovereignty and independence were not so important as was the example of the Dalai Lama's spirit of concession in the resolution of international conflicts. The Strasbourg Proposal had a positive effect upon internation-

---

48. Van Walt, *Population Transfer and the Survival of the Tibetan Identity*, 1.

49. Dawa Norbu, "China's Dialogue with the Dalai Lama 1978-90: Prenegotiation Stage or Dead End?" *Pacific Affairs*, vol. 64, no. 3 (Fall 1991), 360. Having interpreted the Dalai Lama's earlier statements about the happiness of the Tibetan people as signifying his abandonment of any political conditions, the Chinese may have been attempting to return the dialogue to that basis.

50. "Dalai's Threat Seen as Senseless," *Beijing Review*, 26 February 1990, 11.

al interest in and support for the Tibetan cause, ultimately influencing the selection of the Dalai Lama for the Nobel Peace Prize in 1989. However, it had little effect on the progress of Sino-Tibetan dialogue.

Martial Law in Tibet

All pretense of leniency in Tibet was discontinued after the riot of March 1988. Ideological work teams were sent to monasteries and nunneries around Lhasa to root out nationalist monks and nuns. Neighborhood committees and work teams examined Tibetans' ideological conformity and political loyalty as a means of identifying those with nationalist or "splittist" sentiments. Ideological indoctrination was combined with open and intimidating displays of police and military force and the flaunting of Chinese power as a means to impress Tibetans with the futility of their hope for independence. However, Tibetans proved more resistant to ideological coercion and intimidation than in the past. Many refused the demands of ideological work teams that they denounce the Dalai Lama. Tibetans were emboldened to challenge the economic and social justifications for Chinese rule and the "correct view of Tibetan history" propagated by ideological work teams. Tibetans maintained that the traditional Tibetan form of combined religion and politics was actually a more modern political form than "reactionary Chinese communism," and that traditional Tibetan political culture was more consistent with international human rights norms. Renewed repression tended to solidify many Tibetans' sense of communal and nationalist spirit. Collaborators, informers and opportunists were increasingly isolated, while ethnic divisions between Chinese and Tibetans were exacerbated.[51]

Chinese threats to mercilessly repress any further demonstrations materialized on 10 December 1988 on the 40th anniversary of the Universal Declaration of Human Rights, when Chinese PAP troops fired without warning on monks and lay Tibetans circumambulating the Jokhang with Tibetan flags. At least two Tibetans were killed and several wounded.[52] The Panchen Lama was sent to Tibet in January 1989 in another attempt to placate Tibetan sentiments. The Panchen made a

---

51. Ronald Schwartz, "Reform and Repression in Tibet," *Telos*, Summer 1989; "The Anti-Splittist Campaign and the Development of Tibetan Political Consciousness," paper presented at conference on Tibet, School of Oriental and African Studies, University of London, March 1990.

52. *Defying the Dragon*, 26.

speech in Shigatse in which he said that "the price paid by Tibet for its development over the last thirty years has been higher than the gains."[53] Shortly thereafter, in Shigatse, the Panchen suffered a heart attack and died, under what can only be described as very mysterious circumstances.[54]

The Panchen Lama had been a spokesman for the pragmatic faction in Beijing. He was opposed by hardliners, especially Chinese cadres in Tibet who favored a continuation of strict Chinese control in Tibet. His demise reduced the influence of the pragmatic faction and increased the strength of the hardliners. The Dalai Lama was invited by the Chinese Buddhist Association to attend a commemorative ceremony for the Panchen Lama in Beijing, but not to attend the actual funeral in Shigatse. The Dalai Lama declined to attend. China's most recent tactic had been to demand personal participation by the Dalai Lama in any negotiations; the invitation was interpreted by the The Tibetan Government in Exile as an underhanded way to negotiate directly with the Dalai Lama.[55]

In January 1989 Wu Jinghua, the Yi nationality CCP party head in Tibet, was replaced by a Han, Hu Jintao. *Monlam* ceremonies for 1989 were cancelled, but on 5 March 1989 several monks marched around the Barkhor to commemorate the sacrifice of those monks killed and wounded a year earlier. They were again fired on without warning by Chinese policemen. This incident set off three days of rioting during which Tibetan crowds looted and burned 45 Chinese shops. Tibetan crowds were repeatedly allowed to gather without any attempt at control and then were fired upon without warning. Some 80 to 150 Tibetans were killed and many more were wounded; many of the wounded died because they were unable to seek medical care without being arrested. One Chinese policeman was thrown from the roof of the Jokhang and killed. The Chinese expressed tremendous outrage at the death of this one Chinese, mounting a large funeral and dedicating a memorial to his sacrifice, while ignoring the deaths of Tibetans. On the third day, 7 March, martial law was declared; tourists and journalists were expelled from Tibet; Tibetans from rural areas were prohibited from travelling to Lhasa without permission. Public Security Police and PAP conducted house searches in Lhasa; thousands suspected of having played a role in the

---

53. "Political Statements by the Panchen Lama," *Tibet Information Network*, 20 February 1991.

54. The Panchen Lama was 50 years old when he died. Poison was suspected. On the other hand, the Panchen had suffered greatly during his years of imprisonment and his health had undoubtedly been affected.

55. Lodi Gyari, personal communication, Washington, February 1995.

riots were arrested. Further public gatherings were banned. Martial law was in effect in the TAR for more than a year, until 30 April 1990.[56]

Tiananmen and After

Martial law in Tibet proved to be a precursor to a general crackdown on what the CCP considered the deleterious effects of "bourgeois liberalization" in China. Since the end of the Maoist era, Chinese students and intellectuals had rejected Communist philosophy, challenged the legitimacy of one-party rule and demanded greater respect for law by the CCP. CCP policy in the 1980s was to allow economic liberalization while keeping political discourse within the bounds of the "Four Fundamental Principles." However, economic liberalization and the "Four Modernizations" required an "open door" policy in foreign relations, inevitably leading to what the conservatives characterized as "spiritual pollution" by Western capitalist and "humanist" ideologies.

To combat these tendencies, CCP conservatives mounted the "Anti-Spiritual Pollution" campaign of 1983-84 and the "Anti-Bourgeois Liberalization" campaign of 1987-88. Deng Xiaoping defined political liberalization as bourgeois and a threat to political stability and unity: "Liberalization belongs to the bourgeoisie. There is nothing that can be called proletarian or socialist liberalization. Liberalization itself is opposed to our present policies and systems."[57] Bourgeois liberalization was characterized as "refuting socialism, advocating capitalism, and its core is refuting the party's leadership." The campaign against this phenomenon was defined as essential to the fate of both the Party and the nation:

> It has much to do with the fate of our party and nation as well as the future of the socialist cause. In a word, adhering to the Four Fundamental Principles (that is, adhering to socialism, the people's democratic dictatorship, the leadership of the Communist Party, and Marxism-Leninism and Mao Zedong Thought), opposing bourgeois liberalization, and strengthening stability and unity are the foundations of our nation.[58]

---

56. *Defying the Dragon*, 27.

57. Deng Xiaoping's Speech at the Sixth Plenum of the Twelfth Central Committee, 9 January 1987, in "Party Documents on Anti-bourgeois Liberalization and Hu Yaobang's Resignation," in James Tong, ed., *Chinese Law and Government*, vol. 21, no. 1 (Spring 1988), 23.

58. Circular of the CCP Central Committee on Issues of the Current Anti-bourgeois Liberalization Movement, 28 January 1987, in Ibid., 30.

A document adopted by the NPC shortly thereafter laid the basis for suppression of those who did not adhere to the Party's limits on political expression. Noting that not only were the Four Fundamental Principles a part of the PRC Constitution but that they "embody the law of historical development which is independent of man's will," the document attempted to establish these principles within state as well as natural law.[59] The Party thus legalized repression of criticism that "threatened unity and stability." In particular, "those who use counterrevolutionary slogans, leaflets, and other methods to propagate and to incite to overthrow the state power of the proletarian dictatorship and the socialist system" were criminals who should be "investigated and affixed with responsibility according to law."[60]

The CCP identified the "Four Fundamental Principles" as the basis of its legitimacy; however, Chinese students and intellectuals were beginning to identify the same principles as the source of all of China's wrongs. Many challenged the legitimacy of the Fundamental Principles, and correctly opined that no true freedom of thought was possible within this ideological straightjacket. The concept of "democratic dictatorship" was identified as a contradiction in terms. Marxism was belittled as an archaic system of thought little relevant to China's current conditions. The CCP's rule was characterized as feudal and despotic. Chinese intellectuals began to turn to Western "humanist" ideologies and to see that the benefits of Western democracy were not necessarily negated by the inequalities of capitalism:

> As regards the capitalist system of democracy, we used to speak about the rights it denies the people and not the rights it gives to the people. As regards our own system, we only say what it gives to the people and not what it denies the people. In this way we create a false impression of the unmatched superiority of the Chinese political system in the world. We have such a theory that asserts that we practice democracy toward the people and dictatorship toward the enemy. However, we can designate anyone we want to attack into the category of the enemy and deprive him of democratic rights. In fact, the principle of democracy precisely means that we allow not only our own people but also the opposition the right to speak out.[61]

59. "Decision of the Standing Committee of the National People's Congress on Strengthening the Education in the Legal System and Safeguarding Unity and Stability," in Ibid., 40.

60. Ibid., 45.

61. *World Economic Herald*, 15 September 1986, quoted in Ibid., 75.

The death of Hu Yaobang in April 1989 provided a catalyst for the reform movement, much as the death of Zhou Enlai did in 1976. Students' demands for a reappraisal of Hu and for a revival of the reforms that he represented led quickly to a major confrontation between students and the government. The students were joined by older intellectuals and workers, who, taking an example from the autonomous student organizations, formed similar workers' organizations. The support and involvement of the workers was especially threatening to the CCP because it was these same people whose interests the Party claimed to represent. The students were careful to express their loyalty to socialism and the CCP, claiming only that the principles of socialism had been violated by some of those in power. Their inability to identify exactly who in the Party hierarchy were the chief culprits finally led to the realization that it was the system itself, not only the leadership, that was at fault. The eventual violent suppression of the movement in Tiananmen Square on 4 June 1989 further served to convince many Chinese that the problem was not only a few despotic leaders, but that the political system itself was inherently despotic.

After Tiananmen the democracy movement was effectively suppressed, but many of the movement's leaders were able to escape to foreign countries. In exile, the exiled democracy movement's leaders attempted to confront the problem of a political transition in China from the "feudalistic despotism" of CCP rule to a democratic system. They were also confronted for the first time with information about the reality of Chinese rule in Tibet and other minority areas that substantially contradicted what they had been led to believe. Most responded that democracy was the solution to all of China's problems, including that of the national minorities.

The extent of Chinese mis-rule in Tibet and the level of animosity between Tibetans and Chinese was generally unknown to the Chinese democracy leaders, indoctrinated as they were about the benevolence of China's liberation of Tibet from feudalism and barbarism. Most perpetuated an essentially paternalistic attitude toward Tibet, the essence of which was that they, as democratic Chinese, could bestow democracy upon Tibetans and thus satisfy the Tibetans' demands for "self-determination." The first statements of the exiled Chinese "democrats" revealed how little their attitude toward the Tibetan situation differed from that of the CCP. Characterizing the Tibetan struggle as one against Communism, not China (echoing Taiwan's position), Yan Jiaqi, one of the founders of the Democratic Front of China, suggested that the Tibetan uprisings between 1959 and 1989 should not be characterized as "counterrevolutionary," as if a "reversal of verdicts" was a significant issue for Tibetans.

However, Yan also expressed the opinion that Tibet might be accorded federative status within a Chinese democratic state.[62]

The democracy movement's leaders support for Tibetan "self-determination" was criticized by Tibetans as a subterfuge for continued Chinese rule that did not address Tibetans' desires for independence. A few of the exiled Chinese responded with principled support for Tibetan independence, based upon their realization of the fundamental illegitimacy of Chinese rule over Tibetans, while others maintained that democracy in China would satisfy Tibetans' demands for self-determination. Those who supported Tibetan self-determination, even if that were to be manifested as independence, remained a minority within the exile democracy movement, which itself represented only a tiny fraction of opinion among all Chinese.[63]

The exiled Chinese democracy movement leaders eventually proposed a draft "Constitution of the Federal Republic of China" that offered Tibet (as well as Inner Mongolia, Xinjiang, Ningxia, Guangxi and Taiwan) federative status as an "Autonomous State" within a democratic China. Tibet (and only Tibet) was promised the right to a referendum on its status as a part of the Chinese state, after a period of 25 years, not subject to central government approval. Autonomous state status within the proposed "Federal Republic of China" would include the right to participation in international organizations and to establish foreign representative offices. Each autonomous state would have the right to establish entry and exit regulations in order to restrict movement of people into or out of the state. No territorial definition of Tibet was provided, presumably meaning that even Chinese "democrats" regarded the TAR as the extent of "Tibet" and would resist the inclusion of any Tibetan territories in Qinghai, Sichuan, Gansu or Yunnan.[64]

The Dalai Lama's international campaigning combined with the world's revulsion at the repression of demonstrations in Tibet and in China resulted in the award of the Nobel Peace Prize to the Dalai Lama

---

62. *World Journal*, 21 September 1989, in *Tibet Press Watch*, October 1989, 17.

63. "Tibetan Representatives Address First Congress of the Federation for Democracy in China," 23 September 1989, in *Tibet Press Watch*, October 1989, 18; Personal observations at Conference on Sino-Tibetan Dialogue, Washington, October 1992.

64. "Draft Constitution for a Federal China," *Tibet Press Watch*, February 1994, 7. None of the other areas offered federative status is comparable to Tibet: Inner Mongolia is now only 10 percent Mongol, Xinjiang is not a single nationality area, Ningxia's Hui "nationality" is not an ethnic but a religious category, and Guangxi's Chuang nationality is almost completely assimilated. The inclusion of Taiwan in a federative scheme evokes comparisons with the CCP's attempts to propose a "Tibet model" national regional autonomy system for Taiwan.

on 5 October 1989. The Nobel Committee specifically cited the Dalai Lama's consistent opposition to the use of violence and his advocacy of "peaceful solutions based upon tolerance and mutual respect in order to preserve the historical and cultural heritage of his people." He was also credited with having come forward with "constructive and forward-looking proposals for the solution of international conflicts, human rights issues, and global environmental problems."[65]

The award of the Nobel Prize to the Dalai Lama finally overcame international leaders' reluctance to meet with the Dalai Lama. US President George Bush met with the Dalai Lama in Washington on 17 April 1991. In an address to members of Congress (in the Capitol Rotunda, not in the House or Senate chambers), the Dalai Lama spoke of Tibet as a "nation under foreign occupation" and called on the US and other governments to link their relations with China to human rights concerns.[66] The Dalai Lama's visit to Washington was accompanied by a "sense of the Senate" resolution "concerning freedom and human rights for Tibet." The Senate's non-binding resolution repeated the opinion expressed in the International Commission of Jurists' 1960 report that Tibet had demonstrated from 1913 to 1950 the requirements of statehood as generally accepted by international law. The Senate resolved that the PRC should know that "as the Tibetan people and His Holiness the Dalai Lama of Tibet go forward on their journey toward freedom the Congress and the people of the United States stand with them," and that "all Americans are united on the goals of freedom and human rights for Tibet."[67]

Shortly after the Dalai Lama's Washington visit, the US Congress attached a resolution to a Foreign Relations Authorization Act expressing the "sense of the Congress" that:

(1) Tibet, including those areas incorporated into the Chinese provinces of Sichuan, Yunnan, Gansu, and Quinghai [Qinghai], is an occupied country under the established principles of international law;

(2) Tibet's true representatives are the Dalai Lama and the Tibetan Government in exile as recognized by the Tibetan people;

(3) Tibet has maintained throughout its history a distinctive and sovereign national, cultural, and religious identity separate from that of China and,

---

65. Norwegian Nobel Committee Peace Prize Announcement, Oslo, 5 October 1989, in *Government Resolutions on Tibet*, 1.

66. "H.H. The Dalai Lama's Address to Members of the US Congress at the Capital Rotunda, 18 April 1991," in *Tibet Press Watch*, April 1991.

67. Senate Resolution 107, 102nd Congress First Session, *Congressional Record*, vol. 137, no. 57, 18 April 1991, in *Tibet Press Watch*, April 1991.

except during periods of illegal Chinese occupation, has maintained a separate and sovereign political and territorial identity;

(4) historical evidence of this separate identity may be found in Chinese archival documents and traditional dynastic histories, in United States recognition of Tibetan neutrality during World War II, and in the fact that a number of countries including the United States, Mongolia, Bhutan, Sikkim, Nepal, India, Japan, Great Britain, and Russia recognized Tibet as an independent nation or dealt with Tibet independently of any Chinese government;

(5) in 1949-1950, China launched an armed invasion of Tibet in contravention of international law;

(6) it is the policy of the United States to oppose aggression and other illegal uses of force by one country against the sovereignty of another as a means of acquiring territory, and to condemn violations of international law, including the illegal occupation of one country by another; and

(7) numerous United States declarations since the Chinese invasion have recognized Tibet's right to self-determination and the illegality of China's occupation of Tibet.[68]

US Congressional resolutions recognizing Tibet as an occupied country were merely "sense of the Congress" resolutions, non-binding on the US Government. Congressional criticism of China over the Tibet issue was of less significance than the firm policy of the executive branch of the US Government to recognize China's sovereignty over Tibet. In July 1992, the Senate Foreign Relations Committee held hearings on Tibet, the first time that hearings had ever been held on Tibet's political status. State Department spokesman L. Desaix Anderson, Deputy Assistant Secretary of State for East Asian and Pacific Affairs, repeated the US position:

The United States, like all other governments throughout the world, considers Tibet to be a part of China, with the status of an autonomous region. No country recognizes Tibet as independent of China. The United States has never taken the position that Tibet is an independent country, nor has it recognized the Dalai Lama as the leader of a government in exile.[69]

In response to a question in regard to the 1960 US position on Tibet's

---

68. Foreign Relations Authorization Act, Fiscal Years 1992 and 1993, House of Representatives Conference Report 102-238, 3 October 1991, in *Tibet Press Watch*, December 1991.

69. "US and Chinese Policies Toward Occupied Tibet," Hearing before the Committee on Foreign Relations, United States Senate, 28 July 1992, 5.

right to self-determination, Secretary Anderson said, "The question, though, at that time was a discussion of self-determination in the context of Tibet's being an autonomous region, but not the question of whether or not it was an independent country."[70] In regard to the State Department's position on the meaning of self-determination, the Secretary further elaborated:

> We are in favor of self-determination. That's well known. But we do not think that that is equatable necessarily with independence. We see that there are various ways in which to realize self-determination. We have not recognized Tibet as an independent state. We are in favor of their self-determination.[71]

The Dalai Lama's reception in Washington was followed by meetings for the first time with many government officials, including heads of government and heads of state in several countries, including a reception by the British Prime Minister on 2 December 1991. The Tibet issue was also brought up before the United Nations Commission on Human Rights and the Sub-Commission on Prevention of Discrimination and Protection of Minorities. The Sub-Commission passed resolutions condemning China's human rights practices in 1989 and resolutions mentioning such practices in "China, including Tibet" in 1991. In each case, when the resolutions came before the Commission on Human Rights, in 1990, 1992, 1994 and 1996 China, with the support of Pakistan, and, in 1996 with the support of Pakistan, India and Russia, managed to defeat the resolutions on procedural motions.

---

70. Ibid., 8. The statement that the US position on Tibetan self-determination did not imply independence is accurate in the sense that the US was at that time coordinating its policy with that of Nationalist China, which had called for Tibetan self-determination but recognized only Tibetan autonomy. Nevertheless, the US State Department said at the time that the US was not committing itself to ultimate recognition of Tibetan independence, only to "the concept that Tibetans have the right to choose whether or not Tibet is to be independent." State Department Memorandum of Conversation, 3 November 1959, National Archives, 793B.00/11-359.

71. "US and Chinese Policies Toward Occupied Tibet," 11. Senator Moynihan challenged the State Department spokesman on his contention that the previous US position on Tibet's right to self-determination was confined to the context of Tibet as an autonomous region under Chinese sovereignty. This, Senator Moynihan said, was inconsistent with self-determination as defined in the UN Charter: "It was intended to produce independence. . . Self-determination, as a principle in the UN Charter, does not theoretically contemplate independence. It almost assumes that's what the end result is. . . The United Nations General Assembly has said this nation has a right to self-determination. The idea of self-determination arose in exactly, in precisely the setting of indeterminate sovereignties. . . What I mean to say is that self-determination anticipates exactly the kind of situation you have in Tibet." Ibid.

In October 1994 the State Department issued a report mandated by the Foreign Relations Authorization Act of 1994-1995, entitled "Relations of the United States with Tibet," in which the State Department defined the US position on Tibet:

Historically, the United States has acknowledged Chinese sovereignty over Tibet. Since at least 1966, US policy has explicitly recognized the Tibetan Autonomous Region or TAR (hereinafter referred to as "Tibet") as part of the People's Republic of China. This long-standing policy is consistent with the view of the entire international community, including all China's neighbors: no country recognizes Tibet as a sovereign state. Because we do not recognize Tibet as an independent state, the United States does not conduct diplomatic relations with the self-styled "Tibetan government-in-exile." The United States continues, however, to urge Beijing and the Dalai Lama to hold serious discussions at an early date, without preconditions, and on a fixed agenda. The United States also urges China to respect Tibet's unique religious, linguistic and cultural traditions as it formulates policies for Tibet.[72]

In a 7 September 1995 Senate Foreign Relations Committee hearing on Tibet, Deputy Assistant Secretary of State for East Asian and Pacific Affairs, Kent M. Wiedemann, reiterated this policy:

The United States considers the Tibet Autonomous Region or TAR (hereinafter referred to as "Tibet") as part of the People's Republic of China. This longstanding policy is consistent with the view of the entire international community, including all China's neighbors: no country recognizes Tibet as a sovereign state. . . . Because we do not recognize Tibet as an independent state, the United States does not conduct diplomatic relations with the representatives of Tibetans in exile. However, the United States urges China to respect Tibet's unique religious, linguistic and cultural traditions and the human rights of Tibetans.[73]

---

72. "Relations of the United States with Tibet," in *Country Reports on Human Rights Practices for 1994* (Washington D.C.: United States Department of State, October 1994). The State Department was obviously at a quandary to define the history of US relations with Tibet, as is evident from its statement that the US has "historically" acknowledged Chinese sovereignty over Tibet, "at least since 1966." Apparently, a State Department official made a statement in 1966 in regard to the establishment of the TAR in 1965 implying that the US recognized Chinese sovereignty over the TAR.

73. Subcommittee on East Asian and Pacific Affairs, Senate Foreign Relations Committee, Hearing on Tibet, 7 September 1995, 2. The current State Department language urging China to respect Tibet's "unique religious, linguistic and cultural traditions and the human rights of Tibetans" carefully avoids the issue of political autonomy. The United States has been excessively accommodationist in its avoidance of any position on the political rights of Tibetans and in its usage of phrases preferred by the Chinese. For the US to

Western human rights organizations were also limited in their support for Tibet by their self-imposed restriction to individual human rights, a restriction that prevented their dealing with self-determination as a human right. For example, Asia Watch and Amnesty International were limited by their charters to support for political prisoners or "prisoners of conscience."[74] Human rights organizations were able to protest against the arrest of people for nonviolent expression of political ideas and against their abuse while imprisoned, but they were unwilling to address the political issues for which they were arrested or abused. Both human rights organizations and governments chose to treat the Tibetan issue primarily as one of the Chinese Government's mistreatment of Tibetans; they were prevented by their ideological or political interests from consideration of the political sources of that mistreatment.

As Asia Watch acknowledged, "It is difficult to separate the issue of political imprisonment in Tibet from those of freedom of speech and assembly. . . there is one urgent issue around which almost all political activity seems to be centered: the question of Tibet's status and the related questions concerned with the possible return of the Dalai Lama and the withdrawal of the Chinese from Tibet."[75] Asia Watch also criticized the international tendency of "downplaying of human rights violations in Tibet out of suspicion of or disagreement with the main objective of Tibetan protesters: the independence of Tibet."[76] Nevertheless, Asia Watch "takes no position on the status of Tibet."[77]

Despite the limitations of international organizations and governments in addressing the fundamental political issues of Chinese rule in Tibet, the popular international perception was that the issue of Tibet was about the legitimacy of Chinese sovereignty over Tibet. This perception was shared by the immediate protagonists, Tibetans and Chinese, both of whom were fully aware that the fundamental issue was one of sovereignty. Tibetans were disappointed by the lack of official support for their political rights but were greatly encouraged by the dramatic shift since the early 1980s of popular support in their favor.

---

repeat that no country has recognized Tibet is gratuitous, an embarrassment to the United States and an insult to Tibet, which was in fact recognized, in a traditional sense, as independent by its neighbors, China included at one time.

74. Amnesty International, *People's Republic of China: Repression in Tibet 1987-1992* (New York: Amnesty International, 1992); Asia Watch, *Human Rights in Tibet* (Washington: Asia Watch, 1988); *Evading Scrutiny: Violations of Human Rights After the Closing of Tibet* (Washington: Asia Watch, 1988); *Merciless Repression: Human Rights in Tibet* (Washington: Asia Watch, 1990); *Political Prisoners in Tibet* (Washington: Asia Watch and Tibet Information Network, 1992); *Detained in China and Tibet* (Washington: Asia Watch, 1994).

75. Asia Watch, *Human Rights in Tibet*, 25.

76. Asia Watch, *Merciless Repression*, 90.

77. Ibid., 5.

China's Propaganda Offensive

The "internationalization" of the issue of Tibet's political status forced the Chinese reluctantly to return to the fundamental issue of the legitimacy of their rule in Tibet, an issue they had thought buried since 1951 or at least since 1959. The Chinese took some solace in the fact that no foreign government recognized Tibetan independence and official criticism was confined to individual human rights issues, but they tended to regard the human rights issue as a subterfuge for an attack on the legitimacy of Chinese rule in Tibet and, ultimately, of CCP rule in China. The human rights offenses in Tibet for which China was criticized had undeniable political origins. As Dorje Tseten, former chairman of the People's Government of the TAR and director of the China Tibetology Research Center, said, the real purpose of "certain hostile forces abroad" in concocting the human rights issue in Tibet was to "wantonly interfere in China's internal affairs and ultimately to split Tibet from the territory of the People's Republic of China by using human rights as a pretext."[78]

China responded to international criticism of its human rights and Tibet policies with an increase in propaganda on both political and human rights issues. In 1992 the PRC State Council published a White Paper entitled "Tibet—Its Ownership and Human Rights Situation," in which human rights and political issues were linked.[79] The White Paper supported China's claim to "ownership" of Tibet with the usual argument that Tibet had become an integral part of China during the 13th century. Tang Dynasty relations with the Tibetan empire were said to have laid a "solid foundation for the ultimate founding of a unified nation," an argument based on the treaty of 822 in which the Chinese and Tibetans agreed to "unite their territories as one."[80] In substantiating the claim that Chinese rule over Tibet was continuous after the 13th century, the White Paper put an interesting twist on Ming relations with various Tibetan lamas by claiming that the third Ming emperor, Chengzu (reigned 1403-1424), did not desire to rule Tibet directly because he "saw the advantage

---

78. Dorje Tsetan, "Tibet: Human Rights and China's Sovereignty," *Beijing Review*, 2 March 1992, 26. The subtitle of this article was "The so-called Tibet question has nothing to do with human rights, but is a question bearing on the maintenance of China's sovereignty." Ibid., 29.

79. "Tibet—Its Ownership and Human Rights Situation," *Beijing Review*, 28 September 1992, 10-43.

80. Ibid., 10. In Bell's translation of this treaty, the "union" of Tibet and China is clearly in the sense of a union in agreement. The Chinese White Paper fails to mention further sections of this same treaty in which China and Tibet are treated as separate countries, united only by treaty. Bell, *Tibet Past and Present*, 271.

of combined Buddhist religious and political power in Tibet and rivalry between sects occupying different areas."[81]

The White Paper was equally creative in refuting the Tibetan claim to *de facto* independence during the Republican and Nationalist periods. The rules and regulations promulgated by the Republic of China to deal with Tibet were cited, including unilateral declarations that Tibet formed a part of the Republic, the "five races" policy, the Bureau of Mongolian and Tibetan Affairs, and Chinese representatives appointed to handle administrative affairs in Tibet, without mentioning that none of these measures was ever put into effect because China had no control over Tibet at the time. In addition, the central government was said to have supervised and approved the selection and installation of the 14th Dalai Lama. Tibetan representatives were also said to have participated in the Chinese National Assembly in 1946. In 1950, after peacefully liberating the "provinces bordering on Tibet," including Xikang (Sikang), from the rule of the KMT, "in light of the history and reality of Tibet, the central people's government decided to do the same for Tibet."[82]

More interesting interpretations were provided in a separate article attempting to refute the claim that the 17-Point Agreement was concluded by force. The halting of the PLA advance after the capture of Chamdo was alleged to have "greatly encouraged the patriotic forces in Tibet and frustrated imperialist and separatist forces headed by Tagecha [Taktra]." The Dalai Lama's early accession to power was claimed to have represented a "change in the balance of forces" against separatists in favor of "patriotic officials." The Dalai Lama only assumed political power, it was said, after securing approval from the Chinese central government, an approval that, "according to historical practice," he had to seek "before he can lawfully assume government office." This approval was supposedly what Shakabpa and Surkhang went to Delhi in September 1950 to request from the Chinese ambassador to India.[83]

---

81. "Tibet—Its Ownership and Human Rights Situation," *Beijing Review*, 28 September 1992, 11.

82. Ibid., 14; "The Origin of the 14th Dalai Lama," *Beijing Review*, 8 April 1991, 7. The wording of this last statement casts some doubt on how much the Chinese really thought of Tibet as an integral part of China. The CCP made a decision to liberate Tibet because of the "history and reality" of Tibet, conditions which imply that Tibet was considered an area of indeterminate status, not an integral part of China.

83. "Dalai Lama and 17-Article Agreement," *Beijing Review*, 13 May 1991, 18. In fact, Shakabpa delivered a letter from the Dalai Lama to Mao in which the Dalai Lama announced his accession to power and requested that Chinese and Tibetan representatives meet to discuss China's claims to authority over Tibet. The Dalai Lama's announcement of his accession is interpreted in this article as a request for approval. This is a typical Chinese method of pretending to authority over Tibet where none existed in fact. The "change in the

The Chinese claimed that the liberation of Tibet and the 17-Point Agreement had "enjoyed the approval and support" of the Tibetan people and the Dalai Lama. The revolt in Tibet was credited exclusively to the "reactionary clique of the upper social strata," supported by "foreign anti-China forces." According to the Chinese, the Dalai Lama had been against the rebellion but he had been spirited away under duress. Only after reaching India, where he was surrounded by "foreign anti-China forces and separatists," did he "renounce the patriotic stand which he once expressed" and repudiate the 17-Point Agreement. Only then did he claim that Tibet had ever been independent.[84]

China's solution to the dispute with the Dalai Lama was for him to "renounce separatism and return to the stance of patriotism and unity."[85] There could be no discussion about Tibetan "independence, semi-independence or disguised independence" (as the Chinese characterized the Strasbourg formula): "The central government will make not the slightest concession on the fundamental issue of maintaining the motherland's unification." The central government was willing to hold talks with the Dalai Lama at any time, "so long as the Dalai Lama can give up his divisive stand and admit that Tibet is an inalienable part of China."[86]

The Chinese White Paper attacked the "Dalai clique and international anti-China forces" for their championing of human rights in Tibet, when it was they who were responsible for the "dark, savage and cruel feudal serfdom" from which China had liberated Tibet. The Chinese claimed that the human rights issue was a subterfuge by separatist forces "to realize their dream of dismembering China, seizing Tibet and finally subverting socialist China." This attempt, it was said, would be resisted by the Chinese people, including the Tibetan people, because "unity spells common prosperity and separation would mean peril to both parties."[87]

---

balance of forces" claimed to have resulted in the early accession of the Dalai Lama to power (thus portraying the Dalai Lama as a member of the "patriotic forces" in Tibet and as favoring a negotiated settlement with China) was said to have foiled the attempt of "pro-imperialist separatists and some foreign forces to hold negotiations in India or Hong Kong to repeat the plot of `Simla conference.'" Ibid.

84. Ibid., 21.

85. Ibid., 22.

86. Ibid., 24. As in the past, the term "central government" was employed, instead of "Chinese Government," to emphasize that Tibet was an internal issue.

87. Ibid., 43. China addressed the issue of colonization by saying that the central government would continue to send "large numbers of technicians including scientists, engineers, managerial personnel, teachers and medical workers," to Tibet because "Tibet is in short supply of scientific and technical personnel." These personnel would all go there for a "fixed period of time on rotation." Ibid. In a subsequent article, supposedly in response to letters about the White Paper, the PRC claimed that "the status of Tibet is a settled issue," and had been so for 700 years. The reason that Tibet had naturally gravitated toward China,

The CCP's general defense on human rights was set out by the State Council in a White Paper on "Human Rights in China." The PRC claimed that it upheld individual and collective human rights on political and social levels. While claiming to adhere to all international human rights conventions, the position of the Chinese Government was that human rights were within the domestic jurisdiction of states. Respect for sovereignty and the principle of non-interference in states' internal affairs had to take precedence over international human rights concerns or universal human rights principles:

> China has firmly opposed any country making use of the issue of human rights to sell its own values, ideology, political standards and mode of development and to any country interfering in the internal affairs of another country on the pretext of human rights, the internal affairs of developing countries in particular, and so hurting the sovereignty and dignity of many developing countries.[88]

The PRC held that human rights were not universal, but were particular to each country according to different political, economic and social systems as well as different historical, religious and cultural backgrounds.[89] The particular cultural and political traditions defining Chinese human rights doctrine were China's collectivist traditions, its Marxist emphasis upon collectivist material rights, and both Chinese and Marxist anti-imperialism. The liberation of the Chinese people from foreign imperialism and the provision of basic sustenance to all the Chinese people was emphasized by the PRC as its major human rights accomplishments. The Chinese doctrine maintained that individual rights had to take a subordinate position to the rights of the collective. Those individuals defined, by both class and political criteria, as not "of the people" were necessarily subjected to the "dictatorship of the proletariat." The PRC nevertheless claimed that it had no political prisoners:

> In China, ideas alone, in the absence of action which violates the criminal law, do not constitute a crime; nobody will be sentenced to punishment

---

it was said, was because Tibet was walled in on all sides except facing China; this physical characteristic was "one of the most important reasons for Tibet to remain a part of China over the past 700 years." "Tibet's Historical Status," *Beijing Review*, 28 December 1993, 21. Eastern Tibet is no doubt most accessible to China, but central Tibet is far more accessible to India, as is revealed by historical cultural exchanges and trade patterns as well as by China's modern logistical difficulties in supplying Chinese personnel in Tibet.

88. "Human Rights in China," *Beijing Review*, 4 November 1991, 44.

89. Ibid., 9.

merely because he holds dissenting political views. So-called political prisoners do not exist in China. In Chinese Criminal Law "counterrevolutionary crime" refers to crime which endangers state security, i.e., criminal acts
which are not only committed with the purpose of overthrowing state
power and the socialist system, but which are also . . . criminal acts, such as
those carried out in conspiring to overthrow the government or splitting
the country.[90]

National minorities, as members of the Chinese body politic, were subject to the dictatorship of the proletariat (a "proletariat" that was 95 percent Han Chinese). "Discrimination against and oppression of any
nationality are prohibited," but "any acts that undermine the unity and
create splits among the nationalities are also prohibited."[91] Opposition to
the CCP was a criminal offense for national minorities as for the Han
Chinese, but, for minorities, opposition to being forcibly included within
the Chinese state or being identified as Chinese was also a criminal
offense. Minorities, like the Chinese majority, must remain a part of the
collective to benefit from collective rights; rejection of the collective, or,
for minorities, rejection of the Chinese state, made them subject to criminal law. China defined the essence of its human rights achievements as
the "preservation of national independence and state sovereignty and the
freedom from imperialist subjugation."[92]

The Tibetan Government in Exile responded to the Chinese
Government White Paper with a position paper of its own entitled *Tibet:
Proving Truth from Facts*. The Tibetans characterized China's historical
claims to Tibet as imperialist, as was revealed by China's use of the term
"ownership" in the title of its White Paper ("Tibet—Its Ownership and
Human Rights Situation"). They maintained that, no matter how much
China had been able to dominate Tibet in the past, Tibet at no time had
become an integral part of China. Tibet retained, in the past and even
until the present time, all the characteristics of a nation and therefore was
deserving of the right of self-determination. The 17-Point Agreement was
characterized as an unequal treaty of the type that the Chinese typically
condemned as having been imposed upon China by foreign imperialists
in the past.[93]

---

90. Ibid., 24. The PRC has no political prisoners only because opposition to the regime
has been defined as a criminal offense.

91. Ibid., 32.

92. Ibid., 12. This, however, is the same national independence and freedom denied to
the Tibetans.

93. *Tibet: Proving Truth from Facts* (Dharamsala: Department of Information and
International Relations, Central Tibetan Administration, 1993), 3.

The Tibetans maintained that, contrary to China's contention that the Tibetan Government entered into the 17-Point Agreement willingly, they had done so only under the threat of force. In response to China's arguments in regard to Tibet's former social system or the supposed "improvements" made under China's rule, the Tibetan Government in Exile replied that none of those arguments, even if they were true, could justify an invasion and occupation of another country. International law does not accept justifications of this type: "No country is allowed to invade, occupy, annex and colonize another country just because its social structure does not please it." Furthermore, the PRC was responsible for bringing vastly more suffering upon the Tibetan people than was even conceivably possible under the former social system.[94] The Tibetans denied that Tibet's traditional social system was as "dark, savage and cruel" as the Chinese claimed and pointed out that this was typical colonialist propaganda. The PRC was, in contrast, accused of having introduced a form of state feudalism responsible for the very sort of crimes against humanity that they attributed to the former Tibetan social and political system.[95]

In order to refute Chinese claims that Tibetan separatists hoped to reestablish a "feudal serf system," the Dalai Lama in 1992 promulgated new "Guidelines for Future Tibet's Polity and the Basic Features of its Constitution."[96] A free Tibet would have an elected democratic government composed of executive, legislative and judicial branches, in which the Dalai Lama would not accept any political status "on the basis of the traditional system."[97] Tibetans within Tibet were also aware of the need

---

94. Ibid., 44.

95. Ibid., 45. Robert Ford, who lived and worked in Tibet before 1950, put this issue into its proper context: "In the past some of our die-hard British imperialists, forgetful of the doctrine of eventual self-determination, argued their right to hang on because of hospitals, schools, roads, and other such benefits they had brought to the subject peoples. Communist imperialists, whose annexations are openly stated to be forever, make similar capital out of these services. Often non-Communist materialists fall for this line. . . Tibet was backward and feudal, but nobody starved. Most of the people were poor, but there was no hunger and much happiness. Material progress was overdue, but it was beginning to come . . . I am not a medievalist, and I think it is extremely important and beneficial that living standards should be raised. But not at that price. Nothing is worth the extinction of the greatest freedom of all, which is freedom of thought." Robert Ford, *Wind Between the Worlds* (Berkeley: Snow Lion Graphics, 1987), 337.

96. "Guidelines for Future Tibet's Polity and the Basic Features of its Constitution," *Tibet Press Watch*, February 1994, 18.

97. Ibid. The Dalai Lama's "Guidelines" reportedly had a great impact on Tibetan cadres within Tibet; the Chinese purged many Tibetan cadres or replaced them with Chinese and began a new crackdown on support for the Dalai Lama among Tibetan cadres. "Communists Announce Purge of Tibetan Officials Who Support the Dalai Lama," *Tibet Press Watch*, February 1993, 1.

for a democratic constitutional system of government, as was revealed by a manifesto prepared and distributed by a group of Drepung monks in 1988. Entitled "The Meaning of the Precious Democratic Constitution of Tibet," the Drepung manifesto reiterated the principles of the Constitution promulgated by the Dalai Lama in 1963, which would establish a democratic government "embodying both religious and secular principles" but would not restore the previous system of government in Tibet. For this "counterrevolutionary crime," the monks were sentenced to prison for up to 19 years.[98]

A conference in Beijing in March 1993, attended by Chinese and Tibetan representatives from the TAR and Tibetan autonomous districts of Sichuan, Qinghai, Gansu and Yunnan, attempted to combat Tibetan gains in international opinion with a campaign of propaganda exposing the "Dalai Clique's lies" and explaining the "real" situation in Tibet. The main theme of the conference was the "two rights" issues in regard to Tibet—sovereign rights and human rights: China should "declare righteously to the world that Tibet is an inseparable part of Chinese territory" and "use facts to present the human rights situation of Tibet and its progress and to demonstrate that the majority of Tibetan masses support the leadership of the Communist Party, support the socialist system and support the People's Government."[99]

The propaganda battle with the "Dalai Clique" and "international enemy forces" was characterized as one in which the CCP would not compromise, because truth and justice were on its side. The Dalai Lama was accused of using negotiations as a "smoke screen" to "deceive international public opinion" and to "gain some progress in their favor when the old generation of our revolutionaries is still alive." The CCP's position on negotiations remained that Tibet was an internal affair of China and the issue of the Dalai Lama was one "between the Central Government and an exiled religious leader, the purpose of which is to solve the problem of his repatriation and that of the people who follow him." The issue of Tibet, it was said, was "not the same as that of Taiwan. The future of Tibet is national regional autonomy and the realization of socialism."[100]

The conference speakers claimed that there were more and more peo-

---

98. "The Meaning of the Precious Democratic Constitution of Tibet," in *Defying the Dragon*, 115.

99. *China's Public Relations Strategy on Tibet: Classified Documents from the Beijing Propaganda Conference* (Washington: International Campaign for Tibet, 1993), 23.

100. Ibid., 34. The statement in regard to the "old generation of our revolutionaries" seems to imply that the old revolutionaries might be more conducive to making some concessions in Tibet, or to have more authority to do so, than the following generation.

ple in the world who knew the "real situation" in Tibet, which was one of "social stability, market prosperity, national unity, freedom of religion and belief, the development of culture and the full guarantee of the fundamental democratic rights of the people in Tibet" and of "peace and joy" in people's lives. The Dalai Lama's political offensive was said to look strong but to actually have weaknesses since it relied on "rumors and distortions that are void of any truth."[101] International opinion, it was said, had "turned in the direction favorable to us," but the Party propagandists had to admit that the "distorted propaganda and attacks" of the Dalai Clique and its supporters "still enjoy a large market in the world" and "continue to escalate," while "quite a lot of people have deep rooted misunderstanding about us."[102]

Among the CCP's Chinese and Tibetan propagandists there were apparently many true believers, including those who believed that China's sovereignty over Tibet could be proved by historical facts, that exposure of the truth about conditions in Tibet would prove the CCP's case, and that the human rights issue in Tibet was actually a strong point in China's favor. Many of the officials seemed to think that their Tibet White Paper, which, they said, had been rigorously researched and had gone through twelve or thirteen revisions, constituted "convincing proof" and had had a good impact abroad, hitting China's critics "at their fatal point" by revealing the truth and exposing lies.[103]

China's Solution to the Tibet Problem

While the CCP's propaganda offensive was designed for the tactical purpose of countering negative international publicity about Tibet, the economic development program initiated at the 1984 Tibet Work Conference had evolved into a strategy that seemed to hold the potential for permanently resolving the Tibet issue. Since 1984 the CCP had realized that the attempt to convince the Dalai Lama to return had created more difficulties than his return had the potential to resolve; in addition, given the experience with the visits of his representatives, there was considerable uncertainty about the wisdom of allowing his return at all. The decision to abandon negotiations with the Dalai Lama made Chinese policy less dependent upon the approval of Tibetans in exile or of those within Tibet and had allowed the CCP to pursue a policy of development combined with political repression and colonization without regard to Tibetan resistance.

---

101. Ibid., 40.
102. Ibid., 33.
103. Ibid., 18.

The policy of economic development and colonization under the guise of development offered both the political and social solution to the Tibet problem, although this was perhaps not fully realized in 1984 when this policy was decided upon. Economic development would either integrate Tibetans economically or marginalize them if they refused to participate. In addition, they would be demographically and politically marginalized by the transfer of large numbers of Chinese to Tibet. Tibetan resistance would be controlled by strict limits on cultural and religious autonomy and by refined methods of identification and repression of Tibetan nationalists. The Chinese could deny that they were practicing a policy of population transfer or colonization in Tibet because the Han sent to Tibet for development projects or those there independently all retained resident permits in their home provinces and were thus not "residents" of Tibet even though they spent the majority of the time there. The economic development policy for Tibet was even sufficiently politically benign to be presented as deserving of international assistance. However, international development projects in Tibet required the import of additional Chinese.[104]

The influx of Chinese after 1984 eventually contributed to Tibetan discontent and the demonstrations and riots of 1987-89. However, post-Tiananmen China was firmly in the hands of hardliners, and despite international condemnation and sanctions, the PRC proved immune to international criticism. The collapse of the Soviet Union and fears of a similar phenomenon in the PRC determined Chinese hardliners to firmly resist any moves for greater nationality autonomy. The PRC made a rapid economic recovery from Tiananmen and entered a period of the most rapid growth in modern Chinese history. China was therefore relatively immune from international economic sanctions and, in Tibet, able to continue its program of expensive economic subsidies and development. Post-1989 policy in Tibet was characterized by an emphasis upon "security and stability," manifested by an immense security force and immediate repression of any signs of "separatist" or "splittist" activities.

The CCP's new Tibet policy of disguised colonization received its ideological imprimatur from Deng Xiaoping in 1987 in an article entitled "Speeding up Tibet's Development on the Basis of Equality Among Various Nationalities." The origin of this "article" was actually a few

---

104. The Chinese Government managed to limit the number of foreign experts and Tibetans on international development projects in Tibet. The largest international assistance projects were devoted to agricultural development and appeared to be intended to support Chinese colonists. See Ann Forbes and Carole McGranahan, *Developing Tibet? A Survey of International Development Projects* (Cambridge: Cultural Survival, 1992).

remarks made to former President Jimmy Carter during his visit to China in 1987. In reply to a question in regard to China's policy of population transfer to Tibet, Deng said that it was "inappropriate to judge China's nationalities policies and the Tibet issue against the number of Han people in Tibet. . . . The key criteria should be what benefits will accrue to the people of Tibet and how Tibet should be made to develop rapidly and stand at the forefront of China's four modernizations." Deng's remarks, much like the cryptic utterances of emperors in the past, were purported to constitute a "guiding document" on the issue and "an important part of socialism with Chinese characteristics . . . an historical document that directly addresses Tibet's reality" and a "most potent ideological weapon," which "articulated our Party's views on nationalities during the new historical period, and creatively improved upon Marxism-Leninism-Mao Zedong Thought."[105]

The essence of Deng's "guiding document" was that the CCP would no longer restrict the number of Han in Tibet since they were necessary for Tibet to be developed. As the article elaborating Deng's doctrine explained, despite "earth-shaking changes," Tibet "remains in a state of backwardness. . . . The gap between Tibet and the developed regions is growing by the day. Other than the natural environment, this is largely the result of ideological and conceptual differences."[106] What the phrase "ideological and conceptual differences" implied was Tibetans' supposed reliance on economic subsidies and their reversion to religion and the traditional subsistence economy:

> Some people, in particular, will lose confidence in reform because they are poorly educated, cannot adapt to changes in society, are not competitive, and have chronically relied on the free supply system. These people will be unable to cope with the impact of full-scale reform, and because of their inadequate mental preparedness, they can hardly be expected to foster economic and competitive concepts under market economic conditions. All this reflects the differences among various nationalities.[107]

The solution for Tibetans' "inadequate mental preparedness" was declared to be assistance in economic development by the central government and the importation of large numbers of "skilled personnel":

Tibet cannot develop on its own. On the one hand, with the central gov-

---

105. "Tibet Article Urges `Correct' Nationalities Views," Lhasa, *Tibet Daily*, 4 July 1994, in FBIS-CHI-94-137, 18 July 1994, 77.

106. Ibid., 79.

107. Ibid., 78.

ernment's kind attention and economic support, it should carry out some infrastructure projects to create conditions for economic development. On the other hand, it should seek help from fraternal provinces and municipalities in terms of manpower and materials. In the area of manpower, we need to get large numbers of Han comrades into Tibet so that they can impart scientific and technological knowhow, share their scientific management expertise, and help Tibet train scientific, technological, and managerial personnel to speed up its economic development. While Tibet is being helped with its development, no one should unilaterally stress the need to "judge China's nationalities policies and the Tibet issue against the number of Han people in Tibet."[108]

The implication of the new policy was that the CCP would judge the success of its Tibet policy on whether Tibet was economically developed—without regard to who was doing the developing or who were the beneficiaries. Deng and the CCP in essence declared that the Party would no longer adhere to its policy that Tibet was to be an area of exclusive Tibetan "autonomous" rights of any kind. Tibetans would be allowed some cultural autonomy as a minority culture within Tibet as within China as a whole, so long as political issues were not involved, but Tibetans would not have any rights to demographic or cultural homogeneity within their own "autonomous" territory. The CCP was no longer committed to the preservation of Tibet as an area of exclusive Tibetan habitation; instead, Chinese "skilled personnel," not yet admittedly colonists, but colonists nonetheless, would share in the economic development of Tibet as in any other area of China.

The "potent ideological weapon" of Deng's doctrine was an ideological position that was little different from Mao's extremist leftist dictate that "the national question is in essence a class question." The article on "correct" nationalities views reiterated this formula:

All nationalities share identical fundamental interests, politically and economically, in their quest for joint development and common prosperity. Ethnic relations are basically relations between workers, which are socialist relations based on equality, unity, and mutual assistance. By nature, ethnic problems are basically contradictions among workers of all nationalities.[109]

In this formula, ethnic relations are "relations between workers," and

---

108. Ibid., 79.
109. Ibid., 77.

ethnic problems are "contradictions among workers of all nationalities," or, in other words, ethnic relations are class relations without regard to nationality. Mao's ideology on nationality relations had been repudiated by the Party in 1980.[110] The revival of this slogan in a slightly different form signaled a new leftist mentality in nationality relations and an abandonment of Hu Yaobang's reform policy in Tibet in favor of a hardline solution.

In December 1992 Chen Kuiyuan, a hardline leftist, was appointed CCP general secretary in the TAR. Chen immediately affirmed the policy of reliance upon direct Chinese rule in Tibet by purging Tibetans from positions of authority and bringing in Han cadres to take their place. Chen echoed Mao's 1956 dictum that minority nationalities should not be denied the benefits of socialist transformation based upon their presumed backwardness by indicating that Tibet's "special characteristics" would not be allowed to stand in the way of economic development or the opening of Tibet to an influx of Chinese.[111]

In July 1994 the CCP summoned its "Third National Work Forum on Tibet" in Beijing. Attending the conference were Chinese and Tibetan cadres and China's top leaders, including Jiang Zemin and Li Peng. Forum themes were "development and stability," as was evident in the title of the final document, "Decision to Accelerate Development and Maintain Stability in Tibet." Development itself was not discussed so much as the expected "cultural" implications of development, as was indicated in remarks by Jiang Zemin: "While paying attention to promoting Tibet's fine traditional culture, it is also necessary to absorb the fine cultures of other nationalities in order to integrate the fine tradition-

---

110. "Is the National Question Essentially A Class Question?" *Beijing Review*, 25 August 1980, 17. The conclusion of the 1980 article was, "In the ten years of turmoil [Cultural Revolution], Lin Biao and the gang of four made this statement the theoretical basis for pushing an ultra-Left line in areas inhabited by minority peoples and [to] exercise their feudal fascist dictatorship there." Ibid. This policy was actually typical of CCP nationalities policies in the past; the periods of leftist dominance when the national issue was equated with the class issue were essentially all of Chinese Communist history except the short period before 1956 and the reform period from 1980 to 1989.

111. *Cutting Off the Serpent's Head: Tightening Control in Tibet, 1994-1995* (New York: Tibet Information Network, Human Rights Watch/Asia, 1996), 20. As in 1956, minorities' "special characteristics" were regarded as backward; however, Mao had condemned the policy of excluding minorities from socialist development as "rightist," whereas Chen condemned the exclusion of Tibetans from capitalist development as "leftist." Deng's "guiding document" on Tibet policy had characterized Tibetan resistance to the economic development policy as isolationist and communalist, both sins of the "leftist" past. In either case, respect for Tibet's "special characteristics" was inconvenient to Chinese development plans.

al culture with the fruits of modern culture. This will facilitate the development of socialist new culture in Tibet."[112]

The Propaganda Committee of the TAR Communist Party summarized the decisions of the Third Tibet Work Forum in a document for internal distribution among CCP cadres entitled *A Golden Bridge Leading Into a New Era*. This document revealed that the CCP was no longer seriously interested in dialogue with the Dalai Lama or in his return, having characterized the competition with the "Dalai clique" as an "antagonistic contradiction with the enemy."

> The main reason why Tibet could not be made stable is the Dalai clique's splittist activities. The Dalai clique hopes to gain "Tibetan independence" by relying on the hostile forces of western countries, and those western hostile forces use the Dalai clique's demand for "Tibetan independence" to cause disturbances in the hope of splitting our country. To secure stability in Tibet is not only to obtain a peaceful situation in Tibet, but, far more important, is to secure the unity of the whole nation, to safeguard the integrity of our sovereignty, to oppose western hostile forces so that their hopes of "westernizing" China and splitting China disappear into thin air.
> . . .
>
> We must be able to reveal the true colors of the Dalai clique. Due to the traditional religion, Dalai has a certain prestige among monks, nuns, and devotees. But Dalai and the Dalai clique have defected and escaped to a foreign country, and have turned into a splittist political clique hoping to gain Tibet's independence and have become a tool of international hostile forces. The true nature of what Dalai is shouting about when he says "Tibetan independence," "a high standard of autonomy" and "greater Tibet" is to oppose communism, to deny socialism, to overthrow the dictatorship of the people, to split the motherland, to destroy the solidarity of nationalities, and to restore his own authority in Tibet. Although he sometimes says some nice words to deceive the masses, he has never ceased his splittist actions aimed at dividing our motherland. Up to now his standpoint on Tibetan independence has never changed and we must reveal his double-faced true color. The focal point of our region in the struggle against splittism is to oppose the Dalai clique. As the saying goes, to kill a serpent, one must first cut off its head. If we do not do that, we cannot succeed in the struggle against splittism.
>
> The struggle between ourselves and the Dalai clique is not a matter of religious belief nor a matter of the question of autonomy, it is a matter of securing the unity of our country and opposing splittism. It is a matter of antag-

---

112. "Third National Work Conference on Tibet 20-23 July," *NCNA*, Beijing, 26 July 1994, in FBIS-CHI-94-144, 27 July 1994, 19. The first Tibet work meeting was in 1980; the second was in 1984.

onistic contradiction with the enemy, and it represents the concentrated form of the class struggle in Tibet at the present time. This struggle is the continuing struggle between ourselves and the imperialists since they invaded Tibet a hundred years ago. We must safeguard the achievements of the democratic reform and of the Open Reform Policy. As long as the Dalai does not change his splittist standpoint, we have nothing else to do but to continue this struggle right up till the time we achieve victory.[113]

The Third Work Forum also set out an uncompromising line on restriction of religion and the political activities of monks and nuns:

Those monasteries which take sides with the splittists and which are always causing trouble in order to stir up disturbances should be reorganized within a certain time, and if necessary their doors can be closed in order to do so. Those monks and nuns who joined the splittists to cause disturbances and who could not be persuaded to change their attitudes should be punished severely according to the law. This wind of building monasteries and of recruiting new monks and nuns just as they wish should be stopped entirely. In future to build a new monastery, permission must be received from the Religious Affairs Bureau of the TAR. No monastery is allowed to build without its permission. Those monasteries where the numbers of monks have already been set still need to be limited as much as possible, and are not allowed to go beyond that limit. The excess monks should be expelled, and those monasteries which have not set a stipulated number of monks and nuns should set a number as soon as possible. . . .

We must teach and guide Tibetan Buddhism to reform itself. All those religious laws and rituals must be reformed in order to fit in with the needs of development and stability in Tibet, and they should be reformed so that they become appropriate to a society under socialism.[114]

The Third Work Forum document admitted that many Tibetan cadres "were hoodwinked by the propaganda of the Dalai clique about nationalism, and they see people and events from the viewpoint of nationalism. Some cadres act as secret enemy agents and have joined counterrevolutionary organizations. They collect confidential information for the Dalai clique and participate in splittist activities."[115] The document also complained that "counterrevolutionary activities" were spreading, including the distribution of Dalai Lama photos and cassette recordings of his speeches, counterrevolutionary publications smuggled into Tibet, the

---

113. *Cutting Off the Serpent's Head*, 155.
114. Ibid., 158, 165.
115. Ibid., 158.

shouting of counterrevolutionary slogans and singing of counterrevolutionary songs.[116] The recommended solution for these problems on the ideological front was, as usual, more propaganda "showing that Tibet is part of China," revealing the "true colors of the Dalai clique and the dark side of the serf system of old Tibet," and emphasizing the "social developments and achievements" in Tibet under Chinese rule.[117] Tibetan cadres were prohibited from sending their children to India for education in Tibetan exile schools, while those who had been educated in India were not to be employed in official positions, especially as teachers, and were to be carefully observed.[118] Tibetan cadres were not allowed to have religious shrines in their houses or photos of the Dalai Lama.[119]

The Tibet Work Forum ended with the announcement that 62 construction projects would be undertaken to commemorate the 30th anniversary of the TAR in September 1995. These projects were to be in the fields of energy, transportation, telecommunications, agriculture, animal husbandry, forestry, water conservancy, grain and cooking oil processing as well as "social development." Of the total cost of 2.38 billion *yuan* (approx. 270 million US dollars), 75 percent was to be contributed by the central government and 25 percent by various provinces and municipalities.[120] The majority of the projects, as in 1984-85, would be contracted to provincial firms that would import their own workers or hire Chinese already in Tibet.

The importation of Chinese into Tibet was justified as necessary for Tibet's economic development:

> We should intensify opening up to various provinces, municipalities, and regions; encourage and support economic entities and individuals in the hinterland to set up enterprises of all kinds in Tibet; earnestly expand economic cooperation and exchanges with the interior with preferential policies and abundant resources; and establish close organic ties between Tibet's and China's economies.. . . . We should take effective steps to maintain the current ranks of Han cadres and transfer Han and other minority cadres from the hinterland into Tibet. . . . We should introduce special allowances, increase cadres' salaries and fringe benefits, and help cadres

---

116. Ibid., 160.
117. Ibid., 163.
118. Ibid., 160.
119. Ibid., 159.
120. "Third National Work Conference on Tibet," 24. This is five times the amount, 470 million *yuan*, spent in 1984-85 on the 43 projects to commemorate the 20th anniversary of the TAR.

who come to Tibet solve such problems as housing and schooling and employment for their dependents.[121]

The focal point of the policy of opening the door wider in Tibet should be towards the inner part of the country. While depending on our region's own good aspects of policy and production resources, we should combine these with the good aspects of the inner part of the country, its intellectuals, technicians, management personnel, and communications. Mutual economical support and exchange in every field should be broadened. We should encourage traders, investment, economic units, and individuals to enter our region to run different sorts of enterprises. . . .

By learning from the experiences of the past we must practice good methods and take effective measures to obtain a contingent of cadres from different nationalities who will work in Tibet permanently. . . . We must continue the system of sending cadres to Tibet from inner parts of the country. . . . When assigning cadres from the inner parts to work in Tibet we should be farsighted and strive to have cadres living and working long-term in Tibet. We should enroll students by deciding that their future professional work [will be] in Tibet. Universities in the inner areas should enroll those students at their own expense. The TAR military command and the People's Armed Police should transfer their outstanding officers and soldiers to civilian work when their military service is over. In these ways we should strive to have a permanent contingent of cadres in Tibet. The Central Committee has divided the tasks and responsibilities among other provinces within set time limits to support Tibet with people from all walks of life as we have requested. This is a new strategy corresponding to a new era in which we need to sum up our past experiences and find ways to perfect our work.[122]

The Third Tibet Work Forum reaffirmed the policy of relying upon economic development and the importation of large numbers of Han Chinese as the solution to the Tibet problem. Tibet's "special characteristics," the code words for Tibetan autonomy, would no longer be respected even in theory. Autonomy could not be allowed because cultural and religious freedom inevitably led to demands for political freedom; Tibetan cadres' had succumbed to nationalist and splittist propaganda and could not be trusted. Han Chinese would not only be officially transferred to Tibet and given incentives to remain there, but Chinese civilians

---

121. "Tibet to Implement Work Forum Guidelines," Lhasa, *Tibet Daily*, 2 August 1994, in FBIS-CHI-94-159, 17 August 1994, 53.

122. *Cutting Off the Serpent's Head*, 154, 167. The meaning of this last statement was apparently that not only were Chinese cadres and PLA and PAP soldiers to be assigned to Tibet and Chinese civilians attracted with incentives, but each province was to be responsible for sending a certain number of people to Tibet "within set time limits."

would be encouraged, even required, to colonize Tibet. Although the CCP remained officially open to a return of the Dalai Lama "as long as he abandons the advocacy for Tibetan independence and ceases activities to split the motherland,"[123] the language of the Work Forum documents, especially the characterization of the struggle with the "Dalai clique" as an "antagonistic contradiction with the enemy," made it obvious that the CCP was opposed to dialogue with the Dalai Lama or a role for the Dalai Lama in Tibet's future.

Tibetan cadres approved the decisions of the Third Forum without dissent. The Tibet CPPCC added its approval for the Work Forum's emphasis on the inseparability of Tibet from China:

> Attendees particularly mentioned that the principle of two inseparable-nesses maintained by the recent Tibet work forum for solving the national-ity issue in Tibet is an absolute truth, namely the Han nationality is insepa-rable from minority nationalities and vice versa, which has been proven by practices in Tibet. All Attendees said they profoundly experienced the warmth of the big family of the motherland during the forum.[124]

Enthusiastic compliance with the Work Forum's decisions became a loyalty test for Tibetan cadres:

> Leaders of the central authorities have a very clear understanding of Tibet's special nationality and religious situations. The various principles, policies, and guidelines they formulated are completely in keeping with the actual conditions in Tibet. Anyone who is patriotic would be pleased with them without exception. It is only splittists and splittist cliques who are dis-pleased with them, because anyone who is truly patriotic would wish the Tibetan nationality success and prosperity and would support the forum guidelines.[125]

Raidi, secretary of the TAR Party Committee, blamed "splittists," for-eign and domestic, for spreading "reactionary" and "counterrevolution-ary" propaganda into all regions of the TAR and Tibetan areas in "Chinese" provinces, and for having caused Tibetan CCP cadres to waver in their political stand. Raidi blamed the ideological deficiencies of some cadres for "problems and inconsistencies in our work for combatting splittism and stabilizing the situation." Raidi proposed that the test of

---

123. "Third National Work Conference on Tibet," 20.
124. "Tibet CPPCC Forum," *Lhasa Radio*, 4 August 1994, in FBIS-CHI-94-151, 5 August 1994, 46.
125. Ibid.

Tibetan cadres' qualifications should be their stand on the anti-splittist struggle: "The attitude of leading cadres to the anti-splittist struggle is the fundamental political criterion for judging whether they are qualified or not." Raidi conceded that the anti-splittist struggle would go on for a long time but reiterated that it was in fact a class, not a national issue, which would be resolved only when that fact was fully comprehended. Raidi promised resolute efforts to fight against attempts to split the motherland and proclaimed "Tibet is under the rule of the Communist Party and will stay that way forever."[126]

The CCP's new willingness to admit that the cornerstone of Chinese policy in Tibet was colonization was evident in a subsequent article extolling a mixed Han/Tibetan family near Lhasa (husband Han, wife Tibetan). The couple were praised for their vegetable garden, which "prompts us to have a rethink of today's new nationality relations in Tibet: What is it that has strengthened the unity between the Tibetan and Han nationalities under new historical conditions? . . . Extensive economic exchanges and integration are the forces at work behind the strengthening of the relationship between the Han and Tibetan nationalities in Tibet."[127] These relations were part of the natural and inevitable union of nationalities, the article went on, a process which began with the first historical encounter of the two nationalities:

> The Han and Tibetan nationalities have gone through several upsurges of unity in history. Without exception, they were all preceded by extensive exchanges and integration. The marriage of Princess Wencheng of the Tang Dynasty to the Tibetan ruler more than 1,300 years ago raised the curtain of exchanges between the Han and Tibetan nationalities. Among the convoy of Princess Wencheng were a number of Han nationality carpenters. These Han carpenters disseminated their techniques on the snow-covered plateau. They got along swimmingly with the local inhabitants. . . as they exchanged experience with and learned from one another. This whipped up the first upsurge of unprecedented unity between the Han and Tibetan nationalities.

> Today we are witnessing on the plateau another wave of extensive exchanges between different nationalities. This wave is sweeping forward with greater momentum than the one during the days of Princess Wencheng.

> Taking advantage of its favorable geographical position, the "Sichuan

126. "Tibet's Raidi on Antisplittism, Stability," *Tibet Daily*, 24 May 1994, in FBIS-CHI-94-108, 6 June 1994, 79.
127. "Tibet Expanding Ties to Inland Provinces," in FBIS-CHI-95-210, 31 October 1995, 57.

army" had a head start and moved into Tibet in the early 1980s. On its heels came the "Shaanxi army," "Hunan army," "Zhejiang army," and migrant workers from Qinghai, Gansu, Guizhou, Shandong, Henan and other provinces. For these "inland legions," Tibet is a virgin land. . . . In Lhasa today, the food and beverage industry is the exclusive domain of the "Sichuan army," while the garment industry is divided between the "Sichuan army" and the "Wenzhou legion." The furniture and building construction industries are also dominated by self-employed entrepreneurs and migrant workers from the interior. Using the commodity economy as a bridge, a group of travelling inland traders have blended themselves into extensive economic exchanges on the plateau and into the life of the Tibetan people.

The arrival of the "inland legions" has also brought about quiet changes in the life of the Tibetan people. . . . Economic contacts and exchanges have broken down the boundaries between different nationalities and regions and enabled the people of Han, Tibetan and other nationalities to mix naturally in the commodity economy and to cultivate a deeper understanding and friendship. . . .

Only when national unity is established on the basis of common interests will it be a firm unity. . . the extensive economic exchanges and integration now on the surge on the Tibetan Plateau point to a new stage in the relations between the Han and Tibetan peoples in Tibet.[128]

An article in the *Chinese Journal of Population Science* acclaimed the new policy of colonization in Tibet for finally achieving what was admittedly a long-term goal: "In the past 30 years, the Central Government and the local government in Tibet, which designed the policy of mandatory migration, made a tremendous investment in and sent a large number of people to Tibet." However, migration in the past was not very successful because most of the migrants were officials who remained dependent upon central government financial support and many of whom had managed to rotate back to the interior. "The ineffectiveness of the migration [in the past] into Tibet is also related to the composition of migrants. Government officials and their families make up a large proportion of migrants, while there is only a small percentage of those who are able to make free choices [are voluntary migrants] and who are truly qualified in terms of education, occupations, and economic status." The study concluded:

Like other economically backward areas in the country, Tibet lacks the ability to develop by itself, and its economy largely relies on the financial sup-

---

128. Ibid., 58.

port of the Central Government. Tibet's economic dependence also is reflected in its need for migrants from elsewhere. . . . What Tibet needs are not a large number of administrative officials, but artists, teachers, medical workers, scientists, engineers, managers and accountants.[129]

At the end of 1994 the Chinese Government announced that it intended to revive its long-delayed plan to complete a railroad link via Golmud to Lhasa. This project, first announced in the early 1960s and postponed indefinitely thereafter due to difficulties encountered with permanently frozen soil (permafrost) over large sections of the route, was finally to be completed within 5 years at a huge cost of 20 billion yuan (2.36 billion US dollars).[130] This amount compares with a total of 20 billion yuan that the CCP claims to have spent in financial allocations and investments in capital construction projects "in the 43 years since Tibet's peaceful liberation."[131] The completion of a rail line to Tibet would finally overcome Tibet's territorial separation from China and Chinese logistical difficulties in supporting large numbers of Chinese colonists in Tibet. In addition, the Chinese Government announced that the 2.38 billion yuan earmarked for 62 construction projects scheduled for completion in 1995 was only a portion of a total of 10 billion yuan expected to be provided for development in Tibet before the year 2000.[132] The railroad project was put on hold in 1995 due to funding problems, but all of these plans when implemented were certain to accelerate the flood of Chinese officials, workers and petty entrepreneurs to Tibet.[133]

---

129. "An Analysis of the Migration of the Tibetan Population in 1986 and 1987," *Chinese Journal of Population Science*, Vol. 2, No. 1, 1990, 38.

130. "China Announces Construction of Railway to Tibet," *Tibet Press Watch*, October-November 1994, 1.

131. "Tibet Article Urges `Correct' Nationalities Views," in FBIS-CHI-94-137, 18 July 1994, 77.

132. "Construction Boom to Precede 30th Anniversary of the TAR," *Tibet Press Watch*, October-November 1994, 13.

133. A delay in the railroad project was indicated in a speech by Chen Kuiyan in August 1995. Chen revealed that funding had not yet been secured from the central government for the project: "Building railways leading into Tibet is a measure for lifting Tibet out of seclusion once and for all, and it has inestimable significance for Tibet's economic development and social progress. When permitted by its financial resources, the state will surely make a policy decision on building railways leading into Tibet. We should go around touting this cause to ensure that it will be realized at an early date. Moreover, we should do our utmost to expedite the process of feasibility studies and prospecting in connection with the construction of railways leading into Tibet and strive to launch relevant projects at an early date." "Chen Kuiyan Report," in FBIS-CHI-95-168, 30 August 1995, 55. Funding delays were possibly related to difficulties the Chinese had encountered with foreign funding for the controversial Three Gorges Dam project.

Denigration of the Dalai Lama

The new CCP Tibet policy made it evident that the Chinese Government no longer had any intention of negotiating with the Dalai Lama. After the 1994 Tibet Work Forum the Dalai Lama was criticized in the harshest terms and his denunciation was made part of the loyalty test for Tibetan cadres. The contest with the Dalai Lama required that autonomy and religious freedom be restricted because both had led to a rise in Tibetan nationalism and an increase of the Dalai Lama's influence. This was the meaning of the often-repeated formula that the issue with the Dalai Lama was not about autonomy or religion but about the forbidden issue of Tibetan independence.

In a speech in July 1995 Gyaincain Norbu (Gyaltsen Norbu), chairman of the TAR, blamed the "stability" problems in Tibet on external forces headed by the Dalai Lama: "The separatist activities carried out by the Dalai clique are the primary factor affecting Tibet's stability. The struggle between us and the Dalai clique is not over the question of religion or autonomy. Rather it is a matter of safeguarding the motherland's unification and opposing its division: it is in the nature of a struggle between ourselves and the enemy."[134] Tibetan exiles' proposals for what the Chinese labelled as "high-level autonomy" and "self-government of the greater Tibetan region" were condemned as "in essence, aimed at realizing 'Tibetan independence' and splitting the motherland." The PRC's system of national regional autonomy was praised for offering the essential advantage of unity, nationality solidarity and mutual assistance and the "inseparableness" principle that "we cannot live without each other."[135]

The CCP was adamantly opposed to any tinkering with the instruments of its own making that had defined Tibet's autonomous status within China: the 17-Point Agreement, which had apparently so easily attained the perennial Chinese goal of incorporating Tibet within China, or the system of national regional autonomy, a system of nationality relations, as Zhou Enlai said, "never before seen in history," which had theoretically resolved the nationalities question. The system of national regional autonomy could not be altered in Tibet's case without conceding that Tibet was not an integral part of China, past or present:

The type of national regional autonomy found in China is one that suits a

---

134. "Tibet Chairman Presents Government Work Report," *Tibet Daily*, 8 June 1995, in FBIS-CHI-95-140, 74.

135. "Nationality Autonomy Key to Tibet's Success," in FBIS-CHI-95-205, 24 October 1995, 88.

unified, multinational country. Any place where nationality regional autonomy is practiced is an inseparable part of the People's Republic of China. It
is neither "independent autonomy" divorced from the big family of the
motherland, nor is it any kind of political autonomy of a semi-independent
"autonomous state."

The Dalai clique in exile abroad has concocted so-called new recommendations, such as "high-degree autonomy" and "autonomy of the greater
Tibetan region," with the backing of the hostile Western forces. Their real
intention is to separate Tibet from the motherland. The issue between the
CCP and the Dalai clique over the Tibet issue is not about autonomy but
about safeguarding the unity of the motherland and opposing separation.
It concerns the fundamental interests of the state and nation. . . .

It would not work if Tibet went independent, or semi-independent, or independent in disguised form. There is no room for bargaining over the fundamental issue of safeguarding the unity of the motherland.[136]

The fate of Tibet, it was said, was inseparably linked with China:

The 30-year history of the Tibet Autonomous Region is a history of sharing
a common fate with the motherland and achieving common development
in the big family of the motherland. Every bit of progress made in Tibet's
social and economic development was inseparably and vitally linked with
the kind concern of the party Central Committee and the energetic support
rendered by the people of all nationalities. History has demonstrated that
Tibet will only have a bright future if it follows the socialist road under the
leadership of the CCP and that the Tibetan people will only be able to
develop and prosper, enjoy a happy life, and have a beautiful future by
maintaining close unity with other fraternal nationalities in the big family
of the Chinese nation.[137]

The Chinese Government further demonstrated its animosity toward
the Dalai Lama in late 1995 in the affair of the reincarnation of the
Panchen Lama. The 10th Panchen Lama had died in January 1989.
Normally, his reincarnation should have been found in three years, but
the political implications involved delayed the process until 1995. Tibetan
reincarnation politics were traditionally the means by which China had
exerted its pretensions to authority over Tibet. In 1793 the Qing instituted the system of choosing lots from a golden urn to select high incarnations as a means to establish Qing authority over Tibetan religious
and political succession. Since the right to approve reincarnations was

---

136. Ibid., 89.
137. "Tibet Development Said to Depend on Socialism," in FBIS-CHI-95-200, 17 October
1995, 48.

one of the primary aspects of China's claim to political authority over Tibet in the past, it remained so even for the atheistic Chinese Communists. The Chinese Government claimed the authority to recognize the reincarnation of the Panchen Lama "according to the Chinese constitution," a document not known to have anything to say about reincarnation.

A possible precedent was set for the succession of important religious leaders under the Communist regime by the selection of the Karmapa Lama in 1992. The Karmapa's reincarnation was discovered by exiled members of his sect from their headquarters in Gantok, Sikkim, by traditional Tibetan methods. The head of the sect in the absence of the Karmapa, Tai Situ Rimpoche, managed to secure both the Chinese Government's and the Dalai Lama's recognition for his choice, a child born within Tibet near Chamdo. The child was installed at the sect's traditional headquarters at Tsurpu, to the northwest of Lhasa. This procedure was apparently satisfactory for the Chinese, who quickly had the young Karmapa repeating slogans about the "unity of the motherland." The Tai Situ came off somewhat worse for the bargain; the Chinese reneged on their promise to allow the child to go to Sikkim for his religious education.

The precedent of the Karmapa's selection could have been followed in the case of the Panchen to the benefit of both sides in Tibetan reincarnation politics, but was not. The Tashilhunpo selection committee was allowed to search for the incarnation by the traditional Tibetan methods, provided they found the incarnation within the PRC. They did so, discovering a child from Nagchukha, but they secretly conveyed the news to the Dalai Lama and requested his approval. The Dalai Lama announced his recognition of the Panchen's reincarnation in April 1995, setting off furious denunciations from the Chinese, who claimed that the Dalai Lama was violating historical precedent by recognizing the incarnation when that right lay exclusively with the Chinese Government.

In a July 1995 speech to the Tibet Party Congress, Chen Kuiyan criticized the Dalai Lama as "not only reactionary politically, but also a religious renegade who degenerated into betraying Buddhism," and called upon Tibetans to "mercilessly expose and denounce the Dalai Lama's conspiracy and criminal acts."

> Our struggle with the Dalai clique is a full manifestation of the class struggle in Tibet at the present stage, an extension of the struggle between splittism and antisplittism which has long existed in Tibet since the imperialists' invasion of Tibet, and a life-and-death class struggle between the vast number of the masses and the restorationist force of the feudal serf owners. The true nature of our struggle with the Dalai clique is not an issue of whether

one is religious or not religious, of whether there is autonomy or no auton-omy, but an issue that is related to maintaining the motherland's unity and to opposing splittism. As this issue has to do with the Chinese nation's fun-damental interests, there is no room for compromise. . . .

Publicly exposing and denouncing the Dalai Lama is the most natural and just act. All levels of party committees should have the courage and insight of leading the vast number of the party members and the masses to merci-lessly expose and denounce the Dalai Lama's conspiracy and criminal acts and help lay a solid and lasting foundation for Tibet's stability. . . .

Only those who are able to make a clean break with the Dalai clique, take a clear-cut stand on safeguarding the unification of the motherland, and enthusiastically devote themselves to Tibet's development can become true patriotic personages. The employment of patriotic personages of various nationalities and in various circles should be arranged on the basis of the standards of their attitude toward socialism and the safeguarding of the unification of the motherland as well as their contributions to both. . . .
Following the establishment of the socialist market economic system, the Tibetans, Hans and other nationalities are helping and depending on one another, and progressing together. The inseparable relations among them will definitely be strengthened with each passing day. This is an objective need and natural trend. Cadres at all levels must solidly establish the thought that the Han nationality is inseparable from the minority national-ities and vice versa; consolidate the Marxist national viewpoint; and con-scientiously resist the influence of parochial nationalism.[138]

Chen went on to warn against "serious ideological degeneration" of Tibetan cadres who had been found "frequently associating themselves with religious activities." The "disorderly temple construction and recruitment of lamas" should be combatted by democratic management committees and the recruitment of patriotic monks. Tibetan cadres should enthusiastically welcome "incoming Han cadres" since "people from all corners of the land are brothers" and "cadres of any nationality . . . are all cadres of the party." Chen revealed that "the Dalai clique's splittist activities have been spreading in the agricultural and pastoral areas," and promised to "crack down on splittist activities in accordance with the law by bringing into full play the role of organs of dictatorship to maintain social stability."[139] Chen's speech revealed much about the battle against splittism in Tibet, most significantly that the Chinese had substantially lost that battle on the ideological front.

---

138. "Tibet Holds Fifth Regional CPC Party Congress," in FBIS-CHI-95-168, 30 August 1995, 56.
139. Ibid.

Nevertheless, the Dalai Lama's choice for the Panchen's reincarnation was not immediately rejected; the Chinese simply maintained that the choice was theirs to make. For some time, until November 1995, it seemed that an amicable solution could have been worked out, as indeed it could had the Chinese not decided upon confrontation. The Chinese had been embarrassed by the Dalai Lama's preemptive recognition, but this did not necessarily mean that they had to reject his choice. They could easily have ignored his selection as inconclusive while proclaiming their choice of the same child as authoritative and official. In this way, they could have had another pliant tool in their hands, one recognized by the Tibetan people. Nevertheless, they decided to reject the Dalai Lama's and the Tashilhunpo authorities' choice, a child already widely accepted by Tibetans as the legitimate reincarnation, in favor of a child of their own choice whose acceptance would have to be forced upon the Tibetan people. The Chinese choice for Panchen Lama was installed in a ceremony in Lhasa (in secret, in the middle of the night) after a drawing of lots, while the Dalai Lama's choice and his family were retained under arrest in Beijing.

It was apparently not the Dalai Lama's involvement in the process that was so objectionable, the Chinese seemingly were prepared to allow the Dalai Lama a role in order to legitimate the candidate, but his failure to submit to the process of requesting Chinese approval, a failure tantamount to challenging the Chinese Government's final authority in the matter and, therefore, the legitimacy of Chinese authority over Tibet. China's claim to sovereignty over Tibet rested upon its authority to appoint officials, or, in the Tibetan context, to recognize incarnations; therefore the Chinese Government could accept no challenge to that authority. As *Lhasa Radio* admitted, the issue was more political than religious:

> Since the beginning of modern times, the search and identification of reincarnated children for Dalais and Panchens have had close connection with the overall interests of the unification of the motherland and national unity.[140]

> The search for and confirmation of the reincarnated child of the Panchen have never been purely matters of religion and religious rituals; politically, it is a question of subordination to the central government and the safeguarding of its authority."[141]

---

140. "Questions and Answers Regarding the Reincarnated Child of the 10th Panchen," *Lhasa Radio*, 3 November 1995, in FBIS-CHI-95-223, 40.

141. *Lhasa Radio*, 5 November 1995, in FBIS-CHI-95-223, 43.

The Dalai Lama's unilateral action in recognizing the Panchen Lama's reincarnation was condemned as "going against Buddhist doctrine," "infringing upon state sovereignty," and "splitting the motherland through religious means." He was condemned for ignoring historical conventions and religious rites, a reference to the "drawing of lots from the golden urn," a procedure that the Chinese claimed was equivalent to "religious commandments."[142] The Dalai Lama's role in the process was condemned as "no longer a religious issue, but a political plot of the splittists," a characterization indicating that the Chinese Government would no longer cooperate with the Dalai Lama in any way in the selection of reincarnations.[143]

In the wake of the Panchen Lama affair, the Chinese instituted a campaign to eradicate the Dalai Lama's influence in Tibetan religion as well as politics. Tibetan cadres' and religious figures' loyalty was retested by requiring them to denounce the Dalai Lama's interference in the Panchen Lama's recognition, to accept the Chinese choice for Panchen Lama and to reject the Dalai Lama's choice. All members of the Tibet branch of the CPPCC were required to give written and verbal statements condemning the Dalai Lama. The Chinese also attempted to make patriotism to China a requirement for the "freedom" to practice religion: "A qualified believer should, first of all be a patriot. Any legitimate religion invariably makes patriotism the primary requirement for believers."[144] In May 1996 the Chinese reversed their policy of allowing ordinary Tibetans to keep photos of the Dalai Lama; in Lhasa, all images of the Dalai Lama were prohibited and house searches were conducted to confiscate his photos.

China signaled not only a confrontational attitude in Tibet policy but an isolationist and confrontational attitude in international relations by attributing the Dalai Lama's actions in the Panchen Lama affair to foreign imperialist influences. The activities of the "Dalai clique" were identified with the Western challenge to the CCP's legitimacy and China's cultural and political conflicts—past, present and future—with the West:

> This act of the Dalai is supported and instigated by anti-Chinese forces in the West. Having lived in exile for 36 years, the Dalai clique's splittist activities are the continuation of those forces in history. . . . Along with the changes in the overall international climate in the mid- and late 1980s, the Dalai clique's splittist activities are becoming increasingly acute. The Dalai

---

142. "Dalai Lama's Choice for Panchen Lama Rejected," *Xinhua*, 12 November 1995, in FBIS-CHI-95-220, 15 November 1995, 32.

143. "Religious Forum Condemns Dalai for Interference," *Xinhua*, 16 November 1995, in FBIS-CHI-95-222, 17 November 1995, 21.

144. "Why China Picked Its Own Panchen Lama," *Tibetan Review*, January 1996, 5.

intensified his activities and was busy running about, lobbying with a view to internationalizing the Tibet problem. The West, in turn, schemed and plotted for and bought the Dalai clique with cash in an attempt to use the Tibet problem as a breakthrough point for containing, weakening, disturbing, and splitting China. Therefore, on the issue of the Panchen's child reincarnation, our struggle against the Dalai clique is not only an important link in such a struggle, but also an important field in our struggle against hostile forces in the West. This struggle is unavoidable; it will take place sooner or later.[145]

China's disregard for the political capital they might have gained by manipulation of a popularly accepted Panchen Lama demonstrates that the Chinese Government was intent upon confrontation with the Dalai Lama at any cost. The Tibet issue was now identified not only with the legitimacy of the Chinese conquest of Tibet, but with the legitimacy of the Chinese Communist revolution, the current Chinese Government, and the issue of China's role in the world and its cultural and political competition with the West. China's sensitivity on the Tibet issue was revealed by the campaign the PRC began in 1996 to elicit statements from foreign states—a kind of international loyalty test—recognizing that Taiwan and Tibet were both "internal affairs of the People's Republic of China."[146]

---

145. "How Did the Dalai Clique Sabotage the Work for the 10th Panchen's Reincarnation?" *Lhasa Radio*, 3 November 1995, in FBIS-CHI-95-223, 20 November 1995, 41. The "changes in the international climate" refer to the collapse of the Soviet Union, the demise of international Communism and the Tiananmin massacre of 1989. Chinese allegations of foreign imperialism's current attempt to achieve a "breakthrough" into China via Tibet echo similar accusations during the first half of the century, when the British were accused of attempting to enter China through China's "back door" in Tibet. The last sentence in this statement seems to reflect similar concerns in the West about inevitable cultural and political conflicts with China. See Samuel P. Huntington, "The Clash of Civilizations?" *Foreign Affairs*, 1993. Huntington's article and thesis provoked much comment in the Chinese press. A Chinese spokesman rejected the thesis of civilizational or cultural conflict since Marxism had determined that economic factors were the driving force of history. The Chinese saw the thesis as an attempt to rally the West to preserve its economic interests against the rise of China's economic power. "Huntington's `Clash of Civilizations' Rebutted," 15 April 1995, FBIS-CHI-95-185.

146. The first foreign leader to make such a statement was Boris Yeltsin who, in a visit to Beijing in April 1996, recognized that Taiwan and Tibet were "inseparable" and "inalienable" parts of China, in exchange for the PRC's recognition that Chechnya was an internal affair of Russia. "China, Russia Swap Support, Sign Array of Agreements," *Washington Post*, 26 April 1996.

Conclusions

The PRC initiated the dialogue with the Dalai Lama in 1979 for the purpose of securing his return to China, a return which, it was thought, would achieve the final legitimation of Chinese rule in Tibet. Deng's precondition that the Dalai Lama should "give up the idea of independence" was interpreted by Tibetans in exile to mean that they had to accept the present reality of Chinese control over Tibet. This they did in negotiations in the Strasbourg Proposal of 1988, in which they indicated that Tibet would accept some form of autonomy similar to the "one country, two systems" formula being offered by the PRC to Taiwan. The Tibetan Government in Exile interpreted the PRC's frequent statements that "anything could be discussed but independence" to mean that anything but total independence could be discussed. The Tibetans thought that the Strasbourg statement fulfilled Deng's preconditions for negotiations since the Dalai Lama had stated that Tibet would accept some status short of full independence. To the Chinese, however, "giving up the idea of independence" meant nothing short of Tibetan acceptance of full Chinese sovereignty, past, present and future. The Dalai Lama was required to admit that Tibet was an "inalienable part of China," that Tibet was not only not now independent, but had never been independent, at least since Tibet had become an "integral part of China's territory" in the 13th century. The Dalai Lama's agreement to this version of reality was necessary in order to legitimize China's 1950 invasion and to forever eliminate the possibility of Tibetan independence.

The PRC found itself in the position of being unable to exercise any flexibility on the Tibet issue since its most sensitive legitimating ideologies were in question. China was somewhat the victim of its own crime; it could not open a dialogue on Tibet without exposing the illegitimacy of its conquest in 1950 or the facts of its subsequent misrule. Any reopening of the Tibet issue inevitably involved the legitimacy of Chinese sovereignty over Tibet and the CCP's anti-imperialist ideology. The Tibet issue was, in an ethnic sense, even more sensitive than Hong Kong or Taiwan since in neither of those cases was there an issue of Chinese imperialism against a non-Chinese people. China was unwilling and unable to compromise on the Tibet issue and therefore reacted to Tibetan dissent and international criticism with ever more extreme nationalist chauvinism and ideological rigidity. The Tibetan and international challenge to China's sovereignty in Tibet was employed by the hardline leftist faction in Chinese politics to further arouse Chinese nationalism, which, after the *de facto* abandonment of socialism, the CCP had become increasingly reliant upon for political legitimation.

The Chinese Government in 1995 was little disposed to compromise on Tibet since the solution to that problem seemed finally within its grasp. While the Chinese purported to be ready at any time to allow the Dalai Lama to return, his return would have to be unconditional. In fact, it was apparent that the Chinese no longer wanted the Dalai Lama to return at all, having initiated a solution not dependent upon his influence and having, with the Panchen Lama's reincarnation, set the pattern for choosing their own Fifteenth Dalai Lama upon the demise of the Fourteenth. After the Panchen Lama affair, the Chinese attempted to eradicate not only the Dalai Lama's political influence but his religious influence as well.

The brief experiment with limited autonomy in the early 1980s had convinced the CCP that any autonomy, cultural or political, would allow a revival of Tibetan nationalism and Tibetan demands for ever greater autonomy up to and including independence. The visits of Tibetan Government in Exile delegations had revealed that Tibetans still harbored "local nationalist" sentiments and had not transferred their loyalty to the Chinese state; the delegation visits raised the uncomfortable prospects of even greater disruptions and demonstrations of Tibetan rejection of Chinese rule should the Dalai Lama return. Despite Chinese prohibitions, the Tibet issue had been "internationalized"; the exiled Tibetans had not confined discussions to the personal status of the Dalai Lama and had also sought international support. By 1984 Hu Yaobang's liberalization policy in Tibet was under attack for allowing a revival of Tibetan nationalism and issues of Tibet's status thought forever resolved in 1951.

At the 1984 Tibet Work Meeting, a new development strategy was adopted that was dependent upon the influx of large numbers of Chinese. This strategy, combined with limits on cultural autonomy and increased emphasis upon "security and stability" after the riots of 1987-89, seemed to have the potential to finally resolve the Tibet issue by means of a program of colonization under the guise of development. This strategy was accompanied by continuing efforts in education and ideological indoctrination to win over Tibetans, but was not dependent on doing so since Tibetans' opinions became increasingly less important as their demographic majority within Tibet was gradually reduced.[147]

---

147. See Melvyn Goldstein, "Tibet, China, and the United States: Reflections on the Tibet Question," Atlantic Council Occasional Paper, April 1995.

Deng's statement in 1987 that China would "cease to judge the success of Tibet policy by the numbers of Han in Tibet" authorized the colonization policy. The revival of the equivalent of Mao's leftist chauvinist slogan equating nationalism and class justified the abrogation of nationality autonomy and the repression of all aspects of "local nationalism." The economic development and colonization strategy was reconfirmed by the 1994 Third Tibet Work Forum, after which the colonization policy was more openly admitted.

The CCP's ultimate reliance upon a policy of colonization represents both traditional Chinese frontier policy and an admission that the CCP's promise of national minority autonomy was nothing more than a means to achieve the final goal of assimilation. Colonization and assimilationism represents the only unchangeable aspect of the PRC's nationality policy or its policy in Tibet. Mao's intention expressed in 1952 to increase Tibet's population to 10 million represented Mao's faith in the ability of the CCP's nationalities policies to eliminate animosities between nationalities and his belief that colonization would be acceptable to Tibetans because the "new Chinese" were not like the chauvinistic and exploitative Chinese of the past. Mao and other CCP leaders repeatedly justified the union of China and Tibet by pointing out that Tibet had territory and a wealth of resources while China had population capable of filling Tibet's "virgin" territory and exploiting its resources, a bargain the Chinese thought obviously beneficial to both sides.

Traditional Chinese frontier policies, including the assumptions of CCP leaders, and CCP policy on allowing nationality autonomy were obviously contradictory, a fact that led to constant conflicts within the CCP about respect for nationalities' "special characteristics." This contradiction was most apparent in Chinese statements to Tibetans in the early 1950s that they had come to help Tibetans and would leave when Tibet was developed, while at the same time Mao was dreaming of flooding Tibet with Chinese colonists. CCP nationality policy assumed that nationalities' "special characteristics" would gradually disappear along with nationalities' desires or needs for autonomy. "Autonomy" for nationalities was merely a means to reach the ultimate goal of assimilation, not an end in itself. Permanent autonomy was contradictory to all the cultural assumptions of Chinese civilization and all the political assumptions of the Chinese Communists.

The CCP rarely allowed minority nationality autonomy in practice since it more often led to "local nationalism" rather than to a "natural and inevitable merging of nationalities." In Tibet, the CCP allowed a measure of autonomy only in the early 1950s before Chinese control was fully established and after 1979 when the issue of Tibetan nationalism was thought to be forever resolved. The revival of Tibetan nationalism in the 1980s finally convinced the CCP that Tibetan autonomy could not be allowed and that the traditional assimilationist solution would have to be implemented, a solution finally possible because of improvements in China's logistical position in Tibet and in the Chinese economy due to the "reform and opening up" policy.

In the end, the solution to the Tibet question by means of colonization was implemented, not with the cooperation of Tibetans as Mao had anticipated, but against their resistance and as a means of repressing Tibetan resistance. Mao and the Chinese Communists may have overestimated the efficacy of their nationalities doctrines and, like the Chinese nationalists before them, the desire of frontier peoples to partake of the benefits of Chinese civilization; nevertheless, the ultimate solution to the question was always available in the form of the huge preponderance of demographic force at their disposal. Some of the more "liberal" Chinese like Zhou Enlai and Hu Yaobang may have preferred a slower and more voluntary process of assimilation, but all Chinese assumed that assimilation was the final goal.

Hu Yaobang's failed experiment in allowing a modicum of Tibetan cultural autonomy convinced the CCP that autonomy could not be allowed because Tibetans had not accepted Chinese rule and would use any freedom they were allowed to agitate for more, not only within Tibet but internationally. After 1984 the CCP abandoned Hu's promise to reduce and restrict the number of Han in Tibet and essentially abandoned its attempts to secure the return of the Dalai Lama. Autonomy as a goal was abandoned in favor of development, which seemingly coincidentally required the import of Chinese into Tibet. However, the Chinese Government's incentives, exhortations and mandatory requirements to move Chinese to Tibet reveal that the movement of Chinese to Tibet was not merely an incidental aspect of development but an intentional policy of colonization.[148] The "reform and opening up" policy as applied to Tibet implied economic development without political reform and an opening of Tibet to a flood of Chinese. The demographic shift in Tibet, combined with "merciless repression" for "splittist" actions or sentiments, provided the means for repression of Tibetan discontent and anti-Chinese nationalism.

Tibetan optimism accompanying economic and cultural liberalization policies after 1980 had turned to disappointment, resentment and desperation by the end of the Deng era. Tibetans had gained significant inter-

---

148. See *New Majority: Chinese Population Transfer into Tibet* (London: Tibet Support Group UK, 1995).

national sympathy and support but found that it did not translate into political influence capable of affecting Chinese policy in Tibet; Chinese hardliners had used the excuse of foreign interference in Tibet to argue for more repressive measures. Within Tibet, cultural autonomy and religious freedom were highly restricted because of the inextricable connection between culture, religion and politics in Tibet. Tibetans' economic situation had generally improved, but, by the mid-1980s, Tibetans began to see most economic benefits being monopolized by Chinese cadres and by Chinese petty traders and entrepreneurs attracted to Tibet by the economic opportunities created by government subsidies, development projects and tourism.

Tibetans' resentment against past and present repression, resistance to participation in all that the Chinese regarded as development and progress, and their reversion to traditional culture, including the devotion of resources to the restoration of religion, served to marginalize them from economic development. The "development" which China had brought to Tibet included a brutalization of society endemic to Chinese communist culture and society and Chinese colonial rule over Tibet, continuing political and cultural repression, mendacity and sycophancy as a way of life, despair, alcoholism, and the worst of Chinese material culture. The elimination of Tibetan educated and entrepreneurial classes in the past continued to affect Tibetans' ability to compete with newly arrived Chinese. The success of Chinese entrepreneurs in Tibet, compared to the marginalization of many Tibetans, fostered and perpetuated an attitude among many Chinese that hard-working Chinese immigrants were more justified in inheriting Tibet than were the lazy and resentful Tibetans.

Tibetans tended to hope that the hardline course of Chinese policies in Tibet was a temporary phenomenon with its origins in the Chinese succession crisis, rather than a long-term strategy. However, Deng's imprimatur on the colonization policy would tend to argue against that conclusion. Nevertheless, having few options, Tibetans continued their strategy of cultivating international support while awaiting some dramatic political shift in China, perhaps a fall of communism with a breakup of the Chinese empire, or a dramatic change in Chinese leadership or political system after the demise of Deng Xiaoping. This strategy seemed fraught with peril, however, since time and the correlation of political and economic forces, especially demographic forces, appeared to be on the side of the Chinese.

16

Tibetan Self-Determination

Tibet is an ancient nation, but one whose national political consciousness is still in the process of formation. Cultural factors, especially cultural ecology, language and religion, have been of extraordinary importance in the creation and preservation of Tibetan ethnic and national
identity. The particular cultural ecology of the Tibetan plateau was the
defining material characteristic distinguishing Tibetans from their neighbors. A Tibetan political identity corresponding to the boundaries of the
plateau was created during the empire period. Although much of this
political centralization was lost upon the dissolution of the empire after
842, the precedent of a unified Tibetan polity formed the basis for later
Tibetan national identity.

Modern Tibetan nationalism is founded upon a distinct national identity and history, but, like many modern nationalisms, achieved its political manifestation only because of foreign imperialist influences. Tibetan
national consciousness was stimulated by China's threat to transform its
previously vague political domination over Tibet into full sovereignty
and by British support for Tibetan autonomy. Tibet's attempts to achieve
the goals of modern nationalism were hampered by the legacy of ecclesiastical rule and the conservative influence of the Buddhist church.
Ecclesiastical influence was ideologically anti-nationalistic due to the universalist nature of Buddhist doctrine and politically anti-nationalist
because of the church's inherent dependence upon foreign political
patronage. As Samten Karmay has written:

> With the advent of Buddhism and particularly from the eleventh century
> onwards, the national consciousness of the Tibetan people suffered greatly.
> . . . Nationalism requires will, self-assertion, self-identification and self-
> determination and these notions have no place and receive no respect in
> Buddhist education as we know it. . . . If patriotism is the core of nation-
> alism and if it were ever felt it is only expressed in terms of protecting
> Buddhist doctrine and its institutions and not the country as a nation or a
> state.[1]

1. Samten G. Karmay, "The Question of National Identity in Tibet," Paper presented at

Regionalism and indirect political authority within Tibet also hampered the Thirteenth Dalai Lama's attempt to create an independent Tibetan state. Tibet managed to preserve its *de facto* independence from 1912 to 1950 but failed to achieve international recognition. The Chinese skillfully maintained the fiction of their control over Tibet to the outside world during this period through their monopoly on information, negating the Tibetans' achievement of *de facto* independence as far as international recognition of that independence was concerned.

The Chinese invasion and occupation of Tibet since 1950 has seen an increase in Tibetan nationalist consciousness despite the fact that China has devoted intensive efforts at its suppression, including the elimination of most of the upper and educated classes. The CCP's assault on Tibetan civilization has been less effective in creating "class consciousness" and "love of the motherland" than in creating anti-Chinese nationalism and a desperate need among Tibetans for cultural and national survival. Tibetan nationalism has increased in response to the loss of national independence even as Tibet has become more economically and politically integrated with China. Economic liberalization in Tibet after 1980 produced not an alleviation of nationalist animosities as expected, but a cultural and national revival. The existence of a Tibetan exile community beyond the reach of Chinese control has also undoubtedly contributed to the maintenance and growth of Tibetan nationalism.

The contemporary issue of Tibet is not the nature of Tibet's past relationship with China nor the supposed inequalities of Tibet's traditional social and political system. Tibet came under the domination of Mongol Yuan (1260-1368) and Manchu Qing (1644-1911) dynasties of China, but, as the Dalai Lama said, Tibet did not thereby lose its national identity. Tibet was not a "part of China." The argument that Tibet's traditional social system was a "barbarous, cruel, dark, feudal serf system" whose inequalities justified Tibet's "liberation" by the Chinese Communists is nothing but an attempt to obscure the real issue. As the Dalai Lama has said, no country has the right to invade another because it disapproves of that country's social system. In any case, there is no evidence from Tibetans themselves or from foreign observers of traditional Tibet that Tibet's former social system was anything like how the Chinese characterize it; however, there is overwhelming evidence that the social and political system instituted by the Chinese in Tibet has been illegitimate, oppressive, destructive, barbaric and a form of state feudalism that has turned all Tibetans into serfs of the Chinese state.

Forty Years on Tibet Conference (London: School of Oriental and African Studies, March, 1990), 2.

The issue of Tibet is national self-determination. Tibet is a distinct nation whose rightful independence has been denied. The question is: how is Tibet to achieve its goal of self-determination, a goal in fundamental conflict with China's determination to deny that right, or even meaningful autonomy within the Chinese state. This question involves Tibet's status in international law, self-determination in international law, minorities rights in international law and in Chinese practice, and the future of Chinese politics.

Tibet's Legal Status

Tibet first came under the purview of international law at the end of the 19th century when Tibet's status became of interest to competing expansionist empires, British, Russian and Chinese. Imperialist powers sought a "legal" definition of Tibet's status conducive to their own interests. The British definition of China's authority over Tibet as "suzerainty" placed Tibet in a vague category suitable for British intentions. However, as viewed by international law, imperialist interests in Tibet transformed Tibet from a feudal dependency into a protected state. The key word in this new status is *state*; protectorate status implies a similar degree of foreign control and influence as does feudal vassalage, but, unlike vassalage, creates for the protectorate an international identity:

> A number of vassal states, in their striving for independence, attained before complete liberation first a higher status of dependence, that of protectorate. Protected states have, however, not only internal sovereignty, but are able in a number of cases to exercise some of the attributes of external sovereignty, though the latter is in principle vested in the protector state. Not infrequently the relationship between protector and protected was or is of a contractual nature, a feature not inherent in the suzerain-vassal setup. The basic treaty between protector and protected is of an international character and of interest to third Powers. Thus a protected state has to some extent a position within the family of nations, and therefore enters directly the orbit of international law. . . .

> It follows from the above treaties [1904 Lhasa Convention, 1906 Adhesion Agreement, 1907 Anglo-Russian Treaty] that Chinese suzerainty which had been reduced to a nominal right in 1904 tended to be revived with the support of Great Britain. However, this revival, promoted by British policy, could not alter the fact that Tibet through new treaty arrangements had left the narrow framework of exclusively bilateral relations with China and entered the orbit of international law and relations. Great Britain had appeared as an additional guarantor of the territorial integrity of Tibet and as her de facto co-guardian in the same way as China and Russia became

co-guardians in relation to Mongolia. Russia had not been allowed to proceed with the establishment of a protectorate over Tibet, but the multilateral arrangements of the three Powers interested in Tibet, which found their expression in one group of treaties and conventions, had raised Tibet from the status of vassal to that of a protected state.[2]

This theoretical transformation of Tibet's "legal" status reveals at least as much about the nature of international law as about Tibet's actual status. Tibet entered the "orbit of international law," according to this theory, and gained some "position within the family of nations," based not upon its intrinsic national characteristics or even its prior status in relation to Mongol or Manchu empires but due solely to the "interest of third Powers."

The 1904 Younghusband Expedition, the 1904 Lhasa Convention and the 1914 Simla Convention may all be seen as part of a British attempt to alter and redefine Tibet's "legal" status to suit British purposes. British interests dictated that China remain "suzerain" in theory while Britain exercised that role in fact. Had Britain recognized Tibetan independence in 1912 as Russia recognized Mongolia, Tibet might be an independent country today.

British patronage for Tibetan "autonomy" and China's impotence enabled Tibet to achieve *de facto* independence from 1912 to 1950. However, Tibetan nationalists found that their attempts to achieve international recognition were hampered by British recognition of Chinese "suzerainty" over Tibet and international acceptance of China's claim to authority over Tibet. Tibet attempted to establish its claim to independence at Simla in 1914, in negotiations with China in the mid-1930s, and again in 1945, in all of which Tibet expressed the intention to establish and maintain its political independence. However, the lack of international recognition of Tibet's independence was to condemn Tibet's appeal for assistance in 1950. Tibet's most immediate neighbors who had diplomatic relations with Tibet in the past (India, Nepal, Sikkim, Bhutan) had their own reasons for silence on the issue in 1950.[3]

The PRC maintained that its 1950 "peaceful liberation" of Tibet was nothing more than a reassertion of China's authority over its own territory. This claim was essentially unchallenged by the international community due to Tibet's lack of international recognition as an independent state. Tieh-tseng Li, the last KMT representative in Tibet, expressed the

---

2. Charles Henry Alexandrowitz-Alexander, "The Legal Position of Tibet," *American Journal of International Law*, 48 (1954), 266.

3. Michael C. Van Walt van Praag, *The Status of Tibet* (Boulder: Westview Press, 1987), 140.

general Chinese opinion that, not only was Tibet legally a part of China, but that Tibetans had no desire for independence of China:

> Tibet has never declared its wish to be a sovereign state. Nor did the Dalai Lamas and their governments ever express a desire to be independent from China in all their correspondence with the Chinese Government or in their discussions with its numerous missions. . . . However strong outside pressure to secure independence for Tibet may be, the fact remains that the Tibetans are neither willing nor prepared to assume and fulfill international obligations as a new state. . . . A thorough study of the records of Tibet's dealings with the Chinese and Indian governments and the accounts of unbiased observers who have an intimate knowledge of the Tibetan people and government, reveal a keen desire on the part of the Tibetans to preserve their traditional life and their autonomous position, but a lack of any political consciousness aiming at the formation of an independent and sovereign state.[4]

Despite China's claims, Tibetans resisted the Chinese invasion of Tibet in 1950; the "peaceful liberation" of Tibet was accomplished only by the use of force and deceit. The Chinese attack in eastern Tibet compelled the Tibetan Government to send negotiators to Beijing, where the Chinese made it clear that the "liberation" of Tibet and its "return to the Motherland" would be accomplished by the further use of force if no "agreement" were forthcoming. The 1950 invasion of Tibet and the subsequent 17-Point Agreement by which Tibet was incorporated within the People's Republic of China may therefore be held to have been a violation of international law:

> The Chinese view that Tibet legally remained part of the territory of the State of China throughout the years up to and including 1950 is not based upon an objective appreciation of the facts. . . . The events of the 39 years which lay between the ousting of the Chinese garrison from Tibet and the Chinese use of force to "liberate" Tibet belie Chinese assertions of continued rights in Tibet divorced from the use of force. . . . In so far as Chinese claims to authority in Tibet were coupled with actual attempts to assert control, between 1911 and 1950, as has been seen, such attempts were unsuccessful. The most the Chinese statements and actions represent in international law were refusals to recognize a change in legal status between Tibet and China. . . . Thus, with rather technical reservations, it appears that the

---

4. Tieh-tseng Li, "The Legal Position of Tibet," *American Journal of International Law*, 50 (1956), 402. Despite Tieh-tseng Li's claim, Tibet's intention to preserve its independence was repeatedly expressed in negotiations with Chinese representatives, including Mr. Li.

Chinese Communist actions in 1950 might logically be classified as a breach of international law.[5]

International law, however, is limited in its ability to oppose the results of the use of force, or the *fait accompli* presented by China as the result of its successful incorporation of Tibet within the Chinese state:

If the foregoing argument is correct, and the Agreement of 23 May 1951 was void in its inception, it becomes necessary to examine the assertion that this would legally result in returning Tibet to a status of independence. There seem to be two difficulties with that assertion. First, the status of Tibet in 1951 was merely a probable independence, with considerable doubt arising from conflicting legal views as to the function of recognition in international law. Those doubts were certainly not resolved in favor of Tibetan independence by the actions of third states after the "void" agreement was implemented: India in 1954, and Nepal in 1956, recognized Chinese sovereignty over the territory of Tibet. The second point, consequent on the first, is that even if the Agreement of 23 May 1951 is void, the events since 1951 are not a nullity. Although it is doubtful that China could justify its present position in Tibet on the basis of the Agreement, China may be able to justify its position legally by appealing to the general bias for stability of the international legal order. China's administration of Tibet has not been, either in form or in the apparent views of either Chinese or Tibetans, a temporary administration equivalent to a military occupation. It has been, with the active co-operation of all concerned for eight years (1951 to 1959), a constitutional arrangement openly assimilating Tibet into the state of China.

In these circumstances, while it is possible to agree with the contention of the Dalai Lama and his supporters that the 1951 Agreement can be regarded as legally void in its inception, it is difficult to conclude from that voidness that the present status of Tibet is one of rightful independence of China.[6]

China's intention, and the successful achievement of that intention, to "openly assimilate Tibet into the state of China," is then recognized, according to this opinion and in practice, as legal under the principle known as "acquisitive prescription," whereby legitimate title is held to arise from successful incorporation and international acquiescence to that

---

5. Alfred P. Rubin, "The Position of Tibet in International Law," *The China Quarterly* (July-September, 1968), 144. As Rubin commented, "The quality of theoretical doubts surrounding this hesitant classification, which rests so much on theoretical views of statehood, the legal effect of recognition (or the ineffectiveness of non-recognition), and the legal value of stability in the international order, is enough to dismay an impartial observer." Ibid., 140.

6. Ibid., 145.

fact. This principle "derives principally from the need to reconcile tensions between the law and the facts, for there is a limit to the legal system's ability to tolerate significant discrepancies between the two."[7] Ignoring the fact that the 17-Point Agreement was imposed by force and was therefore "illegal" within international law, international law is subsequently willing to accept the forcible incorporation of Tibet within the Chinese state due to the successful achievement of that result. In other words, international law recognizes as "legal" the results of conquest by force if that conquest is successful.

However, the principle of prescription is dependent upon the absence of any effective challenge to the legitimacy of title gained by force: "The principle of prescription rests on silence as an implication of consent, but there can be no implication of consent when dissent is explicit."[8] Tibetan "agreement" to the 17-Point Agreement was based upon specific provisions that guaranteed the preservation of Tibet's political institutions and its traditional autonomy. Despite the Tibetan Government's acceptance of the agreement in 1951, Tibetans violently repudiated its actual implementation as the Chinese interpreted the agreement. Tibet rebelled against Chinese attempts to institute "democratic reforms" and "socialist transformation" in eastern Tibet after 1956. The attempt to transfer governing authority in the TAR from the Tibetan Government to a Chinese-created and controlled Preparatory Committee was regarded by Tibetans as a violation of the provision of the 17-Point Agreement that the political system in Tibet would not be altered. The 1959 revolt, the Dalai Lama's flight, his subsequent repudiation of the agreement and declaration of Tibetan independence, his establishment of a government in exile, as well as continuing Tibetan opposition to the Chinese within Tibet, would seem to constitute adequate evidence of Tibetan opposition to the agreement as interpreted and implemented by China.

Tibetan dissent may have been little known to the outside world but was explicit nonetheless. The principle of prescription should therefore not apply and Tibet should thus retain a status in international law of "rightful independence," or at least an international identity as a disputed territory, or perhaps a case of "residual sovereignty" in which sovereignty continues to reside legally with the Tibetan Government in Exile.[9]

---

7. Van Walt, *Status of Tibet*, 181.

8. Rubin, "The Position of Tibet in International Law," 141.

9. "As Tibet was fully independent prior to 1950, and as no sufficient legal grounds can be found to support the contention that since that time the Tibetan state ceased to exist and was legally incorporated to form an integral part of the People's Republic of China, the State of Tibet still exists at the time of this writing [1987] as an independent legal entity, with a legitimate government, in exile in Dharamsala, to represent it." Van Walt, *Status of Tibet*, 188.

This interpretation is based upon the belief that the use of force is no longer acceptable within international law and that conquest is no longer a valid form of acquisition of territory. However, to maintain this position, Tibet must have been an independent state before being conquered. While that position may be held in international law, based upon Tibet's *de facto* independence, the lack of any international recognition of Tibet's independence inhibits the application of this principle in practice.

The issue of international recognition thus looms finally as the most significant deficiency in Tibet's claim to independence of China, despite the opinion within international law that statehood is dependent upon actual exercise of uncompromised authority over a defined territory and populace, rather than upon international recognition.[10] China's sovereignty over Tibet has been recognized by all states, and is therefore "legal" within the context of international law. Thus, China has been able to deny Tibet's "rightful" independence in practice, and to have its sovereignty over Tibet recognized by all states without exception.

Had the Dalai Lama repudiated the 17-Point Agreement in 1951 and sought exile in India or another country, Tibet's legal position would certainly have been much stronger. This action would have clearly indicated the Tibetan Government's non-acceptance of the 17-Point Agreement and would have defined that agreement as illegal within international law, providing a basis for international support for Tibet by removing the uncertainty about Tibet's acceptance of its incorporation within the Chinese state. Nevertheless, there is little doubt that international law would eventually have recognized the forceful incorporation of Tibet within China, if that were successfully accomplished, despite any Tibetan repudiation, unless the Tibetan case were championed by some third party such as the United States or the United Nations. In other words, politics would have dictated Tibet's "legal" status in any case.

Although the Dalai Lama repudiated the agreement in 1959, stating that it had been imposed by force and had in any case been violated by the Chinese, this had no apparent impact upon the international interpretation of Tibet's legal status.[11] In the eyes of international law, the fact

---

10. "There is a strong school of legal thought which holds that recognition is declaratory, and not constitutive of statehood. Under this view the effectiveness of control by an organized government with no constitutional superior over a defined territory and populace is the only legal criterion of the existence of a state." Rubin, "The Position of Tibet in International Law," 141.

11. Rubin takes the position that although the Chinese may have violated some of the terms of the 17-Point Agreement, this did not constitute a violation of international law because the agreement itself was not an international document (despite Tibet's pre-1950 *de facto* independence). China's intention to completely subsume Tibet within the Chinese state

of China's successful political integration of Tibet within the Chinese state far outweighed the original "illegality" of the 17-Point Agreement, China's violation of the provisions of that agreement, or clear Tibetan opposition to the agreement as it was actually implemented.[12] The Tibetan acceptance of the agreement in 1951 plus the eight years (until 1959) of apparent (to the outside world) Tibetan acceptance of Chinese sovereignty eliminated any recourse Tibet might have had to international law for international recognition or support in 1959 or thereafter.

Self-Determination in International Law

The principle of self-determination is not dependent upon Tibet's historical status or its legal status as interpreted by international law. Tibet does not have to demonstrate an unbroken history of political independence in the past in order to demand the right to independence in the present. Most UN member states could not claim independent statehood if they had to demonstrate a continuous history of independence. Self-determination is a contemporary issue of the Tibetan people's right to self-existence and self-rule and is unaffected by past compromises of Tibetan independence to China's imperial ambitions or the vagaries of an international legal system based upon acquiescence in political *fait accompli*. The principle of self-determination is based upon the political ideal of popular sovereignty, an ideal most commonly expressed within national groups. Self-determination is an issue of the Tibetan nation, and thus involves all Tibetan inhabited territory, not only the area of the current Tibet Autonomous Region. China cannot answer the Tibetan self-determination argument except by a distortion of the facts or of the principle itself.

The "self" of self-determination is, in the fundamental sense, the individual, but individual self-determination is obviously impracticable; self-determination is capable of expression only through social groups.[13] The

---

and its success in doing so makes the 17-Point Agreement, in retrospect, a constitutional, or domestic, document of the PRC, not an international document. Rubin, "The Position of Tibet in International Law," 152.

12. China, of course, does not admit to any violation of the agreement, claiming scrupulous and patient adherence throughout the period up until 1959. However, by its creation of the Preparatory Committee for the TAR, China was clearly in violation of Article 4: "The Central Authorities will not alter the existing political system in Tibet." The contradictory provisions of the agreement, providing both that Tibet should become part of the Chinese state under a system of "national regional autonomy," and that the Tibetan political system should remain unchanged, guaranteed that one or both parties should be in violation of some provisions.

13. Dov Ronen, *The Quest for Self-Determination* (New Haven: Yale University Press, 1979), 25.

definition of those social groups to which the principle of self-determination should apply was a subject of conflict between Wilsonian and Marxist-Leninist doctrines on self-determination. Wilsonian self-determination was derived from American principles of individual rights, democracy and popular sovereignty. It was characterized by an emphasis upon the right of a people to freely choose their form of government, or what has since come to be known as "internal" self-determination. In the Wilsonian view, collective rights are not inherent in groups but are derivative of rights of individuals. American ideology was concerned with issues of non-discrimination against groups that wished to assimilate to the dominant culture, not ethnic groups whose identity was threatened by assimilation. Neither Marxism-Leninism nor Western liberal democracy recognized any intrinsic rights of ethnic nations; both Western individualism (especially in its American form) and socialist internationalism were assimilationist doctrines.

Marxist-Leninist self-determination was aimed at the liberation of all peoples from their class oppressors. Marxism attempted to transcend the chauvinism of nationalism and national self-determination with a universal principle of international class self-determination.[14] Marxism took ethnic nationalism into account while aiming at an ultimate transformation of national consciousness into class consciousness. Marxists supported national self-determination only as a stage in the quest for economic and class self-determination. Support for national liberation struggles of colonies of European states was pursued as a means to defeat European capitalism at its "weakest link." National self-determination for colonies of European imperialism was acceptable as an immediate goal because nationalism was considered a progressive phenomenon for colonies that were in a pre-capitalist or immature capitalist stage.

The efficacy of Leninist national self-determination policy, both in "solving the nationalities question" within the Soviet Union and as an effective weapon against European imperialism, led the Soviet Union to retain the principle of self-determination, including the right of secession (but only against capitalist states) as its policy in international relations.[15] After the Second World War, the Soviet Union championed the principle of self-determination as a strategy against international capitalist imperialism and as a tactic to cultivate favor with African and Asian states.

The terminology of self-determination appeared, at the specific behest of the Soviet Union, in the 1945 Charter of the United Nations (Article 1(2) and Article 55), both of which accorded "respect for the principle of

---

14. Walker Connor, *The National Question in Marxist-Leninist Theory and Strategy* (Princeton: Princeton University Press, 1984), 7.

15. Ibid., 70.

equal rights and self-determination of peoples."[16] Secessionist, or "external" self-determination—supported by Eastern and Western blocs only against each other, and by the Third World not at all—was not legitimized in any form by the UN Charter. Only anti-colonialist self-determination had sufficient support to become an article of the United Nations Charter.

Self-determination did not appear in the 1948 Universal Declaration of Human Rights because it was intended to form a part of the Covenants on Human Rights, negotiations about which began in 1952.[17] The Covenants were not finally adopted until 1966, the delay being in large part due to the controversy over the clause on self-determination. The International Covenant on Civil and Political Rights and the International Covenant on Economic, Social and Cultural Rights (1966) each contains, in Article 1, the provision that "All peoples have the right of self-determination. By virtue of the right they freely determine their political status and freely pursue their economic, social and cultural development."[18] However, the Covenants' rather expansive language did not establish a "right" to self-determination as a legal principle of international law (except within a narrowly defined category of colonial situations), nor did states members of the UN intend that the UN should establish self-determination in its "external," or secessionist form, as a right of all "peoples."

Articles on self-determination in UN resolutions were qualified by other articles requiring respect for the "domestic jurisdiction" and "territorial integrity" of member states and preventing the application of the principle to any sub-state entities of former colonies. In order to limit the definition of colonialism to European colonialism, colonies were defined as geographically or territorially separate from the colonialist state.[19] Continental imperialism was thus excluded; those states that were heirs

---

16. Lee C. Buchheit, *Secession: The Legitimacy of Self-Determination* (New Haven: Yale University Press, 1978), 73; Rupert Emerson, *From Empire to Nation* (Cambridge: Harvard University Press, 1960), 301.

17. United Nations General Assembly, Resolution 217, "Universal Declaration of Human Rights," U.N. Doc. A/810 (1949)

18. United Nations General Assembly, 21st Session, Resolution 2200, "International Covenant on Economic, Social and Cultural Rights, International Covenant on Civil and Political Rights and Optional Protocol to the International Covenant on Civil and Political Rights," in GAOR, 21st Session, Supp. No. 16 (A/6316) (New York: United Nations, 1966).

19. This was the so-called "salt-water" requirement. As Buchheit comments, "International law is thus asked to perceive a distinction between the historical subjugation of an alien population living in a different part of the globe and the historical subjugation of an alien population living on a piece of land abutting that of its oppressors. The former can apparently never be legitimated by the mere passage of time, whereas the latter is eventually transformed into a protected status quo." Buchheit, *Secession*, 18.

to former empires, in particular the Soviet Union and the People's Republic of China, which now styled themselves as multinational states, were immune from categorization as colonialist. This immunity allowed the states of the Socialist bloc to champion self-determination for colonies of capitalist imperialism while denying the same right to their own "minority nationalities."

The 1960 Declaration on the Granting of Independence to Colonial Countries and peoples, placed on the UN agenda by the Soviet Union, specified its goal as "bringing to a speedy and unconditional end colonialism in all its forms and manifestations," but prohibited "any attempt aimed at the partial or total disruption of the national unity and territorial integrity of a country."[20] With the exception of colonies of European imperialism, no issues of self-determination involving member states of the United Nations could expect to be favorably viewed by that body.[21] No states or international organizations composed of states could be expected to favor secessionist self-determination whose goal was the dismemberment of states. As UN Secretary General U Thant stated in 1970:

> So far as the question of secession of a particular section of a Member State is concerned, the United Nations attitude is unequivocal. As an international organization, the United Nations has never accepted and does not accept and I do not believe it will ever accept the principle of secession of a part of its Member State. . . . Self-determination of the peoples does not imply self-determination of a section of a population of a particular Member State . . . . When a State applies to be a Member of the United Nations, and when the United Nations accepts that Member, then the implication is that the rest of the membership of the United Nations recognizes the territorial integrity, independence and sovereignty of this particular Member State.[22]

The conflict between self-determination and territorial integrity, both supposedly "fundamental principles of international law," was addressed in the 1970 Declaration on Principles of International Law concerning Friendly Relations and Co-operation among States. The Declaration began by affirming that "the subjection of peoples to alien subjugation, domination and exploitation constitutes a major obstacle to

---

20. United Nations General Assembly, 15th Session, Resolution 1514, "Declaration on the Granting of Independence to Colonial Countries and Peoples," in GAOR, 15th Session, Supp. No. 16 (A/4684), 66; Buchheit, *Secession*, 85.

21. The People's Republic of China was not admitted to the United Nations until 1972, but China was defended in this regard by the Soviet Union. The Republic of China, which held China's seat in the UN until 1972, also claimed all of the territories included in the PRC and more (Outer Mongolia).

22. U Thant, press conference, Dakar, 9 January 1970, as quoted in Buchheit, *Secession*, 87.

the promotion of international peace and security." On the other hand, "any attempt aimed at the partial or total disruption of the national unity and territorial integrity of a State or country or at its political independence is incompatible with the purposes of the Charter."[23] The conflict between the principles of territorial integrity of states and that of self-determination of peoples was evident throughout the Declaration:

> By virtue of the principle of equal rights and self-determination of peoples enshrined in the Charter of the United Nations, all peoples have the right freely to determine, without external interference, their political status and to pursue their economic and cultural development, and every State has the duty to respect this right in accordance with the provisions of the Charter.

> Every State has the duty to promote, through joint and separate action, realization of the principle of equal rights and self-determination of peoples, in accordance with the principles of the Charter . . . and bearing in mind that subjection of peoples to alien subjugation, domination and exploitation constitutes a violation of the principle, as well as a denial of fundamental human rights.[24]

The Declaration could be interpreted as demanding either self-determination for peoples, including the creation of an independent state, or equal rights for peoples within states. That self-determination could be achieved short of independent statehood was clarified by an explication of the means by which a people might achieve self-determination:

> The establishment of a sovereign and independent State, the free association or integration with an independent State or the emergence into any other status freely determined by a people constitute modes of implementing the right to self-determination by that people.[25]

The Declaration prohibited "any action which would dismember or impair, totally or in part, the territorial integrity or political unity of sovereign and independent States," and was qualified only by the requirement that these states should be "conducting themselves in compliance with the principle of equal rights and self-determination of peoples as

---

23. United Nations General Assembly, 25th Session, Resolution 2625, "Declaration on Principles of International Law concerning Friendly Relations and Co-operation among States in accordance with the Charter of the United Nations," in GAOR, 25th Session, Supp. No. 28 (A/8028) (New York: United Nations, 1971).

24. Ibid.

25. Ibid. This paragraph repeated the language on the means by which a people might achieve self-determination of the 1960 "Declaration of the Granting of Independence to Colonial Countries and Peoples," 14 December 1960, GAOR, 15th Session, Supp. No. 16 (A/4684).

described above and thus possessed of a government representing the whole people belonging to the territory without distinction as to race, creed or colour."[26] The last paragraph, while establishing the principle that a state's claim to territorial integrity is dependent upon its granting "equal rights and self-determination to peoples," and thus establishing, at least in theory, the precedence of the principle of self-determination over that of territorial integrity, also granted that self-determination might be equivalent to "equal rights" based upon non-discrimination according to race, creed or color.[27]

Self-determination of peoples thus attained a status theoretically more fundamental than territorial integrity; however, in practice, the principle of self-determination could be satisfied by the granting of equal rights to all peoples within the state, a claim any state could make without much fear of contradiction from other states beset with similar ethnic national-ist problems. Self-determination thus became in practice an issue legally within the domestic jurisdiction of states, subject only to the qualification that discrimination not be based upon ethnic distinctions (race, creed, color). States were not required to grant self-determination to peoples within their borders if they could claim to provide non-discriminatory representative government.[28]

---

26. Ibid.

27. "Although paragraph 7 is drafted in a somewhat remote manner in the form of a sav-ing clause, a close examination of its text will reward the reader with an affirmation of the applicability of the principle to peoples within existing states and the necessity for govern-ments to represent the governed. The fact that these aspects of the principle must be extract-ed by an *a contrario* reading of the paragraph should not be misunderstood to limit the sweep and liberality of the paragraph." Robert Rosenstock, "The Declaration of Principles of International Law Concerning Friendly Relations: A Survey," *American Journal of International Law*, vol. 65 (1971), 732. A state that denies self-determination may thus be held to have no claim to territorial integrity involving those people; specifically, China's denial of self-determination may be held to invalidate its claim to sovereignty over Tibet. International Committee of Lawyers for Tibet, *Resolving Claims of Self-Determination: A Proposal for Integrating Principles of International Law with Specific Application to the Tibetan People*, 29 December 1992.

28. The qualification concerning representative government was derived from two US proposals relevant to the issue of self-determination versus territorial integrity of states: "The existence of a sovereign and independent state possessing a representative govern-ment, effectively functioning as such to all distinct peoples within its territory, is presumed to satisfy the principle of equal rights and self-determination as regards those peoples," and, "The principle [self-determination] is *prima facie* applicable in the case of the exercise of sovereignty by a State over a territory geographically distinct and ethnically or cultural-ly diverse from the remainder of that State's territory, even though not as a colony or other Non-Self-Governing Territory." UN Doc. A/AC.125/L.75 (15 September 1969). The second proposal was intended to make self-determination applicable outside the (European) colo-nial context, specifically, to "peoples" within communist states, since communist states

The terminology of the 1970 Declaration on Friendly Relations essentially redefined self-determination from a right of nations to independent statehood to the right of individuals to equality and representative government within states. The final emphasis reflected Western liberal doctrines of popular sovereignty, collective rights as derivative of rights of individuals and the ideology of nondiscrimination according to ethnicity or nationality. The doctrine that national self-determination was fundamental to the existence of all human rights was thus replaced by the theory that individual human rights were cumulatively equivalent to national self-determination. The Declaration established that nations could achieve self-determination within multinational states, confirmed the rights of states over nations, and consigned nations within recognized states to the status of minorities. National self-determination would henceforth be presented as an issue of human rights of individuals who happened to be members of a national minority, subject only to the question of whether minority rights were entirely within the domestic jurisdiction of states or were subject to international law.

National self-determination thus ultimately fell victim to East-West competition and the general reluctance of states, many of which had their own separatist problems, to countenance secessionist self-determination. Western states placed their emphasis on individual human rights, which had the advantage of greater compatibility with Western intellectual traditions, and to which, it was thought, socialist states were particularly vulnerable. The socialist states countered the Western campaign for individual political rights with a claim for economic and social rights. Ethnic nations were abandoned to the jurisdiction of states; the right to self-determination was assumed by the state and equated with the principle of sovereign equality of states. Self-determination of "peoples" thus became a right of states rather than of nations:

> The principles of sovereign equality and of equal rights and self-determination of peoples underlie fundamental rights of States, such as sovereignty and independence.[29]

---

were thought incapable of satisfying the requirement of representative government for minority nationalities. The Declaration as adopted did not accept the US position that self-determination might be applicable outside the colonial context; only the qualification in relation to representative government remained in the final document. Buchheit, *Secession*, 119.

29. Aureliu Cristescu, *The Right to Self-Determination, Historical and Current Development on the Basis of United Nations Instruments* (New York: United Nations, 1981), UN Doc. E/CN.4/Sub.2/404/Rev.1, para. 164.

The jurisdiction of States within their frontiers is exercised equally and exclusively over all inhabitants, nationals and aliens alike, and over the whole territory. The principle of sovereign equality on the one hand, and the principle of equal rights and self-determination of peoples on the other, forbid any encroachment upon the authority of the State in these matters.[30]

The state, already semantically confused with nation, subsumed the rights of self-determination due to nations. Secessionist or "external" self-determination, the right of all "peoples" to an independent state, was not accepted in international law:

Where the territorial integrity of the State is involved, the right to self-determination does not in principle apply.[31]

The express acceptance . . . of the principles of the national unity and the territorial integrity of the State implies non-recognition of the right of secession. The right of peoples to self-determination, as it emerges from the United Nations system, exists for peoples under colonial and alien domination, that is to say, who are not living under the legal form of a State. The right to secession from an existing State Member of the United Nations does not exist as such in the instruments or in the practice followed by the Organization, since to seek to invoke it in order to disrupt the national unity and the territorial integrity of a State would be a misapplication of the principle of self-determination contrary to the purposes of the United Nations Charter.[32]

The fact that (external) self-determination, outside the European colonial context, has not achieved any status in international law is not surprising, considering that international law is dominated by states' interests. Nevertheless, self-determination retains some moral authority within international law, based upon the belief that customary international law is founded upon natural law rather than in states' practice. According to this opinion, the principle of self-determination may in some cases take precedence over states' claims to domestic jurisdiction:

However, to avoid any misunderstanding, it is necessary, in the Special Rapporteur's view, to specify that if the national unity claimed and the territorial integrity invoked are merely legal fictions which cloak real colonial and alien domination, resulting from actual disregard of the principle of

---

30. Ibid., para. 171.
31. Hector Gros Espiell, *The Right to Self-Determination, Implementation of United Nations Resolutions* (New York: United Nations, 1980) UN Doc. E/CN.4/Sub.2/405/Rev.1, para. 89.
32. Ibid., para. 90.

self-determination, the subject people or peoples are entitled to exercise, with all the consequences thereof, their right to self-determination.[33]

Self-determination remains, then, a "right" of peoples to revolt against foreign domination, "with all the consequences thereof." International law would neither sanction nor support their cause unless they were successful, in which case the result, even if achieved by violent revolution, would be recognized. International law held no other promise for those nations that considered themselves subjected to unjust foreign domination except the hope that their rights, individual and collective, might be respected by the states of which they were a part.

Minorities' Rights in International Law

The relegation of nations to the status of "minority nationalities" within states effectively denied them the right to (external) self-determination, since it was the express intention of the framers of the UN Charter that only "peoples" should have that right. In the opinion of Gros Espiell, "It is Peoples as such which are entitled to the right to self-determination. Under contemporary international law minorities do not have this right."[34] The Minority Rights Group Report, *Minorities and Human Rights Law*, states that "Self-determination is not a right of minorities. They must look instead to human rights: those which are not the rights of `peoples.'"[35]

Despite the fact that its predecessor, the League of Nations, had considered minorities' issues one of its primary tasks, the Charter of the United Nations did not address minorities' rights.[36] Minorities' issues had plagued the League and had acquired a negative connotation due to Hitler's exploitation of irredentist issues as justification for territorial aggression. The consensus of the drafters of the UN Charter was that minorities' issues would be resolved by the new emphasis on individual human rights, fundamental freedoms, equality and non-discrimination.[37]

The UN never successfully defined minorities, but all references to minorities in UN documents are characterized by scrupulous avoidance

33. Ibid., para. 84, 90.

34. Ibid., para. 56.

35. Patrick Thornberry, *Minorities and Human Rights Law*, (London: Minority Rights Group, 1987), 5.

36. Francesco Capotorti, *Study on the Rights of Persons belonging to Ethnic, Religious and Linguistic Minorities* (New York: United Nations, 1979), UN Doc. E/CN.4/Sub2/384/Rev.1, 26.

37. Ibid.

of the term "peoples," in favor of "groups," which are defined only as "non-dominant" in relation to the majority nationality of the state.[38] The UN did attempt to deal with minorities within the context of human rights. The UN Commission on Human Rights established in 1947 a Sub-Commission on Prevention of Discrimination and Protection of Minorities. Early attempts by the Sub-Commission to address minority issues, however, were rebuffed by members of the Commission.[39]

The Universal Declaration of Human Rights makes no specific mention of minority rights.[40] The UN did attempt to address minority rights in the Covenant on Civil and Political Rights, adopted in 1966. Article 27 provides that: "In those States in which ethnic, religious or linguistic minorities exist, persons belonging to such minorities shall not be denied the right, in community with the other members of their group, to enjoy their own culture, to profess and practice their own religion, or to use their own language."[41] An attempt by the Soviet Union to add language to Article 27 granting the same rights to "national minorities," rather than only to "persons belonging to minorities," was defeated by the Commission, many of whose members were reluctant to recognize collective rights of minorities.[42]

The concept of human rights within the UN was characterized by universality, equality and individualism. The new concept of universal human rights applied to all, not just to minorities; therefore, mention of specific group rights was considered inappropriate: "The first premise of the new system of human rights is that members of minority groups are promised justice in consequence of their basic humanity rather than as members of distinctive groups."[43] Minorities' rights were addressed to individuals rather than to the minority group collectively. This formula, adopted in accordance with the general emphasis on individual rights, avoided giving an international personality to any minority that would have allowed them to bring complaints against a state before an international body.[44]

The fault of this system is that minorities, the most common victims of discrimination as groups, are provided no special status or international protection as groups, only as individuals. The prevailing norms in human rights of individual equality and non-discrimination require an inten-

---

38. Thornberry, *Minorities and Human Rights Law*, 3.

39. Hurst Hannum, *Autonomy, Sovereignty, and Self-Determination* (Philadelphia: University of Pennsylvania Press, 1990), 59.

40. Capotorti, *Ethnic, Religious and Linguistic Minorities*, 27.

41. "International Covenant on Civil and Political Rights," Art. 27.

42. Capotorti, *Ethnic, Religious and Linguistic Minorities*, 32.

43. Thornberry, *Minorities and Human Rights Law*, 6, 7.

44. Capotorti, *Ethnic, Religious and Linguistic Minorities*, 35.

tional disregard of ethnic distinctions; such distinctions thus acquire a pejorative quality:

> A stress on the individual and on the principle of equal treatment tends to promote the view that it is improper even to think about differences of race, sex, language, and religion unless it be to combat discrimination based upon these characteristics. It tends to promote blindness to group differences and a kind of unspoken assumption either that societies are homogeneous or that right-thinking persons will treat them as if they were.[45]

States are not necessarily, or usually, homogeneous, however, and the principle of non-discrimination is not sufficient to guarantee rights of groups. Individual equality does little to preserve the rights of groups and may actually put minority group members at a disadvantage in relation to the majority. Western, particularly American, individualist ideology assumes a homogeneous or at least a non-discriminatory society as reality or as the ultimate goal. Individualism as a political doctrine posits no intermediary groups with legitimate political rights interposed between the individual and the state. As Thornberry has written: "Liberal ideology has a blind spot for minorities. . . . Liberal theory is not completely adequate to the complexity of State reality, and its simple individualism in turn tends to relegate this complexity into a transient precursor of a less complex State."[46]

Democratic ideology based upon majority rule assumes a politically unified country. Where a formerly separate nation has been incorporated as a minority within a majority state this is obviously not the case:

> The prime defect of decision by majority where a mixed or plural society is involved is that it relies upon one of the central instruments of the democratic process despite the absence of the foundations on which democracy rests. . . . Where the issue is one of fundamental national allegiance, and, at least in principle, of permanent subordination of the minority people to the majority nation which wins the state, no such agreement can be read into the situation; and the majority decision carries with it no necessary implication of ethical validity and binding force. If it is legitimate to assume that the sense of common nationality represents the core of the tacit agreement on which modern democracies rest, then the weakness of the majority principle when nations contend against each other is all the greater.[47]

---

45. Vernon Van Dyke, "The Individual, the State, and Ethnic Communities in Political Theory," *World Politics*, vol. XXIX, no. 3 (April 1977), 363.

46. Thornberry, *Minorities and Human Rights Law*, 14.

47. Emerson, *From Empire to Nation*, 330.

To be valid as a theory or as a practical principle, human rights must apply equally to groups as to individuals. In preparation for the drafting of the Universal Declaration on Human Rights in 1948, the American Anthropological Association submitted its opinion that human rights for individuals and for groups were "two facets of the same problem since it is a truism that groups are composed of individuals and human beings do not function outside the societies of which they form a part. ... There can be no individual freedom, that is, when the group with which the individual identifies himself is not free."[48]

Non-discrimination as a principle to be applied to individuals as well as to minorities assumes that discrimination has an exclusively negative and prejudicial meaning, when in fact discrimination may have the entirely neutral meaning of "to distinguish between things." Positive discrimination, or the preservation of distinctions by the group itself, is essential to the very identity of social groups and the preservation of that identity if members of that group so desire. As the report of the Minority Rights Group indicated, a system based upon non-discrimination was "intended in part to function as a substitute for protection of minorities in international law."[49] The former League system, despite the difficulties encountered in practice, had some advantages, both for minorities and for the preservation of peaceful interstate relations:

> The League system and the tradition of legal protection of groups may be assessed as deficient in global human concern and flawed in operation. It was not, however, entirely without virtue. By describing individual rights in a group context it reflected multiple levels of human identity and awareness. It also purported to respect the pragmatic view that injustice to minority groups feeds instability within States and foments international tension. There is the further point that specifying with particularity the beneficiaries of rights is fundamental: the rights of all human beings may degenerate into the rights of none in particular.[50]

In a UN commissioned study on the issue of minority rights, Francesco Capotorti described the reluctance of states to recognize minorities' rights:

> Any international regime for the protection of members of minority groups arouses distrust and fear. It is first seen as a pretext for interference in the

---

48. American Anthropological Association, *American Anthropologist*, Vol. 49, No. 4, October-December, 1947.
49. Thornberry, *Minorities and Human Rights Law*, 8.
50. Ibid., 6.

internal affairs of States. Secondly, the very different situations of minorities in the various countries make States skeptical of a juridical approach to the problem at the world level and they wonder how uniform rules can be applied to profoundly different situations. Moreover, certain States regard the preservation of the identity of minorities as posing a threat to their unity and stability. Another argument put forward is that the special measures of protection aimed at ensuring true equality as between the majority and the minority in each country inevitably lead to differences in treatment; such a situation is thought to contain the seeds of reverse discrimination. In short, Governments would prefer to have a free hand in their treatment of minorities.[51]

Many Third World countries attempting to achieve "national unification" were uncomfortable with mention of minority rights or even claimed to have no minorities. Many were understandably sensitive about any threats, external or internal, to their newly achieved sovereignty and political unity. Concerns of some countries were expressed in such language as the following at the debates of the Sub-Commission on the Prevention of Discrimination and Protection of Minorities:

It is highly desirable that minorities should settle down happily as citizens of the country in which they live, and therefore in any measures that may be taken for the protection of their special traditions and characteristics, including the study [by the Sub-Commission], nothing should be done that is likely to stimulate their consciousness of difference from the rest of the population.[52]

Most new states were vitally interested in creating national—actually state—unity in multinational states. They were aided in this endeavor by modernization theory, of both capitalist and socialist forms, which held that modern systems of communication and bureaucratic state organization would inevitably lead to "national" unity. Socialist theory assumed that modernization within a socialist format would ultimately lead to the predominance of class interests over those of ethnic nationalism. Western, especially American, modernization theory was equally assimilationist; however, as Walker Connor has written, the American experience is not very relevant to that of most multi-ethnic states:

The key factor that differentiates the process of assimilation in the United States is that the impetus for assimilation has come principally from the

---

51. Capotorti, *Ethnic, Religious and Linguistic Minorities*, iv.
52. *Report of the Tenth Session of the Commission on Human Rights*, 18 ESCOR Supp. 7, UN Doc. E/2573 at 48-49 (1954).

unassimilated, not from the dominant group. . . . Ethnic problems within the United States have not been characterized primarily by the resistance of minorities to assimilation, but by the unwillingness or inability of the dominant group to permit assimilation at the rate desired by the unassimilated. . . .

Analogies drawn from the experience of the United States are apt to be specious. A proportionately small number of people who have voluntarily left their cultural milieu to enter an alien politico-cultural environment in which cultural assimilation is conceived positively as indistinguishable to success is one thing; a situation characterized by two or more large groups, each ensconced in a territory it considers its traditional homeland and cultural preserve is something quite different.[53]

Non-ethnic regionalism has indeed been overcome by advances in communication in industrial states, but ethnic differences have remained, even in the United States where the melting-pot ideal has yet to be achieved in reality. Modernization theory is based upon the assumption that improvements in communication between peoples tends to increase realization of what they have in common at the expense of ethnic or regional differences. However, ethnic distinctions may actually be stimulated by unification and modernization of previously unintegrated multi-ethnic states. Attempts at "nation-building" in such situations may result in the elimination of existing autonomy and a consequent exacerbation of ethnic nationalism. Awareness of ethnic differences between the minority and the penetrating majority may be increased rather than diminished as a result of increased physical contact. At the same time, intra-ethnic unity within previously isolated regions of the same nationality may be stimulated by internal contacts or by members of the ethnic group being isolated for education or indoctrination within the majority society. Ethnic nationalism, previously latent due to isolation from state authority, is often stimulated by what is perceived as an outside threat: "Modernity results in—and probably requires—much greater integration of all the parts of the state. A modernizing state is therefore one in which the threat to the survival of the lifeways of the minority ethnic group is much greater than was the threat in the traditional states and colonies."[54]

The persistence of ethnic nationalism has surprised modernists of all types who have had to try to understand why nations have survived as the foci of primary loyalty for much of the world population despite, in

53. Walker Connor, "Nation Building or Nation Destroying? " *World Politics*, 24 (April, 1972), 345.
54. Walker Connor, "Ethnic Nationalism as a Political Force," *World Affairs*, vol. 133, no. 2 (September, 1970), 94.

many cases, loss of many elements thought to be essential to national identity. Cultural components have been changed by modernizing factors without touching the essential elements of self-identity. Even when the persistence of nationalism was recognized, the confusion between ethnic and state nationalism led to the assumption that nationalism would work in favor of the state and "nation-building," actually state-building. Instead, ethnic nationalism has proved resistant to most attempts to create multinational state unity.

Self-determination has not been achieved for nations incorporated within states by individualizing their rights nor have collective identities been subsumed by means of integration and modernization. The opposite has more often been the case; ethnic identities are emphasized and strengthened due to attempts at "national unification" and the autonomous rights of minorities are disregarded. The hope that ethnic nationalism might be overcome by modernization and communication has usually proved futile. Most minority nationalities were, after all, incorporated within majority states by force, a situation unlikely to lead to either equal rights or a diminution of the minority demand for self-government. Nor were rights of individuals often achieved, because rights of minority nationalities were now entirely within the domestic jurisdiction of majority states.

Minorities' Rights in the PRC

The Chinese Communists' system of National Regional Autonomy ostensibly guaranteed minority nationality autonomy. However, this system was contradicted in theory by the Marxist doctrine that class, not ethnicity or nation, was the most fundamental collective social group, and in practice by the extreme centralization of authority under the Marxist-Leninist doctrine of "democratic centralism." Minority autonomy was essentially incompatible with the cultural and political conformity inherent in both Marxist-Leninist doctrine and traditional Chinese political culture.

National minorities incorporated within the Chinese state had no choice in regard to their sovereignty or political system; they were denied the right to both external and internal self-determination and forced to accept both alien rule and alien cultural and political ideologies. National minorities were promised "equality" and a certain degree of autonomous cultural and political rights contingent upon their acceptance of Chinese sovereignty and the Chinese socialist system. However, autonomous rights theoretically guaranteed by the Chinese state were determined and applied not by the minorities themselves but by the Chinese. Resistance to either Chinese rule or the Chinese socialist system was interpreted as "counterrevolutionary." Minorities who opposed the loss of their freedom, individually or collectively, were defined as "enemies of the people."

The autonomous cultural and political status supposedly guaranteed by CCP nationalities policies has not been achieved in practice in the PRC. The minimal rights promised to national minorities were not respected in practice; on the contrary, almost all of China's minority nationalities suffered tremendous cultural destruction and repression. Chinese promises to nationalities of cultural and political autonomy have been fundamentally contradicted and invalidated by the very fact of Chinese rule and the political characteristics of the Chinese Communist state. The PRC has, despite its socialist and "democratic" ideology, achieved greater ideological conformity and has had less tolerance for political or social diversity than even the most monolithic of Chinese imperial dynasties. As Lucian Pye has commented: "Under the Communists the denial of legitimacy to autonomous interest groups is more absolute than at any time in Chinese history."[55]

In conformity with the ideals of Chinese political culture and Marxist-Leninist proletarian internationalist doctrine, the CCP regarded nationality autonomy as merely a transition stage to ultimate cultural and political unity. The autonomy promised to Tibetans and other nationalities within the Chinese state was primarily intended to defuse mistrust while physical and political control was secured. The CCP assumed that nationalities would voluntarily abandon their desire for an isolated and backward cultural autonomy once they had been exposed to the attractions of Chinese culture and the benefits of socialism. Cultural diversity was particularly intolerable within the highly nationalistic atmosphere cultivated by the Chinese Communists. The CCP reacted to minority nationalism as a fundamental rejection of the Chinese revolution and of the Chinese themselves, which indeed it was. Minority nationalists were criticized as anti-socialist rightists and reactionaries, but their most egregious crime was anti-Chinese nationalism. Minority nationalism represented a fundamental rejection of Chinese pretensions to racial and cultural superiority. When the CCP's policies of socialist transformation began to arouse Tibetan "local nationalism," the CCP's reaction, though expressed in socialist terms, was virulently nationalistic.

Genuine minority nationality autonomy has been, and is likely to remain, an extremely doubtful prospect in the PRC. The question remains

---

55. Lucian Pye, *Spirit of Chinese Politics* (Cambridge: Harvard University Press, 1968; 1992), 20.

whether nationality autonomy might be possible under a different regime in China, in particular under a democratic system. Elimination of the communist system *per se* provides no guarantees for minority autonomy; as Hannah Arendt has pointed out, "a legally unrestricted majority rule, that is, a democracy without a constitution, can be very formidable indeed in the suppression of the rights of minorities and very effective in the suffocation of dissent."[56] The key is rule by law, and a constitutional law that provides guarantees of minority nationality autonomy, not just democratic majority rule. However, rule by law has not been achieved in China in the past and has very doubtful prospects for the future considering the authoritarian tendencies of Chinese political culture.

Chinese political culture, even under a democratic system, is likely to retain much of its authoritarian, collectivist and culturally conformist nature. Certain characteristics of Chinese political culture, and the realities of economics, education and the bureaucratic system, would seem to preclude the possibility of meaningful nationality autonomy within the Chinese state. Many of the prerogatives of central state administration as well as modernization and communication are inherently assimilative, especially in terms of language and political culture. The exigencies of centralized administration often preclude actual political autonomy.

All systems of state-imposed autonomy are inherently deficient in their fundamental premise that autonomy will be given by a majority nationality to the minority. No system of nationality autonomy imposed by a majority state can satisfy the fundamental requirement that political loyalty and the political system be *self* determined, not imposed by a state unrepresentative of that group. What can be given can also be taken away, and, as nationality relations within states have demonstrated, usually are when a state's territorial integrity or political unity is threatened. Tibet was guaranteed extensive autonomy, including no alterations in its political system, in the 17-Point Agreement, but those guarantees meant very little in practice. Tibetans' past experience of an almost total absence of any cultural and political autonomy does not lead to confidence in the promises of any Chinese government, democratic or otherwise, to allow meaningful autonomy in the future.

---

56. Hannah Arendt, "Reflections on Violence," *Anthology: Selected Essays from Thirty Years of the* New York Review of Books (New York: New York Review of Books, 1994), 54.

Conclusions: Prospects for Tibetan Self-Determination

International law, while generally supportive of the proposition that the Chinese invasion of Tibet in 1950 was "illegal," eventually condones the result because China subsequently achieved its goal of incorporating Tibet within the Chinese state. Self-determination in its external sense, or secessionist self-determination, is generally not in the interest of states and is therefore not supported by states (except occasionally against one another). International law is therefore deaf to Tibet's appeal that its *de facto* independence or its right to self-determination has been violated.

Given the infeasibility of self-determination as an enforceable "right" for all "peoples," international law has emphasized "internal" self-determination, or autonomy within a majority state, as an alternative capable of satisfying the needs of minorities for cultural and political autonomy. The requirements for internal self-determination are generally interpreted as a democratic system of government and respect for individual human rights and the right of minorities to protect their collective identity and to participate in the overall affairs of the state without discrimination.[57] Were all these requirements achievable in practice, the fundamental requirement of self-determination would still not be met unless a minority has voluntarily chosen to amalgamate with the larger state. Leaving aside the issue of whether the requirements for "internal self-determination" are realistic, most modern self-determination issues involve minorities who have not voluntarily chosen to be included within a majority state. Even proponents of internal self-determination as a solution equivalent to "functional sovereignty" for some minorities admit that internal self-determination may not be capable of resolving the most egregious cases.[58]

International law has proven ineffective in achieving for Tibetans or for many other minorities any semblance of independent or autonomous self-determination. The principle of national self-determination nevertheless retains the popular moral force that lay behind the original attempt to establish a right of all "peoples" to popular sovereignty. Self-determination has attained a popular status that encourages peoples worldwide to pursue political freedom and sympathizers to support them. The idea of a moral right of distinct self-defined "peoples" to pop-

---

57. Hurst Hannum, "Rethinking Self-Determination," *Virginia Journal of International Law*, vol. 34, no. 1 (Fall, 1993), 67.

58. Ibid., 64; Ralph G. Steinhardt, "International Law and Self-Determination," Atlantic Council Occasional Paper, November 1994.

ular sovereignty has achieved the status of an accepted principle, not only among those who feel that their moral right to self-determination has been denied, but within the body of international public opinion. Self-determination remains an issue of political significance since states that repress the desire for self-determination of some portion of their population can hardly claim popular political support.

The ideal of self-determination does not demand that every ethnic group or nation should be in exclusive possession of its own state, only that they should not be forcibly deprived of that opportunity. Self-determination cases resolvable only by independent statehood would number only in the dozens, not hundreds. There would not necessarily be a proliferation effect once the most egregious cases were resolved. As Michael Lind has written: "While there are thousands of ethnic nations in the world, there are at most only dozens of national groups numerous, unified and compact enough conceivably to serve as the nuclei of sovereign nation states. The impossibility of basing nation states on tiny minorities like Sorbs or Wends in Germany or the Amish in the United States in no way discredits the potential for statehood of the Kurds or the Ibo or the Tibetans."[59]

Self-determination is often opposed because of its potential for impeding economic integration and cooperation among states. This point of view assumes that there is some inherent virtue, or at least a tendency to political stability or economic prosperity, in states of large size. However, there is no inherent virtue in size, whether large or small, or in political or economic integration. International cooperation is more likely between self-determined states just as individual cooperation is most likely between persons secure in their individuality. Self-determination may be and usually is manifested as nationalism, but self-determination universally applied may actually be an antidote to chauvinistic nationalism if states are secure in their self-identity and are not threatened by secessionist conflicts. The essence of self-determination is popular sovereignty of voluntarily constituted political entities, not ethnicity or nationalism *per se*. Chauvinistic or aggressive nationalism is not a manifestation of the principle of democracy or popular sovereignty. Many of the sins credited to nationalism are in any case common to multinational states; support for national self-determination is not therefore equivalent to support for nationalism.

Self-determination may be destabilizing to the present international system, but any political system has to be responsive to social and politi-

---

59. Michael Lind, "In Defense of Liberal Nationalism," *Foreign Affairs*, vol 73, no. 3 (May/June 1994), 90.

cal change lest the very rigidity of the system become the source of discontent, disharmony and disorder. Rigidity in the international system leads not to stability, but to an exacerbation of tensions ultimately leading to greater instability. Change, not static rigidity, is characteristic of human social and political evolution, as was recognized in the Chinese *Book of Changes* (*I Ching*). The principle of self-determination represents a social and political evolution from a feudal political system to one based upon popular will. International law is more likely to achieve peace and stability by supporting self-determination, even at the expense of temporary instability, than by supporting states' repression of self-determination in the name of stability. An international community composed of voluntarily constituted political entities has greater potential for ultimate peace and stability than a system in which popular sovereignty is denied. The denial of self-determination is inherently disruptive, potentially leading to greater long-term instability than would have been the case had the issue been resolved, even at the cost of a temporary disruption. It is not self-determination, but self-determination denied, that is the greater threat to international stability.

Tibet remains one of the world's most egregious cases of self-determination denied. Tibet has all the prerequisites for self-determination, including a distinct national, cultural and political identity and a clearly expressed Tibetan desire for national independence. Tibet continues to possess all the characteristics of nationality, and retains, in fact, stronger national, territorial, cultural and political qualifications for independence than do many of the world's recognized states. Tibet's past or present domination by China or the nature of its former social system are irrelevant to the issue of Tibet's contemporary right to self-determination.

While China's claim to Tibet is based upon imperialist domination, Tibet's claim to independence is based upon the principle of popular sovereignty and national self-determination. China has denied Tibetans the fundamental right to choose their political allegiance. The questions that China has to answer concern the legitimacy of China's territorial conquest of Tibet, the consequent depredations perpetrated against Tibetans, and the issue of China's denial of Tibetan self-determination. China's claim to have liberated Tibet from a feudalistic and exploitative social and political system falsely characterizes Tibetan society, falsely conceals China's actual motives in invading Tibet, and fails to acknowledge the brutality contingent upon the conquest of Tibet or the imposition of the Chinese socialist system, a system denounced by many Chinese themselves as state feudalism or even "feudal fascism."

The PRC's primary motive in "liberating" Tibet in 1950 was to substantiate its sovereignty over what was thought to be "Chinese" territory.

The Chinese considered Tibet a part of China, perhaps not an integral part, but a rightful territorial possession nonetheless. The Tibetan plateau was considered a natural extension of Chinese territory whose possession was essential for the defense of the Chinese interior. The PRC was also obviously intent upon gaining access to Tibet's natural resources and the vast territory of Tibet for Chinese expansion and colonization. As Mao and other CCP leaders often pointed out in justifying Tibet's incorporation within China, China would gain access to Tibetan resources necessary for China's development while Tibetans would gain access to Chinese assistance necessary for Tibet's development. However, the CCP's concept of "assistance" differed little in its cultural and political assumptions from traditional Chinese frontier assimilationist policy.

Chinese leaders thought of Tibet not as a political entity, a people, a nation, or a state with political rights, but as a virtually uninhabited territory, a natural area for expansion of the Chinese population, which China had a territorial imperative, or manifest destiny, to populate and exploit. The assumption of a territorial imperative was furthered by the CCP's ideological imperative, which legitimated "liberation" of all the territory of "China" and the export of liberation ideology further afield. The CCP inherited the traditional attitude of most Chinese that Tibetans were legitimately subjects of Chinese rule. The essence of the problem that China has encountered in its attempted absorption of Tibet is that Tibet is indeed a "country" with a national identity and history separate from that of China, not an unpopulated territory suitable for Chinese expansion, whose few barbarian inhabitants' territorial rights could be dismissed as inconsiderable.

China's history of frontier expansionism and the PRC's colonization programs in Inner Mongolia, Xinjiang and Tibet leave little doubt as to the PRC's ultimate solution to the Tibet problem. Mao's 1952 statement to the Dalai Lama that Tibet's population should be increased to 10 million, a prospect that Mao imagined would be acceptable to Tibetans, revealed his and the CCP's assumptions about the policy to be pursued in Tibet. The legitimacy of an assimilationist solution to China's nationalities question, its inevitability, or even the voluntary and enthusiastic acceptance of Chinese culture by those being "allowed" to receive it, have been unquestioned in Chinese history. The TAR has been until recently relatively immune from large-scale colonization of the type promoted in Xinjiang; this has been primarily due to logistical difficulties and, at times, a modicum of respect for Tibet's special status. Nevertheless, eventual assimilation, including colonization, has always been the underlying assumption of Chinese policies in Tibet. The only dispute in Chinese politics has been between proponents of a gradual and voluntary (as much as possible) approach and those who prefer a more rapid cultural and political assimilation of Tibet within the Chinese state. Tibetans' rejection of Chinese rule, their resistance to assimilation and their recent national-ist revival have undoubtedly strengthened Chinese proponents of colo-nization and assimilation. Tibetans' disloyalty to China can be overcome only by overwhelming Tibetans with Chinese; only Chinese colonists can be completely trusted with the defense of China's present frontiers.

The fundamental issue of Tibet remains one of cultural and political survival: will Tibet be subsumed by China's territorial imperative, with "Tibet" becoming little more than a geographic term, or will Tibet finally emerge from its colonial status? Tibetans continue to hope that the justice of their cause will eventually compel the international community to challenge China's sovereignty over Tibet. However, international politi-cal support for Tibet to the extent that Tibetans hope for seems unlikely. China's increasing economic power makes the possibility of official inter-national support ever more remote.

In the absence of any international solution to the Tibetan issue, Tibet's fate depends upon Chinese political developments. Tibetan hopes for a Soviet-type territorial disintegration of China upon the demise of Deng Xiaoping and/or the collapse of communism seem excessively opti-mistic. The Chinese and Soviet cases are significantly different, especial-ly in regard to proportions of nationality populations in relation to the majority. The fact that Tibet is the only former national state incorporat-ed within the PRC may also mean that the PRC will not collapse, at least not in the same manner as did the Soviet Union.[60] The precedent usually cited for a territorial fragmentation of China is the warlord period of recent Chinese history. However, centralized government and territorial unity within the Great Wall is the much more predominant pattern of Chinese history over a period of at least two millennia. In any case, this scenario is not necessarily favorable for Tibet. Chinese residents in Tibet, civilian and military, retain a monopoly on political and military power and, rather than leave Tibet, would be more likely to establish a Chinese warlord-type regime there. The most recent period of warlordism in Chinese history saw Chinese warlords establish regimes in Tibetan areas: Ma Pu-feng in Amdo (Qinghai) and Liu Wen-hui in Kham ("Sikang").

A somewhat more likely scenario involves the creation of a Chinese federative system or a system permitting actual cultural and political autonomy. The exiled Chinese democracy movement's leaders' recogni-

---

60. Tibet's history of independent statehood and other distinguishing characteristics are, however, good reason why Tibetans should emphasize the uniqueness of their case even in comparison with other Inner Asian nationalities incorporated against their will within the PRC.

tion of the factual basis for Tibetan complaints against China represents a rare and potentially significant development. Nevertheless, almost all the Chinese "democrats" have retained patronizing attitudes in regard to China's right to bestow upon Tibetans "self-determination," which they generally equate with equal rights within China. Even some of those who acknowledge that mistakes have been made in Tibet in the past, or even that there is a fundamental injustice in Han rule over Tibetans, imagine that the situation can be rectified with a new "correct" policy and Tibetans made content as one of the nationalities of the great multinational Chinese state.[61]

The Chinese democracy movement leaders' proposals for a federative system and for a referendum on Tibet's political status may offer some hope, assuming China were to institute a system of rule by law under which nationalities would have legal recourse for obtaining their promised cultural and political autonomy. Chinese promises to Tibetans would, as usual, be subject to Chinese prerogatives; any concessions to Tibet, including a promised referendum after 25 years "not subject to central government approval," would remain unilaterally and arbitrarily alterable by the Chinese. All assumptions in regard to the policies a democratic Chinese government might adopt in relation to Tibet are obviously contingent upon the possibility of actually achieving democracy in China. Political movements are famous for promising more than they are able or willing to deliver once in power. There is no assurance that the current Chinese democracy movement leaders will ever achieve power in China, that they are actually democrats, or that they could or would install any semblance of democracy.

The results at Tiananmen give very little reason for optimism in regard to the potential for a transition to democracy in China. China is not like Eastern Europe or the former Soviet Union where alternative political organizations were able to arise in opposition to communist parties and to replace them when communism fell. No such alternative political groupings have so far emerged in the PRC. Post-Tiananmen repression eliminated whatever organized opposition there was in China, and the exiled movement leaders have evidenced little ability to organize a uni-

---

61. See Wei Jingsheng's "Letter to Deng Xiaoping," in which Wei declared that the "peaceful liberation of Tibet" had been a "correct policy," but that later CCP mishandling of the situation had poisoned nationality relations. He favored the revival of negotiations with the Dalai Lama so that Tibet might remain a part of China. Wei repeated many of the arguments of Chinese communist ideology: "The Dalai Lama should know clearly that without alliance with the Han people, he would face the ambitious Indians who are no better than the Han people. . . . The trend of the modern world is that unity is what will happen sooner or later. The advantage of unity overshadows its disadvantage."

fied opposition in exile. The tradition of autocratic government in China is so pervasive that the assumption that China can convert to a democratic system has to be reexamined, especially in light of difficulties in the democratic transition process encountered in the former communist states of Eastern Europe and the former Soviet Union.

Any future government in China would encounter Chinese public opinion in no way enlightened in regard to the history of China's role in Tibet and no doubt still adamantly opposed to Tibetan "splittism." All Chinese have been taught that Tibet is a "part of China" since at least the Qing dynasty. Since the founding of the PRC, Chinese citizens have been told that Tibetans were liberated from a feudal "hell on earth," that they have greatly prospered since then due to the selfless assistance of the Chinese state and that they are boundlessly happy to be part of China and eternally grateful to the CCP and Chairman Mao for liberating them. While many Chinese have since learned to discredit much Party propaganda, most still accept without question the CCP's version of Tibetan history and China's role in Tibet. Many Chinese, even "democratic" Chinese, respond to criticism of China's Tibet policy with a litany of the supposed horrors of Tibet's pre-liberation social and political system. For popular Chinese opinion to shift to a favorable consideration of Tibetans' political rights would require an undoing of the legacy of millennia of Chinese conceptions of history and the distortions and misrepresentations of several decades of CCP propaganda.

The CCP came to power by exploiting Chinese nationalism and has remained in power by the same means; there are no assurances that any Chinese government, democratic or otherwise, would be any less nationalistic. China's contemporary nationalist imperative is not only to maintain China's hold on Tibet but to achieve the reunification of Hong Kong and Taiwan, for which the supposedly "successful resolution" of the Tibet issue is held up as a model. The PRC has not renounced its threat to use force in order to achieve the reunification of Taiwan with the mainland, a threat that the PRC might conceivably employ if Taiwan should declare its independence. China also claims all of the South China Sea up to 15 miles from the coastlines of Vietnam, Malaysia, Brunei and the Philippines (and completely encompassing the island of Taiwan), an area hundreds of miles distant from Chinese shores.[62] These are the territorial imperatives of the Chinese state, not just those of the CCP; China under

---

62. See *Map of the People's Republic of China-South China Sea Islands* (Beijing: Cartographic Publishing House, 1984).

any form of government seems far from voluntarily abandoning any territorial claims, especially those to an area so extensive and important as Tibet, even if that area were confined to the TAR. Lucian Pye points out that China's fear of disunity is "nearly a phobia," and that the compulsion behind the ideal of cultural and political unity cannot be overstated: "Westerners who do not appreciate the impulse behind it have consistently underestimated the cost that China is even now prepared to incur in order to facilitate the recovery of Taiwan and Hong Kong."[63]

A resolution of the Tibetan issue providing for Tibetan cultural and political survival apparently remains entirely dependent upon Chinese benevolence, a benevolence not displayed to this point in Sino-Tibetan relations. Future political events are impossible to predict, but current Chinese nationalist imperatives and continuing chauvinistic attitudes toward Tibetans do not provide much hope that China will refrain from the "natural" and ever more feasible assimilationist solution to the Tibetan problem.[64] The Chinese now feel that they have little reason to compromise and little to gain by negotiations. The Chinese may by now have decided that a return of the Dalai Lama would entail too much political danger, particularly since they may feel that they no longer need him to legitimate their presence or policies in Tibet. The Chinese might reasonably ask why they should reintroduce a role for the Dalai Lama in Tibetan politics and Tibet's future when they are perfectly capable of ruling Tibet without him. Recent Chinese reincarnation politics involving the Panchen Lama reveal what is likely to be China's policy on dealing with the Dalai Lama: the Chinese have only to await the death of the Fourteenth Dalai Lama and then force a Fifteenth of their choice upon the Tibetan people.

Under current conditions, a compromise or negotiated solution to the Tibet issue is unlikely. In his 10 March 1995 speech, the Dalai Lama called for a referendum among Tibetans in exile on the issue of independence or autonomy. Assuming that almost all Tibetans would naturally prefer independence, and considering that this is an issue of Tibetan patriotism, a vote in favor of independence seems a foregone conclusion. The reception that the Strasbourg statement received in the exile community leaves little doubt that the majority of Tibetans in exile would be unwilling to accept anything short of full independence.

---

63. Lucian W. Pye, *Asian Power and Politics* (Cambridge: Harvard University Press, 1985), 64. This compulsion for unity obviously also applies to Tibet.

64. As one Chinese official in Tibet reportedly said in 1994: "Tibet is like California. One needs immigrants from the new world to develop the people of the old world." "Greenpeace Exposes Austrian Government Role in Yamdrok Tso Power Plant," *Tibet Press Watch*, May 1994, 16.

The territorial issue alone is probably sufficient to frustrate any negotiated agreement. Tibetans in exile, many of whom are from Kham and
Amdo, would undoubtedly oppose any agreement which did not either
include Tibetan majority territories in a greater Tibetan autonomous state
or provide a comparable autonomous status for those territories. Chinese
resistance to any Tibetan territorial reunification is certain, not only
because they think that eastern Tibetan areas now part of Chinese
provinces are not "Tibet," but also because a large portion of China's forest and hydropower resources lie in those areas. China's hydrological
development plans include not only exploitation of the huge hydroelectric potential of the upper Yellow, Yangtze and Mekong rivers but ambitious plans for water diversion in Qinghai from the headwaters of the
Yangtze to the Yellow River. Both the Yellow and Yangtze are regarded as
the foundation and sustenance of the Chinese nation, an attitude not conducive to abandonment of their headwaters to an autonomous or independent Tibet. China regards this, like the issue of Tibet as a whole, not
in a rational way, but as an emotional issue of China's sovereignty and
territorial integrity.

Assuming a negotiated solution is not feasible, China will likely continue its current policies in Tibet, Tibet will be demographically transformed and the Tibetan issue will quietly dissolve in a sea of Chinese; or,
Tibetan frustration and despair will lead to violence despite the overwhelming Chinese repressive force at hand. A Tibetan uprising against
the Chinese presence, even one with the implicit blessing of the Dalai
Lama, has little chance of success, and great potential for creating another Tibetan tragedy. Nevertheless, somewhat paradoxically, the outbreak
of violence might be the only way to focus international attention on
Tibet and stimulate international efforts to mediate the Tibet issue.
International attention has been focused on Tibet in the past only when
violence has broken out, in 1950, 1959 and 1987-89; otherwise, Tibet has
been generally ignored. Chinese embarrassment might force one faction
in Chinese politics to seek a negotiated solution (while another faction no
doubt would, as usual, prefer "merciless repression").

International attention, even if provoked by violence, would be a welcome addition to the Tibet issue, but one whose ultimate efficacy is uncertain. China has proven that it is relatively immune from international criticism; however, violence in Tibet would upset Chinese development
plans, create fear among Chinese colonists and decrease China's income
from foreign tourism and international investment. The Chinese response
both to disorder in Tibet and international attempts to mediate would
undoubtedly depend upon which faction in Chinese politics was dominant at the time. Although such a scenario is perilous, only such drastic

actions apparently offer any opportunity for positive, if unpredictable, developments in the situation. The continuation of current Chinese policies in Tibet offers the entirely predictable result of the final demise of Tibetan civilization.

The option of violent resistance has so far been resisted by Tibetans, due to the Buddhist abhorrence of violence, the Dalai Lama's belief that a policy of nonviolence will ultimately prove more efficacious, and the overwhelming preponderance of force in the hands of the Chinese and their demonstrated willingness to use it. This issue remains contentious within Tibetan politics. Proponents of violent resistance point out that only violence has gained international attention and support for the Tibetan cause in the past, and they fault Buddhist non-violence and monastic anti-nationalism and dependence upon Chinese patronage for the loss of Tibetan independence. Nevertheless, those in favor of the use of violent means have so far respected the Dalai Lama's wishes to avoid violence. This issue, like that of Tibet's future in general, is one that can be resolved only by the Tibetans themselves.

The Chinese conquest of Tibet in 1950-51 and the history of Chinese rule of Tibet since that time has been a tragedy for Tibetan and world civilization and a crime of cultural genocide against the Tibetan people. However, the PRC has been unable to eradicate Tibetans' deep sense of national and cultural identity. Chinese repression has in many ways deepened Tibetans' nationalistic sentiments. Despite the horrors of the past, Tibet has survived with a distinct cultural, territorial and even political identity. However, Tibet is currently faced with a tragedy of an even greater magnitude than that of the past. If current Chinese policies continue, Tibet may finally be overwhelmed by Chinese colonists to the extent that Tibetan national territorial identity is lost, Tibetan culture is isolated and marginalized, and Tibetan political identity is overwhelmed as Tibetans become a small minority even in their own land. Tibetans may be engulfed in a sea of Chinese, with areas of Tibetan majority inhabitation continuing to exist only in high altitude and marginal areas. This second Chinese conquest of Tibet has the potential to finally eradicate Tibetan national and cultural identity except as it survives in isolated areas or among Tibetans in exile. The Chinese conquest and assimilation of Tibet would finally be completed and Tibet would survive only in memory, and even the memory would survive only in constant conflict and competition with Chinese distortions of Tibetan history.

Ultimately, the resolution of the Tibetan issue depends upon Chinese political developments, but Tibetans are not totally powerless, as has been demonstrated both by those within Tibet and those in exile. For Tibetan self-determination to remain an issue confronting China, Tibet must remain a distinct culture and nation. The Chinese are well aware of this fact and have since 1951 expended tremendous energy and resources in an attempt to eradicate all trace of Tibetan culture and Tibetan nationalism. Tibetans may have little control over Chinese immigration and other political issues, but only Tibetans themselves can preserve Tibetan culture, the most important contemporary aspect of which is Tibetan language. The Tibetan language, even more so than Buddhism, remains the most important national and cultural characteristic distinguishing Tibetans from Chinese. So long as China cannot regard Tibet as a territory devoid of nationality, Tibet remains a political issue for China conceivably resolvable at some time in the future in Tibet's favor.

Bibliography

Addy, Premen. *Tibet on the Imperial Chessboard*. New Delhi: Academic Publishers, 1984.

Adshead, S.A.M. *Province and Politics in Late Imperial China: Viceregional Government in Szechuan, 1898-1911*. London: Curzon Press, 1984.

Ahmad, Zahiruddin. *Sino-Tibetan Relations in the Seventeenth Century*. Serie Orientale Roma, XL. Roma: Instituto Italiano Per Il Medio Ed Estremo Oriente, 1970.

Aitchison, C.U. *A Collection of Treaties, Engagements and Sanads Relating to India and Neighboring Countries*, vol. XIV. Calcutta: Government of India, 1929.

Alexander, Yonah and Friedlander, Robert A., eds. *Self-Determination: National, Regional and Global Dimensions*. Boulder: Westview Press, 1980.

Alexandrowitz-Alexander, Charles Henry. "The Legal Position of Tibet." *American Journal of International Law*, 48 (1954).

Amnesty International. *People's Republic of China: Repression in Tibet 1987-1992*. New York: Amnesty International, 1992.

Anderson, Benedict. *Imagined Communities: Reflections on the Origin and Spread of Nationalism*. London: Verso, 1983.

Andrugtsang, Gompo Tashi. *Four Rivers, Six Ranges: A True Account of Khampa Resistance to Chinese in Tibet*. Dharamsala: Information and Publicity Office of H.H. The Dalai Lama, 1973.

Arendt, Hannah. *The Origins of Totalitarianism*. New York: Harcourt Brace, 1975.

Aris, Michael. *Bhutan*. London: Aris and Phillips, 1979.

_____, and Aung San Suu Kyi, eds. *Tibetan Studies in Honour of Hugh Richardson*. Proceedings of the International Seminar on Tibetan Studies: Oxford, 1979. Warminister England: Aris and Phillips, Ltd., 1979.

Asia Watch. *Human Rights in Tibet*. Washington: Asia Watch, 1988.

_____. *Evading Scrutiny: Violations of Human Rights After the Closing of Tibet*. Washington: Asia Watch, 1988.

_____. *Merciless Repression: Human Rights in Tibet*. Washington: Asia Watch, 1990.

_____. *Crackdown in Inner Mongolia*. Washington: Human Rights Watch, 1991.

_____. *Continuing Crackdown in Inner Mongolia*. Washington: Human Rights Watch, 1992.

_____, and Tibet Information Network. *Political Prisoners in Tibet*. Washington: Asia Watch, 1992.

_____. *Detained in China and Tibet*. Washington: Asia Watch, 1994.

_____, and Tibet Information Network. *Cutting Off the Serpent's Head: Tightening Control in Tibet, 1994-1995*. Washington: Human Rights Watch/Asia, 1996.

Avedon, John. *In Exile from the Land of Snows*. New York: Vintage Books, 1986.

Aziz, Barbara, and Matthew Kapstein, eds. *Soundings in Tibetan Civilization*. New Delhi: Manohar Publications, 1985.

Bajracharya, Manabajra, and Warren W. Smith. *Mythological History of the Nepal Valley from Svayambhu Purana*. Kathmandu: Avalok Publishers, 1978.

Bakus, Charles. *The Nan-chao Kingdom and T'ang China's Southwestern Frontier*. Cambridge: Cambridge University Press, 1981.

Bao Ruo-wang (Jean Pasqualini). *Prisoner of Mao*. New York: Penguin Books, 1987.

Barber, Noel. *From the Land of Lost Content: The Dalai Lama's Fight for Tibet*. London: Collins, 1969.

Barfield, Thomas. *The Perilous Frontier: Nomadic Empires and China*. Cambridge: Basil Blackwell, 1989.

Barnett, A. Doak. *Communist China: The Early Years, 1949-55*. New York: Praeger, 1968.

_____, ed. *Chinese Communist Politics in Action*. Seattle: University of Washington, 1969.

Barnett, Robert and Shirin Akiner, eds. *Resistance and Reform in Tibet*. Bloomington: Indiana University Press, 1994.

Barth, Fredrik. *Ethnic Groups and Boundaries*. Boston: Little, Brown and Co., 1969.

Bawden, C.R. *The Modern History of Mongolia*. London: Kegan Paul, 1968; 1989.

Beckwith, Christopher. "A Study of the Early Medieval Chinese, Latin, and Tibetan Historical Sources on Pre-Imperial Tibet." Ph.D. diss. Indiana University, 1977.

_____. *The Tibetan Empire in Central Asia: A History of the Struggle for Great Power among Tibetans, Turks, Arabs, and Chinese during the Early Middle Ages*. Princeton: Princeton University Press, 1987.

Bell, Sir Charles. *Tibet Past and Present*. Oxford: Clarendon Press, 1924.

_____. *Portrait of a Dalai Lama: The Life and Times of the Great Thirteenth*. London: William Collins, 1946; London: Wisdom Publications, 1987.

Bennet, Gordon. *Yundong: Mass Campaigns in Chinese Communist Leadership*. Berkeley: University of California, 1976.

Bennigsen, Alexandre A., and S. Enders Wimbush. *Muslim National Communism in the Soviet Union*. Chicago: University of Chicago Press, 1979.

Bianco, Lucien. *Origins of the Chinese Revolution, 1915-1949*. Stanford: Stanford University Press, 1971.

Bibo, Istvan. *The Paralysis of International Relations and the Remedies*. New York: John Wiley and Sons, 1976.

Bishop, Robert L. *Qi Lai! Mobilizing One Billion Chinese: The Chinese Communication System*. Ames: Iowa State University Press, 1989.

Black, Cyril E., et al. *The Modernization of Inner Asia*. Armonk, New York: M.E. Sharpe, 1991.

Bowie, Robert R., and John K. Fairbank, eds. *Communist China 1955-1959: Policy Documents and Analysis*. Cambridge: Harvard University Press, 1962.

The Boundary Question between China and Tibet: A Valuable Record of the Tripartite Conference between China, Britain and Tibet, Held in India, 1913-1914. Peking: 1940.

Bowles, Gordon. "Racial Origins of the Peoples of the Central Chinese-Tibetan Border." Ph.D. diss. Harvard University, 1935.

_____. *The People of Asia*. New York: Charles Scribner's Sons, 1977.

Brandt, Conrad; Schwartz, Benjamin; and Fairbank, John. *A Documentary History of Chinese Communism*. London: Allen and Unwin, 1952.

British Parliamentary Papers: Papers Relating to Tibet, Cd. 1920 (1904), vol. 67. London: His Majesty's Stationery Office, 1904.

British Parliamentary Papers: Further Papers Relating to Tibet, Cd. 2054 (1904), vol. 67. London: His Majesty's Stationery Office, 1904.

British Parliamentary Papers: Further Papers Relating to Tibet, Cd. 2370 (1905), vol. 58. London: His Majesty's Stationery Office, 1905.

British Parliamentary Papers: Further Papers Relating to Tibet, Cd. 5240 (1910), vol. 68. London: His Majesty's Stationery Office, 1910.

Buchheit, Lee C. *Secession: The Legitimacy of Self-Determination*. New Haven: Yale University Press, 1978.

Bushell, F.W. "The Early History of Tibet from Chinese Sources." *Journal of the Royal Asiatic Society*, n.s., 12 (1980).

Capotorti, Francesco. *Study on the Rights of Persons belonging to Ethnic, Religious and Linguistic Minorities*. New York: United Nations, 1979. U.N. Doc. E/CN.4/Sub2/384/Rev.1.

Carnahan, Sumner, and Lama Kunga Rinpoche, eds. *In the Presence of My Enemies: Memoirs of Tibetan Nobleman Tsipon Shuguba*. Santa Fe: Clear Light Publishers, 1995.

Carr, Edward Halett. *Nationalism and After*. MacMillan, 1968.

Carrasco, Pedro. *Land and Polity in Tibet*. Seattle: University of Washington Press, 1959.

Cassinelli, C.W., and Ekvall, Robert B. *A Tibetan Principality: The Political System of Sakya*. Ithaca: Cornell University Press, 1969.

Cell, Charles P. *Revolution at Work: Mobilization Campaigns in China*. New York: Academic Press, 1977.

Chakravarti, B. *A Cultural History of Bhutan*. Chittaranjan, West Bengal: Hilltop Publishers, 1979.

Chan, Anita; Rosen, Stanley; and Unger, Jonathan, eds.. *On Socialist Democracy and the Chinese Legal System: The Li Yizhe Debates*. New York: M.E. Sharpe Inc., 1985.

Chand, Attar. *Tibet: Past and Present: A Select Bibliography with Chronology of Historical Events: 1660-1981*. New Delhi: Sterling Publishers, 1982.

Chang, Gordon H. *Friends and Enemies: The United States, China and the Soviet Union, 1948-1972*. Stanford: Stanford University Press, 1990.

Chang, Jiunn Yih. "A Study of the Relationship Between the Mongol Yuan Dynasty and the Tibetan Sa-skya Sect." Ph.D. diss. Indiana University, 1984.

Chang, Kwang-chih. *The Archaeology of Ancient China*. New Haven: Yale University Press, 1977.

Chen, Lung-chu. "Self-Determination as a Human Right." in *Toward World Order and Human Dignity*. ed. M. Weisman and B. Weston. New York: Free Press, 1976.

Chen, Theodore H.E. *Thought Reform of the Chinese Intellectuals*. Hong Kong: Hong Kong University Press, 1960.

_____. *The Chinese Communist Regime: Documents and Commentary*. New York: Praeger, 1967.

Chiang, Kai-shek. *The Collected Wartime Messages of Generalissimo Chiang Kai-shek: 1937-1945*. comp. Chinese Ministry of Information. New York: John Day Co., 1946.

_____. *China's Destiny*. New York: Roy Publishers, 1947.

Choedon, Dhondub. *Life in the Red Flag People's Commune*. Dharamsala: Information Office of His Holiness the Dalai Lama, 1978.

Chou, En-lai. *Premier Chou En-lai's Letter to the Leaders of Asian and African Countries on the Sino-Indian Boundary Question (November 15, 1962)*. Peking: Foreign Languages Press, 1973.

_____. "Some Questions on Policy Towards Nationalities." *Beijing Review*, March 3, 1980.

Cohen, Roberta. "The People's Republic of China: The Human Rights Exception." *Human Rights Quarterly*, vol 9, no. (4 November 1987).

Connor, Walker. "Self-Determination: The New Phase." *World Politics* XX (October 1967).

_____. "Ethnic Nationalism as a Political Force." *World Affairs*, vol. 133, no. 2 (September 1970).

_____. "Nation-Building or Nation-Destroying?" *World Politics* XXIV (April 1972).

_____. "The Politics of Ethnonationalism." *Journal of International Affairs*. XXVII (1973).

_____. "A Nation is a Nation, is a State, is an Ethnic Group, is a.... *Ethnic and Racial Studies*. vol 1, no. 4 (October 1978).

_____. *The National Question in Marxist-Leninist Theory and Strategy*. Princeton, N.J.: Princeton University Press, 1984.

_____. *Ethnonationalism: The Quest for Understanding*. Princeton: Princeton University Press, 1994.

Concerning the Question of Tibet. Peking: Foreign Languages Press, 1960.

Creele, Herrlee G. *The Origins of Statecraft in China: The Western Chou Empire*. Chicago: University of Chicago Press, 1970.

Cristescu, Aureliu. *The Right to Self-Determination, Historical and Current Development on the Basis of United Nations Instruments*. New York: United Nations, 1981. U.N. Doc. E/CN.4/Sub.2/404/Rev.1.

Current Background. Hong Kong: United States Consulate.

Dalai Lama. *My Land and My People: Memoirs of the Dalai Lama of Tibet*. New York: McGraw Hill, 1962; New York: Potala, 1977.

_____. *The Collected Statements, Interviews and Articles of His Holiness the Dalai Lama*. Dharamsala: Information Office of His Holiness the Dalai Lama, 1982.

_____. *Freedom in Exile*. New York: Harper Collins, 1990.

Dardess, John W. *Conquerors and Confucians*. New York: Columbia University Press, 1973.

Das, Sarat Chandra. *Journey to Lhasa and Central Tibet*. Delhi: Cosmo Publications, 1902, 1988.

Davis, Horace B. *Nationalism and Socialism: Marxist and Labor Theories of Nationalism to 1917*. New York: Monthly Review Press, 1967.

_____. *Toward a Marxist Theory of Nationalism*. New York: Monthly Review Press, 1978.

Declaration on the Granting of Independence to Colonial Countries and Peoples. U.N.G.A. Res. 1514 (1960).

Declaration on Principles of International Law concerning Friendly Relations and Co-operation among States in accordance with the Charter of the United Nations. U.N.G.A. Res. 0605 (1970).

De Crespigny, Rafe. "The Ch'iang Barbarians and the Empire of Han: A Study in Frontier Policy." In *Papers on Far Eastern History*, The Australian National University, Department of Far Eastern History (1977).

_____. *Northern Frontier: The Policies and Strategy of the Later Han Empire*. Faculty of Asian Studies Monographs, n.s., no. 4. Canberra: Australian National University Faculty of Asian Studies, 1984.

Defying the Dragon: China and Human Rights in Tibet. London: Law Association for Asia and the Pacific Human Rights Standing Committee and Tibet Information Network, 1991.

Dikotter, Frank. *The Discourse of Race in Modern China*. Stanford: Stanford University Press, 1992.

Dirlik, Arif. *Revolution and History: Origins of Marxist Historiography in China, 1919-1937*. Berkeley: University of California, 1978.

_____. *The Origins of Chinese Communism*. Oxford: Oxford University Press, 1989.

Donnet, Pierre-Antoine. *Tibet: Survival in Question*. London: Zed Books, 1994.

Dreyer, June Tuefel. *China's Forty Millions: Minority Nationalities and National Integration in the People's Republic of China*. Cambridge: Harvard University Press, 1976.

Dung-dkar, blo-bzang phrim-las. *The Merging of Religious and Secular Rule in Tibet*. Beijing: Foreign Languages Press, 1991.

Durkheim, Emile. *The Elementary Forms of the Religious Life*, trans. Joseph Ward Swain. New York: George Allen and Unwin, Inc., 1915; New York: Free Press, 1965.

Eberhard, Wolfram. *Conquerors and Rulers: Social Forces in Medieval China*. Leiden: E.J. Brill, 1965.

_____. *China's Minorities: Yesterday and Today*. Belmont, California: Wadsworth, 1982.

_____. *A History of China*. 4th ed., rev. Berkeley: University of California Press, 1960; 1987.

Edwards, R. Randle; Henkin, Louis; and Nathan, Andrew J. *Human Rights in Contemporary China*. New York: Columbia University Press, 1986.

Eftimiades, Nicholas. *Chinese Intelligence Operations*. Maryland: Naval Institute Press, 1994.

Ekvall, Robert. *Cultural Relations on the Kansu-Tibetan Border*. Chicago: University of Chicago Press, 1939.

_____. *Religious Observances in Tibet*. Chicago: University of Chicago Press, 1964.

_____. *Fields on the Hoof: Nexus of Tibetan Nomadic Pastoralism*. Prospect Heights, Illinois: Waveland Press, 1968.

_____, and C.W. Cassinelli. *A Tibetan Principality: The Political System of Sa sKya*. Ithaca: Cornell University Press, 1969.

Eliade, Mircea. *Shamanism: Archaic Techniques of Ecstasy*. Princeton: Princeton University Press, 1972.

Ellul, Jacques. *Propaganda: The Formation of Men's Attitudes*. New York: Vintage Books, 1973.

Elvin, Mark. *The Pattern of the Chinese Past*. Stanford: Stanford University Press, 1973.

Emerson, Rupert. *From Empire to Nation*. Cambridge: Harvard University Press, 1960.

d'Encausse, Helene and Schram, Stuart R. *Marxism and Asia*. Penguin Press, 1969.

Epstein, Israel. *Tibet Transformed*. Beijing: New World Press, 1983.

Espiell, Hector Gros. *The Right to Self-Determination, Implementation of United Nations Resolutions*. New York: United Nations, 1980. U.N. Doc. E/CN.4/Sub.2/405/Rev.1.

Eudin, Xenia Joukoff and North, Robert C. *Soviet Russia and the East: 1920-1927*. Stanford University Press, 1964.

Facts About Tibet, 1961-1965. New Delhi: Bureau of His Holiness the Dalai Lama, 1966.

Fairbank, John K., ed. *The Chinese World Order*. Cambridge: Harvard University Press, 1968.

_____. *The Great Chinese Revolution: 1800-1985*. New York: Harper and Row, 1987.

_____, and Ssu-yu Teng. *China's Response to the West: A Documentary Survey, 1839-1923*. Cambridge: Harvard University Press, 1979.

Farquhar, David M. "Emperor as Bodhisattva." *Harvard Journal of Asiatic Studies*, 15.

Feuerwerker, Albert, ed. *History in Communist China*. Cambridge: MIT Press, 1968.

Fleming, Peter. *Bayonets to Lhasa*. Oxford: Oxford University Press, 1961, 1986.

Fletcher, Joseph. "Ch'ing Inner Asia." In *The Cambridge History of China: Late Ch'ing, 1800-1911*, vol 10, ed. John K. Fairbank. Cambridge: Cambridge University Press, 1978.

_____. "The Heyday of the Ch'ing Order in Mongolia, Sinkiang and Tibet." In *The Cambridge History of China: Late Ch'ing, 1800-1911*, vol. 10, ed. John K. Fairbank. Cambridge: Cambridge University Press, 1978.

Forbes, Ann. *Settlements of Hope: Tibetan Refugees in Nepal*. Cambridge: Cultural Survival, 1989.

_____, and Carole McGranahan. *Developing Tibet? A Survey of International Development Projects*. Cambridge: Cultural Survival, 1992.

Forbidden Freedoms: Beijing's Control of Religion in Tibet. Washington: International Campaign for Tibet, 1990.

Ford, Robert. *Wind Between the Worlds*. New York: David McKay, 1957; Berkeley: Snow Lion Graphics, 1987.

Foreign Relations of the United States, 1942, China. Washington: Government Printing Office, 1956.

Foreign Relations of the United States, 1943, China. Washington: Government Printing Office, 1957.

Foreign Relations of the United States, 1947, vol. VII: The Far East: China. Washington: Government Printing Office, 1972.

Foreign Relations of the United States, 1948, vol. VII: The Far East: China. Washington: Government Printing Office, 1973.

Foreign Relations of the United States, 1949, vol. IX: The Far East: China. Washington: Government Printing Office, 1974.

Foreign Relations of the United States, 1950, vol. VI: East Asia and the Pacific. Washington: Government Printing Office, 1976.

Foreign Relations of the United States, 1951, vol. VII: Korea and China. Washington: Government Printing Office, 1983.

Foreign Relations of the United States, 1952-1954, vol. XIV: China and Japan. Washington: Government Printing Office, 1985.

Franke, Herbert. "Tibetans in Yuan China." In *China Under Mongol Rule*, ed. John D. Langlois, Jr. Princeton: Princeton University Press, 1981.

_____. "The Forest Peoples of Manchuria: Kitans and Jurchens," In *The Cambridge History of Early Inner Asia*, ed. Denis Sinor. Cambridge: Cambridge University Press, 1990.

French, Rebecca Redwood. *The Golden Yoke: The Legal Cosmology of Buddhist Tibet*. Ithaca: Cornell University Press, 1995.

Friters, Gerard M. *Outer Mongolia and Its International Position*. Baltimore: Johns Hopkins University Press, 1949.

From Liberation to Liberalization: Views on "Liberalized" Tibet. Dharamsala: Information Office of His Holiness the Dalai Lama, 1982.

Fu, Lo-shu. *A Documentary Chronicle of Sino-Western Relations: 1644-1820*. The Association for Asian Studies: Monographs and Papers, XXII, ed. Delmer M. Brown. Tucson: University of Arizona Press, 1966.

Gashi, Tsering Dorje. *New Tibet: Memoirs of a Graduate of the Peking Institute of National Minorities*. Dharamsala: Information Office of His Holiness the Dalai Lama, 1980.

Gellner, Ernest. *Nations and Nationalism*. Ithaca: Cornell University Press, 1983.

A General Survey of Tibet. Beijing: New World Press, 1988.

Gernet, Jacques. *A History of Chinese Civilization*. Cambridge: Cambridge University Press, 1985.

Ghosh, Suchita. *Tibet in Sino-Indian Relations, 1899-1914*. New Delhi: Sterling Publishers, 1977.

Ginsburgs, George, and Michael Mathos. *Communist China and Tibet: The First Dozen Years*. The Hague: Martinus Nijhoff, 1964.

Gladney, Dru. *Muslim Chinese: Ethnic Nationalism in the People's Republic*. Cambridge: Harvard University Press, 1991.

Glazer, Nathan and Daniel Moynihan, eds. *Ethnicity: Theory and Experience.* Cambridge: Harvard University Press, 1975.

Glimpses of Tibet Today. Dharamsala: Information Office of His Holiness the Dalai Lama, 1978.

Goldman, Merle. *Sowing the Seeds of Democracy in China: Political Reform in the Deng Xiaoping Era.* Cambridge: Harvard University Press, 1994.

Goldstein, Melvyn. "An Anthropological Study of the Tibetan Political System." Ph.D. diss. University of Washington, 1968.

————. *A History of Modern Tibet, 1913-1951.* Berkeley: University of California Press, 1989.

————. "Tibet, China and the United States: Reflections on the Tibet Question." *The Atlantic Council,* April 1995.

————, and Beall, Cynthia M. "The Impact of China's Reform Policy on the Nomads of Western Tibet." *Asian Survey,* vol. XXIX, no. 6 (June 1989).

Gottleib, Gideon. *Nation Against State: A New Approach to Ethnic Conflicts and the Decline of Sovereignty.* New York: Council on Foreign Relations Press, 1993.

Government Resolutions and International Documents on Tibet, 2nd ed. Dharamsala: Office of Information and International Relations, Central Tibetan Secretariat, 1989.

The Great Cultural Revolution in China. Hong Kong: Asia Research Centre, 1967.

Grousset, Rene. *The Empire of the Steppes: A History of Central Asia,* trans. Naomi Walford. New Brunswick, New Jersey: Rutgers University Press, 1970.

Grunfeld, A. Tom. *The Making of Modern Tibet.* London: Zed Books, 1987.

Guibaut, A. and Oliver, G. *Anthropologie des Tibetans Orientaux.* Paris: 1940.

Guillermaz, Jacques. *The Chinese Communist Party in Power, 1949-1976.* Boulder: Westview, 1976.

Haarh, Erik. *The Yar-Lun Dynasty.* Copenhagen: G.E.C. GAD's FORLAG, 1969.

Hannum, Hurst. *Autonomy, Sovereignty, and Self-Determination.* Philadelphia: University of Pennsylvania Press, 1990.

————. "Rethinking Self-Determination." *Virginia Journal of International Law,* vol. 34, no. 1 (Fall, 1993).

————, and Lillich, R.B. "The Concept of Autonomy in International Law." *American Journal of International Law,* 74 (1980):

Harrell, Stevan, ed. *Cultural Encounters on China's Ethnic Frontiers.* Seattle: University of Washington Press, 1995.

Harrer, Heinrich. *Seven Years in Tibet.* London: Rupert Hart-Davis, 1953.

Hoffman, Helmut. "Early and Medieval Tibet." In *The Cambridge History of Early Inner Asia,* ed. Denis Sinor. Cambridge: Cambridge University Press. 1990.

Hollander, Paul. *Political Pilgrims: Travels of Western Intellectuals to the Soviet Union, China and Cuba.* New York: Harper Colophon, 1983.

Hopkirk, Peter. *Setting the East Ablaze: Lenin's Dream of an Empire in Asia.* New York: Norton, 1984.

Horowitz, Donald L. *Ethnic Groups in Conflict.* Berkeley: University of California Press, 1985.

Howells, W.W. "Origins of the Chinese People: Interpretations of the Recent Evidence." In *The Origins of Chinese Civilization,* ed. David N. Keightley. Berkeley: University of California Press, 1983.

Hsiung, James C., ed. *Human Rights in East Asia*. New York: Paragon House Publishers, 1985.

Hsu, Leonard S. *Sun Yat-sen: His Political and Social Ideals*. Los Angeles: University of Southern California Press, 1933.

Indian Committee for Cultural Freedom. *Tibet Fights for Freedom*. New Delhi: Orient Longmans, 1960.

International Commission of Jurists. *The Question of Tibet and the Rule of Law*. Geneva: ICJ, 1959.

_____. *Tibet and the Chinese People's Republic: A Report to the International Commission of Jurists by its Legal Inquiry Committee on Tibet*. Geneva: ICJ, 1960.

International Committee of Lawyers for Tibet. *Resolving Claims of Self-Determination: A Proposal for Integrating Principles of International Law with Specific Application to the Tibetan People*. 29 December 1992.

International Covenant on Civil and Political Rights. U.N. Doc. A/6316 (1966).

International Covenant on Economic, Social and Cultural Rights. U.N. Doc. A/6319 (1966).

Isaacs, Harold R. *The Tragedy of the Chinese Revolution*. Stanford: Stanford University Press, 1951.

Jagchid, Sechin, and Van Jay Symons. *Peace, War, and Trade Along the Great Wall: Nomadic-Chinese Interaction through Two Millennia*. Bloomington: Indiana University Press, 1989.

Jan, George P., ed. *Government of Communist China*. San Francisco: Chandler, 1966.

Jenner, W.J.F. *The Tyranny of History: The Roots of China's Crisis*. New York: Penguin Books, 1992.

Jettmar, Karl. "The Origins of Chinese Civilization: Soviet Views." In *The Origins of Chinese Civilization*, ed. David N. Keightley. Berkeley: University of California Press, 1983.

Johnson, Chalmers A. *Peasant Nationalism and Communist Power: The Emergence of Revolutionary China 1937-1945*. Stanford: Stanford University Press, 1962.

Karan, Pradyumna P. *The Changing Face of Tibet: The Impact of Chinese Communist Ideology on the Landscape*. Kentucky: University of Kentucky, 1976.

Karmay, Samten. "The Question of National Identity in Tibet." Paper presented at the Conference on Tibet, School of Oriental and African Studies, University of London, March 1990.

Keightley, David N., ed. *The Origins of Chinese Civilization*. Berkeley: University of California Press, 1983.

Khazanov, A. M. *Nomads and the Outside World*. Cambridge: Cambridge University Press, 1984.

Kim, Samuel S. *China, the United Nations and World Order*. Princeton: Princeton University Press, 1979.

Kirkland, J. Russell. "The Spirit of the Mountain: Myth and State in Pre-Buddhist Tibet." *History of Religions*, vol. 21, no. 3 (February 1982).

Klieger, P. Christiaan. "Accomplishing Tibetan Identity: The Constitution of a National Consciousness." Ph.D. Diss. University of Hawaii, 1989.

_____. *Tibetan Nationalism: The Role of Patronage in the Accomplishment of a National Identity*. Berkeley: Folklore Institute, 1992.

Kraus, Richard Curt. *Class Conflict in Chinese Socialism*. New York: Columbia University Press, 1981.

Ladhany, Laszlo. *The Communist Party of China and Marxism, 1921-1985*. Stanford: Hoover Institution Press, 1988.

Lamb, Alastair. *British India and Tibet: 1766-1910*, 2nd ed., rev. London: Routledge and Kegan Paul, 1960, 1986.

_____ *The McMahon Line: A Study in the Relations between India, China and Tibet, 1904 to 1914*, 2 vols. London: Routledge and Kegan Paul; Toronto: University of Toronto Press, 1966.

_____ *Tibet, China and India 1914-1950*. Hertingfordbury: Roxford Books, 1989.

Langlois, John D. Jr., ed. *China Under Mongol Rule*. Princeton: Princeton University Press, 1981.

Lattimore, Owen. *Inner Asian Frontiers of China*. The American Geographical Society, 1940; Oxford: Oxford University Press, 1988.

_____. *Studies in Frontier History, Collected Papers 1928-1958*. London: Oxford University Press, 1962.

Lee, Fu-hsiang. "The Turkic-Moslem Problem in Sinkiang: A Case Study of the Chinese Communists' Nationality Policy." Ph.D. diss. Rutgers University, 1973.

Lee, Hong Yung. *The Politics of the Chinese Cultural Revolution*. Berkeley: University of California Press, 1978

The Legal Status of Tibet: Three Studies by Leading Jurists. Dharamsala: Office of Information and International Relations, 1989.

Lenin, V.I. *On Proletarian Internationalism*. Moscow: Progress Publishers, 1976.

_____. "Imperialism, The Highest Stage of Capitalism." *Selected Works*, vol. I. Moscow: Progress Publishers, 1977.

_____. "Preliminary Draft Thesis on the National and the Colonial Questions." *Selected Works*, vol 3. Moscow: Progress Publishers, 1977.

_____. "Report of the Commission on the National and the Colonial Questions." *Selected Works*, vol 3. Moscow: Progress Publishers, 1977.

_____. "The Right of Nations to Self-Determination." *Selected Works*, vol. 1. Moscow: Progress Publishers, 1977.

_____. "Two Tactics of Social-Democracy in the Democratic Revolution." *Selected Works*, vol 1. Moscow: Progress Publishers, 1977.

Levin, M.G. *Ethnic Origins of the Peoples of Northeastern Asia*. Toronto: University of Toronto Press, 1963.

Leys, Simon. *Chinese Shadows*. New York: Penguin Books, 1973.

_____. *The Chairman's New Clothes*. London: Allison and Busby, 1977.

_____. *The Burning Forest: Essays on Chinese Culture and Politics*. New York: Henry Holt and Company, 1987.

Li, Chi. *The Formation of the Chinese People*. Cambridge: Cambridge University Press, 1928.

Li, Tieh-tseng. "The Legal Position of Tibet." *American Journal of International Law*, 50 (1956).

_____. *Tibet: Today and Yesterday*. New York: Bookman Associates, 1960.

Lifton, Robert Jay. *Revolutionary Immortality: Mao Tse-tung and the Chinese Cultural Revolution*. New York: Norton, 1976.

Lind, Michael. "In Defense of Liberal Nationalism." *Foreign Affairs*, vol. 73, no. 3 (May/June 1994).

Liu, William T., ed. *Chinese Society Under Communism: A Reader*. New York: John Wiley, 1967.

Liu, Alan P.L. *The Use of Traditional Media for Modernization in Communist China*. Cambridge: Massachusetts Institute of Technology, 1965.

_____. *Communications and National Integration in Communist China*. Berkeley: University of California Press, 1971.

Lijphart, Arend. *Democracy in Plural Societies: A Comparative Exploration*. New Haven: Yale University Press, 1977.

Liu, Shao-ch'i. "Political Report of the Central Committee of the Communist Party of China," 15 September 1956. In *Communist China 1955-1959: Policy Documents with Analysis*, eds. Robert R. Bowie and John K. Fairbank. Cambridge: Harvard University Press, 1962.

Liu, Tungsheng and Han, Jingtai. "The Role of Qinghai-Xizang Plateau Uplifting in the Shift of Monsoon Patterns over China." *Proceedings of Sino-Japanese Joint Scientific Symposium on the Tibetan Plateau*, Vol 1.

Liu, William T., ed. *Chinese Society under Communism: A Reader*. New York: John Wiley and Sons, 1967.

Louis, Victor. *The Coming Decline of the Chinese Empire*. New York: Times Books, 1979.

Low, Alfred D. *Lenin on the Question of Nationality*, New York: Bookman Associates, 1958.

Lowe, Donald M. *The Function of "China" in Marx, Lenin, and Mao*. Berkeley: University of California Press, 1966.

Luc, Kwanten. "Tibetan-Mongol Relations During the Yuan Dynasty, 1207-1368." Ph.D. diss. University of South Carolina, 1972.

_____. *Imperial Nomads: A History of Central Asia, 500-1500*. Philadelphia: University of Pennsylvania Press, 1979.

Ma, Yin, ed. *Questions and Answers about China's National Minorities*. Beijing: New World Press, 1985.

_____, ed. *China's Minority Nationalities*. Beijing: Foreign Languages Press, 1989.

MacFarquhar, Roderick. *The Origins of the Cultural Revolution: Contradictions Among the People 1956-1957*. New York: Columbia University Press, 1974.

_____. *The Origins of the Cultural Revolution: The Great Leap Forward 1958-1960*. New York: Columbia University Press, 1983.

_____, Timothy Cheek and Eugene Wu, eds. *The Secret Speeches of Chairman Mao*. Cambridge: Harvard University Press, 1989.

Mao, Tse-tung. "On the Correct Handling of Contradictions Among the People." (27 February 1957). In *Communist China 1955-1959: Policy Documents and Analysis*, eds. Robert R. Bowie and John K. Fairbank. Cambridge: Harvard University Press, 1962.

_____. "The Question of Agricultural Cooperation." In *Communist China 1955-1959: Policy Documents with Analysis*, eds. Robert R. Bowie and John K. Fairbank. Cambridge: Harvard University Press, 1962.

_____. *Talks at the Yenan Forum on Literature and Art.* Peking: Foreign
Languages Press, 1967.
_____. "On Contradiction." In *Selected Readings from the Works of Chairman Mao.*
Peking: Foreign Languages Press, 1971.
_____. "On the Policies of Our Work in Tibet." *Selected Works,* vol. 5. Peking:
Foreign Languages Press, 1977.
_____. *On the Ten Major Relationships.* Peking: Foreign Languages Press, 1977.
_____. "On the Correct Handling of Contradictions Among the People."
(Speaking Notes) 27 February 1957. In *The Secret Speeches of Chairman Mao,* eds.
Roderick MacFarquhar, Timothy Cheek and Eugene Wu. Cambridge: Harvard
University Press, 1989.
Maxwell, Neville. *India's China War.* New York: Anchor Books, 1972.
Maybury-Lewis, David, ed. *The Prospects for Plural Societies.* Washington, D.C.:
The American Ethnological Society, 1984.
McMillen, Donald H. *Chinese Communist Power and Policy in Sinkiang, 1949-1977.*
Boulder: Westview Press, 1979.
Mehra, Parshotam. *Tibetan Polity, 1904-37: The Conflict Between the 13th Dalai Lama
and the 9th Panchen.* Wiesbaden: Otto Harrassowitz, 1976.
_____. *The Northeastern Frontier: A Documentary Study of the Internecine Rivalry
between India, Tibet and China.* Delhi: Oxford University Press, 1979.
Meisner, Maurice. *Li Ta-chao and the Origins of Chinese Marxism.* New York:
Athenum, 1974.
_____. *Mao's China and After: A History of the People's Republic.* New York: The
Free Press, 1986.
Michael, Franz. *Rule by Incarnation.* Boulder: Westview Press, 1983.
_____, Yuan-li Wu, et. al. *Human Rights in the People's Republic of China.*
Boulder: Westview Press, 1988.
Mill, John Stuart. *Utilitarianism, Liberty, and Representative Government.* New York:
E.P. Dutton Co., Inc., 1951.
Milosz, Czeslaw. *The Captive Mind.* New York: Vintage, 1981.
Min, Tu-ki. *National Polity and Local Power: The Transformation of Late Imperial
China.* Cambridge: Harvard University Press, 1989.
Mole, Gabriella. *The T'u-Yu-Hun from the Northern Wei to the Time of the Five
Dynasties.* Roma: Instituto Italiano per il Medio ed Estremo Oriente, 1970.
Moore, Charles A., ed. *The Chinese Mind: Essentials of Chinese Philosophy and
Culture.* Honolulu: University of Hawaii Press, 1967.
Moseley, George, trans., and ed. *The Party and the National Question in China.*
Cambridge: Massachusetts Institute of Technology Press, 1966.
_____. *A Sino-Soviet Cultural Frontier: The Ili Kazakh Autonomous Chou.*
Cambridge: Harvard University Press, 1966.
_____. *The Consolidation of the South China Frontier.* Berkeley: University of
California Press, 1973.
Moynihan, Daniel P., and Nathan Glazer, eds.. *Ethnicity: Theory and Experience.*
Cambridge: Harvard University Press, 1975.
Mullik, B.N. *My Years with Nehru: The Chinese Betrayal.* New Delhi: Allied
Publishers, 1971.

The Myth of Tibetan Autonomy: A Legal Analysis of the Status of Tibet. Washington: International Campaign for Tibet and International Human Rights Law Group, 1994.

Narain, A.K. *On the First Indo-Europeans: The Tokharian-Yuezhi and their Chinese Homeland.* Bloomington: Indiana University Press, 1987.

_____. "Indo-Europeans in Inner Asia," in *The Cambridge History of Early Inner Asia*, ed. Denis Sinor. Cambridge: Cambridge University Press, 1990.

Nathan, Andrew J. *Chinese Democracy.* Berkeley: University of California Press, 1985.

Nebesky-Wojkowitz, Rene. *Oracles and Demons of Tibet.* Netherlands: Mouton and Company, 1956.

New Majority: Chinese Population Transfer into Tibet. London: Tibet Support Group UK, 1995.

Ngapo, Jigme. "Behind the Unrest in Tibet." *China Spring*, vol. 2, no. 1 (January/February 1988).

Norbu, Dawa. *Marxism, Nationalism and Revolution: The Rise of Neo-Nationalism in Communist Countries.* Ph.D diss. University of California, Berkeley, 1982.

_____. "An Analysis of Sino-Tibetan Relationships, 1245-1911." In *Soundings in Tibetan Civilization*, eds. Aziz and Kapstein. New Delhi: Manohar Publications, 1985.

_____. *Red Star Over Tibet.* New York: Envoy Press, 1987.

_____. "Changes in Tibetan Economy, 1959-76." *China Report*, 24:3 (1988).

_____. "The Europeanization of Sino-Tibetan Relations, 1775-1907: The Genesis of Chinese `Suzerainty' and Tibetan `Autonomy.'" *Tibet Journal*, vol. XV, no. 4 (1990).

_____. "China's Dialogue with the Dalai Lama 1978-90: Prenegotiation Stage or Dead End?" *Pacific Affairs*, vol. 64, no. 3 (Fall 1991).

Norbu, Jamyang. *Warriors of Tibet.* London: Wisdom Publications, 1986.

_____. *Illusion and Reality: Essays on the Tibetan and Chinese Political Scene From 1978 to 1989.* Dharamsala: Tibetan Youth Congress, 1989.

Norbu, Namkhai. *Drung, Deu and Bon: Narrations, Symbolic Languages and the Bon Tradition in Ancient Tibet.* Dharamsala: Library of Tibetan Works and Archives, 1995.

Norbu, Thupten Jigme (Taktser Rimpoche). *Tibet is My Country.* London: Wisdom Publications, 1986.

North, Robert C., *Moscow and Chinese Communists*, Stanford: Penguin Press, 1969.

Ogden, Suzanne, et al., eds. *China's Search for Democracy: The Student and the Mass Movement of 1989.* Armonk, New York: M.E. Sharpe, 1992.

Paljor, Kunsang. *Tibet the Undying Flame.* Dharamsala: Information and Publicity Office of His Holiness the Dalai Lama, 1977.

The Panchen Lama Speaks: Text of the Panchen Lama's Address to the TAR Standing Committee Meeting of the National People's Congress held in Peking on 28 March 1987. Dharamsala: Department of Information and International Relations, Central Tibetan Administration of HH the Dalai Lama, 1991.

Patt, David. *A Strange Liberation: Tibetan Lives in Chinese Hands.* Ithaca: Snow Lion, 1992.

Patterson, George. *Tibet in Revolt.* London: Faber and Faber, 1960.

_____. *Peking Versus Delhi*. New York: Frederick A. Praeger, 1963.

_____. *Requiem for Tibet*. London: Aurum Press, 1990.

Peissel, Michel. *Cavaliers of Kham: The Secret War in Tibet*. London: Heineman, 1972.

Peiros, Ilya. "The Linguistic Situation in Southeast Asia." In *Explorations in Language Macrofamilies*, ed. Vitaly Shevoroshkin. Bochum: Universitatsverlag Dr. Norbert Brockmeyer, 1989.

Petech, Luciano. *China and Tibet in the Early XVIIIth Century*. Leiden: E.J. Brill, 1972.

_____. "Tibetan Relations with Sung China and with the Mongols." In *China Among Equals*, ed. Morris Rossabi. Berkeley: University of California Press, 1983.

Policy Towards Nationalities of the People's Republic of China. Peking: Foreign Languages Press, 1953.

Political Imprisonment in the People's Republic of China. London: Amnesty International, 1978.

Prusek, Jaroslav. *Chinese Statelets and the Northern Barbarians in the Period 1400-300 B.C.* New York: Humanities Press, 1971.

Pulleyblank, E.G. "Chinese and Indo-Europeans." *Journal of the Royal Asiatic Society* (1966).

_____. "The Chinese and their Neighbors in Prehistoric and Early Historical Times." In *The Origins of Chinese Civilization*, ed. David N. Keightley. Berkeley: University of California Press, 1983.

Pye, Lucian W.. *Spirit of Chinese Politics*. Cambridge: Harvard University Press, 1968.

_____. *Asian Power and Politics*. Cambridge: Harvard University Press, 1985.

Qu, Qingshan. "On the Funeral Reform in Tibet in 1793." *Tibet Studies*, vol. 2, no. 2 (1990).

100 Questions About Tibet. Beijing: *Beijing Review*, 1989.

Ra'anan, Uri. "Ethnic Conflict: Toward a New Typology." *Ethnic and Racial Studies*, vol. 1, no. 4 (October 1978).

Radin, Paul. *Primitive Religion*. Viking Press, 1937; New York: Dover Publications, Inc., 1957.

Ren, Mei'e; Yang, Renzhang and Bao, Haosheng, eds. *An Outline of China's Physical Geography*. Beijing: Foreign Languages Press, 1985.

Ren, Shumin. "The Military Strength of the Tubo Kingdom." *Tibet Studies*, vol. 2, no. 1 (1991).

Richardson, H.E. *Tibetan Precis*. Calcutta: Government of India, 1945.

_____. "The rKong-po Inscription." *Journal of Royal Asiatic Society*, 1972.

_____. "Ministers of the Tibetan Kingdom." *Tibet Journal*, vol. II, no. 1 (1977).

_____. *Tibet and Its History*, rev. 2nd ed. Boston and London: Shambhala, 1984.

_____, and David Snellgrove. *A Cultural History of Tibet*. Boulder: Prajna Press, 1980.

Rinbur Tulku. *The Search for Jowo Mikyoe Dorje*. Dharamsala: Office of Information and International Relations, Central Tibetan Secretariat, 1988.

Rockhill, William Woodville. "Dalai Lamas of Lhasa and Their Relations with The

Manchu Emperors of China: 1644-1908." *Toung Pao*, XI (1910).

_____. *The Land of the Lamas*. New Delhi: Asian Educational Services, 1988.

Roerich, J.N. *The Animal Style Among the Nomad Tribes of Northern Tibet*. Prague: 1930.

_____. "The Epic of King Kesar of Ling." Journal Royal Asiatic Society of Bengal, VIII (1942).

Rona Tas, A. "Social Terms in the List of Grants of the Tibetan Tun-Huang Chronicle." *Acta Orientalia*, no. 1 (1982).

Ronen, Dov. *The Quest for Self-Determination*. New Haven: Yale University Press, 1979.

Rosenstock, Robert. "The Declaration of Principles of International Law Concerning Friendly Relations: A Survey." *American Journal of International Law*, vol. 65 (1971).

Rossabi, Morris. *China and Inner Asia: From 1368 to the Present Day*. New York: Pica Press, 1975.

_____, ed. *China Among Equals*. Berkeley: University of California Press, 1983.

_____. *Khubilai Khan: His Life and Times*. Berkeley: University of California Press, 1988.

Rozman, Gilbert, ed. *The Modernization of China*. New York: The Free Press, 1981.

_____. *A Mirror for Socialism: Soviet Criticisms of China*. Princeton: Princeton University Press, 1985.

Rubin, Alfred P. "The Position of Tibet in International Law." *The China Quarterly* (July-September 1968).

Said, Edward W. *Culture and Imperialism*. New York: Vintage Books, 1993.

Samuel, Geoffrey. "Early Buddhism in Tibet." In *Soundings in Tibetan Civilization*, eds. Aziz and Kapstein. New Delhi: Manohar Publications, 1985.

_____. *Civilized Shamans: Buddhism in Tibetan Societies*. Washington: Smithsonian Institution Press, 1993.

Schein, Edgar H. *Coercive Persuasion: A Socio-psychological Analysis of the "Brainwashing" of American Civilian Prisoners by the Chinese Communists*. New York: Norton, 1961.

Schram, Louis M.J. "The Mongours of the Kansu-Tibetan Frontier." *Transactions of the American Philosophical Society*, n.s., 51 (1961).

Schrecker, John E. *The Chinese Revolution in Historical Perspective*. New York: Praeger, 1991.

Schurman, Franz. *Ideology and Organization in Communist China*. Berkeley: University of California Press, 1968.

Schwartz, Benjamin. *Chinese Communism and the Rise of Mao*. Cambridge: Harvard University Press, 1979.

Schwartz, Henry, ed. *Chinese Policies Towards Minorities: An Essay and Documents*. Bellingham, Washington: Western Washington State College, 1971.

Schwartz, Ronald D. "Reform and Repression in Tibet." *Telos* (Summer 1989).

_____. "The Anti-Splittist Campaign and the Development of Tibetan Political Consciousness." Paper presented at conference on Tibet, School of Oriental and African Studies, University of London. (March 1990).

_____. *Circle of Protest: Political Ritual in the Tibetan Uprising*. New York:

Columbia University Press, 1994.

Selden, Mark. "Cooperation and Conflict: Cooperative and Collective Formation in China's Countryside." In *The Transition to Socialism in China.* eds. Mark Selden and Victor Lippit. Armonk, New York: M.E. Sharpe, Inc., 1982.

_____, and Victor Lippit, eds. *The Transition to Socialism in China.* Armonk, New York: M.E. Sharpe, Inc., 1982.

Sen, Chanakya, comp. and ed. *Tibet Disappears: A Documentary History of Tibet's International Status, the Great Rebellion and Its Aftermath.* New Delhi: Asia Publishing House, 1960.

Serruys, Henry. "The Mongols of Kansu During the Ming." *Melanges Chinois et Bouddhiques,* vol. 10. Bruxelles: l'Institute Belge des Hautes Etudes Chinnoises (1955).

Seton-Watson, Hugh. *Nations and States: An Enquiry into the Origins of Nations and the Politics of Nationalism.* Boulder: Westview Press, 1977.

Shakabpa, W.D. *Tibet: A Political History.* New York: Potala Publications, 1984.

Sharlho, Tseten Wangchuk. "China's Reforms in Tibet: Issues and Dilemmas." *The Journal of Contemporary China,* vol. 1, no. 1 (Fall 1992).

Sharma, Swarn Lata. *Tibet: Self Determination in Politics Among Nations.* New Delhi: Criterion Publications, 1988.

Sinor, Denis, ed. *The Cambridge History of Early Inner Asia.* Cambridge: Cambridge University Press, 1990.

Smil, Vaclav. *The Bad Earth: Environmental Degradation in China.* Armonk, New York: M.E. Sharpe, 1984.

_____. *China's Environmental Crisis: An Inquiry into the Limits of National Development.* Armonk, New York: M.E. Sharpe, 1993.

Smith, Anthony D. *Theories of Nationalism.* London: Duckworth, 1971.

_____. *The Ethnic Origin of Nations.* Oxford: Basil Blackwell, 1986.

Smith, Warren W. "Tibet: An Inside View." *Tibetan Review,* 1983.

_____. "Tibet Transformed." *Tibetan Review,* 1983.

_____. "The Survival of Tibetan Culture." *Cultural Survival Quarterly,* 1986.

_____. "The Ideological Basis of China's Tibet Policy." *Tibetan Review,* 1988.

_____, ed. *China's Tibet: Chinese Press Articles and Policy Statements on Tibet, 1950-1989.* Cambridge: Cultural Survival, 1989.

_____. "China's Tibetan Dilemma." *Fletcher Forum,* 1989.

_____. "Sino-Tibetan Dialogue." *Tibetan Review,* 1992.

_____. "The Socialist Transformation of Tibet." In *Forty Years on Tibet: 1950-1990, School of Oriental and African Studies, University of London Conference on Tibet.* Bloomington: University of Indiana Press, 1993.

_____, and Manabajra Bajracharya. *Mythological History of Nepal Valley from Svayambhu Purana.* Kathmandu: Avalok Publishers, 1977.

Snellgrove, David. *Indo-Tibetan Buddhism.* Boston: Shambhala, 1987.

_____, and Hugh Richardson. *A Cultural History of Tibet.* Boulder: Prajna Press, 1974.

Snelling, John. *Buddhism in Russia: The Story of Agvan Dorzhiev, Lhasa's Emissary to the Tsar.* Rockport, Massachusetts: Element, 1993.

Snow, Edgar. *Red Star Over China.* New York: Grove Press, 1973.

Solomon, Richard H. *Mao's Revolution and the Chinese Political Culture*. Berkeley: University of California Press, 1971.

Sperling, Elliot. "The Chinese Venture in Kham, 1904-11, and the Role of Chao Erh-feng." *Tibet Journal*, vol. 1, no. 2 (1976).

_____. "The 5th Karma-pa and Some Aspects of the Relationship between Tibet and the Early Ming." In *Tibetan Studies in Honour of Hugh Richardson*, eds. Aris and Suu Kyi. Warminster England: Aris and Phillips, Ltd., 1979.

_____. "Early Ming Policy Toward Tibet." Ph.D. diss. Indiana University, 1983.

Stalin, Joseph, *Marxism and the National-Colonial Question*. Moscow: Proletarian Publishers, 1975.

Stein, R.A. "Mi-Nag et Si-Hia," *Bulletin Ecole Francaise d'Extreme Orient XLIV*. 1951.

_____. *Les Tribus Anciennes des Marches Sino-Tibetaines*. Paris: Imprimerie Nationale, 1959.

_____. *Tibetan Civilization*, trans. J.E. Stapelton Driver. London: Faber and Faber, 1972.

_____. "Introduction to the Gesar Epic." *Tibet Journal*, VI, no. 1 (1981).

_____. "Les K'iang des Marches Sino-Tibetaines."

Steinhardt, Ralph G. "International Law and Self-Determination." Atlantic Council Occasional Paper, November 1994.

Strong, Anna Louise. *When Serfs Stood Up in Tibet*. Peking: New World Press, 1960.

Survey of China Mainland Press. Hong Kong: United States Consulate.

Suzuki, Chusei. "China's Relations with Inner Asia." In *The Chinese World Order*, ed. John K. Fairbank. Cambridge: Harvard University Press, 1968.

Suzuki, Eisuke. "Self-Determination and World Public Order." *Virginia Journal of International Law*. vol. 16:4 (1976).

Szerb, Janos. "Glosses on the Oervre of Bla-ma Phags-pa: On the Activity of Sa-skya Pandita." In *Tibetan Studies in Honour of Hugh Richardson*, eds. Aris and Suu Kyi. Warminster England: Aris and Phillips, 1979.

Taaffe, Robert N.. "The Geographic Setting." In *The Cambridge History of Early Inner Asia*, ed. Denis Sinor. Cambridge: Cambridge University Press, 1990.

Tang, Peter S.H. *Russian and Soviet Policy in Manchuria and Outer Mongolia, 1911-1931*. Durham: Duke University Press, 1959.

Teichman, Eric. *Travels of a Consular Officer in Eastern Tibet*. Cambridge: Cambridge University Press, 1922.

Teng, Hsiao-p'ing. "Report on the Rectification Campaign." 23 September 1957. In *Communist China 1955-1959: Policy Documents with Analysis*, eds. Robert R Bowie and John K. Fairbank. Cambridge: Harvard University Press, 1962.

Tewari, Udai Narain. *Resurgent Tibet: A Cause for Nonaligned Movement*. New Delhi: Selectbook, 1983.

Thierry, Francois. "Empire and Minority in China." In *Minority Peoples in the Age of Nation-States*, ed. Gerard Chaliand, 1-11. London: Pluto Press, 1989.

Thomas, F.W. *Tibetan Literary Texts and Documents Concerning Chinese Turkestan*, vol. I. London: Royal Asiatic Society, 1935.

_____. *Nam: An Ancient Language of the Sino-Tibetan Borderland*. Publications of the Philological Society, XIV. London: Oxford University Press, 1948.

_____. *Ancient Folk Literature from North-Eastern Tibet*. Abhandlungen der

Deutschen Akademie der Wissenschaften zu Berlin. Berlin: Akademie Verlag, 1957.

Thomas, Lowell, Jr. *The Silent War in Tibet*. New York: Doubleday, 1959.

Thondup, Tulku. *Buddhist Civilization in Tibet*. New York: Routledge and Kegan Paul, 1987.

Thornberry, Patrick. *Minorities and Human Rights Law*. London: Minority Rights Group, no. 73 (May 1987).

Threadgold, Donald W., ed. *Soviet and Chinese Communism: Similarities and Differences*. Seattle: University of Washington, 1967.

Tibet: 1950-67. Hong Kong: Union Research Institute, 1967.

Tibet in the United Nations. New Delhi: Bureau of His Holiness the Dalai Lama.

Tibet Fights for Freedom: The Story of the March 1959 Uprising as Recorded in Documents, Despatches, Eye-Witness Accounts and World-wide Reactions. New Delhi: Orient Longmans, 1960.

Tibet: From 1951 to 1991. Beijing: New Star Publishers, 1991.

Tibet: The Facts: A Report Prepared by the Scientific Buddhist Association for the United Nations Commission on Human Rights. Dharamsala: Tibetan Young Buddhist Association, 1990.

Tibet Journal. Dharamsala: Library of Tibetan Works and Archives.

Tibet: Proving Truth from Facts. Dharamsala: Department of Information and International Relations, Central Tibetan Administration, 1993.

Tibet: Today and Yesterday. Beijing: Beijing Review, 1983.

Tibet Under Chinese Communist Rule: A Compilation of Refugee Statements: 1958-1975. Dharamsala: Information and Publicity Office of His Holiness the Dalai Lama, 1976.

Tibetans on Tibet. Beijing: China Reconstructs Press, 1988.

Tomimas, Shutaro. *The Open-Door Policy and The Territorial Integrity of China*. Virginia: University Publications of America, 1919, 1976.

Townsend, James R. *Political Participation in Communist China*. Berkeley: University of California Press, 1967.

Trotsky, Leon. *The Permanent Revolution*. New York: Pathfinder Press, 1969.

The True Features of Chinese Communist "Tibet Model." Taipei: Asian People's Anti-Communist League, 1982.

Tsering, Tashi. "Nag-ron mGon-po rNam-gyal: A 19th Century Kham-pa Warrior." In *Soundings in Tibetan Civilization*, ed. Aziz and Kapstein. New Delhi: Manohar Publications, 1985.

Tucci, Guiseppi. *Tibetan Painted Scrolls*. Rome: La Libreria dello Stato, 1949.

_____. *The Religions of Tibet*, trans Geoffrey Samuel. Berkeley: University of California Press, 1980.

Uray, G. "The Four Horns of Tibet According to the Royal Annals." *Acta Orientalia Hungarica*, X (1960).

_____. "The Narrative of Legislation and Organization." *Acta Orientalia Hungarica*, XXVI (1972).

Van den Berghe, Pierre L. "Race and Ethnicity: A Sociobiological Perspective." *Ethnic and Racial Studies*. Vol 1, #4, October, 1978.

_____. *The Ethnic Phenomenon*. New York: Praeger, 1987.

Van Dyke, Vernon. "The Individual, the State, and Ethnic Communities in Political Theory." *World Politics*, vol XXIX, no. 3 (April 1977).

Van Slyke, Lyman P. *Enemies and Friends: The United Front in Chinese Communist History*. Stanford: Stanford University Press, 1967.

Vitali, Roberto. *Early Temples of Central Tibet*. London: Serindia, 1989.

Van Walt van Praag, Michael C. *Population Transfer and the Survival of the Tibetan Identity*. New York: US Tibet Committee, 1986.

_____. *The Status of Tibet*. Boulder: Westview Press, 1987.

Wang, Furen and Suo, Wenqing. *Highlights of Tibetan History*. Beijing: New World Press, 1984.

Wang, James C.F. *Contemporary Chinese Politics*. Englewood Cliffs, N.J.: Prentice Hall Inc., 1989.

Wang, Xiaoqiang and Bai, Nanfeng, trs. Angela Knox. *The Poverty of Plenty*. New York: St. Martin's Press, 1991.

Weber, Max. *Economy and Society*, ed. Guenther Roth and Claus Wittich. Berkeley: University of California Press, 1968.

_____. *The Religion of China*. New York: The Free Press, 1951; Free Press Paperback, 1968.

Whyte, Martin King. *Small Groups and Political Rituals in China*. Berkeley: University of California Press, 1974.

Whyte, Robert Orr. "Evolution of the Chinese Environment." In *The Origins of Chinese Civilization*, ed. David N. Keightley. Berkeley: University of California Press, 1983.

Wilson, Amy Auerbacher; Greenblatt, Sidney Leonard; and Wilson, Richard Whittingham, eds. *Deviance and Social Control in Chinese Society*. New York: Praeger Publishers, 1977.

Wilson, Richard W. *Learning to be Chinese: The Political Socialization of Children in Taiwan*. Cambridge: Massachusetts Institute of Technology Press, 1970.

Wittfogel, Karl A. *Oriental Despotism: A Comparative Study of Total Power*. New Haven: Yale University Press, 1957; New York: Vintage Books, 1981.

Woodman, Dorothy. *Himalayan Frontiers: A Political Review of British, Chinese, Indian and Russian Rivalries*. New York: Frederick A. Praeger, 1969.

Wu, Hongda Harry. *Laogai—The Chinese Gulag*. Boulder: Westview Press, 1992.=

_____. *Bitter Winds: A Memoir of My Years in China's Gulag*. New York: John Wiley and Sons, 1994.

Wylie, Turill, trans. *The Geography of Tibet*. Serie Orientale Roma XXV. Roma: Instituto Italiano per il Medio ed Estremo Oriente, 1962.

_____. "The First Mongol Conquest of Tibet Reinterpreted." *Harvard Journal of Asiatic Studies* (1977).

Yang, Bo. *The Ugly Chinaman and the Crisis of Chinese Culture*. Sydney: Allen and Unwin, 1991.

Younghusband, Francis. *India and Tibet: A History of the Relations which have Subsisted between the Two Countries from the Time of Warren Hastings to 1910; with a Particular Account of the Mission to Lhasa of 1904*. London: John Murray, 1910; Hong Kong: Oxford University Press, 1985.

Yu, Frederick T.C. *Mass Persuasion in Communist China*. New York: Frederick A. Praeger, 1964.

Yu, Ying-shih. "Han Foreign Relations." In *The Cambridge History of China: The Chin and Han Empires*, eds. Denis Twitchett and Michael Loewe. Cambridge: Cambridge University Press, 1966.

_____. *Trade and Expansion in Han China*. Berkeley: University of California Press, 1967.

_____. "The Hsiung-nu." In *The Cambridge History of Early Inner Asia*, ed. Denis Sinor. Cambridge: Cambridge University Press, 1990.

Zhao, Songqiao. *Physical Geography of China*. Beijing: Science Press, 1986.

Zweig, David. *Agrarian Radicalism in China, 1968-1981*. Cambridge: Harvard University Press, 1989.

Zwick, Peter. *National Communism*. Boulder: Westview Press, 1983.

Oral Interviews

Abu Chonga, Khampa resistance fighter; imprisoned 1960-1982.

Abu Gongkar, Khampa resistance fighter; imprisoned 1960-1979.

Ama Adi, resident of Kanze, Kham; imprisoned 1958-1979.

Amdo Rigchok, former official of Cultural Research Center, Sining.

Amdo Some (Tenzin Palgye), resident of Ngaba, Amdo, until 1989.

Ani Gonjo Pachim Dolma, daughter of Tibetan official of Gonjo, Kham; resistance leader 1958-1996; imprisoned 1960-1979.

Drakton, son of former Tibetan Government official.

Jampa Gyaltsen, student at Beijing National Minorities Institute in 1950s.

Jamyang Norbu, former director of Tibetan Institute of Performing Arts and founder and director of Amnye Machen Institute.

Kalsang Wangdu, Khampa resistance fighter; imprisoned 1960-1979.

Kirti Rimpoche, incarnate lama of Kirti Monastery in Ngaba, Amdo.

Lha Gyari, administrator of Lha Gyari estate in Lhoka.

Lobsang Tenzin, former resident of Sok Dzong, Chamdo District.

Lodi Gyari, president of International Campaign for Tibet.

Lhazang Tsering, former president of Tibetan Youth Congress.

Lobsang Wangyal, Lhasa doctor; imprisoned 1959-1967; doctor at prison camps 1967-1983.

Nyima Assam, Khampa resistance fighter 1956-1961; imprisoned 1961-1979.

Rinbur Tulku, incarnate lama of Rinbur Monastery in Kham; head of Tibetan Buddhist Association in 1950s.

Rinchen Paljor, painter, Lhasa resident.

Tashi Tsering, research scholar, Library of Tibetan Works and Archives.

Thupten Norbu, brother of His Holiness the Dalai Lama.

Tinley Phuntsok, former servant of Ling Rimpoche, Lhasa; member of under ground resistance; imprisoned 1970-1984.

Tsayul Tulku, reincarnate lama of Amchok region, Amdo, and Labrang Tashikyil Monastery.

Tsering Dolkar, member of underground resistance, Lhasa, until 1984.

Tseten Namgyal, former manager of Tsarong estate near Shigatse.

Tsering Wangchuk. Tibetan Red Guard during Cultural Revolution.

Abbreviations

APC	Agricultural Producers Cooperative
CCP	Chinese Communist Party
CPPCC	Chinese People's Political Consultative Conference
FBIS	Foreign Broadcast Information Service
FRUS	Foreign Relations of the United States
GAOR	General Assembly Official Records (United Nations)
GOI	Government of India
KMT	Kuomintang
MAT	Mutual Aid Team
MEA	Ministry of External Affairs (India)
MPR	Mongolian People's Republic
NCNA	New China News Agency
NEFA	Northeast Frontier Agency (India)
NPC	National People's Congress
PAP	People's Armed Police
PCTAR	Preparatory Committee Tibet Autonomous Region
PLA	People's Liberation Army
PRC	People's Republic of China
TAR	Tibet Autonomous Region
TIN	Tibet Information Network
UNGA	United Nations General Assembly

Index

Urumchi, 352, 353
U-Tsang (Central Tibet), 89, 92, 216, 221, 361, 502(n155), 609
Uzbek, 115

Van Walt, Michael, 612-614, 615
Victory Congratulations Mission, 251, 254
Vietnam, 531, 690

Wang Ch'i-mei, 547
Wang Feng, 426, 427, 430, 434
Wan Li, 568
Washington Conference, 213, 214
Washington, D.C., 258, 316, 319, 502, 602, 603, 622
Wencheng (Gyalsa), 61, 62, 63, 68, 78, 644
Western Turkestan, 70
White Lotus Rebellion, 137, 138
Wu Chung-hsin, 241
Wu Jinghua, 592, 594, 617
Wu-tai Shan, 165
Wu-ti, 26
Wutitu, 481(n88)

Xinjiang, 362, 687
    See also Sinkiang, East Turkestan
Xi Zhongxun, 573

Yalta, 247(n50), 250
Yamdrok Yumtso, 181
Yangbaijan, 129
Yang Jingren, 568, 572, 573, 574, 575
Yang-shao, 2, 3, 5, 6, 17
Yangtze River (Jinsa Jiang, Dri Chu), xxi, xxii, xxiii, xxiv, xxv, 9, 16, 19, 21, 70, 72, 76(n84), 123, 127, 141, 195(n142), 197, 198, 208, 224, 242, 275, 277, 328, 440(n126), 692
Yan Jiaqi, 620-621
Yao, 337, 339, 340
Yarla Shampo, 50
Yarlung dynasty, 36-40, 50, 51-56, 59,

62, 65, 81
Yatung, 154, 159, 289, 292, 293, 294, 294(n94), 295, 296, 301, 305, 306, 309, 311, 312, 313, 315, 316
Yellow River (Huang Ho, Ma Chu), xxi, xxii, xxiv, 2, 5, 6, 12, 13, 19, 26, 29, 59, 68, 69, 72, 77, 123, 196, 265, 328, 692
Yeltsin, Boris, 653(n146)
Yenan, 340
Yi, 364, 398(n25), 439, 592
Yin Ch'ang-heng, 183
Yin Fatang, 568, 592
Yititu, 481(n88)
Younghusband, Francis, 156-160, 162, 176, 662
Yuan dynasty, 11, 92-100, 103, 141, 171, 327, 328, 455, 660
Yuan Shih-k'ai, 181, 182, 187, 194(n138), 205
Yueh-chih, 3, 9, 10, 14, 29
Yul, 36, 38, 51, 76(n84)
Yul Lha, 38, 45, 46-51
Yulo Dawa Tsering, 608
Yung-cheng, 127-130, 192, 195(n142)
Yung-ho Kung, 166, 167, 220
Yungon Dzasa, 220
Yunnan, xxi, xxvi, 4, 6(n30), 70, 76(n84), 83, 87, 116, 182, 205, 206, 209, 224, 244, 277, 338, 339, 352, 361, 362, 363, 364, 420, 439, 569, 574, 607(n28), 621, 622, 633
Yushu, 363(n77), 400(n30), 406
    See also Jyekundo
Yutok Dzaza, 317(n150), 318

Zayul, 180, 442
Zhangzhung, 12, 15, 39(n14), 59, 61, 63, 64, 65, 66, 69, 76, 76(n84), 77, 81
Zhao Ziyang, 554(n41), 587(n66), 590
Zhou Enlai. *See* Chou En-lai
Zinpoje, 52, 54

About the Book and Author

This detailed history offers the most comprehensive account available of Tibetan nationalism, Sino-Tibetan relations, and the issue of Tibetan self-determination. Warren Smith explores Tibet's ethnic and national origins, the birth of the Tibetan state, the Buddhist state and its relations with China, Tibet's quest for independence, and the Chinese takeover of Tibet after 1950.

Focusing especially on post-1950 Tibet under Chinese Communist rule, Smith analyzes Marxist-Leninist and Chinese Communist Party nationalities theory and policy, their application in Tibet, and the consequent rise of Tibetan nationalism. Concluding that the essence of the Tibetan issue is self-determination, Smith bolsters his argument with a comprehensive analysis of modern Tibetan and Chinese political histories.

Warren W. Smith, Jr., an independent scholar in Alexandria, Virginia, received his Ph.D. in international relations from the Fletcher School of Law and Diplomacy.